1 MONTH OF
FREE
READING

at

www.ForgottenBooks.com

By purchasing this book you are eligible for one month membership to ForgottenBooks.com, giving you unlimited access to our entire collection of over 1,000,000 titles via our web site and mobile apps.

To claim your free month visit:
www.forgottenbooks.com/free921774

ISBN 978-0-260-00738-4
PIBN 10921774

This book is a reproduction of an important historical work. Forgotten Books uses
state-of-the-art technology to digitally reconstruct the work, preserving the original format
whilst repairing imperfections present in the aged copy. In rare cases, an imperfection in
the original, such as a blemish or missing page, may be replicated in our edition. We do,
however, repair the vast majority of imperfections successfully; any imperfections that
remain are intentionally left to preserve the state of such historical works.

THE LAW

OF

PRIVATE CORPORATIONS
IN OHIO

BY

HOWARD A. COUSE

OF THE CLEVELAND BAR

AUTHOR OF THE OHIO FORM BOOK

VOLUME I.

CINCINNATI

THE W. H. ANDERSON CO.

1914

COPYRIGHT, 1913,

BY

THE W. H. ANDERSON COMPANY.

PREFACE

During the ten years since the last work on Ohio Corporations was published, there have been numerous and important changes in the constitution and statutes affecting corporations, as well as many judicial decisions. Among the constitutional and statutory changes are the following:

Abolition of double liability of stockholders (1903) and its restoration as to bank stockholders (1913).

Uniform stock certificate transfer act (1911).

"Blue Sky" law (1913).

Sales of entire corporate property regulated (1906).

Public utilities commission acts (1906, 1911 and 1913).

Tax commission acts (1910 and 1911).

Bank inspection acts (1908 and 1913).

Adoption of the General Code (1910).

Federal income tax (1909 and 1913).

This work contains the constitutional and statutory provisions relating to all corporations, excepting municipal corporations, and the law relating thereto as established by judicial decisions; together with forms and a chapter on organization and management.

Many citations to opinions of the attorneys-general will be found in the following pages. In a work of another character, it might well be considered improper to cite such opinions as authorities; but in this work such opinions are of value. The attorney-general is the official legal adviser of the state departments which have intimate relations with corporations, including the secretary of state, superintendents of insurance and of banks, and the public utility and tax commissions; and precedents are established in such departments by his opinions.

Furthermore, many statutes, which are wholly unadjudicated by the courts, have been construed by the attorney-general. Lawyers, in their study of such statutes, may be much helped by his opinions, whether or not they agree in his conclusions.

HOWARD A. COUSE.

Cleveland, Ohio, October, 1913.

TABLE OF CONTENTS

VOLUME I

OHIO
PRIVATE CORPORATIONS

PART I.

ORGANIZATION AND MANAGEMENT OF PRIVATE CORPORATIONS
FOR PROFIT.

ORGANIZATION AND MANAGEMENT OF PRIVATE CORPORATIONS FOR PROFIT.

§ 1. Scope of chapter. In this chapter it is attempted to treat the subjects from a practical standpoint, and to present in a concise form suggestions and statements of the rules of law which are properly considered before action is taken in the various proceedings of organization and management.

This chapter is intended to be read or used in connection

with the forms immediately following. All of the statements in this chapter are not applicable to banking, insurance, public utility and other corporations which in many respects are governed by special statutes.

§ 2. **Advantages of corporation.** The usual forms under which several individuals may unite for business purposes are the corporation, partnership, limited partnership and the limited partnership association. In practice, corporations greatly outnumber all other forms of business association. Limited partnerships, at one time frequently met with in Ohio, are now comparatively rare. The organization of limited partnership associations is authorized by statute,[1] but these statutes are wholly unadjudicated by the courts and but little advantage has been taken of them.

The corporate form of organization possesses distinct advantages, among which are the following:

a. *Limited liability.* A subscriber to stock in a corporation is liable to the extent of the par value of the stock purchased but no further. Having once paid for his stock, a stockholder is not liable for the debts or obligations of the corporation, nor can the corporation make additional assessments on him. The amount of his subscription is risked in the enterprise, but no more.[2]

When stock is transferred the new holder is not liable for more than the original holder. When stock has once been paid in full no holder is liable.

The liability of a member of a partnership, however, is not limited to the amount of his investment. If a partnership becomes insolvent, the individual property of the partners may be subjected to the payment of firm obligations.

Limited partnerships provide some features of limited liability but a limited partnership must have at least one general partner whose liability is unlimited.

b. *Transferable shares.* The capital stock of a corporation is divided into equal shares, the par value of which may be large or small, so that funds for the enterprise may be contributed by few or by many persons, as may be desired.

Paid up shares in a corporation are evidenced by certificates on which a blank assignment is usually printed. This enables a stockholder to easily transfer his interest in the

G. C., §§ 8059 to 8078.

Stockholders in banks, both national and state, who have paid for their stock, are, in case of insolvency of the bank, liable for an additional amount equal to the par value of their stock. Stockholders in all Ohio corporations were formerly subject to a similar double liability, but this was abolished in November, 1903. The double liability of state bank stockholders was added in 1912, to take effect January 1, 1913.

corporation. A stockholder may not only sell his shares but may use them as collateral security in obtaining loans or credit.

The facility with which a stockholder's interest in a corporation may be transferred and utilized is a feature which is lacking in other forms of organization. The interest of a partner is not easily transferred and can not be pledged as security for loans.

c. *Corporate entity.* A corporation has a separate legal existence without regard to its individual members. Its membership may be completely changed without affecting the corporate existence.[3]

A member of a partnership can not enter into contracts with his firm, nor bring suits against it. A corporation, however, may make contracts with its stockholders, and may sue and be sued by them.

d. *Continuous existence.* The existence of a corporation is not affected by the death of one or more of its stockholders, nor by their bankruptcy, insanity or other incapacity, nor by disagreements between them. The corporate organization continues intact whereas a partnership under such circumstances would in many instances have been dissolved and the enterprise seriously interrupted.

The duration of the life of a corporation is not limited, except in the case of real estate corporations.[4]

Nominally a corporation has a perpetual existence, but it may be terminated, (1) by failure to make annual reports or to pay taxes,[5] (2) by voluntary surrender of its charter by unanimous consent of its stockholders,[6] (3) by dissolution through judicial proceedings, because of insolvency of the corporation or other conditions which render impracticable the accomplishment of its purposes,[7] or (4) by forfeiture of its charter by the state for misuse or nonuse of corporate rights.[8]

Until a corporation has been terminated by one of such methods it continues to exist unaffected by vicissitudes or changing conditions among its stockholders.

e. *Administrative system.* Each member of a partnership is impliedly authorized to act for the firm and to bind it by transactions within the scope of its business. With corpora-

[3] Andres v. Morgan, 62 O. S. 236; Bank v. Trebein, 59 O. S. 316.

[4] Articles of incorporation formed for the purpose of buying or selling real estate expire in twenty-five years. G. C., § 8648.

[5] G. C., §§ 5509 to 5513.

[6] G. C., § 8740. Where no instalments of capital stock have been paid, and there are no investments or unpaid debts, the charter may be surrendered by action of the holders of a *majority* of the stock. G. C., § 8738.

[7] G. C., §§ 11938, 11943.

[8] G. C., § 12323.

tions, however, the rule is different. A stockholder, as such, has no authority to act as agent for the corporation. Representatives of the stockholders are selected, by vote, to conduct the corporate business and affairs.

The stockholders elect a board of directors which has the management and control of the business. It is possible for minority stockholders, by cumulative voting, to elect one or more directors and be represented in the management. The board of directors selects officers and agents who transact the business under the control and supervision of the board.

During their term of office, the directors, acting as a board, are supreme in the management of the corporate business and so long as they in good faith conduct the business lawfully and within the limits of the articles of incorporation, they are not subject to interference or control by the stockholders, even by a majority.

This system of representative management, when properly used, is practical and efficient, and is especially advantageous where the capital stock of a corporation is distributed among numerous holders.

§3. **Disadvantages of corporation.** a. *Expense.* The expense of doing business as a corporation includes (1) the initial incorporation cost, and (2) an annual franchise tax of three-twentieths of one percent on the issued capital stock.

Formerly the sole expense was the initial incorporation cost. In 1902 an annual franchise tax of one-tenth of one percent on the issued capital stock was imposed. In 1910 this was increased to three-twentieths of one percent. In 1909 the federal income tax law was passed by Congress, imposing a tax of one percent of the net income of a corporation in excess of $5,000 per year. At the time this is written an income tax on individuals and partnerships seems certain of passage by Congress, in which event the corporation income tax will no longer be a special corporate disadvantage.

b. *Surveillance of corporate affairs and publicity.* The federal commissioner of corporations has power to investigate a corporation engaged in interstate commerce as to its organization, and the conduct and management of its business. Under the corporation income tax law the tax returns of corporations are filed in the office of the commissioner of internal revenue and constitute a public record, and the books and papers of a corporation may be examined by revenue agents as to the correctness of its tax returns.

In general the advantages of the corporate form largely outweigh its disadvantages. For the conduct of a small business, or a business owned by a few individuals, however, a limited partnership may be preferable.

§ 4. Selection of state for incorporation purposes.

a. *Ohio.* Where the principal business of a proposed corporation is to be transacted in Ohio it should, in general, be organized under the laws of this state. A private business corporation may be organized in another state, and may transact all of its business in Ohio upon compliance with requirements imposed by statute upon foreign corporations. In former years, when stockholders in Ohio corporations were subject to double liability, many companies were incorporated in other states to transact business in this state. But since the abrogation of the double liability in 1903, foreign incorporation is unusual. Foreign incorporation increases the cost. Organization fees and annual franchise taxes must be paid in the state of incorporation and also the license fee and annual franchise tax to the state of Ohio. An additional expense is the maintaining of an office in the state of incorporation, which is required by the laws of many states. Another objection to foreign incorporation is the fact that a state has power to place additional restrictions and conditions on the right of foreign corporations to do business within it, or may wholly exclude them from the state.[1]

Where the stock will be held by residents of Ohio, and the property and business of the corporation will be in another state incorporation in this state may be advantageous. Stock in such foreign corporations, held by residents of Ohio, is taxable in Ohio, while stock in Ohio corporations is exempt from taxation. By Ohio incorporation, tax on the stock is avoided. If the stock is valuable, the entrance and franchise taxes paid by the corporation, in the state where its business is located, are less than the Ohio tax on the stock.

b. *Foreign incorporation.* If the proposed corporation will operate plants or do business in several states, a selection must be made of the state, the laws of which are best adapted to the purposes of the corporation. Among the states having so called liberal incorporation laws are Maine, Delaware, Connecticut, Massachusetts, New York, Nevada, Arizona, South Dakota and New Mexico. Among the subjects for investigation in the choice of a state for incorporation purposes are the following:

Are the laws well adjudicated?

Amount of organization fees and taxes.

Is there an annual franchise tax?

[1] Aetna Iron, etc., Co. v. Taylor,   C. C. 602: 5 C. D. 242. 3 N. P. 152; S. C. 4 Dec. 180: 13

Is the charter perpetual?
Corporate objects and purposes permitted.
Are nonresidents eligible as directors?
May stockholders' and directors' meetings be held outside of the state?
May the principal office be located outside of the state?
Are books required to be kept in the state?
Limitations and restrictions on amount of capital stock.
Can preferred stock be issued?
Amount of capital (subscribed and paid in) with which corporation may commence business.
Amount of capital required to be paid in money.
Power to issue stock in consideration for property, services, etc.
Conclusiveness of judgment of directors as to value of property, services, etc., received by the corporation as payment for stock.
May a voting trust be formed?
Liability of directors.
Liability of stockholders for corporate debts.
Inheritance tax on stock. Does it apply to nonresident stockholders?
Protection of the minority. Cumulative voting.
Publicity of affairs required.
A careful investigation of these questions requires a visit to a law library containing the reports, statutes and most recent session laws of each state. Valuable information, however, may be found in a volume published annually, giving a summary of the corporation laws of every state.[2]

The corporation laws of some of the liberal states require that an office be maintained in the state; that one director be a resident of the state; that the stock book and transfer book be kept in the office, and that stockholders' annual meetings be held in the state. In several of such states there are located incorporating agencies which make a business of furnishing, for a moderate charge, office conveniences to corporations organized therein, but transacting all their business outside. In such cases an officer of the agency usually acts as resident director or agent.

§ 5. **Expense of incorporation.** In estimating the cost of incorporation the yearly fee or tax should be taken into consideration as well as the initial expense of organization.

a. *Initial organization expense.* The expense of organization includes the state filing fees, fees of acknowledgment, etc., equipment of books and seal, and counsel fees.

[2] Parker's Corporation Manual.

In Ohio the state fees required of a corporation with an authorized capital stock of $50,000 or less are reasonable in amount as compared with the fees charged in other states. It is different, however, where the capitalization is large. For instance, the amount required of a corporation having an authorized capital of $1,000,000 in Ohio is $1,002; while in New Jersey it is $210; in Maine $117; in Arizona $40; and in South Dakota $28.

The initial expense of incorporating a company in Ohio with a capital stock of $10,000, or less, may be estimated substantially as follows:

Secretary of State, filing articles of incorporation..................$10.00
Secretary of State, filing certificate of subscription............... 2.00
Notary fee, articles of incorporation............................. .40
Clerk's certificate, articles of incorporation..................... .35
Equipment of record book, stock ledger, transfer book, stock certifi-
      cate book, and seal............................$8.00 and upwards
Attorney's fee ....$50.00 and upwards
      Total...$70.75

Where the capital exceeds $10,000, the fee for filing the articles is one-tenth of one percent of the authorized capital stock ($1 per $1,000).[1]

b. *Annual State franchise tax.* An annual franchise tax, for the privilege of continuing business under the corporate form, popularly known as the Willis law tax, is imposed on Ohio corporations, amounting to three-twentieths of one percent upon the subscribed or issued and outstanding capital stock ($1.50 per $1,000); in no case less than ten dollars.[2]

c. *Federal income tax.* A corporation is subject to an income tax imposed by the federal government amounting to one percent of its net income in excess of $5,000 per annum.[3]

The federal income tax, however, and the state property tax, which is imposed upon the property of corporations at the same rate as on property belonging to individuals, should probably not be classed as "incorporation" expenses.

d. *Foreign corporations. Initial expense of entering State.* There are two laws applying to foreign corporations entering Ohio. To enter the state for the purpose of doing business a foreign corporation must pay a *license* fee according to the amount of its capital stock, ranging from $15 where the capital stock is less than $100.000 to $50 where the capital stock is $1,000,000 or more. If the corporation owns or uses

[1] G. C., § 176.
[2] G. C., § 5498. Southern Gum Co. v. Laylin, 66 O. S. 578.
[3] U. S. Stats. 1909, p. 112, § 38 et seq. This tax is not imposed on labor, agricultural or horticultural corporations, fraternal benefit societies, nor on certain building and loan associations.

a portion of its capital or plant in Ohio, it must pay in addition to the foregoing license fee, an initial *franchise* tax of one-tenth of one percent upon the proportion of property owned and used and business done within the state.[4]

An annual franchise tax is imposed on foreign corporations amounting to three-twentieths of one percent upon the proportion of its authorized capital stock represented by property owned and used and business transacted in Ohio; minimum $10.[5]

§ 6. Transactions before organization.

A corporation is not "organized" until directors have been elected by the stockholders.[1] The business and property of a corporation are conducted and controlled by its board of directors.[2] Prior to organization no one is authorized to bind the corporation by any act or transaction.[3]

Agreements entered into by promoters prior to organization may become binding on the corporation if, after organization, such acts are expressly adopted and ratified by the board of directors, or if the corporation accepts the benefits of the acts.

b. *Contracts by promoters with third persons.* Assuming to represent proposed corporations, promoters frequently enter into agreements with third persons. They engage attorneys to attend to the incorporation; they secure leases on property, and make contracts of purchase, frequently advancing money for such purposes. If, after organization, the corporation accepts the benefit of such a transaction, or expressly assumes it, it becomes the obligation of the corporation.[4]

But if there be a failure to incorporate, or if the corporation after organization neither accepts the benefits of the transaction nor expressly assumes it, the corporation is not bound. The promoter under such circumstances has no redress against the corporation, and may in some cases be personally liable to third persons on the contracts made with them.[5]

Where there are several promoters, one who has been

[4] G. C., §§ 178 to 192.
[5] G. C. § 5503.
[1] An election for directors can not be held until ten percent of the capital stock has been subscribed. G. C., § 8635; Trust Co. v. Floyd, 47 O. S. 525; Telephone Co. v. Cincinnati, 73 O. S. 64, 77; Hessler v. Cleveland, etc. Co., 61 O. S. 621.
[2] G. C., § 8660.

[3] Mosier v. Parry, 60 O. S. 388, 401; Dayton, etc. Co. v. Coy, 13 O. S. 84.
[4] City Bldg. Assn. v. Zahner, 6 W. L. B. 389: 10 Am. L. R. 181; Third Ward Bldg. Assn. v. Lotze, 11 W. L. B. 285.
[5] Mosier v. Parry, 60 O. S. 388, 401.

held liable to third persons on such a contract may compel the others to pay their proportionate share of the losses.

Fraud of a promoter may invalidate his contracts which are adopted by the corporation in ignorance thereof. The corporation may rescind a contract of purchase of property, negotiated on its behalf by the promoter, who received secret commissions from the seller.[6]

c. *Agreements of promoters between themselves.* An agreement between individuals to form a corporation and providing for its future control is valid, as between the parties to it, if the corporation is created according to statutory requirements, and the objects contemplated are lawful and proper.[7]

Such an agreement does not affect the corporation, or future stockholders, unless its provisions are enacted by the stockholders into the corporate regulations.

§ 7. Subscriptions to stock before incorporation. No subscriptions to the capital stock or other preliminary agreements need be made prior to the filing of articles of incorporation with the secretary of state. After the articles have been filed and recorded it is the duty of the incorporators to open books for subscriptions.

It is sometimes desirable, however, to definitely commit, and, if possible, to legally bind the parties interested in a proposed enterprise, before the expense of preparing and filing articles is incurred.

A mutual agreement between individuals to become stockholders in a corporation thereafter to be organized is valid,[1] and has been held to bind the persons executing it from the time it is made, provided incorporation is perfected within a reasonable time.[2]

Such an agreement should be distinguished from an ordinary subscription to capital stock, made before incorporation. The latter is a continuing offer, merely, and not a present contract. Prior to incorporation there is no authority in any person to accept the subscription. There is a want of mutuality. A mere subscription may be withdrawn or cancelled, by the person making it, if he acts before the corporation is organized and his subscription accepted.[3]

[6] Commonwealth Steamship Co. v. American Shipbuilding Co., 10 O. L. R. 427; 197 Fed. 797 (U. S. D. C. 1912) s. c. 10 O. L. R. 395; 197 Fed. 780.

[7] Doan v. Rogan, 79 O. S. 372, 386.

[1] Doan v. Rogan, 79 O. S. 372, 386.

[2] Minneapolis Threshing Machine Co. v. Davis, 40 Minn. 110, 41 N. W. 1026; Knox v. Childersburg Land Co., 86 Ala. 180, 183, 184, 5 So. 578.

[3] Mill Co. v. Felt, 87 Me. 234.; Hudson Real Estate Co. v. Tower, 161 Mass. 10; Auburn Bolt Works v. Schultz, 143 Pa. St. 256; See Wallace v. Townsend, 43 O. S. 537.

If the subscription is not withdrawn, but is permitted to stand until the corporation is organized and the subscription accepted, the contract, according to the rule prevailing in a majority of the states, becomes complete and enforceable by the corporation.[4]

In Ohio, however, it has been held that subsequent incorporation and acceptance of the subscription does not render a prior subscription enforceable.[5]

§ 8. **Stockholders' rights and powers.** a. *In general.* Stockholders have very limited powers and functions in the active management of the affairs of a corporation. The business and property are managed and controlled by the board of directors. Even a majority of stockholders can not interfere with or control the actions of directors so long as the affairs are conducted lawfully, within the limits of the articles of incorporation and in accordance with the lawful regulations. When the holders of a majority of the stock of a corporation become dissatisfied with the management, the usual remedy is to elect other directors at the succeeding annual election. But majority stockholders may bring about an immediate change in the policy of management by increasing the number of directors at a special meeting of the stockholders.[1]

Among the rights and powers possessed by stockholders are the following:

b. *Election of directors.* Directors are elected by the stockholders and every owner of full paid stock has a right to be present at elections and to vote. By cumulative voting minority stockholders are sometimes enabled to elect one or more directors and to secure representation on the board.

c. *Information.* A stockholder has a right to examine the books and records of the corporation at all reasonable times. A corporation is required by statute to make an annual statement of its financial condition and to furnish a copy to each of its stockholders.[2]

d. *Prevention of breach of trust.* Stockholders may, under some circumstances, enjoin the directors from fraudulent dealings with the corporate property or from committing acts beyond the limits of the charter of the corporation.

[4] Nebraska Chicory Co. v. Lednicky, 79 Neb. 587, 113 N. W. 245; McNaught v. Fisher, 96 Fed. Rep. 168; Athol Music Hall Co. v. Carey, 116 Mass. 471; Planters, etc. Packet Co. v. Webb, 144 Ala. 666; Cook on Corporations, § 72 and cases cited.

[5] Dayton, etc. Co. v. Coy, 13 O. S. 84, 91.

[1] G. C., § 8665; Gold Bluff, etc. Co. v. Whitlock, 75 Conn. 669; In re Griffing Iron Co., 63 N. J. L. 168, 357.

[2] G. C., § 8685.

e. *Regulations.* Stockholders have a right to adopt regulations for the government of the corporation. Regulations should not be confused with by-laws, which are adopted by the directors and are for the government of the directors only.[3]

The corporation laws of many other states provide for by-laws only, which are adopted by the stockholders and are similar to the regulations of Ohio corporations.

Although the "corporate powers, business and property must be exercised, conducted and controlled by the board of directors,"[4] the stockholders are expressly authorized by statute to adopt regulations providing for "the duties and compensation of officers" and "the manner of election, or appointment, and the tenure of office, of all officers other than the trustees or directors."[5]

This authorizes the stockholders to place restrictions upon the salaries of the officers and directors, and to reserve the right to elect subordinate officers.

f. *Certificates of stock.* The holders of stock, which has been fully paid, are entitled to certificates evidencing the same. It is the duty of the president and secretary, on demand, to issue such certificates.

Upon any transfer of full paid stock the transferee is entitled to have it transferred to his name on the books of the company and to receive new certificates issued in his name.[6]

g. *Right to dividends and increased stock.* When dividends have been declared by directors each stockholder is entitled to be paid his share. When the capital stock is increased each stockholder has a right to subscribe for and take his pro rata share of the increase.

h. *Certain acts of directors must be ratified by stockholders.* The entire property and assets of a corporation can not be sold unless the proposition has been submitted at a meeting of the stockholders called for the purpose and the proposition ratified by the holders of three-fourths of the stock. In such case minority stockholders who are dissatisfied with the sale are entitled to be paid the value of their stock.[7]

Bonds convertible into stock can not be issued by a corporation without the written assent of three-fourths of the stockholders representing three-fourths of the capital stock actually paid.[8]

i. *Changes in capital stock or corporate name or purposes.*

[3] Morris v. Griffith, 34 W. L. B. 191; State v. Burial Assn. 8 C. C. n. s. 248, 18 C. D. 397.
[4] G. C., § 8660.
[5] G. C., § 8704.
[6] G. C., §§ 8673, 8672.
[7] G. C., §§ 8710 to 8718.
[8] G. C., § 8709.

The capital stock of a corporation can not be increased or reduced, nor can its articles of incorporation be amended, without the favorable action of the holders of at least a majority of its capital stock. Some changes require the consent of the owners of three-fourths or three-fifths of its stock.[9]

§ 9. **Liability of stockholders.** Where stock has been fully paid up, in cash or property, its holder is under no liability (except as to debts incurred by the corporation prior to November 23, 1903). A subscriber to stock is liable to the extent of the par value of his stock but no further. The corporation can not make additional assessments on him, nor is he liable for debts of the corporation.

A person to whom "watered stock" is issued by a corporation may, under some circumstances, be liable to creditors of the corporation for the amount of "water," that is, the difference between the par value of the stock and the amount actually paid for it.[1]

Where "watered stock" is purchased from a stockholder for value, by a person having no notice that the stock is not fully paid up, the purchaser is not liable. The purchaser may rely on the representation of the corporation that the stock is full paid. The statement "full paid and nonassessable" on a stock certificate is a representation by the corporation that the stock has been paid up and the purchaser need not inquire further.[2]

Double liability. Prior to the year 1903 a stockholder in an Ohio corporation who had paid for his stock was, in case of insolvency of the corporation, liable for an additional amount equal to the par value of his stock. This double liability was abolished by an amendment to the constitution. Stockholders are now subject to such double liability for debts incurred prior to November 23, 1903, but are under no liability for debts incurred subsequent to that date,[3] except stockholders in banks, both state and national, who are subject to the double liability. The double liability of State bank stockholders was added by an amendment to the constitution adopted September 3, 1912, to take effect January 1, 1913.[4]

§ 10. **Stock.** The term *"capital stock"* is variously used to indicate (1) the nominal or authorized capital stock, (2)

[9] G. C., §§ 8699, 8720.
[1] Gates v. Tippecanoe Stone Co., 57 O. S. 60.
[3] Roebling Sons Co. v. Shawnee, etc. Co., 4 N. P. n. s. 113, 121: 17 L. D. 8 aff'd no rep. 78 O. S. 408.
[2] G. C., § 8687.
[4] Constitution, Art. XIII, § 3.

the paid up and issued capital stock and (3) the capital or property of the corporation.

a. The *nominal* or *authorized capital stock* is the amount specified in the articles of incorporation as the limit of capital which may be subscribed and paid in by stockholders.[1]

In taxation and certain other statutes the term *capital stock* has been used as meaning the *capital* or property of the corporation.[2]

A clear distinction, however, is now recognized between the *capital stock* and the *capital* of a corporation.

The amount of the capital stock remains fixed while the actual property or capital fluctuates in value and continually increases or dimishes in amount.[3]

b. *A share of stock* is a right which entitles its owner to participate in the profits of the corporation, in its assets upon liquidation, and to vote at elections of directors,. and upon certain matters required by statute to be submitted to stockholders.[4]

In this chapter the term "stock" is used as meaning *shares* of stock which is its generally accepted meaning at the present time. Formerly the word "stock" was used as the equivalent of capital stock.

c. *Issued stock* is that part of the nominal or authorized capital stock which has been subscribed for, or sold, and for which payment has been made. A certificate is not necessary to constitute a person, who has subscribed and paid for stock, a stockholder,[5] as a certificate of stock is not the stock itself, but merely evidence of its ownership. Issued stock, however, is usually represented by certificates, and stockholders who have paid for their stock are entitled to have certificates issued to them.[6]

When originally issued by an Ohio corporation, stock must be fully paid for in cash, services, or property.[7]

d. *Unissued stock* is that part of the nominal or authorized capital stock which has not been subscribed for, or sold. and in which no property rights have been acquired.

Unissued stock is sometimes confused with *treasury stock,* but it differs widely from the latter. Unissued stock is not

[1] See G. C., § 8625.
[2] Lee v. Sturges, 46 O. S. 160; Bradley v. Bauder, 36 O. S. 34; Jones v. Davis, 35 O. S. 476, 477; Railway Co. v. Furnace Co., 49 O. S. 112.
[3] State v. Jones, 51 O. S. 510, 511; Cleveland Trust Co. v. Lander, 62 O. S. 273.
[4] See Jones v. Davis, 35 O. S. 477.
[5] Ry. Co. v. Bank, 1 C. C. 199, 207; 1 C. D. 109.
[6] G. C., § 8672.
[7] Gates v. Tippecanoe Stone Co., 57 O. S. 60.

an asset of the corporation. It is merely the right in the corporation to issue stock.

e. *Treasury stock* is stock originally issued and full paid, which has been acquired by the corporation through gift, in liquidation of a debt, or otherwise, and which is held subject to disposal by the directors.[8]

The term treasury stock is sometimes wrongly applied to unissued stock.

Treasury stock is an asset of the corporation and may be sold below par. Treasury stock can not be voted.

f. *Preferred stock* is that which is given a preference over the other stock of the same corporation. It is issued in many different forms with various preferences and restrictions. The usual preference relates to dividends, and entitles its owner to dividends at a specified rate before any dividends are paid on common stock.

The Ohio statute[9] prohibits the issuing of preferred stock in excess of "two-thirds of the actual capital paid in." The statute limits the priority dividend rate on preferred stock to eight percent. Priority in assets, on liquidation of the corporation, is given by the statute.

Preferred stock may be issued, subject to redemption at a fixed time and price, which must be stated on the certificate of such stock.

The right to vote preferred stock may be limited or entirely withheld.

All preferences and restrictions should be set forth in the articles of incorporation and also on the certificates of stock.

After organization the capital stock of a corporation may be increased by an issue of preferred stock, upon the written assent of three-fourths in number of its stockholders representing three-fourths of its capital stock.[10]

Dividends on preferred stock may be made cumulative or noncumulative. If cumulative, all arrears must be paid in succeeding years before any dividend is paid on common stock. If noncumulative, no deficiency need be made up in subsequent years.

Dividends in excess of the specified rate on preferred stock are paid to the holders of common stock until the common stock holders receive an amount equal to that paid on the preferred stock.

Further surplus profits in any year are divided pro rata among all stockholders, common and preferred, without dis-

[8] Cook on Corporations, § 46; Conyngton on Corporate Organization, § 64; Taylor v. Miami Exporting Co., 6 Ohio 176, 220.

[9] G. C., §§ 8667 to 8671.
[10] G. C., § 8699.

tinction. By an express stipulation, dividends on preferred stock may be limited to the agreed rate and all surplus dividends paid to the holders of common stock.

g. *Common stock* is all the capital stock of a corporation to which no advantage, preference or priority is given over other stock.

h. *Full paid stock* is stock, the entire par value of which has been paid, in money or property, and on which there is no liability to the corporation or to creditors.

i. *"Watered stock"* or *"fictitiously paid stock"* is that which has been issued as full paid stock when in fact the entire par value has not been received by the corporation. The person receiving such stock from the corporation may be held liable to creditors, in the event of insolvency of the corporation, for the amount of the "water," viz., the difference between the par value of the stock and the amount actually paid for it. Because of such possible liability watered stock is usually issued by some method whereby the records of the corporation are made to show that full value has been given for the stock. The method most frequently adopted is that of issuing stock for property or services at an overvaluation. That property has been fraudulently overvalued is usually difficult of proof, and this method appears to be regarded as the most effectual in concealing the real character of the stock.

Occasionally stock is issued as full paid in consideration of a sum of money less than its par value. In such cases the real character of the stock and the amount of "water" are usually easy of proof.[11]

§ 11. Capitalization—Meaning of term. Stock and bonds distinguished. The term "capitalization" is variously used. (1) In one acceptation it includes the entire authorized capital stock of a corporation, both common and preferred, whether issued or not, but does not include bonds. (2) In another acceptation the term capitalization represents the par value of stock which has been issued. (3) In its usual financial acceptation, the term includes both stock and bonds, but only to the extent they have been issued.

In financial practice, stocks and bonds are both treated as securities "issued against" the property of a corporation, but there is an important distinction between them. Bonds are evidences of debt. A bondholder is a creditor of the corporation. An issue of bonds is usually secured by a mort-

[11] For circumstances under which a corporation which has commenced business may sell stock for less than par, see Peter v. Union Mfg. Co., 56 O. S. 181.

gage on all or a part of the property of the corporation. Interest on bonds falls due at fixed intervals, irrespective of whether profits have been earned, and if not paid, the corporate property may be swept away by foreclosure proceedings under the mortgage.

A stockholder, however, is not a creditor. The return on his investment is in the form of dividends, not interest; and dividends even on preferred stock can be declared only out of surplus profits.[1]

§ 12. Amount of capitalization. Considerations affecting.

In this section the term "capitalization" is used as representing the par value of the stock which has been issued.

a. *Actual value.* The basis of capitalization contemplated by the law of Ohio is the amount of cash, or the actual value of property, for which stock is issued.[1]

There are certain classes of corporation, notably banks and financial institutions, which have rigidly adhered to this rule and are capitalized on the basis of actual values. The rule is also followed, in many instances, in the organization of trading or mercantile corporations.

In estimating the actual value of property, as a basis for capitalization, intangible assets may be included. Where an established business is taken over by a corporation, the good will and other intangible property are often exceedingly valuable.

Whether in such cases the valuation placed upon property by directors is conclusive, in the absence of fraud, has not been determined by the supreme court of Ohio. One circuit court has expressed the opinion that the "good faith" rule should prevail.[2]

b. *Exceeding actual value. Earning power.* Numerous corporations have been capitalized not on the amount of money or the value of property invested (including intangible property at a fair appraisement) but on the basis of the prospective earning capacity. Bonds or preferred stock, and sometimes both, were issued up to the cost or value of the property and common stock was issued in such additional amounts as the estimated profits would pay dividends upon.

The practice of capitalizing in excess of property values has been followed, in perhaps a majority of cases, in good faith and without fraudulent intent. It has been defended by authorities upon substantially the following grounds:

[1] G. C., § 8724; Miller v. Ratterman, 47 O. S. 141.
[2] Gates v. Tippecanoe Stone Co., 57 O. S. 60.

[2] Kunz v. National Valve Co., 9 C. C. n. s. 607; 29 C. C. 519.

Capital risked in business enterprises is rightfully entitled to a larger return than capital invested in conservative real estate mortgages or municipal bonds. If a business enterprise, capitalized at actual property values, proves successful it will pay dividends largely in excess of prevailing interest rates. By "a large capitalization dividends are kept low enough to avoid the cupidity of possible competitors and the interference of legislatures."[3] Another reason given is that experience has demonstrated that stock can be sold more easily and for a proportionately higher price where the capitalization is high and the dividend rate fairly low, than where the capitalization is low and the dividend rate high. It has been further suggested by the defenders of capitalizing in excess of property values, that such capitalization injures no one because the practice is so common and well known that neither creditors nor investors rely on the nominal capitalization as representing actual property values.

In Ohio, capitalization at amounts in excess of property values is contrary to the legal requirement that all stock issued must be fully paid for in money, services, or property.[4]

To avoid the liability imposed by this rule resort has been had, in organization proceedings, to fiction, by which it was made to appear that the stock has been fully paid. Usually property or services were accepted in payment by the directors at valuations which were inflated.

As already stated this frequently has been done without fraudulent intent. The persons to whom the stock was so issued, in many cases, derived no personal gain from it, but immediately assigned it to the corporation or to trustees, to be treated as treasury stock and given as a bonus to the purchasers of bonds, or sold at a discount or otherwise used in raising funds for corporate purposes.

If the corporation remains solvent there is but little danger of personal liability arising from the transaction. It is possible that the transaction may be set aside by the corporation, or by dissenting stockholders,[5] but as it has been usually consummated at the time of organization of the corporation and with the consent of the original stockholders, the corporation is bound by the transaction.[6]

If, however, the corporation should become insolvent a

[3] Cook on Corporations, § 46, quoted in Kunz v. National Valve Co., 9 C. C. n. s. 605; 29 C. D. 519.

[4] Gates v. Tippecanoe Stone Co., 57 O. S. 60.

[5] Orton v. Edson Reduction Machinery Co., 5 C. C. n. s. 540; 17 C. D. 107 (affirmed without report 75 O. S. 580).

[6] Old Dominion, etc., Co. v. Lewisohn, 210 U. S. 206.

personal liability to subsequent creditors may result. The persons to whom the stock has been issued may, if it be proved that the property or services were fraudulently overvalued, be held liable for the difference between the actual value of the property and the par value of the stock.[7]

That there has been a fraudulent overvaluation of property is often difficult of proof, especially where the property accepted by the directors includes intangible assets such as good will, etc.[8]

Where the stock will be offered to the public, the "blue sky" law should be taken into consideration by promoters who contemplate capitalization in excess of property values.[9]

c. *Less than actual value.* Where a corporation is organized to conduct a business of comparatively small proportions, and it is intended that the stock shall be held by few persons, and not sold to the public, it is sometimes advantageous to fix the capitalization at less than the actual value of the investment. By this means a saving is effected in the amount of state organization fees and annual franchise (Willis) taxes. In practice the excess of the property values over the capital stock is sometimes covered by a bond issue.

d. *Capitalization of public utility companies and railroads.* Stocks and bonds issued by railroads and public utility companies are void unless the issue is authorized by the public utilities commission of Ohio after a hearing. The application to the commission for authority to issue stock or bonds must specify the amount, character and purpose of the issue, and certain information in detail. The money or property derived from the issue must be applied to the authorized purpose.[10]

The application must be signed and verified by the president and secretary and penalties are provided for false statements.[11]

§ 13. Form of capitalization. Preferred and common stock. Bonds.

In financing a corporation it is often desired to assure or guarantee a specific return on the capital invested. The owner of common stock has no such assurance. He is entitled to his pro rata share of the dividends which have been declared by the directors out of surplus profits. But the directors have discretionary power to declare or to withhold dividends. It is only in exceptional cases that a stockholder can compel the declaration of a dividend, al-

[7] Gates v. Tippecanoe Stone Co., 57 O. S. 60.

[8] See Cook on Corporations, § 35.

[9] See Sec. 14, *Disposal of stock and bonds.*

[10] G. C., §§ 614-53 to 614-55.

[11] G. C., § 614-57.

though there are surplus profits. Directors may, and often do, use the profits to enlarge and develop the business instead of making a division among the holders of common stock.

In cases of bad faith or abuse of discretion on the part of directors, courts will interfere, but not otherwise.

Preferred stock, however, may be issued with a much more definite assurance of dividends, and with priority over common stock in assets in the event of liquidation.[1]

Directors have power, in the exercise of discretion, to withhold dividends on preferred stock, but because of the probable injury to the credit of the corporation arising from nonpayment, such dividends are rarely withheld where surplus profits exist.

The dividend rate on preferred stock is usually fixed at from six to eight percent.[2]

Bonds constitute a debt of the corporation, and are usually secured by a mortgage on the corporate property. The interest rate on bonds is customarily from four to six percent. Where bonds can be sold without sacrifice, the annual interest charge thereon is less than the sum required to pay dividends on preferred stock of the same amount. But if it is uncertain whether the earnings of the corporation will be sufficient to pay interest on the bonds, regularly and promptly when due, in addition to operating expenses, a bond issue is dangerous because of the right of foreclosure of the mortgage upon a default of interest.

Furthermore, preferred stock, held by residents of Ohio, is exempt from taxation, while bonds are taxable.

For these and similar reasons preferred stock is usually chosen as the form of security to be issued, when conditions are such that preferred stock can be sold.

§ 14. **Disposal of stock and bonds. "Blue sky" law.** The sale of corporate stock and bonds is regulated by the so-called "blue sky" law passed in 1913.[1]

In general, this law provides that corporate securities may be disposed of through licensed dealers only. All others are prohibited from obtaining subscriptions to, or selling, securities. But there are a number of exceptions. An Ohio corporation may dispose of securities, issued by it, directly to its own stockholders or by its own officers, without any commission, and at a total expense not exceeding two percent of the proceeds; provided no part of the issue is issued for

[1] G. C., §§ 8668 to 8671.
[2] In Ohio priority dividends are limited to 8 percent. G. C. § 8668.

[1] 103 v. 743, G. C., §§ 6373-1 to 6373-24.

patents, services, good will or for property not located in Ohio. A statement of the above facts must be made by the president and secretary to the commissioner (state superintendent of banks) before the securities are offered for disposition. Unless disposed of by the corporation under the above circumstances corporate securities, with some exceptions, can be disposed of only by persons holding a license.[2]

Licensed dealers are required to file certain information with the commissioner concerning corporate securities to be sold by them, including the name, location and names of officers and directors of the issuer; a financial statement showing, in general detail, its assets and liabilities, capital stock and surplus on or subsequent to the end of its last fiscal year, and its gross income, expenses, net earnings and fixed charges for one year next preceding; also a description of the securities and the purpose of the issue. The above information is dispensed with in certain cases, as where the security has been listed in daily newspaper quotations for a year or more or appears in an approved manual or where the transaction is a single sale for $5,000 or more, or in the case of undefaulted public utility or industrial securities outstanding prior to February 1, 1913, if the issuer was then and is at the time of sale, a going concern.

A special certificate of license from the commissioner is required in the case of promotions, underwriting flotations, etc., as to each issue, to the effect that the commissioner (superintendent of banks) is satisfied that the corporation is solvent, its business properly and legitimately conducted, and that the proposed disposition of securities is not on unfair terms. The application for such certificate must contain detailed information, including:

(a) Certified copies of the articles of incorporation, regulations and by-laws and (b) of all minutes of stockholders and directors relative to the issue. (c) A sworn statement of the president and secretary of the issuing company showing in detail the items of cash, property, services, patents and other consideration for which the securities have been or are to be issued. (d) Certified copies of all contracts between the issuer and underwriters, and all contracts relating to the disposal of the securities. (e) Contracts between underwriters and salesmen, agents or brokers.

A special certificate is not required for the securities of all corporations, exceptions being made in favor of certain public utility, transportation, manufacturing, coal mining, quarrying and real estate companies organized under Ohio

[2] G. C., §§ 6773-1, 6373-2, 6373-14.

laws, whose property covered by such securities is located in Ohio.[3]

A copy of each prospectus, circular, etc., must be filed with the commissioner by dealers.

The "blue sky" law does not apply to certain securities, including:

Securities of a public utility authorized by the public utilities commission and not defaulted or judicially invalidated. Stocks and obligations of banks or building and loan associations which are subject to examination by proper authorities.

A sale to one purchaser of more than fifty percent of an entire issue of corporate bonds, not defaulted, nor judicially invalidated, and secured by mortgage on Ohio real estate for an amount, which with all superior liens, does not exceed the tax value of such real estate.

Isolated sales by an owner (not the issuer) of his own property, or by a pledgee.

Issues of Ohio corporations not for profit.

A statement of only the main features of the law, as affecting disposal of the securities of Ohio corporations, is here given, owing to the lack of space. Full information with blank applications, etc., may be obtained on application to the Superintendent of Banks, Columbus, Ohio.

§ 15. Organization. Outline of procedure. The formal proceedings by means of which a corporation is organized are briefly outlined as follows:

(1) An instrument styled in the Ohio statutes "articles of incorporation," is prepared and executed by five or more incorporators.

(2) This instrument is filed in the office of the secretary of state, where it is recorded and a certified copy furnished to the incorporators.

(3) Books for subscriptions to the capital stock are opened by the incorporators and notice thereof either published or waived by the incorporators.

(4) Subscriptions for stock are received by the incorporators, whose duty it is to then collect from each subscriber ten percent of his subscription.

(5) When ten percent of the entire capital stock has been subscribed the incorporators so certify in writing to the secretary of state.

(6) The first meeting of stockholders is then called by the incorporators, who publish notice of the meeting, unless notice is waived by all the subscribers.

[3] G. C., §§ 6373-14, 6373-16.

(7) At the first meeting of stockholders the number of directors is determined, directors elected and usually a code of regulations adopted and a time fixed for the first meeting of directors.

(8) Before meeting the directors qualify by taking an oath. At their first meeting the directors elect officers and usually enact by-laws. This perfects the organization.

§ 16. **Incorporators.** a. *Qualifications.* Only natural persons may act as incorporators. Corporations, firms, and associations are not qualified.[1] Incorporators must be sui juris. Infants are not competent to act.[2]

At least five incorporators must act in every case. A majority must be citizens of Ohio.

Incorporators are not required to become subscribers to stock or to have any financial interest in the corporation. It is a frequent practice for the attorneys who are employed to incorporate a company, or their clerks, to act as the incorporators. This is sometimes done because the real parties in interest do not desire to be known in that connection. At other times it is for the purpose of convenience or to expedite the organization.

b. *Functions.* Incorporators have in charge the formal organization proceedings. They sign and acknowledge the articles of incorporation, receive subscriptions to the capital stock and receive payment of the first instalment of ten percent. When ten percent has been subscribed they so certify in writing to the secretary of state and call and give notice of the first meeting of stockholders.

c. *Liability.* A person may become involved in liability by acting as an incorporator unless care is taken in one important particular. By signing a "certificate of subscription" and filing it with the secretary of state, the incorporators certify, in effect, not only that ten percent of the capital stock has been subscribed, but also that ten percent on each share subscribed for has been paid, and incorporators may be held personally liable for any deficiency in its actual payment.[3]

d. *Dummy directors.* Persons without financial interest in the corporation, who participate as incorporators in the formal organization proceedings, sometimes go further and act as temporary directors and transact business of importance on behalf of the corporation. When stock is to be is-

---

[1] Rep. Atty. Gen. 1908, p. 72; 2 Opinions Attys. Gen. 109.
[2] State v. Burial Assn., 8 C. C. n. s. 253; 18 C. D. 397.

[3] Hessler v. Cleveland Punch & Shear Works, 61 O. S. 621. G. C., 8634. See below, *Certificate of subscription. Liability of incorporators.*

sued for property, the owners of the property are disqualified from acting as directors in the transaction. In such cases the nominal parties usually subscribe for the small amount of stock necessary to qualify them, are elected directors and pass resolutions authorizing the issuance of stock for the property.

The terms "dummy incorporators" and "dummy directors" are sometimes applied to the persons who act as incorporators and directors without financial interest.

§ 17. Articles of incorporation. "A charter is the instrument which creates the corporation."[1]

In Ohio the formation of corporations is provided for by general laws. The charter of an Ohio corporation consists of the instrument known as "articles of incorporation" together with the general laws of the state.

Persons who fully comply with the general laws are entitled, as a matter of right, to organize a corporation. When articles of incorporation showing compliance with the general laws are presented to the secretary of state, with the proper fee, it is the duty of that officer to file and record the articles. He has no discretion except as to the form of the articles.[2]

Form. The matters to be set forth in articles of incorporation are specified by statute.[3]

The form of the articles is prescribed by the secretary of state. The better practice is to use the blank which is furnished without charge by that officer. If for any reason that is impracticable the language of such blank must be exactly followed.

Suggestions as to filling in and completing the blank forms are given in the paragraphs following.

When completed the instrument must be subscribed by the incorporators and acknowledged by them before a notary public or other officer authorized to take acknowledgments. The official character of such notary public or other officer must be certified by the clerk of the court of common pleas, and the instrument filed in the office of the secretary of state.

§ 18. Articles of incorporation. Statements in. Name of corporation. The name of a corporation for profit must begin with the word "The" and end with the word "Company."[1]

When the business of a corporation is once established

[1] Cook on Corporations, § 2.   [3] G. C., § 8625.
[2] State v. Taylor, 55 O. S. 61.   [1] G. C., § 8625.

its name sometimes becomes of great value. The name is often inseparable from the good will.[2]

It is therefore advisable, in many cases, to select a name for a corporation which is distinctive and in which trade-name rights may be acquired and protected.

When a corporation is formed to take over a partnership business the name of the partnership is usually adopted, with the necessary addition of the words "The" and "Company." Even where partnership assets, including good will, are sold through a receiver, the corporation may adopt the name previously used by the firm.[3]

A corporation can not adopt a name already assumed by an existing Ohio corporation, or so similar thereto as to mislead the public, without the written consent of the existing corporation; nor can a corporation adopt a name which is likely to mislead the public as to the character or purpose of its business.[4]

The action of the secretary of state in filing and record-ing articles of incorporation is not conclusive against another corporation having a similar name. The older company may enforce its rights by injunction.[5]

The use by a corporation of a name which infringes the trade name of an individual, or of another corporation, may be enjoined. The fact of being incorporated by such name is not a defense.[6]

§ 19. Location of corporation.

Articles of incorporation must contain a statement of "the place where" the corporation "is to be located, or where its principal business is to be transacted."[1]

The office building or street address of the corporation need not be specified. The requirement is satisfied by stating, in the articles, the name of the municipality or place where the principal office is to be located. Where a corporation has several offices, the office where the stockholders meetings are held is regarded as the principal office.

Under a former statute, similar in some respects to the present law, it was held that a corporation might, at pleas-

[2] Snyder Mfg. Co. v. Snyder, 54 O. S. 86.

[3] Snyder Mfg. Co. v. Snyder, 54 O. S. 86.

[4] G. C., § 8628.

[5] Cincinnati Vici Shoe Co. v. Cincinnati Shoe Co., 7 N. P. 135; 9 Low. D. 579.

[6] Thayer Carpet Cleaning, etc., Co. v. Geo. A. Thayer Co., 6 N. P. 300; 9 L. D. 288; Backus Oil Co. v. Backus Oil, etc. Co., 5 W. L. B. 546; R. W. Rogers Co. v. Wm. Rogers Mfg. Co., 70 Fed. Rep. 1017; Bissell Chilled Plow Works v. T. M. Bissell Plow Co. 121 Fed. Rep. 357; Chickering v. Chickering, 120 Fed. Rep. 69; Higgins v. Higgins Soap Co., 144 N. Y. 462.

[1] G. C., § 8625.

ure, move its office from one building to another, within the
specified municipality or place, although the motive was to
avoid taxation.[2]

Effect on taxation. The personal property of a corporation
(except property located in other counties) is taxed in the
municipality or township where its principal office is located,[3] although much of its business is carried on elsewhere.

The statement in the articles of incorporation is conclusive as to the location of the office.[4]

Vessel companies and corporations engaged in certain
other kinds of business are able to avoid the higher taxes
of the cities wherein much of their business is actually
transacted, by locating their principal offices in small villages, or rural townships, where the tax rate is low.[5]

The removal of the principal office of a corporation to
another municipality or place is accomplished by an amendment of its articles of incorporation. A vote of at least
three-fifths of the issued capital stock is necessary for this
purpose.[6]

§ 20. **Purpose of corporation.** Corporations may be organized for any purpose for which individuals may lawfully
associate themselves except for carrying on professional
business.[1]

The purpose for which a corporation is formed must be
clearly stated in the articles. The nature of the business to
be transacted must be specified. Where articles of incorporation do not clearly and definitely set forth the corporate
purpose, or where the statement of the purpose is ambiguous,
the secretary of state may refuse to file and record the articles.[2]

It is good practice to state the purpose in general terms.
It is improper to attempt to enumerate incidental powers,
which are conferred upon the corporation by the general
law.[3]

Single purpose. Except where special provision is made by
statute, a corporation can be organized for one main purpose

[2] Pelton v. Transportation Co.,
37 O. S. 450; Mercantile Trust Co.
v. Etna Iron Works, 4 C. C. 585.
[3] G. C., § 5371; Pelton v. Transportation Co., 37 O. S. 450; See
Sims v. Best, 1 C. C. n. s. 41; 15
C. D. 149; Hubbard v. Brush,
61 O. S. 252.

[4] Pelton v. Transportation Company, 37 O. S. 450.
[5] Pelton v. Transportation Company, 37 O. S. 450.
[6] G. C., §§ 8719, 8720.
[1] G. C., § 8623.
[2] 4 Opinions Attys. Gen. 470; 5
Opinions Attys. Gen. 969.
[3] Rep. Atty. Gen. (1909-10) 146.

only. Several different classes of business can not be united in one organization.[4]

But several purposes which are incident to the main purpose of a corporation may be combined. Thus, a corporation organized for the main purpose of operating a street railway by electricity may also furnish electric light and power.[5]

To carry out the main purpose several means may be joined. A corporation organized to furnish light may, in its articles of incorporation, provide for furnishing both gas and electricity for such purpose.[6]

The secretary of state has refused to file and record articles of incorporation in which it was attempted to join several purposes which were unrelated to the main purpose.

§ 21. The capital stock. The amount of the authorized capital stock must be stated in the articles, together with the number of shares.

If preferred stock is to be issued, all preferences and restrictions appertaining thereto should be specified in the articles.[1]

Considerations relating to the amount and form of the capital stock have been discussed elsewhere.[2]

Par value of shares. It is usual to fix the par value of shares at $100 each. Where stock is to be placed in small amounts among numerous holders it is sometimes deemed good policy to make the par value of each share $50 or $10. Shares in mining companies are often given a par value of $1 each.

§ 22. Articles of incorporation. Filing and recording. Articles of incorporation are sent direct to the secretary of state, together with the proper fee. If the instrument is in proper form, and shows compliance with the law, it is the duty of the secretary of state to officially accept, file and record the same. In case of wrongful refusal, mandamus will lie to compel its filing and recording.[1]

But where the instrument is defective in form, or where the corporate purpose is illegal, or unauthorized,[2] or is not clearly stated,[3] or where it is attempted to unite several different classes of business,[4] or the name of the corporation is misleading, or infringes the name of another corporation,[5]

[4] State ex rel. v. Taylor, 55 O. S. 67-68. For discussion of the "single purpose" doctrine, see 3 O. L. R. 187, paper by T. H. Hogsett; 3 O. L. R. 205, paper by C. T. Lewis.
[5] State v. Taylor, 55 O. S. 65; G. C. §§ 9134 to 9136.
[6] Pickard v. Hughey, 58 O. S. 577.

[1] G. C. §§ 8668, 8669.
[2] See *Capitalization* and *Amount of Capitalization*, above.
[1] State v. Taylor, 55 O. S. 61.
[2] State v. Laylin, 73 O. S. 90.
[3] 4 Opinions Attys. Gen. 470.
[4] State v. Taylor, 55 O. S. 61.
[5] G. C. § 8628.

or the law is not complied with in other respects, it is the duty of the secretary of state to refuse to file and record the same.[6]

Correction of defective articles. Where articles of incorporation are refused acceptance and record, the secretary of state returns the same to the incorporators with an explanation of the defects. In such case, it is not proper practice to attempt to alter the original instrument or to correct it by interlineation. A new instrument should be prepared, signed and acknowledged by the incorporators.[7]

Effect of filing. The filing and recording of articles of incorporation do not create the corporation; they are merely authority to the incorporators to do so. The corporate existence does not commence until the requisite stock has been subscribed and paid and the directors chosen.[8]

Certified copy of articles. A certified copy of articles of incorporation, which have been filed and recorded, is furnished by the secretary of state to the incorporators. Such copy is by statute made "prima facie evidence of the existence of the corporation."[9]

In appropriation proceedings in addition to such certified copy it is necessary for the corporation to prove the legal and proper organization including the subscription and payment of the requisite stock and the legal election of directors. This would be the safe course to pursue in any case where it is necessary to prove the legal existence of a corporation.[10]

§ 23. Articles of incorporation. Amendments. Articles of incorporation may be amended in the following respects:

(1) The corporate name may be changed.

(2) The location of the corporation may be changed.

(3) The corporate purposes may be modified, enlarged or diminished.

(4) There may be added matters omitted from the articles, or which might lawfully have been provided for in the original articles.

Limitations. A corporation can not, by amendment, change substantially the original purposes of its organization, nor can the capital stock, by amendment, be increased or diminished.

The restrictions upon the selection of the original corporate name apply also to a change of name.[1]

Procedure. Amendments to articles of incorporation may be

[6] Trust Co. v. Ford, 75 O. S. 335.
[7] 2 Opinions Attys. Gen. 243.
[8] State v. Insurance Co., 49 O. S. 440.
[9] G. C. § 8629.
[10] Telephone Co. v. Cincinnati, 73 O. S. 64.
[1] G. C. § 8719.

made only at a meeting of the stockholders, by a vote of the owners of at least three-fifths of its capital stock then subscribed. For the notices, or waivers of notices, required in connection with the stockholders' meeting, and for the certificate of amendment to be filed with the secretary of state, see *Forms*.

§ 24. **Record or minute book.** One book is usually sufficient to contain the record of the organization proceedings and also of the proceedings of the stockholders and directors.

A loose-leaf book is used to a considerable extent for this purpose, the advantage being that all records and minutes may be typewritten. Formerly loose-leaf books were subject to the objection that the records could be easily changed by the removal of pages and the substitution of others. At the present time loose-leaf books are made for this purpose, with the pages consecutively numbered and permanently marked, so that the risk of substitution is little if any greater than in the case of a bound book.

Many corporations, however, use a bound book, the minutes being written with pen, or typewritten on thin paper and pasted in the book. In the latter case, substitutions are possible. If, however, each page is attested by the signatures of the president and secretary, no substitution can be made without the aid of such officers.

For the purposes of a small corporation a book of 100 pages is adequate. Corporations whose directors hold frequent meetings keep separate books for stockholders and directors minutes.

Preparation of organization record in advance. In the case of small and close corporations where the directors, officers and organization details have been agreed upon in advance by the parties in interest, it is a not uncommon practice for attorneys in charge of the incorporation to prepare in advance the entire organization record including the minutes of the first stockholders' and directors' meetings and the certificates of stock. By this method the minutes as well as all waivers, certificates, subscriptions, consents, etc., are ready for signature, and the organization proceedings may be consummated and the record completed with a considerable saving of time. If the meetings are actually held and the formal procedure actually carried out the practice is believed to be valid.

Contents of record. Organization proceedings should be recorded in full so that the due and complete organization and legal existence of the corporation may be readily proved, should occasion require.

Upon receiving from the secretary of state the certified copy of the articles of incorporation, the record book should be opened. On the title page should be entered, "Record of proceedings of the Incorporators, Stockholders and Directors of The .... Company."

The following matters should be recorded in the order given:

Proceedings of incorporators.
(1) Copy of the articles of incorporation, with all certificates.
(2) Order for opening books of subscription, with notice or waiver.
(3) Order designating one incorporator to receive payment of first instalment on stock.
(4) Subscription agreement.
(5) Certificate of subscription.
(6) Order for first stockholders' meeting.
(7) Notice, or waiver of notice, of first meeting of stockholders.

Proceedings of stockholders.
(1) Minutes of first meeting of stockholders.
(2) Regulations.
(3) Assent to adoption of regulations.
(4) Certificate (by incorporators) of election of directors.

Proceedings of directors.
(1) Oath of directors.
(2) Minutes of first meeting of directors.
(3) By-laws.

Forms for the above entries are given in detail elsewhere in this work.[1]

All orders, subscriptions, certificates, waivers, etc., should be signed in the record book. This places the record of the entire organization proceedings in a compact and convenient form.

§ 25. Subscriptions to stock. a. *Opening books.* After a certified copy of the articles of incorporation is received from the secretary of state the first important duty of the incorporators relates to subscriptions to the capital stock.[1]

All of the incorporators need not act. A majority may open the subscription book and sign the certificate of subscription. But thirty days' previous notice of the opening

[1] See *Forms.*
[1] For formal proceedings of incorporators including order for, and waiver of notice of, opening of subscription books, notice of opening, subscription agreement, etc., see Forms.

of the subscription book must be published where only a majority act. Publication can not be waived unless all of the incorporators sign the waiver.[2]

Whether an incorporator may act by proxy has not been judicially determined in Ohio.

b. *By whom received.* Before the election of directors, subscriptions are received by the incorporators. The right to dispose of whatever stock remains unsubscribed after the directors are elected and qualified vests in the board of directors.[3]

The "blue sky" law should be considered before subscriptions are sought from the public.[4]

c. *Requisites.* A subscription for stock must be in writing. A verbal agreement to take shares is not enforceable, in the absence of facts constituting an estoppel.[5]

It is not essential to the validity of a subscription that it be made in the book provided for that purpose by the incorporators. A subscription is not invalid because made on a separate sheet of paper.[6]

The form of the subscription is not prescribed by statute. The subscription need not contain a statement of the times of payment, as this is provided for by the statute.[7]

d. *Ten percent payable with subscription.* An instalment of ten percent on each share is payable at the time the subscription is made. The incorporators are authorized to receive payment of this instalment.[8]

It is good practice for the incorporators to designate one of their number, by an order entered in the record of their proceedings, to receive payment.[9]

Payment is frequently made in the form of certified checks payable to the order of the corporation, which are turned over to the treasurer of the corporation upon his election.

e. *Payable in cash.* The incorporators have no authority to receive anything but money in payment of the first instalment.[10]

It is clear that ten percent of the original capital stock

---

[2] G. C. § 8631.
[3] Sims v. Street Railroad Co., 37 O. S. 565.
[4] See Sec. 14, *Disposal of stock and bonds.*
[5] Fanning v. Insurance Co., 37 O. S. 339; Hanes v. Dayton, etc., R. R. Co., 40 O. S. 98.
[6] Ashtabula, etc., R. R. Co. v. Smith, 15 O. S. 328.
[7] Chamberlain v. R. R. Co., 15

O. S. 225, 249; Ashtabula, etc., R. R. Co. v. Smith, 15 O. S. 328, 336.
[8] Sims v. Street Railroad Co. 37 O. S. 565.
[9] Cincinnati v. Queen City Telephone Co., 2 N. P. n. s. 349, 364; 15 L. D. 43 (affirmed 73 O. S. 64).
[10] Dayton, etc., R. Co. v. Hatch. 1 Disney 96; See Gates v. Tippecanoe Stone Co., 57 O. S. 74.

is required to be paid in cash. Where the capital stock is increased, however, it is doubtful whether ten percent of the new or increased stock need be paid in cash. A practice sometimes followed, where it is desired to take over property of considerable value and to pay in the least possible amount of cash, is to originally organize with a small capital stock, one-tenth of which is paid in cash. After organization the capital stock is increased and all the increased stock issued for property.[11]

f. *Effect of nonpayment.* A subscriber who has not paid the first instalment of ten percent may be excluded from voting at elections for directors.[12]

But failure to pay the first instalment does not release the subscriber from liability on his subscription.[13]

If the incorporators certify to the secretary of state that ten percent of the capital stock has been subscribed, when ten percent has not been paid, the incorporators may incur a personal liability.[14]

g. *Release or withdrawal.* The incorporators being authorized to receive subscriptions,[15] a subscription received by the incorporators after books have been opened is binding.[16]

Such subscriptions should be distinguished from subscriptions made before articles of incorporation have been filed, which have been held to be lacking in mutuality and not enforceable.[17]

A subscription received by the incorporators is a contract, which can not be dissolved without the consent of both parties. The subscriber can not relieve himself from liability by attempting to withdraw or cancel his subscription. The corporation can not release the subscriber to the prejudice of any intervening creditor.[18]

Directors have no power to release or cancel a subscription, except with the unanimous consent of the other subscribers.[19]

But the directors may compromise with and release a

---

[11] See *Increase of capital stock,* below.

[12] G. C. § 8636; Queen City Telephone Co. v. Cincinnati, 73 O. S. 77.

[13] Henry v. Vermillion, e·c., R. R. Co., 17 Ohio 187; See Chamberlain v. R. R. Co., 15 O. S. 225 (249); Ashtabula, etc., R. R. Co. v. Smith, 15 O. S. 328 (336).

[14] Hessler v. Cleveland Punch & Shear Works, 61 O. S. 621.

[15] Sims v. Street Railroad Co., 37 O. S. 565.

[16] Milford, etc., Turnpike Co. v. Brush, 10 Ohio 113, 114; Ashtabula, etc., R. R. Co. v. Smith, 15 O. S. 334, 336.

[17] Dayton, etc., Co. v. Coy, 13 O. S. 84 (91).

[18] Gaff v. Flesher, 33 O. S. 107; Royce & Pulling v. Tyler, 2 C. C. 175; 1 C. D. 428; Niles v. Olszak, 87 O. S. 229.

[19] Cook on Corporations, §§ 168, 169; See Warner v. Callender, 20 O. S. 198; Royce & Pulling v. Tyler, 2 C. C. 187; 1 C. D. 428.

subscriber where there is a controversy as to his liability, or where the subscriber is insolvent.[20]

Subscriptions obtained through fraud by promoters or representatives of a corporation may be rescinded, if the subscriber acts promptly upon discovery of the fraud.[21]

h. *Payment.* As already stated, ten percent on each share is payable to the incorporators when the subscription is made. The balance is payable as required by the directors,[22] who may require the entire amount to be paid immediately, or may levy assessments as money is needed for the purposes of the corporation. Directors have power to accept property in payment of such balance.

After the first instalment of ten percent has been paid, nothing is due on a subscription until a call has been made by the directors specifying the person to whom, and the time and place where the instalment is payable.[23]

A suit to collect an instalment can not be brought until sixty days after the time of payment designated in the call.[24]

Where subscriptions are paid by instalments it is customary to issue transferable receipts for payments, the receipts being exchanged for certificates of stock when all the instalments are paid.

§ 26. Certificate of subscription. Liability of incorporators.

As soon as ten percent of the capital stock has been subscribed and paid, it is the duty of the incorporators, or a majority of them, to so certify in writing to the secretary of state. A blank form of such certificate is furnished to the incorporators by the secretary of state.

Incorporators sometimes fail to appreciate the full significance of the certificate of subscription, as, in the form provided, no mention is made of payment. Incorporators are by statute made liable for the amount of any deficiency in the actual payment of ten percent on each share of stock subscribed for.[1]

In other words, by signing a certificate of subscription, incorporators become guarantors of the corporation to future creditors.

A number of interesting questions relating to the liability of incorporators under a certificate of subscription have not been adjudicated. It has not been determined whether there is any liability where the directors subsequently accept prop-.

[20] Cook on Corporations, § 171; Warner v. Callender, 20 O. S. 198.
[21] See Armstrong v. Karshner, 47 O. S. 294; Nugent v. R. R. Co., 2 Dis. 302; Jewett v. Railway, 34 O. S. 609.
[22] G. C. § 8632.
[23] G. C. § 8632; Railroad Co. v. Fink, 41 O. S. 329.
[24] G. C. § 8674.
[1] G. C. § 8634.

erty in payment of the entire subscription, no cash having been paid by the subscriber; or whether the liability can be enforced under any circumstances by subsequent stockholders.

It is settled, however, that this liability is a security for the creditors of the corporation, and may be enforced by creditors although they have no knowledge of the certificate.[2]

It is not difficult for incorporators to effectually guard against liability. They may, by order entered on the record of proceedings, designate one of their number to receive payment of the first instalment; and may refuse to accept any subscription unless the first instalment accompanies it.

It is probable that incorporators may refuse to call the first meeting of stockholders until the requisite sum is in the possession of the designated incorporator. If a first meeting is called, the incorporators have the right to act as inspectors or tellers of the first election of directors and may refuse to permit a subscriber to vote until he has paid the first instalment.[3]

All of the incorporators need not sign the certificate of subscription. A majority is sufficient.

Avoiding liability of incorporators under large capitalization. Where it is desired to issue a large part of the stock for property and to pay in the least possible cash for stock, a practice sometimes followed is to originally organize with a small capital stock, one-tenth of which is paid in cash. After organization the capital stock is increased to the desired amount. Incorporators have nothing to do with the increase, their duties and functions having ended with the organization and election of directors. All the increased stock is subsequently issued for property by the directors.[4]

§ 27. **First meeting of stockholders.** The first meeting of stockholders is called by the incorporators after ten percent of the capital stock has been subscribed.

This meeting should be held within the state.[1]

A notice of such meeting is required to be published thirty days before the time designated, but the notice may be, and in practice almost invariably is, waived in writing by all of the subscribers.[2]

[2] Hessler v. Cleveland Punch & Shear Works Co., 61 O. S. 621; Ames v. McGaughey, 88 O. S. ——.
[3] G. C. § 8636; Cincinnati v. Queen City Telephone Co., 2 N. P. n. s. 364; 15 L. D. 43 (affirmed 73 O. S. 64).

[4] See *Increase of Capital Stock,* below.
[1] See Myers v. Manhattan Bank, 20 Ohio 283; Cook on Corporations, § 589.
[2] G. C. § 8631.

For the routine of the first meeting of stockholders, see *Forms*.

The important business transacted at the first meeting consists of (1) the adoption of regulations, and (2) the election of directors.

§ 28. Regulations.

a. *Distinguished from by-laws.* Provisions are contained in the Ohio statutes for *regulations,* which are adopted by the stockholders for the government of the corporation and for *by-laws* which are adopted by the directors for the government of the directors.[1]

In many States the corporation laws provide for by-laws only, which are adopted by the stockholders and correspond to the regulations of an Ohio corporation.

A corporation is not required to adopt regulations, but a carefully prepared code of regulations is important, as it provides for many details which would otherwise, in all probability, be entirely omitted.

Regulations must be consistent with the constitution and laws of the state. Regulations are intended to supplement the general provisions of the statutes and to provide permanent rules relating to the administration of the affairs of a corporation, and also relating to organization, in matters of detail.

b. *Provisions in.* Certain matters are specified by statute,[2] as proper subjects to be provided for in the regulations. It seems that there is no authority to make regulations upon other subjects, although other regulations have been sustained as contracts.[3]

The number of directors is fixed by the stockholders, within the statutory limitation that the number shall not be less than five nor more than thirty. As a matter of convenience the determination of the number of directors is usually in the form of a provision in the regulations. Where the regulations provide that more than a majority vote is necessary for amendments thereto,[4] the provision relating to the number of directors should be omitted from the regulations, and a separate resolution should be passed fixing the number. By statute, the number of directors may be changed by a vote of *a majority* of the stock at a stockholders' meeting.[5] For customary provisions of regulations, see *Forms*.

c. *Directors and officers, regulations relating to.* Stock-

---

[1] State v. Burial Assn., 8 C. C. n. s. 248; 18 C. D. 397.
[2] G. C. § 8704.
[3] Nicholson v. Franklin Brewing Co., 82 O. S. 94, 110, 111.

[4] Wangerien v. Aspell, 47 O. S. 260.
[5] G. C. § 8665.

holders are authorized by statute to provide in the regulations for (a) "the duties and compensation of officers" and (b) "the manner of election, or appointment, and the tenure of office, of all officers other than the trustees or directors."[6]

This confers important rights upon the stockholders, viz., the right to control (1) the salaries, (2) and duties of officers, and (3) the election and term of subordinate officers.[7]

A complaint not infrequently made against the management of corporations, is that dividends are improperly diminished by the payment of extravagant salaries to the officers.[8]

The stockholders, through appropriate regulations, may remove the temptation to such abuse of power by the directors. It is sometimes provided in regulations that each director shall receive a certain sum (ranging from $1 to $20) for his attendance at any directors' meeting, and that he shall receive no other compensation as director.

The salaries of other officers may be specified in the regulations; or it may be provided that such salaries shall be fixed yearly in advance by the stockholders at the annual meeting. Or the regulations may merely place maximum limits on salaries, leaving the exact amount to be determined by the directors.

In the absence of regulations on the subject, the president, vice-president, secretary, treasurer and other subordinate officers are chosen by the board of directors. Stockholders may, in the regulations, reserve the right to elect all of such officers,[9] with the exception of the president.[10]

This right is infrequently exercised except in the case of the secretary. As these officers perform their duties under the supervision of the directors, it is generally deemed better policy to lodge the appointing power in the directors also.

d. *How adopted.* Regulations may be adopted, or amended, by the written assent of two-thirds of the stockholders, or by a majority of the stockholders at a meeting called for the purpose.[11]

§ 29. **Election of directors.** *Qualifications and term of office.* All directors must be the holders of stock in the corporation in an amount to be fixed by the by-laws, and a majority of the directors must be citizens of Ohio.[1]

[6] G. C. § 8704; Morris v. Griffith, 34 W. L. B. 191.
[7] Belting Co. v. Gibson, 68 O. S. 449; Morris v. Griffith, 34 W. L. B. 191.
[8] Dissette v. Publishing Co., 9 C.
C. n. s. 118; 19 C. D. 168; Cook on Corporations, § 657.
[9] G. C. § 8704.
[10] G. C. § 8664.
[11] G. C. § 8703.
[1] G. C. § 8661.

The voting at elections for directors must be by ballot. Directors elected at the first meeting of stockholders hold office until the next annual election, or until their successors are elected and qualified. Thereafter directors are elected for the term of one year.[2]

a. *The procedure* at elections is usually as follows: Nominations are called for by the presiding officer. When the nominations are closed, if there is a contest, tellers or inspectors of election are chosen, who take charge of the balloting.

If there is no contest, the secretary or some other officer may be instructed by motion to cast the ballot of all stockholders present for the persons nominated.

b. *Tellers or inspectors of election.* Stockholders are entitled to have the election conducted by tellers or inspectors of election. Where such officials are appointed, they, and not the president or chairman of the meeting, have the right to decide who may vote.

At the first election of directors the incorporators have a right to act as tellers or inspectors of election.[3]

At subsequent elections the right to choose the inspectors is vested in the stockholders, and not in the directors.[4]

Upon application by stockholders owning at least a one-tenth interest in the stock of a corporation, made prior to a stockholders' meeting, a court of common pleas may appoint three disinterested inspectors of election.[5]

c. *Who may vote.* In general, only persons who appear as stockholders on the books of the corporation are entitled to vote, in person or by proxy, at stockholders' meetings. The officers in charge of the election are governed by the stock books of the corporation. They can not take notice of the rights of third persons in the stock, nor can they refuse to permit a registered stockholder to vote.[6]

It is sometimes provided in the corporate regulations that only those persons may vote who appear on the books as stockholders for a certain period, usually ten days, prior to the meeting.[7]

Where stock is transferred during such period, it is cus-

---

[2] See Lutterby v. Herancourt Brewing Co., 12 N. P. Dec. 67. For term of office of directors of Building and Loan and certain Insurance Companies, see G. C. §§ 9646, 9515.
[3] G. C. § 8637; Queen City Telephone Co. v. Cincinnati, 2 N. P.

n. s. 364; 15 Low. D. 43 (affirmed 73 O. S. 64).
[4] State v. Merchant, 37 O. S. 251.
[5] G. C. §§ 8640 to 8645.
[6] Hafer v. Railway Co., 14 W. L. B. 68, 72 (1885); Franklin Bank v. Commercial Bank, 36 O. S. 355 (1881); See G. C. §§ 8642, 8643.
[7] See G. C. § 8642.

tomary for the transferrer to give a proxy enabling the transferee to vote at the meeting.

No person may vote on any stock on which an instalment is due and unpaid.[8]

Holders of preferred stock may vote unless by the terms of its issue the voting right is withheld.

d. *Proxies.* Where a stockholder, in writing, authorizes another person to vote his stock at one or more stockholders' meetings, the written authorization is called a "proxy." The term "proxy" is also applied to the person to whom the authority is given.

A proxy may be revoked at any time by the stockholder, although by its terms "irrevocable."[9]

A stockholder who attends the meeting is entitled to vote, although he has given a proxy.

e. *Cumulative voting.* A stockholder in an Ohio corporation has the right to cast his votes under the socalled cumulative system. He may vote "the number of shares owned by him for as many persons as there are directors to be elected, or . . . cumulate said shares and give one candidate as many votes as the number of directors multiplied by the number of his shares of stock equals, or . . . distribute them on the same principle among as many candidates as he thinks fit."[10]

Cumulative voting is authorized for the purpose of enabling minority stockholders to secure representation on the board of directors.

For each director to be elected a stockholder is entitled to one vote per share of stock registered in his name on the books of the corporation. Under the cumulative system a stockholder may cast all of his votes for one candidate, or he may divide them among a part, or all, of the candidates.

Where there are five directors, a person owning one share is entitled to five votes, all of which may be cast for one candidate. Or one vote may be cast for each of five candidates, or the votes may be divided among the candidates in any other other manner desired.

If 500 shares of stock have been issued and are represented at a stockholders' meeting at which five directors are to be elected, a minority which controls 85 shares is enabled, under the cumulative system, to elect one director. The 85 shares are entitled to 425 votes. The balance of 415 shares is entitled to 2,075 votes. If the 425 minority votes

[8] G. C. § 8636.   [10] G. C. § 8636.
[9] Griffith v. Jewett, 15 W. L. B. 419.

are cast solidly for one candidate, it is impossible for the majority to defeat him.

Under the cumulative system it is impossible for a minority to obtain control of the board of directors, if the majority act together and cumulate their votes. But if the majority scatter their votes, a strong minority of stockholders may be able to secure a majority of the board.[11]

§ 30. Regular meetings of stockholders. a. *When held.*

An annual meeting of stockholders is usually provided for in the regulations, which specify the time, place and manner of calling and conducting the meeting and for the number of stockholders necessary to constitute a quorum.

In the absence of a regulation on the subject, the annual meeting should be held on the first Monday in January of each year.[1]

Meetings of stockholders should be held within the State.

b. *Notice.* Where the time and place of the annual meeting are provided for in the regulations, notice of the meeting, or of the business to be transacted, is not required to be given unless the regulations provide for notice.[2]

Regulations sometimes require notice to be mailed to the stockholders, but stipulate that failure to give the notice shall not invalidate proceedings at the meeting.

In such case the secretary should observe the requirement. The notices should be signed by the secretary and a copy preserved, with the date of mailing.

If any business, other than the routine of the annual meeting, is to be considered at the meeting, it is prudent to mention it in the notice.

c. *Closing of stock records.* It is sometimes provided in the regulations that only those persons may vote who appear as stockholders on the stock books for a certain number of days before the meeting. Where the regulations contain such a provision it is customary to so state in the notice.

This provision is not, in effect, a closing of the transfer books. Transfers of stock may be made at any time, but the transferee can not vote as a stockholder unless the transferrer gives a proxy enabling the transferee to vote at the meeting.

d. *Presiding officer, etc.* The regulations usually provide that the president shall preside at meetings of the stockholders, and that the secretary shall keep a record of the proceedings of stockholders. In the absence of the president,

---

[11] See Schwartz v. State, 61 O. S. 497.

[1] G. C. § 8647.

[2] State v. Bonnell, 35 O. S. 10.

the vice-president should preside. In the absence of both president and vice-president, a chairman of the meeting should be chosen by the stockholders. In the absence of the secretary, a secretary pro tem should be chosen.

e. *Quorum.* A quorum at a stockholders' meeting is the number of shares of stock necessary to be represented by the holders, or proxies, in order that business may legally be transacted. This is usually provided for in the regulations, the customary requirement being a majority of the stock issued and outstanding.

If there is no regulation on the subject, the stockholders present in person or by proxy, at a duly called meeting, may transact the business of that meeting although a majority of the stock is not represented.[3]

Where a quorum is required by the regulations, it is important to determine at the outset of the meeting, whether a quorum is present. This may be ascertained by a roll call, or by requesting the stockholders and holders of proxies to report to the secretary.

Proxies should be filed with the secretary.

If a quorum is present, that fact should be noted on the minutes.

If a quorum is not present, the meeting may be adjourned to a specified time when, if a quorum is secured, the meeting may proceed.

f. *Procedure at meetings.* Stockholders' meetings are usually conducted according to the rules of parliamentary law. It is sometimes provided in the regulations that meetings shall be conducted according to Robert's Rules of Order or some other handbook on parliamentary law.

g. *The order of business* at stockholders' meetings is usually prescribed in the regulations as follows:

(1). *Reading of minutes.* The minutes of the preceding annual meeting, and of all special meetings of the stockholders held subsequent thereto, should be read by the secretary.

This is not always an unimportant part of the meeting. As minutes are proper evidence of the proceedings,[4] all incomplete or ambiguous statements, or errors, should be corrected before the minutes are approved. The record, or form of statement of the previous proceedings, is approved by an approval of minutes at a subsequent meeting.[5]

(2). *Reading of reports and statements.* Reports are frequently made by the president, treasurer, and sometimes by

[3] See Lutterby v. Herancourt Brewing Co., 12 L. D. 67, 72, 73.
[4] See Cook on Corporations, § 714.
[5] Bank v. Iron Co. 30 W. L. B. 382.

other officers. After being read, the reports may, on motion, be ordered received and placed on file. Some reports may properly be referred to special committees or to the incoming board of directors for attention.

(3). *Unfinished business.* This includes matters which may have been considered at previous meetings, but not disposed of and also matters which have been referred to committees for attention.

(4). *The election of directors* has been discussed elsewhere in this chapter.

(5). *New or miscellaneous business.*

(6). *Adjournment.* The meeting may on motion be adjourned *sine die,* or to a definite time. An adjourned meeting is merely a continuation of the original meeting and notice of the adjourned meeting need not be given to the stockholders.[6] For authentication of the minutes by the officers, see *Forms.*

§ 31. Special meetings of the stockholders. Unless waived by all stockholders of the corporation, two preliminaries are required for a special meeting of stockholders. (1) The meeting must be ordered or called by competent authority, and (2) Notice, specifying the time, place and object of the meeting must be given to all stockholders.

It is frequently provided in the regulations (1) that special meetings may be called by the board of directors or by a certain number of stockholders, and (2) that notice of the meeting may be given to the stockholders by mail.

No business can be legally transacted at a special meeting except that which is specified in the call and notice of the meeting.

Where a special meeting is held by consent of all the stockholders these rules do not apply. As a precautionary measure in such cases a waiver should be signed by all stockholders.[1]

There are numerous statutory provisions for stockholders' meetings to take action on special matters. The provisions of the statute relating to the call for and notice of the meeting should be carefully followed in each case. Among the subjects specially provided for are the following: election of directors where, for any cause, directors have not been elected at the regular meeting; change in the number of directors; amendment of the articles of incorporation; amendment of the regulations; increase of capital stock; sale of entire assets of the corporation, and dissolution of the corporation.

[6] State v. Bonnell, 35 O. S. 10.   [1] See *Forms.*

§ 32. Minutes. The minutes of stockholders' meetings do not differ materially from the minutes of directors' meetings, except that the names of the directors present at the meeting are entered in the minutes, which is not the usual practice in making up the minutes of stockholders' meetings.

Matters are properly brought before a meeting in the form of motions or resolutions. Important matters are usually presented in the form of written resolutions. Other matters are brought up by motion, usually presented orally.

During a meeting the secretary, as a rule, takes notes of the proceedings and subsequently from his notes writes out the minutes in full. It is advisable to make up the full minutes within a short time after the meeting, before the circumstances are forgotten.

All motions and resolutions passed upon should be recorded in the minutes with the action taken thereon, whether favorable or adverse. It is not customary to mention the names of the persons by whom motions are made; but the names of the persons by whom important resolutions are offered are usually entered.

As motions are made verbally, care should be taken by the secretary to enter accurately the substance of every motion. When the secretary is in doubt as to the meaning of a motion, the person making it may be requested to repeat his motion, or to place it in writing.

The discussions over motions and resolutions are usually not entered, although the names of persons taking part in the debate are sometimes mentioned.

Reports, contracts and other instruments are frequently presented and acted upon at corporate meetings. Where the matter is important the document should be copied into the minutes. In other cases it is sufficient to describe the instrument so as to identify it, and to file the original.

For specimens and forms of minutes see *Forms*.

§ 33. Directors. a. *Qualifications.* A majority of the directors must be citizens of Ohio, and all directors must be holders of stock in the amount fixed by the by-laws.[1]

A person not a stockholder may be elected a director and may, after election, qualify himself by acquiring stock.[2]

Where a director ceases to own stock, but continues to act as a director, he may be recognized as a *de facto* director and his acts as to third persons held valid.[3]

It has been held that a person does not become properly

[1] G. C. § 8661.
[2] Greenough v. Railroad Co., 64 Fed. Rep. 22.
[3] Campbell Printing Press Co. v. Belman Bros. Co., 11 C. C. 360; 5 C. D. 389.

qualified where a share of stock is transferred to him merely for the purpose of qualifying him as a director; he having no real interest in the stock.[4]

An oath, faithfully to discharge his duties as director, is required to be taken by each director before entering upon his duties.[5]

b. *Number.* The number of directors of a corporation is fixed by the holders of a majority of its stock, within the statutory limitation that the number must be not less than five nor more than thirty.[6]

Within the same limitations, the number of directors may be changed at a regular or special meeting of the stockholders. When majority stockholders become dissatisfied they may bring about a change in the policy of management by increasing the number of directors at a special meeting of stockholders.[7]

A director can not be ousted from his office by a decrease in the number of directors. In other words, a decrease in the number of directors can not become effective until the expiration of the terms of the directors then serving.

In practice the minimum number is usually the most satisfactory for small corporations. Where the stock of a corporation is equally divided between two separate interests, the number of directors is sometimes fixed at six, or some other even number, so that each interest may have an equal representation on the board.

In the case of large corporations, especially consolidated companies, a large directorate is not infrequently chosen in order that several interests may be represented on the board.

Where the number of directors is large, the work of the board is performed, to a considerable extent, through committees.

c. *Term.* The term of directors chosen at the first election continues until the time fixed for the annual election.[8]

Thereafter directors are elected for one year.[9]

But, if no election is held at the time fixed for the annual meeting, or if an attempted election is invalid, the directors previously elected hold over and continue in office until their successors are properly elected and qualified.[10]

---

[4] Bartholomew v. Bentley, 1 O. S. 37.
[5] G. C. § 8663.
[6] G. C. § 8635.
[7] G. C. § 8665; Gold Bluff, etc., Co. v. Whitlock, 75 Conn. 669; In re Griffing Iron Co., 63 N. J. L. 168, 357.
[8] G. C. § 8635.
[9] Lutterby v. Herancourt Brewing Co., 12 N. P. Dec. 67. The terms of directors of Building and Loan, certain Insurance and other Companies, may in the regulations or by-laws, be fixed at from one to three years. G. C. §§ 9646, 9515.
[10] State v. Bonnell, 35 O. S. 10, 17; State v. Smalley, 7 C. C. 400; 4 C. D. 653.

d. *Vacancies* on the board of directors caused by death, resignation, disqualification, etc., may be filled by the remaining directors, unless the by-laws otherwise provide.[11]

e. *Meetings.*[12] Individual directors, as such, have no authority to represent the corporation. To bind the corporation the directors must act together as a board.[13]

Regular meetings of the board are usually provided for in the by-laws, usually being held monthly or quarterly. No notice of regular meetings need be given to the directors unless notice is required by the regulations or by-laws.[14]

Notice of *special meetings* should in general be given all directors. But transactions at special meetings within the powers of the board of directors have been upheld, where a quorum was present, although a minority of the board were not personally notified of the meeting and were absent, but no objection was subsequently made by the absent members.[15]

Notice of a special meeting may be waived by all directors.

Where all the directors attend a meeting, failure to give notice does not invalidate the proceedings of the meeting, although notice is required by the by-laws.

f. *Quorum.* A majority of the entire board of directors constitutes a quorum.[16]

Directors must be present in person. A director can not act by proxy.[17]

Where a quorum is assembled, a majority of those present may bind the board and the corporation, although they constitute a minority of the entire board.[18]

The acts of directors at a meeting at which a quorum is not present are voidable, but may be ratified by the acquiescence of the full board.[19]

g. *Minutes.* The minutes of directors' meetings do not differ materially from the minutes of the meetings of stockholders.

Where important business is transacted at a meeting, a practice sometimes followed is to insert below the minutes an approval thereof signed by all the directors.

[11] G. C. § 8662.

[12] For proceedings at the first meeting of directors and for specimen minutes of other directors meetings including notices, waivers, etc., see *Forms.*

[13] McCortle v. Bates, 29 O. S. 422; State v. Peoples, etc., Assn., 42 O. S. 583; State v. O. & M. Ry., 6 C. C. 412; 3 C. D. 516; 49 O. S. 668; Schott, etc., Co. v. Security, etc., Ins. Co., 7 N. P. n. s. 548; 19 L. D. 249, affirmed 11 C. C. n. s. 401; 20 C. D. 656; 83 O. S. 507.

[14] State v. Bonnell, 35 O. S. 15.

[15] Bank v. Flour Co., 41 O. S. 552, 559.

[16] See G. C. § 8664.

[17] Bank v. Iron Co., 30 W. L. B. 382.

[18] See Kalb v. American Nat'l Bank, 21 C. C. 1, 7, 8; 11 C. D. 437.

[19] See Rolling Stock Co. v. Railroad, 34 O. S. 450.

h. *Compensation.* If the compensation of directors is provided for in the regulations of the corporation, directors are not entitled to additional compensation without the consent of the stockholders. Where no provision for compensation is made in the regulations, directors are probably entitled to reasonable compensation for their time and reimbursement for the expense incurred in attending meetings.[20]

A director, who is also elected or appointed an executive officer of the corporation is entitled to reasonable compensation for his services *as such officer* although no agreement was made in advance regarding compensation, where the circumstances show that the intention of both parties was that he should be paid.[21]

Where directors have accepted compensation for a period of service they can not subsequently vote themselves "back pay" for the same period.[22]

i. *Resignation.* A director has the right to resign at any time.[23] His resignation may be oral or in writing.

It is doubtful whether all the directors can resign at one time leaving the corporation helpless.

Where no directors are elected within a reasonable time after the expiration of the terms of those duly elected, and the corporation discontinues business, it is presumed that the offices have been abandoned.[24]

j. *Powers.* The corporate powers, business and property of corporations are exercised, conducted and controlled by the board of directors.

Within the limitations of the articles of incorporation, and the regulations of the corporation, the board of directors is supreme in the management of its affairs.[25]

By express statutory provision, certain acts of unusual importance, such as a sale of the entire assets and property of the corporation, and the issuance of convertible bonds, are required to be ratified by stockholders.

It has already been stated that directors must act together as a board. One director as such has no authority to represent the corporation. The business transactions of the corporation are carried out through the executive officers or other agents; but the authority of such officers and agents must be traced to the board of directors in all cases, except

[20] State v. Peoples, etc., Assn., 42 O. S. 579, 583; See Cook on Corporations, § 657.

[21] Dalton v. Brush Electric Light Co., 13 C. C. 505; 7 C. D. 141.

[22] State v Peoples, etc., Assn., 42 O. S. 579.

[23] Briggs v. Spaulding, 141 U. S. 132, 154.

[24] Bartholomew v. Bentley, 1 O. S. 37, 42.

[25] Bradford Belting Co. v. Gibson, 68 O. S. 442.

where the officers' authority has been defined by the stockholders in the regulations.[26]

The executive officers and other agents are chosen by the board of directors, unless by the regulations the stockholders have reserved the right to select them. Directors are eligible to become executive officers.[27]

k. *Directors' contracts with corporation.* Although a contract made by a corporation with a director, who participated in the directors' meeting at which the contract was authorized, is not wholly void,[28] yet it may be avoided by the corporation upon a showing of its unfairness. It is the duty of a director to act in entire good faith, and to have no personal interest adverse to the corporation.

In all cases of directors' contracts with the corporation, including the fixing of the salary of a director as an executive officer, the interested director should not participate in the vote, and the minutes should so indicate. In fact the better practice is for him to remain away from the meeting, or at least to withdraw from the room while his contract is being discussed and voted upon.

l. *By-laws.* Directors may adopt by-laws for their government, consistent with the laws of the State and the regulations adopted by the stockholders.[29]

m. *Power to issue stock for property.* A corporation may exchange its stock for property.[30]

This power is undoubtedly vested in the board of directors, as the board controls the business and property of the corporation,[31] is authorized to dispose of its unissued stock,[32] and controls the payment of the original subscriptions to its stock, except as to the first instalment of ten percent.[33]

It may be stated generally that the board of directors of a corporation has power (a) to accept property in payment for the original stock subscriptions (except the ten percent payable in cash), (b) to exchange for property any stock which remains unissued after organization, and (c) upon an increase of the capital stock to exchange for property that part of the increased stock which is not subscribed for by existing stockholders. Directors may accept property in payment of such subscriptions by existing stockholders.

The general rules of law governing such transactions re-

[26] Bradford Belting Co. v. Gibson, 68 O. S. 442.
[27] Dalton v. Brush Electric Light Co., 13 C. C. 505; 7 C. D. 141.
[28] Rolling Stock Co. v. Railroad, 34 O. S. 450.
[29] G. C. § 8702.
[30] See Gates v. Tippecanoe Stone Co., 57 O. S. 75; Orton v. Edson, etc., Co., 5 C. C. n. s. 540; 17 C. D. 107 (affirmed 75 O. S. 580).
[31] G. C. § 8660.
[32] Sims v. Street Railway Co., 37 O. S. 565.
[33] G. C. § 8632.

quire (1) that the property be taken at a fair valuation; (2) that the directors have no personal interest in the property or transaction; (3) that the directors act in good faith, and (4) that the property be such as may be purchased by the corporation in the prosecution of its business.

The practice of issuing stock for overvalued property is frequent. Stock thus issued is termed "watered stock." As to the consequences of violating the rule that property must be taken at a fair valuation, the law is not well settled. If it can be proved that the property was fraudulently overvalued, the persons to whom the stock was issued may be held personally liable to subsequent creditors for the difference between the actual value of the property and the par value of the stock.[34]

The corporation itself can not recover this amount from the stockholders, but may, if not estopped, set aside the transaction and recover the stock itself, upon returning the property.[35]

Where no fraud is proved in the issuance of stock for property, there is some conflict of authority in the various jurisdictions. In many jurisdictions it is held that a valuation placed upon property by the directors is conclusive in the absence of fraud. The "good faith" rule has received the approval of one circuit court in Ohio.[36]

That property has been fraudulently overvalued is sometimes difficult of proof, especially in cases where the property received by the corporation includes good will, patents, etc.

In cases where it is possible to prove the actual value of the property, fraud may sometimes be implied. "A gross and obvious overvaluation of property would be strong evidence of fraud."[37]

Where corporations are organized to "take over" a "property" or business, a common procedure is to have the company incorporated by "dummy incorporators," sometimes clerks in the employ of the real parties in interest, or clerks in the office of the attorneys employed to attend the incorporation. The "dummy incorporators" subscribe for the minimum amount of stock necessary, pay the amount required to be paid in cash with certified checks or drafts furnished by the real parties and made payable to the order of the corporation. The incorporators are then elected direc-

[34] Gates v. Tippecanoe Stone Co., 57 O. S. 60.
[35] See Orton v. Edson, etc., Co., 5 C. C. n. s. 540; 17 C. D. 107 (affirmed no rep. 75 O. S. 580).
[36] Kunz v. National Valve Co., 9 C. C. n. s. 607; 19 C. D. 519 (1907).
[37] Coit v. North Carolina, etc., Co., 119 U. S. 313.

tors, hold a directors' meeting, elect officers and adopt a resolution accepting a written proposition, made by the real parties in interest, to exchange property for stock. The "dummy directors" and officers then resign their positions. one by one, and the vacancies are filled by the election of the real parties in interest.

When it is desired to pay in the least possible cash for the stock the corporation is sometimes organized with a small capital stock, ten percent of which is paid by certified check as already described. After organization the capital stock is increased, the original stockholders waive their right to subscribe for the new stock, and all the new or increased stock is issued for the property.

Where any part of an issue of stock is issued for patents, services, good will or property not located in Ohio, the issue can, as a rule, be disposed of only through a licensed dealer. on a special certificate obtained from the commissioner as to the issue.[38]

n. *Liability.* Directors may become personally liable: by incurring debts before ten percent of the capital stock has been paid in;[39] by issuing false statements concerning the financial condition of the corporation; by engaging in a business not authorized by the articles of incorporation, and wholly foreign thereto; by gross negligence whereby assets of the corporation are lost, by fraudulently dealing with the property of the corporation, and for false statements in a prospectus or advertisement of the stock or bonds of the corporation.[40]

By statute directors are also made personally liable for declaring dividends otherwise than out of surplus profits determined as directed by the statute; for advertising a greater dividend than has been actually earned and paid; and for advertising a larger amount of capital stock than has actually been subscribed and paid in.[41]

The trustees of a corporation not for profit are liable for all corporate debts by them contracted.[42]

As business men are often unwilling to assume such liability, clubs and other organizations are frequently incorporated as corporations for profit, although their purposes are really not for profit.

§ 34. Committees of the board. Executive committee.

An executive committee is provided for in the regulations of

---

[38] See § 14 *Disposal of stocks and bonds.* G. C. §§ 6373-2, 6373-14.
[39] Trust Co. v. Floyd, 47 O. S. 525.
[40] See notes to G. C. § 8660.
[41] G. C. § 8728.
[42] G. C. § 8666.

many corporations. In larger corporations a finance committee is not uncommon. A loan or discount committee is usually appointed by the directors of banks.[1]

These are permanent or standing committees of directors appointed to exercise certain powers of the board of directors during intervals between meetings of the board. The object of such committees is to render unnecessary frequent meetings of the board and to provide authority in cases where action must be taken quickly. Standing committees are more frequent in large corporations having numerous directors than in the case of small corporations. A small committee is more easily convened than a large board and its decisions are more promptly and definitely reached.

The membership of a standing committee is determined by the regulation by which it is authorized. In many cases the president, treasurer and sometimes one other officer, *ex officio*, constitute the executive committee. The treasurer is usually *ex officio* a member of the finance committee. In other cases the members of the committee are chosen by the board. All members of standing committees must be directors.

Powers. The supervision and control of transactions in the usual course of business may undoubtedly be delegated to an executive committee.[2]

Whether the discretionary powers conferred upon directors by statute[3] may be delegated to a committee has not been decided in Ohio. In other jurisdictions there is some conflict of authority upon the subject. It is said that, by the weight of authority, such powers may be delegated to an executive committee composed of directors, and that its acts and contracts are binding on the corporation.[4]

Where the acts of an executive committee are subsequently approved by the board of directors, no question can arise as to the powers of the committee. The question may arise, however, where the acts are not brought to the attention of the board, or, being brought to its attention, are repudiated.

In view of the unsettled condition of the law regarding the powers of an executive committee, it is advisable to clearly define in the regulations the duties and powers of the executive committee and to limit its functions so far as possible to transactions arising in the usual course of business.[5]

---

[1] See G. C. §§ 9728, 9729.
[2] Bank v. Iron Co., 30 W. L. B. 382; Cincinnati v. Cameron, 33 O. S. 336, 364.
[3] G. C. § 8660, 8704.
[4] Cook on Corporations, § 715; Thompson on Corporations (2 ed.) § 1207; Lutterby v. Herancourt Brewing Co., 12 L. D. 74.
[5] See Bank v. Iron Co., 30 W. L. B. 382; Morris v. Griffith, 34 W. L. B. 191.

Where no executive committee is provided for in the regulations the board of directors may appoint such a committee, at least with limited powers, through a by-law provision or a resolution.

A standing committee should transact its business at meetings of which all members should have notice.[6] A record of its proceedings and acts should be kept and frequent reports thereof made to the board for approval.

A standing committee is sometimes used as a device for the purpose of excluding minority directors from participation in the active management. An executive committee authorized to exercise "all the powers of the board" during intervals between meetings may (in jurisdictions where such powers may legally be delegated to the committee) become in effect the real managing body of the corporation.

This may be guarded against by inserting, in the regulation by which the committee is authorized, a provision requiring the members of the committees to be elected by the unanimous vote of the board of directors.

§ 35. Executive officers. a. *Who are.* A director is an "officer,"[1] but not an "executive officer."[2]

The executive officers are the president, secretary and treasurer,[3] and probably also the chairman of the board, vice-president, managing director, etc., where such officers are provided for in the corporate regulations.[4]

b. *Qualifications.* The president must be a director.[5] The other executive officers are not required to be members of the board of directors, but all executive officers must be holders of stock in an amount fixed by the by-laws.[6]

In practice the vice-president and treasurer are usually chosen from among the members of the board. The secretary is in many cases not a director. In small corporations two offices are frequently held by the same person.

c. *By whom elected or appointed.* The executive officers are chosen by the board of directors except where, in the regulations, the stockholders have otherwise provided for their selection. The stockholders may, in the regulations, reserve the right to elect all of the officers,[7] with the exception of the president.[8]

[6] Hayes v. Canada, etc., Co., 181 Fed. Rep. 289.
[1] Railway Co. v. McCoy, 42 O. S. 253; G. C. § 8704.
[2] See G. C. § 8661; State ex rel. v. Peoples, etc., Assn., 42 O. S. 583; Schott, etc., Co. v. Insurance Co., 7 N. P. n. s. 548; 19 L. D. 249 affirmed in 11 C. C. n. s. 401; 20 C. D. 656: 83 O. S. 507.
[3] G. C. § 8664.
[4] G. C. § 8704.
[5] G. C. § 8664.
[6] G. C. § 8661; See Bonnell v. Brown, 11 C. C. n. s. 58.
[7] G. C. § 8704.
[8] G. C. § 8664.

d. *Powers and duties.* The powers of executive officers are derived from (1) statute, (2) the regulations adopted by the stockholders, and (3) the board of directors.[9]

By statute, the president and secretary are authorized and required to execute stock certificates[10] and certain certificates and reports to the state.

The regulations may, and usually do, contain provisions defining the duties of officers. All other powers of the executive officers are derived from the board of directors. The active business of a corporation is managed and controlled by the board of directors. Corporate contracts are usually negotiated and executed by the executive officers, but the authority of the officers to do so should, in some manner, be traced to the board of directors.[11]

The executive officers are agents merely. Authority is conferred upon them in the same manner in which the authority of agents is bestowed in other cases. It may be given by the directors expressly in the form of by-laws, or by motion or resolution; or the authority may be given informally, by consent or acquiescence of the board. Unauthorized acts of officers may be ratified by the board of directors.[12]

In general, the burden of proof of an officer's authority rests on the party who affirms it.[13]

But in some cases the authority may be presumed. Written contracts and other instruments are usually executed in the name of the corporation by one or more of the executive officers. It is usually provided in corporate regulations that "the president shall sign all contracts, notes, and other papers executed by this company." In the absence of such a regulation instruments are generally executed by the president, with the consent or acquiescence of the directors. It has been held that an instrument or contract, executed in proper form by the president and delivered, with the corporate seal affixed, is presumed to have been authorized by the directors, and that the burden of proof rests on the party denying such authority.[14]

This presumption is applied only to matters within the

[9] See Morris v. Griffith, 34 W. L. B. 191.

[10] G. C. § 8672.

[11] Belting Co. v. Gibson, 68 O. S. 442; Minor v. Board of Control, 20 C. C. 4; 11 C. D. 16.

[12] Smead Foundry Co. v. Chesbrough, 18 C. C. 783: 6 C. D. 670; East Cleveland R. R. Co. v. Everett, 19 C. C. 205: 10 C. D. 493; Armstrong v. Chemical, N. B., 83 Fed. Rep. 556; Sun, etc., Assn. v. Moore, 183 U. S. 642.

[13] Belting Co. v. Gibson, 68 O. S. 442.

[14] Bank v. Flour Co., 41 O. S. 557; C. H. & D. R. Co. v. Harter, 26 O. S. 426; Dexter Sav. Bank v. Friend, 90 Fed. Rep. 703.

usual authority of the president. There is no presumption
that the president is authorized to convey the entire property of a corporation,[15] to make an assignment for creditors;[16] to execute a cognovit note,[17] to sell a bond issue of
the corporation, and to employ a broker for that purpose,[18]
or to make promissory notes payable to himself.[19]

A certificate of stock issued to the president or secretary
personally is valid in the hands of a bona fide holder, although issued fraudulently, the president and secretary being
authorized by statute to execute such certificates.[20]

e. *Compensation.* The stockholders, by appropriate provisions in the regulations, have the right to fix or limit the
salaries of officers, or to provide that such salaries shall be
fixed by the stockholders from time to time. In the absence
of such a regulation the salaries may be fixed by the directors.

An executive officer is entitled to reasonable compensation for his services although no agreement was made in advance for compensation, where the circumstances show that
it was the intention of all the parties that he should be
paid.[21]

In practice certain officers serve without the expectation
of compensation.[22]

In view of the foregoing, it is advisable to insert provisions regarding salaries in the regulations or by-laws, fixing in advance the salaries which are to be paid, and, where
certain officers are to serve without salary, specifically stating that such officers shall receive no compensation.

f. *Resignation or removal.* An officer may usually resign
at any time, unless he has entered into a contract with the
corporation to serve for a certain time, in which case he may
be liable for damages in the event of resignation. Where an
officer has been appointed or elected for a certain term, and
has accepted the appointment, a contract for that term is
consummated. The officer can not be removed without liability for damages, unless the right of removal is reserved
in the regulations or by-laws; or unless the removal is for
cause,[23] such as embezzlement or breach of trust.

[15] DeLaVergne, etc., Co. v. German Sgs. Inst., 175 U. S. 40.
[16] Commercial N. B. v. Cincinnati N. B., 3 C. C. 513 (517) 2 C. D. 295.
[17] Smead Foundry Co. v. Chesbrough, 18 C. C. 783: 6 C. D. 673.
[18] East Cleveland R. R. Co. v. Everett, 19 C. C. 205: 10 C. D. 493.
[19] In re Continental Iron Co., 2 O. L. R. 563; Arnkens v. Rouse, 26 W. L. B. 221.
[20] Railway Co. v. Bank, 56 O. S. 351.
[21] Dalton v. Brush, etc., Co., 13 C. C. 505: 7 C. D. 141.
[22] See Fitzgerald, etc., Co. v. Fitzgerald, 137 U. S. 98 (111).
[23] See State v. Bryce, 7 Ohio pt. 2, 82.

g. Liability. Officers are not personally liable on corporate contracts within their authority, and within the powers of the corporation. But when they exceed their authority, officers may be held personally liable.[24]

Officers should make all contracts in the name of the corporation.[25]

Where an officer make a contract or signs promissory notes, in his own name, he may be held personally liable thereon, although he has no personal interest in the transaction and did not intend to bind himself. Where he signs "John Doe, Treasurer," he is still personally liable. To relieve himself from liability the signature should be "The A. B. Company, by John Doe, Treasurer."[26]

An officer may be personally liable for negligence or misconduct in the discharge of his duties. He may also be held personally liable for fraudulent or reckless and careless misrepresentations as to the financial condition of the corporation which are relied on by other persons to their injury.[27]

h. President. The president must be chosen from the members of the board of directors. He has, by virtue of his office, only such powers as are given him by statute, viz., to sign stock certificates and to make certain reports and certificates to the state. All other powers of the president are derived from the regulations or from the directors.

His duties as usually defined in the regulations are to preside at meetings of the stockholders and directors, to sign all bonds, contracts, notes, etc., of the corporation, and to perform other duties assigned to him by the directors.

As to the authorization by directors of the acts of the president see *"Powers"* above.

i. Chairman of the board. This office is sometimes created by the regulations of large corporations. The duties of the incumbent are usually limited to presiding at the meetings of the directors.

j. The vice-president performs the duties of the president in the absence or disability of the latter. In large corporations several vice-presidents are provided for, termed first vice-president, second vice-president, etc., and in some cases active executive duties are prescribed for the incumbents.

k. The secretary keeps the records of the meetings of the stockholders and directors, has charge of the corporate seal and the stock books, and together with the president exe-

[24] Medill v. Collier, 16 O. S. 610.
[25] Norris v. Dains, 52 O. S. 215.
[26] Aungst v. Creque, 72 O. S. 551; Titus v. Kyle, 10 O. S. 444; Eells v. Shea, 20 C. C. 527: 11 C. D. 304 (affirmed 66 O. S. 683).
[27] Cable v. Bowlus, 21 C. C. 53 11 C. D. 563 (affirmed 69 O. S. 563).

cutes certificates of stock,[28] and certain reports and certificates to the state.

As in the case of other executive officers the secretary has only such powers as are given him by statute, regulations, or the board of directors.[29]

He has no implied authority to bind the corporation by statements to the effect that the corporation had refused to perform a contract,[30] nor has he implied authority to sign a petition for a street improvement, making the property of the corporation liable for an assessment.[31]

The secretary must obey the orders of a court of competent jurisdiction respecting the books of the corporation in his possession, and may be held for contempt of court for wilful disregard of such orders. It is no defense that he is acting under the orders of the directors.[32]

l. *Treasurer.* The customary duties of the treasurer include the receipt and custody of all moneys and securities of the corporation, and the supervision of its accounts and financial affairs.

Usually the by-laws require all moneys received to be promptly deposited in some specified bank. All bank accounts should be kept in the name of the corporation. If a deposit of corporate money is made under the name of the treasurer, any loss by reason of the failure of the bank may fall upon the treasurer personally.

The treasurer is usually required to give bond in an amount sufficiently large to protect the corporation against loss.

Where a corporation is a creditor of a bankrupt, the claim should be proved by the oath of the treasurer. If that is impossible owing to his absence or disability, the proof may be made by another person having knowledge of the facts, but in such case the reason why the proof is not made by the treasurer must be stated.

m. *General manager.* The duties of a general manager, when such officer is provided for in the regulations, are usually to have charge of the transactions occurring in the usual course of the business of the corporation.[33]

Transactions not occurring in the ordinary course of business are usually beyond his authority. It has been held that a general manager has no authority to sign a petition

[28] G. C. §§ 8672, 8673.
[29] Belting Co. v. Gibson, 68 O. S. 442; Trustees v. Deposit Co., 76 O. S. 267.
[30] Belting Co. v. Gibson, 68 O. S. 442.
[31] Minor v. Board of Control, 20 C. C. 4: 11 C. D. 16.
[32] Arbuckle v. Woolson Spice Co., 21 C. C. 356: 11 C. D. 727.
[33] See Washington Gas Light Co. v. Lansden, 172 U. S. 534, 547.

for a street improvement, making the corporate property liable for an assessment.[34]

n. *Managing director.* The office of managing director is sometimes provided for in the regulations. A director appointed to this office usually performs the duties of the general manager, but he is given larger powers. He is regarded as the direct representative of the directors and, in the active management of the business, as the highest executive officer.

§ 36. **Certificates of stock.** a. *In general.* A holder of stock which has been paid in full is entitled to a certificate, signed by the president and secretary of the corporation, showing the number of shares owned by him.[1]

A certificate of stock is not the stock itself but merely evidence of its ownership.[2] A person may be a stockholder without a certificate. The person who appears on the books of the corporation as the owner of stock is entitled to vote and to receive dividends. He is entitled to these rights although no certificates have been issued by the corporation, or although his certificates have been lost.[3] Certificates of stock, however, are valuable as evidence of title. They enable the stockholder to readily dispose of his stock, or to use it as collateral security.[4]

A stockholder is not entitled to a certificate until his stock is paid in full.[5]

Where stock subscriptions are paid by instalments it is customary to issue transferable receipts for the payments; the receipts being exchanged for certificates when all the instalments are paid.

b. *Negotiability.* Certificates of stock issued after July 1, 1911, are negotiable, under the Uniform Stock Transfer Act.[6]

Certificates of stock issued prior to July 1, 1911, do not possess the legal essentials of negotiable instruments, but as a general rule, the corporation itself and former owners of the stock are estopped from setting up claims to stock evidenced by such certificates in the hands of an innocent purchaser for value.[7]

---

[34] Minor v. Board of Control, 20 C. C. 4: 11 C. D. 16.

[1] G. C. § 8672.

[2] Bank v. Towle Mfg. Co., 67 O. S. 314.

[3] Railroad Co. v. Robbins, 35 O. S. 502; Franklin Bank v. Commercial Bank, 36 O. S. 355; Norton v. Norton, 43 O. S. 522.

[4] Railway Co. v. Bank, 56 O. S. 351; National Bank v. National Bank, 37 O. S. 215.

[5] Cincinnati, etc., Ry. Co. v. Bank, 1 C. C. 208; 1 C. D. 109, 207.

[6] G. C. §§ 8673-1, 8673-5.

[7] Dueber, etc., Co. v. Dougherty, 62 O. S. 589, 595; Railway Co. v. Bank, 56 O. S. 351; Railroad Co. v. Robbins, 35 O. S. 483.

Liability of transferee. Where stock represented by certificates has not been fully paid, a purchaser who has notice of that fact may be liable to creditors for the amount unpaid. But a purchaser for value without notice that the stock is unpaid is not liable. The statement "full paid and non-assessable," printed on a stock certificate, is a representation by the corporation that the stock has been fully paid and the purchaser need not inquire further.[8]

c. *Transfers.* When stock is assigned the assignee is entitled to have the stock transferred to his name on the books of the corporation, and to have a new certificate issued to him.[9]

The regulations of most corporations contain provisions relating to the transfers of stock and the issue of new certificates. It is usually provided that old certificates must be surrendered before new certificates are issued in their place. In such a case where a corporation issues a new certificate without requiring a return of the old certificate which is subsequently presented by an innocent purchaser, the corporation is liable and must replace the stock or account for its value to the purchaser.[10]

d. *Method of transfer.* A form of assignment is customarily printed on the back of each stock certificate. In practice a stockholder usually transfers his stock by affixing his signature to the blank without filling in the name of the assignee or of the attorney to make the transfer on the books of the corporation. Certificates thus assigned in blank may be transferred by delivery only until the name of an assignee is filled in, in which case it should be presented for transfer on the corporate books. The name of the secretary is usually filled in as the attorney to make the transfer on the books. When surrendered for transfer a certificate should be marked "cancelled" by the secretary and pasted on the stub from which it was detached.[11]

Trust companies are frequently employed by large corporations to act as *transfer agents* or *registrars*. This is for the purpose of guarding against an overissue of stock and as a guaranty to the public of the genuineness and regularity of certificates.

A transfer agent usually has possession of the stock certificate book, cancels surrendered certificates, fills out new certificates and, after they are signed by the president and

[8] Roebling Sons Co. v. Shawnee, etc., Co., 4 N. P. n. s. 113, 121; 17 L. D. 8 (aff'd no rep. 78 O. S. 408).

[9] Railroad Co. v. Fink, 41 O. S. 321.

[10] Railroad Co. v. Robbins, 35 O. S. 483; Lee v. Citizens N. Bank, 2 C. S. R. 298.

[11] Herrick v. Wardwell, 58 O. S. 294.

secretary, the transfer agent endorses or otherwise authenticates the certificates.

Doubt has been expressed as to whether a trust company or other corporation can legally be appointed a transfer agent of an Ohio corporation with the usual powers of a transfer agent.[12]

A registrar keeps a record or register of all stock issued and transferred, and countersigns the new certificates as issued.

e. *Consequences of failure to transfer.* On the books of the corporation stock appears in the name of the original stockholder until the certificates are presented for transfer. A purchaser or pledgee of stock who merely holds the certificates endorsed in blank, and does not present them for transfer, is not entitled to vote and incurs the risk that the dividends may be paid to the transferrer. Furthermore, notices of stockholders' meetings and of proposed corporate action on important matters, such as a sale of the entire corporate property, or a consolidation, are sent to the person registered on the books as the owner. In some instances purchasers and pledgees of stock have suffered losses which might have been averted by a prompt transfer.[13]

f. *Pledged stock.* When stock is used as collateral security for a loan or credit, the certificates are usually assigned in blank and delivered to the pledgee together with a "collateral note." The pledgee is entitled to have the stock transferred to his name on the corporate books,[14] the word "pledgee" usually being entered on the stock record after his name.

If the stock was issued by a foreign corporation and is taxable in Ohio, it is taxed in the name of the pledgor, where it has not been transferred to the pledgee on the corporate books.[15]

By holding the endorsed certificates, without a transfer on the corporate books, the pledgee does not avoid taxation on the note, or debt due him, but does avoid taxation on the stock.

Before the double liability of stockholders was abolished in the year 1903 there were good reasons why a pledgee

[12] Burch v. Cincinnati Trust Co., 12 N. P. n. s. 87 (1911) s. c. 14 C. C. n. s. 346.

[13] See Stafford v. Banking Co., 61 O. S. 160; Railway Co. v. Bank, 68 O. S. 582; Railroad Co. v. Robbins, 35 O. S. 502; Schmuck v. Crume, etc., Co., 7 N. P. n. s. 24: 19 L. D. 819 (aff'd 78 O. S. 409).

[14] Railway Co. v. Bank, 68 O. S. 599; Dayton N. B. v. Merchants N. B., 37 O. S. 215; Railway Co. v. Rawson, 16 W. L. B. 423.

[15] Ratterman v. Ingalls, 48 O. S. 468, 491; See *Taxation of stock* below, as to what stock is taxable in Ohio.

should not have the stock transferred to his name. Where the stock was transferred the pledgee became the stockholder and became subject to the double liability; while such liability was avoided by merely holding the assigned certificates without a transfer.[16]

Since the abolishment of the double liability (except as to bank stockholders) this reason no longer exists. If the pledgee desires to collect the dividends, to vote and to receive notices of corporate meetings he should have the stock registered in his name.

g. *Lost certificates* are usually provided for in corporate regulations, new certificates being issued in place of those lost, the corporation taking a bond of indemnity from the stockholder as security against loss from the reappearance of the old certificate in the hands of an innocent purchaser.[17]

The loss of a certificate does not deprive a stockholder of his right to vote and receive dividends, but without a certificate it is difficult for him to dispose of his stock.

By statute it is provided that an owner of a lost certificate may, by a proceeding in the probate court, require the corporation to issue a new certificate, upon the giving of a bond.[18]

§ 37. Taxation of stock. a. *In Ohio corporations.* No person is required to list for taxation shares of stock in any Ohio corporation.[1]

b. *In foreign corporations.* As a general rule, shares of stock in foreign corporations held by residents of Ohio are taxable in Ohio and the holders of such stock are required to list the same for taxation.[2]

But to this rule there is an important exception. Where all the property of a foreign corporation is taxed in the name of the corporation in Ohio, the stock of such corporation is exempt from taxation.[3]

Stock in a foreign corporation is also exempt from taxation where its holder furnishes satisfactory proof to the taxing authorities that at least two-thirds of the property of such corporation is taxed in Ohio and the remainder in

[16] Henkle v. Salem Mfg. Co., 39 O. S. 547.

[17] G. C. § 8673-17; See Hof v. Western German Bank, 6 W. L. B. 665 (697).

[18] G. C. §§ 8673-17, 8677 to 8681.

[1] G. C. §§ 192, 5372; Jones v. Davis, 35 O. S. 474; Prior to the amendment of R. S. 148c in 1904 (97 O. L. 496) stock in Ohio corporations was exempt from taxation only when the property of the corporation was taxed in its name in Ohio; Lander v. Burke, 65 O. S. 532 (1901).

[2] G. C. § 5372; Bradley v. Bauder, 36 O. S. 28; Lee v. Sturges, 46 O. S. 153.

[3] G. C. §§ 192, 5372; Hubbard v. Brush, 61 O. S. 252.

other states; providing the corporation pays, as an annual franchise tax, the same percentage on its entire authorized capital stock that is required of a domestic corporation on its subscribed or issued stock.[4]

§ 38. Increase of capital stock. When the original capital stock is fully subscribed for, and ten percent on each share paid in, a corporation may increase its capital stock or the number of shares into which it is divided.

a. *Before organization,* the increase may be effected by the unanimous written consent of all the original subscribers.

b. *After organization,* the increase is affected by the vote of the holders of a majority of its stock.[1]

c. *Disposition of new stock.* Each stockholder is entitled to subscribe for and take new stock in proportion to his holdings of the old stock. This right may be waived by a stockholder. If a stockholder fails to subscribe within a reasonable time, after opportunity is afforded him, he is deemed to have waived his right and the directors may dispose of the stock to others.[2]

Where capital stock is increased, there is no requirement that a certificate of subscription be filed with the secretary of state.[3]

Directors and stockholders may, however, incur a personal liability by acting as if it had been subscribed. In one case where an increase of capital stock was properly authorized by stockholders, a certificate of such action filed with the secretary of state, and a bond issue put forth on the faith of such increased stock and no effort was made to sell the new stock, it was held that an intention was thereby shown on the part of the stockholders to take new stock in proportion to their original holdings, and a judgment against the stockholders was rendered accordingly.[4]

When the original capital stock is subscribed for ten percent of the subscriptions are payable in cash. It is doubtful whether the same requirement applies in the case of an increase of capital stock.[5]

Where it is desired to incorporate a company to take over property of considerable value, and to pay in the least possible cash for the stock, a practice sometimes followed is for the corporation to be originally organized with a small

[4] G. C. § 192.
[1] G. C. § 8698; For the notice, or waiver of notice of the stockholders' meeting, and the certificate of increase, see *Forms.*
[2] Hall v. Hall, 11 C. C. n. s. 335: 20 C. D. 826 (aff'd 79 O. S. 456).

[3] Rep. Atty. Gen. 1911-1912 p. 66.
[4] Kreisser v. Ashtabula Gas Light Co., 2 C. C. n. s. 597; 14 C. D. 313.
[5] Rep. Atty. Gen. 1911-1912 p. 66; Rep. Atty. Gen. 1906-1907 p. 52.

capital stock, ten percent of which is paid in cash. After organization the capital stock is increased to the desired amount, and the new stock is by the directors exchanged for the property. The validity of this practice, however, has not been recognized by judicial decisions in Ohio.

d. *Stock dividend.* Where a surplus of corporate assets, in excess of all debts and of the capital stock, has been earned, the capital stock may be increased to the amount of the surplus, and the new stock distributed among the stockholders in the form of a stock dividend.

e. *Increase by preferred stock.* Upon the written assent of three-fourths in number of the stockholders, representing at least three-fourths of the capital stock, a corporation may increase its capital stock by an issue of preferred stock.[6]

§ 39. Reduction of capital stock. With the written consent of the persons in whose names a majority of the stock stands on the books of a corporation, the directors may reduce the amount of its capital stock and the nominal value of all the shares.[1]

The statute provides that the rights of corporate creditors can not be affected by a reduction of the capital stock. Where the subscriptions to the original capital stock have not been entirely called in, or assessed to the full amount, before the reduction of the stock, the subscribers will remain liable to existing creditors in the original amount.

Where corporate assets have been reduced by losses, the capital stock is sometimes reduced to bring it to the level of the assets, and to make the book value of the stock approximately par.

The annual franchise (Willis law) tax is assessed not on corporate assets but on the issued and outstanding stock. By a reduction of the capital stock, a saving is effected in such tax. The credit of the corporation is not affected, in many instances, by the reduction, as the nominal capital stock is not often relied upon in extending credit to a corporation.

§ 40. Organization of corporation to take over business of partnership or another corporation.[1]

Corporations are frequently organized to take over the business of a partnership or of another corporation. Pay-

[6] G. C. § 8699.
[1] G. C. 8700; For forms of written consent of stockholders, resolution of directors, and certificate of reduction, see *Forms.*

[1] The consolidation of corporations, authorized by special statutes, is not considered in this paragraph.

ment for the property and business transferred is usually made in the form of stock in the new corporation.[2]

One of the important things to be provided for in such cases is the indebtedness of the partnership or old corporation, if any indebtedness exists. Where partnership property is transferred to a new corporation, organized to continue the business, payment being made wholly in stock of the new corporation, the new corporation may be liable for the debts of the partnership.[3]

This rule does not, of course, apply where the new corporation purchases the assets for cash, unless the transaction is a fraudulent one.

Where the partnership, or old corporation, is solvent and the change is made to obtain the advantages of the corporate form of organization or for other good reasons, the debts may be assumed by the new corporation as a part of the transaction.

Where the partnership or old corporation is insolvent or in serious financial embarrassment, there are grave objections to assuming its debts and it is difficult, if not impossible, to acquire its assets except for cash.

In case of insolvency the assets may be purchased for cash from the trustee in bankruptcy or assignee for creditors. But the value of the good will of the old concern will be largely destroyed by bankruptcy or an assignment. It is often possible for the old concern to effect a private settlement or composition with the creditors, without the financial difficulties becoming publicly known and without any cessation of business.

A corporation can not dispose of its entire property, except by the action of three-fourths of its directors, ratified at a stockholders' meeting by a vote of the holders of three-fourths of its stock.[4]

Where the property of a corporation is taken over, the foregoing proceedings should be taken.

Where a partnership is succeeded by a corporation the partnership name is usually adopted by the corporation, with such changes as are necessary to make it conform to the statutory requirement that a corporate name must commence with the word "The" and end with the word "Company."[5]

---

[2] See Gas & Fuel Co. v. Dairy Co., 60 O. S. 96, 105-106.

[3] Andres v. Morgan, 62 O. S. 236; Creditors may recover a judgment against the new corporation *ib.* Or they may, by other proceedings, reach the property transferred.

Bank v. Trebein, 59 O. S. 316; Cook on Corporations §§ 672, 673.

[4] G. . §§ 8710 to 8718.

[5] For right to adopt partnership name, see Snyder Mfg. Co. v. Snyder, 54 O. S. 86.

Many matters to be taken into consideration in incorporating a business or partnership are discussed elsewhere.[6]

§ 41. Foreign corporations. A foreign corporation is one that has been organized under the laws of another state or of a foreign government.[1]

A State has power to wholly exclude foreign corporations from doing business within its borders, or it may admit them under any reasonable conditions or limitations.[2] Corporations engaged in interstate commerce, however, can not be excluded or restricted by a state.[3]

Foreign corporations are permitted to do business in Ohio upon compliance with certain conditions. There are two laws imposing conditions upon foreign corporations entering the State: (a) the license fee law and (b) the franchise tax law.

a. *The license fee law* applies to nearly all private business corporations and requires the procurement of a certificate or license from the secretary of state.[4]

In order to procure a certificate from the secretary of state a corporation is required to file a sworn copy of its charter or articles of incorporation, and a statement showing the amount of its authorized capital stock, the kind of business proposed to be carried on, and to designate a principal office or place of business and a person upon whom process may be served, and to pay a small license fee based on its authorized capital stock.[5]

b. *Initial franchise tax.* Corporations which own or use a part or all of their capital or plant in Ohio must procure the certificate already mentioned and are further required to pay a franchise tax of one-tenth of one percent "upon the proportion of the authorized capital stock of the corporation represented by property owned and used and business transacted in Ohio."[6]

c. *Method of computing franchise tax.* This tax is based, not upon the *property* owned and used and business transacted in this state, but upon the *proportion of the total authorized capital stock* represented by such property and business. The proportion which the property owned and used and business transacted in Ohio bears to the entire property and business of the corporation is the proportion of the capital stock on which the

[6] See *Amount of Capitalization; Form of Capitalization;* and *Directors (number, power to issue stock for property).*
[1] Cook on Corporations, § 7.
[2] Humphrey v. State, 70 O. S. 87, 88; W. U. Tel. Co. v. Mayer, 28 O. S. 521.
[3] Toledo Commercial Co. v. Glen Mfg. Co., 55 O. S. 221.
[4] G. C. §§ 178, 179, 180.
[5] G. C. §§ 179, 180.
[6] G. C. §§ 183, 184.

tax is based. Thus, where the property owned and used and business transacted in Ohio is $25,000, the entire corporate property and business $50,000, and the authorized capital stock $100,000, the tax is based on one-half of its authorized capital stock, or $50,000, the Ohio property and business being one-half of the total property and business. If all of its property and business were in Ohio the tax would be based upon its total authorized capital stock.[7]

d. *What corporations are subject to law.* A foreign corporation organized to carry on professional business is not entitled to a certificate from the secretary of state as foreign corporations are permitted to enter the state to carry on only such business as may lawfully be carried on by Ohio corporations.[8]

The franchise tax law[9] does not apply to banking, insurance, building and loan or bond investment corporations or to corporations engaged in interstate commerce. A foreign corporation engaged in interstate commerce which is not subject to the laws gains no advantage by voluntary compliance with their requirements.[10]

A foreign corporation organized to deal in real estate may be admitted to do business in Ohio, but the application for admission should expressly limit its life in Ohio to twenty-five years.[11]

e. *Failure to comply with law—Consequences of.* A foreign corporation can not maintain an action upon a contract made by it in this state until it has complied with the statutory requirements.[12]

A contract made by a foreign corporation, before complying with the statutory requirements, is void on its behalf but is enforceable against it.[13]

The property of a foreign corporation "doing business" in Ohio without complying with the statutory requirements is subject to attachment.[14]

A foreign corporation engaged in interstate commerce which is not subject to the law does not become exempt from attachment by a voluntary compliance with the requirements.[15]

Certain penalties and fines are provided in the acts for

[7] Opinion of Wade H. Ellis, Atty. Gen., 5 O. L. R. 163; Aetna Iron & Steel Co. v. Taylor, 13 C. C. 602: 5 C. D. 242, s. c. 3 N. P. 152: 4 Low. D. 180; 4 Opins. Attys. Gen. 621-624 (1894); Rep. Atty. Gen. 1910-1911, p. 600.

[8] State v. Laylin, 73 O. S. 90; See 5 Opin. Attys. Gen. 975 (1903).

[9] G. C. §§ 183, 184.

[10] Bigalow v. Armour, 74 O. S. 168.

[11] 5 Opin. Attys. Gen. 1002.

[12] G. C. §§ 178, 187.

[13] G. C. § 5508.

[14] G. C. §§ 11819, 10253, 186.

[15] Bigalow v. Armour, 74 O. S. 168.

noncompliance with the requirements, but in this respect the acts appear to be wholly unadjudicated.[16]

f. *What is "doing business" in the State.* A foreign corporation which maintains a stock of goods within the state, from which deliveries are made of goods sold, is doing business in the state.[17]

But a foreign corporation is not doing business in the state where it maintains no stock of goods in the state and limits its business to shipping goods into the state, upon orders, and it need not register as a foreign corporation. This is true whether the orders are obtained through traveling salesmen or correspondence,[18] or a resident broker,[19] or whether the corporation maintains an office in the state with a resident agent in charge, for the purpose of soliciting orders.[20]

Nor is it doing business in a state to consign goods to a commission merchant, located in the state, where the commission merchant conducts all the business in the state and pays all expenses of receiving, handling and storing the goods.[21]

A single and isolated transaction is not doing business in the state.[22]

g. *Annual franchise tax.* A foreign corporation is required to file an annual report with the secretary of state and to pay an annual franchise tax of "three-twentieths of one percent upon the proportion of the authorized capital stock of the corporation represented by property owned and used and business transacted in Ohio, and to be not less than ten dollars in any case."[23]

§ 42. Syndicates. A syndicate is an unincorporated combination of persons united for the purpose of an enterprise too large for successful accomplishment by a single individual.[1]

Syndicates are frequently formed for the purpose of promoting or financing large corporations, or of holding corporate stocks and bonds.

[16] G. C. §§ 182, 186.

[17] People v. Wample, 131 N. Y. 64; 29 N. E. 1002; Singer Mfg. Co. v. Adams, 165 Fed. 877.

[18] Commercial Co. v. Mfg. Co., 55 O. S. 217.

[19] McBath v. Jones Cotton Co., 149 Fed. 383; Doe v. Mfg. Co., 104 Fed. 684.

[20] Textbook Co. v. Pigg, 217 U. S. 91.

[21] Butler Bros. Shoe Co. v. U. S. Rubber Co., 155 Fed. 1 (C. C. A.).

[22] Cooper Mfg. Co. v. Ferguson, 113 U. S. 727.

[23] G. C. § 5503; See Opinion by Wade H. Ellis, Atty. Gen., 5 O. L. R. 163.

[1] 27 American & English Ency. of Law (2d ed.) 562; Anderson's Dictionary of Law; Baltimore Trust & Guarantee Co. v. Hambleton, 84 Md. 456; 40 L. R. A. 216.

Before an enterprise is incorporated, or its securities are offered to the public, it is often necessary or advantageous to obtain options on property, or to purchase property, and sometimes to develop and improve the property and place the enterprise in the situation of a going concern. For such purposes large amounts of money are often required. Where a syndicate is formed, its members contribute funds with which the property is acquired or developed. The property is subsequently turned over to the corporation and the stocks, bonds or money received from the corporation for the property are distributed among the members of the syndicate in proportion to the amounts contributed by each.[2]

Where, after the organization of a corporation, an issue of bonds, or of preferred stock is to be offered to the public, it is often desirable that there be some assurance or guaranty to the corporation that all of the securities will be sold. This is sometimes accomplished through an "underwriting syndicate," which agrees to purchase all of the bonds or stock which remain unsold at the end of a certain period.

The agreement. A syndicate agreement usually recites the purposes of syndicate and, where the syndicate is formed to raise funds, binds the members who are usually termed "syndicate subscribers," to pay in the amounts set opposite their respective names. The mutual promises of the parties to the agreement constitute the consideration. A subscriber to an interest in a syndicate formed to purchase the property of a corporation can not defend against a note given for his subscription on the ground that the property was fraudulently overvalued, where the valuation was made by representatives of the syndicate and not of the vendor corporation.[3]

A syndicate agreement usually appoints a treasurer to receive and disburse the funds, and one or more "syndicate managers" to act as agents or attorneys in fact for the syndicate and to take active charge of the business.

The powers of the syndicate managers are usually defined in detail. Extensive discretionary powers are sometimes conferred.

Legal status. Judicial decisions as to the legal status of syndicates and the liabilities of syndicate members have not been entirely harmonious. This is perhaps due to the fact that individuals have united under the name "syndicate" for widely different purposes, and under agreements containing entirely dissimilar provisions. Whether the members

[2] Knickerbocker Trust Co. v. Evans, 188 Fed. 549 (C. C. A. 1911).

[3] Tradesmen's N. B. v. Looney, 99 Tenn. 278; 42 S. W. Rep. 149.

of a syndicate are liable as partners has been variously decided. In a number of cases they have been held to be partners.[4]

In one case syndicate members were said to be "quasi partners" with the syndicate manager, whose relation to the members was "analogous to that of a partner to his copartner."[5]

The true rule probably is that a syndicate is not necessarily a partnership, but the liability of its members for the acts of the syndicate managers or agents depends upon whether there exists "a basis of fact for the legal implication of agency."[6]

[4] Bank v. Wehrmann, 69 O. S. 160; 202 U. S. 295: 4 O. L. R. 344; Wehrman v McFarlan, 6 N. P. 333; Horner v. Meyers, 29 W. L. B. 403; Lape v. Parvin, 2 Disney 560; Baltimore Trust & Guarantee Co. v. Hambleton, 84 Md. 456; 40 L. R. A. 216, 230; See note 18 L. R. A. n. s. 1094; See also Mooney v. Nagel, 14 C. C. n. s. 228 (1911) affirming 9 N. P. n. s. 385.

[5] Runkle v. Burrage, 202 Mass. 98 (1909).

[6] Hornblower v. Crandall, 7 Mo. App. 220, affirmed 78 Mo. 581; Lane v. Fenn, 120 N. Y. Suppl. 256 (1909); Merrill v. Milliken, 101 Me. 56: 63 Atl. Rep. 299 (1905).

PART II.

FORMS.

LIST OF FORMS.

Articles of Incorporation.

Form No.
1. Of corporation for profit.
2. Preferred stock clauses.
3. Provision limiting each stockholder to one vote.

Purpose Clauses.

4. Abstract company.
5. Advertising novelty company.
6. Agency company.
7. Air cooling company.
8. Amusement park company.
9. Architectural company.
10. Audit company.
11. Baking company.
12. Band company.
13. Bank and trust company.
14. Baseball club company.
15. Building and loan association.
16. Building company.
17. Business college.
18. Butchering company.
19. Car company.
20. Clay and brick company.
21. Coal company.
22. Coal company. Another form.
23. Collateral loan company.
24. Commercial school.
25. Common carrier company.
26. Construction company.
27. Construction company. Another form.
28. Construction company. Another form.
29. Cooperage company.
30. Co-operative store company.
31. Dairy company.
32. Directory company.
33. Dock and warehouse company.
34. Driving park company.
35. Drugstore company.
36. Drygoods and notions company.
37. Electric light and power company.
38. Elevator company.
39. Embalming fluid company.
40. Engineering and construction company.
41. Express company.
42. Fence company.
43. Foundry company.
44. Fish company.
45. Freight loading company.
46. Gas and electric company.

Form No.
47. Natural gas company.
48. Artificial gas company.
49. General store company.
50. Glassware company.
51. Green house and nursery company.
52. Heating company.
53. Hotel and restaurant.
54. House furnishing company.

Insurance companies.

55. Employers' libility accident and health company.
56. Fidelity and guarantee company.
57. Fire insurance company.
58. Mutual protective insurance association (fire, etc.).
59. Life, accident, etc., insurance company.
60. Mutual protective association (life and accident).
61. Live stock insurance company.
62. Live stock mutual protective association.
63. Credit insurance company.
64. Interurban and street railway company.
65. Iron company.
66. Light, heat and power company.
67. Live stock company.
68. Lodge building company.
69. Lumber company.
70. Mail order company.
71. Mail tube company.
72. Manufacturing company.
73. Market house company.
74. Mausoleum company.
75. Meat market company.
76. Men's furnishing company.
77. Mercantile agency company.
78. Mercantile or trading company.
79. Messenger service company.
80. Millinery company.
81. Milling company.
82. Mineral springs company.
83. Mining company.
84. Motion picture company.
85. Motion picture company. Another form.
86. Musical instrument company.
87. Ohio river bridge company.

Form No.
189. Special clauses for preferred stock certificates.
190. Certificate of stock reserving lien to secure indebtedness to corporation.
191. Corporation calendar.
192. Stock transfer book.
193. Stock ledger.
194. Proxy, one specified meeting.
195. Proxy, all meetings within a specified time.
196. Proxy, general.
197. Revocation of proxy.

Annual meetings of stockholders.

198. Notice of annual meeting.
199. Minutes of annual meeting.
200. Ballot.
201. Inspector's certificate of election.

Special meetings of stockholders.

202. Waiver of call and notice.
203. Call, by stockholders.
204. Call, by resolution of directors.
205. Notice of special meeting.
206. Minutes of special meeting (including resolutions (a) for increase in number of directors and (b) for committee to inspect books).

Amendment of regulations.

207. Assent of stockholders to.
208. Resolution of stockholders for.

Directors' meetings.

209. Notice of regular meeting.
210. Call for special meeting.
211. Notice of special meeting.
212. Waiver of notice of special meeting.
213. Minutes of directors' meeting, including (a) motion authorizing compromise of claim and (b) resolution declaring dividend.
214. Certificate to transcript of minutes.
215. Certificate by secretary to resolution.
216. Resolution filling vacancy caused by disqualification.
217. Resignation of director or officer.
218. Resolution accepting donation of treasury stock.
219. Donation of stock to treasury.
220. Resolution ratifying unauthorized act of officer.
221. Resolution declaring stock dividend.

Miscellaneous.

222. Dividend order.
223. Permanent dividend order.

Form No.
224. Railroad consolidation agreement.
225. Railroad consolidation agreement, another form.
226. Lease of railroad.
227. Release, by property owner, to railroad company of damages for occupation of street.
228. Deed of land to interurban traction company for railroad purposes.
229. Deed of right of way to railroad company.
230. Consolidation of religious societies.
231. Agreement to subscribe for stock in corporation not yet organized.
232. Stock pooling agreement.
233. Voting trust agreement.
234. Consent to use of similar name by new corporation.
235. Deed of corporation, with certificate of acknowledgment.
236. Bill of sale by corporation of assets, with agreement of officers not to reengage in business.
237. Option on manufacturing plant.
238. Option, by corporation, on manufacturing plant.
239. Option to purchase stock in corporation.
240. Option to purchase stock at "book value"; certificates to be deposited.
241. Option contract to purchase stock if vendee desire to resell.
242. Put.
243. Call.
244. Bond to corporation issuing new certificate of stock in lieu of lost or destroyed certificate.
245. Bond of treasurer of corporation.
246. Collateral note.
247. Collateral note, another form.
248. Syndicate agreement.
249. Underwriting agreement.
250. Underwriting agreement, another form.
251. Power of attorney to managing agent.

Bond Issues.

252. Resolution of directors authorizing.
253. Resolution of stockholders ratifying.
254. Written assent of stockholders to convertible bonds.
255. Deed of trust, or corporate mortgage, securing bonds.
256. Bond pooling agreement.
257. Bondholders' agreement, corporation in default for interest.

ARTICLES OF INCORPORATION.

NOTE.—The following forms are prepared for use under the general corporation law for manufacturing and business corporations. (G. C. §§ 8623 to 8743.) The special statutory provisions relating to the incorporation of banks, insurance, building and loan, and public utility corporations should be carefully followed; but the forms and procedure are generally similar to those here given.

No. 1.

Corporation for Profit.

(G. C. § 8625.)

These Articles of Incorporation

of

The .... Company

Witnesseth, that we, the undersigned, all (or a majority) of whom are citizens of the State of Ohio, desiring to form a corporation, for profit, under the general corporation laws of said State, do hereby certify:

FIRST. The name of said corporation shall be The........ Company.

SECOND. Said corporation is to be located at .... in .... county, Ohio, and its principal business there transacted.

THIRD. Said corporation is formed for the purpose of .... (*for statements of purposes of various corporations, see purpose clauses, form No. 4 et seq.*).

FOURTH. The capital stock of said corporation shall be ... . dollars ($......), divided into .... (......) shares of .... dollars ($......) each.

(*If preferred stock is to be issued omit the foregoing "Fourth" and use such parts of Form No. 2, as may be desired.*)

In witness whereof, we have hereunto set our hands this .... day of ...., A. D. 19....

....

....

The State of Ohio, County of ...., ss.

Personally appeared before me, the undersigned, a *Notary Public,* in and for said county, this ...... day of ...., A. D. 19.., the above named ...., ..., ..., and ...., who each severally acknowledged the signing of the foregoing articles of incorporation to be his free act and deed, for the uses and purposes therein mentioned.

Witness my hand and official seal on the day and year last aforesaid.

........................,

Notary Public.

The State of Ohio, County of ...., ss.

I, ..., Clerk of the Court of Common Pleas, within and for the county aforesaid, do hereby certify that ...., whose name is subscribed to the foregoing acknowledgment as a *Notary Public,* was at the date thereof a *Notary Public,* in and for said county, duly commissioned and qualified, and authorized as such to take said acknowledgment; and further, that I am well acquainted with his handwriting, and believe that the signature to said acknowledgment is genuine.

In witness whereof, I have hereunto set my hand and affixed the seal of said court, at ...., this ...... day of ...., A. D. 19.....

................,
Clerk.

No. 2.

Preferred Stock Clauses.

NOTE.—If preferred stock is to be issued omit the "Fourth" paragraph of the foregoing form and use such of the following provisions as may be desired.

FOURTH. The capital stock of said corporation, common and preferred, shall be .... dollars ($........), consisting of .... (........) shares of common stock of the par value of .... dollars ($......) each and .... (.........) shares of preferred stock of the par value of .... dollars ($......) each. The holders of the preferred stock shall be entitled to a dividend of .... percent per annum, payable (*quarterly, semiannually or annually*) out of the surplus profits of the company for each year in preference to all other stockholders, and such dividends shall be cumulative (*or noncumulative*).

PREFERRED STOCK NOT TO PARTICIPATE IN EXCESS PROFITS.

The holders of preferred stock shall not be entitled to any dividends in excess of .... percent per annum and the arrears thereof.

NOTE.—If the following paragraph is used, omit the foregoing paragraph.

PREFERRED STOCK TO PARTICIPATE IN EXCESS DIVIDENDS.

When dividends of .... percent have been paid for any year on the entire preferred and common capital stock, issued and outstanding, further dividends for that year shall be paid on all stock without distinction.

PREFERRED STOCK NOT ENTITLED TO VOTE.

The holders of preferred stock shall not be entitled to vote thereon at meetings of the stockholders of said corporation.

PREFERRED STOCK TO BE VOTED, UPON DEFAULT OF DIVIDENDS.

The holders of preferred stock shall not be entitled to vote thereon at meetings of the stockholders of said corporation so long as dividends at the rate above specified are paid; but in case of default in the payment of such dividends, then and thereafter the holders of preferred stock may vote thereon at any and all stockholders' meetings.

PROVISION FOR REDEMPTION.

Such preferred stock may be redeemed at the option of the corporation on the ...... day of ...., 19...., or on the ...... day of .... of any year thereafter, upon payment of .... dollars ($....) per share and all accumulated dividends.

OPTION TO CONVERT PREFERRED INTO COMMON STOCK.

The holder of any number of shares of preferred stock may, at his election, on surrender of his certificates thereof, convert the same into an equal number of shares of common stock.

No. 3.

Provision in Articles of Incorporation Limiting Each Stockholder to One Vote Irrespective of Stock Owned.

(G. C. § 8638.)

NOTE.—The following may be added to the "Fourth" paragraph of the form No. 1, above.

Provided, that each stockholder, irrespective of the amount of stock he may own, shall be entitled to one vote, and no more, at any election of directors, or upon any subject submitted at a stockholders' meeting.

PURPOSE CLAUSES. CORPORATIONS FOR PROFIT.

No. 4.

Abstract Company.

THIRD. Said corporation is formed for the purpose of making and furnishing abstracts and certificates of title to real property and to do a general searching of records.

No. 5.

Advertising Novelty Company.

THIRD. Said corporation is formed for the purpose of manufacturing, improving, buying, selling and dealing in, at wholesale and retail, calendars, signs and all kinds of advertising novelties, articles and devices, and the doing of all things necessary or incident thereto.

No. 6.

Agency Company.

THIRD. Said corporation is formed for the purpose of acting as an Agency for general insurance, bonding, negotiating loans and transfers of real estate, and doing all things incident thereto.

No. 7.

Air-Cooling Company.

THIRD. Said corporation is formed for the purpose of ventilating, purifying and regulating the humidity of air and of manufacturing and dealing in all kinds of apparatus, devices and inventions designed for said purposes.

No. 8.

Amusement Park Company.

THIRD. Said corporation is formed for the purpose of furnishing to the public facilities for holding musical, theatrical and other entertainments, providing social entertainments and other means of recreation and amusement; to acquire, lease, own and maintain such real estate, buildings and personal property as may be necessary or proper for the objects and purposes aforesaid, and the doing of all things necessary or incident thereto.

No. 9.

Architectural Company.

THIRD. Said corporation is formed for the purpose of making plans, specifications and drawings, making estimates, superintending work, designing and building all kinds of structures and of carrying on and conducting a general architectural business.

No. 10.

Audit Company.

THIRD. Said corporation is formed for the purpose of auditing accounts and books, and appraising and valuing the assets of individuals, firms and corporations, both public and private, and the doing of all things necessary or incident thereto.

No. 11.

Baking Company.

THIRD. Said corporation is formed for the purpose of manufacturing, buying, selling and dealing in bread, crackers, cakes, biscuits, candies, confectionery and kindred products and all materials for the same, and doing all things necessary or incident thereto.

No. 12.

Band Company.

THIRD. Said corporation is formed for the purpose of furnishing band and orchestra music and generally to do and carry out all things incident to band and orchestra organizations, including the purchase of all necessary music and instruments, uniforms and other necessary paraphernalia.

No. 13.

Bank and Trust Company.

(G. C. § 9703.)

THIRD. Said corporation is formed for the purpose of conducting a commercial bank, savings bank, safe deposit company and trust company; exercising all of the powers which may be exercised by a corporation engaged in such business, and the doing of all things necessary or incident thereto.

NOTE.—The above form combines all the four classes of business authorized by G. C. §§ 9702 and 9703. Omit such classes of business as it is not desired to engage in, if any.
Minimum capital stock see G. C. § 9704.

No. 14.

Baseball Club Company.

THIRD. Said corporation is formed for the purpose of acquiring, owning, leasing, equipping, improving and maintaining suitable grounds for a baseball park, the exhibition of baseball games and the giving of other exhibitions therein, and the doing of all things necessary or incident thereto.

No. 15.

Building and Loan Association.

(G. C. § 9643 et seq.)

THIRD. Said corporation is formed for the purpose of raising money to be loaned to its members, and others, and generally the doing of all things and the transaction of all business authorized by the laws of Ohio to be done and transacted by building and loan associations.

No. 16.

Building Company.

(G. C. § 10210.)

THIRD. Said corporation is formed for the purpose of constructing and maintaining buildings to be used for hotels, storerooms, offices, warehouses and factories, and to acquire by purchase or lease and to hold, use, mortgage and lease all such real estate and personal property as may be necessary for such purpose, and the doing of all things necessary or incident thereto.

No. 17.

Business College.

THIRD. Said corporation is formed for the purpose of conducting a general business college, including instruction in bookkeeping, banking, penmanship, office practice, shorthand and typewriting, and all branches of study pertaining to a thorough business education, and the doing of all things necessary or incident thereto.

No. 18.

Butchering Company.

THIRD. Said corporation is formed for the purpose of carrying on a general wholesale and retail butcher, provision and food product business, manufacturing of meat foods and a general butcher business in all its branches.

No. 19.

Car Company.

THIRD. Said corporation is formed for the purpose of owning, leasing, operating and furnishing cars for the transportation of freight on and over railroad lines, within or without the state of Ohio, or partly within and partly without said state, and the transaction of such other business as is incident thereto.

No. 20.

Clay and Brick Company.

(See G. C. § 10137.)

THIRD. Said corporation is formed for the purpose of leasing, buying, owning, holding and operating clay, shale, limestone, coal and mineral properties; mining, selling and dealing in clay, shale, limestone, coal and other minerals, the manufacturing therefrom of brick, cement and other products, and the doing of all things necessary or incident thereto.

No. 21.

Coal Company.

(See G. C. § 10137.)

THIRD. Said corporation is formed for the purpose of leasing, buying, owning, holding and operating coal mines and coal properties in Ohio and other states, manufacturing coke, buying, selling and dealing in coal and coke and the products thereof, and the doing of all things necessary or incident thereto.

No. 22.

Coal Company, Another Form.

THIRD. Said corporation is formed for the purpose of mining coal and dealing in coal, coke and kindred products, by wholesale and retail, and the transaction of all business incidental thereto and connected therewith; with power and authority to purchase, sell or lease mineral lands and to purchase, own, lease or control suitable real estate for the transaction of its business.

No. 23.

Collateral Loan Company.

(G. C. § 9857 et seq.)

THIRD. Said corporation is formed for the purpose of making loans on pledges of goods and chattels, and upon mortgages thereof, and the doing of all things necessary or incident thereto.

No. 24.

Commercial School.

THIRD. Said corporation is formed for the purpose of carrying on the ordinary work of a business or commercial school, and of acquiring and holding the property, whether real or personal, necessary to carry on such work.

No. 25.

Common Carrier Company.

(G. C. § 10170.)

THIRD. Said corporation is formed for the purpose of making and performing contracts for the carriage of persons and the storage, forwarding, carriage and delivery of property, and doing all things incident thereto and necessary for the convenient dispatch of its business, and authorized by law.

No. 26.

Construction Company.

THIRD. Said corporation is formed for the purpose of carrying on the general work of a construction company, such as grading, laying track, ballasting, building bridges, and doing any and all work necessary in making and preparing roadbeds for steam, electric and 'other railroads, and all contract work relating thereto; also construction and contract work of every kind for cities and towns; also the construction and erection of buildings, and in general, doing construction and contract work of every kind.

No. 27.

Construction Company. Another Form.

THIRD. Said corporation is formed for the purpose of carrying on a general contracting, construction and building business with and for individuals, firms, private and public corporations and public authorities and bodies, and for that purpose to manufacture, buy, sell and deal in materials and furnish labor, and generally to do all things necessary or incident thereto.

No. 28.

Construction Company. Another Form.

THIRD. Said corporation is formed for the purpose of doing a general contracting and construction business, building, constructing, manufacturing, installing, operating and repairing power plants, bridges, dams, sewers, buildings, machinery and structures of all kinds; buying, selling and dealing in the materials therefor and the doing of all things necessary or incident thereto.

No. 29.

Cooperage Company.

THIRD. Said corporation is formed for the purpose of manufacturing, buying, selling and dealing in barrels, boxes and all kinds of cooperage stock and all things incident thereto.

No. 30.

Co-operative Store Company.

THIRD. Said corporation is formed for the purpose of conducting a general store, buying, selling and dealing in groceries, provisions, dry goods, clothing and general merchandise; distributing merchandise to its stockholders at prices not greater than the cost thereof, with expense of distribution, and the doing of all things necessary or incident thereto.

No. 31.

Dairy Company.

THIRD. Said corporation is formed for the purpose of manufacturing, buying, selling and dealing in butter, cheese, cream and all other dairy products, and the doing of all things necessary or incident thereto.

No. 32.

Directory Company.

THIRD. Said corporation is formed for the purpose of printing and publishing city, county and state directories and of doing a general printing and publishing business.

No. 33.

Dock and Warehouse Company.

(See G. C. § 10207.)

THIRD. Said corporation is formed for the purpose of establishing, constructing, acquiring, owning, leasing and operating docks, wharves and warehouses in the city of ....
and elsewhere in and adjacent to *Lake Erie,* and of receiving, shipping and forwarding merchandise and property of all kinds, issuing warehouse receipts therefor and the doing of all things necessary or incident thereto.

No. 34.

Driving Park Company.

THIRD. Said corporation is formed for the purpose of erecting and maintaining a park and grounds, containing drive and speedways for the purpose of recreation and amusement and holding meets therein with horses and vehicles.

No. 35.

Drug Store Company.

THIRD. Said corporation is formed for the purpose of carrying on a wholesale and retail drug, cigar and tobacco business, buying and selling drugs, druggists' sundries, cigars and tobacco, and also for the purpose of manufacturing, compounding and selling pharmaceutical preparations.

No. 36.

Dry Goods and Notions Company.

THIRD. Said corporation is formed for the purpose of buying, selling and dealing in dry goods, notions, furnishing goods and general merchandise in all their varieties at wholesale and retail, also acquiring by purchase or lease such property, both real and personal, as may be deemed necessary or convenient for the aforesaid purposes; also doing all such other things and business as may be necessary, convenient or incident to the main purpose of such corporation.

No. 37.

Electric Light and Power Company.

THIRD. Said corporation is formed for the purpose of manufacturing or otherwise acquiring, transmitting, distributing, selling and supplying electricity to public or private consumers, for light, heat and power purposes; constructing, maintaining and operating all necessary plants, poles, wires, conduits and structures for the transmission and distribution of electricity in the counties of .... in the municipalities and townships of said counties, and for lighting the streets and public and private buildings therein and the doing of all things necessary or incident thereto.

No. 38.

Elevator Company.

(G. C. § 10172.)

THIRD. Said corporation is formed for the purpose of purchasing and holding real and personal estate, erecting or purchasing and owning the necessary buildings, offices and machinery for the purpose of carrying on the business of receiving, storing, delivering and forwarding grain of all kinds, and the doing of the business of general storage, warehousemen and forwarders of all kinds of produce and merchandise. Said corporation shall not deal as buyer or seller, on its own account or for others.

No. 39.

Embalming Fluid Company.

THIRD. Said corporation is formed for the purpose of manufacturing, compounding, buying, selling and trading in embalming fluids, embalming instruments, embalming tables, disinfectants, antiseptics, deodorizers and anything pertaining to the business of embalming, preserving and caring for the human dead.

No. 40.

Engineering and Construction Company.

THIRD. Said corporation is formed for the purpose of doing a general engineering and contracting business; grading, macadamizing and all other work connected with or incident to road and street building, ballasting, railroad construction and concrete work of all kinds, acquiring by lease, purchase or otherwise, real estate and other property necessary or convenient for such purposes and the doing of all things necessary or incident thereto.

No. 41.

Express Company.

THIRD. Said corporation is formed for the purpose of doing a general express business within said state, carrying and delivering express matter.

No. 42.

Fence Company.

THIRD. Said corporation is formed for the purpose of growing and manufacturing hedge and wire fences, dealing in wire, hedge plants, tools, fence machines, patents pertaining to the same, and such other business as may grow out or on account of the said business.

No. 43.

Foundry Company.

THIRD. Said corporation is formed for the purpose of carrying on the business of a foundry and machine shops, for purchasing and owning the necessary real estate, buildings, machinery, tools, fixtures, supplies, for manufacturing and selling the products of said foundry and machine shop, including iron and steel castings, machinery, and generally to carry on a manufactory in iron and steel products.

No. 44.

Fish Company.

THIRD. Said corporation is formed for the purpose of operating fisheries, buying, selling and dealing in, at wholesale and retail, fish, fisheries, materials and supplies; acquiring, owning, holding and disposing of all necessary or convenient real estate, docks, wharves, tugs and other boats, and other property and equipment, and the doing of all things necessary or incident thereto.

No. 45.

Freight Loading Company.

THIRD. Said corporation is formed for the purpose of loading coal, iron ore, freight, merchandise, materials and property of all kinds from docks or cars to boats, scows, lighters or other vessels, or therefrom to docks, or cars, conducting a general stevedore business and the doing of all things necessary or incident thereto.

No. 46.

Gas and Electric Company.

(See also Light, Heat and Power Company.)

THIRD. Said corporation is formed for the purpose of manufacturing, producing, distributing, furnishing and selling gas and electricity, or either, for light, heat, power and other purposes, and for doing all things incident to said purpose.

No. 47.

Natural Gas Company.

(See Oil and Gas Company.)

No. 48.

Artificial Gas Company.

THIRD. Said corporation is formed for the purpose of manufacturing gas for light, heat and power, to be made from any and and all substances, or a combination thereof, from which gas can be obtained, and for the purpose of selling and disposing of the same in the city of .... and elsewhere, with full power to lay pipes and conductors therefor, through the avenues, streets, lanes and alleys thereof, and in such other places as may be necessary or convenient to supply said avenues, streets, lanes and alleys, and any manufactories, public places, buildings, houses or any other place or building whatsoever with gas, for light, heat and power, together with the power to hold, occupy and employ such real and personal estate and to do such other things as may be necessary or convenient to carry out the objects of this corporation, and to manufacture and sell coke and all other products used in the manufacture of gas.

No. 49.

General Store Company.

THIRD. Said corporation is formed for the purpose of doing a general merchandise business at wholesale and retail and of buying, selling and dealing at wholesale and retail in dry goods, notions, clothing, gentlemen's furnishing goods, hats, caps, boots, shoes, carpets, groceries, queensware, glassware, wool, live stock, grain, butter, eggs and other country produce.

No. 50.

Glassware Company.

THIRD. Said corporation is formed for the purpose of manufacturing, selling, buying and dealing in, glass bottles, glass jars and all other forms and kinds of glassware; and of doing all other acts and things in any way incidental to or connected with such business.

No. 51.

Greenhouse and Nursery Company.

THIRD. Said corporation is formed for the purpose of growing, raising, buying, selling and dealing in any and all kinds of trees, shrubs, vines, plants, flowers, seeds, grains, roots, vegetables, bulbs and fruits; acquiring, holding, owning and selling all real estate and personal property necessary or convenient in carrying out of said purpose and the doing of all things necessary or incident thereto.

No. 52.

Heating Company.

THIRD. Said corporation is formed for the purpose of making and supplying steam and steam heat for both public and private consumption and use; also the supplying of hot water for said use; and the purchase and use of such tools, engines, pipes and other apparati necessarily incident to said business; and to acquire franchises and privileges to so supply said steam, steam heat and hot water.

No. 53.

Hotel and Restaurant.

THIRD. Said corporation is formed for the purpose of doing a general hotel, restaurant, catering and cafe business, and the doing of all things necessary or incident thereto.

NOTE.—For hotel building company, see *Building Company.*

No. 54.

House Furnishing Company.

THIRD. Said corporation is formed for the purpose of manufacturing, leasing, buying, selling and dealing in house, store and other furniture and furnishings and cabinet work of all kinds and to do all things incident thereto, including selling said goods on installments.

INSURANCE COMPANIES.

No. 55.

Employers' Liability, Accident and Health Company.

(G. C. § 9510.)

THIRD. Said corporation is formed for the purpose of making insurance on the health of individuals and against personal injury, disablement or death, resulting from traveling or general accidents by land and water; making insurance against loss or damage resulting from accident to property, from cause other than by fire or lightning; making insurance to indemnify employers against loss or damage for personal injury or death resulting from accidents to employes or persons other than employes and of indemnifying persons and corporations other than employers against loss or damage for personal injury or death resulting from accidents to other persons or corporations.

No. 56.

Fidelity and Guarantee Company.

(G. C. § 9510.)

THIRD. Said corporation is formed for the purpose of guaranteeing the fidelity of persons holding places of public or private trust, who may be required to, or do, in their trust capacity, receive, hold, control, disburse public or private moneys or property; of guaranteeing the performance of contracts other than insurance policies; executing and guaranteeing bonds and undertakings required or permitted in all actions or proceedings, or by law allowed; and indemnifying bank depositors against loss by reason of bank suspension and failure, and doing any and all things necessary or incident thereto.

No. 57.

Fire Insurance Company.

(G. C. §§ 9510, 9556.)

THIRD. Said corporation is formed for the purpose of insuring houses, buildings and all other kinds of property in and out of the state, against loss or damage by fire, lightning and tornadoes, and explosions from gas, dynamite, gunpowder, and other like explosives, and against loss or damage by water, caused by the breakage or leakage of sprinklers, pumps, tanks, water pipes and fixtures connected therewith, and insuring against loss by the theft of automobiles and accessories, and against damage thereto from this cause, and the making of all kinds of insurance on goods, merchandise and other property in the course of transportation, on land, water or on a vessel, boat or wherever it may be.

No. 58.

Mutual Protective Insurance Association (Fire, etc.).

(G. C. §§ 9593, 9594.)

(Insert in articles of incorporation of corporation not for profit, Form No. 138.)

THIRD. Said corporation is formed for the purpose of enabling its members to insure each other against loss by fire and lightning, cyclones, tornadoes, or wind storms, hail storms and explosions from gas, to enforce any contract by them entered into whereby the parties thereto agree to be assessed specifically for incidental purposes and for the payment of losses which occur to its members on property in this state, subject to the limitations of section 9593 of the General Code of Ohio.

No. 59.

Life, Accident, etc., Insurance Company. (Corporation for Profit.)

(G. C. §§ 9339, 9385, 9340).

THIRD. Said corporation is formed for the purpose of making insurance on the lives of individuals, and every insurance appertaining thereto or connected therewith, in Ohio and elsewhere, *on the stock plan,* and granting, purchasing and disposing of annuities, and, further, of insuring against accidents to, and sickness, temporary or permanent physical disability, of, individuals, and the doing of all things necessary or incident thereto.

(As to the following special provisions, see G. C. § 9340.)

FOURTH. The corporate powers of said corporation are to be exercised according to the provisions of Chapter 1, Subdivision 1 of Division III, Title IX, Part Second, of the General Code of Ohio, and of the regulations and by-laws of said corporation.

FIFTH. The number of directors of said corporation shall be *twenty-one* (21) all of whom shall be stockholders and a majority of whom shall be citizens of the state of Ohio. The directors shall be elected at the annual meeting of the stockholders of the corporation on the *second Monday in January* in each year and shall hold office until the next annual meeting of the stockholders and until their successors are chosen and qualified. The other officers of said company shall be elected annually by the board of directors at the first regular meeting or special meeting of the board after such annual election. In the event of a vacancy occurring in said board by death or otherwise, the same shall be filled by the affirmative vote of a majority of the members of the board of directors.

SIXTH. Regulations for the government of the business and affairs of the company, not inconsistent with law, may be adopted, changed or amended by a majority vote of the shareholders at any annual meeting or at any special meeting, provided notice of such special meeting shall show that an amendment of the regulations will be proposed. The board of directors of the corporation may from time to time adopt, change, amend or repeal by-laws not inconsistent with law, governing the transaction of its business and affairs.

SEVENTH. The capital stock of said company and the amount of capital to be employed shall be *one hundred thousand* ($100,000) dollars divided into ten thousand (10,000) shares of ten dollars ($10.00) each.

No. 60.

Mutual Protective Association. (Life and Accident.)

(G. C. § 9427 et seq.)

(Insert in articles of incorporation of corporation not for profit, Form No. 138.)

THIRD. Said corporation is formed for the purpose of transacting the business of life (*and accident*) insurance, on the assessment plan, under sections 9427, 9428 and 9429 of the General Code of Ohio, and of doing all things necessary and incident thereto.

No. 61.

Live Stock Insurance Company.

(G. C. §§ 9510, 9524.)

THIRD. Said corporation is formed for the purpose of making insurance on the lives of horses, cattle and other live stock against loss by death caused by accident, disease, fire or lightning, and against loss by theft and damage by accident, and the doing of all things necessary and incident thereto.

No. 62.

Live Stock Mutual Protective Association.

(G. C. §§ 9608, 9609.)

(Insert in articles of incorporation of coporation not for profit, Form No. 138.)

THIRD. Said corporation is formed for the purpose of enabling its members to insure each other against loss from death of domestic animals, and to enforce any contract by them entered into, whereby they specifically agree to be assessed for the payment of losses and incidental expenses.

No. 63.

Credit Insurance Company.

(G. C. § 9621.)

THIRD. Said corporation is formed for the purpose of guaranteeing and indemnifying merchants, manufacturers, traders and those engaged in business, and giving credit, from loss and damage by reason of giving and extending credit to their customers and those dealing with them, and the doing of all things necessary and incident thereto.

FOURTH. (*Add paragraphs Fourth, Fifth, Sixth and Seventh, of Articles of Life, Accident, etc., Insurance Company, Form No. 59.*) See G. C. Secs. 9621, 9340, 9341.

No. 64.

Interurban and Street Railway Company.

(G. C. § 9117.)

THIRD. Said corporation is formed for the purpose of constructing, building, acquiring, by purchase, lease or otherwise, and owning, maintaining and operating a line of railroad with rights of way, roadbed, single or double tracks, side tracks, switches, spurs, turnouts, branches, extensions, stations, depots, terminals, way stations, freight houses, power houses, lines for the transmission of electric power, telegraph and telephone lines, and all other necessary or convenient appurtenances and appliances incidental to the operation of a railroad; said railroad to be operated by electric or other motive power except animal power; of acquiring and holding real estate and personal property and all equipment and accessories necessary, convenient and proper to carry out the purposes herein mentioned, of constructing, owning and operating power plants for the generating of electricity by steam, water or other motive power, the same to be used in propelling its cars, rolling stock and machinery; of using, supplying and selling electricity so generated, for heat, light, power and other purposes, and receiving compensation therefor; for transporting passengers, packages, express matter, United States mail, baggage and freight, and engaging in the general business of a common carrier upon its railroad, or lines of railway, telegraph and telephone lines; and with full right to purchase, lease, sublease or otherwise acquire electricity or other motive power.

Said line of railroad shall have the city of ...., county of ...., state of Ohio, for one terminus, and the city of ...., county of ...., state of Ohio, for its other terminus, and shall pass through the following named counties in the state of Ohio, to wit: ....

No. 65.

Iron Company.

(G. C. § 10143.)

THIRD. Said corporation is formed for the purpose of manufacturing, buying, selling and dealing in iron and steel and the various products and forms thereof.

No. 66.

Light, Heat and Power Company.

THIRD. Said corporation is formed for the purpose of producing, acquiring, buying, leasing, using, furnishing, supplying, selling, transmitting, and distributing light, heat and power, generated by means of gas, electricity, steam or hot water, or any or all of them, and in connection therewith, of constructing, acquiring, purchasing, using, leasing or purchasing plants, works, constructions, or parts thereof for the production, use, transmission, distribution, regulation, control or application of gas, electricity, steam or hot water, and the doing of all things necessary or incident thereto.

No. 67.

Live Stock Company.

THIRD. Said corporation is formed for the purpose of buying, breeding, raising, selling and dealing in horses, cattle and all other kinds of live stock, vehicles, harness and other equipment therefor, and the doing of all things necessary or incident thereto.

No. 68.

Lodge Building Company.

(G. C. § 10196.)

THIRD. Said corporation is formed for the purpose of erecting, equipping and maintaining a building, to be used and occupied by .... (*specify two or more lodges which will occupy the building*) as a lodge room and club house; of acquiring, owning, holding and disposing of real estate and personal property necessary or convenient to carry out the purpose aforesaid and the doing of all things necessary or incident thereto.

No. 69.

Lumber Company.

THIRD. Said corporation is formed for the purpose of doing a general manufacturing and wholesale lumber business; manufacturing wood products of every description; buying, selling and dealing in lumber, at wholesale or retail, in its own behalf and as agent, factor, or broker; acquiring, by lease, purchase or otherwise, and holding and disposing of such timber lands and other real and personal property as is necessary or convenient for carrying out the foregoing purpose and the doing of all things necessary or incident thereto.

No. 70.

Mail Order Company.

THIRD. Said corporation is formed for the purpose of conducting a mail order business in a general line of .... (*specify articles to be dealt in*) and the doing of all things necessary or incident thereto.

No. 71.

Mail Tube Company.

(See G. C. § 3645-1.)

THIRD. Said corporation is formed for the purpose of establishing and carrying on the business of transporting and delivering United States mail, messages, packages, commercial bundles, and merchandise; conducting a general forwarding business by and through subways, underground tubes, tunnels, conduits and other similar means, operated by air, electricity or other motive power, and also by vehicles, and motor vehicles; transmitting and supplying power along the line of its subways, mail tubes, tunnels, or conduits; acquiring, holding, owning, leasing, and disposing of inventions, letters patent and patent rights relating to such tubes, tunnels, or conduits and the motive power thereof, and the doing of all things necessary or incident thereto.

No. 72.

Manufacturing Company.

(See G. C. §§ 10137 to 10141.)

THIRD. Said corporation is formed for the purpose of manufacturing, buying, selling and dealing in .... (*specify articles to be manufactured*) ; of acquiring, owning, holding and selling real estate and personal property necessary or convenient to carry out the purpose aforesaid and the doing of all things necessary or incident thereto.

No. 73.

Market House Company.

(G. C. § 10151.)

THIRD. Said corporation is formed for the purpose of constructing and maintaining a market house in ...., Ohio, and exercising all the powers which may be exercised by such corporations under the laws of Ohio.

No. 74.

Mausoleum Company.

THIRD. Said corporation is formed for the purpose of erecting, maintaining, operating and selling mausoleums, crypts, vaults and burial places for the dead; caring for, preserving and protecting dead bodies and the doing of all things necessary or incident thereto.

No. 75.

Meat Market Company.

THIRD. Said corporation is formed for the purpose of buying, selling and dealing in meats, fish, fowl and provisions and the doing of all things necessary or incident thereto.

No. 76.

Men's Furnishing Company.

THIRD. Said corporation is formed for the purpose of dealing in woolens, trimmings and fabrics used in connection with the tailoring business; in the manufacture, purchase and sale of custom made and ready made clothing of every kind and nature and for the purpose of dealing in furnishing goods.

No. 77.

Mercantile Agency Company.

THIRD. Said corporation is formed for the purpose of compiling, collecting, publishing and selling commercial credit rating and other directories, collecting accounts, furnishing reports and abstracts and certificates of titles and the performing of such other business as usually pertains to the publishing of reference and other directories, making collections and furnishing financial reports and abstracts and certificates of titles with the right to acquire and hold by lease or purchase, such real and personal estate as may be necessary to the carrying on of said business.

No. 78.

Mercantile or Trading Company.

THIRD. Said corporation is formed for the purpose of buying, selling and dealing in, at wholesale or retail, ... (*specify kinds of merchandise to be dealt in, as "cigars, tobacco, pipes and smokers' supplies"*) and the doing of all things necessary and incident thereto.

No. 79.

Messenger Service Company.

THIRD. Said corporation is formed for the purpose of constructing, maintaining, leasing and operating lines of telegraph for the private use of individuals, firms, corporations, municipal and otherwise, for general business, for police, fire and burglar alarm telegraph service, and in connection therewith for constructing, owning and operating a general messenger, delivery and district telegraph service, a general collection, storage and delivery of packages, freight and other properties, for the constructing, owning and operating of a local system of electrical call-boxes for messages, messengers, fire and burglar alarm signals and signals for police and fire patrol and night watchmen, and for any other purpose or purposes in connection therewith or incident thereto; also the manufacture and sale of any and all electrical or other appliances, supplies and fixtures necessary or incidental to the carrying on of said business, and also to carry on a general electrical construction and supply business, and to generate and supply electricity for any and all purposes.

Said company may also act as advertisers, distributors and general agents for handling the business and collecting and remitting funds in connection therewith, of corporations, firms or individuals. It may engage in the business of furnishing stationery and advertising matter, devices and novelties of all kinds.

No. 80.

Millinery Company.

THIRD. Said corporation is formed for the purpose of manufacturing, importing, buying, selling, jobbing and dealing in millinery of every description and doing all things incident thereto, and for owning and holding such real and personal property as may be necessary or convenient therefor.

No. 81.

Milling Company.

THIRD. Said corporation is formed for the purpose of owning, controlling and operating flour and grist mills, and for buying and selling, at wholesale and retail, and dealing in, grain, seed, flour, feed and kindred merchandise, and for the purpose of owning all machinery, privileges, real estate and other property needed in carrying on such business, and for doing all things incident to such purposes and business.

No. 82.

Mineral Springs Company.

THIRD. Said corporation is formed for the purpose of preparing, manufacturing, bottling, buying, selling, vending, dealing in and furnishing to dealers and consumers, drinking and table water; carbonated water, carbonated and other nonintoxicating beverages, and to do all things incident thereto, and for the further purpose of manufacturing, buying, selling and dealing in such machinery, tanks, fountains, bottles and other material as may be used in connection with or in or about the preparation, manufacture, dealing in or furnishing such water or beverages and to do all things incident thereto.

No. 83.

Mining Company.

(See G. C. §§ 10137, 10139, 10142 and 10143.)

THIRD. Said corporation is formed for the purpose of mining, manufacturing and dealing in any and all kinds of ores, minerals and metals, and acquiring and selling any and all real estate and personal property in the state of Ohio and elsewhere necessary or convenient for the better transaction of the business of the company, and to insure or aid in the carrying out of the general powers of the company, and the doing of all things necessary or incident thereto.

No. 84.

Motion Picture and Vaudeville Theater Company.

THIRD. Said corporation is formed for the purpose of purchasing, renting and holding real estate and constructing buildings thereon for the purpose of operating and conducting motion picture and vaudeville entertainments and the doing of all things necessary or incident thereto.

No. 85.

Motion Picture and Vaudeville Theater. Another Form.

THIRD. Said corporation is formed for the purpose of buying, leasing or otherwise acquiring and owning, holding, operating and conducting motion picture and vaudeville theaters and the doing of all things necessary or incident thereto.

No. 86.

Musical Instrument Company.

THIRD. Said corporation is formed for the purpose of manufacturing, purchasing, selling and dealing in all kinds of pianos, organs, automatic pianos, instruments of all kinds, appliances, supplies and all things incident thereto.

No. 87.

Ohio River Bridge Company.

(G. C. § 9310 et seq.)

THIRD. Said corporation is formed for the purpose of constructing, owning, maintaining and operating a toll bridge over the Ohio River, with one or more tracks, for railway and highway traffic from a point in .... Township, ... County, Ohio, on the northerly side of said river to a point in .... Township, ... County, State of ...., on the southerly side of said river, with suitable avenues and approaches thereto, and for such purposes and objects to have the powers enumerated and conferred on such companies by sections 9310 to 9313 of the General Code of Ohio and the doing of all things necessary or incident thereto.

No. 88.

Oil and Gas Company.

(See G. C. §§ 10137, 10139.)

THIRD. Said corporation is formed for the purpose of drilling for and accumulating petroleum oil and natural gas, buying and selling oil and gas rights, privileges and leases, and oil and gas and the products thereof, leasing oil and gas territory, refining, manufacturing and dealing in oil, dealing in land containing oil and other minerals and the doing of all things necessary or incident thereto.

No. 89.

Oil and Gas Company. Another Form.

THIRD. Said corporation is formed for the purpose of leasing, acquiring, holding, operating and disposing of petroleum oil and natural gas properties, drilling for petroleum oil and natural gas, producing, accumulating and disposing of petroleum oil and natural gas, and the products thereof; manufacturing, distilling, refining and otherwise converting such oil and gas and the products thereof, and marketing and disposing of the same, and the doing of all things necessary or incident thereto.

No. 90.

Orchard Land Company.

THIRD. Said corporation is formed for the purpose of buying, selling and dealing in orchard lands, and the products thereof, cultivating and maintaining orchards and nurseries, and the doing of all things necessary or incident thereto. Said corporation is formed subject to the provisions of section 8648 of the General Code of Ohio.

No. 91.

Pipe Line Company.

(G. C. § 10128.)

THIRD. Said corporation is formed for the purpose of transporting oils and other fluids through tubing and pipes and for handling and storing the same in tanks or otherwise and exercising all the powers which may be exercised by such corporations under the laws of Ohio.

No. 92.

Plumbing and Heating Company.

THIRD. Said corporation is formed for the purpose of doing the business of plumbing, heating, gas fitting, sewer building and buying, selling and dealing in all kinds of material and supplies used by or in said above trades or business; of owning, manufacturing, selling, leasing for hire and dealing in mechanical devices, machinery and articles of all kinds made and connected and in accordance with any or all letters patent of the United States or foreign countries heretofore or hereafter granted pertaining to said above trades or business. Also to purchase, own and control patents whether domestic or foreign pertaining to said above trades or business and of licensing others to use the same for hire.

No. 93.

Pottery Company.

THIRD. Said corporation is formed for the purpose of manufacturing, buying and selling china pottery and earthenware; to decorate and embellish the same; to mine and manufacture and deal in china clay, flint and feldspar and all materials of any nature used in the manufacture of said wares and to acquire, hold and possess and sell real estate and other property necessary for the proper and convenient conduct of said business for profit.

No. 94.

Printing and Publishing Company.

THIRD. Said corporation is formed for the purpose of doing a general printing, publishing, binding, engraving, electrotyping and lithographing business, and the doing of all things necessary and incident thereto.

No. 95.

Publishing Company.

THIRD. Said corporation is formed for the purpose of printing and publishing newspapers, magazines, periodicals; conducting a general advertising and printing business and the doing of all things necessary or incident thereto.

No. 96.

Railroad Company.

THIRD. Said corporation is formed for the purpose of building, constructing, acquiring by purchase, lease or otherwise, and owning, maintaining and operating a railroad with rights of way, roadbed, tracks, side tracks, spurs, switches, stations, depots, terminals, way stations, freight houses, power houses, lines for the transmission of electric power, telegraph and telephone lines, and all necessary, useful and convenient buildings and structures, having the city of ...., county of ...., state of Ohio, for one terminus and the city of ...., county of ...., state of Ohio, for its other terminus, and passing through the following named counties in the state of Ohio, to wit: .... and ...., and with branches from said main line to towns or places within the limits of said counties, or to connections with other railroads within the state, or to mines, clay banks, quarries, manufacturing establishments, elevators, warehouses and navigable waters; said railroad to be operated by steam, electric or other motive power; and of building, constructing, manufacturing and acquiring, by purchase, lease or otherwise, the necessary engines, locomotives, motors, cars, coaches, rolling stock and equipment of all kinds necessary, sufficient and convenient for the proper and profitable operation of such railroad; of owning real estate in all the said counties sufficient and proper for maintaining such stations, depots, terminal facilities, way stations, freight houses, power houses and yards necessary, sufficient and convenient for the proper and profitable operation of a complete railroad system; of owning real estate, with buildings, structures, machinery, tools and other appliances sufficient for shops and repair shops, for the purpose of making, manufacturing, building and repairing engines, locomotives, motors, cars, coaches and rolling stock and equipment of all kinds.

No. 97.

Real Estate Company.

(G. C. §§ 8648-8650).

THIRD. Said corporation is formed for the purpose of buying, selling and dealing in real estate and the doing of all things incident thereto, subject to the provisions of sections 8648, 8649 and 8650 of the General Code of Ohio and is to exist for the term of twenty-five years.

No. 98.

Sales Agency Company.

THIRD. Said corporation is formed for the purpose of doing a general agency and commission business, buying, selling and dealing in .... (*specify articles*) for itself and as agent, factor and broker and the doing of all things necessary or incident thereto.

No. 99.

Sand and Gravel Company.

THIRD. Said corporation is formed for the purpose of acquiring, by dredging, purchase, or otherwise, selling and dealing in sand, gravel, crushed stone and building materials and supplies, and the doing of all things necessary or incident thereto.

No. 100.

Sanitorium Company.

(G. C. § 8624.)

THIRD. Said corporation is formed for the purpose of erecting, owning and conducting sanitoriums for the receiving of and caring for patients and for the medical, surgical and hygienic treatment of such patients, and for instruction of nurses in the treatment of disease and hygiene.

No. 101.

Sanitorium and Drug Company.

THIRD. Said corporation is formed for the purpose of manufacturing, compounding, using, buying, selling and dealing in drugs, medicines, surgical instruments, chemicals and formulae; erecting, owning and conducting sanitoriums or hospitals for the receiving and caring for patients, and for the medical, surgical and hygienic treatment of the diseases of such patients, and for the instruction of nurses in the treatment of disease and in hygiene, and of doing all things necessary to carry out, or incident to, said purpose.

No. 102.

Scenic Railway Company.

THIRD. Said corporation is formed for the purpose of manufacturing, operating and selling scenic and pleasure railways of improved construction covered by letters patent of the United States; to acquire the control of said and future patents upon or in relation to such railways; to introduce said structures into public use; and, in connection with said business, to manufacture, use and vend such articles as may be conveniently and profitably dealt with in that connection; and to acquire and use such property as may be necessary or convenient for the aforesaid business of the company.

No. 103.

Securities Company.

THIRD. Said corporation is formed for the purpose of acquiring, owning, holding and disposing of stocks in other kindred but not competing private corporations, bonds, notes, bills of exchange, mortgages, bills of lading, warehouse receipts and other securities, as owner, agent, factor or broker; promoting, financing, developing and otherwise furthering the lawful enterprises of others and the doing of all things necessary or incident thereto.

No. 104.

Securities Company. Another Form.

THIRD. Said corporation is formed for the purpose of carrying on a general brokerage business, dealing in stocks, of other kindred and not competing corporations, bonds and other kinds of securities and commercial paper; acting as financial agent for corporations, firms and persons, and the doing of all things necessary or incident thereto.

No. 105.

Sewerage Company.

((G. C. § 10157 et seq.)

THIRD. Said corporation is formed for the purpose of constructing, maintaining and operating a sewer on ....

Avenue, ... Ohio, draining the streets, alleys, buildings and grounds lying contiguous and adjacent to said avenue, and the doing of all things necessary or incident thereto.

No. 106.

Stock-Yard Company.

(G. C. § 10211).

THIRD. Said corporation is formed for the purpose of erecting and maintaining pens, buildings and other structures for the safe keeping of live stock intrusted to it on sale or otherwise, and to purchase or lease such real estate as may be necessary for the convenient prosecution of said business.

No. 107.

˙ Taxicab and Garage Company.

THIRD. Said corporation is formed for the purpose of doing a general taxicab and automobile livery business, acquiring, owning, operating, letting and renting automobiles, taxicabs, motor and other vehicles for hire, in the transportation of persons and property; the conducting of a general automobile garage and repair business; buying, selling and dealing in automobile supplies, parts and accessories, and the doing of all things necessary or incident thereto.

No. 108.

Telephone Company.

THIRD. Said corporation is formed for the purpose of building, purchasing, equipping, maintaining and operating telephone exchange systems and furnishing telephone service in .... and neighboring townships and villages. One terminus of said improvement will be in .... county of ...., Ohio, and the other terminus will be in ...., county of ...., Ohio, with lines extending into .... (*specify route*).

No. 109.

Telephone Company. (Local.)

THIRD. Said corporation is formed for the purpose of constructing, maintaining and operating a telephone exchange system in the city of ...., Ohio, and in the county of ...., in said state.

No. 110.

Telephone Company. (Mutual.)

THIRD. Said corporation is formed for the purpose of giving its members, together with their families and help in business relations, free telephone service over any of its lines and to enforce any of its contracts which may be by them entered into by which those entering shall agree to be assessed specifically for incidental purposes and for the payment of exchange services.

No. 111.

Tennis Club Company.

THIRD. Said corporation is formed for the purpose of promoting the game of tennis; acquiring, by lease, purchase or otherwise, owning, holding and selling such real estate and personal property as may be necessary or convenient for constructing, equipping and maintaining tennis courts and club houses for its members and guests, and the doing of all things necessary or incident thereto.

No. 112.

Theater Company.

THIRD. Said corporation is formed for the purpose of operating theaters for the exhibition of motion pictures, shows and theatrical performances, the providing of other forms of public entertainment and amusement; of constructing, buying, leasing, owning, maintaining and selling such real estate, buildings and personal property as may be necessary or convenient to the carrying out of said purpose, and the doing of all things necessary or incident thereto.

No. 113.

Title Guarantee and Trust Company.

(G. C. § 9850.)

THIRD. Said corporation is formed for the purpose of preparing and furnishing abstracts and certificates of title to real estate, bonds, mortgages and other securities; guaranteeing such titles, the validity and due execution of such securities, and the performance of contracts incident thereto; making and negotiating loans for itself and as agent or trustee for others, and guaranteeing the collection of interest and principal of such loans; taking charge of and selling, mortgaging, renting or

otherwise disposing of real estate for others, and performing all
the duties of an agent relative to property deeded or otherwise
entrusted to it; owning real estate, as a place for carrying on
its business, and to do any and all things necessary or incidental to an abstract, title guarantee and loaning business, and
the transaction of any and all business incidentally or necessarily
connected with each or all of the foregoing provisions.

No. 114.
Towel Supply Company.

THIRD. Said corporation is formed for the purpose of
buying, selling, leasing and otherwise supplying white coats,
aprons, towels, napkins and other linen, soap, combs, brushes and
other toilet articles, with cabinets therefor, to persons, firms and
corporations, in offices, stores, factories and other places, conducting a laundry, and the doing of all things necessary or incident thereto.

No. 115.
Trade Secrets and Patents Company.

THIRD. Said corporation is formed for the purpose of
applying for, acquiring, leasing, purchasing, registering, holding,
owning and using any and all trade secrets, processes, inventions
and improvements whether secured by letters patent in the
United States or elsewhere, or otherwise; operating, manufacturing and using the same; selling, assigning, granting of licenses
in respect of, and otherwise disposing of the same and the doing
of all things necessary or incident thereto.

No. 116.
Transfer Company.

THIRD. Said corporation is formed for the purpose of
transferring, moving and delivering baggage, household goods
and other personal property, the carrying of passengers and property by automobiles, trucks and other vehicles in the city of
.........., Ohio, and in the vicinity thereof and the doing
of all things necessary or incident thereto.

No. 117.
Undertaking Company.

THIRD. Said corporation is formed for the purpose of
engaging in the undertaking business; buying, selling, renting,
supplying and furnishing caskets, coffins and burial and funeral

supplies and furnishings; owning and operating an ambulance and coach service and the doing of all things necessary or incident thereto.

No. 118.

Union Interurban Depot and Terminal Company.

(G. C. § 9169-1 et seq.)

THIRD. Said corporation is formed for the purpose of constructing, owning, maintaining and operating a union electric interurban terminal depot and connecting tracks, with all necessary and proper yards, tracks, buildings and structures for the use of interurban and street railways, with all the rights, privileges and powers incident thereto or connected therewith, and with all the properties, rights, privileges and powers given or granted to such a corporation under any general or special law of the state of Ohio, including the power to purchase, appropriate or condemn private lands for the purpose aforesaid and to hold and improve the same, and also the power of acquiring all necessary, proper or desirable rights of way or franchises for electric interurban railways to enter said interurban terminal and depot buildings and grounds. Said union electric interurban terminal and depot and connecting tracks and the improvements connected therewith shall be located in the city of ...., county of ...., and state of ....

NOTE.—Articles of union depot company, see form No. 127.

No. 119.

Vessel Company.

THIRD. Said corporation is formed for the purpose of purchasing, building, leasing, chartering, acquiring, owning, operating and selling steamboats and all other kinds of vessels and water craft, the doing of a general freight and passenger business, and towing; of acquiring, by purchase or otherwise, such real estate, docks, wharfs, equipment, appliances and other properties as may be necessary or convenient to carry out such purpose and the doing of all things necessary or incident thereto.

No. 120.

Warehouse Company.

THIRD. Said corporation is formed for the purpose of establishing, maintaining and conducting warehouses for the storage, receipt, custody, shipment and forwarding of personal property and chattels of all kinds; issuing warehouse receipts therefor; acquiring, holding, owning and selling real estate and personal property, including trucks and moving vans, necessary or convenient in the carrying out of said purpose and the doing of all things necessary or incident thereto.

No. 121.

Waste Paper and Junk Company.

THIRD. Said corporation is formed for the purpose of buying and otherwise acquiring, selling and dealing in waste paper, rags, bottles, broken glass, zinc, iron, rubber, brass, junk and other kindred articles and the doing of all things necessary or incident thereto.

No. 122.

Water Transportation Company.

THIRD. Said corporation is formed for the purpose of purchasing, chartering, acquiring, owning, handling or operating steamships, vessels and other vessel property or interest therein; purchasing, constructing or owning all necessary or proper terminal facilities, including all real estate and personal property as may be suitable or necessary thereto and doing all such things as may be properly incident to the above enumerated purposes.

No. 123.

Water Transportation Company.   Another Form.

THIRD. Said corporation is formed for the purpose of building, buying, selling, leasing and renting boats, barges and all kinds of water craft and operating the same in towing, freighting and transporting, by water, of any and all kinds of merchandise and property, and the doing of all things necessary or incident thereto.

No. 124.

Waterworks Company.

THIRD. Said corporation is formed for the purpose of supplying the city of .... and the inhabitants thereof and individuals, firms, corporations, townships and municipalities within said city and in the vicinity thereof with water for domestic, sanitary, manufacturing, fire and other purposes; of acquiring, erecting, maintaining, owning and operating all necessary, expedient or convenient pumping stations, settling basins, filtering galleries, reservoirs, water towers, buildings, structures, engines, machinery, appliances and equipment; of acquiring, laying and maintaining in public streets, alleys, lanes, highways and public and private grounds, pipe lines, conduits and connections through which to distribute water; and of acquiring, by lease, purchase or otherwise, owning, selling and conveying all such real estate, water rights, easements and franchises as may be necessary or convenient to carry into effect the corporate purposes aforesaid and the doing of all things necessary or incident thereto.

No. 125.

Wine or Liquor Company.

THIRD. Said corporation is formed for the purpose of manufacturing and selling at wholesale and retail spirituous, malt and vinous, distilled or fermented liquors, wines and other beverages.

To acquire and own all such real estate and personal property as may be necessary or convenient to the successful accomplishment of the above objects and purposes.

No. 126.

Wrecking Company.

THIRD. Said corporation is formed for the purpose of erecting, purchasing, moving, wrecking, selling and erecting buildings and structures and building material and the doing of all things necessary or incident thereto.

No. 127.

Union Depot Company. Articles of Incorporation.

(G. C. § 9160 et seq.)

The undersigned, A. B., president of The E. F. Railroad Company, and C. D., president of The G. H. Railroad Company, having been thereto duly authorized and directed by resolutions of the boards of directors of said railroad companies, respectively, duly passed, hereby associate said companies to become a body corporate, in accordance with the laws of the state of Ohio, under the following articles:

1. The name of said corporation shall be "The . . . . Union Depot Company."

2. The names of said companies are The E. F. Railroad Company and The G. H. Railroad Company, and said corporation is formed for the purpose of purchasing depot grounds, and locating, constructing and maintaining a common or union station house, passenger and freight depot and terminals, and a union railroad, by two or more tracks, connecting the railroads of said companies for business purposes.

Said depot, terminals and connection tracks are to be constructed in the city of ....,Ohio.

3. The amount of capital stock necessary to obtain a site, and construct and maintain such depot, terminals and tracks is .... dollars ($....).

In witness whereof, the presidents of said companies, on behalf of said companies, have hereunto set their hands and caused the seals of said companies, respectively, to be hereto affixed this .... day of ...., A. D. 19...

(Corporate seal.)   The E. F. Railroad Company.
Attest ...., Secretary.   By A. B., President.
(Corporate seal.)   The G. H. Railroad Company.
Attest ...., Secretary.   By C. D., President.

NOTE.—For articles of interurban depot and terminal company, see form No. 118.

No. 128.

Record of Organization Proceedings of Corporations for Profit.

NOTE.—Every corporation should have a permanent record book containing a record of the proceedings of the incorporators, stockholders and directors. On the title page should be entered "Record of Proceedings of the Incorporators, Stockholders and Directors of The .... Company."

On the first page an entry substantially as follows should be made:

On the .... day of ...., 19...., ..., ..., ..., ... and ...., the persons named below as subscribers of articles of incorporation, desiring for themselves, their associates, successors and assigns, to become a body corporate, in accordance with the general corporation laws of Ohio, under the name and style of The .... Company, and with all the corporate rights, powers, privileges and liabilities provided for by such laws, did subscribe and acknowledge, as required by law, articles of incorporation as follows, to wit:

(*Copy in full the articles of incorporation, together with the certificate of acknowledgment and certificate of the clerk as to the official character of the officer taking the acknowledgment. A copy of the articles is furnished by the secretary of state, and the certificate of the secretary of state as to the filing and recording of the articles should also be copied into the record.*)

(1) PROCEEDINGS OF INCORPORATORS.

On this .... day of ...., 19...., all (or "a majority") of the incorporators of The .... Company met at .... to order the opening of books of subscription to the capital stock of said The .... Company; to fix the time and place for such opening and to waive the notice of such opening required by law to be given; and having agreed upon the same the following order for, and waiver of notice of, the opening of such books of subscription was made in writing by all the subscribers to the articles of incorporation.

(a)

ORDER FOR, AND WAIVER OF NOTICE OF, OPENING OF BOOKS OF SUBSCRIPTION.

.........., Ohio, ..., 19...

The undersigned, being .... (all, *or*, a majority) of the subscribers to the articles of incorporation of The .... Company, do hereby order that books be opened for subscriptions to the capital stock of said Company at the office of ...., in the city of ...., ..., county, Ohio, on the .... day of ...., 19.., at .... o'clock .. M., and we do hereby in writing waive (*or* order) the notice by publication of the time and place of such opening of books of subscription, required by law.

.............,
.............,
.............,
.............,
.............,
Incorporators.

NOTE.—If all the incorporators are not present to waive notice, or if publication is deemed best, the foregoing forms should be changed in such particulars and the following notice must be published at least thirty days before the time set for opening in a newspaper published or generally circulated in the county where the books of subscription are to be opened:

(b)

NOTICE OF OPENING BOOKS FOR SUBSCRIPTIONS TO CAPITAL STOCK OF THE .... COMPANY.

Pursuant to an order this day made by the undersigned, books for subscriptions to the capital stock of The .... Company will be opened at the office of ...., in the city of ...., ... county, Ohio, on ...., 19.., at ..... o'clock .. M. ...., Ohio, ..., 19...

.............,
.............,
.............,
.............,
.............,
Incorporators.

(c)

ORDER DESIGNATING ONE INCORPORATOR TO RECEIVE PAY-
MENT OF INSTALMENTS OF SUBSCRIPTIONS.

We, the undersigned, do hereby designate and appoint ......
to receive payment, from the subscribers to the capital stock of
The .... Company, of the instalments required by law to be
paid on their respective subscriptions; the same to be paid to the
treasurer of said corporation as soon as a treasurer is elected and
qualified.

.............,.
.............,.
.............,.
.............,.
.............,.

Incorporators.

(d)

SUBSCRIPTION BOOK.

Subscriptions to the Capital Stock
of
The .... Company.

We, the undersigned, do hereby severally subscribe for the
number of shares of the capital stock of The .... Company
set opposite our respective names, and do agree to pay therefor
the sum of .... dollars ($......) per share.

Names.	Shares.

(e)

SEPARATE SUBSCRIPTION FOR STOCK.

Subscription for Stock.

The .... Company.

Suite ...., ... Building, ..., Ohio.

Capital Stock, $..........

................, Ohio, ..., 19...

The undersigned applies for ...... shares of the capital stock of The .... Company, of ...., Ohio, and hereby agrees to accept such portion thereof as may be allotted and to pay therefor the sum of One Hundred Dollars ($100) per share.

Name ....

Address ....

Number of shares ....

(f)

CERTIFICATE OF SUBSCRIPTION OF TEN PERCENT.

The .... Company.

Certificate of Subscription.

.........., Ohio, ..., 19...

To the Secretary of State, Columbus, Ohio:

We, the undersigned, all (*or,* a majority) of the incorporators of The .... Company, do hereby certify that on the .... day of ...., 19.., all the incorporators of said Company did order, in writing, that books be opened for subscriptions to the capital stock of said Company at ...., on the .... day of ...., 19.., at .... o'clock .. M. and, at the same time, did waive, in writing, the notice by publication of the time and place of such opening of books of subscription, required by law; and further, said books having been opened at the time and place ordered, that ten percent of the capital stock of said Company has been subscribed.

................,
................,
................,
................,
................,

Incorporators.

NOTE.—If the notice by publication was not waived, the certificate should be changed accordingly, to show publication.

The incorporators are personally liable for any deficiency in the actual payment of ten percent of the stock subscribed for. G. C. § 8634.

It is imprudent for the incorporators to permit an election for directors to be held until such payment has been made. It is proper for the incorporators to designate one of their number to receive payments.

(g)

ORDER FOR FIRST STOCKHOLDERS' MEETING

.........., Ohio, ..., 19...

We, the undersigned, do hereby certify that the foregoing is a true and correct record of the proceedings by us had as subscribers to the articles of incorporation of The .... Company in the organization of said corporation, and we do hereby appoint the office of .... in the city of ...., Ohio, as the place, and ...., 19.., at .... o'clock .. M., as the time, for holding the first meeting of stockholders of said corporation for the election of directors and the transaction of such other business as may come before said meeting.

................,
................,
................,
................,
................,
　　　　　　Incorporators.

(2) PROCEEDINGS OF STOCKHOLDERS.

(a)

NOTICE OF FIRST MEETING OF STOCKHOLDERS.

Notice is hereby given that the first meeting of the stockholders of The .... Company will be held at the office of .... in the city of ......, Ohio, on the .... day of ......, 19.., at .... o'clock .. M. for the election of directors and the transaction of such other business as may come before said meeting.

................,
................,
................,
................,
................,
　　　　　　Incorporators.

NOTE.—The above notice should be published for at least thirty days before the time set for the meeting. The notice, however, may be waived in writing in case all subscribers to the capital stock are present in person or by proxy.

(b)

WAIVER OF NOTICE OF FIRST MEETING OF STOCKHOLDERS.

.........., Ohio, ..., 19...

We, the undersigned, being all of the subscribers to the capital stock of The .... Company and being all this day, at .... o'clock ..M., present, in person or by proxy, at the first meeting of stockholders of said Company, at the office of .... in the city of ...., Ohio, do hereby waive the notice of such meeting required by law, and agree that the same may be held forthwith.

Stockholders.	Proxies.	Shares.
....	....	....
....	....	....
....	....	....
....	....	....
....	....	....

(c)

MINUTES OF FIRST STOCKHOLDERS' MEETING.

.........., Ohio, ..., 19...

Pursuant to the foregoing waiver and agreement the stockholders of The .... Company met at the time and place therein mentioned, being the time and place designated by the incorporators for the holding of the first meeting of stockholders.

On motion of ...., duly seconded and carried, Mr. ..... was chosen chairman and Mr. .... secretary of the meeting.

Mr. .... presented and read the proposed code of regulations hereinafter set forth for the government of this corporation and moved their adoption. The motion was duly seconded and ...... shares, being the entire capital stock of said corporation being cast in the affirmative and no shares of stock being cast in the negative, it was resolved that the code of regulations hereinafter set forth be adopted as the code of regulations governing this corporation, and that the written assent of the stockholders favoring the adoption of such resolutions be recorded in the minutes of the meeting.

NOTE.—Minutes of the first meeting of stockholders are continued on page 125. Provisions and suggestions for regulations are given in the intermediate pages.

(d)

REGULATIONS OF A CORPORATION FOR PROFIT.

Regulations of The .... Company.

ARTICLE I. STOCK.

(a). *Certificates of stock.* Each stockholder of this Company, whose stock has been paid up, shall be entitled to a certificate or certificates showing the amount of stock registered in his name on the books of the Company. Each certificate shall be issued in numerical order from the stock certificate book, and be signed by the president and secretary. A full record of each certificate, as issued, shall be entered on the stub thereof.

(b). *Transfers of stock.* Transfers of stock shall be made only on the books of the Company, and must be accompanied by the surrender of the certificates, properly assigned, evidencing the stock so transferred. Certificates so surrendered shall be cancelled and attached to the stubs corresponding thereto in the stock certificate book.

(c). *Lost, destroyed or mutilated certificates.* If any certificate of stock in this Company becomes worn, defaced or mutilated, the directors, upon production and surrender thereof, may order the same cancelled and may issue a new certificate in lieu of the same. If any certificate of stock be lost or destroyed, the directors, upon the giving of a proper bond of indemnity with surety to their satisfaction, may issue a new certificate in lieu thereof to the person entitled to such lost or destroyed certificate.

ARTICLE II. MEETINGS OF STOCKHOLDERS.

(a). *Annual meeting.* The annual meeting of the stockholders of this Company shall be held at the principal office of the Company in ...., Ohio, on the first Monday in January of each year at 10 o'clock A. M., if not a legal holiday, but if a legal holiday, then on the day following at the same hour.

(b). *Special meetings* of the stockholders may be held at any time pursuant to a resolution of the board of directors, or by a call signed by *two* stockholders. Calls for special meetings shall specify the time, place and object or objects thereof, and no business other than that specified in the call shall be considered at any such meeting.

(c). *Notice of meetings.* A written or printed notice of every regular or special meeting of the stockholders, stating the time and place, and in case of special meetings, the objects thereof shall be given each stockholder appearing on the books of the company by mailing the same to his last known address at least ten days before any such meeting. Provided, however, no failure or irregularity of notice of any regular meeting shall invalidate the same or any proceeding thereat.

(d). *Quorum.* A majority in amount of stock issued and outstanding shall constitute a quorum for the transaction of business.

ARTICLE III. DIRECTORS.

The number of directors shall be five. The election of directors shall be held at the annual meeting of the stockholders, or at a special meeting called for that purpose. Directors shall hold office for one year, or until their successors are elected and qualified.

Directors chosen at the first election shall hold office until the time fixed for the next annual meeting, or until their successors are elected and qualified. All directors must be holders of at least one share of the capital stock of this Company.

A majority of the directors must be citizens of the state of Ohio.

ARTICLE IV. OFFICERS.

The officers of the Company shall be a president, vice-president, secretary, and treasurer. Two offices may be held by one person. Said officers shall be chosen by the board of directors by a majority ballot, and shall hold office for one year or until their successors are elected and qualified, except that officers elected at the first meeting of the directors shall hold office until the next annual meeting of directors, or until their successors are chosen and qualified, provided, however, any REMOVAL. officer may be removed at any time by a vote of two-thirds of the members of the board of directors.

All officers must be holders of at least one share of the capital stock of this Company.

ARTICLE V. DUTIES OF OFFICERS.

(a). *President.* The president shall preside at all meetings of stockholders and directors, sign the records thereof, and, together with the secretary, shall sign all certificates of stock and all other written contracts and obligations of the Company except checks, and perform generally all the duties incident to the office, and such further and other duties as may be from time to time required of him by the stockholders or directors.

(b). *Vice-President.* The vice-president shall perform all the duties of the president in case of the absence or disability of the latter. In case both president and vice-president are absent or unable to perform their duties, the stockholders or directors, as the case may be, may appoint a president pro tempore.

(c). *Secretary.* The secretary shall keep minutes of all the proceedings of the stockholders and directors of this Company and make a proper record of the same, which shall be attested by him. He shall keep such books as may be required by the board of directors, and shall have charge of the seal and stock books of the Company and shall issue and attest all certificates of stock, and generally perform such duties as may be required of him by the stockholders or directors.

(d). *Treasurer.* The treasurer shall receive and have in charge all money, bills, notes, bonds, and similar property belonging to the Company, and shall do with the same as may be ordered by the board of directors. He shall sign all checks and shall keep such financial accounts as may be required, and shall generally perform such duties as may be required of him by the stockholders and directors. On the expiration of his term of office, he shall turn over to his successor, or to the board of directors, all property, books, papers and money of the Company in his hands.

ARTICLE VI. COMPENSATION OF OFFICERS.

The compensation of directors shall be such as the stockholders may from time to time determine. The compensation of other officers shall be fixed by the board of directors.

The treasurer and other officers, if required by the board of directors, shall furnish bonds for the faithful performance of their duties in such amount, and with such sureties, as may be fixed and required by the board of directors.

(NOTE.—For substitute Article VI, see *special provisions* following:)

ARTICLE VII. SEAL.

The corporate seal of this Company shall be circular with the words "The .... Company" and "........, Ohio," surrounding the word "seal."

ARTICLE VIII. ORDER OF BUSINESS.

Unless changed by a majority vote at all stockholders' meetings the order of business shall be as follows:

(1) Reading of the minutes.
(2) Reading of reports and statements.
(3) Unfinished business.
(4) Election of directors.
(5) New or miscellaneous business.

ARTICLE IX. AMENDMENTS.

These regulations may be adopted, amended or repealed by the written assent of the owners of two-thirds of the stock of this Company, or by the vote of the owners of a majority of the stock at a meeting called and held for that purpose.

SPECIAL PROVISIONS.

NOTE.—The following provisions may be included in the regulations, if desired.

ARTICLE ——. WHO MAY VOTE AT STOCKHOLDERS' MEETINGS.

At all meetings of stockholders, only such persons shall be entitled to vote who appear as stockholders upon the books of the corporation for ten days next prior to such meeting.

ARTICLE ——. PROXIES.

The instrument appointing a proxy shall be in writing and subscribed by the person making the appointment.

The instrument appointing a proxy shall be deposited at the office of the Company not less than twenty-four hours before the time for holding the meeting at which the person named in such instrument proposes to vote.

No instrument appointing a proxy shall be valid after the expiration of six months from the date of its execution, and no proxy shall be used at an adjourned meeting which could not have been used at the original meeting.

A vote in accordance with the terms of a proxy shall be valid, notwithstanding the previous death of the principal or revocation of the appointment, or the transfer of the share on which the vote was given, unless notice in writing of the death, revocation or transfer shall have been received at the office of the Company at least twenty-four hours before the meeting.

ARTICLE ——. ADDITIONAL OFFICERS. DUTIES AND SALARIES.

(NOTE.—The following may be added to Article V of the Code of Regulations, supra. The titles of the offices should also be inserted in Article IV.)

(e). *General manager.* The general manager shall, under the supervision of the board of directors and the president, have charge of and manage the active business operations of the Company. He shall perform such further duties and make such reports as may be required of him by the board of directors, and shall receive such salary, not exceeding .... dollars per annum, as may be fixed by the board of directors.

(f). *Counsel.* Counsel of the company shall prepare all such contracts required in the business of the Company, and shall examine and pass upon all such instruments presented to the

Company as may be referred to him by its officers. He shall advise with the officers of the Company in all such matters pertaining to its affairs as may require his consideration. He shall receive such annual retainer, not exceeding ...... dollars per annum, as may be fixed by the board of directors.

(g) *Auditor.* The auditor shall have supervision over the account books, and over all books and papers relating thereto, and shall examine all vouchers and audit all accounts. He shall keep such records as will at all times show the condition of the business, finances and accounts of the Company. At least twice during each year he shall verify the assets of the Company, and shall make such reports and statements as may be required by the board of directors.

ARTICLE ——. COMPENSATION OF OFFICERS.

Note.—The following may be used as a substitute for Article VI of the Code of Regulations, supra.

Directors. Each director shall receive the sum of *five* dollars as compensation for his attendance at any regular or special meeting of the board of directors, and shall receive no other compensation for his services as a director of the Company.

The *president* shall receive such compensation, not exceeding .... dollars per annum, as may be fixed by the board of directors.

The *vice-president* shall receive no compensation whatever.

The *secretary* shall receive such salary, not exceeding ...... dollars per annum, as may be fixed by the board of directors.

The *treasurer* shall receive such compensation, not exceeding .... dollars per annum, as may be fixed by the board of directors.

ARTICLE ——. DUTIES OF OFFICERS MAY BE DELEGATED.

In case of the absence of any officer of the corporation, or for any other reason which the directors may deem sufficient, the directors may delegate the powers or duties of such officer to any other officer, or to any director, for the time being, provided a majority of the entire board concur therein.

ARTICLE ——. REGULAR MEETINGS OF DIRECTORS.

The board of directors shall hold regular meetings at the office of the Company at two o'clock P. M. on the *first Tuesday* of each month, if not a legal holiday. If a legal holiday, then on the day following at the same hour.

ARTICLE ——. EXECUTIVE COMMITTEE.

The president, secretary and treasurer shall together constitute an executive committee which shall, in the interim between meetings of the directors, exercise all the powers of that body in accordance with the general policy of the Company and the instructions of the board of directors. Meetings of the executive committee shall be held on call of the president or of any two members of the committee. All members of the committee shall be notified of its meetings and a majority of its members shall constitute a quorum. The executive committee shall keep a record of its meetings and transactions which shall at all times be open to the inspection of any director.

ARTICLE ——. EXECUTIVE COMMITTEE. (ANOTHER FORM.)

The board of directors may appoint, at their discretion, an executive committee of not less than two members from their own number, who shall have charge of the management of the business and affairs of the Company in the interim · between meetings of directors, with power to fix prices for the Company's products, determine credits, and generally to discharge the duties of the board of directors, but not to incur debts excepting for current expenses, and to replace stock or raw materials in the usual course of business, unless specially authorized. Such executive committee shall at all times act under the direction and control of the board of directors and shall make report of their acts and transactions to the board, which shall form part of the records of the Company.

ARTICLE ——. LIEN OF COMPANY ON STOCK.

(a) The Company shall have a first and paramount lien upon all shares registered in the name of each stockholder, whether held solely or jointly with others, for his debts, liabilities and engagements, solely, or jointly with any other person, to or with the Company, whether the period for the payment, fulfillment or discharge thereof shall have actually arrived or not. And such lien shall extend to all dividends declared on such shares. A memorandum of this article shall be printed on each certificate.

(b) *Sale to satisfy lien.* After default on any debt, liability or engagement above referred to, on ten days' notice by mail or publication, the directors may sell the shares of the stockholder so in default at either public or private sale and may purchase the same on behalf of the Company, if the same can not be otherwise satisfactorily sold. The net proceeds of any such sale shall be applied in or towards satisfaction of the debts, liabilities or engagements of such stockholder, and the residue, if any, paid to him or his executors, administrators or assigns.

Article ——. Annual Audit and Appraisal.

In the month of *December* of each year an audit of the books of account and an appraisal of all the property and assets of the Company shall be made by a competent and responsible Audit Company or Accountant, selected by the board of directors.

The report of such Audit Company or Accountant shall be printed and a copy thereof mailed by the secretary to each stockholder appearing on the books of the Company at least *five* days before the date of the annual meeting of stockholders.

(e)
REGULATIONS OF A CLUB.
Article I.   Name and Location.

1. The name of this corporation shall be The .... Club Company.

2. It shall be located within the corporate limits of the city of ...., Ohio.

Article II.   Officers.

The officers of the Club shall be a president, a vice-president, a secretary and a treasurer.

Article III.   Duties of Officers.

1. The president shall preside at all the meetings of the Club. He shall, with the secretary, sign all certificates of stock and all other written contracts and obligations of the Club, except checks, and in general perform all duties incident to the office. He shall be ex-officio president of the board of directors.

2. In the absence of the president, the vice-president shall perform all the duties of the president.

3. The secretary shall give notice of all meetings of the Club, and shall keep minutes of such meetings. He shall be ex-officio secretary of the board of directors. He shall keep a roll of members, and notify the treasurer of the election of new members. He shall conduct the correspondence of the Club and be the custodian of its records, documents and seal. Together with the president, the secretary shall sign all certificates of stock and all the written contracts and obligations of the Club, except checks, and in general perform all the duties incident to the office. He shall be exempt from payment of the annual dues.

4. The treasurer shall collect the assessments on stock, annual dues, and other sums due the Club. He shall sign all checks and pay the bills for authorized expenses when they are certified by the person empowered to make the expenditure. He shall keep the books of the Club. The treasurer shall be exempt from payment of the annual dues.

ARTICLE IV. DIRECTORS.

1. The board of directors shall consist of the president, vice-president, treasurer, secretary and chairman of the entertainment committee, all ex-officio, and nine others, three of whom shall be elected at each annual meeting of the Club, to hold office for three years.

2. The board of directors shall have general charge of the affairs, finances and property of the Club and general control of all committees, and shall present a report at the annual meeting.

3. The board of directors shall be empowered to fill a vacancy in any office, or in any committee, or in its own body, by the appointment of a member to serve until the next annual election.

4. The board of directors shall hold stated meetings on the Monday following the annual election and on the third Monday of April, June, October, December and February, and such special meetings as may be called by the president or secretary.

5. Seven of its members shall constitute a quorum.

6. At its regular February meeting the board of directors shall appoint a nominating committee of five members, not more than two of whom shall be members of the board, which shall prepare and post on the bulletin in the club-house, not less than twenty days prior to said annual meeting, a list consisting of a candidate for each of the offices and places upon committees to be filled at such annual meeting. Other names may be proposed for any of the positions to be filled at such annual meeting by any twenty members of the Club causing the same, with their signatures, to be presented to the nominating committee not less than five days prior to such annual meeting, whereupon such committee shall post the same on the bulletin board as candidates. From the ticket proposed by such nominating committee, together with such other candidates, as shall be posted as hereinbefore provided, shall be elected at such annual meeting the officers and members of committees for the ensuing year.

ARTICLE V. HOUSE COMMITTEE.

There shall be a house committee, consisting of three members, appointed for one year by the board of directors, at least one of whom shall be a member of such board. The committee shall have charge of the club-house, shall arrange for catering and have the oversight and control of the prices of the same; shall receive complaints, appoint and dismiss all employees, and in general have supervision over the internal economy and regulation of the club-house, its premises and other property, except such property as is assigned to the supervision of other officers or committees. The house committee shall provide rules, not inconsistent with these regulations, governing the use of the Club property.

ARTICLE VI. ENTERTAINMENT COMMITTEE.

1. There shall be an entertainment committee, consisting of a chairman and four others elected annually by the Club.

2. The committee shall arrange for such social and literary entertainment as in its opinion will promote best the interests and purposes of the Club.

ARTICLE VII. COMMITTEE ON LITERATURE AND ART.

1. There shall be a committee on literature and art, consisting of three members, elected annually by the Club.

2. The committee shall have charge of the acquisition of all books, periodicals and works of art; and no book, periodical or work of art shall be deposited in the club-house without the committee's approval.

ARTICLE VIII. AUDITING COMMITTEE.

1. There shall be an auditing committee, consisting of three members, elected annually by the club.

2. The committee shall audit the accounts of the treasurer at least once each year, shall report each audit to the board of directors and shall report at the annual meeting of the Club.

3. No officer, member of the board of directors, or of any other standing committee shall be eligible to membership.

4. The committee shall be empowered to engage the assistance of an expert bookkeeper.

ARTICLE IX. ATHLETICS COMMITTEE.

1. There shall be an athletics committee, consisting of three members appointed for one year by the board of directors, at least one of whom shall be a member of such board.

2. The committee shall have charge of all property of the Club used in connection with athletics and shall arrange all tournaments and interclub contests.

ARTICLE X. ADMISSION COMMITTEE.

1. There shall be an admission committee, consisting of nine members, to serve three years, three of whom shall be appointed annually by the board of directors at its first meeting. The names of the appointees shall not be posted or published.

2. The committee shall investigate the eligibility and act upon the names of all candidates for admission that shall be presented, as hereinafter provided. When the name of a person proposed for membership has been forwarded to the admission committee as provided in Article XIV, Section 1, the committee shall determine whether to post such name, and if it decides to post the same, the name shall then be posted as provided in said article.

3. Five members shall constitute a quorum of the admission committee.

ARTICLE XI. MEETINGS AND ELECTION OF OFFICERS.

1. The members of the Club shall meet annually at 8 P. M. on the third Monday of March for the election of officers, directors and elective committees and for the transaction of other business. Notice of such meeting shall be posted in the club-house and mailed to each member at least one week prior thereto. Officers and members of committees thus elected shall serve until their successors are elected and qualified.

2. All elections shall be by ballot. The ballots shall contain the names of all candidates regularly nominated. The ballots shall be prepared and furnished by the secretary.

3. At the annual meeting of the Club, the order of business shall be:

(a) Reading of minutes of last meeting.
(b) Report of the secretary.
(c) Report of the treasurer and auditors.
(d) Report of the board of directors.
(e) Reports of the committees.
(f) Election of officers.
(g) General business.

4. Special meetings of the Club members may be called at any time by the board of directors and shall be called by them upon written request of twenty members or more. Notice of any special meeting and the object of the same shall be given in the same manner as for the annual meeting, and no business not thus announced shall be transacted at such special meeting.

5. A majority of the resident members, present either in person or by proxy, shall constitute a quorum at any meeting of the Club.

ARTICLE XII. MEMBERSHIP.

1. Any man residing or having a place of business in ......
county shall be eligible to membership, subject, however to section
3 of this article.

2. The resident membership shall not be increased above
...... hundred except by resolution of the board of directors,
and shall in no case exceed ...... hundred in number.

3. No person may become a resident member until he has
become a stockholder in this corporation, and prior to final consideration of his application by the admission committee, he shall
deposit with the treasurer a sum sufficient to meet any assessments
on his stock then due.

4. The admission committee may extend the privileges of the
Club to commissioned officers of the United States army and
navy, and to such men of public distinction as the committee
may designate; and those to whom privileges are so extended
shall pay half resident dues.

ARTICLE XIII. NONRESIDENT MEMBERS.

1. Any person not residing, or having a place of business in
.... county, who is eligible under the provisions of Article XII, may become a nonresident member, subject to the
same conditions of proposal and election as obtain in the case
of resident members, except that in lieu of the purchase of a
share of stock, he shall be required to pay an initiation fee of
.... dollars.

2. Nonresident members shall not be permitted to vote or
to hold office in the Club.

3. A nonresident member becoming a resident of ....
county may become a resident member if, or as soon as there is
a vacancy, by becoming a stockholder and paying resident dues,
and failing so to do, within three months after written notice of
such vacancy has been given him by the secretary, his membership shall be terminated. When any resident member shall
cease to have a residence or place of business in .... county,
he may, upon written request to the secretary, become a nonresident member, and shall then pay nonresident dues.

ARTICLE XIV. ELECTION OF MEMBERS.

1. Candidates for membership must be proposed and seconded by members of the Club, by letters addressed to the admission committee. These letters must state the name, residence
and present occupation of the candidate and they must set forth
fully the grounds of recommendation. If the committee determines to post the name of the candidate as provided in Article

X, Section 2, the facts constituting his eligibility, together with the names of his proposer and seconder, shall be posted on the bulletin board in the club-house and remain posted for at least two weeks before final action may be taken thereon by the committee. Letters, except those of the proposer and seconder, relating to candidates whose names have been acted upon finally shall forthwith be destroyed.

2. Two negative ballots shall be sufficient to reject, and at least five affirmative ballots shall be necessary to elect a candidate.

3. No member of the admission committee shall propose or second a candidate for admission.

ARTICLE XV. STOCK.

1. The capital stock shall consist of ...... hundred shares of the par value of fifty dollars each, until the same be increased in the manner provided by law.

2. Each candidate elected to resident membership shall become a stockholder before he shall be entitled to the privileges of the Club, but no person shall be entitled to such privileges until he has been regularly elected to membership.

3. The Club shall have first lien on transferable shares of the stock to secure all indebtedness of a stockholder to the Club. This lien may be enforced after sixty days from the date at which the indebtedness became due, by the sale, in such manner as the board of directors shall determine, of such stock registered in the name of the debtor on the books of the Club. As much of the proceeds of such sale as may be required to liquidate such indebtedness shall be applied thereto, and any balance shall be paid by the treasurer to the former holder, or his legal representative.

4. All certificates of stock shall contain a statement that the same is issued to and held by such stockholder subject to the regulations and rules of the Club, together with a statement that such stock upon the resignation, expulsion or death of the holder, shall be forfeited to the Club, except that in the case of transferable shares, it shall be subject to the lien provided for in the preceding section.

5. Transfers of stock to be valid must be registered on the books of the Club, and no stock shall be transferred until all indebtedness of the former holder has been discharged; nor in any case where such former holder has waived his right to transfer.

ARTICLE XVI. DUES.

1. The annual dues of the Club shall be .... dollars, payable quarterly in advance on the first day of March, June,

September and December. Any resident member intending to be absent from the city for twelve consecutive months, but intending to reside again in ...., may give notice of such intention to the treasurer and thenceforth he shall be exempt from the payment of dues for one year, provided his absence continues for such period. If his absence continues beyond one year he may again give notice as above provided and again obtain exemption from the payment of dues for one year; but not longer except by vote of the board of directors.

2. Nonresident members shall pay an initiation fee of ..... dollars, which, if the nonresident member becomes a resident of .... county, shall be applied upon the annual dues of such member for the next succeeding year after he becomes a resident member. If such member fails to become a resident member, as provided in Article XIII, Section 3, his initiation fee shall be forfeited to the Club.

3. The annual dues of nonresident members shall be ...... dollars, payable on the first day of March.

4. Bills for supplies furnished by the Club to its members shall be presented before the fifth of each month.

5. If the quarterly dues or the bills for supplies of any member remain unpaid on the twentieth day of the month in which they become due, the treasurer shall notify the delinquent that, unless payment is made in the meantime, his name with the amount of his indebtedness will be posted in the club-house on the first day of the following month, and in due time the treasurer shall post the delinquent according to the notice given. No supplies shall be sold to delinquents while thus posted. If the debt remain unpaid for thirty days after such posting the membership of such delinquent member may be terminated, and his stock forfeited or sold as provided in Article XV, Sections 3 and 4.

On the written application of such delinquent and on the payment by him of all dues and other indebtedness to date, the board of directors may, upon such terms as it deems proper, remit the penalties of Articles XV and XVI.

ARTICLE XVII. RESIGNATION AND EXPULSION.

1. Resignation of membership shall be made in writing to the secretary and shall be accepted by the board of directors, provided the member resigning is not indebted to the Club.

2. Any member of the Club may be censured, suspended or expelled by a majority vote of the board of directors after opportunity for a hearing has been given. Notice of the hearing and of the charges preferred shall be sent to the member against whom such action is proposed at least ten days before the date appointed for the hearing.

ARTICLE XVIII. VISITORS.

At the request of any member, the Club may give to any non-resident of .... county a visitor's card entitling the recipient to the privileges of the Club for a period of ten days, but no more than three such cards may be given to one recipient within any period of sixty days. The date of introduction and the name and residence of the visitor must be entered upon the visitor's book of the Club, together with the name of the introducing member, who will be held responsible for any debts to the Club incurred by the recipient of the card.

ARTICLE XIX. AMENDMENTS.

1. To make amendments to the regulations it shall be necessary to post the proposed amendment in the club-house and mail a copy of the same to each member at least thirty days before the meeting at which the amendment is to be voted upon; but nothing herein shall be construed to prevent the amending at such meeting of any such proposed amendment. A two-thirds vote of the members present shall be necessary to pass amendments.

2. Article XII, Section 2, of the Regulations, shall be amended only by a four-fifths vote of all the members of the Club present in person or by proxy.

ARTICLE XX. CONSTRUCTION OF THE REGULATIONS.

1. The construction of the regulations shall rest with the board of directors.

2. The board of directors shall determine also, *pro tempore*, any matters not provided for by these regulations, and shall have full power to appoint any special committee and approve its acts.

ARTICLE XXI. SEAL.

The seal of the corporation shall be circular, two inches in diameter, with the name of the corporation engraved around the margin, and in the center the word "Seal," with such other device as may be adopted by the board of directors.

MINUTES OF STOCKHOLDERS' MEETING—Continued from page 111.

NOTE.—The code of regulations as adopted should be copied in full on the minutes.

Thereupon the subscribers to the capital stock of The ...... Company duly executed the following written assent to the adoption of the foregoing code of regulations as follows:

(f)

ASSENT TO ADOPTION OF REGULATIONS.

.........., Ohio, ..., 19...

We, the undersigned, being the owners of the number of shares of the capital stock of The .... Company set opposite our respective names, do hereby assent in writing to the adoption of the code of regulations hereinbefore set forth, for the government of this corporation.

Stockholders.	Proxies.	Shares.
....	....	....
....	....	....
....	....	....
....	....	....
....	....	....

Thereupon the chairman declared the election of a board of directors to be next in order. The incorporators of the Company were requested by the chairman to act as inspectors of election. An election for directors was then held.

The names of ...., ..., ..., ..., and .... were placed in nomination as candidates for the office of directors. No other names were proposed. A ballot was then had with the following result, as announced by the inspectors of election.

.... received .... votes.

      "   "

      "   "

      "   "

      "   "

Thereupon the following certificate of election was here made upon this record of proceedings by the inspectors of election, and appointing a time and place for holding the first meeting of directors:

(g)

CERTIFICATE OF ELECTION OF DIRECTORS.

.........., Ohio, ..., 19...

We, the undersigned, being the only subscribers to the articles of incorporation of The .... Company present at the first meeting of the stockholders of said corporation, held at the office of .... in the city of ...., Ohio, on ...., 19.., at .... o'clock .. M., do hereby certify that at the election for directors held at such meeting, and at which we acted as inspectors of election, ... shares of the capital stock of said corporation were cast in favor of the election of ...., ..., ..., ..., and ...., and no votes were cast in favor of the election of any other person. And we do further certify that at said election, ..., ..., ..., ..., and .... were each duly elected to the office of director of said corporation, to hold their said offices until the next annual election of directors, or until their successors are elected and qualified; and we do hereby appoint ...., the ...... day of ...., 19.., at .. o'clock .. M., as the time, and .... as the place, for the holding of the first meeting of said directors.

................,
................,
................,
................,
................,
    Incorporators.

There being no further business, the meeting adjourned on motion of ....
Attest:
.........., ...,
    Secretary.   Chairman.

(3) PROCEEDINGS OF DIRECTORS.

(NOTE—For regular and special meetings of directors see forms Nos. 209-221.)

(a)

MINUTES OF FIRST DIRECTORS' MEETING.

........, Ohio, ..., 19...

Pursuant to the order made at the first meeting of the stockholders of The .... Company, held on ...., 19.., the directors of said company met at the office of ...... on ......, the ...... day of ...., 19.., at .... o'clock .. M. Present Messrs. ...., ..., ..., ..., and ....
· An oath faithfully to discharge their duties as directors of said Company was then taken, as follows:

(b)

OATH OF DIRECTORS.

State of Ohio, ..., County, ss.

We, the undersigned, being duly sworn, say that we will faithfully discharge our duties as directors of The .... Company.

................,

................,

................,

................,

................,

Sworn to and subscribed before me this .... day of ....,
19...

................,
Notary Public.

.... was chosen chairman and .... secretary of said meeting.

On motion of ...., duly seconded, the following code of by-laws was adopted:

(c)

BY-LAWS OF THE .... COMPANY.

ARTICLE I. MEETINGS.

(a) The directors shall meet *annually* at the office of the Company on the first Monday of January of each year at 9 o'clock A. M.

(b) *Regular monthly meetings* of the board of directors shall be held at two o'clock P. M. on the first Monday of each month, if not a legal holiday. If a legal holiday, then on the day following at the same hour.

(c) *Special meetings* of the board of directors may be held at the office of the company at any time pursuant to a written call by the president or by any two members of the board, or may be held at any time and place, without notice, by the unanimous written consent of all members, or by the presence of all members at such meeting.

(d) *Notice of meetings.* A written or printed notice of every regular or special meeting, stating the time and place, and in case of special meetings, the objects thereof, shall be mailed to each director at least three days before such meeting, or be telegraphed at least two days before the same. **Provided, however,** no failure or irregularity of notice of any regular meeting shall invalidate the same or any proceeding thereof. Only the business specified in such notice shall be transacted at any special meeting.

(e) *Quorum.* A majority of the board shall constitute a quorum at all meetings.

ARTICLE II. VACANCIES.

In case of any vacancy in the board of directors caused by death, resignation or otherwise, such vacancy shall be filled for the unexpired term by a majority of the board of directors.

ARTICLE III. EXECUTIVE COMMITTEE.

The management and conduct of the routine business of this company shall be vested in an executive committee composed of two members. The persons holding the offices of president and .... shall ex officio constitute such executive committee. Such executive committee is authorized to hire and discharge employes and make all contracts in the ordinary course of business, and to do all things necessary and incident thereto. In case of disagreement between the members of said committee as to the making or not making of a contract, such contract shall not be entered into without special authority from the board of directors. The executive committee shall make a full report at each regular meeting of the board of directors, and at other times when requested by the board, of all business transacted by it.

ARTICLE IV. BONDS.

The treasurer of this Company shall furnish a bond, conditioned for the faithful performance of his duties in the penal sum of $...... with sureties, to be approved by the board of drectors.

ARTICLE V. BANK DEPOSITS.

All moneys of this Company shall be deposited by the treasurer, as the same are received by him, in the .... Bank of ...., Ohio, in the name of this Company, and shall be withdrawn only by check signed by the treasurer and countersigned by the president.

ARTICLE VI. AMENDMENTS.

These by-laws may be amended or repealed by a majority vote of the board at any regular meeting or at any special meeting called for that purpose.

MINUTES OF DIRECTORS' MEETING—CONTINUED.

An election of officers was then held by the board, resulting in the unanimous choice of the following:

........, president.
........, vice-president.
........, secretary.
........, treasurer.

The chairman thereupon declared said persons to be duly elected to said offices, and said persons thereupon entered upon the performance of their duties.

(d)

RESOLUTION OF DIRECTORS ACCEPTING PROPERTY IN PAYMENT FOR STOCK.

The secretary read the following written proposition:

............, Ohio, ..., 19...

To The .... Company.

Gentlemen:

We hereby offer to sell to your Company the following property: (*description of property*)

for the sum of $......, payable in the stock of your Company; the same to be received as full payment of the subscription to the capital stock of your Company heretofore made by us; said stock to be issued as fully paid.

Respectfully,   A. B.
C. D.

On motion of ...., duly seconded, it was resolved to accept said proposition, and that the president and secretary be instructed to issue and deliver certificates for ...... shares of the capital stock of this Company to said *A. B.* and *C. D.*, in the amounts respectively subscribed by each; the same to be issued as fully paid up; and that said property be received in full payment of the subscriptions to the capital stock made by said *A. B.* and *C. D.;* said certificates of stock to be delivered upon the delivery of said property to the Company, free of incumbrances, with proper instruments of conveyance thereof. The vote of the directors on said resolution was as follows: Mr. ......, yea, Mr. ......, yea, etc.

NOTE.—Directors selling property to the corporation in payment for stock can not act for the corporation in the transaction.

Thereupon the board adjourned on motion duly seconded.

........,
Chairman.
Attest:

........,
Secretary pro tem.

We hereby approve the foregoing minutes.

........,
President.
Attest:

........,
Secretary.

............,
............,
............,
Directors.

No. 129.

Amendments to Articles of Incorporation; Proceedings For.

(G. C. §§ 8719 to 8723.)

(a)

WAIVER OF NOTICE OF STOCKHOLDERS' MEETING.

.........., Ohio, ..., 19.....

We, the undersigned, being all the stockholders [or *members*] of [*name of the corporation*], do hereby waive the giving of the notice required by law of the meeting to be held by the stockholders [or *members*] of said [*name of the corporation*], on [*time of the meeting*], at [*place of the meeting*], which meeting has been called by a majority of the board of directors [or *trustees*] of said [*name of the corporation*] for the purpose of considering the subject of amending the articles of incorporation of said [*name of the corporation*]. *[*The proposed amendment may also be set forth in the waiver*]; thus, beginning at the*, "so as to change the name of said corporation from [*its present name*], to [*the name proposed*]."

Names.	Shares.
....	....
....	....
....	....
....	....
....	....

NOTE.—If not waived by all the stockholders or members a notice substantially as follows must be published for at least thirty days prior to the meeting:

(b)

NOTICE OF STOCKHOLDERS' MEETING.

Notice is hereby given to the stockholders [or *members*] of [*name of the corporation*], that on ...., the ...... day of ...., 19.., at [*the place of meeting*], there will be a meeting of the stockholders [or *members*] of [*name of the corporation*], to consider the subject of amending the articles of incorporation of said [*name of the corporation*]. [*The contemplated amendment may be set forth in the notice, but it is probably unnecessary*].

. . . .,

. . . .,

. . . .,

Directors (or Trustees).

(The notice must be given by a majority of directors or trustees.)

NOTE.—The waiver, or copy of notice with proof of publication, should be entered on the record.

(c)

MINUTES OF STOCKHOLDERS' MEETING.

. . . ., Ohio, ..., 19. . .

A meeting of the stockholders (or members) of The . . . . . . Company was held at . . . . . . on . . . . . ., 19. ., at . . . . . . o'clock .. M., the time and place specified in the foregoing waiver (or notice). . . . ., president of the Company, presided.

Mr. . . . . presented the following resolution:

(d)

RESOLUTION FOR AMENDMENT OF ARTICLES OF INCORPORATION.

"Resolved, that the articles of incorporation of The . . . . . . Company be, and the same are hereby amended, so that

(*Copy proposed amendment, as*

"the corporate name be changed from The . . . . Company to The . . . . Company,"

or "the place where said corporation is to be located, and its principal business transacted be changed from . . . ., ... county, Ohio, to . . . ., ... county, Ohio.")

Mr. . . . . moved the adoption of said resolution. The motion was duly seconded and a vote thereon was had by ballot. . . . . shares of the capital stock of said Company were cast in favor of the adoption of said resolution and . . . . shares were cast against its adoption. (*If the corporation has no capital stock, the minutes should be changed accordingly.*)

More than three-fifths of the capital stock (or members) of said corporation having *been* voted in favor of the adoption of said resolution the same was declared duly adopted. Thereupon the following written assent and waiver was executed by all the stockholders (*or members*) of said corporation, as follows:

(e)

WAIVER OF NOTICE OF AMENDMENT.

We, the undersigned, being all of the stockholders (or members) of The .... Company, do hereby consent in writing that the notice by publication, required by law, of the amendment made to the articles of incorporation of said The .... Company at a meeting of its stockholders (or members) held on ...., the .... day of ...., 19.., at the office of ......, be and the same is hereby waived.

Names.	Shares.
....	....
....	....
....	....
....	....
....	....

There being no further business, the meeting adjourned on motion.

Attest:

.........., Secretary.   ...., President.

NOTE.—Unless waived by all stockholders or members, a notice substantially as follows should be published for three consecutive weeks.

(f)

NOTICE.

To whom it may concern:

Notice is hereby given that on ...., the ...... day of ...., 19.., at a meeting of the stockholders (or members) of The .... Company, held at the office of ...., it was, by a vote of more than three-fifths of the stockholders (or members) resolved, that

(Copy resolution in full.)

........, Secretary of ....
(Name of Corporation.)

(g)

CERTIFICATE OF AMENDMENT TO BE FILED WITH THE SECRETARY OF STATE.

(Copy of resolution in full.)

To the Secretary of State,

    Columbus, Ohio.

    The .... Company, acting by its president and secretary, hereby certifies that the foregoing is a true copy of the original amendment to the articles of incorporation of The .... Company which was adopted by the votes of the owners of more than three-fifths of its capital stock (or members) at a meeting thereof, held on ...., the ...... day of ...., 19.., at ...., notice of which meeting was duly waived in writing as authorized by law (or, pursuant to notice duly given according to law).

    In testimony whereof, the president and secretary of The .... Company, acting for and on behalf of said corporation, have hereunto set their hands and caused the seal of said corporation to be affixed (if the corporation has a seal) this ...... day of ...., 19...

                                         The .... Company.

(Corporate seal.)   By ...., President.

                                By ...., Secretary.

No. 130.

Increase of Capital Stock; Proceedings For.

(G. C. § 8698.)

(1) Before Organization.

(a)

CONSENT TO INCREASE OF CAPITAL STOCK.

    We, the undersigned, being all the subscribers to the capital stock of The .... Company, all of the authorized capital stock having been subscribed and an installment of ten percent having been paid thereon, do hereby unanimously consent that the capital stock of said company be increased from $......, its present capital stock, to $......, divided into ...... shares of $...... each.

Names of Subscribers.	Shares.	
....	....	....
....	....	....
....	....	....
....	....	....
....	....	....

(b)

CERTIFICATE OF INCREASE, BEFORE ORGANIZATION, TO BE FILED WITH THE SECRETARY OF STATE.

We, the undersigned, being all the original subscribers to the capital stock of The .... Company, do hereby certify that on the ...... day of ...., 19.., the original capital stock was fully subscribed for and an installment of ten percent on each share of stock was paid; and that on said day, by unanimous written consent, it was agreed to increase the capital stock of said The .... Company from $......, its original capital stock, to $......, divided into ...... shares of $...... each.

In witness whereof, we have hereunto set our hands this .... day of ...., 19...

....

....

....

....

....

(2) After Organization.

(a)

WAIVER AND AGREEMENT FOR PURPOSE OF INCREASING CAPITAL STOCK.

........, Ohio, ..., 19...

We, the undersigned, being the holders of all the capital stock of The .... Company, and being this day all present, in person or by proxy, at a meeting of the stockholders of said Company, *called by a majority of its directors, to consider the subject of increasing the capital stock of said Company, (*If the meeting has not been so called, and at any meeting at which all*

the stockholders are present, in person or by proxy, it is decided
unanimously to make an increase of capital, that portion of the
*above beginning at the * should be omitted)*, do hereby waive
in writing the notice of such meeting, by publication and by
letter, required by law; and we do also agree, in writing, that
the capital stock of said Company may be increased from $......,
its present capital stock, to $......, divided into ...... shares,
of $...... each.

Name of Stockholder.	Name of Proxy.	No. of Shares.
....	....	....
....	....	....
....	....	....
....	....	....
....	....	....

NOTE.—If the notice of meeting is not waived, a notice substantially
as follows must be given by publication, and by mail, to each stockholder
at least thirty days before the time of the meeting:

(b)

NOTICE OF STOCKHOLDERS' MEETING.

Notice is hereby given that a meeting of the stockholders of
The .... Company will be held at ...., on ...... the
...... day of ...., 19.., at .... o'clock .. M., for the
purpose of considering a proposed increase of the capital stock
of said Company from $...... to $......, or such other amount
as may be fixed at said meeting.
........, Ohio, ..., 19...

....
....
....
....
....
Directors.

NOTE.—At the meeting at which such increase is considered a resolution must be adopted. If the increase is to be common stock, the resolution may be in the following form:

(c)

RESOLUTION FOR INCREASE.

"Resolved, that the capital stock of said The .... Company be increased from $......, its present capital stock, to $......, divided into ...... shares, of $...... each; and further, that the president and secretary of said Company be instructed to file a certificate of such increase with the secretary of state."

(d)

CERTIFICATE OF INCREASE OF CAPITAL STOCK.

........, president, and ...., secretary of The .... Company, duly authorized in the premises, and acting on behalf of said Company, do hereby certify, that on the ...... day of ...., A. D. 19.., the capital stock of said Company was fully subscribed for, and an installment of ten percent on each share of stock had been paid; that on said day, by a vote of the holders of a majority of the stock of said Company, at a meeting called by a majority of its directors, and held at the office of the Company, in the .... of ...., ... county, Ohio, and at which meeting all the holders of the capital stock of said Company were present in person or by proxy, and waived in writing the notice, by publication and by letter, of the time, place and object of such meeting required by law, and also agreed in writing to the increase of capital stock hereinafter set forth, it was, on motion, "Resolved, that the capital stock of said The .... Company, be increased from $......, its present capital stock, to $......, divided into ...... shares of $...... each; and further, that the president and secretary of said Company be instructed to file a certificate of such increase with the secretary of state;" which is done accordingly.

In witness whereof, the aforesaid ......, president, and ...., secretary of The .... Company, acting for and on behalf of said Company, have hereunto set their hands this .... day of ...., A. D. 19...

(Corporate Seal)

The .... Company.

By ...., President.

..........., Secretary.

Increase by preferred stock.

(e)

WRITTEN ASSENT OF STOCKHOLDERS TO INCREASE BY PREFERRED STOCK.

(G. C. § 8699.)

We, the undersigned, being the owners of the number of shares of the capital stock of The .... Company set opposite our respective names, hereby assent to the increase of the capital stock of said Company from $...... to $...... ($..... or the whole) of said increase to consist of preferred stock in ...... shares of the par value of .... dollars ($......) each.

The holders of such preferred stock shall be entitled to a dividend, etc.

(*Set out terms of preference, etc., for which see Preferred Stock Clauses, Form No. 2.*)

Names.	Shares.
....	....
....	....
....	....
....	....
....	....

NOTE.—The written assent of three-fourths in number of the stockholders, representing three-fourths of the capital stock, is required. G. C. § 8699.

(f)

RESOLUTION FOR INCREASE BY PREFERRED STOCK.

"Resolved, that the capital stock of said The .... Company be and the same is hereby increased from $..... to $....., and that .... ($...... or the whole) of said increase be issued and disposed of as preferred stock, in .... shares of $...... each, and that the holders thereof be entitled to receive a dividend on said preferred stock of ...... percent per annum, payable .... out of the surplus profits of the Company for each year, in preference to all other stockholders and such dividends shall be ...... cumulative.

Such preferred stock may be redeemed at not less than par at the time and price hereby fixed, and to be also expressed in the stock certificates thereof, to wit:

(*Set out terms of redemption, preference, voting powers, restrictions or qualifications, if any, for which see Preferred Stock Clauses, Form No. 2.*)

And further, that the president and secretary of said Company be instructed to file a certificate of such increase with the secretary of state."

NOTE.—As G. C. § 8699 does not specify the procedure for an increase by preferred stock, it is prudent to hold meetings of both the stockholders and the directors and to have the foregoing resolution passed at each meeting.

Where the articles of incorporation do not provide for preferred stock, the articles should be amended. See G. C. §§ 8668 and 8669.

(g)

CETIFICATE OF INCREASE OF CAPITAL STOCK (PREFERRED).

The .... Company hereby certifies that on the .... day of ...., A. D. 19.., the capital stock of said Company was fully subscribed for, and an installment of ten percent on each share of stock has been paid; that at a meeting of its directors, held at the office of said Company, on the .... day of ...., A. D. 19.., the assent in writing of three-fourths in number of the stockholders, representing more than three-fourths of the capital stock of said Company, having been first previously obtained, the following resolution was adopted, viz.:

"Resolved, that the capital stock of said The .... Company be and the same is hereby increased from $..... to $..... and that ($...... *or the whole*) of said increase be issued and disposed of as preferred stock, in .... shares of $...... each, and that the holders thereof be entitled to receive a dividend on said preferred stock of .... percent per annum, payable .... out of the surplus profits of the Company for each year, in preference to all other stockholders, and such dividends shall be ...... cumulative.

"Such preferred stock may be redeemed at not less than par at the time and price hereby fixed, and to be also expressed in the stock certificates thereof, to wit:

(*Here state the terms of redemption and also the designations, preferences, voting powers, restrictions or qualifications, if any, created.*)

"And further, that the president and secretary of said Company be instructed to file a certificate of such increase with the secretary of state," which is done accordingly.

In witness whereof, said The .... Company has
(Seal.)   caused its corporate seal to be affixed and its president
and secretary to subscribe this certificate, this ......
day of ...., A. D. 19...

The .... Company.

By ...., President.

.........., Secretary.

(h)

WAIVER BY STOCKHOLDERS OF RIGHT TO TAKE INCREASED STOCK.

.........., Ohio, ..., 19...

We, the undersigned stockholders of The .... Company,
do hereby release and waive our right to subscribe for or purchase any part of the new or increased capital stock of said Company authorized by resolution of the stockholders passed ......
19.., and we hereby authorize the directors of said Company to
sell or otherwise dispose of the same for the best interest of said
Company, as in their discretion they may deem proper.

No. 131.

Reduction of Capital Stock; Proceedings For.

(G. C. § 8700.)

(a)

CONSENT OF STOCKHOLDERS TO REDUCTION OF CAPITAL STOCK.

........, Ohio, ..., A. D. 19...

The undersigned, in whose names a majority of the shares
of the capital stock of The .... Company stands on the
books of the Company, hereby consent that the capital stock of
said Company may be reduced from $......, its present author-
ized capital, to $......, and the nominal value of each share
from $...... to $......, and that the board of directors may
take such action as may be necessary to carry such reduction
into effect.

Names of Stockholders.	No. Shares Owned.
....	....
....	....
....	....

(b)

RESOLUTION OF BOARD OF DIRECTORS FOR REDUCTION OF
CAPITAL STOCK.

"Resolved, that the capital stock of The .... Company be
and the same is hereby reduced from $......, the present
amount of its authorized capital, to $......, divided into ......
shares of $...... each; and further, that the president and sec-
retary are hereby instructed, on surrender of the original certificates, to issue new certificates therefor, and also to file a certificate of such reduction in the office of the secretary of state, as
required by law."

(c)

CERTIFICATE OF REDUCTION TO BE FILED WITH THE SECRETARY
OF STATE.

Certificate of Reduction of Capital Stock
of
The .... Company.

To the Secretary of State, Columbus, Ohio:

The .... Company hereby certifies that, at a meeting of
the directors of said Company, held on ...., 19.'., the written consent of the persons in whose names a majority of the
shares of the capital stock of said Company stood on the books
of the Company having first been obtained, the capital stock of
said Company was reduced from .... dollars ($......) to
.... dollars ($......), and the nominal value of each share
from $...... to $...... each, and new certificates in accordance
therewith directed to be issued on surrender of the original certificates.

In witness whereof, The .... Company
has caused its name to be hereto sub-
(Corporate Seal)   scribed by its president and secretary and
its corporate seal to be hereunto affixed
this ...... day of ...., A. D. 19...

The .... Company.

By ...., President.

.........., Secretary.

No, 132.

Sale of Entire Property and Assets of Corporation; Proceedings For.

(G. C. §§ 8710 to 8718.)

(a)

MINUTES OF DIRECTORS' MEETING.

........, Ohio, ..., 19...

A meeting of the directors of The .... Company was held at the office of the Company at ...... o'clock ..M., ..., 19... Present, Messrs. ...., ..., ..., ... and ....

The meeting was called to order by ...., president of the Company.

Mr. .... presented the following resolution:

"Whereas, an offer of $...... has been made by ...., for the entire property and assets of The .... Company, payable in *("cash," or, "stock of ......," or "bonds of ......,")*, and whereas, all the terms, considerations and conditions of said proposed sale are contained in the following proposed agreement, to wit:

(Copy proposed amendment in full.)

"Therefore be it resolved, that said offer be and is hereby accepted subject to the action thereon of the stockholders of this corporation; and that the president and secretary of this Company be and are hereby authorized and instructed to execute the foregoing agreement upon the adoption of the same by the stockholders; and that a meeting of the stockholders of this Company be called for the purpose of taking into consideration the execution of said proposed agreement to be held at the office of the Company on ...., ..., 19.., at ...... o'clock .. M., and the secretary is hereby directed to give notice thereof to all the stockholders of this Company according to law."

Mr. .... moved the adoption of said resolution. The motion was duly seconded and was put by the president and the following was the vote:

Mr. .... yea.
Mr. .... yea.
Mr. .... yea.
Mr. .... yea.
Mr. .... yea.

Thereupon the president declared said motion duly carried and said resolution duly adopted.

There being no further business, the meeting adjourned on motion duly seconded.

Attest:

............., ...,
Secretary.   President.

We approve the foregoing minutes.

....

....

                        ....

                                              Directors.

(*Three-fourths of the directors must authorize a sale of the entire assets of a corporation.*)

(b)

NOTICE OF STOCKHOLDERS' MEETING.

A meeting of the stockholders of The .... Company will be held at the office of said Company on ...., the .... day of ...., 19.., at .... o'clock .. M. for the purpose of considering and acting upon a proposed agreement for the sale of the entire property and assets of said The .... Company.

........, Ohio, ..., 19...

                                              ....,
                                              ....,
                                              ....,
                                              ....,
                                              ....,
                                              Directors.

NOTE.—Ten days' notice of the time and place of holding the meeting and the object thereof must be given by registered letter containing a written or printed notice addressed to each of the persons in whose names the capital stock stands on the books of the corporation; and also by like notice published in some newspaper in the city or town where the corporation has its principal office or place of business. The notice may, however, be waived in writing in case all the stockholders are present in person or by proxy.

(c)

WAIVER OF NOTICE OF STOCKHOLDERS' MEETING.

........, Ohio, ..., 19...

We, the undersigned, being the holders of all the capital stock of The .... Company and being all present, in person or by proxy as appears below, at a meeting of stockholders called by the board of directors for the purpose of considering a proposed agreement for the sale of the entire property and assets of said corporation, do hereby waive notice of said meeting required by law.

Stockholders.	Proxies.	No. of Shares.
. . . .	. . . .	. . . .
. . . .	. . . .	. . . .
. . . .	. . . .	. . . .
. . . .	. . . .	. . . .
. . . .	. . . .	. . . .

(d)

MINUTES OF STOCKHOLDERS' MEETING.

. . . ., Ohio, ..., 19. . .

Pursuant to the foregoing notice (or waiver) a meeting of the stockholders of The . . . . Company was held at the office of the Company on . . . ., 19. ., at . . . . o'clock . . M. Mr. . . . ., president of the Company, presided.

Mr. . . . . presented the following resolution:

"Whereas, an offer of $. . . . . . has been made by . . . . for the entire property and assets of The . . . . Company, payable in . . . ., and

Whereas, all the terms, considerations and conditions of said proposed sale are contained in the following proposed agreement, to wit:

(*Copy proposed agreement in full.*)

And whereas, the directors of this corporation at a meeting held . . . ., 19. ., by a vote of more than three-fourths, authorized the execution of said agreement;

Therefore be it resolved, that the action of the board of directors be and is hereby ratified; and that said agreement be and is hereby adopted; and the president and secretary of this corporation are hereby authorized and directed to execute said agreement and all good and sufficient deeds and transfers of all the property and assets of this Company upon the terms and conditions in said agreement provided."

Mr. . . . . moved the adoption of said resolution and agreement. The motion was seconded by Mr. . . . . The president appointed . . . . and . . . . as tellers. The president thereupon put said motion and a vote by ballot was taken with the following results:

. . . . votes were cast for the adoption of said resolution and agreement.

. . . . votes were cast for the rejection of said resolution and agreement.

Thereupon the tellers announced the foregoing result of the vote and the president declared said motion duly carried and said resolution and agreement duly adopted, more than three-fourths of all the votes cast at the meeting having been cast in favor of such adoption.

There being no further business, the meeting adjourned on motion.

Attest:

.........., ...,
    Secretary.   President.

No. 133.

Dissolution of Corporations.

(G. C. §§ 8738 to 8743.)

(a)

CALL FOR STOCKHOLDERS' MEETING.

(G. C. §§ 8738, 8740.)

........, Ohio, ..., 19...

To ....,

    Secretary of The .... Company.

I (or we) .... (president or directors) of The .... Company do hereby call and order a meeting of the stockholders of said Company, to be held at ......, ... Street, ..., Ohio, on the ...... day of ...., 19.., at .... o'clock .. M. for the purpose of considering and acting upon the proposed dissolution of said corporation and the surrender and abandonment of its corporate authority and franchises and for the transaction of any and all business necessary or incident thereto, and you are hereby instructed to give notice of such meeting to the stockholders pursuant to law.

....

(b)

NOTICE OF STOCKHOLDERS' MEETING

(G. C. § 8740.)

........, Ohio, ..., 19...

A meeting of the stockholders of The .... Company will be held at ...., ..., Ohio, on the ...... day of ...., 19.., at .... o'clock .. M. for the purpose of considering and acting upon the proposed dissolution of said corporation and the surrender and abandonment of its corporate authority and franchises, and the transaction of any and all business necessary or incident thereto.

. . . . ,

Secretary.

NOTE.—The statute does not authorize a waiver of this notice by the stockholders. It must be given by publication for four weeks in a newspaper published and of general circulation in the county wherein the principal office of the corporation is located, and by mailing to each stockholder.

(c)

CERTIFICATE OF DISSOLUTION OF A CORPORATION FOR PROFIT.

(Where installments of its capital stock have been paid.)

(G. C. §§ 8740, 8741.)

. . . . , president, and . . . . , secretary, of The. . . . . . . Company, duly authorized in the premises, and acting on behalf of said corporation, do hereby certify that said corporation has completely closed its business, and paid all its debts and liabilities; that a majority of the directors of said corporation, desiring to surrender its corporate authority and franchises, duly called a meeting of the stockholders of said corporation, by publication for four weeks in the . . . . , a newspaper of general circulation in . . . . county, and by written notice to each stockholder, whose residence is known of the object, time and place thereof, to be held at the office of said corporation, at . . . . , in . . . . county, Ohio, on the . . . . . . day of . . . . , A. D. 19..; that at said meeting of said stockholders held on said date, in pursuance of said notice, it was, by the vote of all of the stockholders of said corporation present, in person or proxy.

"Resolved, that The . . . . Company, having completely closed its business, and paid all its debts and liabilities, hereby surrenders and abandons its corporate authority; and further, that the president and secretary of said corporation be instructed to file a certificate thereof with the secretary of state;" which is done accordingly.

In witness whereof, the aforesaid . . . . , president, and . . . . , secretary, of The . . . . Company, acting for and on behalf of said corporation, have hereunto set their hands, and caused the seal of said corporation to be affixed this . . . . . . day of . . . . , A. D. 19. . .

(Seal)

The . . . . Company.

By . . . . , President.

. . . . , Secretary.

(d)

CERTIFICATE OF VOLUNTARY DISSOLUTION OF A CORPORATION FOR PROFIT.

(Where no installments of its capital stock have been paid in.)

(G. C. §§ 8738, 8739.)

........, president, and ...., secretary, of The ......
Company, duly authorized in the premises, and acting on behalf
of said corporation, do hereby certify that no installments of the
capital stock of said corporation have been paid in, no investments
have been made, and no debts incurred which are unpaid, and
that a majority of the directors of said corporation, having become satisfied that the objects of said corporation can not be
accomplished, and desiring to abandon the corporate existence
of said corporation, duly called a meeting of the stockholders
of said corporation, by publication for two weeks in the ....,
a newspaper of general circulation in .... county, to be held
at the office of said corporation, at ...., in .... county,
Ohio, on the .. ..day of ...., A. D. 19..; that at said
meeting of said stockholders held on said date, in pursuance of
said notice, it was, by the vote of a majority in amount of the
stockholders of said corporation present, in person or by proxy,

"Resolved, that The .... Company, having decided that
the objects of said corporation can not be accomplished, and
having fully paid all its debts and liabilities, hereby abandons
and dissolves its corporate existence; and, further, that the president and secretary of said corporation be instructed to file a
certificate thereof with the secretary of state;" which is done accordingly.

In witness whereof, the aforesaid ...., president, and
........, secretary, of The .... Company, acting for and
on behalf of said corporation, have hereunto set their hands, and
caused the seal of said corporation to be affixed this ...... day of
........, A. D. 19...

(Seal)

The .... Company.

By ...., President.

.........., Secretary.

(e)

CERTIFICATE OF VOLUNTARY DISSOLUTION OF A CORPORATION NOT FOR PROFIT.

(G. C. § 8738.)

........, president, and ...., secretary, of The ......,
duly authorized in the premises, and acting on behalf of said

corporation, do hereby certify that no debts incurred by said corporation are unpaid, and that a majority of the trustees of said corporation, desiring to abandon the corporate existence of said corporation, duly called a meeting of the members of said corporation, by publication for two weeks in the ...., a newspaper of general circulation in .... county, to be held at the office of said corporation, at ...., in .... county, Ohio, on the ...... day of ...., A. D. 19..; that at said meeting of said members held on said date, in pursuance of said notice, it was, by the vote of a majority of the members of said corporation present, at said meeting,

"Resolved, that The .... having decided that the objects of said corporation can not be accomplished and having fully paid all its debts and liabilities, hereby abandons and dissolves its corporate existence; and, further, that the president and secretary of said corporation be instructed to file a certificate thereof with the secretary of state;" which is done accordingly.

In witness whereof, the aforesaid ...., president, and ...., secretary, of The ...., acting for and on behalf of said corporation, have hereunto set their hands this ...... day of ...., A. D. 19...

(Seal)

The ....

By ...., President.

............, Secretary.

FOREIGN CORPORATIONS.

No. 134.

Statement by Foreign Corporation Entering State.

(G. C. §§ 178 to 182.)

(Attach copy of articles of incorporation here.)
To the Secretary of State,
    Columbus, Ohio.

........, a corporation organized and existing under the laws of the state of ......, with its principal office located at ......, in .... county, ..., desiring to conform to the laws of Ohio, regulating foreign corporations doing business therein, does hereby make the following statement:

FIRST. The amount of its authorized capital stock is .....

SECOND. The business or objects of the corporation which it is engaged in carrying on, or which it purposes to engage in or carry on, in the state of Ohio is ....

THIRD. The principal place of business of said corporation in Ohio is to be located at ...., in .... county.

FOURTH. We hereby appoint ...., of ...., in .... county, Ohio, as the person upon whom process may be served in all actions that may be brought against this Company in any of the courts of the state, and designate his office ...., in said city, as the principal office of the Company in the state of Ohio.

In witness whereof, said corporation has caused its corporate seal to be hereto attached, and this certificate to be executed by its president and secretary, this ...... day of ...., A. D. 19...   ....

By ...., President.

............, Secretary.

State of ...., ..., county, ss.

........, and ...., being first duly sworn, depose and say that they all did execute and sign the foregoing certificate for and on behalf of said corporation, and that the same is their free act and deed, and is the free act and deed of said ...., of which they are respectively the president and secretary; that the statements therein are true, and that the seal attached thereto is the genuine seal of said corporation; they further declare, on oath, that the charter or certificate of incorporation hereto attached is a true copy of the articles of incorporation or charter of said ....

....

....

Sworn to before me and subscribed in my presence, this .... day of ...., A. D. 19...

....

(L. S.)

....

State of ...., County of ...., ss.

I, ..., within and for the county aforesaid, do hereby certify that ...., whose name is subscribed to the foregoing acknowledgment as a Notary Public, was at the date thereof a Notary Public in and for said county, duly commissioned and qualified, and authorized as such to take said acknowledgment; and further, that I am well acquainted with his handwriting, and believe that the signature to the same is genuine.

In witness whereof, I have hereunto set my hand and affixed the seal of said court, at ...., this .... day of ...., A. D. 19...

....

(L. S.)

. . . .

. . . .

Gentlemen: I hereby accept the appointment as the representative of your Company upon whom process may be served, and agree to the designation of my office . . . ., as your principal office in the state of Ohio.

. . . .

State of Ohio, County of . . . ., ss.

Personally appeared before me, the undersigned, a notary public in and for said county, this . . . . . . day of . . . ., A. D. 19.., the above named . . . ., who acknowledged the signing of the foregoing to be his free act and deed for the uses and purposes therein mentioned.

Witness my hand and official seal on the day and year last aforesaid.

(Seal)

. . . .

Notary Public in and for . . . . County, Ohio.

No. 135.

Statement by Foreign Corporation Entering State.

(G. C. §§ 183 to 192.)

. . . .

. . . ., 19. . .

To the Secretary of State,
    Columbus, Ohio.

. . . ., a foreign corporation organized and existing under and by virtue of the laws of the state of . . . ., with its principal office located at . . . . . ., in . . . . . . county, ..., in compliance with Sections 183 and 184 of the General Code of the state of Ohio, passed February 14, 1910, approved February 15, 1910, requiring a foreign corporation organized for purposes of profit, and owning or using, or which proposes to own or use, a part or all of its capital stock or plant in said state of Ohio, before being permitted to do business, exercise its franchises, or maintain an action therein, under the oath of its president, secretary or other officer, to make and file with the secretary of state a statement of facts and pay a certain stipulated fee, hereby makes the following declaration:

FIRST. The authorized capital stock of said corporation is . . . . dollars ($. . . . . .), divided into . . . . (. . . . . .) shares of the par value of . . . . dollars ($. . . . . .) each.

SECOND. The value of the property owned and used in Ohio, situate at . . . ., is . . . . dollars ($. . . . . .).

THIRD. The value of the property of the Company owned and used outside of Ohio is . . . . dollars ($. . . . . .).

FOURTH. The proportion of the capital stock of the Company represented by property owned and used and by business transacted in Ohio is ....

FIFTH. The location of its office or offices in Ohio is at ....

SIXTH. The names and addresses of the officers or agents of the Company in charge of its business in Ohio are as follows:

Name of president, ...

     Address,   .

Name of secretary, ...

     Address,   .

Name of treasurer, ...

     Address, ...

Names and addresses of managers or agents, other than as above enumerated: ....

In witness whereof, said .... has caused its corporate seal to be affixed and its corporate name to be hereunto attached by an officer thereof, to wit, its ...., this .... day of ...., A. D. 19...

....
By ....,

(L. S.)

State of ...., County of ...., ss.

........, being duly sworn, deposes and says that he is an officer, to wit, the ...., of ....; that he executed the foregoing statement in the name and on behalf of said corporation and caused its corporate seal to be thereto affixed; that he was authorized to make such statement and to execute the same by authority of the corporation, and that the statements therein are true.

....

Sworn to before me and subscribed in my presence, this .... day of ...., A. D. 19...

............,
....

(L. S.)

State of ...., ... County, ss.

I, ..., within and for the county aforesaid, do hereby certify that ...., whose name is subscribed to the foregoing acknowledgment as a .... was at the date thereof a .... in and for said county, duly commissioned and qualified, and authorized as such to take said acknowledgment; and further, that I am well acquainted with his handwriting, and believe that the signature to the same is genuine.

In witness whereof, I have hereunto set my hand and affixed

the seal of said court, at ...., this .... day of ....,
A. D. 19...

.............,
....

(L. S.)

Office of the Secretary of State.
Columbus, Ohio, ..., 19...

From the facts thus reported by the said .... I find the
proportion of the capital stock of the Company represented by its
property and business in Ohio to be ...... percent of its authorized capital stock, to wit: the sum of .... dollars, on
which I have assessed a fee of one-tenth of one percent, amounting to the sum of .... dollars.

.............,

(L. S.)   Secretary of State.

NOTE.—The franchise tax is based upon the proportion of the entire
authorized capital stock represented by the property owned and used and
business transacted in Ohio. The proportion which the property owned
and used and business transacted in Ohio bears to the total property and
business of the corporation is the proportion of the capital stock on which
the tax is based. For instance, if the property owned and used and business transacted in Ohio is $5,000, the total corporation property and
business $10,000, and the authorized capital stock $20,000, the proportion
(of the capital stock represented by Ohio property and business) required
to be stated in the "Fourth" paragraph of the above form is one-half or
the capital stock, or $10,000, the Ohio property and business being one-
half of the total corporate property and business. If all of the corporate
property and business were in Ohio the tax would be based on the total
authorized capital stock.

See 5 O. L. R. 163 (Opinion by Wade H. Ellis, Atty. Gen.); Aetna
Iron & Steel Co. v. Taylor, 13 C. C. 602; 5 C D. 242, s. c. 3 N. P. 152;
4 L. D. 180.

No. 136.

Certificate of a Foreign Corporation Retiring From Business in This State.

(G. C. § 11976.)

........, president, and ...., secretary, of The ....
Company, a corporation organized under the laws of the state of
........, having been duly authorized to do business in this state,
in compliance with the provisions of sections 178 to 192 of the
General Code, do hereby certify that on the .... day of ....,
19.., the said corporation, by action of its board of directors
duly authorized, has fully retired from business in the state of
Ohio, authorizing hereby the cancellation of the certificate of
authority to do business in said state, heretofore issued in the
office of the secretary of state.

In witness whereof, the aforesaid ...., president, and
........, secretary, of The .... Company, acting for and

on behalf of said corporation, have hereunto set their hands and caused the seal of said corporation to be hereto affixed this .... day of ...., A. D. 19...

(Seal)

The .... Company.
By ...., President.
........, Secretary.

No. 137.

Statement of Increase of Proportion of Capital Stock by Foreign Corporation.

(G. C. § 185.)

........, 19...

To the Secretary of State,
    Columbus, Ohio:
    ...., a foreign corporation organized and existing under and by virtue of the laws of the state of ...., with its principal office located at ...., in .... county, ..., in compliance with section 185 of the General Code of Ohio, requiring a foreign corporation, which has filed statements as required by sections 183 and 184 of the General Code of Ohio, and which has increased the proportion of its capital stock represented by property used and business done in Ohio, under the oath of its president, secretary or other officer, to make and file with the secretary of state an additional statement of facts and pay a certain additional fee, hereby makes the following declaration:

    FIRST. The present authorized capital stock of said corporation is .... dollars ($......), divided into ...... (....) shares of the par value of .... dollars ($......) each.

    SECOND. The value of the property owned and used in Ohio, situate at ...., is .... dollars ($......).

    THIRD. The value of the property of the Company owned and used outside of Ohio is .... dollars ($......).

    • FOURTH. The increase in the proportion of the capital stock of the Company represented by property owned and used and by business transacted in Ohio is ....

    FIFTH. The location of its office or offices in Ohio is at ....

    SIXTH. The names and addresses of the officers or agents of the Company in charge of its business in Ohio are as follows:
Name of president, ...
    Address,   .
Name of secretary, ...
    Address,   .
Name of treasurer, ...
    Address,   .

Names and addresses of managers or agents, other than as above enumerated: ....

In witness whereof, said .... has caused its corporate seal to be affixed and its corporate name to be hereunto attached by an officer thereof, to wit: its ...., this ...... day of ...., A. D. 19...

........................,

(L. S.)

By ....

State of ...., County of ...., ss.

........, being duly sworn, deposes and says that he is an officer, to wit: the ...., of ....; that he executed the foregoing statement, in the name and on behalf of said corporation, and caused its corporate seal to be thereto affixed; that he was authorized to make such statement and to execute the same by authority of the corporation, and that the statements therein are true.

Sworn to before me and subscribed in my presence this .... day of ...., A. D. 19...

........................,

(L. S.)

....

State of ...., County of ...., ss.

I, ..., within and for the county aforesaid, do hereby certify that ...., whose name is subscribed to the foregoing acknowledgment as a ...., was at the date thereof a ......, in and for said county, duly commissioned and qualified, and authorized as such to take said acknowledgment; and further, that I am well acquainted with his handwriting, and believe that the signature to the same is genuine.

In witness whereof, I have hereunto set my hand and affixed the seal of said court, at ...., this ...... day of ...., A. D. 19...

........................,

(L. S.)

....

No. 138.

Articles of Incorporation of Corporation not for Profit.

These articles of incorporation of ....

Witnesseth, that we, the undersigned ("all" or "a majority") of whom are citizens of the state of Ohio, desiring to form a corporation, not for profit, under the general corporation laws of said state, do hereby certify

FIRST. The name of said corporation shall be ....

SECOND. Said corporation is to be located at ...., in .... county, Ohio, and its principal business there transacted.

THIRD. 'Said corporation is formed for the purpose of (*for statements of corporate purpose see the forms immediately following*).

In witness whereof, we have hereunto set our hands this .... day of ...., A. D. 19..

.............,
.............,
.............,
.............,
....

The State of Ohio, County of ...., ss.

Personally appeared before me, the undersigned, a notary public in and for said county, this .... day of ...., A. D. 19.., the above named ...., ..., ..., ... and ...., who each severally acknowledged the signing of the foregoing articles of incorporation to be his free act and deed, for the uses and purposes therein mentioned.

Witness my hand and official seal on the day and year last aforesaid.

.............,
....

The State of Ohio, County of ...., ss.

I, ... Clerk of the Court of Common Pleas, within and for the county aforesaid, do hereby certify that ...., whose name is subscribed to the foregoing acknowledgment as a notary public, was at the date thereof a notary public, in and for said county, duly commissioned and qualified, and authorized as such to take said acknowledgment; and further, that I am well acquainted with his handwriting, and believe that the signature to said acknowledgment is genuine.

In witness whereof, I have hereunto set my hand and affixed the seal of said court at ...., this .... day of ...., A. D. 19..

.............,
Clerk.

PURPOSE CLAUSES. CORPORATIONS NOT FOR PROFIT.

No. 139.

Associated Charities.

THIRD. Said corporation is formed for the purpose of investigating, assisting, providing relief and promoting the gen-

eral welfare of the poor and needy, in the city of ....,
Ohio, and including the establishment and maintenance of a
registration bureau for fostering co-operation between all charitable organizations and agencies in said city; receiving funds by
gift or bequest, disbursing the same and the doing of all things
necessary or incident thereto.

No. 140.

Association for Apprehending Horse Thieves. Protective Association.

(G. C. § 10200.)

THIRD. Said corporation is formed for the purpose of
the apprehension and conviction of horse thieves and other felons.

No. 141.

Athletic Club.

THIRD. Said corporation is formed for the purpose of
providing means and facilities for exercise tending to promote
physical culture, also rowing, football, baseball, foot racing, wrest-
ling, boxing and other athletic sports, for the recreation and
amusement of the members and guests.

No. 142.

Athletic Club.   Another Form.

THIRD. Said corporation is formed for the purpose of
the mutual benefit of all its members by promoting an interest
among themselves in all athletics, both indoor and outdoor athletics, and to promote social intercourse among its members.
This association is formed not for profit.

No. 143.

Builders' Exchange.

THIRD. Said corporation is formed for the purpose of
maintaining and conducting a society, the general object and
design of which shall be to cultivate friendly, social and business
relations among persons connected with building trades in the
city of ...., Ohio, and vicinity; to provide facilities for the
interchange of views, and the avoidance or amicable settlement
of controversies and differences amongst its members and their
employees; and, in general, to advance and promote all legitimate
interests of the building trades of the city of ...., Ohio,
and vicinity.

No. 144.

Canoe Club.

THIRD. Said corporation is formed for the purpose of encouraging and promoting an interest in canoeing and other aquatic and athletic sports, by providing means and facilities for the recreation, physical culture, amusement, and social intercourse of its members and their guests, and the acquiring by purchase, lease or otherwise, of club-house, club-rooms and other equipment.

This corporation is nonmutual in character.

No. 145.

Cemetery Association.

THIRD. Said corporation is formed for the purpose of acquiring land, by purchase or otherwise, for cemetery purposes; establishing and maintaining a cemetery for public burial; the sale of burial lots; accepting endowment funds by gift or bequest, investing the same, disbursing the income thereof in maintaining and beautifying the lots and cemetery grounds; and the doing of all things necessary or incident thereto.

No. 146.

Chamber of Commerce.

(See G. C. § 10144 et seq.)

THIRD. Said corporation is formed for the purpose of collecting and circulating valuable and useful information relating to the manufacturing, industrial and mercantile interests of the city of ...., Ohio; to oppose the enactment of laws prejudicial to said interests; to encourage wise and useful legislation; to investigate transportation systems and endeavor to correct the abuses and evils existing therein; to secure reasonable and fair rates of freight to and from said city; to aid in the adjustment of controversies and misunderstandings between its members and others; and generally to promote and maintain the general welfare of the manufacturing, industrial and mercantile interests of said city.

No. 147.

To Administer Charitable Trust.

(G. C. § 10092-1.)

THIRD. Said corporation is formed for the purpose of administering a certain trust provided by the last will and testament of ...., deceased, which has been duly proven and recorded in volume ......, page ......, of the probate records of .... county, Ohio, a certified copy of which said will is filed herewith.

NOTE.—See also form No. 177.

No. 148.

Chautauqua Assembly.

(G. C. § 5888.)

THIRD. Said corporation is formed for the purpose of holding annual Chautauqua assemblies, encouragement of religion, art, science and literature, the general dissemination of knowledge, and to provide social entertainments and other means of recreation and amusements.

No. 149.

Church or Religious Society.

(G. C. § 10010.)

THIRD. Said corporation is formed for the purpose of providing a place of worship for its members and conducting the same according to the rules, regulations and customs of the ..... Church; of promoting the cause of the Christian religion; and of receiving, holding and disbursing gifts, bequests and funds arising from other sources; of owning and maintaining suitable real estate and buildings, and the doing of all things necessary or incident thereto.

No. 150.

Club House Corporation.

THIRD. Said corporation is formed for the purpose of acquiring by purchase, lease or otherwise, real estate, for a club house, and owning, improving and holding the same for the accommodation, convenience and pleasure and entertainment of members of the .... Society.

No. 151.

College.

THIRD. Said corporation is formed for the purpose of establishing, maintaining and conducting an institution of learning for the purpose of promoting education in all departments of learning and knowledge, and especially in those branches usually comprehended in academic, collegiate and university courses; to acquire and hold for said purposes money, real estate and other property necessary or proper to carry out said objects; and to do any and all things reasonable and necessary to be done to carry out said purposes.

NOTE.—A schedule of property must be filed with the secretary of state. See G. C. § 9922.

No. 152.
Consumers' League.   (Ruling Organization.)

THIRD. Said corporation is formed for the purpose of being a ruling or principal organization over subordinate organizations associated not for profit and located in municipalities in the state of Ohio. The purpose of this corporation, and of the subordinate and affiliated organizations is to further the welfare of persons engaged in the making and distribution of commodities, and of working women and children, by investigation, discussion, dissemination of information, legislation and appeal to public sentiment.

No. 153.
Deaconess Home.

THIRD. Said corporation is formed for the purpose of caring for the sick, the spiritually and physically destitute and needy and engaging in such other forms of charitable and benevolent work which may commend itself from time to time to the association; to promote the interests of the Christian religion; to receive and disburse donations, to receive and hold bequests and all funds arising from other sources for the benefit of said corporation.

No. 154.
Family Association.

THIRD. Said corporation is formed for the purpose of promoting and perpetuating the general welfare of the family of *John Doe,* mentally, physically, socially and morally, and of receiving and holding real estate and personal property by gift, devise or otherwise, and disposing of the same to carry out the purpose aforesaid, and the doing of all things necessary or incident thereto.

No. 155.

Farmers' Institute Society.

(G. C. § 9916.)

THIRD. Said corporation is formed for the purpose of teaching better methods of farming, stock raising, fruit culture and business connected with agriculture and the doing of all things necessary or incident thereto.

NOTE.—Twenty or more incorporators are required.

No. 156.

Farm Laborers' Association.

(G. C. § 10179.)

THIRD. Said corporation is formed for the purpose of promoting the interests of agriculture and for the relief of distressed farm laborers, or their orphans, whether such widows and orphans are members of the association or not, and the doing of all things necessary or incident thereto.

No. 157.

Free Loan Association.

THIRD. Said corporation is formed for the purpose of loaning money to poor and needy persons, without interest or compensation, and the doing of all things necessary or incident thereto.

No. 158.

Home for Indigent and Aged Women.

THIRD. Said corporation is formed for the purpose of establishing and maintaining a home for indigent and aged women; acquiring, by purchase, lease or otherwise, real estate necessary or convenient for said purpose, and constructing, improving and maintaining buildings thereon, disposing of the same; receiving, holding, investing and disbursing gifts and bequests and funds, and the doing of all things necessary or incident thereto.

No. 159.

Hospital.

THIRD. Said corporation is formed for the purpose of establishing, maintaining and conducting a hospital for medical and surgical treatment of persons, conducting a training school for nurses, the granting of diplomas to nurses graduating therefrom, engaging in research work in medicine, surgery and kindred subjects; receiving funds by donation, bequest or otherwise; holding, investing and disbursing the same; charging and receiving compensation for treatment, services and accommodations, all for the purpose of maintaining said hospital and not for profit; and the doing of all things necessary or incident thereto.

No. 160.

Improvement Association.

THIRD. Said corporation is formed for the purpose of promoting the general welfare of the *residence districts* of said city, by giving special attention to public improvements and all that relates to the betterment thereof and the convenience and comfort of the residents thereof, encouraging social intercourse among its members, and the doing of all things necessary or incident thereto.

No. 161.

Law and Order League.

THIRD. Said corporation is formed for the purpose of promoting the enforcement of laws and ordinances *regulating the sale of intoxicating liquors* in said county, and assisting, in all proper ways, the public authorities in the prevention, discovery and punishment of violations of such laws and ordinances.

No. 162.

Merchants' Exchange.   (Leaf Tobacco.)

(G. C. § 10144 et seq.)

THIRD. Said corporation is formed for the purpose of collecting and recording local and general statistical information relating to the tobacco trade; establishing uniformity in its usages and customs; adjusting and settling, in a proper and equitable manner, controversies, disputes and differences as to contracts, accounts, customs and usages that may arise; the appointment of inspectors and weighers of leaf tobacco; guarding, protecting and promoting the general interests of the tobacco trade and of its members, and the doing of all things necessary or incident thereto.

No. 163.

Musical Club.

THIRD. Said corporation is formed for the purpose of the study and culture of vocal and instrumental music, and the promotion of social intercourse of its members and all things incident thereto.

No. 164.

Musical Club. Another Form.

THIRD. Said corporation is formed for the purpose of the vocal study, the rehearsal and the private and public rendition of concerted music for male and mixed voices, also the employment and presentation of musical artists.

No. 165.

Mutual Benefit Association of Employees.

THIRD. Said corporation is formed for the purpose of mutual protection and relief of the employees of the .... Company, who become members, and their families and relatives, exclusively; receiving and raising funds by donation and by assessment on its members; giving financial aid to members when disabled by sickness or accident, and payment of benefits, on the death of members.

No. 166.

Benevolent Mutual Aid Association.

THIRD. Said corporation is formed for the purpose of assisting the members of said corporation in sickness or distress, by voluntary contributions of its members, and is organized strictly for charitable and benevolent purposes.

No. 167.

Political Club.

THIRD. Said corporation is formed for the purpose of organizing a political and social club; to promote the study of political institutions and the science of government and to provide a place where its members may enjoy the society of each other and their friends.

No. 168.

Public Library.

THIRD. Said corporation is formed for the purpose of owning, maintaining and conducting a public library in the village of ...., Ohio; to lease, purchase and maintain suitable real estate and buildings for said purpose; to receive, hold and disburse donations, bequests and other funds for the purposes of said corporation and to do all things necessary and incident thereto.

No. 169.

Retail Merchants' Association.

THIRD. Said corporation is formed for the purpose of fostering and extending the retail trade of said city; encouraging wise and needful legislation, and opposing the enactment of laws and ordinances prejudicial to the mercantile interests of said city; giving and exchanging information among its members; promoting the social intercourse among persons engaged in the retail trade and the doing of all things necessary or incident thereto.

No. 170.

Salvage.

(G. C. §§ 9873, 9875.)

SECOND. Said corporation is to be located at ...., in .... County, Ohio, and shall prosecute its business within the .... (*municipality or other subdivision*) of ...., Ohio.

THIRD. Said corporation is formed for the purpose of discovering and preventing fires and of saving property and life from conflagration and exercising all of the powers which may be exercised by such corporations under the laws of Ohio.

No. 171.

Social and Improvement Club.

THIRD. Said corporation is formed for the purpose of promoting friendly social intercourse and to encourage education and investigation in matters pertaining to the *plumbing trade;* of providing social entertainment and amusement for its members and their families and friends and of providing a meeting place for its members.

No. 172.

Social Settlement Association.

THIRD. Said corporation is formed for the purpose of providing a place and facilities for social, physical, civic, educational and moral instruction and improvement, and for such work as is now, or may be hereafter, commonly associated with "settlement work;" and for such purpose of acquiring, by purchase, lease, or otherwise, necessary and convenient real estate, buildings and rooms; the holding, improving and disposing of the same; the receiving of funds by bequest or gift, disbursing the same and the doing of all things necessary or incident thereto.

No. 173.

Yacht Club.

THIRD. Said corporation is formed for the purpose of the encouragement of yachting, the designing and building of yachts, and the promotion of social relations of those interested in yachting.

No. 174.

Young Men's Christian Association.

(Must be approved by State Association: G. C. §§ 10031, 10024.)

THIRD. Said corporation is formed for the purpose of developing the Christian character and usefulness of its members and of promoting the spiritual, mental, social and physical welfare of young men.

No. 175.

Agricultural Society. Articles of Incorporation.

(G. C. §§ 9880, 9885.)

The undersigned, being residents of .... county (*or* of a district embracing the counties of .... and ....), Ohio, hereby organize themselves into a society for the improvement of agriculture within said county (*or district*), subject to the rules of the Agricultural Commission of Ohio, and in accordance with the laws of Ohio governing corporations so organized for said purpose.

The name of said society shall be .... Said society shall be located at ....

In witness whereof, we hereunto set our hands this ...... day of .... , 19...

NOTE.—Thirty or more incorporators are necessary. A copy of the printed rules may be obtained, on application, from the Agricultural Commission, Columbus, Ohio.

No. 176.

Township Agricultural Society. Articles of Incorporation.

(G. C. § 9911.) .

The undersigned residents of .... Township, ... County, Ohio, hereby form a society for the promotion of agriculture in such township and, desiring to become incorporated under the laws of Ohio and the following agreement, do hereby certify:

1. The name of said society shall be ....

2. The object of its formation is not for profit, but for the promotion of agriculture in said township.

3. Said society shall be located in said township of ....

In witness whereof, we hereunto set our hands and seals this ...... day of ...., 19...

```
..........  (Seal)
..........  (Seal)
..........  (Seal)
..........  (Seal)
..........  (Seal)
```

(Certificate of acknowledgment.)

NOTE.—The acknowledgment should be made before a justice of the peace.

No. 177.

Charitable Trust; Corporation to Administer.

(G. C. § 10086.)

These articles of incorporation of The ....

Witnesseth: That ...., executor of the last will and testament of ...., deceased, and .... and ...., citizens and residents of .... county, Ohio, desiring to form a corporation for the administration of a certain trust provided by the last will and testament of said decedent, hereby certify:

1. That the following is a copy of the last will and testament of said ...., deceased, which has been duly proven and recorded in volume ......, page ......, of the probate records of .... county, Ohio.

2. The name of said corporation shall be .... (*name of testator should be included, unless the will otherwise provides*).

3. Said corporation shall be located at ...., in .... county, Ohio.

In witness whereof, we have hereunto set our hands this .... day of ...., A. D. 19...

```
............,
............,
............,
```

(Add certificate of acknowledgment.)

NOTE.—See also form No. 147.

No. 178.

Endowment Fund Corporation.
Board of Trustees.   Articles of.

(G. C. § 10011.)

It is hereby certified by the undersigned that at a regular session of the .... Conference of the .... Conference, of the .... Church, held at ...., in .... county, Ohio, the following named persons, to wit: ...., members of said denomination, one or more of whom are resident freeholders in this state, were duly elected a board of trustees for ...., the .... Conference of the .... Church, and who are to serve as such until successors shall be elected and who with their said successors in office shall exist and become and be an incorporated board of trustees and a corporation not for profit for the purpose of acquiring in trust and of so controlling and disposing of all such real and personal property as from time to time the said society may deem it desirable to have acquired, controlled and disposed of for church and benevolent purposes. The said board of trustees, however, shall hold all such property in trust for said society and church at all times and acquire, control and dispose of the same under the supervision and control of said church and subject to its directions and order.

That the uses to which the said property so to be acquired and holden shall be applied are all such uses as it may be and is lawful for the said church and society to apply the same as a religious organization and body under the laws of Ohio.

In witness whereof, we have hereunto set our hands this .... day of ...., A. D. 19...

........, ..., and officer presiding over the said ...... Conference.

........, secretary, of the said .... Conference.

The State of Ohio, ... County, ss.

On this ...... day of ...., A. D. 19.., personally appeared before me, a notary public in and for said county and state, ... and ...., who acknowledged that they did make and sign the foregoing statement as and for the uses and purposes therein set forth, and that they are still satisfied therewith.

(Seal)

............,
Notary Public in and for ...., Ohio.

No. 179.

Fraternal Benefit Society.

(G. C. § 9473.)

Articles of Association
of
The A. B. Society.

The undersigned persons, all of whom are citizens of the United States and a majority of whom are citizens of the state of Ohio, desiring to form a fraternal benefit society as defined by the Act of the General Assembly of the State of Ohio entitled "An act for the regulation and control of fraternal benefit societies, passed May 31, 1911, hereby certify:

1st.   The proposed name of the society is The *A. B. Society.*

2d.   The purpose for which the society is formed and the mode in which its corporate powers are to be exercised are as follows:

Said corporation is formed not for profit, but for the purpose of carrying on a fraternal benefit society for the mutual benefit of its members and their beneficiaries, having a lodge system with ritualistic form of work and representative form of government, and providing for the payment of benefits in accordance with section 9466 of the General Code of Ohio.

The corporate powers of said corporation are to be exercised according to the provisions of Chapter 4, Subdivision 1, of Division III, Title IX, Part second of the General Code of Ohio and of the constitution and laws, rules and regulations of said corporation.

Said corporation shall have no capital stock.

3.   The names, residences and official titles of all the officers, trustees, directors and other persons who are to have and exercise general control and management of the affairs and funds of the society for the first year or until the ensuing election at which all such officers shall be elected by the supreme legislative or governing body are as follows: ....

4th.   The place of the principal office of the society shall be ...., in the state of Ohio.

In testimony whereof, we have hereunto set our hands this ...... day of ...., A. D. 19...

(*Signatures and addresses of seven or more incorporators.*)

The State of Ohio, ..., County, ss.

Personally appeared before me, the undersigned authority within and for said county, on this ...... day of ...., A. D. 19.., the above named ...., all of whom I hereby certify are citizens of the United States, and of whom I hereby certify the following named are citizens of the state of Ohio

........, and each of them severally acknowledged the signing
of the foregoing articles of association to be his free act and
deed for the uses and purposes therein mentioned.

Witness my hand and official seal on the day and year last
aforesaid.

.............,

....

No. 180.

Society for the Prevention of Cruelty to Animals.

(G. C. § 10068.)

Record of proceedings had at a meeting held at ....,
Ohio, for the organization of a society for the prevention of
cruelty to animals.

At a meeting of .... (*state number*) citizens held at
........, in ...., Ohio, on ...., 19.., for the purpose of organizing a society for the prevention of cruelty to
animals, ... was elected temporary chairman and ....
secretary. A permanent organization was then effected, as follows: ...., president; ...., secretary; ....,
........, directors.

On motion duly seconded and unanimously carried, it was
resolved that the persons present associate themselves together
as a society for the prevention of acts of cruelty to animals under
the name of the .... Society.

The secretary was instructed to file, certify and forward to
the secretary of state a true record of the proceedings of the
meeting. On motion the meeting adjourned.

..............., ...,
        President.   Secretary.

        ...., Ohio, ..., 19...

I, the undersigned, do hereby certify that the foregoing is a
true and exact copy of the proceedings of a meeting held ......,
19.., at ...., Ohio, for the purpose of effecting an organization for the prevention of cruelty to animals.

.............,

Secretary.

No. 181.

Organization Record of Corporations not for Profit.

NOTE.—Every corporation should have a blank book suitable for
the record of all its proceedings. A membership book may be convenient,
but most corporations not for profit use the first few pages of the record
of proceedings for the membership roll. On the first page should be
entered:

(a) **Record Book.**

"Record of proceedings of the incorporators, members and trustees of .... (*name of corporation*)."

(*Under the above heading an entry substantially as follows should be made:*)

On this ...... day of ...., 19.., ..., ..., ..., ..., and ...., the persons named below as subscribers of articles of incorporation, desiring for themselves, their associates and successors, to become a body corporate, in accordance with the general corporation laws of the state of Ohio, under the name and style of .... (*name of corporation*), and with all the corporate rights, powers, privileges and liabilities enjoyed under or imposed by such laws, did subscribe, acknowledge and afterward, to wit: on the ...... day of ...., 19.., file in the office of the secretary of state at Columbus, in the state of Ohio, articles of incorporation, as follows, to wit:

(*Copy in full the articles of incorporation, with acknowledgment and certificate of the secretary of state.*)

(*Persons may become members by subscribing their names to a copy of the articles (G. C. § 8653), which may be done in the following form:*)

We, the undersigned, having the qualifications prescribed by its regulations and desiring to become members of thereof, do hereby subscribe our names to the foregoing copy of the articles of incorporation of .... (*name of corporation*).

(*Leave sufficient space for the signatures of all persons who are likely to become members.*)

(b)

MINUTES OF MEETING OF INCORPORATORS FOR ELECTION OF FIRST TRUSTEES.

(G. C. § 8655.)

........, Ohio, ..., 19...

A meeting of the subscribers to the articles of incorporation of the .... (*name of corporation*) was held at ...., in ...., Ohio, on the .... day of ...., 19... Present: Messrs. .... Mr. .... was chosen chairman and Mr. .... secretary of said meeting.

An election for trustees, to hold their offices until the next annual meeting, or until their successors are elected and qualified, was then held, resulting in the choice of the following: .... (*five or more trustees are required*).

There being no further business, the meeting adjourned on motion.

Attest:

............., ...,
    Secretary.   Chairman.

(c)

OATH OF TRUSTEES.

State of Ohio, ... County, ss.

We, the undersigned, being duly sworn, say that we will faithfully discharge our duties as trustees of .... (*name of corporation*).

.............,
.............,
.............,
.............,
....

Subscribed and sworn to before me this .... day of ...., 19...

.............,
    Notary Public.

(d)

REGULATIONS OF CORPORATION NOT FOR PROFIT.

ARTICLE I. MEETINGS OF MEMBERS.

(a). *Annual meeting.* The annual meeting of the members of this association shall be held at .... on the first Monday in January of each year at ...... o'clock .. M.

(b). *Periodical meetings.* —— (monthly, quarterly, etc.), meetings shall be held at .... on the ...... at ...... o'clock .. M.

(c). *Special meetings* of the members may be called by the trustees, or by any two members, by giving notice in writing to each member by mail at his last known address, or by publication in some newspaper published in ...., Ohio, for ...... days. At all meetings .... shall constitute a quorum.

ARTICLE II. TRUSTEES.

The number of trustees shall be .... The election of trustees shall be held at the annual meeting of members, or at a special meeting called for that purpose.

Trustees shall hold office for one year or until their successors are elected and qualified. Trustees chosen at the first election shall hold office until the time fixed for the next annual meeting, or until their successors are elected and qualified.

At all meetings ...... shall constitute a quorum.

ARTICLE III.   OFFICERS.

The officers of the association shall be a president, vice-president, secretary and treasurer.   Said officers shall be chosen by the trustees by a majority ballot, and shall hold office for one year or until their successors are elected and qualified, except that officers elected at the first meeting of the trustees shall hold office until the next annual meeting of the trustees, or until their successors are elected and qualified.

NOTE.—The president must be chosen by the trustees; but the regulations may provide for the election of other officers by the members. G. C. § 8664.

ARTICLE IV.   DUTIES OF OFFICERS.

(a). *President.* The president shall preside at all meetings of the members and trustees, sign the records thereof, and perform generally all the duties usually performed by presidents of like associations, and such further and other duties as may be from time to time required of him by the members or trustees.

(b). *Vice-president.* The vice-president shall perform all the duties of the president in case of the absence or disability of the latter. In case both president and vice-president are absent or unable to perform their duties, the members or trustees, as the case may be, may appoint a president pro tempore.

(c). *Secretary.* The secretary shall keep minutes of all the proceedings of the members and trustees of this association and make a proper record of the same, which shall be attested by him, and generally perform such duties as may be required of him by the members or trustees.

(d). *Treasurer.* The treasurer shall receive and have in charge all moneys belonging to the association and shall disburse the same as may be ordered by the board of trustees. He shall keep an accurate account of the moneys received and disbursed by him, and shall generally perform such duties as may be required of him by the members and trustees. On the expiration of his term of office he shall turn over to his successor, or to the board of trustees, all money and property of the association in his hands.

ARTICLE V.   QUALIFICATIONS OF MEMBERS.

Any person may become a member of this association upon election by three-fourths of the members present at any regular meeting, and by signing the membership roll and agreeing to be bound by the regulations and by-laws of the association, and by payment of the initiation fee specified in these regulations.

ARTICLE VI.   INITIATION FEE AND DUES.

Each member shall pay an initiation fee of .... dollars within .... days after election, and in case of failure so to do, said election shall be void. The annual dues of the members shall be .... dollars, payable semiannually. Failure to pay dues within thirty days after the same are due and payable shall be a cause for expulsion.

ARTICLE VII.   SUSPENSION AND EXPULSION OF MEMBERS.

Any member may be suspended or expelled by the board of trustees for failure to pay dues, or for conduct unbecoming a member. Before any member is suspended or expelled he shall be notified in writing by mail at his last known address of the charges against him, and of the time and place of the trustees, meeting at which the same are to be considered, at least five days before said meeting; and shall be given an opportunity to defend, and shall have the right to appeal from the decision of the board of trustees to the members, and, at his request, the secretary shall call a special meeting of the members to consider said appeal.

ARTICLE VIII.   ORDER OF BUSINESS.

Unless changed by a majority vote, at all members' meetings, the order of business shall be as follows:
(1) Reading of the minutes.
(2) Reading of reports and statements.
(3) Unfinished business.
(4) Election of trustees.
(5) New or miscellaneous business.

ARTICLE IX.   AMENDMENTS.

These regulations may be amended or repealed by the written assent thereto of the members of this association, or by a majority vote of the members at a meeting called for that purpose.

(e)

WRITTEN ASSENT TO ADOPTION OF REGULATIONS.
(G. C. § 8703.)

We, the undersigned, being more than two-thirds of the members of .... (*name of corporation*), do hereby assent in writing to the adoption of the foregoing code of regulations for the government of this association.

........, Ohio, ..., 19...

MISCELLANEOUS FORMS.
RELATING TO ORGANIZATION AND MANAGEMENT.

No. 182.

Resolution of Directors for Call or Assessment on Stock Subscriptions.

(G. C. § 8632.)

Upon motion of Mr. ...., duly seconded, the following resolution was unanimously adopted:

"Resolved, that an assessment of .... percent on subscriptions to the capital stock of this Company be, and the same hereby is, called for and required to be paid to ...., the treasurer of this Company, at No. .... Street, ... Ohio, on or before the ...... day of ...., 19..."

No. 183.

Notice of Call or Assessment on Stock Subscriptions.

The .... Company.

........, Ohio, ..., 19...

By resolution of the board of directors an assessment of .... percent on subscriptions to the capital stock of this Company is called for and required to be paid to ...., treasurer, at No. ...... Street, ..., Ohio, on or before the ...... day of ...., 19...

............,
Secretary.

NOTE.—The manner of giving notice of calls is not provided by statute. Notice by registered mail is probably sufficient.

No. 184.

Notice of Sale of Stock for Nonpayment of Call.

(G. C. § 8675.)

Public notice is hereby given that .... shares of the capital stock of The .... Company will be sold at public auction by the directors of said Company at the office of said Company, No. .... Street, ..., Ohio, on the ...... day of ...., 19.., at 10 o'clock A. M.

Said sale will be made pursuant to the statute in such case made and provided because of the nonpayment by ...., subscriber for said stock, of a call for the payment of an installment on the same for sixty days after said installment was required to be paid, due notice thereof having been given.

The .... Company.
By ....,
Secretary.

........, Ohio, ..., 19...

· NOTE.—Publish as required by G. C. § 8675.

No. 185.

Receipt for Installment Payment on Stock.

Stub.	Receipt.
	No. .... $..... ...... Shares
	The .... Company,
	.... Building,
No.	........, Ohio.
Name	Received of .... the sum of ......
Amount $......	dollars, being installment payment No. ...
Installment No......	of ..... percent on his subscription for
Number shares	.... shares of the capital stock of The
Date	.... Company.
	........,
	Treasurer.
	........, 19...

No. 186.

Transferable Receipt for Installment Payment on Stock.

No. .... $........   ....Shares.

Transferable Receipt.   .
The .... Company.
.... Building, ... Ohio.

Received of .... the sum of .... dollars on account of his subscription for .... shares of the capital stock of The .... Company at the par value of *one hundred* dollars per share.

Upon payment of the balance of said subscription, in accordance with its terms, and upon surrender of this receipt, certificates for said .... shares of stock will be issued to the order of said subscriber.

........, 19...   ...., Treasurer.

ASSIGNMENT OF SUBSCRIPTION, ENDORSED ON FOREGOING RECEIPT.

For value received, I hereby sell, assign and transfer to ......
my subscription for ...... shares of the capital stock of The
.... Company, together with all payments made thereon,
as shown by the within receipt, and I hereby direct and authorize
said The .... Company, upon full payment of said subscription, to issue certificates for said stock to the order of said assignee.

........, 19...   ....

In presence of

    ....

No. 187.

Certificate of Common Stock.

(G. C. § 8672.)

Stub.	Certificate.
	Incorporated under the laws of the state of Ohio.
	No. ...... Number of shares .....
Certificate No.	Capital stock, $300,000.
For ...... shares.	Common stock, $200,000.
Issued to	Preferred stock, $100,000.
....	The .... Company.
Dated ......, 19...	This certifies that ...... is the holder
Transferred from ..	of .... shares of *one hundred* dollars
....	each, full paid and nonassessable, of the
Dated ......, 19...	capital stock of The .... Company,
No. original certifi-	transferable only on the books of the cor-
cate............	poration, in person or by attorney, on sur-
No. shares transfer-	render of this certificate, properly en-
red............	dorsed.
Received certificate	
No. .... for	Witness the seal of the
shares this	(Corporate Seal) corporation and the sig-
........., 19.....	natures of its duly au-
....	thorized officers this ...
	day of ......, 19...
	........., ...,
	Secretary. President.
	Shares, $100 each.

ASSIGNMENT TO BE ENDORSED ON CERTIFICATE.

For value received, ... hereby sell, transfer and assign
to .... (*all, or specify number of shares transferred*) of

the shares of stock evidenced by the within certificate and hereby irrevocably constitute and appoint ...., ... attorney, with full power of substitution, to transfer the same on the books of the corporation.

Dated ...., 19...   ....

In presence of

....

NOTE.—The person to whom a certificate is issued, or his duly authorized agent or attorney, should sign the receipt on the corresponding stub.

No. 188.

Certificate of Preferred Stock.

(G. C. § 8667 et seq.)

Stub as in preceding form, inserting word "Preferred" on top line.

Incorporated under the laws of the state of Ohio.

No. ...... Number of shares ......

Capital stock, $300,000.

Common stock, $200,000.

Preferred stock, $100,000.

The .... Company.

This certifies that ...... is the holder of .... shares of one hundred dollars each, fully paid, of the preferred stock of The .... Company, transferable only on the books of the corporation, in person or by attorney, on the surrender of this certificate properly endorsed. The holder of this certificate is entitled to cumulative (*or noncumulative*) dividends in each year at the rate of *six* percent per annum, payable out of the surplus profits of said Company, in preference to any dividend on the common stock. (*Insert here such of the special clauses following as may be desired.*)

Witness the seal of the corporation and the signatures of its duly authorized officers at ...., Ohio, this .... day of ...., 19...

.........., ...,

Secretary.   President.

Shares, $100 each.

(Corporate Seal)

No. 189.

Special Clauses for Preferred Stock Certificates.

DIVIDENDS LIMITED TO SPECIFIED RATE.

The holder of this certificate shall not be entitled to any dividends in excess of six percent per annum and the arrears thereof.

PREFERRED STOCK TO PARTICIPATE IN EXCESS DIVIDENDS.

When dividends of six percent have been paid for any year on the entire preferred and common capital stock, issued and outstanding, the holder of this certificate shall be entitled to share in all further dividends for that year.

RIGHT TO VOTE WITHHELD.

The holder of this certificate shall not be entitled to vote at meetings of the stockholders of said Company.

PREFERRED STOCK TO BE VOTED UPON DEFAULT FOR DIVIDENDS.

The holder of this certificate shall not be entitled to vote at meetings of the stockholders of said Company so long as dividends at the above rate are paid; but in case of default in the payment of such dividends, then and thereafter the holder hereof may vote at any and all stockholders' meetings.

OPTION TO CORPORATION TO REDEEM STOCK.

The preferred stock represented by this certificate is subject to redemption at the option of the Company on the ......day of ...., 19.., or on the ...... day of .... of any year thereafter, upon payment of ...... dollars ($......) per share and all accumulated dividends.

OPTION TO HOLDER TO CONVERT INTO COMMON STOCK.

The holder hereof may, at his election, on surrender of this certificate, convert the same into an equal number of shares of common stock.

No. 190.

Certificate of Stock Reserving Lien to Secure Indebtedness to Corporation.

Stub as in preceding forms.	Incorporated under the laws of the state of Ohio. No. ....shares. The .... Company. Capital stock $.... Shares $.... each. This certifies that .... is the owner of ...... shares of ...... dollars each, fully paid, of the capital stock of The .... Company, transferable only on the books of the corporation, in person or by attorney, on surrender of this certificate and the payment of all indebtedness of the above owner to said The .... Company. The .... Company has a first lien on the shares of stock represented by this certificate to secure all indebtedness of the above owner to it. (Seal) In witness whereof, the duly authorized officers of this Company have hereunto subscribed their names and caused the corporate seal to be hereto affixed at ...., Ohio, this .... day of ...., 19... ...., President. ...., Secretary.

NOTE.—See G. C. §§ 8673-15, 9761. Stafford v. Produce Exchange Banking Co., 61 O. S. 160.

No. 191.

Corporation Calendar.

NOTE.—During the course of a year many things require attention by the officers of a corporation on certain specified dates. As a reminder, the secretaries of many corporations enter memoranda of such matters in the "tickler" system regularly used by their respective companies. The secretaries of other corporations prepare a calendar which is hung in a conspicuous place. The following specimen calendar, which is printed merely to suggest the general nature of the entries, is prepared for the year 1914 for a corporation of which the annual meeting of stockholders is held on the first Monday in January, with monthly meetings of directors on the first Tuesday of each month. If any regular meeting day is a legal holiday, the meeting is held on the day following. Notice of stockholders' meetings of this corporation are required to be mailed ten days, and of directors' meetings at least three days, before the day of the meeting.

Calendar of The .... Company.
1914.

January

5   Stockholders' annual meeting 10 A. M.

     (If directors elected at this meeting are all present hold regular monthly meeting of directors immediately after adjournment of stockholders' meeting. All directors should sign a waiver of notice of this meeting.)

30   Send out notices of the directors' meeting of February 3.

February

3   Directors' meeting 2 P. M.

16   Federal income tax return must be made on or before March 1 to U. S. Collector of Internal Revenue, ..., Ohio.

27   Send income tax return to U. S. Collector of Internal Revenue.

     Send out notices of the directors' meeting of March 3.

March

3   Directors' meeting 2 P. M.

April

3   Send out notices for directors' meeting of April 7.

7   Directors' meeting 2 P. M.

May

1   Send out notices for directors' meeting of May 5.

5   Directors' meeting 2 P. M.

15   Property tax return to county auditor due by May 31; franchise tax statement to tax commission of Ohio due by May 31.

29   Mail franchise tax statement to state tax commission. Make return of property for taxation to county auditor.

     Send out notices for directors' meeting of June 2.

June

2   Directors' meeting 2 P. M.

July

3   Send out notices for directors' meeting of July 7.

7   Directors' meeting 2 P. M.

31   Send out notices of the directors' meeting of August 4.

August

4   Directors' meeting 2 P. M.

28   Send out notices for the directors' meeting of September 1.

September
    1   Directors' meeting 2 P. M.
   October
    2   Send out notices for the directors' meeting of October 6.
    6   Directors' meeting 2 P. M.
   30   Send out notices for the directors' meeting of November 3.
November
    3   Directors' meeting 2 P. M.
   27   Send out notices for the directors' meeting of December 1.
December
    1   Directors' meeting 2 P. M.
        Get tax bills from county treasurer.
   19   Pay property taxes to county treasurer.
   24   Send out notices for stockholders' annual meeting January 4, 1915, at 10 A. M.

STOCK BOOKS.

NOTE.—By statute every corporation is required to keep a book in which it is the duty of the secretary to register all subscriptions and transfers of stock. G. C. § 8673.

The form of the book is not prescribed. Harpold v. Stobart, 46 O. S. 397 (400).

Many corporations keep no stock book, but attempt to keep on the stubs of the stock certificate book a record of the stock issued and transferred. This is not a compliance with the statute; although where the certificates representing transferred stock are cancelled and pasted on the stubs from which they were originally detached, and proper entries are made on such stubs showing the transfers and issue of new certificates, and where the outstanding certificates are properly receipted for on the stub, the certificate book undoubtedly contains a complete record. See, Herrick v. Wardwell, 58 O. S. 294 (311-312).

The better practice is to keep two books: (1) a stock transfer book and (2) a stock ledger. The following forms of stock books are suggested:

No. 192.
Stock Transfer Book.

Date 1911	By whom sold	Certificates Canceled			To whom transferred	Certificates Issued				
		Ledger folio	Number of certificate	Number of shares transferred		Ledger folio	Number of certificate	Number of shares	Par value of shares	We, the undersigned, acting by the undersigned attorney, do hereby, sell, transfer and assign to the transferees named herein, the number of shares of stock of The .... Company set opposite our respective names, all as set forth. Signature of Attorney
Jan. 4	Original issue	...	...	...	William Brown	1	1	10	$1,000	Herbert Jones
" 4	"	...	...	...	Thomas White	2	2	10	1,000	Herbert Jones
" 4	"	...	...	...	Franklin Green	3	3	10	1,000	Herbert Jones
" 4	"	...	...	...	George Black	4	4	20	2,000	
" 4	"	...	...	...	Edward Irwin	5	5	50	5,000	
Feb. 1	William Brown	1	1	5	{ Peter Smith	6	6	5	500	
					{ William Brown (reissue)	1	7	5	500	
Mar. 1	Thomas White	2	2	10	Joseph Miller	7	8	10	1,000	
Apr. 1	Franklin Green	3	3	10	William Brown	1	9	10	1,000	

No. 193.
Stock Ledger.
WILLIAM BROWN, CLEVELAND, OHIO.

Date	From or to whom transferred	Transfer book folio	Certificate numbers		Number of shares		Par value of shares		Balance	
			Canceled	Issued	Received	Disposed of	Received	Disposed of	No. of shares	Par value
1911										
Jan. 4	Original issue	1	..	1	10	..	$1,000	....	10	$1,000
Feb. 1	To Peter Smith	1	1	6	..	5	.....	$500	5	500
	To William Brown (reissue)	1	..	7	..	..	.....	....		
Apr. 1	From Franklin Green	1	3	9	10	..	1,000	....	15	1,500

NOTE.—*Stock transfer book.* The hypothetical entries in the above form of stock transfer book represent the following transactions:

(1) An issue to the original subscribers of certificates representing 100 shares of stock, as follows:

To William Brown   10 shares
" Thomas White   10   "
" Franklin Green   10   "
" George Black   20   "
" Edward Johnson 50   "

(2) A transfer of five shares by William Brown to Peter Smith; the original certificate issued to William Brown being surrendered and cancelled and two certificates being issued in its stead; one to Peter Smith for five shares and one to William Brown (a reissue) for five shares.

(3) A transfer of ten shares by Thomas White to Joseph Miller.

(4) A transfer of ten shares by Franklin Green to William Brown.

Stock ledger. In the above form only one ledger account is given which will illustrate the character of entries required. When a certificate is issued to a new stockholder a new ledger account should be opened in his name. When all stock of a stockholder is transferred to other persons his account should be closed.

These forms may be changed to meet the individual taste of any bookkeeper; but whatever be the forms adopted, the facts set out in the last two forms should appear in some shape or other in the forms adopted.

No. 194.

Proxy.   One Specified Meeting.

Know all men by these presents, that I, the undersigned stockholder in The .... Company, do hereby appoint .... my true and lawful attorney, substitute and proxy (with power of substitution) for me and in my name to vote at the annual meeting of stockholders of said Company, to be held on ......, the ...... day of ...., 19.., or at any adjournment of said meeting, with all powers I should have if personally present, hereby revoking all proxies heretofore given.

Dated at ...., on this ...... day of ...., 19...

Witness, ...

No. 195.

Proxy.   All Meetings Within a Specified Time. '

Know all men by these presents, that I, ... of ...., hereby appoint .... to be my substitute and proxy, for me, and in my name, place and stead, to vote at any election held by the stockholders of The ...... Company for directors within .... months from the date hereof, and to vote on all matters considered at any stockholders' meeting, annual or special, held during said period, as fully as I might do if personally present.

In witness whereof, I have hereunto set my hand and seal at
........, this .... day of ...., 19...
Witness,
.... (Seal)

NOTE.—A seal is not required in Ohio but is required in some
States. It is prudent to execute proxies under seal, when intended for
use in another State, or when the corporation is organized under the laws
of another State.

No. 196.

Proxy. General.

Know all men by these presents, that I, ..., do hereby
constitute and appoint .... my attorney and substitute (with
power of substitution) for me and in my name, place and stead,
to vote as my proxy at any annual or special meeting of the
stockholders of The .... Company for the election of directors, and upon such other questions as may come before any
such meeting, according to the number of votes I should be entitled to cast if then personally present.
In witness whereof, I have hereunto set my hand and seal this
...... day of ...., A. D. 19...
                                   .... (L. S.)
Sealed and delivered in presence of

No. 197.

Revocation of Proxy.

Know all men by these presents, that, whereas, in and by
my proxy dated ...., 19.., I, A. B., did constitute
and appoint C. D. my attorney, substitute and proxy, for
me and in my name, place and stead to vote at (*insert reference
to meeting or meetings, and other authority, of any, given to
proxy*) as will more fully appear by reference to said proxy.
Now I, the said A. B., do hereby revoke, countermand, annul
and make void the said proxy above mentioned, and all power
and authority thereby given, or intended to be given, to the said
C. D.
Witness my hand this ...... day of ...., 19...
In presence of   A. B.

ANNUAL MEETINGS OF STOCKHOLDERS.

NOTE.—For record and minutes of first meeting of stockholders see pages 111, 125 and 126. See also page 39.

No. 198.

Notice of Annual Meeting.

The .... Company.

No. .... Building.

........, Ohio, ...19...

The annual meeting of the stockholders of The .... Company will be held in the office of the Company, No. .... Building, ..., Ohio, on ...., the .... day of ...., 19.., at .... o'clock .. M. for the election of directors for the ensuing year and for the transaction of such other business as may come before said meeting.

NOTE.—If the regulations provide that only those persons may vote who are stockholders of record a certain number of days before the annual meeting, add the following:

At said meeting only such persons shall be entitled to vote who appear as stockholders on the books of the Company on the ...... day of ...., 19...

............,
Secretary.

No. 199.

Minutes of Annual Meeting.

NOTE.—If the regulations of the corporation provide for notice of the annual meeting, it is good practice to insert a copy of the notice above the minutes of the meeting, with the following certificate appended:

I hereby certify that a true copy of the foregoing notice was, on the .... day of ...., 19.., by me mailed, postage prepaid, to each and every stockholder registered on the books of this Company.

............,
Secretary.

Annual Stockholders' Meeting.

........, 19...

The stockholders of The .... Company met in annual meeting at the office of the Company in ...., Ohio, at .... o'clock .. M., ..., 19...

The meeting was called to order by ...., president of the Company, who presided over the meeting. ...., secretary of the Company, acted as secretary of the meeting.

The president directed the secretary to call the roll of the stockholders, and requested all persons holding proxies to deposit the same with the secretary, which was accordingly done. Thereupon the secretary announced that out of 500 shares of outstanding stock entitled to vote at the meeting, 450 shares were represented at the meeting; 300 shares by stockholders in person, and 150 shares by proxy.

The minutes of the preceding annual meeting of stockholders were read and approved. The minutes of special stockholders' meetings held ...., 19.., and ...., 19.., were read and approved.

The annual report of the president was then read by him, and, on motion duly made and seconded and unanimously carried, was ordered received and placed on file.

The annual report of the treasurer was then presented and, upon motion duly made and seconded and unanimously carried, was ordered received and placed on file.

There being no unfinished business, the president thereupon declared nominations of persons to serve as directors for the ensuing year to be in order.

The following persons were placed in nomination: Messrs. ....

(X) On motion duly made, seconded and carried, Messrs. .... and .... were appointed inspectors of election. Thereupon the secretary delivered to the inspectors of election the proxies on file and a list showing the stockholders entitled to vote at the meeting, and the number of shares owned by each.

Thereupon a ballot was had, and the inspectors of election presented a certificate of the result thereof, showing that Messrs. .... had received a majority of the votes cast.

NOTE.—If there is no contest, only the number of directors to be elected having been nominated, omit the foregoing paragraph beginning at (X) and insert the following:

"There being no other nominations, upon motion duly made, seconded and unanimously carried, the secretary was instructed to cast the ballot of all stockholders present for the candidates for directors so placed in nomination. The secretary accordingly cast said ballot."

Whereupon said persons were declared by the president to be duly elected as directors for the ensuing year and until their successors are elected and qualified.

There being no further business, the meeting was duly adjourned on motion.

............,
President.

Attest:
............,
Secretary.

No. 200.

Ballot.

The .... Company.

Annual meeting ...., 19...

The undersigned hereby votes the number of shares set opposite his signature below for the following persons to serve as directors for the ensuing year.

................, ...,

................, ...,

....

Name   Number of Shares.

                in person

....   or   ....

                proxy for

....

No. 201.

Inspectors' Certificate of Election.

See G. C. § 8644.

We, the undersigned, duly appointed inspectors of election to conduct the election of directors of The .... Company, held ...., 19.., do hereby certify that we duly conducted said election by ballot, and received and counted the votes cast, with the result that the following named directors were elected by the majority vote set opposite their respective names:

Names.	Votes Received.	Majority.
....	....	....
....	....	....
....	....	....
....	....	....
....	....	....

In witness whereof, we hereunto set our hands at ...., Ohio, this ...... day of ...., 19...

SPECIAL MEETINGS OF STOCKHOLDERS.

NOTE.—The following forms are not applicable in all respects where a special meeting of the stockholders is held to act upon matters which are specially provided for by statute, such as a sale of the entire assets of the corporation, amendment of the articles of incorporation, increase of number of directors, increase of capital stock, amendment of the regulations, etc. In such cases the special statutory provisions, if any, for calling and giving notice of the meeting should be followed. Forms therefor, including motions and resolutions are included under the special titles.

No. 202.

Waiver of Call and Notice of Special Stockholders' Meeting.

.........., Ohio, ..., 19...

We, the undersigned, being all the stockholders of The ...... Company, of ...., Ohio, do hereby consent that a special meeting of the stockholders of said corporation may be held at the office of the Company, No. .... Street, ..., Ohio, on the ...... day of ...., 19.., at ...... o'clock .. M. for the purpose of considering and acting upon .... (*state object of meeting, as "a proposed increase in the number of directors of this company from five, the present number, to ten."*)

We hereby waive any and all requirements of law, or of the regulations of said Company, as to the making of a call for, and the giving of notice of said meeting, and we hereby agree to the transaction at said meeting of any and all business within the powers of said Company.

Stockholders.   Proxies.   Shares.

No. 203.

Call for Special Meeting of Stockholders.

........, Ohio, ..., 19...

To ....

Secretary of The .... Company.

We, the undersigned, ... (*directors, or stockholders*) .... of The .... Company, do hereby call and order a special meeting of the stockholders of said Company to be held in the office of the Company, No. .... Street, ..., Ohio, on the .... day of ...., 19.., at .... o'clock .. M. for the purpose of considering and acting upon .... (*state object of meeting*) .... and for the transaction of any and all business necessary or incident thereto, and we do hereby instruct you to give notice of such meeting to the stockholders pursuant to law and to the regulations of this Company.

..............,

..............,

....

NOTE.—The foregoing call should be signed by the number of stockholders authorized by the regulations; or by all the directors. If not signed by all the directors, a director's meeting should be held and a resolution similar to the following should be adopted:

No. 204.

Call for Special Stockholders' Meeting by Resolution of Directors.

"Resolved, that a special meeting of the stockholders of this Company be and is hereby called and ordered, to be held in the office of the Company, No. .... Street, ..., Ohio, on the .... day of ...., 19.., at .... o'clock .. M. for the purpose of considering and acting upon .... (*state object of meeting*)........ and for the transaction of any and all business necessary or incident thereto; and the secretary is hereby instructed to give notice thereof to the stockholders pursuant to law and to the regulations of this Company."

No. 205.

Notice of Special Meeting of Stockholders.

The .... Company.

Notice of Special Stockholders' Meeting.

........, Ohio, ..., 19...

A meeting of the stockholders of The .... Company will be held at the office of the Company, No. ....

Street, ..., Ohio, on the .... day of ...., 19.., at
.... o'clock .. M. for the purpose of considering and acting
upon (*state object of meeting*) .... and the transaction of
any and all business necessary or incident thereto.

.............,
Secretary.

No. 206.

Minutes of Special Stockholders' Meeting.

NOTE.—The call for the meeting should be copied or pasted into the
minute book above the minutes of the meeting; followed by a copy of the
notice of the meeting, with the certificate of the secretary thereto, for
which see *Minutes of Annual Meeting*.

If notice is waived by all the stockholders, the waiver should be inserted in place of the call and notice.

Special Stockholders' Meeting.

.... 19...

Pursuant to the foregoing call and notice (*or waiver*) the
stockholders of The .... Company met in the office of the
company in ...., Ohio, at .... o'clock .... M. ......
...... 19...

The meeting was called to order by Mr. ...., president
of the company, who presided over the meeting. Mr. ....,
secretary of the company, acted as secretary of the meeting.

The president directed the secretary to call the roll of the
stockholders and requested all persons holding proxies to deposit
the same with the secretary, which was accordingly done. Thereupon the secretary announced that out of .... shares entitled
to vote .... shares were represented at the meeting; .... shares
by stockholders in person and .... shares b ;

The call for the meeting was then read by the secretary.

(The business transacted at the meeting should here be recorded.
Only the business specified in the call and notice can be transacted
at a special meeting of the stockholders, unless by consent of all the
stockholders.)

The following form may be used in entering a resolution on the
minutes:

Mr. .... presented, read and moved the adoption of the
following resolution:

(*Copy resolution in full as*)

RESOLUTION FOR INCREASE IN NUMBER OF DIRECTORS.

"Resolved, that the number of directors of this Company be
increased from *five*, the present number, to *ten;* that the five
new directors shall be elected at this meeting and shall hold
office until the next annual meeting."

The motion was seconded by Mr. ...., and was duly carried (*by a unanimous vote, or,* .... *shares being cast in favor of said resolution and* .... *shares being cast against its adoption.*

Whereupon the president declared said resolution duly adopted.

(For election of directors, see *minutes of annual meeting* above). A motion may be entered on the minutes in the following form:

"Upon motion duly made and seconded and (unanimously) carried .... (*enter the substance of the motion, as, the president was authorized to appoint a committee composed of three stockholders, to examine the books and records of the company and to report to the stockholders at a subsequent meeting to be held* ...., 19...., *at* ...... *o'clock* ..*M.*")

There being no further business the meeting was duly adjourned on motion.

Attest:

....

   Secretary.   President.

AMENDMENT OF REGULATIONS.

NOTE.—The provisions of the regulations as to the manner in which amendments may be made should be carefully followed.

No. 207.

Assent of Stockholders to Amendment.

........, Ohio, ..., 19...

We, the undersigned, being the owners of the number of shares of the capital stock of The .... Company set opposite our respective names do hereby assent in writing that Article .... of the Regulations of said The .... Company be amended so that as amended it shall read as follows:

(*Insert article as amended*)

Stockholders.   *Shares.*

No. 208.

Resolution of Stockholders for Amendment.

Resolved that Article .... of the Regulations of The .... Company be amended so that as amended it shall read as follows:

(*Insert article as amended*)

DIRECTORS' MEETINGS.

No. 209.

Notice of Regular Meeting.

NOTE.—For record and minutes of first meeting of directors see page 127. That record is applicable to all first meetings held after annual elections.

The regular (*monthly*) meeting of the board of directors of The .... Company will be held in the office of the Company on Saturday, ..., 19.., at .... o'clock .. M.

............,
Secretary.

No. 210.

Special Meeting of Directors. Call For.

........, Ohio, ..., 19...

To ....
Secretary of The .... Company.
The undersigned, president (*or, directors*) of The ....
Company, does (*or, do*), hereby call a special meeting of the directors of said company, to be held at the office of the company on the ...... day of ...., 19.., at ...... o'clock ..M. for the purpose of considering and acting upon .... (*state object of meeting*) .... and for the transaction of any and all business necessary or incident thereto, and you are hereby instructed to give notice of such meeting to the directors pursuant to the by-laws of this Company.

....
....

No. 211.

Special Meeting of Directors. Notice.

........, Ohio, ..., 19...

A special meeting of the directors of The .... Company will be held at the office of the Company on the .... day of ...., 19.., at .. o'clock .. M. for the purpose of considering and acting upon .... (*state object of meeting*) .... and the transaction of any and all business necessary or incident thereto.

............,
Secretary.

No. 212.

Special Meeting of Directors. Waiver of Notice.

........, Ohio, ..., 19...

We, the undersigned, being all the directors of The .... Company, do hereby consent that a special meeting of the directors of said Company may be held at the office of the Company on the .... day of ...., 19.., at .... o'clock, .. M. for the purpose of considering and acting upon .... (*state object of meeting*) ....

We hereby waive notice of said meeting and agree to the transaction at said meeting of any and all business within the powers of said board.

....

....

....

No. 213.

Directors' Meeting. Minutes.

NOTE.—The following form may be used for either a regular or special meeting. If a special meeting, the call and notice, or waiver, should be pasted or entered in the minute book above the minutes. The call, or waiver, may be originally entered and signed in the minute book.

DIRECTORS' MEETING.

............, 19...

SPECIAL MEETING.

Pursuant to the foregoing waiver (or call and notice) a special meeting of the board of directors of The .... Company was held at the office of the Company at .... o'clock, .. M., ..., 19...

NOTE.—If a regular meeting, omit the foregoing statement, and use the following:

REGULAR MEETING.

The regular (monthly) meeting of the board of directors of this Company was held at the office of the Company at .... o'clock, .. M. ...., 19...

MINUTES CONTINUED.

Present, Messrs. ....
The meeting was called to order by the president, Mr. ....
...., who presided. Mr. ...., secretary of the Company
acted as secretary of the meeting.

The business transacted at the meeting should be recorded here. .
A motion may be entered in the following form:

"Upon motion duly made and seconded and (unanimously)
carried (here enter *the substance* of the motion, as 'the treasurer
was authorized and instructed to compromise the claim of John
Doe against this Company by the payment to John Doe of
$500.')"

A *resolution* may be entered as follows:

"Mr. .... presented, read and moved the adoption of
the following resolution:
(*Copy resolution in full, as*)

RESOLUTION DECLARING DIVIDEND.

"Resolved, that the sum. of .... dollars ($......) be
and is hereby appropriated and set aside from the surplus profits
arising from the business of this Company for the payment of
a (*or the annual, semi-annual, or quarterly*) dividend of ....
percent upon its issued and outstanding capital stock; the same
to be due and payable on ...., 19.., to stockholders as
shown by the books of the Company at the close of the business
on the .... day of ...., 19..; and that the treasurer of
this Company be directed and authorized to give notice of said
dividend and to pay the same on said date."
The motion was seconded by Mr. ...., and was duly
carried (by a unanimous vote).
, Whereupon said resolution was declared duly adopted.
There being no further business the meeting adjourned on
motion.
Attest:

............, ...,
Secretary.   President.

We approve the foregoing minutes.

                                                ....,
                                                ....,
                                                ....,
                                                ....,
                                                Directors.

No. 214.

Certificate to Transcript of Minutes.

(Copy of such portion of minutes as is desired.)

We hereby certify that the foregoing is a true and correct transcript from the minutes of a meeting of the Board of Directors of The .... Company, duly called and held on the .... day of ...., 19. ., (and recorded on pages ...., ..., of the minute book of said Company.)

In witness whereof we have hereunto set our hands and affixed the corporate seal of said Company this .... day of ...., 19...

............,
President.
............,
Secretary.

(Corporate seal)

No. 215.

Certificate by Secretary to Resolution.

(Copy of Resolution.)

I hereby certify that the foregoing resolution was duly adopted at a meeting of the directors of The .... Company, duly called and held on the .... day of ...., 19.., at which a quorum was present.

In witness whereof I have hereunto set my hand and affixed the corporate seal of said company this .... day of ...., 19...

............,
Secretary of The .... Company.

(Corporate seal)

No. 216.

Resolution of Directors Filling Vacancy Caused by Disqualification of Director.

Whereas ...., having ceased to be the holder of any share or shares of the capital stock of this corporation, is thereby disqualified as a director, be it resolved that the office of said .... as such director be and the same hereby is declared to be vacant, and .... is, for the unexpired term, hereby appointed a director to fill the vacancy so caused and declared.

No. 217.

Resignation of Director (or Officer).

.........., Ohio, ..., 19...

To the Board of Directors of The .... Company.

Gentlemen:

I hereby tender my resignation as a director (*or, president*) of The .... Company, the same to take effect immediately (*or, upon acceptance, or on the* ...... *day of* .... 19....).

Yours respectfully,

....

NOTE.

How vacancy in board is filled.

(G. C. § 8662.)

A vacancy in the board of directors is filled, for the unexpired term, by appointment by the board of directors, and not by the stockholders, unless the regulations so provide.

Where owing to a change in the stock ownership and control, a new board of directors is to be elected, if accomplished by appointment by the board, a quorum of qualified directors must act in each case. Stock should be transferred to the new directors, before the meeting, if possible.

The resignations of the old directors should be presented and accepted one at a time, and a new director immediately elected, who should take his oath of office and immediately assume his duties and participate in accepting the next resignation and the filling of the vacancy, so that a quorum is constantly maintained.

If all the resignations are presented at one time, a stockholders' meeting should be held to elect the new board.

No. 218.

Resolution of Directors, Accepting Donation of Treasury Stock.

Mr. .... presented, read and moved the adoption of the following resolution:

"Whereas, A. B. has offered to assign and transfer to this Company, without consideration, ... shares of the full paid common stock of this corporation, heretofore issued to him, to be deemed and regarded as treasury stock, and to be sold at such prices, whether above or below the par value thereof, as the directors in their discretion may deem best, or to be given as a bonus to purchasers of the bonds (or preferred stock) of this Company, or otherwise used for the benefit of this Company;

"Now therefore be it resolved, that this Company accept such assignment and transfer and that said shares be held in the treasury subject to further action of the directors."

The motion was seconded by Mr. ...., and was duly carried by a unanimous vote. Whereupon said resolution was declared duly adopted.

No. 219.

Donation of Stock to Treasury.

To the Board of Directors of The .... Company:

By duly assigned certificates, I herewith transfer to The .... Company .... shares of the full paid capital stock of said Company, to be deemed and regarded as treasury stock, and to be sold, in the discretion of the directors for prices either above or below par, or to be given as a bonus to purchasers of the bonds (or preferred stock) of the Company, or otherwise used for the benefit of the Company,. as the directors, in their discretion, may deem best.

Respectfully,

....

........, Ohio, ..., 19...

No. 220.

Resolution of Directors Ratifying Unauthorized Act of Officer or Agent.

Resolved, that the act of ...., president (*or other officer or agent*) of this company in .... (*recite action of officer or agent*) .... be and the same is hereby ratified, approved and confirmed as the act of this corporation.

No. 221.

Resolution of Directors Declaring Stock Dividend.

(NOTE.—For resolution declaring cash dividend see page 194.)

Whereas, the surplus profits of this Company amounting to more than $......, have, from time to time, been invested in extensions and betterments to the plant and property of the Company, and in providing additional facilities for its business, and in that manner a large addition has been made to the value of the assets of the Company by withholding from the stockholders moneys which have been fairly earned, and but for the above mentioned expenditures would have been paid to them; and

Whereas, upon a just and fair estimate, the assets of the Company have been in such manner increased in value over the amount of the capital stock, now issued and outstanding, by at least the said sum of $......; and

Whereas, the stockholders desire to realize without impairing the property of the Company, or profits which have been so invested, and to make the same more available;

Now, therefore, be it resolved, that from the surplus profits so invested, a dividend of $...... for each share of the present issued and outstanding capital stock of this Company be and is hereby declared, payable, on the .... day of ...., 19.., in the capital stock of this Company, to stockholders as shown by the books of the Company at the close of business on the .... day of ...., 19..; and that the president and secretary be directed to issue proper stock certificates representing the same to such stockholders on said date.

NOTE.—See Adams v. Shields, 17 C. C. 129: 9 C. D. 558 (aff'd no report, 61 O. S. 643).
If there is not sufficient unissued stock for the purposes of the stock dividend, the capital stock should be increased before the dividend is declared.

No. 222.

Order to Pay Single Dividend to Third Person.

(DIVIDEND ORDER.)

........, Ohio, ..., 19...

To the Treasurer of The .... Company.

Pay to ...., or order, dividend due ...., 19.., on .... shares of stock in your company, standing in my name, and this shall be your sufficient voucher.

No. 223.

Permanent Dividend Order.

........, Ohio, ..., 19...

To the Treasurer of The .... Company.

Until this order is revoked in writing please remit by mail to ...., (give mail address) ...., all dividends now due or which may hereafter be declared on all shares of the capital stock of The .... Company, now or hereafter standing in the name of ....

Witness

No. 224.

Railroad Consolidation Agreement.

(G. C. §§ 9028, 9121, 9127, 9190, 10139.)

• Agreement of Consolidation
of
The A. B. Railroad Company
and
The C. D. Railroad Company.

s agreement made and concluded this .... day of ....,
19.. by and between The A. B. Railroad Company and The C.
D. Railroad Company, witnesseth:

That whereas, both parties hereto are corporations duly organized and existing under the laws of the State of Ohio, and desire to consolidate;

Now therefore, said corporations, acting herein by authority of resolutions of their respective boards of directors, and subject to the ratification of their respective stockholders, as required by law, in consideration of their mutual agreements, covenants, provisions, and grants herein contained and of the benefits to accrue to the parties hereto, do hereby agree to consolidate their business, property, franchises and rights, so as to become one corporation, and, by these presents, do merge and consolidate their capital stock, franchises, and property into one corporation to be known by the name of The E. F. Railroad Company, upon the following terms and conditions, to wit:

FIRST. All the rights, franchises, privileges, property, and appurtenances of every kind and description, credits, choses in action, debts, claims and demands of each of the parties hereto shall vest in the consolidated Company.

SECOND. The consolidated Company shall assume and be bound by all the liabilities and obligations of each of the corporations, parties hereto.

THIRD. The capital stock of the consolidated Company shall be $......, divided into .... shares of $...... each.

FOURTH. The directors of the consolidated Company shall be .... in number, and the officers shall be a president, vice-president, secretary and treasurer.

The names and residences of the first directors of said consolidated Company are as follows:

Names.   Residences.

The names and residences of the first officers are as follows:

Names.   Residences.

President,

Vice-president,

Secretary,

Treasurer,

FIFTH. The manner of converting the capital stock of each of the constituent companies parties hereto shall be as follows:

(a) For each share of the capital stock of The A. B. Railroad Company surrendered to the consolidated Company shall be issued to the holder thereof .... shares of the capital stock of the consolidated company.

(b) For each share of the capital stock of The C. D. Railroad Company surrendered to the consolidated company shall be issued to the holder thereof .... shares of the capital stock of the consolidated Company.

SIXTH. Each of the constituent Companies, parties hereto, for itself and not for the other, in consideration of the premises, does hereby grant, convey, assign, set over and vest in the said consolidated Company for the purpose of such consolidation, all of the property, rights, franchises, privileges and powers by it now held or in or to which it has any right, title, interest, or claim in law or equity; and each of said constituent companies hereby agrees to execute and deliver all instruments of conveyance and assignment necessary to vest in said consolidated Company the legal title to all of said property, rights, franchises, and privileges.

In witness whereof, said The A. B. Railroad Company, by its board of directors, has caused its corporate seal to be hereunto affixed and these presents to be signed by its president and secretary and by a majority of its board of directors, the day and year first above written.

And said The C. D. Railroad Company, by its board of directors, has caused its corporate seal to be hereunto affixed and these presents to be signed by its president and secretary, and by a majority of its board of directors, the day and year first above written.

In presence of

....

....

(Seal)   The A. B. Railroad Company.

.... President.

.... Secretary.

....

....

Directors.

The C. D. Railroad Company.
(Seal)   .... President.
                          .... Secretary.

.

                                        Directors.

CERTIFICATE OF CONSOLIDATION.

I, ..., secretary of The A. B. Railroad Company duly authorized in the premises, do hereby certify that at a meeting of the stockholders of said Company, duly called and held at ...... in the city of ...., ... county, Ohio, on the .... day of ...., 19.., at which meeting all the stockholders of said Company were present in person or by proxy and waived, in writing, the notice of the time and place of holding the same and consented in writing that said meeting should be then and there held, the original agreement of consolidation, of which the foregoing is a true copy, was submitted for consideration and considered, and on a vote by ballot being taken for the adoption or rejection of the same, all the issued and outstanding capital stock of said company, to wit: .... shares were cast in favor of the adoption of said agreement and no vote was cast for its rejection.

In witness whereof I have hereunto set my hand officially and affixed the corporate seal of said company this .... day of ...., 19...

                              ....,
(Seal)   Secretary of The A. B. Railroad Company.

NOTE. — Add similar certificate by secretary of the other constituent company. See G. C. § 9028.

No. 225.

Railroad Consolidation Agreement. Another Form.

Between
The A. B. Railroad Company
and
The C. D. Railroad Company
Under the name of
The X. Y. Railroad Company.

Whereas, The A. B. Railroad Company, a corporation duly organized under the laws of Ohio, is the owner of a railroad constructed and in operation from ...., Ohio, to ...., Ohio, and

Whereas, The C. D. Railroad Company, a corporation duly

organized under the laws of Ohio, is the owner of a railroad constructed and in operation from ...., Ohio, to ...., Ohio, and

Whereas, the lines of road of both of said Companies are so constructed as to admit the passage of passenger and freight cars over said railroads, continuously, without break or interruption, and the interest of both of said Companies will be promoted and their ability to perform their duty to the public as common carriers will be increased by a merger and consolidation of the capital stock, franchises, railroads and properties of the said two Companies into one consolidated Company, and

Whereas, said railroads are not parallel or competing and will, when consolidated as proposed, form a continuous line of railroad between .... and ...., all in the state of Ohio, and

Whereas, such merger and consolidation is authorized by the laws of the state of Ohio, in which said railroads are respectively situated and from which they respectively derive corporate powers;

Therefore, the boards of directors of said Companies, acting in pursuance of resolutions duly adopted by them respectively and subject to ratification by the stockholders of said Companies, as required by law, do hereby enter into the following agreement in respect to such merger and consolidation:

FIRST. The capital stock, franchises, railroads and estates, real, personal and mixed, of said The A. B. Railroad Company and said The C. D. Railroad Company, together with all the rights, privileges, exemptions and immunities owned or enjoyed by each of said Companies, shall be and they are hereby united, merged and consolidated, to be known, owned and controlled as and by one Railroad Company.

SECOND. The name of said Company shall be The X. Y. Railroad Company.

THIRD. The directors of the consolidated Company shall be .... in number, and the names and residences of the first directors are as follows:

Names.	Residences.
....	....
....	....
....	....
....	....
....	....

Said first directors shall continue in office until the first election of the consolidated Company as provided by law.

The annual meeting of the stockholders of the consolidated Company shall be held at the principal office of the Company on the ...... Tuesday in ...., of each year at .... o'clock ... M., at which time directors shall be elected by ballot and the officers shall be chosen by the directors as soon thereafter as possible; but the time and place of the annual meeting may be changed from time to time by the stockholders at any regular meeting thereof.

The officers of said consolidated Company shall consist of a president, vice-president, secretary and treasurer, and such other officers and agents as may be prescribed by the regulations, or by-laws, or as in the judgment of the directors may from time to time be deemed necessary.

The name and residences of the first officers of the Company are as follows:

Names.   Residences.

President, ...

Vice-president, ...

Secretary, ...

Treasurer ....

FOURTH. The capital stock of the consolidated Company shall be $...... divided into ...... shares of $...... each.

FIFTH. The capital stock of the consolidated Company shall be issued in exchange for the outstanding capital stock of the constituent Companies, on the following basis:

1. To the holders of the stock of The A. B. Railroad Company, ... shares of new stock for each share of old stock.

2. To the holders of the stock of the C. D. Railroad Company,....... shares of new stock for each share of old stock.

SIXTH. The consolidated Company shall assume and pay the bonded indebtedness, and all other lawful indebtedness, claims, charges and liens against the several constituent Companies as the same shall become due, without any extension of time.

SEVENTH. The principal office of said consolidated Company will be in ...., Ohio.

In witness whereof, each of said corporations has caused its respective seal to be hereunto affixed and its corporate name subscribed, by its president and secretary, and a majority of the directors of each Company have hereunto set their hands, to duplicates hereof, this .... day of ...., 19...

The A. B. Railroad Company.

(Seal)   By ...., President.

Attest ...., Secretary.

....
....
....
....
....

Directors of The A. B. Railroad Company.

The C. D. Railroad Company.

(Seal)   By ...., President.

Attest ...., Secretary.

....
....
....
....
....
Directors of the C. D. Railroad Company.

CERTIFICATE OF CONSOLIDATION.

........, Ohio, ..., 19...

I, ..., secretary of The A. B. Railroad Company do hereby certify that the execution of the foregoing agreement of consolidation on the part of The A. B. Railroad Company was authorized by resolution, duly entered on its minutes, by its directors, at a meeting duly called and held at ...., on the .... day of ...., 19..; and also that said agreement was submitted to the stockholders of said Company, at a meeting called for the purpose of considering said agreement, on the .... day of ...., 19.., statutory notice of said meeting having been waived, in writing, by all stockholders of said Company, and all stockholders being present at said meeting in person or by proxy; that at said stockholders' meeting said agreement was adopted, approved, ratified and confirmed by unanimous vote of the holders of all the stock of said company.

In witness whereof, I have hereunto set my hand officially and affixed the corporate seal of said Company this .... day of ...., 19...

.............,

(Seal)   Secretary of the A. B. Railroad Company.

NOTE.—Annex corresponding certificate of the secretary of the other constituent company.

No. 226.

Lease of Railroad.

(G. C. §§ 8807-8814.)

This indenture of lease made this .... day of ...., 19.., by and between The A. B. Railroad Company, a corporation of the State of Ohio, party of the first part, and The C. D. Railroad Company a corporation of the State of ...., party of the second part, witnesseth:

Whereas, the party of the first part is the owner of the railroad property and franchises hereinafter mentioned and described, and whereas the railroad so owned by the party of the first part extends from .... in the State of .... to .... in the State of '...., where it connects with the railroad of the party of the second part and includes various branches and leased lines, appurtenances, easements, rights of way, rolling stock, and all other equipment commonly possessed by railroad Companies, all of which is hereinafter more particularly described; and, whereas, the party of the second part owns and operates a railroad which together with leased lines and branches constituting what is known as the X. Y. system extends from .... in the City of .... to .... aforesaid where it connects with the railroad of the party of the first part, the said railroads being non-competitive, and with their connections constituting a through line from ....· to ....;

And whereas, the stockholders of The A. B. Railroad Company at a meeting duly called for the purpose by its directors, and held on the .... day of ...., A. D. 19.., by resolution duly passed by the affirmative vote of the holders of more than two-thirds of the capital stock of said Company, instructed its directors to lease its said railroad to said The C. D. Railroad Company, in the terms and form of this indenture, and duly assented to this lease, and whereas, the board of directors of said The A. B. Railroad Company, at a meeting duly held in the City of ...., Ohio, on the .... day of ...., 19.., at which all of its directors were present, duly resolved to lease its said railroad to said The C. D. Railroad Company, in the terms and form of this indenture and as instructed by the stockholders of said A. B. Railroad Company.

And whereas, the stockholders of The C. D. Railroad Company at a meeting duly called for the purpose by its directors and held on the .... day of ...., A. D. 19.., by resolution duly passed by the affirmative vote of the holders of more than two-thirds of the capital stock of said Company instructed its directors to lease the railroad of said The A. B. Railroad Company, in the terms and form of this indenture, and duly assented to this lease, and whereas the board of directors of said The C. D. Railroad Company, at a meeting duly held in the City of ...., Ohio, on the .... day of ...., A. D. 19.., at which all of its directors were present, duly resolved to lease said railroad from said The A. B. Railroad Company in the terms and form of this indenture and as instructed by the stockholders of said The C. D. Railroad Company.

Now, therefore, in consideration of the premises and of the rent to be paid and the covenants and undertakings to be performed by the party of the second part hereinafter set forth, the party of the first part doth hereby demise and lease unto the party of the second part, its successors and assigns, for the term of ninety-nine (99) years, commencing on the .... day of ...., 19.., the aforesaid railroad of the party of the first part extending from .... aforesaid to .... aforesaid, with all the tenements, hereditaments, and appurtenances, rights of way, easements and all other rights appertaining thereto, also the . . . . Branch and

.... Branch together with all other branch roads of the party of the first part; also all telegraph lines and property and all rights of the party of the first part therein for the term of years for which they are respectively held by the party of the first part, and for any renewal or renewals of such term and terms, also the following leasehold interests and estates; that is to say, the leasehold estate of the party of the first part in and to the railroads, property and franchises of The E. F. & G. H. Railway Company including all rights and property heretofore acquired by the last mentioned Company and the party of the first part under and through the following railroad Companies, to wit: ....

Also any and all other lands, docks or property now held by the party of the first part for any term of years, also all and singular the rolling stock and equipment of every kind and description in the possession of the party of the first part, wherever the same may be situated, also all the buildings, houses, machine shops, other shops, machinery, tools, implements and all other property of every kind and description in the possession of the party of the first part for use upon or in connection with the railroads aforesaid or any of them, also all the corporate franchises of the party of the first part necessary and proper to be held and enjoyed by the party of the second part to efficiently possess, enjoy and protect the premises and property herein and hereby demised. All railroad supplies on hand when this lease takes effect shall be turned over to the party of the second part and the party of the first part does hereby assign to the party of the second part all executory contracts held by the party of the first part relating to the use and operation of the railroad and property hereby leased.

In consideration of the premises, as rental of and for the premises hereby demised, the party of the second part covenants and agrees to assume the aforesaid leases under which part of the premises aforesaid are held and possessed by the party of the first part, and to perform all the obligations thereof according to their tenor; to assume and perform according to the tenor thereof the obligations of the following equipment trusts of which the party of the second part has and takes full notice, namely, the so-called .... Equipment trust of 19.., and the .... Equipment trust of 19..; to assume and pay the interest as and when it becomes payable upon the existing prior lien mortgage of and upon the above described premises to The .... Trust Company, Trustee, securing a bond issue of .... dollars ($....): to maintain, at its own expense the corporate organization of the party of the first part, to pay all taxes due or to become due in respect to the herein demised premises, and to perform all the obligations now or hereafter imposed by law upon the party of the first part: to pay, in addition to the sums of money to be paid in fulfillment of the obligations assumed as aforesaid, the further sum of .... dollars ($....) in gold coin per annum, as net rental, payable semi-annually on the first day of January and July of each year. The party of the second part further covenants and agrees at its own expense to maintain, by all needful repairs and renewals, the plant, rolling stock and equipment of the demised premises up to its present standard of efficiency and repair, and to render to the trustees of the Equipment trusts hereinbefore mentioned an annual statement of the condition of the property included in the said trusts, with a detailed list of all property included therein, showing the cars, engines and hoists destroyed and replaced each year with the numbers of each affixed thereto, and generally in respect of all matters relating to the operation and maintenance of railroads to keep the demised premises up to the standard of efficiency generally prevailing from time to time on trunk lines in respect of roadbed, rolling stock and otherwise.

Provided, however, that if said rent, or any part thereof, shall at any time be in arrear and unpaid, and without any demand being made therefor, or if said party of the second part, its successors or assigns, shall fail to keep and perform any of the covenants, agreements or conditions of this lease, on its part to be kept and performed, said party of the first part, its successors or assigns, may enter into and upon said premises and again have, repossess and enjoy the same as if this lease had not been made, and thereupon this lease and everything herein contained on the part of said party of the first part to be done and performed shall cease, determine and be utterly void; without prejudice, however, to the right of said party of the first part to recover from said party of the second part, its successors or assigns, all rent due up to the time of such entry.

In witness whereof the said The A. B. Railroad Company and said The C. D. Railroad Company have caused their corporate seals to be affixed and their corporate names to be subscribed to duplicates hereof by their respective presidents, the day and year first above written.

Signed, sealed and acknowledged
in presence of   The A. B. Railroad Company.
....   By ...., President.
                    (corporate seal.)
                                    Attest ...., Secretary.
                          The C. D. Railroad Company.
                                    By ...., President.
                    (corporate seal.)
                                    Attest ...., Secretary.
          (Certificates of acknowledgment.)

No. 227.

Release, by Property Owner to Railway Company, of Damages for Occupation of Street.

(G. C. § 8765.)

We, the undersigned A. B. and M. B., (husband and wife) of the City of ...., County of .... and State of Ohio, in consideration of one dollar ($1.) received to our full satisfaction of The .... Railway Company, as well as in consideration of the benefits to be derived by us from the construction of *two* railroad tracks on the .. side of .... Street in said City of ...., Ohio, do, for ourselves and our heirs and assigns, hereby release and discharge the said Railway Company, its successors and assigns, and also said City of ...., Ohio, from any and all claims or demands which we may have against them, or either of them, for or on account of damages or injury to our adjoining premises, known as

(description of property)

or to our right of access to and from said premises, or in any manner growing out of the construction, maintenance or use of said tracks on said street; provided, however, that said tracks, including clearance, shall not occupy more than twenty-five feet in width of said street on said .... side thereof.

Witness our hands this .... day of ...., 19...

Signed and acknowledged

in presence of

....   A. B.

                                                               M. B.

(Certificate of acknowledgment.)

No. 228.

Deed of Land to Interurban Traction Company for Railroad Purposes.

Know all men by these presents, that whereas, The .... Railroad Company is now constructing an interurban railroad from ...., Ohio, to .... Ohio, which will pass through the land hereinafter described, and,

Whereas, the undersigned is desirous of assisting said railroad by furnishing to it a right of way through said property, in view of the benefits to be derived from its construction and operation.

Now therefore, A. B., the grantor, in consideration of ...... dollars ($....) and other valuable considerations paid to him by said The .... Railroad Company, the grantee, the receipt of which is hereby acknowledged, does hereby give, grant, bargain, sell, assign and convey unto said The .... Railroad Company, its successors and assigns, the following described premises, to wit: situated in the township of ...., county of .... and State of Ohio,

(description of property, *as*

and known as being a strip of land twenty (20) feet wide along the south side of .... road, extending from the land of .... on the east to the land of .... on the west, all of said lands being situated in original lot number .... of said township).

Should the above land cease to be used for railroad purposes it shall revert to said grantor.

To have and to hold said premises unto the said The .... Railroad Company, its successors and assigns forever, for railroad purposes only: and the said grantor does, for himself and his heirs, executors, administrators and assigns, covenant and agree with said grantee, its successors and assigns, that the said grantor is the true and lawful owner of said premises and is well seized of the same in fee simple, and has good right and full power to bargain, sell, and convey the same in manner aforesaid, and that the same are free and clear from all incumbrances,

and that said grantor will warrant and defend the same against the claims of all persons whomsoever.

In witness whereof, the said A. B. has hereunto set his hand this .... day of ...., A. D. 19...

Signed and acknowledged
in presence of

....   A. B.

(Certificate of acknowledgment.)

No. 229.

Deed of Right of Way to Railway Company.

Know all men by these presents, that whereas, The .... Railroad Company is constructing a railroad from ...., to ...., which will pass through the land hereinafter described,

Now, therefore, A. B., the grantor, in consideration of .... dollars ($....) and the advantages which may or will result to the public in general, and said grantor in particular, by the construction of said railroad as now surveyed, or as the same may be finally located, and for the purpose of facilitating the construction and completion of said work, does hereby, for himself, his heirs, administrators, executors, and assigns, grant and release unto said The .... Railroad Company, the grantee, its successors and assigns, the right of way for so much of said railroad as may pass through the following described real estate, to wit:

(description of way.)

Said right of way to be one hundred feet wide and to extend across the above described premises.

To have and to hold the same unto the said grantee, its successors and assigns, for a right of way for its tracks, side tracks, switches, and the operation of its railroad over the same.

(Add covenants, release of dower, etc., as usual form of deeds.)

NOTE.—See Railway Co. v. Wachter, 70 O. S. 113.

No. 230.

Consolidation of Religious Societies.

(G. C. § 10004 et seq.)

AGREEMENT.

Whereas, the .... Church of ...., Ohio, a corporation duly organized under the laws of Ohio, and the .... Church of ...., Ohio, a corporation duly organized under the laws of Ohio, both of which are religious societies and churches, recognizing the same ecclesiastical jurisdiction, form of faith, government and discipline, and desire to be consolidated or united as a single corporation:

Therefore we, the subscribers, *A. B., C. D., and E. F.,* elders, *G. H., H. I., and I. J.,* deacons, and *L. M., N. O., and P. Q.,* trustees, of the .... Church; and *Q. R., R. S., and S. T.,* elders, *T. V. and U. V.,* deacons, and *V. W., W. X., and Y. Z.,* trustees of the .... Church, have and do hereby enter into an agreement for such union or consolidation, and do hereby prescribe the following terms and conditions thereof, to wit:

FIRST.   The property, real, personal and mixed, of the .... Church, and the .... Church shall become and be the property of the new corporation.

SECOND.   The new corporation shall assume and pay all the debts and liabilities remaining unpaid by either or both of said churches.

THIRD.   The corporate name of the united church shall be the .... Church of ...., Ohio.

FOURTH.   The time for holding the first meeting of the new corporation shall be ...., 19.., at .... o'clock P. M., and the place shall be .... at No. ...... Street, in the city of ...., Ohio.

FIFTH.   The number of members of each constituent church to be chosen as elders, deacons and trustees of the new corporation, to succeed to the rights, trusts, duties and obligations of such officers of the constituent churches, shall be as follows:

From members of the .... Church *three* elders, *three*

deacons, *three* trustees. From members of the ....
Church *three* elders, *three* deacons, and *three* trustees.

Signed at ...., Ohio, this .... day of ...., 19...

....

....

....
Elders of the ...... Church.   Elders of the ...... Church.

....

....

....
Deacons of the ..... Church.   Deacons of the ..... Church.

....

....

....
Trustees of the ..... Church.   Trustees of the ..... Church.

To the Secretary of State,
      Columbus, Ohio:

I, ..., Clerk of the first meeting of the united corporation, held in pursuance of the above agreement, ..., 19.., at .... o'clock P. M., at .... Street, in the city of ...., Ohio, to which meeting the foregoing agreement and the proceedings and acts of the several churches and parties thereto, were submitted, and at which meeting a board of trustees were duly elected in accordance with the terms of said agreement, do hereby certify that the foregoing agreement, or terms of union were by a unanimous vote at said meeting, duly approved, ratified and confirmed.

In witness whereof, I have hereunto set my hand this ......
day of ...., A. D. 19...

                    ...., Clerk.

No. 231.

Agreement to Subscribe for Stock in Corporation Not Yet Organized.

This agreement, made and concluded at ...., Ohio, this'.... day of ...., 19.., witnesseth:

That, whereas, it is proposed to organize, under the laws of Ohio, a corporation under the name of The .... Company, or such other name as may be hereafter determined upon by the parties in interest, and

Whereas, it is proposed that said corporation shall have a capital stock of .... dollars ($....) divided into shares of .... dollars ($....) each, which corporation shall be organized for the purpose of .....

Now therefore the undersigned, in consideration of their

mutual promises and agreements, do severally agree to and with each other, and with ...., the promoter of said corporation, that they will subscribe for and take and they do hereby severally subscribe for the number of shares of the capital stock of said Company set opposite their respective names.

This agreement is conditional upon the procuring by said .... of valid agreements of subscription to at least .... shares of .... dollars ($....) each of said capital stock.

In witness whereof the parties have hereunto set their hands the day and year first above written.

Names.   Number of shares.

. . . .
. . . .

No. 232.

Stock Pooling Agreement.

Know all men by these presents, that the undersigned, the owners of the number of shares of the capital stock of The .... Company, a corporation organized and existing under the laws of Ohio, set opposite their names, respectively, hereby agree, one with the other, to place and deposit their certificates evidencing the number of shares of said stock set opposite their respective names, with .... of ...., to be kept, held and possessed by said .... for and during a period of .... years from and after ...., 19.., upon the following terms and subject to the following restrictions, to wit:

(1) All certificates of said stock shall be endorsed in blank by the owners thereof prior to depositing the same as aforesaid, and the stock represented by the certificates so deposited shall, upon deposit as aforesaid, be pooled, and shall not be sold or in any manner disposed of, except as herein provided.

(2) Each of the parties hereto does hereby promise and agree, one with the other, that if, during said period of .... years, he desires to sell or dispose of his shares of stock so deposited and pooled, he will give notice in writing of such desire to all of the other parties hereto, whereupon all of said other parties hereto shall jointly have the option and right to purchase the same within ....days after receipt of such notice for the price and upon the terms following, to wit: The amount to be paid for such shares under said option shall be the "book value" thereof at the time said notice is given, to wit: that proportionate value of the net assets of said corporation which the number of shares proposed to be sold bears to the entire issued capital stock of said corporation.

In determining the value of said net assets of the corporation, all patents or copyrights owned or held by the corporation and the good will of its business shall be excluded and not taken into consideration; all materials and stock, finished, semi-finished and raw, shall be valued at the actual cost thereof with suitable allowance for depreciation; and the plant, machinery, equipment, fixtures and furnishings, and all accounts, claims, notes and choses in action receivable shall be valued at their value in money. From the total of said tangible property, valued as aforesaid, shall be deducted the total amount of the indebtedness of the corporation.

The terms of sale under said option shall be as follows ....:

(3) It is mutually agreed that if all the parties hereto, to whom any notice of a desire to sell is given as hereinbefore provided, shall be unwilling to join in a purchase under said option, that said option may be exercised by such of the parties as may desire so to do, who shall make such purchase under such option jointly; but each and every party hereto shall be entitled to participate in such purchase if he desire so to do.

(4) Any and all stock purchased under the provisions of this agreement shall be owned jointly by the parties participating in its purchase; the same shall not be sold or disposed of except with the written consent of the parties owning eighty percent thereof and all dividends on the same shall be paid to ...., who shall distribute the same among the parties participating in its purchase.

(5) This pool and agreement may be terminated at any time upon the unanimous consent of the parties hereto.

In witness whereof the parties have hereunto set their hands this .... day of ...., 19....

.... owning .... shares of said stock .....

.... owning .... shares of said stock .....

NOTE.—An agreement between stockholders whereby they bind themselves not to dispose of any stock during a certain period without their joint consent has been held to be valid. Hey v. Dolphin, 92 Hun 230 (N. Y.). Also an agreement between two or more stockholders binding themselves to offer their stock to the other, in case they desire to sell. Scruggs v. Cotterill, 67 N. Y. App. Div. 583; Jones v. Brown, 171 Mass. 318; Cook on Corporations, § 622c.

No. 233.

Voting Trust Agreement.

NOTE.—For the validity of the following agreement, see Railway Co. v. State, 49 O. S. 668. Such an agreement, however, may be revoked by any one of the stockholders, although it is in terms irrevocable. Griffith v. Jewett, 15 W. L. B. 419. For voting trust agreement held invalid, see State ex rel· v. Standard Oil Co., 49 O. S. 137. See also, Hafer v. Railway Co., 14 W. L. B. 68, and article by W. P. Rogers, 7 O. L. R. 561.

(a)

DEPOSIT BLANK.

The .... Trust Company,
     .... Ohio.

Depositary for A. B., C. D. and E. F., trustees for stock-holders of The .... Company.

The undersigned, holder of the certificates of the capital stock of The .... Company listed below, hereby deposits the same with said trustees, duly assigned to said trustees, to be exchanged for certificates of deposit issued by said The .... Trust Company, on behalf of said trustees, for the purposes and subject to the terms and conditions endorsed hereon, and also endorsed on said certificates of deposit.

Number of stock certificate.	Date of issue.	Name of person to whom issued.
....	....	....

(Signature of depositor) ....
              (Address) ....
........, Ohio, ..., 19...

(b)

CERTIFICATE OF DEPOSIT.

No. ...., Ohio, ..., 19...

The .... Trust Company of .... hereby certifies that it has received from .... certificate number .... for .... shares of $100 each of the common stock of The .... Company, which certificate is deposited under and subject to the terms and conditions endorsed hereon, to which the holder hereof assents and agrees to be bound by receiving this certificate.

The interest represented by this certificate is transferable only on the books of said trustees in person or by attorney and the surrender of this certificate, under rules established by the trustees hereunder.

                        The .... Trust Company
                            By .... Secretary.

For A! B.
    C. D.
    E. F. Trustees.

(c)

TERMS AND CONDITIONS ENDORSED ON DEPOSIT BLANK, AND ON
CERTIFICATE OF DEPOSIT.

(1) This deposit is made for the purpose of enabling widely separated stockholders of said The .... Company to actively and effectively participate in the control and management of its affairs for the benefit of both said corporation and said stockholders.

(2) By the deposit of the within mentioned shares with said The .... Trust Company of ...., hereinafter termed the depositary, the within named trustees are vested with the same powers, in all respects as to voting or otherwise, as if the trustees were the absolute owners thereof.

(3) The genuineness of the certificates of stock deposited, in respect to which this certificate of deposit is issued, is not guaranteed, and the trustees reserve the right to call in this certificate upon returning to the holder thereof the certificate so deposited by him in case the genuineness of such certificate is disputed or doubtful.

(4) All proceedings of the trustees shall in case of difference be decided by a majority of the votes of the trustees present at a meeting.

(5) In case of the death or resignation of any of the trustees, or in case of a vacancy through any cause, the remaining trustees are authorized to fill such vacancy or vacancies, and the person or persons so selected shall have the same powers as if he or they had been originally a trustee hereunder. Any trustee absent or incapacitated through illness may, with the consent of the other trustees, appoint a proxy or substitute who shall represent him and perform his duties hereunder.

(6) Said trustees shall not, without the consent of a majority of the certificate holders at a meeting called for that purpose, agree or vote at any stockholders' meeting in favor of increasing or reducing the capital stock of said The .... Company, or in favor of issuing preferred stock, or of executing any mortgage on the property of said corporation except as a renewal or refunding of the loans now secured by mortgage.

(7) Meetings of the certificate of deposit holders may be convened by the trustees on ten days' notice to each certificate holder mailed to his last known address. The place and time of meetings shall be fixed by the trustees and mentioned in such notice.

(8) Each trustee is responsible only for the bona fide exercise of his judgment on the matters and things done by said trustee. No trustee shall be liable for the act or omission of any

agent hereunder, nor by reason of any error of law or of any matter or thing done or omitted under this agreement, except for his own malfeasance.

(9) Any and all dividends declared and paid upon the shares deposited hereunder shall be paid to the persons appearing by the transfer books of said trustees to be the owners thereof.

(10) A charge of .... per share is to be paid to the depositary on deposit of the within shares for the purpose of defraying the expenses of such deposit and of said trustees.

No. 234.

Consent by Corporation to Use of Similar Name by New Corporation.

(G. C. § 8628).

The *C. D.* Company consents to the use of the name, The *C. & D.* Company, by a corporation proposed to be formed by *A. B., E. F., G. H., I. J.,* and *L. M.,* whose articles of incorporation are filed herewith.

In witness whereof, said The *C. D.* Company has caused its seal to be hereto affixed and its name signed hereto this ......
day of ...., 19...

The *C. D.* Company,
By *N. O.,* President.
P. Q., Secretary.

No. 235.

General Warranty Deed by a Corporation.

Know all men by these presents, that The *A. B.* Company, a corporation duly organized and existing under and by virtue of the laws of Ohio, the grantor, in consideration of ...... dollars ($......) to it paid by C. D., the grantee, the receipt of which is hereby acknowledged, does hereby grant, bargain, sell and convey unto the said grantee, his heirs and assigns forever, the following described real property, situated in the .... of ...., county of ...., and State of Ohio, and
   (*description of property*)
and all the estate, title and interest of said grantor in and to said premises.

To have and to hold said premises, with the appurtenances thereunto belonging, to the said grantee, his heirs and assigns forever, subject, however, to all legal highways and subject to the conditions herein contained.

And the said grantor, for itself and its successors, hereby covenants with the said grantee, his heirs and assigns, that said grantor is the true and lawful owner of said premises, and is well seized of the same in fee simple, and has good right and full power to bargain, sell and convey the same in manner aforesaid, and that the same are free and clear from all incumbrances (except taxes for the year 19.., etc.).

And further, that said grantor will warrant and defend the same against all claims of all persons whomsoever.

In witness whereof, said The A. B. Company has caused its corporate name to be subscribed, and its corporate seal to be affixed to these presents by its president and secretary this .....
day of ...., in the year of our Lord, one thousand nine hundred and ....

Signed, sealed and acknowledged   The A. B. Company.
in presence of   By P. R., President.
I. J.   S. T., Secretary.
L. N.
(Seal)

ACKNOWLEDGMENT.

State of Ohio, ... County, ss.

Before me, a Notary Public, in and for said county, personally appeared ...., president (*or other officer*) of The .... Company, the corporation which executed the foregoing instrument, who acknowledged that the seal affixed to said instrument is the corporate seal of said corporation; that he did sign and seal said instrument as president (*or other officer*) in behalf of said corporation and by authority of its board of directors; and that said instrument is the free act and deed of said The .... Company.

In testimony whereof, I have hereunto subscribed my name at ...., this .... day of ...., 19...

                         ....,
                         Notary Public.

NOTE.—See Hays v. Galion Gas Light & Coal Co., 29 O. S. 330 (334). For execution of deeds by railway companies, see G. C. § 8761.

The officer of a corporation having authority to execute an instrument, is the proper person to acknowledge the same. Sheehan v. Davis, 17 Ohio St. 571.

In deeds to corporations the words "its successors" should be used, following the word "grantee" instead of the word "heirs" which is used in deeds to individuals and which is printed in most blank deeds.

No. 236.

Bill of Sale by Corporation of Fixtures, Lease, Good Will and Stock: (Book Accounts, Etc., Excepted), with Agreement of Officers not to Reengage in Business.

Know all men by these presents, that The .... Company, a corporation duly organized and existing under the laws of Ohio, the grantor, for the consideration of .... dollars ($......) paid by The .... Company, the grantee, the receipt of which is hereby acknowledged, does hereby grant, bargain, sell, transfer and deliver unto the said grantee, its successors and assigns, the following described goods, chattels and effects, to wit: all stock in trade, fixtures and property now owned and used by said The .... Company in connection with its .... business in the city of ...., including ...., and all contracts, excepting outstanding book accounts, bills receivable and claims for money.

Also the good will established by said grantor in connection with said business of .... in the city of .... Said grantor hereby agrees to assign and transfer to said grantee, by proper instruments of conveyance, all its interest as lessee in the premises occupied by it as ....

It is the purpose of this instrument to convey to said grantee all stock in trade, fixtures and personal property now owned and used by said grantor in connection with its ...... business, whether or not specifically described herein, excepting the book accounts, bills receivable and claims for money.

In consideration of the foregoing, and of the sum of .... dollars ($......) received by A. B. and C. D. individually, the receipt of which is hereby acknowledged, and as an inducement to said grantee to pay the purchase price aforesaid, said grantor agrees that it will not as a corporation, and the said A. B. and C. D. hereby agree that they will not as individuals, either directly or indirectly, engage in the business of ...... in the city of ...., for a period of ...... years from and after the date hereof; and during said time said The (grantor) Company and A. B. and C. D. individually, agree that they will not, directly or indirectly, either in firms, corporations or as individuals, come into competition with said grantee, and will not interfere in any way or manner with the business, trade, good will or customers of said grantee.

To have and to hold the same unto the said grantee, its successors and assigns, forever. And the said grantor hereby covenants to and with the said grantee, its successors and assigns, that said grantor is the lawful owner of the above described goods, chattels and effects, and has good right to sell the same as aforesaid; that the same are free and clear from all incumbrances whatsoever; and that said grantor will warrant and defend the same against all lawful claims and demands whatsoever.

In witness whereof, the name of said grantor is hereunto subscribed and its corporate seal hereunto affixed by its president and secretary, and said *A. B.* and *C. D.* individually hereunto set their hands, at ...., Ohio, this .... day of ......, 19...

The .... Company.

By *A. B.*, President.

C. D., Secretary.

Signed, sealed and delivered

In presence of   A. B.

(Corporate Seal.)   C. D.

NOTE.—See Davis v. Booth, 2 O. L. R. 310 as to agreement of officers not to re-engage in business.

No. 237.

Option on Manufacturing Plant.

In consideration of *one dollar* and of other good and valuable consideration, the receipt of which is hereby acknowledged, the undersigned hereby gives and grants unto C. D., of ...., the right and option to purchase, as a going concern, the (*paint, oil and varnish*) manufacturing business conducted by the undersigned, including all the real estate, machinery, fixtures, materials, both unfinished and finished, and supplies used in connection with said business, and also the good will, trade rights, trade marks, inventions, patents, formulae, recipes, trade names, patterns and all other property of every kind and nature used in connection with said business, excepting only money on hand and in bank and accounts and bills receivable, which are to be and remain the property of the undersigned. All of said property to be, at the time of such sale, free and clear of all liens and incumbrances whatsoever, including taxes and assessments.

The consideration for said sale to be .... dollars ($....) and, in addition, the inventory value of stock on hand at the time of completion of the sale.

This option shall expire on the .... day of ...., 19.., unless the said C. D., or his assigns, shall on or before said day give notice in writing of his acceptance thereof, in which case the sale shall be completed, the purchase money paid, and said property delivered within ...... days after the date of such acceptance.

The undersigned hereby agrees, upon receipt of notice of the exercise of this option, to furnish a full abstract of the title to all of said real estate, showing a good title thereto.

This option may be assigned by the said 'C. D., and in case of such assignment before acceptance, said C. D. shall be free from any liability hereunder, the same as if the assignee had originally been named herein.

Dated at ...., Ohio, this .... day of ...., 19...

....

No. 238.

Option, by Corporation, on Manufacturing Plant.

For and in consideration of .... dollars ($....) and of other good and valuable considerations, the receipt of which is hereby acknowledged, The .... Company, a corporation duly organized and existing under the laws of the State of Ohio, does hereby give and grant unto C. D. of ...., or assigns, the exclusive right and option to purchase, as a going concern, the following property to wit:

All of the real estate, buildings, improvements, easements, plant and machinery belonging to it, and situated in the City of ...., County of .... and State of Ohio: also all of the railroad tracks, switches, boilers, engines, forges, steam and water pipes, tanks, trucks, cars, extra parts of machinery, shafting, belting, pulleys, gears, tools, dies, patterns, horses, wagons, implements, materials and property of every kind and nature now being used, or intended to be used, in connection with the manufacture and sale of ....: excepting raw and partly finished material and manufactured product hereinafter mentioned, and excepting cash on hand and in bank and bills and accounts receivable:

also, all the good will, trade rights, trade marks, brands, inventions, patents, formulæ, recipes and trade names now owned and used by it.

All of said property to be, at the time of said sale, free and clear from all liens and incumbrances whatsoever, including taxes and assessments.

The consideration for said sale to be .... dollars ($....), payable as follows: $.... on notice of the exercise of this option and the balance of $.... at the time of the completion of said sale.

This option shall expire on the .... day of ...., 19...

Notice of the exercise of this option shall be in writing signed by said C. D., or assigns, and mailed to said The .... Company, or delivered to its president or secretary.

Said The .... Company further agrees, that, on notice of the

exercise of this option and on payment of said sum of $....
to apply on said purchase price, it will, within .... days after
said payment, furnish to said C. D., or assigns, for examination,
full abstracts showing clear title of record to all of its said real
estate.

Upon final consummation of said sale said The .... Company
agrees to convey all of said real estate and appurtenances by
good and sufficient deed or deeds of general warranty, and to
execute and deliver such bills of sale and other instruments as
may be necessary or proper for effectually conveying and transferring all of said property, both real and personal: and further,
said The .... Company agrees to procure and cause to be
executed and delivered, together with said instruments of conveyance, the agreement or agreements of said The .... Company, and of ...., ..., and ...., its president, secretary and
treasurer, respectively, binding said The .... Company and
said ...., ..., and ...., for a period of .... years after the
completion of said sale, not to engage, or be interested, directly
or indirectly, either individually, or in firms, corporations, or as
stockholders, directors, officers, clerks, agents or employees, in the
business of manufacturing, buying and selling .... or any kindred products, or by-products, in said City of .... or within
.... miles therefrom.

By the exercise of this option, it is expressly agreed, on the
part of said C. D., or assigns, that, in addition to the purchase
of the property above mentioned, he, or they, will further purchase all raw and partly finished materials, on hand or in transit,
at the cost thereof to said The .... Company, also all finished
product at the inventory thereof; also all unexpired policies of
fire, liability, or other insurance then in force, at the pro rata
value thereof.

Payment for said raw and partly finished materials, finished,
product and insurance policies to be made in cash upon completion of said sale.

It is further agreed on the part of said C. D., or assigns, by
the acceptance of this option, that he or they will assume and
be bound by all bona fide contracts theretofore made by said
The .... Company for the purchase or sale of raw materials and
supplies and finished product.

Said The .... Company agrees that this option may be assigned, and that the same shall inure to the assignee or assignees thereof, and that in case of such assignment before the
exercise of this option, said C. D. shall be under no liability
hereunder.

In witness whereof, said The .... Company has caused its
corporate name to be signed hereto by its president by authority
of its board of directors, duly ratified by its stockholders, as

required by law, and its corporate seal to be hereto affixed attested by its secretary this .... day of ...., 19...

The .... Company,
By ...., President.

(Corporate seal.)
Attest.

...., Secretary.

NOTE.—See G. C. §§ 8710 to 8718.

No. 239.

Option to Purchase Stock in Corporation.

........, Ohio, ..., 19...

In consideration of .... dollars ($....), the receipt of which is hereby acknowledged, I hereby give to C. D. the right and option to purchase from me at any time within .... days from the date hereof .... shares of the .... (common or preferred) stock of The .... Company at $.... per share, payable in cash.

All dividends, for which the transfer books close during said time, go with the stock. One day's notice of the exercise of this option is required, except on the last day.

A. B.

No. 240.

Option to Purchase Stock at "Book Value"; Certificates to be Deposited with a Trust Company.

NOTE.—This plan is sometimes adopted where the option covers a large block of stock and runs for a considerable period of time, the transferable receipts of the trust company enabling the person granting the option to use his stock as collateral, etc., meanwhile. For stock pooling agreement with option, see form No. 232.

This agreement made this .... day of ...., 19.., by and between A. B. of ...., party of the first part; C. D. of ...., party of the second part, and The E. F. Trust Company, of ...., hereinafter called the Trustee, party of the third part, witnesseth:

(1) That in consideration of .... dollars ($....), received to his full satisfaction of said party of the second part, said party of the first part hereby gives and grants to said party of the second part the exclusive right and option to purchase, at any time prior to ...., 19.., ... shares of the *common* stock of The X. Y. Company, in the manner and for the price hereinafter set forth.

(2) Said party of the first part has this day deposited with said Trustee certificates for said .... shares of stock, duly endorsed in blank for transfer, to be held by that depositary as trustee for the purposes hereinafter set forth.

(3) The price to be paid for said stock under said option shall

be an amount in cash equal to its "book" or "net" value at the time the notice hereinafter mentioned is given, to wit: that proportion of the value of the net assets of said corporation which the number of shares to be purchased bears to the entire issued capital stock of said corporation. In determining the value of said net assets the merchandise, stock and materials shall be valued at the actual cost thereof with suitable allowance for depreciation; the plant, machinery, equipment and fixtures shall be taken at a fair inventory value, with a suitable allowance for depreciation, and the accounts and notes receivable shall be taken at their face value, less a suitable allowance for prospective losses. From the total value of all the assets of said corporation, ascertained as aforesaid, shall be deducted all debts and liabilities of the corporation (if preferred stock is outstanding add "and an amount in cash equal to the value of the total issued preferred stock of said corporation,") and the remainder shall be divided by the total number of shares of the *common* stock of the Company, issued and outstanding, and the quotient shall be the "book" or "net" value per share of said stock, and the price per share at which said common stock under this option may be obtained.

(4) Said party of the second part, or his assigns, may exercise said option at any time during said period by notice in writing to the party of the first part by registered mail, at his last known usual place of residence and to the Trustee at its office. Within ..... days after the date of the mailing of such notice, the party of the first part shall furnish, or cause to be furnished to the Trustee and the party of the second part, or his assigns, a statement of the net value of the *common* stock of said corporation, ascertained as aforesaid, certified to by the treasurer of said corporation.

If the party of the first part fails or refuses to furnish such statement of the net value of said stock, within the time herein limited, or in case the net value of such stock is, in the opinion of the party of the second part or his assigns, incorrect, then the net value of said stock shall be determined by arbitration as follows: The party of the second part shall choose an arbitrator, giving notice thereof by mail to the Trustee and to party of the first part.

Within *thirty* days after the mailing of said notice said party of the first part shall choose an arbitrator and give notice thereof by mail to the Trustee and to party of the second part. In case party of the first part shall fail to choose an arbitrator and give notice thereof within the time above limited the Trustee is hereby authorized and directed, upon the request in writing of the party of the second part, or his assigns, to choose a disinterested person as arbitrator in behalf of the party of the first part. The two arbitrators so chosen shall choose a third arbitrator and the three so chosen shall proceed to fix the value of said stock in the method hereinbefore prescribed. The award in writing signed by any two of said arbitrators shall be final and conclusive as to the net value of said stock. The expense of said arbitration shall be borne by the party of the .... part.

Unless arbitration be requested by party of the second part, as aforesaid, the statement furnished by party of the first part, certified by the treasurer of said corporation, shall fix the value of said stock. At any time within .... days after the net value of the stock is fixed by either of the aforesaid methods, the party of the second part may request of the Trustee, and the Trustee upon such request and upon receiving a certified copy of the certificate of said treasurer, or of the award of the arbitrators, is hereby authorized to deliver to said party of the second part, or his assigns, the certificates of stock deposited with the Trustee hereunder, upon payment in cash of the value of the stock, fixed as aforesaid. The Trustee shall pay the avails of said sale to said party of the first part, or to the holders of the transferable receipts of the Trustee hereinafter mentioned, but only upon surrender of said transferable receipts properly endorsed for cancellation.

(5) The Trustee shall issue to said party of the first part transferable deposit receipts in the following form:

No. .   .... Shares.

TRANSFERABLE DEPOSIT RECEIPT.
THE X. Y. COMPANY.

The E. F. Trust Company certifies that .... has deposited with it certificates for .... shares of the *common* stock of the X. Y. Company to be held subject to the terms of a certain agreement, dated ...., 19.., which said agreement provides that the holder hereof will be entitled to the return of said certificates or to payment of the avails thereof as therein provided, but only upon surrender of this receipt properly endorsed for cancellation.

The E. F. Trust Company,
By ....

........, 19...
(Endorsed)   ...., 19...
For value received .... hereby sell, assign and transfer to ....the within certificate and all rights and interests thereunder.

Witness:

(6) If said option shall not be exercised within the time and in the manner herein provided, then and in that event, the Trustee shall return the certificates to party of the first part, or to the holders of the transferable deposit receipts hereinbefore mentioned, but only on the surrender of said receipts properly endorsed for cancellation.

(7) Said Trustee shall be and is hereby appointed the true and lawful attorney of the party of the first part, in his name and stead, to make all necessary transfers of stock deposited hereunder and for him, the said Trustee may execute all necessary acts of assignment and transfer, the party of the first part hereby ratifying and confirming all that his said attorney shall lawfully do by virtue hereof.

(8) It is mutually agreed between the parties hereto:

(a) That all charges for the services and expenses of the Trustee hereunder shall be paid by the party of the *second* part;

(b) That this agreement shall inure to, and shall be binding upon, the executors, administrators, successors and assigns of the parties hereto;

(c) That this agreement is signed in triplicate, and any one copy may be used as an original;

(d) That the recitals in this agreement are not made by the Trustee and shall not be construed to impose any obligation or responsibility upon it in respect thereof; and that the Trustee shall not be liable in respect to any act performed or omitted to be performed by it hereunder save and except for its own wilful default.

(e) That unless written notice of a change of address be given any notice hereunder may be given to party of the first part by mailing the same to *A. B.* at ....; to party of the second part or his assigns, by mailing the same to *C. D.* at ...., and to the Trustee by mailing the same to it at its office in .....

In witness whereof the parties of the first and second parts have hereunto set their hands and said party of the third part has caused its corporate name to be signed and its corporate seal to be affixed hereto the day and year first above written.

Witnesses:

....   *A. B.*
....   *C. D.*
                     The E. F. Trust Company,
                          By ....

No. 241.

Option Contract to Purchase Stock, if Vendee Desires to Resell.

Whereas, A. B. has this day purchased ...... shares of the .... (*common or preferred*) stock of The .... Company, for the price of .... dollars per share;

Now I, the undersigned, in consideration of said sale, and in consideration of one dollar ($1) paid to me by said A. B., the receipt of which is hereby acknowledged, do hereby agree that if, at the expiration of one year from the date hereof, the said A. B. shall desire to sell said stock at the price paid by him therefor, I will purchase the same and pay to him the amount paid by him therefor, together with interest thereon at the rate of .... **percent per annum.**

........, Ohio, ..., 19....

....

No. 242.

Option to Deliver Stock (A "Put").

........, Ohio, ..., 19...

For value received, the bearer may deliver me .... shares of the .... (common *or* preferred) stock of The .... Company at .... percent, at any time in .... days from date. The undersigned is entitled to all dividends or extra dividends declared during said time.

Expires ...., 19.., at .... P. M.

No. 243.

Option to Purchase Stock (A "Call").

........, 19...

For value received the bearer may call on me on one day's notice, except last day, when notice is not required, for .... shares of the .... (common or preferred) stock of The .... Company at .... at any time within .... days from date. All dividends, for which transfer books close during said time, go with the stock.

Expires ...., 19.., at 3 P. M....................

Note.—See Treat v. White, 181 U. S. 264.

No. 244.

Bond to Corporation Issuing New Certificate of Stock in Lieu of Lost or Destroyed Certificate.

(G. C. § 8673-17.)

Know all men by these presents, that we, A. B. as principal and E. F. as surety, are held and firmly bound unto The .... Company in the sum of .... dollars ($....) for which payment well and truly to be made we bind ourselves firmly by these presents.

Dated this .... day of ...., 19...

The condition of this obligation is such, that whereas, a certificate for .... shares of the capital stock of said The .... Company, being certificate number ...., owned by and standing on the books of said corporation in the name of said A. B., has been lost or destroyed, and can not be produced by him, and whereas, at his request, and upon his promise to indemnify and save harmless said The .... Company in the premises and to surrender said certificate when found to said The .... Company, to be cancelled, said The .... Company has this day issued to said A. B. a new certificate for .... shares in lieu of said certificate so lost or destroyed:

Now if said A. B. shall well and truly indemnify and save harmless said The .... Company, its successors and assigns, from and against said certificate of stock and from and against any and all damages, costs, charges and expenses, including attorney's fees, and all actions and suits, whether groundless or otherwise, by reason of said certificate of stock, and shall surrender or deliver the same, as soon as the same shall be found, to be cancelled, then this obligation shall be void; otherwise to remain in full force and effect.

In presence of   A. B.
....   E. F.

No. 245.

Bond of Treasurer of Corporation.

Know all men by these presents, that we, A. B. as principal and E. F. as surety, are held and firmly bound unto The C. D. Company, a corporation duly organized and existing under and by virtue of the laws of Ohio, with its principal office in the City of ...., Ohio, in the sum of .... dollars ($....) for which payment well and truly to be made we do bind ourselves firmly by these presents.

Dated this .... day of ...., 19...

The condition of this obligation is such that, whereas, the said A. B. has been elected treasurer of said The C. D. Company

for the period of one year from the .... day of ...., 19..,
and thereafter until his successor is elected and qualified. Now
if the said A. B. shall well, honestly and faithfully perform and
discharge his duties as such treasurer and shall account to said
The C. D. Company, its successors or assigns, for all money and
property that may come into his possession or under his control,
and shall well and faithfully pay and deliver said money and
property as required or directed by said corporation, then this
obligation to be void, otherwise to remain in full force and
effect.

Provided that any forbearance on the part of The C. D. Company toward the said A. B. in respect to his failure or neglect
in the performance and discharge of his duties as such treasurer,
or any extension or extensions by said corporation of the time or
times of said payments of money or deliveries of property shall
not in any manner operate to release or discharge the said E.
F. from his liability under the foregoing obligation.

Signed and delivered
in presence of   A. B.
. . . .   E. F.

No. 246.

Collateral Note.

$.....   ...., Ohio, ..., 19...
.... days after date .... promise to pay to the order of ....
Bank, ... dollars, for value received, at the office of said Bank
with interest at .... percent per annum, having deposited with
said Bank as collateral security for payment of this or any other
liability or liabilities of .... to said Bank, due or to become
due, or that may be hereafter incurred, the following property:
(description of property)
the market value of which is now $....: in case of depreciation
of the same, or of any other securities which may be hereafter
pledged for this loan, a payment shall forthwith be made on
account, or additional securities given, satisfactory to said Bank,
so that the market value of the collateral shall always be at least
.... percent in excess of the amount unpaid on this note. In
case of failure so to do, this note shall be deemed to be due and
payable on demand, with full power and authority to sell, assign
and deliver the whole of said property, or any part thereof, at
public or private sale at the option of said Bank, or its assigns,
and with the right to themselves become the purchasers thereof
at public sale, freed and discharged from any equity of redemption, on the nonperformance of this promise or the nonpayment
of any of the liabilities hereinbefore mentioned, at any time or
times thereafter, without advertisement or notice. All legal or

other costs and expenses for collection, sale and delivery to be deducted from the proceeds of such sale, and the residue applied on any or all of the liabilities under this note and agreement: the overplus, if·any, to be returned to the undersigned.

. . . .

No. 247.

Collateral Note. Another Form.

$.....   ...., Ohio, ..., 19...

.... days after date .... promise to pay to the order of .... Bank .... dollars, for value received, at the office of said Bank with interest at .... percent per annum, having deposited with said Bank as collateral security for payment of this or any other liability or liabilities of .... to said Bank, due or to become due, or that may be hereinafter incurred, the following property:

(description of property)

the market value of which is now $.... with the right on the part of said Bank from time to time to demand such additional collateral security as it may deem sufficient should the market value thereof decline, and also give said Bank a lien for the amount of all said liabilities upon all the property or securities given unto or left in its possession by the undersigned, and also upon any balance of the account of the undersigned with it. Upon failure to comply with any such demand, this obligation shall forthwith become due, will full power and authority to it, or its assigns, in case of such default or of the nonpayment of any of the liabilities above mentioned at maturity, to sell, assign and deliver the whole or any part of such securities, or any substitutes therefor or additions thereto, at any brokers' board, or at public or private sale, at its option, at any time or times thereafter without advertisement or notice to the undersigned, and with the right on the part of said bank to become purchaser thereof at any public sale thereof or at any sale thereof at brokers' board, freed and discharged of any equity of redemption. And after deducting all legal or other costs and expenses for collection, sale and delivery, to apply the residue of the proceeds of such sale or sales so made, to the payment of any, either or all of said liabilities, as it may deem proper, rendering the overplus, if any, to the undersigned: and the undersigned will remain liable for any amount remaining unpaid after such sale. The undersigned do hereby authorize and empower said Bank, at its option, at any time, to appropriate and apply to the payment and extinguishment of any of the above named obligations or liabilities, whether now existing or hereafter contracted, any and all moneys now or hereafter in its possession, on deposit or otherwise, to the credit of or belonging to the undersigned, whether said obligations or liabilities are then due, or not due.

. . . .

No. 248.

Syndicate Agreement.

A. & B. RAILWAY SYNDICATE.

An a eemen made and entered into this .... day of ...., 19gr, by and between L. M. and S. T., parties hereto of the first part, hereinafter sometimes called "Syndicate Managers," and the individuals, firms and corporations other than the Syndicate Managers subscribing hereto severally, parties hereto of the second part, hereinafter sometimes called "Syndicate Subscribers," and all of whom together with the Syndicate Managers constitute the "Syndicate."

Whereas, The O. & P. Traction Company is a corporation organized under the laws of the State of Ohio for the purpose of constructing and operating an electric street railroad property, to wit, from the City of .... in .... County, Ohio, to the City of .... in .... County, Ohio, with the right to make extensions and branches from said street railroad; and

Whereas, It is proposed by the Syndicate to acquire as large an amount as possible of the outstanding capital stock of said Traction Company, and also all outstanding claims against said Traction Company and the assets thereof, and after having acquired the same to construct certain electric street railways over the route authorized by the charter of said Traction Company, with extensions and branches therefrom; and

Whereas, For accomplishing said purposes and providing the necessary funds therefor, and for the other purposes herein set forth, the parties hereto desire to form a Syndicate, to be known as A. & B. Railway Syndicate.

Now, therefore, this agreement witnesseth: that in consideration of the premises and the mutual promises and agreements herein made, and the sum of one dollar ($1.00) by each of the parties hereto in hand paid to the other, the Syndicate Managers and the Syndicate Subscribers hereto agree as follows:

FIRST. The parties hereto hereby form a Syndicate for the purpose of acquiring as large an amount as possible of the capital stock of said Traction Company, together with the claims against said Traction Company and the assets thereof, and after having acquired the same, of financing said Traction Company and constructing an electric street railroad, as authorized by the charter of said Traction Company, with extensions and branches therefrom, and of bringing the property of said Traction Company to successful operation and of doing and performing such other things as may, in the judgment of the Syndicate Managers, be necessary or proper in connection therewith.

SECOND. The Syndicate Managers are hereby authorized, as attorneys and agents for the Syndicate Subscribers severally, to purchase on their behalf and for them, as large an amount as possible of the capital stock of said Traction Company together with its assets, at such a price and upon such terms and conditions as may be deemed advisable by the Syndicate Managers.

THIRD. The Syndicate Managers, for the purposes contemplated by this agreement, are authorized to proceed with the construction of the street railway system of the Traction Company with extensions and branches therefrom, and for that purpose to have the capital stock of the said Traction Company increased or if deemed advisable to organize a corporation under the laws of the State of Ohio with such name and capitalization as may be designated by the Syndicate Managers, for the purpose of taking over the stock, property and assets of, and claims against, said Traction Company.

Wherever the designation "Traction Company" occurs in this agreement, the same shall be held and deemed to apply to either The O. & P. Traction Company by the present corporate name or by any change of name, or to said new corporation to be organized as the context may require or indicate.

The Syndicate Managers are given full power, authority and discretion to determine all matters relating to the capitalization of The Traction Company, and of the stocks, bonds, or securities to be issued thereby, and are also authorized to acquire any or all of the stocks, bonds or securities issued by said Traction Company, for the benefit of the Syndicate.

FOURTH. The Syndicate Managers agree to proceed with reasonable diligence to carry out and consummate, in so far as they may be able to do so, the purposes for which this Syndicate is organized, in such manner as in their judgment may be best to that end, and to do all things and perform all acts which in their judgment shall be deemed for the best interests of the Syndicate.

FIFTH. Each Syndicate Subscriber shall set opposite his name as signed hereto or to any counterpart hereof, the amount of his subscription to the Syndicate, and shall pay as herein provided the amount thereof as called by the Syndicate Managers. All funds received by the Syndicate Managers from the Syndicate Subscribers shall be expended and disposed of in the following manner:

(a) The payment of all expenses of the Syndicate and the Syndicate Managers, including incorporation expenses and charges, counsel and attorney's fees, brokers' commissions, interest, charges, expenses and commissions on Syndicate loans, and other necessary and proper disbursements and expenses made or incurred in connection with the carrying out of this agreement.

(b) The payment of and for such amount of the capital stock of the Traction Company, and the assets thereof, as the Syndicate Managers may be able to acquire; the constructing, building and equipping of said street railway system, and the purchasing and acquiring of stocks, bonds and securities of said Traction Company, or any of said purposes which may be deemed advisable by the Syndicate Managers.

SIXTH. The Syndicate Subscribers irrevocably nominate and appoint the Syndicate Managers, and their survivors, as their agents and attorneys, with full power to do any and all acts and to enter into and execute all agreements or other instruments necessary or proper or by the Syndicate Managers deemed expedient in the premises and for the purposes of this Syndicate Agreement, and to that end, to absolutely control the stock, claims and assets of the Traction Company so to be acquired, together with all stocks, bonds and securities of the Traction Company now or hereafter issued or authorized and acquired by the Syndicate, as fully in all respects as if the Syndicate Managers were the owners thereof, and to pledge any or all of said stocks, claims, assets, bonds and securities, or any portion thereof, or this contract and the several obligations of the Syndicate Subscribers hereunder, as security for the repayment of money borrowed on behalf of the Syndicate.

It is further agreed that if the Syndicate Managers pledge the stocks, bonds and securities of the Traction Company, or this agreement and the several obligations of the Syndicate Subscribers, as security for the payment of the Syndicate's obligations, the person, firm or corporation to whom the same are pledged shall have the right and power, in order to secure payment of such obligations, to make calls upon the subscriptions hereunder in case the Syndicate Managers neglect or refuse to make the same.

SEVENTH. The Syndicate Subscribers agree that they will from time to time, and at any time on call of the Syndicate Managers, and to the amount of such call or calls, make cash payments on account of their respective subscriptions hereunder, upon ten (10) days written notice by mail from the Syndicate Managers; all payments hereunder by the Syndicate Subscribers shall be made to The .... Trust Company, ..., Ohio, for the account of the Syndicate Managers. Each Subscriber shall, at the time of making each of the payments called hereunder, receive a certificate issued by said Trust Company, certifying to the amount of such payment and the interest of such Subscriber in said Syndicate, subject to the terms and conditions of this agreement; said certificate shall be in assignable form, and be transferable only on the books of said Trust Company by due assignment and surrender of such certificate, and upon due assignment and surrender thereof, a new certificate may be issued in the name of the transferee. No such assignment or transfer or issue of a new certificate to a transferee shall release any Subscriber hereto from his obligations assumed hereunder. Every Syndicate Subscriber and any and all owners, holders, transferees or pledgees of said certificates, or of the bonds, stocks or securities represented thereby, or deliverable thereunder, hereby ratify and approve the action of the Syndicate Managers and of the officers and directors of said Traction Company in the matter of issuing, paying for and disposing of the stocks, bonds and securities issued by said Traction Company.

EIGHTH. The Syndicate Managers shall have the sole direction, management and the entire conduct of the Syndicate, and the enumeration of particular or specific powers in this agreement shall not be considered as in any way limiting or abridging the general power or discretion intended to be conferred upon and reserved to the Syndicate Managers in order to authorize them to do any and all things proper, necessary or expedient in their discretion to carry out the purposes of this agreement; neither shall they, or either of them, be liable under any of the provisions of this agreement, or in or for any matter connected therewith, except for want of good faith or malfeasance.

NINTH. The Syndicate Managers may be Subscribers to the Syndicate and to the extent of any subscription or reservation by them, they are to participate in the profits and losses and the securities purchased or acquired, to the same extent as the other Subscribers.

TENTH. Each Syndicate Subscriber hereby ratifies, assents to and agrees to be bound by any action of the Syndicate Managers taken under this agreement, and agrees to perform all of his undertakings hereunder from time to time, on call of the Syndicate Managers, to the full extent of the amount set opposite his name or allotted to him, but he shall be liable hereunder solely to the Syndicate Managers or their successors or assigns, or to the Traction Company issuing any bonds, stocks and securities purchased hereunder, or to the person owning the same, and only to the extent of his individual subscription to the Syndicate.

ELEVENTH. The failure of any Syndicate Subscriber to perform any of his undertakings hereunder shall not affect or release any other Subscriber. The Syndicate Managers may, in their discretion, by written consent, release any Syndicate Subscriber. In case any Syndicate Subscriber shall fail to perform any of his undertakings hereunder or be released by the Syndicate Managers, other Subscribers may be received by the Syndicate Managers and take the share of the Subscriber so failing to perform his undertakings or so released. Upon failure of any Syndicate Subscriber to perform any of his undertakings hereunder, the Syndicate Managers shall have the right at their option to exclude such Syndicate Subscriber from further interest and participation in the Syndicate, and to hold him liable for all damages caused by his failure.

Nothing contained in this agreement or otherwise shall constitute the Syndicate Subscribers partners with the Syndicate Managers or with one another, or render them liable to contribute more than the amounts of their subscriptions, as aforesaid, or entitle them to any participation in the results or profits of said Syndicate other than as specified in this agreement.

TWELFTH. This agreement shall bind and benefit ratably according to the amount of the several subscriptions, not only the parties hereto but their respective successors, survivors, assigns and personal representatives. Two originals hereof are to be signed by the Syndicate Managers and one original is to be deposited with The .... Trust Company, and counterparts may be signed by the Syndicate Subscribers and retained by the Syndicate Managers, or by said Trust Company, and all shall be taken and deemed to be one original instrument.

THIRTEENTH. All notices issued by the Syndicate Managers hereunder shall be mailed to the adresses of subscribers as given below opposite their respective names. The holding of certificates issued by said Trust Company in pursuance thereof, shall constitute such holders parties to this agreement, as fully to all intents and purposes as signing the same.

FOURTEENTH. It is mutually agreed that during the term of this agreement the Syndicate Managers shall have full power of sale, or exchange for other stocks and bonds, or either, of any other Company or corporation, of all stocks, bonds and securities acquired and received by them on behalf of the Syndicate Subscribers, and also of any stocks, bonds or securities received in exchange therefor, upon sale to or consolidation with any other corporation upon such terms, prices and conditions as may be deemed by them to be for the interests of the Syndicate, and that until the distribution of said stocks, bonds, or securities to the Subscribers hereto, all stocks of said Traction Company, and all other stocks, bonds or securities belonging to the Syndicate, shall be held by and in the name of the Syndicate Managers, or their nominees, with full power in the Syndicate Managers or their nominees, to vote the same at any and all meetings of the stockholders of the corporation issuing said stocks, bonds or securities.

FIFTEENTH. Should the Syndicate Managers in carrying out this agreement sell and dispose of the holdings of the Syndicate hereunder for cash or securities, the Syndicate Managers shall be entitled to hold and retain .... (..) percentum of the profits of the Syndicate, either in cash or securities, the same to be in full as compensation to the Syndicate Managers for their services performed hereunder. After the deduction of the said .... (..) percentum of said profits as compensation to the Syndicate Managers as above, the balance of said profits shall be distributed pro rata to the Syndicate Subscribers from time to time, in the discretion of the Syndicate Managers.

Should the Syndicate Managers not sell or dispose of the holdings of the Syndicate hereunder, but distribute the same to the Syndicate Subscribers, the Syndicate Managers at the time of such distribution shall be entitled to hold and retain .... (..) percentum, in par amount, of any and all common corporate stocks at that time owned by the Syndicate, the same to be in full compensation to the Syndicate Managers for their services performed hereunder; and after the deduction of said .... (..) percentum of said common corporate stocks as aforesaid, the balance of said ordinary corporate stock, together with any bonds or other securities owned by the Syndicate shall be distributed pro rata, to the subscribers from time to time, in the discretion of the Syndicate Managers.

Whenever any partial distribution is made to the Syndicate Subscribers hereunder, said subscribers shall present the certificates, representing their interests, to said Trust Company, and have said distribution endorsed thereon, and upon such final distribution hereunder, the Syndicate Subscribers shall surrender their said certificates.

All expenses and obligations of the Syndicate shall be a charge against the cash, securities or property at any time owned by the Syndicate.

SIXTEENTH. In case of the death, resignation or inability to act of either of the Syndicate Managers, the survivor shall have power subject to the approval of The .... Trust Company, to designate, by writing, filed with the said Trust Company, a person to fill the place so made vacant; and in case said survivor fails to fill said vacancy within thirty (30) days after such death, resignation or inability to act, and to give a written notice of such designation to said Trust Company, and to secure the approval of said Trust Company, then the said

Trust Company shall have power to designate a person to fill the place so made vacant.

In case of the death, resignation or inability to act of both of said Syndicate Managers, The .... Trust Company shall have power to designate persons to fill the places so made vacant. In case said Trust Company fails to fill said vacancy or vacancies within thirty (30) days after the date of the accruing of its right to fill said vacancy or vacancies, a majority in amount of the Subscribers hereto, who have paid the full amount of all calls made, shall have power to name and designate, in writing, a successor or successors, and such successor or successors chosen in any manner as above provided shall, upon acceptance in writing endorsed upon this agreement, be clothed with all the powers and be subject to all the duties conferred and enjoined upon the Syndicate Managers herein.

SEVENTEENTH. It is mutually agreed that the obligations of the Syndicate Subscribers under this contract are several and not joint, and that no one of said subscribers shall be liable for a breach of this contract by any other Subscriber than himself.

Each and every party hereto will, upon reasonable request, execute and deliver all further writings which may be necessary or proper to carry this agreement into effect.

EIGHTEENTH. No calls shall be made by the Syndicate Managers upon the subscriptions of the Syndicate Subscribers until the total subscriptions hereto shall equal the sum of .... dollars ($....).

NINETEENTH. The Syndicate Managers shall have power to reduce the subscription or subscriptions of any or all of the Syndicate Subscribers for any reason deemed by the Syndicate Managers to be for the benefit of the Syndicate.

TWENTIETH. All action taken by the Syndicate Managers hereunder shall be in pursuance of unanimous agreement of the Syndicate Managers. In case the Syndicate Managers are unable to agree, either or both of the Syndicate Managers may make statements in writing to The .... Trust Company of the matters in dispute or the proposed action, and the said Trust Company is hereby given full power, right and authority to settle and determine the dispute submitted or the action proposed, and its decision of any such matters shall be final and binding on all the parties hereto, and the action of the Syndicate Managers shall in such event be in accord and compliance with the decision of the Trust Company.

Each of said Syndicate Managers hereby agrees to be bound by such decision of the Trust Company and to execute any and all deeds, transfers, contracts, or assignments as may by the Trust Company be deemed necessary, proper or convenient to carry out and make effective the decision of the Trust Company.

TWENTY-FIRST. This agreement shall continue in force and operation for a period of .... (..) years from and after ...., 19..; provided, however, that if the Syndicate Managers deem it to be for the best interests of the Syndicate to extend the term of the Syndicate for one (1) year from and after the expiration of said period of .... (..) years, they may do so, by giving notice in writing of such intention to the Syndicate Subscribers, at any time on or before thirty (30) days prior to the expiration of the said period of .... (..) years; and the Syndicate Managers may, if they deem best to do so, terminate this Syndicate at any time, upon written notice of such intention to the Syndicate Subscribers.

IN WITNESS WHEREOF, the Syndicate Managers, parties hereto of the first part, and the Syndicate Subscribers, parties hereto of the second part, have subscribed an original or counterpart hereof, as of the day and year first above written.

L. M............

S. T............

Syndicate Managers.

Syndicate Subscribers.

Name	Address	Amount of Subscription
....	....	$............
....	....	$............
....	....	$............

No. 249.

Underwriting Agreement.

We, the undersigned, each for himself severally and not jointly, do hereby agree to and with each other, and with the .... Trust Company of ...., for itself and The *A. B.* Company, to subscribe to, receive and pay for the amount of .... (*bonds* or *stock*) of The *A. B.* Company, set opposite our respective signatures below, at the price of .... dollars ($......) for each .... (*bond or share of stock*), ... percent of which price shall be payable upon allotment and the remainder on demand of The .... Trust Company.

We further agree to receive and pay for any smaller amount than that subscribed for which may be allotted to us.

The conditions of this underwriting agreement are as follows:

(1). This agreement shall not be binding upon the undersigned unless the entire amount of .... dollars ($......) of .... (*bonds* or *stock*) shall have been underwritten.

(2). Within such reasonable time as shall be fixed by The .... Trust Company, the entire amount of .... dollars ($......) of .... (*bonds* or *stock*), less any amount taken and withdrawn by the underwriters as hereinafter set forth, shall be offered to the public, through such brokers or bankers as shall be designated by The .... Trust Company, for subscription at not less than the price of .... dollars ($......) for each .... (*bond* or *share of stock*).

(3). If the amount of .... (*bonds* or *stock*) subscribed and paid for, upon said public offering, shall be equal to, or exceed, the amount of .... (*bonds* or *stock*) so offered to the public, then all liability under this agreement shall cease.

(4). If the amount of .... (*bonds* or *stock*) subscribed for, upon said public offering, shall be less than the total amount of .... (*bonds* or *stock*) so offered to the public, or if the .... (*bonds* or *stock*) subscribed for, on such public offering, shall not be paid for in full at the minimum price above specified, then the deficiency in subscriptions and payments shall be made good by the underwriters, on demand of said The .... Trust Company, pro rata, in the proportion which the subscriptions of each underwriter, less any amount taken and withdrawn by him, shall bear to the total amount of .... (*bonds* or *stock*) so offered to the public.

(5). Each underwriter shall receive preferred and common stock of The *A. B.* Company, in an amount, at par, equal to .... percent of the par value of the .... (*bonds* or *stock*) hereby underwritten by him, in each class of stock, and all the proceeds, not exceeding *five* (5) percent, realized from the sale of .... (*bonds* or *stock*) at public issue in excess of *ninety* (90) percent, after deducting issue expenses, shall belong to the underwriters.

(6). Any underwriter shall have the option of withdrawing, from the public offering, any of the .... (*bonds* or *stock*) hereby underwritten by him, provided that he notify The ...... Trust Company *five* days prior to the date fixed for the public issue, that he elects to purchase said .... (*bonds* or *stock*) and provided that, in the proportion of .... (*bonds* or *stock*) so purchased, he shall be deemed to have waived his right to participate in the cash proceeds realized from the public issue.

(7). No underwriter shall sell or offer for sale the .... (*bonds* or *stock*) so purchased, nor any of the bonus shares received by him, until .... months after the date of payment by him for the .... (*bonds* or *stock*) so purchased, without the consent of The .... Trust Company.

.........., Ohio, ... 19...

Names.	Addresses.	Bonds (or stock) Underwritten.
....	....	....
....	....	....
....	....	....
....	....	....
....	....	....

No. 250.

Underwriting Agreement. Another Form.

This agreement made at ...., Ohio, this ...... day of ...., 19.., Witnesseth:

Whereas, *A. B.,* hereinafter sometimes called "promoter," proposes to organize a corporation under the laws of Ohio to be called The .... Company, or such other name as may hereafter be selected by the parties in interest, hereinafter sometimes called "the corporation" for the purpose of .... (*state purpose of new corporation*).

The corporation shall have a capital stock of .... dollars ($.....) consisting of .... dollars ($......) of preferred stock, divided into .... shares of the par value of .... dollars ($......) each, the dividends on said preferred stock to be .... percent, cumulative; and .... dollars ($.....) of common stock, divided into ...... shares of the par value of .... dollars ($......) each, and

Whereas, the promoter has acquired options and contracts for the purchase of certain properties, desirable for the business of the corporation, at certain prices, to be paid for in part in cash, and partly in stock of the corporation, and

Whereas, it will be necessary to raise at least .... dollars ($......) in cash to complete said purchases and provide the necessary working capital for the corporation, and

Whereas, it is advisable to form a syndicate for the purpose of furnishing the cash so required, by underwriting a subscription to the preferred stock of the corporation, at par, such syndicate to be composed of The .... Trust Company of .... as "syndicate manager" together with the persons, other than the promoter and The .... Trust

Company, subscribing hereto severally, hereinafter sometimes called "syndicate subscribers," and

Whereas, the syndicate, for underwriting said stock and furnishing said cash, is to receive, as a commission therefor from the promoter, ... dollars ($....) par value of the common stock of said corporation, full paid and non-assessable, which commission, after paying the fees of The .... Trust Company, is to be divided among the syndicate subscribers, in proportion to the amount of their subscriptions.

Now, therefore, in consideration of the premises and of the mutual promises and agreements herein made, each syndicate subscriber, for himself, severally and not jointly, does hereby subscribe for the amount of the preferred stock of said corporation set opposite his signature below, and does hereby agree to pay to said The .... Trust Company therefor the full par value thereof, in cash, on ...... days' notice from said The .... Trust Company. On such payments said Trust Company shall issue transferable receipts therefor, which shall be exchangeable for certificates of said preferred stock.

This agreement shall not be binding upon any of the parties hereto unless the entire amount of $...... of preferred stock shall have been underwritten. hereunder, but shall immediately become operative when said amount is subscribed.

The .... Trust Company may enforce this agreement by suit on the subscriptions, or by forfeiting payments made thereon, by any other proper remedies.

The cash paid in by the subscribers hereto shall be, by said The .... Trust Company, paid over to the Treasurer of the corporation, upon his election and qualification as such officer.

................, **Promoter.**
The .... Trust Company.

Names	Addresses	Number shares of preferred stock
....	....	....
....	....	....
....	....	....
....	....	....
....	....	....

No. 251.

Power of Attorney to Managing Agent.

Know all men by these presents: That The A. B. Company, a corporation duly organized under the laws of ...., and having its principal office in the City of ......, State of ....., does hereby make, constitute and appoint C. D., of ....., its true and lawful attorney, for it, and in its name, place and stead, to conduct and carry on its .... (*specify kind of business*) .... business in the city of ......, state of ......; to open a bank account in its name at some bank in said city; to endorse, for deposit to its credit in said bank, checks, drafts, notes and other evidences of value, to draw and sign checks in its name against said deposits for such moneys as may be necessary from time to time in the transaction of said business, or for remittance to its principal office in the city of ......; to hire and discharge employes; to purchase (*for cash*) goods, wares, merchandise, supplies and materials connected with its said business; to sell goods, wares and merchandise connected with its said business for cash or on credit, and generally to do all things necessary or proper in its interest in the usual course of its business in said city; giving and granting unto its said attorney full power and authority to do and perform all and every act and thing whatsoever, requisite, necessary and proper to be done in and about the premises, as fully, to all intents and purposes, as it might or could do, hereby ratifying and confirming all that its said attorney shall lawfully do, or cause to be done, by virtue hereof.

In witness whereof, said The A. B. Company has caused its corporate name to be subscribed hereto by its president, and its corporate seal to be affixed attested by its secretary, this ...... day of ......, A. D. 19...

Signed, sealed and
   acknowledged in presence of   The A. B. Company,

....   By ...., President.

....   (Corporate Seal)

                        Attest ...., Secretary.

STATE OF OHIO, ⎱ SS.
..........County, ⎰

   Before me, a notary public in and for said county, personally appeared ...., president and ...., secretary of The A. B. Company, the corporation which executed the foregoing instrument, who acknowledged that the seal affixed to said instrument is the corporate seal of said corporation; that they did sign and seal said instrument in behalf of said corporation and by authority of its board of directors; and that said instrument is the free act and deed of said corporation.

In testimony whereof I have hereunto subscribed my name and affixed my seal at ...., this .... day of ...., 19...

....

BOND ISSUES.

No. 252.

Resolution of Directors Authorizing Bond Issue and Corporate Mortgage or Deed of Trust.

(G. C. § 8705.)

Mr. .... presented and read the following resolution:

"Whereas, it is necessary to provide for the procuring of funds for the purpose of .... (*insert purpose of bond issue,* as "providing for the redemption of its outstanding obligations, the acquisition of additional property, the making of additions, extensions and betterments to the plant and property now owned or hereafter acquired by it, and for its other proper corporate uses and purposes")

Therefore be it resolved, that the president and secretary of this Company be and are hereby authorized to execute and deliver to The .... Trust Company of ......, Ohio, ready for certification by it, the coupon bonds of this company to an aggregate amount not exceeding .... dollars dated the ......day of ...... 19.., maturing on the ...... day of ......, 19.., bearing interest at rates not exceeding *five* per centum per annum, payable semi-annually on the first day of January and the first day of July in each year evidenced by coupons attached to said bonds executed by the engraved facsimile of the signature of the Treasurer of this company, all of said bonds to be of like date, tenor and effect, and are to be in the principal sum of $1,000, each, and to be subject to redemption on ......, 19.., and at any interest date thereafter at 105% plus accrued interest, said bonds to be issued from time to time as may be determined by the Board of Directors and in the manner set forth in the mortgage or deed of trust hereinafter mentioned; and be it further resolved, that to secure said bonds and interest the President and Secretary of this company be and they are hereby authorized and directed to execute, acknowledge and deliver to said The .... Trust Company of ......, Ohio, a mortgage, or deed of trust, upon all of the property, plant, rights, franchises and privileges of this company, now owned or hereafter acquired, which said mortgage is submitted herewith, and a copy thereof is on file with the secretary of this company, together with the form of bonds and coupons to be executed, all the provisions, terms and conditions of which said mortgage or deed of trust and bonds and coupons are hereby approved and authorized.

And be it further resolved that a meeting of the stockholders of this company be and is hereby called and ordered to meet at the office of the company on the ...... day of ......, 19.., at ...... o'clock ..M., for the purpose of considering and acting upon said proposed issue of bonds, secured by mortgage or deed of trust as aforesaid, and the transaction of any and all business necessary or incident thereto, and the secretary is hereby instructed to give notice thereof to the stockholders pursuant to law and to the regulations of this company."

Mr. .... moved the adoption of the foregoing resolution.

The motion was duly seconded by Mr. .... Thereupon the president put said resolution and the following was the vote of the directors thereon.

............, yea.
............, yea.
............, yea.
............, yea.
............, yea.

No director voted nay. Thereupon said resolution was declared carried.

No. 253.

Resolution of Stockholders Ratifying Bond Issue, Etc.

NOTE.—Action by stockholders is not required except (a) in the case of certain building companies, mortgages by which companies must be consented to by a vote of the holders of two-thirds of the stock (G. C. § 10210) and (b) except where convertible bonds are to be issued, in which case the written assent of three-fourths of the stockholders representing three-fourths of the paid up stock is required. (G. C. § 8709.)

In any case, however, ratification by stockholders will estop those voting.

For notices and minutes of meeting, see forms for special meetings of stockholders, supra.

"Whereas at a meeting of the Board of Directors of this company duly called and held on the ...... day of ......, 19.., the following resolution was duly adopted:

(*Copy directors' resolution in full.*)

Now therefore be it resolved that said action of the Board of Directors and the issue of said bonds, secured by mortgage or deed of trust, be and the same is hereby consented to, ratified, approved and confirmed in all respects."

No. 254.

Written Assent of Stockholders to Issue of Convertible Bonds.

(G. C. § 8709.)

We, the undersigned stockholders of The .... Company, do hereby assent in writing to the issue of convertible bonds as provided by the resolution of the board of directors of this company adopted the ...... day of ...., 19...

Names.	Shares.
....	....
....	....
....	....
....	....
....	....

NOTE.—Three-fourths of the stockholders and three-fourths of the stock must be represented in the written assent.

No. 255.

Deed of Trust, or Mortgage, by Corporation to Secure Bonds.

The A. B. Electric Light Company
                    to
The C. D. Trust Company
              and
E. F.   Trustees.

Indenture dated for convenience this ...... day of ......, A. D. 19.., but actually made and entered into this .... day of .... ,A. D. 19.., by and between The A. B. Electric Light Company, a corporation duly organized and existing under and by virtue of the laws of the state of Ohio, hereinafter called the "Company" party of the first part, and The C. D. Trust Company, a corporation duly organized and existing under and by virtue of the laws of the state of Ohio, and E. F., of the city of ......, as Trustees, the said The C. D. Trust Company, Trustee, being sometimes hereinafter referred to as the "Corporate Trustee," and the said E. F., Trustee, being sometimes hereinafter referred to as the "Individual Trustee," parties of the second part.

Whereas, under the laws of the state of Ohio, the Company

is authorized to borrow money and issue its negotiable bonds
therefor and secure the payment thereof by mortgage upon its
property, rights, franchises and privileges; and whereas the Company, desiring to provide for the redemption of its outstanding
obligations, the acquisition of additional property, the making
of additions, extensions and betterments to the property now
owned or hereafter to be acquired by it, and money for its other
proper corporate uses and purposes, the Board of Directors of
the Company at their meeting duly called and held in the city of
.............., Ohio, on the ...... day of ......, A. D. 19..,
duly authorized its President, or Vice-President, and Secretary,
or Assistant Secretary, to execute and deliver to the Corporate
Trustee, ready for certification by it, the coupon bonds of the
Company to an aggregate amount not exceeding *Five Million* dollars, dated the ...... day of ......, 19.., maturing on the
...... day of ......, 19.., bearing interest at rates not exceeding five per centum per annum, payable semi-annually on the
first day of *January* and the first day of *July* in each year,
evidenced by coupons attached to said bonds, executed by the
engraved fac-simile of the signature of the Treasurer of the
Company, all of which bonds are of like date and except as to the
rate of interest thereon, of like tenor and effect and are to be in
the principal sum of $1,000 each and consecutively numbered
from one upwards, and shall be subject to redemption on ......,
19.., and on any interest date thereafter, at 105 percent plus
accrued interest, said bonds to be issued from time to time for the
purposes and in the manner hereinafter set forth, but at no time
to exceed in the aggregate *Five Million* dollars of principal, and
for the purpose of securing the prompt and punctual payment
of the principal and interest of said bonds as the same become
due, said Board of Directors at their said meeting so called and
held as aforesaid, duly authorized and directed the President,
or Vice-President, and Secretary, or Assistant Secretary, of the
Company to execute, acknowledge and deliver to the Trustee a
mortgage or deed of trust upon all of the property, plant, rights,
franchises and privileges of the Company, whether now owned
or hereafter acquired; and whereas the stockholders of the Company at a meeting duly called and held on the ...... day of
......, 19.., by resolution duly passed by the vote of the holders
of a majority of the capital stock consented to, ratified, approved and confirmed the aforesaid action of the Board of Directors and authorized the issue of said bonds and the securing
of the same by mortgage as aforesaid, and whereas, pursuant to
said action of said Directors and said stockholders so had and
taken as aforesaid, the President, or Vice-President, and Secretary, or Assistant Secretary, of the Company have executed
and delivered to the *C. D.* Trust Company; the Corporate Trustee,

for authentication, as hereinafter provided, *one million five hundred thousand dollars,* of principal of said bonds, which said *one million five hundred thousand dollars* of bonds bear interest at the rate of five per centum per annum, payable semi-annually as aforesaid, and said officers will from time to time hereafter, in accordance with the provisions hereinafter set forth, execute and deliver to the Corporate Trustee, ready for authentication, as hereinafter provided, bonds' of the issue hereinafter described, bearing a rate or rates of interest not exceeding five per centum per annum, payable semi-annually as aforesaid, and including said $1,500,000 of bonds aggregating an amount not exceeding *five million* dollars ($5,000,000) each of which said bonds shall be in substantially the words and figures following, subject only to the necessary variations in the distinguishing numbers and rates of interest thereon, to wit:

No. .... $1,000.

United States of America,
State of Ohio.
The *A. B.* Electric Light Company,
First Mortgage Gold Bond.

Know all men by these presents, that the *A. B.* Electric Light Company, a corporation duly organized and existing under the laws of the state of Ohio, for value received, promises to pay to bearer, or, if registered, to the registered holder hereof, the sum of one thousand dollars, in gold coin of the United States of America of the standard of weight and fineness existing on the ...... day of ...., 19.., at the office of The *C. D.* Trust Company, in the city of ...., Ohio, on the ...... day of ...., 19.., with interest thereon at the rate of .... percentum per annum, payable semiannually on the first day of *January* and the first day of *July* in each year until said principal sum is paid, in like gold coin at the office of said Trust Company or at its fiscal agency in the city of New York, New York, upon the presentation and surrender of the coupons evidencing the same, hereto attached, as they respectively become due and payable as provided therein. In case of default in the payment of any of said coupons attached to this bond, in the manner provided in the trust deed or mortgage hereinafter mentioned, or in the performance of certain covenants and agreements as contained in said trust deed or mortgage, then the principal sum of this bond shall become due in the manner and with the effect provided in said trust deed or mortgage. This bond is one of an authorized issue of bonds, the amount whereof is limited so that there shall never be at any one time outstanding bonds of said issue for an aggregate principal sum exceeding *five million* dollars, all of which bonds are of like date, and except as to the rate of interest thereon, of like tenor and effect, may bear interest at rates not exceeding *five* percentum per annum, and are numbered from one upwards. All of said bonds are issued or are to be issued under and are equally and ratably secured, without priority or preference by reason of priority of date of issue, or otherwise, by a trust deed or mortgage, dated the ...... day of ...., 19.., duly executed, acknowledged and delivered by the Company, and recorded in the office of the Recorder of .... County, Ohio, conveying to said Trust Company and *E. F.*, of the city of ...., in trust, all of the corporate property, real and personal, rights, franchises and privileges, as described in said mortgage, now owned by the Company or hereafter acquired by it. This bond is subject to all and every the provisions, conditions and agreements and entitled to all and every the benefits and privileges in said trust deed or mortgage recited and set forth. The Company reserves to itself and its successors the right to pay and retire this bond on the ...... day of .... ,19.., and on any interest date thereafter at 105% and accrued interest, upon giving *eight* weeks' notice by publication of its desire to so pay and retire this bond, as provided in said trust deed or mortgage, and notice of such desire to so pay and retire this bond having been given in the manner provided in said trust deed or mortgage, this bond shall cease to draw interest from the date of retirement fixed in said notice, unless upon such date, this bond being presented for payment, default in payment be made. This bond, unless registered, shall pass by delivery, but may be registered, and such registration certified hereon upon presentation to said Trust Company, at its office in the city of ...., as provided in said mortgage. After registration certified hereon, no transfer hereof, unless made on the books of the Trust Company at said office in said city, shall be valid, unless the last registration shall have been to bearer, and this bond shall be subject to successive registration and transfers to bearer at the option of each holder. After such registration only such registered holder, or the legal representatives of such holder, shall be entitled to receive the principal hereof, but the registry of this bond shall not restrain the negotiability of the coupons by delivery merely, but the coupons may be surrendered and the interest made payable only to the registered owner hereof. No recourse shall be had for the payment of the principal and interest of this bond against any incorporator, stockholder, officer or director of the Company, past, present or future, either directly or through the Company, by virtue of any statute or constitution, or by the enforcement of any assessment of any penalty or otherwise howsoever, any and all liability of such incorporators, stockholders, directors and officers of the Company being hereby released. This bond shall not become obligatory until it shall have been authenticated by the execution by either one of the said trustees of the certificate endorsed hereon.

In witness whereof, said The *A. B.* Electric Light Company has caused these presents to be signed by its president and secretary, and its corporate seal to be hereto affixed and the coupons hereto annexed to be executed by the fac-simile of the signature of its treasurer, as of the ...... day of ...., 19...

The A. B. Electric Light Company,

By ...., President.

Attest ...., Secretary.

Coupon. $..........

The *A. B.* Electric Light Company will pay to bearer at the office of The *C. D.* Trust Company, in the city of ...., Ohio, or at its fiscal agency in the city of New York, on the ...... day of ...., 19. ., ... dollars, in United States gold coin, being six months' interest then due on its First Mortgage Gold Bond No. ....

.............., Treasurer.

TRUSTEE'S CERTIFCATE.

It is hereby certified that the within bond is one of the series and issue described in the trust deed or mortgage therein mentioned.

The C. D. Trust Company, Trustee.

By ...., President.

Now, therefore, this indenture, witnesseth: The *A. B.* Electric Light Company, for and in consideration of the premises and of the sum of one dollar, lawful money of the United States of America, to it in hand paid by said The *C. D.* Trust Company, and *E. F.*, Trustees, at or before the ensealing and delivery of these presents, the receipt whereof is hereby acknowledged, and in pursuance of the direction and authority of its directors and stockholders, given as above recited, and in order to secure equally and ratably the prompt and punctual payment of the principal and interest of all its bonds aforesaid at any time outstanding, and the fulfillment of the promises, covenants and agreements herein and in said bond so contained, hath granted, bargained, sold, aliened, conveyed, assigned, transferred, set over, released and confirmed, and by these presents doth grant, bargain, sell, alien, convey, assign, transfer, set over, release and confirm unto said The *C. D.* Trust Company and *E. F.*, Trustees, and to their successors in the trust hereby created, and assigns forever, the following described property, rights, franchises and privileges, to wit:

I.

(Description of Real Estate.)

II.

(Description of Personal Property.)

General Description.—Also all other property, real, personal and mixed, of the Company, wheresoever situate, now owned by the Company, and all which it may hereafter acquire, excepting money, bills and accounts receivable, stock supplies and securities, all of which are expressly reserved by the Company, and excepted from the lien of this mortgage. Provided, however, and it is expressly agreed, that upon the entry and possession by the trustees or by a receiver all money, bills and accounts receivable, stock supplies and securities shall thereupon become and be subject to the lien of this mortgage, and shall on demand be delivered to the trustees or to such receiver. And also all corporate property, rights, franchises and privileges of the Company now owned or controlled, or that may be hereafter owned or acquired by it. And also all present and after acquired rights of way, licenses, easements, leases, leasehold interests, buildings, erections, superstructures, machine shops, tools, implements and machinery and all contracts. And also all property, real, personal or mixed, chattels, fixtures, rights, franchises and privileges of whatsoever nature or description, hereafter acquired by the Company. And also all and singular the tenements, hereditaments and appurtenances now or hereafter belonging, or in any wise appertaining unto the aforesaid property, rights, franchises and privileges and the reversions, remainders, rents, issues and profits, income, revenues and proceeds thereof.

And also all the present and hereafter acquired estate, right, title, interest, property, possession, claim and demand, whatsoever, as well in law as in equity of the Company, of, in and to the above described premises, property, rights, franchises and privileges, and every part thereof, with the appurtenances. All of the foregoing property, rights, franchises and privileges mentioned and described under headings I and II constitutes and is hereafter referred to as the "trust estate."

To have and to hold the above described premises, property, rights, franchises and privileges with the appurtenances thereunto belonging or in any wise appertaining, unto the said trustees, their successors and assigns, for its, his and their own use, but in trust, nevertheless, for the equal pro rata benefit and security of any and all persons and parties and their respective successors, executors, administrators or assigns, who may at any time hold any of the bonds or coupons to be issued hereunder, without any discrimination, preference or priority in favor of any one bond over any other by reason of priority in time of issue thereof, or otherwise, and with the powers and upon the terms, conditions and covenants hereinafter expressed and declared of and concerning the same, that is to say:

ARTICLE I. AUTHENTICATION AND ISSUE OF BONDS.

Section 1. The amount of bonds hereby secured which may be executed by the Company and which may be authenticated by the *corporate trustee*, is limited, so that never at one time shall there be outstanding bonds of the issue hereby secured for an aggregate principal sum exceeding *five million* dollars, but no bonds shall be authenticated and delivered hereunder at any time in excess of the issued or authorized capital stock of the Company, so long as the laws of the state of Ohio impose such limitation.

Section 2. All bonds issued hereunder shall be signed by the president or one of the vice-presidents and secretary or an assistant secretary of the Company and the corporate seal of the company shall be affixed thereto. In case the officers who shall sign and seal any of such bonds as aforesaid shall cease to be such officers of the Company before said bonds so signed and sealed shall have been actually authenticated and delivered by the corporate trustee, as hereinafter provided, such bonds may nevertheless be issued, authenticated and delivered as though the persons who signed and sealed such bonds had not ceased to be officers of the Company. The coupons attached to said bonds shall be authenticated by the engraved signature of the present treasurer or any future treasurer of the Company, it being intended that the Company may adopt and use for that purpose the engraved signature of any such treasurer, notwithstanding that he may have ceased to be the treasurer of the Company at the time that such bonds shall be actually authenticated and delivered.

Section 3. Said bonds when executed by the Company shall be delivered to the corporate trustee to be authenticated by it and the corporate trustee shall authenticate and deliver the same only as provided in this article. Only such bonds as shall bear thereon a certificate substantially in the form hereinbefore recited, duly executed by the corporate trustee, shall be secured by this indenture or be entitled to any lien or benefit hereunder, and every such certificate of the corporate trustee upon any bond executed by the Company shall be conclusive and only evidence that the bond so authenticated was duly issued hereunder and is entitled to the benefit of the trust hereby created. Before authenticating and delivering any bonds hereby secured the corporate trustee shall detach and shall cancel all coupons thereon then matured.

Section 4.   No bonds shall be authenticated and delivered by the corporate trustee hereunder until this instrument shall have been filed for record in the office of the recorder of .... County, Ohio.

Section 5.   Upon compliance with the provisions of section 4, the corporate trustee shall be, and is hereby authorized and directed to authenticate and deliver, upon the order of the board of directors of the Company, and to such person or persons as the said board may direct from time to time any of the bonds authorized hereunder.   Each and every of such orders shall be evidenced by a duly attested copy of the resolutions of the board of directors made in that behalf, and such resolutions shall recite the disposition to be made of the bonds so ordered to be delivered, which shall be for some or all of the purposes hereinafter set forth.   Such authentications and deliveries shall be made as follows:

(a) $500,000 principal of said bonds forthwith upon compliance with said section 4 and $500,000 principal of said bonds from time to time thereafter as the board of directors may by resolution request.

(b) $1,000,000, principal of said bonds for the purpose of paying or redeeming the certain bonds of the Company issued under its first mortgage to The X. Y. Trust Company of ...., Ohio, as trustee, dated *January* 1, 1895, under which there are now outstanding $1,000,000 of bonds under a total authorized issue of $1,500,000, and which bonds are subject to redemption on the ...... day of ...., 19.., or at any time thereafter, upon payment of the principal thereof and a premium of 5% thereon.   And whenever and as often as the Company shall deliver to the corporate trustee any one or more of said bonds of *January* 1, 1895, with all coupons thereto belonging then in the future to become due, the corporate trustee shall authenticate and deliver an amount of bonds of the issue in this instrument described equal in principal to 105% of the principal of such bonds of *January* 1, 1895, so surrendered to the corporate trustee, or the corporate trustee shall, on the request of the Company authenticate and deliver in lots of $5,000 of principal, or in some multiple thereof, upon the receipt of par and interest accrued since the last interest paying date, to the Company or its nominee, any of the bonds mentioned in this subdivision.   The corporate trustee shall hold the money so received by it, and allow interest thereon at the same rate and upon the same terms as it allows on like deposits in its trust department and shall use said money in or toward the retirement of the first mortgage bonds in this subdivision mentioned at the maturity thereof or when said bonds are presented to it therefor. In the event said fund is insufficient to pay in full said first mortgage bonds so maturing or presented, the Company agrees, upon demand of the corporate trustee, to pay to it sufficient money to complete the retirement of said first mortgage bonds. In the event of any surplus remaining after the payment of said first mortgage bonds the corporate trustee shall pay over such surplus to the company.

(c) The remainder of said bonds for the purpose of paying for, or providing in advance the means to pay for, or reimbursing the Company for moneys expended for, additional property (not including capital stock or securities of any corporation) the making of extensions, additions, improvements or betterments to the property now owned or hereafter acquired by the Company, but the Company covenants and agrees that no bond shall be certified for any of the purposes mentioned in this subdivision (c) of section 5 except upon the following terms and conditions and the facts required to be shown by the resolutions, certificates and statements hereinafter set forth shall exist at the time of the passage or making thereof: The board of directors of the Company shall adopt a resolution requesting the corporate trustee to authenticate the bonds which the Company desires to be issued, stating, 1. The officer of the Company, or the person, or persons, to whom the same are to be delivered. 2. The purpose or purposes for which the bonds or their proceeds are to be used, which shall be one or more of the purposes named in this subdivision (c). 3. That no bonds have been issued in respect to such particular property, extensions, additions, improvements or betterments. 4. The estimated (or, if such property, extensions, additions, improvements or betterments have been theretofore acquired or made, the actual) cost thereof to the Company in money. 5. The gross income of the property of the Company for one year of *three hundred and sixty-five days out of the thirteen calendar months* immediately preceding the date of the adoption of such resolution. 6. The expense of manufacture and distribution, including such expense for repairs, maintenance and replacements as are incurred or made in the ordinary course of business, and the general expenses of management incurred or made in the ordinary course of business, together with all taxes and assessments of the Company or upon the property thereof, and all premiums for insurance for such period, not including in the foregoing any item for amortization or property or capital. 7. The net income after deducting from such gross income such expenses, taxes, assessments and insurance premiums. 8. The principal amount of the issue of bonds hereby secured at the time outstanding. 9. The principal amount of any bonds or secured debt which this Company has assumed or become obligated

to pay and which are secured by lien upon property acquired
subsequent to the date of this indenture, prior to the lien hereof;
and the rate of interest upon such bonds or debt; provided, however, that in the event any property to be acquired by the Company and in respect to which bonds are requested to be authenticated and delivered, or any property hereafter acquired by the
Company shall have had an earning capacity for such period, such
property, and its income and expenses as above defined, shall be
treated for such period as if the same had been owned by the
Company for the purpose of determining the net earnings of the
Company as the basis for the authentication and delivery of
bonds as herein provided. Said resolution shall be certified by
the secretary of the Company and delivered to the corporate trustee. There shall also be delivered to the corporate trustee a
certificate by the president or chief engineer of the Company,
showing the truth of the facts set forth in said directors' resolution. There shall also be delivered to the corporate trustee a
certificate of counsel, believed by said trustee to be competent,
that the good and unincumbered title to any real property for
the acquisition of which bonds are to be issued has been vested
in the Company and subjected to the terms and conditions of this
mortgage. And the foregoing having been done, if it shall appear
that the net income ascertained in the manner aforesaid shall
equal or exceed twice the interest charge for one year upon the
bonds of the Company at the time.outstanding and on the bonds
requested to be authenticated pursuant to the foregoing provisions, and on the bonds and debt which the Company has assumed or become obligated to pay and which are secured by lien
upon property acquired subsequent to the date of this indenture
prior to the lien hereof, then the corporate trustee shall authenticate and deliver to the person or party named in said resolution
of said board of directors, bonds of the issue herein described of
an amount of principal equal to 80% of such cost of such additional property, additions, extensions, improvements or betterments. Provided, however, if any such bonds are issued upon the
basis of estimated cost of such property, extensions, additions,
betterments or improvements, prior to the acquisition or making
thereof, then, in making delivery of such bonds the corporate
trustee shall only deliver such bonds from time to time, at the rate
aforesaid, as such property, extensions, additions, betterments or
improvements are paid for, as shown by certificate of the president or chief engineer or other officer of the Company believed
by the corporate trustee to have knowledge of the facts, and in
the event the actual cost shall be less than such estimated cost,
any balance of said bonds in the hands of the corporate trustee
undelivered shall be held by it subject to future delivery hereunder the same as the remainder of the unauthenticated bonds

authorized to be issued hereunder: All or any part of such estimated amount of bonds may be sold by the Company at a price for any one bond or lot of bonds which will result in the loan thereon costing the company a rate of interest not exceeding *six* percentum per annum for the remainder of the term of such bond or bonds, and the proceeds from such sale shall be deposited with the corporate trustee. The corporate trustee shall pay over said proceeds to or upon the order of the Company upon receipt of a statement sworn to by an officer of the Company showing expenditures made or indebtedness incurred and then due on account of property, extensions, additions, betterments or improvements for the purchase or making of which said bonds were issued and said money deposited, to an amount not exceeding 80% of the amount of such indebtedness or expenditures. Or, at the election of the Company it may make and deliver drafts upon the corporate trustee each of which drafts shall be given for the purpose and shall show upon the face that the same is given for the purpose of paying not exceeding 80% of the indebtedness incurred or created on account of such property, extensions, additions, betterments or improvements, or some portion thereof. The Company reserves the right to deposit the proceeds of the sale of any of said bonds in some bank or banks of good standing in the city of ...., Ohio, or in the city of New York, N. Y., in the name of the corporate trustee, in which event said proceeds· shall be payable for the purposes hereinbefore set forth only upon the order of the corporate trustee, and the corporate trustee shall make such payments from time to time upon delivery to it of sworn statements as hereinabove mentioned. If the estimated cost of such property, extensions, additions, betterments or improvements shall exceed the actual cost thereof in money and a balance of the proceeds of the sale of bonds shall remain on deposit with said corporate trustee or said bank, or banks, the same shall be thereafter paid out only in the manner and at the rate hereinbefore provided, for some one or more of the purposes for which bonds may be issued as in this article provided, or at the request of the company, may be used in or towards the retirement and cancellation of the bonds issued under this indenture. The corporate trustee shall be under no obligation to see to the application of said bonds or their proceeds to the purpose or purposes for which they are authenticated and delivered and shall be entitled to rely upon any resolution of said board of directors, statements and certificates of said officers and counsel and vouchers of the Company with reference to the authentication and delivery of bonds, payment of money, title of property and lien of this instrument and shall be absolutely protected in so doing; provided, however, that the corporate trustee may, at the expense of the

Company, require additional evidence of the facts set forth in such resolution, certificates, vouchers or statements, but is not obligated so to do; and that the trustees, or either of them, if they deem best so to do, may, at the expense of the Company, require an examination, by a competent person satisfactory to the trustees, of the books and accounts of the Company and of any such additional property, additions, extensions, betterments or improvements, and shall be absolutely protected in relying upon any report which such person shall make to them.

Section 6. In case any bond issued hereunder, with the coupons thereto appertaining, shall become mutilated, or be lost or destroyed, the Company, in its discretion, may execute, and thereupon the corporate trustee shall authenticate and deliver a new bond of like tenor and date, including the unmatured coupons thereon, bearing the same serial number, in exchange and substitution for, and upon cancellation of the mutilated bond and its coupons, or in lieu of or substitution for said bond or its coupons, upon receipt of satisfactory evidence of the destruction or loss of such bond and its coupons and upon receipt also of satisfactory indemnity.

Section 7. In the event of the resignation, removal, dissolution or unfitness to act of the corporation trustee, or any corporation successor to it, all of the powers and authority vested by this article in the corporate trustee may be exercised by the individual trustee hereinbefore named, or his successor.

ARTICLE II.   COVENANTS BY THE COMPANY.

The Company hereby covenants as follows:

Section 1. That it has a good and indefeasible estate in fee simple or in possession absolute, according to the nature of the property conveyed, in and to all of the property and rights hereinbefore described as being now owned by it; that the franchises hereinbefore described as now owned by it are valid and subsisting franchises, and that it has good right and lawful authority to convey, assign and transfer said premises, rights and franchises as provided in and by this indenture.

Section 2. That it will punctually pay the principal and interest of every bond issued hereunder and secured hereby, in gold coin of the United States of America of the present weight and fineness, or its equivalent, at the date and place and in the manner specified in said bonds, and in the coupons thereto belonging, according to the true intent and meaning thereof, without deduction from either principal or interest for any tax or taxes imposed by the United States of America or by any state, territory, county, city or other municipality or governmental subdivision, and which the Company may be required to pay thereon and deduct or retain therefrom under or by reason of any present or future law, the Company hereby agreeing to pay all such taxes. That after coupons evidencing interest are paid said coupons shall be forthwith cancelled. The principal of each bond shall be payable only upon the presentation and surrender of the bond and the principal of registered bonds shall be payable only to the registered holders thereof. Each bond when paid shall forthwith be duly cancelled.

Section 3. That it will not issue, sell or dispose of any bonds issued hereunder in any manner other than in accordance with the provisions of this indenture and the covenants and agreements in that behalf herein contained and that it will in good faith use or expend said bonds or their proceeds only for the purposes provided in this indenture, according to the true intent and meaning thereof.

Section 4. That at all times until the full payment of the principal of the bonds secured by this indenture, the Company will keep an office in the city of ...., Ohio, where bonds and interest coupons may be presented for payment and where notices and demands with respect to said bonds and coupons or other notices and demands hereunder may be served, and an office or agency in the city of New York where coupons may be presented for payment and from time to time the Company will give written notice to the trustees of the location of such offices or agencies. In case the Company shall fail to do so, presentation and demand may be made, and notices may be served at the office of the corporate trustee or its successors.

Section 5. That at the office of the corporate trustee, or at some Bank or Trust Company in the city of ...., Ohio, it will keep books for registration of bonds issued hereunder (which books at all reasonable times shall be open to the inspection of the trustees) under such reasonable regulations as the Company may prescribe. The ownership of any bond issued under this indenture, which shall be presented for that purpose, may be registered in such book or books free of charge by the Company. Upon presentation to the bond registrar or transfer agent, at the place where such books of registry are kept, of any bond which shall have been registered as aforesaid and delivery of a written instrument of transfer, in form approved by the Company, executed by the registered holder for the time being, such bond shall be transferred upon such registry. The registered holder shall also have the right to cause the same to be registered as payable to bearer, in which case transferability by delivery shall be restored, and thereafter the principal of such bond shall be payable to any person presenting the same, but any such bond registered as payable to bearer may be registered again in the name of the holder with the same effect as in the case of the first registration thereof. Successive registrations and transfers as aforesaid may be made from time to time as desired. Each registration shall be noted by the bond registrar or transfer agent of the Company upon the bond. The *C. D.* Trust Company, the corporate trustee hereinbefore mentioned, is hereby constituted and appointed the bond registrar and transfer agent of the Company for the purpose of registration as hereinbefore set forth. The registration of any bond, however, shall not restrain the negotiability of any coupon thereto belonging, but every such coupon shall continue to pass by delivery merely and shall remain payable to bearer. The holder of any bond may, however, register the same and surrender the coupons thereto belonging to the corporate trustee, who shall forthwith cancel such coupons, and thereafter the interest on such bond shall be payable only to the registered holder thereof.

Section 6. The Company will, from time to time, duly and punctually pay and discharge all real estate, personal, franchise and other taxes, water rates, assessments, imposts and governmental and other charges, lawfully imposed upon the property now or hereafter subject to the lien and operation of this indenture, and also upon all other property at any time subject to this indenture, and upon each and every part thereof, and upon the income and profits thereof and with respect to the carrying on or doing business by the Company, so that the lien and priority of this indenture shall be fully preserved in respect to the real and personal property, rights, franchises and privileges now or hereafter subject to the lien and operation of this indenture; provided, however, that nothing in this section shall require the Company to pay any such taxes, assessments, imposts or other charges so long as the Company shall in good faith and by proper legal proceedings contest the validity thereof or its being a charge upon the property covered by this indenture. If the Company shall fail to keep this covenant, the trustees, in addition to any other remedy or remedies which they may have hereunder, and without prejudice to any rights of the trustees by reason of any such default and upon request of one or more of the holders of said bonds secured hereby, and upon being provided with adequate funds for that purpose and ample indemnity in the premises, shall pay such taxes, assessments and charges, and all amounts so paid, with interest thereon at the rate of six percentum per annum shall be a charge upon the trust estate prior to the bonds hereby secured, and the trustees may forthwith sue for and recover from the Company any such amount in a proper action therefor.

Section 7. That it will not create or suffer to be created any lien or charge having priority to or preference over the lien of this indenture upon the trust estate, or any part thereof, or upon the income thereof, and that within three months after the same shall have accrued it will pay or cause to be discharged or will make adequate provision for the satisfaction and discharge of all lawful claims and demands of mechanics, laborers and others which might by law be given precedence as a lien or charge upon the trust estate, or any part thereof or the income thereof; provided, however, that nothing in this instrument contained shall require the Company to pay any claim or demand so long as the Company shall in good faith and by proper legal proceedings contest the validity thereof, provided however, that nothing in this section contained shall apply to purchase money, or other assumed liens upon after acquired property.

Section 8. That it will from time to time upon written demand of the Trustees and at its own expense record and re-record, file and refile these presents, whether as a chattel mortgage or a mortgage on real estate, and make, do, execute, acknowledge and deliver, or cause to be made, done, executed, acknowledged and delivered all such other acts, deeds, transfers, assignments, conveyances and assurances in the law as may by said Trustees or their counsel be reasonably advised or required for effectuating the intention of these presents or for the better assuring and confirming unto the Trustee upon the trusts and for the purposes herein expressed, of the trust estate and any part or parts thereof, and also all and singular the property, rights, franchises and privileges which may hereafter be acquired by the Company.

Section 9. That it will, except as herein otherwise provided, at all times actively conduct and carry on the business for which it was incorporated and which it is now or may hereafter be carrying on or conducting; that it will maintain and keep in good repair and condition its plants and properties, make all necessary renewals and replacements thereof or therein, diligently preserve, observe and protect all licenses under patents or otherwise owned or held, and will at all times, so long as the bonds issued hereunder or any of them remain outstanding and unpaid, diligently preserve and maintain its corporate existence and all franchises now or hereafter granted to it, and do or cause to be done all other acts and things necessary or proper to maintain and keep in full force and effect the lien and incumbrance hereby created.

Section 10. The Company shall also furnish to the trustees, at any time that they may in writing so request, a written statement containing a summary of all its then assets and liabilities, its gross receipts, expenses and net income, determined as hereinbefore provided and shall permit the Trustees or their agents, upon like request at any time to examine its premises, property or books of account; provided, however, that the Company shall not be obliged to furnish such statement or permit such examination unless it is furnished with satisfactory evidence by the trustees that the holders of not less than 15 per centum of the bonds secured hereby at any time outstanding demanded that they request such statement or make such examination.

Section 11. The Company shall and will at all times, so long as any of the bonds issued hereunder remain outstanding and unpaid, at its own cost and expense, insure and keep insured against loss or damage by fire, in responsible insurance Companies, all its property usually insured by like Companies similarly situated and in the same manner and to the same extent. Said policies for such insurance shall be made payable, in case of loss, to the trustees as their interest may appear, provided, however, that the Company may, if it elects so to do, pay to the corporate trustee the sum of .... dollars ($....) in money or, in lieu thereof, deliver to the corporate trustee bonds of the issue herein provided for equal in principal sum to said amount, or part thereof in said bonds at par and the remainder in money, in which event it shall not be required to insure its property as hereinabove provided, unless said deposit (hereinafter called "insurance fund") shall be depleted by payment of losses to less than $..... The money in said fund shall, at the request of the Company, be invested in the bonds of the Company of the issue hereby secured or in other securities in which Trust Companies organized under the laws of the State of Ohio may invest money or property received by them in trust, or in such other interest bearing securities as may be approved by the Company and the trustees. The securities in which such investment may be made shall, except as hereinbefore provided, be chosen by the Company. The corporate trustee agrees to allow interest upon moneys remaining on deposit with it in said insurance fund, at the same rate and upon the same terms that it allows upon like deposits in its trust department. Until default the Company shall be entitled to all income earned by the insurance fund or the securities in which the same is invested, whether the same be bonds of the Company, or otherwise. In the event of loss occurring by fire, the corporate trustee shall from time to time at the request of the Company pay over to it such amount of money out of the insurance fund as shall be necessary to repair, restore or replace such lost or destroyed property; such payments to be made from time to time upon receipt of vouchers showing the expenditure by the Company of the amount called for in any such vouchers, or that an indebtedness has been incurred for such purposes of repair, restoration or replacement equal to the amount called for by such vouchers. In the event sufficient moneys are not on hand in the insurance fund to pay any such loss, the corporate trustee shall, on request of the Company, sell sufficient of the securities belonging to said fund to provide for the payment of said loss. In the event said fund is reduced below the sum of $75,000 by the payment of any such loss, the Company shall make good such deficiency by making payments to the corporate trustee for the account of said fund at the rate of $5,000, per annum until said fund and the accummulations thereof shall again equal the sum of $75,000. In the event said insurance fund is depleted by payment of losses to less than $75,000, then the Company shall effect and maintain insurance as hereinabove first provided, until said fund shall again equal $75,000. Upon the maturity of the bonds issued hereunder, any bonds of the issue hereby secured then remaining in said fund shall be cancelled, and any other securities and moneys then in said fund shall be applied toward the payment of the bonds issued hereunder at the time outstanding and unpaid. The Company covenants to at all times keep the corporate trustee informed as to the amounts of insurance carried by it, when it is required to carry insurance, furnishing said corporate trustee with lists of the Companies, policy numbers and amounts, and in the event the Company shall fail at any time when required by the terms hereof to carry insurance deemed by the trustees to be sufficient, the trustees may, but shall be under no obligation to, insure the property of the Company as they may deem best for the benefit of the bondholders, and the cost of the same, with five percent interest thereon from the date of payment of the respective premiums, shall be repaid to them by the Company on demand, and until so paid shall be a charge upon the trust estate prior in lien to the bonds issued hereunder.

Section 12. That the Company will duly call for redemption and retire all bonds issued and outstanding under the mortgage described in Section 5 of Article 1 hereof, as soon as the same may be redeemed under the terms of said respective mortgages, and will, as soon as all of the bonds issued under said respective mortgages have been paid, cause said mortgages to be duly cancelled of record.

ARTICLE III.   RETIREMENT OF BONDS.

Section 1. The Company reserves to itself, its successors and assigns, the right at its or their election to retire the whole or any part of the bonds issued hereunder, on the .... day of ...., 19.., and on any interest maturing date thereafter, at 105% of par plus accrued interest. In the event the Company elects to retire the whole or any part of said bonds on any such interest maturing date, it shall at least *ten weeks* prior to the date of retirement notify the corporate trustee of such election and the corporate trustee shall, if the amount of bonds to be retired be less than the entire amount outstanding, choose the bonds to be retired by lot and notify the Company of the numbers of the bonds so chosen within one week after receipt of such notice. The Company shall in all cases of retirement of bonds hereunder give notice by publication in some newspaper of general circulation published in the City of ...., Ohio, and in some newspaper of general circulation published in the City of New York, N. Y., which notice shall state that the Company will retire the bonds chosen for retirement, on the date fixed therefor, naming the price at which same are to be retired, upon presentation and surrender of such bonds, with all unpaid coupons thereto belonging, at the office of the corporate trustee in the City of ...., Ohio. Such notice shall be published once each week for eight weeks prior to the date fixed for such retirement. In all cases in which less than the entire amount of bonds are chosen for retirement the published notice of retirement shall contain the numbers of the bonds so chosen. In all cases of retirement of bonds the Company shall, on or before the date fixed for retirement, deposit with the corporate trustee sufficient money to pay the retirement price of said bonds and accrued interest on the principal thereof to date of retirement. Said notice having been given in the manner aforesaid and sufficient money to retire all bonds called for retirement at the rate specified having been deposited with the corporate trustee, if the holder or holders of any bond or bonds so called for retirement fails to present the same for retirement at the time and place in said notice specified, such bond or bonds shall thereafter cease to bear interest and the corporate trustee shall credit to each of such bonds as may not be so presented, designated by the number thereof, a sum of money equal to such retirement price plus the interest accrued thereon to the date fixed for retirement as aforesaid and remaining unpaid and said credit shall be treated as full payment for each such bond and the coupons thereto belonging as between the Company and the holder thereof, and said sum so credited by the corporate trustee to bonds which have not been presented for retirement shall bear no interest, and thereupon and thereafter said bonds and all coupons thereto belonging shall be excluded from participation in the lien and security afforded by these presents and the holder thereof shall look for the payment of such bonds and accrued interest only to sums so credited thereto in the hands of the corporate trustee and in no event to the Company, and the Company shall, as to all such bonds be released from liability in respect thereof, but said sums so deposited shall be held by the corporate trustee to the credit and for the payment of said bonds and the interest thereon and shall be paid by the corporate trustee to the holders thereof on presentation and delivery to it of said respective bonds, together with all outstanding coupons thereto belonging.

Section 2. Upon presentation to the corporate trustee, cancelled, of all said authorized issue of bonds and coupons which at the time shall have been issued and outstanding, or upon presentation of a portion thereof, cancelled, all of said bonds having been called for retirement under the provisions of this article and the corporate trustee having credited to all such bonds as have not been presented for retirement the retirement price thereof and the interest thereon, the trustees shall cancel and discharge this mortgage or deed of trust as fully and to the same effect as if the total issue of said bonds and coupons had been duly paid by the Company at maturity thereof. All bonds retired under this article, together with the coupons thereto belonging, shall be forthwith cancelled by the corporate trustee. All costs, charges and expenses incurred by the corporate trustee hereunder with respect to the retirement of bonds shall be paid by the Company.

ARTICLE IV. REMEDIES OF TRUSTEES AND BONDHOLDERS.

Section 1. The Company covenants and agrees that it will not directly or indirectly extend, or consent to the extension of, the time of payment of any coupon or claim for interest upon any of the bonds issued hereunder and that it will not directly or indirectly be a party to or approve any arrangement therefor by purchasing or funding the same in any other manner. In case the payment of any such coupon shall be extended by or with the consent of the Company, such coupon or claim for interest so extended shall not be entitled, in case of default hereunder, to the benefit or security of this indenture except subject to the prior payment in full of the principal of all outstanding bonds, and of all coupons of such bonds the payment of which has not been so extended, the intention being to prevent any accumulation after maturity of coupons upon the bonds issued hereunder.

Section 2. In case default shall be made (a) in the payment of any interest upon any bond or bonds secured hereby, and outstanding, and such default shall continue for the period of three months, or (b) in the performance or observance of any other covenant or condition herein contained to be performed or observed by the Company and such default shall have continued for a period of four months after demand by the trustees of performance or observance, then and in either such case the trustees may, and upon the written request of the holders of 35% of the bonds hereby secured and then outstanding, shall, by notice in writing delivered to the Company declare the principal of all the bonds secured hereby and then outstanding to be due and payable immediately, and upon any such declaration the same shall become and be due and payable immediately, anything in this indenture or in said bonds to the contrary notwithstanding. This provision, however, is subject to the condition that if at any time after the principal of said bonds shall have been declared due and payable, the default for which such declaration was made and all other defaults, if any, shall be cured, before any sale of the trust estate, then and in every such case the holders of a majority in value of bonds hereby secured and then outstanding, by written notice to the Company and to the trustees, may waive such defaults and their consequences, but no such waiver shall extend to or affect any subsequent default or impair any right consequent thereon. In case the trustees shall have proceeded to enforce any right under this indenture by foreclosure or otherwise, and such proceedings shall have been discontinued or abandoned because of such waiver or for any other reason, or shall have been determined adversely to the trustees, then and in every such case the Company and the trustees shall be restored to their former position and rights hereunder in respect to the trust estate and all rights, remedies and powers of the trustees shall continue as though no such proceeding had been taken.

Section 3. In case (1) default shall be made in the payment of any principal of any bonds hereby secured, or in case (2) default shall be made in the due and punctual payment of interest upon any bonds secured hereby, and such default shall continue for the period of three months, or in case (3) default shall be made in the due observance or performance of any other covenant or condition hereby required to be observed or performed by the Company and such default shall continue for four months after written demand by the trustees, then and in every such case the trustees, personally or by attorneys, in their discretion may (a) enter in, into and upon and take possession of the trust estate and every part thereof, and may exclude the Company therefrom, and have and hold the same and use, operate, manage and control the trust estate, and manufacture, supply and sell electricity and all articles, things, and products manufactured, produced or supplied by the Company in its business, execute any and all contracts, leases and undertakings, and in general conduct and carry on the business of the Company as fully as it could do if in possession thereof, and exercise all lawful franchises and powers of the Company, and upon every such entry the trustees at the expense of the trust estate from time to time, by purchase, repair or construction, may maintain, restore and repair the trust estate, and any part or parts thereof and in the same manner and to the same extent as is usual with Companies of like character similarly situated, and make all necessary and proper renewals, replacements, alterations, additions, betterments and improvements thereto and thereon as to the trustees may seem judicious or convenient, and in such case the trustees shall be entitled to collect and receive all tolls, earnings, incomes, revenues, rents, issues and profits of the trust estate and of every part thereof and of the business thereof and after deducting the expenses of operating the trust estate and conducting the business thereof and of all repairs, renewals, replacements, alterations, additions, betterments and improvements, and all payments which may have been made for taxes, assessments and other prior or proper charges upon the trust estate, or any part thereof, and all liability incurred by the trustees hereunder, as well as just and reasonable compensation for the services of said trustees, and for the services of their attorneys and all agents, clerks, servants and other employees by them engaged and employed, they shall apply the moneys arising as aforesaid as follows: In case the principal of the bonds hereby secured shall not have become due by declaration or otherwise, then to the payment of the accrued and unpaid interest upon said bonds in the order of the maturity of the respective installments thereof, with interest thereon at the same rate of interest as borne by the bonds upon which such interest shall be in default, such payments to be made ratably to the persons entitled thereto without distinction or preference; in case the principal of the bonds hereby secured shall have become due by declaration or otherwise, then to the payment of the principal and accrued interest in the manner provided in Section 12 of this Article, and upon the payment of whatever may be due for principal and interest upon such bonds and payment of other charges required to be paid by the Company under the terms of this indenture, the premises shall be returned to the Company, subject however to the lien, covenants and conditions of this mortgage, in all respects, as if said entry had never been made. This power of entry may be exercised as often as occasion therefor may arise during the continuance of the trust created hereby; or (b) sell to the highest bidder all or any part of the trust estate, and all right, title, interest, claim and demand therein and right of redemption thereof in one lot as an entirety or in separate lots as the trustees may deem best, and in one sale or in any number of separate sales, held at one time or any number of times, which said sale or sales shall be made at public auction at such place in the City of ...., Ohio, and at such time or times and upon such terms as the trustees may fix and briefly specify in the notice of sale to be given as herein provided, or as may be provided by law, provided, always, that such sale or sales may be at such place or places and in such other manner as may be authorized or required by law; or (c) and upon request of the holders of 35% in value of the bonds outstanding hereunder shall proceed to protect and enforce their rights and the rights of the bondholders under this indenture but a suit or suits in equity or at law, whether for specific performance of any covenant or agreement contained herein, or in aid of the execution of any power herein granted, or for any foreclosure hereunder, or for the enforcement of any other proper legal or equitable remedy as the trustees, being advised by their counsel learned in the law, shall deem most effectual to protect and enforce the rights aforesaid.

Section 4. Nothing in this indenture contained, or otherwise, shall be construed as requiring the trustees or bondholders to resort to any particular property mortgaged hereunder or to waive any particular remedy for the purpose of procuring the satisfaction of the indebtedness hereby secured, but the trustees and the bondholders may resort to all or any part of the trust estate, or enforce all or any of the rights herein provided or which may be given by statute, law or equity or otherwise, in the absolute discretion of the trustees or the bondholders as the case may be.

Section 5. Notice of any sale by the trustees pursuant to any provision of this indenture shall state the time when and place where the same is to be made and shall contain a brief general description of the property to be sold and shall be sufficiently given if published once each week for six consecutive weeks prior to such sale in one daily newspaper published in the City of ...., Ohio, and once each week for six consecutive weeks in one daily newspaper published in the City of New York, N. Y.; provided that if other or different notice shall be provided by law the notice thus required shall be given.

Section 6. The trustees from time to time may adjourn any sale or sales to be by them made under any provision of this indenture by announcement at the time and place appointed for such sale or adjourned sale or sales, and without further notice or publication they may make such sale or sales at the time and place to which the same may be adjourned.

Section 7. Anything in this indenture contained to the contrary notwithstanding, the holders of a majority in value of the bonds hereby secured and then outstanding, from time to time, shall have the right to direct, subject to the limitations above described, the method and place of conducting any and all proceedings for the sale of the trust estate, or for the foreclosure of this indenture or for the appointment of a receiver, or the taking of any other proper action hereunder.

Section 8. Upon the completion of any sale or sales under this indenture the trustees shall execute and deliver to the accepted purchaser or purchasers all such deeds, conveyances, bills of sale or other instruments in writing as may be requisite, convenient, necessary or desirable to vest in the purchaser or purchasers the complete title to the property sold. The trustees and their successors are hereby appointed the true and lawful attorneys irrevocable of the Company, in its name and stead, or otherwise, to make, execute, acknowledge and deliver all such deeds, conveyances, bills of sale and other written instruments as may in the judgment of the trustees be necessary or proper to vest title in such purchaser or purchasers, the Company hereby ratifying and confirming all that its said attorneys shall lawfully do by virtue hereof.

Section 9. Any such sale or sales made under or by virtue of this indenture, whether under the power of sale hereby granted and conferred, or under and by virtue of judicial proceedings, shall operate to divest all right, title, interest, claim and demand whatsoever either at law or in equity of the Company of, in and to the property so sold and shall be a perpetual bar both at law and in equity against the Company, its successors and assigns, and against any and all persons claiming or to claim the property sold or any part thereof by, from, through or under the Company, its successors or assigns.

Section 10. The receipt of the trustees shall be a sufficient discharge to any purchaser of the trust estate, or any part thereof, sold as aforesaid, for the purchase money, and no such purchaser, or his representatives, grantees or assigns, after paying such purchase money and receiving such receipt, shall be bound to see to the application of such purchase money upon or for any trust or purposes of this indenture, or in any manner whatsoever be answerable for any loss, misapplication or nonapplication of such purchase money, or any part thereof or be bound to inquire as to the authorization, necessity, expediency or regularity of any such sale.

Section 11. In case of any such sale, whether under the power of sale hereby granted or pursuant to judicial proceedings, the principal sums of all bonds hereby secured, if not previously due, immediately thereupon shall become due and payable anything in said bonds or in this indenture contained to the contrary notwithstanding.

Section 12. The purchase money, proceeds and avails of any such sale, whether under the power of sale hereby granted or pursuant to judicial proceedings, together with all other sums which may then be held by the trustees as part of the trust estate or the proceeds thereof shall be applied as follows: (1) To the payment of the costs and expenses of such sale including the reasonable compensation of the trustees, their agents, attorneys and counsel, and all expenses, liabilities and advances made or incurred by the trustees, and all other charges which by the terms hereof, are prior to the bonds hereby secured; (2) to the payment of the whole amount then owing and unpaid upon the bonds hereby secured for principal and interest, with interest at the respective rates borne by the principal debt on the overdue installments of interest, and in case such proceeds shall be insufficient to pay in full the whole amount then due and unpaid upon said bonds, then to the payment of such principal and interest without preference or priority of principal over interest or of interest over principal or any installment of interest over any other installment of interest ratably to the aggregate amount of such principal and the accrued and unpaid interest subject, however, to the provisions of Section 1 of this Article; (3) to the payment of the surplus, if any, to the Company, its successors or assigns, or to whomsoever may be lawfully entitled to receive the same.

Section 13. At any sale or sales of the trust estate, or any part thereof, any purchaser, for the purpose of making settlement or payment for the property purchased shall be entitled to turn in any bond and any unmatured and unpaid coupons hereby secured in order that there may be credited as paid thereon the sums payable out of the net proceeds of such sale to the holder of such bonds and coupons as his ratable share of such net proceeds after allowing for the proportion of the total purchase price required to be paid in cash to pay the costs and expenses of the sale or otherwise, and any such purchaser shall be credited on account of the purchase price of the property so purchased with the sums payable out of such net proceeds on the bonds and coupons so turned in, and in the event such net proceeds are less than the amount due on such bonds and coupons, such credit shall be made by stamping on each bond the amount to be credited thereon, and the said bonds shall thereafter be returned to such purchaser. And at any such sale the trustees or any of the bondholders may bid for and purchase said property and may make payment therefor as aforesaid, and upon compliance with the terms of sale may hold, retain and dispose of such property without further accountability therefor.

Section 14. In case the Company shall make an assignment for the benefit of creditors, or in case in any judicial proceeding by any party other than the trustees, a receiver, assignee or trustee in bankruptcy shall be appointed by or for the Company, or a judgment or order entered for the sequestration of its property, or the greater part of its property be seized under any writ of attachment or other legal process, and it shall not cause said property to be released or discharged therefrom by giving bond or otherwise within twenty days after being requested so to do by the trustees, then and in every such case the trustees shall be entitled forthwith to exercise the right of entry and sale herein conferred, without awaiting the prescribed default period and may also and upon the request of the holders of 35% in value of the bonds at the time outstanding hereunder shall proceed to exercise any of the rights and powers herein conferred and provided to be exercised by the trustees upon the occurrence and continuance of default as hereinbefore provided, including the right to declare the principal of the bonds hereby secured to be due and payable and as matter of right the trustees shall thereupon be entitled to the appointment of a receiver, or receivers, of the trust estate, and of the earnings, income, rents, issues and profits thereof, with such powers as the court making such appointment shall confer.

Section 15. The Company covenants that (1) in case default shall be made in the payment of any interest upon any of the bonds at any time outstanding and secured by this indenture, and such default shall continue for the period of three months, or (2) in case default shall be made in the payment of the principal of any such bonds when the same shall become due and payable whether at the maturity of said bonds or by declaration as authorized by this indenture, or by a sale of the trust estate, as herein provided, then upon demand of the trustees, the Company will pay to the trustees for the benefit of the holders of the bonds and coupons hereby secured and then outstanding, the whole amount due and payable on all such bonds and coupons then outstanding for interest or principal or both, as the case may be, with interest at the respective rates borne by the principal obligations upon the overdue installments of interest, and in case the Company shall not pay the same forthwith upon any such demand the trustees, in their own names and as trustees of an express trust, shall be entitled to recover judgment for the whole amount so due and unpaid. The trustees shall be entitled to recover judgment as aforesaid either before or after or during the pendency of any proceedings for the enforcement of the lien of this indenture upon the trust estate, or any part thereof, and the right of the trustees to recover any such judgment shall not be affected by any sale hereunder or by the exercise of any other right, power or remedy or for the enforcement of the provisions of this indenture for the foreclosure of the lien hereof, and in case of a sale of the trust estate, or any part thereof, and of the application of the proceeds of the sale to the payment of the debt, the trustees in their own names and as trustees of an express trust shall be entitled to enforce payment of and to receive all amounts then remaining due and unpaid upon any and all of the bonds issued hereunder and then outstanding for the benefit of the holders thereof and shall be entitled to recover judgment for any portion of the debt remaining unpaid, with interest. No recovery of any such judgment by the trustees and no levy under any execution upon any such judgment upon the property subject to the lien of this indenture, or upon any other property, shall in any manner or to any extent affect the lien of the trustees upon the trust estate or any part thereof or any rights, powers or remedies of the trustees hereunder or any rights, powers or remedies of the holders of the bonds hereby secured, but such lien, rights, powers and remedies shall continue unimpaired as before. Any moneys collected by the trustees under this section shall be applied by the trustees toward the payment of the amounts then due and unpaid upon such bonds and coupons respectively, without any preference or priority of any kind except as provided in Section 1 of this Article, but ratably according to the amounts due and payable upon such bonds and coupons respectively, on the date fixed by the trustees for the distribution of such moneys.

Section 16. The holders of a majority in value of the bonds issued and outstanding hereunder at any time shall have and are hereby given the absolute right to direct the action of the trustees in and about the enforcing or waiving of any of the provisions of this indenture except the payment of the principal and interest of such bonds at the time when they become due, and the holders of a majority in value of such bonds shall have the right to direct the trustees to waive any default which may occur in the performance of any of the covenants and conditions herein contained except the payment of the principal and interest of the bonds secured hereby at the time and place provided therein, and the holders of a majority in value of said bonds shall further have the right to direct the trustees to discontinue any proceedings which they may have taken to foreclose this mortgage or deed of trust or to enforce in any way the provisions hereof, or to direct the trustees to restore to the Company the trust estate, in the event the said trustees shall have taken possession thereof, or to waive any other act or thing done or omitted to be done by the Company in violation of the terms hereof, or of any covenant on the part of the Company, under this indenture, except the payment of the principal and interest of the bonds secured hereby at the time and place provided herein. Such request of the holders of a majority in amount of bonds issued and outstanding shall be made in writing, and upon the same being made in accordance with the provisions hereof, any action by said trustees in declaring the principal of said bonds due and payable for any default so waived, shall forthwith cease and determine and become null and void and any and all proceedings commenced by said trustees to foreclose this indenture shall forthwith abate and said trustees shall forthwith surrender and redeliver to the Company the trust estate, or such part thereof, if any, as said trustees shall have become possessed of, by reason of such default, and to the extent expressed in said request any and all acts done or omitted to be done by the Company in violation hereof shall be waived and the right to take any action hereunder by reason thereof shall immediately cease and determine, but no such waiver shall extend to or affect any subsequent default or impair any right consequent thereon.

Section 17. The Company will not at any time insist upon or plead or in any manner claim or take the benefit of any stay of execution or extension law now or at any time hereafter in force, nor will it take or insist upon any benefit or advantage of any law now or hereinafter in force providing for the valuation or appraisement of the trust estate, or any part thereof, prior to any sale or sales thereof to be made pursuant to any provision herein contained or to the decree of any court of competent jurisdiction nor, after any such sale or sales, will it claim or exercise any right under any statute or otherwise to redeem the property so sold or any part thereof, and it hereby expressly waives the benefit and advantage of any such law or laws, and it covenants that it will not hinder, delay or impede the execution of any power herein granted and delegated to the trustees and that it will suffer and permit the execution of every such power as though no such law or laws had been made or enacted.

Section 18. In the event the trustees shall commence any proper proceedings at law or in equity for the purpose of foreclosing the security of this mortgage or deed of trust, or the enforcement of any right or remedy hereunder, the said trustees shall as a matter of right be entitled to the appointment, *ex parte* and without notice, of a receiver or receivers, of and for all and singular the trust estate and by and through said receiver or receivers, to take possession thereof, and of the business of the Company, and operate the same and receive the tolls, rents, revenues, issues and profits thereof.

Section 19. No holder of any bond or coupon hereby secured shall have any right to institute any suit, action or proceeding in equity or at law for the foreclosure of this indenture, or for the execution of any trust hereof, or for the appointment of a receiver or for any other remedy hereunder, unless such holder shall have previously given to the trustees written notice of such default and of the continuance thereof as hereinbefore provided, nor unless the holders of 35% in value of the bonds hereby secured and then outstanding shall have made written request upon the trustees and shall have offered them a reasonable opportunity either to proceed to exercise the powers hereinbefore granted or to institute such action, suit or proceeding in their own names, nor unless they shall have offered to the trustees adequate security and indemnity against the costs, expenses and liabilities to be incurred therein or thereby, and such notification, request and offer of indemnity are hereby declared, in each and every such case, at the option of the trustees, to be conditions precedent to the execution of the powers and trusts in this indenture and to any action or causes of action for foreclosure, or for the appointment of a receiver, or for any other remedy hereunder, it being understood and intended that no one or more of the holders of the bonds and coupons hereby secured shall have any right in any manner, by his or their action, to affect, disturb, or prejudice the lien of this indenture or to enforce any right hereunder except in the manner herein provided, and that all proceedings at law or in equity shall be instituted, had and maintained in the manner herein provided and for the equal proportionate benefit of all holders of such outstanding bonds and coupons.

Section 20.   Except as herein expressly provided to the contrary, no remedy herein conferred upon or reserved to the trustees, or to the holders of bonds hereby secured, is intended to be exclusive of any other remedy, but each and every such remedy shall be cumulative and shall be in addition to every other remedy given hereunder or now or hereafter existing at law, in equity or by statute.

Section 21.   No delay or omission of the trustees, or of any holder of bonds hereby secured, to exercise any right or power accruing upon any default continuing as aforesaid shall impair any such right or power or shall be construed to be a waiver of any such default, or acquiescence therein; and every power and remedy given by this article to the trustees or to the bondholders may be exercised from time to time and as often as may be deemed expedient by the trustees or by the bondholders.

ARTICLE V.   IMMUNITY OF INCORPORATORS, OFFICERS, DIRECTORS AND STOCKHOLDERS.

No recourse under or upon any obligation, covenant or agreement of this indenture, or upon any bond or coupon hereby secured, shall be had against any incorporator, stockholder, director or officer of the Company, past, present or future, or of any successor corporation, or any corporation in which the Company may be merged or consolidated, either directly or through the Company, or any other such corporation, by the enforcement of any assessments, penalty or contractual obligation, or by any legal or equitable proceedings by virtue of any statute or otherwise, it being expressly agreed and understood that this indenture and the obligations hereby secured are solely corporate obligations and no personal liability whatsoever shall attach to or be incurred by the incorporators, stockholders, directors or officers of the Company, past, present or future, or of any successor corporation, or corporation in which the Company may be consolidated or merged, or any of them, because of the incurring of the indebtedness hereby authorized or under or by reason of any obligations, covenants or agreements contained in this indenture or in any of the bonds or coupons hereby secured or implied therefrom, and that any and all personal liability of every name and nature, either at common law or in equity, or by statute or constitution, of every such incorporator, stockholder, director or officer is expressly waived, as a condition of and in consideration for the execution of this indenture and the issuing of such bonds and coupons.

ARTICLE VI. SALE OF MORTGAGED PROPERTY.

Section 1. In case any real property, part of the trust estate, can not be advantageously used in the proper and judicious operation of the business of the Company, or if the sale, exchange or disposition thereof has become necessary or advisable for any cause, the same, or any interest therein, may be sold or exchanged for other property; and upon request of the Company, expressed by resolution of its Board of Directors, the trustees shall have authority to release said property from the lien and effect of this indenture upon the following terms and conditions: (a) This section shall not be construed as authorizing the trustees to release the trust estate as an entirety or the substantial or greater part thereof. (b) In case of any such sale of any part of the trust estate, the price or proceeds of sale, if in excess of $1,000, or a sum equal to such price or proceeds, shall be deposited with the corporate trustee, to be held for the further security of the bonds hereby secured until paid over or applied as hereinafter provided. (c) In case of any exchange, the property received in exchange for that released shall be forthwith subjected to the lien of this indenture. (d) The consideration received for the property released shall be substantially equal to the value of the released property and whenever the trustees shall be requested to release any property pursuant to this article, the Company shall deliver to them a certified copy of the resolution of the Board of Directors above mentioned, and a written instrument, signed by the president, vice-president, secretary or treasurer of the Company, certifying that the consideration to be received for such property is substantially equal to the value thereof as above provided in this subdivision, and such resolution and instrument shall be conclusive in favor of the trustees. (e) In the event any portion of the trust estate shall be taken by the exercise of the right of eminent domain, the trustees shall, upon payment to the corporate trustee of the entire compensation awarded to the Company and the trustees, release the same from the lien and operation of this indenture. (f) All moneys received by the corporate trustee upon any such sale or release shall be applied as and when directed by the Company as follows: (1) Said corporate Trustee shall pay over to the Company out of any such proceeds sums equal to any expenditures that shall have been made by the Company for any of the purposes for which the Company is authorized to issue additional bonds as specified in Section 5 of Article 1 hereof, and all such property so purchased shall forthwith become subject to the lien of this indenture, or (2) at the option of the Company, the corporate trustee shall apply such proceeds, or any part thereof, to the purchase and retirement of bonds secured by this mortgage, and such bonds so purchased and retired shall thereupon be cancelled and delivered to the Company. (g) The resolutions, certificates, reports, and statements referred to and provided for by this section shall be full warrant to the trustees for their action on the faith thereof, and they shall incur no liability for anything done pursuant to this article; but the trustees may in their discretion, at the expense of the Company, make such other and further investigation of the facts as they may deem advisable, and may rely, and shall be absolutely protected in acting upon the results of such investigation in releasing or refusing to release any property under the provisions of this article.

Section 2. While in possession of the mortgaged premises the Company shall also have full power, in its discretion from time to time, to dispose of, free from lien of this indenture, any portion of the implements, machinery, tools, appliances, furniture and other movable property embraced within the trust estate which may have become unfit for use, replacing the same by, or substituting for the same, new implements, machinery, tools, appliances, furniture and property, which shall become subject to the lien of this indenture; provided, however, that no such sale shall substantially impair the security afforded by these presents, and that if the proceeds of such sales shall in any one year ending December 31, amount to $15,000, or more, the excess over $15,000, shall be paid to the corporate trustee and applied by it as provided in Section 1 of this Article. Settlement and payment for any such excess shall be made as of the 31st day of December on or before the 20th day of January of the ensuing year. The trustees shall have the right to require the Company at any time to furnish them satisfactory evidence of the compliance by the Company with the covenants and agreements of this and the preceding section contained.

ARTICLE VII.   EFFECT OF MERGER, CONSOLIDATION, ETC.

Section 1. Nothing in this indenture shall prevent any consolidation or merger of the Company with or into, or any conveyance, transfer or lease (subject to this indenture) of the trust estate as an entirety to any corporation lawfully entitled to acquire or lease and operate the same, provided, however, and the Company covenants and agrees that such consolidation, merger, conveyance, transfer or lease shall be upon such terms as fully to preserve, and in no respect to impair the lien, security or efficiency of this indenture, or any of the rights or powers of the trustees, or the bondholders hereunder, and provided further that any such lease shall be made expressly subject to immediate termination by the Company or by the trustees at any time during the continuance of any default hereunder, and also by the purchaser of the property so leased at any sale thereof hereunder, whether such sale be made under the power of sale herein conferred or under judicial proceedings, and provided further that upon any such consolidation, merger, conveyance, transfer or lease, the due and punctual payment of the principal and interest of all said bonds according to their tenor, and the due and punctual observance and performance of all of the covenants and conditions of this indenture to be kept and performed by the Company, shall be assumed by the corporation formed by such consolidation or into which such merger shall have been made, or to which the trust estate as an entirety as aforesaid shall be so conveyed, transferred or leased.

Section 2. In case the Company, pursuant to Section 1 of this Article, shall be consolidated with or merged into any other corporation or shall convey or transfer (subject to the lien of this indenture) the trust estate as an entirety, the corporation formed by such consolidation or into which the Company shall have been merged or which shall have received a conveyance or transfer as aforesaid, upon executing and causing to be recorded an indenture with the trustees, satisfactory to the trustees, whereby such consolidated, merged, or vendee corporation shall assume and agree to pay duly and punctually the principal and interest of the bonds issued hereunder and secured hereby in accordance with the provisions of said bonds and coupons and this indenture, and shall agree to perform and fulfil all the covenants and conditions of this indenture binding upon the Company, shall succeed to and be substituted for the Company with the same effect as if it had been named herein as party of the first part, and such consolidated, merged or vendee corporation thereupon may cause to be signed, issued and delivered, either in its own name or in the name of The *A. B.* Electric Light Company any and all such bonds which shall not theretofore have been signed by the Company and authenticated by the corporate trustee, and upon the order of such consolidated, merged or vendee corporation, in lieu of the Company, subject to the terms, conditions and restrictions of this indenture prescribing and touching the authentication and issuance of bonds, the corporate trustee shall authenticate and deliver any of such bonds which shall have been previously signed and delivered by the officers of the Company to the corporate trustee for authentication, and any of such bonds which such consolidated, merged or vendee corporation shall thereafter in accordance with the provisions of this indenture cause to be signed and delivered to the corporate trustee for such purpose shall have the same legal right and security as the bonds theretofore or thereafter issued in accordance with the terms of this indenture and as though all of said bonds had been issued at the date of the execution hereof; provided, however, that as a condition precedent to the execution of such consolidated, merged or vendee corporation and the authentication by the corporate trustee of any such additional bonds in respect to the purchase of additional property, or the making by such consolidated, merged or vendee corporation of any betterments, improvements, extensions or additions to or about its plant and property, the indenture with the trustees to be executed and caused to be recorded by the consolidated, merged or vendee corporation as in this section provided, shall contain a conveyance or transfer and mortgage in terms sufficient to include such additional property. betterments, improvements, extensions, or additions, and provided further that the lien created thereby shall have similar force, effect and standing as the lien of this indenture would have if the Company had not been consolidated with or merged into such other corporation, or had not conveyed or transferred, subject to the lien of this indenture, the trust estate as an entirety as aforesaid to such vendee corporation and had itself purchased such additional property or had made such betterments, improvements, additions or extensions and requested the authentication and delivery of bonds under the provisions of this indenture in respect thereof. The trustees may receive the certificate of any counsel selected by them as conclusive evidence that any such indenture complies with the foregoing conditions and provisions of this section.

Section 3. In case the Company pursuant to Section 1 of this Article shall be consolidated with or merged into any other corporation or shall transfer or convey, subject to the lien of this indenture, the trust estate as an entirety as aforesaid, neither this indenture nor the indenture with the trustees to be executed and caused to be recorded by such consolidated, merged or vendee corporation as in Section 2 of this Article, provided, shall become or be a lien upon any of the property or franchises of such consolidated, merged or vendee corporation, except that acquired by it from the Company and any additional property, betterments, extensions or additions thereto, and the betterments, improvements, extensions or additions to or about the plant and property of such consolidated, merged or vendee corporation made and used by it as the basis for additional bonds under this indenture, as herein provided, and such franchises, repairs and additional property as may be acquired by such consolidated, merged or vendee corporation in pursuance of the covenants herein contained, to maintain, renew and preserve the franchises covered by this indenture and to keep and maintain the property covered by this indenture in good repair or working order or in pursuance of some other covenant or agreement hereof to be kept and performed by the Company.

Section 4. The word "Company" as used in this indenture shall include such consolidated, merged or vendee corporation so complying with the provisions hereof and in such case the certificates or resolutions of the Board of Directors or officers of the Company required by Article 1, may be made by like officials of such consolidated, merged or vendee corporation.

Section 5. At any time prior to the exercise of any power by this article reserved to the Company or to a consolidated, merged or vendee corporation, the Company may surrender any power reserved to the Company, or to such consolidated, merged or vendee corporation, by delivering to the trustees an instrument in writing, executed by its president or vice-president, under its corporate seal, attested by its secretary or assistant secretary, accompanied by the affidavit of its secretary or assistant secretary, that the execution of such instrument was authorized by the vote of a majority of its entire Board of Directors at a meeting duly called and held, and thereupon the power so surrendered shall cease.

ARTICLE VIII. CONCERNING BONDHOLDERS.

Any request or other instrument required by this indenture to be signed and executed by the bondholders may be in any number of concurrent instruments of similar tenor, and may be signed or executed by such bondholders in person or by agent appointed in writing. Proof of the execution of any such request or other instrument, or of a writing appointing any such agent, and of the holding by any person of bonds transferable by delivery, shall be sufficient for any purpose of this indenture, if made in the following manner: (a) The fact and date of the execution by any person of any such request, or other instrument in writing, may be proved by the certificate of any notary public or other officer authorized to take acknowledgment of deeds, that the person signing such request or other instrument acknowledged to him the execution thereof, or by an affidavit of a witness of such execution. (b) The amount and issue numbers of bonds transferable by delivery, held by any person executing any such request or other instrument as a bondholder, and the date of his holding the same, may be proved by a certificate executed by any trust company, bank, banker, or other depositary, wherever situated, if such certificate shall be deemed by the trustees to be satisfactory, showing therein that at the date therein mentioned, such person had on deposit with such depositary the bonds described in such certificate. The ownership of registered bonds shall be proved by the register of such bonds, as provided in Section 5 of Article II hereof. Such proof shall be conclusive in favor of the trustees with regard to any action taken by them under such request or other instrument. (c) The bearer of any bond hereby secured at the time which shall not be registered as hereinbefore authorized, and the bearer of any coupon for interest on any bond, issued hereunder, whether the same shall be registered or not, may be deemed and treated by the Company and the trustees as the absolute owner of such bond or coupon, as the case may be, for the purpose of receiving payment thereof and for all other purposes, and no notice to the contrary shall affect the Company or the trustees.

ARTICLE IX. POSSESSION OF PRORERTY AND DEFEASANCE.

Section 1. Until some default shall have been made in the due and punctual payment of the interest or of the principal of the bonds hereby secured, or of some part of such interest or of the principal of the bonds hereby secured, or of some part of such interest or principal, or in the due and punctual performance or observance of some covenant or condition hereof obligatory upon the Company, and until such default shall have continued beyond the period of grace herein provided, if any, the Company shall be suffered and permitted to retain the actual possession of the trust estate and to manage, operate and enjoy the same and every part thereof, with the rights and privileges thereunto belonging, and to collect, receive, take, use and enjoy the tolls, revenues, rents, incomes, issues and profits thereof as if this indenture had not been made.

Section 2. If, when the bonds hereby secured shall have become due and payable, whether by lapse of time or by reason of the same being called for retirement, the Company shall well and truly pay or cause to be paid the whole amount of the principal moneys and interest due upon all of the bonds and coupons for interest thereon hereby secured then outstanding, or shall provide for such payment by depositing with the corporate trustee hereunder the entire amount then due thereon for principal and interest, and shall also pay or cause to be paid all other sums payable hereunder by it, and shall well and truly keep and perform all things required hereunder to be kept and performed by it according to the true intent and meaning of this indenture, then and in that case all right, title and interest of the trustees in and to the trust estate, and each and every part thereof, shall thereupon cease and determine and become void, and the trustees in such case upon demand of the Company and at the Company's cost and expense, shall execute and deliver to the Company proper instruments acknowledging satisfaction of this indenture and such deeds of release or conveyance as shall be necessary, proper or requisite to revest the Company with the trust estate, as it then exists, free and discharged from the lien of this indenture.

ARTICLE X.   CONCERNING THE TRUSTEES.

Section 1. The trustees, for themselves and their successors hereby accept the trusts and assume the duties, herein created and imposed, upon the terms and conditions following, to wit: (a) The trustees, and each of them, shall be protected, in any action taken by them, or either of them, upon any notice, resolution, vote, request, consent, certificate, affidavit, statement, bond, or other paper or document believed by the trustees, or either of them so acting, to have been passed or signed by the proper parties. (b) The trustees shall have no responsibility for the validity of this instrument or for the execution or acknowledgment thereof or for the validity of any bond issued hereunder, nor shall they, or either of them, be in anywise responsible for the breach of any covenant hereof by the Company. (c) The trustees, or either of them acting, may select and employ in and about the execution of this trust, suitable agents and attorneys, whose reasonable compensation shall be paid by the Company, or in default of such payment shall be a charge upon the trust estate and the income and proceeds thereof paramount to said bonds. (d) It shall be no part of the duty of the trustees, or either of them, to file or record this indenture as a mortgage or conveyance of real estate, or as a chattel mortgage, or as a conveyance or transfer of personal property, or to renew such mortgage or to procure any further or additional instruments of further assurance, or do any other act which may be necessary to be done for the continuance of the lien hereof, or for the giving of notice of the existence of any such lien, or for extending or supplementing the same. Neither of the trustees shall be liable for the exercise of any discretion or power hereunder or mistake or errors in judgment, nor shall any trustee be answerable for the acts or defaults of any other trustee or trustees, or otherwise in connection with this trust, except for its or his own wilful misconduct or gross negligence. (e) The trustees shall have a first lien upon the trust estate and the income and proceeds thereof for their reasonable compensation, expenses, counsel fees and compensation, and for all liabilities incurred in and about the execution of the trusts hereby created, and the exercise and performance of their powers and duties hereunder, which expenses, counsel fees and compensation the Company covenants and agrees to pay. (f) The trustees shall be under no obligation or duty to perform any act hereunder or to defend any suit in respect hereof unless reasonably indemnified, nor to take notice of any default, until they receive notice thereof, request and indemnity in the manner provided in Section 19 of Article IV hereof. The trustees shall not be bound to recognize any person as a bondholder unless and until his bonds are submitted to the trustees for inspection if required, and his title satisfactorily established, if disputed. (g) The recitals of fact herein and in said bonds contained shall be taken as statements made by the Company and shall not be construed as made by the trustees, or either of them. (h) The trustees shall not be personally liable for the debts contracted by them or either of them, nor for damages to person or property injured, nor for salaries or non-fulfillment of contracts, during any period in which the trustees shall manage or operate the trust estate upon entry as herein-before provided. (i) The trustees shall not be required at any time, before or after proceedings, to sell any part of the trust estate or take any action which they or either of them may be authorized to take hereunder, whether pursuant to the terms of this instrument, or otherwise, to give or file any bond as such trustee or trustees, the Company for itself, its successors and assigns, and the holders of any and all bonds at any time to be issued hereunder hereby forever waiving and releasing any and all right to require the trustees, or either of them, to give any such bond. (j) In case at any time it shall be necessary or proper for the trustees, or either of them, or any successor or successors of them, or either of them, to make any investigation respecting any fact preparatory to taking or not taking action or doing or not doing anything under this indenture as such trustees or trustee, the certificate of the Company over its cor-porate seal, sworn to by its president, vice-president, secretary or treasurer, shall, except as herein otherwise expressly provided, be sufficient evidence of such facts to protect the trustees, or either of them, or their successor or successors in any action, such trustees, or either of them, or their successor or successors, may take or refrain from taking by reason of the supposed existence of such fact, but the trustees may nevertheless, make such other or further investigation as they may deem proper.

Section 2. The trustees, or either of them, or any successor or successors hereafter appointed, may resign and be discharged of the trusts hereby created by written notice to the Company and by publication at least once each week for four successive weeks in a daily newspaper published in the City of ...., Ohio, and for a like number of times in a daily newspaper published in the City of New York, N. Y., and by due execution of ·the conveyance herein required.

Section 3. The trustees, or either of them, or any trustee hereafter appointed, may be removed at any time by an instrument, or concurrent instruments, in writing, signed by the holders of not less than a majority in value of the bonds hereby secured and then outstanding, upon payment of the trustees compensation and expenses to the date of such removal.

Section 4. In case at any time the trustees, or either of them, or any trustee hereafter appointed, shall resign or shall be removed or otherwise shall become incapable of acting, a successor shall be appointed by the holders of a majority in value of the bonds hereby secured, and then outstanding, by an instrument, or concurrent instruments, signed by such bondholders, or their attorneys in fact duly authorized. Provided, nevertheless, and it is hereby agreed and declared that in case at any time there shall be a vacancy in the office of any trustee hereunder, the Company, by an instrument executed by order of its Board of Directors, may appoint a trustee to fill such vacancy until a new trustee shall be appointed by the bondholders as herein authorized. The Company shall publish notice of any such appointment by it made once a week for four consecutive weeks in a daily newspaper published in the City of ...., Ohio, and for a like number of times in a daily newspaper published in the City of New York, N. Y., and any new trustee appointed by the Company shall immediately and without further act be superseded by a trustee appointed by the bondholders in the manner above provided. During any such vacancy, the remaining trustee shall have full power and authority to act and to perform all duties of the trustees hereunder, and be entitled to all their rights, authority and remedies. Any successor to the corporate trustee may be an individual, anything herein contained to the contrary notwithstanding.

Section 5. Any new trustee appointed hereunder, shall execute, acknowledge and deliver to the retiring trustee, and also to the Company, an instrument accepting such appointment and thereupon such new trustee without any further act, deed or conveyance, shall become vested with all of the estates, property, rights, powers, trusts, duties and obligations as if originally named as trustee herein; but the trustee ceasing to act shall nevertheless upon the written request of the Company or any new trustee, execute and deliver an instrument transferring to such new trustee, upon the trusts herein expressed, all of the estates, property, rights, powers and trusts of the trustee ceasing to act, and shall duly assign, transfer and deliver all properties and moneys held by it or him to the new trustee. Should any deed, conveyance or instrument in writing from the Company be required by any new trustee for more fully and certainly vesting in and confirming to such new trustee such estate, rights, powers and duties, any and all such deeds, conveyances and instruments in writing shall upon request be made, executed and delivered to it.

ARTICLE XI.   SUNDRY PROVISIONS AND DEFINITIONS.

Section 1. Nothing in this indenture expressed or implied is intended or shall be construed to confer upon any person, firm or corporation, other than the parties hereto and the holders of the bonds issued under and secured by this indenture, any right, remedy, or claim, legal or equitable, under or by reason of this indenture or any covenant, condition or stipulation thereof, this indenture, and all of its covenants, conditions and stipulations being intended to be and being for the sole and exclusive benefits of the parties hereto and of the holders from time to time of the bonds hereby secured.

Section 2. All of the covenants, stipulations, terms, undertakings and agreements herein contained by or on behalf of the Company shall bind its successors and assigns whether so expressed or not.

Section 3. For every purpose of this indenture, including the execution, issue and use of any and all bonds hereby secured, the term "Company" includes and means not only the party of the first part hereto, but also its successors and assigns and any corporation into which it may be consolidated or merged.

Section 4. The word "trustee" or "trustees" means the trustee or trustees for the time being, whether original or new.

Section 5. The word "trustee," "bond" and "bondholder" shall include the plural as well as the singular number, unless otherwise expressly indicated. The word "coupon" refers to the interest coupons attached to the bonds. secured hereby. The word "person" used with reference to a bondholder shall include associations or corporations owning such. bonds. Whenever any officer of the Company is referred to herein it shall be taken and held to mean the person who shall hold such office for the time being. The words "trust estate" shall be held to mean and include all of the property, rights, franchises and privileges at any time subject to the lien and operation of this indenture, whether the same be now owned or hereafter acquired.

In witness whereof The *A. B.* Electric Light Company by its president and secretary, thereunto lawfully authorized by action of its directors and stockholders, has hereunto set its corporate name and seal, and The *C. D.* Trust Company, by its president and secretary, thereunto lawfully authorized by action of its directors, has hereunto set its corporate name and seal, and the said *E. F.* has hereunto set his hand and seal, as of the day and year aforesaid.

The A. B. Electric Light Company,

Signed, sealed, acknowledged   By ......, **President.**
  and delivered in presence   ......, Secretary.
  of ....   (Corporate seal)
....
As to The A. B. Electric Light
  and **Power** Company.
....   The C. D. Trust Company,
....   By ......, **President.**
As to The C. D. Trust   ......, Secretary.
  Company.   (Corporate seal)
....
....   E. F.
As to E. F.

State of Ohio, ... County, ss.

Personally appeared before me a notary public in and for said county and state ...., president, and ...., secretary, of The A. B. Electric Light Company, the corporation which executed the foregoing instrument as party of the first part, to me known, and known to me to be such president and secretary, who severally acknowledged that they did sign and seal the foregoing instrument as such president and secretary for and on behalf of said corporation, and that the same is their free act and deed individually, and as such president and secretary, and the free and corporate act and deed of said The A. B. Electric Light Company. In testimony whereof I have hereunto set my hand and official seal at ...., Ohio, this .... day of ...., A. D. 19...

(Notarial seal)

                 ....,
                 Notary **Public.**

State of Ohio, ... County, ss.

Personally appeared before me, a notary public in and for said county and State, ..., president, and ...., secretary, of The

C. D. Trust Company, the corporation which executed the foregoing instrument as a party of the second part, to me known and known to me to be such president and secretary, who severally acknowledged that they did sign and seal the foregoing instrument as such president and secretary for and on behalf of said corporation and that the same is their free act and deed individually and as such president and secretary and the free and corporate act and deed of The C. D. Trust Company.

In tertimony whereof I have hereunto set my hand and official seal at ...., Ohio, this .... day of ...., A. D. 19...

(Notarial seal)   ....,
                                                  Notary Public.

State of Ohio, ... County, ss.

Personally appeared before me, a notary public in and for said county and State, the above named E. F. who acknowledged that he did sign the foregoing instrument as a party of the second part, and that the same is his free act and deed.

In testimony whereof I have hereunto set my hand and official seal at ...., Ohio, this .... day of ...., A. D. 19...

(Notarial seal)   ....,
                                                  Notary Public.

No. 256.

Bond Pooling Agreement, Authorizing Managing Committee to Sell.

Agreement made under date of ...., 19.., by and among A. B., C. D. and E. F. first parties, hereinafter sometimes called the "Managing Committee;" the signers hereof (other than the first parties, as such Managing Committee, and the Depositary hereinafter named), and any first mortgage bondholders of The ....Railway Company who may hereafter deposit their bonds and accept the certificates of deposit hereinafter provided for, second parties, hereinafter sometimes called the "Bondholders," and The .... Trust Company, third party, hereinafter sometimes called the "Depositary."

Whereas, the undersigned second parties are, severally, owners of first mortgage bonds of The .... Railway Company, of the par amount set opposite their respective names as said Bondholders as signed hereto; and,

Whereas, said Bondholders are desirous of disposing of said bonds on the terms hereinafter set forth, and to accomplish said result desire to confer and vest power and authority with reference thereto upon the Managing Committee; and,

Whereas, G. H. and Company, of ...., Ohio, have requested that they be given an option for the purchase of the bonds owned by the bondholders as hereinafter set forth, at the price of .... (..) percent of the par value of said bonds, plus accrued interest;

Now, therefore, this agreement witnesseth, that the parties hereto, for and in consideration of the premises and of the sum of one dollar ($1.00) to each in hand paid by the other, the receipt whereof is hereby acknowledged, do hereby promise and agree to and with each other as follows:

FIRST. The Bondholders do hereby deposit with the Depositary first mortgage bonds of The .... Railway Company, of the par value set opposite the name of each of the Bondholders as their signatures appear hereto, said bonds being a part of a total authorized issue of .... million dollars ($....), par value, and secured by a first mortgage or deed of trust dated ...., 19.., to The .... Trust Company, of ...., as Trustee, said bonds so deposited to be by said Depositary held to and for the uses and purposes, and with the powers and duties in relation thereto as follows:

(a) To hold the same until ...., 19.., unless sooner sold by the Managing Committee as hereinafter provided at a price not less than ...., (..) percent of the par value of said bonds, plus accrued interest to date of sale.

(b) To distribute the proceeds thereof upon the receipt of the same, in the event of a sale by said Managing Committee, among the persons and parties entitled thereto, in accordance with the provisions of this agreement.

(c) To distribute the interest collected upon said bonds among the persons and parties entitled thereto, in accordance with the provisions of this agreement.

SECOND. It is mutually understood and agreed that said Managing Committee shall have power and authority, during the term of this agreement, to sell said bonds, or any or all thereof, so delivered to said Depositary, at a price not less than .... (..) percent of the par value of said bonds, plus accrued interest to date of sale, by the unanimous agreement of the members of said Managing Committee, and in the event of a sale being made as aforesaid, the proceeds thereof shall be paid to the said Depositary.

The Managing Committee shall have authority and power to enter into contracts or to give options for the sale of said bonds, at not less than the price aforesaid, during the term of this agreement.

THIRD. The Depositary, upon the deposit of bonds hereunder, agrees to issue to said Bondholders certificates showing the interest of said Bondholders in and to said bonds, or the proceeds thereof, and the said certificates to be issued by the Depositary shall be in such form and contain such terms as the Depositary shall decide, subject at all times to the terms of this agreement. Said certificates, however, shall be in assignable form, subject to such rules with reference thereto as the Depositary may establish.

FOURTH. It is further understood and agreed that the Depositary shall have authority, during the term of this agreement, to collect and receive all moneys due and paid upon said interest coupons attached to said bonds aforesaid, and as and when such interest is paid to it, shall distribute the same, within ten (10) days after the receipt thereof by the Depositary, to the persons entitled thereto, as evidenced by said certificate of deposit aforesaid. The persons entitled to such interest, or to the proceeds of the sale of said bonds in case of their sale as herein provided, or to any bonds in the possession of the Depositary remaining unsold at the expiration or termination of this agreement, shall be the certificate holders of record at the date of the maturity of said coupons, or of the sale of said bonds, or any part thereof, or of the expiration or termination of this agreement.

FIFTH. It is further understood and agreed that the said Depositary shall not, until the expiration or termination of this contract, deliver any of the bonds so placed in its hands, or any part thereof, to any of the parties hereto, except to said Managing Committee, and to said Managing Committee only for the purpose of sale as herein provided, and then only upon receipt by said Depositary of the proceeds of the sale of said bonds, in the event of any such sale, and that in case said bonds, or any thereof, are sold as herein provided, said Depositary shall deliver the same to the Managing Committee, upon receiving the proceeds of the sale of said bonds; and that in case said bonds are not sold on or before the expiration or termination of this agreement, the said Depositary shall deliver said bonds to the holders entitled thereto, according to the provisions of this contract and the certificates issued in pursuance hereof, upon the surrender of said certificates by the holders thereof.

SIXTH. In case of the death, resignation or inability to act of either or any of said members of the Managing Committee, during the term hereof, the surviving member or members of said Managing Committee shall have the power to appoint a successor or successors; and in case of the death, resignation or inability to act of all the members of said Managing Committee, the said Depositary shall have authority to choose and appoint a Managing Committee.

SEVENTH. The certificates of deposit to be issued under this agreement shall be transferable only by assignment in writing on the back thereof, which assignment shall be witnessed, and shall transfer all interest in said certificate so assigned, which assignment may be transferred subject to the rules and regulations of the Depositary and registered on its books, and a new certificate or certificates evidencing a like interest in said bonds, may be issued by the Depositary in lieu of the certificate so assigned.

EIGHTH. It is expressly understood and agreed that there shall be no charge made against the depositing Bondholders hereunder for any costs, expenses or services of the Depositary or the Managing Committee.

NINTH. This agreement shall be binding upon the heirs, executors, administrators and assigns of the parties hereto, and as to the said Bondholders, the agreement of each is several and individual, and shall be binding upon such of said Bondholders as sign this agreement, without regard to the fact that the same may not be signed by all the owners of the first mortgage bonds of The .... Railway Company. The deposit of bonds or the acceptance, by assignment or otherwise, of certificates of deposit as herein provided, shall constitute the persons, firms or corporations depositing said bonds or so accepting such certificates of deposit, parties hereto for all purposes, as fully as though such persons, firms or corporations had signed this agreement, or a duplicate hereof.

TENTH. The Managing Committee agrees to act as such, and to faithfully discharge the duties imposed upon them as such Managing Committee; and the Depositary agrees to perform the duties herein delegated to it; it being understood and agreed, however, that no liability hereunder shall attach to the Managing Committee, or either member thereof, or to said Depositary, on account of any representation, statement or recital herein contained or made, or for the genuineness, regularity or authenticity of the bonds deposited hereunder, or for the lien or interest created thereby, and that beyond the obligation to perform their direct obligations assumed hereunder, said Managing Committee and the Depositary shall be liable to the Bondholders only for want of good faith or failure to exercise reasonable care.

ELEVENTH. All actions to be taken hereunder by the Managing Committee shall be in pursuance of the unanimous agreement of the members of said Committee.

TWELFTH. This agreement shall be in force and effect until ...., 19.., but may be terminated at any time by the Managing Committee, by written notice thereof signed by the Managing Committee and by the Depositary, and upon the expiration or termination of this agreement the bonds, or the proceeds thereof, or both, represented by the certificates of deposit issued hereunder, shall then be distributed to the persons entitled thereto, as herein provided.

THIRTEENTH. It is further agreed that, for convenience in executing the same, several copies of this agreement may be made, each of which shall be treated as an original, and that the signing of any of said copies shall constitute an execution of this contract by the person, firm or corporation signing the same, to the same extent as if all the signatures made in the execution of this agreement were affixed to a single copy thereof.

In witness whereof, the Managing Committee and the Depositary have subscribed to an original hereof, and the said Bondholders, parties of the second part, have subscribed said original or a counterpart thereof, all as of the day and year first above written.

A. B.
C. D.
E. F.
Managing Committee.
The .... Trust Company,
Depositary,
By ...., Treasurer.
Par Amount of Bonds.

Bondholders.

....
....
....
....

....
....
....
....

No. 257.

Bond Holders' Agreement; Corporation in Default for Interest on Mortgage Bonds.

This agreement made and concluded at .·... this .... day of ...., 19.., by and between A. B., C. D. and E. F., hereinafter termed the "Committee" parties of the first part, and such holders of the first mortgage bonds of The .... Electric Railway Company secured by its mortgage dated ...., 19.., as shall become parties hereto in the manner hereinafter provided, hereinafter termed "Bondholders," parties of the second part, witnesseth, that

Whereas, said The .... Electric Railway Company issued its first mortgage bonds dated ......, 19.., secured by a mortgage executed by said Electric Railway Company to The .... Trust Company of .... as trustee and recorded ...., and said Electric Railway Company has made default in the payment of certain of its obligations, including the interest due on said bonds ......, 19.., and receivers have been appointed for the property of said Electric Railway Company, and it is necessary that the holders of said bonds unite for the protection of their common interests: Now, therefore, the depositing bondholders, said parties of the second part, do hereby severally agree, each with the other and others and with the committee, as follows, to wit:

FIRST. This agreement shall be signed by the memebers of said committee and deposited with The .... Trust Company of ...., hereinafter termed the "Depositary." The holders of any of such mortgage bonds may become parties to this agreement and obtain the benefits thereof by depositing, on the terms of this agreement, on or before such date as the committee may fix or limit, their bonds with the coupons for interest thereon due ...., 19.., and subsequent thereto. Registered bonds must be accompanied by suitable transfers thereof.

Such depositing bondholders shall receive certificates of deposit issued by said depositary for the bonds and coupons deposited, which certificates shall be in such form, and shall be transferable, subject to this agreement, in such manner as the committee shall approve. Upon the transfer of any certificate the transferee shall for all purposes be substituted for the prior holder under this agreement. Each depositor hereunder, and each holder of a certificate of deposit issued hereunder, and each transferee of any such certificate, shall be bound by all the provisions of this agreement as fully as if he had signed the same. The committee and the depositary may treat each certificate of deposit as a negotiable instrument and the holder for the time being as the absolute owner thereof, and shall not be affected by any notice to the contrary.

The committee in its discretion, with or without prior publication of notice, may fix or limit a date after which holders of such bonds shall not be entitled to deposit their bonds hereunder: and any such holders who fail to deposit their bonds and coupons on or before any date so fixed or limited will not be entitled to deposit the same or to become parties to this agreement or to share in the benefits thereof, and shall acquire no rights hereunder; but the committee, in its discretion, either generally or in special instances, and on such terms and conditions as it shall prescribe, may, by a written direction filed with said depositary, extend the time for receiving deposits or authorize the receipt of any deposit at a later date, or waive any default.

Each depositing bondholder, for himself, but not for the others, by the deposit of his bonds, assigns and transfers the bonds and coupons deposited by him, to the committee and their survivors and their successors, as joint tenants, and agrees that the committees shall be vested with all the rights and powers of owners thereof; and all bonds and coupons deposited shall be received and held by the depositary subject to the order of the committee.

SECOND. The depositing bondholders authorize and request

the committee in its discretion, as owners and holders of said deposited bonds, to demand, receive and collect the interest and principal of the deposited bonds; to declare due the principal of said bonds, and to revoke any such declaration; to request the trustee of said mortgage to institute foreclosure or other proceedings; to institute or become parties to any legal proceedings which any of the depositing bondholders may institute or become parties to, and to become parties to, or exercise control over, all legal proceedings now pending or hereafter instituted in which the holders of said bonds are or may be interested, including the right to apply for receivers or for the removal of receivers and the substitution of other receivers; to exercise every right and power conferred upon owners or holders of said bonds by the terms thereof, or by the mortgage securing the same or otherwise; and generally to do any and all things which the committee in its discretion may deem necessary or expedient for any of the foregoing purposes, or for the protection of the interests of the depositing bondholders, or of the holders of the certificates issued hereunder, or for the purpose of carrying out any of the provisions of this agreement; it being hereby expressly declared that the specification of particular powers shall not be construed as limiting any of the general powers hereby conferred.

THIRD. The committee may borrow such sums of money not exceeding in the aggregate three percent of the par value of the bonds which shall be deposited hereunder, as may be required for the purpose of paying the expenses incurred by the committee hereunder, and the reasonable compensation of the committee, and it may charge or pledge the deposited bonds pro rata for the redemption of any sums borrowed; and if any sum shall be collected by the committee upon the deposited bonds and coupons the committee may apply such moneys to the payment of any sums so borrowed, and to the payment of such expenses and compensation.

FOURTH. The committee is hereby authorized and empowered to adopt, or approve of, a plan or agreement for the reorganization or readjustment of the interests of all or any of the bondholders and other creditors and parties interested in said railway company, which plan or agreement may provide for the purchase of all or any of the property of said railway company at any foreclosure or other sale and for the organization of a new Company to acquire such property and for the issue, disposition and distribution of all or any of the stock and bonds of such new Company, and for raising any sums in cash deemed necessary for improvements, working capital, expenses and other purposes. Any such plan or agreement may contain any terms and provisions and may confer upon the committee, or upon any other committee designated in such plan or agreement any powers which the committee hereunder may deem reasonable and proper; and full power and discretion in that behalf is hereby conferred upon the committee, subject to the right of dissent and withdrawal next hereinafter referred to. When the committee shall have adopted or approved of any such plan or agreement, a copy thereof shall be lodged with the depositary hereunder, at its office in the city of ...., with the written adoption or approval thereof endorsed thereon by majority of the members of the committee, and thereupon a brief notice of the fact of the adoption or approval of a plan or agreement of reorganization or readjustment shall be published by the committee at least twice in each week for two successive weeks in two newspapers published in the city of ...., and such lodgement of said plan or agreement and publication of notice thereof shall be conclusive notice to all depositing bondholders and to all holders of certificates of deposit of the adoption or approval of such plan or agreement by the committee. Any then holders of certificates of deposit, who, within thirty days after the first publication of such notice, shall surrender their certificates and pay a ratable amount of the obligations and expenses and reasonable compensation of the committee to the date of such surrender (not exceeding in the aggregate three percent of the par value of the deposited bonds), shall thereupon be entitled to withdraw from such plan or agreement and to receive from the depositary the respective bonds in respect of which such certificates were issued (or a like amount of bonds of the same issue) and any sums realized thereon remaining in the hands of the committee and such certificate holders by such withdrawal shall thereupon and without any further act be released from this agreement and cease to have any rights hereunder or under such plan or agreement. All holders of certificates who shall not exercise such right within said thirty days after such first publication to withdraw the bonds in respect of which their certificates were issued shall be conclusively deemed to have finally assented to and adopted such plan or agreement (whether they had actual notice or not), and shall be bound by all the terms and provisions thereof without further act or notice and the committee shall be fully authorized to carry out such plan or agreement irrespective of the parties withdrawing, and shall have full power and authority to use, transfer or deliver, under or in accordance with such plan or agreement, the deposited bonds and coupons, which shall not have been withdrawn as aforesaid, as fully as though such plan or agreement were a part hereof and had been expressly assented to by the depositing bondholders and the holders of the certificates of deposit issued hereunder.

FIFTH. The committee undertakes in good faith to endeavor to protect the interests of the depositing bondholders under this agreement, but the members of the committee assume no further responsibility. In case the committee for any cause should deem it inexpedient to proceed further under this agreement, it shall cause notice thereof to be published at least twice in two newspapers in the city of ...., and shall return to the holders of certificates of deposit issued hereunder the bonds represented by such certificates (or like amount of bonds of the same issue) and any sums realized thereon remaining in the hands of the committee, upon surrender of the respective certificates of deposit and payment of ratable amounts of the obligations, expenses and reasonable compensation of the committee.

SIXTH.   The committee may employ such counsel, attorneys and agents as it may deem necessary and may fix the compensation for their services and may make such other expenditures as it shall deem necessary for any of the purposes of this agreement, and it may procure the performance of any of the matters herein provided for by agents, trustees or substitutes.

In all cases a majority of the members of the committee, present in person or by proxy, shall constitute a quorum, but no action shall be taken except with the assent of the majority of the whole committee, such assent being given in person or by proxy at a meeting, or in writing without a meeting. Such action of a majority shall constitute the action of the committee, and shall have the same effect as if assented to by the whole committee.

The committee shall keep a record of its acts and proceedings. Any member of the committee, by written appointment, may empower any other member of the committee, or any person approved by a majority of the remaining members of the committee, to vote and to act as his proxy with all the powers of the member making the appointment. Any member of the committee may at any time resign by giving notice in writing to the chairman or secretary of the committee, and the committee may settle any account or transaction with such member or with the personal representatives of a deceased member and give a full release and discharge upon any such resignation. Any vacancy in the committee caused by resignation, death, or otherwise, may be filled by appointment in writing by a majority of the remaining members; and the committee may in like manner add to its number by appointing an additional member or additional members. All title, rights, duties and powers vested in the committee hereunder shall from time to time vest in the members of the committee for the time being without any further appointment, transfer or assignment whatsoever. The present or future members of the committee may be or become pecuniarily interested in any of the bonds or matters which are the subject of this agreement including the right to become members of any syndicate formed in connection therewith.

SEVENTH. No member of the committee shall be liable in any case for the acts of the other members or of the depositary, nor for the acts of any attorney, trustee or agent selected in good faith, nor shall any member be personally liable for any error of judgment, or mistake of law, but each shall be liable for his own willful malfeasance. The members of the committee shall be entitled to receive reasonable compensation for their services. The holders of certificates of deposit, by receipt of any securities or cash distributed by the committee and surrender of their certificates, release and discharge the committee from all liability.

This agreement shall extend to and be obligatory upon the respective heirs, executors, administrators, successors and assigns of the parties hereto.

In testimony whereof, the members of the committee have hereunto set their hands the day and year first above written and the parties of the second part have executed this agreement by depositing their bonds and coupons and accepting certificates of deposit therefor.

PART III.

CONSTITUTION OF OHIO.

PROVISIONS AFFECTING CORPORATIONS.

Art. VIII. § 4. Credit of state. The state shall not become joint owner or stockholder.—The credit of the state shall not, in any manner, be given or loaned to, or in aid of, any individual association or corporation whatever; nor shall the state ever hereafter become a joint owner, or stockholder, in any company or association in this state, or elsewhere, formed for any purpose whatever.

Under the constitution of 1802 the general assembly was authorized to aid in the construction of internal improvements by subscriptions to the stock of corporations created for such purpose, and to levy taxes to pay therefor; and to authorize political subdivisions of the state to subscribe to such stock, and to levy taxes to pay therefor.

See Cincinnati, etc., R. R. Co. v. Commissioners, 1 O. S. 77 (1852); Stubenville, etc., R. R. Co. v. Trustees, 1 O. S. 105 (1852); Loomis v. Spencer, 1 O. S. 153 (1853); Cass v. Dillon, 2 O. S. 607 (1853); Thompson v. Kelly, 2 O. S. 647 (1853); State ex rel. v. Commissioners, 6 O. S. 280 (1856); State ex rel. v. Van Horne, 7 O. S. 327 (1857); State ex rel. v. Trustees, 8 O. S. 394 (1858); Weaver v. Cherry, 8 O. S. 564 (1858); State ex rel. v. Commissioners, 11 O. S. 183 (1860); State ex rel. v. Commissioners, 12 O. S. 596 (1861); Trustees v. Springfield, etc., R. R. Co., 12 O. S. 624 (1861); Commissioners v. Nichols, 14 O. S. 260 (1863); Fosdick v. Perrysburg, 14 O. S. 472 (1863); Walker v. Cincinnati, 21 O. S. 14 (1871).

A county agricultural society is of a public character, not for profit, and public aid is not prohibited by this section.

Commissioners v. Brown, 1 N. P. n. s. 357; 14 L. D. 241 (1903).

§ 5. No assumption of debts by the state.—The state shall never assume the debts of any county, city, town, or township, or of any corporation whatever, unless such debt shall have been created to repel invasion, suppress insurrection, or defend the state in war.

See Walker v. Cincinnati, 21 O. S. 14, 52 (1871).

§ 6. Counties, cities, towns or townships not authorized to become stockholders.

—No laws shall be passed authorizing any county, city, town or township, by vote of its citizens, or otherwise, to become a stockholder in any joint stock company, corporation, or association whatever; or to raise money for, or to loan its credit to, or in aid of, any such company, corporation, or association; provided, that nothing in this section shall prevent the insuring of public buildings or property in mutual insurance associations or companies. Laws may be passed providing for the regulation of all rates charged or to be charged by any insurance company, corporation or association organized under the laws of this state or doing any insurance business in this state for profit. (As amended 1912, in effect January 1, 1913.)

This section prohibits business partnership with private corporations, but does not prohibit the state or its subdivisions from making improvement on its or their sole account.
Walker v. Cincinnati, 21 O. S. 14, 54, 55 (1871).

Acts held invalid under this section. Authorizing counties, etc., to levy certain taxes to build a railroad, to be used as a part of the system of a private corporation (69 v. 84).
Taylor v. Commissioners, 23 O. S. 22 (1872). See Wyscaver v. Atkinson, 37 O. S. 80 (1881).
Authorizing municipalities to contract with a private corporation to build a waterworks and lease it back to the municipality.
Alter v. Cincinnati, 56 O. S. 47 (1897).
A municipality can not purchase land for the purpose of donating it to a corporation or person as an inducement to build and operate a manufacturing plant therein.
Markley v. Mineral City, 58 O. S. 430 (1898). Rep. Atty. Gen. 1911-1912, p. 388.

Laws and transactions held valid under this section. Authorizing county commissioners to purchase toll roads (G. C. § 7405).
Ferris v. Commissioners, 9 C. C. n. s. 169; 19 C. D. 622 (1907); affd. no rep. 80 O. S. 755.
Authorizing county commissioners to construct roads (64 v. 80).
State v. Commissioners, 17 O. S. 558 (1867).
Ordinance authorizing appropriation of land, to enable county commissioners to build an avenue thereon.
Purcell v. Riverside, 1 C. C. 12; 1 C. D. 7 (1885).
Authorizing municipalities to build railroads within their municipal limits (66 v. 80).
Walker v. Cincinnati, 21 O. S. 14 (1871).
See Cincinnati v. Taft, 63 O. S. 141 (1900).
Trustees v. Insurance Co., 138 U. S. 69; 6 O. F. D. 686 (1891).
Providing for the sale of a railroad owned by a municipality.
Cincinnati v. Dexter, 55 O. S. 93 (1896).
A lease by a municipality of terminal facilities of a railroad owned by it.
Cincinnati v. Ferguson, 12 L. D. 439 (1902); affd. no rep. 66 O. S. 658.
Operation by private company of municipal owned railroad, under a lease.

Railway v. Railway, 3 N. P. n. s. 109; 16 L. D. 777 (1904).
Deposit of public funds in public depositories.
State v. Bowers, 4 C. C. n. s. 345; 16 C. D. 326 (1903); aff'd, no rep. 70 O. S. 423.
Public aid to agricultural societies.
Commissioners v. Brown, 1 N. P. n. s. 357; 14 L. D. 241 (1903).

Art. XIII. § 1. Corporate powers.—The general assembly shall pass no special act conferring corporate powers.

Scope of section. No distinction can be made between private and municipal corporations, and the inhibition extends as well to the conferring of additional powers on an existing corporation as to the creation of a new one. State ex rel. v. Mitchell, 31 O. S. 592, 607 (1877).

Sections are prospective only. The sections of Art. XIII are prospective and not retrospective in their intent and application.
Citizens Bank v. Wright, 6 O. S. 318 (1856).
State ex rel. v. Roosa, 11 O. S. 16 (1860).
State ex rel. v. Trustees, 8 O. S. 394 (1858).

Acts held to be in violation of this section. Authorizing the reorganization of one corporation.
Atkinson v. M. & C. R. R. Co., 15 O. S. 21 (1864).
Authorizing one municipality to issue bonds for repair of a hospital and to levy a tax for their payment.
Cincinnati v. Trustees, 66 O. S. 440 (1902).
See also State ex rel. v. Cincinnati, 23 O. S. 445 (1872).
State ex rel. v. Davis, 23 O. S. 434 (1872).
Dividing cities, having substantially the same conditions and characteristics, into classes and grades so that each city is placed in a class or grade by itself, and conferring corporate power on a single city by such classification.
State ex rel. v. Jones, 66 O. S. 453 (1902).
State ex rel. v. Beacom, 66 O. S. 491 (1902).

Acts held not to violate this section. Permission to surrender corporate powers.
P. & O. Canal Co. v. Commissioners, 27 O. S. 14 (1875).
An ordinance of a municipality permitting a street railway company to extend its tracks.
Sims v. Street Railroad Co., 37 O. S. 556 (1882).
A fair and reasonable classification of street railway corporations, to which an extension of franchises might be granted by municipalities.
Railway v. Horstman, 72 O. S. 93, 105-107 (1905).
Permission to building and loan associations to receive, under some circumstances, usurious rates for loans.
Brooklyn, etc., Co. v. Desnoyers, 4 C. C. n. s. 337, 343; 16 C. D. 352 (1904).
Cramer v. Loan & Tr. Co., 72 O. S. 395 (1905).
Providing for the abandonment of a state canal and for leasing it to a specified railroad company.
Vought v. Railroad Co., 58 O. S. 123 (1898).

§ 2. Corporations; how formed.—Corporations may be formed under general laws; but all such laws may, from time to time, be altered or repealed. Corporations may be classified and there may be conferred upon proper boards,

commissions or officers, such supervisory and regulatory powers over their organization, business and issue and sale of
stocks and securities, and over the business and sale of the
stocks and securities of foreign corporations and joint stock
companies in this state, as may be prescribed by law. Laws
may be passed regulating the sale and conveyance of other
personal property, whether owned by a corporation, joint
stock company or individual. (As amended 1912, in effect
January 1, 1913.)

This section must be construed in connection with section 2, article
1, which provides that "no special privileges or immunities shall ever be
granted that may not be altered or repealed."
Shields v. State, 26 O. S. 86, 94 (1875).

What are general laws. See State ex rel. v. Sherman, 22 O. S. 411
(1872).

Consolidated companies subject to this section. Consolidated companies organized in pursuance of the general laws are subject to this
section.
Shields v. State, 26 O. S. 86 (1875); (affirmed 95 U. S. 319).

Power to regulate rates of fare. Under this section the general
assembly has power to alter and regulate rates of fare chargeable by common carrier companies.
Shields v. State, 26 O. S. 86 (1875); (affirmed 95 U. S. 319).

Right to alter or repeal. The property of a corporation can not be
taken without due process of law under authority of this section.
State v. Lake Erie Iron Co., 33 W. L. B. 6; 51 O. S. 632 (1894).
A corporation is a "person" within the 14th amendment of the federal constitution forbidding the deprivation of property without due
process of law.
Covington, etc., Co. v. Sandford, 164 U. S. 578 (1896).
See generally Milan, etc., Road Co. v. Husted, 3 O. S. 578, 583
(1854); Bank of Toledo v. Bond, 1 O. S. 622 (1853); Lake Shore, etc.,
Ry. Co. v. Cincinnati, etc., Ry. Co., 30 O. S. 604 (1876); State ex rel.
v. Columbus Gas Co., 34 O. S. 572 (1878); Zanesville v. Gas Light Co.,
47 O. S. 1 (1889); Harper v. Ampt, 32 O. S. 291 (1877).

Vested rights. The inalienable right to acquire, hold and dispose
of property, and to make contracts relating thereto, appertains to cor-
porations as well as to individuals.
Stewart v. Gardner, 10 C. C. n. s. 408; 20 C. D. 218 (1907); affd.
no rep. 78 O. S. 451.
Shaw v. Railway Co., 173 Fed. 746, 751; 8 O. L. R. 43, 49 (C. C.
A. 1909).
Ohio ex rel. v. Neff, 52 O. S. 375 (1895).

§ 3. Dues from corporations; how secured.—Dues from
private corporations shall be secured by such means as
may be prescribed by law, but in no case shall any stockholder be individually liable otherwise than for the unpaid
stock owned by him or her; except that stockholders of corporations authorized to receive money on deposit shall be
held individually responsible, equally and ratably, and not

one for another, for all contracts, debts, and engagements of such corporations, to the extent of the amount of their stock therein, at the par value thereof, in addition to the amount invested in such shares. No corporation not organized under the laws of this state, or of the United States, or person, partnership or association shall use the word "bank", "banker" or "banking", or words of similar meaning in any foreign language, as a designation or name under which business may be conducted in this state unless such corporation, person, partnership or association shall submit to inspection, examination and regulation as may hereafter be provided by the laws of this state. (As amended September 1912, in effect January 1, 1913.)

Prior to 1903 a double liability was imposed on stockholders of all corporations. In 1903 the double liability was abolished, but was restored as to bank stockholders in 1912.

The amendment of 1903 (see 95 v. 961) was held to be self-executing so as to repeal by implication the statutes then in force and to relieve stockholders from double liability for debts incurred by the corporation subsequent to November 23, 1903.

Sheets Mfg. Co. v. Neer Mfg. Co., 4 N. P. n. s. 201; 17 L. D. 119 (C. P. 1906).

See G. C. § 8687 and notes.

The former provision imposing a double liability on stockholders in all corporations was held not to be self-executing so as to sustain an action to enforce liability in federal courts against nonresidents, where no proceeding had been brought in Ohio under G. C. § 8690 et seq.

Middletown N. B. v. Railway Co., 197 U. S. 394 (1905).

Irvine v. Elliott, 203 Fed. 82 (D. C. 1913).

For decisions under this section prior to amendment of 1903 see:

State ex rel. v. Sherman, 22 O. S. 411 (1872).

Kreisser v. Ashtabula, etc., Co., 2 C. C. n. s. 597; 14 C. D. 313 (1901).

§ 4. Corporate property subject to taxation.—The property of corporations, now existing or hereafter created, shall forever be subject to taxation, the same as the property of individuals.

Double taxation prohibited. The limitation in this section and in article 12, section 3 of the constitution prohibit the double taxation of corporations.

Cleveland Trust Co. v. Lander, 62 O. S. 266, 280 (1900).

But such limitations apply only to the taxation of property, not of privileges and franchises. An additional tax may be imposed upon franchises.

Southern Gum Co. v. Laylin, 66 O. S. 578, 596 (1902).

Property. What constitutes. A corporate franchise is not property.

Exchange Bank v. Hines. 3 O. S. 1, 7 (1853).

Baker v. Cincinnati, 11 O. S. 540 (1860).

Ashley v. Ryan, 49 O. S. 525.

Power to surrender right to tax. See Milan, etc., Road Co. v. Husted, 3 O. S. 578 (1854); Debolt v. Ohio, etc., Trust Co., 1 O. S. 563 (1853); Mechanics' Bank v. Debolt, 1 O. S. 591 (1853); Knoup v. Piqua Bank, 1 O. S. 603 (1853); Bank of Toledo v. Bond, 1 O. S. 622 (1853); Matheny v. Golden, 5 O. S. 361 (1856); State ex rel. v. Moore, 5 O. S. 444 (1856); Ross County Bank v. Lewis, 5 O. S. 447 (1856); Piqua Bank v. Knoup, 16 How. (U. S.) 369 (1854).

Exemptions from taxation by general laws operating alike on corporations and individuals.
See Const. article XII, § 2.
Little v. Seminary, 72 O. S. 417 (1905).
Humphreys v. State, 70 O. S. 67, 85 (1904).
Watterson v. Halliday, 77 O. S. 150 (1907).

§ 5. Right of way.—No right of way shall be appropriated to the use of any corporation, until full compensation therefor be first made in money, or first secured by a deposit of money, to the owner, irrespective of any benefit from any improvement proposed by such corporation; which compensation shall be ascertained by a jury of twelve men, in a court of record, as shall be prescribed by law.

See Const., article I, § 19. G. C. §§ 8759, 8760, 11038 et seq.

§ 7. Associations with banking powers.—No act of the general assembly, authorizing associations with banking powers, shall take effect until it shall be submitted to the people, at the general election next succeeding the passage thereof, and be approved by a majority of all the electors, voting at such election.

The words "banking powers" in this section relate only to the power to issue notes and bills intended to circulate as money. The incorporation of banks of deposit and discount may be authorized by the legislature without a referendum.
Dearborn v. Bank, 42 O. S. 617 (1885).
Bates v. Peoples, etc., Ass'n, 42 O. S. 655 (1885).
See also Forest City, etc., Ass'n v. Gallagher, 25 O. S. 208, 216 (1874).

PART IV.

Section 31-1. (Seal.) The commission shall have an official seal, with the words "The Tax Commission of Ohio" and such other design as the commission may prescribe engraved thereon, by which it shall authenticate its proceedings and of which the courts shall take judicial notice. (June 2, 1911, 102 v. 225, § 8; 101 v. 400.)

Section 32. (Seal; of what it may consist.) Where an official or a corporate seal is required to be affixed to an instrument of writing, an impression of such seal upon either wax, wafer or other adhesive substance, or upon the paper or material on which such instrument is written, shall be alike valid and sufficient. Private seals are abolished, and the affixing of what has been known as a private seal to an instrument shall not give such instrument additional force or effect, or change the construction thereof. (R. S. Sec. 4; April 14, 1884, 81 v. 198; 80 v. 79; Rev. Stat. 1880; 29 v. 349, § 1; S. & C. 1385.)

Section 121. (Bankers, etc., ineligible to act as notaries in certain cases.) No banker, broker, cashier, director, teller or clerk of a bank, banker or broker, or other person holding an official relation to a bank, banker, or broker, shall be competent to act as notary public in any matter in which such bank, banker, or broker is interested. (R. S. Sec. 111; March 23, 1893, 90 v. 119; April 11, 1876, 73 v. 206.)

Liability of bank for default of notary.
Bank v. Butler, 41 O. S. 519 (1885); s. c. 153 U. S. 436.

Section 176. (Fees to be collected by secretary of state.) The secretary of state shall charge and collect the following fees for official services:

1. For filing articles of incorporation of a corporation whose capital stock is ten thousand dollars or under, ten dollars; of a corporation whose capital stock is over ten

thousand dollars, one-tenth of one per cent upon the authorized capital stock of such corporation.

2. For filing certificate of increase of capital stock of a corporation, if the increase is ten thousand dollars or under, ten dollars; if the increase is over ten thousand dollars, one-tenth of one per cent upon the proposed increase of capital.

3. For filing articles of agreements of consolidation of corporations having a capital stock, one-tenth of one per cent upon the authorized capital stock of the new corporation, created by such articles of agreements of consolidation, but not less than ten dollars in any case; but no credit shall be allowed for fees previously paid by any of the constituent corporations, parties to such consolidation.

4. For filing articles of incorporation of a mutual life insurance corporation having no capital stock, or of other mutual corporations not organized strictly for benevolent or charitable purposes and having no capital stock, twenty-five dollars, except as hereinafter provided.

5. For filing articles of incorporation formed for religious, benevolent or literary purposes; or of corporations not organized for profit and not mutual in their character, or of religious or secret societies; or societies or associations composed exclusively of any class of mechanics, express, telegraph, railroad or other employes, and formed exclusively for the mutual protection and relief of members thereof and their families, two dollars.

6. For filing articles of incorporation of a building and loan association, ten dollars; for filing certificate of increase of the capital stock of such a corporation, five dollars.

7. For filing certificate of reduction of capital stock of a corporation, five dollars.

8. For filing certified copy of the acceptance of any provision of existing law by a corporation incorporated prior to the adoption of the present constitution, five dollars.

9. For filing an amendment to articles of incorporation, twenty cents for each hundred words, but in no case less than five dollars.

10. For filing certificates of extension of line of a railroad corporation, certificate of change of termini, certificate of intention of a corporation to construct a branch line, or certificate of change of route, twenty cents for each one hundred words, but in no case less than five dollars.

11. For filing certificate of extension of purpose, or change of domicile of a corporation, five dollars.

12. For filing certificates not herein enumerated, twenty cents for each one hundred words, but in no case less than

five dollars, except certificates of election for which no charge shall be made.

13. For filing copy of papers evidencing the incorporation of a municipal corporation, or of annexation of territory by a municipal corporation, five dollars, to be paid by the corporation, the petitioners therefor, or their agent.

14. For filing certificate of subscription to ten per cent of the capital stock of a corporation, two dollars.

15. For filing name, or names or initials filed by manufacturers, bottlers and dealers in ginger ale, seltzer-water, soda water, mineral water and other beverages, as provided by law, five dollars.

16. For making certificates under the great seal of the state, one dollar.

17. For recording miscellaneous records, papers, or other documents, required by law to be recorded in the office of the secretary of state, twenty cents for each one hundred words.

18. For making copies of articles of incorporation, and for making copies of a document or a part thereof, ten cents for each one hundred words; for affixing seal of office to copies, fifty cents, except copies of documents required by state officers for official purposes, for which no charge shall be made. (R. S. Secs. 148, 148a. February 12, 1889, 86 v. 33; March 14, 1888, 85 v. 80; May 15, 1886, 83 v. 165; March 18, 1884, 81 v. 52; April 18, 1881, 78 v. 186; 73 v. 227, § 2; 44 v. 65, § 4.)

This act is constitutional, and applies to a consolidation of an Ohio and a foreign corporation, as well as to consolidation of Ohio corporations.

Ashley v. Ryan, 49 O. S. 504 (1892); 153 U. S. 436.

Where the business of a corporation substantially amounts to insurance, the filing fee for its articles is $25.00. Such a corporation is not a society organized for benevolent purposes under § 176.

Rep. Atty. Gen. 1911-1912, pp. 57, 88, 90, 112. 3 Opins. Atty. Gen. 504.

Section 177. (Fees to be paid before filing or record.) The secretary of state shall not file or record articles of incorporation or consolidation, certificates or other papers referred to in the preceding section, unless the fee therein prescribed has been paid. (R. S. Sec. 148a; Febrary 12, 1889, 86 v. 33; March 14, 1888, 85 v. 80; May 15, 1886, 83 v. 165; March 18, 1884, 81 v. 52.)

PART V.

FOREIGN CORPORATIONS.

Section 178. (Certificate of admission of foreign corporation.) Before a foreign corporation for profit transacts business in this state, it shall procure from the secretary of state a certificate that it has complied with the requirements of law to authorize it to do business in this state, and that the business of such corporation to be transacted in this state, is such as may be lawfully carried on by a corporation, organized under the laws of this state for such or similar business, or if more than one kind of business, by two or more corporations so incorporated for such kinds of business exclusively. No such foreign corporation doing business in this state without such certificate shall maintain an action in this state upon a contract made by it in this state until it has procured such certificate. This section shall not apply to foreign banking, insurance, building and loan, or bond investment corporations. (R. S. Sec. 148d; April 23, 1898, 93 v. 227; May 19, 1894, 91 v. 355; April 25, 1893, 90 v. 261.)

Cross references. Noncompliance with act, effect of: note to § 194.
Right to maintain action: note to § 187.
Retirement from state, certificate, etc., on: §§ 5521, 11976 to 11978.
Foreign corporations generally: note to § 194.

Classification of foreign corporation acts. There are two laws imposing conditions upon foreign corporations entering the state to transact business: (1) the license fee law (G. C. § 178 to 182) which applies to all corporations except the classes specified in § 178, and (2) the franchise tax law (G. C. § 183 to 192) which (except as to the classes specified in § 188) applies to corporations which own or use a part or all their capital or plant in Ohio.

An annual franchise tax is imposed by G. C. § 5503.

Constitutionality. These acts are constitutional.

Aetna Iron & Steel Co. v. Taylor, 3 N. P. 152; 4 L. D. 180; s. c. 13 C. C. 602; 5 C. D. 242 (1896).

See also Express Co. v. State, 55 O. S. 69 (1896).

Southern Gum Co. v. Laylin, 66 O. S. 595 (1902).

Corporations engaged in interstate commerce. This section does not exempt foreign corporations engaged in interstate commerce, from its requirements, as in § 188.

Rep. Atty. Gen. 1910-1911, p. 240.

See note to § 194. *Right of state to exclude or impose conditions upon foreign corporations.*

Foreign corporations may enter Ohio only to do such business as may be lawfully carried on by Ohio corporations. A foreign corporation organized for the purpose of carrying on professional business is not entitled to a certificate authorizing it to do business in Ohio, such business being prohibited to corporations by G. C. § 8623.

State v. Laylin, 73 O. S. 90 (1905).

5 Opins. Atty. Gen. 975.

A foreign corporation authorized to acquire and deal generally in the stock of other corporations can not be admitted to do business in Ohio, since under § 8683 a corporation may acquire stock in kindred and not competing corporations only.

5 Opins. Atty. Gen. 924, 969 (1903).

Rep. Atty. Gen. 1910-1911, p. 246.

Rep. Atty. Gen. 1911-1912, p. 61.

Unless it expressly renounces the right to exercise such corporate power in Ohio.

Rep. Atty. Gen. 1911-1912, p. 78.

A corporation organized to deal in real estate may be admitted to do business in Ohio but the articles should expressly limit its life in Ohio to twenty-five years.

5 Opins. Atty. Gen. 1002.

What corporate powers may be exercised in Ohio.

See note to § 194, *powers of foreign corporations.*

Acting as a stockholder in an Ohio corporation, or giving assent to changes in its regulations, is not "doing business" in Ohio within the meaning of G. C. §§ 178 or 5508.

Toledo T. L. & P. Co. v. Smith, 58 Bull. 201 (U. S. D. C. 1913).

Section 179. (Statement required before admission.)

Before granting such certificate, the secretary of state shall require such foreign corporation to file in his office a sworn copy of its charter or certificate of incorporation, and a statement under its corporate seal setting forth the following: The amount of capital stock of the corporation, the business in which it is engaged or in which it proposes to engage within this state; the proposed location of its principal place of business within this state; and the name of a person designated as provided by law, upon whom process against the corporation may be served within this state. The person so designated must have an office or place of business at the proposed location of the principal place of business of the corporation. (R. S. Sec. 148d; April 23, 1898, 93 v. 227; May 19, 1894, 91 v. 355; April 25, 1893, 90 v. 261.)

In a suit brought by a resident of Ohio upon a cause of action arising in another state, service of process upon the agent designated by the foreign corporation in its statement is sufficient to give the Ohio courts jurisdiction.

Burke v. McClintic-Marshall Co., 9 N. P. n. s. 577 (1910).

Madison v. Pittsburg Construction Co., 11 N. P. n. s. 634; 21 L. D. 369 (1911).

See Handy v. Insurance Co., 37 O. S. 366 (1881).

Jurisdiction over a foreign corporation may be acquired in federal court by service of process on the agent designated in its statement.

Runkle v. Insurance Co., 2 Fed. 9; 5 W. L. B. 217; 4 O. F. D. 620 (C. C. 1880).

Barrow Steamship Co. v. Kane, 170 U. S. 100, 107 (1898).

Process issued from one county may be served upon the designated agent in another county.

Blanton v. Burroughs, etc., Co., 13 N. P. n. s. 423 (C. P. 1912).

For service of process on foreign corporations see also notes to G. C. § 11290 and § 10244.

Section 180.   (Fees to be paid before delivery of certificates.) For issuing such certificate the secretary of state shall be entitled to receive from a foreign corporation the following fees:

A corporation having an authorized capital stock of one hundred thousand dollars or less, fifteen dollars.

A corporation having an authorized capital stock of more than one hundred thousand dollars, and not exceeding three hundred thousand dollars, twenty dollars.

A corporation having an authorized capital stock of more than three hundred thousand dollars, and not exceeding five hundred thousand dollars, twenty-five dollars.

A corporation having an authorized capital stock of more than five hundred thousand dollars, and less than one million dollars, thirty dollars.

A corporation having an authorized capital stock of one million dollars, or more, fifty dollars.

Whereupon such foreign corporation shall be entitled to receive from the secretary of state the certificate provided in the second preceding section. (R. S. Sec. 148d; April 23, 1898, 93 v. 227; May 19, 1894, 91 v. 355; April 25, 1893, 90 v. 261.)

Compliance with §§ 178 and 179 and the payment of a fee under § 180 do not constitute a contract which will prevent the state from thereafter imposing other fees.

Aetna Iron & Steel Co. v. Taylor, 3 N. P. 152; 4 L. D. 180; 13 C. C. 602; 15 C. D. 242 (1896).

Compare American, etc., Co. v. Colorado, 204 U. S. 103 (1906).

Southern Railway Co. v. Greene, 216 U. S. 400 (1910).

The secretary of state has no discretionary power to investigate and determine the legality of the manner in which a foreign corporation is conducting its business, with a view to rejecting the application, where the application is in proper form and shows the business to be legal.

Rep. Atty. Gen. 1910-1911, p. 202.

Section 181. (Person upon whom process to be served.)
If a person designated by a foreign corporation as its agent
within this state dies or removes from the principal place of
business of the corporation within this state, the corporation,
within thirty days after such death or removal, shall designate in like manner another person upon whom process may
be served within this state. On failure so to do, the secretary of state shall revoke the authority of the corporation
to do business within this state and process against such
corporation in an action upon the liability incurred within
this state before such revocation may be served upon the
secretary of state after such death or removal and before
another designation is made. At the time of such service the
plaintiff shall pay to the secretary of state a fee of two
dollars, which shall be included in the taxable costs of the
action, and the secretary of state shall forthwith mail a copy
of the service to the corporation if its address or the address
of any officer is known to him. (R. S. Sec. 148d; April 23,
1898, 93 v. 227; May 19, 1894, 91 v. 355; April 25, 1893, 90
v. 261.)

Where the agent removes from the state, the duty of the secretary
of state to revoke the authority of the corporation is mandatory.
Rep. Atty. Gen. 1910-1911, p. 264.

Service of process by mail.
'Mohr Distilling Co. v. Fireman's Ins. Co., 12 Am. L. R. 168 (1883).
Heart v. Lycoming Ins. Co., 26 O. S. 594 (1875); s. c. 2 Am. L.
R. 355.

**Section 182. (Penalty for noncompliance with previous
section.)** Whoever solicits or transacts business in this state
for a foreign corporation which is subject to the provisions
of the preceding four sections, before it has complied with
the provisions of such sections, shall be fined not less than
ten dollars nor more than five hundred dollars, or imprisoned
not less than ten days nor more than six months, or both.
Upon direction of the attorney general, the prosecuting
attorney shall prosecute any person charged with a violation
of the provisions of such section. (R. S. Sec. 148d; 93 v. 227;
91 v. 355; 90 v. 261.)

See §§ 5523, 5524, 191.

Section 183. (Statement required before doing business.)
Before doing business in this state, a foreign corporation
organized for profit and owning or using a part or all of its
capital or plant in this state shall make and file with the
secretary of state, in such form as he may prescribe, a statement under oath of its president, secretary, treasurer, super-

intendent or managing agent in this state, containing the following facts:

1. The number of shares of authorized capital stock of the corporation and the par value of each share.

2. The name and location of the office or offices of the corporation in Ohio and the names and addresses of the officers or agents of the corporation in charge of its business in Ohio.

3. The value of the property owned and used by the corporation in Ohio, where situated, and the value of the property of the corporation owned and used outside of Ohio.

4. The proportion of the capital stock of the corporation represented by property owned and used and by business transacted in Ohio. (R. S. Sec. 148c; April 27, 1904, 97 v. 496; May 10, 1902, 95 v. 539; April 14, 1900, 94 v. 225; April 23, 1898, 93 v. 225; May 16, 1894, 91 v. 272.)

What constitutes "doing business."
See notes to §§ 194 and 188.
Effect of noncompliance, see note to § 194.

Section 184. (Payment of franchise fee and certificate.) From the facts thus reported and any other facts coming to his knowledge, the secretary of state shall determine the proportion of the capital stock of the corporation represented by its property and business in this state, and shall charge and collect from such corporation for the privilege of exercising its franchise in this state, one-tenth of one per cent upon the proportion of its authorized capital stock represented by property owned and used and business transacted in this state, but not less than ten dollars in any case. Upon the payment of such fee the secretary of state shall make and deliver to such foreign corporation a certificate that it has complied with the laws of Ohio and is authorized to do business therein, stating the amount of its authorized capital stock and the proportion of such authorized capital stock represented in this state. (R. S. Sec. 148c; April 27, 1904, 97 v. 496; May 10, 1902, 95 v. 539; April 14, 1900, 94 v. 225; April 23, 1898, 93 v. 225; May 16, 1894, 91 v. 272.)

The secretary of state has no discretionary power to investigate and determine the legality of the manner in which a foreign corporation is conducting its business, with a view to rejecting the application, where the application is in proper form and shows the business to be legal.
Rep. Atty. Gen. 1910-1911, p. 202.

Method of computing tax. This tax is not based upon the *property* owned and used and *business* transacted in Ohio, but is based upon the *proportion of the total authorized capital stock* represented by such property and business. The proportion which the property owned and used and business transacted in Ohio bears to the entire property and business of the corporation is the proportion of the capital stock on which the tax is based. If the property owned and used and business transacted in Ohio is $10,000, the entire corporate property and business $20,000, and the authorized capital stock $50,000, the tax would be based upon one-half of its authorized capital stock ($25,000) the Ohio property and business being one-half of the total property and business.

If the entire corporate property and business is in Ohio the tax would be based upon the entire authorized capital stock.

5 O. L. R. 163 (Atty. Gen. 1907).

Aetna, etc., Co. v. Taylor, 13 C. C. 602; 5 C. D. 242 (1896).

4 Opins. Atty. Gen., 621-24 (1894).

Rep. Atty. Gen. 1910-1911, p. 600.

Payment of the fee under protest does not render it an involuntary payment, unless the other circumstances under which it is paid would justify its recovery back.

Aetna Iron & Steel Co. v. Taylor, 3 N. P. 152; 4 L. D. 180 (1896).

See § 194.

For annual franchise tax, see § 5499 et seq.

Section 185. (Fee for increase of capital stock.) A corporation which has filed its statement and paid the fee prescribed by the preceding two sections and which thereafter shall increase the proportion of its capital stock, represented by property used and business done in this state, shall file within thirty days after such increase an additional statement with the secretary of state, and pay a fee of one-tenth of one per cent upon the increase of its authorized capital stock represented by property owned and business transacted in this state. (R. S. Sec. 148c; April 27, 1904, 97 v. 496; May 10, 1902, 95 v. 539; April 14, 1900, 94 v. 225; April 23, 1898, 93 v. 225; May 16, 1894, 91 v. 272.)

Where the capital stock of a foreign corporation is increased, a statement thereof must be filed with the secretary of state.

Rep. Atty. Gen. 1909-1910, p. 101.

Section 186. (Exemption from penalty.) If a foreign corporation complies with the provisions of the preceding three sections, it shall not be subject to process of attachment under any law of this state upon the ground that it is a foreign corporation, or non-resident of the state. A foreign corporation subject to the provisions of such sections which shall neglect or refuse to comply with the requirements thereof shall forfeit and pay one thousand dollars and an additional penalty of one thousand dollars for each month that it continues to transact business in this state without complying with such sections, to be recovered by an action in the name of the state, and on collection paid into the state treasury to the credit of the general revenue fund. (R. S. Secs. 148c, 148d; April 27, 1904, 97 v. 496; May 10, 1902, 95

v. 539; April 14, 1900, 94 v. 225; April 23, 1898, 93 v. 225, 227; May 16, 1894, 91 v. 272; April 15, 1893, 90 v. 261.)

Cross references. Remission of penalty, §§ 191, 5523.
Attachment and garnishment of foreign corporations.
In court of common pleas, § 11819 et seq.
Before justice of the peace, § 10253 et seq.

Attachment. The exemption from attachment provided for in this section is constitutional.
Puerrung v. Carter Crume Co., 16 C. C. 629; 9 C. D. 411 (1898); s. c. 35 W. L. B. 2.

Affidavit for (a) Before justice of the peace. An affidavit for attachment under G. C. § 10253 need not aver noncompliance with foreign corporation laws.
Rosenham Co. v. Cohen & Mack, 13 C. C. n. s. 102 (1910).

(b) In court of common pleas. An affidavit for attachment under G. C. § 11819 should allege noncompliance.
Edwards Mfg. Co. v. Ashland Sheet Mill Co., 6 N. P. n. s. 1; 18 L. D. 413 (1907); affirmed 11 C. C. n. s. 479; 20 C. D. 414.
Leavitt, etc., Co. v. Rosenberg, etc., Co., 83 O. S. 230 (1910).

Transportation company. A foreign transportation corporation engaged in interstate commerce does not, by a voluntary compliance with G. C. § 183, become exempt from attachment.
G. C. § 188.
Bigalow v. Armour, 74 O. S. 168 (1906) reversing 5 C. C. n. s. 161; 16 C. D. 496.

A sleeping car is an instrumentality of interstate commerce, and when actually employed in interstate transportation is immune from attachment under process from a state court. A sheriff who seizes such immune property is liable as for conversion. An attaching creditor and his attorney who actively assist in the seizure may also be liable.
Pullman Co. v. Linke, 11 O. L. R. 63; 203 Fed. 1017 (D. C. 1913).

Foreign corporation as garnishee. A foreign corporation which neither transacts business nor exercises its corporate powers within the state can not be made a garnishee in an action against another foreign corporation. But a corporation which has complied with the foreign corporation acts, and is capable of suing and being sued in the state, may be made a garnishee in such an action.
Ritter-Conley Mfg. Co. v. Mzik, 3 C. C. n. s. 125; 13 C. D. 164 (1901).
Compare, Kelley Co. v. Garvin Machine Co., 6 N. P. 350; 4 L. D. 374 (1896).

Section 187. (Must comply herewith before certain actions can be brought.) A foreign corporation which has violated such preceding sections shall not maintain an action in this state upon contract made by it in this state, until it has complied with the requirements of such sections and procured the requisite certificate from the secretary of state. (R. S. Sec. 148c; April 27, 1904, 97 v. 496; May 10, 1902, 95 v. 539; April 14, 1900, 94 v. 225; April 23, 1898, 93 v. 225; May 16, 1894, 94 v. 272.)

See § 178.
Before the enactment of § 5508 (May 31, 1911) it was held that a

contract made by a foreign corporation, without complying with §§ 178 to
192, was not void.

Fergus v. Columbus, 6 N. P. 82; 8 L. D. 290 (1898).

Union, etc., Ins. Co. v. McMillan, 24 O. S. 67 (1873).

But the right of action on such contract in the state courts was
suspended until the conditions of the law were complied with.

Simplex Dairy Co. v. Cole, 86 Fed. 739 (1898).

Crefeld Miller v. Goddard, 69 Fed. 141 (1895).

Suit thereon might be brought in federal court.

Johnson v. Breweries Co., 178 Fed. 513 (1910).

By § 5508 a contract made by a foreign corporation, before compliance with § 178 is void in its behalf, but is enforceable against it.

Construction of section. The inhibition of this section is as to
actions upon contracts, and not transactions, and as to maintaining
actions and not the institution of actions. It is a technical defense and
should be technically considered. An answer setting up a defense under
this section should show that the plaintiff corporation came within the
provisions of the act at the time of the filing of the answer, and was
not included in any of its exceptions.

Automatic, etc., Co. v. Schlemmer Co., 6 O. L. R. 72; 18 L. D. 788
(C. P. 1908).

**Noncompliance with laws, no defense to prosecution for crime
against property of foreign corporation.** On the trial of an indictment
for embezzlement of funds coming into the possession of the defendant as
agent for a foreign corporation, it is no defense that the corporation has
not complied with these acts.

State v. Pohlmeyer, 59 O. S. 491 (1898).

See Starkey v. State, 6 O. S. 266 (1856).

Pleading compliance or noncompliance. A foreign corporation bringing suit need not allege compliance with laws. Want of compliance is a
matter of defense. The answer of the defendant must set forth specifically facts bringing the foreign corporation within the provisions of the
statute, and show that it is not among the classes exempted by §§ 188
and 178.

Brady v. Palmer, 19 C. C. 687; 10 C. D. 27 (1899); affd. 64 O. S.
267 (1901).

Toledo Commercial Co. v. Glen Mfg. Co., 55 O. S. 217 (1896); affmg.
11 C. C. 153; 5 C. D. 131.

Automatic, etc., Co. v. Schlemmer Co., 6 O. L. R. 72; 18 L. D. 788
(1908).

Illinois, etc., Co. v. Whitman, 13 N. P. n. s. 362; 23 L. D. 12 (1911).

Pleading corporate capacity and powers. A foreign corporation
bringing suit need not aver in its petition that it is a corporation, or the
terms of its charter showing its capacity to maintain the action. If such
averment is made, it will be held to be immaterial and mere surplusage.
A general denial to a petition containing such averment will not raise
an issue as to corporate capacity.

To raise the issue of corporate capacity of the plaintiff, it must be
specially pleaded by the defendant.

Brady v. National Supply Co., 64 O. S. 267 (1901); affirming 19 C.
C. 687; 10 C. D. 27.

Smith v. Weed Sewing Machine Co., 26 O. S. 562 (1875).

Elektron Mfg. Co. v. Jones Bros. Elec. Co., 8 C. C. 311; 4 C. D. 555
(1894).

A person who has dealt with a foreign corporation and received the
benefits of the contract, is estopped to deny its legal existence and power
to make the contract.

Newburgh Petroleum Co. v. Weare, 27 O. S. 343 (1875).

But where a foreign corporation seeks to appropriate private property, the rule is otherwise. The corporation must allege in its petition and prove its incorporation according to law, including the due and legal election of directors, and its charter power to appropriate property.

Central Union Tel. Co. v. Columbus, 8 C. C. n. s. 81; 28 C. D. 131 (1905).

Queen City Tel. Co. v. Cincinnati, 73 O. S. 64 (1905).

And where a corporation is made a defendant, and its charter, powers or franchise become the foundation of the action, they must be specially pleaded in the petition, including the name of the state of incorporation, and the substantial terms in which the charter, powers and franchises were granted.

Devoss v. Gray, 22 O. S. 159 (1871).

Brady v. National Supply Co., 64 O. S. 267 (1901).

Proof of legal existence and powers. The law of the state under which a foreign corporation is organized constitutes a part of its charter. Courts of this state do not take judicial notice of the laws of other states. To establish the legal existence and powers of a foreign corporation it is necessary to prove the laws of its home state conferring its powers, as well as the articles of incorporation, subscriptions to capital stock, election of officers, etc.

Niagara County Bank v. Baker, 15 O. S. 68 (1864).

James v. C. H. & D. R. R., 2 Disney 261, 266 (1858).

See notes to § 11046.

Section 188. (Certain corporations excepted.) The preceding five sections shall not apply to foreign insurance, banking, savings and loan, building and loan, or bond investment corporations, or to express, telegraph, telephone, railroad, sleeping car, transportation, or other corporations engaged in Ohio in inter-state commerce; or to foreign corporations entirely non-resident soliciting business or making sales in this state by correspondence or by traveling salesmen. (R. S. Sec. 148c; April 27, 1904, 97 v. 496; May 10, 1902, 95 v. 539; April 14, 1900, 94 v. 225; April 23, 1898, 93 v. 225; May 16, 1894, 91 v. 272.)

Section 178, unlike this section, does not exempt foreign corporations engaged in interstate commerce.

Rep. Atty. Gen. 1910-1911, p. 240.

Interstate commerce "strictly considered, consists in intercourse and traffic, including in these terms navigation and the transportation of persons and property, as well as the purchase, sale and exchange of commodities."

Mobile County v. Kimball, 102 U. S. 691, 702 (1881).

An incorporated correspondence school which maintained in another state an office with a resident agent in charge for the purpose of soliciting students, and collecting and forwarding their payments, for instruction sent by mail, was held to be engaged in interstate commerce upon which no license tax or conditions could be imposed by a state.

International Text Book Co. v. Pigg, 217 U. S. 91 (1910); reversing 76 Kans. 328.

Property used in interstate commerce may be taxed by the state in which it is situated, although the business of, or the right to engage in, interstate commerce may not.

Adams Express Co. v. Ohio State Auditor, 165 U. S. 194, 220 (1896); affirming 51 O. S. 492.

See also note to § 194, "doing business" in state.

Transportation company. A foreign corporation engaged in furnishing refrigerator cars and ice therefor, for transportation purposes partly within and partly without and across Ohio, is, under this section, not subject to § 183 et seq.

Bigalow v. Armour, 74 O. S. 168 (1906); reversing 5 C. C. n. s. 161.

Insurance corporation. A foreign corporation which sells to physicians a contract whereby it agrees to defend any malpractice suits brought within a specified time, but which does not agree to assume or pay any judgments, is not engaged in the business of insurance.

State v. Laylin, 73 O. S. 90 (1905).

See also, State v. Railway Co., 68 O. S. 9 (1903).

Section 189. (Right of hearing before secretary of state.) On application, a foreign corporation shall have the right to be heard by the secretary of state in the matter of the determination of the proportion of its capital stock represented by property used and business done in this state. (R. S. Sec. 148c; April 27, 1904, 97 v. 496; May 10, 1902, 95 v. 539; April 14, 1900, 94 v. 225; April 23, 1898, 93 v. 225; May 16, 1894, 91 v. 272.)

Section 190. (Right of appeal.) A corporation aggrieved by the decision of the secretary of state under the preceding section may, within ten days, appeal to the auditor of state, the treasurer of state and the attorney general, whose decision shall be final. (R. S. Sec. 148c; April 27, 1904, 97 v. 496; May 10, 1902, 95 v. 539; April 14, 1900, 94 v. 225; April 23, 1898, 93 v. 225; May 16, 1894, 91 v. 272.)

The remedy provided by this section must be exhausted.

Aetna Iron & Steel Co. v. Taylor, 3 N. P. 152, 155; 4 L. D. 180; s. c. 13 C. C. 602; 5 C. D. 242 (1896).

See also, State ex rel. v. Jones, 51 O. S. 492 (1894); affirmed 165 U. S. 194.

Section 191. (Actions against foreign corporation; remission of penalties.) On request of the secretary of state, the attorney general shall prosecute an action against a foreign corporation under the provisions of this chapter in the court of common pleas of Franklin county or in any county in which the corporation has an office or place of business. On good cause shown, the governor and secretary of state may remit the penalty or part thereof incurred by a foreign corporation under this chapter. (R. S. Sec. 148c; 97 v. 496; 95 v. 539; 94 v. 225; 93 v. 225; 91 v. 272.)

Section 192. (Shares of stock of certain corporations not taxable.) No person shall be required to list for taxation a share of the capital stock of an Ohio corporation; or a share of the capital stock of a foreign corporation, the property of which is taxed in Ohio in the name of such corporation; or a share of the capital stock of any other foreign corporation, if the holder thereof furnishes satisfactory proof to the taxing authorities that at least two-thirds of the property of such corporation is taxed in Ohio and the remainder is taxed in another state or states, provided such corporation, as a fee for the privilege of exercising its franchise in Ohio, pays annually the same percentage upon its entire authorized capital stock that is required by law to be paid by a domestic corporation on its subscribed or issued capital stock. (R. S. Sec. 148c; April 27, 1904, 97 v. 496; May 10, 1902, 95 v. 539; April 14, 1900, 94 v. 225; April 23, 1898, 93 v. 225; May 16, 1894, 91 v. 272.)

Taxation of property of foreign corporation. Choses in action, whether book accounts, promissory notes, or the like, of foreign corporations that are kept in this state and arise out of the corporate business transacted here are subject to taxation under the provisions of G. C. §§ 5404, 5405 and 5406.
Hubbard v. Brush, 61 O. S. 252 (1899).
Scottish, etc., Ins. Co. v. Bowland, 196 U. S. 611, 627 (1905).
Western Assur. Co. v. Halliday, 126 Fed. 257 (C. C. A. 1903).
Sims v. Best, 1 C. C. n. s. 41; 15 C. D. 149 (1903).
Deposits of insurance companies, made as required by law, are not taxable: §5437.

Taxation of stock in Ohio corporations. Prior to the amendment of this section in 1904 (97 O. L. 496) stock in an Ohio corporation was exempt from taxation only when the property of the corporation was taxed in its name in Ohio.
Lander v. Burke, 65 O. S. 532 (1901).

Stock in foreign corporations. Under former laws, see:
Hubbard v. Brush, 61 O. S. 252 (1899).
Lee v. Sturges, 46 O. S. 153 (1889).
Bradley v. Bauder, 36 O. S. 28 (1880).
Worthington v. Sebastian, 25 O. S. 1 (1874).
Sturges v. Carter, 114 U. S. 511 (1885).

Stock in a foreign corporation (when not exempted under §§ 192 or 5372) is taxable in Ohio, although the certificates evidencing such stock are in the possession of an agent in another state where taxes are paid thereon.
Rep. of Atty. Gen. 1906, p. 257.
A statute imposing a tax on stock in foreign corporations held by residents of Ohio is constitutional.
Worthington v. Sebastian, 25 O. S. 1 (1874).
Bradley v. Bauder, 36 O. S. 28 (1880).
Sturges v. Carter, 114 U. S. 511 (1885).
A state may tax stock in a foreign corporation, whose capital consists wholly of patent rights, which are exempt under federal laws.
Scott v. Smith, 2 N. P. n. s. 617; 15 L. D. 590 (1905).

Section 193. (Record of fees.) The secretary of state shall keep a record of all fees collected under the provisions of this chapter and pay them into the state treasury to the credit of the general revenue fund. (R. S. Sec. 148; April 18, 1881, 78 v. 186; R. S. 1880; 73 v. 227, § 2; 44 v. 65, § 4; S. & C. 1394.)

Section 194. (Fees paid under protest.) If fees are paid under protest to recover which while held by him an action would lie against the secretary of state, and such fees are paid into the state treasury in compliance with the preceding section, actions to recover them shall be brought against the state and not against the secretary of state. For such purposes permission is hereby given to maintain actions against the state in the cases and to the extent that such actions might be maintained against the secretary of state, if the fees were held by him. Service of process shall be made on the attorney-general who shall represent the state. (R. S. Sec. 148b; 89 v. 325.)

FOREIGN CORPORATIONS GENERALLY.

I. What are foreign corporations.
    A. Definition.
    B. Incorporation in more than one state.
    C. Domestic corporation qualifying to do business in another state.

II. "Doing" or "transacting" business in state.
    A. In general.
    B. Sales of goods.
    C. Sale through commission merchants.
    D. Miscellaneous
        (1) Held not doing business.
        (2) Held doing business.

III. Noncompliance with requirements. Effect.
    A. On contracts.
    B. Attachment.
    C. Ouster by quo warranto.
    D. Penalties.

IV. Liability of stockholders.
    A. As partners.
    B. Statutory liability may be enforced in Ohio.

V. Power of Ohio courts over internal affairs.
    A. Calling stockholders' meeting.
    B. Inspection of books.

VI. Legal existence.
    A. Where no business transacted in home state.
    B. Corporation or partnership, how determined.

VII. Powers.
    A. Limited to charter powers.
    B. Effect of general law of home state.
    C. Must be exercised in accordance with Ohio laws.

1. WHAT ARE FOREIGN CORPORATIONS.

A. Definition. A foreign corporation is one that has been organized under the laws of another state or of a foreign government.

Cook on Corporations, § 7.

Horn Silver Min. Co. v. New York, 143 U. S. 305, 314 (1891).

Boley v. Ohio, etc., Co., 12 O. S. 139 (1861).

B. Incorporation in more than one state. A corporation incorporated in several states has a legal domicile in each state. In each state it is regarded as a domestic and not a foreign corporation.

Gerling v. B. & O. R. R. Co., 151 U. S. 673, 677 (1894).

Graham v. Boston, etc., R. R., 118 U. S. 161, 168 (1886).

Covington, etc., Bridge Co. v. Mayer, 31 O. S. 317 (1877).

Sebastian v. Covington, etc., Bridge Co., 21 O. S. 451 (1871).

State v. Covington, etc., Bridge Co., 6 N. P. n. s. 55; 18 L. D. 273 (1907).

A corporation incorporated in several states, including the one in which suit is brought against it, must be regarded as a citizen of the latter state for the purpose of determining the jurisdiction of a federal court.

L. S. & M. S. Ry. v. Eder, 174 Fed. 944; 8 O. L. R. 386 (C. C. A. 1909).

C. Domestic corporation does not become foreign by qualifying to do business in another state. An Ohio corporation does not cease to be such nor become a foreign corporation by obtaining a license and transacting business elsewhere.

Lander v. Burke, 65 O. S. 532 (1901).

Railway Co. v. Stringer, 32 O. S. 468, 472 (1877).

A foreign corporation, after compliance, may remove a suit to federal court.

Lee v. Insurance Co., 3 O. F. D. 663.

A foreign railroad company, by leasing and operating in this state the property of an Ohio corporation, does not thereby become an Ohio corporation.

B. & O. R. R. Co. v. Cary, 28 O. S. 218 (1876).

Railway v. Stringer, 32 O. S. 468 (1877).

B. & O. R. R. Co. v. Koontz, 104 U. S. 5 (1881).

II. "DOING" OR "TRANSACTING" BUSINESS IN THE STATE; WHAT CONSTITUTES.

See also note to § 188.

A. **In general.** The words "doing business" or "transacting business" refer to the transaction of the ordinary business for which the corporation was organized, and do not include acts not a part of the ordinary business, such as bringing a suit;

Alpena Cement Co. v. Jenkins, etc., Co., 244 Ill. 354; 91 N. E. 480.
Trust Co. v. Railroad Co., 7 N. P. n. s. 497 (1908).

or soliciting and obtaining subscriptions to the capital stock of the foreign corporation.

First Nat. Bk. v. Leeper, 121 Mo. App. 688; 97 S. W. 636.
Payson v. Withers, 5 Biss (U. S.) 269.
Galena Mining, etc., Co. v. Frazier, 20 Pa. Super. Ct. 394.
Bartlett v. Chouteau Ins. Co., 18 Kans. 369.
5 Opins. Atty. Gen. 830.

A single and isolated transaction does not constitute "doing business" in a state.

Cooper Mfg. Co. v. Ferguson, 113 U. S. 727 (1885).

B. **Sales of goods.** A foreign corporation which maintains a stock of goods in the state, from which deliveries are made of goods sold, is doing business in the state.

People v. Wemple, 131 N. Y. 64; 29 N. E. 1002.
Singer Mfg. Co. v. Adams, 165 Fed. 877 (1909).
Thomas Mfg. Co. v. Knapp, 101 Minn. 432; 112 N. W. 989.
Fay Fruit Co. v. McKinney, 103 Mo. App. 304; 77 S. W. 160.
See also Muskegon v. Zeeryp, 134 Mich. 181; 96 N. W. 502.

But where goods are shipped into the state to fill orders previously obtained, the transaction constitutes interstate commerce, upon which no license tax or restriction may be imposed by a state. A foreign corporation which maintains no stock of goods within the state and limits its business to shipping goods into the state, upon orders, need not obtain a license or certificate or comply with the conditions imposed by state laws. This is true whether the orders are obtained through traveling salesmen or correspondence;

Toledo Commercial Co. v. Glen Mfg. Co., 55 O. S. 217 (1896).
Haldy v. Tomoor-Haldy Co., 3 N. P. 43; 4 L. D. 118 (1896).
General Electric Co. v. Lima, etc., Co., 4 N. P. 167 (1897).
Aultman Miller & Co. v. Holder, 34 W. L. B. 92 (1895).
Bruner v. Plow Co., 168 Fed. 218 (C. C. A. Okl. 1909).
See U. S. v. Tucker, 188 Fed. 741 (1911).

or a resident broker;

McBath v. Jones Cotton Co., 149 Fed. 383 (1906).
Doe v. Springfield, etc., Mfg. Co., 104 Fed. 684 (1900).

or whether the foreign corporation maintains an office in the state with a resident agent in charge, for the purpose of soliciting orders.

International Text Book Co. v. Pigg, 217 U. S. 91 (1910); reversing 76 Kans. 328.
Case v. Smith, etc., Co., 152 Fed. 730 (1907).
Cummer Lumber Co. v. Assd. Mfgrs., etc., Corp., 73 N. Y. Suppl. 668; 67 N. Y. App. Div. 151; affirmed 173 N. Y. 633.
Contractor Pub. Co. v. Nocenti Co., 139 N. Y. Supp. 853.
See 4 Opins. Atty. Gen. 826.

It is not necessary, to constitute a transaction interstate commerce, that the goods, to fill orders previously obtained, be shipped direct to the purchaser. The goods may be sent to the agent for delivery by him to the purchaser,

Caldwell v. North Carolina, 187 U. S. 622 (1903).

Norfolk, etc., Co. v. Sims, 191 U. S. 441, 450 (1903).

and the work of installing the goods upon premises or property when incident to the sale, may be performed by agents of the corporation.

U. S. v. U. S. Fidelity & G. Co., 178 Fed. Rep. 721 (1910).

For definition of interstate commerce, see note to § 188.

C. **Sales through commission merchants.** A foreign corporation which has no warehouse, office or place of business in the state to which it consigns goods to a factor, the factor conducting all the business in such state, and paying all expenses of receiving, handling and storing the goods, is not doing business in such state.

Butler Bros. Shoe Co. v. U. S. Rubber Co., 156 Fed. 1 (C. C. A. Colo. 1907); writ of certiorari denied 212 U. S. 577.

Atlas Engine Co. v. Parkinson, 161 Fed. 223 (D. C. 1908).

Allen v. Tyson-Jones Buggy Co., 91 Tex. 22; 40 S. W. 393, 714.

Lasater v. Purcell, etc., Co., 22 Tex. Civ. App. 33; 54 S. W. 425.

Hovey's Estate, 198 Pa. St. 385; 48 Atl. 311.

Bertha, etc., Zinc, etc., Co. v. Clute, 27 N. Y. S. 342.

Brookford Mills v. Baldwin, 139 N. Y. Supp. 195.

See Gibbin v. Coal Co., 2 C. S. C. R. 75 (1870).

Contra, Wilson-Moline Buggy Co. v. Priebe, 123 Mo. App. 521; 100 S. W. 558.

Milsom, etc., Co. v. Kelly, 10 Pa. Super. Ct. 565.

Compare Milburn Wagon Co. v. Commonwealth, 31 Ky. Law Repr. 937; 104 S. W. 323.

D. **Miscellaneous.** (1). *Held not to constitute "doing business."* The maintaining of a resident agent to solicit and make contracts for traffic, by a foreign railroad corporation, the lines of which are wholly outside of the state, none of the contract of carriage being performed in the state.

Green v. C. B. & Q. R. R. Co., 205 U. S. 530 (1907).

Berger v. Penna. R. Co., 27 R. I. 583; 65 Atl. 261.

Abraham v. So. R. Co., 149 Ala. 547; 42 So. Rep. 837.

West v. Cincinnati, etc., R. Co., 170 Fed. 349 (1909).

Arrow Lumber & Shingle Co. v. U. P. R. Co., 53 Wash. 629; 102 Pac. 650.

Compare Central of Ga. R. Co. v. Eichberg, 107 Md. 363; 68 Atl. 690.

Acting as a stockholder in an Ohio corporation, or giving assent to changes in its regulations.

Toledo T. L. & P. Co. v. Smith, 58 Bull 201 (U. S. D. C. 1913).

The ownership of a controlling interest in the stock of a domestic corporation.

Mannington v. H. V. Ry. Co., 183 Fed. 133; 8 O. L. R. 451; 16 O. F. D. 522 (C. C. Ohio 1910).

The discounting by a corporation in its own state of a note sent to it for such purpose from another state.

Bamberger v. Schoolfield, 160 U. S. 149 (1895).

The loaning of money by a foreign insurance company on property in Ohio is not the doing of "banking or other business" in Ohio.

Hall v. Kummero, 7 N. P. 394; 5 L. D. 176 (1883).

For one person to supply the means to another to do business with or on is not the doing of such business by the former.

U. S. v. American Bell Telephone Co., 29 Fed. 17 (C. C. Ohio 1886).

Foreign trust company accepting a trust relating to land in Ohio.

Rep. Atty. Gen'. 1906-1907, p. 49.

See, Trust Co. v. Railway, 7 N. P. n. s. 497 (1908).

(2) *Held to constitute "doing business."* The supervision by a for-

eign corporation of plans for a factory to be built in the state by a resident, and the management and operation of the plant for such resident owner.

Diamond Glue Co. v. U. S. Glue Co., 187 U. S. 611 (1903).

The purchasing and assembling, within the state, of machinery and parts for a manufacturing plant, by a foreign corporation engaged in engineering and contracting (case distinguished from that of a foreign manufacturing corporation).

Buffalo Refrigerating Mach. Co. v. Penn. H. & P. Co., 178 Fed. 696 (C. C. A. Pa. 1910).

The maintaining of an office in Ohio, by a foreign insurance company, where insurance is written on property situated in other states is doing business in Ohio, although no contracts are made relating to property situated in Ohio.

State v. Amazon Insurance Co., 1 C. C. n. s. 4; 14 C. D. 387 (1903).

See notes to G. C. § 9559.

III. NONCOMPLIANCE WITH REQUIREMENTS. EFFECT OF.

A. **On contracts.** Before the enactment of § 5508 (1911) it was held that a contract entered into in Ohio by a foreign corporation, which had not complied with secs. 178 to 192 was not void.

Fergus v. Columbus, 6 N. P. 82; 8 L. D. 290.

Union, etc., Ins. Co. v. McMillen, 24 O. S. 67 (1873).

Manhattan Ins. Co. v. Ellis, 32 O. S. 388 (1877).

See Johnson v. N. Y. Breweries Co., 178 Fed. 513 (C. C. A. 1910).

But the right of action thereon was suspended until a certificate was secured.

Simplex Dairy Co. v. Cole, 86 Fed. 739 (1898).

Crefeld Miller v. Goddard, 69 Fed. 141 (1895).

G. C. § 187.

Under § 5508 such a contract is void in behalf of the corporation, but is enforceable against it.

B. **Attachment.** The property of a foreign corporation which has not complied with the statutory requirements is subject to attachment.

G. C. §§ 11819, 10253, 186.

C. **Ouster by quo warranto.** A foreign corporation which exercises its franchises in the state in contravention of its laws, may be ousted by quo warranto proceedings.

State v. W. U. M. Ins. Co., 47 O. S. 167 (1890).

State v. Ins. Co., 49 O. S. 440 (1892).

D. **Penalties** for doing business without compliance.

G. C. §§ 182, 186.

IV. LIABILITY OF STOCKHOLDERS IN FOREIGN CORPORATIONS.

A. **As partners.** When a foreign corporation engages in a business not authorized by its charter, all of its stockholders do not become individually liable. Only those stockholders who engage in or sanction the same may be held.

Paul v. Groene, 4 O. L. R. 632 (1907).

Bank v. Hall, 35 O. S. 158, 166 (1878).

B. **Statutory liability may be enforced in Ohio.** An individual liability for corporate debts, imposed upon stockholders by the statutes of the state in which a foreign corporation is organized, may be enforced in Ohio, where such liability is contractual in its nature and not penal.

Kulp v. Fleming, 65 O. S. 321 (1901).

Blair v. Newbegin, 65 O. S. 425 (1902).

V. POWER OF OHIO COURTS OVER INTERNAL AFFAIRS OF FOREIGN CORPORATIONS.

A. Calling stockholders' meeting. The courts of Ohio have no visitorial or supervisory jurisdiction with regard to the internal affairs of a foreign corporation. The calling of an annual meeting of stockholders of a foreign corporation can not be enforced in Ohio, although its office is located, and its directors and secretary reside, in this state.

State ex rel. v. Unida, etc., Co., 13 C. C. n. s. 100; 22 C. D. 54 (1910).

B. Inspection of books. Where the books of a foreign corporation were kept in an office maintained by it in Ohio, it was held that the right of stockholders to inspect its books, granted by a statute of its home state, could be enforced in the courts of this state.

State v. Farmer, 7 C. C. 429 (1892).
Compare Riggs v. Whippey, etc., Co., 7 O. L. R. 446 (1909).

VI. LEGAL EXISTENCE OF FOREIGN CORPORATION.

Allegation and proof of, see note to § 187.

A. The legal existence of a foreign corporation is not invalidated by the fact that it has transacted all its business in other states, and has done no business, beyond its mere organization, in its home state.

Hanna v. International Petroleum Co., 23 O. S. 622 (1873).

B. Corporation or partnership. How determined. If an organization possesses the properties, rights, attributes, privileges and immunities of a corporation, it will be regarded as such. The designation or classification, by the statute of another state, of organizations as joint stock associations or partnerships is not conclusive.

Express Co. v. State, 55 O. S. 69 (1896).
State ex rel. v. Ackerman, 51 O. S. 163, 197 (1894).
State v. U. S. Express Co., 1 N. P. 259; 2 N. P. 98 (1895).
Andrews Bros. Co. v. Youngstown Coke Co., 86 Fed. 585 (1898).

VII. POWERS OF FOREIGN CORPORATIONS.

For corporate powers generally see note to § 8627.

A. Charter powers can not be exceeded. A corporation has no greater powers in a foreign state than in the state of its creation. A contract in excess of its charter powers, made in another state, is not validated by the fact that such contract is within the powers of a domestic corporation of such state.

Ewing v. Bank, 43 O. S. 31, 37 (1885).
Larwell v. Hanover Sgs. Fund Soc., 40 O. S. 274 (1883).
Curtis v. Hutchinson, 10 W. L. J. 134 (1852).

B. Effect of general law of home state. Where the charter powers of a foreign corporation are sufficiently broad to include a certain act, a general law of its home state restricting corporations in doing such acts will not affect it in other states. The power of a New York corporations to take land by devise is not affected by the New York statute of wills.

American Bible Soc. v. Marshall, 15 O. S. 537 (1864).

C. Powers must be exercised in accordance with laws of Ohio. A corporation doing business in Ohio must transact its business and exercise its powers in accordance with the laws of this state. It waives the powers and privileges of its charter which are contrary to the positive enactments of this state, or to the general spirit and policy of its law.

Manington v. Railway Co., 9 N. P. n. s. 641, 665 (1910).

Kit Carter Cattle Co. v. McGillin, 21 C. C. 210; 11 C. D. 413; s. c. 7 N. P. 575; 10 L. D. 146 (1900).

D. Powers not greater than powers of similar Ohio corporations. Foreign corporations have no greater powers than are possessed by Ohio corporations of like character.

G. C. § 5508.

See State v. Aetna Life Ins. Co., 69 O. S. 327 (1903).

Mannington v. H. V. Ry. Co., 8 O. L. R. 451, 484; 183 Fed. 133; 16 O. F. D. 552 (C. C. 1910).

E. To hold stock in Ohio corporations. See also note to § 8683.

A foreign corporation organized for the sole purpose of holding the stock and securities of an Ohio corporation may exercise in Ohio all the incidents of such ownership, such as voting at stockholders' meetings and giving assent to change of regulations, provided the exercise of such incidents does not tend to foster monopoly or suppress competition.

Toledo T. L. & P. Co. v. Smith, 58 Bull 201 (U. S. D. C. 1913).

F. To sue as a taxpayer. Where a foreign corporation is a taxpayer it may, under G. C. § 4314, bring suit to enjoin a municipality from abuse of its corporate powers.

United Cigars Stores Co. v. Von Bargen, 7 N. P. n. s. 420; 19 L. D. 120 (1908).

G. To hold land. Until forbidden by express legislation or the general policy of the law, a foreign corporation may hold land in Ohio.

State v. Sherman, 22 O. S. 411, 433 (1872).

It may acquire property by devise.

American Bible Soc. v. Marshall, 15 O. S. 537 (1864).

H. To appropriate property. A foreign corporation can not exercise the right of eminent domain in the absence of express statutory provisions conferring it.

Central Union Tel. Co. v. Columbus Grove, 8 C. C. n. s. 81; 18 C. D. 131 (1905).

Under the provisions of G. C. § 9090 a foreign railroad corporation may appropriate property in this state.

State v. Sherman, 22 O. S. 411, 434 (1872).

I. To acquire property by devise or bequest. A foreign corporation may acquire property by devise or bequest, in the absence of a prohibitory statute.

American Bible Soc. v. Marshall, 15 O. S. 537 (1864).

But such devise or bequest is in general liable to the collateral inheritance tax.

Humphreys v. State, 70 O. S. 67 (1904).

VIII. FOREIGN CORPORATIONS AS "PERSONS" AND "CITIZENS" UNDER FEDERAL CONSTITUTION AND LAWS.

A foreign corporation is a "person" within the provisions of the 14th amendment that no state shall deprive any person of property without due process of law, nor deny to any person within its jurisdiction the equal protection of the laws.

Southern Railway Co. v. Greene, 216 U. S. 400 (1910).

Blake v. McClung, 172 U. S. 239, 259 (1898).

Santa Clara County v. So. Pac. R. R. Co., 118 U. S. 394, 396 (1886).

The "liberty" guaranteed by the 14th amendment is the liberty of natural persons, not corporations.

Western Turf Assn. v. Greenberg, 204 U. S. 359, 363 (1907).

A foreign corporation is not a "citizen" within the provision of article IV, section 2, that "The citizens of each state shall be entitled to all privileges and immunities of citizens in the several states."

Western Union Tel. Co. v. Mayer, 28 O. S. 521 (1876).

Humphreys v. State, 70 O. S. 67, 86 (1904).

Blake v. McClung, 172 U. S. 239, 259 (1898).

For certain jurisdictional purposes, including diverse citizenship as a ground for the jurisdiction of federal courts, a corporation is to be regarded as a citizen of the state under the laws of which it was created and organized.

Railroad Co. v. Koonz, 104 U. S. 5, 12 (1881).

Shelby v. Hoffman, 7 O. S. 450 (1857).

Humphreys v. State, 70 O. S. 86 (1904).

IX. RIGHTS OF FOREIGN CORPORATIONS IN ABSENCE OF STATUTES.

In the absence of statutes, a foreign corporation may transact business, exercise its powers and sue or be sued in this state.

Newburg Petroleum Co. v. Weare, 27 O. S. 343 (1875).

State v. Sherman, 22 O. S. 412 (1872).

B. & O. R. R. Co. v. Cary, 28 O. S. 213, 214 (1876).

Hanna v. International Petroleum Co., 23 O. S. 622 (1873).

Bank v. Hall, 35 O. S. 167 (1878).

Lewis v. Bank, 12 Ohio 132 (1843).

But this right or privilege exists only by comity or legislative consent.

Western Union Tel. Co. v. Mayer, 28 O. S. 521 (1876).

X. RIGHT OF STATE TO EXCLUDE, OR IMPOSE CONDITIONS UPON, FOREIGN CORPORATIONS.

A. Foreign corporations may be wholly excluded from the state, or their admission to operate in the state may be made subject to such reasonable terms and conditions as the general assembly may impose.

Ashley v. Ryan, 153 U. S. 436; affirming 49 O. S. 504 (1894).

Western Union Co. v. Mayer, 28 O. S. 521 (1876).

Humphreys v. State, 70 O. S. 79, 80 (1904).

See papers (E. J. Marshall) 32 W. L. B. 166, 177; (F. E. Loughran) 34 W. L. B. 334.

There are limited exceptions to this rule. A state can not exclude or impose conditions upon a corporation in the employ of the federal government, nor a corporation engaged in interstate commerce.

Pembina, etc., Co. v. Pennsylvania, 125 U. S. 181, 190 (1883).

McClellan v. Chipman, 164 U. S. 347, 357, 359 (1896).

Toledo Commercial Co. v. Glen Mfg. Co., 55 O. S. 217 (1896).

A foreign corporation engaged in interstate commerce can not be required to pay, as a license fee for doing its intrastate business, a percentage on its entire capital stock, whether employed in the state or elsewhere. Such a tax is a burden on interstate commerce.

Ludwig v. Western Union Tel. Co., 216 U. S. 146 (1910).

Pullman Car Co. v. Kansas, 216 U. S. 56 (1910).

Western Union Tel. Co. v. Kansas, 216 U. S. 1 (1910).

A state can not require a foreign corporation, as a condition precedent to admission, to waive its right to remove actions to the federal courts; such a waiver is illegal and void, the requirement being repugnant to the federal constitution.

Railway v. Stringer, 32 O. S. 468 (1877).

B. & O. Ry. v. Cary, 28 O. S. 208 (1876).

Assurance Co. v. Pierce, 27 O. S. 155 (1875).

Herndon v. Chicago, etc., Co., 218 U. S. 135 (1910).
Roach v. A. T. & S. F. Ry., 218 U. S. 159 (1910).

But where a foreign corporation enters a state in which a statute (see §§ 9384, 9563) provides for a revocation of its license for removing actions to federal courts, the state may enforce such provision and revoke the license of the corporation.

Doyle v. Insurance Co., 94 U. S. 535 (1876).

It has been held that where a foreign railroad company entered a state, in compliance with its laws, and acquired a large amount of property within the state, its license could not be revoked, under authority of a statute subsequently enacted, for removing an action to federal court.

Herndon v. Railway Co., 218 U. S. 135 (1910).
Roach v. Railway Co., 218 U. S. 159 (1910).

B. Privilege of doing business is not property.
W. U. Tel. Co. v. Mayer, 28 O. S. 521 (1876).

XI. PERMISSION TO ENTER STATE AS A CONTRACT.

Aetna Iron & Steel Co. v. Taylor, 3 N. P. 152; 4 L. D. 180; 13 C. C. 602; 5 C. D. 242 (1896).

Compare American Smelting, etc., Co. v. Colorado, 204 U. S. 103 (1906).

XII. INSOLVENT FOREIGN CORPORATIONS.

A. Subject to involuntary bankruptcy. When. A petition in involuntary bankruptcy may be filed against a foreign corporation in the district in which it has had its principal place of business for the greater portion of the preceding six months,

Dressel v. North State Lumber Co., 107 Fed. 255; 5 A. B. R. 744 (1901).

In re Magid-Hope Silk Mfg. Co., 110 Fed. 352; 6 A. B. R. 610 (1901).
White Mountain Paper Co. v. Morse, 127 Fed. 643; 11 A. B. R. 633 (1904).

although the corporation has not obtained a license from the state permitting it to do business therein.

In re Duplex Radiator Co., 142 Fed. 906; 15 A. B. R. 324 (1906).

B. Preferences. A preferential transfer of property by a foreign corporation to one creditor, is not void but voidable. Ohio creditors can not levy on such property, but may have the transfer treated and enforced as an assignment for all of its creditors.

Bryant v. Johnson, 12 C. C. 102; 5 C. D. 333 (1896).

C. Foreign assignment for creditors. Effect on property in Ohio. A deed of assignment for creditors executed by a foreign corporation in its home state can not be filed in a probate court, or court of insolvency, under G. C. §§ 11092 and 11093; but it may be treated as a conveyance of property, and the trust enforced in equity.

Keystone Bank v. Union Oil Co., 2 C. C. n. s. 420; 15 C. D. 464 (1903).

Wright v. Franklin Bank, 59 O. S. 80, 95 (1898).
Compare Hall v. Ohio, etc., Co., 24 W. L. B. 310 (1890).

D. Jurisdiction of Ohio courts to wind up business. The courts of Ohio have jurisdiction to wind up a part of the business of a foreign corporation which has been interdicted by the laws of this state.

Everhardt v. U. S. Inv. Red. Co., 8 N. P. 525; 11 L. D. 688. ·

PART VI.

PUBLIC UTILITIES COMMISSION.

Section 487. (The public utilities commission of Ohio; appointment, term, vacancies.) There shall be and there is hereby created a public utilities commission of Ohio and by that name the commission may sue and be sued. The public utilities commission shall consist of three members, who shall be appointed by the governor with the advice and consent of the senate, and shall possess the powers and duties herein specified as well as all powers necessary and proper to carry out the purposes of this chapter. Immediately after this act shall take effect, the governor shall, with the advice and consent of the senate, appoint a member whose term shall expire on the first day of February, 1915; another whose term shall expire on the first day of February, 1917, and another whose term shall expire on the first day of February, 1919; and thereafter each member shall be appointed and confirmed for a term of six years. Vacancies shall be filled in the same manner for unexpired terms. One of such commissioners, to be designated by the governor, shall, during the term of the appointing governor, be the chairman of the commission. Not more than two of said commissioners shall belong to or be affiliated with the same political party. (May 5, 1913, 103 v. 804, § 1, in effect August 8, 1913; April 2, 1906, 98 v. 342, § 1; R. S. Sec. 244-11.)

The original railroad commission act (98 v. 342) was held constitutional.

Coal Co. v. Railroad Commission, 8 N. P. n. s. 585; 19 L. D. 783.

B. & O. R. R. Co. v. Railroad Commission, 10 N. P. n. s. 665; 21 L. D. 468; affd. no rep. 86 O. S. 365.

The railroad commission act was, in part, adapted from the Wisconsin railroad commission act.

Commission v. Railway Co., 79 O. S. 419, 424.

A governor has no power to appoint a commissioner whose term of office is to begin after the expiration of the term of office of such governor.

State v. Sullivan, 81 O. S. 79.

State v. Morris, 11 C. C. n. s. 547; 20 C. D. 119.

The restrictions, limitations and prohibitions of this act are matters between the state and railroad companies. Where a railroad return ticket is not made non-transferable, the act does not prohibit the sale of unused coupon.

Knecht v. Railway Co., 6 N. P. n. s. 13; 18 L. D. 202.

Section 488. (Removal; filing record of proceedings and decision.) The governor may remove any commissioner for inefficiency, neglect of duty, or malfeasance in office, giving to him a copy of the charges against him and an opportunity to be publicly heard, in person or by counsel, in his own defense, upon not less than ten days' notice. If such commissioner shall be removed the governor shall file in the office of the secretary of state a complete statement of all charges made against such commissioner, and his findings thereon, together with a complete record of the proceedings, and his decision therein shall be final. (May 5, 1913, 103 v. 804, § 2; G. C. § 491 (original number); April 2, 1906, 98 v. 341, § 1; R. S. 244-11b.)

Section 489.   (Oath.)   Before entering upon the discharge of the duties of his office each commissioner shall take and subscribe to an oath of office, which oath in writing shall be filed in the office of the secretary of state. (May 5, 1913, 103 v. 804, § 3; G. C. § 490 (original number); April 2, 1906, 98 v. 343, § 1; R. S. Sec. 244-11e.)

Section 490.   (Salary.)   Each of the members of the public utilities commission shall receive from the state an annual salary of six thousand dollars ($6,000.00), payable in the same manner as other state officers are paid. (May 5, 1913, 103 v. 805, § 4.)

Section 491.   (Qualifications.)   Each commissioner shall be a bona fide resident of this state and shall not, during the term of his office, hold any other office under the government of the United States, or of this state, or of any political subdivision thereof, either of trust or profit; nor shall he engage in any occupation or business inconsistent with his duties as such commissioner, but devote his entire time to the duties of his office. (May 5, 1913, 103 v. 805, § 5; G. C. § 488 (original number); April 2, 1906, 98 v. 342, § 1; R. S. Sec. 244-11a.)

Section 492.   (Bond.)   Before entering upon the duties of his office each member shall give a bond in the sum of five thousand dollars ($5,000.00) with a sufficient surety or sureties which shall be approved by the treasurer of state; and after such approval such bond shall be filed with the secretary of state. If such bond is executed by a surety company the premiums thereon shall be paid out of the funds appropriated for the expense of the commission. (May 5, 1913, 103 v. 805, § 6.)

Section 493.   (Quorum; transaction of business.)   A majority of the commission shall constitute a quorum for the transaction of any business, for the performance of any duty or for the exercise of any power of the commission. No vacancy in the commission shall impair the right of the remaining commissioners to exercise all the powers of the commission. The act of a majority of the commission, when in session as a board, shall be deemed to be the act of the commission; but any investigation, inquiry or hearing which the commission has power to undertake or to hold may be undertaken or held by or before any commissioner designated for the purpose by the commission, and every finding, order or decision made by a commissioner so designated, pursuant to such investigation, inquiry or hearing, approved and confirmed by the commission and ordered filed in its office, shall be and be deemed to be the finding, order or decision of the commission. (May 5, 1913, 103 v. 805, § 7; G. C. § 493 (original number); April 2, 1906, 98 v. 343, § 1.)

Section 494. (Location of office; sessions.) The office of the commission shall be at the seat of government in the city of Columbus, in suitable quarters to be provided by the state, and shall be open between the hours of eight-thirty a. m. and five-thirty p. m. throughout the year, Sundays and legal holidays excepted. The commission shall hold its sessions at least once in each calendar month in said city of Columbus, but may also meet at such other times and at such other places as may be necessary for the proper performance of its duties. For the purpose of holding session in places other than the seat of government the commission shall have power to rent quarters or offices, and the expense thereof, in connection thereith, shall be paid in the same manner as other expenses authorized by this chapter. (May 5, 1913, 103 v. 805, § 8; G. C. § 498 (original number); April 2, 1906, 98 v. 344, § 1.)

Section 495. (Equipment and supplies.) The commission is authorized to procure all necessary books, maps, charts, stationery, instruments, office furniture, apparatus and appliances, including telephone and telegraph service (and to purchase from the interstate commerce commission blank forms for the use of railroads and other utilities in making their annual reports) necessary for the proper administration of the affairs of said commission as provided in this chapter, and the same shall be audited and paid as other expenses are audited and paid. (May 5, 1913, 103 v. 806, § 9; G. C. § 498 (original number); April 2, 1906, 98 v. 344, § 1.)

Section 496. (Secretary; duties.) The commission shall

G. C· § 498   OHIO PRIVATE CORPORATIONS.   328

appoint a secretary who shall hold office during the pleasure of the commission. It shall be the duty of the secretary to keep a full and true record of all proceedings of the commission, to issue all necessary process, writs, warrants and notices, to keep all books, maps, documents and papers ordered filed by the commission, and of all orders made by a commissioner, or by the commission, or approved and confirmed by it and ordered filed; and he shall be responsible to the commission for the safe custody and preservation of all such documents in its office. Under the direction of the commission the secretary shall have general charge of its office, superintend its clerical business and perform such other duties, as the commission may prescribe. He may administer oaths in all parts of the state, so far as the exercise of such power is properly incidental to the performance of his duty or that of the commission. The secretary shall designate from time to time, with the approval of the commission, one of the clerks appointed by the commission to perform the duties of secretary during his absence, and during such time the clerk so designated shall, at the office, possess the powers of the secretary of the commission. (May 5, 1913, 103 v. 806, § 10; G. C. §§ 494, 495 (original numbering); April 2, 1906, 98 v. 343, § 1.)

Section 497. (Legal adviser; special counsel.) The attorney general shall be the legal adviser of the commission, but shall designate, subject to the approval of the governor, one or more of his special counsel, to perform the services and discharge the duties of attorney to the commission. Such specially designated counsel shall receive such salary as may be fixed by the commission and approved by the governor, such salary to be paid in the same manner as that of the members of the commission. (May 5, 1913, 103 v. 806, § 11.)

Section 498. (Employment of other officers, experts, etc.) The commission shall have power to employ, during its pleasure, such other officers, and experts, engineers, statisticans, accountants, inspectors, clerks, stenographers and other employes as it may deem necessary to carry out the provisions of this chapter or to perform the duties and exercise the powers conferred by law upon the commission. All officers, experts, engineers, statisticians, accountants, inspectors, stenographers, clerks and other employes of the commission shall receive such salaries and compensation as may be fixed by the commission, with the approval of the governor; said salaries and compensation to said officers and employes to be paid out of the state treasury upon the warrant of the auditor, upon presentation of vouchers signed by the chairman and secretary of the commission. (May 5, 1913, 103 v. 806, § 12; May 31, 1911, 102 v. 574, § 85; G. C. § 614-81 (original number); G. C. § 496 (original number); April 2, 1906, 98 v. 343, § 1.)

Section 499. (Expenses; how paid.) All expenses incurred by the commission pursuant to the provisions of this chapter, including the actual and necessary traveling and other expenses and disbursements of the commission, their officers and employes, incurred while on the business of the commission shall be paid from funds appropriated for the use of the commission after being approved by the commission. An itemized statement of traveling expenses shall be sworn to by the person incurring same before payment is made. (May 5, 1913, 103 v. 807, § 13; G. C. § 499 (original number); April 2, 1906, 98 v. 344, § 1; G. C. § 614-81 (original number); May 31, 1911, 102 v. 574, § 85.)

Section 499-1. (Right of commission, employes, etc., to pass on vehicles of common carrier.) The commissioners, their attorney, secretary, or other officers and employes of the commission shall, when in the performance of their official duties, have the right to pass, free of charge, on all railroads, cars, vessels and other vehicles of every common carrier, as said term is defined in this chapter, subject, in whole or in part, to the control or regulation by the commission, between points within this state, and such persons shall not be denied the right to travel upon any railroad, car, vessel or other vehicle of such common carrier, or any part thereof, whether such railroad, car, vessel or other vehicle be used for the transportation of passengers or freight, and regardless of its class. (May 5, 1913, 103 v. 807, § 14.)

See § 608.

Section 499-2. (Seal.) The commission shall have a seal, bearing the following inscription: "The Public Utilities Commission of Ohio". The seal shall be affixed to all writs and authentications of copies of records and to such other instruments as the commission shall direct. All courts shall take judicial notice of said seal. (May 5, 1913, 103 v. 807, § 15; G. C. § 31-2 (original numbering); May 31, 1911, 102 v. 573, § 79.)

Section 499-3. (Who eligible to the office of commissioner.) No person in the employ of or holding any official relation to any person, corporation or utility, which said person, corporation or utility is subject, in whole or in part, to regulation by the commission, and no person holding stocks or bonds of any such corporation or utility or who is in any manner pecuniarily interested therein shall be appointed to or hold the office of commissioner or be appointed or employed by the commission; provided, that if any such person shall become the owner of such stocks or bonds, or become pecuniarily interested in such corporation or utility otherwise than voluntarily he shall, within a reasonable time, divest himself of such ownership or interest; failing to do so, his office or employment shall become vacant. (May 5, 1913, 103 v. 807, § 16; G. C. § 488 (original number); April 2, 1906, 98 v. 342, § 1.)

Section 499-4. (Commissioner, attorney, employe, etc., prohibited from accepting gifts, etc.) Each commissioner, attorney to the commission, the secretary to the commission and every person employed or appointed to office, either by the commission or by the attorney to the commission, is hereby forbidden and prohibited from accepting any gift, gratuity, emolument or employment from any public utility or railroad or any officer, agent or employe thereof, or to solicit, suggest, request or recommend, directly or indirectly, to any person, corporation or utility subject to the supervision of the commission, or to any officer, attorney, agent or employe thereof, the appointment of any person to any office, place, position or employment. Any commissioner, attorney to the commission, the secretary thereof, or any person employed or appointed to office by the commission violating any provision of this section, shall be removed from the office held by him. (May 5, 1913, 103 v. 807, § 17.)

Section 499-5. (Annual report to governor.) All proceedings of the commission and all documents and records in its possession shall be public records. The commission shall make and submit to the governor, on or before the fifteenth day of December of each year a report containing a full and complete account of its transactions and proceedings for the preceding fiscal year together with such other facts, suggestions and recommendations as it may deem of value to the people of the state; which report shall be published as the reports of the heads of other departments of the state, for the; use of the general assembly and the public. (May 5, 1913, 103 v. 808, § 18; G. C. § 614-80 (original number); April 22, 1913, 103 v. 176; May 31, 1902, 102 v. 574, § 84;

G. C. § 614 (original number); R. S. Sec. 264; February 27, 1877, 74 v. 33, § 12.)

Whether a railway company has complied with the terms of a certain statute must, in an action between the railroad company and an individual, be proved. Judicial notice will not be taken of a statement in a report of the commissioner of railroads that such statute has been complied with. Railroad Co. v. Hoffhines, 46 O. S. 643.

Section 499-6. (Publication of rules governing proceedings.) The commission may adopt and publish rules to govern its proceedings, and to regulate the mode and manner of investigations and hearings of railroads and other parties before it. All hearings shall be open to the public. (May 5, 1913, 103 v. 808, § 19; G. C. § 497 (original number); April 2, 1906, 98 v. 344, § 1.)

Section 499-7. (The public service commission of Ohio superseded.) The public utilities commission shall succeed to and be possessed of the rights, authority and powers now exercised by the public service commission of Ohio and perform all the duties now imposed upon the public service commission of Ohio, and said powers and authority shall be exercised and enforced and said duties performed in the manner now provided by law for the said public service commission. Said public service commission of Ohio shall on and after the time when this act shall take effect have no further legal existence, and the public utilities commission is hereby authorized and directed to assume and continue as successor of said public service commission of Ohio. Wherever in the General Code the terms railroad commission or public service commission occur, the term public utilities commission shall be substituted therefor. (May 5, 1913, 103 v. 808, § 20.)

Section 499-8. (Valuation of property to determine justice of rates. Assistance by public utility required.) The commission, for the purpose of ascertaining the reasonableness and justice of rates and charges for the service rendered by public utilities or railroads of this state, or for any other purpose authorized by law, shall investigate and ascertain the value of the property of every public utility or railroad in the state, used and useful for the service and convenience of the public. At the request of the council of any municipality the commission shall also investigate and ascertain the value of the property of any public utility used and useful for service and convenience of the public where the whole or major portion of such utility is situated in such municipality. Every public utility or railroad shall furnish to the commission, its engineers, experts or other assistants from time to time and as the commission may require maps, profiles, contracts, reports of engineers and other documents, records and papers or copies of any or all of the same, in aid of any investigation and ascertainment of the value of its property, and shall grant to the commission or its agents free access to all of its premises and property and its accounts, records and memoranda whenever and wherever requested by any such duly authorized agent, and every public utility or railroad is hereby directed and required to co-operate with and aid the commission in the work of the valuation of its property in such further particulars and to such extent as the commission may require and direct. The commission shall have such power to make all rules and regulations, as to it may seem necessary, to ascertain the value of each and every utility or railroad in the state. (May 5, 1913, 103 v. 808, § 21; G. C. §§ 614-24 (original number); May 31, 1911, 102 v. 557, § 26.)

Section 499-9. (Facts; commission has authority to ascertain and report in the valuation of property.) The commission shall prescribe the details of the inventory of the property of each public utility or railroad in the state; and such inventory shall include all the kinds and classes of property, with the value of each, owned by each public utility or railroad, used and useful for the service and convenience of the public. In ascertaining the value of the various kinds and classes of property of each public utility or railroad, the commission shall have authority to ascertain and report in such detail as it may deem necessary as to each piece of property owned or used by such public utility or railroad to show separately the following facts:

A. The original cost, if any, of each parcel of land owned and used by such public utility or railroad, and a statement of the conditions of acquisition; whether by direct purchase, by donation, by exercise of the power of eminent domain or otherwise.

B. The value as of a date certain, of each parcel of land owned and used by such public utility or railroad, by comparison with the value of contiguous and neighboring parcels of land, and land of similar character as to location and use.

C. If there shall be any additional value to such utility or railroad by reason of the ownership by it of one or more parcels of land and its use as a continuous right of way for transportation purposes, or for other purpose, such additional value shall be separately and specifically set forth for each parcel.

D. The cost of new production as of a date certain, of all physical property other than land, owned and used by such public utility or railroad, showing the values of the separate items comprising such property, together with the unit basis of such valuation.

E. Depreciation, if any, from the new reproductive cost as of a date certain, for existing mechanical deterioration, for age, for obsolescence, for lack of utility or for any other cause, the percentage and amount of each class of depreciation, if any, to be specifically set forth in detail.

F. The net value as of a date certain, of all physical property other than land owned by such utility or railroad, to be derived by deducting the sum of the amounts of depreciation from the sum of the new reproductive costs.

G. If there shall be any additional value given to the value of the property of a public utility or railroad due to the possession of a franchise to perform a public service, or for good will or for financing, such additional value shall be separately and specifically set forth, together with the basis for the computation or estimate of such additional value.

H. A duplicate copy of the record of every physical valuation of a public utility or railroad shall be furnished to the Ohio tax commission, on request, for its use in ascertaining the value of the property of such utility or railroad for purposes of taxation, and upon demand any person or corporation owning or operating a public utility or railroad shall be furnished with a copy of the valuation of his or its property.

Such investigations and report shall show separately the property used and useful to such utility or railroad in the furnishing of the service to the public, and the property held by such utility or railroad for other purposes, and such other items concerning values and methods of making valuations as the commission may deem proper; which said inventories and reports shall be filed in the office of the commission for the information of the governor and the general assembly. (May 5, 1913, 103 v. 809, § 22.)

Section 499-10. (What additional facts report may show.) Such investigation and report shall also show whenever the commission may deem necessary, the amounts and dates and rates of interest of all bonds, outstanding against each public utility or railroad, the property upon which they are a lien, the amounts paid therefor; and, in such detail as may be necessary, the original capital stock and the moneys

received by any such utility or railroad by reason of any
issue of stock, bonds or other securities. Such report shall
also show the net and gross receipts of such utility or railroad and the method by which moneys were expended or
paid out and the purpose of such payments. The commission shall have the power to prescribe the method of procedure to be followed in making the investigation and valuation and the form in which the results of the ascertainment
of the value of each utility or railroad shall be submitted,
and the classifications of the elements that constitute the
ascertained value. Such investigation shall also show the
value of the property of every public utility or railroad as
a whole; and, in case such utility or railroad has property
in more than one county, the value of its property in each
of such counties. (May 5, 1913, 103 v. 810, § 23.)

Section 499-11. (Revision and correction of valuations.)
The commission, during the making of the valuation herein
provided for, and after the completion thereof, shall thereafter in like manner keep itself informed through its engineers, experts and other assistants of all extensions and improvements or other changes in the condition and value of
the property of all public utilities or railroads and shall
ascertain the value of such extensions, improvements and
changes and shall from time to time, as may be required for
the proper regulation of such public utilities or railroads,
revise and correct its valuations of property, showing such
revisions and corrections as a whole and as to each county
in the state. Such revisions and corrections shall be filed
in the same manner as is provided for original reports. (May
5, 1913, 103 v. 811, § 24.)

**Section 499-12. (Notice to public utility before valuation
becomes final; protest, hearing.)** The commission, whenever
it shall have completed the valuation of the property of any
public utility or railroad and before such valuation shall
have become final, shall give notice by registered letter to
such public utility or railroad, or if the whole or the major
portion of said utility or railroad is situated in any municipality, then to the mayor of such municipality, stating the
valuations placed upon the several kinds and classes of
property of such public utility or railroad and upon the
property as a whole. If within thirty days after such
notification no protest shall have been filed with the commission then said valuation shall be and become final. If
notice of protest shall have been filed, however, by any public utility or railroad, the commission shall fix a time for

hearing the same and shall consider at such hearing any matter material thereto presented by such public utility or railroad or municipality, in support of its protest or by any representative of the public against such protest. If after the hearing of any protest of any valuation so fixed, the commission shall be of the opinion that its inventory is incomplete or inaccurate or that its valuation is incorrect it shall make such changes as may be necessary and shall issue an order making such corrected valuations final. A final valuation by the commission and all classifications made for the ascertainment of such valuations shall be public and shall be prima facie evidence relative to the value of the property. (May 5, 1913, 103 v. 811, § 25; May 31, 1911, 102 v. 557, § 27; G. C. § 614-25 (original number).

Section 499-13. (Ohio state university engineers and experts may be employed.) In the employment of engineers, experts or other assistants the commission may make use of such engineers and experts as may be employed in the Ohio state university in such manner as may be provided by mutual arrangement between the commission and the trustees and faculty of such university, and any information, data and equipment of such university shall be placed at the disposal of the commission. Whenever the authority is conferred or the obligation imposed by law upon the commission to ascertain the value of any public utility or railroad, such valuation under such authority or obligation shall be made in accordance with the provisions of this act. (May 5, 1913, 103 v. 811, § 26.)

Section 499-14. (System of accounts may be established for public utilities.) The commission shall have power to establish a system of accounts to be kept by the public utilities or railroads (including municipally owned or operated utilities), or to classify said public utilities or railroads and to establish a system of accounts for each class, and to prescribe the manner in which such accounts shall be kept; and such system shall when practicable conform to the system prescribed by the tax commission of Ohio. It may also in its discretion prescribe the forms of accounts, records and memoranda to be kept by such public utilities or railroads, including the accounts, records and memoranda of the movement of traffic as well as the receipts and expenditures of moneys, and any other forms, records and memoranda which in the judgment of the commission may be necessary to carry out any of the provisions of this chapter. The system of accounts established by the commission and the forms of accounts, records and memoranda prescribed by it shall not be inconsistent, in the case of corporations subject to the provisions of the act of congress entitled "An act to regulate commerce" approved February fourth, eighteen hundred and eighty-seven, and the acts amendatory thereof and supplementary thereto, with the systems and forms from time to time established for such corporations by the interstate commerce commission, but nothing herein contained shall affect the power of the commission to prescribe forms of accounts, records and memoranda covering information in addition to that required by the interstate commerce commission. The commission may, after hearing had upon its own motion or upon complaint, prescribe by order the accounts in which particular outlays and receipts shall be entered, charged or credited. Where the commission has prescribed the forms of accounts, records or memoranda to be kept by any public utility or railroad for any of its business, it shall thereafter be unlawful for such public utility or railroad to keep any accounts, records or memoranda for such business other than those so prescribed, or those prescribed by or under the authority of any other state or of the United States, excepting such accounts, records or memoranda as shall be explanatory of and supplemental to the accounts, records or memoranda prescribed by the commission. The commission shall at all times have access to all accounts kept by such utilities or railroads and may designate any of its officers or employes to inspect and examine any and all such accounts. It shall be the duty of the auditor or other chief accounting officer of any such utility to keep such accounts and make the reports provided for in section 614-48 of the General Code. Whoever being such auditor, or chief accounting officer violates or fails to comply with the provisions of this section shall upon conviction thereof be subject to the penalties provided for in section 614-65 of the General Code. It shall be the duty of the attorney general to enforce the provisions of this section upon request of the commission, by mandamus or other appropriate proceedings. (May 5, 1913, 103 v. 812, § 27.)

Section 499-15. (Hearing to ascertain value of property; notice.) For the purpose of ascertaining the value of the property of every public utility or railroad in this state, including municipally owned or operated utilities, the commission may cause a hearing or hearings to be held at such time or times and place or places as the commission may designate. Before any hearing is had, the commission shall give the public utility or railroad affected thereby, or if the whole or the major portion of said utility or railroad is situated in any municipality, then to the mayor of such municipality, at least thirty days' written notice specifying the time and place of hearing, and such notice shall be sufficient to authorize the commission to inquire into the matters designated in this section, but this provision shall not prevent the commission from making any preliminary examination or investigation into the matters herein referred to, or from inquiring into such matters in any other investigation or hearing. All public utilities or railroads affected, and any municipality in which the whole or the major portion of said utility or railroad is located, shall be entitled to be heard and to introduce evidence at such hearing or hearings. The commission is empowered to resort to any other source of information available. The evidence introduced at such hearing shall be reduced to writing and certified under the seal of the commission. (May 5, 1913, 103 v. 813, § 28; May 31, 1911, 102 v. 557, § 27; G. C. § 614-25 (original numbering).)

Section 499-16. (Filing finding of facts; review.) The commission shall make and file its findings of fact in writing upon all matters concerning which evidence shall have been introduced before it which in its judgment have bearing on the value of the property of the public utility or railroad affected. Such findings shall be subject to review by the supreme court of this state in the same manner and within the same time as other orders and decisions of the commission. (May 5, 1913, 103 v. 813, § 29.)

Section 499-17. (Admissibility in evidence of finding.) The findings of the commission so made and filed, when properly certified under the seal of the commission, shall be admissible in evidence in any action, proceeding or hearing before the commission or any court, in which the commission, the state or any officer, department or institution thereof, or any county, city, municipality or other body politic and the public utility railroad affected may be interested, whether arising under the provisions of this chapter or otherwise, and such findings, when so introduced, shall be evidence of the facts therein stated as of the date therein stated under conditions then existing. (May 5, 1913, 103 v. 813, § 30.)

Section 499-18. (Further hearings.) The commission may from time to time cause further hearings and investigations to be had for the purpose of making revaluations or ascertaining the value of any betterments, improvements, additions or extensions made by any public utility or railroad subsequent to any prior hearing or investigation, and

may examine into all matters which may change, modify or
affect any finding of fact previously made, and may at such
time make findings of fact supplementary to those theretofore made. Such hearings shall be had upon the same notice
and be conducted in the same manner and the findings so
made shall have the same force and effect as is provided
herein for such original notice, hearing and findings; provided, that such findings made at such supplemental hearings
or investigations shall be considered in connection with and
as a part of the original findings except in so far as such
supplemental findings shall change or modify the findings
made at the original hearing or investigation. (May 5, 1913,
103 v. 813, § 31.)

**Section 500. (May confer with railroad commissioners
of other states.)** The commission may confer on any matters relating to railroads by correspondence or by attending
conventions, or otherwise, with the railroad commissioners
of other states, and with the interstate commerce commission.
(98 v. 344, § 1; April 2, 1906; R. S. Sec. 244-11m.)

Section 501. ("Railroad" defined. Other companies.)
The term "railroad" as used in this chapter shall include
all corporations, companies, individuals, associations of individuals, their lessees, trustees, or receivers appointed by a
court, which owns, operates, manages or controls a railroad
or part thereof as a common carrier in this state, or which
owns, operates, manages or controls any cars or other equipment used thereon, or which owns, operates, manages or controls any bridges, terminals, union depots, side tracks, docks,
wharves, or storage elevators used in connection therewith,
whether owned by such railroad or otherwise. Such term
"railroad" shall mean and embrace express companies, water
transportation companies and interurban railroad companies,
and all duties required of and penalties imposed upon a railroad or an officer or agent thereof insofar as they are applicable, shall be required of and imposed upon express companies, water transportation companies and interurban railroad companies, their officers and agents. The commission
shall have the power of supervision and control of express
companies, water transportation companies and interurban
railroad companies to the same extent as railroads. (May
31, 1911, 102 v. 549; April 2, 1906, 98 v. 344, § 2; R. S.
Sec. 244-12.)

For definitions of "railroad." See Commissioners v. Traction Co.
75 O. S. 548, 559; In re Avon Beach, etc., Co. 3 N. P. n. s. 561; 16 L.
D. 87.

A state court is without power to enforce payment of a statutory penalty against a railroad, out of funds, in the hands of a receiver appointed by a federal court, but the commission probably has a right to apply to the federal court, which has appointed a receiver for the railroad, for an order compelling the receiver to execute an order of the commission, requiring the receiver to perform the statutory duty.

Rep. Atty. Gen. 1911-1912, p. 724.

Section 502. (Application of act.) This chapter shall apply to the transportation of passengers and property between points within this state, to the receiving, switching, delivering, storing and handling of such property, and to all charges connected therewith, including icing charges and mileage charges, to all railroad companies, sleeping car companies, equipment companies, express companies, car companies, freight and freight line companies, to all associations of persons, whether incorporated or otherwise, which do business as common carriers, upon or over a line of railroad within this state, and to a common carrier engaged in the transportation of passengers or property wholly by rail or partly by rail and partly by water or wholly by water. In addition thereto the provisions of this act shall apply to the regulation of any and all other duties, services, practices and charges, of the railroad company, incident to the shipping and receiving of freight, which are proper subjects of regulation, excepting only, that they shall not apply to the regulation of commerce with foreign nations, and among the several states, and with the Indian tribes. (May 31, 1911, 102 v. 549; May 20, 1910, 101 v. 327; April 2, 1906, 98 v. 345, § 2; R. S. Sec. 244-12a.)

Before the amendment of this section it was held that the railroad commission had no power to regulate car service or demurrage charges as to cars employed in interstate commerce.

Railroad Commission v. Ann Arbor R. R Co., 12 C. C. n. s. 317; 21 C. D. 340, affirming 8 N. P. n. s. 233; 19 L. D. 691.

A state court has no jurisdiction to enjoin the putting into effect of an increased rate on interstate traffic, pending a determination by the Interstate Commerce Commission of the reasonableness of the proposed rate.

Ohio Dairy Co. v. Railway, 7 N. P. n. s. 451; 19 L. D. 97.

An order of the commission requiring a railroad to cease and desist from requiring shippers of milk, between points within the state, to load the same into cars, is not an interference with interstate commerce.

B. & O. R. R. v. Railroad Commission 10 N. P. n. s. 665; 21 L. D. 468, aff'd, no rep., 86 O. S. 365, s. c., 88 O. S. —.

Section 503. (To what this chapter shall not apply.) This chapter shall not apply to street and electric railroads engaged solely in the transportation of passengers within the limits of cities, or other private railroads not doing business as common carriers. (98 v. 345, § 2; R. S. Sec. 244-12b.)

Section 504. (Railroad required to furnish adequate service and facilities.) Each railroad shall furnish reasonably adequate service and facilities. The charges made for any service rendered or to be rendered in the transportation of passengers or property, or for any service in connection therewith, or for the receiving, switching, delivering, storing or handling of such property, shall be reasonable and just. Every unjust and unreasonable charge for such service is prohibited and declared to be unlawful. (April 2, 1906, 98 v. 345, § 3; R. S. Sec. 244-13.)

See further as to rates and service note to § 535.

Competition is an element to be considered in determining whether rates are reasonable and just.

Between competitive points a railroad may reduce its rates below those of its competitors.

Commission v. Railway Co., 82 O. S. 25, affirming 5 N. P. n. s. 265; 18 L. D. 21.

Abandonment of line. Will not be prevented by commission, when. Bickerstaff v. Steubenville, etc., Co., 5 O. L. R. 539; 53 B. 29.

Power of commission to enforce contracts. The commission has no power to enforce a contract made by an interurban railroad to stop its cars at a certain platform, in consideration of such platform being constructed by the complainant; or to award damages for its violation.

Ashley v. Sandusky, etc., Co., 5 O. L. R. 359, 361; 52 B. 498 (Railroad Commission).

Section to be construed as a part of entire act. This section and § 567 are to be operative only as a part of the whole legislative plan. They can not be segregated either in the interpretation of the act or in its application.

Warner v. Railway, 11 N. P. n. s. 487 (C. P. 1911).

Adequate service and facilities.

See notes to §§ 535 and 519.

Section 505. (Railroad required to file schedules with commission.) Each railroad shall print in plain type and file with the commission, within a time fixed by the commission, schedules which shall be open to public inspection, showing all rates, fares and charges for transportation of passengers and property, and any service in connection therewith, which such railroad has established and which are in force at such time between all points in this state upon its line, or any line controlled or operated by it. (April 2, 1906, 98 v. 345, § 4; R. S. Sec. 244-14.)

The commission has no discretion as to the filing of tariffs by industrial roads which are common carriers as defined by § 501.

Rept. Atty. Gen. 1911-1912, p. 706.

Section 506. (What schedules shall contain and where posted.) The schedules shall plainly state the places upon the line of such railroad or upon any line controlled or operated by it in this state between which passengers and property will be carried, and there shall be filed with such schedule the classification of freight in force. As a part of such schedules, each railroad shall publish the rules and regulations affecting the rates charged or to be charged for transportation of passengers or property; also its charges for delay in loading or unloading cars, for track and car service, rental, demurrage, switching, terminal or transfer service, or for any other service in connection with transportation of persons or property. Two copies of such schedules, in such form and place as to be accessible for inspection by the public, shall be filed and kept on file in every depot, station and office of such railroad where passengers or freight are received for transportation. (R. S. Sec. 244-14; April 2, 1906, 98 v. 345, § 4.)

Section 507. (Schedules of joint rates.) When passengers or property are transported over connecting lines in this state operated by two or more railroads, and such railroads establish joint rates, fares and charges, a schedule thereof, compiled as provided in the next preceding section, shall be printed, filed with the commission and filed in every depot, station and office of such railroads where passengers or property are received for transportation. (R. S. Sec. 244-14; April 2, 1906, 98 v. 345, § 4.)

Section 508. (Changes in schedules.) No change thereafter shall be made in any schedule, including schedule of joint rates, or in any classification, except upon ten days' notice to the commission. All such changes shall be plainly indicated upon existing schedules, or by filing new schedules ten days prior to the time they are to take effect, but the commission, upon application of any railroad, may prescribe a less time within which a reduction may be made. Copies of all new schedules shall be filed as provided in the preceding section in every depot, station and office of such railroad ten days prior to the time they are to take effect, unless the commission shall prescribe a less time. (April 2, 1906, 98 v. 346, § 4; R. S. Sec. 244-14a.)

Section 509. (Posting changes in schedules.) When a change is made in an existing schedule, including schedules of joint rates, the railroad shall post a notice in a conspicuous place in every depot, station and office, stating that changes

have been made in the schedules on file, specifying the class
or commodity affected and the date when such changes will
take effect. (April 2, 1906, 98 v. 346, § 4; R. S. Sec. 244-14b.)

Section 510. (Charges shall conform to schedule.) No
railroad shall charge, demand, collect or receive a greater
or less compensation for the transportation of passengers or
property, or for any service in connection therewith, than is
specified in such printed schedules, including schedules of
joint rates, as being then in force. The rates, fares and
charges named therein shall be the lawful rates, fares and
charges until they are changed as provided in this chapter.
(R. S. Sec. 244-14c; April 2, 1906, 98 v. 346, § 4.)

Where a railroad company, by mistake, collected less than its published rate, it may recover the deficiency from the consignee.
Railway Co. v. Magnus Co. 13 C. C. n. s. 305 (1910).
Store Fixture Co. v. Railway Co., 1 N. P. n. s. 242; 13 L. D. 648.
A rate scheduled and established pursuant to the statute is the
lawful rate. If unjust or discriminatory it may be changed by the
commission, but a railroad charging such established rate is not liable
in damages under § 569.
Warner v. Railway, 11 N. P. n. s. 487 (C. P. 1911).

Section 511. (Commission shall prescribe forms.) The
commission may prescribe such changes in the form in which
schedules are issued by a railroad as may be found expedient. Such schedules, as far as practicable, shall conform to
the forms prescribed by the interstate commerce commission.
(April 2, 1906, 98 v. 346, § 4; R. S. Sec. 244-14d.)

Section 512. (Rates shall be just and reasonable.) When
passengers or property are transported over two or more
connecting lines of railroad between points in this state, and
the railroad companies have made joint rates for the transportation of such passengers or property, such rates and all
charges in connection therewith shall be just and reasonable,
and every unjust and unreasonable charge is prohibited and
declared to be unlawful; but a less charge by each of such
railroads for its proportion of such joint rates than is made
locally between the same points on their respective lines
shall not for that reason be construed as a violation of the
provisions of this chapter, nor render such railroads liable
to any of the penalties thereof. (April 2, 1906, 98 v. 346,
§ 5; R. S. Sec. 244-15.)

Section 513. (Special contract rates.) Nothing in this
chapter shall prevent concentration, commodity, transit and
other special contract rates, but all such rates shall be sub-

ject to the provisions of this chapter as to their printing and filing, shall be open to all shippers for a like kind of traffic under similar circumstances and conditions, and shall be under the supervision and regulation of the commission. (April 2, 1906, 98 v. 346, § 6; R. S. Sec. 244-16.)

Section 514.   (Classification of freight shall be uniform.) The classification of freight in the state shall be uniform on all railroads.   (98 v. 347, § 7; R. S. Sec. 244-17.)

Section 515.   (Exceptions as to freight rates.)   Nothing in this chapter shall prevent the carriage, storage or handling of freight free or at reduced rates, for the United States, the state, any political subdivision or municipality thereof, for charitable purposes, to and from fairs and expositions for exhibition thereat, or the property of railway employees for their own exclusive use or consumption or that of their families; or the issuance of mileage, commutation or excursion passenger tickets, if obtainable by any person applying therefor without discrimination, or of party tickets, if obtainable by all persons applying therefor under like circumstances and conditions.   (May 20, 1910, 101 v. 322; R. S. Sec. 244-18; April 21, 1908, 99 v. 128, § 8; April 2, 1906, 98 v. 347, § 8.)

The issuance of mileage, excursion, etc., tickets is permissive only. Ordinarily railroads cannot be required to issue such tickets.

The giving of more favorable commutation rates to children attending public school, as a class, than to children traveling for other purposes, is not an arbitrary selection or unjust discrimination.

Shryock v. B. & O. R. R., 6 O. L. R. 19; 53 B. 86; s. c., 4 O. L. R. 614; 52 B. 23.

This section does not prevent the holder of an excursion ticket, sold at a reduced rate, from selling the unused return coupon where the ticket is not, in terms, nontransferable.

Knecht v. Railway, 6 N. P. n. s. 13; 18 L. D. 202 (C. P. 1907).

This section is applicable to express companies (§ 501).   A railroad or express company may carry free, or at reduced rates, the property of employes of other railroads or express companies.

Rept. Atty. Gen. 1910-1911, p. 624.

Section 516.   (Prohibiting free transportation by railroad company. Exceptions. Definitions.)   No railroad company, owning or operating a railroad wholly or partly within this state, shall, directly or indirectly, issue or give a free ticket, free pass, or free transportation for passengers, except to its employes and their families, its officers, agents, surgeons, physicians, and attorneys at law; to ministers of religion, traveling secretaries of railroad young men's christian associations, inmates of hospitals and charitable and eleemosynary institutions, and persons exclusively engaged in charitable and eleemosynary work; to indigent, destitute and homeless persons, and to such persons when transported by charitable societies or hospitals, and the necessary agents employed in such transportation; to inmates of the national homes or state homes for disabled volunteer soldiers, and soldiers' and sailors' homes, including those about to enter and those returning home after discharge, and boards of managers of such homes; to necessary caretakers of live stock, poultry and fruit; to employes on sleeping cars, express cars, and to linemen of telegraph and telephone companies; to railway mail service employes, postoffice inspectors, custom inspectors and immigration inspectors; to newsboys on trains, baggage agents, witnesses attending any legal investigation in which the railroad is interested, persons injured in wrecks and physicians and nurses attending such persons. Provided, that the term "employes" as used in this paragraph shall include furloughed, pensioned, and superannuated employes, persons who have become disabled or infirm in the service of any such common carrier, and the remains of a person killed in the employment of a carrier and ex-employes traveling for the purpose of entering the service of any such common carrier; and the term "families" as used in this paragraph shall include the families of those persons named in this proviso and also the widows and dependent children of employes who died while in the service of any common carrier. (April 29, 1911, 102 v. 85; R. S. Sec. 244-18; April 21, 1908, 99 v. 128, § 8; April 2, 1906, 98 v. 347, § 8.)

See 4 O. L. R. 667.

Section 517. (Passes may be interchanged.) The next preceding section shall not be construed to prohibit the interchange of passes for the officers, agents, and employees and their families; nor to prohibit any railroad company from carrying passengers free in order to provide relief in cases of general epidemics, pestilence, or other calamitous visitation. (R. S. Sec. 244-18; April 21, 1908, 99 v. 128, § 8; April 2, 1906, 98 v. 347, § 8.)

Section 518. (Penalty.) Any railroad company violating a provision of the preceding three sections, for each offense, shall be fined not less than fifty dollars nor more than five hundred dollars, and any person other than the persons excepted in such sections, who uses such free ticket, free pass, or free transportation, shall be subject to a like penalty. (R. S. Sec. 244-18; April 21, 1908, 99 v. 128, § 8; April 2, 1906, 98 v. 347, § 8.)

Section 519. (Depots, switches and sidetracks.) Each railroad shall provide and maintain adequate depots and depot buildings at its regular stations for the accommodation of passengers, and such depot buildings shall be kept clean, well lighted and warmed, for the comfort and accommodation of the traveling public. Each railroad shall provide and maintain adequate and suitable freight depots, buildings, switches and sidetracks for receiving, handling and delivering freight, transported or to be transported by such railroads; but this section shall not be construed as repealing any existing law on the subject. (April 2, 1906, 98 v. 347, § 9; R. S. Sec. 244-19.)

This section does not require a railroad company to open its public or team tracks to other companies.

Rheinstrom v. Railway, 4 O. L. R. 755 (Railroad Commission).

The commission has power to order and require reasonably adequate depot facilities.

Greenwich v. N. O. Ry. Co., 6 O. L. R. 51 (Railroad Commission).

See G. C. §§ 8926, 8927 and notes to § 535.

Section 520. (Supply of cars.) If within its power so to do, and upon reasonable notice, each railroad shall furnish suitable cars for all persons who may apply therefor, for the transportation of any and all kinds of freight in car load lots. In case of insufficiency of cars at any time to meet all requirements, such cars as are available shall be distributed among the applicants therefor in proportion to their respective immediate requirements, without discrimination between shippers or competitive or non-competitive places; but preference may be given to shipments of live stock and perishable property. (April 2, 1906, 98 v. 347, § 10; R. S. Sec. 244-20.)

Railroad fuel cars should not be ordered distributed to coal mines when. See Coal Co. v. Railroad Commission, 8 N. P. n. s. 585; 19 L. D. 783; enjoining order of railroad commission reported in Carbon Coal Min. Co. v. M. C. & C. R. R., 7 O. L. R. 196; s. c., 6 O. L. R. 528.

When an industry is uncertain and irregular in its requirements as to cars, the shipper must give reasonable notice thereof to the railroad.

Greer, etc., Co. v. Penna. Co., 6 O. L. R. 133 (Railroad Commission).

See also notes to §§ 535 and 567.

Section 521. (Commission shall enforce regulations as to cars.) The commission may enforce reasonable regulations for furnishing cars to shippers, switching, loading and unloading them, and the weighing of cars and freight offered for shipment over any line of railroad. (April 2, 1906, 98 v. 348, § 10; R. S. Sec. 244-20a.)

The commission has no power to promulgate an arbitrary rule as to the distribution of cars in the future, and thereby determine a future judicial question.

Coal Co. v. Railroad Commission, 8 N. P. n. s. 585; 19 L. D. 783.

Demurrage Charges.. Right of railroad to enforce.

Phillips Co. v. Erie R. R. Co., 6 C. C. n. s. 505; 17 C. D. 486; affirming 14 L. D. 706, 709.

Troy, etc., Co. v. C. H. & D. Ry. Co., 3 N. P. n. s. 412; 16 L. D. 111; affirmed, no report, 72 O. S. 612.

Cincinnati, etc. Co. v. N. &. W. Ry. Co., 8 C. C. n. s. 134; 18 C. D. 543.

Pittsburg, etc., Co. v. Mooar Lumber Co., 6 C. C. n. s. 638; 17 C. D. 588.

Weighing freight, Duty of railroads as to.

Nimishilling, etc., Co. v. C. T. & V. R. R., 5 O. L. R. 455; 52 B. 569 (Railroad commission).

Section 522. (Interchange of traffic.) Steam railroad companies as between themselves, and interurban and electric railroads as between themselves, shall afford reasonable and proper facilities for interchange of traffic between their respective lines, for forwarding and delivering passengers and property, and shall transfer and deliver without unreasonable delay or discrimination cars, loaded or empty, freight or passengers, destined to a point on its own or connecting lines; but precedence over other freight may be given to live stock and perishable freight. (April 2, 1906, 98 v. 348, § 11; R. S. Sec. 244-21.)

This section and § 614-42 authorize the public service commission to make an order requiring two or more railroad companies to construct a connecting track between their lines.

Penna. Co. v. Public Service Com., 14 N. P. n. s. 262; 58 Bull. 185 (C. P. 1913).

An order requiring three railroad companies, whose tracks intersect in a city, to construct transfer or connecting tracks at a cost of $14,000, in order to accommodate manufacturers and other shippers whose traffic approximates two thousand cars per year, is not so unreasonable as to violate a constitutional right.

Penna. Co. v. Commission, 14 N. P. n. s. 262, 58 Bull. 185 (C. P. 1913).

Section 523. (Control over private tracks.) The commission shall have the same control over private tracks, so far as such tracks are used by common carriers in connection with a railroad for the transportation of freight, as it has over the tracks of such railroad. (R. S. Sec. 244-21a; April 2, 1906, 98 v. 348, § 11.)

Section 524. (Complaints and hearings.) Upon complaint of a person, firm, corporation or association, or of a mercantile, agricultural or manufacturing society, or of a body politic or municipal organization, that any of the rates, fares, charges or classifications, or any joint rate or rates are in any respect unreasonable or unjustly discriminatory, or that any regulation or practice, affecting the transportation of persons or property, or any service in connection therewith, are in any respect unreasonable or unjustly discriminatory, or that any service is inadequate, the commission may notify the railroad complained of that complaint has been made, and ten days after such notice proceed to investigate such charges as provided in this chapter. Before proceeding to make such investigation, the commission shall give the railroad and the complainants ten days' notice of the time and place such matters will be considered and determined, and such parties shall be entitled to be heard and to have process to enforce the attendance of witnesses. (April 2, 1906, 98 v. 348, § 12; R. S. Sec. 244-22.)

See § 535.
This act provides an adequate remedy for discrimination and unjust or unreasonable rates and classifications, and courts have no original jurisdiction with reference thereto.
Publishing Co. v. Express Co., 13 N. P. n. s. 403 (1911).
The franchise of an interurban railway granted by county commissioners can not be forfeited because excessive rates of fare are charged. The remedy for unreasonable charges is by complaint to the public service commission.
State v. Northern Ohio, etc., Co., 1 C. of App. —, (1913).

Section 525. (Railroad may be complainant.) The next preceding section shall be construed to permit a railroad to make complaint with like effect as though made by any person, firm, corporation or association, mercantile, agricultural or manufacturing society, body politic or municipal organization. (April 2, 1906, 98 v. 349, § 12; R. S. Sec. 244-22c.)

Section 526. (May separate complaint.) When complaint is made of more than one rate or charge, the commission may order separate hearings thereon, and may consider and determine the matters complained of separately, and at such times as it may prescribe. No complaint shall necessarily be dismissed because of the absence of direct damage to the complainant. (April 2, 1906, 98 v. 349, § 12; R. S. Sec. 244-22a.)

Section 527. (Commission may change unreasonable rate.) Upon an investigation, if the rate or rates, or any regulation, practice or service complained of is found to be unreasonable or unjustly discriminatory, or the service inadequate, the commission may fix and order substituted therefor, such rate or rates, fares, charges or classification as it shall have determined to be just and reasonable, which shall be charged, imposed and followed in the future. It also may make such orders respecting such regulation, practice or service as it shall have determined to be reasonable, which shall be observed and followed in the future, but no rates fixed shall exceed the maximum rates prescribed by any statute of this state in force at the time the commission fixes such rates. (April 2, 1906, 98 v. 348, § 12; R. S. Sec. 244-22.)

Both a finding and an order are requisite to give effect to any action by the commission. A finding is the ascertainment of facts, and results from investigation. A judgment is the application of the law to ascertained facts, and results from consideration.

Warner v. Railway, 11 N. P. n. s. 487 (C. P. 1911).

See § 535 and note.

This act provides an adequate remedy for discrimination and unjust or unreasonable rates and classifications, and courts have no original jurisdiction with reference thereto.

Publishing Co. v. Express Co., 13 N. P. n. s. 403 (1911).

Section 528. (Commission may investigate on its own motion.) If the commission believes that any rate or rates, or charge or charges, may be unreasonable or unjustly discriminatory, and that an investigation relating thereto should be made, it may investigate them upon its own motion. Before such investigation it shall present to the railroad a statement in writing setting forth the rate or charge to be investigated. Thereafter, on ten days' notice to the railroad of the time and place of such investigation, the commission may proceed to investigate such rate or charge in the same manner and make like orders in respect thereto, as if such investigation had been made upon complaint. (April 2, 1906, 98 v. 349, § 12; R. S. Sec. 244-22b.)

Section 529. (Record of certain investigation.) A full record shall be kept of the proceedings before the commission on such investigations. All testimony shall be taken by the stenographer appointed by the commission. (April 2, 1906, 98 v. 350, § 13; R. S. Sec. 244-23c.)

Section 530. (Power of commissioners to administer oaths.) Each of the commissioners, for the purposes mentioned in this chapter, may administer oaths, certify to official acts, issue subpoenas, compel the attendance of witnesses, and the production of papers, way-bills, books, accounts, documents and testimony. (April 2, 1906, 98 v. 349, § 13; R. S. Sec. 244-23.)

Section 531. (Witnesses may be compelled to testify.) If a person disobeys an order of the commission or a commissioner, or a subpoena, or if a witness refuses to testify to any matter regarding which he may be lawfully interrogated, on application of a commissioner, the court of common pleas of a county or a judge thereof shall compel obedience by attachment proceedings for contempt, as in the case of disobedience of the requirements of a subpoena issued from such court, or a refusal to testify therein. The commission also shall have the powers vested in justices of the peace or notaries public to compel witnesses to testify and to produce books and papers. (April 2, 1906, 98 v. 349, § 13; R. S. Sec. 244-23.)

Section 532. (Witness fees and mileage.) Each witness who appears before the commission by its order shall receive for his attendance the fees and mileage provided for witnesses in civil cases in courts of record, which shall be audited and paid by the state as other expenses are audited and paid, upon the presentation of proper vouchers sworn to by such witnesses and approved by the chairman of the commission. No witness subpoenaed at the instance of parties other than the commission shall be entitled to compensation from the state for attendance or travel, unless the commission certify that his testimony was material to the matter investigated. (April 2, 1906, 98 v. 349, § 13; R. S. Sec. 244-23a.)

Section 533. (Depositions may be taken.) In an investigation, the commission or any party may cause the depositions of witnesses residing within or without the state to be taken in the manner prescribed by law for depositions in civil actions in the court of common pleas. (April 2, 1906, 98 v. 349, § 13; R. S. Sec. 244-23b.)

Section 534. (Transcribed copy certified by stenographer is evidence.) A transcribed copy of the evidence and proceedings on an investigation, or a specific part thereof, taken by a stenographer appointed by the commission, certified by such stenographer to be a true and correct transcript thereof, carefully compared by him with his original notes, shall be received in evidence as if such reporter was present and testified to the facts as certified. A copy of such transcript shall be furnished on demand, free of cost, to a party to an investigation, and to all other persons, on payment of a reasonable amount therefor. (R. S. Sec. 244-23c; April 2, 1906, 98 v. 350, § 13.)

Section 535. (Commission may change rate or service.) If, upon an investigation under the provisions of this chapter, the commission finds that any existing rate or rates, fares, charges or classification, any joint rate or rates, or any regulation or practice affecting the transportation of persons or property, or service in connection therewith, are unreasonable or unjustly discriminatory, or that any service is inadequate, it shall determine and by order fix a reasonable rate, fare, charge, classification, joint rate, regulation, practice or service to be imposed, observed and followed in the future, in place of that so found to be unreasonable, unjustly discriminatory, or inadequate, as the case may be. A certified copy of each such order shall be delivered to an officer or station agent of the railroad affected thereby, and such order shall of its own force take effect and become operative thirty days after service thereof. (R. S. Sec. 244-24; April 21, 1908, 99 v. 129, § 14; April 2, 1906, 98 v. 350, § 14.)

See §§ 527, 564, 567, 572.
The functions of the commission are administrative or executive in their character and not judicial or legislative.
Penna. Co. v. Commission, 14 N. P. n. s. 262 (C. P. 1913).
Railroad v. Commission, 10 N. P. n. s. 665; 21 L. D. 468; aff'd. no rep., 86 O. S. 365.
See Prentis v. Atlantic Coast Line, 211 U. S. 210 (1908).

Freight rates. That a rate has been in effect a long period of time has a bearing upon its reasonableness.
Nat'l. Refg. Co. v. Penna. Co., 7 O. L. R. 192, 193.
Factors in rate making.
See Akron Sand & Gravel Co. v. B. & O., 8 O. L. R. 263.
Natl. Refg. Co. v. Penna. Co., 7 O. L. R. 192, 195.
Rates in less than car load lots.
Interstate Commerce Commission v. C. H. & D. Ry., 3 O. L. R. 497, (U. S. C. C. Ohio).
To justify a finding that a classification rating is wrong, when the result would be to disturb the entire system of rates, the evidence should be clear and convincing and not merely speculative.
Nat'l. Refg. Co. v. Penna. Co., 7 O. L. R. 192.

Reasonable Rates.
(Coal) Pittsburg, etc., Assn. v. W. & L. E. R. R. Co., 8 O. L. R. 1.
Warner v. B. & O., 8 O. L. R. 251.
See also §§ 564, 567.

Discrimination. In distribution of cars.
Greer, etc., Co. v. Penna. Co., 6 O. L. R. 133.
Coal Co. v. Railroad Commission, 8 N. P. n. s. 585; 19 L. D. 783.
Haring, etc., Co., v. W. & L. E. R. R., 4 O. L. R. 639.
Oeffler v. Ry. Co., 4 O. L. R. 709; 52 B. 134; aff'd 6 N. P. n. s. 273; 18 L. D. 519.
Railway Co. v. Wren, 78 O. S. 137 (1908).
In coal rates.
Warner v. B. & O., 8 O. L. R. 251.
Against locality in passenger rates.

Ransbottom, etc., Co. v. S. E. Ohio, etc., Co., 6 O. L. R. 159.
Shryock v. B. & O. R. R., 6 O. L. R. 19; 52 B. 88.
See § 567.
In rates on piling as compared with logs other than piling.
Callahan v. C. C. C. & St. L. Ry., 6 O. L. R. 523.
In rating of coal mines.
Nimishilling, etc., Co. v. C. T. & V. R. R., 5 O. L. R. 455; 52 B. 569.
H. V. Ry. Co. v. Railroad Commission, 18 L. D. 519; 6 N. P. n. s. 273; affirming 4 O. L. R. 709; 52 B. 134.
In switching service.
Johnson, etc., Co. v. Railroad Co., 1 N. P. n. s. 385; 14 L. D. 209 (1910).
Gill v. H. V. Ry. Co., 6 O. L. R. 140.
Pierce, etc., Co. v. C. N. R. R. Co., 6 O. L. R. 147; 53 B. 285.
Rheinstrom v. P. C. C. & St. L. Ry., 4 O. L. R. 755.
Railway v. Scofield, 2 C. C. 305 (1887).
See G. C. § 8998.
Against irregular shippers.
H. V. Ry. Co. v. Railroad Commission, 6 N. P. n. s. 273; 18 L. D. 519; affirming 4 O. L. R. 709; 52 B. 134.
In terminal facilities.
Coal Co. v. Railway, 1 C. C. n. s. 333; 14 C. D. 289 (1902).

Adequate service and facilities. Stops of passenger trains at small village.
Cloppert v. B. & O. S. W., 5 O. L. R. 431; 52 B. 520.
Stops of interurban cars other than at crossings.
Ashley v. Railway Co., 5 O. L. R. 359; 52 O. L. B. 498.
By interurban railway. Duty to furnish seats to passengers.
Falls, etc., Co. v. No. Ohio, etc., Co., 5 O. L. R. 364; 52 B. 506.
Unprofitableness of operation of interurban railway. Effect of.
Ferguson v. Dayton, etc., Co., 4 O. L. R. 750; 52 B. 197.
In receiving shipments of milk.
West Jefferson, etc., Co. v. B. & O. R. R. Co., 8 O. L. R. 10.
Establishment of stations.
Good v. T. & O. C. Ry., 8 O. L. R. 260; s. c., 55 O. L. B. 301.
Leedon & Co. v. N. & W. Ry., 7 O. L. R. 474.
Rule requiring shipper to load milk into car.
West Jefferson, etc., Co. v. B. & O. R. R. Co., 8 O. L. R. 10.
B. & O. R. R. v. Railroad Commission, 10 N. P. n. s. 665; s. c., 21 L. D. 468; 86 O. S. 365; modified, 88 O. S. —.
Section 504 does not require a railroad company to open its public or team tracks to other railroads.
Rheinstrom v. Railway, 4 O. L. R. 755.

Section 536. (**Railroads shall correct schedules.**) All railroads to which the order applies shall make such changes in their schedules on file as are necessary to conform to such order, and no change shall thereafter be made by any railroad in any such rates, fares, or charges, or in any joint rate or rates, without the approval of the commission. (R. S. Sec. 244-24; April 21, 1908, 99 v. 129, § 14; April 2, 1906, 98 v. 350, § 14.)

Section 537. (**Copies of orders to be supplied railroad.**) Certified copies of all other orders of the commission shall be delivered to an officer or station agent of each railroad affected thereby, and shall take effect within such time thereafter as the commission prescribes. (R. S. Sec. 244-24; April 21, 1908, 99 v. 129, § 14; April 2, 1906, 98 v. 350, § 14.)

Section 538. (Commission may rescind or amend an order.) Upon application of any person or any railroad and after notice to the parties in interest and opportunity to be heard as provided in this chapter for other hearings, has been given, the commission may rescind, alter or amend an order fixing any rate or rates, fares, charges or classification, or any other order made by the commission. Certified copies of such orders shall be served and take effect as provided for original orders. (R. S. Sec. 244-24a; April 21, 1908, 99 v. 130, § 14; April 2, 1906, 98 v. 350, § 14.)

Section 539. (Supplemental order.) Whenever a joint rate or charge is ordered substituted by the commission, and the railroads party thereto fail to agree within twenty days after the service of such order upon the apportionment thereof, the commission may after a hearing, issue a supplemental order declaring the apportionment of such joint rate or charge, which shall take effect of its own force as part of the original order. (May 2, 1910, 101 v. 166; R. S. Sec. 244-24b; April 21, 1908, 99 v. 130, § 14; April 2, 1906, 98 v. 350, § 14.)

Section 540. (When commission may fix joint rate.) Whenever railroads refuse or neglect to establish a joint rate or rates for the transportation of persons or property, the commission may, upon notice to the railroads and after opportunity to be heard, fix and establish such joint rate or rates. If the railroads party thereto fail to agree upon the apportionment thereof within twenty days after service of such order, the commission may, upon a like hearing, issue a supplemental order declaring the apportionment of such joint rate or rates which shall take effect of its own force as part of the original order. (R. S. Sec. 244-24c; April 21, 1908, 99 v. 130, § 14; April 2, 1906, 98 v. 350, § 14.)

This section empowers the commission to require railroads to fix joint passenger rates.
Rep. Atty. Gen. 1910-1911, p. 623.

Section 541. (Rates, fares, etc., fixed by commission, prima facie lawful.) All rates, fares, charges, classifications and joint rates fixed by the commission shall be in force and be prima facie lawful for one year from the day they take effect, or until changed or modified by the commission, or by an order of a competent court in an action under the provisions of this chapter. (April 2, 1906, 98 v. 351, § 15; R. S. Sec. 244-25.)

Section 542. (Regulations, practices, etc., prescribed by commission prima facie reasonable.) All regulations, practices and service prescribed by the commission shall be in force and be prima facie reasonable, unless suspended or found otherwise in an action brought for that purpose pursuant to the provisions of this chapter, or until changed or modified by the commission. (April 2, 1906, 98 v. 351, § 15; R. S. Sec. 244-25.)

Section 543. (Rehearing; who may have. Time of hearing, when granted without suspension of order.) After any order or decision has been made by the commission, any party to the action or proceeding, or any stockholder or bondholder or other party pecuniarily interested in the public utility affected, may apply for a rehearing in respect to any matters determined in said action or proceeding and specified in the application for rehearing, and the commission may grant and hold such rehearing on said matters, if in its judgment sufficient reason therefor be made to appear. No cause of action arising out of any order or decision of the commission shall accrue in any court to any corporation or person unless such corporation or person shall have made, before the effective date of said order or decision, application to the commission for a rehearing. Such application shall set forth specifically the ground or grounds on which the applicant considers said decision or order to be unreasonable or unlawful. No corporation or person shall in any court urge or rely on any ground not so set forth in said application. Any application for a rehearing made ten days or more before the effective date of the order as to which a rehearing is sought, shall be either granted or denied before such effective date, or the order shall stand suspended until such application is granted or denied. Any application for a rehearing made within less than ten days before the effective date of the order as to which a rehearing is sought, and not granted within twenty days, may be taken by the party making the application to be denied, unless the effective date of the order is extended for the period of the pendency of the application.

If an application for a rehearing be granted without suspension of the order involved, the commission shall forthwith proceed to hear the matter with all dispatch and shall determine the same within twenty days after final submission and if such determination is not made within said time, it may be taken by any party to the rehearing that the order involved is affirmed.   An application for rehearing shall not excuse any corporation or person from complying with and obeying any order or decision, or any requirement of any order or decision of the commission theretofore made, or operate in any manner to stay or postpone the enforcement thereof, except in such cases and upon such terms as the commission may by order direct.   If, after such rehearing and a consideration of all the facts, including those arising since the making of the order or decision, the commission shall be of the opinion that the original order or decision or any part thereof is in any respect unjust or unwarranted, or should be changed, the commission may abrogate, change or modify the same.   An order or decision made after such rehearing, abrogating, changing or modifying the original order or decision shall have the same force and effect as an original order or decision, but shall not affect any right or the enforcement of any right arising from or by virtue of the original order or decision unless so ordered by the commission. (May 5, 1913, 103 v. 814, § 32.)

Section 544.   (Order may be reversed.)   A final order made by the commission shall be reversed, vacated or modified by the supreme court, on a petition in error, if upon consideration of the record such court is of the opinion that such order was unlawful or unreasonable.   May 5, 1913, 103 v. 815, § 33; G. C. § 543 (original numbering); R. S. Sec. 244-26; April 2, 1906, 98 v. 351, § 16.)

As erroneously printed in 103 v. 815, the last three words of this section read "unlawful *and* unreasonable."

This section and the sections following, providing for judicial review of the orders of the commission, preserve the validity of the act.

Railroad v. Railroad Commission, 10 N. P. n. s. 665; aff'd no rep. 86 O. S. 365; s. c., 88 O. S. —.

Coal Co. v. Railroad Commission, 8 N. P. n. s. 585; 19 L. D. 783.

Under the railroad commission act, empowering common pleas courts to vacate "unlawful or unreasonable" orders of the commission, it was held that the court was authorized to vacate only orders which were so unreasonable as to amount to a taking of private property without due process of law or without just compensation.

Penna. Co. v. Commission, 14 N. P. n. s. 262 (C. P. 1913).

See Railroad v. Commission, 6 N. P. n. s. 273; 18 L. D. 519, affirming 4 O. L. R. 709; 52 Bull. 134.

Section 545.   (Proceedings in error.)   The proceeding to obtain such reversal, vacation or modification shall be by petition in error, filed in the supreme court, by any party to the proceeding before the commission, against the public utilities commission of Ohio, setting forth the errors com-

plained of. Thereupon unless the same is duly waived a
summons shall issue and be served, as in other cases, upon
the chairman of the commission, or, in the event of his absence, upon any member of the commission, or by leaving a
copy at the office of the commission at the city of Columbus.
The court may permit any interested party to intervene by
cross-petition in error. (May 5, 1913, 103 v. 815, § 34; G.
C. § 544 (original numbering); April 2, 1906, 98 v. 350, §§ 13,
16.)

Section 546. (Transcript.) Upon service or waiver of
the summons in error the commission shall forthwith transmit to the clerk of the supreme court a transcript of the
journal entries, original papers or transcripts thereof and a
certified transcript of all evidence adduced upon the hearing
before the commission in the proceeding complained of, which
shall be filed in said court. (May 5, 1913, 103 v. 815, § 35;
G. C. § 544 (original numbering); April 2, 1906, 98 v. 350,
§§ 13, 16.)

Section 547. (When proceeding commenced.) No proceeding to reverse, vacate or modify a final order of the
commission shall be deemed commenced unless the petition
therefor is filed within sixty days after the entry of the final
order complained of upon the journal of the commission.
(May 5, 1913, 103 v. 815, § 36; G. C. § 543 (original numbering); April 2, 1906, 98 v. 351, § 16.)

Under the original railroad commission act, orders of the commission
were reviewed by the common pleas court. Under that act it was held
that the limitation of sixty days applied exclusively to the judgment
of the court of common pleas, and did not apply to an error proceeding
in the supreme court to review a judgment of the circuit court.
Commission v. Railway Co., 79 O. S. 419.

Section 548. (Stay of execution.) No proceeding to reverse, vacate or modify a final order rendered by the commission shall operate to stay execution thereof unless the
supreme court or a judge thereof in vacation, on application
and three days' notice to the commission, shall allow such
stay, in which event the plaintiff in error shall be required
to execute an undertaking, payable to the state of Ohio, in
such a sum as the court may prescribe, with surety to the
satisfaction of the clerk of the supreme court, conditioned
for the prompt payment by the plaintiff in error of all damages arising from or caused by the delay in the enforcement
of the order complained of, and for the repayment of all
moneys paid by any person, firm or corporation for transportation, transmission, produce, commodity or service in

excess of the charges fixed by the order complained of, in the event such order be sustained. (May 5, 1913, 103 v. 815, § 37; G. C. § 551 (original numbering); April 2, 1906, 98 v. 351, § 16.)

Section 549. (Jurisdiction.) No court other than the supreme court shall have power to review, suspend or delay any order made by the commission, or enjoin, restrain or interfere with the commission or any member thereof in the performance of official duties. Nor shall the writ of mandamus be issued against the commission or any member thereof by any court other than the supreme court. (May 5, 1913, 103 v. 816, § 38.)

Section 550. (Order as to payment of money in case of stay, etc.) The supreme court, in case it stays or suspends the order or decision of the commission in any matter affecting rates, joint rates, fares, tolls, rentals, charges or classifications, may also by order direct the public utility or railroad affected to pay into the hands of a trustee to be appointed by the court, from time to time, to be held until the final determination of the proceeding, under such conditions as the court may prescribe, all sums of money collected in excess of the sums payable if the order or decision of the commission had not been stayed or suspended. (May 5, 1913, 103 v. 816, § 39.)

Section 551. (Order to keep excess accounts pending review.) In case the supreme court stays or suspends any order or decision lowering any rate, joint rate, fare, toll, rental, charge or classification, the commission, upon the execution and approval of said suspending bond may require the public utility or railroad affected, under penalty of the immediate enforcement of the order or decision of the commission, pending review, to keep such accounts, verified by oath, as may, in the judgment of the commission, be sufficient to show the amounts being charged or received by such public utility or railroad, in excess of the charges allowed by the order or decision of the commission, together with the names and addresses of the corporations or persons to whom overcharges will be refundable in case the charges made by the public utility or railroad, pending review, be not sustained by the supreme court. (May 5, 1913, 103 v. 816, § 40.)

Section 551-1. (Disposition of moneys charged in excess.) Upon the final decision by the supreme court, all moneys which the public utility or railroad may have collected, pending the appeal, in excess of those authorized by such final decision, shall be promptly paid to the corporations or persons entitled thereto, in such manner and through such methods of distribution as may be prescribed by the court. If any such money shall not have been claimed by the corporations or persons entitled thereto within one year from the final decision of the supreme court, the trustees appointed by the court shall cause notice to such corporations or persons to be given by publication, once a week for two consecutive weeks, in a newspaper of general circulation, printed and published in the city of Columbus, Franklin county, Ohio, and such other newspaper or newspapers as may be designated by such trustee, said notice to state the names of the corporations or persons entitled to such moneys and the amount due each corporation or person. All moneys not claimed within three months after the publication of said notice shall be paid by the public utility or railroad, under the direction of such trustee, into the state treasury for the benefit of the general fund, and the court may make such order with respect to the compensation of the trustee as it may deem proper. (May 5, 1913, 103 v. 816, § 41.)

Section 551-2. (Act shall not affect pending actions.) This act shall not affect pending actions or proceedings brought by or against the state of Ohio, the railroad commission of Ohio, the public service commission of Ohio, or by any other person or corporation, but the same may be prosecuted and defended with the same effect as though this act had not been passed or said commission abolished. Any investigation, hearing or examination undertaken, commenced, instituted or prosecuted prior to the taking effect of this act may be conducted and continued to a final determination in the same manner and with the same effect as if it had been undertaken, commenced, instituted or prosecuted in accordance with the provisions of this act. All proceedings hitherto taken by the commissions above named in any such investigation, hearing or examination and hereby ratified, approved, validated and confirmed, and all such proceedings shall have the same force and effect as if they had been undertaken, commenced, instituted and prosecuted under the provisions of this act and in the manner herein prescribed. (May 5, 1913, 103 v. 817, § 42; in effect August 8, 1913.)

Section 551-3. (Abatement.) No cause of action arising under the laws of Ohio shall abate by reason of the passage of this act, whether a suit or action has been instituted there-

on at the time of the taking effect of this act or not, but
actions may be brought upon such causes in the same manner, under the same terms and conditions, and with the same
effect as though said laws in force at the time this act takes
effect had not been repealed. (May 5, 1913, 103 v. 817, § 43.)

Section 551-4. (Orders, decisions, etc., remain in force.)
All orders, decisions, rules or regulations heretofore made,
issued or promulgated by the commission above named shall
continue in force and have the same effect as though they
had been lawfully made, issued or promulgated under the
provisions of this act. (May 5, 1913, 103 v. 817, § 44.)

Section 551-5. (Each section independent.) Each section of this act and every part thereof is hereby declared to
be an independent section, and part of a section, and the
holding of a section or part thereof to be void or ineffective
for any cause shall not be deemed to affect any other section
or part thereof. (May 5, 1913, 103 v. 817, § 45.)

**Section 551-6. (Order of disposition of cases under
chapter.)** All actions and proceedings in the supreme court,
under this chapter, and all actions or proceedings to which
the commission or the state of Ohio may be parties, and in
which any question arises under this chapter, or under or
concerning any order or decision of the commission, to reverse, vacate or modify an order of the commission, shall be
taken up and disposed of by the court out of its order on
the docket. (May 5, 1913, 103 v. 817, § 46; G. C. § 545 (original numbering); April 2, 1906, 98 v. 351, § 16.)

Section 552. (Rules of practice.) Except when otherwise provided by law, all processes in actions and proceedings in a court arising under the provisions of this chapter
shall be served, and the practice and rules of evidence be
the same, as in civil actions. A sheriff or other officer empowered to execute civil processes shall execute process issued under the provisions of this chapter and receive compensation therefor as prescribed by law for like services.
(April 2, 1906, 98 v. 352, § 17; R. S. Sec. 244-27.)

Section 553. (Witnesses compelled to testify.) A person
shall not be excused from testifying or from producing books
and papers in a proceeding based upon or growing out of
violation of the provisions of this chapter, on the ground
that the testimony or evidence, documentary or otherwise,
required of him may tend to incriminate him or subject him

to a penalty or forfeiture; but no person having so testified shall be prosecuted or subjected to a penalty or forfeiture for, or on account of, any transaction, matter or thing concerning which he may have testified or produced documentary evidence. A person so testifying shall not be exempt from prosecution or punishment for perjury. (April 2, 1906, 98 v. 352, § 17; R. S. Sec. 244-27a.)

Section 554. (Certified copy shall be evidence.) Upon application, the commission shall furnish certified copies under its seal or any order made by it, which certified copy shall be prima facie evidence in a court or proceeding of the facts stated therein. (April 2, 1906, 98 v. 352, § 17; R. S. Sec. 244-27b.)

Section 555. (Commission may inquire into management of railroads.) The commission may inquire into the management of the business of any railroad, and shall keep itself informed as to the manner and method in which it is conducted. It may obtain from a railroad the information necessary to enable it to perform the duties and carry out the objects for which it was created. (April 2, 1906, 98 v. 353, § 18; R. S. Sec. 244-28.)

Section 556. (Commission shall prepare blanks for railroad.) The commission shall cause blanks to be prepared suitable for the purposes designated in this chapter which shall conform as nearly as practicable to the forms prescribed by the interstate commerce commission, and, when necessary, furnish such blanks to each railroad. (April 2, 1906, 98 v. 353, § 18; R. S. Sec. 244-28a.)

Section 557. (Railroads shall file blanks and verify answers.) A railroad receiving blanks from the commission shall cause them to be properly filled, answering fully and correctly each question therein. In case it is unable to answer any question, such railroad shall give a good and sufficient reason therefor. Such answers shall be verified under oath by the proper officer of the railroad and returned to the commission within the time fixed by it. The making or filing of a false affidavit shall be deemed perjury and punishable as such. (R. S. Sec. 244-28a; April 2, 1906, 98 v. 353, § 18.)

Section 558. (Commission may make examinations.) Upon demand, the commission, a commissioner, or any person or persons employed by it for that purpose, may inspect the books and papers of a railroad and examine under oath any officer, agent or employe thereof, in relation to any matter which is the subject of complaint and investigation. A person other than one of the commissioners, who makes such demand shall produce his authority to make such inspection, under the hand of a commissioner, or of the secretary, and under the seal of the commission. (April 2, 1906, 98 v. 353, § 18; R. S. Sec. 244-28b.)

Section 559. (Commission may require production of books and papers.) By order or subpoena, served on a railroad as a summons is served in a civil action in the court of common pleas, the commission may require at such time and place within this state as it designates the production of books, papers or accounts relating to any matter which is the subject of complaint or investigation, kept by such railroad in any office or place outside of this state, or verified copies thereof, in order that an examination of such books, papers or accounts may be made by the commission or under its direction. Such subpoena may issue to a sheriff of any county of the state. (April 2, 1906, 98 v. 353, § 18; R. S. Sec. 244-28c.)

Section 560. (Forfeiture for refusal to comply with subpoena.) A railroad failing or refusing to comply within a reasonable time with such order or subpoena from the commission shall forfeit and pay into the state treasury, for each day it so fails or refuses, not less than one hundred dollars nor more than one thousand dollars, to be recovered in a civil action in the name of the railroad commission of Ohio. (R. S. Sec. 244-28c; April 2, 1906, 98 v. 353, § 18.)

Section 561. (Commission may demand copies of transportation contracts.) When required by the commission· and within a time fixed by it, each railroad shall deliver to the commission for its use copies of all contracts which relate to the transportation of persons or property or any service in connection therewith, made or entered into by such railroad with any other railroad, terminal, depot, car or equipment company, express or other transportation company, bridge company, or any shipper or shippers, producers or consumers or other person or persons doing business with it. (April 2, 1906, 98 v. 353, § 19; R. S. Sec. 244-29.)

Section 562. (Report of free transportation.) On the first Monday in February in each year and oftener if required by the commission, each railroad shall file with the commission a verified list of all railroad tickets, passes and mileage books issued free or for other than actual bona fide money consideration at full established rates during the preceding year, together with the names of the recipients thereof, the amount received therefor and the reason for issuing them. This provision shall not apply to the sale of tickets at reduced rates open to the public, or tickets, passes, or mileage books issued to persons not residents of the state, or tickets, passes or mileage books issued free pursuant to authority conferred in this chapter. (April 2, 1906, 98 v. 354, § 19; R. S. Sec. 244-29a.)

Section 563. (Investigation into violations of the inter-state commerce law.) The commission shall have power and, on complaint, it is hereby made its duty to investigate any freight rates on interstate traffic on railroads in this state, and, if in its opinion they are excessive or discriminatory or are levied in violation of the interstate commerce law, or in conflict with the rulings, orders or regulations of the inter-state commerce commission, it shall present the facts to the railroad with the request to make such changes as the com-mission may advise. If such changes are not made within a reasonable time, the commission shall apply by petition to the interstate commerce commission for relief. All freight tariffs issued by any such railroad relating to interstate traf-fic in this state shall be filed in the office of the commission when issued. (April 2, 1906, 98 v. 354, § 21; R. S. Sec. 244-31.)

This section does not empower the commission to make rules relating to car service or demurrage in interstate commerce.

Railroad Commission v. Railroad Co., 12 C. C. n. s. 317; 21 C. D. 337; affirming 8 N. P. n. s. 233; 19 L. D. 691.

Section 564. (Unjust discriminations, forfeiture.) If a railroad, or an agent or officer thereof, by special rate, re-bate, drawback, or by means of false billing, false classifica-tion, false weighing, or other device, shall charge, demand, collect or receive, either directly or indirectly, from any per-son, firm or corporation, a greater or less compensation for service rendered or to be rendered by it for the transporta-tion of persons or property or any service in connection therewith, than that prescribed in the published tariffs then in force, or established as provided herein, or a greater or less compensation than it charges, demands, collects or re-ceives from any other person, firm, or corporation for a like and contemporaneous service in the transportation of a like kind of traffic, under substantially similar circumstances and conditions, it shall be deemed guilty of unjust discrimination, which is hereby prohibited and declared unlawful, and upon conviction thereof shall forfeit and pay into the state treasury not less than one hundred dollars nor more than five thousand dollars for each offense. (R. S. Sec. 244-32; April 2, 1906, 98 v. 354, § 22.)

Decisions of commission as to discriminations, see note to § 535.

Charging less than minimum carload rate, where car does not contain minimum weight of freight, constitutes a rebate.

Hisylvania Coal v. T. & O. C. Ry., 7 O. L. R. 467, 468 (Railroad Commission).

Where a lower rate is given by a common carrier to a favored shipper, which is intended to give and necessarily gives an exclusive monopoly to the favored shipper, affecting the business and destroying the trade of other shippers, the latter have the right to require an equal rate for all under like circumstances. An injunction may be obtained to prevent discrimination.

Scofield v. Railway Co., 43 O. S. 571 (1885).

Where a railway company, as a common carrier, in consideration of the fact that a shipper furnished a greater quantity of freights than other shippers during a given term, agrees to make a rebate from the published tariff on such freights to the prejudice of the other shippers of like freights under the same circumstances, the contract so made is an unlawful discrimination in favor of the larger shipper, tending to create monopoly, destroy competition, injure, if not destroy, the business of smaller operators, contrary to public policy, and will be declared void at the instance of parties injured thereby.

And such a contract can not be upheld simply because the favored shipper may furnish for shipment during the year a larger freightage in the aggregate than any other shipper, or more than all others combined. A discrimination resting exclusively on such a basis will not be sustained. And such a contract will not be upheld simply because the business to be done under it is "largely profitable" to the company.

Scofield v. Railway Co., 43 O. S. 571 (1885).

A railroad company is not warranted in making a contract whereby it binds itself to carry for one shipper crude petroleum, or other article, at half the rate it agrees to charge all others for the same service, at the same time, and as part of the agreement, binding itself to charge all others double the amount as a fixed open rate, and to pay such favored shipper one-half of it when collected, in consideration of his agreeing to establish and maintain a system of pipe lines to its road. Money so paid by a shipper, in ignorance of the agreement, and received by the favored shipper, may be recovered back in an action for money had and received by the former against the latter.

Brundred v. Rice, 49 O. S. 640 (1892).

Action to enforce rebate. A railroad company whose line extends to a point of intersection with a canal of the state can not make a valid contract to repay to a shipper a portion of the freight paid by him, it being the regular rate posted by the company and received from other shippers, such contract being prohibited by § 8981. An action can not be maintained to enforce a promise of such repayment.

Baltimore, etc., R. R. Co. v. Diamond Coal Co., 61 O. S. 242 (1899).

Remedy by quo warranto. A corporation created by this state, and engaged in carrying goods for hire as a common carrier, has no franchise, privilege, or right to discriminate in its freight rates in favor of one shipper, even when it is necessary to do so to secure his custom, if the discriminating rate will tend to create a monopoly by excluding from their proper markets the products of the competitors of the favored shipper.

State ex rel v. Railway, 47 O. S. 130 (1890).

Rights of shipper when agent fraudulently overcharges.

Maple v. Railroad Co., 40 O. S. 313 (1883).

When consignee can not sue. Consignee can not sue when he has a delivered price on the goods.

Thompson v. Cleveland, etc., Ry. Co., 11 W. L. B. 211 (1884).

Section 565. (Penalty against agent or officer.) Whoever, being an agent or officer of a railroad, violates any provision of the next preceding section shall be fined not less than fifty dollars nor more than one thousand dollars for each offense. (April 2, 1906, 98 v. 355, § 22; R. S. Sec. 244-32.)

Section 566. (Illegal concessions.) No railroad shall demand, charge, collect or receive from a person, firm or corporation a less compensation for the transportation of property or for a service rendered or to be rendered by it in consideration of such person, firm or corporation furnishing a part of the facilities incident thereto; but nothing herein shall prohibit a railroad from procuring facilities or service incident to transportation and paying a reasonable compensation therefor. (April 2, 1906, 98 v. 355, § 22; R. S. Sec. 244-32a.)

Section 567. (Unlawful preference.) No common carrier subject to the provisions of this chapter shall make or give undue or unreasonable preference or advantage to a particular person, company, firm, corporation or locality, or to any particular description of traffic, in any respect whatsoever, or subject any particular person, company, firm, corporation or locality, or any particular description of traffic to any undue or unreasonable prejudice or disadvantage in any respect whatsoever. (R. S. Sec. 244-33; April 2, 1906, 98 v. 355, § 23.)

See §§ 8981, 8988, 8990 and note to § 535.

Charging a rate, between competitive points, lower than the rates of competitors, does not of itself constitute undue or unreasonable discrimination against other localities. Such discrimination must be ascertained from all the facts and circumstances of each case.

Commission v. Railway Co., 82 O. S. 25; affirming 5 N. P. n. s. 265; reversing 5 O. L. R. 69 (Railroad Commission).

Discrimination against locality in passenger rates.

See Ransbottom, etc., Co. v. S. E. Ohio, etc., Co., 6 O. L. R. 159 (Railroad Commission).

To establish commutation, party rate, etc., rate tickets between certain stations and to refuse to establish like rates between other stations is not, of itself, a discrimination against such other localities.
Shryock v. B. & O. R. R., 6 O. L. R. 19; 53 B. 88.
This section to be construed as part of the entire act.
Warner v. Railway, 11 N. P. n. s. 487 (C. P. 1911).
A lease of ground by a railroad company to a shipper, for a term of five years with an option to renew, at a rent much less than its rental value, the reduction being a concession on freight charges, is an illegal preference or advantage and invalid; but the railroad company was held not to be precluded from maintaining a suit for a cancellation of the lease at the end of the five year term, the renewal being executory. The company was held not entitled to an accounting for rents accrued prior to the commencement of the suit.
Railway Co. v. Hirsch, 204 Fed. 849 (C. C. A. 1913).

Section 568.   (Giving rebate or concession.) Whoever, being a person, firm or corporation, knowingly accepts or receives a rebate, concession or discrimination in respect to transportation of property wholly within this state or for service in connection therewith, whereby such property by false billing, false classification, false weighing or other device, is transported at a less rate than that named in the published tariffs in force, or whereby any service or advantage is received other than that therein specified, shall be fined not less than fifty dollars nor more than one thousand dollars.   (April 2, 1906, 98 v. 355, § 24; R. S. Sec. 244-34.)

Section 569.   (Punitive damages.) If a railroad does, causes or permits to be done any matter, act or thing in this chapter prohibited or declared to be unlawful, or omits to do an act, matter or thing required to be done by this chapter, such railroad shall be liable to the person, firm, or corporation injured thereby in treble the amount of damages sustained in consequence of such violation. A recovery provided by this section shall not affect a recovery by the state of the penalty prescribed for such violation.   (April 2, 1906, 98 v. 355, § 25; R. S. Sec. 244-35.)

A railroad is not liable in treble damages for charging the rate which has been established and scheduled, although such rate may be unjust or discriminatory.
Warner v. Railway, 11 N. P. n. s. 487 (C. P. 1911).

Section 570.   (Penalty for refusal to fill blanks.) Whoever, being an officer, agent or employe of a railroad company, wilfully fails or refuses to fill out and return a blank required by the commission, or by law, or wilfully fails or refuses to answer a question therein propounded, or knowingly gives false answer to such question or evades the answer to it, if the fact inquired of is within his knowledge, or, upon proper demand, wilfully fails or refuses to exhibit a book, paper or account of such railroad, which is in his possession or under his control, to a member of the railroad commission or other person authorized to examine it, shall be fined not less than one hundred dollars nor more than one thousand dollars; and a penalty of not less than five hundred dollars nor more than one thousand dollars shall be recovered from the railroad for each such offense when such officer, agent or employe acted in obedience to the direction, instruction or request of such railroad or a general officer thereof. (April 2, 1906, 98 v. 356, § 26; R. S. Sec. 244-36.)

Section 571. (Forfeiture for failure or neglect to comply with this chapter.) If a railroad fails or refuses to perform a duty enjoined upon it by the provisions of this chapter or does any act prohibited by such provisions, for which no penalty has been provided by law, or fails, neglects or refuses to obey a lawful requirement or order made by the commission or order of any court upon its application for each violation, failure, or refusal, such railroad shall forfeit and pay into the state treasury not less than one hundred dollars nor more than ten thousand dollars. In construing and enforcing the provisions of this section, the act, omission or failure of any officer, agent or other person acting for or employed by a railroad, while acting within the scope of his employment, shall be the act, omission or failure of the railroad. (April 2, 1906, 98 v. 356, § 27; R. S. Sec. 244-37.)

Section 572. (Power of commission to regulate in cases not designated.) If, after hearing and investigation as provided by this chapter, the commission finds any charge, regulation or practice affecting the transportation of passengers or property, or any service in connection therewith, not hereinbefore specifically designated, unreasonable or unjustly discriminatory, it may regulate it as herein provided in such cases. (April 2, 1906, 98 v. 356, § 28; R. S. Sec. 244-38.)

See § 535.

Section 573. (Duty of railroad to report certain accidents.) Whenever an accident attended with loss of human life occurs within this state upon the line of any railroad or on the depot grounds or yards thereof, such railroad shall give immediate notice thereof to the commission. (April 2, 1906, 98 v. 356, § 29; R. S. Sec. 244-39.)

Section 574. (Duty of the commission to investigate such

accident.) In case of such accident, the commission, if it deems the public interest requires it, shall cause an investigation to be made forthwith, which shall be held in the locality of the accident, unless, for greater convenience of those concerned, it shall order it held at some other place. Such investigation may be adjourned from place to place as it may be found necessary and convenient. The commission shall give reasonable notice to an officer or station agent of the company of the time and place of the investigation. (April 2, 1906, 98 v. 356, § 29; R. S. Sec. 244-39.)

Section 575. (Costs of investigation.) The cost of such investigation shall be certified by the chairman of the commission, and audited and paid by the state as other expenses. A record or file of the proceedings and evidence shall be kept by the commission. (April 2, 1906, 98 v. 357, § 29; R. S. Sec. 244-39.)

Section 576. (Commission shall inquire into violation of laws.) The commission shall inquire into any neglect or violation of the laws of this state by a railroad doing business in this state, by its officers, agents or employes or by any person operating a railroad. It shall enforce the provisions of this chapter, as well as all other laws relating to railroads and report violations thereof to the attorney general. (April 2, 1906, 98 v. 357, § 30; R. S. Sec. 244-40.)

Section 577. (Counsel for commission.) Upon request of the commission, the attorney general or the prosecuting attorney of the proper county shall aid in an investigation, prosecution, hearing or trial had under the provisions of this chapter, and shall institute and prosecute necessary actions or proceedings for the enforcement of such provisions and of other laws of this state relating to railroads and for the punishment of all violations thereof. (April 2, 1906, 98 v. 357, § 30; R. S. Sec. 244-40.)

Section 578. (Action for forfeiture by attorney general.) An action for the recovery of a forfeiture provided for in this chapter, when prosecuted by the attorney general, may be brought in the court of common pleas of Franklin county, or of any county having jurisdiction of the defendant. (April 2, 1906, 98 v. 357, § 30; R. S. Sec. 244-40.)

Section 579. (Damage claims. Verification. Burden of proof.) All claims, charges or demands against a railroad for loss of, or damage to property occurring while in the custody of such railroad and unreasonable delay in transportation and delivery, or for overcharges upon a shipment, or for any other service in violation of this chapter, if not paid within sixty days from the date of the filing thereof with such railroad, may be submitted to the commission by a formal complaint to be made upon blank forms which it is hereby made the duty of the commission to provide upon demand of the claimant. Such complaint shall be verified as petitions in civil actions and may be accompanied by the sworn statements of any witnesses who have knowledge of any fact material to the inquiry. Upon the filing of such complaint the commission shall forthwith cite the railroad to answer the complaint, and the citation shall be accompanied with a brief statement of the claim. The answer of the railroad shall be filed within three weeks from the service of the citation and shall be verified as answers in civil cases and may be accompanied with the affidavits of any witnesses having knowledge of facts material to the inquiry. The burden of proof shall be upon the railroad to show that loss or damage to property was not due to its negligence. The railroad to which property is delivered for shipment shall prima facie be liable for loss or damage occurring to such property in transit notwithstanding it may be delivered to other railroads before reaching its destination. The claim referred to in this section for loss of or damage to property may be made to any carrier over whose lines the lost or damaged property has been consigned, and such claimant may at his option join all of such railroads as parties defendant in his complaint before said commission. The railroad shall furnish the claimant with a copy of its answer and affidavits, if any, and within two weeks from the filing of such answers the claimant may file his reply with affidavits in support thereof, verified as replies in civil cases. At the expiration of said period of two weeks the commission shall proceed summarily to examine the complaint, answer, the reply and affidavits and shall determine the existence and validity of the claim presented. If it find in favor of the claimant it shall certify its findings to the clerk of the court of common pleas of the county in which the claimant resides or where the railroad or any of its offices is maintained. (May 9, 1910, 101 v. 173; R. S. Sec. 244-41; April 21, 1908, 99 v. 130, § 31; April 2, 1906, 98 v. 357, § 31.)

The commission has no power to award damages for the violation of a contract to make stops at a platform.

Ashley v. Sandusky, etc., Co., 5 O. L. R. 359; 52 B. 498 (Railroad Commission).

A carrier is liable for negligence in weighing coal and in furnishing incorrect weight certificates to shipper.

Nimishilling, etc., v. C. T. & V. R. R., 5 O. L. R. 455; 52 B. 569; (Railroad Commission).

Consignor is real party in interest, when.

Hisylvania Coal Co. v. T. & O. C. Ry., 7 O. L. R. 467 (Railroad Commission).

Compare State v. Mullin 78 O. S. 358.

Exemption from liability, in bill of lading. A carrier can not, by contract exempt itself from liabilty for negligence.

Hisylvania Coal Co. v. T. & O. C. Ry., 7 O. L. R. 467 (Railroad Commission).

Section 580. (Immediate trial. Costs.) Within thirty days from the receipt of such findings by said clerk, the railroad may by motion cause the same to be docketed as a civil action in said court in which case the original pleadings shall be used and the case shall be advanced for immediate trial. If no such motion is filed the clerk shall enter up the finding of the commission as a judgment and the same shall be in all respects treated as a judgment at law with all the incidents thereof and upon which execution may issue as in other cases. If said matter is docketed for trial the action shall proceed as in other civil actions for damages except that upon trial thereof a copy of the findings and order of the commission, duly certified by the secretary thereof, shall be competent testimony and shall be prima facie evidence of the facts therein stated, and except that the plaintiff shall not be liable for any costs unless they accrue upon his appeal. (May 9, 1910, 101 v. 174; R. S. Sec. 244-41; April 21, 1908, 99 v. 130, § 31; April 2, 1906, 98 v. 357, § 31.)

Section 581. (Construction to be placed on provisions of this chapter.) A substantial compliance by the commission with the requirements of this chapter shall be sufficient to give effect to all its rules, orders, acts and regulations, and they shall not be declared inoperative, illegal or void for an omission of a technical nature in respect thereto. Nothing in this chapter shall be construed as affecting, modifying or repealing any law, fixing the rate which a company operating a railroad may demand and receive for the transportation of passengers. (April 2, 1908, 98 v. 357, §§ 32, 38; R. S. Sec. 244-42.)

Section 582. (Forfeiture shall be cumulative.) All forfeitures accruing under this chapter shall be cumulative, and a suit for and recovery of one shall not bar the recovery of any other forfeiture. (April 2, 1906, 98 v. 358, § 33; R. S. Sec. 244-43.)

Section 583. (Actions by mandamus, etc., in certain cases.) In addition to the other remedies provided in this chapter for the prevention and punishment of violations of the provisions thereof and orders of the commission, the commission may compel compliance with such provisions and its orders by proceedings in mandamus, injunction, or by other appropriate civil remedies. (April 2, 1906, 98 v. 358, § 34; R. S. Sec. 244-44.)

Section 584. (Sections of this chapter independent.) Each section of this chapter and every part thereof is hereby declared to be an independent section, and part of a section, and the holding of a section or part thereof to be void or ineffective for any cause shall not be deemed to affect any other section or part thereof. (April 2, 1906, 98 v. 358, § 37; R. S. Sec. 244-47.)

TRACKS AND CROSSINGS.

Section 585. (Duty of commission as to dangerous track, bridges, etc.) If, on complaint or otherwise, the commission has reasonable grounds to believe that any of the tracks, bridges, or other structures of a railroad are in a condition which renders them dangerous or unfit for the transportation of passengers, it shall forthwith inspect and examine them, and, if of opinion that they are unfit for the transportation of passengers with safety, it shall immediately give to the superintendent, or other executive officer of the company operating such road, notice of the condition thereof, and of the repairs or reconstruction necessary to place them in a safe condition. The commission may prescribe the time within which such repairs or reconstruction must be made, and the rate of speed for trains passing over such dangerous or defective track, bridge or other structure, until the repairs or reconstruction required are made. If of opinion that it is needful and proper, it may forbid the running of passenger trains over such defective track, bridge or other structure. (R. S. Sec. 247; April 5, 1867, 64 v. 111, § 6, S. & S. 77.)

Section 586. (Penalty for neglect to repair defective track, etc.) Whoever, being the superintendent or other executive officer of a company operating a railroad, receives from the railroad commission notice of a prescribed rate of speed for trains passing over a defective track, bridge or other structure, or forbidding the running of passenger trains over such defective track, bridge or other structure, neglects for two days after receiving such notice to direct the proper subordinate officers to run the passenger trains over such defective track, bridge or other structure, at a speed not greater than that so prescribed, or, if the running of a passenger train is so forbidden, to stop running passenger trains over it, or, an engineer, conductor or other employe who knowingly disobeys such order shall be fined not exceeding five hundred dollars or imprisoned in the county jail not exceeding one year, or both.   (R. S. Sec. 247; April 5, 1867, 64 v. 111, § 6; S. & S. 77.)

Section 587.   (Forfeiture in case of noncompliance.)   If the company operating such road neglects or without good cause fails to make the repairs or reconstruction prescribed by the commission within the time limited by it, for each day that such repairs or reconstruction is delayed beyond the time prescribed, such company shall forfeit and pay to the state the sum of óne hundred dollars.   (R. S. Sec. 247; April 5, 1867, 64 v. 111, § 6; S. & S. 77.)

Section 588.   (Gates, bells, devices, or flagmen at crossing.)   If, in its opinion, the public safety requires that a gate or gates, automatic alarm-bell, or other mechanical device be erected and maintained at any place where a public road or street is crossed at the same level by a railroad, and the crossing has been declared by the commission to be dangerous, or the public safety requires that a flagman be stationed and maintained at such dangerous crossing, the commission shall give the superintendent, manager or other officer in charge of such railroad, a written notice of what is required, and such company, person or corporation owning or operating such railroad shall erect such mechanical device or station such flagman within the time prescribed by the commission.   (R. S. Sec. 247a; April 15, 1889, 86 v. 367; May 19, 1894, 91 v. 353.)

This section requires flagmen to be maintained only at crossings which have been found dangerous to the public.
    Akron, etc., Co. v. Erie R. R. Co., 7 C. C. n. s. 199; 18 C. D. 36.
    Duty of company to maintain gates or flagmen, in absence of order of the railroad commission.
    Railway Co. v. Schneider, 45 O. S. 678.
    Weaver v. Railway Co., 76 O. S. 164, 176.
    C. C. & I. Ry. Co. v. Reiss, 13 C. C. 405; 7 C. D. 450; B. & O. S. W. Ry. Co. v. Maloney, 7 C. C. n. s. 437, 442.
Duty of gatemen.
    Railway Co. v. Schneider, 45 O. S. 678.
    Toledo, etc., Co. v. Fuller, 17 C. C. 562, 571; 9 C. D. 123.
Defective gates.   Not proximate cause of injury, when.

B. & O. R. R. Co. v. Anderson, 37 W. L. B. 54.
A municipal corporation has no power, by ordinance, to compel a railroad company to maintain a watchman at a street crossing, in the absence of a special staute.
Ravenna v. Penna. Co., 45 O. S. 118.

Section 589. (Forfeiture for failure to comply with notice of commission.) Any person, company, or corporation neglecting or refusing to erect or maintain such gate or gates, automatic alarm-hell or other mechanical device, or to maintain such flagman, when required by the commission, shall forfeit and pay to the state, for every such neglect or refusal, one hundred dollars, and in addition ten dollars for each day such neglect or refusal continues. (R. S. Sec. 247a; May 19, 1894, 91 v. 353; April 15, 1889, 86 v. 367.)

Section 590. (Regulations as to gates, bells, and devices.) All gates, bells or devices erected under the direction of the commission shall be built within the time, in the manner and of materials approved by the commission. Such gates shall be located in the highway or street on one or both sides of the railroad track or tracks, as the commission deems the public safety requires, and shall be so constructed that when closed, they shall obstruct or prevent passage across such railroad or railroads from the side on which a gate is located. Such bell must be so constructed that it will ring before the approach of every train of cars or locomotive within three hundred feet or more of such crossing, and continue to ring until such train or locomotive has reached the crossing. A person shall be in charge of such gate who shall close it at the approach of each train or locomotive, and keep it open at all other times. If an automatic bell or other mechanical device is required at such crossing, the railroad shall keep such bell or device at all times in good working order, and for every neglect of duty imposed by this section such railroad shall forfeit and pay the sum of twenty-five dollars. (R. S. Sec. 247b; May 19, 1894, 91 v. 353; April 15, 1889, 86 v. 367.)

Section 591. (Cost of gates, bells, and devices in certain cases.) When two or more railroads cross a public highway or street at a dangerous crossing, the expenses incurred in the erection and maintenance of gates, bells or other device, and of necessary gate-keepers or flagmen shall be shared equally by such railroads; but nothing in this chapter shall prevent the use of automatic bells or other mechanical device by a railroad at a public crossing not declared dangerous by the commission. If a gate is erected or a flagman is stationed and maintained by a railroad, such gate or flagman shall not be abandoned nor an automatic bell or other mechanical device substituted therefor. (R. S. Sec. 247b; May 19, 1894, 91 v. 353; April 15, 1889, 86 v. 367.)

Section 592. (When engines or trains may pass crossings without stopping.) When two or more railroads, or a railroad and an electric railroad, erect a system of interlocking works or fixtures at the place where such railroads cross each other at a common grade, or when a railroad erects such works or fixtures at a swing or draw-bridge where it crosses a stream, and such works or fixtures render it safe for engines or trains to pass over such crossing or bridge without stopping, such railroad or railroads may run engines or trains over such works or fixtures without stopping, and any law to the contrary shall not apply in such case; but such system of interlocking works or fixtures shall have been approved by the commission, and a plan thereof shall have been prepared by such railroad or railroads and filed with the commission. (R. S. Sec. 247d; April 27, 1896, 92 v. 315, § 1.)

See §§ 8826, 8827 and 8833.

Section 593. (Unsafe interlocking works or fixtures.) If in its opinion any such system of interlocking works or fixtures proves to be unsafe or impracticable, the commission may order that no engines or trains shall pass over any such crossing or bridge without stopping, and the laws regulating the running of engines and trains shall apply. Before such order is made or enforced the commission shall give such railroad or railroads opportunity to be heard as to the propriety of the order. (April 27, 1896, 92 v. 315, § 1; R. S. Sec. 247d.)

Section 594. (Safety devices at grade crossings.) When two steam railroads, a steam railroad and an inter-urban, electric or street railway, two inter-urban railroads, or a steam or electric railroad and a street or highway cross at grade, if, in its opinion, public safety requires protection, the railroad commission, upon its own motion or upon complaint, after notice to the railroads interested and full investigation, may make an order requiring the railroads so intersecting and crossing to install such device or devices as in the opinion of the commission will properly protect such crossing. (R. S. Sec. 247e; May 9, 1908, 99 v. 390, § 2; April 27, 1896, 92 v. 315.)

See note to § 597.

Section 595. (Commission may make order as to a crossing.) The railroad commission may make any further or other orders regulating the speed and running of trains or of cars and the switching of cars over such crossing or street, and it shall apportion the expense of installation or maintenance of such device or devices between the railroad companies whose tracks are thus protected. (R. S. Sec. 247e; May 9, 1908, 99 v. 390, § 2; April 27, 1896, 92 v. 315.)

Section 596. (Hearing as to necessity of safety device.) At the time and place named for hearing, unless continued for good cause, the railroad commission shall try the question of whether or not such crossing shall be protected by interlocking or other safety devices and shall give all companies or parties interested an opportunity to be fully heard. (R. S. Sec. 247e; May 9, 1908, 99 v. 390, § 2; April 27, 1896, 92 v. 315.)

Section 597. (What order of commission shall contain.) After such hearing, the railroad commission shall enter upon a record book or docket kept for that purpose an order granting or denying the petition. In case the petition is granted, such order shall prescribe the inter-locking or other safety devices for such crossing and all other matters deemed proper for the efficient protection of such crossing, the proportion of the cost of construction and of the expense of maintaining and operating such device which each company or person concerned shall pay. The order shall also fix the time within which such appliance shall be put in and the time within which such order shall be complied with. (R. S. Sec. 247e; May 9, 1908, 99 v. 390, § 2; April 27, 1896, 92 v. 315.)

When one railway company desires to cross the tracks of another railway company, it is competent for the companies to agree between themselves upon the terms of crossing, including the compensation for the right to cross, the cost of constructing and maintaining an interlocking system, and as to which company shall employ, control and pay the employe by whom the interlocking system is operated. Such a contract is not prohibited by Secs. 594 to 597.

Hydell v. Railway 74 O. S. 138 (1906).

Section 598. (Compulsory interlocking.) If a railroad or electric railroad with its track or tracks shall cross at grade the track or tracks of a railroad or electric railroad previously constructed, the former shall provide at such crossing interlocking works or other fixtures satisfactory to the commission, and pay the costs of such fixtures and the expenses of installing them. The maintenance and operation thereof shall be apportioned equally between the railroads by the commission; but this section shall not apply to crossings of side-tracks only. (R. S. Sec. 247f; April 25, 1898, 93 v. 334, § 3; April 27, 1896, 92 v. 315.)

See Street Railway v. Railway 21 C. C. 391; 12 C. D. 113.
Railway Co. v. Railway Co. 5 N. P. 83; 7 L. D. 558.
Railway Co. v. Traction Co. 1 N. P. n. s. 218; affirmed 4 C. C. n. s. 329, reversed on other grounds, 72 O. S. 429.

Section 599. (Crossing without stopping.) Whenever interlocking works or other fixtures are constructed and maintained in compliance with law by railroads and electric railroads where such road or roads cross each other, engines and trains or cars of an electric railroad may be run over such crossing without stopping; any law to the contrary shall not apply to such case. (April 27, 1896, 92 v. 316, § 4; R. S. Sec. 247g.)

Section 600. (Forfeiture for noncompliance with order.) A railroad or electric railroad refusing or neglecting to comply with an order of the commission, concerning the protection of persons and property from danger at grade crossings of any such railroad over another, or over a swing or drawbridge and at junction points, by providing interlocking works or other fixtures, shall forfeit and pay five hundred dollars per week for each week such railroad refuses or neglects to obey such orders. Such forfeiture shall be recovered in an action of debt in the name of the state, and, when collected, paid into the treasury of the county in which such suit was brought. (April 27, 1896, 92 v. 317, § 5; R. S. Sec. 247h.)

MISCELLANEOUS.

Section 601. (Examinations into alleged violations of law.) If upon complaint, or otherwise, the commission has reason to believe that a railroad or any officer, agent, or employe thereof has violated or is violating any law of the state, or if it has reason to believe that differences have arisen between citizens of the state and any railroad operating as a common carrier within the state, it shall examine into the matter. (R. S. Secs. 248, 248a; May 18, 1886, 83 v. 206; April 15, 1867, 64 v. 111, § 5; S. & S. 76.)

Section 602. (List of officers and directors must be furnished by railroad or telegraph company.) Within thirty

days after the election of the directors of a railroad, or telegraph company, now doing business, or whose line is in process of construction, or which hereafter may be organized in
the state, the secretary of such companies shall make and
forward to the commission a list of the officers and directors
thereof, giving the place of residence and post office address
of each. If a change occurs in the organization of the officers
or board of directors of a railroad or company, the secretary
shall notify the commission of such change and the residence
and post office address of each of the officers and directors.
(R. S. Sec. 260; April 24, 1873, 70 v. 155, § 1.)

**Section 603. (Commission shall be furnished copies of
certain leases, contracts, and agreements.)** On demand of
the commission, each railroad within this state shall furnish
it copies of all leases, contracts and agreements with express,
sleeping car, freight or rolling stock companies, or other
companies doing business upon or in connection with such
road. The commission or its duly authorized agent may
examine any officer, agent or employe of a railroad or of
such other companies, under oath, relative to the stock which
he has in any of such companies, and his pecuniary interests
direct or indirect therein. (R. S. Sec. 256; May 5, 1873, 70
v. 276, §§ 2, 3.)

Section 604. (Map and profile of new railroad.) Within
a reasonable time after the construction of a railroad, or at
any time when required by the commission, such railroad
shall make and file with the commission a map and profile
of such railroad, which shall be drawn on a scale, and certified and signed by the president or engineer of such railroad. (R. S. Sec. 250-1; April 19, 1894, 91 v. 154, § 1.)

Section 605. (Annual report of railroad.) On or before
the fifteenth day of September in each year, each railroad
or telegraph company incorporated or doing business in this
state shall make and transmit to the commission a full and
true statement under oath of the proper officers of such corporation, of the affairs of such corporation relative to the
state of Ohio for the year ending on the thirtieth day of
June preceding. Such statement shall be similar in character and detail to the annual report required to be made by
railroad companies to the interstate commerce commission.
The commission may submit additional interrogatories to a
railroad or telegraph company at any time. If such report
is defective or erroneous, the commission may require the
railroad or telegraph company to correct or amend it within

fifteen days. (R. S. Secs. 244-30, 250-1; April 19, 1894, 91 v. 154, § 1; April 2, 1906, 98 v. 354, § 20.)

Reports of accidents, made by railroad companies under this section, are not admissible in evidence in personal injury actions by employes. C. C. C. & St. L. Ry. Co. v. Ullom 20 C. C. 512; 11 C. D. 321; affirmed no report 64 O. S. 582.

Section 606. (Assessment for maintaining commission, and how apportioned.) For the purpose of maintaining the department of the public service commission of Ohio, and the exercise of police supervision of railroads and public utilities of the state by it, a sum not exceeding seventy-five thousand dollars each year shall be apportioned among and assessed upon the railroads and public utilities within the state, by the commission, in proportion to the intra state gross earnings or receipts of such railroads and public utilities for the year next preceding that in which the assessments are made.

On or before the first day of August next following, the commission shall certify to the auditor of state the amount of such assessment apportioned by it to each railroad and public utility and he shall certify such amount to the treasurer of state, who shall collect and pay the same into the state treasury to the credit of a special fund for the maintenance of the department of such public service commission. (May 31, 1911, 102 v. 550; April 19, 1894, 91 v. 155, § 2; R. S. Sec. 250-2.)

The requirement of this section that the commission shall certify the assessment by August 1 is directory and not mandatory for the reason that under § 605 railroads need not file their reports until September 15.
Rep. Atty. Gen. 1911-1912, p. 714.

Section 607. (Penalty.) A railroad company or telegraph company violating a provision of the preceding three sections shall forfeit and pay to the state one thousand dollars, and twenty-five dollars for each day such company refuses, neglects or fails to comply with a requirement of such sections, which forfeiture shall not release such company from the assessment provided in the next preceding section. (April 15, 1894, 91 v. 155, § 3; R. S. Sec. 250-3.)

Section 608. (Commission may pass free over all railroads.) In the performance of its duties, the commission may pass free of charge on all railroads and upon all trains or any part thereof within this state. (R. S. Sec. 250; April 5, 1867, 64 v. 111, § 4; S. & S. 76.)

See § 499-1.

Section 609. (Penalty for refusing to answer questions in examination.) Whoever, being an officer, agent, or employe of a railroad company, refuses to answer a question propounded to him by a member of the commission in the course of an examination authorized by this chapter shall be fined not less than fifty dollars nor more than five hundred dollars. The property of the railroad company of which he is an officer, agent or employe, shall be liable to be taken in execution to satisfy the fines and costs in such cases. (R. S. Sec. 259; May 5, 1873, 70 v. 276, § 3.)

Section 610. (Form of action for forfeitures and penalties.) Unless otherwise provided by law, all prosecutions against a railroad or telegraph company or an officer, agent or employe thereof for forfeitures under the provisions of this chapter and other provisions of law shall be by civil action in the name of the state. All prosecutions for penalties involving imprisonment shall be by indictment. (R. S. Sec. 262; April 25, 1893, 90 v. 299; April 5, 1867, 64 v. 111, § 7; May 5, 1873, 70 v. 276, § 3.)

Section 611. (Action for forfeiture by prosecuting attorney.) If the commission, the officer requested by it, or a city solicitor, when the cause of action arises in a municipality, fails or neglects to prosecute a civil action for forfeiture against a railroad, telegraph company, officer, agent or employe thereof as provided by law, the prosecuting attorney of the county in which a cause of action for forfeiture arises, upon the request of any taxpayer thereof, and on being furnished with evidence which in his judgment will sustain it, shall bring such action. If such action fails the costs thereof shall be adjudged against the county. (R. S. Sec. 263; April 25, 1893, 90 v. 299; April 5, 1867, 64 v. 111, § 8.)

Section 612. (Action for forfeiture by city solicitor.) If a cause of action for forfeiture arises within a municipality, and the commission, the officer requested by it or the prosecuting attorney as above provided, fails or neglects to prosecute such action, the city solicitor of such municipality, when required by resolution of the council, shall institute such action and prosecute it to final judgment. If such action fails, the costs therefore shall be adjudged against the municipality. The time for notice of appeal and giving a bond shall not apply to cases within the meaning of this and the preceding section. (R. S. Sec. 263; April 25, 1893, 90 v. 299; April 5, 1867, 64 v. 111, § 8.)

Section 613. (Moneys arising from prosecutions and actions for forfeiture.) All moneys arising from prosecutions or from actions for forfeiture in the name of the state against a railroad or telegraph company, or against an officer or employee thereof, for violations of the provisions of law relating to railroads or telegraph companies shall be paid into the state treasury. (R. S. Sec. 265; April 5, 1867, 64 v. 111, § 7.)

Section 614. Repealed 103 v. 804. (February 27, 1877, 74 v. 33, § 12; R. S. Sec. 264.)

PUBLIC UTILITIES COMMISSION ACT.

Section 614-1. (Name.) The railroad commission of Ohio shall hereafter be known as the public service commission of Ohio. In addition to the powers, duties, and jurisdiction conferred and imposed upon said commission by chapter one, division two, title three, part first, of the General Code, and the acts mandatory or supplementary thereto, the public service commission of Ohio shall have and exercise the powers, duties, and jurisdiction provided for in this act. (May 31, 1911, 102 v. 550, § 2.)

Section 614-2. (Definitions.) The following words and phrases used in this act, unless the same be inconsistent with the text shall be construed as follows:

The term "commission" when used in this act, or in chapter one, division two, title three, part first, of the General Code and the acts amendatory or supplementary thereto means "The Public Service Commission of Ohio."

The term "commissioner" means one of the members of such commission.

Any person or persons, firm or firms, co-partnership or voluntary association, joint stock association, company or corporation, wherever organized or incorporated:

When engaged in the business of transmitting to, from, through or in this state, telegraphic messages, is a telegraph company;

When engaged in the business of transmitting to, from, through, or in this state, telephonic messages, is a telephone company and as such is declared to be a common carrier;

When engaged in the business of supplying electricity for light, heat or power purposes to consumers within this state, is an electric light company;

When engaged in the business of supplying artificial gas

for lighting, power or heating purposes to consumers within this state, is a gas company;

When engaged in the business of supplying natural gas for lighting, heating, or power purposes to consumers within this state, is a natural gas company;

When engaged in the business of transporting natural gas or oil through pipes or tubing, either wholly or partly within this state, is a pipe line company;

When engaged in the business of supplying water through pipes or tubing, or in a similar manner to consumers within this state, is a water works company;

When engaged in the business of supplying water, steam, or air through pipes or tubing to consumers within this state for heating or cooling purposes, is a heating or cooling company;

When engaged in the business of supplying messengers for any purpose, is a messenger company;

When engaged in the business of signalling or calling by an electrical apparatus, or in a similar manner, for any purpose, is a signalling company;

When engaged in the business of operating, as a common carrier, a railroad, wholly or partly within this state, with one or more tracks upon, along, above or below any public road, street, alley, way or ground, within any municipal corporation, operated by any motive power other than steam, and not a part of an interurban railroad, whether such railroad be termed street, inclined plane, elevated, or underground railroad, is a street railroad company;

When engaged in the business of operating as a common carrier, whether wholly or partially within this state, a part of a street railway constructed or extended beyond the limits of a municipal corporation, and not a part of an interurban railroad is a suburban railroad company;

When engaged in the business of operating a railroad, wholly or partially within this state, with one or more tracks from one municipal corporation or point in this state to another municipal corporation or point in this state, whether constructed upon the public highways or upon private rights-of-way, outside of municipalities, using electricity or other motive power than animal or steam power for the transportation of passengers, packages, express matter, United States mail, baggage and freight, is an interurban railroad company, and included in the term "railroad" as used in section 501 of the General Code. The term "railroad," when used in this act, includes all railroads, interurban railroad companies, express companies, freight line companies, sleeping car companies, equipment companies, car companies, water transportation companies, and all persons and associations of persons, whether incorporated or not, operating such agencies for public use in the conveyance of persons or property within this state. (May 31, 1911, 102 v. 552, § 3.)

The public service commission is superseded by the public utilities commission, G. C. § 499-7.

In enacting the public service commission act (102 v. 552), it was the intention of the legislature to keep alive all of the former powers, prerogatives, jurisdiction and purposes of the previous railroad commission act.

Rep. Atty. Gen. 1911-1912 p. 712.

Section 614-2a. (**"Public utility" defined.**) The term "public utility" as used in this act, shall mean and include every corporation, company, co-partnership, person or association, their lessees, trustees or receivers, defined in the next preceding section, except such public utilities as operate their utilities not for profit, and except such public utilities as are, or may hereafter be owned or operated by any municipality, and except such utilities as are defined as "railroads" in sections 501 and 502 of the General Code and these terms shall apply in defining "public utilities" and "railroads" wherever used in chapter one, division two, title three, part first of the General Code and the acts amendatory or supplementary thereto or in this act. (May 31, 1911, 102 v. 552, § 4.)

The construction of a private telephone line and station for the use of a number of persons associated together for that purpose does not constitute a public utility, and the persons using such a line are not subject to control by the public service commission.

Gratiot etc. Co. v. Brownsville etc. Co. 15 C. C. n. s. 508 (1912); affirming 13 N. P. n. s. 429.

Section 614-3. (**Jurisdiction to regulate "public utilities" and "railroads."**) The public service commission of Ohio is hereby vested with the power and jurisdiction to supervise and regulate "public utilities" and "railroads" as herein defined and provided and to require all public utilities to furnish their products and render all services required by the commission, or by law. (May 31, 1911, 102 v. 552, § 5.)

This act provides an adequate remedy for discrimination and unjust or unreasonable rates and classifications, and courts have no original jurisdiction with reference thereto.

Publishing Co. v. Express Co. 13 N. P. n. s. 403 (1911).

Section 614-4. (**Powers of commission.**) The jurisdiction, supervision, powers and duties of the public service commission shall extend to every public utility and railroad, the plant or property of which lies wholly within this state and when the property of a public utility or railroad lies partly within and partly without this state to that part of such plant or property which lies within this state, and to the persons or companies owning, leasing or operating the same, and to the records and accounts of the business thereof done within this state. (May 31, 1911, 102 v. 552, § 6.)

Section 614-5. (Rules governing proceedings.) The commission shall have power to adopt and publish rules to govern its proceedings and to regulate the mode and manner of all valuations, tests, audits, inspections, investigations and hearings which shall be open to the public. (May 31, 1911, 102 v. 552, § 7.)

Section 614-6. (Examination of witnesses and production of records.) The commission shall have power, either through its members or by inspectors or employes duly authorized by it, to examine under oath, at any time and for assisting the commission in the performance of any powers or duties of the commission, any officer, agent or employe of any public utility or railroad or any other person, in relation to the business and affairs of such utility and to compel the attendance of such witness for the purpose of such examination. In case of disobedience on the part of any person or persons to comply with any order relating to the production or examination of books, contracts, records, documents and papers or in case of the refusal of any person to testify to any matter regarding which he may be lawfully interrogated by any such member, employe or inspector of the commission at any time or place, it shall be the duty of the common pleas court of any county or any judge thereof, on application of any member of the commission, to compel obedience by contempt proceedings as in the case of the disobedience of the requirements of a subpoena issued from such court or a refusal to testify therein. (May 31, 1911, 102 v. 552, § 8.)

Section 614-7. (Examination of records.) The commission shall have power, either through its members or by inspectors or employes duly authorized by it, to examine all books, contracts, records, documents and papers of any public utility, and by subpoena duces tecum to compel the production thereof, or of duly verified copies of the same or any of them, and to compel the attendance of such witnesses as the commission may require to give evidence at such examination. (May 31, 1911, 102 v. 552, § 9.)

Section 614-8. (General supervision.) The commission shall have general supervision over all public utilities within its jurisdiction as hereinbefore defined, and shall have the power to examine the same and keep informed as to their general condition, their capitalization, their franchises and the manner in which their properties are leased, operated, managed, and conducted with respect to the adequacy or accommodation afforded by their service, and also with respect to the safety and security of the public and their employes, and with respect to their compliance with all provisions of law, orders of the commission, franchises and charter requirements. The commission, either through its members or inspectors or employes, duly authorized by it, may enter in or upon, for the purpose of inspection, any property, equipment, building, plant, factory, office, apparatus, machinery, device and lines of any public utility. (May 31, 1911, 102 v. 553, § 10.)

Section 614-9. (May require copy of contract.) Every public utility shall file with the commission, when and as required by it, a copy of any contract, agreement or arrangement, in writing, with any other public utility relating in any way to the construction, maintenance or use of its plant or property, or any service, rate or charge. (May 31, 1911, 102 v. 553, § 11.)

Section 614-10. (System of accounts. Form of records. Changes in accounts.) The commission may establish a system of accounts to be kept by public utilities, or classify utilities and prescribe a system of accounts for each class and prescribe the manner in which such accounts shall be kept. Such system shall when practicable conform to the system prescribed by the tax commission of Ohio. It may also, in its discretion, prescribe the form of records to be kept by public utilities, and the commission may require that no other records be kept except as may be required by the laws of the United States or as may hereafter be required by the laws of this state. The commission shall, at all times, have access to all accounts kept by public utilities, and may designate any of its officers or employes to inspect and examine any and all such accounts.

The commission, may, if it shall determine that any expenditures or receipts have been improperly charged or credited, order the necessary changes in such accounts. (May 31, 1911, 102 v. 553, § 12.)

Section 614-11. (Penalty for divulging information.) Except in his report to the commission or when called on to testify in any court or proceeding, any such employe or agent who shall divulge any information acquired by him in respect to the transaction, property, or business of any public utility, while acting or claiming to act as such employe or agent shall be fined not less than fifty dollars, and not more than one hundred dollars, and shall thereafter be disqualified from acting as agent, or in any other capacity under the appointment or employment of the commission. (May 31, 1911, 102 v. 553, § 13.)

Section 614-12. (Unreasonable charge prohibited.) Every public utility shall furnish necessary and adequate service and facilities which shall be reasonable and just, and every unjust or unreasonable charge for such service is prohibited and declared to be unlawful. (May 31, 1911, 102 v. 553, § 14.)

Section 614-13. (Facilities and charges.) Every public utility shall furnish and provide with respect to its business such instrumentalities and facilities as shall be adequate and in all respects just and reasonable. All charges made or demanded for any service rendered, or to be rendered, shall be just and reasonable, and not more than allowed by law or by order of the commission. Every unjust or unreasonable charge made or demanded for any service, or in connection therewith, or in excess of that allowed by law or by order of the commission, is prohibited and declared to be unlawful. (May 31, 1911, 102 v. 554, § 15.)

See State v. Union etc. Co. 13 C. C. n. s. 12 (1910).
Nivison etc. Co. v. Union etc. Co. 7 O. L. R. 243 (C. P. 1909).

Section 614-14. (Rebates, special rates, free service, etc., prohibited.) No public utility shall directly or indirectly, or by any special rate, rebate, drawback or other device or method, charge, demand, collect or receive from any person, firm, or corporation, a greater or less compensation for any services rendered, or to be rendered, except as provided in this act, than it charges, demands, collects, or receives from any other person, firm, or corporation for doing a like and contemporaneous service under the same, or substantially the same circumstances and conditions. Nor shall free service or service for less than actual cost be furnished for the purpose of destroying competition, and such free service and every such charge is prohibited and declared unlawful. (May 31, 1911, 102 v. 554, § 16.)

See State v. Union etc. Co. 13 C. C. n. s. 12 (1910).
Nivison etc. Co. v. Union etc. Co. 7 O. L. R. 243 (1909).

Section 614-15. (Undue advantage.) No public utility shall make or give any undue or unreasonable preference or advantage to any person, firm, corporation, or locality, or subject the same to any undue or unreasonable prejudice or disadvantage in any respect whatsoever. (May 31, 1911, 102 v. 554, § 17.)

Section 614-16. (Printed schedules of rates must be filed.) Every public utility shall print and file with the commission, within ninety days after this act takes effect, schedules, showing all rates, joint rates, rentals, tolls, classifications and charges for service of each and every kind by it rendered or furnished, which were in effect at the time this act takes effect and the length of time the same has been in force, and all rules and regulations in any manner affecting the same. Such schedules shall be plainly printed and kept open to public inspection. The commission shall have power to prescribe the form of every such schedule, and may, from time to time, prescribe, by order, changes in the form thereof. The commission may establish rules and regulations for keeping such schedule open to public inspection, and may, from time to time, modify the same. A copy of such schedules or so much thereof as the commission shall deem necessary for the use and information of the public, shall be printed in plain type and kept on file or posted in such places and in such manner as the commission may order. (May 31, 1911, 102 v. 554, § 18.)

Section 614-17. (Reasonable arrangements allowed. Approval.) Nothing in this act shall be taken to prohibit a public utility from entering into any reasonable arrangement with its customers, consumers or employes for the division or distribution of its surplus profits or providing for a sliding scale of charges or providing for a minimum charge for service to be rendered, unless such minimum charge is made or prohibited by the terms of the franchise, grant or ordinance under which such public utility is operated, a classification of service based upon the quantity used, the time when used, the purpose for which used, the duration of use, and any other reasonable consideration, or providing any other financial device that may be practicable or advantageous to the parties interested. No such arrangement, sliding scale, minimum charge, classification or device shall be lawful unless the same shall be filed with and approved by the commission. Every such public utility is required to conform its schedules of rates, tolls and charges to such arrangement, sliding scale, classification or other device.

Every such arrangement, sliding scale, minimum charge, classification or device shall be under the supervision and regulation of the commission, and subject to change, alteration or modification by the commission. (May 31, 1911, 102 v. 554, § 19.)

Section 614-18. (Schedule rate collected. Refunder or remitter not allowed.) No public utility shall charge, demand, exact, receive or collect a different rate, rental, toll or charge for any service rendered, or to be rendered, than that applicable to such service as specified in its schedule filed with the commission and in effect at the time. Nor shall any public utility refund or remit directly or indirectly, any rate, rental, toll or charge so specified, or any part thereof, nor extend to any person, firm or corporation, any rule, regulation, privilege or facility except such as are specified in such schedule and regularly and uniformly extended to all persons, firms and corporations under like circumstances for the like, or substantially similar, service. (May 31, 1911, 102 v. 555, § 20.)

Section 614-19. (Prior contract.) The furnishing by any public utility of any product or service, at the rates, and upon the terms and conditions provided for in any existing contract, executed prior to the passage of this act, shall not be construed as constituting a discrimination, or undue or unreasonable preference, or advantage within the meaning specified.

Provided, however, that when any such contract or contracts are or become terminable by notice, the commission shall have power, in its discretion, to direct by order, that such contract or contracts shall be terminated as and when directed by such order. (May 31, 1911, 102 v. 555, § 21.)

Section 614-20. (Change of rates. 30 days' notice.) Unless otherwise ordered by the commission, no change shall be made in any rate, joint rate, toll, classification, charge or rental, in force at the time this act takes effect, or as shown upon the schedules which shall have been filed by a public utility in compliance with the requirements of this act, or by order of the commission, except after thirty days' notice to the commission, which notice shall plainly state the changes proposed to be made in the schedule then in force, and the time when the change, rate, charge, toll, classification or rental shall go into effect; and all proposed changes shall be plainly indicated upon existing schedules, or by filing new schedules thirty days prior to the time they are to take effect, but the commission may prescribe a less time when they may take effect. (May 31, 1911, 102 v. 555, § 22.)

Section 614-21. (Complaint. Notice of complaint and time and place of hearing. Rights of parties.) Upon complaint in writing, against any public utility, by any person, firm or corporation, or upon the initiative or complaint of the commission that any rate, fare, charge, toll, rental, schedule, classification or service, or any joint rate, fare, charge, toll, rental, schedule, classification or service rendered, charged, demanded, exacted or proposed to be rendered, charged, demanded, or exacted, is in any respect unjust, unreasonable, unjustly discriminatory, or unjustly preferential or in violation of law, or that any regulation, measurement or practice affecting or relating to any service furnished by said public utility, or in connection therewith, is, or will be, in any respect unreasonable, unjust, insufficient or unjustly discriminatory or unjustly preferential, or that any service is, or will be, inadequate or can not be obtained, the commission shall notify the public utility complained of that complaint has been made, and of the time and place when the same will be considered and determined, which notice shall be served upon the public utility not less than fifteen days before such hearing, and shall plainly state the matters or things complained of. The commission shall, if it appear that there are reasonable grounds for the complaint, at such time and place proceed to consider such complaint and may adjourn the hearing thereof from time to time. The parties thereto shall be entitled to be heard, represented by counsel and to have process to enforce the attendance of witnesses. A public utility may make complaint as to any matter affecting its own product or service with like effect as though made by a person, firm or corporation, in which event the commission shall publish notice thereof for ten days prior to such hearing in a newspaper of general circulation at the situs of such public utility. (May 31, 1911, 102 v. 556, § 23.)

Section 614-22. (Separate hearings.) When complaint is made of more than one rate, charge, or service, the commission may order separate hearings thereon and may consider and determine the matters complained of separately and at such times and places as it may prescribe. No complaint shall necessarily be dismissed because of the absence of direct damage to the complainant. (May 31, 1911, 102 v. 556, § 24.)

Section 614-23. (May fix reasonable rate.) Whenever the commission shall be of the opinion, after hearing, that any rate, fare, charge, toll, rental, schedule, classification or service, or any joint rate, fare, charge, toll, rental, schedule, classification, or service rendered, charged, demanded, exacted or proposed to be rendered, charged, demanded, or exacted, is, or will be, unjust, unreasonable, unjustly discriminatory or unjustly preferential or in violation of law, or the service inadequate, or that the maximum rates, charges, tolls or rentals chargeable by any such public utility are insufficient to yield reasonable compensation for the service rendered, and are unjust and unreasonable, the commission shall, with due regard among other things, to the value of all of the property of the public utility actually used and useful for the convenience of the public, excluding therefrom the value of any franchise or right to own, operate or enjoy the same in excess of the amount, (exclusive of any tax or annual charge) actually paid to any political subdivision of the state or county, as the consideration for the grant of such franchise or right; and exclusive of any value added thereto by reason of a monopoly or merger and to the necessity of making reservation out of the income for surplus, depreciation and contingencies, and all such other matters as may be proper, according to the facts in each case, fix and determine the just and reasonable rate, fare, charge, toll, rental or service to be thereafter rendered, charged, demanded, exacted or collected for the performance or rendition of the service, and order the same substituted therefor; and thereafter, no change in the rate, fare, toll, charge, rental, schedule, classification or service, shall be made, rendered, charged, demanded, exacted or changed by such public utility without the order of the commission and any other rate, fare, toll, charge, rental, classification or service shall be deemed and held to be unjust and unreasonable, prohibited and unlawful. Upon application of any person or any public utility, and after notice to the parties in interest and opportunity to be heard as provided in this act for other hearings, has been given, the commission may rescind, alter or amend an order fixing any rate or rates, fare, toll, charge, rental, classification or service, or any other order made by the commission. Certified copies of such orders shall be served and take effect as provided for original orders. (May 31, 1911, 102 v. 556, § 25.)

This act provides an adequate remedy for discrimination and unjust or unreasonable rates and classifications, and courts have no original jurisdiction with reference thereto.

Publishing Co. v. Express Co. 13 N. P. n. s. 403 (1911).

Section 614-24. Repealed 103 v. 804. Enacted 102 v. 557, § 26.

Section 614-25. Repealed 103 v. 804. Enacted 102 v. 557, § 27.

Section 614-26. Repealed 103 v. 804. Enacted 102 v. 557, § 28.

Section 614-27. (Power to change rules and prescribe equipment.) Whenever the commission shall be of the opinion, after hearing had upon complaint, as in this act provided, or upon its own initiative or complaint, served as in this act provided, that the rules, regulations, measurements or practices of any public utility with respect to its public service are unjust or unreasonable, or that the equipment or service thereof is inadequate, inefficient, improper or insufficient, or can not be obtained, it shall determine the regulations, practices and service thereafter to be installed, observed, used and rendered, and fix and prescribe the same by order to be served upon the public utility. It shall thereafter be the duty of such public utility and all of its officers, agents and official employes to obey the same and do everything necessary or proper to carry the same into effect and operation; provided, that nothing herein contained shall be so construed as to give to the commission power to make any order requiring the performance of any act or the doing of anything which is unjust or unreasonable or in violation of any law of the state or the United States. (May 31, 1911, 102 v. 557, § 29.)

Section 614-28. (May order repairs, improvements, etc.) Whenever the commission shall be of the opinion, after hearing had, as in this act provided, or upon its own initiative or complaint, as in this act provided, that repairs or improvements to the plant or equipment of any public utility, should reasonably be made, or that any additions thereto should reasonably be made, in order to promote the convenience or welfare of the public, or of employes, or in order to secure adequate service or facilities, the commission may make and serve an appropriate order with respect thereto, directing that such repairs, improvements, changes or additions be made within a reasonable time, and in a manner to be specified therein. Every such public utility, its officers agents and official employes shall obey such order and make such repairs, improvements, changes and additions required of such public utility by such order. (May 31, 1911, 102 v. 558, § 30.)

Section 614-29. (Use of equipment over street, etc., by other public utility.) Every public utility having any equipment on, over or under any street, or highway, shall, subject to the provisions of section 9103 of the General Code, for a reasonable compensation, permit the use of the same by any other public utility whenever the commission shall determine as provided in section 32 hereof that public convenience, welfare and necessity require such use, or joint use, and such use or joint use will not result in irreparable injury to the owner or other users of such equipment, nor in any substantial detriment to the service to be rendered by such owners or other users. (May 31, 1911, 102 v. 558, § 31.)

Section 614-30. (Application on failure to agree.) In case of failure to agree upon such use or joint use or the conditions or compensation for such use or joint use, any public utility may apply to the commission, and if after investigation the commission shall ascertain that the public convenience, welfare and necessity require such use or joint use and that it would not result in irreparable injury to the owner or other users of such property or equipment, nor in any substantial detriment to the service to be rendered by such owner or other users of such property or equipment, said commission shall by order direct that such use or joint use be permitted and prescribe reasonable conditions and compensation for such joint use. (May 31, 1911, 102 v. 558, § 32.)

Section 614-31. (Conditions and compensation.) Such use or joint use so ordered shall be permitted and such conditions and compensation so prescribed shall be the lawful conditions and compensation to be observed, followed and paid, subject to recourse to the courts by any interested party as provided in this act. Any such order made by the commission may be revoked or from time to time revised by the commission. (May 31, 1911, 102 v. 558, § 33.)

Section 614-32. (Power to amend, alter or suspend schedule of rates.) The commission shall have power, when deemed by it necessary to prevent injury to the business or interests of the public or any public utility of this state in case of any emergency to be judged by the commission, to temporarily alter, amend, or with the consent of the public utility concerned suspend any existing rates, schedules or order relating to or affecting any public utility or part of any public utility in this state. Such rates so made by the commission shall apply to one or more of the public utilities in this state or to any portion thereof as may be directed by the commission, and shall take effect at such time and remain in force for such length of time as may be prescribed by the commission. (May 31, 1911, 102 v. 559, § 34.)

Section 614-33. (Construction accounts.) The commission shall keep informed of all new construction, extensions and additions to the property of such public utilities and may prescribe the necessary forms, regulations and instructions to the officers and employes of such public utilities for the keeping of construction accounts, which shall clearly distinguish all operating expenses and new construction. (May 31, 1911, 102 v. 559, § 35.)

Section 614-34. (Standard units.) The commission shall ascertain and prescribe suitable and convenient standard commercial units of the product or service of any public utility, when the character of its product or service is such that it can be determined, and such units shall be the lawful units for the purposes of this act. (May 31, 1911, 102 v. 559, § 36.)

Section 614-35. (Report, etc.) Each such utility shall furnish to the commission in such form and at such times as the commission may require such accounts, reports and information as shall show completely and in detail the entire operation of the public utility in furnishing the unit of its product or service to the public. (May 31, 1911, 102 v. 559, § 37.)

Section 614-36. (Standards of measurement.) The commission may ascertain and fix adequate and serviceable standards for the measurement of quality, pressure, initial voltage or other condition pertaining to the supply or quality or the product or service rendered by any public utility and prescribe reasonable regulations for examination and testing of such product or service and for the measurements thereof. It may establish reasonable rules, regulations, specifications and standards to secure the accuracy of all meters and appliances for measurements, and every public utility is required to carry into effect all orders issued by the commission relative thereto. (May 31, 1911, 102 v. 559, § 38.)

Section 614-37. (Examination and test.) The commission may provide for the examination and testing of any and all appliances used for the measurement of any product or service of a public utility. Any consumer or user may have any such appliance tested upon payment of the fees fixed by the commission. The commission may declare and establish reasonable fees to be paid for testing such appliances on the request of the consumers or users, the fees to be paid by the consumer or user at the time the request is made, but to be paid by the public utility and repaid to the consumer or user if the appliance be found commercially defective or incorrect to the disadvantage of the consumer or user. (May 31, 1911, 102 v. 559, § 39.)

Section 614-38. (Facts shall be public and records open.) All facts and information in the possession of the commission shall be public, and all reports, records, files, books, accounts, papers and memoranda of every nature whatsoever in their possession shall be open to inspection by the public at all reasonable times, except when the commission shall determine it to be necessary to withhold for a reasonable time from the public any facts or information in its possession. (May 31, 1911, 102 v. 560, § 40.)

Section 614-39. (Incrimination no excuse.) No person shall be excused from testifying or from producing accounts, books and papers, in any hearing before the commission, or any member thereof, or any person appointed by it to investigate any matter or thing under its jurisdiction, on the ground or for the reason that the testimony or evidence might tend to incriminate him, or subject him to a penalty or forfeiture, but no such person shall be prosecuted or subjected to any penalty or forfeiture for, or on account of, any transaction, matter or thing concerning which he may have testified or produced any documentary evidence; provided, that no person so testifying shall be exempted from prosecution or punishment for perjury in so testifying. (May 31, 1911, 102 v. 560, § 41.)

Section 614-40. (Supplemental order.) Whenever any rate, toll, charge or service, ordered substituted by the commission, shall be a joint rate, toll, charge or service, and the public utilities parties thereto, fail to agree upon the apportionment thereof within twenty days after the service of such order, the commission may, after hearing, make and issue a supplemental order fixing the apportionment of such joint rate, toll, charge or service between such public utilities, and the same shall take effect of its own force as a part of the original order. (May 31, 1911, 102 v. 560, § 42.)

Section 614-41. (All orders take effect, when.) All orders made by the commission shall, of their own force, take effect and become effective operative thirty days after service thereof, unless a different time be provided in the order. (May 31, 1911, 102 v. 560, § 43.)

Section 614-42. (Railroad track connection. Complaint on failure. Hearing—order. Interchange of traffic.) When the tracks of a steam railroad, the tracks of an interurban or suburban railroad cross, connect or intersect and such tracks are of the same gauge, the companies owning such roads may connect the tracks of the roads so connecting, crossing or intersecting, so as to admit the passage of cars from one road to the other with facility. If any such road or roads fail, neglect or refuse to make such connection, upon complaint of any party authorized by the provisions of this chapter to file complaint, the commission shall proceed to hear and determine the same in a manner provided for making investigations, upon complaint. If upon such hearing the commission shall find it is practicable and reasonably necessary to accommodate the public to connect such tracks and that when so connected, it will be practicable to transport over such road, cars without endangering the equipment, tracks or appliances of either company, then the commission shall make an order requiring such railroads to make connection, describing the terms and condition, and apportion the cost thereof between the railroads. When such connection is made, the railroads parties thereto, according to their respective powers, shall afford all reasonable and proper facilities for the interchange of traffic between their respective lines for forwarding and delivering passengers and property, and without unreasonable delay or discrimination shall transfer, switch and deliver cars, freight or passenger, destined to a point on its own or connecting lines; but precedence may be given to live stock and perishable freight over other freight. Whenever a derailing device is required at the intersection of any railroads herein mentioned the same shall be installed, maintained and operated as required by such commission, which shall have full power and authority to prescribe the necessary rules and regulations for the operation of the same, and designate the company or companies that shall be responsible for the operation thereof. (May 31, 1911, 102 v. 560, § 44.)

This section authorizes the public service commission to make an order requiring two or more railroad companies to construct a connecting track between their lines.

Penna. Co. v. Public Service Commission, 14 N. P. n. s. 262; 58 Bull. 185 (C. P. 1913).

An order requiring three railroad companies, whose tracks intersect in a city, to construct transfer or connecting tracks at a cost of

$14,000 in order to accommodate manufacturers and other shippers whose traffic approximates two thousand cars per year, is not so unreasonable as to violate a constitutional right.

Penna. Co. v. Commission, 14 N. P. n. s. 262 (C. P. 1913).

Section 614-43. (Rehearing.) Upon the application of any person, public utility or railroad aggrieved thereby, the commission may, upon written petition therefor, filed within thirty days after any order made by the commission shall have been entered upon its records, grant a rehearing of the matter upon which such order was based. Notice of such rehearing shall be given as required with respect to original hearings, of the time and place for the rehearing thereon. Upon such rehearing any party may offer additional evidence which could not, with reasonable diligence, have been offered on the former hearing. Upon such rehearing, the commission may change, modify, vacate or affirm its former order and make and enter such new order as may be deemed necessary. (May 31, 1911, 102 v. 561, § 45.)

Section 614-44. (Power of municipality to fix rate, etc. Complaint—hearing. Accepted rate becomes operative, when.) Any municipal corporation in which any public utility is established, may, by ordinance, at any time within one year before the expiration of any contract entered into under the provisions of sections 3644, 3982 and 3983 of the General Code between the municipality and such public utility with respect to the rate, price, charge, toll, or rental to be made, charge, demanded, collected or exacted, for any commodity, utility or service, by such public utility, or at any other time authorized by law proceed to fix the price, rate, charge, toll, or rental that such public utility may charge, demand, exact or collect therefor for an ensuing period, as provided in sections 3644, 3982 and 3983 of the General Code. Thereupon, the commission, upon complaint in writing, of such public utility, or upon complaint of one per centum of the electors of such municipal corporation, which complaints shall be filed within sixty days after the passage of such ordinance, shall give thirty days' notice of the filing and pendency of such complaint to the public utility and the mayor of such municipality, of the time and place of the hearing thereof, and which shall plainly state the matters and things complained of.

If any public utility shall have accepted any rate, price, charge, toll, or rental fixed by ordinance of such municipality, the same shall become operative, unless within sixty days after such acceptance there shall have been filed with the commission, a complaint, signed by not less than three per centum of the qualified electors of such municipality. Upon such filing, the commission shall forthwith give notice of the filing and pendency of such complaint to the mayor of such municipality and fix a time and place for the hearing thereof. The commission shall at such time and place, proceed to hear such complaint, and may adjourn the hearing thereof from day to day.

The filing of a complaint by a public utility, as herein provided, shall be taken and held to be the consent of such public utility to continue to furnish its product or service, and devote its property engaged therein to such public use during the term so fixed by ordinance or by the provisions of this act. Parties thereto shall be entitled to be heard, represented by counsel, and to have process to force the attendance of witnesses. (May 31, 1911, 102 v. 561, § 46.)

This section is prospective in its operation. The commission has no jurisdiction to entertain an appeal from an ordinance passed prior to the enactment of this section, although the ordinance was not to take effect, and was not accepted by the public utility, until after its enactment.

Rep. Atty. Gen. 1911-1912, p. 725.

Section 614-45. (Rate will not be suspended or vacated, etc., without bond.) No such complaint or appeal to the commission shall suspend, vacate, or set aside the rate, price, charge, toll or rental fixed by ordinance unless such public utility shall elect to charge the rate, price, charge, toll or rental in force and effect immediately prior to the taking effect of the regulation complained of and appealed from, and shall give an undertaking in such amount as the commission shall determine. The undertaking shall be filed with the commission and shall be payable to the state of Ohio for the use and benefit of the consumers affected by the regulation in question. The condition of the undertaking shall be that such public utility shall refund to each of its consumers, public or private, the amount collected by it in excess of the amount which shall finally be determined it was authorized to collect from such consumers. The commission shall make all necessary orders in respect to the form of such undertaking and the manner of making such refunders. (May 31, 1911, 102 v. 562, § 47.)

Section 614-46. (Finding as to rate.) If the commission, after such hearing, shall be of the opinion that the rate, price, charge, toll or rental, so fixed by ordinance is or will be unjust or unreasonable, or insufficient to yield reasonable compensation for the service, the commission shall, with due regard to the value of all the property of the public utility actually used and useful for the convenience of the public, excluding therefrom the value of any franchise or right to own, operate or enjoy the same in excess of the amount (exclusive of any tax or annual charge) actually paid to any political subdivision of the state or county as a consideration or the grant of such franchise or right; and exclusive of any value added thereto by reason of a monopoly or merger and to the necessity of making reservations from the income for surplus, depreciation and contingencies, and such other matters as may be proper, according to the facts in each case, fix and determine the just and reasonable rate, price, charge, toll or rental to be charged, demanded, exacted or collected by such public utility, during the period so fixed by ordinance, which shall not be less than two years, and order the same substituted for the rate, price, charge, toll or rental so fixed by ordinance or the commission may find and declare that the rate, price, charge, toll or rental, so fixed by ordinance, is just and reasonable, and ratify and confirm the same.

No such rate, price, charge, toll or rental so determined by the commission shall become effective or valid until after the commission shall have ascertained and determined the valuation upon which such price, charge, toll or rental is based as provided in this act. And such valuation so determined shall be, at all times, open to public inspection. Thereupon the commission shall make inquiry and investigation with respect to the ability of such public utility to furnish its product during such period, if it be found that it is able so to do, the commission shall order the public utility in question to continue to furnish the same for the period and at the rate, price, charge, toll or rental so fixed and determined, and such public utility shall continue to furnish its product as provided in such order. (May 31, 1911, 102 v. 562, § 48.)

Section 614-47. (When act not applicable.) This act shall not apply to any rate, fare or regulation now or hereafter prescribed by any municipal corporation granting a right, permission, authority or franchise, to use its streets, alleys, avenues or public places, for street railway or street railroad purposes, or to any prices so fixed under sections 3644, 3982 and 3983 of the General Code, except as provided in sections 46, 47 and 48 of this act. (G. C. §§ 614-44, 614-45 and 614-46.) (May 31, 1911, 102 v. 563, § 49.)

Section 614-48. (Annual report.) Every public utility shall file with the commission, at such times and in such form as it may prescribe, an annual report, duly verified, covering the yearly period fixed by the commission. The commission shall prescribe the character of the information to be embodied in such annual report, and shall furnish to each public utility a blank form therefor. If any such report is defective or erroneous, the commission may order the same to be amended within a prescribed time. Such annual reports shall be preserved in the office of the commission. The commission may, at any time, require specific answers to questions upon which it may. desire information. (May 31, 1911, 102 v. 563, § 50.)

Section 614-49. (Depreciation account.) Every public utility shall carry a proper and adequate depreciation or deferred maintenance account, whenever the commission after investigation shall determine that a depreciation account can be reasonably required. The commission shall ascertain, determine and prescribe what are proper and adequate charges for depreciation of the several classes of property for each public utility. The charge for depreciation shall be such as will provide the amount required over and above the cost and expense of maintenance to keep the property of the public utility in a state of efficiency corresponding to the progress of the art or industry. The commission may prescribe such changes in such charges for depreciation from time to time as it may find necessary. (May 31, 1911, 102 v. 563, § 51.)

Section 614-50. (Depreciation fund.) The moneys for depreciation charges thus provided for shall be set aside out of the earnings and carried as a depreciation fund. The moneys in such fund may be expended in new construction, extensions or additions to the property of the public utility, or invested, and if invested, the income from the investment shall also be carried in the depreciation fund. Such fund and the proceeds thereof, may be used for the purpose of renewing, restoring, replacing or substituting depreciated property in order to keep the plant in a state of efficiency. Such fund and the ·proceeds or income therefrom shall be used for no purpose other than as provided in this section, except upon the approval of the commission. (May 31, 1911, 102 v. 564, § 52.)

Section 614-51. (Power to require additions and extensions.) The council of any municipality shall have the power upon filing of an application therefor by any person, firm or corporation, to require of any public utility, by ordinance or otherwise, such additions or extensions to its distributing plant within such municipality as shall be deemed reasonable and necessary in the interest of the public, and, subject to the provisions of section 9105 of the General Code, to designate the location and nature of all such additions and extensions, the time within which they must be completed, and all conditions under which they must be constructed and operated. Such requirements and orders of the council shall be subject to review by the commission, as provided in sections 46 and 48 hereof. (G. C. §§ 614-44 and 614-46.) The council and commission in determining the practicability of such additions and extensions, shall take into consideration the supply of the product furnished by such public utility available, and the returns upon the cost and expense of constructing said extension and the amount of revenue to be derived therefrom, as well as the earning power of the public utility as a whole. (May 31, 1911, 102 v. 564, § 53.)

This section and section 614-28 do not authorize the commission to compel a street railway company to extend its line beyond its terminal points, but merely to compel additions and facilities between such points. Rep. Atty. Gen. 1911-12, p. 716.

Section .614-52. (Company not permitted to exercise right of franchise where another is giving adequate service.) No telephone company shall exercise any permit, right, license or franchise that may have been heretofore granted but not actually exercised or that may hereafter be granted to own or operate a plant for the furnishing of any telephone service, thereunder in any municipality or locality, where there is in operation a telephone company furnishing adequate service, unless such telephone company first secures from the commission a certificate after public hearing of all parties interested that the exercising of such license, permit, right or franchise is proper and necessary for the public convenience. (May 31, 1911, 102 v. 564, § 54.)

A telephone company can not extend its lines into territory, already occupied by another company, without a certificate from the public service commission. An attempt to so extend its lines may be enjoined by the other company.
Telephone Co. v. Telephone Co. 13 N. P. n. s. 61 (1912).
Proof of the incorporation of a telephone company and purchase of telephone equipment is not sufficient to sustain an allegation that the company is about to exercise a franchise and engage in public service, as distinguished from providing private lines for the use of stockholders and others residing within a short distance.
Gratiot, etc., Telephone Co. v. Brownsville, etc., Co., 13 N. P. n. s. 429 (C. P. 1911); affirmed, 15 C. C. n. s. 508.
An allegation by an existing telephone company that it is rendering adequate service must be proved, when traversed by the defendant.

Gratiot etc. Co. v. Brownsville etc. Co. 13 N. P. n. s. 429 (C. P. 1911); affirmed 15 C. C. n. s. 508.

A telephone company, upon which both primary and secondary franchises had been conferred prior to the enactment of this section, need not secure a certificate from the commission.

Gratiot etc. Co. v. Brownsville etc. Co. 15 C. C. n. s. 508 (1912); affirming 13 N. P. n. s. 429.

Section 614-53. (When public utility may issue stocks, bond, notes, etc.   How and for what purposes commission may authorize issue.) A public utility or a railroad, as defined in this act, may, when authorized by order of the commission, and not otherwise, issue stocks, bonds, notes and other evidences of indebtedness, payable at periods of more than twelve months after date thereof, when necessary for the acquisition of property, the construction, completion, extension or improvement of its facilities or for the improvement or maintenance of its service, or for the reorganization or readjustment of its indebtedness and capitalization, or for the discharge or lawful refunding of its obligations, or for the reimbursement of moneys actually expended from income or from any other moneys in the treasury of the public utility or railroad not secured or obtained from the issue of stocks, bonds, notes or other evidences of indebtedness of such public utility or railroad within five years next prior to the filing of an application therefor as herein provided, or for any of the aforesaid purposes except maintenance of service and except replacements in cases where the applicant shall have kept its accounts and vouchers of such expenditures in such manner as to enable the commission to ascertain the amount of money so expended and the purposes for which said expenditure was made.

The commission may, by order duly made, authorize the issue of bonds, notes, or other evidences of indebtedness, for the reimbursement of money heretofore actually expended from income for any of the aforesaid purposes, except maintenance of service and replacements prior to five years next preceding the filing of an application therefor, if such application for such consent be made prior to January 1, 1913. Any bonds, notes, or other evidences of indebtedness, payable at periods of more than twelve months after date thereof, may be issued as herein provided, regardless of the amount of the capital stock of the public utility or railroad, subject to the approval of the commission to the excess of such bonds, notes, or other evidences of indebtedness above the amount of the capital stock of such public utility or railroad, notwithstanding any provisions of the General Code of Ohio now in force to the contrary.

Provided, however, that it shall be the duty of the commission to authorize on the best terms obtainable, such issues of stocks, bonds and other evidence of indebtedness as shall be necessary to enable any public utility to comply with the provisions of any contract heretofore made between such public utility and any municipality. (May 9, 1913, 103 v. 841; May 31, 1911, 102 v. 565, § 56.)

Section 614-54. (Proceedings to obtain authority to issue stocks, bonds, etc.) The proceedings for obtaining the consent and authority of the commission for such issue as provided in the next preceding section of this act, shall be as follows:

(a) In case the stocks, bonds, notes, or other evidence of indebtedness are to be issued for money only, the public utility or railroad shall file with the commission a statement, signed and verified by the president and secretary thereof, setting forth:

(1) The amount and character of the stocks, bonds or other evidence of indebtedness.

(2) The purposes for which they are to be issued. ·

(3) The terms upon which they are to be issued.

(4) The total assets and liabilities of the public utility or railroad in such detail as the commission may require.

(5) If the issue is desired for the purpose of the reimbursement of money expended from income, as herein provided, the amount expended, when and for what purposes expended.

(6) Such other facts and information pertinent to the inquiry as the commission may require.

(b) If the stocks, bonds, notes or other evidence of indebtedness are to be issued, partly or wholly for property or services or other consideration than money the public utility or railroad shall file with the commission a statement, signed and verified by its president and secretary, setting forth:

(1) The amount and character of the stocks, bonds or other evidence of indebtedness proposed to be issued.

(2) The purposes for which they are to be issued.

(3) The description and estimated value of the property or services for which they are to be issued.

(4) The terms on which they are to be issued or exchanged.

(5) The amount of money, if any, to be received from the same in addition to the property, service or other consideration.

(6) The total assets and liabilities of the public utility or railroad in such detail as the commission may require.

(7) Such other facts and information pertinent to the inquiry as the commission may require. Provided, however, that this section or the preceding section shall not apply to union depot companies heretofore organized and under contract until the same are completed. (May 31, 1911, 102 v. 565, § 57.)

Section 614-55. (Hearings. Order. Application of proceeds. Issue without authority, void.) For the purpose of enabling the commission to determine whether it should issue such order, it shall hold such hearings, make such inquiries or investigation, examine such witnesses, books, papers, documents and contracts as it may deem proper. The order of the commission shall fix the amount, character and terms of any such issue, and the purposes to which the issue or any proceeds thereof shall be applied, and recite that the money, property, consideration or labor procured or to be procured or paid for by such issue, has been, or is reasonably required for the purposes specified in the order, and the value of any property, consideration or service as the case may be, as found by the commission for which in whole or in part, such issue is proposed to be made. No such public utility or railroad shall, without the consent of the commission, apply any such issue or its proceeds to any purpose not specified in the order. Such public utilities or railroads may issue notes for proper corporate purposes, and not in violation of any provision of this act, payable at periods of not more than twelve months without the consent of the commission, but no such notes shall, in whole or in part, directly or indirectly, be refunded by any issue of stocks or bonds, or by any evidence of indebtedness, running for more than twelve months without the consent of the commission. All stocks, bonds, notes or other evidence of indebtedness, issued by any public utility or railroad without the consent or permission of the commission, as herein provided, shall be void and of no effect. No interstate railroad or public utility shall be required, however, to apply to the commission for authority to issue stock, bonds, notes or other evidence of indebtedness for the acquisition of property, the construction, completion, extension or improvement of its facilities or the improvement or maintenance of its service outside the state, or for the discharge or refunding of obligations issued or incurred for such purposes or for reimbursement of moneys actually expended for such purposes outside of the state. (May 31, 1911, 102 v. 566, § 58.)

Section 614-56. (Public utility in hands of receiver, etc., exempt from this act.) Where a public utility or railroad is, at the time this act takes effect, in the possession of one or more receivers or its property is under foreclosure, and a reorganization thereof is pending, any new company or companies that may hereafter be organized to acquire such property or any part thereof, shall be exempt from all the provisions of this act with respect to the issue of bonds, stocks and evidences of debt, provided that the total debts, obligations and securities of such new or reorganized company or companies exclusive of bonds, obligations, stocks, and other securities that may be issued or authorized for additional capital shall not exceed the debts, obligations, stocks and other securities of the existing company or companies, and provided further that from and after its organization and the issue of such bonds, obligations, stocks and other securities as hereby permitted, all the provisions of this act shall apply to such new or reorganized company or companies. (May 31, 1911, 102 v. 567, § 59.)

Section 614-57. (Penalty for false statement.) Any director, president, secretary, manager, officer or other official of any public utility or railroad who shall knowingly make any false statement to secure the issue of any stock, bond, note or other evidence of indebtedness, or who shall, by such false statement, procure the order of the commission for the issue of any stock, bond, note or other evidence of indebtedness, or issue with knowledge of such fraud, negotiate, or cause to be negotiated any such stock, bond, or other evidences of indebtedness in violation of this act, shall upon conviction thereof, be fined not less than five hundred dollars, or be imprisoned in the penitentiary for not less than one year or more than ten years. (May 31, 1911, 102 v. 567, § 60.)

Section 614-58. (Dividend must be authorized.) No public utility or railroad shall declare any stock, bond or scrip dividend or divide the proceeds of the sale of any stock, bond, or scrip among its stockholders, unless authorized by the commission so to do. (May 11, 1911, 102 v. 567, § 61.)

Section 614-59. (Capitalization.) The commission shall not have power to authorize the capitalization of any franchise or right to own, operate or enjoy any franchise whatsoever in excess of the amount (exclusive of any tax or annual charge) actually paid to any political subdivision of the state or county as the consideration for the grant of such franchise or right, nor shall the capital stock of a corporation formed by the merger or consolidation of two or more corporations exceed the sum of the capital stock of the corporation or corporations so consolidated or merged, at the par value thereof, and such sum or any additional sum actually paid in cash; nor shall any contract for consolidation or lease be capitalized in the stock of any corporation whatever; nor shall any such corporation hereafter issue any bonds against or as a lien upon any contract for consolidation or merger; nor shall the aggregate amount of the debt of such consolidated companies by reason of such consolidation be increased. (May 31, 1911, 102 v. 567, § 62.)

Section 614-60. (Consent and approval of commission. Petition. Hearing.) With the consent and approval of the commission, but not otherwise:

(a) Any two or more public utilities, furnishing a like service or product and doing business in the same municipality or locality within this state, or any two or more public utilities whose lines intersect or parallel each other within this state, may enter into contracts with each other that will enable such public utilities to operate their lines or plants in connection with each other.

(b) Any public utility may purchase, or lease the property, plant or business of any other such public utility.

(c) Any such public utility may sell or lease its property or business to any other such public utility.

(d) Any such public utility may purchase the stock of any other such public utility.

The proceedings for obtaining the consent and approval of the commission for such authority, shall be as follows:

There shall be filed with the commission a petition, joint or otherwise, as the case may be, signed and verified by the president and secretary of the respective companies, clearly setting forth the object and purposes desired, stating whether or not it is for the purchase, sale, lease or making of contracts or for any other purpose in this section provided and also the terms and conditions of the same. The commission shall, upon the filing of such petition, if it deem the same necessary, fix a time and place for the hearing thereof. If, after such hearing or in case no hearing is required, the commission is satisfied that the prayer of such petition should be granted and the public will thereby be furnished adequate service for a reasonable and just rate, rental, toll, or charge therefor, it shall make such order in the premises as it may deem proper and the circumstances require, and thereupon it shall be lawful to do the things provided for in such order. (May 31, 1911, 102 v. 568, § 63.)

A valuation of properties by the commission is probably not a condition precedent to granting an application under this section, but the commission may make such valuation at any time.
Rep. Atty. Gen. 1911-12, p. 729, 739.
See G. C. § 499-8.
This section applies to physical connections and is independent of § 614-61.
Rep. Atty. Gen. 1911-12, p. 729.

Section 614-61. (Merger. Petition. Order. Valuation, rates, etc.) With the consent and approval of the commission, but not otherwise, any two or more telephone companies, defined in this act, and doing business in this state or partly within and partly without this state, may consolidate with each other, when such telephone companies shall have complied with the orders and requirements of the commission and the provisions of this act.

Such telephone companies shall file with the commission a joint petition for such consolidation, signed and verified by the president and secretary of the respective companies, in which shall be set forth in detail, all of the terms, conditions and proceedings pertaining to such consolidation and in such form as the commission may require, and thereupon the commission shall fix a time and place for the hearing of such petition.

If, after such hearing, the commission is satisfied that such consolidation will promote public convenience, and will furnish the public adequate service for a reasonable rate, rental, toll or charge therefor, it shall make an order authorizing such consolidation, which order before taking effect shall be filed with the secretary of state. Other proceedings relating to such consolidation shall be in the manner and with the effect, not inconsistent with the provisions of this act, as is provided for in the consolidation of railroad companies under the laws of this state.

No consolidation, purchase, lease or contract by which two or more telephone companies merge or operate their lines or plants jointly or in connection with each other, shall become valid or effective until after the commission shall have ascertained and determined the valuation as provided in this act upon which the rates, tolls, charges and rentals are based and also shall have fixed and determined such rates, tolls, charges and rentals so to be charged.

All valuations so ascertained and determined shall be at all times open to public inspection. (May 31, 1911, 102 v. 568, § 64.)

See § 9190.
The terms "consolidation' and "merger" are not synonymous.
Rep. Atty. Gen. 1911-12, p. 729.
A valuation of properties by the commission is a condition precedent
to the granting of an application under this section.
Rep. Atty. Gen. 1911-12, p. 729.

Section 614-62. (Void contracts.) All such contracts,
leases, purchases, sales or consolidations not made pursuant
to the provisions of this act or contrary hereto shall be void
and of no effect. (May 31, 1911, 102 v. 569, § 65.)

**Section 614-63. (Power to form continuous line. Charges,
rates, etc.)** The commission shall have the power upon complaint, in writing, by any person, or on its own initiative,
by order, to require any two or more telephone companies
whose lines or wires form a continuous line of communication, or could be made to do so by the construction and
maintenance of suitable connections or the joint use of equipment, or the transfer of messages at common points, between
different localities which can not be communicated with or
reached by the lines of either company alone, where such
service is not already established or provided for, unless
public necessity requires additional service, to establish and
maintain through lines within the state between two or more
such localities. The joint rate or charges for such service
shall be just and reasonable and the commission shall have
power to establish the same, and declare the portion thereof
to which each company affected thereby shall be entitled and
the manner in which the same shall be secured and paid.
All necessary construction, maintenance and equipment in
order to establish such service shall be constructed and
maintained in such manner and under such rules, with such
division of expense and labor as shall or may be required
by the commission. (May 31, 1911, 102 v. 569, § 66.)

**Section 614-64. (Penalty on failure to comply with or-
ders.)** Every public utility or railroad and every officer
thereof, shall obey, observe, and comply with every order,
direction and requirement of the commission, made under authority of this act, so long as the same shall be and remain
in force. Any public utility or railroad herein defined which
violates any provision of this act, or which after due notice
fails, omits or neglects to obey, observe or comply with any
order or any direction or requirement of the commission
officially promulgated shall forfeit and pay to the state not
to exceed one thousand dollars for each such failure, omission
or neglect and each day's continuance thereof shall be

deemed and held to be a separate offense. (May 31, 1911, 102 v. 570, § 67.)

Section 614-65. (Penalty.) Whoever being an officer, agent or employe in an official capacity, of a public utility or railroad defined in this act, knowingly violates any provisions of this act, or wilfully fails, omits or neglects to obey, observe or comply with any lawful order or direction of the commission made with respect to any public utility or railroad shall be fined not less than one hundred dollars nor more than one thousand dollars, or imprisoned not more than two years, or both, and each day's continuance of such failure, omission or neglect shall constitute a separate offense. (May 31, 1911, 102 v. 570, § 68.)

Section 614-66. (Title of action.) Actions to recover penalties and forfeitures provided for in this act, shall be prosecuted in the name of the state and may be brought in the court of common pleas of any county in which the public utility or railroad may be located. Such action shall be commenced and prosecuted by the attorney general, when directed so to do by the commission. Moneys recovered by such action shall be deposited in the state treasury to the credit of the general revenue fund. (May 31, 1911, 102 v. 570, § 69.)

Section 614-67. (Mandamus—injunction.) Whenever the commission shall be of the opinion that any public utility or railroad has failed, omitted or neglected to obey any order made with respect thereto, or is about to fail or neglect so to do, or is permitting anything, or about to permit anything contrary to, or in violation of law, or an order of the commission, duly authorized under the provisions of this act, the attorney general, upon the request of the commission, shall commence and prosecute such action, actions, or proceedings in mandamus or by injunction in the name of the state, as may be directed by the commission, against such public utility or railroad, alleging the violation complained of and praying for proper relief, and in such case the court may make such order as may be proper in the premises. (May 31, 1911, 102 v. 570, § 70.)

Section 614-68. (Treble damages on violations.) If any public utility or railroad does, or causes to be done, any act, matter, or thing prohibited by this act, or declared to be unlawful, or shall omit to do any act, matter or thing required by this act, or by order of the commission, such public utility or railroad shall be liable to the person, firm or corporation injured thereby in treble the amount of damages sustained in consequence of such violation, failure or omission; provided, that any recovery under this section shall in no manner affect a recovery by the state for any penalty provided for in this act. (May 31, 1911, 102 v. 570, § 71.)

Section 614-69. Repealed 103 v. 804. (May 31, 1911, 102 v. 571, § 72.)

Section 614-70. Repealed 103 v. 804. (May 31, 1911, 102 v. 571, § 73.)

Section 614-71. (Service of order.) Every order provided for in this act, shall be served upon every person or corporation to be affected thereby, either by personal delivery or a certified copy thereof, or by mailing a certified copy thereof, in a sealed package with postage prepaid, to the person to be affected thereby, or in the case of a corporation, to any officer or agent thereof, upon whom a summons may be served. It shall be the duty of every person and corporation to notify the commission forthwith, in writing, of the receipt of the certified copy of every order so served, and in the case of a corporation such notification must be signed and acknowledged by a person or officer duly authorized by the corporation to admit such service. Within a time specified in the order of the commission every person or corporation upon whom it is served must if so required in the order notify the commission in like manner whether the terms of the order are accepted and will be obeyed. (May 31, 1911, 102 v. 572, § 74.)

Section 614-72. (Free service or reduced rates valid, when.) Nothing in this act contained shall prevent any public utility or railroad from granting the whole or any part of its property for any public purpose, or granting reduced rate or free service of any kind to the United States government, the state government or any political division or subdivision thereof, or for charitable purposes or for fairs or expositions or to any officer or employe of such public utility or railroad or his family and all contracts and agreements made or entered into by such public utility or railroad for such use, reduced rates, or free service shall be valid and enforcible at law. (May 31, 1911, 102 v. 572, § 75.)

Section 614-73. (Limitation.) No franchise, permit, license or right to own, operate, manage or control any public utility, herein defined as an electric light company, gas company, water works company or heating and cooling company, shall be hereafter granted or transferred to any corporation not duly incorporated under the laws of Ohio. (May 31, 1911, 102 v. 572, § 76.)

A foreign corporation may hold and vote a majority of the capital stock of an Ohio public utility corporation. Such stock control is not equivalent to a transfer of its franchise to the foreign corporation prohibited by this section.

Toledo T. L. & P. Co. v. Smith 58 Bull. 201 (U. S. D. C. 1913).

Section 614-74. (Companies subject to act.) Companies formed to acquire property or to transact business which would be subjected to the provisions of this act, and companies owning or possessing franchises for any of the purposes contemplated in this act, shall be deemed and held to be subject to the provisions of this act, although no property may have been acquired, business transacted or franchises exercised. (May 31, 1911, 102 v. 572, § 77.)

Section 614-75. (Liability for act of officer, etc.) The act, omission or failure of any officer, agent or other person, acting for or employed by a public utility or railroad, while acting within the scope of his employment, shall be deemed and held to be the act or failure of the public utility or railroad. (May 31, 1911, 102 v. 572, § 78.)

Section 614-76. (Fees.) The commission shall charge and collect for furnishing any copy of any paper, record, testimony or writing made, taken or filed under the provisions of this act, except such transcripts and other papers as are required to be filed in any court proceedings herein authorized, whether under seal and certified to or otherwise, the same fees now charged by the secretary of state, and such fees itemized shall be paid into the state treasury on the first day of each month. Upon application of any person, and payment of the proper fee therefor, the commission shall furnish certified copies under the seal of the commission, of any order made by it, which shall be prima facie evidence in any court of the facts stated therein. The copies of schedules and classifications and tariffs of rates, tolls, prices, rentals, regulations, practices, services, fares and charges, and of all contracts, agreements and arrangements between public utilities and railroads, or either, filed with the commission as herein provided, and the statistics, tables and figures contained in the annual or other reports of such companies made to the commission as required under the provisions of this act, shall be preserved as public records in the custody of the commission and shall be received as prima facie evidence of what they purport to be, for the purpose of investigations and prosecutions by the commission and in all judicial proceedings; and copies of and extracts from any of such schedules, classifications, tariffs, contracts, agreements, arrangements, or reports, made public records as aforesaid, certified by the commission under the seal of such commission, shall be received in evidence with like effect as the originals. Also copies of any order made by such commission certified under the seal of such commission, shall be furnished to any person upon application. (May 31, 1911, 102 v. 573, § 80.)

Section 614-77.   (Information furnished by commission.) The commission shall, whenever called upon by any officer, board or commission now existing or hereafter created in the state or any political subdivision thereof, furnish any data or information to such officer, board or commission and shall aid or assist any such officer, board or commission in performing the duties of his or its office, and all officers, boards or commissions now existing or hereafter created in the state or any political subdivision thereof, shall furnish to the commission, upon request, any data or information which will assist such commission in the discharge of the duties imposed upon it by this act. (May 31, 1911, 102 v. 573, § 81.)

Section 614-78.   (Costs and expenses.) If the commission after investigating shall find that any rate, joint rate, fare, charge, toll, rental, schedule or classification of service is unjust, unreasonable and insufficient or unjustly discriminatory or unjustly preferential or in violation of law or otherwise in violation of any provisions of this act or that any service is inadequate or can not be obtained the public utility found to be at fault shall pay the expenses incurred by the commission upon such investigation.

All fees, expenses and costs of or in connection with any hearing or investigation may be imposed by the commission upon any party to the record, or may be divided between any or all parties to the record in such proportion as the commission may determine. (May 31, 1911, 102 v. 574, § 82.)

Section 614-79.   (Penalty for wilful over or under valuation.) Whoever, being a member of the commission, shall wilfully overvalue the property of a public utility for the purpose of enabling such public utility to exact a higher rate for service than could lawfully be exacted, or, shall wilfully undervalue such property for the purpose of preventing such public utility from charging a lawful rate for such service shall be fined not to exceed one thousand dollars or be imprisoned not more than two years or both. (May 31, 1911, 102 v. 574, § 83.)

Section 614-80. Repealed 103 v. 804. (103 v. 176; 102 v. 574, § 84.)

Section 614-81. Repealed 103 v. 804. (102 v. 574, § 85.)

Section 614-82. (Each section of act independent.) Each section of this act, and every part thereof, is hereby declared to be independent sections and parts of sections and the holding of any section or part thereof to be void or ineffective for any cause, shall not be deemed to affect any other section or part thereof. (May 31, 1911, 102 v. 574, § 86.)

PART VII.

SUPERINTENDENT OF INSURANCE.

Section 615. (Superintendent of insurance, appointment and term.) The governor, with the advice and consent of the senate shall appoint a superintendent of insurance, who shall serve for a term of three years and have an office at the state capitol. No person shall be appointed to such office who has any official connection with an insurance company, owns any stock therein, or is interested in the business thereof, except as a policy holder. (May 9, 1913, 103 v. 842; R. S. Secs. 266, 270; May 12, 1902, 95 v. 549; May 1, 1885, 82 v. 202; Rev. Stat. 1880; March 12, 1872, 69 v. 32, § 4.)

Section 616. (Bond.) Before entering upon the discharge of the duties of his office, the superintendent of insurance shall give a bond to the state in the sum of one hundred thousand dollars with two or more sureties approved by the governor, conditioned for the faithful discharge of the duties of his office. Such bond, with the approval of the governor and the oath of office indorsed thereon, shall be deposited with the secretary of state and kept in his office. (R. S. Sec. 267; April 26, 1904, 97 v. 433; March 12, 1872, 69 v. 32, § 3.)

Section 617. (Duties of superintendent.) The superintendent of insurance shall see that the laws relating to insurance are duly executed and enforced. When violation of a law relating to insurance is reported to him, he shall take or cause to be taken the testimony under oath of any and all persons supposed to have knowledge of such violation, and cause such testimony to be reduced to writing. If of opinion that there is sufficient evidence, he shall cause the person suspected of such violation to be arrested and charged with such offense, and furnish the proper prosecuting attorney all information obtained by him, the names of witnesses and a copy of all material testimony taken in the case. (R. S. Sec. 268; April 2, 1906, 98 v. 265; March 12, 1872, 69 v. 32, § 3.)

Section 618. (Deputy superintendent.) The superintendent of insurance may appoint a deputy superintendent who shall have the same qualifications as the superintendent and whose appointment shall be evidenced by a certificate under the official seal of the superintendent. (R. S. Sec. 269; April 2, 1906, 98 v. 265; May 12, 1902, 95 v. 549; April 26, 1898, 93 v. 292; March 12, 1872, 69 v. 32, § 4.)

Section 619. (Bond of deputy.) Before entering upon the discharge of the duties of his office, the deputy superintendent of insurance shall give a bond to the superintendent in the sum of ten thousand dollars with two or more sureties approved by the superintendent, conditioned for the faithful discharge of the duties of his office. (R. S. Sec. 269; April 2, 1906, 98 v. 265; May 12, 1902, 95 v. 549; April 26, 1898, 93 v. 292; March 12, 1872, 69 v. 32, § 4.)

Section 620. (Duties of deputy.) Subject to the control of the superintendent of insurance, the deputy superintendent shall have power to perform the duties of his principal, except that during the absence or inability of the superintendent such deputy shall have the powers and perform the duties of the superintendent. (R. S. Sec. 269; April 2, 1906, 98 v. 265; May 12, 1902, 95 v. 549; April 26, 1898, 93 v. 292; March 12, 1872, 69 v. 32, § 4.)

Section 621. (Warden.) The superintendent shall appoint a warden who shall investigate all reported violations of law relating to insurance. (May 6, 1913, 103 v. 543; R. S. Sec. 269; April 2, 1906, 98 v. 265; May 12, 1902, 95 v. 549; April 26, 1898, 93 v. 292; March 12, 1872, 69 v. 32, § 4.)

Section 622. (Actuary, clerks and experts; compensation.) The superintendent of insurance may employ, with the approval of the governor, an actuary and such additional clerks as the prompt dispatch of business requires, and skilled and competent persons to examine and report the business and affairs of insurance companies. The compensation of such deputy superintendent, actuary, warden, clerks and examiners shall be fixed by the superintendent with the approval of the governor. (May 6, 1913, 103 v. 543; R. S. Sec. 269; April 2, 1906, 98 v. 265; May 12, 1902, 95 v. 549; April 26, 1898, 93 v. 292; March 12, 1872, 69 v. 32, § 4.)

Section 623. (Powers to compel the attendance of witnesses.) The superintendent of insurance, or when directed by him under his official seal, the deputy superintendent or warden, may summon and compel by order or subpoena the attendance of witnesses to testify in relation to any matter, which, by the laws of this state relating to insurance, is the subject of inquiry and investigation, and require the production of any book, paper or document pertaining to such matter. For such purpose they shall have the same power which is by law vested in justices of the peace to compel the attendance of witnesses and punish them for refusal to testify. Sheriffs and constables are required to serve and return any such process, and shall receive the same fees therefor as are allowed by law for like services. Witnesses shall receive the fees and mileage allowed in civil actions in courts of common pleas. All such fees, upon the presentation of proper vouchers approved by the superintendent of insurance, shall be paid out of the appropriation for the contingent fund of the insurance department. The fees and mileage of witnesses not summoned by the superintendent of insurance, deputy superintendent or warden shall not be paid by the state. (May 6, 1913, 103 v. 543; R. S. Sec. 269; April 2, 1906, 98 v. 265; May 12, 1902, 95 v. 549; April 26, 1898, 93 v. 292; March 12, 1872, 69 v. 32, § 4.)

Section 623-1. (Salary and compensation.) The provision of section 622 of the General Code, as amended by this act, relating to compensation, shall be deemed to supersede the provisions of any existing law fixing the salary or compensation of any such officer or employee. (May 6, 1913, 103 v. 544, § 2.)

Section 624. (Instruments under seal of the superintendent.) A certificate, assignment or conveyance executed in pursuance of law by the superintendent of insurance with the seal of his office thereto affixed shall be received as evidence and may be recorded in the same manner and with like effect as a deed duly acknowledged by an officer au-

thorized by law. In all cases copies of papers in the office
of the superintendent, certified by him under the seal of his
office, shall be equal to the original as evidence. (R. S. Sec.
271; March 12, 1872, 69 v. 32, § 5.)

Section 625. (Examination of insurance companies.) The
superintendent of insurance, or a person appointed by him
for that purpose, may make an examination of the affairs of
any insurance company doing business in this state. Such
company, its officers and agents shall submit their books and
business to such examination and in every way facilitate it.
The superintendent shall make or cause to be made each year
an examination of the assets of every life insurance company
organized under the laws of this state, and ascertain whether
such assets are invested in the manner prescribed by law at
the date such investments were made, and whether the last
preceding annual statement of assets and unpaid death
claims was correct. (R. S. Sec. 272; April 25, 1904, 97 v.
415; May 12, 1902, 95 v. 549; May 15, 1878, 75 v. 576, § 7;
March 12, 1872, 69 v. 32, § 12.)

Insurance companies organized under special charters prior to the
constitution of 1851 are subject to this section.
State v. Eagle Insurance Co. 50 O. S. 252 affirmed 153 U. S. 446.

Section 626. (Authority of examiners.) For the purpose
of such examination, the superintendent, or other person so
appointed, shall have authority to administer oaths to and
examine the officers and agents of such insurance company
relating to its business and affairs. If he deems it to the
interest of the public, the superintendent may publish the
result of such investigation in a newspaper printed at the
seat of government and of general circulation in the state,
and also a newspaper printed in the county where the principal office of such company is located. (R. S. Sec. 273;
March 12, 1872, 69 v. 32, § 8.)

Section 627. (Expenses of examiners.) The actual expenses incurred in making such examination shall be paid
by the treasurer of state on the warrant of the auditor of
state, upon the certificate of the superintendent of insurance;
but, if an examination of an insurance company is made
upon the demand of the company, the expenses thereof shall
be paid by such company and if the laws of another state,
district, territory or nation require or permit the insurance
department or other authority thereof to make examinations
of insurance companies of this state at the expense of such
companies, the expenses of the superintendent of insurance

of this state in making an examination of an insurance company of such other state, district, territory or nation, shall be charged to and collected from such company. (R. S. Sec. 272; April 25, 1904, 97 v. 415; May 12, 1902, 95 v. 549; May 15, 1878, 75 v. 576, § 7; March 12, 1872, 69 v. 32, § 12.)

Section 627-1. (Authority and power of superintendent of insurance.) The superintendent of insurance is authorized and empowered to make written requisitions upon the officers or directors of any national bank, state bank, state bank and trust company or private bank, of this state, for such information as he may require relating to the financial transactions of any of such institutions with any insurance company, fraternal beneficiary association or assessment association authorized to do business in this state. (May 14, 1910, 101 v. 102, § 1.)

Section 627-2. (Duty of bank officers.) It shall be the duty of any officer or director of any such bank or trust company upon the receipt of such requisition, or within five days thereafter, to furnish to such superintendent in writing all the information called for in such requisition and in such manner and form as therein directed. (April 14, 1910, 101 v. 102, § 2.)

Section 627-3. (Penalty.) Any officer or director of any such bank or trust company who fails, neglects or refuses to comply with the provisions of section two of this act shall be guilty of a misdemeanor and on conviction shall be fined not more than $500.00 nor less than $25.00. (April 14, 1910, 101 v. 103, § 3.)

Section 628. (Unsound companies.) If it appears to the superintendent of insurance upon satisfactory evidence that the assets of an insurance company organized under the laws of this state after deducting therefrom all liabilities including reinsurance, reserve or unearned premium fund, computed according to the laws of this state, are reduced twenty per cent or more below the capital required by law, he shall require such company to restore such deficiency within such period as he designates in such requisition. (R. S. Sec. 274; April 25, 1904, 97 v. 416; April 26, 1873, 70 v. 165, § 9.)

This section and § 629 confer powers and duties upon the superintendent of insurance, but do not confer power upon a court of equity, in the first instance, at the suit of stockholders and creditors, to wind up the affairs of an insurance company.

Benson v. Columbia Life Ins. Co., 7 N. P. n. s. 113.

Illegal method of restoring impaired capital. An insurance com-

pany can not make good its impaired capital stock by organizing a
holding company, transferring its stock to the holding company, and
having the holding company borrow the amount of the impairment on
the stock so transferred.
   Rep. Atty. Gen. 1910-1911, pp. 558, 561.

   **Unpaid assessment on stock. Right of company to withhold div-
idends.** Where a stockholder, liable to assessment on his stock, failed
to pay an assessment under this section, it was held that the insurance
company had a right to withhold dividends subsequently declared, and to
credit them on the unpaid assessment.
   Rhodes v. Equitable, etc., Co., 3 C. C. 501; 2 C. D. 288.

   A **reinsurance reserve fund** is not a debt which may be deducted
in making returns for taxation.
   Insurance Co. v. Cappellar, 38 O. S. 560.

Section 629. (Restrictions on unsound companies.)   If
such deficiency is more than forty per cent of the capital
required by law, such company shall not thereafter issue any
new policies or transact any new business until it receives
from the superintendent of insurance a license authorizing
it to do business, or until so authorized by a court in a
proper proceeding therein.   If the deficiency is more than
twenty per cent and less than forty per cent of the capital
required by law, and the officers of the company certify that
the deficiency will be restored by the company, such company may continue business for thirty days from the date
of such requisition.   If at the expiration of the thirty days
any portion of the deficiency is not restored, the company
shall not thereafter issue new policies or transact new business until authorized by the superintendent or by a court in
a proper proceeding therein.   (R. S. Sec. 274; April 25, 1904,
97 v. 416; April 26, 1873, 70 v. 165, § 9.)

Section 630. (Unsound mutual companies.)   If it appears
to the superintendent of insurance upon satisfactory evidence
that the funds and assets, other than contingent liability, of
any company organized on the plan of mutual insurance
after deducting therefrom a reinsurance reserve fund computed in accordance with law, are less than its liabilities,
such company shall be deemed to have impaired its capital.
If such impairment exceeds twenty-five per cent of such
reinsurance reserve fund, the superintendent shall require
such company to make an assessment as provided by law in
case of impairment of its capital by a mutual company, for
the amount needed to pay its incurred losses and expenses
and to make good the reinsurance reserve fund required by
law.   The assessment shall be paid within such period as the
superintendent names in the requisition.   (R. S. Sec. 275;
April 25, 1904, 97 v. 416; April 26, 1873, 70 v. 165, § 10.)

Section 631. (Restrictions on unsound mutual companies.) If the impairment is more than forty per cent of such reinsurance reserve fund, it shall be unlawful for the company to issue new policies or transact new business until the superintendent of insurance issues the company a license authorizing it to resume business, or until so authorized by a court in a proper proceeding therein. If the impairment is more than twenty-five per cent and less than forty per cent of such reinsurance reserve fund, and the officers of the company certify that the impairment will be restored, the company may continue business for thirty days from the date of such requisition. If at the expiration of the thirty days any portion of the impairment is not restored, the company shall not thereafter issue new policies or transact new business until authorized by the superintendent, or until so authorized by a court in a proper proceeding therein. (R. S. Sec. 275; April 25, 1904, 97 v. 416; April 26, 1873, 70 v. 165, § 10.)

Section 632. (Liability of trustees or directors.) The trustees or directors of any such company shall be personally liable for any losses upon risks taken after the superintendent of insurance has issued the requisition to restore any deficiency in the assets, and before such deficiency is restored. Nothing herein shall be construed as requiring a mutual fire insurance company to keep on hand a cash reinsurance reserve or funds invested in securities, other than its premium notes, when such premium notes amount in gross to three per cent of the amount at risk by the company. (R. S. Sec. 275; April 25, 1904, 97 v. 416; April 26, 1873, 70 v. 165, § 10.)

Section 633. (Action by attorney general.) Upon default of a company to comply with such requisition of the superintendent of insurance, the superintendent shall communicate the fact to the attorney general, who shall apply to the court of common pleas of the county in which the principal office of the company is located for an order requiring such company to show cause why its business should not be closed. The attorney general shall give the company such notice of the pendency of the application as the court directs, and thereupon the court shall hear the allegations and proof of the respective parties, or refer the application of the attorney general to a referee. (R. S. Sec. 276; April 25, 1904, 97 v. 416; April 26, 1873, 70 v. 165, § 11.)

Section 634. (Dissolution of unsound companies.) If it

appears to the satisfaction of the court that the assets of such company are reduced below the amount so required by law, or that the interest of the public so requires, the court shall decree a dissolution of the company and a distribution of its assets. A transfer of stock of a company made during the pendency of such investigation shall not release the party making the transfer from his liability for losses which have occurred previous to the transfer. (R. S. Sec. 276; April 25, 1904, 97 v. 416; April 26, 1873, 70 v. 165, § 11.)

Section 634-1. (Application of sections 634-1 to 634-7.) This act shall apply to all domestic corporations, associations, societies and orders to which any insurance law of this state is applicable; the words "corporation" or "corporations" herein shall also include all such associations, societies or orders. (April 12, 1910, 101 v. 114, § 1.)

Section 634-2. (Superintendent to take charge of property in certain cases. Attorney general to represent superintendent.) Whenever any such corporation (a) is insolvent; or (b) has refused to submit its books, papers, accounts or affairs to the reasonable inspection of the superintendent of insurance of this state, or his deputy or examiner; or (c) has neglected or refused to observe an order of the superintendent to make good within the time prescribed by law any deficiency, whenever its capital, if it be a stock corporation, or its reserve, if it be a mutual corporation, shall have become impaired to the extent of twenty per cent.; or (d) has, by contract or reinsurance or otherwise, transferred or attempted to transfer substantially its entire property or business, or entered into any transaction the effect of which is to merge substantially its entire property or business in the property or business of any other corporation, association, society or order, without having first obtained the written approval of the superintendent; or (e) is found, by the superintendent of insurance to be in such condition that its further transaction of business will be hazardous to its policy holders, or to its creditors, or to the public; or (f) has willfully violated its charter or any law of the state; or (g) whenever any officer thereof has refused to be examined under oath by the superintendent of insurance touching its affairs, the superintendent may, the attorney general representing him, apply to the supreme court or any judge thereof or to the court of appeals of Franklin county or to the court of appeals of the county in which the principal office of such corporation is located for an order directing such corporation to show cause why the superintendent should not take possession of its property and conduct its business, and for such other relief as the nature of the case and the interests of its policy holders, creditors, stockholders or the public may require. (May 6, 1913, 103 v. 407; April 12, 1910, 101 v. 115, § 2.)

Section 634-3. (Injunction.) On such application or at any time thereafter, such court may, in its discretion, issue an injunction restraining such corporation from the transaction of its business or disposition of its property until the further order of the court. On the return of such order to show cause, the court shall either deny the application or direct the superintendent forthwith to take possession of the property and conduct the business of such corporation, and retain such possession and conduct such business until, on the application either of the superintendent, the attorney general representing him, or of such corporation, it shall, after a like hearing, appear to the court that the ground for such order directing the superintendent to take possession has been removed and that the corporation can properly resume possession of its property and the conduct of its business, and such corporation shall have the right to prosecute appeal or error from such order as provided in other cases. (April 12, 1910, 101 v. 115, § 3.)

Section 634-4. (Order of liquidation.) If, on a like application and order to show cause, and after a full hearing, the court shall order the liquidation of the business of such corporation, such liquidation shall be made by and under the direction of the superintendent, who may deal with the property and business of such corporation in his own name as superintendent or in the name of the corporation, as the court may direct, and shall be vested by operation of law with title to all of the property, contracts and rights of action of such corporation as of the date of the order so directing him to liquidate. The filing or recording of such order in any record office of the state shall impart the same notice that a deed, bill of sale or other evidence of title duly filed or recorded by such corporation would have imparted. (April 12, 1910, 101 v. 116, § 4.)

Section 634-5. (Special deputy, clerks, etc. Special counsel.) For the purposes of this act, the superintendent shall have power to appoint, under his hand and official seal when necessary, a special deputy superintendent of insurance, as his agent, and to employ such clerks as may by him be deemed necessary, and give each of such persons such powers to assist him as he may consider wise. The compensation of such special deputy superintendent, and clerks, and all expenses of taking possession of and conducting the business or of liquidating any such corporation shall be fixed by the superintendent, subject to the approval of the court, and shall, on certificate of the superintendent, be paid out of the funds or assets of such corporation. The attorney general shall act as counsel for the superintendent under this act and neither shall receive any compensation therefor in addition to their regular salary as fixed by law. Provided, however, that the attorney general may, whenever it shall become necessary in the course of his duties hereunder, employ special counsel to aid him, and the compensation of such special counsel shall be fixed by the attorney general, subject to the approval of the court and shall, on certificate of the superintendent of insurance, be paid out of the funds or assets of such corporation. (April 12, 1910, 101 v. 116, § 5.)

Section 634-6. (Rules and regulations.) For the purposes of this act, the superintendent shall have power, subject to the approval of the court, to make and prescribe such rules and regulations as to him shall seem proper, provided however that summons as in other cases shall first be served upon such corporation. (April 12, 1910, 101 v. 116, § 6.) !

Section 634-7. (Report of special deputy.) The superintendent shall transmit to the legislature, in his annual report, the names of the corporations so taken possession of, whether the same have resumed business or have been liquidated, and such other facts as shall acquaint the policyholders, creditors, stockholders and the public with his proceedings under this section; and, to that end, the special deputy superintendent in charge of any such corporation shall file annually with the superintendent a report of the affairs of such corporation similar to that required by law to be filed by such corporation. (April 12, 1910, 101 v. 116, § 7.)

Section 634-8. (Unpaid losses are preferred claims.) When a domestic fire insurance company, whether stock or mutual becomes insolvent, or is unable to pay in full its liabilities, unpaid losses arising from the contingencies insured against by the contracts shall, in the distribution of its assets, whether liquidation is affected by a receiver or otherwise, be deemed and treated as preferred claims over claims for return premiums on uncompleted contracts. **But**

nothing in this act shall impair the obligations imposed by
law upon the officers of a mutual company to make assessments to pay all legal obligations of the company. (April
12, 1910, 101 v. 108.)

**Section 635. (Authority of unsound insurance company
revoked.)** If it appears to the superintendent of insurance
upon satisfactory evidence that the affairs of an insurance
company, partnership, or association, not organized under
the laws of this state, are in an unsound condition, he shall
revoke the authority granted to such company to do business
in this state, and cause a notice thereof to be published in
at least one newspaper published at the seat of government,
and in a newspaper published in the county of this state
where the general agency is located. After the publication
of such notice, it shall be unlawful for the agents of such
company to procure applications for insurance or to issue
policies. (R. S. Sec. 277; March 12, 1872, 69 v. 32, § 12.)

See State v. Moore 42 O. S. 103, 106.
Injunction, not mandamus, is the proper remedy to prevent wrongful
revocation of the license of an insurance company.
State v. Hahn 50 O. S. 714, 718.

Section 636. (Annual valuation of policies.) Each year
the superintendent of insurance shall make or cause to be
made net valuations of all outstanding policies, additions
thereto, unpaid dividends, and all other obligations of each
life insurance company transacting business in this state.
For the purpose of such valuations, and for making special
examinations of the condition of life insurance companies,
as provided in the laws of this state relating to life insurance
companies, and for valuing all policies of whatever description, and for any purpose whatever, the rate of interest shall
be four per cent per annum, and the rate of mortality shall
be established by the table known as the American Experience Table, but such valuations may be made according to
the standards of valuation adopted by the company for the
obligations to be valued, if the total valuation determined by
any such standards for the obligations for which they have
been adopted shall not be less than that determined by the
legal minimum standard herein prescribed, and if such standards of valuation adopted by the company for the obligations
to be valued shall not be less than the standards adopted
by the company in computing its premiums and guarantees.
(R. S. Sec. 279; April 22, 1908, 99 v. 178; April 26, 1904,
97 v. 437; February 7, 1889, 86 v. 11; Rev. Stat. 1880; May
15, 1878, 75 v. 580, § 14.)

Section 637. (When valuation of an officer of another state shall be received.) When the laws of any other state of the United States authorize a valuation of life insurance policies by some designated state officer, according to the standard prescribed in the next preceding section, or according to any other standard which makes the value of the policy not less than that of the standard so prescribed, the valuation made according to such standard, by such officer of the policies and other obligations of any life insurance company not organized under the laws of this state, and certified by such officer, shall be received as true and correct and the superintendent shall require no further valuation of such policies, if such officer accepts a like certificate from the superintendent of insurance of this state of the valuation of the policies of any life insurance company incorporated under the laws of this state. (R. S. Sec. 279; April 22, 1908, 99 v. 178; April 26, 1904, 97 v. 437; February 7, 1889, 86 v. 11; Rev. Stat. 1880; May 15, 1878, 75 v. 580, § 14.)

Section 638. (When valuation of an officer of another state shall not be received.) If such officer of another state of the United States is prohibited by law from accepting the certificate of valuation of the superintendent of insurance of this state, the superintendent shall require the officers of all companies located in such state to submit to him within a reasonable time the description of the policies thereof for valuation, and shall make, or cause to be made, a valuation thereof according to the standard prescribed. If such descriptions are not submitted to the superintendent within the time fixed by him, he shall revoke the license of such company and shall not renew it until such descriptions are submitted and a valuation by him is completed. (R. S. Sec. 279; April 22, 1908, 99 v. 178; April 26, 1904, 97 v. 437; February 7, 1889, 86 v. 11; Rev. Stats. 1880; May 15, 1878, 75 v. 580, § 14.)

Section 639. (When valuation of an officer of another state or country shall be received.) If by the laws of any other state or country an annual valuation of the policies of life insurance companies of such state or country is required to be made by a state officer of such state or by an officer of such country, the valuation so made by such state officer or officer of such country of the policies of any company organized under the laws of the state or country in which such valuation is made in accordance with the standards prescribed by the laws of such state or country may be accepted by the superintendent of insurance of this state, and if so accepted by the superintendent of insurance, such valuation shall stand in the place of any valuation of such policies required to be made by the superintendent of insurance of this state. (R. S. Sec. 279; April 22, 1908, 99 v. 178; April 26, 1904, 97 v. 437; February 7, 1889, 86 v. 11; Rev. Stats. 1880; May 15, 1878, 75 v. 580, § 14.)

See State v. Reinmund, 45 O. S. 214.

Section 640. (Securities to be deposited with state treasurer.) All securities deposited with the superintendent of insurance shall be deposited by him with the treasurer of state, and the treasurer shall not deliver such securities or coupons attached thereto, except upon the written order of the superintendent. No security shall be accepted for deposit by the superintendent unless it is of par and market value of one thousand dollars or more. (R. S. Sec. 281; April 25, 1904, 97 v. 410; April 26, 1873, 70 v. 165, § 16.)

For exceptions see §§ 9459 to 9461.
Attachment of securities. See 3 Opins. Attys. Gen. 531.
Taxation of securities deposited by foreign companies, see § 5437.

Section 641. (Sale and distribution of securities of defaulting companies.) If any company, corporation, or association required by law to make a deposit with the superintendent of insurance, or other state officer, to secure the contracts of such company, corporation, or association, or for any other purpose, fails to pay any of its liabilities upon such contracts, or other obligations, according to the terms thereof after the liability thereon has been determined, or if such company, corporation, or association, having ceased to do business within this state, leaves unpaid any such liability or has become insolvent, the attorney general of the state, on behalf of the superintendent of insurance, or such other officer, and upon the application of any person entitled to participate in such deposit, or the proceeds arising therefrom, shall commence a civil action in the court of common pleas of Franklin county, making the company, corporation, or association, a party defendant, to determine the rights of all parties claiming any interest in such deposit, to subject the deposit to the payment or satisfaction of all liabilities and to distribute such fund among the persons entitled thereto. (R. S. Sec. 281-1; 95 v. 480, § 1.)

See 3 Opins. Attys. Gen., 531.

Section 642. (Notice to claimants.) Upon the filing of the petition in such case, the superintendent of insurance, or other officer, shall cause to be published for six consecutive weeks in three papers of general circulation within the state, one of which shall be published at the seat of government, a notice containing a succinct statement of the object and prayer of the petition in such action, and the time within which persons claiming to have an interest in such fund shall be required to answer. (95 v. 481, § 2; R. S. Sec. 281-2.)

Section 643. (Procedure in such case.) The clerk of such court shall forward a copy of such notice to the last known address of such company, corporation or association. The code of civil procedure shall govern such proceedings in so far as it is applicable, and upon the hearing of the cause, such order, judgment or decree shall be entered by the court as is deemed just and equitable. (95 v. 481, §§ 2, 3; R. S. Secs. 281-2, 281-3.)

Section 644. (Agents license.) No person, company or corporation in this state, shall procure, receive, or forward applications for insurance in any company or companies not organized under the laws of this state, or in any manner aid in the transaction of the business of insurance with any such company, unless duly authorized by such company and unless duly licensed by the superintendent of insurance. (R. S. Sec. 283; April 25, 1904, 97 v. 411; March 12, 1872, 69 v. 32, § 18.)

Where a life insurance agent promises to pay another person a commission upon the first premiums paid by persons recommended by him to the agent, this section does not bar a recovery on such promise.
Connelly v. Pickard, 4 N. P. n. s. 294; 17 L. D. 116.
The superintendent of insurance has discretion to refuse a license to an agent who has previously solicited insurance without a license and offered rebates of premium.
Vorys v. State, 67 O. S. 15.
Agent of foreign assessment or co-operative life associations.
See 4 Opins. Attys. Gen., 329.
License refused because of objectionable agency contract.
See Rep. of Atty. Gen., 1908, p. 163.
5 Opins. Attys. Gen., 942.
Insurance policies may be sold by means of automatic vending machines, providing sample copies of policies are displayed and all persons in charge of the machines are licensed as agents.
Rep. Atty. Gen., 1910-1911, p. 563.
A "life insurance club," the members of which receive compensation for procuring new members, and additional compensation if such new members take insurance, can not act as agent without a license.
Rep. Atty. Gen., 1904-1905, p. 112.
In the articles of incorporation of an insurance agency company, the corporate purpose can not be expressed as a "business of general insurance underwriters."
Rep. Atty. Gen., 1911-1912, p. 60.

Section 645. (When non-residents may not act as agent.) The superintendent of insurance shall issue no license to any person as agent of an insurance company if such person is a resident of a state which by its laws, prohibits residents of this state from acting as agents of insurance companies in such state, and if the superintendent is satisfied that any person holding a license as such agent is a resident of such state, he shall revoke such license. (R. S. Sec. 283a; April 22, 1904, 97 v. 152.)

Section 646. (Certificate of compliance.) Upon the filing of each of its annual statements or as soon thereafter as practicable, the superintendent of insurance shall issue to each insurance company or association authorized to do business in this state, a certificate that it has complied with the laws of this state. Such certificate of compliance shall also contain a statement of the amounts of its paid up capital stock, assets, liabilities, income and expenditures for the preceding year, as shown by its annual statement for that year. The superintendent shall issue to each newly applying company or association which he finds should be authorized to do business in this state, a certificate that it has complied with the laws of this state, which certificate shall contain a statement of the amounts of its paid up capital stock, assets, liabilities, income and expenditures as shown by a financial statement submitted by it under the oath of its officers. (R. S. Sec. 284; April 25, 1904, 97 v. 405; March 12, 1872, 69 v. 32, §§ 19, 21; S. & S. 227.)

It is said that the superintendent of insurance should refuse a certificate to an insurance company, the majority of whose stock is owned by a holding company.
Rep. Atty. Gen. 1910-1911, pp. 540, 558, 561.
Discretion of superintendent in refusing to issue certificate.
State v. Moore 42 O. S. 103.
Vorys v. State 67 O. S. 15.
See also note to § 9365.
Expiration of certificates.
See § 667.
Sections 646 et seq., 9365 et seq. and 9559 et seq. are statutes in pari materia and should be construed together.
5 Opins. Atty. Gen. 658 (1902).
Citing State v. Guilbert 58 O. S. 637.

Section 647. (Copy of certificate to be filed with county recorder.) Each insurance company and association not incorporated under the laws of this state, before it does any business under authority of its certificate of compliance in any county of this state in which it has an agency, shall file a copy of such certificate duly certified by the superintendent with the recorder of such county. For filing each certificate of compliance and each license, the recorder shall receive ten cents. (R. S. Sec. 284; April 25, 1904, 97 v. 405; March 12, 1872, 69 v. 32, §§ 19, 21; S. & S. 227.)

Section 648. (Publication of certificate.) Annually, and before the time of making its report to the superintendent of insurance as hereafter provided, such company or association shall publish its certificate of compliance in every county, where it has an agency, in a newspaper published and of general circulation in such county. (R. S. Sec. 284; April 25, 1904, 97 v. 405; March 12, 1872, 69 v. 32; §§ 19, 21; S. & S. 227.)

This section applies to assessment associations as well as to companies doing business on the stock or mutual plan; but does not apply to fraternal benefit societies.
5 Opin. Attys. Gen., 343 (1900).
The publication should be in a newspaper published in the English language.
4 Opins. Attys. Gen., 922 (1899).

Section 649. (When newspaper deemed of general circulation.) No newspaper shall be deemed to be a newspaper of general circulation as defined in the preceding section unless it has been established for at least one year, is printed in the English language and has a circulation in the county in which it is published as follows: In a county having at the last preceding federal census a population not more than thirty thousand, six hundred; in a county having a population of over thirty thousand and not more than fifty thousand, eight hundred; in a county having a population of over fifty thousand and not more than one hundred thousand, twelve hundred; in a county having a population of over one hundred thousand and not more than one hundred and fifty thousand, two thousand; in counties having a population of more than one hundred and fifty thousand, three thousand. (R. S. Sec. 284; April 25, 1904, 97 v. 405; March 12, 1872, 69 v. 32, §§ 19-21; S. & S. 227.)

Section 650. (Certificate as to circulation of newspaper.) Before publication of any such certificate, the manager, editor or proprietor of a newspaper shall certify under oath on a prepared blank, furnished him on application by the superintendent of insurance, the information prescribed in the preceding section, and if such affidavit shows that such newspaper is one of general circulation under the provisions of such section, the superintendent shall deliver to him a certificate that such newspaper is one of general circulation, as defined by the preceding section. (R. S. Sec. 284; April 25, 1904, 97 v. 405; March 12, 1872, 69 v. 32, §§ 19, 21; S. & S. 227.)

Section 651. (Report of publication by foreign company.) On or before October first of each year, each insurance company and association doing business in this state which is not incorporated under the laws thereof, shall file with the superintendent of insurance, upon blanks prepared and upon application furnished by him, a report in writing under oath of its president and secretary showing the counties in which publication of its certificate of authority to do business was made, the counties in which it had agencies at the time of such publication, and the names of the newspapers in which the publication was made, with a copy of the certificate so published attached thereto. (R. S. Sec. 284; April 25, 1904, 97 v. 405; March 12, 1872, 69 v. 32, §§ 19, 21; S. & S. 227.)

Section 652. (Penalty for failure to make publication.) If any such company or association fails to comply with the laws relating to the publication of such certificate, the superintendent shall suspend its authority to do business in any county where such publication has not been made, until such publication is made; provided that if it appears that through mistake or oversight such publication has not been made in any county, such authority shall not be suspended in such county if such publication is made within a time designated by the superintendent. (R. S. Sec. 284; April 25, 1904, 97 v. 405; March 12, 1872, 69 v. 32, §§ 19, 21; S. & S. 227.)

Section 653. (Approval of publication.) Publication in a newspaper shall not be approved by the superintendent of insurance unless prior to such publication he has certified that such newspaper is one published and of general circulation in the county, but if publication has been made in any such newspaper without such certificate and a report as herein provided filed and such certificate of the superintendent is procured within such time as he designates, publication in such newspaper shall be approved. The superintendent shall keep a book in which shall be recorded the names of the newspapers so certified as newspapers of general circulation, which book shall be open to inspection, and every such certificate of circulation shall remain in force until revoked, provided that whenever he deems proper the superintendent may demand further certificates as to the circulation of any such newspaper. (R. S. Sec. 284; April 25, 1904, 97 v. 405; March 12, 1872, 69 v. 32, §§ 19, 21; S. & S. 227.)

A certificate from the superintendent of insurance certifying that a newspaper is of general circulation is conclusive evidence of that fact. Rep. Atty. Gen., 1910-1911, p. 559.

Section 654. (Foreign company may appoint general and other agents.) By resolution of its board of directors or managers, an insurance company not organized under the laws of this state may appoint one or more general agents with authority to appoint other agents in this state. A certified copy of such resolution and appointment shall be filed with the superintendent of insurance, and agents so appointed by such general agents, shall be deemed to be the agents of such company as if directly appointed by such company. Agents for such company may be appointed in writing by the president, vice-president, chief manager or secretary thereof, and when so appointed shall be deemed to be the agents of such company as fully as if appointed by the board of directors or managers thereof. (R. S. Sec. 285; April 22, 1904, 97 v. 152; March 12, 1872, 69 v. 32, § 20.)

Section 655. (Discontinuance of business by life insurance company.) When a life insurance company doing business in this state decides to discontinue its business, the superintendent of insurance upon application of such company or association shall give notice, at its expense, of such intention at least once a week for six weeks in a paper published and of general circulation in the county in which such company or its general agency is located. After such publication the superintendent shall deliver to such company or association its securities held by him, if he is satisfied on an exhibition of its books and papers, and on an examination made by himself or by some competent disinterested person or persons appointed by him, and upon the oath of the president, or principal officer, and the secretary or actuary of such company, that all debts and liabilities due or to become due upon any contract or agreement made with any citizen or resident of the United States are paid and extinguished; but the superintendent from time to time may deliver to such company or association or its assigns any portion of such securities on being satisfied that an equal proportion of the debts and liabilities due or to become due upon any such contract or agreement have been satisfied, if the amount of securities retained by him is not less than twice the amount of the remaining liabilities. (R. S. Sec. 286; March 12, 1872, 69 v. 32, § 22.)

Section 656. (Discontinuance of insurance companies other than life. Notice. Superintendent may deliver securities to companies under certain conditions.) When any insurance company or corporation other than life, which has made a deposit with the superintendent of insurance, intends to discontinue its business in this state, the superintendent upon application of such company or corporation, shall give notice at its expense of such intention at least once a week for six weeks in three newspapers of general circulation in the state. After such publication, the superintendent shall deliver to such company or association its securities held by him, if he is satisfied by the affidavits of the principal officers of the company and on an examination made by him or by some competent, disinterested person or persons appointed by him, if he deems it necessary, that all liabilities and obligations which said deposit has been made to secure have been paid and extinguished; but the superintendent may, from time to time, deliver to such company or its assigns, under like condition, any portion of such securities on being satisfied that an equal proportion of said liabilities and obligations have been satisfied, if the amount of securities retained by him is not less than twice the amount of the remaining liabilities and obligations. (March 21, 1913, 103 v. 135; April 28, 1910, 101 v. 147; R. S. Sec. 286a; March 22, 1893, 90 v. 103.)

Securities deposited prior to the amendment of this section (101 v. 147) can not be withdrawn until its liabilities on contracts with non-residents, incurred prior to the amendment, are satisfied.
Rep. Atty. Gen. 1910-1911, pp. 554, 556.
The amendment of this section (101 v. 147) did not repeal §§ 9373 and 9565.
Rep. Atty. Gen., 1911-1912, p. 817.

Section 657. (Fees of superintendent.) There shall be paid to the superintendent of insurance the following fees:
By each insurance company doing business in this state;
For filing copy of its charter or deed of settlement, twenty-five dollars;
For filing each statement, twenty dollars;
For each certificate of authority or license, and certified copy thereof, two dollars;
For each copy of a paper filed in his office, twenty cents per folio;
For affixing the seal of office and certifying any paper, one dollar.
By each life insurance company doing business in this state;

For annual valuation of its policies, one cent on every one thousand dollars of insurance.

By foreign insurance companies doing business in this state;

For making and forwarding annually, semi-annually and quarterly the interest checks and coupons accruing upon bonds and securities deposited, twenty-five dollars each year, on each one hundred thousand dollars so deposited. (R. S. Secs. 269, 282; April 2, 1906, 98 v. 265; May 12, 1902, 95 v. 549; April 26, 1898, 93 v. 292; March 30, 1892, 89 v. 167; March 25, 1891, 88 v. 196; March 12, 1872, 69 v. 32, §§ 4, 17.)

Valuation of policies.
State v. Reinmund, 45 O. S. 214.

Section 658. (Retaliatory provision.) When by the laws of any other state, district, territory or nation, any taxes, fines, penalties, license fees, deposits of money, securities, or other obligations, or prohibitions are imposed on insurance companies of this state doing business in such state, district, territory or nation, or upon their agents therein, the same obligations and prohibitions shall be imposed upon insurance companies of such other state, district or nation doing business in this state and upon their agents. (R. S. Sec. 282; May 12, 1902, 95 v. 549; March 30, 1892, 89 v. 167; March 25, 1891, 88 v. 196; March 12, 1872, 69 v. 32, § 17.)

See § 5436.
The provisions of this section are retaliatory and must, therefore, be confined to such cases as fairly fall within the letter of the statute.
State v. Insurance Co., 49 O. S. 440.
See also State v. Reinmund, 45 O. S. 214.
3 Opins. Attys. Gen. 199.

Section 659. (Forms of statements to be furnished.) In November of each year, the superintendent of insurance shall furnish each insurance company doing business in this state two or more printed copies of the forms of statements required by law to be made by them, and from time to time he may make such changes in such forms or such additions thereto as he deems best adapted to secure a true statement of the condition of such companies. (R. S. Sec. 280; April 25, 1904, 97 v. 410; March 12, 1872, 69 v. 32, § 15.)

Section 660. (Licenses to solicit certain insurance.) The superintendent of insurance may issue licenses to citizens of this state, subject to revocation at any time, permitting the person named therein to solicit and issue fire, lightning, tornado, explosion or marine insurance on property in this state in insurance companies not authorized to transact business in this state. Each such license shall expire on the thirty-first day of March next after the year in which it is issued, and may be then renewed. (R. S. Sec. 3656-1; April 22, 1904, 97 v. 157, § 1.)

Section 661. (Fee.) For each such license and renewal, the superintendent of insurance shall collect ten dollars, and such licenses and renewals shall be filed with the recorder and published annually in the county where such agent's office is located in the same manner as certificates of compliance are filed and published. (R. S. Sec. 3656-1; April 22, 1904, 97 v. 157, § 1.)

Section 662. (Affidavit to be filed before issuing such insurance.) Before the person named in such license shall solicit or issue any insurance in such companies on any such property, he shall in every case file with the superintendent of insurance his own affidavit and the affidavit of the person, or of the president or secretary of the corporation, owning the property on which the insurance is to be placed, which shall have force and effect one year only from the date thereof, that such owner is unable to procure from companies authorized to do business in this state the amount of insurance necessary to protect such property. (R. S. Sec. 3656-1; April 22, 1904, 97 v. 158, § 1.)

Section 663. (Separate accounts.) Each person so licensed shall keep a separate account of the business done under his license, a certified copy of which account he shall forthwith, on issuing any such policy, file with the superintendent of insurance, showing the amount of such insurance, the name of the owner, brief description and location of the property, gross premium charged, name of company in which the insurance is placed, date of policy and term thereof, and, also, a report in the same detail of all such policies cancelled and gross return premiums thereon. (R. S. Sec. 3656-2; April 22, 1904, 97 v. 158, § 2.)

Section 664. (Bond, where filed.) Before receiving such license such person shall execute and deliver to the superintendent of insurance a bond in the sum of two thousand dollars, payable to the state, with at least two sureties, approved by the superintendent and conditioned that he will faithfully comply with all the requirements of this law, and will annually file with the superintendent of insurance in January, a sworn statement of the gross premiums charged for insurance procured or placed, and the gross premiums on such insurance cancelled under such license during the year ending on the thirty-first day of December last preceding and at the time of filing such statement will pay to the superintendent of insurance an amount equal to five per cent. of the balance of such gross premiums after deducting such return premiums so reported. Such bond shall be deposited with the secretary of state and kept in his office. (May 6, 1913, 103 v. 530; R. S. Sec. 3656-2; April 22, 1908, 97 v. 158, § 2.)

Section 664-1. (Unauthorized insurance company provision. Tax of 5 per cent.) That all persons, companies, associations or corporations residing or doing business in this state that enter into any agreements with any insurance company, association, individual, firm, underwriter or Lloyd, not authorized to do business in this state, whereby said person, company, association or corporation shall enter into contracts of insurance covering risks within this state, with said unauthorized association, individual, firm, underwriter, or Lloyd, for which there is a premium charged or collected, the said person, company, association or corporation so insured shall, annually on the first day of July or within ten days thereafter return to the superintendent of insurance of this state, a statement under oath of all actual cost of indemnity and gross premiums paid or payable for the twelve months preceding on policies or contracts of insurance taken by the said person, company, association or corporation and shall at the same time pay to said superintendent of insurance a tax of five per centum of the actual cost of indemnity paid or payable to any such association, firm, or individual, or a tax of five per centum of the gross premiums paid or payable to any such insurance company, underwriter or Lloyd. All taxes collected under the provisions of this section by the superintendent of insurance shall be paid by him, upon the warrant of the state auditor, into the general revenue fund of the state. (May 10, 1910, 101 v. 373, § 1.)

Section 664-2. (Penalty.) Any person, company, association or corporation failing or refusing to make the report required in section one of this act and to furnish all the data and information that may be required by the superintendent of insurance to determine the amount due, shall be deemed guilty of a misdemeanor and upon conviction, be fined not less than one hundred dollars, nor more than five hundred dollars for each offense. (May 10, 1910, 101 v. 373, § 2.)

Section 664-3. (Citizens, etc., exempt from § 664-1 to 664-3.) No provision of this act shall be construed as extending to private citizens, firms or corporations, residents of this state, who seek to provide indemnity among themselves from fire loss or other casualty, by exchange of private contracts for protection only and not for profit. Nor shall any provision of this act be construed as extending to fraternal beneficiary associations or members thereof. (May 10, 1910, 101 v. 374, § 3.)

Section 665. (Insurance business must be authorized.) No company, corporation, or association whether organized in this state or elsewhere, shall engage either directly or indirectly in this state in the business of insurance, or enter into any contracts substantially amounting to insurance, or in any manner aid therein, or engage in the business of guaranteeing against liability, loss or damage, unless it is expressly authorized by the laws of this state, and the laws regulating it and applicable thereto, have been complied with. (R. S. Sec. 289; April 9, 1908, 99 v. 131; April 23, 1904, 97 v. 287; May 12, 1902, 95 v. 533; March 12, 1872, 69 v. 32, § 25.)

This section applies to foreign insurance companies, whether incorporated or not.
State v. Ackerman 51 O. S. 163, 169.

"Business of insurance." An insurance contract, other than that of life and accident, where the injury results in death, is one of indemnity.
State v. Laylin 73 O. S. 97.
For various definitions see
State v. Railway Co. 68 O. S. 9, 30 (Life and accident).
State v. Laylin 73 O. S. 90, 97.
State v. Amazon Insurance Co., 1 C. C. n. s. 4, 9; 14 C. D. 387.
Keckley v. Coshocton Glass Co., 86 O. S. 213 (Life).

Physicians' defense company. A foreign corporation the sole business of which is to defend physicians against civil actions for malpractice, but which does not assume or agree to pay any judgment which may be rendered against its contract holders, is not engaged in the business of insurance.
State v. Laylin 73 O. S. 90.

Railway relief association. An association established by a railway company, composed of employes and the company, to maintain a relief fund created by voluntary contributions is not engaged in the insurance business.
State v. Railway Co. 68 O. St. 9.
See also as to what constitutes the business of insurance.
Rep. Atty. Gen. 1906, p. 40.
5 Opins. Attys. Gen. 975.
Rep. Atty. Gen., 1911-1912, p. 803.

Transacting business in the state. What constitutes. A foreign fire insurance company which maintains an office in Ohio in which contracts of insurance are made respecting property in other states, is engaged in the insurance business in Ohio, although it insures no property in Ohio and makes no contracts with citizens of this state.

State v. Amazon Insurance Co. 1 C. C. n. s. 4; 14 C. D. 387.

The acceptance by a foreign insurance company in its home state of an application for insurance sent by mail by a resident of Ohio is not the transaction of business in Ohio.

Rep. Atty. Gen. 1904-1905, p. 121.
Rep. Atty. Gen. 1906, p. 146.

Failure to obtain authority. Effect on contracts.
See Insurance Co. v. McMillen 24 O. S. 67.
Insurance Co. v. Ellis 32 O. S. 388.

Suit by unlicensed company for premiums. A foreign insurance company issuing polices in another state, upon property in Ohio, can not maintain an action in the state courts of Ohio to recover premiums on such policies.

Bankers Casualty Co. v. Richland County Banking Co. 12 C. C. n. s. 200; 21 C. D. 428 (1908).

Suit brought in another state.
See Insurance Co. v. Parks, 1 C. S. C. R. 574 (1871).

Section 666.   (Insurance of burial and funeral expenses.) No company, corporation or association engaged in the business of providing for the payment of the funeral, burial or other expenses of deceased members, or certificate holders therein or engaged in the business of providing any other kind of insurance shall contract to pay or pay such insurance or its benefits or any part of either to any official undertaker or to any designated undertaker or undertaking concern or to any particular tradesman or business man, so as to deprive the representative or family of the deceased from, or in any way to control them in, procuring and purchasing such supplies and services in the open market with the advantages of competition, unless expressly authorized by the laws of this state and all laws regulating such insurance or applicable thereto have been complied with. (R. S. Sec. 289; April 9, 1908, 99 v. 131; April 23, 1904, 97 v. 287; May 12, 1902, 95 v. 533; March 12, 1872, 69 v. 32, § 25.)

This section is constitutional.
Robbins v. Hennessey, 86 O. S. 181 (1912).
The assignment of the benefit certificate or policy to an undertaker or to any particular tradesman or business man is in violation of this section and void.
Robbins v. Hennessey, 86 O. S. 181 (1912).
This section does not prohibit organization of funeral benefit associations, but prohibits merely the designation of an undertaker.
Rep. Atty. Gen. 1908, p. 178.
See also Rep. Atty. Gen. 1909, p. 340.
State v. Burial Assn., 8 C. C. n. s. 233; 18 C. D. 397.

Section 667. (When certificates shall expire.) All certificates of authority and licenses of companies, organized or admitted to do business under the provisions of the revised statutes relating to life insurance companies and of their agents, shall expire on the first day of April next after they are issued, and all certificates of authority and licenses of companies organized or admitted to do business under the provisions of the revised statutes relating to insurance companies other than life, and of their agents, shall expire on the first day of March next after they are issued. (R. S. Sec. 284; April 25, 1904, 97 v. 405; March 12, 1872, 69 v. 32, §§ 19, 21; S. & S. 227.)

Section 668. (How certain provisions shall apply.) The provisions of this chapter, relating to insurance companies organized under the laws of any other state of the United States shall apply to any company organized under the laws of the United States, for any of the purposes specified in this chapter. The provisions of this chapter relating to agents of companies organized under the laws of any state shall apply to the agents of such companies organized under the laws of the United States. Any violation of the provisions of this chapter by any person, or agent, in the employment of any such company, organized under the laws of the United States, shall subject the offender to the same penalties provided by this chapter for a violation of its provisions by persons acting for similar companies organized under the laws of any other state of the United States. (R. S. Sec. 287; March 12, 1872, 69 v. 32, § 23.)

Section 669. (To what associations insurance laws shall not apply.) No law of this state pertaining to insurance shall be construed to apply to the establishment and maintenance by individuals, associations or corporations, of sanatoriums or hospitals for the reception and care of patients for the medical, surgical or hygienic treatment of any and all diseases, or for the instruction of nurses in the care and treatment of diseases and in hygiene, or for any and all such purposes, nor to the furnishing of any or all such services, care or instruction in or in connection with any such institution, under or by virtue of any contract made for such purposes, with residents of the county in which such sanatorium or hospital is located. (R. S. Sec. 289; April 9, 1908, 99 v. 131; April 23, 1904, 97 v. 287; May 12, 1902, 95 v. 533; March 12, 1872, 69 v. 32, § 25.)

See Rep. of Atty. Gen. 1909, p. 108.

Section 670. (How provisions of this chapter shall apply.) The provisions herein relating to the superintendent of insurance shall apply to all persons, companies and associations, whether incorporated or not, engaged in the business of insurance. (R. S. Sec. 289; April 9, 1908, 99 v. 131; April 23, 1904, 97 v. 287; May 12, 1902, 95 v. 533; March 12, 1872, 69 v. 32, § 25.)

Section 671. (Superintendent of insurance; annual report.) The superintendent of insurance shall keep and preserve a full record of his proceedings, including a concise statement of the condition of each insurance company or association, authorized to transact business in this state. Each year at the earliest practicable date after their annual statements are received, he shall make a report to the governor of their general conduct and condition, including the information contained in the statements required of them, arranged in tabular form in two separate reports, one pertaining to life insurance companies and the other to insurance companies other than life, and in such report the superintendent may make such suggestions as he deems expedient. He shall also include therein the names and compensations of the clerks employed by him, the amount of receipts and the sources from which derived, and the amount of expenses in detail during the year ending the thirty-first day of December. (May 21, 1910, 101 v. 347; R. S. Sec. 278; March 12, 1872, 69 v. 32, § 13.)

Section 672. (Penalty.) Whoever violates any provision herein relating to the superintendent of insurance or any provision of an insurance law of this state, for the violation of which no penalty is elsewhere provided, shall be fined not more than one thousand dollars or imprisoned not more than six months or both. (R. S. Sec. 288; May 19, 1894, 91 v. 331; April 17, 1885, 82 v. 138; 69 v. 32, § 24.)

This section does not preclude a quo warranto proceeding against an unauthorized association.
State v. Ackerman 51 O. S. 163.

Section 673. (Forfeiture.) Any association, company or corporation which violates any provision herein relating to the superintendent of insurance or any insurance law of this state, for the violation of which no forfeiture or penalty is elsewhere provided, shall forfeit and pay not less than one hundred dollars nor more than one thousand dollars to be recovered by an action in the name of the state and on collection paid to the superintendent of insurance to be paid by him into the state treasury. (R. S. Sec. 288; May 19, 1894, 91 v. 331; April 17, 1885, 82 v. 138; 69 v. 32, § 24.)

This section does not preclude a quo warranto proceeding against an unauthorized association.
State v. Ackerman 51 O. S. 163.

BUREAU OF BUILDING AND LOAN ASSOCIATIONS.

Section 674. (Inspector of building and loan associations.) The governor with the advice and consent of the senate, shall appoint an inspector of building and loan associations, who shall serve for a term of three years. No such inspector of building and loan associations shall have any official connection with a building and loan association, or be interested in the business thereof, except as a stockholder. (April 23, 1913, 103 v. 181, § 1; May 11, 1908, 99 v. 532, §§ 27, 28, 30; see R. S. Sec. 3836-8; May 1, 1891, 88 v. 469.)

Section 675. (Bond, oath and approval.) Before entering upon the discharge of the duties of his office the inspector of building and loan associations shall give a bond to the state in the sum of ten thousand dollars with two or more sureties or with a surety company authorized to do business in the state of Ohio, approved by the governor, conditioned for the faithful discharge of the duties of his office. Such bond, with the approval of the governor and the oath of office endorsed thereon, shall be deposited with the secretary of state and kept in his office. (April 23, 1913, 103 v. 181, § 2; May 11, 1908, 99 v. 532, § 28; see R. S. Sec. 3836-9; May 1, 1891, 88 v. 469.)

Section 676. (Duties of inspector.) The inspector of building and loan associations shall see that the laws relating to building and loan associations are duly executed and enforced. When a violation of a law relating to building and loan associations is reported to him he shall take, or cause to be taken, the testimony, under oath, of any and all persons supposed to have any knowledge of such violation, and cause such testimony to be reduced to writing. If he be of the opinion that there is sufficient evidence, he shall cause the person suspected of such violation to be arrested and charged with such offense, and shall furnish the attorney general or the proper prosecuting attorney with the information obtained by him, the names of the witnesses and a copy of all material testimony taken in the case. (April 23, 1913, 103 v. 181, § 3; May 11, 1908, 99 v. 532, § 30.)

Section 677. (Deputies.) With the approval of the governor, the inspector of the building and loan associations may employ from time to time, the necessary deputies, assistants, clerks and examiners, to assist him in the discharge of the duties imposed upon him by law. With such approval he may remove any such clerk or examiners at any time. (April 23, 1913, 103 v. 181, § 4; original G. C. § 676; May 11, 1908, 99 v. 532, § 28; see R. S. Sec. 3836-9; May 1, 1891, 88 v. 469.)

Section 677-1. (Salary of inspector.) The salary of the inspector of building and loan associations shall be three thousand six hundred dollars, per annum, and shall be paid at the same time as the heads of other state departments. (April 23, 1913, 103 v. 182, § 5.)

Section 677-2. (Salary of deputies, assistants, etc.) The inspector of building and loan associations shall fix the salaries of the deputies, assistants, clerks and examiners at such rates per annum as the governor shall approve. Upon vouchers approved by the inspector of building and loan associations, such salaries shall be paid by the treasurer of state, upon the warrant of the auditor of state. (April 23, 1913, 103 v. 182, § 6.)

Section 677-3. (Expenses.) The actual and necessary traveling expenses of the inspector of building and loan associations, and of the deputies, assistants, clerks and examiners, incurred in the discharge of their official duties shall be paid monthly by the treasurer of state, upon the warrant of the auditor of state. Vouchers therefor shall be fully itemized, approved by the inspector of building and loan associations, and countersigned by the auditor of state. (April 23, 1913, 103 v. 182, § 7.)

An examiner absent from his home city on official business is entitled to his traveling expenses. Street car fare from his residence to the office of a building and loan association, outside of an examiner's regular place of work, is a proper item of expense.

The domicile of an examiner is his official residence, but the inspector may assign an examiner to another city, and the latter would be his permanent headquarters.

Rep. Atty. Gen. 1911-1912, pp. 140, 142, 811, 815.

Section 677-4. (Salaries and expenses; how paid.) All expenses incurred by the inspector of building and loan associations, in the performance of the duties imposed upon him by law, including the salary of such inspector, his deputies, assistants, clerks and examiners, shall be paid from funds appropriated therefor. (April 23, 1913, 103 v. 182, § 8.)

Section 677-5. (Seal.) The seal of the inspector of building and loan associations shall be one and three-fourths inches in diameter, shall have engraved thereon the coat of arms of the state, and shall be surrounded by the words, "Inspector of Building and Loan Associations of Ohio." (April 23, 1913, 103 v. 182, § 9.)

Section 677-6. (All instruments sealed with the seal, received in evidence.) Every certificate or other instrument executed, or order made, by the inspector of building and loan associations, in pursuance of any authority conferred upon him by law, and sealed with the seal of his office, or copies thereof duly authenticated under such seal, shall be received in evidence in all courts of this state. (April 23, 1913, 103 v. 182, § 10.)

Section 677-7. (Place of office.) The inspector of building and loan associations shall be furnished by the state with suitable rooms, at the seat of the government, for conducting the business of his office. (April 23, 1913, 103 v. 182, § 11; original G. C. § 677; May 11, 1908, 99 v. 533, § 29; see R. S. Sec. 3836-10; May 1, 1891, 88 v. 469.)

Section 678. (Requirements from foreign associations.) Foreign building and loan assiciations doing business in this state shall conduct such business in accordance with the laws governing domestic associations. No foreign building and loan association shall do business in Ohio until it procures from the inspector of building and loan associations a certificate of authority to do business in this state after complying with the following provisions:

1. It shall deposit with the inspector one hundred thousand dollars, in cash or bonds of the United States or this state, or of a county or municipal corporation therein, satisfactory to the inspector.

2. It shall file with the inspector a certified copy of its charter, constitution and by-laws, and other rules and regulations showing its manner of conducting business together with a statement such as is required annually from all associations.

3. It shall also file with the inspector a written instrument, duly executed, agreeing that a summons may issue against it from any county in this state directed to the sheriff of the county in which the office of inspector is situated, commanding him to serve it by certified copy personally upon the inspector or by leaving a copy thereof at his office. The inspector shall mail a copy of any papers served on him to

the home office of such association. (May 11, 1908, 99 v. 533, § 31; see R. S. Sec. 3836-12; May 1, 1891, 88 v. 469.)

Section 679. (Certificate of authority to do business.) When a foreign building and loan association has complied with the provisions of the preceding section, and the inspector is satisfied that it is doing business according to the laws of Ohio and is in sound financial condition, he shall issue his certificate of authority to the association to do business in this state. Annually thereafter, upon filing the annual statement herein provided for, if the inspector is satisfied as herein provided, he shall issue a renewal of such certificate. (May 11, 1908, 99 v. 533, § 32; see R. S. Sec. 3836-13; May 1, 1891, 88 v. 469.)

Section 680. (Collection of interest and exchange of securities.) A foreign building and loan association may collect and use the interest on securities deposited as provided by law so long as it fulfills its obligations and complies with the laws of this state. It may also exchange them for other securities of equal value satisfactory to the inspector. (May 11, 1908, 99 v. 534, § 33; see R. S. Sec. 3836-14; May 1, 1891, 88 v. 469.)

Section 681. (Securities liable for claimants.) The deposit made by a foreign building and loan association with the inspector of building and loan associations shall be held as a security for all claims of residents of this state against such association, and be liable for all judgments or decrees thereon, and subjected to the payment thereof in the same manner as the property of other non-residents. Should an association cease to do business in this state, the inspector may release securities in his discretion, retaining sufficient to satisfy all outstanding liabilities. (May 11, 1908, 99 v. 534, § 34; see R. S. Sec. 3836-15; May 1, 1891, 88 v. 469.)

Section 682. (Annual report.) Every building and loan association doing business in this state, annually, at the end of each fiscal year or within forty days thereafter, shall make a full and detailed report in writing of the affairs and business of the association for the preceding year, and showing its financial condition at the end thereof. With the first report made by an association it shall file a certified copy of its constitution and by-laws, or other rules and regulations, showing its manner of doing business. (May 11, 1908, 99 v. 534, § 35; see R. S. Sec. 3836-16; May 1, 1891, 88 v. 469.)

Section 683. (Form of report.) The report required in the preceding section shall be the form and contain such information as is prescribed by the inspector of building and loan associations. It shall be sworn to by the secretary and its correctness attested by at least three directors or an auditing committee appointed by the board. The original shall be filed with the inspector of building and loan associations within forty days after the close of the fiscal year. Such an abstract thereof as the inspector requires shall be posted for sixty days in the office or meeting place of such association, and published in a newspaper regularly issued in the county in which it is located. (May 11, 1908, 99 v. 534, § 36; see R. S. Sec. 3836-17; May 1, 1891, 88 v. 469.)

Section 684. (Annual examination.) At least once each year the inspector of building and loan associations shall make an examination into the affairs of each such association, or cause it to be made by a person appointed by him for that purpose. (May 11, 1908, 99 v. 534, § 37; see R. S. Sec. 3836-18; May 12, 1902, 95 v. 614; May 1, 1891, 88 v. 469.)

Section 685. (Expenses of examination.) The expenses of all examinations shall be paid by the state, except that when, by the laws of any other state, district, territory or nation, examinations of such associations of this state are required or permitted to be made by any official or other authority of such other state, district, territory or nation at the expense of such associations, then the expenses of all such examinations made by the inspector of this state, of such associations of that state, district, territory or nation, must be respectively charged to and collected from such associations so examined. (May 11, 1908, 99 v. 534, § 37; see R. S. Sec. 3836-18; May 12, 1902, 95 v. 614; May 1, 1891, 88 v. 469.)

Section 686. (Revocation of charter for illegal practices.) If upon examination, the inspector of building and loan associations finds any domestic association conducting its business in whole or part contrary to law, or failing to comply therewith, he shall notify the board of directors of such association of such fact in writing. If, after thirty days, such illegal practices or failure continues, he shall communicate the facts to the attorney general, who shall cause proceedings to be instituted in the proper court to revoke the charter of such association. (May 11, 1908, 99 v. 535, § 38;

see R. S. Sec. 3836-18; May 12, 1902, 95 v. 614; May 1, 1891, 88 v. 469.)

Section 687. (Dissolution if condition unsound.) If, upon examination, the inspector of building and loan associations finds that the affairs of a domestic building and loan association are in an unsound condition, and that the interests of the public demand its dissolution and the winding up of its business, he shall so report to the attorney general, who shall institute the proper proceedings for that purpose. (May 11, 1908, 99 v. 535, § 39; see R. S. Sec. 3836-18; May 12, 1902, 95 v. 614; May 1, 1891, 88 v. 469.)

Where the inspector finds the affairs of an association in an unsound condition it is improper for him to permit an officer of the association to personally advance funds to declare and pay a dividend.

Webb v. Stasel 4 N. P. n. s. 587, 589; 17 L. D. 317 (C. P. 1906).

Section 688. (Powers of examiners.) An examiner appointed by the inspector of building and loan associations under the provisions herein relating to such associations, shall have access to and may compel the production of all books, papers, securities, moneys and other property of an association under examination. He may administer oaths to, and examine the officers and agents of such association as to its affairs. (May 11, 1908, 99 v. 535, § 40; see R. S. Sec. 3836-19; May 1, 1891, 88 v. 469.)

Section 689. (Inspector may publish result.) If the inspector of building and loan associations deems it to the interest of the public, he may publish the results of such examination in a newspaper of general circulation in the county in which such association is located, if it is a domestic association, and in some newspaper in the city of Columbus if it is a foreign association. (May 11, 1908, 99 v. 535, § 41; see R. S. Sec. 3836-20; May 1, 1891, 88 v. 469.)

Section 690. (May cancel authority of foreign association.) If upon examination the inspector of building and loan associations finds that a foreign association does not conduct its business in accordance with law, or that its affairs are in an unsound condition, or if it refuses to permit an examination to be made, he may cancel its authority to do business in this state, and cause a notice thereof to be mailed to the home office of the association and published in at least one newspaper published in the city of Columbus. After the publication of such notice no such association or agent thereof shall receive further stock deposits from members residing in this state, except payments on stock on which a loan has been taken. (May 11, 1908, 99 v. 535, § 42; see R. S. Sec. 3836-21; May 1, 1891, 88 v. 469.)

Section 691. (Fees to be paid to inspector.) Foreign building and loan associations shall pay to the inspector of building and loan associations the following fees:

For filing an application for admission to do business in this state five hundred dollars;

For each certificate of authority and annual renewal thereof, two hundred dollars.

Every building and loan association doing business in this state, whether foreign or domestic, shall pay to the inspector of building and loan associations, for filing each annual report, at the time said annual report is filed, the sum of twenty dollars, and in addition thereto, one one-hundredth of one per cent. of its assets, as shown in such report. All such fees collected shall be paid into the general revenue fund. (April 23, 1913, 103 v. 191; May 11, 1908, 99 v. 535, § 43; see R. S. Sec. 3836-22; May 12, 1902, 95 v. 615; May 1, 1891, 88 v. 469.)

Section 692. (Securities to be deposited with treasurer of state.) All securities or cash deposited with the inspector of building and loan associations shall be deposited with the treasurer of state, who, with his sureties, shall be responsible for the safe keeping thereof. The treasurer shall deliver such securities only upon the written order of the inspector. (May 11, 1908, 99 v. 536, § 44; see R. S. Sec. 3836-23; May 1, 1891, 88 v. 469.)

Section 693. (Dissolution or consolidation of building and loan associations.) A building and loan association or a savings association may provide in its constitution and by-laws for the time and terms of its dissolution and for its consolidation with one or more of such corporations on terms and conditions to be determined upon by their board of directors. In case of the dissolution of such a corporation, its board of directors by a majority vote may be authorized to sell and transfer its mortgage securities or other property, or both, to another corporation, person or persons, subject to the vested and accrued rights of the mortgagors. (May 11, 1908, 99 v. 537, § 48; see R. S. Sec. 3836-27; April 27, 1893, 90 v. 315; May 1, 1891, 88 v. 469; April 11, 1889, 86 v. 238, § 3835j.)

See § 9665.

Section 694. (Forfeiture for non-compliance.) A building and loan association which does business in this state without first complying with the provisions herein or which violates or fails to comply with provisions of law relating to building and loan associations shall forfeit and pay not less than fifty dollars nor more than one thousand dollars, to be recovered by an action in the name of the state and on collection paid into the state treasury. (May 11, 1908, 99 v. 536, § 45; see R. S. Sec. 3836-24; May 1, 1891, 88 v. 469.)

Section 695. (Building and loan; annual report.) The inspector of building and loan associations shall keep and preserve in permanent form a full record of his proceedings, including a concise statement of each association examined, and make an annual report to the governor of the general conduct and condition of the building and loan associations doing business in this state, with such suggestions as he deems proper. Such report shall include the information contained in the statements required of the associations in tabulated form. He shall also report the names and compensation of the clerks employed by him, the whole amount of the income of his office, the source thereof, and the expenditures of his department during the year ending the thirty-first day of December. (May 21, 1910, 101 v. 348; May 11, 1908, 99 v. 537, § 47; see R. S. Sec. 3836-26; May 1, 1891, 88 v. 469.)

SUPERVISOR OF BOND INVESTMENT COMPANIES.

Section 696. (Supervisor of bond investment companies.) By virtue of his office, the deputy inspector of building and loan associations shall be the supervisor of bond investment companies. He shall see that the laws of this state relating to such companies are strictly enforced. (R. S. Sec. 3821x; May 12, 1902, 95 v. 642; April 14, 1900, 94 v. 149; April 25, 1898, 93 v. 403.)

Section 697. (Definition.) Every corporation, partnership or association other than a building and loan association, which places or sells certificates, bonds, debentures or other investment securities of any kind, on the partial payment or installment plan, and every investment guaranty company doing business on the service dividend plan shall be deemed a bond investment company. (R. S. Sec. 3821r; April 25, 1898, 93 v. 402; April 14, 1900, 94 v. 147, § 1.)

A corporation which, in consideration of installment payments, delivers a bond entitling the payer upon conditions named, to receive an article of value, and requiring the payer to contribute to the expenses of the corporation, is a bond and investment company.

State ex rel. v. Tontine Surety Co. 62 O. S. 428.
Eee also Rep. Atty. Gen. 1908, p. 65.
5 Opins. Attys. Gen. 32, 1048.

Section 698. (Deposit with treasurer of state.) Before doing business in this state, every bond investment company shall deposit with the treasurer of state on hundred thousand dollars in cash or bonds of the United States or of the state of Ohio, or of any county or municipal corporation in Ohio, for the protection of investors in the securities of such company. Such deposit shall be made out of the paid-up capital stock of such bond investment company. (R. S. Sec. 3821r; April 14, 1900, 94 v. 147, § 1; April 25, 1898, 93 v. 402.)

Penalty for violation of this act, G. C. § 13151.
Construction of former act.
State v. Matthews 62 O. S. 147.

Section 699. (Purpose of such deposit.) The deposit made by a bond investment company with the treasurer of state shall be held as security for all claims of residents of this state against such company, and shall be liable for all judgments and decrees thereon, and subject to the payment of such decrees in the same manner as the property of other non-residents. If such company ceases to do business in this state, the treasurer of state may release securities, in his discretion, retaining sufficient to satisfy all outstanding liabilities. (R. S. Sec. 3821r; April 14, 1900, 94 v. 147, § 1; April 25, 1898, 93 v. 402.)

Taxation of deposit of foreign companies. See § 5437 and cases cited in note.
Collection of claims from deposit, § 641.
Power of a court of equity to appoint a receiver and wind up an unlawful or fraudulent business.
See Woods v. Equitable etc. Co. 8 N. P. 125; 11 L. D. 154.
Stevens v. Times-Star Co. 72 O. S. 112.
Shaw v. Interstate etc. Co. 5 N. P. 411; 8 L. D. 510.
The state treasurer is a necessary party to an action to wind up a bond and investment company.
Everhardt v. U. S., etc., Co., 8 N. P. 525.

Section 700. (Interest on securities.) A bond investment company may collect and use the interest on any securities deposited as required by the preceding section so long as it fulfills its obligations and complies with the provisions herein relating to such companies. It may exchange such securities for others of equal value and satisfactory to the treasurer of state. (R. S. Sec. 3821u; April 14, 1900, 94 v. 149, § 4; April 25, 1898, 93 v. 402.)

Section 701. (Requirements before doing business.) Before doing business in this state every bond investment company shall comply with the following conditions:

1. It shall file with the supervisor of bond investment companies certified copies of its charter and articles of incorporation, constitution and by-laws, and other rules and regulations showing its manner of doing business.

2. It shall file with the supervisor a statement, under oath of its president and secretary, or other managing officer of its business for the preceding year, in a form required by the supervisor.

3. It shall file with the supervisor a written instrument, duly executed, agreeing that a summons may issue against it from any county in this state, directed to the sheriff of the county in which the office of the supervisor is situated, commanding the sheriff to serve such summons by certified copy, personally upon the supervisor, or by leaving a copy thereof at his office. The supervisor shall mail a copy of any papers served on him to the home office of such bond investment company. (R. S. Sec. 3821s; April 14, 1900, 94 v. 148, § 2; April 25, 1898, 93 v. 401.)

Section 702. (Certificate of authority to do business.) When a bond investment company has complied with the provisions herein relating to such companies, and the supervisor of bond investment companies is satisfied that it is doing business in accordance with law, he shall issue it a certificate of authority to do business in Ohio. Thereafter, upon the filing of its annual statement, as herein provided, if the supervisor is satisfied that such company has complied with all the provisions of law, he shall issue a renewal of such certificate. (R. S. Sec. 3821t; April 14, 1900, 94 v. 148, § 3; April 25, 1898, 93 v. 402.)

A certificate of authority to do business does not authorize the transaction of unlawful or fraudulent business.
State v. Investment Co., 64 O. S. 283, 318.
See also Shaw v. Interstate etc. Co. 5 N. P. 411; 8 L. D. 510.

Lottery contracts. Contracts of investment security which contain elements of chance and prize constituting a lottery are unlawful.
State v. Investment Co. 64 O. S. 283.

Fraudulent contracts. Contracts of investment security, etc., which can not reasonably be expected to accumulate a reserve fund equal to the stipulated endowment values, without aid from lapses or premiums on new business, are fraudulent and unlawful.
State v. Investment Co. 64 O. S. 283.
See also Woods v. Equitable Debenture Co. 8 N. P. 125; 11 L. D. 154.

Section 703. (Revocation of certificate.) The supervisor of bond investment companies shall revoke the authority of such a company to do business, if, on investigation or examination, he finds that it is not transacting its business in accordance with law, or that its statement of the condition and affairs required under the provisions herein relating to such companies, are false and fraudulent, or for its failure to file an annual statement. (R. S. Sec. 3821t; April 14, 1900, 94 v. 148, § 3; April 25, 1898, 93 v. 402.)

Section 704. (License fees.) A bond investment company shall pay to the supervisor of such companies the following fees:

For filing each application for admission to do business in this state, one hundred dollars;

For filing each certificate of authority and annual renewal of certificate, fifty dollars;

For filing each annual statement, twenty-five dollars;

For issuing license to each agent, two dollars;

For each copy of paper filed in his office, fifty cents per folio;

For affixing seal and certifying any paper, one dollar.

The fees provided for herein shall be deposited by the supervisor with the treasurer of state, upon the certificate of the auditor of state. (R. S. Sec. 3821y; May 12, 1902, 95 v. 642; April 14, 1900, 94 v. 150; April 25, 1898, 93 v. 403.)

Section 705. (Annual statement of companies.) On or before the tenth day of January of each year, each bond investment company doing business in this state shall file with the supervisor of bond investment companies, under oath of its president, secretary or other managing officer, and in a form required by the supervisor, a statement of its business for the twelve months next preceding the thirty-first day of December. Such abstract thereof as the supervisor may require shall be posted for sixty days in the principal office of such company and published in a newspaper of general circulation in the county in which its principal office is situated. (R. S. Sec. 3821w; May 12, 1902, 95 v. 642; April 14, 1900, 94 v. 149; April 25, 1898, 93 v. 402.)

Section 706. (Supervisor may verify statements.) The supervisor of bond investment companies shall verify the annual statement required by the preceding section, by an examination of the affairs of such company. He may make quarterly examinations of the affairs of such company if he deems it necessary. (R. S. Sec. 3821w; May 12, 1902, 95 v. 642; April 14, 1900, 94 v. 149; April 25, 1898, 93 v. 402.)

Section 707. (Proceedings in quo warranto.) If, upon examination of a bond investment company by the supervisor of bond investment companies, it appears that such company is not carrying on its business in accordance with law, or that its affairs are being improperly managed, the supervisor, after ten days' notice to such company, shall institute proceedings in quo warranto against it in the manner provided by law. (R. S. Sec. 3821w; May 12, 1902, 95 v. 642; April 14, 1900, 94 v. 149; April 25, 1898, 93 v. 402.)

See State v. Investment Co. 64 O. S. 283.

Section 708. (Expenses of examination.) The expenses of all examinations provided for by the laws relating to bond investment companies shall be paid by the state of Ohio, except that, if by the laws of any other state, district, territory or nation, examinations of such companies of this state are required or permitted to be made by any officer or other authority of such state, district, territory or nation at the expense of such company, then the expenses of such examination made by the supervisor of this state of a bond investment company of such state, district, territory or nation, shall be charged to and collected from such company. (R. S. Sec. 3821w; May 12, 1902, 95 v. 642; April 14, 1900, 94 v. 149; April 25, 1898, 93 v. 402.)

Section 709. (Agent must be licensed.) An agent of a bond investment company shall not transact business in this state without being first regularly appointed by such company and licensed by a certificate of authority issued by the supervisor of bond investment companies. (R. S. Sec. 3821v; April 14, 1900, 94 v. 149; April 25, 1898, 93 v. 402.)

Penalties for violation of this act, G. C. § 13151.

PART VIII.

SUPERINTENDENT OF BANKS.

Section 710. (Superintendent of banks, appointment and term.) The governor, with the advice and consent of the senate, shall appoint a superintendent of banks, who shall hold his office for the term of four years and until his successor is appointed and qualified. The superintendent may be removed by the governor at any time. (May 5, 1908, 99 v. 287, § 78.)

Sections 710 to 744 together with 9702 to 9797 compromise what is popularly known as the Thomas Banking Act of 1908.

Section 711. (General duties.) The superintendent of banks shall execute the laws in relation to banking companies, savings banks, savings societies, societies for savings, savings and loan associations, savings and trust companies, safe deposit companies and trust companies and every other corporation or association having the power to receive, and receiving money on deposit, chartered or incorporated under the laws of this state. Nothing in this chapter contained shall apply to building and loan associations. (May 5, 1908, 99 v. 287, § 79.)

Section 712. (Appointment and removal of examiners and clerks.) With the approval of the governor, the superintendent of banks may employ from time to time necessary clerks and examiners to assist in the discharge of the duties imposed upon him by law. With such approval, he may remove any such clerks or examiners. He shall summarily remove the deputy superintendent of banks, and any examiner, clerk or deputy connected with the department of the superintendent of banks upon the violation by any such officer, examiner or clerk of any of the provisions of section 717 of the General Code. (May 2, 1913, 103 v. 384, § 12; March 7, 1913, 103 v. 61, § 1; May 5, 1908, 99 v. 287, § 81.)

Section 713. (Salaries.) The superintendent of banks shall fix the salaries of the deputies, assistants, clerks and examiners at such rates per annum as the governor approves. Upon vouchers approved by the superintendent of banks, such salaries shall be paid monthly by the treasurer of state upon the warrant of the auditor of state. (May 18, 1910, 101 v. 276; May 5, 1908, 99 v. 288, § 82, 83.)

This section confers on the superintendent the right to fix the salaries of his assistants. Where the legislature fails to appropriate sufficient funds to pay salaries so fixed, the assistants have a valid claim against the state for the deficiency.

Rep. Atty. Gen. 1911-1912, pp. 749, 751.

Section 714. (Traveling expenses.) The actual and necessary traveling expenses of the superintendent of banks and of the deputies, assistants, clerks and examiners incurred in the discharge of their official duty shall be paid monthly by the treasurer of state upon the warrant of the auditor of state. Vouchers therefor shall be fully itemized, approved by the superintendent of banks and countersigned by the auditor of state. (May 18, 1910, 101 v. 277; May 5, 1908, 99 v. 288, § 84.)

Section 715. (Expenses.) All expenses incurred by the superintendent of banks in the performance of the duties imposed upon him by law, including the salary of such superintendent, his deputies, assistants, clerks and examiners, shall be paid from funds appropriated therefor. (May 18, 1910, 101 v. 277; May 5, 1908, 99 v. 289, § 92.)

Section 716. (Bond of superintendent, where filed.) Before entering upon the discharge of his duties, the superintendent of banks shall give bond to the state in the sum of fifty thousand dollars with sureties approved by the governor, conditioned for the faithful discharge of his official duties. Such bond, with the approval of the governor and the oath of office indorsed thereon, shall be filed with the secretary of state and kept in his office. (May 6, 1913, 103 v. 530; May 5, 1908, 99 v. 287, §§ 85, 86.)

Section 717. (Superintendent and examiners shall not be interested in or borrow money from banks.) Neither the superintendent of banks nor the examiners appointed by him shall be interested directly or indirectly in any national banking association or in any bank or other corporation or association under their supervision, or be engaged in the business of banking. Neither the superintendent of banks, the deputy superintendent of banks, or any examiner, deputy or clerk connected with the department of the superintendent of banks shall directly or indirectly borrow money from any corporation, person or association under the supervision of the superintendent of banks. (May 2, 1913, 103 v. 384, § 12; May 5, 1908, 99 v. 288, § 87.)

Section 718. (Certificates and copies, evidence.) Each certificate or other instrument executed or ordered made by the superintendent of banks in pursuance of authority conferred upon him by law, and sealed with the seal of his office, or copies thereof duly authenticated under such seal, shall be received in evidence in all courts of the state. (May 5, 1908, 99 v. 288, § 89.)

Section 719. (Office.) The superintendent of banks shall be furnished by the state suitable rooms at the seat of government for conducting the business of his office. May 5, 1908, 99 v. 288, § 90.)

As this section does not specify the officer having power to contract for an office, it is presumed that the superintendent is vested with such power. The amount and term of a lease for such purpose is dependent on the amount which the legislature appropriates therefor and the superintendent should not execute a lease dependent on future action of the legislature.
Rep. Atty. Gen. 1911-1912, p. 755.

EXAMINATIONS.

Section 720. (Expenses of special examination.) In case a corporation, company, society or association requests the superintendent of banks to make a special examination under the provisions of this chapter, the expenses thereof shall be paid by the corporation, company, society or association making the request. (May 5, 1908, 99 v. 289, § 92.)

Section 721. (Examination upon request.) When requested in writing upon the authority of the board of directors or the stockholders of any banking institution to make an examination of such bank, the superintendent of banks shall comply therewith, if in his opinion such examination is desirable. (May 5, 1908, 99 v. 289, § 93.)

Section 722· (Moneys received for special examinations, how deposited.) The moneys received by the superintendent of banks for special examinations shall be deposited and paid by him into the state treasury to the credit of the banking department fund to reimburse all sums advanced from the treasury for such expenses. (May 5, 1908, 99 v. 289, § 94.)

Section 723. (Restrictions as to compensation.) Neither the superintendent of banks nor any examiner, clerk or person employed in his office shall take or receive directly or indirectly compensation for services or extra services rendered in the banking department other than that allowed by law. (May 5, 1908, 99 v. 289, § 95.)

Section 724. (Examinations twice each year.) At least twice each year, and also when requested by the board of directors or trustees thereof, the superintendent of banks or an examiner appointed for that purpose shall thoroughly examine the cash, bills, collaterals or securities, books of account and affairs of each bank, savings bank, safe deposit and trust company, savings and loan society or association incorporated under any law in this state. Such examination shall be made in the presence of the members of the executive committee or a majority thereof. He shall also ascertain if any such corporation, company, society or association is conducting its business in the manner prescribed by law and at the place designated in its articles of incorporation. (May 5, 1908, 99 v. 289, § 96.)

Banks incorporated prior to the enactment of this section must submit to examination.
G. C. § 9794.
Rep. Atty. Gen. 1908-1909, p. 191.
Rep. Atty. Gen. 1909-1910, p. 332.

Section 725. (Superintendent or examiner may administer oaths.) For the purpose of such examination, the superintendent of banks or such examiner may administer oaths to and examine any officer, agent, clerk, customer, depositor or share holder of such corporation, company, association or society touching its affairs and business. (May 5, 1908, 99 v. 289, § 96.)

Section 726. (May summon witnesses.) The superintendent of banks may summon in writing under his seal any such officer, agent, clerk, customer, depositor, share holder or any person resident of the state to appear before him and testify in relation thereto. Whoever, being so summoned, neglects or fails to appear at the time and place specified in the summons, or, having appeared, refuses to be sworn or refuses to answer any pertinent and legal question, shall forfeit and pay one hundred dollars to be recovered with costs by the superintendent of banks and paid into the state treasury to the credit of the banking fund. (May 5, 1908, 99 v. 290, § 97.)

Section 727. (Proceedings for refusal to attend and testify.) If a person summoned to appear before the superintendent of banks and give testimony under the provisions of this chapter neglects or refuses to answer any pertinent or legal question that may be put to him by the superintendent touching the matter under examination, the superintendent shall apply to the probate court or court of insolvency of the county in which such inquiry is conducted to issue a subpoena to such person to appear before him. (May 5, 1908, 99 v. 290, § 98.)

Section 728. (Penalty.) Upon such application, the probate judge or judge of the court of insolvency shall issue a subpoena for the appearance of such person or persons forthwith before him to give testimony. Whoever, being so subpoenaed, fails to appear, or appearing, refuses to testify, shall be subject to like proceedings and penalties for contempt as witnesses in actions pending in the probate court or court of insolvency. (May 5, 1908, 99 v. 290, § 98.)

Section 729. (Liquidation by superintendent of banks.) The officers of any such corporation, company, society or association shall submit its books, papers and concerns to the inspection and examination of the superintendent of banks or any deputy, or duly appointed examiner, and on refusal so to do or to be examined on oath touching the affairs of such corporation, company, society or association, the superintendent of banks may forthwith take possession of the property and business of such corporation, company, society or association and liquidate its affairs and remain in possession of its property and business until its affairs be finally liquidated, as hereinafter provided. (May 18, 1910, 101 v. 277; May 5, 1908, 99 v. 290, § 99.)

Section 730. (Deficiency to be made good.) Whenever it appears from the report of such corporation, company, society or association, or the superintendent of banks has reason to believe that its capital is impaired or reduced below the amount required by law, he shall make examination thereof and ascertain the facts. If he finds such impairment or reduction of capital, he shall require such corporation, company, society or association to make good such deficiency. (May 5, 1908, 99 v. 291, § 100.)

Where directors, in order to make good a loss, execute a note to the bank and the bank in consideration thereof executes a note of the same amount to the directors, one obligation offsets the other.
Rep. Atty. Gen. 1911-1912, p. 765.

Section 731. (Superintendent may take possession on refusal.) If such corporation, company, society or association refuses or fails after written notice to make good the deficiency appearing or found to exist, the superintendent of banks may forthwith take possession of the property and business of such corporation, company, society or association until its affairs be finally liquidated by him, as hereinafter provided. (May 18, 1910, 101 v. 277; May 5, 1908, 99 v. 291, § 101.)

Under §§ 729, 730 and 731 the superintendent may, in his discretion, permit the voluntary liquidation of a bank, although its capital stock is impaired, if he is satisfied that it is solvent.
Rep. Atty. Gen. 1910-1911, p. 568.

Section 732. (How proceedings shall be brought.) All suits or proceedings brought by the superintendent of banks under authority of law, or to collect any penalty or forfeiture, shall be brought in the name of the state upon his relation, and shall be conducted under the direction and supervision of the attorney-general. (May 5, 1908, 99 v. 291, § 102.)

Suits to collect notes and claims of a bank under liquidation by the superintendent should under this section be brought in the name of the state on relation of the superintendent.
Rep. Atty. Gen. 1911-1912, p. 759.

Section 733. (Copies of records and papers evidence.) Copies of all records and papers in the office of the superintendent of banks, certified by him, and authenticated by his seal of office shall be evidence in all cases equally and with like effect as the original. (May 5, 1908, 99 v. 291, § 103.)

Section 734. (Examinations shall be made without previous notice.) All examinations required to be made by the superintendent of banks under the provisions of this chapter shall be made without previous notice to the corporation, company, society or association to be examined. (May 5, 1908, 99 v. 291, § 104.)

Section 735. (Expenses of special examination.) When an examination is made at the special instance and request of such corporation, company, society or association, the expense incurred and the services performed shall be paid by the one examined, and the charges collected shall be paid into the state treasury by the superintendent of banks to the credit of the banking fund. (May 5, 1908, 99 v. 291, § 105.)

Section 736. (Fees to be paid to superintendent of banks.) That for the purpose of maintaining the department of the superintendent of banks and the payment of expenses incident thereto, and especially the expenses of inspection and examination, the following fees shall be paid to the superintendent of banks of Ohio:

(a) Each company, firm, corporation, person, association and co-partnership which under the laws of Ohio is subject to inspection and examination by the superintendent of banks, shall pay to the superintendent of banks on or before the fifteenth day of November in each year the sum of thirty dollars, and in addition thereto one seventy-fifth of one per cent. of the total aggregate resources of such company, firm, corporation, person, association or co-partnership in excess of one hundred thousand dollars as shown by the report of the condition of each such company, firm, corporation, person, association or co-partnership made last before October fifteenth of such year; provided, however, that in no event is such total fee to exceed the sum of twelve hundred and fifty dollars in any one year.

(b) Each company, firm, corporation, person, association and co-partnership desiring and intending to transact business in this state, which will be subject to inspection and examination by the superintendent of banks, shall pay to the superintendent of banks for the preliminary examination required by law to be made by the superintendent of banks a fee of thirty dollars, such fee to be paid before a certificate is granted to such company, firm, corporation, person, association or co-partnership, authorizing it to commence business in this state.

(c) Each foreign trust company desiring and intending to do business in this state shall pay to the superintendent of banks a fee of fifty dollars for issuance to it of a certificate authorizing it to transact business in this state. Such fee to be paid before such certificate is issued. (April 23, 1913, 103 v. 180, § 1; former section 736 repealed May 18, 1910, 101 v. 285. Enacted May 5, 1908, 99 v. 292, § 107.)

The superintendent may issue a certificate authorizing a foreign trust company to accept trusts in Ohio, upon compliance by it with § 9778 and other requirements.
Rep. Atty. Gen. 1911-1912, p. 789.
G. C. §§ 744-2, 744-3.

Section 736-1. (Penalty.) Every company, firm, corporation, person, association or co-partnership which fails or neglects to pay the fee provided by paragraph "a" of section 1 of this act (G. C. § 736) on or before the fifteenth day of November of each year shall be subject to a penalty of one hundred dollars for each day after said date that such fee remains unpaid. The superintendent of banks shall maintain an action against the delinquent company, firm, corporation, person, association or co-partnership in the common pleas court of Franklin county, Ohio, or of the county in which the business of such company, firm, corporation, person, association or co-partnership is carried on, for the collection of such fee and the penalty herein imposed. (April 23, 1913, 103 v. 180, § 2.)

Section 736-2. (Receipts credited to general revenue fund.) The superintendent of banks shall pay all money received by him under the provisions of this act into the state treasury to the credit of the general revenue fund of the state. (April 23, 1913, 103 v. 180, § 2.)

REPORTS.

Section 737. (Reports of banking companies to the superintendent of banks.) Not less than four times during each calendar year each banking company, savings bank, savings and trust company, safe deposit and trust company, society for savings, or savings society, chartered or incorporated under any law of this state, and every person or co-partnership doing a banking business shall make a report to the superintendent of banks. Such reports shall be made at such times as required by the superintendent on forms prescribed and furnished by him, and, so far as possible, they shall be made on the same day on which reports are required from national banking associations by the comptroller of the currency. (May 5, 1908, 99 v. 292, § 108.)

Under a former statute (R. S. §§ 3817, 3818) which required "every banking institution" to make reports to the auditor of state it was held that a banking partnership was not an "institution."
State v. Kilgour 8 N. P. n. s. 617; 19 L. D. 670 (C. P. 1909)
A former statute (R. S. §§ 2759 to 2761) which required banks to make statements to the county auditor, was held constitutional.
Treasurer v. Bank 47 O. S. 503 (1890).
Collett v. Springfield Sgs. Soc. 13 C. C. 131; 7 C. D. 146 (1896); affirmed 56 O. S. 776.
This statute was construed in
Exchange Bank v. Hines 3 O. S. 1 (1853).
Ellis v. Linck 3 O. S. 66 (1853).
Bank v. McGregor 6 O. S. 45.
Patton v Bank, 7 N. P. 401; 10 L. D. 321 (1900).
Chapman v. Bank 56 O. S. 310, 329 (1897); 173 U. S. 205.
Cleveland Trust Co. v. Lander 19 C. C. 271; 10 C. D. 451; s. c. 62 O. S. 266; 184 U. S. 111.

Section 738. (How reports shall be verified.) Such reports shall be verified by the oath or affirmation of the president, vice-president, cashier, secretary or treasurer thereof, and shall exhibit in detail, and under appropriate heads, a true statement of the resources, assets and liabilities of such banking company, savings bank, society or association, at the close of business of any past day by him specified, which day shall be the same for all corporations required to make such reports. (May 5, 1908, 99 v. 292, § 109.)

Section 739.   (Report shall be published in newspaper.) Such reports shall be transmitted to the superintendent within ten days after the receipt of the request therefor from him, and shall be published in a newspaper in the city, town or county where the company is located, and, if there is none, then in a newspaper of general circulation in an adjoining county. A copy of such publication shall be furnished to the superintendent of banks. (May 5, 1908, 99 v. 292, § 110.)

Section 740.   (Special reports.) The superintendent of banks may call for special reports whenever in his judgment they are necessary to inform him fully of the conditions of any companies, societies and corporations, which reports shall be verified as provided by this chapter for other reports to the superintendent. (May 5, 1908, 99 v. 292, § 111.)

Section 741.   (Penalty for failure to make reports.) Every company, corporation, society or association failing to make and transmit to the superintendent of banks any of the reports required by this chapter, or failing to publish the reports as required by law shall forthwith be notified by the superintendent, and, if such failure continues for ten days after the receipt of such notice, such delinquent company, society or association shall be subject to a penalty of one hundred dollars for each day after the time required for making such report. In case of delay or refusal to pay the penalty herein imposed for failure to make and transmit a report, the superintendent shall maintain an action against the delinquent company, society or association, for the recovery of such penalty, and all sums collected by such action or paid as such penalty shall be paid into the state treasury to the credit of the banking fund. (May 5, 1908, 99 v. 292, § 112.)

Under a former statute (R. S. § 3818) it was held that a proceeding to recover penalties for failure to make reports must be brought in the name of the state and not in the name of the state officer.

Guilbert v. Bank 5 N. P. n. s. 209; 18 L. D. 115 (C. P. 1907).

See § 732.

The penalty of this section relates to a failure to make the reports required by § 737 and not the report of the "examining committee" under § 9736.

Rep. Atty. Gen. 1911-1912, p. 786.

Section 742. (Liquidation by superintendent.) Whenever in this act it is provided that the superintendent of banks may take possession of the property and business of any corporation, company, commercial bank, savings bank, safe deposit company, trust company, or any combination of two or more of such 'classes of business or society for savings, or banking asociation, doing business under the provisions of the banking laws of this state to liquidate its affairs, the superintendent of banks shall take possession of and administer the assets of such company or association as herein provided. (May 18, 1910, 101 v. 277; May 5, 1908, 99 v. 294, § 117.)

Section 742-1. (Written notice to holders of assets.) Upon taking possession of the property and business of any such corporation, company, society or association, the superintendent of banks shall forthwith give written notice of such fact to all banks, trust companies, associations and individuals holding or in possession of any assets of such corporation, company, society or association. No bank, trust company, association or individual knowing that the superintendent of banks has taken possession of such company or association, shall have a lien or charge for any payment advanced or any clearance thereafter made, or liability thereafter incurred against any of the assets of the corporation, company, society or association of whose property and business the superintendent of banks shall have taken possession. Such corporation, company, society or association may, with the consent of the superintendent of banks, resume business upon such conditions as may be approved by him. (May 18, 1910, 101 v. 277.)

Section 742-2. (Collections. Special deputies. Bonds of agents, where filed.) Upon taking possession of the property and business of such corporation, company, society or association, the superintendent of banks is authorized to collect money due to such corporation, company, society or association, and do such other acts as are necessary to preserve its assets and business, and shall proceed to liquidate the affairs thereof, as hereinafter provided. The superintendent of banks shall collect all debts due and claims belonging to it, and upon the order of the common pleas court in and for the county in which the office of such corporation, company, society or association was located may sell or compound all bad or doubtful debts, and on like order may sell all the real estate and personal property of such corporation, company, society or association, on such terms as the court shall direct; and the superintendent of banks upon the terms of sale or compromise directed by the court, shall execute and deliver to the purchaser of such real or personal property, such deeds or instruments as shall be necessary to evidence the passing of the title; and if said real estate is situated outside of the county in which the office of the corporation, company, society or association was located, a certified copy of such order authorizing and ratifying said sale shall be filed in the office of the recorder of the county within which said property is situated; and may, if necessary to pay the debts of such corporation, company, society or association, enforce the individual liability, if any, of the stockholders. The superintendent of banks may under his hand and official seal appoint one or more special deputy superintendents of banks as agent or agents, to assist him in the duty of liquidation and distribution, a certificate of appointment to be filed in the office of superintendent of banks and a certified copy in the office of the clerk of the county in which the office of such corporation, company, society or association was located. The superintendent of banks shall require from such agent or agents such surety for the faithful discharge of their duties as he may deem proper. All bonds given shall be deposited with the secretary of state and kept in his office. (May 6, 1913, 103 v. 530; May 18, 1910, 101 v. 278.)

Actions to collect claims should, under G. C. § 732, be brought in the name of the state on relation of the superintendent.

Rep. Atty. Gen. 1911-1912, p. 759.

Where public deposits are secured by bonds exceeding in value the amount of such deposits, the superintendent is authorized by this section to pay such deposits and redeem the bonds, in order to prevent loss by a forced sale therof.

Rep. Atty. Gen. 1911-1912, p. 785.

. Where loans are secured by assignments of construction contracts, the superintendent is authorized by this section to make further advances to the contractors if necessary to preserve the securities. It is possible that under this section, the superintendent may obtain the approval of the common pleas court to such action. The court has power to order a sale of "doubtful debts" and perhaps has power to authorize proper steps to preserve the same.

Rep. Atty. Gen. 1911-1912, p. 767.

A special deputy can not be appointed by the superintendent to act as attorney. Special counsel can under G. C. §§ 333, 336, be appointed only by the attorney general. The fees of counsel so appointed may be paid under § 742-4.

Rep. Atty. Gen. 1911-1912, p. 795.

Use, by the superintendent of banks, for payment of a private debt, of funds belonging to a bank in his possession for liquidation, does not constitute a crime under the embezzlement statute, where the funds so taken were soon afterward returned to the depository with interest.

State v. Baxter, 14 N. P. n. s. 223 (C. P. 1913).

Section 742-3. (Notice by advertisement. Rejected claims.) The superintendent of banks shall cause notice to be given by advertisement in such newspaper as he may direct weekly for three consecutive months, calling on all persons who may have claims against such corporation, company, society or association, to present the same to the superintendent of banks, and to make legal proof thereof at a place and within a time not earlier than the last day of publication to be therein specified. The superintendent of banks shall mail a similar notice to all persons whose names appear as creditors upon the books of the corporation, company, society or association. If the superintendent of banks doubts the justice and validity of any claim, he may reject the same and serve notice of such rejection upon the claimants, either by mail or personally, and an affidavit of the service of such notice, which shall be prima facie evidence thereof, shall be filed in his office. An action upon a claim so rejected must be brought within six months after such service. Claims presented and allowed after the expiration of the time fixed in the notice to creditors, shall be entitled to be paid the amount of all prior dividends therein if there be funds sufficient therefor and share in the distribution of the remaining assets in the hands of the superintendent of banks equitably applicable thereto. (May 18, 1910, 101 v. 278.)

Interest accrued on deposits, not entered on the books of the bank, should be credited by the superintendent up to the interest date preceding the time possession was taken by the superintendent.
Rep. Atty. Gen. 1911-1912, p. 753.
Creditors are entitled to legal interest on book accounts from the date of suspension of payment.
Rep. Atty. Gen. 1911-1912, p. 797, citing Richmond v. Irons 121 U. S. 27.

Section 742-4. (Attorney fees. Expense of liquidation; how paid.) The expenses incurred by the superintendent of banks in the liquidation of any bank in accordance with the provisions of this act, shall include the expenses of deputy or assistants, clerks and examiners employed in such liquidation, together with reasonable attorney fees for counsel employed by said superintendent of banks in the course of such liquidation. Such compensation of counsel, of deputies or assistants, clerks, and examiners in the liquidation of any corporation, company, society or association, and all expenses of supervision and liquidation shall be fixed by the superintendent of banks, subject to the approval of the common pleas court of the county in which the office of such corporation, company, society or association was located, on notice

to such corporation, company, society or association. The
expense of such liquidation shall be paid out of the property
of such corporation, company, society or association in the
hands of said superintendent of banks, and such expenses
shall be a valid charge against the property in the hands of
said superintendent of banks and shall be paid first, in the
order of priority. (May 18, 1910, 101 v. 279.)

> The notice to the corporation should state the time when the state-
> ment of expenses will be submitted to the common pleas court for
> approval. Such notice may be served upon an officer of the bank cor-
> poration in accordance with the method prescribed for service of sum-
> mons on corporations (G. C. § 11288).
> Rep. Atty. Gen. 1911-1912, p. 757.

Section 742-5. (Inventory. Supplemental lists.) Upon
taking possession of the property and assets of such corporation, company, society or association, the superintendent of
banks shall make an inventory of the assets of such corporation, company, society or association in duplicate,—one to be
filed in the office of the superintendent of banks, and one in
the office of the clerk of the county in which the office of
such corporation, company, society or association was located; upon the expiration of the time fixed for the presentation of claims, the superintendent of banks shall make in
duplicate a full and complete list of the claims presented, including and specifying such claims as have been rejected by
him, of which one shall be filed in the office of the superintendent of banks, and one in the office of the clerk of the
county in which the office of such corporation, company, society or association was located. And the superintendent of
banks shall in like manner make and file supplemental lists
showing all claims presented subsequent to the filing of the
first list,—such supplemental lists to be filed at least fifteen
days before the declaration of any dividend, and in any
event such supplemental lists shall be filed at intervals of
not exceeding six months. Such inventory and list of claims
shall be open at all reasonable times for inspection. (May
18, 1910, 101 v. 279.)

Section 742-6. (Deposits.) The moneys collected by the
superintendent of banks shall be from time to time deposited in one or more state banks of deposit, savings banks, or
trust companies, subject to his order as herein provided.
(May 18, 1910, 101 v. 280.)

Section 742-7. (Dividends.) At any time after the expiration of the date fixed for the presentation of claims, the
superintendent of banks may, out of the funds remaining in

his hands after the payment of expenses, declare one or more dividends, and after the expiration of one year from the first publication of notice to creditors, he may declare a final dividend,—such dividends to be paid to such persons and in such amounts and upon such notice as may be directed by the common pleas court of the county in which the office of such corporation, company, society or association was located. (May 18, 1910, 101 v. 280.).

Section 742-8. **(Filing objections.)** Objection to any claim not rejected by the superintendent of banks may be made by any party interested by filing a copy of such objection with the superintendent of banks, who shall present the same to the common pleas court of the county in which the office of such corporation, company, society or association was located, upon written notice to the party filing the same, said notice setting forth the time and place of the presentation. The court upon return day of said notice shall hear the objections raised to said claim, or refer the determination of said objections to a referee for report, or upon demand of either the superintendent of banks or the party filing the objections direct that the issues be tried before a jury. The court may make proper provision for unproved or unclaimed deposits. (May 18, 1910, 101 v. 280.)

Section 742-9. **(Application to C. P. Court.)** Whenever any such corporation, company, society or association of whose property and business the superintendent of banks has taken possession, as aforesaid, deems itself aggrieved thereby, it may at any time within ten days after taking such possession apply to the common pleas court of the county in which the office of such corporation, company, society or association was located, to enjoin further proceedings, and said court, after citing the superintendent of banks to show cause why further proceedings should not be enjoined, and hearing the allegations and proofs of the parties and determining the facts, may, upon the merits, dismiss such application or enjoin the superintendent of banks from further proceedings, and direct him to surrender such business and property to such corporation, company, society or association. (May 18, 1910, 101 v. 280.)

Section 742-10. **(Duty of superintendent of banks after service of notice.)** No receiver shall be appointed by any court, nor shall any deed of assignment for the benefit of creditors be filed in any probate court or court of insolvency, within this state, for any incorporated bank, savings bank, savings and trust company, safe deposit and trust company, society for savings, savings society, or any combination of same doing business under the laws of this state except upon notice to the superintendent of banks, unless in case of urgent necessity it becomes in the judgment of the court necessary so to do in order to preserve the assets of such corporation, company, society or association. The superintendent of banks may within five days after the service of such notice upon him take possession of such corporation, company, society or association, in which case no further proceedings shall be had upon such application for the appointment of receiver or under such deed of assignment, or, if a receiver has been appointed or such assignee shall have entered upon the administration of his trust, such appointment shall be vacated or such assignee shall be removed upon application of the superintendent of banks to the proper court therefor, and the superintendent of banks shall proceed in all such cases to administer the assets of such corporation, company, society or association as herein provided. (May 18, 1910, 101 v. 281.)

Section 742-11. (Stockholders' meeting.) Whenever the superintendent of banks shall have paid to each depositor and creditor of such corporation, company, society or association (not including stockholders) whose claim or claims as such depositor or creditor shall have been duly proved and allowed, the full amount of such claims, and shall have made proper provision for unclaimed or unpaid deposits or dividends, and shall have paid all the expenses of the liquidation, the superintendent of banks shall call a meeting of the stockholders of such corporation, company, society or association, by giving notice thereof for thirty days in one or more newspapers published in the county wherein the office of such corporation, company, society or association was located. (May 18, 1910, 101 v. 281.)

Section 742-12. (Distribution.) At such meeting the stockholders shall determine whether the superintendent of banks shall continue to administer its assets and wind up the affairs of such corporation, company, society or association, or whether an agent or agents shall be elected for that purpose; and in so determining the said stockholders shall vote by ballot in person, or by proxy, each share entitling the holder to one vote and the majority of the stock shall be necessary to a determination. In case it is determined to continue the liquidation under the superintendent of banks, he shall complete the liquidation of the affairs of such corporation, company, society or association, and after paying the expenses thereof shall distribute the proceeds among the stockholders in proportion to the several holdings of stock, in such manner and upon such notice as may be directed by the comon pleas court of the county in which the office of such corporation, company, society or association was located. (May 18, 1910, 101 v. 281.)

Section 742-13. (Agent's bond.) In case it is determined to appoint an agent or agents to liquidate, the stockholders shall thereupon select such agent or agents by ballot,—a majority of the stock present and voting, in person or by proxy, being necessary to a choice. Such agent or agents shall file with the superintendent of banks a bond to the state of Ohio in such amount and with such sureties as shall be approved by the superintendent of banks for the faithful performance of all the duties of his or their trust, and thereupon the superintendent of banks shall transfer to such agent or agents all the undivided or uncollected or other assets of such corporation, company, society or association then remaining in his hands; and upon such transfer and delivery the said superintendent of banks shall be discharged from all further liability to such corporation, company, society or association and its creditors. (May 18, 1910, 101 v. 282.)

Section 742-14. (Expenses.) Such agent or agents shall convert the assets coming into his or their possession into cash, and shall account for and make distribution of the property of such corporation, company, society or association as herein provided in the case of distribution by the superintendent of banks, except that the expenses thereof shall be subject to the direction and control of the common pleas court of the county in which the office of such corporation, company, society or association was located. (May 18, 1910, 101 v. 282.)

Section 742-15. (Successor of agent.) In case of death or removal or refusal to act of any such agent, or agents, the stockholders may elect a successor as hereinbefore provided who shall have the same powers and be subject to the same liabilities and duties as the agent, or agents originally elected. (May 18, 1910, 101 v. 282.)

Section 742-16. (Unclaimed deposits, etc. Application to C. P. court.) Dividends and unclaimed deposits remaining in the hands of the superintendent of banks for six months after the order for final distribution shall be by him deposited in one or more state banks of deposits, savings banks or trust companies to the credit of the superintendent of banks in his name of office, in trust for the several depositors or creditors entitled thereto. The superintendent of banks may pay over the moneys so held by him to the persons respectively entitled thereto, upon being furnished satisfactory evidence of their right to the same. In cases of doubt or conflicting claims he may apply to the common pleas court of the county in which the office of such corporation, company, society or association was located for an order authorizing and directing the payment thereof. He may apply the interest earned by the money so held by him towards defraying the expenses of the payment and distribution of such unclaimed deposits or dividends to the depositors and creditors entitled to receive the same, and he shall include in his annual report to the governor a statement of the amount of interest earned by such unclaimed dividends. (May 18, 1910, 101 v. 282.)

Section 743. (Annual report. Summary, showing financial condition. Deputies.) At the end of each fiscal year, the superintendent of banks shall make an annual report to the governor, which report shall exhibit:

(a) A summary of the state and condition of every incorporated bank, savings bank, savings and trust company, safe deposit and trust company, society for savings, savings society, or other corporation included within this chapter, from which reports have been received during the year, with an abstract of the whole amount of capital returned by them, the whole amount of their debts and liabilities, the total amount of means and resources, separating the reports of the various kinds of corporations, and specifying the amount of lawful money held by them at the time of their several returns, and such other information in relation to such banks, societies and associations as in his judgment may be required;

(b) A statement of the banks, societies or associations whose business has been closed during the year, the amount of their resources and liabilities, and the amount paid to the creditors thereof;

(c) The names and compensation of the deputies, assistants, clerks and examiners employed or appointed by him, and the whole amount of expenses of the banking department during the year;

(d) The amount of fees and charges received from such

banks, societies and associations, and penalties collected and paid into the state treasury;

(e)   A statement of the banks, societies or associations liquidated or in process of liquidation by the superintendent of banks, and the status of affairs of each of said banks, societies or associations at the time of said report, including the amount of their resources and liabilities and the nature of the same and the amounts paid the creditors. (May 18, 1910, 101 v. 283; May 5, 1908, 99 v. 293, § 114.)

Section 744.   (Report shall be printed.)   Such reports shall be printed in like manner and the expenses thereof paid as provided by law for the publication of the reports of state officers.   (May 18, 1910, 101 v. 348; May 5, 1908, 99 v. 293, § 115.)

Section 744-1.   (Certain corporations, persons, etc., prohibited from using the word "bank," "banker," etc., unless they submit to examination and regulation.)   That no corporation not organized under the laws of this state, or of the United States, or person, partnership or association, shall use the word "bank," "banker" or "banking" or "trust" or "trust company," or words of similar meaning in any foreign language, as a designation or name under which business may be conducted in this state unless such corporation, person, partnership or association shall submit to inspection, examination and regulation, as provided in this act.   The superintendent of banks shall execute all laws in relation to corporations organized under the laws of this state or of the United States, persons, partnerships and associations using the word "bank," "banker" or "banking," or "trust" or "trust company," or words of similar meaning in any foreign language as a designation or name under which business is conducted in this state.   (May 2, 1913, 103 v. 379, § 1.)

See Constitution, Art. 13, Sec. 3.

Sections 744-2.   (Filing of detailed statement; contents thereof.)   Every corporation not organized under laws of this state, or of the United States, or person, partnership or association using the word "bank," "banker" or "banking" or "trust" or "trust company" or words of similar meaning in any foreign language as a designation or name under which business may be conducted in this state, now transacting or hereafter desiring to transact a banking business in this state, shall, under oath file with the secretary of state a full, complete detailed statement of,

1.   Name of the bank or proposed bank.

2. A copy of the articles of co-partnership or agreement, under which the business of the bank is being or is to be conducted, which shall be executed and acknowledged by all of the parties interested therein, and at least one of whom shall be at all times a resident of the state of Ohio. If the banking business is being or is to be transacted or carried on by an individual, such individual shall at all times, while engaged in such banking business, be a resident of the state of Ohio, and the statement herein required shall show such.

3. The county and city or village in which the bank is to be located, and the business carried on.

4. A statement of the responsibility and the net worth of the individual members of such corporation, person, partnership or association.

5. If not disclosed in the articles of co-partnership or agreement, then the name of the officers, agents or employes in active charge of the management of the business of the bank, every such corporation, person, partnership or association now doing a banking business in this state shall on or before January 1, 1914, file with the secretary of state a detailed statement as provided herein. The secretary of state in filing said statements shall be governed by the provisions of sections 9705 and 9706 of the General Code of Ohio.

No such corporation, person, partnership or association shall transact business except such as is essential or necessarily preliminary to its organization until it has been authorized by the superintendent of banks.

In authorizing said banks to commence business and issuing a certificate to that effect, the superintendent of banks and such corporation, person, partnership or association shall be governed by the provisions of sections 9720, 9721, 9722 and 9723 of the General Code. (May 2, 1913, 103 v. 379, § 2.)

Foreign corporations prohibited from transacting banking business, § 9796.

Foreign trust companies, power to execute trusts, § 9778.

Section 744-3. (Certificate of authority to commence business.) If upon examination of the facts which may come to the knowledge of the superintendent of banks, whether by means of a special commission appointed by him for the purpose of inquiring into the conditions of such applicants or otherwise, the superintendent of banks finds that such person or firm is lawfully entitled to commence business, he shall give a certificate under his hand and official seal that they or he have complied with the law, and are authorized to commence business. But the superintendent of banks may withhold such certificate when he has reason to believe that such person or firm has formed for any other purpose than the legitimate business herein contemplated, or that the character and general fitness of the person or firm named in the application are not such as to command the confidence of the community in which such bank is proposed to be located, or that the public convenience and advantage will not be promoted by its establishment. If the superintendent of banks withholds a certificate for any of the reasons named in this section, an appeal may be made to a board composed of the governor, attorney general and superintendent of banks, whose decision shall be final. (May 2, 1913, 103 v. 380, § 3.)

Foreign corporations prohibited from transacting banking business, § 9796.

Foreign trust companies, power to execute trusts, § 9778.

Section 744-4. (**When superintendent authorized to take possession of property and business of a corporation, person, etc., for liquidation.**) Upon becoming satisfied that a corporation not organized under the laws of this state, or of the United States, or person, partnership or association, using the word "bank," "banker" or "banking" or "trust" or "trust company," or words of similar meaning in any foreign language, as a designation or name under which business is conducted in this state, has refused to pay its depositors in accordance with the terms on which such deposits were received, or that such corporation, person, partnership, or association has become otherwise insolvent, or that it is conducting its business in an unsafe or unauthorized manner, or from any report or examination provided for by law, the superintendent shall have reason to conclude that such corporation, person, partnership or association is in an unsound or unsafe condition to transact the business for which it was organized, or that it is unsafe for it to continue business, the superintendent of banks forthwith may take possession of the property and the business of such corporation, person, partnership, or association, until its affairs be finally liquidated as provided by law. The superintendent of banks shall not take possession of the property and business of any such corporation, person, partnership or association which was doing business in this state prior to the time of the passage of this act for the failure to comply with the provisions of this act, as to transactions made prior to the passage of this act or renewals or settlements and adjustments of such transactions, where the examination provided for in this act discloses, or any such corporation, person, partnership, or association, shows to the satisfaction of the superintendent

of banks, that the interests of its depositors, creditors and
stockholders will not be endangered by permitting it to transact its regular business.   (May 2, 1913, 103 v. 380, § 4.)

**Section 744-5.   (Posting of notice that bank is private
bank.)** Every such corporation, person, partnership or association shall post in the room in which it transacts its business, and in plain view of its customers, a printed list of all
the owners of, and parties interested in, such bank, and statement that the bank is a private bank.   Should the interests
of any member of such corporation, partnership or firm, or
of an individual doing a banking business under the provisions of this act, change either by death, devise, sale or otherwise, then and in that case the superintendent of banks of
the state of Ohio shall be notified of such change and notice
printed and posted in the room of any such bank as herein
provided.   No such bank shall advertise by newspaper, let-
terhead, or in any other way, a larger capital than has been
actually paid in.   (May 2, 1913, 103 v. 381, § 5.)

**Section 744-6.   ("Unincorporated" shall be printed upon
stationery and advertising matter.   Depositors shall have first
lien on assets; reserve.)** That all persons, partnerships or
associations that shall engage in business under the purview
of this act, shall have printed on all their advertising matter and business stationery, the word "unincorporated" immediately following the name of the firm or business title.

The depositors in any bank shall have first lien on the
assets of such bank, in case it is wound up to the amount
of their several deposits, and for any balance remaining unpaid, such depositors shall share in the general assets of the
owner or owners alike with the general creditors.   Every
such corporation, person, partnership, or association shall
keep as a reserve at least fifteen per cent. of the total deposits; such reserve may be in lawful currency kept in the
vaults of the bank, or may be invested in the securities
named in the paragraphs b and c of section 9758, or the
bonds of any city of county within this state, or kept subject to demand in other banks or trust companies designated
by such bank with the approval of the superintendent of
banks of Ohio.   (May 2, 1913, 103 v. 381, § 6.)

**Section 744-7.   (Reports filed in the office of superintend-
ent.)** That all reports received from persons, partnerships
and associations engaged in, and all applications received
from persons, partnerships or associations desiring to engage in business within the purview of this act, shall be kept

on file in the office of the superintendent of banks, and open
to the inspection of all persons, at the discretion of the superintendent of banks. (May 2, 1913, 103 v. 382, § 7.)

Section 744-8. (Dissolution.) Upon the failure of any
person, persons, partnership or association coming within the
purview of this act, to comply with it in any particular, the
superintendent of banks shall proceed at once to take charge
of their affairs and proceed with their dissolution with full
power and authority as provided for other cases in section 4
of this act. (G. C. § 744-4.) (May 2, 1913, 103 v. 382, § 8.)

**Section 744-9. (Laws governing the conduct and busi-
ness of banking institutions.)** Sections 720, 724, 725, 729,
734, 735, 737, 738, 740, 741, 742, 742-1, 742-2, 742-3, 742-4,
742-5, 742-6, 742-7, 742-8, 742-9, 742-10, 742-11, 742-12, 742-13,
742-14, 742-16 and 743 of the General Code of Ohio shall
refer to and include every and all corporations not organized under the laws of this state or of the United States, persons, partnerships and associations using the word "bank,"
"banker" or "banking" or "trust" or "trust company" or
words of similar meaning in any foreign language as a designation or name under which business is or may be conducted in this state, and every such corporation, person,
partnership or association shall be governed by and shall
conduct all their business and transactions as provided in
said sections in the same manner as if such corporations,
persons, partnerships or associations were specifically mentioned in each of said sections; and every such corporation,
person, partnership or association shall do and perform all
things required by each and all said sections, and the superintendent of banks shall have the power and authority over
such corporations, persons, partnerships and associations, as
is given to him over banking corporations in Ohio by said
sections; and each and every other section of the General
Code of Ohio providing for the inspection, examination and
regulation of banking corporations, except the provisions as
to capital stock and the amount of loans and investments
computed on the basis of capital stock, and except the provisions for the publication of reports, shall be held to apply
to each and every such corporation, person, partnership or
association so far as the said sections and parts of sections
may be applicable. (May 2, 1913, 103 v. 383, § 9.)

**Section 744-10. (Penalty for certifying check without
deposit, or resort to device to evade law.)** Whoever, being
connected with or serving, or being an officer, employe,

agent or director of a corporation not organized under the
laws of this state, or the United States, or person, partnership or association using the word "bank," "banker," or
"banking" or "trust" or "trust company," or words of
similar meaning in any foreign language as a designation or
name under which business is conducted in this state, wilfully certifies a check drawn on such corporation, person,
partnership or association and fails forthwith to charge the
amount thereof against the account of the person, firm or
corporation drawing it, or wilfully certifies a check drawn
upon such corporation, person, partnership or association,
unless the person, firm or corporation drawing it has on deposit with such corporation, person, partnership or association an amount of money subject to the payment of such
check and equal to the amount specified therein, or resorts to
a device, receives a fictitious obligation in order to evade that
provision of this section, or certifies a check before the
amount thereof has been regularly entered to the credit of
the drawer thereof upon the books of such corporation, person, partnership or association, shall be fined not more than
five thousand dollars or imprisoned in the penitentiary not
less than one year nor more than five years, or both. (May
2, 1913, 103 v. 383, § 10.)

**Section 744-11. (Penalty for receiving deposits with
knowledge of insolvency, issuing fraudulent certificate of
deposit, etc.)** Whoever, being connected with or serving, or
being an officer, employe, agent or director, of a corporation
not organized under the laws of this state, or of the United
States, or person, partnership or association, using the word
"bank," "banker" or "banking" or "trust" or "trust company" or words of similar meaning in any foreign language,
as a designation or name under which business is conducted
in this state, receives, or permits an employe to receive
money, checks, drafts or other property as a deposit therein
when he has knowledge that it is insolvent, or wilfully and
fraudulently issues or puts forth a certificate of deposit,
draws an order or a bill of exchange, makes an acceptance,
assigns a note, bond, draft, bill of exchange, mortgage, judgment of decree, or makes a false entry in a book, report or
statement of such corporation, person, partnership or association, or fictitiously borrows or solicits, obtains or receives
money for said corporation, person, partnership or association not in good faith intended to be and not the property
of such corporation, person, partnership, or association, with
intent to defraud or injure such corporation, person, partnership or association, or another corporation or person, or

to deceive an officer of such corporation, person, partnership or association or an agent appointed to examine the affairs of such corporation, person, partnership or association, or publishes a false statement or report relating to the financial condition of such corporation, person, partnership or association, with intent to defraud or injure it or another corporation or person, shall be fined not more than five thousand dollars or imprisoned in the penitentiary for more than ten years, or both. (May 2, 1913, 103 v. 383, § 11.)

Section 744-12. (Institutions prohibited as depositories of state funds.) That whenever any of the funds of the state, or any of the political subdivisions of the state, shall be deposited under any of the depository laws of the state, every corporation, person, partnership and association coming within the purview of this act shall be permitted to bid upon and be designated as depositories of such funds, upon furnishing such surety or securities therefor as is prescribed by the laws of the state of Ohio; provided, however, that there shall not be deposited with any such corporation, person, partnership, or association by any such political subdivision an amount in excess of $500,000, nor in any event an amount in excess of fifty (50) per cent. of the amount of the funds of such political subdivision so at any time to be deposited. (May 2, 1913, 103 v. 384, § 13.)

Section 744-13. (When act shall take effect). This act (G. C. §§ 744-1 to 744-13) shall go into effect July first, 1914, except that every corporation not organized under the laws of this state or of the United States, person, partnership or association, using the word "bank," "banker" or "banking" or "trust" or "trust company" or words of similar meaning in any foreign language, as a designation or name under which business is conducted in this state, shall, on and after September first, 1913, make reports to the superintendent of banks of Ohio in the manner and form as provided in sections 737, 738, and 741 of the General Code of Ohio which shall apply to and govern all such corporations, persons, partnerships or associations; provided further that at any time after September first, 1913, the superintendent of banks of Ohio, when he has reason to believe from any report made by any such corporation, person, partnership or association, or otherwise, that such corporation, person, partnership or association is in a failing or insolvent condition he may make an examination of any such corporation, person, partnership or association as provided by section 730 of the General Code, and upon his finding any such corporation, person, partnership, or association to be insolvent or in a failing condition he may take charge of the same and proceed to liquidate its affairs as provided by law for the liquidation of banking corporations of this state; provided further that section 2 of this act (G. C. § 744-2) shall go into effect on January first, 1914; provided further that section 12 of this act (G. C. §§ 712 and 717) shall go into effect at the earliest date allowed by law. (May 2, 1913, 103 v. 384, § 15.)

Section 841. (Tax on insurance companies for fire marshal's department.) For the purpose of maintaining the department of state fire marshal and the payment of the expenses incident thereto, each fire insurance company doing business in this state shall pay to the superintendent of insurance in the month of November each year, in addition to the taxes required by law to be paid by it, one-half of one per cent on the gross premium receipts of such companies on all business transacted by it in Ohio during the year next preceding, as shown by its annual statement under oath to the insurance department. The superintendent of insurance shall pay the money so received into the state treasury to the credit of a special fund for the maintenance of the office of state fire marshal. If any portion of such special fund remains unexpended at the end of the year, for which it was required to be paid, and the state fire marshal so certifies, it shall be transferred to the general revenue fund of the state. (R. S. Sec. 409-56; April 25, 1904, 97 v. 418; 95 v. 474; 94 v. 388.)

PART IX.

TAX COMMISSION.

Section 1465-1. (Appointment.) Between the first day and the second Monday of February, 1913, and biennially thereafter, the governor shall appoint one member of the tax commission of Ohio for the term of six years from the second Monday of February of such year. (June 2, 1911, 102 v. 224.)

This act is constitutional.
Railway v. Dittey 203 Fed. 537 (D. C. 1913).
Establishment of tax commission. See § 5445.
Former laws.
Board of appraisers and assessors of railroads, etc.
R. S. § 2770. G. C. § 5415 (original number).
Railway Co. v. Hynicka, 4 N. P. n. s. 345; 17 L. D. 163.
Board of equalization for banks.
R. S. § 2808. G. C. § 5602. (original number).
State v. Jones 51 O. S. 492.
State v. Board 65 O. S. 544.
Cummings v. Bank, 101 U. S. 153.
Whitbeck v. Bank, 127 U. S. 193.
Banking Co. v. Hubbard 22 C. C. 20; 12 C. D. 279.
State board of equalization for real property.
R. S. § 2818. G. C. § 5612.

State v. Raine 47 O. S. 447.
State v. Morris, 63 O. S. 496.
Scarborough v. Gibson 1 N. P. n. s. 73; 13 L. D. 738.
State v. Godfrey, 13 L. D. 536; affirmed 14 C. D. 455.

Section 1465-2. (Removal.) The governor shall at any time remove any commissioner for inefficiency, neglect of duty or malfeasance in office. (June 2, 1911, 102 v. 224; May 10, 1910, 101 v. 399, § 2.)

Section 1465-3. (Entire time of officers required.) Each commissioner and each employe shall devote his entire time to the duties of his office, and shall not hold any position of trust or profit, engage in any occupation or business interfering with or inconsistent with his duty as such commissioner or employe, or serve on or under any committee of any political party. (June 2, 1911, 102 v. 224, § 3; 101 v. 399, § 3.)

Section 1465-4. (Continuous session. Record of proceedings.) The commission shall be in continuous session and open for the transaction of business during all the business hours of each and every day, excepting Sundays and legal holidays. All sessions shall be open to the public, and sessions of the commission shall stand and be adjourned without further notice thereof on its records. All of the proceedings of the commission shall be shown on its record of proceedings, which shall be a public record, and all voting shall be by calling each member's name by the secretary and each member's vote shall be recorded on the record of proceedings as cast. (June 2, 1911, 102 v. 224, § 4; 101 v. 399, § 4.)

The proceedings of the tax commission constitute a public record, and, subject to proper regulations, are open to inspection by any person. State v. Dittey, 12 N. P. n. s. 319; 23 L. D. 31 (C. P. 1911).

Section 1465-5. (Oath.) Before entering upon the duties of his office each commissioner shall take and subscribe the constitutional oath of office and shall swear or affirm that he holds no other office of profit, or any position under any committee of a political party; which oath or affirmation shall be filed in the office of the governor. (June 2, 1911, 102 v. 224, § 5; 101 v. 399, § 5.)

Section 1465-6. (Quorum. Hearings, decisions, orders, etc.) A majority of the commission shall constitute a quorum to transact business, and any vacancy shall not impair the right of the remaining commissioners to exercise all the powers of the commission so long as a majority remains. Any investigation, inquiry or hearing which the commission is authorized to hold or undertake may be held or undertaken by or before any one member of the commission. All investigations, inquiries, hearings, and decisions of the commission, and every order made by a commissioner, when approved and confirmed by the commission, and so shown on its record of proceedings shall be deemed to be the order of the commission. (June 2, 1911, 102 v. 224, § 7; 101 v. 400, § 7.)

Section 1465-7. (Place of office.) The commission shall keep its office in the city of Columbus, and shall provide a suitable room or rooms, necessary office furniture, supplies, books, periodicals and maps. All necessary expenses shall be audited and paid as other expenses are audited and paid. The commission may hold sessions at any place within the state. (June 2, 1911, 102 v. 225, § 9; 101 v. 400, § 9.)

Section 1465-8. (Secretary, examiners, clerks, etc. Expenses.) The commission is authorized to employ a secretary, examiners, experts, clerks, accountants, stenographers and other assistants and to fix their compensation. Such employments and compensation therefor shall be first approved by the governor. The commissioners, secretary, experts, clerks, accountants, stenographers and other assistants that may be employed, shall be entitled to receive from the state their actual and necessary expenses while traveling on the business of the commission. Such expenses shall be itemized and sworn to by the person who incurred the expense and allowed by the commission. (June 2, 1911, 102 v. 225, § 10; 101 v. 400, § 10.)

Section 1465-9. (Attorney general or prosecuting attorney shall aid in investigations or hearings.) Upon the request of the commission the attorney general, or under his direction, the prosecuting attorney of any county, shall aid in any investigation, hearing or trial had under the laws which the commission is required to administer, and to institute and prosecute all necessary actions or proceedings for the enforcement of such laws, and for the punishment of all violations thereof, arising within the county in which he was elected. (June 2, 1911, 102 v. 225, § 11; 101 v. 400, § 11.)

Section 1465-10. (Rules and regulations.) The commission shall adopt reasonable and proper rules and regulations to govern its procedings and to regulate the mode and manner of all valuations of real or personal property, apportionments, investigations, inspections and hearings not otherwise specifically provided for. (June 2, 1911, 102 v. 225, § 12; 101 v. 401, § 12.)

Section 1465-11. (Conferences.) The commission may confer and meet with officers of other states and officers of the United States on any matter pertaining to its official duties. (June 2, 1911, 102 v. 225, § 13; 101 v. 401, § 13.)

Section 1465-12. (Inspection of books, records, etc.) To carry out the purposes of the laws which it is required to administer, the commission, or any commissioner, or any person or persons employed by the commission for that purpose, shall, upon demand, have the right to inspect books, accounts, records and memoranda of any company, firm, corporation, person, association, co-partnership or public utility, subject to the provisions of such laws, and to examine under oath any officer, agent or employe of any such company, firm, corporation, person, association, co-partnership or public utility. Any person, other than one of such commissioners, who shall make such demand, shall produce his authority to make such inspection. (June 2, 1911, 102 v. 225, § 14; 101 v. 401, § 14.)

Officers of banks may be required to testify concerning their depositors.

Rep. Atty. Gen. 1911-1912, p. 663.

Section 1465-13. (Power to require production of books, etc., by order or subpoena. Penalty.) The commission may require, by order or subpoena, to be served on any such company, firm, corporation, person, association, co-partnership or public utility, in the same manner that a summons is served in a civil action in the court of common pleas, the production, within this state, at such time and place as it may designate, of any books, accounts, papers or records kept by it in any office or place within or without the state of Ohio, or verified copies in lieu thereof, if the commission shall so order, in order that an examination thereof may be made by the commission or under its direction. Any such company, firm, corporation, person, association, co-partnership or public utility, failing or refusing to comply with any such order or subpoena, shall, for each day it so fails or refuses, forfeit and pay into the state treasury a sum of not less than fifty dollars nor more than five hundred dollars. (June 2, 1911, 102 v. 226, § 15; 101 v. 401, § 15.)

Section 1465-14. (Agent.) For the purpose of making any investigation with regard to any company, firm, corporation, person, association, co-partnership or public utility, subject to the provisions of the laws which the commission is required to administer, the commissioner shall have power to appoint, by an order in writing, an agent whose duties shall be prescribed in such order. (June 2, 1911, 102 v. 226, § 16; 101 v. 401, § 16.)

Section 1465-15. (Powers of agent.) In the discharge of his duties such agent shall have every power whatsoever of an inquisitorial nature granted by law to the commission and the same powers as a notary public, with regard to the taking of depositions; and all powers given by law to a notary public relative to depositions are hereby given to such agent. (June 2, 1911, 102 v. 226, § 17; 101 v. 401, § 17.)

Section 1465-16. (Penalty for disclosure of information.) Except in his report to the commission, or when called on to testify in any court or proceeding, any such agent who shall divulge any information acquired by him in respect to the transactions, property or business of any company, firm, corporation, person, association, co-partnership, or public utility, while acting or claiming to act under such order, shall be fined not less than fifty dollars nor more than one hundred dollars, and shall thereafter be disqualified from acting as agent or in any other capacity under the appointment or employment of the commission. (June 2, 1911, 102 v. 226, § 18; 101 v. 401, § 17.)

Section 1465-17. (Decision.) The commission may conduct any number of such investigations, contemporaneously, through different agents, and may delegate to any agent the taking of all testimony bearing upon any investigation or hearing. The decision of the commission shall be based upon its examination of all testimony and records. The recommendations made by an agent shall be advisory only, and shall not preclude the taking of further testimony, if the commission so order, nor further investigation. (June 2, 1911, 102 v. 226, § 19; 101 v. 402, § 18.)

Section 1465-18. (Returns and answers by firm, company, corporation, etc.) Each company, firm, corporation, person, association, co-partnership or public utility, shall furnish the commission in the form of returns prescribed by it all information required by law and all other facts and information, in addition to the facts and information in this act specifically required to be given, which the commission may require to enable it to carry into effect the provisions of the laws which the commission is required to administer, and shall make specific answers to all questions submitted by the commission. (June 2, 1911, 102 v. 226, § 20; 101 v. 402, § 19.)

Section 1465-19. (Reason in writing for failure to answer.) Any such company, firm, corporation, person, association, co-partnership or public utility, receiving from the commission any blanks with directions to fill them, shall cause them to be properly filled out so as to answer fully and correctly each question therein propounded, and in case it is unable to answer any question, it shall, in writing, give a good and sufficient reason for such failure. (June 2, 1911, 102 v. 227, § 21; 101 v. 402, § 20.)

Section 1465-20. (Verification of answers.) The answers to such questions shall be verified under oath by such person or by the president, secretary, superintendent, general manager, principal accounting officer, partner or agent, and returned to the commission at its office, within the period fixed by the commission. (June 2, 1911, 102 v. 227, § 22; 101 v. 402, § 20.)

Section 1465-21. (Who empowered to administer oath.) Each commissioner, the secretary and every agent provided for in this act, for the purposes therein mentioned, shall have power to administer oaths, certify to official acts, issue subpoenas, compel the attendance of witnesses and the production of books, accounts, papers, records, documents and testimony. (June 2, 1911, 102 v. 227, § 23; 101 v. 402, § 22.)

Section 1465-22. (Proceedings for contempt, for refusal or disobedience.) In case of disobedience on the part of any person or persons, to comply with an order of the commission or a commissioner, or subpoena, or on the refusal of a witness to testify to any matter regarding which he may be lawfully interrogated before the commission, or its agents, authorized as provided by law, the court of common pleas of the county in which the person resides, or a judge thereof, on application of a commissioner, shall compel obedience by attachment proceedings as for contempt as in the case of disobedience of the requirements of a subpoena issued from such court or a refusal to testify therein. (June 2, 1911, 102 v. 227, § 24; 101 v. 402, § 22.)

Section 1465-23. (Fees, mileage, etc.) Each officer who
serves a summons or subpoena shall receive the same fees as
a sheriff, and each witness who shall appear before the commission, by its order, shall receive for his attendance the fees
and mileage now provided for witnesses in civil cases in
courts of common pleas, which shall be audited and paid by
the state in the same manner as other expenses are audited
and paid, upon the presentation of proper vouchers approved
by the chairman of the commission. No witness subpoenaed
at the instance of parties other than the commission, shall
be entitled to compensation from the state for attendance
or travel, unless the commission shall certify that his testimony was material to the matter investigated. (June 2,
1911, 102 v. 227, § 25; 101 v. 403, § 23.)

Section 1465-24. (Expenses, witness fees, etc.; how paid.)
A person who shall appear before the commission, by its
order, with respect to the appraisement of property in any
taxing district, shall be allowed and paid out of the treasury of the proper county, if an officer of any such taxing
district or a member of any annual or quadrennial county
board of equalization or county board of revision, or city
board of review, his actual and necessary traveling expenses,
such expenses to be itemized and sworn to by the person
who incurred the expense; and if other than any such
officer or member of any such board, he shall receive for his attendance the fees and mileage provided in the next preceding
section. Such traveling expenses and witness fees shall be
audited and paid out of the county treasury of the proper
county, in the same manner as other expenses are audited
and paid, upon the presentation of a certificate from the
commission certifying to the fact of such attendance. (June
2, 1911, 102 v. 227, § 26.)

Section 1465-25. (Depositions.) In an investigation the
commission, or any party, may cause depositions of witnesses, residing within or without the state, to be taken in
the manner prescribed by law for like depositions in civil
actions in courts of common pleas. (June 2, 1911, 102 v.
228, § 27; 101 v. 403, § 24.)

**Section 1465-26. (Stenographer's copy of testimony and
proceedings shall be received in evidence.)** A transcribed
copy of the evidence and proceedings, or any specific part
thereof, on any investigation, taken by the stenographer appointed by the commission, being certified by such stenographer to be a true and correct transcript of all the testi-

mony on the investigation, or of a particular witness, or of
a specific part thereof, carefully compared by him with his
original notes, and to be a correct statement of the evidence
and proceedings had on such investigations so purporting
to be taken and transcribed, shall be received in evidence
with the same effect as if such reporter were present and
testified to the facts so certified. A copy of such transcript
shall be furnished on demand to any party upon the payment of the fee therefor, as provided for transcripts in
courts of common pleas. (June 2, 1911, 102 v. 228, § 28;
101 v. 403, § 25.)

Only parties to hearings and investigations are entitled to demand
transcripts of evidence. The fee therefor is eight cents per one hundred
words.
Rep. Atty. Gen. 1910-1911, p. 619.

Section 1465-27.   (Production of testimony.)   No person
shall be excused from testifying or from producing accounts,
books and papers in any proceedings based upon or growing
out of any violation of the provisions of the laws which the
commission is required to administer, on the ground or for
the reason that the testimony or evidence, documentary or
otherwise, required of him, may tend to incriminate him or
subject him to penalty or forfeiture, but no person having
so testified shall be prosecuted or subjected to any penalty
or forfeiture for, or on account of any transaction, matter
or thing concerning which he may have testified or produced any documentary evidence; but no person so testifying shall be exempted from prosecution or punishment for
perjury in so testifying. (June 2, 1911, 102 v. 228, § 29; 101
v. 403, § 26.)

Section 1465-28.   (Blanks. Extension of time.)   The
commission shall cause to be prepared suitable blanks for
carrying out the purposes of the laws which it is required
to administer, and, on application, furnish such blanks to
each company, firm, corporation, person, association, co-partnership or public utility, subject thereto.
   The commission, when it deems the same necessary or
advisable, may extend to any corporation or public utility a
further specified time not to exceed ninety days within which
to file any report required by law to be filed with the commission in which event the attaching or taking effect of any
penalty for failure to file such report or pay any tax or fee
shall be extended or postponed accordingly. (June 2, 1911,
102 v. 228, § 30; 101 v. 426, § 109.)

Section 1465-29. (Other information.) If any company, firm, corporation, person, association, co-partnership or public utility, subject to the provisions of this act, fails or refuses to make out and deliver to the commission any statement required by law, or furnish the commission with any information requested, the commission shall inform itself as best it may on the matters necessary to be known in order to discharge its duties. (June 2, 1911, 102 v. 229, § 31; 101 v. 428, § 114.)

Section 1465-30. (Service.) Every order or notice, service of which is required, shall be served upon the person or corporation to be affected thereby, either by personal delivery of a certified copy thereof, or by mailing a certified copy thereof, by registered mail, to the person to be affected thereby, or in case of a corporation, to any officer or agent thereof upon whom a summons may be served. Within the time specified in the order of the commission every person or corporation upon whom it is served, if so required by the order, shall notify the commission, in like manner, whether the terms of the order are accepted and will be obeyed. (June 2, 1911, 102 v. 229, § 32; 101 v. 429, § 118.)

Section 1465-31. (Injunction.) No injunction shall issue suspending or staying any order, determination or direction of the commission, or any action of the auditor of state, treasurer of state, or attorney general, required by law to be taken in pursuance of any such order, determination or direction, but nothing herein shall affect any right or defense in any action to collect any tax or penalty. (June 2, 1911, 102 v. 229, § 33; 101 v. 429, § 119.)

Under this section injunction will not lie to restrain the tax commission from certifying the gross earnings of a railway company to the auditor of state to be used as a basis for an excise tax. Where a constitutional right is infringed, the company has other adequate remedies.

Ohio River, etc., v. Dittey, 12 N. P. n. s. 93 (C. P. 1911).

Before the amendment of 1911 (102 v. 229) it was held that improper taxation of corporations by the tax commission might be enjoined.

Railway v. Poland, 10 N. P. n. s. 617 (1910).

Involuntary payment.

See Ratterman v. Express Co., 49 O. S. 608 (1892).

Western Union Co. v. Mayer, 28 O. S. 521 (1876).

Section 1465-32. (Mandamus.) In addition to the other remedies provided for by law for the prevention and punishment of any violation of the laws which it is required to administer, and the orders of the commission, the provisions of such laws and such orders may upon the application of the commission be enforced by proceedings in mandamus, injunction or other appropriate proceedings. (June 2, 1911, 102 v. 229, § 34; 101 v. 429, § 120.)

Section 1465-33. (Further powers of commission. Board of appraisers and assessors, shall appoint boards of review.) All powers, duties and privileges imposed and conferred upon any state board, which board was abolished or its powers in whole or in part conferred upon the tax commission of Ohio, by an act of the general assembly, passed May 10, 1910, or any power or duty theretofore conferred upon any state or county officer or board, which power and duty by such act was conferred upon such commission, is hereby imposed and conferred upon the commission created by such act.

Provided further that the auditor of state, treasurer of state, attorney general and secretary of state shall constitute a board of appraisers and assessors with the power to appoint boards of review in municipalities as provided in sections fifty-six hundred and eighteen to fifty-six hundred and twenty-four inclusive of the General Code. (June 2, 1911, 102 v. 229, § 35; May 10, 1910, 101 v. 428, § 115.)

This act does not divest county auditors of the power to correct assessments made by them prior to the passage of the act, and before appointment of the tax commission.
Railway v. Edmondson, 13 N. P. n. s. 377; 57 Bull 434; 23 L. D. 33 (C. P. 1912).

Section 1465-34. (Transcript of records for commission.) When called upon by any officer, board or commission, now existing or hereafter created, of the state or any political division thereof, the commission shall furnish any data or information to such officer, board or commission, and shall, so far as possible, aid and assist such officer, board or commission in performing the duties of his or its office. All state, county and local officers shall make and forward to the commission, upon its written order, such transcripts of records, or parts thereof and other information on file in their respective offices or in their possession, as are deemed necessary by the commission to properly and effectually carry into operation the provisions of the laws which the commission is required to administer. (June 2, 1911, 102 v. 230, § 36; 101 v. 428, § 116.)

Section 1465-35. (Report to governor and general assembly.) Annually, on or before the fifteenth day of December, the commission shall make and deliver to the governor a full report of the operation and execution of all laws which it is required to administer, one thousand copies of which shall be printed in book form for the use of the general assembly and the public. The commission shall report to the governor and general assembly its recommendations of such changes and alterations, as in its opinion, should be made in the tax laws of the state. (June 2, 1911, 102 v. 230, § 37; 101 v. 429, § 122.)

Section 1465-36. (Definitions.) The term ''commission'' or the term ''tax commission'' when used in this act or in the laws which the commission is required to administer, means the tax commission of Ohio. The term ''commissioner'' means one of the members of such commission. (June 2, 1911, 102 v. 230, § 38; 101 v. 403, § 27.)

PART X.

CEMETERY ASSOCIATIONS.

Section 3450. (No levy on lots.) No lot held by any individual in a cemetery, in any case shall be levied on or sold on execution. (R. S. Sec. 1469; April 15, 1857, 54 v. 187, § 4; S. & C. 228.)

Section 3461. (Buildings upon grounds of cemetery.) Where the township owns a burial-place within the grounds of a cemetery association, the trustees of the township may levy a tax not exceeding five mills on the dollar of the tax duplicate of the township for the purpose of erecting permanent buildings upon and within such cemetery grounds. (R. S. Sec. 1465-1; April 20, 1893, 90 v. 218, § 1.)

Section 3462. (Application of tax.) When such tax has been assessed and collected it shall be paid to the officers of such cemetery association, and by them applied to the erection of such permanent buildings as in their judgment may be requisite for the accommodation of the patrons of the cemetery. (R. S. Sec. 1465-2; April 20, 1893, 90 v. 218, § 2.)

Section 3463. (Bonds in anticipation of tax.) In anticipation of such tax, the officers of such cemetery association may issue and sell bonds to bear interest at a rate not to exceed six per cent per annum. (R. S. Sec. 1465-3; April 20, 1893, 90 v. 218, § 3.)

Section 3465. (Abandoned burial ground. Removal of bodies and stones.) When any burial ground, public or private, has been abandoned, or when the trustees of a township, or the trustees or directors of a cemetery association, are of the opinion that the further use for burial purposes of any cemetery or burial ground will be detrimental to the public welfare or health, and a cemetery or burial ground in the near vicinity thereof is open for public use, such township trustees in every such case, or, in case of a cemetery association, the trustees or directors thereof, may order such cemetery or burial ground to be discontinued, and provide for the removal of all bodies therein buried, and for the removal of all stones and monuments marking the graves thereof, and for the re-interment of such bodies and the re-erection of such stones and monuments in suitable and public ground in the near vicinity, and pay therefor from the township treasury. They shall before providing for any such removal, first cause notice to be given to the family, friends or kindred of the deceased, if known to them of such order and of the time within which, not less than thirty days, such removal must be made, and that it is desired that such removal be made by the friends or kindred of the dead. If at the expiration of such time such removals have not been made, the trustees or the board, as the case may be, may cause them to be made as hereinbefore provided. May 13, 1910, 101 v. 201; R. S. Sec. 1470-1; March 15, 1876, 73 v. 33, § 1.)

Section 3466. (May sell burial grounds at public sale.) After due notice thereof has been first given in two newspapers of the county, of general circulation, township trustees and trustees and boards of directors of cemetery associations may dispose of, at public sale, and make conveyance of any burial grounds under their control that they have determined to discontinue as burial grounds, but possession thereof shall not be given to a grantee until after the dead therein buried, together with stones and monuments, have been removed as hereinbefore provided. (R. S. Sec. 1470-2; March 15, 1876, 73 v. 33, § 2.)

Section 3467. (Disinterment of body buried in cemetery.) The trustees or board of any cemetery association, or other officers having control and management of a cemetery, shall disinter or issue a permit for disinterment, and deliver any body buried in such cemetery, on application of the next of kin of the deceased, being of full age and sound mind, to such next of kin, on payment of the reasonable cost and expense of disinterment. No such disinterment shall be made during the months of April, May, June, July, August and September, and in no event if the deceased died of a contagious or infectious disease, until a permit has been issued by the local health department. (R. S., Sec. 1470-3; May 14, 1874, 91 v. 231, § 1.)

Brothers and sisters are next of kin of minor children deceased;

but where these brothers and sisters are minors, the parents are next of
kin and competent to make the application.

State, ex rel., v. Shonhoft, 14 C. C. 354; 7 C. D. 716 (1897).

Section 3468.   (Form of application.)   Such application
shall be in writing and shall state the relation of the applicants to the deceased, that the applicants are the next of
kin of the deceased, of full age and sound mind, the disease
of which the deceased died, where the body shall be re-in-
terred, and shall be subscribed and verified by oath.   (R. S.
Sec. 1470-4; May 14, 1874, 91 v. 231, § 2.)

Section 3469.   (Writ of mandamus.)   If such trustees or
board or other officers in charge of the cemetery refuse to
issue a permit for disinterment, there shall be issued by the
court of common pleas of the county wherein the cemetery
is situated, a writ of mandamus requiring such trustees or
board or other officers to issue such permit.   (R. S. Sec.
1470-5; May 14, 1874, 91 v. 231, § 3.)

PART XI.

MISCELLANEOUS PROVISIONS OF THE MUNICIPAL CODE RELAT-
ING TO PRIVATE CORPORATIONS.

Section 3615. (General powers of municipalities.) Each municipal corporation shall be a body politic and corporate, which shall have perpetual succession, may use a common seal, sue and be sued, and acquire property by purchase, gift, devise, appropriation, lease, or lease with the privilege of purchase, for any municipal purpose authorized by law,

and hold, manage and control it and make any and all rules
and regulations, by ordinance or resolution, that may be
required to carry out fully all the provisions of any conveyance, deed or will, in relation to any gift or bequest, or
the provisions of any lease by which it may acquire property. (March 7, 1911, 102 v. 40; January 24, 1908, 99 v. 5,
§ 7; April 27, 1904, 97 v. 504, § 7; October 22, 1902, 96 v.
21, § 7; Bates Stats. § 1536-100.)

Section 3616. (Powers by ordinance or resolution.) All
municipal corporations shall have the general powers mentioned in this chapter, and council may provide by ordinance
or resolution for the exercise and enforcement of them.
(January 24, 1908, 99 v. 5, § 7; 96 v. 26, § 8; 97 v. 504, § 7;
Bates §§ 1536-100, 1536-101; October 22, 1904, 96 v. 21, 26,
§§ 7, 8.)

**Section 3618-1. (Gas; power to purchase. Ten-year
limit.)** That any municipal corporation owning a municipal
gas plant or system of gas distribution shall have the power
to purchase gas, natural or artificial, and to furnish the same
to said municipality and the inhabitants thereof for the purposes of light, power and heat. To carry out the power
herein conferred, any such municipality is hereby authorized
to make and execute a contract to purchase such gas through
its appropriate boards or officers for any period not exceeding ten years, upon the council of such municipality authorizing and directing such contract to be made. Any such
municipality may furnish and supply to its inhabitants any
gas, natural or artificial, so purchased, on such terms and
under such regulations as may be determined by the proper
officers and authorities of said municipality. (March 29,
1910, 101 v. 36.)

Section 3632. (Vehicles, and use of streets.) To regulate the use of carts, drays, wagons, hackney coaches, omni-
buses, automobiles, and every description of carriages kept
for hire or livery stable purposes; to license and regulate
the use of the streets by persons who use vehicles, or solicit
or transact business thereon; to prevent and punish fast
driving or riding of animals, or fast driving or propelling of
vehicles through the public highways; to regulate the transportation of articles through such highways and to prevent
injury to such highways from overloaded vehicles, and to
regulate the speed of interurban, traction and street railway
cars within the corporation. (January 24, 1908, 99 v. 6, § 7i;
97 v. 505, § 7-9; 96 v. 23, § 7-9; Bates § 1536-100.)

Speed ordinances. See § 3781.

In the absence of a speed ordinance the speed must be reasonable in view of all the facts and circumstances.

Cincinnati St. R. Co. v. Lewis, 3 C. C. n. s. 115; 13 C. D. 127 (1901; s. c., 8 N. P. 417; 10 L. D. 53.

A provision in an ordinance that the speed of cars shall not exceed fourteen miles per hour, including stops, requires that at the end of the run the average speed should not have exceeded that rate.

Columbus Ry. v. Connor, 6 C. C. n. s. 361; 17 C. D. 229 (1905).

This section does not authorize a municipality, by penal ordinance, to require interurban cars to stop and take on or discharge passengers.

Townsend v. Circleville, 78 O. S. 122 (1908).

Effect of violation of speed ordinance in negligence cases, see

Ulrich v. Street Ry. Co., 10 C. C. 635; 5 C. D. 111 (1895).

Becker v. Street Ry. Co., 1 N. P. 359; 2 L. D. 137 (1894).

Stephens v. Traction Co., 12 C. C. n. s. 385; 21 L. D. 439 (1909).

Section 3637. (Erection of fences, signs; construction and repair of wires, poles, plants; licensing, house movers, electrical contractors, plumbers, etc.) To regulate the erection of fences, billboards, signs and other structures, within the corporate limits, and to provide for the removal and repair of, insecure billboards, signs and other structures; to regulate the construction and repair of wires, poles, plants and all equipment to be used for the generation and application of electricity; to provide for the licensing of house movers, electrical contractors, plumbers and sewer tappers and vault cleaners. (March 14, 1913, 103 v. 93; January 24, 1908, 99 v. 6, § 7m; 97 v. 506, § 7-13; 96 v. 23, § 7-13; R. S. Sec. 1536-100.)

See Toledo v. Winters, 10 N. P. n. s. 661; 21 L. D. 171 (1910).

Section 3643. (Street cars.) To require the employment of conductors on all street cars within the corporate limits. (January 24, 1908, 99 v. 9, § 7bb; 97 v. 509, § 7-28; 96 v. 25, § 7-28; Bates § 1536-100.)

See Thornhill v. Cincinnati, 4 C. C. 354; 2 C. D. 592 (1890).

A municipality can not, by penal ordinance, prescribe the qualifications of motormen or conductors.

Columbus, etc., Co. v. Columbus, 10 N. P. n. s. 161; 20 L. D. 555; (1910).

Section 3644. (Hot water and steam heating.) To use, or by ordinance grant, for periods not exceeding twenty-five years, the use of, its streets, avenues, alleys, lanes and public places, to lay pipes, conduits, manholes, drains, and other necessary fixtures and appliances, under the surface thereof, to be used for supplying such municipality and its inhabitants with steam or hot water, or both, for heat or power purposes, or both, but in all such grants, such municipal corporations shall reserve the right to regulate, at intervals of not less than five years, the prices which the grantee or grantees may charge for such heat or power. (January 24, 1908, 99 v. 7, § 7r; 97 v. 507, § 7-18; Bates § 1536-100.)

See §§ 614-44 to 614-46.
A similar statute was held constitutional.
Kumler v. Silsbee, 38 O. S. 445 (1882).
Validity of former act containing curative provisions.
Columbus v. Lighting Co., 16 L. D. 311 (1905).
Where a franchise has been granted by the council for steam pipes under sidewalks and such use is made under the direction of the board of public service, the court can not inquire as to the propriety or mode of the use.
Stone v. Cuyahoga Light Co., 9 N. P. n. s. 545; 20 L. D. 130 (1909).
This section does not place restrictions on a natural gas company which furnishes light.
Columbus v. Gas & Fuel Co., 10 N. P. n. s. 305; 21 L. D. 179 (1910).

Section 3645. (Movable and rolling roads.) To use or grant, for periods not exceeding twenty-five years, the use of its streets, avenues, alleys, lanes and public places for the construction of inclined movable or rolling roads, for the conveying or moving of freight, vehicles, animals and other property, and those in charge thereof, upon such terms as the council of the municipal corporation may deem proper, but in all such grants, the municipal corporations shall reserve the right to regulate, at intervals of not less than five years, the prices which the grantee or grantees may charge for the conveying or moving of such freight, vehicles, animals, and other property. No such grant shall be made until there is produced to such council the written consent of the private property owners of more than two-thirds of the feet front of the lots and lands abutting on the street, avenue, alley, lane or public place, or part thereof, upon or over which it is proposed to construct the inclined movable or rolling road. (January 24, 1908, 99 v. 7, § 7r.)

Section 3645-1. (U. S. mail subways.) To use, or by ordinance grant to any person, company or corporation, for periods not exceeding twenty-five years, the use of its streets, avenues, alleys, lanes and public places for the purpose of constructing, laying, maintaining and operating subways and underground conduits, together with manholes and all other necessary appliances for transmitting United States mail matter under or beneath such streets, avenues, alleys, lanes and public places. (April 14, 1910, 101 v. 101.)

Section 3677. (Appropriation of property. Street improvement, etc. Canal improvement. Water supply. Change

of venue. **Street, interurban, suburban railways or terminals,
etc.**) Municipal corporations shall have special power to appropriate, enter upon and hold real estate within their corporate limits. Such power shall be exercised for the purposes, and in the manner provided in this chapter.

1. For opening, widening, straightening, changing the grade of, and extending streets, and all other public places, and for this purpose the corporation may appropriate the right of way across railway tracks and lands held by railway companies, when such appropriation will not unnecessarily interfere with the reasonable use of the property so crossed by such improvement, and for obtaining material for the improvement of streets and other public places;

2. For parks, park entrances, boulevards, market places, and children's playgrounds;

3. For public halls and offices, and for all buildings and structures required for the use of any department;

4. For prisons, workhouses, houses of refuge and correction, and farm schools;

5. For hospitals, pesthouses, reformatories, crematories and cemeteries;

6. For levees, wharves and landings;

7. For bridges, aqueducts, viaducts and approaches thereto;

8. For libraries, university sites and grounds therefor;

9. For constructing, opening, excavating, improving or extending any canal, or water course, located in whole or in part within the limits of the corporation or adjacent and contiguous thereto, and which is not owned in whole or in part by the state, or by a company or individual authorized by law to make such improvement;

10. For sewers, drains, ditches, public urinals, bathhouses, water closets and sewage and garbage disposal plants and farms;

11. For natural and artificial gas, electric lighting, heating and power plants, and for supplying the product thereof;

12. For establishing esplanades, boulevards, park ways, park grounds, and public reservations in, around and leading to public buildings, and for the purpose of reselling such land with reservations in the deeds of such resale as to the future use of such lands, so as to protect public buildings and their environs, and to preserve the view, appearance, light, air and usefulness of public grounds occupied by public buildings and esplanades and parkways leading thereto.

13. For providing for a supply of water for itself and its inhabitants by the construction of wells, pumps, cisterns,

aqueducts, water pipes, dams, reservoirs, reservoir sites and water works, and for the protection thereof; and to provide for a supply of water for itself and its inhabitants, any municipal corporation may appropriate property within or without the limits of the corporation; and for this purpose any such municipal corporation may appropriate in the manner provided in this chapter, any property or right or interest therein, theretofore acquired by any private corporation for any purpose by appropriation proceedings or otherwise. Either party to such appropriation proceedings shall have the same right to a change of venue as is now given by law in the trial of civil actions.

14. For the construction or operation of street, interurban, suburban or other railways or terminals and the necessary tracks, way stations, depots, terminals, workshops, conduits, elevated structures, subways, tunnels, offices, sidetracks, turnouts, machine shops, bridges and other appurtenances for the transportation of persons, packages, express matter, freight and other matter, in, from, into or through the municipal corporation; and for such purpose or purposes any municipal corporation may appropriate any property within or without its corporate limits; any municipal corporation may appropriate any property or right or interest therein theretofore acquired by any private or public utility corporation for any purpose by appropriate proceedings, as well as the right to cross on, over or under any street, avenue, alley, way or public place or part thereof of any other municipality, township or country. (May 3, 1913, 103 v. 496; March 10, 1910, 101 v. 15; April 27, 1908, 99 v. 207, § 10; April 25, 1904, 97 v. 333, § 10; October 22, 1902, 96 v. 26, § 10; Bates §§ 1536-102, 1536-103.)

Right of way across railway tracks. Where a municipal corporation is about to file an application in court for the assessment of compensation for the extension of a street over railway tracks, a suit for injunction may be maintained by the railway company, in which suit it may be determined whether such street extension will unnecessarily interfere with the reasonable use of the railway property.
P. C. C. & St. L. Ry. Co. v. Greenville, 69 O. S. 487 (1903).
See Cleveland, etc., R. Co. v. Akron, 1 C. C. n. s. 174 (1903); s. c.;
    4 C. C. n. s. 632 (1904); affirmed, 74 O. S. 457; s. c., 6 N. P. n.
    s. 81; 18 L. D. 231 (1907).
That the street crossing will inconvenience the railroad company, and cause it additional expense in operation, is no defense, providing the use of the property by the railroad company is not "unnecessarily" interfered with and the municipality acts in good faith.
Railroad Co. v. Akron, 6 N. P. n. s. 81; 18 L. D. 231 (1907).
    Railroad Co. v. Dayton, 23 O. S. 510 (1872).
    Railroad Co. v. Bellaire, 4 W. L. B. 201 (1872).
    Railroad Co. v. Hyde Park, 4 N. P. 296; 7 L. D. 156 (1897).
    A municipality can not open a new street, or extend an existing

street, across a railroad track without acquiring the right to do so
by agreement or appropriation proceedings.

In re Avon Beach, etc., Ry., 3 N. P. n. s. 561, 567; 16 L. D. 87
(C. P. 1905).

Railway Co. v. Troy, 68 O. S. 510 (1903).

Railroad Co. v. Commissioners, 63 O. S. 23 (1900).

The railroad company is entitled to compensation for the cost of a
bridge or viaduct to carry its trains over the street.

Railway Co. v. Troy, 68 O. S. 510 (1903).

Estoppel of railroad company. Where a railroad company obtains
the right to cross certain streets on condition that when it becomes
necessary to open or extend the same it shall grant a right of way, it
is estopped from denying the right to make such opening or extension.

Chicago, etc., Co. v. Hamilton, 3 C. C. 455; 2 C. D. 259 (1888).

Pleading and procedure. See

Toledo, etc., Ry. Co. v. Fostoria, 7 C. C. 293; 4 C. D. 602 (1893);
aff'd, no rep., 56 O. S. 726.

P. C. C. & St. L. Ry. Co. v. Greenville, 69 O. S. 487.

Railroad Co. v. Hyde Park, 4 N. P. 296; 7 L. D. 156 (1897).

Appropriation of railroad property for other purposes.
Public offices and prison.

Railroad Co. v. Belle Center, 48 O. S. 273 (1891).

Parks.

Toledo, etc., Co. v. Toledo, 7 N. P. 285; 5 L. D. 306 (1894).

Ditches.

Railroad Co. v. Commissioners, 63 O. S. 23 (1900).

Lake Erie, etc., Co. v. Seneca Co., 57 Fed. 944 (1893).

Appropriation of private property for railroad use. A municipality can not appropriate private property for the use of a railroad
company.

Morehouse v. Norwalk, 6 W. L. B. 267 (C. P. 1881).

See White v. Cleveland, 12 N. P. n. s. 225 (1911); aff'd, 14 C. C.
n. s. 369.

Title of railway company extinguished when. The title to land
not used or needed for railway purposes is wholly extinguished by the
establishment of a street. But if the land is so used, such use is not
superseded.

Railway Co. v. Railway Co., 5 C. C. n. s. 583; 16 C. D. 180 (1903);
aff'd, no rep., 73 O. S. 364.

Dedication of street by railroad. An intention by a railroad company to dedicate a street is not clearly shown by proof that a way over
its tracks and unenclosed lands was used for forty years by the public,
when during the entire time the way was maintained by the company
and was used by its patrons, and the use by the public was merely
permissive.

Railroad v. Roseville, 76 O. S. 108 (1907).

**Section 3699-1. (Municipal leases. Terms, fixed by ordi-
nance.)** All municipal corporations shall have power to construct, maintain, use and lease, or grant the right to construct,
maintain and use, any pier, dock, wharf or landing for use
by passenger or freight carriers, with buildings and appurtenances necessary to such use, on any land belonging to the

corporation, and on and over any made or submerged land, whose title is in the corporation or the state of Ohio, in front of land belonging to the corporation. All municipal corporations shall also have power to construct, maintain, use and lease, or grant the right to construct, maintain and use, on and over any land belonging to the corporation and such made or submerged land, any steam, electric or street railroad tracks and appurtenances, necessary for the use of any pier, dock, wharf or landing as aforesaid. Such lease or grant may be made by the passage of an ordinance fixing its terms and conditions and by the acceptance thereof by the lessee or grantee. Land belonging to the corporation shall be construed to include also any land heretofore or hereafter appropriated or held by the corporation for streets, parks or other public purposes; but this section shall not be construed to authorize the taking of reversionary or other property rights without such compensation and proceedings as are authorized by law. (May 17, 1910, 101 v. 236.)

This section is constitutional.
White v. Cleveland, 14 C. C. n. s. 369 (1911); affirming 12 N. P. n. s. 225; 21 L. D. 311.

Section 3700. (Procedure when for passenger railroad station.) When a municipal corporation owns real estate suitable for the location of a passenger railroad station, and council by ordinance declares that it is necessary that such land be devoted to such use, the municipality may sell, lease, or exchange such land to such railroad or railroads for such purpose in the manner provided in the next section. (March 31, 1906, 98 v. 165, § 24.)

Section 3701. (What ordinance shall contain; election.) An ordinance authorizing the mayor of the municipality to deed or lease the land shall be passed. In the ordinance council shall fix by metes and bounds the amount of land to be sold, leased or exchanged, the quantity of interest sold, leased or exchanged, and the consideration to be paid or exchanged therefor by such railroad or railroads, and in the ordinance shall call thereon a special election, to be held upon a day fixed by such ordinance, not less than thirty days from the passage thereof. (March 31, 1906, 98 v. 165, § 24.)

Section 3702. (How such election conducted.) A majority of all the votes cast on such proposition shall be necessary to its ratification. When so ratified, the ordinance shall be effective, and the mayor shall proceed to execute a deed of conveyance or lease of the property as therein pro-

vided. In holding such special election, the provisions of
law for submission of the question of issuing bonds in excess
of four per cent of the taxable property of the municipality,
shall apply. (March 31, 1906, 98 v. 165, § 24.)

Section 3714. (Council to have care, supervision and control.) Municipal corporations shall have special power to
regulate the use of the streets, to be exercised in the manner
provided by law. The council shall have the care, supervision
and control of public highways, streets, avenues, alleys, sidewalks, public grounds, bridges, aqueducts, and viaducts, within the corporation, and shall cause them to be kept open, in
repair, and free from nuisance. (October 22, 1902, 96 v. 26,
§ 9; 96 v. 31, § 28; Bates §§ 1536-131, 1536-102.)

Additional burdens. Rights of abutting owners.

Railroads. See note to § 8765.
Street and interurban railways. See note to § 9105.
Gas pipes. See note to § 9320.
Telegraph and telephone lines. See notes to §§ 9170 and 9178.

Index to note.

I. Miscellaneous.
II. Franchises generally.
   A. Must emanate from legislature.
   B. Defective franchise. Validity of curative act.
   C. Ordinance granting; requisites.
      1. Must contain but one subject.
      2. Reading on three different days.
      3. Publication.
   D. By grant of franchise, municipality not divested of
      control of part of street occupied by street railway.
   E. Permission to occupy streets, when acted upon, a
      vested property right in the nature of a franchise
      or easement.
   F. Franchise as a contract.
   G. Council has no power to grant exclusive franchise,
      in absence of power clearly conferred.
   H. Grant silent as to duration. Franchise continues by
      consent of parties.
   I. Grants of franchises; how construed.
      1. Rule of strict construction.
      2. Exception. Provisions for forfeiture.
      3. Conditions precedent or subsequent.
      4. Provisions as to time for beginning or completing construction work.
   J. Invalid conditions in valid franchise. That grantee
      shall not exercise one of its corporate powers.
   K. Invalid franchises.
      1. Injunction against exercise of.
      2. Limitation of action to enjoin.
      3. What defects render franchise invalid.
      4. Estoppel of municipality permitting expenditures
         in reliance upon grant.
      5. Estoppel of grantee.

I. MISCELLANEOUS.

This section does not authorize a municipality, by penal ordinance, to prescribe the qualifications of motormen and conductors.

Columbus, etc., Co. v. Columbus, 10 N. P. n. s. 161; 20 L. D. 555 (1910).

This section authorizes a municipality to establish regulations for the operation of a street railway, which promote public safety, and which do not unreasonably interfere with its franchise.

Millcreek, etc., Co. v. St. Bernard, 8 N. P. 288; 11 L. D. 454 (1901).

The control of streets is vested exclusively in the council. Directions by the mayor, regarding improvements, are unauthorized.

Cincinnati, etc., Ry. Co. v. Carthage, 36 O. S. 631 (1881).

II. FRANCHISES.

Electric light, gas and water companies.

§§ 3982 to 3994 and 9320 to 9338, 9192 to 9198.

For street and interurban railways, §§ 3768 to 3780 and 9100 to 9149.

Railroads, § 8763.

Telegraph and telephone companies, §§ 9170 to 9191.

A. **Must emanate from legislature.** A franchise must emanate either directly or indirectly from the legislature.

State v. Cincinnati Gas, etc., Co., 18 O. S. 262, 291 (1868).

State v. Railway, 1 C. C. n. s. 145; 14 C. D. 609 (1903); aff'd no rep., 73 O. S. 363.

A municipality has no inherent power to grant a franchise to a street railway.

Woodland Ave., etc., Co. v. Cleveland, 7 N. P. n. s. 161; 17 L. D. 763.

Raynolds v. Cleveland, 2 C. C. n. s. 139; 14 C. D. 215; aff'd no rep. 76 O. S. 619.

Grant under statute subsequently declared unconstitutional. A franchise granted under a statute which had been upheld by the supreme court, but was subsequently held to be unconstitutional, is valid.

State v. Oakwood St. Ry. Co., 11 C. C. n. s. 263; 20 C. D. 632 (1908); aff'd, no rep., 81 O. S. 502.

B. Defective franchise. Validity of curative act.

The legislature may by a subsequent law validate acts or contracts made ultra vires by a municipality, if the act might have been authorized by prior law.

    Mill Creek, etc., Ry. Co. v. Carthage, 18 C. C. 216; 9 C. D. 833 (1899);
        aff'd, no rep., 62 O. S. 636.
    See Cincinnati, etc., Co. v. Horstman, 72 O. S. 93, 666 (1905).
    Burgett v. Norris, 25 O. S. 308 (1874).
    Kumler v. Silsbee, 38 O. S. 445 (1882).
    State v. Hoffman, 35 O. S. 435 (1880).

C. Ordinance granting. Requisites of.

    Generally, see G. C. §§ 4224 to 4235.
    Street railways, § 3768 et seq.

1. Must contain but one subject. "No ordinance, resolution or by-law shall contain more than one subject which shall be clearly expressed in its title . . ."
    G. C. § 4226.
Where a granting ordinance contains but one subject matter, which is clearly expressed in its title, other provisions contained in the ordinance which are merely incident to the main subject matter do not render the ordinance invalid.

    Belle v. Glenville, 5 C. C. n. s. 461; 17 C. D. 181 (1904); affirmed,
        no rep., 73 O. S. 392, 397; 75 O. S. 574.

A provision in a franchise for a waterworks system, for a lease of the system to the municipality and for an option to purchase, does not render the ordinance invalid as containing more than one subject.

    Moore v. Elmore, 13 N. P. n. s. 651; 23 L. D. 50 (C. P. 1910).

2. Reading on three different days.

    G. C. §4224.
    Smith v. Columbus, etc., Co., 8 N. P. 1; 10 L. D. 441.
    Contra under former law, State v. Oakwood St. R. Co., 11 C. C. n. s.
        263; 20 C. D. 632 (1908); aff'd, no rep., 81 O. S. 502.

3. Publication. The duty of publishing an ordinance rests upon the municipality. In an action to oust a street railway company from its franchise, the burden of proof as to defective publication rests upon the municipality.

    State v. Oakwood St. Ry. Co., 11 C. C. n. s. 263; 20 C. D. 632
        (1908); aff'd, no rep., 81 O. S. 502.
Estoppel by recital in ordinance as to publication.

    Raynolds v. Cleveland, 8 C. C. n. s. 278; 18 C. D. 463 (1906); aff'd,
        no rep., 77 O. S. 631.

D. By grant of franchise municipality not divested of control of part of street occupied by street railway. A municipality is not divested of its control of streets by the grant of a franchise to a street railway company, by the terms of which the company is required to keep in repair that part of the streets between the rails, and which further provides that failure to comply with the terms of the grant, or with any general ordinances of the municipality regulating the use of the streets, should render the company liable for damages.

    Columbus v. Street Railroad Co., 45 O. S. 98 (1887).
    Gas Co. v. Columbus, 50 O. S. 65.
    See New Orleans, etc., Co. v. Drainage Commission, 197 U. S. 453,
        462.
    Union, etc., Co. v. Railway Co., 14 N. P. n. s. 171 (1913).

E. **Permission to occupy streets, when acted upon, a vested property right in the nature of a franchise or easement.** When accepted by the grantee, and acted upon, a grant of the right to occupy streets for a street railway is more than a license; "it is a vested property right, in the nature of a franchise or easement in or to the particular portion of the street designated in the grant itself."

> Hamilton, etc., Traction Co. v. Hamilton, etc., Transit Co., 69 O. S. 402, 410 (1903).

F. **Franchise as a contract.** The grant of a right to construct street railway tracks in the streets of a municipality, when accepted by the grantee, is a contract, which can not be rescinded by one party without consent of the other.

> Cincinnati Street Railway Co. v. Smith, 29 O. S. 291 (1876).
> Columbus v. Street Railroad Co., 45 O. S. 98 (1887).
> Cincinnati, etc., Ry. Co. v. Carthage, 36 O. S. 631 (1881)
> Cleveland v. Cleveland City Railway Co., 194 U. S. 517, 534 (1904).
> Hamilton, etc., Co. v. Hamilton, etc. Co., 69 O. S. 402, 410 (1903).
> Hattersly v. Waterville, 4 C. C. n. s. 242; 16 C. D. 226 (1904); affirmed, no rep., 74 O. S. 446.
> See also, Columbus v. Columbus Gas Co., 76 O. S. 309 (1907).

The same rule applies to a renewal grant.

> Street Ry. v. Cleveland, 7 N. P. n. s. 161; 17 L. D. 763.

And to a grant by county commissioners.

> State, ex rel., v. C. E. Ry. Co., 15 C. C. 200; 8 C. D. 474 (1897).

A franchise can not be abrogated by the vacation of the street.

> Union, etc., Co. v. Railway Co., 14 N. P. n s. 171 (1913).

G. **Council has no power to grant exclusive franchise, in the absence of power clearly conferred.** The council of a municipality can not grant an exclusive franchise in its streets in the absence of power expressly conferred upon the municipality by the legislature, or so far necessary to the execution of express powers as to make its existence free from doubt.

> Columbus v. Columbus Gas Co., 76 O. S. 309, 339 (1907).
> State, ex rel., v. Cincinnati Gas, etc., Co., 18 O. S. 262 (1868); approved in 115 U. S. 659.
> State ex rel., v. Hamilton, 47 O. S. 52, 70, 71 (1890).
> Cincinnati St. R. R. Co. v. Smith, 29 O. S. 291 (1876).

But the grantee of a franchise for a street railway over a right of way already occupied by a street railway, under a prior franchise, can not, without appropriation proceedings, take possession of the right of way, where the new use will materially interfere with and abridge the use of the prior franchise.

> Hamilton, etc., Co. v. Hamilton, etc., Co., 69 O. S. 402, 409 (1903).
> Isom v. Low Fare Ry. Co., 10 C. C. n. s. 89, 101; 19 C. D. 583 (1907); aff'd, no rep., 77 O. S. 638.

H. **Grant silent as to duration. Franchise continues merely by consent of parties.** Where the grant is silent as to its duration, the franchise is not perpetual, but exists only so long as the parties mutually agree thereto. The grantee may wholly withdraw from the exercise of its franchise.

> East Ohio Gas Co. v. Akron, 81 O. S. 33 (1909).
> Compare State, ex rel., v. Columbus Ry. Co., 1 C. C. n. s. 145; 14 C. D. 609 (1903); aff'd, no rep., 73 O. S. 363.
> State v. Northern, etc., Co., 1 Ct. of Ap. — (1913).

I. **Grants of franchises; how construed.**

1. **Rule of strict construction.** Every grant in derogation of the

rights of the public in the streets will be construed strictly against the grantee and liberally in favor of the public, and never extended beyond its express terms when not indispensable to give effect to the grant.

Railroad Co. v. Defiance, 52 O. S. 262, 307 (1895).

East Ohio Gas Co. v. Akron, 81 O. S. 33, 52 (1909).

Cleveland Electric Railway Co. v. Cleveland, 204 U. S. 116 (1907).

Columbus v. Columbus Gas Co., 76 O. S. 339 (1907).

Central Trust Co. v. Municipal Traction Co., 7 O. L. R. 413 (1909).

2. Exception. Provisions for forfeiture.

Toledo v. Toledo Ry. & Light Co., 2 C. C. n. s. 97; 15 C. D. 441 (1903).

3. Conditions precedent or subsequent. Where the conditions of a franchise do not clearly appear to be conditions precedent, they will be regarded as conditions subsequent.

State, ex rel., v. Boyce, 43 O. S. 46 (1885).

Toledo v. Toledo Ry. & Light Co., 2 C. C. n. s. 97, 105; 15 C. D. 441 (1903).

4. Provisions as to time for beginning or completing construction work. A requirement that the road be completed within a specified time does not prevent the laying of additional switches, etc., thereafter.

Chambers v. C. & S. W. Tr. Co., 5 C. C. n. s. 298; 17 C. D. 193 (1904); aff'd, no rep., 73 O. S. 348.

Where work is delayed by an injunction suit, involving the validity of the franchise, the time for commencing work, as required by the ordinance, should be computed from the date of judgment in the injunction suit.

State, ex rel., v. Boyce, 43 O. S. 46 (1885).

Where a street railway grant required the road to be in operation within six months after the city had completed certain grading, the completion of such grading dates, not from acceptance of work by city from contractor, but from time when the street so graded is in condition for railway to be safely built thereon.

Toledo v. Toledo Ry. & Light Co., 2 C. C. n. s. 97; 15 C. D. 441 (1903).

J. Invalid conditions in valid franchise. That grantee shall not exercise one of its corporate powers.

A condition in a franchise prohibiting the grantee corporation from exercising one of its corporate powers is invalid.

A provision, in an ordinance granting a franchise to a natural gas company, that natural gas shall not be furnished for illuminating purposes, but for heat and power only, is void, and the company may be compelled to furnish natural gas for illuminating purposes.

Springfield v. Springfield Gas Co., 12 C. C. n. s. 392; 21 C. D. 446 (1907); affirmed, no rep., 81 O. S. 537.

See comment, 58 Bull. 125.

Condition in franchise for a street railway that it should not transport freight held invalid.

State v. Dayton Traction Co., 18 C. C. 490; 10 C. D. 212 (1899); affirmed, 64 O. S. 272.

K. Invalid franchises.

1. Injunction against exercise of.

See notes to §§ 9101 and 9105.

2. Limitation of action to enjoin.

See Defiance Water Co. v. Defiance, 68 O. S. 520 (1903).

Defiance v. McGonigale, 150 Fed. 689 (1907); affirming 140 Fed. 621.

3. What defects render franchise invalid. To render a grant invalid the defects or irregularities must be in some respect which is jurisdictional to the grant, or of such a nature that equity and justice require interference by the courts.

Sloane v. People's, etc., Ry. Co., 7 C. C. 84; 3 C. D. 674 (1891).

Defects in a street railway franchise can not be cured by an amendment to the granting ordinance which merely sets forth the facts as to the publication of notice before bids were received, and declares that the publication was sufficient to meet the requirements of the granting ordinance.

Raynolds v. Cleveland, 8 C. C. n. s. 278; 18 C. D. 463 (1906);
   aff'd on the ground of laches, 77 O. S. 631.

Invalid conditions, not constituting moving consideration for the grant, do not invalidate grant; when.

See Columbus v. Federal Gas & Fuel Co., 2 N. P. n. s. 277 (1903);
   aff'd, no rep., 72 O. S. 632.

4. Estoppel of municipality permitting expenditures in reliance on grant. Where the grantee of a franchise has expended a large amount of money in reliance thereon, a suit in equity to enjoin the enjoyment thereof, on the ground that the contract was *ultra vires*, can not be maintained. The municipality will be left to its remedy at law.

Pugh v. Edison, etc., Co., 19 C. C. 594; 10 C. D. 573 (1900).

Columbus v. Federal Gas & Fuel Co., 2 N. P. n. s. 277 (1903);
   aff'd, no rep., 72 O. S. 632.

Raynolds v. Cleveland, 8 C. C. n. s. 278; 18 C. D. 463 (1906);
   aff'd, no rep., 77 O. S. 631.

Darby v. Norwood, 4 O. L. R. 536; 17 L. D. 253 (1906).

Mill Creek, etc., Ry. Co. v. Carthage, 18 C. C. 216; 9 C. D. 833
   (1899); aff'd, no rep., 62 O. S. 636.

See Bunning v. Cincinnati St. Ry. Co., 1 C. C. 323; 1 C. D. 178
   (1886).

Mt. Vernon v. State, 71 O. S. 428 (1904).

Detwiler v. Toledo, etc., Co., 6 N. P. 485; 8 L. D. 166.

Estoppel by recital in ordinance as to publication of notice.

Raynolds v. Cleveland, 8 C. C. n. s. 278; 18 C. D. 463 (1906);
   aff'd, no rep., 77 O. S. 631.

5. Estoppel of grantee. A gas company which accepts franchise ordinances, and lays and maintains pipes in the streets pursuant thereto, is estopped from questioning the validity of the ordinances.

Columbus v. Federal Gas & Fuel Co., 13 N. P. n. s. 394 (C. P.
   1910).

L. Forfeiture of franchises.

1. In general. Must be declared by council, before suit will lie.

Toledo v. Toledo Ry. & Light Co., 2 C. C. n. s. 97; 15 C. D. 441
   (1903).

The declaration of forfeiture must be unconditional.

State v. Northern Ohio, etc., Co., 1 Ct. of Ap. — (1913).

Judicial declaration of forfeiture not essential, when ordinance authorizes municipality to remove tracks.

Stewart v. Ashtabula, 36 W. L. B. 46 (1896).

Stewart v. Ashtabula, 98 Fed. 516, 520 (1899).

But when the right to remove tracks is not reserved in the grant, the right to remove tracks must be exercised by due process of law.

Mill Creek, etc., Co. v. Carthage, 18 C. C. 216; 9 C. D. 833 (1899);
   aff'd, no rep., 62 O. S. 636.

Cleveland, etc., Co. v. Cleveland, 4 N. P. 21; 6 L. D. 33.

Akron, etc., Co. v. Bedford, 6 N. P. 276; 8 L. D. 142 (1899).

Forfeiture must be expressly provided for in the franchise. No conditions of forfeiture can be implied.

State v. Northern Ohio, etc., Co., 1 Ct. of Ap. — (1913).

The franchise of an interurban railroad granted by county commissioners can not be forfeited because excessive rates of fare are charged. The remedy for unreasonable charges is by complaint to the public service commission.

State v. Northern Ohio, etc., Co., 1 Ct. of Ap. — (1913).

Notice must be given as a condition precedent to forfeiture, where the franchise ordinance provides that failure to comply with its terms and conditions, after twenty days' notice from the council, shall operate as a forfeiture.

Akron v. Northern Ohio, etc., Co., 6 C. C. n. s. 445; 17 C. D. 536 (1905); aff'd, no rep., 75 O. S. 565.

Forfeiture for delay in construction.

State, ex rel., v. Boyce, 43 O. S. 46 (1886).

Toledo v. Toledo Ry. & Light Co., 2 C. C. n. s. 97; 15 C. D. 441 (1903).

A forfeiture may be waived by the municipality and neither a competing company nor an abutting owner may bring suit to enforce the forfeiture and thus prevent the municipality from exercising its right of waiver.

Hamilton, etc., Co. v. Hamilton, etc., Co., 5 C. C. 319; 3 C. D. 158 (1890).

Barney v. Mt. Adams, etc., Co., 30 W. L. B. 286.

See Moore v. Elmore, 13 N. P. n. s. 651; 23 L. D. 50 (1910).

2. Defenses. Compliance with terms of franchise delayed or prevented by injunction.

State, ex rel., v. Boyce, 43 O. S. 46 (1886).

State v. Cincinnati, etc., Co., 6 C. C. n. s. 167 (1905).

M. Abandonment of franchise. The failure for over twenty years to operate a railway on certain streets raises a presumption of abandonment of the grant as to such streets.

Louisville Trust Co. v. Cincinnati, 76 Fed. 296 (1896).

N. Expired franchise.

1. Rights of corporation in streets. After the expiration of its franchise, a gas company has no right to further use of the streets without a new grant. In making such new grant the municipality is not limited to regulating the price of gas but may impose other reasonable regulations.

Columbus v. Columbus Gas Co., 76 O. S. 331 (1907).

The municipality may require the company to remove its equipment from the streets within a reasonable time.

Detroit United Ry. v. Detroit, 229 U. S. 39 (1913); affirming 156 Mich. 106.

Right of telephone or telegraph company to renewal of franchise.

See State v. Telephone Co., 14 C. C. 273; 7 C. D. 536 (1897); § 9178.

2. Title to property. After the expiration of a franchise of a street railway company, the title to the rails, poles, etc., is in the company. The right to take possession of such property can not, by ordinance, be conferred upon another company.

C. E. Ry. Co. v. Cleveland, 204 U. S. 116 (1907).

3. Duty to continue service. After the expiration of its contracts with a municipality, a gas company may wholly withdraw therefrom. It is under no obligation to continue service.

East Ohio Gas Co. v. Akron, 81 O. S. 33, 56 (1909).

4. Renewal of franchise as surrender of rights and obligations under prior franchise.

See Cleveland v. C. C. Ry. Co., 194 U. S. 517 (1904).

C. E. Ry. Co. v. Cleveland, 137 Fed. 111; 3 O. L. R. 75 (1905); aff'd, 204 U. S. 116 (1907).

O. Remedies.

1. Injunction against street railway involving validity of franchise.

See notes to §§ 9101 and 9105.

2. Of muncipality to compel performance of contract obligations. The solicitor may, under G. C. § 4311 et seq. (R. S. § 1777), bring suit in the name of the municipality to enjoin a public utility company from violating its obligations to the municipality and to compel it to perform its duty.

Gaslight Co. v. Zanesville, 47 O. S. 35 (1889).

Springfield v. Springfield Gas Co., 12 C. C. n. s. 392; 21 C. D. 446 (1907); aff'd, no rep., 81 O. S. 537.

Milford v. C. M. & L. Tr. Co., 4 C. C. n. s. 191; 16 C. D. 271 (1904); aff'd, no rep., 71 O. S. 529.

Toledo v. N. W., etc., Gas Co., 5 C. C. 557; 3 C. D. 273 (1890); affirming 6 N. P. 531; 8 L. D. 277.

Specific performance is not a proper remedy.

Matthews v. So. Ohio Tr. Co., 5 C. C. n. s. 179; 15 C. D. 652 (1903); aff'd, no rep., 70 O. S. 436.

Nor is mandamus.

State, ex rel., v. Cleveland El. Ry. Co., 15 C. C. 200; 8 C. D. 474 (1897).

See State v. Union Gas & Electric Co., 14 N. P. n. s. 97 (1913).

Negligent operation of system causing injury to municipal water pipes may be enjoined.

Dayton v. City Ry. Co., 6 C. C. n. s. 41; 16 C. D. 736 (1904).

It is probable that quo warranto will lie to oust a railway company from the exercise of the franchise, the terms of which it has violated.

State v. Toledo Ry. & L. Co., 3 C. C. n. s. 285; 13 C. D. 603 (1902); reversed, no rep., 73 O. S. 356.

State v. Traction Co., 18 C. C. 490 (1899); aff'd, 64 O. S. 272.

State v. Oakwood St. Ry., 11 C. C. n. s. 263, 265; 20 C. D. 632 (1908); aff'd, no rep., 81 O. S. 502.

State v. Cincinnati, etc., Co., 6 C. C. n. s. 167 (1905).

State v. Telephone Co., 11 C. C. 55; 5 C. D. 311 (1895).

Ohio v. Railway Co., 53 O. S. 189 (1895).

A municipality, having granted a franchise for a street railway including all necessary switches, etc., can not by force prevent the construction of a switch on the ground that it is unnecessary or that the railway has not complied with the terms of the franchise. It can not take the law into its own hands, but must seek its legal remedy.

Akron, etc., Ry. v. Bedford, 6 N. P. 276; 8 L. D. 142 (1899).

Cleveland City Ry. v. Cleveland, 4 N. P. 21; 6 L. D. 33.

3. Of municipality, where streets used without franchise. A street railway company occupying streets without a franchise may be treated as a trespasser, or as committing a nuisance, and may be enjoined under G. C. § 4311.

Rogers v. Railway Co., 12 L. D. 136 (1901).

County commissioners may recover damages under G. C. § 2424 from a street railway occupying a county road without a franchise.

Railway v. Commissioners, 56 O. S. 1 (1897).

4. Forfeiture of deposit, made by grantee of franchise, as security for performance. A deposit made by the successful bidder for a street railway franchise, to secure performance, may, on total failure to construct the railway within the specified time, and on abandonment of the enterprise, be forfeited as liquidated damages.

Hattersly v. Waterville, 4 C. C. n. s. 242; 16 C. D. 226 (1904); aff'd, no rep., 74 O. S. 266.

5. Remedy of holder of franchise. The holder of a franchise may enjoin acts of the municipality, other public service companies, or individuals which materially and injuriously interfere with the exercise of the franchise, or which violate contract obligations.

Hamilton, etc., Traction Co. v. Hamilton, etc. Transit Co., 69 O. S. 402 (1903).

Cleveland v. Cleveland City Ry. Co., 194 U. S. 517 (1904).

Millcreek, etc., R. Co. v. Carthage, 18 C. C. 216; 9 C. D. 833 (1899); affirmed, 62 O. S. 636.

Millcreek, etc., R. Co. v. St. Bernard, 8 N. P. 288; 11 L. D. 454 (1901).

Woodland Ave., etc., Co. v. Cleveland, 7 N. P. n. s. 161; 17 L. D. 763.

Suit may be brought in federal court where the acts of the municipality violate contract obligations.

Cleveland v. Cleveland City Ry. Co., 194 U. S. 517 (1904).

Where a gas company laid pipes in a street, under a franchise, and subsequently the street was vacated and the abutting owner, a railroad company, changed the grade of the former street in order to lay tracks, and in so doing exposed the gas pipes, and made it necessary that the same be relaid, the railroad company is liable to the gas company for the cost thereof.

Union, etc., Co. v. Cincinnati, etc., Ry. Co., 14 N. P. n. s. 171 (1913).

6. Remedy of third persons under contracts. A street railway company may be enjoined from increasing fares in violation of a contract with private parties.

Humphrey Co. v. Cleveland Ry. Co., 9 N. P. n. s. 609 (1910).

But contracts with a street railway company are made in contemplation of existing laws and ordinances.

Cemetery v. Cincinnati St. Ry. Co., 11 C. C. n. s. 429; 21 C. C. 429 (1908).

7. Remedy of citizen to obtain service. A citizen may, by mandamus, compel a public service corporation to furnish him service in compliance with the terms of its franchise.

State v. Union Gas & El. Co., 14 N. P. n. s. 97 (1913).

But citizens can not maintain an action at law for failure to furnish service.

Blunk v. Dennison, etc., Co., 71 O. S. 250 (1904).

STREET RAILROADS.

See § 9100 et seq.

Section 3748. (Tax levy therefor; railway companies to pay portion of cost.) To provide a fund to pay all or part of the cost of such sprinkling, the board or officer having charge of the repair of streets in the corporation, each year may estimate the cost thereof, and cause to be levied a tax therefor upon the general tax duplicate of the corporation, in the same manner and subject to the same conditions as other levies for municipal purposes, except that the levy may be in addition to the amount authorized for municipal purposes. Upon such estimate, the levy shall be made by the council in the corporation. Street railroad companies operating within such corporation shall annually pay into the treasury of the municipal corporation one cent per lineal foot of track upon sprinkled streets as their part of the cost of such sprinkling. (95 v. 448, § 4; R. S. Bates § 1536-175.)

Section 3749. (Council may require street railway company to sprinkle its right of way.) The council of a municipality by resolution may require any interurban or street railway company to sprinkle with water its right of way on any street, alley or public highway, or any portion thereof lying within the limits of the municipality. (February 9, 1906, 98 v. 5, § 1; Bates § 1536-175a.)

Section 3750. (Municipality may contract, when. Costs and penalty; a lien.) Upon failure of any interurban or street railway company after sixty days' notice to the person having charge or management of such interurban or street railway company in such municipality, to comply with the provisions of such resolution, the municipality may do such sprinkling or contract therefor, through its proper officials in accordance with the laws relating to contracts, and the cost thereof shall be charged against such interurban or street railway company so directed to sprinkle, and shall be a lien upon all the real estate and leasehold interest of such interurban or street railway company within the county wherein such municipality is situate, and such charge and cost together with a penalty of twenty-five dollars for each and every day of failure on the part of such interurban or street railway company to sprinkle as required, may be collected in any court of competent jurisdiction or the lien enforced in the manner provided by law. All charges, costs and penalties collected under the provisions of this section shall be paid into the general fund of the municipality to be disposed of as the council thereof may direct. (February 9, 1906, 98 v. 5, § 2; April 11, 1911, 102 v. 48; R. S. Bates § 1536-175b.)

LIGHTING BRIDGES AND RAILROADS.

Section 3762. (Council may require bridge or railway to be lighted.) When deemed necessary by the council of a municipality to have a bridge or railway, located in whole or in part in such corporation, owned, possessed, or operated by an individual, company, association or corporation, or any portion thereof, lighted, the council shall pass an ordinance for that purpose, requiring such individual, company, association, or corporation, to light such bridge or railway within a specified time, but it shall not require such railway or portion thereof to be lighted with electric arc lights. (R. S. Sec. 2494; May 7, 1902, 95 v. 419; March 23, 1872, 69 v. 47, § 429; R. S. Bates § 1536-175.)

This act is constitutional, being a police regulation.
C. H. & D. R. R. Co. v. Sullivan, 32 O. S. 152 (1877).
C. C. C. & St. L. Ry. Co. v. St. Bernard, 15 C. C. 588; 8 C. D. 385 (1898).
This section applies only to steam railroads. A street or interurban railway can not be compelled to light its bridge or railroad.
Ohio Electric Railway v. Ottawa, 85 O. S. 229 (1912); reversing 13 C. C. n. s. 562; 22 C. D. 197.
A company operating a railroad, the track of which extends within the municipality, is subject to this act, although it is neither the owner nor lessee.
C. H. & D. R. R. Co. v. Bowling Green, 57 O. S. 336 (1897) affirming 9 C. C. 524; 6 C. D. 531.
No notice to the railway company of the intention of the council to pass an ordinance is required. The only notice provided is under § 3764.
C. C. C. & St. L. Ry. Co. v. St. Bernard, 19 C. C. 299; 10 C. D. 415 (1898).
See also Ravenna v. Penna. Co., 45 O. S. 118, 123 (1887).

Section 3763. (Specifications in ordinance. Removal of lights and fixtures obstructing view of fixed signal.) The ordinance shall specify the manner in which such bridge or railway shall be lighted, the number and style of lamp posts, gas posts, electric lights or other lights and fixtures, and the time such lights shall be kept burning in each twenty-four hours; but no such lights, poles or fixtures, nor any lights, poles or fixtures, located by any municipal corporation on its streets, alleys or public grounds shall be required to be so placed as to interfere with a clear view of any fixed signal used in the operation of such railroad from such points thereon as such view is required for safe operation. And all lights, poles or fixtures heretofore placed so as to interfere with such clear view shall, within a reasonable time, be re-located to conform to this act. Provided, however, that nothing herein contained shall be construed as excusing any railway company from lighting its bridges and tracks, when required so to do or from paying any reasonable assessment or charge therefor. (May 3, 1913, 103 v. 470; April 13, 1894, 91 v. 147; May 7, 1869, 66 v. 220, § 430.)

The municipality has authority to prescribe the kind of light that shall be employed, and where an electric light plant is in operation within such city or village lighting its streets and furnishing light to its inhabitants, an ordinance is not unreasonable because it requires a railroad company to use the particular kind of lamp and illuminating material in use for lighting the streets of such municipality.
> Railway Co. v. Bowling Green, 57 O. S. 336 (1897); affirming 9 C. C. 524; 6 C. D. 531.
> See also s. c., 10 C. C. 63; 4 C. D. 39.

An ordinance under this section should receive a reasonable construction. The instrument should be reasonably certain in its requirements, but no particular form of words is necessary. It will not be held defective as failing to fix a specified time for the performance of such requirement by the company, if its language, taking the ordinance altogether, is sufficiently definite to inform the company that such lighting is required to be done, how and when it is to be done.
> St. Mary's v. Railroad Co., 60 O. S. 136 (1899); reversing 14 C. C. 202; 7 C. D. 661.

A requirement that the company proceed to do the lighting by electricity within twenty days after notice of the passage of the ordinance is not necessarily unreasonable.
> St. Mary's v. Railroad Co., 60 O. S. 136 (1899); reversing 14 C. C. 202; 7 C. D. 661.

An ordinance prescribing that "the number of hours that said electric lights shall be required to be lighted during each period of twenty-four hours shall be the same as the said council does now or may hereafter require for electric lamps within the limits of said village for lighting streets, shall be lighted," is sufficiently definite.
> Railroad Co. v. Bowling Green, 57 O. S. 336 (1897); affirming 9 C. C. 524; 6 C. D. 531.

It is a good defense that the ordinance is unreasonable in that the light required will obscure headlights and endanger the service of the company.
> Railway Co. v. St. Bernard, 15 C. C. 588; 8 C. D. 385 (1898).

An electric light company in a municipality is bound to furnish light impartially to all applicants, including railroad companies, at a reasonable price.
> Railway Co. v. Bowling Green, 57 O. S. 336 (1897); affirming 9 C. C. 524; 6 C. D. 531.

Section 3764. (Notice of requirement shall be given; time and manner.) Notice of such requirement shall be given at least twenty days before penalty or charge shall be imposed for default, and such notice may be given by delivering a written or printed copy of the ordinance to an owner or part owner, or any person having possession, charge or management of such bridge or railway. When such ordinance requires the lighting of a railway, service of such written or printed copy of the ordinance upon a ticket or freight agent of such railway company in such municipality, and if there is no such ticket or freight agent therein, upon any ticket or freight agent of such railway company in the county wherein such municipality is located, shall be sufficient, and shall charge the person, company, corporation, or partnership, owning or operating such railway with notice of the passage of the ordinance and the requirements thereof. (R. S. Sec. 2496; May 6, 1902, 95 v. 369; May 7, 1869, 66 v. 220.)

For insufficient service of notice under former law, see
Dayton v. C. C. C. & St. L. Ry. Co., 46 W. L. B. 287 (1901).
C. C. C. & St. L. Ry. Co. v. De Graff, 20 C. C. 710; 10 C. D. 825 (1899).
No notice to the railway company of the intention of the council to pass an ordinance is required. The only notice required is under this section.
Railway Co. v. St. Bernard, 19 C. C. 299; 10 C. D. 45 (1900).
A requirement that the company proceed to do the lighting by electricity within twenty days after the passage of the ordinance is not necessarily unreasonable.
St. Mary's v. Railroad Co., 60 O. S. 136 (1899).

Section 3765. (Procedure on failure to light bridge or railway.) If the person, company, or corporation, owning, possessing or operating such railway or bridge, neglects or fails to do such lighting in conformity with the provisions of the ordinance, for twenty days after such notice, the council may immediately cause the lighting to be done at the expense of such person, company, or corporations. (R. S. Sec. 2497; March 23, 1872, 69 v. 47, § 432.)

Although the lamps were not placed by the municipality on the track, the municipality may recover where the lamps lighted the tracks, although the street was incidentally lighted as well.
Railway Co. v. St. Bernard, 19 C. C. 299; 10 C. D. 415 (1900).

Section 3766. (Assessment for expense of such lighting.) The council may direct the manner in which the expense of lighting such bridge or railway shall be assessed and collected. When so assessed, the amount shall be a debt due against and payable by such person, company, or corporation, and shall be a lien to be enforced as any other lien on such bridge and the land on which it is built, or upon the real estate of the railway company or leasehold interest within the county wherein such municipality is located. (R. S. Sec. 2498; March 23, 1872, 69 v. 47, § 433.)

When, on default of the railway company, such lighting is procured to be done by the council, the expense of such lighting may, by the council, be assessed or declared a lien upon any of the real estate of the railway company within the muncipality.

C. H. & D. R. R. Co. v. Sullivan, 32 O. S. 152 (1877).

The liability of the railway company to pay such expenses can only be enforced by suit or action, or in the language of the constitution, "by due course of law." It is not a tax or an assessment in the nature of a tax for local improvements, and can not therefore be summarily placed upon the county duplicate and collected as a tax or assessment proper.

C. H. & D. R. R. v. Sullivan, 32 O. S. 152 (1877).

Where an assessing ordinance, fixing the expense of such lighting, has been enacted in conformity with this section, such ordinance of itself furnishes prima facie evidence ot the expense of the lighting.

St. Mary's v. Railroad Co., 60 O. S. 136 (1899).

Section 3767. (How lien may be enforced.) The charge may be collected or the lien enforced in the manner provided for the assessment of damages and expenses for making public improvements. (R. S. Sec. 2499; May 7, 1869, 66 v. 221, § 434.)

The mode of collecting such charge or enforcing the lien thereof, prescribed by this section, is by suit in the name of the municipal corporation, in a court of competent jurisdiction.

C. H. & D. R. R. Co. v. Sullivan, 32 O. S. 152 (1877).

MUNICIPAL CODE PROVISIONS AFFECTING STREET RAILWAYS AND RAILROADS.

STREET RAILWAYS.

Section 3768. (Terms and conditions of construction and operation to be fixed by council; renewal of grant.) No corporation, individual or individuals shall perform any work in the construction of a street railroad, until application for leave is made to the council in writing, and the council by ordinance has granted permission, prescribed the terms and conditions upon, and the manner in which, the road shall be constructed and operated, and the streets and alleys to be used and occupied therefor, but the council may renew any such grant at its expiration upon such conditions as may be considered conducive to the public interest. (R. S. Sec. 2501; April 21, 1896, 92 v. 206; March 4, 1887, 84 v. 40; R. S. 1880; June 12, 1879, 76 v. 156, § 4; May 7, 1869, 66 v. 217, § 411.)

Sections 3768 to 3780 apply to street railway lines wholly within municipalities. Sections 9100 et seq. relate to street railways wherever located.

In case of conflict between the special provisions of § 3768 et seq. and the general provisions of § 9100 et seq., the more specific provisions of § 3768 et seq. will prevail.

Railway Co. v. Railway Co., 5 C. C. n. s. 583; 16 C. D. 180 (1903); aff'd, no rep., 73 O. S. 364.

See, Raynolds v. Cleveland, 2 C. C. n. s. 139, 150; 14 C. D. 215 (1902); aff'd, no rep., 76 O. S. 619.

Hamilton v. Railway, 5 N. P. 457; 8 L. D. 174.

Use of streets by street railways.

See also note to § 3714.

A street railway company occupying or using a street, without a grant of the right to do so, may be treated as a trespasser or as committing a nuisance.

Rogers v. Railway, 12 L. D. 136 (1901).

In re Avon Beach, etc., Ry., 3 N. P. n. s. 561, 564; 16 L. D. 87 (1905).

See Horstman v. Railway, 1 N. P. n. s. 25; 13 L. D. 670; 14 L. D. 545; reversed, 72 O. S. 93.

A street car is a vehicle.

Ry. Co. v. Ry. Co., 5 C. C. n. s. 583, 588 (1903); aff'd, no rep., 73 O. S. 364.

Cincinnati, etc., Co. v. Snell, 54 O. S. 197 (1896).

Difference between use of streets by street railways, and by other passenger vehicles.

See Isom v. Low Fare Ry. Co., 10 C. C. n. s. 90; 19 C. D. 583 (1907); aff'd, no rep., 77 O. S. 638.

Street Railway v. Cumminsville, 14 O. S. 545 (1863).

Akron, etc., Co. v. Erie R. R. Co., 7 C. C. n. s. 199, 203; 18 C. D. 36 (1905).

Franchise.

Generally. See note to § 3714.

Outside of municipalities. § 9101 et seq.

Permission to occupy streets is a franchise and easement. When accepted by the grantee, and acted upon, permission to occupy streets for a street railway is more than a license; "it is a vested property right, in the nature of a franchise or easement in or to the particular portion of the street designated in the grant itself."

Hamilton, etc., Traction Co. v. Hamilton, etc., Transit Co., 69 O. S. 402, 410 (1903).

State v. Dayton Traction Co., 18 C. C. 490, 499; 10 C. D. 212 (1899).

Application.

Is a condition precedent to passage of final grant.

Raynolds v. Cleveland, 2 C. C. n. s. 139, 152; 14 C. D. 215 (1902); affirmed, without report, 76 O. S. 619.

The presentation to the council of an ordinance for a street railway grant is a sufficient written application.

Sanfleet v. Toledo, 10 C. C. 460; 8 C. D. 711 (1893); affirmed, no rep., 54 O. S. 620.

The application may be for two routes in the alternative, leaving it to the municipality to grant either one.

Simmons v. Toledo, 5 C. C. 124, 141; 3 C. D. 64 (1889).

See Somers v. Cincinnati, 8 Am. L. R. 612, 622.

A grant to a corporation is not invalid because the application was filed before the articles of incorporation had reached the secretary of state, where the corporation was fully organized before the grant was made.

Sloane v. People's, etc., Co., 7 C. C. 84; 3 C. D. 674 (1891).

Grant must be made by council. A street railway franchise within a municipality can only be granted by the council, by ordinance. G. C. § 9101.

The authority to grant a franchise can not be delegated by the council to a board or officer.

State v. Bell, 34 O. S. 194 (1877).

Sommers v. Cincinnati, 8 Am. L. R. 612, 622.

Hamlet trustees, under the former municipal code, were authorized to grant a street railway franchise.

Commissioners v. Railway Co., 21 C. C. 769; 11 C. D. 664 (1896).

See In re Newburgh Twp., 15 C. C. 78; 8 C. D. 24 (1897).

Ordinance. Preliminary or establishing ordinance under former statute.

See note to § 3769.

Granting ordinance, requisites, etc. See note to § 3714.

As a contract. When accepted by the grantee, a franchise ordinance constitutes a contract.

Hattersly v. Waterville, 4 C. C. n. s. 242; 16 C. D. 226 (1904); affirmed, no rep., 74 O. S. 466.

Cincinnati St. Ry. Co. v. Smith, 29 O. S. 291 (1876).

Cleveland v. Ry. Co., 194 U. S. 517, 534 (1904).

Hamilton, etc., Co. v. Hamilton, etc., Co., 69 O. S. 402, 410 (1903).

Columbus v. Street Railroad Co., 45 O. S. 98 (1887).

The repeal of a granting ordinance is of no effect after acceptance.

Cincinnati, etc., Co. v. Carthage, 36 O. S. 631 (1881).

Terms and conditions of franchise. See also note to § 3770.

The council may, in the grant, reserve the right to thereafter impose terms and conditions other than those expressly stipulated.

Kinsman, etc., Co. v. Broadway, etc., Co., 36 O. S. 239 (1880).

Payments to municipality. Car license fees, etc. Car license fees can not be imposed, where the franchise requires the company to repair, clean and sprinkle streets between tracks. .

Columbus v. Jeffrey, 1 N. P. n. s. 265; 12 L. D. 756 (1903).

But when provided for in the grant, such fees are a valid obligation.

Cincinnati v. Mt. Auburn, etc., Co., 28 W. L. B. 276 (1892).

Cincinnati St. Ry. Co. v. Cincinnati, 8 N. P. 80; 11 L. D. 15.

Cincinnati v. Cincinnati St. R. Co., 6 N. P. 140; 9 L. D. 235 (1899).
Cincinnati v. Cincinnati, etc., Co., 22 L. D. 723 (1911).
It has been held that liability for car license fees ceases on expiration of the franchise.
Cincinnati v. Cincinnati, etc., Co., 30 W. L. B. 321.
Such fees are the property of the municipality and not of the state.
Cincinnati St. Ry. Co. v. Smith, 29 O. S. 291, 296, 306 (1876).
Percentage of gross receipts. See § 14770.
A contract, providing that whenever the municipality should desire to reinforce a viaduct so that it would be safe for heavy vehicular traffic or electric cars, the railway company would pay a stipulated sum toward the expense, was held to render the company liable whenever the viaduct was so reinforced, although the company had ceased to use the viaduct, with the consent of the municipality.
Cincinnati v. Cincinnati St. Ry. Co., 9 O. L. R. 190 (C. P. 1911).

Route. The council can not make a grant of two or more routes in the alternative, leaving the choice of routes to the company.
Somers v. Cincinnati, 8 Am. L. R. 612, 622.
See Cincinnati, etc., Co. v. Smith, 29 O. S. 291 (1876).
But the application may be for two routes in the alternative, leaving it to the municipality to grant either one.
Simmons v. Toledo, 5 C. C. 124, 141; 3 C. D. 64 (1889).
The grant must be of the route as published under § 3769. A grant can not be made of only a part of such route, nor can another street be included.
Raynolds v. Cleveland, 2 C. C. n. s. 139, 152, 154; 14 C. D. 215 (1902); aff'd, no rep., 76 O. S. 619.
But the grant may include only a part of the route described in the application.
Simmons v. Toledo, 5 C. C. 124; 3 C. D. 64 (1889); aff'd, no rep., 30 W. L. B. 392.
A line may fork and be but one route.
Aydelott v. Cincinnati, 11 C. C. 11, 17; 4 C. D. 86 (1893).
Belle v. Glenville, 5 C. C. n. s. 461; 17 C. D. 181; aff'd, no rep., 73 O. S. 392, 397; s. c., 75 O. S. 574.

Paving. See § 3776 and note.

Limitation of time for beginning or completing construction work. See note to § 3714.

Rate of fare. See note to § 3770.

Transfers. A provision requiring transfers is valid; although a company operating intersecting lines is placed at a disadvantage in bidding.
Raynolds v. Cleveland, 8 C. C. n. s. 278; 18 C. D. 463 (1906); aff'd, no rep., on ground of laches, 77 O. S. 631.
Where by the negligence of a conductor a passenger is given a defective transfer and is wrongfully ejected from a car for refusing to pay an additional fare, he may recover damages for the tort.
Railway v. Conner, 74 O. S. 225 (1906).

Exclusive franchise. The council can not by express grant give exclusive right of way in streets to one company.
Hamilton, etc., Traction Co. v. Hamilton, etc., Transit Co., 69 O. S. 402, 409 (1903).
Cincinnati St. Ry. Co. v. Smith, 29 O. S. 291 (1876).

Kinsman, etc., Ry. Co. v. Broadway, etc., R. Co., 36 O. S. 239, 250
(1880).

Toledo, etc., Co. v. Toledo, etc., Co., 6 C. C. 362; 3 C. D. 493 (1892);
aff'd, 50 O. S. 603.

See Columbus v. Columbus Gas Co., 76 O. S. 309, 339 (1907).

A provision that "only one set of wires and poles shall be erected
upon any one street" was construed not to give grantee a monopoly of
the street, but to limit the grantee to one set of poles and wires on a
street.

Mulhenny v. Toledo Central St. Ry., 20 C. D. 686.

Grant over right of way of another company. Straddle tracks.
The grantee of a street railway franchise in streets already occupied
and used under a prior franchise can not, without appropriation proceedings, take possession of the streets, where the new use will materially
interfere with the use under prior franchise.

Hamilton, etc., Traction Co. v. Hamilton, etc., Transit Co., 69 O. S.
402, 409 (1903).

Isom v. Low Fare Ry. Co., 10 C. C. n. s. 89, 101; 19 C. D. 583
(1907); aff'd, no rep., 77 O. S. 638.

Hamilton, etc., Co. v. Hamilton, etc., Co., 5 C. C. 319; 3 C. D. 158
(1890).

Toledo Consol. St. Ry. v. Toledo, Elec., etc., Co., 6 C. C. 362; 3 C. D.
493 (1892); aff'd, 50 O. S. 603.

See §§ 9103, 9108.

Duplication of grant over same right of way by consent. Consent of the stockholders of the corporation holding the prior grant is
necessary to a grant over the same right of way to other persons.

Isom v. Low Fare Ry. Co., 10 C. C. n. s. 89, 101; 19 C. D. 583
(1907); aff'd, no rep., 77 O. S. 638.

Joint use of tracks by other street railways. Under a franchise
stipulating that another company, then in existence, should have the right
to jointly use the tracks of the grantee, upon a reasonable compensation,
and stipulating that the franchise was subject to such other terms and
conditions as the council might thereafter prescribe, it was held that
a subsequent grant of franchise over the route of the grantee, to a
company subsequently organized, subject to the payment of a reasonable
compensation, was valid.

Kinsman, etc., Co. v. Broadway, etc., Co., 36 O. S. 239 (1880).
Broadway, etc., Co. v. Brooklyn, etc., Co., 10 W. L. B. 72.
See §§ 9103, 9108.

Construction of terms and conditions. See also note to § 3714.
The grant of a street railway franchise is strictly construed in
favor of the public.

C. E. Ry. Co. v. Cleveland, 204 U. S. 116 (1907).
Railroad Co. v. Defiance, 52 O. S. 262, 307 (1895).
E. Ohio Gas Co. v. Akron, 81 O. S. 33, 52 (1909).
Central Trust Co. v. Municipal Traction Co., 7 O. L. R. 413 (1909).

A renewal or extension of the term of grants by implication is not
favored.

C. E. Ry. Co. v. Cleveland, 137 Fed. 111; 3 O. L. R. 75 (1905);
affirmed, 204 U. S. 116.

Central Trust Co. v. Municipal Traction Co., 7 O. L. R. 413 (1909).
Cleveland v. C. E. Ry. Co., 201 U. S. 529 (1906).

A franchise for an extension of tracks, to terminate with the franchise for the main line, should be construed with reference to the main
line franchise at that time, and not as subsequently extended.

C. E. Ry. Co. v. Cleveland, 204 U. S. 116 (1907).

The words "other appliances" in a grant for "all necessary side tracks, curves, switches, and other appliances," do not include a shelter house in the middle of the street.

Hamilton, etc., Transit Co. v. Hamilton, 1 N. P. 366; 4 L. D. 10.

A provision prohibiting the carriage of freight has been held invalid.

State v. Dayton Traction Co., 18 C. C. 490; 10 C. D. 212 (1899); affirmed, 64 O. S. 272.

Where the provisions of the ordinance are plain and unambiguous, the practical construction of the contract by conduct of the parties is without effect.

Cincinnati v. Cincinnati St. Ry. Co., 6 N. P. 140; 9 L. D. 235 (1899).

Grantee of franchise. The grantee must be expressly named in the granting ordinance.

State v. Bell, 34 O. S. 194, 198 (1877).

A grant may be made to a person describing him as trustee.

Simmons v. Toledo, 5 C. C. 124; 3 C. D. 64 (1889); aff'd, no rep., 30 W. L. B. 392.

A franchise may be assigned by the grantee, although the word "assignee" or "assigns" is not used.

State v. Northern Ohio, etc., Co., 1 Ct. of App. —, (1913).

Misnomer of grantee. Use of the word *Railroad* instead of *Railway* in the name of grantee company does not invalidate a grant where there is no such *Railroad* company, and the grant was accepted by the grantee and expenditures made thereunder.

State v. Oakwood St. Ry. Co., 11 C. C. n. s. 263; 20 C. D. 632 (1908); aff'd, no rep., 81 O. S. 502.

See note to § 3770.

Renewal of grant by implication. A renewal or extension of the term of a grant by implication is not favored in law.

C. E. Ry. v. Cleveland, 137 Fed. 111; 3 O. L. R. 75 (1905); affirmed, 204 U. S. 116.

Cleveland v. C. E. Ry. Co., 201 U. S. 529 (1906).

Central Trust Co. v. Municipal Traction Co., 7 O. L. R. 413; 169 Fed. 308 (1909).

An ordinance consenting to the consolidation of several companies on condition that but one fare should be charged for a continuous ride does not extend the franchise of any line.

C. E. Ry. Co. v. Cleveland, 204 U. S. 116 (1907); affirming 137 Fed. 111; 3 O. L. R. 75.

Central Trust Co. v. Municipal Traction Co., 169 Fed. 308; 7 O. L. R. 413 (1909).

Permission by the municipality that the motive power be changed to electricity does not have the effect of renewing the franchise.

Cincinnati v. Railway Co., 30 W. L. B. 321; affirmed, no rep., 52 O. S. 609.

Renewal by extension of route.

See Belle v. Glenville, 5 C. C. n. s. 461; 17 C. D. 181 (1904); aff'd, no rep., 73 O. S. 392, 397; 75 O. S. 574.

Isom v. Low Fare Ry. Co., 10 C. C. n. s. 89, 95; 19 C. D. 583 (1907); aff'd, no rep., 77 O. S. 638.

C. E. Ry. Co. v. Cleveland, 204 U. S. 116 (1907); affirming 137 Fed. 111; s. c., 3 O. L. R. 75.

Central Trust Co. v. Municipal Traction Co., 7 O. L. R. 413; 169 Fed. 308 (1909).

Renewal before or after expiration of original franchise.
A grant may be renewed before its expiration.
State, ex rel., v. East Cleveland Ry. Co., 6 C. C. 318, 323; 3 C. D.
  471 (1891); aff'd, no rep., 27 W. L. B. 64.
Cleveland v. C. E. Ry. Co., 201 U. S. 529 (1906).
Cleveland v. C. C. Ry. Co., 194 U. S. 517 (1904).
Belle v. Glenville, 5 C. C. n. s. 461, 470; 17 C. D. 181, aff'd, no rep.,
  73 O. S. 392, 397; 75 O. S. 574.
Lima v. Cramer, 5 N. P. n. s. 113; 17 L. D. 245 (1906).
Cincinnati v. St. Ry. Co., 31 W. L. B. 308; 1 L. D. 591 (1894).
A renewal grant is not invalid because made after expiration of
original franchise, where negotiations therefor were begun before expira-
tion and not abandoned, but by agreement the grant was deferred until
enabling legislation was enacted.
State v. Oakwood St. Ry. Co., 11 C. C. n. s. 263; 20 C. D. 632 (1908);
  aff'd, no rep., 81 O. S. 502.

To holder of original franchise only. The council may renew a grant
only to the grantee of the original franchise, or its assigns.
Isom v. Low Fare Ry. Co., 10 C. C. n. s. 89, 95; 19 C. D. 583
  (1907); aff'd, no rep., 77 O. S. 638.

Renewal of part of grant. The council may renew a grant as to one
part of the route only.
Lima v. Cramer, 5 N. P. n. s. 113, 121; 17 L. D. 245 (1906).

Terms and conditions of renewal grant. A municipality, in granting
an extension of a franchise, may require the railroad company to widen
a bridge occupied by it, or in lieu thereof, to pay a stipulated sum.
Elyria v. Traction Co., 8 N. P. n. s. 85; 19 L. D. 294 (1908).
A requirement in a renewal grant that fares to certain points outside
the municipality be increased, is inoperative as to points where a contract
as to fares is in effect between the railway company and others.
Humphrey Co. v. Cleveland Ry. Co., 9 N. P. n. s. 609; 20 L. D.
  510 (1910).
See Cemetery v. Cincinnati, etc., Co., 11 C. C. n. s. 429; 21 C. D.
  51 (1908).
Where a company accepted a renewal grant in which the municipality reserved the right to grant the use of its track to any other
company, on such terms as the municipality should deem equitable, and
the municipality exercised its right, the court will not interfere if the
terms are reasonable. Nor can the company object because a part of its
business will be taken away.
Broadway, etc., Co. v. Brooklyn, etc., Co., 10 W. L. B. 72.
See § 9103.

Ordinance, renewing all rights, covers unconstructed lines. An
ordinance which provides that the rights, privileges and franchises granted
under former ordinances "be and the same are hereby renewed and
extended," continues and renews the right of the grantee to lay tracks
on a portion of the territory covered by the original ordinance in which
no tracks had been laid, although such territory is not specifically mentioned in the renewing ordinance.
Akron v. Northern Ohio, etc.. Co., 6 C. C. n. s. 445; 17 C. D. 536
  (1905); aff'd, no rep., 75 O. S. 565.

Renewal grant as a contract. A renewal grant, when accepted and
acted upon, is a contract.
Street Ry. v. Cleveland, 7 N. P. n. s. 161; 17 L. D. 763.
See note to § 3714.

Renewal grant as a waiver of rights under prior grant. A renewal grant, when accepted, operates as a waiver of rights under the prior grant.

> C. E. Ry. Co. v. Cleveland, 137 Fed. 111; 3 O. L. R. 75 (1905); affirmed, 204 U. S. 116.
> Cleveland v. C. C. Ry. Co., 194 U. S. 517 (1904).

Where the grantee of a franchise failed to construct tracks on one street specified in the grant, the right of the municipality to forfeit the franchise as to such street is waived by a new grant renewing all the rights, privileges and franchises of the original grant.

> Akron v. No. Ohio, etc., Co., 6 C. C. n. s. 445; 17 C. D. 536 (1905); aff'd, no rep., 75 O. S. 565.

G. C. §§ 3769 and 3770 not applicable to renewals. The provisions of §§ 3769 and 3770 do not apply to the renewal of a grant. A renewal is not invalid because made without the publication of notice, consents of property owners and competitive bidding.

> State, ex rel., v. East Cleveland R. R. Co., 6 C. C. 318; 3 C. D. 471 (1891); aff'd, no rep., 27 W. L. B. 64.
> Clement v. Cincinnati, 16 W. L. B. 355 (1886).
> Haskins v. Cincinnati, etc. Co., 4 W. L. B. 1126 (1880).
> Pelton v. East Cleveland R. R. Co., 22 W. L. B. 67.
> Lima v. Cramer, 5 N. P. n. s. 113; 17 L. D. 245 (1906).
> See §§ 3770 and 9106.

Remedies. Of municipality to compel performances of contract obligations. See note to § 3714.

Of municipality and abutting owners, involving validity of franchise. See note to §§ 9101 and 9105.

Of holder of franchise. See note to § 3714.

Municipal ownership of street railways. A municipality is not authorized to own or operate a street railway.

> Cleveland v. C. C. Ry., 3 C. C. n. s. 563, 566; 13 C. D. 373 (1902).

Section 3769. (Proceedings to establish a street railway route.) Nothing mentioned in the preceding section shall be done, no ordinance or resolution to establish or define a street railroad route shall be passed, no action inviting proposals to construct and operate such railroad shall be taken by the council, and no ordinance for the purpose specified in such section shall be passed, until public notice of the application therefor has been given by the clerk of the council once a week, for the period of at least three consecutive weeks in one or more of the daily papers, if there be such, and if not, then in one or more weekly papers published in the corporation. (April 15, 1908, 99 v. 103, § 30; October 22, 1902, 96 v. 32, § 30; Bates Stats. § 1536-185; see R. S. Sec. 2502.)

Publication of notice.

Is jurisdictional to grant. A written application and publication of notice are conditions precedent to passage of final grant.

> Raynolds v. Cleveland, 2 C. C. n. s. 139, 152; 14 C. D. 215 (1902); affirmed, no rep., 76 O. S. 619.

Not required for extension of tracks or renewal of franchise. Publication of notice is not required for an extension of tracks.

State v. Cincinnati, etc., Co., 19 C. C. 79; 10 C. D. 418 (1889).

Somers v. Cincinnati, 8 Am. L. Rec. 612.

See also, Ry. Co. v. Ry. Co., 5 C. C. n. s. 583, 596; 16 C. D. 180 (1903); affirmed, without report, 73 O. S. 364.

Nor on renewal of grant.

State v. E. Cleveland R. R., 6 C. C. 318; 3 C. D. 471 (1891); affirmed, without report, 27 W. L. B. 64.

Lima v. Cramer, 5 N. P. n. s. 113; 17 L. D. 245.

In one newspaper. Effect of general ordinance regulating publication. Publication in one newspaper is sufficient where the council, acting under the notice, passes an ordinance granting a franchise, although a general ordinance requires publication in two newspapers.

Simmons v. Toledo, 5 C. C. 124; 3 C. D. 64 (1889); affirmed, 30 W. L. B. 392.

Aydelot v. Cincinnati, 11 C. C. 11; 4 C. D. 486 (1893).

See G. C. § 4229.

Defective publication, rendering franchise invalid, can not be cured by an amendment to the granting ordinance declaring the publication sufficient.

Raynolds v. Cleveland, 8 C. C. n. s. 278; 18 C. D. 463 (1906); affirmed, without report, 77 O. S. 631.

The duty of publishing an ordinance rests upon the municipality. In an action by a city solicitor to oust a street railway company from its franchise, it is incumbent on the municipality to establish the omission. In the absence of evidence, a presumption arises that publicawas regularly made.

State v. Railway, 11 C. C. n. s. 263; 20 C. D. 632 (1908); affirmed, without report, 81 O. S. 502.

Estoppel of municipality. A recital in a granting ordinance that proper publication had been made, when relied upon by the grantee of the franchise and expenditures made on the faith thereof, estops the municipality from maintaining an action to invalidate the grant because of defective publication.

Raynolds v. Cleveland, 8 C. C. n. s. 278; 18 C. D. 463 (1906); aff'd, no rep., on ground of laches, 77 O. S. 631.

Mandamus to compel. An owner of land, abutting on the proposed line, can not by mandamus compel the clerk to publish notice.

State v. Henderson, 38 O. S. 644 (1883).

Grant must be of route as advertised. A grant can not be made of a part only of route as advertised; nor can a street not included in advertisement or bids be embraced in grant.

Raynolds v. Cleveland, 2 C. C. n. s. 139, 152, 154; 14 C. D. 215 (1902); aff'd, no rep., 76 O. S. 619.

Compare Simmons v. Toledo, 5 C. C. 124; 3 C. D. 64.

Action by council prior to publication. "Establishing ordinance." Former law. Former statute construed as to necessity and propriety of action by the council prior to publication. ("Establishing" ordinance or resolution.)

Raynolds v. Cleveland, 2 C. C. n. s. 139, 151-153; 14 C. D. 215 (1902); affirmed, without report, 76 O. S. 619.

Aydelot v. Cincinnati, 11 C. C. 11; 4 C. D. 486.

Sloane v. People's, etc., Co., 7 C. C. 84, 93; 3 C. D. 674 (1891).

Hamilton v. C. & H., etc., Ry., 5 N. P. 457; 8 L. D. 174.

State v. Henderson, 38 O. S. 644 (1883).

Section 3770. (When consent of property owners neces-sary.) No such grant shall be made, except to the corporation, individual or individuals, that agree to carry passengers upon such proposed railroad at the lowest rates of fare, and shall have previously obtained the written consent of a majority of the property holders upon each street or part thereof, on the line of the proposed street railroad, represented by the feet front of the property abutting on the several streets along which such road is proposed to be constructed. When within the year preceding, a street railway has been operated upon such street or part thereof, under a grant or renewal of a grant which has expired or will expire within two years, it shall not be necessary to obtain the consent of the property holders abutting thereon, if the number of tracks on the street, public way or part thereof is not increased beyond the number for which consents were originally obtained. (April 15, 1908, 99 v. 103, § 30; October 22, 1902, 96 v. 32, § 30; Bates Stats. § 1536-185.)

Consents of property owners. See notes to §§ 9105 and 9106.

Lowest rates of fare. The council is not authorized to grant a franchise to the company which will bid "the lowest price of commutation tickets in packages." Such a bid is not in compliance with this section.
Cincinnati St. R. R. Co. v. Smith, 29 O. S. 291 (1876).
Rates of fare fixed in a granting ordinance, with no reservation of the right to change the fare, can not be reduced by the council during the life of the grant.
Cleveland v. C. C. Ry. Co., 194 U. S. 517 (1904); affirming 94 Fed. 385.

Ordinance or resolution inviting bids.

Takes effect when. Council may fix time for taking effect.
Sloane v. Peoples, etc., Co., 7 C. C. 84, 93; 3 C. D. 674 (1891).
See State v. Henderson, 38 O. S. 644 (1883).
G. C. § 4227.

Provisions in.

Held valid. Requirement that fare shall entitle passenger to transfer.
Raynolds v. Cleveland, 8 C. C. n. s. 278; 18 C. D. 463 (1906);
aff'd, no rep., on ground of laches, 77 O. S. 631.
Requiring each bidder to accompany his bid with a bond, or cash deposit, to secure performance of bid.
Compton v. Johnson, 9 C. C. 532; 6 C. D. 110 (1895).
Simmons v. Toledo, 5 C. C. 124; 3 C. D. 64 (1889).
See Raynolds v. Cleveland, 8 C. C. n. s. 278, 279; 18 C. D. 463 (1906); aff'd, no rep., 77 O. S. 631.
Sloane v. Peoples, etc., Co., 7 C. C. 84; 3 C. D. 674 (1891).
Limiting time for the filing of bids and bonds.
Simmons v. Toledo, 5 C. C. 124; 3 C. D. 64 (1889).
Establishing route through private property of president of applicant corporation. Competitive bidding is not prevented where owner of the property is estopped.
Harrison v. Mt. Auburn Cable Co., 17 W. L. B. 265.

Held invalid. A requirement that controversies between the grantee of the franchise and its employes shall be settled by arbitration.

Raynolds v. Cleveland, 2 C. C. n. s. 154; 14 C. D. 215 (1902); aff'd no rep., 76 O. S. 619.

Inviting bids for the lowest price of commutation tickets in packages.

Cincinnati St. R. R. v. Smith, 29 O. S. 291, 308 (1876).

Waiver of conditions in. A requirement as to a bond may be waived by the council, if no favoritism is practiced and no injury results to city.

Sloane v. Peoples, etc., Co., 7 C. C. 84; 3 C. D. 64 (1891).
Simmons v. Toledo, 5 C. C. 124; 3 C. D. 110 (1889).

Bids and bidding.

By whom made. A bid by an individual "for himself and associates" not named is the bid of the individual. The reference to associates does not invalidate the bid.

Compton v. Johnson, 9 C. C. 532, 542; 6 C. D. 110 (1895).
Gallagher v. Johnson, 30 W. L. B. 139 (1893).

Right of council to reject bids.

May reject all bids. The council can not be compelled to grant a franchise, even to the lowest bidder.

State v. Bell, 34 O. S. 194, 199 (1877).
State v. Henderson, 38 O. S. 644, 650 (1883).
Sloane v. People's, etc., Co., 7 C. C. 84, 93; 3 C. D. 674 (1891).

Rejection of part of bids. The council may reject a sham or fraudulent bid.

Compton v. Johnson, 9 C. C. 532; 6 C. D. 110 (1895).

Or a bid not accompanied by a bond when required, or not filed within the time limited.

Simmons v. Toledo, 5 C. C. 124; 3 C. D. 64 (1889).

But it may not reject a bid which substantially complies with the establishing ordinance and is not shown to be collusive or fraudulent.

Compton v. Johnson, 9 C. C. 532; 6 C. D. 110 (1895).
Gallagher v. Johnson, 31 W. L. B. 24.
Gallagher v. Johnson, 30 W. L. B. 139 (1893).
Knorr v. Miller, 5 C. C. 609; 3 C. D. 297 (1891); aff'd 27 W. L. B. 64.

Irregularities in bids, bonds, and in the opening of bids. Informalities in a bid, or a bond filed by a bidder, which do not go to the substance, may be disregarded.

Compton v. Johnson, 9 C. C. 532; 6 C. D. 110 (1895).
Simmons v. Toledo, 5 C. C. 124; 3 C. D. 64 (1889); aff'd, no rep., 30 W. L. B. 392.

Irregularities on the part of the council in opening and considering bids do not, under all circumstances, invalidate the award.

Sloane v. Peoples, etc., Co., 7 C. C. 84; 3 C. D. 784 (1891).
Simmons v. Toledo, 5 C. C. 124; 3 C. D. 64 (1889); aff'd, no rep., 30 W. L. B. 392.

Grant must conform to advertisement and bid. A grant can not include a street not advertised or bid for.

Raynolds v. Cleveland, 2 C. C. n. s. 139, 154; 14 C. D. 215 (1902); aff'd, no rep., 76 O. S. 619.

Injunction against grant to person not lowest bidder. A grant to a person not the lowest bidder may be enjoined.

Knorr v. Miller, 5 C. C. 609; 3 C. D. 297 (1891); affirmed, 27
W. L. B. 64.
Compton v. Johnson, 9 C. C. 532; 6 C. D. 110 (1895).
State v. Bell, 34 O. S. 194, 199 (1877).
But only on clear proof that the council erred in determining which
bid was the lowest.
Simmons v. Toledo, 5 C. C. 124; 3 C. D. 64 (1889).

Renewal grant.

Competitive bidding and consents not required. A renewal grant
is not rendered invalid because made without competitive bidding or
consents.
State, ex rel., v. East Cleveland R. R. Co., 6 C. C. 318; 3 C. D. 471
(1891); aff'd, no rep., 27 W. L. B. 64.
Clement v. Cincinnati, 16 W. L. B. 355 (1886).
Haskins v. Cincinnati, etc., Co., 4 W. L. B. 1126 (1880).
Pelton v Railroad, 22 W. L. B. 67.
See Isom v. Low Fare Ry. 10 C. C. n. s. 89; 19 C. D. 583 (1907);
aff'd, no rep., 77 O. S. 638.

Deposit to secure bid regarded as liquidated damages. A certified
check, to secure performance of a bid, deposited by a bidder to whom a
franchise is awarded, is supported by a consideration. On abandonment
of the enterprise, the deposit may be deemed liquidated damages and
forfeited to the municipality.
Hattersly v. Waterville, 4 C. C. n. s. 242; 16 C. D. 226 (1904);
aff'd, no rep., 74 O. S. 466.

**Section 3771. (Grant not valid for more than twenty-
five years.)** No grant or renewal of a grant for the construction or operation of a street railroad, shall be valid for
a greater period than twenty-five years from the date of
such grant or renewal, and after such grant or renewal of
a grant is made, whether by special or general ordinance, the
municipality shall not, during the term of such grant or renewal, release the grantee from any obligation or liability
imposed by the terms of such grant or renewal of a grant.
(April 15, 1908, 99 v. 103, § 30; October 22, 1902, 96 v. 32,
§ 30; Bates Stats. § 1536-185.)

See § 9102.
Franchises generally, see notes to § 3714.

Twenty-five year limitation. A grant made for a period exceeding
twenty-five years is valid to the extent of twenty-five years.
Sommers v. Cincinnati, 8 Am. L. R. 612.
An unlimited franchise granted prior to enactment of this section
was held to be perpetual.
State v. Columbus Ry. Co., 1 C. C. n. s. 145; 14 C. D. 609 (1903);
aff'd, 73 O. S. 363.
See Louisville Trust Co. v. Cincinnati, 76 Fed. 296 (1896); 73 Fed.
716.
Compare East Ohio Gas Co. v. Akron, 81 O. S. 33.
Duration of extensions of route.
See Belle v. Glenville, 5 C. C. n. s. 461; 17 C. D. 181 (1904);
aff'd, no rep., 73 O. S. 392, 397; 75 O. S. 574.

C. E. Ry. Co. v. Cleveland, 137 Fed. 111; 3 O. L. R. 75 (1905);
   aff'd, 204 U. S. 116.
Rights of parties after expiration of franchise.
   C. E. Ry. Co. v. Cleveland, 204 U. S. 116 (1907).
   East Ohio Gas Co. v. Akron, 81 O. S. 33, 56 (1909).
   Columbus v. Columbus Gas Co., 76 O. S. 331 (1907).

   Release of obligation or liability. A modification of the contract,
made in good faith for the better accommodation of the public, is not
void under this section.
   Clement v. Cincinnati, 16 W. L. B. 355 (1886); aff'd, 19 W. L. B. 74.
   Cleveland v. Cleveland City Ry. Co., 194 U. S. 517 (1904).
   Cleveland v. Cleveland Electric Ry. Co., 201 U. S. 529 (1906).
   Cincinnati v. Cincinnati St. Ry. Co., 2 N. P. 298; 2 L. D. 468 (1893).
   A sum due a municipality as car license fees can not be released
except on payment of the full amount. The principles of account stated
and accord and satisfaction, based on a less amount, do not apply.
   Cincinnati St. Ry. Co. v. Cincinnati, 8 N. P. 80; 11 L. D. 15.

**Section 3772. (When franchise shall be submitted to
vote.)** If, within thirty days after the passage of an ordinance granting a franchise, extension or renewal thereof,
to a street railroad, there is presented to the council or filed
with its clerk a written petition signed by fifteen per cent
of the qualified electors of such municipality, to be determined by the highest number of votes cast for the mayor
of the municipality at the last preceding municipal election,
requesting such ordinance to be submitted to a vote of the
electors thereof, the ordinance shall not become operative
until it has been so submitted and has received a majority
of the votes cast thereon. (April 15, 1908, 99 v. 104, § 30a.)

Section 3773. (How the election shall be conducted.)
The council by resolution shall provide that such vote be
taken at a special election or at the next municipal election,
and shall cause a copy of such resolution to be certified to
the board of deputy state supervisors of the county in which
such municipal corporation is situated, which board shall
thereupon prepare the ballots and make all other necessary
arrangements for the submission of such question at the time
fixed in the resolution. Such election shall be held at the
regular place or places of voting in such municipality and
shall be conducted, canvassed and certified in the same
manner as the election of officers thereof. (April 15, 1908,
99 v. 104, § 30a.)

Section 3774. (Notice of the election; form of ballots.)
Thirty days' notice of such submission shall be given by the
mayor of the municipality in two newspapers of opposite
politics printed therein, once a week for four consecutive
weeks, stating the object and purpose, and the time and place

of holding such election. Those voting in favor of the propo-
sitiou shall have written or printed on their ballots the words
"For the franchise," and those voting against it shall have
written or printed on their ballots the words "Against the
franchise." (April 15, 1908, 99 v. 104, § 30a.)

**Section 3775. (Grade of streets when street railroad is
constructed.)** Before a street railroad shall be constructed
on any street less than sixty feet in width, with a roadway
of thirty-five feet or under, the council shall provide that
the crown of the street shall be made a nearly flat uniform
curve from curb to curb, without ditch gutters, and in such
manner as to give wheeled vehicles the full use of the roadway up to the face of the curb. When the tracks of two
street railroads, or of a street railroad and a steam railroad,
cross each other at a convenient grade on a street, the crossings shall be made with crossing-frogs of the most approved
pattern and materials, and kept up and in repair at the joint
expense of the companies owning such tracks. (R. S. Sec.
2503; April 20, 1881, 78 v. 296; R. S. 1880; May 7, 1867, 66
v. 217 § 413.)

The grade may be established in the granting ordinance.
Cincinnati, etc., Ry. Co. v. Carthage, 36 O. S. 631 (1881).

Crossing-frogs. This requirement is constitutional. It applies to
all companies, whether their lines were constructed before or after its
passage. All companies are under the duty of renewing with crossing
frogs which may be found of a more approved pattern.
Cincinnati St. R. Co. v. C. H. & D. R. R., 32 W. L. B. 4 (1894).

Grade crossing over steam railroad. A street railway company
will not be enjoined from constructing a crossing over a steam railroad
at grade, under a franchise from the municipality. It is for the council
to determine the grade.
Railway Co. v. Railway Co., 5 C. C. n. s. 583; 16 C. D. 180 (1903);
    aff'd, no rep., 73 O. S. 364.
See note to § 9108.
This section, and not § 592 et seq., govern the crossing of railroads
and street railways at grade.
Railway Co. v. Railroad Co., 21 C. C. 391; 12 C. D. 113 (1898);
    aff'd, no rep., 64 O. S. 550.

**Section 3776. (Pavement of streets where railroads are
constructed.)** The council may require any part or all of
the track, between the rails of any street railroad constructed
within the corporate limits, to be paved with stone, gravel,
boulders, or wooden or asphaltic pavement, as may be deemed
proper, but without the corporate limits, paving between the
rails with stone, boulders, wooden or asphaltic pavement
shall not be required. (R. S. Sec. 2504; April 21, 1890, 87
v. 246; May 7, 1867, 66 v. 217, § 414.)

Under this section the council may require a street railway to pave between the rails, although the franchise is silent in regard thereto.
Rep. Atty. Gen. 1911-1912, p. 1571.

Franchise obligation to repair. When the granting ordinance provides that the company shall repair the street between rails, and that in case of default the city may do the work and recover the cost; the city is not divested of its right to control the street, and it may cause new improvements to be made and determine the kind of improvement. The company, in accepting the grant, incurs the obligation to repair.
Columbus v. Street R. R. Co., 45 O. S. 98 (1887).
Cincinnati, etc., Ry. Co. v. Carthage, 36 O. S. 631 (1881).

Recovery by municipality for paving.
Cleveland v. Cleveland, etc., R. R., 1 Cleve. L. R. 304 (1878).
Cleveland v. C. E. Ry., 1 N. P. 413; 3 L. D. 92; reversed, 60 O. S. 586.
On failure of railway company to pave, as required by its franchise, within a reasonable time, a cause of action accrues to the municipality, without notice or demand on the company.
Cincinnati, etc., Ry. Co. v. Carthage, 36 O. S. 631 (1881).
Unless the franchise ordinance provides for notice.
Columbus v. Street Ry. Co., 45 O. S. 98 (1887).
Measure of damages is the reasonable cost of the work. *Ib.*

Miscellaneous. A requirement to pave "between the rails" does not include the "devil strip," nor require paving to the end of the ties.
Street Ry. v. Cleveland, 7 N. P. n. s. 161; 17 L. D. 763.
Car license fees can not be imposed by a municipality where franchise requires company to repair, sprinkle, etc., streets between tracks.
Columbus v. Jeffrey, 1 N. P. n. s. 265; 13 L. D. 639 (1903).
A provision in a franchise requiring the company to pay paving assessments is valid.
Railway Co. v. Columbus, 3 N. P. n. s. 438; 16 L. D. 102 (1905).
Columbus v. Railroad, 45 O. S. 98 (1887).
Such a provision does not make the railway company liable to the municipality for any part of the damages awarded to property owners as caused by the improvement of the street.
Railway v. Dayton, 1 Dayton (Iddings), 165.
Acceptance of franchise requiring railway company to pay paving assessment precludes railway company from certain defenses otherwise available.
Ry. Co. v. Columbus, 3 N. P. n. s. 438; 16 L. D. 102 (1905).
Right to pay paving assessments in installments as an abutting owner.
See 35 W. L. B. 345.
Repayment by the company to property owners, of assessments, under terms of franchise. The owner at time of repayment is entitled thereto.
Harkness v. Schiely, 13 C. C. 177; 7 C. D. 108 (1896).
An action against a street railway company for a tortious injury to a pavement, requiring a paving contractor to repair the same under its contract with the city, is barred in four years under G. C. § 11224.
Barber, etc., Co. v. N. O. T. & L. Co., 202 Fed. 817 (C. C. A. 1913).

Section 3777. (Council may grant extension of street railroad.) The council of a municipality may grant permission, by ordinance, to any corporation, individual, or company, owning, or having the right to construct, a street railroad, to extend the track, subject to the provisions of law relating to the construction, operation and extension of street railways, within or without, or partly within or without any municipal corporation, on any street or streets where council deems such extension beneficial to the public. When such extension is made, the charge for carrying passengers on a street railroad so extended and its connections made with any other road or roads, by consolidation, shall not be increased by reason of such extension or consolidation. (R. S. Sec. 2505; Bates Stats. § 1536-188; March 9, 1880, 77 v. 43; R. S. 1880; May 7, 1869, 66 v. 140, § 1.)

The reference to passengers in this section does not prohibit the transportation of freight.
State v. Traction Co., 18 C. C. 490; 10 C. D. 212; aff'd, 64 O. S. 272.

What constitutes an extension.
See Sommers v. Cincinnati, 8 Am. L. R. 612, 623, 624.
An extension can only be predicated of an existing line, or a present right to construct a line.
Cleveland, etc., Co. v. Urbana, etc., Ry., 5 C. C. n. s. 583, 595; 16 C. D. 180 (1903); aff'd, no rep., 73 O. S. 364.
An extension is not a new route; it has no independent life; it depends upon, and is a part of, the line to which it is added.
C. E. Ry. Co. v. Cleveland, 137 Fed. 111, 130, 132; 3 O. L. R. 75, 102, 106 (1905); aff'd, 204 U. S. 116.

May be by branches from main line. The extension need not begin at terminus of line, or run in same general direction. It may be by branches from the main line.
Belle v. Glenville, 5 C. C. n. s. 461; 17 C. D. 181 (1904); affirmed, no rep., 73 O. S. 392, 397; 75 O. S. 574.
Cincinnati v. Cincinnati St. Ry., 31 W. L. B. 308 (1894).
Sommers v. Cincinnati, 8 Am. L. R. 612, 623.
Aydelott v. Cincinnati, 11 C. C. 11, 17; 4 C. D. 486 (1893).

Over existing tracks. The council may grant a franchise for an extension over existing tracks of another company, but the grantee must appropriate the right to use such tracks before taking possession.
Street Ry. Co. v. Street Ry. Co., 50 O. S. 603 (1893).
Kinsman, etc., Co. v. Broadway, etc., Co., 36 O. S. 239 (1880).
Broadway, etc., Co. v. Brooklyn, etc., Co., 10 W. L. B. 72.
Lima v. Cramer, 5 N. P. n. s. 113, 117 (1906).
See G. C. § 9103.

Additional switches. Old switches can not be enlarged or extended, nor additional switches laid, without new authority from the municipality.
Harner v. Columbus, etc., Ry., 29 W. L. B. 387 (1893).
Chestnut v. Railway, 15 L. D. 336 (1905); affirmed, 76 O. S. 567.
Chambers v. Cleveland, etc., Co., 5 C. C. n. s. 298; 17 C. D. 193 (1904); aff'd, no rep., 73 O. S. 348.

Consents. See notes to § 9105.
Consents of abutting owners, as required by G. C. § 9105, must be procured for each street to be occupied by the extension.
Mt. Auburn, etc., Co. v. Neare, 54 O. S. 153 (1896); affirming 29 W. L. B. 171.
Sommers v. Cincinnati, 8 Am. L. R. 612.

Harner v. Railway, 29 W. L. B. 387 (1893).

But when the extension is over existing tracks of another company, consents need not be procured.

State v. Cincinnati, etc., Co., 19 C. C. 79; 10 C. D. 418 (1899).

Broadway, etc., Co. v. Brooklyn, etc., Co., 10 W. L. B. 72.

Mt. Auburn Cable R. Co. v. Neare, 54 O. S. 153 (1896).

Lima v. Cramer, 5 N. P. n. s. 113; 17 L. D. 245 (1906).

Compare, Sanfleet v. Toledo, 10 C. C. 460; 8 C. D. 711 (1893).

Where existing tracks occupy the street without right, the franchise having expired, consents are requisite.

Isom v. Low Fare Ry. Co., 10 C. C. n. s. 89; 19 C. D. 583 (1907);
    aff'd, no rep., 77 O. S. 638.

See G. C. §§ 9106, 3770.

Consents for an extension inure to persons to whom given and assigns, only, and can not be used by others.

Isom v. Low Fare Ry. Co., 10 C. C. n. s. 89, 99; 19 C. D. 583 (1907);
    aff'd, no rep., 77 O. S. 638.

See Forest City Ry. Co. v. Day, 73 O. S. 83 (1905).

A consent given for one specified extension is not available as a consent for a different extension.

Neare v. Mt. Auburn, etc., Co., 29 W. L. B. 171; 4 L. D. 475;
    aff'd, 54 O. S. 153.

Publication of notice not required for an extension.

State, ex rel., v. Cincinnati, etc., Co., 19 C. C. 79; 10 C. D. 418 (1899).

Sommers v. Cincinnati, 8 Am. L. Rec. 612.

See also Railway Co. v. Railway Co., 5 C. C. n. s. 583, 596, 597;
    16 C. D. 180 (1903); aff'd, no rep., 73 O. S. 364.

Period for which extensions may be made.

Belle v. Glenville, 5 C. C. n. s. 461; 17 C. D. 181 (1904); aff'd,
    no rep., 73 O. S. 392, 397; 75 O. S. 574.

C. E. Ry. Co. v. Cleveland, 137 Fed. 111, 132; 3 O. L. R. 75, 106
    (1905); affirmed, 204 U. S. 116.

Isom v. Low Fare Ry. Co., 10 C. C. n. s. 89, 95; 19 C. D. 583 (1907);
    aff'd, no rep., 77 O. S. 638; § 3771.

Change of motive power. Where animal power was specified in the original grant, an extension is not rendered invalid by the specification of electricity, where the line had been operated for years by electricity.

Belle v. Glenville, 5 C. C. n. s. 461; 17 C. D. 181 (1904); aff'd, no
    rep., 73 O. S. 392, 397; 75 O. S. 574.

Discretion of council. The discretion of the council in authorizing an extension will not be interfered with by the courts except upon a showing of fraud or bad faith.

Sims v. Street R. Co., 37 O. S. 556 (1882).

Cincinnati v. Cincinnati, etc., Co., 31 W. L. B. 308 (1894).

The extension may be granted upon conditions.

Cincinnati v. Cincinnati, etc., Co., 31 W. L. B. 308 (1894).

The council may, in its discretion, grant a franchise for an extension over several routes, leaving the choice of route to the company.

Sommers v. Cincinnati, 8 Am. L. R. 612, 622.

Miscellaneous. An ordinance granting permission for an extension is not a grant of corporate power, but a permit to exercise powers already granted.

Sims v. Street R. Co., 37 O. S. 556 (1882).

A steam railroad can not be extended under this section.

Cincinnati Inc. Plane Ry. v. Cincinnati, 7 N. P. 541; 5 L. D. 562
    (1897).

An extension may be granted beyond the termini specified in the articles of incorporation of the company.
Sims v. Street Railway, 37 O. S. 556 (1882).

INTERURBAN RAILROADS.

Section 3778. (Franchises to interurban railroads for the purpose of securing terminals.) The council of any municipality may grant a franchise upon such terms and conditions as it may prescribe for the building of any interurban railroad having, constructing, or building, ten miles or more of track outside of such municipality, to any company or companies using electric or other motive power, save steam, for the purpose of securing to such company or companies access to or terminals within such municipality. The council may authorize such company to build and construct tracks and to operate cars thereon, on any street or streets, or parts of streets, of such municipality, upon which tracks have not already been laid and where the consent of the owners of a majority foot frontage has already been obtained by such company. (April 2, 1906, 98 v. 253, § 1.)

Cited, Railway v. Poland, 10 N. P. n. s. 621.

Section 3779. (Condemnation proceedings when they can not agree.) The council may permit such interurban railroad to make use of the tracks or such parts of the tracks of any existing street railroad company within the limits of the municipality by agreement with such existing company. If no such agreement can be arrived at, the interurban railroad company may be authorized by council to condemn the right to make use of the tracks of such existing company upon the payment of proper compensation. But the interurban railroad company shall be permitted to condemn and make use of not more than one-eighth of the trackage of such company within the municipality, or so much as may be necessary to give the interurban company access to terminals within the municipality, or to enable such company to secure a right of way over such tracks through such municipality. The interurban railway company seeking permission to enter or pass through a municipality shall not be required to submit to competitive bidding on such routes. (April 2, 1906, 98 v. 253, § 1.)

Contracts for use of city tracks.
See § 9130.
Appropriation of use of tracks.
See notes to § 9108.

Section 3780. (**Competitive bidding shall not be required.**) No grant or franchise shall be made to such interurban company for a period longer than twenty years, and no franchise so granted shall be used for the purpose of operating a municipal street car system, it being the only intent hereof to provide a method whereby bona fide interurban railroads may gain access to, and a terminal within, and an exit from, a municipality. (April 2, 1906, 98 v. 253, § 1.)

STEAM RAILROADS.

Section 3781. (**Regulation of rate of speed.**) When a railroad track is laid in a municipal corporation, the council by ordinance may regulate the speed of all locomotives and railroad cars within the corporate limits, but such ordinance shall not require a less rate of speed than four miles an hour, and in villages having a population of two thousand or less, it shall not require a less rate than eight miles an hour. The corporate authorities, by civil action, may recover from an engineer, conductor, or company, violating such ordinance, not less than five dollars nor more than fifty dollars for each offense. (R. S. Sec. 2500; April 27, 1877, 74 v. 132, § 1.)

For regulation of speed of street cars see § 3632.
Cited, Ravenna v. Penna. Co., 45 O. S. 118, 124.
An ordinance regulating the speed of trains is rendered invalid by a provision for its enforcement by criminal proceedings.
Caskey v. Belle Center, 8 N. P. n. s. 153; 19 L. D. 726 (1908).

Violation of speed ordinance; effect of in negligence cases. In an action to recover for an injury alleged to have been caused by cars moving on a railroad track, proof that the company was moving its cars in violation of a city ordinance at the time the injury was inflicted, while not sufficient per se to create a liability, is yet competent to go to the jury as tending to show negligence and to excuse contributory negligence.
Meek v. Pennsylvania Co., 38 O. S. 632 (1883).
Hart v. Devereux, 41 O. S. 565 (1885).
Becker v. Cincinnati Street Ry. Co., 1 N. P. 359; 2 L. D. 137 (1894).
Cincinnati, etc., R. R. Co. v. Murphy, 18 C. C. 298; 10 C. D. 195 (1899).
Pennsylvania Co. v. Trainer, 18 C. C. 716; 7 C. D. 567.
Railway Co. v. Herrick, 49 O. S. 25, 32 (1892).
Engleman v. Lake Shore, etc., Ry. Co., 34 W. L. B. 229 (1895).

Signals by bell and whistle at crossings.
G. C. § 8853.

Section 3809. (**Council may provide for light, water and certain public necessaries.**) The council of a city may authorize, and the council of a village may make, a contract with any person, firm or company for lighting the streets, alleys, lands, lanes, squares and public places in the municipal corporation, or for furnishing water to such corporation, or for the collection and disposal of garbage in such corporation, or for the leasing of the electric light plant and equipment, or the waterworks plant, or both, of any person, firm, company or municipality or for the purchase of electric current for furnishing light, heat or power to such municipality or the inhabitants thereof for a period not exceeding ten years, and the requirement of a certificate that the necessary money is in the treasury, shall not apply to such contract, and such requirement shall not apply to street improvement contracts extending for one year or more, nor to contracts made by the board of health, nor to contracts made by a village for the employment of legal counsel, nor to contracts by a municipality for the leasing or acquisitiou of the electric light plant and equipment, or the waterworks plant, or both, of any person, firm or corporation therein situated. (May 6, 1913, 103 v. 526; October 22, 1902, 96 v. 37, § 45; Bates Stats. § 1536-205.)

See also notes to §§ 3983, 3994 and 9324.
Power to lease a waterworks plant is expressly granted to villages by this section.
Moore v. Elmore, 13 N. P. n. s. 651; 23 L. D. 50 (C. P. 1910).
A village prevented from constructing a waterworks system, by inability to vote sufficient bonds, may grant a franchise to an individual to construct the system, and at substantially the same time lease the same, as provided by this section.
Moore v. Elmore, 13 N. P. n. s. 651; 23 L. D. 50 (C. P. 1910).

Section 3981. (Municipalities may contract for a water supply; contract to be submitted to a vote.) A municipal corporation may contract with any individual or individuals or an incorporated company for supplying water for fire purposes, or for cisterns, reservoirs, streets, squares and other public places within the corporate limits, or for the purpose of supplying the citizens of such municipal corporation with water for such time, and upon such terms as may be agreed upon. But such contract shall not be executed or binding upon the municipal corporation until it has been ratified by a vote of the electors thereof, at a special or general election, and the municipal corporation shall have the same power to protect such water supply and prevent the pollution thereof as though the water works were owned by such municipal corporation. (R. S. Sec. 2434; Bates Stats. § 1536-545; 71 v. 93, § 54; R. S. 1880; 78 v. 42; 80 v. 71; 82 v. 11.)

See notes to §§ 3983, 3994 and 9324.

MUNICIPAL CODE PROVISIONS AFFECTING GAS, WATER AND
ELECTRIC LIGHT COMPANIES.

Section 3982. (Council may regulate price of electric light, gas and water.) The council of a municipality in which electric lighting companies, natural or artificial gas companies, gas light or coke companies, or companies for supplying water for public or private consumption, are established, or into which their wires, mains or pipes are conducted, may regulate from time to time the price which such companies may charge for electric light, or for gas for lighting or fuel purposes, or for water for public or private consumption, furnished by such companies to the citizens, public grounds, and buildings, streets, lanes, alleys, avenues, wharves, and landing places, or for fire protection. Such companies shall in no event charge more for electric light, natural or artificial gas, or water, furnished to such corporation or individuals, than the price specified by ordinance of council. The council may regulate and fix the price which such companies shall charge for the rent of their meters, and such ordinance may provide that such price shall include the use of meters to be furnished by such companies, and in such case meters shall be furnished and kept in repair by such companies and no separate charge shall be made, either directly or indirectly, for the use or repair of them. (R. S. Sec. 2478; March 31, 1906, 98 v. 170; April 20, 1904, 97 v. 114; March 1, 1889, 86 v. 62; March 4, 1887, 84 v. 39; R. S. 1880; May 7, 1869, 66 v. 218, § 415.)

Appeal to public utilities commission from price fixed. §§ 614-44 to 614-46.

Gas and water companies, powers, etc., §§ 9320 to 9338.

Limitations on power to regulate price. The intention of the legislature was to permit councils to limit gas companies to fair and reasonable prices. The power is discretionary, but must be exercised in good faith and for the purpose for which it was given.

An ordinance fraudulently passed, fixing the price at a rate for which council knew gas could not be manufactured and sold without loss, would be invalid.

State v. Cincinnati, etc., Co., 18 O. S. 262, 301 (1868).

Cleveland, etc. Co. v. Cleveland, 35 W. L. B. 155; 71 Fed. 610; 9 O. F. D. 258 (1891).

Peoria Gas & Electric Co. v. Peoria, 200 U. S. 48 (1906).

The council has no power to compel a gas company to furnish gas in a manner and at a rate entirely at the option of the consumer.

Logan, etc., Co. v. Chillicothe, 65 O. S. 186 (1901); reversing 8 N. P. 88; 11 L. D. 24.

An ordinance attempting to fix rates on both a meter and flat basis, and to give consumers the privilege of changing from one to the other, at their option, is not enforceable.

Granville v. Crawford, etc., Co., 14 C. C. n. s. 421 (1911); reversing 11 N. P. n. s. 641.

The council has no power to make a contract that for an indefinite period delegates to other parties the regulation of the price, quality and quantity of gas.

Cincinnati, etc., Co. v. Avondale, 43 O. S. 257 (1885).

Section § 3983 is a limitation on the general power of regulation conferred by this section.

Logan, etc., Co. v. Chillicothe, 65 O. S. 186, 209 (1901).

Provisions in an ordinance which fixed the price of gas according to the use to which the heat produced by the gas was applied, and which provided that consumers having a flat rate prior to the passage of the ordinance should not be compelled to receive gas by meter, were held unreasonable.

Toledo v. Gas Co., 5 C. C. 557; 3 C. D. 273 (1890); s. c., 6 N. P. 631; 8 L. D. 277.

Provision as to price in franchise ordinance. Where a maximum price is fixed in the franchise ordinance, which is accepted by the grantee, it is a legislative regulation of the price of gas, and a limitation upon the franchise, and must stand as such until changed by subsequent legislation.

Manhattan Trust Co. v. Dayton, 59 Fed. 327; 9 O. F. D. 310 (1893).

Ordinance regulating price presumed to be valid. The presumption is in favor of the good faith and validity of the action of the council in passing an ordinance regulating prices. Inadequacy of the price fixed by the council is not the subect of inquiry in the absence of facts showing fraud or bad faith on the part of the council.

State, ex rel., v. Ironton Gas Co., 37 O. S. 45 (1881).

Central Ohio, etc., v. Columbus, 16 L. D. 359, 365 (1905).

Rates for varying quantities used. Rent of meters. The council may fix maximum rates for varying quantities used.

Van Wert v. Van Wert Public Service Co., 11 N. P. n. s. 91 (1910).

And may fix the charge for rent of meters.

State v. Columbus, etc., Co., 34 O. S. 572 (1878).

Power to regulate price after expiration of contract. After the expiration of a contract with a gas company, a municipal corporation may regulate the price of gas so long as the gas company continues to exercise its franchise within the municipal corporation. But where the franchise in the streets has expired. the gas company may wholly withdraw, and the municipality can not prevent it from removing its property.

East Ohio Gas Co. v. Akron, 81 O. S. 33 (1909).

Gaslight Co. v. Zanesville, 47 O. S. 35 (1889).

Where no action taken by council, reasonable price only may be charged. Where no action has been taken by the council of a municipality towards fixing the price of electric light, and the electric light company and a consumer are unable to agree as to a price, the company may be compelled to furnish light at a reasonable price.

C. H. & D. R. R. Co. v. Bowling Green, 57 O. S. 336, 346 (1898).

Council may regulate prices of company chartered under former constitution. A gas company chartered by an act of the legislature, passed before the adoption of the present constitution, is subject to this section, unless the right to fix its own prices is expressly conferred in its charter.

Zanesville v. Gaslight Co., 47 O. S. 1, 35 (1889).
State, ex rel., v. Columbus, etc., Co., 34 O. S. 572 (1878).
State, ex rel., v. Cleveland etc., Co., 3 C. C. 251; 2 C. D. 142 (1888).
See Cleveland, etc., Co. v. Cleveland, 35 W. L. B. 155; 17 Fed. 610 (1891).

Price. Natural and artificial gas furnished by same company. A gas company authorized by ordinance to supply natural gas, and, under certain conditions, artificial gas at a higher price, the existence of such conditions to be determined by the board of public service of the muncipality, can not be compelled, at the suit of a property owner, to furnish artificial gas for the price of natural gas, where the board has found that the conditions exist under which artificial gas may be furnished.

Feckler v. Union Gas, etc., Co., 6 O. L. R. 658; 19 L. D. 658 (1909).

A charge for "readiness to serve" in addition to charge for electricity used, at rates fixed by ordinance, can not be imposed.

Van Wert v. Van Wert Public Service Co., 11 N. P. n. s. 91 (1910).

Power to require information from gas companies. As an incident to its power to regulate the price of gas, a municipal corporation may require gas companies to furnish information relative to the cost of gas.

Cline v. Springfield, 7 N. P. 626; 10 L. D. 389.

Remedy to enforce.

Where it is the duty of a gas company to furnish gas at rates fixed by the council, it may be compelled by a mandatory injunction to perform its duty.

A suit for such purpose may be brought by the city solicitor under G. C. § 4312 (R. S. 1777).

Gaslight Co. v. Zanesville, 47 O. S. 35 (1889).
Toledo v. N. W., etc., Co., 5 C. C. 557; 3 C. D. 273 (1890).
Springfield v. Springfield Gas Co., 12 C. C. n. s. 392; 21 C. D. 446 (1907); aff'd, 81 O. S. 537.

A citizen may, by mandamus, compel a gas company to supply him gas in accordance with its franchise. Such remedy is not provided by § 3982 but exists without express statutory provision.

State v. Union Gas & El. Co., 14 N. P. n. s. 97 (1913).

Section 3983. (Minimum price not to be reduced during term agreed upon.) If council fixes the price at which it shall require a company to furnish electricity or either natural or artificial gas to the citizens, or public buildings or for the purpose of lighting the streets, alleys, avenues, wharves, landing places, public grounds or other places or for other purposes, for a period not exceeding ten years, and the company or persons so to furnish such electricity or gas assents thereto, by written acceptance, filed in the office of the auditor or clerk of the corporation, the council shall not require such company to furnish electricity or either natural or artificial gas, as the case may be, at a less price during the period of time agreed on, not exceeding such ten years. (R. S. Sec. 2479; April 23, 1904, 97 v. 263; May 7, 1869, 66 v. 218, § 416.)

Appeal to public utilities commission by electors. See §§ 614-44 to 614-46.

Term for which municipalities may contract for public lighting under § 3994 is limited to ten years by this section.

Lima Gas Co. v. Lima, 4 C. C. 22; 2 C. D. 396 (1889).

This section a limitation on § 3982. This section is a limitation on the power of regulation conferred by § 3982.

Logan, etc., Co. v. Chillicothe, 65 O. S. 186, 209 (1901).

Acceptance of ordinance constitutes a contract. Where an ordinance, granting a franchise in streets of a municipality upon certain terms and conditions, has been accepted in writing by a gas company, such action constitutes a contract which determines the rights of the parties.

Columbus v. Columbus Gas Co., 76 O. S. 309 (1907); reversing 2 N. P. n. s. 37.

Logan, etc., Co. v. Chillicothe, 65 O. S. 186 (1901).
East Ohio Gas Co. v. Akron, 81 O. S. 33 (1909).
State, ex rel., v. Cincinnati, etc., Co., 18 O. S. 262 (1868).

Provision as to price in franchise ordinance. Where a maximum price is fixed in the franchise ordinance, which is accepted by the grantee, it is a legislative regulation of the price of gas, and a limitation upon the franchise, and must stand as such until changed by subsequent legislation.

Manhattan Trust Co. v. Dayton, 59 Fed. 327; 9 O. F. D. 310.

If ordinance not accepted, power of council to regulate continues. A provision in an ordinance fixing the price of gas for a specified period operates as a proposition to the gas company. If not accepted the power of the council to regulate during such period remains as if the ordinance contained no such provision.

State, ex rel., v. Ironton Gas Co., 37 O. S. 45.

Contract for more than ten years, or for indefinite time, void. An ordinance, accepted by the company, fixing the price of gas for an indefinite time, or for a period exceeding ten years, is void as an agreement.

Manhattan Trust Co. v. Dayton, 59 Fed. 327, 335 (C. C. A. 1893); affirming 55 Fed. 181.

Wellston v. Morgan, 59 O. S. 147, 156, 157 (1898).
Cincinnati, etc., Co. v. Avondale, 43 O. S. 257 (1885).
State. ex rel., v. Ironton Gas Co., 37 O. S. 45 (1881).
See Toledo v. Gas Co., 5 C. C. 557; 3 C. D. 273 (1890).

Council can not change the standard during term of the contract. Where an ordinance fixing the price has been accepted by a gas company, it can not be altered without the consent of the company by fixing another standard which may affect the price previously fixed.

Logan, etc., Co. v. Chillicothe, 65 O. S. 186 (1901).

Contract with one company not impaired by ordinance fixing price for new company at lower rate.

Central Ohio, etc., Co. v. Columbus, 16 L. D. 359 (1905).

See Home Telephone, etc., Co. v. Los Angeles, 211 U. S. 264; 6 O. L.
R. 610.

Construction.   Contract to furnish electric "light" includes lamps.
A contract by an electric light company to "furnish light" at certain
prices, includes the supplying of lamps or globes as well as electric
current.
Newark v. Licking, etc., Co., 4 O. L. R. 351; 3 O. L. R. 644 (1906);
16 L. D. 669.

Invalid contract.   Limitation of action to enjoin payments under.
An action to enjoin payments by a municipality under an invalid contract is barred in ten years from the time the parties attempted to
enter into the contract and to act under it.
Water Co. v. Defiance, 68 O. S. 520 (1903).

Expired contract.   Rights of parties.
See East Ohio Gas Co. v. Akron, 81 O. S. 33 (1909).-
An artificial gas company, whose contract has expired, can not enjoin
a natural gas company from furnishing gas for illuminating purposes,
although the franchise of the natural gas company was for fuel purposes
only.
Circleville, etc., Co. v. Buckeye Gas Co., 69 O. S. 259 (1903);
affirming 1 C. C. n. s. 526.

**Section 3984.   (When council may occupy streets for gas
purposes.)** If at any time any such company required by the
council to lay pipes and light a street, alley, avenue, wharf,
landing place, public ground or building, refuses or neglects
for six months after being notified by authority of the council to comply with such requirement, the council may lay
pipes and erect gas works for lighting such streets, alleys, or
public grounds, and all other streets, alleys, and public
grounds not already lighted, and such company shall thereafter be precluded from using or occupying any of the
streets, alleys, public grounds or buildings not already furnished with gas pipes of such company, and council may
open any street for the purpose of so conveying gas. (R. S.
Sec. 2480; May 7, 1869, 66 v. 218, § 417.)

This section does not authorize a municipality to engage in the
business of selling natural gas.
Central, etc., Co. v. Columbus, 16 L. D. 359 (1905).
See note to § 3990.

**Section 3985.   (Gas companies may be permitted to oc-
cupy streets.)** At any time after the default mentioned in
the preceding section, the council may permit such companies
to use and occupy the streets, alleys, and public grounds of
such corporation for the purpose of lighting them and furnishing gas to the citizens and public buildings. (R. S. Sec.
2481; May 7, 1869, 66 v. 218, § 418.)

Section 3986. (Forfeiture of charter for neglect to furnish gas.) A neglect to furnish gas to the citizens and other consumers of gas or to the corporation by any company in accordance with the prices fixed and established by the council from time to time shall forfeit all rights of such company under the charter by which it has been established, and the council may proceed to erect, or, by ordinance, empower any person to erect gas works, for the supply of gas to such corporation and its citizens. (R. S. Sec. 2482; May 7, 1869, 66 v. 218, § 419.)

A person who installed electric light in his premises and thereafter used gas only occasionally or in cases of emergency is not a "consumer" of gas under this section, and the company is not bound to continue gas connections with his premises.

Adams Exp. Co. v. Cincinnati, etc., Co., 21 W. L. B. 18 (1888).

A municipality may erect a gas plant, although the gas company has not been negligent in furnishing gas.

State v. Hamilton, 47 O. S. 52 (1890).

A natural gas company may be compelled to furnish natural gas for illuminating purposes although its franchise prohibited such use.

Springfield v. Gas Co., 12 C. C. n. s. 392; 21 C. D. 446 (1907); aff'd, no rep., 81 O. S. 537.

Section 3987. (A temporary failure shall work no forfeiture.) A temporary failure to furnish gas shall not operate as a forfeiture, unless such failure is through the neglect or misconduct of such gas-light or gas-light and coke company. (R. S. 2483; May 7, 1869, 66 v. 219, § 420.)

Section 3988. (Council may provide for electric current and gas inspection.) In a municipality in which gas works are constructed, council may provide, by ordinance, for the appointment of an officer, to be known as inspector of gas, whose duty it shall be to inspect all gas and gas meters, and certify the correctness of all bills against consumers of gas, make photometric tests, and perform such other duties as may be prescribed by ordinance, and the council shall fix his compensation. Council may also provide for the inspection and testing of meters used for measuring electric current for electric light, power or other purposes, furnished by any individual or company within the corporation, and may prescribe a suitable charge for such inspection and testing, and the manner of collecting it. (R. S. Sec. 2484; May 18, 1894, 91 v. 300; April 12, 1876, 73 v. 227, § 4; May 7, 1869, 66 v. 219, § 421.)

Constitutionality.

See Cincinnati, etc., Co. v. State, 18 O. S. 237 (1868).

A provision in a franchise requiring the grantee to pay a reasonable sum annually to compensate the municipality for supervision and inspection is valid. A clause in the franchise ordinance providing that the payments are "for the benefit of the gas and light fund of said city" does not render the ordinance invalid, as a means to raise revenue, the clause being subordinate to the principal obligation.

Columbus v. Columbus Gas Co., 76 O. S. 309 (1907).

Section 3989. (Exclusive monopoly shall not be allowed to gas companies.) Council shall not agree by ordinance, contract, or otherwise, with any person or persons for the construction or extension of gas works for manufacturing or supplying the corporation or its inhabitants with gas, which gives or continues to such person or persons the exclusive privilege of using the streets, lanes, commons, or alleys, for the purpose of conveying gas to the corporation, or the citizens thereof, or which deprives council of the right to designate, inspect or regulate the kind of meter to be used for the correct measurement of the gas furnished under such agreement, or which does not specify the exact quality of the gas to be furnished, and reserve to the council the right to enforce an exact compliance with such specification, under such rules as the council may prescribe, nor shall the council make any such agreement which does not secure to the council the right to purchase such works, and all the appurtenances belonging thereto, at any time within the existence of such contract or agreement   (R. S. Sec. 2485; May 7, 1869, 66 v. 219, § 422.)

This section does not apply to natural gas companies.

Logan, etc., Co. v. Chillicothe, 65 O. S. 186, 208, 209 (1901).

The words "persons or persons" include a gas company or other private corporation.

Cincinnati, etc., Co. v. Avondale, 43 O. S. 257 (1885).

The right to use the streets of a municipality for the laying of gas pipes is a franchise, and must emanate either directly or indirectly from the legislature.

State, ex rel., v. Cincinnati Gas, etc., Co., 18 O. S. 262, 291 (1868).

The council of a municipality has no power to grant an exclusive gas franchise in its streets. Such power must have been expressly conferred by the legislature, or be so far necessary to the execution of express powers as to make its existence free from doubt.

Columbus v. Columbus Gas Co., 76 O. S. 309, 339 (1907).

State, ex rel., v. Cincinnati Gas Co., 18 O. S. 262, 289 (1868); approved, 115 U. S. 659.

State, ex rel., v. Hamilton, 47 O. S. 52, 70, 71 (1890).

See, Circleville, etc., Co. v. Buckeye Gas Co., 69 O. S. 259, 271 (1903).

A contract by a gas company to furnish gas to a municipality for public lighting under § 3994 is valid, although it fails to secure to the municipality the right to purchase the plant.

Lima Gas Co. v. Lima, 4 C. C. 22; 2 C. D. 396 (1889).

Section 3990. (Council may erect or purchase gas or electric works.) The council of a municipality may, when it is deemed expedient and for the public good, erect gas works or electric works at the expense of the corporation, or purchase any gas or electric works already erected therein, but in villages where gas works or electrical works have already been erected by any person, company of persons, or corporation, to whom a franchise to erect and operate gas works or electric works has been granted, and such franchise has not yet expired, the council shall, with the consent of the owner or owners, purchase such gas works or electric works already erected therein. If the council and owner or owners of such gas or electric works are unable to agree upon the compensation to be paid therefor, the council may file in the probate court of the county where such gas works or electric works are located, a petition to appropriate such gas works or electric works, and thereupon the same proceedings of appropriation shall be had as is provided for the appropriation of private property by a municipal corporation. A municipal contract existing between any village and such person, company of persons or corporation for the public or street lighting shall be considered as an element of value in fixing the compensation to be paid for such gas works or electric works. (R. S. Sec. 2486; 95 v. 599; 93 v. 59; 66 v. 219, § 423.)

A franchise granted to a gas company does not confer vested rights which are violated by the municipality erecting its own gas plant.
State, ex rel., v. Hamilton, 47 O. S. 52 (1890).
Hamilton, etc., Co. v. Hamilton, 146 U. S. 258 (1892).
This section is constitutional.
Hamilton, etc., Co. v. Hamilton, 146 U. S. 258 (1892).
See Fellows v. Walker, 39 Fed. 651; 6 O. F. D. 362 (1889).
Application of section to natural gas plants.
See Central, etc., Co. v. Columbus, 16 L. D. 359 (1905).
Bellaire Goblet Co. v. Findlay, 5 C. C. 419; 3 C. D. 205 (1891).
Fellows v. Walker, 39 Fed. 651; 6 O. F. D. 362 (1889).
Findlay Gas Light Co. v. Findlay, 2 C. C. 237; 1 C. D. 463 (1887).
A municipality can not enjoin a gas company from laying new pipes in its streets, on the ground that a gas plant owned by the municipality will be injured by the competition.
Hamilton v. Gas Light & Coke Co., 8 N. P. 319; 11 L. D. 513.
An option, in a franchise, giving the municipality the right to purchase the electric light plant upon the establishment of a municipal plant. is a mere offer, and the municipality may build its own plant, without offering to purchase the private plant under the option.
Rep. Atty. Gen. 1911-1912, p. 1642.

Section 3994. (Contracts to supply municipality with electric light or gas.) A municipal corporation may contract with any company for supplying, with electric light, natural or artificial gas, for the purpose of lighting or heating the streets, squares and other public places and buildings in the corporation limits.   (R. S. Sec. 2491; March 31, 1906, 98 v. 150; March 1, 1889, 86 v. 62; March 4, 1887, 84 v. 39; Bates Stats. § 1536-581; R. S. 1880.)

See § 9324.

A contract for public lighting under this section need not contain a provision under G. C. § 3989 securing to the municipality the right to purchase the plant.

Lima Gas Co. v. Lima, 4 C. C. 22; 2 C. D. 396 (1889).

Term of contract. The power of a municipality to contract under this section is by § 3983 limited to ten years.

Lima Gas Co. v. Lima, 4 C. C. 22; 2 C. D. 396 (1889).

A contract for public lighting for a period exceeding ten years is ultra vires and void. Neither party can enforce the same. There can be no recovery for light furnished to the municipality thereunder.

Wellston v. Morgan, 59 O. S. 147 (1898).

Nor is the municipality liable therefor on an account or on a quantum meruit.

Wellston v. Morgan, 65 O. S. 219 (1901).

In Defiance v. McGonigale, 150 Fed. 689; 15 O. F. D. 291 (1907); affirming 140 Fed. 621; 15 O. F. D. 100 (Petition for writ of certiorari denied, 207 U. S. 585), a water company was permitted to recover for water furnished to the municipality, under a contract for a period which exceeded the legal limit, where the contract was acquiesced in by the municipality, and no action taken to rescind or annul the contract until the statute of limitations had barred such action.

See also Defiance Water Co. v. Defiance, 68 O. S. 520 (1903).

Defiance Water Co. v. Defiance, 90 Fed. 753.

Municipality not liable in absence of contract. One who has furnished gas to a municipality can not recover therefor in the absence of a contract.

There is no implied liability to pay, on the part of the municipality.

Wellston v. Morgan, 65 O. S. 219 (1901).

Limitation of action to restrain performance of invalid contract. An action to enjoin payments by a municipal corporation under an invalid contract is barred in ten years from the time the parties attempted to enter into it and act upon it.

Defiance Water Co. v. Defiance, 68 O. S. 520 (1903).

See Defiance v. McGonigale, 150 Fed. 689 (1907).

Purchase by municipality to supply inhabitants. A municipality may, under § 3618, purchase electric current from a private corporation for the purpose of supplying its inhabitants, customers of its municipal plant, as well as for public lighting.

Rep. Atty. Gen., 1910-1911, p. 1026.

Construction of contract for "lowest averaged price" of gas furnished to private consumers in certain other cities. Cincinnati v. Gas Light & Coke Co., 53 O. S. 278.

MISCELLANEOUS.

LIBRARY ASSOCIATIONS.

Section 4019. (Compensation to private company for maintaining library.) The council of each city may levy and collect a tax not to exceed one mill on each dollar of the taxable property of the municipality each year, and pay it to a private corporation or association maintaining and furnishing a free public library for the benefit of the inhabitants of the municipality, as and for compensation for the use and maintenance thereof. Without change or interference in the organization of such corporation or association, the council shall require the treasurer of such corporation or association to make an annual financial report, setting forth all the money and property which has come into its hands during the preceding year, and the disposition thereof, together with recommendation as to its future necessities. (March 15, 1904, 97 v. 35, § 218.)

ART GALLERIES.

Section 4020. (Compensation to private company for maintaining free art gallery.) The council of each city may levy and collect a tax not to exceed one-quarter of one mill on each dollar of the taxable property of the municipality each year, and pay it to a private corporation or association maintaining and furnishing a free museum or gallery for the exhibition of paintings, sculpture and other works of art, and, in connection therewith, an academy for advancing, improving and promoting painting, sculpture, drawing, architecture and other fine arts, and furnishing instruction therein by lectures and otherwise, for the benefit of the inhabitants of the municipality, as and for compensation for the use and maintenance thereof. Without change or interference in the organization of such corporation or association, the council shall require the treasurer of such corporation or association to make an annual financial report, setting forth all the money and property which has come into its hands during the preceding year, and its disposition thereof, together with recommendation as to future necessities. (March 29, 1906, 98 v. 146, § 218a.)

Section 4022. (Council may agree with a corporation for hospital service.) Such council may agree with a corporation or association organized in the municipality for charitable purposes, for the erection and management of a hospital for the sick and disabled, and a permanent interest therein to such extent and upon such terms and conditions as may be agree upon between them. The council shall provide for the payment of the amount agreed upon for such interest, either in one payment or installments or so much each year as the parties may stipulate. (R. S. Sec. 2166.)

Constitutionality.
   See Crossland v. Zanesville, 8 C. C. 652; 4 C. D. 363; reversed,
       56 O. S. 735.
   Cincinnati v. Trustees, 66 O. S. 440.

Section 4198. (Purchase of lands; improvements.) The council of a municipality, and the trustees of a township, may purchase of an incorporated cemetery association the lands, lots, and improvements of such cemetery association remaining unsold, for cemetery purposes, and take a conveyance thereof, but the purchase money in such cases shall be applied to the payment of the legal debts of the association, and to the embellishment and preservation of the land purchased, and such other purposes as the trustees of the cemetery may direct. (R. S. Sec. 2545; 66 v. 213, § 388; R. S. of 1880.)

Section 4199. (Municipality or township may transfer cemetery property to cemetery association.) The council of a municipality, and the trustees of a township, may transfer to an incorporated cemetery association, the lands, lots and improvements of a cemetery, owned and controlled by the municipality or township for cemetery purposes. The cemetery association shall assume all legal debts on the cemeteries so transferred. (R. S. Sec. 2545a; April 22, 1904, 97 v. 165.)

Section 4200. (Rights and titles inviolate.) The rights and titles of lot owners, purchased prior to such sale and conveyance, shall not be questioned, and such lot owners shall continue to hold and occupy their lots, under such rules and regulations as shall be adopted for the government and regulation of the cemetery by the authorities making the purchase. (R. S. Sec. 2546; 66 v. 214, § 389; R. S. 1880.)

MUNICIPAL CODE PROVISIONS. INDETERMINATE FRANCHISES OF
STREET RAILWAYS.

Section 4000-1. ("Public utility" defined. "Indeterminate permit" defined.) Wherever in this act and for the purpose of this act, the term "public utility" shall be taken to mean and include any street railroad operated in whole or in part under the act passed April 22, 1896, commonly known as "The Rogers Law" and entitled "An act to amend and supplement sections 2505a and 2505b of the Revised Statutes of Ohio enacted May 1, 1891, and amended April 18, 1892" or any street railroad operated in connection with or upon the tracks of any such street railroad and any corporation which owns, operates or leases any such street railroads.

The term "indeterminate permit" as used in this act, shall mean and embrace any grant of a municipality to any person, association of persons, company or corporation, of power, right or privilege to own, operate, manage or control any plant or equipment or any part of a plant or equipment within this state of any public utility created under said acts as herein defined, which by the terms thereof is to continue in force until such time as the municipality shall exercise its right to purchase the property of such public utility, in accordance with the terms of this act or until it shall be otherwise terminated according to law. (May 6, 1913, 103 v. 726, § 1; in effect August 8, 1913.)

Section 4000-2. (Authority to surrender franchise and accept indeterminate permit. Purchase by municipality of public utility; how amount of payment determined.) Any such public utility is hereby authorized to surrender any existing license, permit, grant or franchise, and to accept in lieu thereof any indeterminate permit, and the munici-

pality in which all or the major part of the property of such
public utility is situated may accept such surrender and
grant an indeterminate permit, and at the time or times provided in the grant of such permit, or, if no time be provided
in such grant, then at any time after such grant, the municipal corporation may purchase all the property of such public
utility actually used and useful for the convenience of the
public, upon paying therefor just compensation as determined or agreed upon in accordance with the terms of this
act. Any such municipality is authorized to purchase and
operate such property, and every such public utility is hereby required to sell such property for the compensation determined or agreed upon in accordance with the terms of
this act. The amount to be paid for the property may be
determined, first, by condemnation proceedings, or second, by
proceedings as hereinafter described before the public utilities commission of Ohio, or third, by agreement between the
municipality and the public utility as hereinafter described.
In the ascertainment of the compensation to be paid by any
municipality for the property of any public utility, either
by condemnation proceedings before the public utilities commission, the compensation shall be made and awarded only
for such property of the public utility as is used and useful
for the convenience of the public, excluding therefrom the
value of any franchise or right to own, operate or enjoy the
same, in excess of the amount actually paid to such municipal
corporation as the consideration for the grant of such indeterminate permit. (May 6, 1913, 103 v. 727, § 2; in effect
August 8, 1913.)

**Section 4000-3. (Authority to grant indeterminate per-
mit.)** Any municipality may grant an indeterminate permit
to any such public utility upon such terms and conditions as
may be considered conducive to the public interests, and as
provided in this act. (May 6, 1913, 103 v. 727, § 3; in effect
August 8, 1913.)

Section 4000-4. (How compensation determined.) When
the municipality determines to acquire the property by condemnation, the compensation therefor shall be determined in
the manner provided by law for the appropriation of private
property by a municipal corporation. (May 6, 1913, 103 v.
728, § 4; in effect August 8, 1913.)

**Section 4000-5. (Procedure when municipality desires to
acquire public utility.)** When the municipality so desires,
as expressed in the ordinance determining to acquire the

property of any such public utility, to have the compensation determined by the public utilities commission of Ohio,
the municipality shall make a request in writing to such
commission in accordance with the provisions of section 21
[G. C. § 499-8] of an act passed April 28, 1913, entitled "An
act to create the public utilities commission of Ohio, to prescribe its organization, its powers and its duties, and to
repeal sections 487 to 499 inclusive, sections 543 to 551 inclusive, sections 614-24, 614-25, 614-26, 614-69, 614-70, 614-80,
614-81, and 614-83 of the General Code". Thereupon the public utilities commission shall proceed to make an inventory
and valuation of the property of such public utility in accordance with the provisions of said act. The proceedings
for a review of such valuation shall be as prescribed in section 29 of said act [G. C. § 499-16.]   Such valuation shall
not become binding upon the municipality, however, unless
the council thereafter passes an ordinance accepting the
same, which ordinance shall be subject to a referendum in
accordance with the provisions of law relating to referenda
upon municipal ordinances. If not accepted, the municipality shall reimburse the public utility for its expenses reasonably incurred in the valuation proceedings, the amount
to be ascertained and fixed by the commission.   In the
absence of agreement as to compensation as provided in
section 6 hereof [G. C. § 4000-6] the acceptance of an indeterminate permit shall be construed as a consent on the
part of the public utility to the procedure provided for in
this section.   (May 6, 1913, 103 v. 728, § 5; in effect August
8, 1913.)

Section 4000-6. (Agreement by municipality with public
utility as to compensation and time of purchase; proceedings.) Any municipal corporation may contemporaneously
with or at any time after the grant of an indeterminate
permit, as provided in sections 2 and 3 of this act [G. C.
§§ 4000-2, 4000-3], agree with the public utility upon the
compensation to be paid for its property, and the time or
times for the exercise of the privilege of purchase; provided,
however, that no period between the times fixed for such
purchase shall exceed five years.   Upon the determination
of the municipality to acquire the property of such public
utility, the amount to be paid by the municipality and the
terms and conditions of the acquisition shall be as· thus
agreed upon.   The agreement of the municipality shall be
by ordinance.   In the same or other ordinances, the municipality and public utility may agree upon the amount of or
basis of calculating the amount of annual payment, if any,

to be made to the city to be treated as operating expenses of the utility or otherwise; also upon the basis of a division of earnings between the utility and the city; also the purposes for which and the amounts or the basis for calculating the amounts in which new stock, bonds or other securities may be issued; also the minimum net earnings or basis of or device for calculating the minimum net earnings which the utility may earn as a condition precedent to a reduction of fares or rates, and as a test of the reasonableness of extensions; also the initial rates, fares and charges, and the dates of revision of rates, fares or charges, but no period between dates fixed for revision shall exceed five years; also the obligations of the utility with reference to minimum maintenance, renewal and depreciation reserve funds; also for arbitration of differences, also any other terms and conditions relative to the construction, maintenance, financing, operation and control of service of the utility consistent with the terms and conditions of this act and an indeterminate permit. (May 6, 1913, 103 v. 728, § 6; in effect August 8, 1913.)

Section 4000-7. (Ordinance shall not take effect until **submission of question to electors; notice of election.)** No ordinance passed pursuant to the provisions of section 6 hereof [G. C. § 4000-6], shall take effect until submitted to the electors of the municipality, at a special or general election held in the municipality at such time as council may determine, and approved by a majority of the electors voting thereon. The ordinance shall be duly passed by an affirmative vote of not less than a majority of the members elected or appointed to the council, and shall be subject to the approval of the mayor as provided by law. The ordinance shall specify the form or phrasing of the question to be placed upon the ballot. Thirty days' notice of the election shall be given by publication once a week for four consecutive weeks in two daily or weekly newspapers published or circulated in the municipality, which notice shall contain the full form or phrasing of the question to be submitted. The clerk of the council shall certify the passage of such ordinance to the officers having control of elections in such municipality, who shall cause such question to be voted on at the general or special election as specified in the ordinance. (May 6, 1913, 103 v. 729, § 7; in effect August 8, 1913.)

Section 4000-8. (Time of continuance of indeterminate permit; effect of acceptance.) Any indeterminate permit granted under the terms of this act shall continue in force until such time as the municipality shall acquire the property of the public utility as provided in this act, or until otherwise terminated according to the terms and conditions of the permit. The acceptance of an indeterminate permit shall be deemed to deprive the public utility of all rights under any license, permit, grant or franchise or granted in any municipal ordinance or resolution existing at the time of the granting of the permit. From the time of such grant, the rates, fares, charges, service, accounts, equipments, repairs, additions, extensions, improvements, transfers, joint use, depreciation, capitalization, bonded or other indebtedness and all other terms and conditions relating to the financing, construction, maintenance, and operation of such utility shall be subject to municipal regulation; provided, however, that such power of municipal regulation shall not be exercised in a manner inconsistent with the express terms of the ordinance granting the permit.

Provided, also, that the capitalization and bonded or other indebtedness for improvement and other purposes beyond the limits of the municipality granting the permit shall remain subject to regulation by the state public utilities commission as provided by law; but no such capitalization or indebtedness shall be given effect as a basis for purchase price to or rate regulation by the municipality contrary to the agreement of the municipality and public utility as expressed in the ordinance granting the permit.

Nothing in this act shall be construed as conferring upon any municipality, officer, department, or commission thereof any power to grant an indeterminate permit to any such public utility in any other manner than by ordinance, or to prescribe that such ordinance shall take effect in any other manner than by acceptance by the public utility to which it is granted by filing a written acceptance thereof with the clerk of the city council or other officers named in such permit. (May 6, 1913, 103 v. 729, § 8; in effect August 8, 1913.)

Section 4000-9. (Rates, tolls or charges.)

In the absence of agreement as to rates, fares or charges, as provided in section 6 hereof [G. C. § 4000-6], all rates, fares, tolls and charges for services rendered and commodities furnished by any public utility shall be sufficient to yield a reasonable compensation to the public utility operating under an indeterminate permit, and in the ascertainment of what shall constitute such reasonable rates, fares, tolls, and charges, the municipal corporation shall have due regard, among other things, to the value of all the property of the public utility actually used and useful for the convenience of the public, excluding therefrom the value of any franchise or right to own, operate or enjoy the same, in excess of the amount actually paid to such municipal corporation as the consideration for the grant of such indeterminate permit and exclusive of any value added thereto by reason of a monopoly or merger, and also with due regard to the necessity of making reservation out of the income for surplus, depreciation and contingencies.   (May 6, 1913, 103 v. 730, § 9; in effect August 8, 1913.)

Section 4000-10.   (Department may be created to exercise the powers conferred; procedure before department.)   In the event that any municipality shall establish any department for the purpose of exercising any of the powers herein conferred, such department is hereby granted such powers of supervision and regulation of any public utility operating under an indeterminate grant, as are provided by law and in the ordinance granting the permit, and as may be from time to time prescribed by the terms of any ordinance not inconsistent with the express provisions of the ordinance granting the permit.   It is hereby made the duty of every such public utility to comply with all orders and regulations of such department issued by virtue of the powers herein granted. The procedure of, by and before such department shall be as ordained by the council of the municipality in the permit and other ordinances.   The council shall also have power to prescribe the penalties for non-compliance with and the methods of enforcement of the orders and regulations of such department, not inconsistent with the express provisions of the ordinance granting the permit.   The provisions of the permit or of any ordinance or order of the municipality passed or issued under this act shall be binding upon all public officers and commissions.   (May 6, 1913, 103 v. 730, § 10; in effect August 8, 1913.)

Section 4000-11.   (Appeals, when ordinance contains no provisions.)   When the ordinance granting the permit contains no provisions whatever relative to appeal from or arbitration concerning the orders of the municipality, the utility may appeal to the public utilities commission of Ohio from any order of the municipality which is in violation of law or of the permit, or from any unreasonable order concerning matters upon which the parties have not agreed in the permit itself.   Such appeal shall be by petition filed within thirty days from the issuance of the order.   The filing of any such appeal shall not suspend the operation of the order appealed from unless the public utility shall give an undertaking payable to the municipality in such amount and containing such conditions as may be fixed by said commission. (May 6, 1913, 103 v. 731, § 11; in effect August 8, 1913.)

Section 4000-12. (Procedure on appeals to public utilities commission.) In the event that the ordinance granting the permit provides for an appeal to or arbitration by the state public utilities commission, then such commission shall determine such appeal or arbitration according to the procedure, methods, terms and conditions provided for in such ordinance. The provisions of law specially providing for judicial review of the orders of the public utilities commission shall not apply to actions of the commission upon such appeals or arbitration. Except as provided in this and the next preceding section, the provisions of law relating to appeals, complaints, or applications to the public utilities commission shall not apply to public utilities operating under indeterminate permits. (May 6, 1913, 103 v. 731, § 12; in effect August 8, 1913.)

Section 4000-13. (How duties shall be enforced.) In addition to the methods of enforcement herein provided, the duties herein imposed upon public utilities shall be enforceable by mandamus and all other judicial proceedings provided by law for the enforcement of the duties of public utilities. (May 6, 1913, 103 v. 731, § 13; in effect August 8, 1913.)

Section 4000-14. (Other methods unaffected.) Nothing in this act shall be construed to deprive any municipality of its rights to prescribe, by charter, any other methods, terms or conditions according to and upon which indeterminate permits may be granted in such municipality. (May 6, 1913, 103 v. 731, § 14; in effect August 8, 1913.)

Section 4000-15. (Independent sections.) The invalidity of any section or any part of this act shall not be deemed to affect the validity of any other section or part thereof. (May 6, 1913, 103 v. 731, § 15; in effect August 8, 1913.)

Section 4560. (Jurisdiction over railroad forming part of boundary line.) When the line of a railroad adjoins or forms a part of the boundary line of a municipal corporation, such municipal corporation shall have jurisdiction over the entire width of the right of way of the line of railroad, so adjoining or forming a part of the boundary line of such municipal corporation, for the punishment of the violation of the ordinances of such municipal corporation.   (92 v. 428, § 1; Bates Stats. § 1536-884.)

PART XII.

TAXATION OF CORPORATIONS AND STOCK.

Section 5324. ("**Investment in stocks.**") The term "investment in stocks" as so used, includes all moneys invested in the capital or stock of a bank whether incorporated under the laws of this state or the United States, or an association, corporation, joint stock company, or other company, the capital or stock of which is or may be divided into shares, which are transferable by each owner without the consent of the other partners or stockholders, for the taxation of which no special provision is made by law, held by persons residing within this state, either for themselves or others. (R. S., Sec. 2730; 95 v. 533; R. S. 1880; S. & C. 1439; 76 v. 28, § 1; 75 v. 436, § 1; 71 v. 96, § 78; 56 v. 175, § 1.)

Taxation of bank stock, § 5408.
Exemption of stock in Ohio corporations, §§ 192, 5372 and notes.
Stock in foreign corporations, when exempt, §§ 192, 5372.
Stock in a national bank is an "investment in stocks" under this section and not a "credit" under § 5327. Its owner can not deduct his debts from the value of the stock.
Chapman v. Bank, 56 O. S. 310 (1887); aff'd, 173 U. S. 205.
Niles v. Shaw, 50 O. S. 370 (1893).
See notes to §§ 5372 and 5412.

Section 5325. ("**Personal property.**") The term "personal property" as so used, includes first, every tangible thing being the subject of ownership, whether animate or inanimate, other than money, and not forming part of a parcel of real property, as hereinbefore defined; second, the capital stock, undivided profits, and all other means not forming part of the capital stock of every company, whether incorporated or unincorporated, and every share, portion, or interest in such stocks, profits, or means, by whatsoever name designated, inclusive of every share or portion, right, or interest either legal or equitable, in and to every ship, vessel, or boat, of whatsoever name or description, used or designed to be used either exclusively or partially in navigating any of the waters within or bordering on this state, whether such ship, vessel, or boat is within the jurisdiction of this state or elsewhere, and whether it has been enrolled, registered, or licensed at a collector's office, or within a collection district in this state, or not; third, money loaned on pledge or mortgage of real estate, although a deed or other instrument may have been given for it, if between the parties thereto it is considered as security merely. (R. S. Sec. 2730; 95 v. 533; R. S. 1880; S. & C. 1439; 76 v. 28, § 1; 75 v. 436, § 1; 71 v. 96, § 78; 56 v. 175, § 1.)

Section 5327. ("Credits.") The term "credits" as so used, means the excess of the sum of all legal claims and demands, whether for money or other valuable thing, or for labor or service due or to become due to the person liable to pay taxes thereon, including deposits in banks or with persons in or out of the state, other than such as are held to be money, as hereinbefore defined, when added together, estimating every such claim or demand at its true value in money, over and above the sum of legal bona fide debts owing by such person. In making up the sum of such debts owing, there shall not be taken into account an obligation to a mutual insurance company, nor an unpaid subscription to the capital stock of a joint stock company, nor a subscription for a religious, scientific, literary, or charitable purpose; nor an acknowledgement of indebtedness, unless founded on some consideration actually received, and believed at the time of making such acknowledgement to be a full consideration therefor; nor an acknowledgement made for the purpose of diminishing the amount of credits to be listed for taxation; nor a greater amount or portion of a liability as surety, than the person required to make the statement of such credits believes that such surety is in equity bound, and will be compelled to pay, or to contribute, in case there are no securities. Pensions receivable from the United States shall not be held to be credits; and no person shall be required to take into account in making up the amount of credits, a greater portion of any credits than he believes will be received or can be collected, or a greater portion of an obligation given to secure the payment of rent than the amount that has accrued on any lease and remains unpaid. (R. S. Sec. 2730; 56 v. 175, § 1 (§ 2); 71 v. 96, § 78; 75 v. 436, § 1; 76 v. 28, § 1; S. & C. 1439; 95 v. 533.)

A foreign corporation may deduct from the claims due to it, arising out of its Ohio business, such of its debts as arise out of the same source.

Hubbard v. Brush, 61 O. S. 252 (1899).

The surplus dividend fund of an insurance company is not a "debt" under this section.

French v. Insurance Co., 12 L. D. 183 (1901).

A life insurance company can not deduct its accumulated deferred divident and reserve fund.

Insurance Co. v. Hynicka, 5 N. P. n. s. 255; 18 L. D. 1 (1907).

Reinsurance is not a debt of an insurance company under this section.

Insurance Co. v. Cappelar, 38 O. S. 560 (1883).

See also as to deductions, note to G. C. § 5412.

Where government bonds, delivered by the owner to a national bank to be deposited as security for its circulating notes, under an agreement whereby the bonds were to be returned on demand, or to be paid for as the owner might elect, and whereby the bank agreed to pay the interest received thereon, together with a stipulated annual sum, it was held to be a bailment of bonds to the bank, and not a taxable credit.

Clark v. Gault, 77 O. S. 497 (1908).

An owner of bonds is not entitled to deduct his debts therefrom.

Payne v. Watterson, 37 O. S. 121 (1881).

Credits, arising out of machines rented or leased to persons outside of Ohio, are taxable in this state.

Rep. Atty. Gen. 1911-1912, p. 676.

Where an Ohio corporation has ordered machinery to be constructed for it in another state, such machinery is not taxable in Ohio until it reaches this state, but the right to such machinery may be a taxable "credit."

Rep. Atty. Gen. 1911-1912, p. 676.

Section 5328. (Property subject to taxation.) All real or personal property in this state, belonging to individuals or corporations, and all moneys, credits, investments in bonds, stocks, or otherwise, of persons residing in this state, shall be subject to taxation, except only such property as may be expressly exempted therefrom. Such property, moneys, credits, and investments shall be entered on the list of taxable property as prescribed in this title. (R. S. Sec. 2731; 56 v. 175, § 1; 71 v. 96, § 78; S. & C. 1438; S. & S. 757.)

Bank stock, § 5408.
Stock in Ohio corporations, §§ 192. 5372.
Stock in foreign corporations, §§ 192, 5372.

Provisions in special charter limiting rate of taxation. A provision in a special charter, granted under a former constitution, providing for a tax rate in lieu of the rate which might be imposed by general taxation, was held to constitute a contract, which could not be impaired by subsequent legislation.

Bank v. Knoop, 16 How. (U. S.) 369.
Dodge v. Woolsey, 18 How. 331.
Bank v. Debolt, 18 How. 380.
State v. Auditor, 5 O. S. 444.
Bank v. Lewis, 5 O. S. 447.
Sebastian v. Bridge Co., 21 O. S. 451.
State v. Bank, 5 Ohio (pt. 1) 125.
See Debolt v. Trust Co., 1 O. S. 563.
Bank v. Debolt, 1 O. S. 591.
Bank v. Toledo, 1 O. S. 622.
Plank Road Co. v. Husted, 3 O. S. 578.
Bank v. Wilbor, 7 O. S. 481.
Skelly v. Bank, 9 O. S. 606.
Insurance Co. v. Debolt, 16 How. (U. S.) 416.

Section 5364. (Property of certain societies.) Real or personal property belonging to an incorporated post of the grand army of the republic, union veterans union, grand lodge of free and accepted masons, grand lodge of the independent order of odd fellows, grand lodge of the knights of Pythias, association for the exclusive benefit, use and care of aged, infirm and dependent women, a religious or secret benevolent organization maintaining a lodge system, an incorporated association of ministers of any church, or incorporated association of commercial traveling men, an association which is intended to create a fund or is used or intended to be used for the care and maintenance of indigent soldiers of the late war, indigent members of said organizations, and the widows, orphans and beneficiaries of the deceased members of such organizations, and not operated with a view to profit or having as their principal object the issuance of insurance certificates of membership, and the interest or income derived therefrom, shall not be taxable, and the trustees of any such organizations shall not be required to return or list such property for taxation. (R. S. Sec. 2732-3; 94 v. 371; 93 v. 219; 87 v. 141.)

This section is, at least in part, unconstitutional.
Rep. Atty. Gen. 1911-1912, p. 692.

Section 5365-1. (Funds exempt from taxation.) Every fraternal benefit society organized or licensed under this act is hereby declared to be a charitable and benevolent institution, and all of its funds shall be exempt from all and every state, county, district, municipal and school tax, other than taxes on real estate and office equipment. (May 31, 1911, 102 v. 546, § 30.)

Section 5370. (Who shall list personal property.) Each

person of full age and sound mind shall list the personal property of which he is the owner, and all moneys in his possession, all moneys invested, loaned, or otherwise controlled by him, as agent or attorney, or on account of any other person or persons, company or corporation, and all moneys deposited subject to his order, check, or draft; all credits due or owing from any person or persons, body corporate or politic, whether in or out of such county; and all money loaned on pledge or mortgage of real estate, although a deed or other instrument may have been given for it, if between the parties, it is considered as security merely. The property of a ward shall be listed by his guardian, of a minor child, idiot, or lunatic having no guardian, by his father, if living, if not, by his mother, if living, and if neither father nor mother is living by the person having such property in charge; of a person for whose benefit property is held in trust, by the trustees; of an estate of a deceased person, by his executor or administrator; of corporations whose assets are in the hands of receivers, by such receivers; of a company, firm, or corporation, by the president or principal accounting officer, partner or agent thereof; and all surplus or undivided profits held by a society for savings or bank having no capital stock, by the president or principal accounting officer. (R. S. Sec. 2734; March 7, 1879, 76 v. 28, § 2; May 11, 1878, 75 v. 441, § 1; April 8, 1865, 62 v. 105, § 4.)

In listing bank deposits, outstanding checks which have not been certified can not be deducted.
Insurance Co. v. Hynicka, 5 N. P. n. s. 255; 18 L. D. 1 (Super. Ct., Cin., 1907); affirming 4 N. P. n. s. 297; 17 L. D. 80.
The receiver of a corporation appointed in a dissolution proceeding must return for taxation the property in his possession.
In re Patent Wood Keg Co., 13 N. P. n. s. 321; 23 L. D. 381 (C. P. 1912).

Section 5371.   (Where personal property shall be listed.)
A person required to list property, on behalf of others, shall list it in the township, city, or village in which he would be required to list it if such property were his own. He shall list it separately from his own, specifying in each case the name of the person, estate, company, or corporation, to whom it belongs. Merchants' and manufacturers' stock, and personal property upon farms shall be listed in the township, city or village in which it is situated. All other personal property, moneys, credits, and investments, except as otherwise specially provided, shall be listed in the township, city, or village in which the person to be charged with taxes thereon resides at the time of the listing thereof, if

such person resides within the county where the property is listed, and if not, then in the township, city, or village where the property is when listed. (R. S. Sec. 2735; April 8, 1865, 62 v. 105, § 4.)

The location of a corporation designated in its articles of incorporation is the situs of the corporation for taxation purposes. The statement in the articles of incorporation is conclusive, although much of the business of the corporation is transacted elsewhere.

A corporation located in a township outside of the limits of a city may, when the city limits are extended to include the site of its office, remove its office and location to another part of the township and avoid municipal taxation.

Pelton v. Transportation Co., 37 O. S. 450 (1882).
Booth v. Wonderly, 36 N. J. L. 250.
Union Steamboat Co. v. Buffalo, 82 N. Y. 351.

Tangible personal property, actually located in another state, is not taxable in Ohio, although belonging to an Ohio corporation.

Rep. Atty. Gen. 1911-1912, p. 676.

Machines leased or rented by an Ohio manufacturer to persons outside of Ohio are not taxable in Ohio, but the credits arising therefrom are taxable.

Rep. Atty. Gen. 1911-1912, p. 676.

Foreign corporation. The residence of a foreign corporation, having its principal office in a county in Ohio where all of its business is transacted, is, for taxation purposes, in such county.

Sims v. Best, 1 C. C. n. s. 41; 15 C. D. 149 (1903).
Deduction of debts from credits. See § 5327.

Section 5372.   (In whose name listed.) Personal property of every description, moneys and credits, investments in bonds, stocks, joint stock companies, or otherwise, shall be listed in the name of the person who was the owner thereof on the day preceding the second Monday of April, in each year. No person shall be required to list for taxation any shares of the capital stock of a company, the capital stock of which is taxed in the name of such company. (R. S. Sec. 2746; May 5, 1859, 56 v. 175, § 59.)

"Investment in stocks" defined, § 5324.
"Credits" defined, § 5327.

Capital stock. The "capital stock" of a company under this section means its capital or property. Where a corporation is required to list its property, the shares of its stock are exempt from taxation, whether or not the corporation has actually listed its property.

Lee v. Sturges, 46 O. S. 153, 160, 175 (1889).
Jones v. Davis, 35 O. S. 474, 476, 477 (1880).

Pledged stock, if taxable, is taxed in the name of the pledgor, where it has not been transferred to the pledgee on the corporate books.

Ratterman v. Ingalls, 48 O. S. 468, 491 (1891).

Scrip certificates not taxable, when.

Adams v. Shields, 17 C. C. 129; 9 C. D. 558 (1898); aff'd, 61 O. S. 643.
State v. Franklin, 10 Ohio 91 (1840).

Void or illegal stock is not taxable.
McDonald v. Haggerty, 7 C. C. 508; 4 C. D. 702 (1893).
"False return of stock," what constitutes.
Ratterman v. Ingalls, 48 O. S. 468 (1891).
Ratterman v. Phipps, 7 C. C. 458; 4 C. D. 678 (1893).

Exemptions from taxation. An exemption from taxation must be expressed in clear and unmistakable terms.
Lee v. Sturges, 46 O. S. 160 (1889).
Scott v. Smith, 2 N. P. n. s. 617; 15 L. D. 590 (C. P. 1905).

Stock in Ohio corporations. Shares of stock in Ohio corporations are exempt from taxation.
G. C. § 192.
Prior to the amendment of § 192 in 1904 (97 v. 496), stock in an Ohio corporation was exempt only when the property of the corporation was taxed in its name in Ohio.
Lander v. Burke, 65 O. S. 532 (1901).
No distinction is made in this section between preferred and common stock.
Miller v. Ratterman, 47 O. S. 141 (1890).

Stock in foreign corporations. As a general rule stock in foreign corporations owned by residents of Ohio is taxable in Ohio, although the corporate property is taxed in its home state.
Bradley v. Bauder, 36 O. S. 28 (1880).
Worthington v. Sebastian, 25 O. S. 1 (1874).
Lee v. Sturges, 46 O. S. 153 (1889).
Sturges v. Carter, 114 U. S. 511 (1885).
And although certificates representing the stock are in the possession of an agent in another state where taxes are paid thereon.
Rep. of Atty. Gen., 1906, p. 257.
But where all the property of the corporation is taxed in Ohio in the name of the corporation, the shares of its stock are exempt under §§ 192 and 5372.
Hubbard v. Brush, 61 O. S. 252 (1899).
Stock in a foreign corporation is also exempt where its holder furnishes satisfactory proof to the taxing authorities that at least two-thirds of its property is taxed in Ohio and the remainder in other states, providing the corporation also pays, as an annual franchise tax, the same percentage on its entire authorized capital stock that is required of an Ohio corporation on its subscribed or issued stock.
G. C. § 192.
Shares of stock in a foreign corporation are taxable, although its capital is wholly invested in patent rights, which are exempt under federal law.
Scott v. Smith, 2 N. P. n. s. 617; 15 L. D. 590 (C. P. 1905).

Other exemptions. The exemption from taxation of the first $100 of personal property applies only to natural persons and not to corporations.
Rep. Atty. Gen., 1911-1912, p. 656.
Charitable institutions, lodges, etc., G. C. § 5364.
Churches, colleges, etc., G. C. §§ 5349, 7915-1.
See Watterson v. Halliday, 77 O. S. 150 (1907).
Humphreys v. State, 70 O. S. 68 (1904).
Little v. Seminary, 72 O. S. 417.
Cleveland, etc., Ass'n. v. Pelton, 36 O. S. 253 (1880).
Humphries v. Little Sisters, 29 O. S. 201 (1876).
Morning Star Lodge v. Hayslip, 23 O. S. 144 (1872).

New Jerusalem Soc. v. Richardson, 10 N. P. n. s. 214 (C. P. 1910).
Y. W. C. A. v. Spencer, 9 C. C. n. s. 351; 19 C. D. 249 (1907).

Section 5404. (Corporation returns.) The president, secretary, and principal accounting officer of every incorporated company, except banking or other corporations whose taxation is specifically provided for, for whatever purpose they may have been created, whether incorporated by a law of this state or not, shall list for taxation, verified by the oath of the person so listing, all the personal property thereof, and all real estate necessary to the daily operations of the company, moneys and credits of such company or corporation within the state, at the true value in money. (April 12, 1911, 102 v. 61; April 8, 1876, 73 v. 139, § 16; R. S. Sec. 2744.)

Stock in corporations. See §§ 192, 5372 and notes.
Banks, § 5407 et seq.

Excise or privilege tax does not exempt corporation. The imposition of a franchise or privilege tax does not bring a corporation within the exception of this section relating to corporations whose taxation is otherwise provided for.
Scottish, etc., Ins. Co. v. Bowland, 196 U. S. 610; 2 O. L. R. 515 (1904).
Western Assur. Co. v. Halliday, 127 Fed. 830 (C. C. 1903).
See Southern Gum Co. v. Laylin, 66 O. S. 578 (1902).

Credits of foreign corporation. Choses in action, whether book accounts, notes, etc., of foreign corporations that are kept in Ohio and rise out of the corporate business transacted here are taxable in Ohio under §§ 5404 to 5406.
Hubbard v. Brush, 61 O. S. 252 (1899).
Rep. Atty. Gen. 1911-1912, p. 676.
But if the books, notes, etc., are kept at its home office in another state, and all collections made from the home office, the credits are not taxable in Ohio.
Rep. Atty. Gen., 1911-1912, p. 630.
Where a foreign corporation loans money on mortgages in this state, through a resident agent, the agent holding the notes and mortgages in this state, such credits are taxable in Ohio.
Rep. Atty. Gen., 1911-1912, p. 630.
Conditional sale contracts or leases, owned by a foreign corporation, covering goods sold by sample and shipped into Ohio to fill orders, are not taxable in Ohio.
4 Opins. Atty. Gen., 826 (1898).
See note to § 194 "doing business" in Ohio.
Rep. Atty. Gen., 1911-1912, p. 676.
Bonds deposited with state officers pursuant to statutory requirements.
See § 5437.
Sims v. Best, 1 C. C. n. s. 41; 15 C. D. 149 (1903).
Scottish, etc., Ins. Co. v. Bowland, 196 U. S. 611; 2 O. L. R. 515 (1904).
Western, etc., Co. v. Halliday, 126 Fed. 257 (1903).

Miscellaneous. Franchise to be a corporation.
Exchange Bank v. Hines, 3 O. S. 1, 7 (1853).

Southern Gum Co. v. Laylin, 66 O. S. 578 (1902).
Unpaid stock subscriptions.
Farmers Ins. So. v. La Rue, 22 O. S. 630 (1872).
Interest in unincorporated company.
Pomeroy Salt Co. v. Davis, 21 O. S. 555 (1871).
How value of property ascertained.
State v. Jones, 51 O. S. 492, 511 (1894).

Insurance companies are required to make returns of taxable property under this section.
Scottish, etc., Ins. Co. v. Bowland, 196 U. S. 610; 2 O. L. R. 515 (1904).

A mutual insurance company, incorporated in Ohio, is required to return for taxation notes and cash, in the possession of its agents in other states, although it is required to pay an excise tax for the privilege of doing business in such states.
Insurance Co. v. Hard, 8 N. P. 36; 10 L. D. 469 (1900); s. c., 59 O. S. 248 (1898).

Section 5405. (**Returns. Valuation by county auditor. Apportionment.**) Return shall be made to the several auditors of the respective counties where such property is situated, together with a statement of the amount thereof which is situated in each township, village, city, or taxing district therein. Upon receiving such returns, the auditor shall ascertain and determine the value of the property of such companies, and deduct from the aggregate sum so found of each, the value as assessed for taxation of any real estate included in the return. The value of the property of each of such companies, after so deducting the value of all the real estate included in the return, shall be apportioned by the auditor to such cities, villages, townships, or taxing districts, pro rata, in proportion to the value of the real estate and fixed property included in the return, in each of such cities, villages, townships, or taxing districts. The auditor shall place such apportioned valuation on the tax duplicate and taxes shall be levied and collected thereon at the same rate and in the same manner that taxes are levied and collected on other personal property in such township, village, city or taxing district. (April 12, 1911, 102 v. 61; April 8, 1876, 73 v. 139, § 16; R. S. Sec. 2744.)

Corporation returns are made under § 5404 and bank returns under § 5411. In both cases real estate must be included in the return, and the deductions for real estate values are made by the auditor.
Rep.. Atty. Gen., 1911-1912, p. 1352.

Section 5406. (**Duty of county auditor.**) The auditor of each county, on or before the first Monday of May, annually, shall furnish the president, secretary, principal accounting officer, or agent as provided in the next two preceding sections, the necessary blanks for the purpose of making such returns, but neglect or failure on the part of the county auditor to furnish such blanks shall not excuse such president, secretary, accountant, or agent, from making the returns within the time specified herein. If the county auditor to whom returns are made is of the opinion that false or incorrect valuations have been made, that the property of the corporation or association has not been listed at its full value, or that it has not been listed in the location where it properly belongs, or if no return has been made to the county auditor, he must have the property valued and assessed. This section and the next preceding section shall not tax any stock or interest held by the state in a joint stock company. (R. S. Sec. 2744; April 8, 1876, 73 v. 139, § 16.)

See Ohio, etc., Co. v. Hard, 59 O. S. 248 (1898).
State v. Halliday, 61 O. S. 352 (1899).

BANKS AND BANKERS.

Section 5407. ("Bank" and "bankers" defined.) A company, association, or person, not incorporated under a law of this state or of the United States, for banking purposes, who keeps an office or other place of business, and engages in the business of lending money, receiving money on deposit, buying and selling bullion, bills of exchange, notes, bonds, stocks, or other evidences of indebtedness, with a view to profit, is a bank, or banker, within the meaning of this chapter. (R. S. Sec. 2758; 64 v. 204, § 12; S. & S. 765.)

See Robinson v. Ward, 13 O. S. 293.
A society for savings incorporated under a special charter (see § 9812 et seq.), having no capital stock is not taxable under this chapter. Rep. Atty. Gen., 1911-1912, p. 645.
A firm or corporation engaged in a general merchandising business, not incorporated for banking purposes, which accepts deposits subject to check and pays interest thereon, but does not loan money or buy and sell evidences of indebtedness, is not a bank within the meaning of this section and is not required to make returns under this chapter. Rep. Atty. Gen., 1911-1912, p. 662.

Section 5408. (Shares or capital of banks, incorporated or unincorporated.) All the shares of the stockholders in an incorporated bank or banking association, located in this state, incorporated or organized under the laws of the state or of the United States, and all the shares of the stockholders in an unincorporated bank, located in this state, the capital stock of which is divided into shares held by the owners of such bank, and the capital employed, or the property representing it, in an unincorporated bank the capital stock of which is not divided into shares, located in this state, shall be listed at the true value in money, and taxed only in the city, ward, or village where such bank is located. (R. S. Sec. 2762; April 23, 1904, 97 v. 279; April 16, 1900, 94 v. 348; April 16, 1867, 64 v. 204, § 1.)

Investment in stocks defined, § 5324.

Shares, not corporate property, taxed. Under §§ 5408 to 5414 the shares of the stockholders are taxed, and not the property of the bank except its real estate.

Cleveland Trust Co. v. Lander, 62 O. S. 266 (1900); aff'd, 184 U. S. 111.

Frazer v. Siehern, 16 O. S. 614 (1866).

The shares are taxed in the name of the stockholders and not the bank.

Miller v. First N. B., 46 O. S. 424 (1889).

National bank stock. The state has power to tax shares in national banks located in Ohio, subject to the limitations of U. S. Rev. Stats. § 5219, that such tax shall not exceed the rate imposed upon other moneyed capital of individuals, nor that imposed upon shares in state banks.

Frazer v. Siebern, 16 O. S. 614 (1866).

See Lander v. Mercantile N. B., 186 U. S. 458 (1902).

The restriction of § 5219 R. S. U. S. requires that both the tax rate and the assessed value of shares shall not be greater than on moneyed capital of individuals.

Cleveland Trust Co. v. Lander, 62 O. S. 266 (1900); aff'd, 184 U. S. 111.

Where a tax upon national bank shares exceeds the restrictions of § 5219 R. S. U. S. its collection will be enjoined only upon payment of a sum which is a fair equivalent for the tax on state banks.

Frazer v. Siebern, 16 O. S. 614 (1866).

Where other moneyed capital is systematically and intentionally valued for taxation far below its true value while national bank shares are assessed at their true value, the state taxing authorities may be enjoined, in federal court, upon tender of an amount equal to the tax on other property, from collecting the excess, although the state statutes require all property to be taxed at its true value.

Pelton v. Commercial N. B., 101 U. S. 144; 4 O. F. D. 573 (1880).

Cummings v. Merchants N. B., 101 U. S. 153; 4 O. F. D. 578 (1880).

Exchange N. B. v. Miller, 19 Fed. 372; 4 O. F. D. 578 (1884).

Stock in national banks belonging to nonresidents is taxable in Ohio.

Rep. Atty. Gen., 1911-1912, pp. 592, 610.

Miscellaneous. Deductions. See § 5412 and note.

Value of shares.

Chapman v. First N. B., 56 O. S. 310 (1897); s. c., 173 U. S. 205; 12 O. F. D. 446.

Tax a lien on shares, § 5672.

Bank to collect tax from stockholders. See §§ 5672, 5673.

See Miller v. First N. B., 9 W. L. B. 353 (C. P. 1883); aff'd, 46 O. S. 424.

Miller v. Fourth N. B., 12 W. L. B. 66 (Dist. Ct. 1884).

A bank is not required to make return for taxation until actively engaged in doing business. Money paid on stock subscriptions before business is commenced should be listed by the subscribers.

Rep. Atty. Gen., 1909-1910, p. 158.

Corporation returns are made under § 5404 and bank returns under § 5411. In both cases real estate must be included in the return, and the deductions for real estate values are made by the auditor.

Rep. Atty. Gen., 1911-1912, p. 1352.

Section 5409. (Tax on real estate of bank.) The real estate of a bank or banking association shall be taxed in the place where it is located, in like manner as the real estate of persons is taxed. (R. S. Sec. 2763; April 16, 1867, 64 v. 204, § 2.)

Section 5410. (Names of stockholders and shares of each.) There shall be kept in the office at all times where the business of such bank or banking association is transacted, a full and correct list of the names and residences of the stockholders therein, and the number of shares held by each, which at all times during business hours shall be open to the inspection of all officers who are or may be authorized to list or assess the value of such shares for taxation. (R. S. Sec. 2764; April 16, 1867, 64 v. 204, § 3.)

Cited, Cleveland Trust Co. v. Lander, 62 O. S. 266.

Section 5411. (Return made by cashier, etc., to auditor.) The cashier of each incorporated bank, and the cashier, manager or owner of each unincorporated bank, shall return to the auditor of the county in which such bank is located, between the first and second Mondays of May, annually, a report in duplicate under oath, exhibiting in detail, and under appropriate heads, the resources and liabilities of such bank at the close of business on the Wednesday next preceding the said second Monday, with a full statement of the names and residences of the stockholders therein, the number of shares held by each and the par value of each share, and of the amount of capital employed by unincorporated banks, not divided into shares, and the name, residence and proportional interest of each owner of such bank. (R. S. Sec. 2765; April 23, 1904, 97 v. 279; April 16, 1900, 94 v. 347; April 12, 1877, 74 v. 88, § 1.)

The shares must be listed in the names of the stockholders, not in the name of the bank.

Miller v. First N. B., 46 O. S. 424 (1889).

Correction of returns is provided for by § 5413 and not § 5401.

Miller v. First N. B., 46 O. S. 424.

Bank to pay tax, § 5673.

The return of bank stock should be made by the cashier, and not by the stockholders.

Lander v. Mercantile N. B., 118 Fed. 785; 14 O. F. D. 54; 55 C. C. A. 523 (1902).

Former statute requiring return by savings societies.

See Collett v. Springfield Sgs. Soc., 13 C. C. 131; 7 C. D. 146 (1896).

Section 5412. (Auditor to fix value of bank shares or property.) Upon receiving such report the county auditor shall fix the total value of the shares of such banks, and the value of the property representing the capital employed by unincorporated banks, the capital stock of which is not divided into shares, each, according to their true value in money, and deduct from the aggregate sum so found, of each, the value of the real estate included in the statement of resources as it stands on the duplicate. Thereupon he shall make and transmit to the annual state board of equalization for banks a copy of the report so made by the cashier, manager or owner with the valuation of such shares or property representing capital employed as so fixed by the auditor. (R. S. Sec. 2766; April 23, 1904, 97 v. 279; March 9, 1883, 80 v. 54; April 13, 1880, 77 v. 191; April 12, 1877, 74 v. 88, § 2; April 16, 1867, 64 v. 204, § 5.)

Deductions. Stockholders are not entitled to a deduction, from the value of their shares, of the amount of the capital stock of the bank which is invested in United States bonds.

Cleveland Trust Co. v. Lander, 62 O. S. 266 (1900); aff'd, 184 U. S. 111.

Frazer v. Siebern, 16 O. S. 614 (1866).

Nor is a stockholder entitled to a deduction of his debts from the value of his shares.

Chapman v. First N. B., 56 O. S. 310 (1897); aff'd, 173 U. S. 205.
Niles v. Shaw, 50 O. S. 370 (1893).
See Whitbeck v. Mercantile N. B., 127 U. S. 193 (1888).
Mercantile N. B. v. Shields, 59 Fed. 952 (1894).
Lander v. Mercantile N. B., 186 U. S. 458 (1901).
State v. Akins, 63 O. S. 182 (1900).

Nor can a deduction be made for the franchise.

Frazer v. Siebern, 16 O. S. 614 (1866).

Assessed value less than actual value. Discriminations. A stockholder, whose shares are valued at eighty percent of their true value in money, can not enjoin the collection of the tax thereon on the ground that other property in the county is valued at only forty percent of its value.

Wagoner v. Loomis, 37 O. S. 571 (1881).

But where national bank stock is assessed at its actual value, while other moneyed capital is intentionally and systematically valued far below its true value, under U. S. Rev. Stats. § 5219 the state taxing authorities may be enjoined from collecting the excess.

Pelton v. Commercial N. B., 101 U. S. 144; 4 O. F. D. 573 (1880).
Cummings v. Merchants N. B., 101 U. S. 153; 4 O. F. D. 578 (1880).
See Exchange N. B. v. Miller, 19 Fed. 372; 4 O. F. D. 578 (1884).
First N. B. v. Treasurer, 25 Fed. 749; 5 O. F. D. 467 (1885).

Section 5413. (When bank fails to make return.) If a bank fails to make and furnish to the county auditor the statement required, within the time herein fixed, the auditor shall examine the books of the bank; and also any officer or agent thereof under oath, with such other persons as he deems proper, and make such statement. The auditor shall have like powers, and the probate judge of the county shall exercise like powers, and perform like duties in aid of the auditor in the performance of his duties under this section, as are authorized by law in cases where the county auditor is informed, or has reason to believe, that any person has failed to make a return, or has made a false return for taxation. The statement so made out by the auditor shall stand as the statement required to be made by the cashier. (R. S. Sec. 2769; April 16, 1867, 64 v. 204, § 9.)

The correction of returns made by the cashier of a bank is provided for by this section, and not by § 5401.
Miller v. First Nat. Bank, 46 O. S. 424 (1889).
See State v. Akins, 63 O. S. 182 (1900).

Section 5414. (Penalty for making false return.) A bank officer who fails to make out and furnish to the county auditor the return required by section fifty-four hundred and eleven, or wilfully makes a false statement in such return, shall forfeit not more than one hundred dollars together with the costs and other expenses incurred by the auditor or other proper officer in obtaining such statement. (R. S. Sec. 2769; April 16, 1867, 64 v. 204, § 9.)

PUBLIC UTILITIES.

Section 5415. (Public utility defined.) The term "public utility" as used in this act means and embraces each corporation, company, firm, individual and association, their lessees, trustees, or receivers elected or appointed by any authority whatsoever, and herein referred to as express company, telephone company, telegraph company, sleeping car company, freight line company, equipment company, electric light company, gas company, natural gas company, pipe line company, waterworks company, messenger company, signal company, messenger or signal company, union depot company, water transportation company, heating company, cooling company, street railroad company, railroad company, suburban railroad company, and interurban railroad company, and such term "public utility" shall include any plant or property owned or operated, or both, by any such companies, corporations, firms, individuals or associations. (June 2, 1911, 102 v. 230, § 39; 101 v. 429, § 121.)

Section 5416. (Definitions.) That any person or persons, firm or firms, co-partnership or voluntary association, joint stock association, company or corporation, wherever organized or incorporated:

When engaged in the business of conveying to, from, or through the state, or part thereof, money, packages, gold, silver, plate or other article, by express, not including the ordinary lines of transportation of merchandise and property in this state, as an express company;

When engaged in the business of transmitting to, from, through, or in this state, telephonic messages, is a telephone company;

When engaged in the business of transmitting to, from, through, or in this state, telegraphic messages, is a telegraph company;

When engaged in the business of operating cars for the transportation, accommodation, comfort, convenience, or safety of passengers, on or over any railway line or lines, in whole or in part within this state, such line or lines not being owned, leased or operated by such company, whether such cars be termed sleeping, palace, parlor, chair, dining or buffet cars, or by another name, is a sleeping car company;

When engaged in the business of operating cars for the transportation of freight, whether such freight is owned by such company, or any other person or company, over any railway line or lines in whole or part within this state, such line or lines not being owned, leased or operated, by such company, whether such cars be termed box, flat, coal, ore, tank, stock, gondola, furniture or refrigerator cars, or by another name, is a freight line company;

When engaged in the business of furnishing or leasing cars, of whatsoever kind or description, to be used in the operation of any railway line or lines, wholly or partly within this state, such line or lines not being owned, leased or operated, by such company, is an equipment company;

When engaged in the business of supplying electricity for light, heat or power purposes, to consumers within this state, is an electric light company;

When engaged in the business of supplying artificial gas for lighting or heating purposes, to consumers within this state, is a gas company;

When engaged in the business of supplying natural gas

for lighting, heating or power purposes, to consumers within this state, is a natural gas company;

When engaged in the business of transporting natural gas or oil through pipes or tubing, either wholly or partially within this state, is a pipe line company;

When engaged in the business of supplying water through pipes or tubing, or in a similar manner to consumers within this state, is a waterworks company;

When engaged in the business of supplying messengers for any purpose in a messenger company;

When engaged in the business of signalling or calling by electrical apparatus, or in a similar manner, for any purpose is a signal company;

When engaged in the business of operating a union depot or station for railroad, suburban or interurban railroad purposes, is a union depot company;

When engaged in the transportation of passengers or property, by boat or other water craft, over any water way, whether natural or artificial, from one point within this state to another point within this state, or between points within this state and points without this state, is a water transportation company:

When engaged in the business of supplying water, steam or air through pipes or tubing, to consumers within this state, for heating purposes, is a heating company;

When engaged in the business of supplying water, steam or air through pipes or tubing, to consumers within this state, for cooling purposes, as a cooling company;

When engaged in the business of operating a street, suburban or interurban railroad company, wholly or partially within this state, whether cars used in such business are propelled by animals, steam, cable, electricity, or other motive power, is a street, suburban or interurban railroad company;

When engaged in the business of operating a railroad, either wholly or partially within this state, on rights-of-way acquired and held exclusively by such company, or otherwise, is a railroad company. (June 2, 1911, 102 v. 230, § 40; May 10, 1910, 101 v. 404, 406, 409, §§ 28, 29, 30, 39, 46; April 24, 1904, 97 v. 324; R. S. Secs. 2777, 2780-7, 2780-12, 2780-17; April 15, 1902, 95 v. 136; March 19, 1896, 92 v. 79.)

Under this section an interurban railroad is classed as a street railroad.

Electric St. R. Co. v. Lohe, 68 O. S. 110 (1903).

For definitions of public utilities in Public Utilities Act, see §§ 614-2. 501.

Railroad or interurban railroad company. Whether a railroad is a commercial or an interurban road is determined, not exclusively by its charter, but from its method of operation and the character of its business.

Railway v. Poland, 10 N. P. n. s. 617; 21 L. D. 630 (C. P. 1910); aff'd, no rep., 88 O. S. —.

See note to § 9117.

Pipe line company. The power to own and operate pipe lines can not be joined in the articles of incorporation of a company formed to bore for oil, gas, etc.

Rep. of Atty. Gen., 1909-10, p. 147.

Rep. of Atty. Gen., 1908, p. 69-79.

A corporation engaged in drilling and operating gas wells, which sells part of its gas to a manufacturer, is not a pipe line company merely by reason of the fact that it owns and uses the pipe through which such gas passes.

Rep. Atty. Gen., 1911-1912, p. 630.

Natural gas company. A corporation engaged in drilling and operating gas wells which sells a part of its gas to a manufacturing company is a natural gas company under this section, as it sells to a "consumer" for "power purposes."

Rep. Atty. Gen., 1911-1912, p. 630.

Messenger company. An association of individuals engaged in the special delivery business, handling parcels and packages from stores and factories, furnishing guides to strangers, delivering letters and packages in connection with a taxicab and auto livery business is a messenger company under this section.

Rep. Atty. Gen., 1911-1912, p. 644.

Section 5417. ("Gross receipts" defined.) The term "gross receipts" shall be held to mean and include the entire receipts for business done by any person or persons, firm or firms, co-partnership or voluntary association, joint stock association, company or corporation, wherever organized or incorporated, from the operation of any public utility, or incidental thereto or in connection therewith. The gross receipts for business done by an incorporated company, engaged in the operation of a public utility, shall be held to mean and include the entire receipts for business done by such company under the exercise of its corporate powers, whether from the operation of the public utility itself or from any other business done whatsoever. (June 2, 1911, 102 v. 232, § 41.)

Section 5418. ("Gross earnings" defined.) The term "gross earnings" shall be held to mean and include the entire earnings for business done by any person or persons, firm or firms, co-partnership or voluntary association, joint stock association, company or corporation, wherever organized or incorporated, from the operation of any public utility, or incidental thereto, or in connection therewith. The gross earnings for business done by an incorporated company, engaged in the operation of a public utility, shall be held to mean and include the entire earnings for business done by such company under the exercise of its corporate powers, whether from the operation of the public utility itself or from any other business done whatsoever. (June 2, 1911, 102 v. 232, § 42.)

Section 5419. (Definitions.) The property owned or operated by a public utility, required to make return to the commission of its property to be assessed for taxation by the commission, shall be deemed and held to include such utility's plant or plants and all real estate necessary to the daily operations of the public utility and all other property, moneys and credits owned or operated, or both, by it wholly or in part within this state, used in connection with or as incidental to the operation of the public utility, whether the same be held in common or by the individuals operating such public utility. In the case of incorporated companies, all the real estate, personal property, moneys and credits owned and held by such corporation within this state in the exercise of its corporate powers, or as incidental thereto, whether such property, or any portion thereof, is used in connection with such public utility business or not, shall be conclusively deemed and held to be the property of such public utility. (June 2, 1911, 102 v. 232, § 43.)

The scheme of taxation of the property of a public utility adopted by this act is termed "the unit rule or rule of entirety," and is similar to the plan previously in effect applying to express, telegraph and telephone companies (R. S. §§ 2777 to 2780), upheld in State v. Jones, 51 O. S. 492; Express Co. v. Auditor, 165 U. S. 194 and 166 U. S. 183.
Rep. Atty. Gen., 1911-1912, p. 603.

Section 5420. (Exceptions.) Each public utility, as defined in this act, except express, telegraph and telephone companies, shall annually, on or before the first day of March, make and deliver to the tax commission of Ohio, in such form as the commission may prescribe, a statement, with respect to such utility's plant or plants and all property owned or operated, or both, by it wholly or in part within this state. (June 2, 1911, 102 v. 233, § 44.)

Section 5421. (Statement under oath.) Such statement shall be signed and sworn to under the oath of the person constituting such public utility, if a person or under the oath of the president, secretary, treasurer, superintendent or principal accounting officer or person of such firm, association or corporation, if a firm, association or corporation. (June 2, 1911, 102 v. 233, § 45.)

Section 5422. (Shall contain, what. Real estate, value and separate statement. Personal property inventory and statement. Property outside of state. Bonded indebtedness. Statement by street and other railroad companies. Pipe line, gas and other companies.) Such statement shall contain:

1. The name of the company.

2. The nature of the company, whether a person or persons, firm, association or corporation, and under the laws of what state or country organized.

3. The location of its principal office.

4. The name and postoffice address of the president, secretary, auditor or the principal accounting officer or person, treasurer, and superintendent or general manager.

5. The name and postoffice address of the chief officer or managing agent of the company in this state.

6. The number of shares of the capital stock.

7. The par value and market value, or if there is no market value, the actual value of its shares of stock on the first day of the month of January in which the statement is made; the amount of capital stock subscribed, and the amount thereof, actually paid in.

8. A detailed statement of the real estate owned by the company in this state, where situated, and the value thereof as assessed for taxation, making separate statements of that part used in connection with the daily operations of the company, and that part used otherwise, if any such there be.

9. An inventory of the personal property, including moneys, investments and credits, owned by the company, in this state, on the first day of the month of January in which the statement is made, where situated, and the value thereof, making separate statements of that part used in connection with the daily operations of the company, and that part used otherwise if any such there be.

10. The total value of the real estate owned by the company and situated outside of this state, making separate statements of that part used in connection with the daily operations of the company, and that part used otherwise if any such there be.

11. The total value of the personal property owned by the company and situated outside of this state, making separate statements of that part used in connection with the daily operations of the company, and that part used otherwise if any such there be.

12. The total amount of bonded indebtedness and of indebtedness not bonded; the gross receipts for the preceding calendar year from any and all sources, and the gross expenditures for the preceding calendar year.

13. In the case of street, suburban or interurban railroad companies, and railroad companies, such statements shall also give:

(a) The whole length of their lines and the length of so much of their line as is without and is within this state, including branches in and out of the state, which shall include lines and branches such companies control and use under lease or otherwise.

(b) The railway track in each county in the state, through which it runs; giving the whole number of miles of road in the county, including the track and its branches and side and second tracks, switches, and turnouts therein and the true and actual value per mile of such railway in each county, stating the valuation of main track, second or other main tracks, branches, sidings, switches and turnouts, separately.

(c) Such statement as to character, classes, number, amounts, values, locations, ownership or control and use of rolling stock, as the commission may require.

(d) The depots, station houses, section houses, freight houses, machine and repair shops and machinery therein, and all other buildings, structures and appendages connected thereto or used therewith, including tool houses, and the tools usually kept therein, together with telegraph and telephone lines owned or used, and the true and actual value of all buildings and structures, and all such machinery, tools and appendages, including such telegraph and telephone lines; and the true and actual value thereof in each county in this state in which it is located.

(e) The gross earnings for the year, including earnings from telegraph lines, which shall be stated separately, on the whole length of the road, including the branches thereof, in and out of the state, and also such earnings within this state on way freight and passengers.

14. In case of pipe line, gas, natural gas, waterworks and heating or cooling companies, such statement shall also show:

(a) The number of miles of pipe line owned, leased or operated within this state, the size or sizes of the pipe composing such line, and the material of which such pipe is made;

(b) ,If such pipe line be partly within and partly without this state, the whole number of miles thereof within this state and the whole number of miles without this state, including all branches and connecting lines in and out of this state;

·(c) The length, size and true and actual value of such

pipe line in each county of this state, including in such valuation the main line, branches and connecting lines, and stating the different value of the pipe separately;

(d) Its pumping stations, machine and repair shops and machinery therein, tanks, storage tanks and all other buildings, structures and appendages connected or used therewith, including telegraph and telephone lines and wires, and the true and actual value of all such stations, shops, tanks, buildings, structures, machinery and appendages and of such telegraph and telephone lines, and the true and actual value thereof in each county in this state in which it is located; and the number and value of all tank cars, tanks, barges, boats and barrels. (June 2, 1911, 102 v. 233, § 46; May 10, 1910, 101 v. 414, § 72.)

Section 5423. (Assessment; when made.) On the second Monday of June of each year, the commission shall ascertain and assess, at its true value in money, all the property in this state of each such public utility, subject to the provisions of this act, other than express, telegraph and telephone companies. (June 2, 1911, 102 v. 235, § 47; 101 v. 417, § 73.)

Section 5424. (How assessment shall be made.) In determining the value of the property of each such public utility to be assessed and taxed within the state, the commission shall be guided by the value of the property as determined by the information contained in the sworn statements made by the public utility to the commission and such other evidence and rules as will enable it to arrive at the true value in money of the entire property of such public utility within this state, in the proportion which the value of such property bears to the value of the entire property of such public utility. (June 2, 1911, 102 v. 235, § 48; 101 v. 417, § 73.)

Section 5425. (Property to be assessed.) The property of such public utilities to be so assessed by the commission shall be all the property thereof, as defined in section forty-three (G. C. § 5419) of this act. (June 2, 1911, 102 v. 235, § 49; 101 v. 417, § 73.)

Section 5426. (Hearing.) Before the assessment of such property each of such public utilities shall have the right, upon written application, to appear before the commission and to be heard in the matter of the valuation of its property for taxation. (102 v. 235, § 50; 101 v. 417, § 74.)

Section 5427. (Corrections.) Between the date herein

fixed for the assessment of the property of any such public
utility for taxation by the commission, and the date herein
fixed for the certification by it of the apportioned value to
the county, or to the several counties as herein provided, the
commission may, on the application of such public utility or
any person interested therein, or on its own motion, correct
the assessment or valuation of its property in such manner as
will in its judgment make the valuation thereof just and
equal. (June 2, 1911, 102 v. 235, § 51; May 10, 1910, 101 v.
417, § 74.)

This act does not divest county auditors of the power to correct
assessments made by them prior to the passage of the act, and before
appointment of the tax commission.
  Railway v. Edmondson, 13 N. P. n. s. 377; 57 Bull 434; 23 L. D.
    33 (C. P. 1912).

Section 5428. (Deductions.) The commission shall deduct from the total value of the property of each of such
public utilities in this state, as assessed by it, the value of
the real property owned by such public utilities, if any there
be, as otherwise assessed for taxation in this state, and shall
justly and equitably equalize the relative values thereof.
(June 2, 1911, 102 v. 236, § 52; 101 v. 417, § 74.)

Section 5429. (Valuation of railroad properties.) The
commission shall ascertain all of the personal property, road-
bed, stations, power houses, poles, wires, water and wood
stations and real estate necessary to the daily running operations of the road, moneys and credits of each railroad company and each suburban or interurban railroad company,
having any line, or road, or part thereof in this state and
the undivided profits, reserved or contingent fund of the
company, whether in moneys, credits, or in any manner invested, and the actual value thereof in money, and also locomotives, motors and cars not belonging to the company, but
hired for its use or run under its control on its road by a
sleeping car company or other company. Such rolling stock
not belonging to it, but under its control, may be returned
by such public utility separate from its own property, and
if so returned the commission shall fix the valuation of such
property separately, but must include the amount in the
aggregate valuation. (June 2, 1911, 102 v. 236, § 53; 101
v. 418, § 75; R. S. Sec. 2772; 64 v. 114, § 3.)

Personal property under this section includes the road bed, water
stations, moneys, credits and undivided profits.
  Lee v. Sturges, 46 O. S. 153, 166 (1889).
  The "roadbed" and "real estate necessary to the daily running

operations of the road" are by this section made personal property for taxation purposes.

Railway Co. v. Hynicka, 4 N. P. n. s. 345, 349; 17 L. D. 163 (Super. Ct. Cin. 1906) ; aff'd, no rep., 77 O. S. 628.

The bridge of the Cincinnati Southern Railway which spans the Ohio River, together with the viaduct or trestle leading up to it, constitutes with the underlying ground, a part of the roadbed, and is property necessary to the daily operation of the road, and there being no additional charge to shippers or passengers on account of the use thereof, it should be taxed with the remainder of the road as a unit and "averaged" over the entire road.

Railway Co. v. Hynicka, 4 N. P. n. s. 345; 17 L. D. 163 (Super. Ct. Cin. 1906) ; aff'd, 77 O. S. 628.

Side tracks, in daily use for loading and unloading of freight, and land purchased for the purpose of establishing a connection track with another railroad do not constitute real estate, structures or stationary personal property to be "localized" for taxation but should likewise be "averaged" for taxation over the entire road. After such property has been valued under this section, it can not again be taxed as omitted property, nor as property which has escaped taxation.

Railway Co. v. Hynicka, 4 N. P. n. s. 345; 17 L. D. 163 (Super. Ct. Cin. 1906) ; aff'd, 77 O. S. 628.

Where a railroad of this state which terminated at low water mark on the Ohio River was leased to a company owning a railroad on the Kentucky side of the river, and connected by a bridge and an approach on the Ohio side owned by the lessee which extended back from low water mark, and an additional charge was made for freight and passengers crossing the bridge, it was held that the approach on the Ohio side was subject to taxation as a separate "structure" belonging to the lessee, although the roadbed, etc., to the low water mark had been averaged for taxation.

Cowan v. Aldridge, 114 Fed. 44; 14 O. F. D. 21 (C. C. A. 1902).

Taxation of terminals of railroad owned by a municipality.

See Railway v. Roth, 13 N. P. n. s. 633 (1913).

Section 5430. (Apportionment.) The value of such property, moneys and credits of each such street, suburban and interurban railroad and railroad companies, as found and determined by the commission, shall be apportioned· by the commission among the several counties through which the road, or any part thereof, runs, so that to each county and to each taxing district therein, shall be apportioned such part thereof as will equalize the relative value of the real estate, structures and stationary personal property of such company therein, in proportion to the whole value of the real estate, structures and stationary personal property of the company in this state; and so that the rolling stock, main track, roadbed, power houses, poles, wires, supplies, moneys and credits of the company shall be apportioned in like proportion that the length of the road in such county, bears to the entire length thereof in all the counties, and to each city, village and district or part thereof therein. (June 2, 1911, 102 v. 236, § 54; 101 v. 418, § 77; R. S. Sec. 2774; 82 v. 160; R. S. 1880; 64 v. 58; 59 v. 88, § 5.)

This section is valid. A railroad passing through a taxing district created under the "one mile assessment pike law," is subject to taxation in such district, in the proportion fixed under this section.

Railroad Co. v. Commissioners, 48 O. S. 249 (1891).

Railway Co. v. Hynicka, 4 N. P. n. s. 345; 17 L. D. 163 (1906); aff'd, 77 O. S. 628.

See State v. Jones, 51 O. S. 492, 508 (1894).

Construction of former act.

Wabash, etc., Ry. Co. v. Kelsey, 11 W. L. B. 234 (1884).

In entering for taxation the property of a railroad which lies partly within and partly without the state, sections 5445, 5423 and 5429, should govern and not this section or sec. 5431.

Railway Co. v. Hynicka, 4 N. P. n. s. 345; 17 L. D. 163 (Super. Ct. Cin. 1906); aff'd, no rep., 77 O. S. 628.

Section 5431. (Apportionment.) If the line of such company is divided into separate divisions or branches, so much of the rolling stock thereof as belongs to or is used solely upon such divisions or branches shall be apportioned in like manner to the county, or counties, and to each taxing district therein, through which such branch or division runs. The commission shall certify to each such county auditor such apportionment. (June 2, 1911, 102 v. 236, § 55; 101 v. 417, § 77; R. S. Sec. 2774; 82 v. 160; R. S. 1880; 64 v. 58; 59 v. 88, § 5.)

The phrase "belongs to . . . such division or branches" has reference to cases in which a division or branch is separately equipped.

State v. Aldridge, 66 O. S. 598 (1902).

FOREIGN INSURANCE COMPANIES.

Section 5432. (Annual statements of foreign insurance companies.) Every insurance company incorporated by the authority of another state or government, in its annual statement to the superintendent of insurance, shall set forth the gross amount of premiums received by it from policies covering risks within this state during the preceding calendar year. without deductions for commissions, return premiums, considerations paid for reinsurance or any deductions whatever. It shall also set forth therein in separate items, return premiums paid for cancellations and considerations received from other companies for reinsurances in this state during such year. If the superintendent of insurance has reason to suspect the correctness of such statement he may make an examination, at the expense of the state, of the books of such company or its agents for the purpose of verifying them. (R. S. Sec. 2745; March 9, 1909, 100 v. 67; April 26, 1904, 97 v. 401; April 29, 1902, 95 v. 290; March 27, 1894, 91 v. 91; April 19, 1893, 90 v. 201; April 12, 1889, 86 v. 274; April 11, 1888, 85 v. 183; R. S. 1880; April 8, 1876, 73 v. 138.)

Construction of section before amendment (100 v. 67).
　　Insurance Co. v. State, 79 O. S. 305 (1909).
　　Same case upon amended petition, 13 C. C. n. s. 113; 22 C. D. 51
　　　　(1910) reversed, 83 O. S. 469.
　　Rep. Atty. Gen., 1909-1910, p. 346.
　　A casualty insurance company may not deduct estimated cost of inspection of boilers, etc., from premiums in making annual statement.
　　Rep. Atty. Gen., 1908, p. 166.
　　This section does not apply to foreign mutual protective associations admitted to do business in Ohio under § 9435 et seq.; nor to assessment companies doing business under § 9445 et seq.; nor to fraternal benefit societies.
　　5 Opins. Attys. Gen., 343 (1900).
　　It does apply to mutual fire companies admitted under § 9559.
　　5 Opins. Attys. Gen. 343, 347 (1900).

Section 5433. (Payment of tax to superintendent of insurance.) If the superintendent of insurance finds such report to be correct, prior to the month of November in each year, he shall compute an amount of two and one-half per cent on the balance of such gross amount after deducting such return premiums and considerations received for reinsurances as shown by the next preceding annual statement and charge them to such company as a tax upon the business done by it in this state for the period shown by such annual statement. He shall forthwith mail to the last known address of the principal office of such company, a statement of the amount so charged against it, which amount, in the month of November next succeeding, the company shall pay to the superintendent of insurance at his office. All taxes collected by the superintendent of insurance under this section shall be paid by him, upon the warrant of the state auditor, into the general revenue fund of the state. (R. S. Sec. 2745; March 9, 1909, 100 v. 67; April 26, 1904, 97 v. 401; April 29, 1902, 95 v. 290; March 27, 1894, 91 v. 91; April 19, 1893, 90 v. 201; April 12, 1889, 86 v. 274; April 11, 1888, 85 v. 183; R. S. 1880; April 8, 1876, 73 v. 138.)

The tax imposed by this section is a privilege or excise tax. Such tax does not relieve a corporation from the taxation of its property.
Scottish, etc., Ins. Co. v. Bowland, 196 U. S. 610 (1904).
Western Assur. Co. v. Halliday, 127 Fed. 83; 1 O. L. R. 643 (1903).
Amount under former law.
State v. Hahn, 50 O. S. 714 (1893).

Section 5433-1. (Term "gross premiums" defined for taxation purposes. What annual statement shall show.) For the purpose of computing franchise taxes, on gross premiums, to be paid under any law of this state, now or hereafter in force, by any mutual fire insurance company authorized to do business under the laws of this state, the amount of premium deposits received by such company upon any risk within this state in excess of the net cost of insurance to the insured, shall not be included where such excess deposit is returned ratably by such company to its policy holders; but the amount of gross or aggregate premiums received by any such company shall be deemed to be the balance remaining after deducting from the gross amount of premium deposits received or collected by it on risks in this state during the preceding calendar year ending on the thirty-first day of December, that portion of gross premium deposits returned by it to policy holders during said preceding calendar year, upon the cancellation or expiration of risks upon property situated within this state. In addition to the matters of return required to be made by insurance companies for the purpose of computing taxes, any such company shall also return for such purpose in its annual statement:

(a) The total gross amount of premium deposits received or collected by it on risks in this state during the preceding calendar year ending on the thirty-first day of December;

(b) The total amount of gross premium deposits returned to policy holders during such preceding calendar year upon cancellation and upon expiration of risks upon property situated within this state. (May 7, 1913, 103 v. 713; in effect August 8, 1913.)

Section 5434. (Failure to pay tax or make true statement.) If a company fails or refuses to pay such tax, after a statement thereof has been made and mailed to it, or if the statement required to be made by it under section fifty-four hundred and thirty-two is false or incorrect, the superintendent of insurance may revoke the license of such company doing business in this state. Upon failure or refusal to pay the tax, the superintendent of insurance shall certify that fact to the attorney-general, who shall thereupon begin an action against the company in the court of common pleas of Franklin county, or of any other county, as he may elect, to recover the amount of the tax. If such company ceases to do business in this state, it shall thereupon make report to the superintendent of insurance of the gross amount of premiums, not theretofore ᵣreported as provided in section fifty-four hundred and thirty-two, received by it from policies covering risks within this state, prior to such discontinuance of business after deducting return premiums˙ and considerations received for reinsurance, not theretofore so reported, and shall forthwith pay to the superintendent of insurance a like per cent of tax thereon. (R. S. Sec. 2745; March 9, 1909, 100 v. 67; April 26, 1904, 97 v. 401; 95 v. 290; 91 v. 91; 90 v. 201; 86 v. 274; 85 v. 183; 73 v. 138.)

The license of an insurance company may be revoked although an action to recover the tax is pending.
State v. Matthews, 58 O. S. 1 (1898).
Injunction is the proper remedy to test the amount of the tax and to prevent a revocation of the license.   Mandamus is not a proper remedy.
State v. Hahn, 50 O. S. 714 (1893).

Section 5435. (Penalty for non-payment of taxes.) If such company refuses to pay such tax, upon demand being made therefor, it shall be liable to the state of Ohio at the suit of the attorney-general, to a penalty of not more than five hundred dollars per month for each month it has failed, after demand therefor, to pay the tax. Service of process in such action shall be made acording to the requirements of law governing suits brought against such companies by a policy holder therein. (R. S. Sec. 2745.)

Section 5436. (Retaliatory provision.) If the laws of another state, territory or nation authorize charges for the privilege of doing business therein, or taxes against insurance companies organized in this state, exceeding the charges provided in this chapter, like amounts shall be charged against all insurance companies of such state, territory or nation, doing business in this state, instead of the charges herein provided. (R. S. Sec. 2745; 100 v. 67; 97 v. 401; 95 v. 290; 91 v. 91; 90 v. 201; 86 v. 274; 85 v. 183; 73 v. 138.)

See § 658.
State v. Reinmund, 45 O. S. 214 (1887).
State v. Insurance Co., 49 O. S. 440 (1892).

Section 5437. (Deposits with superintendent of insurance not taxable.) Neither insurance companies and associations,

incorporated by the authority of another state or government, nor the superintendent of insurance, shall be required
to make returns for taxation of the deposits of such companies or associations, made as required by law, with the
superintendent of insurance, for the benefit and security of
policy holders; nor be governed with respect to such deposits,
by the provisions of law relating to the listing of personal
property or to the making of tax returns by corporations.
(R. S. Sec. 2745; March 9, 1909, 100 v. 67; April 26, 1904, 97
v. 401; April 29, 1902, 95 v. 290; March 27, 1894, 91 v. 91;
90 v. 201; 86 v. 274; 85 v. 183; R. S. 1880; 73 v. 138.)

See Sims v. Best, 1 C. C. n. s. 41; 15 C. D. 149 (1903).
Scottish, etc., Ins. Co. v. Bowland, 196 U. S. 611 (1904).
Western Ins. Co. v. Halliday, 126 Fed. 257 (C. C. A. 1903).

**Section 5438. (Where policy on Ohio property to be
placed.)** An insurance company or agent legally authorized
to transact insurance business in this state shall not write,
place, or cause to be written or placed, a policy, renewal of
policy or contract for insurance upon property, situated or
located in this state, except through a legally authorized
agent in this state, who shall countersign all policies so issued
and enter the payment of the premium upon his record. The
writing, renewal, placing or causing to be written or placed
of a policy of insurance in any other manner or form is a
violation of the law providing for the payment of taxes by
foreign insurance companies doing business in the state of
Ohio, as set out and provided in this chapter. (R. S. Sec.
2745a; April 16, 1900, 94 v. 299; 88 v. 487.)

Insurance against damage in transportation of goods transported
from a place without the state to a place within the state need not
be written or placed through an agent residing in Ohio.
5 Opins. Attys. Gen., 432 (1901).

**Section 5439. (Reinsuring, etc., risk with unauthorized
foreign company.)** No fire insurance company or association, authorized to do business in this state, shall reinsure,
dispose of, cede, pool, divide or in any manner or form, reduce a portion of its risk or liability, covering property
wholly or partially located in this state, in or with a company, association, person or persons, incorporated or otherwise, not authorized by law to do the business of fire insurance in this state, or to reinsure, or assume as a reinsuring
company or otherwise, in any manner or form, the whole or
part of a risk or liability, covering property wholly or partially located in this state, of or for an insurance company, association, person or persons, incorporated or other-

wise, not authorized by law to do business of fire insurance in this state. (R. S. Sec. 2745a; April 16, 1900, 94 v. 299; 88 v. 487.)

Section 5440. (Annual report required of chief officer.) The superintendent of insurance of this state annually, and at such times as he may see fit, shall require the president or other chief officer of each company or association, to file a statement under oath, showing the names of each fire insurance company, or association, with whom or for whom liability for insurance on property located wholly or partially in this state has been reinsured, disposed of, ceded, pooled, divided, or in any manner or form reduced or increased. (R. S. Sec. 2745a; April 16, 1900, 94 v. 299; 88 v. 487.)

Section 5441. (When authority of insurance company revoked.) Any company violating any of the provisions of the next three preceding sections, upon notice and satisfactory proof thereof being made to the superintendent of insurance of this state, shall have its authority to transact business in this state revoked for a period of not less than ninety days. Any insurance company whose license to do business in this state is so revoked, shall not be again permitted to do business in this state, until all taxes and penalties due from it have been paid, together with any expense that may be due under the provisions of this chapter. Such company shall only be re-admitted to transact business in this state upon a complete re-compliance with the laws in regard to the admission of such company. (R. S. Sec. 2745b; May 1, 1891, 88 v. 488.)

Section 5442. (When superintendent to inspect company.) When notice of a violation of any provision of the next four preceding sections is received by the superintendent of insurance, he shall forthwith in person, or by deputy, visit the office of the company where such contract of insurance has been written or made, and demand an inspection of the books and records thereof. Any company refusing to exhibit its books and records for his inspection shall be guilty of violating such provisions, and the penalties provided by law shall forthwith be enforced against such company by the superintendent of insurance. (R. S. Sec. 2745c; April 2, 1906, 98 v. 242; May 1, 1891, 88 v. 488.)

Section 5443. (When foreign insurance company not admitted in state.) When application is made by a foreign insurance company to the superintendent of insurance of this state for admission to do business in this state, it shall not be admitted until it has paid all taxes and penalties assessed against it for the violation of the laws relating to insurance. If such foreign company has been reported to the superintendent of insurance as having violated any of the laws of this state relating to insurance, he shall make or cause to be made an examination of the books and records of the company seeking admission, and before granting license to do business in this state, he shall require it to pay into the office of the state treasurer a penalty equal to twenty per cent of all premiums written in this state, for the six years next preceding the date of request for admission, and upon whi·h such taxes have not already been paid. (R. S. Sec. 2745c; April 2, 1906, 98 v. 242; May 1, 1891, 88 v. 488.)

Section 5444. (Expenses of inspection to be paid by company.) The superintendent of insurance shall receive, as compensation for services rendered under the provisions of this chapter, his necessary expenses. Such sum shall be charged against the company or companies so visited by him, and be collected by suit in any court of competent jurisdiction. (R. S. Sec. 2745d; May 1, 1891, 88 v. 488.)

PUBLIC UTILITIES.

Property Taxes. Excise Taxes.

Section 5445. (Tax Commission of Ohio. Appointment of commissioners; terms of office, etc. Vacancy.) A tax commission is hereby created, to be known as the tax commission of Ohio, to be composed of three commissioners, electors of the state, not more than two of whom at any time shall be of the same political party. On or before July first, 1910, the governor shall appoint such commissioners as follows: the term of one such appointee, who shall belong to the same political party as one of the other members appointed on such commission, if there be two appointees from the same political party, shall terminate on the second Monday of February, 1911; the term of the second such appointee shall terminate on the second Monday of February, 1912; the term of the third such appointee shall terminate on the second Monday of February, 1913. In February, 1911, and annually thereafter, in the month of February, there shall be appointed in the same manner, one commissioner for the term of three years, from the second Monday of February of such year. Each commissioner so appointed shall hold his office until a successor is appointed and qualified. Any vacancy on the commission shall be filled by appointment of the governor for the unexpired term. No appointee shall be qualified to act until after his appointment has been confirmed by the senate, unless appointed during a recess or adjournment of the senate. (May 10, 1910, 101 v. 399.)

There are two sections numbered § 5445.
See G. C. § 1465-1.

Section 5445. (Valuation when part of road in another state.) When a street, suburban or interurban railroad or railroad company has part of its road in this state and part thereof in another state or states, the commission shall take the entire value of such property, moneys and credits of such public utility so found and determined, in accordance with the provisions of this act, and divide it in the proportion the length of the road in this state bears to the whole length thereof, and determine the principal sum for the value of the road in this state accordingly, equalizing the relative value thereof in this state. (June 2, 1911, 102 v. 237, § 56; 101 v. 419, § 78; G. C. § 5431 (original number); R. S. Sec. 2776; 59 v. 88, § 8.)

The words "such property" refer back to §§ 5423 and 5429.
> Railway Co. v. Hynicka, 4 N. P. n. s. 345, 349; 17 L. D. 163 (Super. Ct. Cin. 1906) ; aff'd, no rep., 77 O. S. 628.

Where property of a railroad lies partly within and partly without the state this section—§ 5423 and § 5429 should govern, and not §§ 5430, 5431.
> Railway Co. v. Hynicka, 4 N. P. n. s. 345; 17 L. D. 163 (Super. Ct. Cin. 1906) ; aff'd, no rep., 77 O. S. 628.

Section 5446. (Apportionment.) The commission shall apportion the value of the property of all other public utilities assessed according to the provisions of this act as follows:

(a) When all the property of such public utility is located within the limits of a county, the assessed value thereof shall be apportioned by the commission between the several taxing districts therein, in the proportion which the property located within the taxing district in question, bears to the entire value of the property of such public utility, as ascertained and valued as herein provided, so that, to each taxing district there shall be apportioned such part of the entire valuation as will fairly equalize the relative value of the property therein located, to the whole value thereof.

(b) When the property of such public utility is located in more than one county in this state, the assessed value thereof shall be apportioned by the commission between the several counties and the taxing districts therein, in the proportion which the property located therein, bears to the entire value of the property of such public utility as ascertained and valued, as herein provided, so that to each county and each taxing district therein, there shall be apportioned such part of the entire valuation as will fairly equalize the relative value of the property therein located to the whole value thereof.

(c) When the property of such public utility, required to be assessed by the provisions of this act, is located in more than one state, the assessed value thereof shall be apportioned by the commission in such manner as will fairly and equitably determine the principal sum for the value thereof in this state, and after ascertaining such value it shall be apportioned by the commission, as herein provided. (102 v. 237, § 57; 101 v. 419, § 79.)

Section 5447. (Certified to county auditors.) On the second Monday of July, the commission shall certify such apportionment to the auditor of each county in which any of the property of the public utility is located. (102 v. 237, § 58.)

Section 5448. (Entry on tax duplicate.) The county auditor shall place the apportioned value on the tax list and duplicate and taxes shall be levied and collected thereon, in the same manner and at the same rate, as other personal property in the taxing district in question. (102 v. 237, § 59.)

Section 5449. (Verified statement by express, telephone and telegraph Co.'s.) On or before the first day of August, annually, every express, telegraph and telephone company, doing business in this state, under the oath of the person constituting such company, if a person, or under the oath of the president, secretary, treasurer, superintendent or chief officer in this state of such association or corporation, if an association or corporation shall make and file with the commission a statement, in such form as the commission may prescribe. (102 v. 238, § 60; 101 v. 404, § 31; R. S. Sec. 2778; 91 v. 220; 90 v. 330; 62 v. 174, § 1.)

Section 5450. (Contents.) Such statement shall contain:
1. The name of the company.
2. The nature of the company, whether a person or persons, or association or corporation, and under the laws of what state or country organized.
3. The location of its principal office.
4. The name and postoffice address of the president, secretary, auditor, treasurer and superintendent or general manager.
5. The name and postoffice address of the chief officer or managing agent of the company in this state.
6. The number of shares of the capital stock.
7. The par value and market value, or if there is no market value, the actual value of its shares of stock on the thirtieth day of the month of June in which the statement is made, the amount of its capital stock subscribed and the amount thereof actually paid in.
8. A detailed statement of the real estate owned by the company in this state, where situated, and the value thereof as assessed for taxation.
9. A full and correct inventory of the personal property, including moneys and credits, owned by the company in this state on the thirtieth day of the month of June in which the statement is made, where situated and the value thereof.
10. The total value of the real estate owned by the company and situated outside of this state.
11. The total value of the personal property owned by the company and situated outside of this state.

12. The total amount of bonded indebtedness and of indebtedness not bonded; the gross receipts from whatever source derived of business wherever done, for the year ending on the thirtieth day of June next preceding; and the total gross expenditures for such year.

13. In the case of telegraph and telephone companies, such statement shall also set forth, the whole length of their lines, and the length of so much of their lines as is without and is within this state, which shall include the lines such telegraph and telephone companies control and use under lease or otherwise and the miles of wire in each taxing district in this state.

14. In the case of telegraph and telephone companies, such statement shall also contain the entire gross receipts, including all sums earned or charged, whether actually received or not, for the year ending the thirtieth day of June, from whatever source derived, whether messages, telephone tolls, rentals, or otherwise, for business done within this state, including the company's proportion of gross receipts for business done by it within this state in connection with other companies, firms, corporations, persons or associations excluding therefrom all receipts derived wholly from interstate business or business done for the federal government. Such statement shall also contain the total gross receipts of such company, for such period, from business done within this state.

15. In the case of express companies, such statement shall also contain the entire receipts, including all sums earned or charged, whether actually received or not, from whatever source derived, for business done within this state, for the year ending the thirtieth day of June, for and on account of such company, including the company's proportion of gross receipts for business done by it within this state in connection with other companies, firms, corporations, persons or associations, excluding therefrom all receipts derived wholly from interstate business or business done for the federal government. Such statement shall also contain the total gross receipts of such company, for such period, from business done within this state.

16. In the case of express companies, the gross receipts for the year ending the thirtieth day of June, from whatever source derived, of each office within this state, giving the name of each office in this state.

17. In the case of express companies, such statement shall also contain the whole length of the lines of rail and water routes, over which the company did business on the thirtieth day of June, and the length of so much of such

lines of land and water transportation as is without and within this state, naming the lines within this state. (June 2, 1911, 102 v. 238, § 61; May 10, 1910, 101 v. 404, § 32; R. S. Sec. 2778; May 10, 1894, 91 v. 220; April 27, 1893, 90 v. 330; April 13, 1865, 62 v. 174, § 1.)

Constitutionality. The act of 90 v. 330 taxing the *property* of express, telephone and telegraph companies held constitutional.

> State v. Jones, 51 O. S. 492 (1894); affirmed in Adams Express Co.
> v. Ohio State Auditor, 165 U. S. 194 (1896); s. c., 166 U. S.
> 185 (1897).

The act imposing an *excise tax* on the gross receipts of express and other companies, held constitutional.

> Express Co. v. State, 55 O. S. 69 (1896).
> Western Union Telegraph Co. v. Mayer, 28 O. S. 521 (1876).
> See Southern Gum Co. v. Laylin, 66 O. S. 578 (1902).

Section 5451. (Assessment of values.) On the first Monday in September, of each year, the commission shall ascertain and assess the value of the property of the express, telegraph and telephone companies in this state. (102 v. 239, § 62; 101 v. 405, § 34.)

Section 5452. (How determined.) In determining the value of the property of such companies in this state, to be taxed within the state and assessed as herein provided, the commission shall be guided by the value of the property as determined by the value of the entire capital stock of the companies, and such other evidence and rules as will enable such commission to arrive at the true value, in money, of the entire property of such companies within this state, in the proportion which such property bears to the entire property of the companies, as determined by the value of the capital stock thereof, and such other evidence and rules. (June 2, 1911, 102 v. 239, § 63; May 10, 1910, 101 v. 405, § 34; R. S. Sec. 2778a; May 10, 1894, 91 v. 220; April 27, 1893, 90 v. 330.)

Held constitutional.

> Western Union Tel. Co. v. Poe, 64 Fed. 9 (C. C. 1894).
> Adams Express Co. v. Auditor, 165 U. S. 194; 166 U. S. 185.
> State v. Jones, 51 O. S. 492 (1894).

Section 5453. (Hearing.) Before the assessment of the property of any express, telegraph or telephone company is determined, any company or person interested shall have the right, on written application to appear before the commission and be heard in the matter of the valuation of the property of any company for taxation. (June 2, 1911, 102 v. 239, § 64; 101 v. 405, § 35; R. S. Sec. 2778a; 91 v. 220; 90 v. 330.)

Section 5454. (Corrections.) Between the date herein fixed for the assessment of the property of any such company for taxation by the commission, and the date herein fixed for the certification by the commission of the apportioned valuation to the several counties, the commission may, on the application of any interested person or company, or on its own motion, correct the assessment or valuation of the property of any such company, in such manner as will, in its judgment, make the valuation thereof just and equal. (102 v. 240, § 65; 101 v. 405, § 35; R. S. Sec. 2778a; 91 v. 220; 90 v. 330.)

Remedies provided by statute for the correction of errors must be exhausted before resort to the courts.
State v. Express Companies, 2 N. P. 98; 3 L. D. 326; affirmed, 55 O. S. 69.

Section 5455. (Deductions.) The commission shall deduct from the total value of the property of each express, telegraph and telephone company in this state, the value, as assessed for taxation of any real estate situated within this state and owned by such company. (102 v. 240, § 66; 101 v. 406, § 36; R. S. Sec. 2780; 91 v. 223; 90 v. 332; 60 v. 11, § 1.)

Section 5456. (Apportionment.) The value of the property of telegraph and telephone companies of this state, after deducting the value of the real estate, shall be apportioned by the commission among the several counties through or into which the lines of such telegraph or telephone companies run, so that to each county shall be apportioned such part of the entire valuation as will equalize the relative value of the property of the company therein, in proportion to the whole value of the property of the company in the state, and in the proportion that the length of the lines of wire owned by the company in the county, bears to the whole length of the lines of wire in all the counties in the state, and to each city, village and taxing district, or part thereof, therein. (102 v. 240, § 67; 101 v. 406, § 36; R. S. Sec. 2780; 91 v. 223; 90 v. 332; 60 v. 11, § 1.)

Section 5457. (Apportionment.) The value of the property of express companies shall be apportioned by the commission among the several counties in which the company does business, in the proportion that the gross receipts in each county, bear to the entire gross receipts in all the counties in the state, and to each city, village and taxing district, or part thereof, therein. (102 v. 240, § 68; 101 v. 406, § 37; R. S. Sec. 2780; 91 v. 223; 90 v. 332; 60 v. 11, § 1.)

Section 5458. (Certified to county auditors.) On the third Monday of September, the commission shall certify to the county auditor the amount apportioned to his county and to each city, village, township or other taxing district therein. (102 v. 240, § 69; 101 v. 406, § 38; R. S. Sec. 2780; 91 v. 223; 90 v. 332, 60 v. 11, § 1.)

Section 5459. (How taxes levied.) The county auditor shall place the apportioned valuation on the tax list and duplicate, and taxes shall be levied and collected thereon, at the same rate and in the same manner, as taxes are levied and collected on other personal property in the taxing district in question. (102 v. 240, § 70; 101 v. 406, § 38; R. S. Sec. 2780; 91 v. 223; 90 v. 332; 60 v. 11, § 1.)

Section 5460. (Public utilities not required to make returns under certain sections.) Public utilities shall not be required to make returns under, nor be governed by the provisions of sections fifty-four hundred and four, fifty-four hundred and five and fifty-four hundred and six of the General Code. (June 2, 1911, 102 v. 240, § 71.)

Section 5461. (How valuations determined on failure of report or statement. Domestic corporations. Foreign corporations. Sleeping car or freight line. Power extends to preceding years.) When a public utility or corporation fails to make any report or furnish any statement, which it is required to make or furnish, to the commission, or makes a return or statement of a portion only of the gross receipts or gross earnings, which it is required by law to make or return, and fails to make return or statement of the remainder, or fails to report a part or all of its taxable property, or report the same, or part thereof, according to its true value in money, the commission shall ascertain, as nearly as practicable, the gross receipts or gross earnings, or omitted portion of the same, or taxable property, or omitted part of the same, or such as was not reported according to its true value in money, that should have been reported or returned by such public utility or corporation, and certify such gross receipts or gross earnings, or the value of such property, so ascertained, as required in this act, with respect to its gross receipts, gross earnings and property of public utilities and corporations. When a domestic corporation makes a report of a portion only of its subscribed or issued and

outstanding capital stock, the commission shall ascertain, as
nearly as practicable, the omitted portion thereof, that should
have been reported by such corporation, and certify such
additional amount, as required in this act, with respect to
the certification of the subscribed or issued and outstanding
capital stock of domestic corporations. When a foreign corporation makes a report to the commission of a portion only
of the property owned and used or business done by it in
this state, or makes a report of a fictitious or excessive
amount of property owned and used or business done by it
outside of this state, or makes a report of a portion only
of its total authorized capital stock, which it is required by
law to make, the commission shall ascertain, as nearly as
practicable, the total amount of property owned and used
and business done by such foreign corporation in this state,
and the total amount of property owned and used and business done by such foreign corporation outside of this state,
and the proportion of the total authorized capital stock of
such corporation, represented by property owned and used
and business done in this state, and certify such corrected
amount, or the difference between such corrected amount
and the amount that may have previously been certified, as
required in this act, with respect to the certification of the
proportion of the authorized capital stock of foreign corporations, represented by property owned and used and
business done by such corporations in this state. When a
sleeping car, freight line or equipment company fails to
make any report or statement, which it is required to make
or furnish, to the commission, or makes a return or statement of a portion only of its total authorized capital stock,
or of the value of its shares of stock, or of its real estate
owned either within or without this state, or of the number
and value of the cars owned or leased by it and the daily
average number of cars operated in this state, or the length
of the lines of railway over which the company runs its
cars within this state, or makes a return or statement of a
fictitious or excessive length of lines of railway over which
the company runs its cars without this state, the commission
shall ascertain, as nearly as practicable, the amount of the
capital and property of any such company owned and used
in this state, and the amount of capital and property of such
company owned and used outside of this state, and the proportion of the capital stock of any such company representing capital and property thereof owned and used in this
state, as provided in this act, and shall certify such amount
so ascertained, as required in this act, with respect to the
certification of the amount and value of the proportion of

the capital stock of such companies representing capital and property owned and used by them in this state. The power and duty of the commission, above provided for, shall extend to preceding years in such manner as that the commission shall, for such year or years preceding the year in which the inquiries are made, and omissions ascertained, certify such omitted amounts, so ascertained, as required in this act, with respect to such companies, in which event such omitted amounts shall be taxed at the rate of taxation belonging to the year or years in which the failure or omission occurred, in the case of property, and in all other cases the amount of the tax or fee upon such omitted amounts shall be calculated upon the amount so ascertained by the commission, at the rate provided by law, for such year or years; provided, however, that the power and duty of the commission with respect to property shall extend only to the five years next preceding the year in which such inquiries and corrections are made, and not in any event prior to the year 1911, except where no property of a company has been returned or assessed in any such year or years. (June 2, 1911, 102 v. 240, § 72; 101 v. 399, § 114; R. S. Sec. 2778a; 91 v. 221; 90 v. 331.)

Section 5462. (Verified statement.) Annually, between the first and thirty-first days of May, every sleeping car, freight line and equipment company, doing business or owning cars which are operated in this state, shall under the oath of the person constituting such company, if a person, or under the oath of the president, secretary, treasurer, superintendent or chief officer in this state of such association or corporation, if an association or corporation, make and file with the commission a statement in such form as the commission may prescribe. (June 2, 1911, 102 v. 242, § 73; May 10, 1910, 101 v. 407, § 40; R. S. Secs. 2780-8, 2780-13; March 30, 1896, 92 v. 89; May 24, 1894, 91 v. 408.)

Section 5463. (Statement shall contain; what.) Such statement shall contain:
1.   The name of the company.
2.   The nature of the company, whether a person or persons or association or corporation, and under the laws of what state or country organized.
3.   The location of its principal office.
4.   The name and postoffice address of the president, secretary, auditor, treasurer and superintendent or general manager.

5. The name and postoffice address of the chief officer and managing agent of the company in this state.

6. The number of shares of capital stock.

7. The par and market value, or, if there is no market value, the actual value of the shares of stock on the first day of May.

8. A detailed statement of the real estate owned by the company in this state, where situated, and the value thereof as assessed for taxation.

9. The total value of the real estate owned by the company and situated outside of this state.

10. The whole length of the lines of railway over which the company runs its cars, and the length of so much of such lines as is without and is within this state.

11. The whole number and value of the cars owned or leased by the company classifying the cars according to kind, and the daily average number of cars operated in this state. (June 2, 1911, 102 v. 242, § 74; 101 v. 407, § 41; R. S. Secs. 2780-8, 2780-13; 92 v. 89; 91 v. 408.)

Section 5464. (Equipment company.) In the case of an equipment company, such statement shall also contain the whole number and value of the cars owned and leased by the company, classifying the cars according to kind; the whole length of the lines of railway, wherever located, operated by the companies, naming them, to which cars owned by such equipment company are leased, and the length of so much of such lines as is without and within this state, giving the name and location of the lines wholly or partially within this state. (June 2, 1911, 102 v. 243, § 75; 101 v. 408, § 42; R. S. Sec. 2780-8; 92 v. 89.)

Section 5465. (Valuation.) On the first Monday in July, the commission shall ascertain and determine the amount and value of the proportion of the capital stock of sleeping car, freight line and equipment companies, representing capital and property of such companies owned and used in this state, and in so determining shall be guided in each case by the proportion of the capital stock of the company representing rolling stock, which the miles of railroad over which such company runs cars, or its cars are run in this state, bear to the entire number of miles in this state and elsewhere over which such company runs cars, or its cars are run, and such other rules and evidence as will enable the commission to determine, fairly and equitably, the amount and value of the capital stock of such company representing capital and property owned and used in this state. (102 v. 243, § 76;

101 v. 408, § 44; R. S. Secs. 2780-9, 2780-14; 92 v. 89; 91 v. 408.)

Section 5466. (Hearing.) Before the amount and value of the capital stock of any company representing capital and property owned and used in this state is determined, any company or person interested shall have the right, on written application, to appear before the commission and be heard in the matter of such determination. (102 v. 243, § 77; 101 v. 408, § 44; R. S. Sec. 2780-9; 92 v. 89; R. S. Sec. 2780-14; 91 v. 408.)

Section 5466-1. (Witness fees, mileage, etc.) A person who shall appear before the tax commission, by its order, with respect to the appraisement of property in any taxing district, shall be allowed and paid out of the treasury of the proper county, if an officer of any such taxing district or a member of any board mentioned in section 5542-9a, his actual and necessary traveling expenses, such expenses to be itemized and sworn to by the person who incurred the expense, and if other than any such officer or member of any such board he shall receive for his attendance the fees and mileage now provided for witnesses in civil cases in the courts of common pleas. Such traveling expenses and witness fees shall be audited and paid out of the county treasury of the proper county in the same manner as other expenses are audited and paid, upon the presentation of a certificate from the tax commission certifying to the fact of such attendance. (102 v. 30.)

Section 5467. (Corrections.) Between the date herein fixed for fixing the amount and value of the capital stock of any company representing capital and property owned and used in this state, and the date herein fixed for the certification to the auditor of state of such amount, the commission may, on the application of any person or company interested, or on its own motion, review and correct its action in such manner as it deems just and proper. (102 v. 243, § 78; 101 v. 408, § 44; R. S. Sec. 2780-9; 92 v. 89, § 3; R. S. Sec. 2780-14; 91 v. 408, § 3.)

Section 5468. (Certified to auditor of state. Excise tax.) On the first Monday in August, of each year, the commission shall certify such amount to the auditor of state, who shall charge a sum in the nature of an excise tax, to be collected from each sleeping car, freight line and equipment company, doing business or owning cars which are operated in this state, to be computed by taking one and two-tenths per cent. of the amount fixed by the commission as the value of the portion of the capital stock representing the capital and property of each company owned and used in this state. (102 v. 243, § 79; 101 v. 408, § 45; R. S. Sec. 2780-11; 92 v. 89, § 5; R. S. Sec. 2780-16; 91 v. 408, § 5.)

Constitutionality of excise tax.
  Express Co. v. State, 55 O. S. 69 (1896).
  Western Union Tel. Co. v. Mayer, 28 O. S. 521 (1876).
  See Southern Gum Co. v. Laylin, 66 O. S. 578 (1902).

Section 5469. (Collection by treasurer of state.) On or before the first day of September of each year, the auditor of state shall certify to the treasurer of state, as herein provided, for collection from each sleeping car, freight line and equipment company, doing business or owning cars which are operated in this state, the amount so charged. (102 v. 244, § 80; 101 v. 408, § 45; R. S. Sec. 2780-11; 92 v. 89, § 5; R. S. Sec. 2780-16; 91 v. 408, § 5.)

Section 5470. (Verified statement.) Each public utility, except express, telegraph and telephone companies, and street, suburban and interurban railroad and railroad companies, doing business in this state, shall, annually, on or before the first day of August, and each street, suburban and interurban railroad and railroad company, shall, annually, on or before the first day of September, under the oath of the person constituting such company, if a person, or under the oath of the president, secretary, treasurer, superintendent or chief officer in this state, of such association or corporation, if an association or corporation, make and file with the commission a statement in such form as the commission may prescribe. (102 v. 244, § 81; 101 v. 409, § 47; R. S. Sec. 2780-18: 97 v. 325; 95 v. 137; 92 v. 79.)

Section 5471. (Statement; what shall contain.) The statement, provided for in the preceding section, shall contain:

1. The name of the company.
2. The nature of the company, whether a person or persons or association or corporation, and under the laws of what state or country organized.
3. The location of its principal office.
4. The name and postoffice address of the president, secretary, auditor, treasurer and superintendent or general manager.
5. The name and postoffice address of the chief officer

or managing agent of the company in this state. (102 v. 244, § 82; 101 v. 410, § 48; R. S. Sec. 2780-18; 97 v. 325; 95 v. 137; 92 v. 79.)

Section 5472. (Further statement by railroad company.) In the case of each railroad company, such statement shall also contain the entire gross earnings, including all sums earned or charged, whether actually received or not, for the year ending on the thirtieth day of June next preceding, from whatever source derived, for business done within this state, excluding therefrom all earnings derived wholly from interstate business or business done for the federal government. Such statement shall also contain the total gross earnings of such company for such period in this state from business done within this state. (102 v. 244, § 83; 101 v. 410, § 51; R. S. Sec. 2780-18; 97 v. 325; 95 v. 137; 92 v. 79.)

Section 5473. (Further statement by street, suburban or interurban railroad company.) In the case of each street, suburban or interurban railroad company, such statements shall also contain the entire gross earnings, including all sums earned or charged, whether actually received or not, for the year ending on the thirtieth day of June next preceding, from whatever source derived, for business done within this state, excluding therefrom all earnings derived wholly from interstate business or business done for the federal government. Such statement shall also contain the total gross earnings of such company for such period in this state from business done within this state. (102 v. 244, § 84; 101 v. 411, § 52; R. S. Sec. 2780-18; 97 v. 325; 95 v. 137; 92 v. 79.)

Section 5474. (What statement shall contain.) In the case of all such public utilities except railroad, street, suburban and interurban railroad companies, such statement shall also contain the entire gross receipts of the company, including all sums earned or charged, whether actually received, or not, from whatever source derived, for business done within this state for the year next preceding the first day of May, including the company's proportion of gross receipts for business done by it within this state in connection with other companies, firms, corporations, persons or associations, but this shall not apply to receipts from interstate business, or business done for the federal government. Such statement shall also contain the total gross receipts of such company for such period in this state from business done within this state. (102 v. 245, § 85; 101 v. 411, § 53; R. S. Sec. 2780-18; 97 v. 325; 95 v. 137; 92 v. 79.)

The phrase "entire gross receipts" does not include receipts which pass through the hands of a company but do not belong to it. Where a local gas company obtains its supply from another company, under a contract by which the receipts are divided on a percentage bases, the local company may be assessed only on its proportion of the recipts. State v. Coshocton Gas Co., 12 N. P. n. s. 570; 22 L. D. 412 (C. P. 1912).

See Rep. Atty. Gen., 1910, 1911, p. 603.

Section 5475. (Valuation determined.) On the first Monday of September the commission shall ascertain and determine the entire gross receipts of each electric light, gas, natural gas, pipe line, waterworks, messenger or signal, union depot, heating, cooling and water transportation company for business done within this state for the year then next preceding the first day of May, and of each express, telegraph and telephone company for business done within this state for the year ending on the thirtieth day of June, excluding therefrom, as to each of the companies named in this section, all receipts derived wholly from interstate business or business done for the federal government. (102 v. 245, § 86; 101 v. 411, § 55; R. S. Sec. 2780-19; 97 v. 326; 95 v. 138; 92 v. 79.)

Section 5476. (Gross receipts of electric light, gas, etc., companies.) The amount so ascertained by the commission, in such instance, for the purposes of this act, shall be the gross receipts of such electric light, gas, natural gas, pipe line, waterworks, express, telegraph, telephone, messenger or signal, union depot, heating, cooling or water transportation companies for business done within this state for such year. (102 v. 245, § 87; 101 v. 411, § 55; R. S. Sec. 2780-19; 97 v. 326; 95 v. 138; 92 v. 79.)

Section 5477. (Gross earnings.) On the first Monday of October, the commission shall ascertain and determine the gross earnings as herein provided, of each railroad company whose line is wholly or partially within this state, for the year ending on the thirtieth day of June next preceding, excluding therefrom all earnings derived wholly from interstate business or business done for the federal government. The amount so ascertained by the commission shall be the gross earnings of such railroad company for such year. (102 v. 245, § 88; 101 v. 412, § 56; R. S. Sec. 2780-19; 97 v. 326; 95 v. 138, 92 v. 79.)

Section 5478. (Gross earnings.) On the first Monday of October, the commission shall ascertain and determine the gross earnings, as herein provided, of each street, suburban and interurban railroad company whose line is wholly or partially within this state, for the year ending on the thirtieth day of June next preceding, excluding therefrom, as to each of the companies named in this section, all earnings derived wholly from interstate business or business done for the federal government. The amount so ascertained by the commission shall be the gross earnings of such street, suburban or interurban railroad company for such year. (102 v. 245, § 89; 101 v. 412, § 57; R. S. Sec. 2780-19; 97 v. 326; 95 v. 138; 92 v. 79.)

Section 5479. (Hearing.) Before the gross receipts or earnings of any such public utility are determined, any company, or person interested, shall have the right, on written application, to appear before the commission and be heard in the matter of such determination. (102 v. 246, § 90; 101 v. 412, § 58; R. S. Sec. 2780-19; 97 v. 326; 95 v. 138; 92 v. 79.)

Section 5480. (Corrections.) Between the dates herein fixed for the determination of the amount of the gross receipts or earnings of any such public utility, and the dates herein fixed for the certification to the auditor of state of such amount, as provided in this act, the commission may, on the application of any person or company interested, or on its own motion, review and correct its findings. (102 v. 246, § 91; 101 v. 412, § 59; R. S. Sec. 2780-19; 97 v. 326; 95 v. 138; 92 v. 79.)

Section 5481. (Certified to auditor of state.) On the first Monday of October the commission shall certify to the auditor of state, the amount of the gross receipts so determined, of electric light, gas, natural gas, pipe line, waterworks, express, telegraph, telephone, messenger or signal, union depot, heating, cooling and water transportation companies, for the year covered by its annual report to the commission, as required in this act.. (102 v. 246, § 92; 101 v. 412, § 60; R. S. Sec. 2780-21; 97 v. 329; 95 v. 138; 92 v. 79.)

Section 5482. (Gross earnings certified to auditor of state.) On the first Monday of November the commission shall certify to the auditor of state the amount of the gross earnings so determined of each street, suburban and interurban railroad and railroad company for the year ending on the thirtieth day of June next preceding. (102 v. 246, § 93;

101 v. 412, § 60; R. S. Sec. 2780-21; 97 v. 329; 95 v. 138; 92 v. 79.)

Section 5483. (Excise tax.) In the month of October, annually, the auditor of state shall charge, for collection from each electric light, gas, natural gas, waterworks, telephone, messenger or signal, union depot, heating, cooling and water transportation company, a sum in the nature of an excise tax, for the privilege of carrying on its intra-state business, to be computed on the amount so fixed and reported by the commission as the gross receipts of such company on its intra-state business for the year covered by its annual report to the commission, as required in this act, by taking one and two-tenths per cent. of all such gross receipts, which tax shall not be less than ten dollars in any case. (102 v. 246, § 94; 101 v. 412, § 61; R. S. Sec. 2780-21; 97 v. 329; 95 v. 138; 92 v. 79.)

That different rates are imposed on various classes of public utilities does not render the tax unconstitutional.
Railway Co. v. Dittey, 203 Fed. 537 (D. C. 1913).
Constitutionality of statutes imposing an excise tax on gross receipts.
Express Co. v. State, 55 O. S. 69 (1896).
Western Union Tel. Co. v. Mayer, 28 O. S. 521 (1876).
Southern Gum Co. v. Laylin, 66 O. S. 578 (1902).
See State v. Jones, 51 O. S. 492 (1894); affirmed, 165 U. S. 194; 166 U. S. 185.

Section 5484. (Excise tax on street, etc., railway companies.) In the month of November, the auditor of state, shall charge, for collection from each street, suburban and interurban railroad company, a sum in the nature of an excise tax, for the privilege of carrying on its intra-state business, to be computed on the amount so fixed and reported to him by the commission as the gross earnings of such company on its intra-state business for the year covered by its annual report to the commission, as required in this act, by taking one and two-tenths per cent. of all gross earnings, which tax shall not be less than ten dollars in any case. (102 v. 246, § 95; 101 v. 413, § 62; R. S. Sec. 2780-21; 97 v. 329; 95 v. 138; 92 v. 79.)

See Railway v. Poland, 10 N. P. n. s. 617 (1910).
That different rates are imposed on various classes of public utilities does not render the tax unconstitutional.
Railway Co. v. Dittey, 203 Fed. 537 (D. C. 1913).

Section 5485. (Excise tax on express and telegraph companies.) In the month of October, the auditor of state shall charge for collection, from each express and telegraph company, a sum in the nature of an excise tax, for the privilege of carrying on its intra-state business, to be computed on the amount so fixed and reported to him by the commission as the gross receipts of such company on its intra-state business for the year covered by its annual report to the commission, as required in this act, by taking two per cent. of all such gross receipts, which tax shall not be less than ten dollars in any case. (102 v. 247, § 96; 101 v. 413, § 63; R. S. Sec. 2780-21; 97 v. 329; 95 v. 138; 92 v. 79; 91 v. 237.)

Act of 91 v. 237 held constitutional.
    Express Co. v. State, 55 O. S. 69 (1896).
    See Western Union Tel. Co. v. Mayer, 28 O. S. 521 (1876).
Taxation of receipts from interstate commerce.
    Ratterman v. Express Co., 49 O. S. 608 (1892).
    Western Union Tel. Co. v. Mayer, 28 O. S. 521 (1876).
    Express Co. v. State, 55 O. S. 69 (1896).
    Adams Express Co. v. Ohio State Auditor, 165 U. S. 194 (1896);
        (s. c., rehearing denied 166 U. S. 185); affirming State v.
        Jones, 51 O. S. 492 (1894).
Where an express company paid a tax illegally imposed on gross receipts from interstate business, under protest and with notice of an intention to bring action to recover back the amount paid, such payment is involuntary and an action may be maintained to recover back the same.
    Ratterman v. Express Co., 49 O. S. 608 (1892).
That different rates are imposed on various classes of public utilities does not render the tax unconstitutional.
    Railway Co. v. Dittey, 203 Fed. 537 (D. C. 1913).

Section 5486. (Excise tax on railroads.) In the month of November, the auditor of state shall charge for collection, from each railroad company, a sum in the nature of an excise tax, for the privilege of carrying on its intra-state business, to be computed on the amount so fixed and reported to him by the commission, as the gross earnings of such company on its intra-state business for the year covered by its annual report to the commission, as required in this act, by taking four per cent. of all such gross earnings, which tax shall not be less than ten dollars in any case. (102 v. 247, § 97; 101 v. 413, § 64; R. S. Sec. 2780-21; 97 v. 329; 95 v. 138; 92 v. 79.)

The tax imposed by this section is an excise tax for the privilege of doing business. Being on intrastate business only it is not unconstitutional as imposing a burden on interstate commerce. That various public utilities are taxed at different rates does not render the tax unconstitutional as wanting in uniformity of operation.
    Railway Co. v. Dittey, 203 Fed. 537 (D. C. 1913).
Commercial or interurban road: how determined.
    Railway v. Poland, 10 N. P. n. s. 617; 21 L. D. 630 (1910); aff'd,
        no rep., 88 O. S. —.
A former statute which required every corporation operating a rail-

road within the state to pay a fee of $1.00 per mile was held unconstitutional.

Railway v. State, 49 O. S. 189 (1892).

Section 5487. (Excise tax on pipe line companies.) In the month of October, the auditor of state shall charge for collection, from each pipe line company, a sum in the nature of an excise tax, for the privilege of carrying on its intra-state business, to be computed on the amount so fixed and reported to him by the commission, as the gross receipts of such company on its intra-state business for the year covered by its annual report to the commission, as required in this act, by taking four per cent. of all such gross receipts, which tax shall not be less than ten dollars in any case. (102 v. 247, § 98; 101 v. 413, § 65; R. S. Sec. 2780-21; 97 v. 329; 95 v. 138; 92 v. 79.)

Section 5488. (Collection by treasurer of state. Notice of taxes.) After determining the amount of taxes or fees payable to the state, as provided in this act, the auditor of state shall thereupon prepare proper duplicates and reports, and certify them to the treasurer of state for collection.

Upon the receipt of such duplicate, the treasurer shall notify each company charged with taxes or fees thereon, of the amount due from it. (102 v. 247, § 99; 101 v. 413, § 66; R. S. Sec. 2780-21; 97 v. 329; 95 v. 138; 92 v. 79.)

Section 5489. (Daily statement to auditor.) The treasurer of state shall proceed to collect such taxes and render a daily itemized statement to the auditor of state of the amount of taxes or fees collected and the name of the company from whom collected, under all provisions of this act. (102 v. 247, § 100; 101 v. 413, § 66; R. S. Sec. 2780-21; 97 v. 329; 95 v. 138; 92 v. 79.)

Section 5490. (Other companies not exempt.) Nothing contained in this act shall exempt or relieve electric light, gas, natural gas, pipe line, waterworks, street, suburban or interurban railroad, express, telegraph, telephone, messenger or signal, union depot, railroad, heating, cooling, sleeping car, freight line, equipment and water transportation companies from the assessment and taxation of their property in the manner authorized and provided by law. (102 v. 247, § 101; 101 v. 413, § 67; R. S. Sec. 2780-21; 97 v. 329; 95 v. 138; 92 v. 79.)

See Railway v. Poland, 10 N. P. n. s. 617; 21 L. D. 630 (C. P. 1910)

That a corporation pays a property tax does not render an excise tax unconstitutional.

Railway Co. v. Dittey, 203 Fed. 537 (D. C. 1913).

Section 5491. (Tax credited to general revenue fund. Penalty.) All taxes received by the treasurer of state, under the provisions of this act, shall be credited to the general revenue fund. If any public utility fails or refuses to pay, on or before the fifteenth day of December, the tax assessed against it, or if any corporation fails or refuses to pay, on or before the dates fixed, in this act, the fee charged against it, the treasurer of state shall certify the list of such utilities or corporations, so delinquent, to the auditor of state, who shall add to the tax or fee due, a penalty of fifteen per cent. thereon. The auditor of state shall thereupon forthwith prepare proper duplicates and reports of such taxes and fees and penalties thereon and certify them to the treasurer of state for collection. Thirty days after he receives such duplicates of delinquent taxes and fees and penalties thereon from the auditor of state, the treasurer of state shall certify to the commission a list of such public utilities and corporations as have failed to pay such taxes or fees and penalties thereon. (102 v. 248, § 102; 101 v. 414, § 68; R. S. Sec. 2780-21; 97 v. 329; 95 v. 138; 92 v. 79.)

It is said that the delinquent list, certified under this section, should include corporations which have not been notified of the amount of the tax, as required by § 5488.

Rep. Atty. Gen., 1910-1911, p. 485.

Section 5492. (Action for recovery may be brought, where.) Such taxes or fees and penalties thereon may be recovered by an action in the name of the state, which may be brought in the court of common pleas of Franklin county, or of any county, in which such corporation has an office or place of business, or in which such public utility is doing business, or the line of any street, suburban or interurban railroad company or railroad company is located, and such court of common pleas shall have jurisdiction of such action regardless of the amount involved therein. The attorney general, on request of the commission, shall institute such action in the court of common pleas of Franklin county, or of any of such counties as the commission may direct. In any such action it shall be sufficient to allege that the tax, fee or penalty sought to be recovered, stands charged on the delinquent duplicate of the treasurer of state, and that the same has been unpaid for a period of thirty days after having been placed thereon. Sums recovered in any such action shall be paid into the state treasury, to the credit of the general revenue fund. (102 v. 248, § 103; 101 v. 414, § 68; R. S. Sec. 2780-21; 97 v. 329; 95 v. 138; 92 v. 79.)

Section 5493. (Effect when tax charged invalid.) In case the tax or fee herein authorized to be charged and collected against any class of corporations or public utilities, defined in this act, shall for any reason, be declared invalid, such invalidity shall in no wise affect the validity of the law, as applicable to any other class or classes of corporations or public utilities, defined in this act, nor shall the abrogation or repeal of any section or clause of this act be held to abrogate or repeal any other section or clause thereof. (102 v. 248, § 104; 101 v. 414, § 69; R. S. Sec. 2780-21; 97 v. 329; 95 v. 138; 92 v. 79.)

Section 5494. (Municipal corporation exempt.) This act shall not be so construed as to require any municipal corporation within this state to make any return or pay any taxes under any provisions of this act. (102 v. 248, § 105; 101 v. 414, § 71; R. S. Sec. 2780-22; 97 v. 331; 95 v. 143; 92 v. 79.)

This act was not intended to give the tax commission any control over the property of municipal corporations.
Railway v. Roth, 13 N. P. n. s. 633 (1913).

FRANCHISE TAX ON CORPORATIONS. WILLIS LAW.

§ 5495. Report of corporations for profit.
§ 5496. Verified.
§ 5497. Report shall contain, what.
§ 5498. Amount of capital stock determined. Certified to auditor of state. Fee. Minimum.
§ 5499. Foreign corporations reports.
§ 5500. Verified.
§ 5501. Contents.
§ 5502. Valuation certified to auditor of state.
§ 5503. Collection. Fee, minimum.
§ 5504. Hearing. Corrections.
§ 5505. Receipt.
§ 5506. First lien.
§ 5507. Penalty.
§ 5508. Liabilities of foreign corporations. Insurance companies not included in this act.
§ 5509. Failure to report or pay tax, or fee, effect of. Cancellation of articles.
§ 5510. Penalty.
§ 5511. Reinstatement.
§ 5512. Action by attorney general.
§ 5513. Quo warranto proceedings.

§ 5514. Certified list of new corporations each month by secretary of state to commission.
§ 5515. Information by county auditors.
§ 5516. Fees, power of commission as to.
§ 5516-1. Extension of time.
§ 5517. Hearing. Review. Corrections. Mistake.
§ 5518. Public utility, insurance, etc., companies excepted.
§ 5519. Report not required until lapse of six months from date of incorporation.
§ 5520. Dissolution no exemption from payment or filing report.
§ 5521. When certificate of dissotion may be filed.
§ 5522. Affidavits as to use of money or property in aid of elections.
§ 5523. Certificate of secretary of state as to foreign corporation doing business without compliance with laws. Prosecution.
§ 5524. Compromise.
§ 5525. Application of preceding sections. Independent sections. Pending actions not affected.

Section 5495. (Report of corporations for profit.) Between the first day of May and the first day of July, 1911, and annually thereafter during the month of May, each corporation, organized under the laws of this state, for profit, shall make a report, in writing, to the commission, in such form as the commission may prescribe. (June 2, 1911, 102 v. 249, § 106; May 10, 1910, 101 v. 421, § 82; April 11, 1902, 95 v. 124, § 1.)

§ 5495 and succeeding sections, popularly known as the Willis law, were originally G. C. §§ 5522 to 5542. The fee or tax imposed is a franchise or privilege tax and not a tax on property.
Southern Gum Co. v. Laylin, 66 O. S. 578 (1902).

Constitutionality. The state may impose a tax on privileges or franchises, not to exceed the reasonable value of the privilege or franchise originally conferred, or its continued annual value thereafter. Act of 95 v. 124 held constitutional.
Southern Gum Co. v. Laylin, 66 O. S. 578 (1902).
State v. Covington, etc., Co., 6 N. P. n. s. 55; 18 L. D. 273 (C. P. 1907).

Franchise tax does not affect property tax. The imposition of a franchise or privilege tax does not relieve corporations from the taxation of their property.
Scottish, etc., Ins. Co. v. Bowland, 196 U. S. 611 (1905).

Company incorporated in several states. A corporation, organized by concurrent legislation of two or more states, is a domestic corporation in each state. Such a corporation is subject to the franchise tax as a domestic corporation.
State v. Covington, etc., Bridge Co., 6 N. P. n. s. 55; 18 L. D. 273 (C. P. 1907).

Miscellaneous. A receiver, assignee or trustee for creditors must file reports and pay fees until the corporation is dissolved or its charter revoked by a court of competent jurisdiction, and until a certificate of dissolution under § 11975 is received and filed by the secretary of state.
Rep. Atty. Gen. 1911-1912, p. 699.
Rep. Atty. Gen. 1904-1905, pp. 68, 69.
See § 5520.
A corporation not yet organized is not liable for the tax. A corporation is not organized until ten percent of its capital stock has been subscribed and its directors chosen.
5 Opins. Attys. Gen., 999 (1903).
Citing State, ex rel., v. Insurance Co., 49 O. S. 440.

Section 5496. (Verified.) Such report shall be signed and sworn to before an officer authorized to administer oaths, by the president, vice-president, secretary or general manager of the corporation, and forwarded to the commission. (June 2, 1911, 102 v. 249, § 107; May 10, 1910, 101 v. 421, § 82; April 11, 1902, 95 v. 124, § 1.)

Section 5497. (Report shall contain, what.) Such report shall contain:

1. The name of the corporation.

2. The location of its principal office.

3. The names of the president, secretary, treasurer and members of the board of directors, with the postoffice address of each.

4. The date of the annual election of officers.

5. The amount of authorized capital stock and the par value of each share.

6. The amount of capital stock subscribed, the amount of capital stock issued and outstanding, and the amount of capital stock paid up.

7. The nature and kind of business in which the corporation is engaged and its place or places of business.

8. The change or changes, if any, in the above particulars, made since the last annual report. (June 2, 1911, 102 v. 249, § 108; May 10, 1910, 101 v. 421, § 83; April 11, 1902, 95 v. 124, § 1.)

The statement required by paragraph 7 of this section does not, by inference, relieve corporations not engaged in business from making reports and paying taxes.

State v. C. & P. R. R., 13 N. P. n. s. 671 (C. P. 1913).

Section 5498. (Amount of capital stock determined; certified to auditor of state. Fee. Minimum.) Upon the filing of the report, provided for in the last three preceding sections, the commission, after finding such report to be correct, shall, on the first Monday of July, determine the amount of the subscribed or issued and outstanding capital stock of each such corporation. On the first Monday in August, the commission shall certify the amount so determined by it to the auditor of state, who shall charge for collection, on or before August fifteenth, as herein provided, from such corporation, a fee of three-twentieths of one per cent. upon its subscribed or issued and outstanding capital stock, which fee shall not be less than ten dollars in any case. Such fee shall be payable to the treasurer of state on or before the first day of the following October. (June 2, 1911, 102 v. 249, § 109; May 10, 1910, 101 v. 422, § 84; April 11, 1902, 95 v. 124, § 1.)

Where the subscribed capital stock is more than the issued and outstanding capital stock, the tax should be assessed on the subscribed, and not on the issued and outstanding, capital stock.

5 O. L. R. 122 (Atty. Gen. Opin. 1907).

The fee is for the year next ensuing after the filing of the annual report, and not for the past enjoyment of the franchise. The fee or tax is not entitled to priority under Bankruptcy Act § 64a, where the petition in bankruptcy was filed prior to the time when the tax became due.

In re Emmerman v. Ohio, etc., Co., 14 O. F. D. 289.

(Referee in Bk'ry, 1904; aff'd, without report, by District Court.)
In re Bank v. Aultman, 14 O. F. D. 298.
Rep. Atty. Gen., 1906-1907, p. 59.
The tax is for the entire year. The act does not provide for consideration of fractional parts of a year, nor does it provide for remitting part of the tax where a corporation discontinues business during a year.
Rep. Atty. Gen. 1904-1905, pp. 69, 70.

Section 5499. (Foreign corporations report.) Annually, during the month of July, each foreign corporation for profit, doing business in this state, and owning or using a part or all of its capital or plant in this state, and subject to compliance with all other provisions of law, and in addition to all other statements required by law, shall make a report in writing to the commission in such form as the commission may prescribe. (June 2, 1911, 102 v. 249, § 110; May 10, 1910, 101 v. 422, § 85; April 11, 1902, 95 v. 124, § 2.)

Section 5500. (Verified.) Such report shall be signed and sworn to before an officer, authorized to administer oaths, by the president, vice-president, secretary, superintendent or managing agent in this state, and forwarded to the commission. (June 2, 1911, 102 v. 249, § 111; May 10, 1910, 101 v. 422, § 85; April 11, 1902, 95 v. 124, § 2.)

Section 5501. (Contents.) Such report shall contain:

1. The name of the corporation and under the laws of what state or country organized.

2. The location of its principal office.

3. The names of the president, secretary, treasurer and members of the board of directors, with the postoffice address of each.

4. The date of the annual election of officers.

5. The amount of authorized capital stock, and the par value of each share.

6. The amount of capital stock subscribed, the amount of capital stock issued, and the amount of capital stock paid up.

7. The nature and kind of business in which the company is engaged and its place or places of business, both within and without the state.

8. The name and location of its office or offices in this state, and the name and address of the officers or agents of the corporation in charge of its business in this state.

9. The value of the property owned and used by the company in this state, where situated, and the value of the property owned and used outside of this state, and where situated.

10. The change or changes, if any, in the above particulars, made since the last annual report. (June 2, 1911, 102 v. 249, § 112; May 10, 1910, 101 v. 422, § 86; April 11, 1902, 95 v. 124, § 2.)

Section 5502. (Valuation certified to auditor of state.) Upon the filing of the report, provided for in the last three preceding sections, the commission, from the facts thus reported and any other facts coming to its knowledge bearing upon the question, shall, on the first Monday in September, determine the proportion of the authorized capital stock of the company represented by its property and business in this state. On the first Monday of October, the commission shall certify the amount of the proportion of the authorized capital stock of each such company represented by its property and business in this state, as determined by it, to the auditor of state. (June 2, 1911, 102 v. 250, § 113; May 10, 1910, 101 v. 422, § 87; April 11, 1902, 95 v. 124, § 2.)

A company organized by concurrent legislation of two states is a domestic corporation in each state. A finding by the taxing officers that such a company is a foreign corporation, and the acceptance of annual reports, does not bar the state from collection of the proper tax.
State v. Covington, etc., Co., 6 N. P. n. s. 55; 18 L. D. 273 (C. P. 1907).

The tax commission *is* invested with a reasonable discretion in making the determination. Rep. Atty. Gen., 1910-1911, p. 600.

Effect of erroneous compliance with G. C. §§ 178 to 192. Where a foreign corporation, which neither owned nor used property in the state, by error, in complying with G. C. §178 et seq., reported its entire capital stock as used in the state, the tax commisssion may permit an amended report to be filed, and, under the authority to consider "other facts coming to its knowledge bearing on the question," may accept the minimum annual fee, and release the corporation from liability for the balance.
Rep. of Atty. Gen., 1909-1910, p. 84.

Method of computing tax. This tax is not based upon the *property* owned and used and *business* transacted in Ohio, but is based upon the *proportion of the total authorized capital stock* represented by such property and business. The proportion which the property owned and used and business transacted in Ohio bears to the entire property and business of the corporation is the proportion of the capital stock on which the tax is based. If the property owned and used and business transacted in Ohio is $10,000, the entire corporate property and business $20,000, and the authorized capital stock $50,000, the tax would be based upon one-half of its authorized capital stock ($25,000), the Ohio property and business being one-half of the total property and business.

If the entire corporate property and business is in Ohio the tax would be based upon the entire authorized capital stock.
5 O. L. R. 163 (Atty. Gen. 1907).
Aetna, etc., Co. v. Taylor, 13 C. C. 602; 5 C. D. 242 (1896).
4 Opins. Atty. Gen., 621-624 (1894).
Rep. Atty. Gen., 1910-1911, p. 600.

Section 5503. (Collection. Fee. Minimum.) On or before October fifteenth, the auditor of state shall charge for collection, as herein provided, annually, from such company, in addition to the initial fees otherwise provided for by law, for the privilege of exercising its franchises in this state, a fee of three-twentieths of one per cent. upon the proportion of the authorized capital stock of the corporation represented by property owned and used and business transacted in this state, which fee shall not be less than ten dollars in any case. Such fee shall be payable to the treasurer of state on or before the first day of the following December. (June 2, 1911, 102 v. 250, § 114; May 10, 1910, 101 v. 422, § 87; April 11, 1902, 95 v. 124, § 2.)

Section 5504. (Domestic corporations. Hearing. Corrections.) Between the dates herein fixed for the determination of the amount of the subscribed or issued and outstanding capital stock of a domestic corporation and the proportion of the authorized capital stock of a foreign corporation, represented by property owned and used and business transacted by it in this state, and the dates herein fixed for the certification to the auditor of state of such amount or proportion, the commission may, on the application of any person or company interested, or on its own motion, review and correct its findings. (June 2, 1911, 102 v. 250, § 115; May 10, 1910, 101 v. 425, § 100; April 25, 1904, 97 v. 382, § 6; April 11, 1902, 95 v. 124, § 6.)

Section 5505. (Receipt.) Upon the payment of the tax or fee, provided for in this act, to the treasurer of state, the treasurer of state shall make out and deliver to the public utility or corporation so paying a receipt for the payment by such public utility or corporation of the tax or fee herein provided for. (June 2, 1911, 102 v. 251, § 116; May 10, 1910, 101 v. 424, § 92; April 11, 1902, 95 v. 126, § 4.)

Section 5506. (First lien.) The fees, taxes and penalties, required to be paid by this act, shall be the first and best lien on all property of the public utility or corporation, whether such property is employed by the public utility or corporation in the prosecution of its business or is in the hands of an assignee, trustee or receiver for the benefit of the creditors and stockholders thereof. (June 2, 1911, 102 v. 251, § 117; May 10, 1910, 101 v. 424, § 93; April 25, 1904, 97 v. 381, § 5; April 11, 1902, 95 v. 124, § 5.)

Section 5507. (Penalty.) If a public utility or corporation, required to file a report by any provision of this act, fails or neglects to make such report, as required herein, it shall be subject to a penalty of ten dollars per day for each day's omission after the time limited in this act for making such report. (June 2, 1911, 102 v. 251, § 118; May 10, 1910, 101 v. 424, § 94; April 25, 1904, 97 v. 381, § 5; April 11, 1902, 95 v. 126, § 5.)

Compromise of penalty, G. C. § 5524.

Section 5508. (Liabilities of foreign corporations. Insurance companies not included in this act.) All foreign corporations, and the officers and agents thereof, doing business in this state, shall be subjected to all the liabilities and restrictions that are, or may be imposed upon corporations of like character, organized under the laws of this state, and shall have no other or greater powers. Every contract made by or on behalf of any such foreign corporation, affecting the liability thereof or relating to its property within this state, before it shall have complied with the provisions of section one hundred and seventy-eight of the General Code, shall be wholly void on its behalf and on behalf of its assigns, but shall be enforceable against it or them. Nothing contained in this section shall be held or construed to apply to insurance corporations, fraternal beneficiary associations, or building and loan associations required by law to report to the superintendent of insurance, nor to repeal, change or modify the provisions of section one hundred and eighty-eight of the General Code. (June 2, 1911, 102 v. 251, § 119.)

Acting as a stockholder in an Ohio corporation, or giving assent to changes in its regulations, is not "doing business" in Ohio within the meaning of G. C. §§ 178 or 5508.
Toledo T. L. & P. Co. v. Smith, 58 Bull. 201 (U. S. D. C. 1913).
Powers of foreign corporations prior to enactment of § 5508.
See State v. Insurance Co., 69 O. S. 327 (1903).
Mannington v. Ry. Co., 8 O. L. R. 451, 484; 183 Fed. 133; 16 O. F. D. 552 (C. C. 1910).

Effect on contracts of noncompliance with § 178 et seq. Before the enactment of § 5508 it was held that a contract made by a foreign coroporation which had not complied with § 178 to 192 was not void.
Fergus v. Columbus, 6 N. P. 82; 8 L. D. 290.
Ins. Co. v. Ellis, 32 O. S. 388 (1877).
Ins. Co. v. McMillen, 24 O. S. 67 (1873).
But the right of action thereon was suspended until a certificate was secured.
Simplex Dairy Co. v. Cole, 86 Fed. 739 (1898).
Crefeld Miller v. Goddard, 69 Fed. 141 (1895).

Section 5509. (Failure to report or pay tax or fee; effect

of. Cancellation of articles.) If a corporation, wherever organized, required by the provisions of this act, to file any report or returns or to pay any tax or fee, either as a public utility or as a corporation, organized under the laws of this state, for profit or as a foreign corporation for profit doing business in this state and owning or using a part or all of its capital or plant in this state, or as a sleeping car, freight line or equipment company, fails or neglects to make any such report or return or to pay any such tax or fee for ninety days after the time prescribed in this act for making such report or return or for paying such tax or fee, the commission shall certify such fact to the secretary of state. The secretary of state shall thereupon cancel the articles of incorporation of any such corporation which is organized under the laws of this state, by appropriate entry upon the margin of the record thereof, or cancel the certificate of authority of any such foreign corporation to do business in this state by proper entry. Thereupon all the powers, privileges and franchises conferred upon such corporations, by such articles of incorporation or by such certificate of authority, shall cease and determine. The secretary of state shall immediately notify such domestic or foreign corporation of the action taken by him. (June 2, 1911, 102 v. 251, § 120; May 10, 1910, 101 v. 424, § 97; April 25, 1904, 97 v. 381, § 5.)

See § 5525.

Section 5510. (Penalty.) Any person or persons who shall exercise, or attempt to exercise, any powers, privileges or franchises, under the articles of incorporation or certificate of authority, after the same are cancelled, as provided in section one hundred and twenty of this act [G. C. § 5509], shall be fined not less than one hundred dollars nor more than one thousand dollars. (June 2, 1911, 102 v. 252, § 121.)

See § 5525.

Section 5511. (Reinstatement.) Any corporation whose articles of incorporation or certificate of authority, to do business in this state, has been cancelled by the secretary of state, as provided in section one hundred and twenty of this act [G. C. § 5509], upon the filing, within two years after such cancellation, with the secretary of state, of a certificate from the commission that it has complied with all the requirements of this act and paid all taxes, fees or penalties due from it, and upon the payment to the secretary of state of an additional penalty of one hundred dollars, shall be entitled again to exercise its rights, privileges and franchises in this state, and the secretary of state shall cancel the entry made by him under the provisions of section one hundred and twenty of this act [G. C. § 5509], and shall issue his certificate entitling such corporation to exercise its rights, privileges and franchises. (June 2, 1911, 102 v. 252, § 122.)

See § 5525.

Section 5512. (Action by attorney general.) In addition to all other remedies for the collection of any taxes or fees due, under the provisions of this act, the attorney general, shall, upon the request of the commission, whenever any taxes, fees or penalties due, under this act, from any public utility or corporation, shall have remained unpaid for a period of ninety days, or whenever any corporation or public utility has failed or neglected for ninety days to make or file any report or return, required by this act, or to pay any penalty for failure to make or file such report or return, apply to the common pleas court of Franklin county, or of any county in the state in which such public utility or corporation is located or has an office or place of business, for an injunction to restrain such public utility or corporation from the transaction of any business within this state, until the payment of such taxes or fees and penalties thereon, or the making and filing of such report or return and payment of penalties for failure to make or file such report or return, and the costs of such application, which shall be fixed by the court. Such petition shall be in the name of the state, and if it is made to appear to the court, upon hearing, that such public utility or corporation has failed and neglected, for ninety days, to pay such taxes, fees or penalties thereon, or to make or file such reports or returns, or to pay such penalties for failure to make or file such reports or returns, such court of common pleas shall grant and issue such injunction. All actions brought under this act shall have precedence over any civil cause of a different nature pending in such court, and the court of common pleas shall always be deemed open for the trial of any such action brought therein. (June 2, 1911, 102 v. 252, § 123.)

See § 5525.

Section 5513. (Quo warranto proceedings.) If any corporation fails or neglects to make and file the reports or returns, required by this act, or to pay the penalties provided in this act for failure to make and file such reports or returns, for a period of ninety days after the time prescribed in this act, the attorney general, on the request of the commission, shall commence an action in quo warranto, in the circuit court of Franklin county, or of any county in this state in which such corporation is located or has an office or place of business, to forfeit and annul its privileges and franchises. If the court is satisfied that any such corporation is in default as aforesaid, it shall render judgment ousting such corporation from the exercise of its privileges and franchises within this state, and shall otherwise proceed as provided in Chapter One of Title VIII, Part 3 of the General Code. (June 2, 1911, 102 v. 253, § 124; May 10, 1910, 101 v. 424, § 97; April 25, 1904, 97 v. 382, § 5; April 11, 1902, 95 v. 126, § 5.)

See § 5525.

Section 5514. (Certified list of new corporations each month by secretary of state to commission.) The secretary of state shall prepare and keep a correct list of all corporations, subject to the provisions of this act, engaged in business within this state. Each month he shall file with the commission a certified report showing all the new corporations, the increase or decrease of the capital stock, or the dissolution of existing corporations, and such other information as the commission requires. For the purpose of obtaining the necessary information, the secretary of state or the commission, shall have access to the records of the offices of the county auditors of the state. (June 2, 1911, 102 v. 253, § 125; May 10, 1910, 101 v. 425, § 98; April 25, 1904, 97 v. 382, § 6.)

Section 5515. (Information by county auditors.) Upon request of the secretary of state or the commission, any county auditor shall furnish such information as is shown by the records of his office concerning corporations located within his county, and subject to the provisions of this act. (June 2, 1911, 102 v. 253, § 126; May 10, 1910, 101 v. 425, § 99; April 25, 1904, 97 v. 382, § 6; April 11, 1902, 95 v. 126, § 6.)

Section 5516. (Fees; power of commission as to.) For the purpose of determining the amount of fees due from any such corporation, the commission may investigate and determine the facts showing the proportion of the authorized capital stock of the company represented by its property and business in this state. (June 2, 1911, 102 v. 253, § 127.)

Section 5516-1. (Extension of time.) The tax commission of Ohio, when it deems the same necessary or advisable, may extend to any corporation or public utility, a further specified time within which to file any report required by law to be filed with the tax commission, in which event the attaching or taking effect of any penalty for failure to file such report or pay its tax or fee into the state treasury shall be extended or postponed accordingly. (March 2, 1911, 102 v. 31.)

Section 5517.   (Hearing.   Review.   Corrections.   Mistake.)   Any bank, public utility or corporation may be heard by the commission upon the question as to the correctness of any determination, finding or order of the commission after the same has been made.   Application to the commission for a review of any determination, finding or order by it made, must be filed within sixty days after the passage of this act, or within sixty days from the date of the certification thereof by the commission to the proper officer.   The commission, upon such application, may make such correction in its determination, finding or order, as it may deem proper, and its decision in the matter shall be final.   Such correction shall be certified to the proper official, who shall correct his records and duplicates in accordance therewith. In case any such bank, public utility or corporation has paid the tax or fee assessed against it under mistake, and such mistake is corrected by the commission, upon application so filed, so that the amount due from such bank, public utility or corporation, under such corrected determination, finding or order, is less than the amount of the taxes or fees paid, the county auditor or the auditor of state, as the case may be, shall upon certificate of such correction, as herein provided, draw his warrant on the treasurer, in favor of the bank, public utility or corporation, for the amount so erroneously paid by it.   The county treasurer or the treasurer of state, as the case may be, shall pay such warrant; and there is hereby appropriated from the general revenue fund of any such county and from the general revenue fund of the state, not otherwise appropriated, such amount as may be necessary to pay such warrants.   (June 2, 1911, 102 v. 253, § 128; May 10, 1910, 101 v. 425, § 100.)

The "proper officer" to whom the tax commission should certify corrections is the auditor of state.   The state treasurer should also be notified of corrections.
Rep. Atty. Gen. 1911-1912, pp. 164, 451.
That part of this section which provides for an appropriation for a refunder of taxes overpaid is said to be in conflict with Art. 2, Sec. 22 of the constitution in that it is not specific and not limited to two years. This does not affect the remainder of the section.
Rep. Atty. Gen. 1911-1912, p. 148.

Section 5518. (Insurance companies excepted.) An incorporated company, whether foreign or domestic, owning or operating a public utility in this state, and as such required by law to file reports with the tax commission and to pay an excise tax upon its gross receipts or gross earnings as provided in this act, and insurance, fraternal beneficial, building and loan, bond investment and other corporations, required by law to file annual reports with the superintendent of insurance, shall not be subject to the provisions of sections one hundred and six to one hundred and fifteen, inclusive, of this act [G. C. §§ 5495 to 5504]. June 2, 1911, 102 v. 254, § 129; May 10, 1910, 101 v. 425, § 101; April 25, 1904, 97 v. 382, § 7; April 11, 1902, 95 v. 127, § 7.)

Public utility companies not engaged in active business should file reports under § 5495 et seq.
Rep. Atty. Gen., 1906-1907, pp. 45, 41.
A railroad corporation which owns a line of railroad which is operated under a long term lease by another railroad company is not relieved by this section from making reports and paying taxes, although the lessee company pays an excise tax on its gross receipts, where the lessor company maintains its corporate organization, collects the rent, pays dividends, and issues stock and bonds for extensions and betterments.
State v. C. & P. R. R., 13 N. P. n. s. 671 (C. P. 1913).
A railroad company, having sold all of its property and shares of stock to another company, but which maintains a corporate organization, is required to make reports and pay taxes on its capital stock under § 5495 et seq.
Rep. Atty. Gen., 1911-1912, p. 694.

Section 5519. (Report not required until lapse of six months from date of incorporation.) A corporation shall not be required to file its first annual report under sections one hundred and six to one hundred and fifteen [G. C. §§ 5495 to 5504] inclusive, of this act, until the proper month, hereinbefore provided, for the filing of such report, next following the expiration of six months from the date of its incorporation or admission to do business in this state. (June 2, 1911, 102 v. 254, § 130; May 10, 1910, 101 v. 425, § 102; April 25, 1904, 97 v. 382, § 7; April 11, 1902, 95 v. 127, § 7.)

Where its capital stock is increased within six months prior to the time of filing the report, a corporation is not required to pay a fee on the increased stock.
5 Opins. Attys. Gen., 865 (1903).
"Date of incorporation" is the date of filing the articles of incorporation, not the certificate of subscription.
Rep. Atty. Gen., 1908, p. 85.
A consolidated corporation need not file a report until after the expiration of six months following the filing of its certificate of consolidation.
Rep. Atty. Gen., 1908, p. 83.

Section 5520. (Dissolution no exemption from payment or filing report.) The mere retirement from business or voluntary dissolution of a domestic or foreign corporation, without filing the certificate, provided for in sections eleven thousand nine hundred and seventy-four, eleven thousand nine hundred and seventy-five and eleven thousand nine hundred and seventy-six of the General Code, shall not exempt it from the requirements to make reports and pay fees or taxes in accordance with the provisions of this act. (June 2, 1911, 102 v. 254, § 131; April 25, 1904, 97 v. 383, § 8; April 11, 1902, 95 v. 127, § 8.)

A receiver, assignee or trustee for creditors must file reports and pay fees until the corporation is dissolved or its charter revoked by a court of competent jurisdiction, and until a certificate of dissolution under § 11975 is received and filed by the secretary of state.
Rep. Atty. Gen., 1911-1912, p. 699.
Rep. Atty. Gen., 1904-1905, pp. 68, 69.
See note to § 5498.

Section 5521. (When certificate of dissolution may be filed.) In case of dissolution or revocation of its charter, on the part of a domestic corporation, or of the retirement from business in this state, on the part of a foreign corporation, the secretary of state shall not permit a certificate of such action to be filed with him unless the commission shall certify that all reports, required to be made to it, have been filed in pursuance of law, and that all taxes or fees and penalties thereon due from such corporation have been paid. (June 2, 1911, 102 v. 254, § 132; April 25, 1904, 97 v. 383, § 8; April 11, 1902, 95 v. 127, § 8.)

Corporations not for profit are not required to procure certificates from the tax commission, except corporations organized more than six months prior to November, 1910. Under the former law reports were required from corporations not for profit.
Rep. Atty. Gen., 1911-1912, p. 697.
This section does not apply to insurance, fraternal benefit and other corporations required to file reports with the superintendent of insurance.
G. C. § 5518.
Rep. Atty. Gen., 1911-1912, p. 697.

Section 5522. (Affidavits as to use of money or property in aid of elections. Form prescribed by commission and made part of return.) Every corporation or public utility required, by the provisions of this act, to make returns, statements or reports to the commission, shall file therewith, in such form as the commission may prescribe, an affidavit subscribed and sworn to by a person or officer having knowledge of the facts therein set forth, setting forth that such corporation or public utility has not, during the preceding year, directly or indirectly paid, used or offered, consented or agreed to pay or use, any of its money or property for, or in aid of any political party, committee or organization, or for, or in aid of any candidate for political office or for nomination for any such office, or in any manner used any of its money or property for any political purpose whatever, or for the reimbursement or indemnification of any person or persons for moneys or property so used. Such forms of affidavit as the commission may prescribe shall be attached to or made a part of the return, statement or report required to be made by such corporation or public utility under any provision of this act. (June 2, 1911, 102 v. 255, § 133.)

See §§ 8729, 8730.

Section 5523. (Certificate of secretary of state as to foreign corporation doing business without compliance with laws. Prosecution.) When the secretary of state has knowledge that a foreign corporation, organized for profit, and owning or using a part or all of its capital and plant in this state, is doing business in this state without having complied with the laws thereof, he shall certify such fact to the commission. The commission, when it ascertains from such certificate of the secretary of state, or otherwise, that any such foreign corporation is doing business in this state without having complied with the laws thereof, shall certify the same to the attorney general, with the request that he prosecute an action against such foreign corporation for the penalties provided by law, in the court of common pleas of Franklin county, or in any county in which the corporation has an office or place of business. It shall be the duty of the attorney general, upon receipt of such request, to commence and prosecute such an action. On good cause shown, the commission may remit the penalty, or part thereof, incurred by a foreign corporation under the provision of Chapter 2, of Division 1, Title III, Part First, General Code. (June 2, 1911, 102 v. 255, § 134.)

See §§ 182, 186, 191.

Section 5524. (Compromise.) With the advice and consent of the commission, the attorney general may, before or after any action for the recovery of fees, taxes or penalties certified to him, as delinquent, under the provisions of this act, compromise or settle any claim for delinquent taxes, fees or penalties so certified.

And all claims compromised or settled as herein provided shall be set forth in the annual report of the tax commission to the general assembly and governor, giving in detail the terms and conditions of such compromise or settlement. (June 2, 1911, 102 v. 255, § 135; April 25, 1904, 97 v. 381, § 5; April 11, 1902, 95 v. 126, § 5.)

Section 5525. (Application of preceding sections.) The provisions of sections one hundred and twenty, one hundred and twenty-one, one hundred and twenty-two, one hundred and twenty-three and one hundred and twenty-four of this act [G. C. §§ 5509, 5510, 5511, 5512 and 5513] shall apply to any public utility or corporation which for two years prior to, and for ninety days from and after, the passage of this act, shall fail to pay any taxes or fees or penalties thereon, due from it to the state of Ohio, or to make or file any report or return, required by law, or to pay any penalty provided by law for failure to make or file any report or return required by law. (June 2, 1911, 102 v. 259, § 159.)

MISCELLANEOUS.

§ 5650. Levy to pay bonds given for railroad subscription.
§ 5672. Tax a lien on bank shares. Collection of tax. Penalty.
§ 5673. Banks may deduct taxes paid from shareholders, when. Lien.

§ 5675. Agent of express or telegraph company to pay taxes thereof.
§ 5676. Unlawful to act as agent, etc., for certain companies when taxes are unpaid.
§ 5677. Railroad shall not transport anything for such company.

Section 5650. (Levy to pay bonds given for railroad subscription.) The lawful authorities of a county, city, or township which have subscribed to the capital stock of a railroad company and have issued its bonds or other securities for the payment of such subscription, may levy or cause to be levied, annually, on the taxable property thereof, within five years next before the principal of such bonds, or other securities are payable, if the market price of the stock of such railroad company is less than seventy-five per cent on its par value, such tax, not exceeding one mill on the dollar, as will be sufficient to balance the discount on the railroad stock held by such county, city or township, by the time such bonds may become due. The proceeds of such taxes shall form, with such stock, a sinking fund, and be invested in the purchase of the bonds issued by such county, city or township, or in other safe and productive securities, and be applied only to the payment of the bonds so issued. (R. S. Sec. 2831; 56 v. 175, § 80; S. & C. 1466.)

Section 5672. (Tax a lien upon bank shares. Collection of tax. Penalty.) Taxes assessed on shares of stock, or the value thereof, of a bank or banking association, shall be a lien on such shares from the first Monday of May in each year until they are paid. It shall be the duty of every bank or banking association to collect the taxes due upon its shares of stock from the several owners of such shares, and to pay the same to the treasurer of the county, in which such bank or banking association is located, as other taxes are paid, and any bank or banking association failing to pay the said taxes as herein provided, shall be liable by way of penalty for the gross amount of the taxes due from all the owners of the shares of stock, and for an additional amount of one hundred dollars for every day of delay in the payment of said taxes. (May 2, 1911, 102 v. 91; R. S. Sec. 2839; 64 v. 204, § 6.)

Stock in national banks belonging to nonresidents is taxable in Ohio.
    Rep. Atty. Gen., 1911-1912, pp. 592, 610.

Section 5673. (Banks may deduct taxes paid from shareholders; when. Lien.) Such bank or banking association paying to the treasurer of the county in which it is located, the taxes assessed upon its shares, in the hands of its shareholders respectively, as provided in the next preceding section, may deduct the amount thereof from dividends that are due or thereafter become due on such shares, and shall have a lien upon the shares of stock and on all funds in its possession belonging to such shareholders, or which may at any time come into its possession, for reimbursement of the taxes so paid on account of the several shareholders, with legal interest; and such lien may be enforced in any appropriate manner. (May 2, 1911, 102 v. 91; R. S. Sec. 2840; 64 v. 204, § 7.)

Section 5675. (Agent of express or telegraph company to pay taxes thereof.) The agent of an express or telegraph company shall retain in his hands and pay to the county treasurer, the amount of all taxes assessed against such company. In default of such payment, the treasurer shall collect the tax as in other cases of delinquent personal property tax. When there is more than one such agent of the same company in one county, the agent thereof in the principal city, or village of such county, may assume the payment of such tax, and upon so doing, the other agents in the county shall not be required to retain funds to pay the tax. (R. S. Sec. 2842; 59 v. 91, § 6.)

Section 5676. (Unlawful to act as agent, etc., for certain companies when taxes are unpaid.) If the taxes assessed against an express, telegraph, telephone, or insurance company, in any county in this state, remains due and unpaid to the treasurer of the county, for twenty days after the time provided by law for the payment thereof, no person or corporation, shall act as agent, or transact any business for such company so in default, until the tax, interest, and penalty are paid. (R. S. Sec. 2843; 82 v. 92; R. S. 1880; 59 v. 91, § 7.)

Section 5677. (Railroad company shall not transport anything for such company.) After the default in payment of taxes named in the next preceding section, a railroad company which, directly or indirectly, conveys or carries for such defaulting express, telegraph, telephone, or insurance company, a package of money, merchandise, or other articles, or transmits a telegraphic message, after having notice of such default, for each offense shall forfeit and pay a sum equal to the amount of such tax due and unpaid, with the interest and penalty thereon, to be recovered by an action in the name of the state, in the county where the tax is assessed, with costs of suit. (R. S. Sec. 2843; 82 v. 92; R. S. 1880; 59 v. 91, § 7.)

Section 5888. (Chautauqua assemblies may make rules for government of grounds.) A corporation, organized under the laws of this state, for holding Chautauqua assemblies, or encouraging religion, art, science, literature, the general dissemination of knowledge, or two or more of such purposes, occupying grounds and holding meetings or entertainments thereon for advancing the purpose of its incorporation, through its board of directors or trustees, may make such rules and regulations for the government of such grounds, not inconsistent with the laws of this state, as will promote the purposes for which it is incorporated. (April 10, 1908, 99 v. 90, § 1; R. S. Sec. 7017-10.)

NOTE.—Sections 5889 to 5893, which authorize Chautauqua assemblies. etc., to appoint special police and define their powers, are omitted.

When a corporation which has for its object the owning and holding of land, for the purpose of carrying on religious exercises and meetings on the same, leases a part of such land with restrictive covenants in the lease that lessees "during all meetings would be subject to the rules and regulations of said meeting," and "would use such premises for the purpose of a private dwelling or residence only, except on a special permit from the company," such covenants are valid and binding on the lessees.

Where such lessees make a business of renting rooms, in their buildings on such leased premises, to temporary occupants, and refuse to obtain a special permit from the lessor and refuse to comply with the reasonable requirements of the lessor, in regard to the privilege of so using the leasehold, such use is a breach of the covenant to "use such premises for the purpose of a private dwelling or residence only, except on a special permit from the company."

The refusal to pay a gate fee, during the meetings, for admission to the grounds of the plaintiff on which the buildings of the defendant are situated, the same as charged to all other persons, is a breach of the covenant that the lessees "during all meetings would be subject to the rules and regulations of said meetings."

Park Co. v. Van Dusen, 63 O. S. 183 (1900).

PART XIII.

REGULATION OF SALE OF BONDS, STOCKS AND SECURITIES
("BLUE SKY LAW").

Section 6373-1. (Providing license for dealers in securities.) Except as otherwise provided in this act, no dealer shall, from and after the first day of August, A. D., 1913, within this state, dispose or offer to dispose of any stocks, bonds, mortgages or other instruments evidencing title to or interest in property or other securities of any kind or character (all hereinafter termed "securities"), issued or executed by any private or quasi-public corporation, copartnership or association (except corporations not for profit, organized under the laws of this state) or by any taxing subdivision of any other state, territory, province or foreign government, without first being licensed so to do as hereinafter provided. (May 6, 1913, 103 v. 743, § 1; in effect August 8, 1913.)

Sections 6373-1 to 6373-24 are popularly known as the "Blue Sky Law."

Section 6373-2. (Term "securities" shall not include what. Term "dealer" defined. Exceptions. Definitions.) The term "securities," as used in this act, shall not be deemed to include conveyances of real estate located in Ohio, book accounts, or commercial paper, or other evidences of indebtedness running not more than one year; or, where the same have not been judicially declared invalid, and where, at the time of such sale, there is no default in payment of any part of the interest or principal of the same:

a. Mortgage bonds and notes (other than corporate bonds where more than fifty per cent. of the entire issue is not included in a sale to one purchaser) secured by mortgage on real estate in the state of Ohio; provided, that such mortgage and all superior subsisting liens upon said real estate shall not aggregate more than the appraised value thereof, for taxation;

b. Securities of quasi-public corporations, the issuance of which has been authorized by the public service commission of this state;

c. The stock, note or other obligation of any national bank, or of any bank, trust company or building and loan association, organized under the laws of this state and subject to examination and supervision by the proper authorities thereof; or any instrument for the unconditional payment of a certain sum of money, the full payment of the principal and interest of which shall be unconditionally guaranteed, through endorsement or otherwise, by such national bank or such other bank, company or association.

The term "dealer", as used in this act, shall be deemed to include any person or company, except national banks, disposing, or offering to dispose, of any such security, through agents or otherwise, and any company engaged in the marketing or flotation of its own securities either directly or through agents or underwriters or any stock promotion scheme whatsoever; except:

a. An owner, not the issuer of the security, who disposes of his own property, for his own account, when such disposal is not made in the course of continued or successive transactions of a similar nature by such owner;

b. One who, in a trust capacity created by any law of the United States or of this or any other state or by judicial authority, lawfully disposes of any property embraced within such trust;

c. A bank or trust company, organized under the laws of this state and subject to examination and supervision by the proper authority thereof, selling a security for a licensee, other than the issuer or underwriter thereof, at a commission of not more than two per cent., where such bank or trust company is not a regular dealer in securities;

d. One, not the issuer, who disposes of securities to a licensee under this act or to a company which, as a part of its regular business, deals in or holds such securities;

e. A pledgee selling, in the ordinary course of business and not in continued or successive transactions, a security pledged to him as security for debt in good faith and not for the purpose of avoiding the provisions of this act;

f. An issuer, organized under the laws of this state, where the disposal, in good faith and not for the purpose of avoiding the provisions of this act, is made directly to its stockholders or by its own officers, without any commission and at a total expense of not more than two per centum of the proceeds realized therefrom and where no part of the issue is issued, directly or indirectly, in payment for patents, services, good will, or for property not located in this state; provided that the president and secretary of the issuer shall, prior to such disposal, file with the "commissioner" a written statement setting forth the existence of all of such facts.

As used in this act, the term "company" shall include any corporation, co-partnership or association, incorporated or unincorporated, and whenever and wherever organized; "dispose of" shall be construed to mean "sell, barter, pledge or assign for a valuable consideration or obtain subscriptions for"; "issuer", the original issuer; and where the context demands it, words in the present tense include the future tense; in the masculine gender include the feminine and neuter gender; in the singular number include the plural, and in the plural, the singular number; the word "whoever" includes all persons, natural and artificial, principals, agents and employes; "and" may be read "or", and "or", "and". (May 6, 1913, 103 v. 743, § 2.)

Section 6373-3. (Filing fee, application for license and information required.) Before such license shall be issued to any dealer, there shall be filed by him with the superintendent of banks, herein termed the "commissioner", together with a filing fee of ten dollars, an application for such license, together with information, in such form as shall be determined by such "commissioner," setting forth:

a. Names and addresses of the directors and officers if such applicant be a corporation or association, and of all partners if it be a partnership, and of the person if the applicant be an individual, together with the names and addresses of all agents of such applicant assisting in the disposal of such securities;

b. Location of the applicant's principal office and of his principal office in the state, if any;

c. The general plan and character of the business of said applicant, together with references, which the "commissioner" shall confirm by such investigation as he may deem necessary, establishing the good repute in business of such applicant, directors, officers, partners and agents;

If the applicant be a corporation organized under the laws of any other state, territory or government, or have its principal place of business therein, it shall also file a copy of its articles of incorporation, certified by the proper officer of such state, territory or government, and of its regulations and by-laws; and if it be a co-partnership or unincorporated association, a certified copy of its articles of co-partnership or association, or deed of settlement.

The applicant at the same time shall also file with said "commissioner" a duly executed written instrument, irrevocable, consenting that any action brought against such applicant, arising out of the disposal of such securities by him or his agents, may be brought in Franklin county, and that, in the event that proper service of process cannot be had upon such applicant in such county, service of process made therein by the sheriff of such county, by sending a copy thereof by registered mail, at least thirty days prior to taking judgment in such case, addressed to such applicant at the place of his principal office named in his application or such other place as the applicant may thereafter designate in writing filed with the "commissioner", shall have the same effect as if personally made upon the applicant, according to the laws of this state. (May 6, 1913, 103 v. 745, § 3.)

Section 6373-4. (Publication of notice of applications for registration.) Notice of all applications for registration as a licensed dealer in such securities shall be published in a daily newspaper of general circulation in the city where the applicant's principal place of business in the state is located, or in the city of Columbus if the applicant has no place of business in the state and no such application shall be acted on by the "commissioner" until the expiration of one week from the date of such publication, but shall be acted upon within twenty days after proof of such publication has been filed with him. If the "commissioner" be satisfied of the good repute in business of such applicant, directors, officers, partners and agents, he shall, upon the payment of an annual fee of fifty dollars, and five dollars additional for each agent named in the application, register the applicant as a licensed dealer in such securities, and issue to him a license, containing the name of the applicant and all such agents, renewable annually upon the payment of such annual fee, unless revoked as herein provided. The expense of all publications provided for in this act shall be paid by the applicant for license. (May 6, 1913, 103 v. 746, § 4.)

Section 6373-5. (When license shall be taken out; fee. Revocation and amendment of license; fee.) Such license shall be taken out at the beginning of each calendar year, but it may be issued at any time for the remainder of a calendar year, and in such case the annual fee shall be reduced pro rata but in no case shall it be less than twenty-five dollars. Upon the payment of a fee of ten dollars for each specified agent not named in such license, when issued, the same may at any time be amended or supplemented to include such agent. Upon the written request of such applicant, accompanied by a fee of two dollars, such license shall be revoked as to any agent or agents of such applicant, and an amended license shall thereupon be issued for such applicant and his remaining agents; and thereafter the applicant shall not be bound by the acts of the agent whose license has been revoked. Notice of such amendments shall also be published as aforesaid. (May 6, 1913, 103 v. 746, § 5.)

Section 6373-6. ("Commissioner" may revoke license, when.) Such "commissioner" may at any time revoke any such license, or refuse to renew the same, upon ascertaining that the licensee:

a. Is insolvent or is of bad business repute;

b. Has violated any provision of this act; or

c. Has engaged, or is about to engage, under favor of such license, in illegitimate business or in fraudulent transactions; and, he shall at once lay before the prosecuting attorney of the proper county any evidence which shall come to his knowledge of criminality under this act.

No dealer whose license has been revoked shall be relicensed within one year from the date of such revocation. (May 6, 1913, 103 v. 746, § 6.)

Section 6373-7. (Notice of revocation or refusal of license.) At least five days before refusing or revoking a license, or refusing upon proper application presented on or before the 10th day of December to renew at expiration a license previously issued, the "commissioner" shall send by registered mail to the licensee, at the address named in the application for license, written notice of his intention so to do, specifying therein the reasons for the refusal or revocation of such license. (May 6, 1913, 103 v. 747, § 7.)

Section 6373-8. (Providing suit against commissioner in case of refusal or revocation. Answer.) Any one whose license shall be refused or revoked, or to whom a renewal of license previously issued may be denied, may file, within thirty days thereafter in the court of common pleas of Franklin county, a petition against the commissioner, officially, as defendant, alleging therein in brief detail the plaintiff's qualifications to be licensed, and praying for a reversal of the official action complained of. Upon service of summons upon said defendant, returnable within three days from its date, but otherwise made as in civil actions, he shall, within one week from such return day, file an answer, in which he shall allege by way of defense the grounds previously assigned in his notice to such applicant or licensee, and such other grounds as shall, in the meantime, accrue or be discovered. All allegations of the answer shall be deemed · to stand denied without further pleading and, upon application of either party, the cause shall be advanced and heard without delay. Merely technical irregularities in the procedure of such "commissioner," shall be disregarded and the burden shall rest upon the plaintiff to disprove the grounds assigned and specified in the official action complained of. The court's decision shall consult only the rights of plaintiff and protection of the public and shall be final and shall not be subject to modification, vacation or reversal; but its judgment sustaining the refusal of the "commissioner" to grant or renew a license shall not bar, after thirty days, a new application by plaintiff for a license, nor shall its judgment in favor of the plaintiff prevent such "commissioner" from thereafter revoking such license for any cause which may thereafter accrue or be discovered. (May 6, 1913, 103 v. 747, § 8.)

Section 6373-9. (Information required to be filed before disposal of securities.) Before such licensee shall dispose, or offer to dispose, of any of such securities, within this state, he shall file with such "commissioner," in such form as shall be determined by him, the following information concerning such securities if issued by any company;

(a). The name, location of principal office of the issuer and the names of its officers and directors, or if a co-partnership, the partners;

(b). A statement of the issuer, showing, in general detail, the assets and liabilities, surplus and capital stock of

the issuer, as of a date as late as the close of its last fiscal
year, and of its gross income, expenses, net earnings and
fixed charges, for one year last prior thereto, or for such
time as the issuer has been in business, if less than one year.

(c). A pertinent description of such securities, and the
purpose of said issue;

(d). If the securities be of a taxing subdivision of any
other state, territory, province or foreign government, and
are not an obligation of the entire taxing subdivision and
payable out of the proceeds of a general tax, there shall be
filed the information required by paragraphs (c) and (e)
of this section and, in addition thereto a statement of the
licensee, setting forth the nature of the obligation of such
securities, how payment of the same is secured and that, to
the best of his knowledge, there is no default in the payment
of any part of the interest or principal of such securities and
are no adjudications adversely affecting, or pending suits
questioning the validity of the same; and

(e). Unless the foregoing information be excused under
the provisions of the following section, the approximate price
at which the licensee purposes to dispose of such securities.
(May 6, 1913, 103 v. 747, § 9.)

Section 6373-10.   (When information need not be filed.)
The information required in the preceding section need not
be filed:

(a). Unless required by the "commissioner," if the
same has been filed by any other licensee; or

(b). If actual current sales of the securities, at prices
quoted, shall have been, from time to time, for not less than
one year next preceding such disposal, published in the
tabulated market reports of the news columns of a daily
newspaper published and of general circulation in this state;
or

(c). Where there is a disposal of securities, the price
paid or consideration rendered for which, in a single transaction, by one disposee, shall amount to five thousand dollars or more; or

(d). Where the securities disposed of are those of manufacturing or transportation companies, or of common carriers or other public utilities, issued and outstanding in the
hands of bona fide purchasers for value, prior to February
1st, 1913, where such companies were on said date, and
shall be at the time of sale, actual going concerns, either
directly or through lessees, and where there shall be at the
time of sale no default in payment of any part of the interest or principal of such securities; or

e. Where the information required, other than the approximate selling price, is contained in any standard manual of information, approved by such "commissioner;" or

f. Where the disposal is made for a commission of less than one percentum of the par value thereof, by a licensee who is a member of a regularly organized and recognized stock exchange and who has an established and lawfully conducted place of business in this state, regularly open for public patronage as such. (May 6, 1913, 103 v. 747, § 10.)

Section 6373-11. (Filing prospectus of advertisements and sales.) Every dealer, before or at the time of issuing or circulating the same, shall file with the "commissioner" one copy of each prospectus, circular or other document of like nature and of each advertisement, issued or circulated by him in connection with the sale of any such securities of the classes referred to in section nine hereof (G. C. § 6373-9); which documents shall each bear a serial number. (May 6, 1913, 103 v. 747, § 11).

Section 6373-12. (Contract of subscription or disposal; contents.) No person or company shall, for the purpose of organizing or promoting any insurance company, or of assisting in the flotation of its stock after organization, dispose or offer to dispose, within this state, of any such stock, unless the contract of subscription or disposal shall be in writing, and contain a provision substantially in the following language:

"No sum shall be used for commission, promotion and organization expenses on account of any share of stock in this company in excess of .... per cent. of the amount actually paid upon separate subscriptions (or, in lieu thereof there may be inserted, '$.............. per share from every fully paid subscription,') and the remainder of such payments shall be invested as authorized by the law governing such company and held by the organizers (or trustees as the case may be) and the directors and officers of such company after organization, as bailees for the subscriber, to be used only in the conduct of the business of such company after having been licensed and authorized therefor by proper authority."

The amount of such commission, promotion and organization expenses shall in no case exceed fifteen per cent. of the amount actually paid upon subscription.

Funds and securities held by such organizers, trustees, directors or officers, as bailees, shall be deposited with a bank or trust company of this state or invested as provided in sections ninety-five hundred and eighteen and ninety-five hundred and nineteen of the General Code until such company has been licensed as aforesaid. (May 6, 1913, 103 v. 748, § 12.)

Section 6373-13.   (Liability of one who counsels or advises the purchase without disclosing agency.) Whoever counsels, advises or procures any person to purchase any security and receives for such advice or services any commission or reward from the owner or salesman, without disclosing to the purchaser the fact of his agency or his interest in the sale of such security, shall be liable to the purchaser for the amount paid by him for such security, with interest, upon the tender of such security to such advisor within one year subsequent to the transaction. (May 6, 1913, 103 v. 748, § 13.)

Section 6373-14.   (Additional statement of information by dealer.   Securities to which section does not apply.) No dealer, for the purpose of organizing or promoting any company, or assisting in the flotation of the securities of any company after organization, shall, within this state for or on behalf of the issuer or any underwriter thereof, dispose or attempt to dispose of any such security unless each dealer be licensed as provided herein and until, together with the filing fee of five dollars, there be filed with the "commissioner" the application of such issuer for the certificate provided for in section sixteen of this act, (G. C. § 6373-16) and, in addition to the other information hereinbefore required.

(a) A certified copy of the articles of incorporation, or association of the issuer, its regulations and by-laws;

(b) Certified copies of all minutes of stockholders and directors relative to the issue of such securities;

(c) A sworn statement made by the president and secretary of the issuer, showing in detail the items of cash, property, services, patents, good will, and any other consideration for which such securities have been or are to be issued in payment;

(d) Like certified copies of all contracts or agreements between the issuer and any underwriter of such securities, and, if disposed of by the issuer, all contracts and agreements relative to the sale and disposition thereof, and any such contracts or agreements made subsequent thereto shall be filed immediately upon the execution thereof;

(e) All contracts made between such underwriter and

any salesman, agent or broker; and until such "commissioner" shall issue his certificate, as provided in section sixteen hereof. (G. C. § 6373-16.)

This section shall not apply where the issuance of the securities has been approved by the public service commission or like body of any state of the United States or any province of the Dominion of Canada, or where the disposal is made by or on behalf of an underwriter who, in good faith and not for the purpose of avoiding the provisions of this act, purchases the securities disposed of and pays therefor in cash or its equivalent, before attempting to dispose of the same, not less than 90 percentum of the price at which such securities are thereafter disposed of. The certificate provided for in section 16 of this act (G. C. § 6373-16), shall not be required where the securities are those of a common carrier or of a company organized under the laws of this state and engaged only in the business of manufacturing, transportation, coal mining or quarrying, and the whole or a part of the property covered by such securities, is located within this state; nor of a real estate or building company all of whose property covered by such securities is located in this state; nor in cases where information is dispensed with under the provisions of paragraphs (d) and (f) of section ten hereof. (G. C. § 6373-10).

The information required by paragraphs (d) and (e) of this section shall be for the information of the "commissioner" only, and shall not be disclosed by him, except when lawfully required in a judicial proceeding. (May 6, 1913, 103 v. 750, § 14.)

Section 6373-15. (Licensed dealers only shall deal in real estate not located in Ohio. Transactions to which section does not apply.) No person or company, other than a dealer licensed as hereinbefore provided, shall within this state, in repeated or successive transactions, deal in real estate not located in Ohio; and, unless so licensed and the "commissioner" shall issue his certificate as provided in the following section, and, prior to such issuance, there shall, together with a filing fee of ten dollars, be filed with the "commissioner" an application for such certificate and a written statement of the dealer containing a pertinent description of the real estate the disposal of all or a part of which is sought to be made, the nature and source of title of the owner thereto, and the amount or value and the nature of the consideration paid or allowed by him therefor, it shall, within this state, be unlawful:

(a) For any corporation or any person, association or

co-partnership doing business under any name other than the name or names of such person or of all the members of such association or co-partnership to dispose or offer to dispose of any real estate not located in Ohio.

(b) For any person or company to sell or offer for sale any such real estate, the owner of which is, or is represented to the purchaser to be, a corporation, or any person or company of the character described in the foregoing paragraph, where such corporation, person or company is engaged in the business of dealing in real estate.

This section shall apply where the title to such property is held in the name of a trustee for any corporation or for any such described person or company; but it shall not be deemed to prohibit the disposal by an owner of his own property, in good faith and not for the purpose of avoiding the provisions of this act, where the transaction is not one of repeated transactions of a similar nature, performed as a part of the business of dealing in real estate; nor shall it be deemed to prohibit a railroad company having an immigration bureau or department from advertising either directly or through its accredited representatives, the fact that there are along its route lands for colonization or sale; provided that such advertising be not of specific tracts of real estate, and not for the purpose of avoiding the provisions of this act. (May 6, 1913, 103 v. 751, § 15.)

Section 6373-16. (Examination of issuer of securities or owner; certificate. Right of review.) Said "commissioner" shall have power to make such examination of the issuer of the securities or the owner of the property, named in the two preceding sections, and of such securities or property, as he may deem advisable; and if he shall find that the law has been complied with, and is satisfied that said company is solvent, that its business is properly and legitimately conducted, and that its proposed disposal of its securities or other property is not on unfair terms, upon the payment of a fee of twenty dollars he shall issue his certificate to that effect, authorizing such disposal; but if he shall not affirmatively so find, and is not so satisfied, he shall notify the applicant, in writing, of such finding and of his refusal to issue such certificate. Said applicant shall have the right of review of such finding given to a dealer by section eight hereof. [G. C. § 6373-8.]   (May 6, 1913, 103 v. 751, § 16.)

Section 6373-17. (Certificate must state, commissioner in no wise recommends securities.) Such certificate shall recite in bold type that the "commissioner" in no wise recommends such securities or other property; and no person or company shall advertise, in connection with the sale of such securities, the fact that such certificate has been issued unless such advertisement also contains in bold type a copy of such recital. (May 6, 1913, 103 v. 752, § 17.)

Section 6373-18. (Liability of seller to purchaser. Limitation of action.) In addition to the liability now imposed by law, any person or company that, by written or printed circular, prospectus, statement or advertisement of any kind, shall offer for subscription or purchase any security, or receive the profits accruing from the disposal of securities so advertised, shall be liable to any person who, on the faith of such advertisement or document, acquires such security, for the loss or damage sustained by him by reason of any untrue statement contained therein, unless such person or company shall establish that he or it had no knowledge or notice of the publication of such advertisement prior to the transaction complained of, or had just and reasonable grounds to believe the statements thereof to be true. Wherever any corporation shall be so liable, the directors thereof shall also be, under like limitations, jointly and severally liable. Any such director, upon the payment of a judgment so obtained against him, shall be subrogated to the rights of the plaintiff against such corporation and shall have the right of contribution for the payment of such judgment, under like limitations, against any of his fellow directors. Lack of reasonable diligence to ascertain the fact of such publication the falsity of any statement therein contained, shall be deemed to be knowledge of such publication and of the falsity of any untrue statement thereof. Any action brought against such director, based upon the liability hereby imposed, shall be brought within two years after the acquisition of the security by any person so damaged or after payment of the judgment for which contribution is sought. (May 6, 1913, 103 v. 752, § 18.)

Section 6373-19. (Duties of superintendent of insurance.) If the issuer of such securities be a company incorporated, organized or formed to make any insurance named in subdivisions I and II, division III, title IX of the General Code, the "commissioner," for all the purposes named in sections 14 and 16 of this act [G. C. §§ 6373-14, 6373-16], shall be the superintendent of insurance of this state. In addition to the powers given to, and the duties prescribed to be performed by, such "commissioner," under said sections, the superintendent of insurance shall have, over any such company disposing or attempting to dispose of any of its securities within this state, the powers of regulation, supervision and examination conferred on him by law, with reference to companies licensed to transact the business of insurance within this state. . (May 6, 1913, 103 v. 752, § 19.)

Section 6373-20.   (Penalty for violations.)   Whoever knowingly makes any false statement of fact in any statement or matter of information required by this act to be filed with the "commissioner," or in any advertisement, prospectus, letter, circular or other document, containing an offer to dispose or solicitation to purchase, or commendatory matter concerning, such securities or real estate, with intent to aid in the disposal of the same, or whoever knowingly violates any of the provisions of sections 12, 14 or 15 of this act [G. C. §§ 6373-12, 6373-14, 6373-15], or for the purpose or aiding in the disposal of any security or real estate, knowingly makes any false statement or representation concerning any license or certificate issued under the provisions hereof, shall be fined not less than one hundred dollars nor more than five thousand dollars, or imprisoned in the penitentiary not more than one year or both; and whoever violates any of the other provisions of this act shall be fined not less than fifty dollars nor more than one thousand dollars, or imprisoned in the county jail or workhouse not more than sixty days, or both. (May 6, 1913, 103 v. 753, § 20.)

Section 6373-21.   (When accused presumed to have knowledge.)   In any prosecution brought under this act, the accused shall be deemed to have had knowledge of any matter of fact where, in the exercise of reasonable diligence, he should, prior to the commission of the offense complained of, have secured such knowledge. Information and indictments under this act need not negative any of the exceptions enumerated in sections two, ten and fourteen hereof. [G. C. §§ 6373-2, 6373-10, 6373-14.]   (May 6, 1913, 103 v. 753, § 21.)

Section 6373-22.   (Act does not limit other liability imposed.)   Nothing herein contained shall limit or diminish the liability of any person or company now imposed by law, or prevent the prosecution of any person or company violating any of the provisions of this act, for the violation of any other statute or of any other provision hereof. (May 6, 1913, 103 v. 753, § 22.)

Section 6373-23. (Contract obligations unimpaired.) Nothing herein contained shall be so construed as to impair the obligation of prior contracts. (May 6, 1913, 103 v. 753, § 23.)

Section 6373-24. (Clerks, salaries, fees, appropriation.) The superintendent of banks is hereby authorized to appoint such clerks as are actually necessary to carry out the provisions of this act and to fix their salaries; such appointments and salaries to be subject to the approval of the governor. All fees received hereunder by the "commissioner" shall be deposited by him with the treasurer of state upon warrant of the auditor of state. The sum of seven thousand five hundred dollars is hereby appropriated out of any money in the state treasury to the credit of the general fund, not otherwise appropriated, for the payment of the salaries and expenses necessary to carry out the provisions of this act. (May 6, 1913, 103 v. 753, § 24.)

PART XIV.

TRUSTS.

Section 6390. (Definition of terms.) The word "person" or "persons" as used in this chapter includes corporations, partnerships and associations existing under or authorized by any state or territory of the United States, or a foreign country. (April 19, 1898, 93 v. 146, § 12; R. S. Sec. 4427-12.)

Section 6391. (Definition of trusts.) A trust is a combination of capital, skill or acts by two or more persons, firms, partnerships, corporations or associations of persons, for any or all of the following purposes:

1. To create or carry out restrictions in trade or commerce.

2. To limit or reduce the production or increase, or reduce the price of merchandise or a commodity.

3. To prevent competition in manufacturing, making, transportation, sale or purchase of merchandise, produce or a commodity.

4. To fix at a standard or figure, whereby its price to the public or consumer is in any manner controlled or established, an article or commodity of merchandise, produce or commerce intended for sale, barter, use or consumption in this state.

5. To make, enter into, execute or carry out contracts, obligations or agreements of any kind or description, by which they bind or have bound themselves not to sell, dispose of or transport an article or commodity, or an article of trade, use, merchandise, commerce or consumption below a common standard figure or fixed value, or by which they agree in any manner to keep the price of such article, commodity or transportation at a fixed or graduated figure, or by which they shall in any manner establish or settle the

price of an article, commodity or transportation between
them or themselves and others, so as directly or indirectly
to preclude a free and unrestricted competition among themselves, purchasers or consumers in the sale or transportation
of such article or commodity, or by which they agree to
pool, combine or directly or indirectly unite any interests
which they have connected with the sale or transportation
of such article or commodity, that its price might in any
manner be affected. Such trust as is defined herein is unlawful, against public policy and void. (April 19, 1898, 93
v. 143, § 1; R. S. Sec. 4427-1.)

The original act included in §§ 6390 to 6402, popularly known as the
Valentine Anti-trust Act, was adopted from the Texas Anti-trust Law.
  State v. Bovee, 6 N. P. n. s. 337, 343; 17 L. D. 663.

  Constitutionality. Original act (93 v. 143) held constitutional.
  State v. Buckeye, etc., Co., 61 O. S. 520 (1899).
  State v. Gage, 72 O. S. 210 (1905); reversing 1 C. C. n. s. 221;
    14 C. D. 724.
  Lemmon v. State, 77 O. S. 427, 432 (1908).
  State v. Jacobs, 7 N. P. 261; 17 L. D. 515.
  Salt Co. v. Salt Co., 12 L. D. 386.
  Quo warranto was held to be a proper method of testing the
constitutionality of the act.
  State v. Pipe Line Co., 61 O. S. 520 (1899).

  Corporation, its officers and stockholders as a combination. A corporation and its own officers, stockholders and agents, without the participation of others, may be guilty of forming a trust and conspiracy
in violation of this act, and all, including the corporation, may be counted
in making up the two or more necessary parties.
  State v. National Cash Register Co., 13 C. C. n. s. 73; 21 C. D.
    637 (1910).
  The combination does not lose its identity by the dissolution of
the corporation and the formation of a new corporation by the same
parties to continue the unlawful purpose.
  State v. National, etc., Co., 13 C. C. n. s. 73; 21 C. D. 637 (1910).

  "Trade and commerce." Combinations of insurance agents. A
combination of insurance agents is not a violation of the anti-trust act.
  State v. Bovee, 6 N. P. n. s. 337; 17 L. D. 663 (C. P. 1907).
  Runck v. Cloud, 8 N. P. 436; 11 L. D. 444 (Super. Ct. Cin. 1901).
  Contra, State v. Ross, 4 N. P. n. s. 377; 16 L. D. 704 (C. P. 1906).
  See G. C. § 9563.

  Combinations fixing prices, pooling interests, etc. An indictment
charging that defendants were members of a combination formed to carry
out restraint in trade and commerce, increasing the price and preventing
competition in the sale of lumber, and knowingly acted in pursuance of
such combination, binding themselves not to sell lumber for use in
a certain locality below a common standard in prices, and agreeing to pool,
combine and unite their interests in such lumber trade states a violation
of this section and not of § 6392.
  Arnsman v. State, 11 C. C. n. s. 113; 20 C. D. 445 (1908).
  An organization of manufacturers which raises a fund with which it
"leases down" competing factories, and allots the trade of such factories
among its members, controls the output and prices of its members and

binds them not to sell to specified customers except by consent of its members, is an unlawful combination.

Fisher v. Flickinger Wheel Co., 7 C. C. n. s. 533; 18 C. D. 501 (1906).

A contract between two mercantile houses engaged in the same line of business, by which each acquires an interest in the gross profits made by the other is not on its face illegal, as tending to create a monopoly and void as against public policy either under this act or at common law.

Fechteter v. Palm Bros. & Co., 133 Fed. 462; 14 O. F. D. 369 (C. C. A. 1904).

An association organized for the purpose of increasing the price and decreasing the production of a commodity in general use, such as candles, is contrary to public policy.

Emery v. Ohio Candle Co., 47 O. S. 320 (1890).

Labor union, the by-laws of which prohibited members from working at non-union shops, limiting amount of work to be performed in a certain time, etc., held an illegal association.

Kealey v. Faulkner, 7 N. P. n. s. 49; 18 L. D. 498 (C. P. 1907).

Agrements to maintain prices, etc.

See Graf v. Masters, etc., Assn., 1 N. P. n. s. 423; 11 L. D. 18 (Super. Ct. Cin. 1904).

Needles v. Bishop, etc., Co., 2 N. P. n. s. 77; 14 L. D. 445 (C. P. 1904).

State v. Standard Oil Co., 51 Bull 563 (Probate Ct. 1906).

Agreement to furnish employment if competitor discontinues business. An agreement to furnish employment to a competitor, if such competitor will discontinue business is not a violation of this act.

Kevil v. Standard Oil Co., 8 N. P. 311; 11 L. D. 114 (Super. Ct. Cin. 1901).

Monopoly at common law. Stock control of competing line, by railway.

State v. Railway Co., 12 C. C. n. s. 49; 21 C. D. 175 (1909); s. c., 12 C. C. n. s. 145.

Gould v. Railway, 10 N. P. n. s. 313 (1910).

Manufacturer fixing prices of resale by wholesale and retail dealers.

Freeman v. Miller, 9 N. P. n. s. 26 (Super. Ct. Cin. 1909).

Section 6392. (Owning trust certificate or entering into a combination prohibited.) It shall not be lawful for a person, partnership, association or corporation, or an agent thereof, to issue or own trust certificates, or for a person, partnership, association or corporation, or an agent, officer or employe thereof, or a director or stockholder of a corporation, to enter into a combination, contract or agreement with any person or persons, corporation or corporations, or a stockholder or director thereof, the purpose and effect of which is to place the management or control of such combination or combinations, or the manufactured product thereof, in the hands of a trustee or trustees with the intent to limit or fix the price or lessen the production and sale of an article of commerce, use or consumption, or to prevent, restrict or diminish the manufacture or output of such article. (April 19, 1898, 93 v. 145, § 10; R. S. Sec. 4427-10.)

Section construed.

Arnsman v. State, 11 C. C. n. s. 113, 118; 20 C. D. 445 (1908).

Control of several corporations by trustees, issuing trust certificates to stockholders.

See State v. Standard Oil Co., 49 O. S. 137 (1892).

Section 6393. (Illegal contract.) A contract or agreement in violation of any provision of this chapter is void and not enforceable either in law or equity. (April 19, 1898, 93 v. 145, § 8; R. S. Sec. 4427-8.)

A covenant in a lease of saloon property by a brewing company, lessor, prohibiting the sale on the premises of beer other than that of the manufacture of the lessor is not invalid under this section.

Diehl Brewing Co. v. Konst, 12 C. C. n. s. 577; 20 C. D. 782 (1905); aff'd, no rep., 79 O. S. 469.

Brewing Co. v. Demko, 9 C. C. n. s. 130; 19 C. D. 102 (1907).

See Huebner, etc., Breweries v. Singlar, 8 C. C. n. s. 49; 18 C. D. 329; reversed, no report, 77 O. S. 626.

Where a combination purchased all the machinery of one of its constituent members, stipulating that the vendor corporation should not compete with its members, and providing employment for the president of the vendor company; and it appeared that the machinery was purchased without a plan for its use and location and remained unused for eight months, the agreement was held to be void. Where possession was not taken of the machinery the contract was not an executed contract although the full purchase price was paid.

Fisher v. Flickinger Wheel Co., 7 C. C. n. s. 533; 18 C. D. 501 (1906).

See Standard Distilling Co. v. Block. 5 N. P. n. s. 386; 17 L. D. 601; reversed, without report, 78 O. S. 448.

A contract monopolistic in its character is illegal at common law.

Crawford v. Wick, 18 O. S. 190 (1868).

Central, etc.. Co. v. Guthrie, 35 O. S. 666 (1880).

Emery v. Ohio Candle Co., 47 O. S. 320 (1890).

Action by member of a combination to recover price of goods sold. In an action to recover the purchase price of goods sold it is no defense that the plaintiff is a member of an unlawful trust or combination.

Corn, etc., Co. v. Roser, etc., Co., 10 N. P. n. s. 596; 22 L. D. 663 (1910).

See Kinner v. Ry. Co., 69 O. S. 339, 344 (1903).

Continental Wall Paper Co. v. Voight, 212 U. S. 227 (1909); affirming 148 Fed. 939; 15 O. F. D. 401.

Agreement by vendor of business not to re-engage in business. An agreement by which one sells his business, agreeing not to enter into a similar business, within certain time and territorial limits, is valid if the prohibited territory is not more extensive than necessary to enable the vendee to enjoy the fruits of the contract.

Kevil v. Standard Oil Co., 8 N. P. 311; 11 L. D. 114 (Super. Ct. Cin. 1901).

But an agreement by the seller that he will not directly or indirectly engage in the same business in the state or United States for a period of twenty-five years necessarily tends to create a monopoly and is void.

Lufkin Rule Co. v. Fringeli, 57 O. S. 596 (1898).

Such agreements are valid only when the restraint of trade is partial and reasonable and not oppressive.

Grasseli v. Lowden, 11 O. S. 349 (1860).
Lange v. Werk, 2 O. S. 528.
Carr v. Walker Brewing Co., 3 O. L. R. 618; 17 L. D. 222 (Super.
Ct. Cin. 1906).

Rescission of contract to form combination. Non-consenting stock-holders of a corporation, which has entered. a prohibited combination, are not in *pari delicto*, and may, after demand upon the corporate officers and their refusal to take steps to rescind, bring suit for a rescission. Nat'l. Salt Co. v. United Salt Co., 12 L. D. 386 (C. P. 1902).

Where the illegal acts are wholly unexecuted, a party to the contract may abandon the contract and recover back the money paid.
Nat'l Salt Co. v. United Salt Co., 12 L. D. 386 (C. P. 1902).

Section 6394. (Foreign corporations must comply with anti-trust acts. Revocation of certificate.) A foreign corporation or foreign association exercising any of the powers, franchises or functions of a corporation in this state, violating any provision of this chapter shall not have the right, of and shall be prohibited from, doing any business in this state. The attorney general shall enforce this provision by proceedings in quo warranto in the supreme court, or the court of appeals of the county in which the defendant resides or does business, or by injunction or otherwise. The secretary of state shall revoke the certificate of such corporation or association theretofore authorized by him to do business in this state. (May 6, 1913, 103 v. 424; May 18, 1910, 101 v. 274; R. S. Sec. 4427-3; April 19, 1898, 93 v. 144, § 3.)

Section 6395. (Violation, penalty.) A person, firm, partnership, corporation or association violating any provision of this chapter shall forfeit and pay to the state, for the use of the general revenue fund thereof, the sum of fifty dollars for each day that such violation is committed or continued after due notice given by the attorney-general or a prosecuting attorney. Such sum may be recovered in the name of the state in any county where the offense is committed or where any of the offenders reside; and the attorney-general, or the prosecuting attorney of any county upon the order of the attorney-general, shall prosecute for the recovery thereof. When such action is prosecuted by the attorney-general he may begin the same in the court of common pleas of Franklin county or of any county in which the defendant resides or does business. (May 18, 1910, 101 v. 275; R. S. Sec. 4427-7; April 19, 1898, 93 v. 145, § 7.)

The probate court has concurrent jurisdiction with the court of common pleas of offenses under this section, which are misdemeanors under G. C. § 12372.

State v. Standard Oil Co., 51 Bull 563 (Prob. Ct. 1906).
. Prosecutions may be brought by information as well as by indictment.
State v. Standard Oil Co., 51 Bull 563 (Prob. Ct. 1906).
One party to an unlawful combination is liable for the acts of other parties done under the agreement.
State v. Standard Oil Co., 51 Bull 563 (Prob. Ct. 1906).
Two or more corporations charged with conspiracy are properly joined in one information.
State v. Standard Oil Co., 51 Bull 563.

Section 6396. (Criminal penalty. Penalty when Violation relates to bread, meat, vegetables, etc.) A violation of any or all of the provisions of this chapter is a conspiracy against trade, and a person engaged in such conspiracy or taking part therein, or aiding or advising in its commission, or, as principal, manager, director, agent, servant or employer, or in any other capacity, knowingly carrying out any of the stipulations, purposes, prices or rates, or furnishing any information to assist in carrying out such purposes, or orders thereunder, or in pursuance thereof, or in any manner violating a provision of this chapter, shall be fined not less than fifty dollars nor more than five thousand dollars or imprisoned not less than six months nor more than one year, or both. Provided, however, that when the violation of the provisions of this chapter consists of a combination to control the price or supply, or to prevent competition in the sale of bread, butter, eggs, flour, meat or vegetables or any one of said articles, the person or persons thus engaged shall upon conviction thereof be fined in any sum not less than five hundred dollars and be imprisoned in the penitentiary not less than one nor more than five years. Each day's violation of any of the provisions of this chapter shall constitute a separate offense. (April 27, 1913, 103 v. 254; R. S. Secs. 4427-4, 4427-10; April 19, 1898, 93 v. 144, 145, §§ 4, 10.)

Venue of criminal prosecution. The illegal combination must have been entered into in the county where the prosecution is brought, or some act must have been committed in such county in furtherance of the unlawful purpose.
Hughes v. State, 9 C. C. n. s. 369; 19 C. D. 237 (1907); aff'd, 77 O. S. 640.
Compare, State v. Ice Delivery Co., 5 N. P. n. s. 89; 17 L. D. 515 (C. P. 1907).
State v. King Bridge Co., 7 C. C. n. s. 557; 18 C. D. 147 (1906).

Indictment. An indictment charging defendants with being an unlawful combination from March 10, 1900, and continuing until March 9, 1903, and further charging violations during such period, is valid, although each day's violation constitutes a separate offense.
Hughes v. State, 9 C. C. n. s. 369; 19 C. D. 237 (1907); aff'd, no rep., 77 O. S. 640.

Arnsman v. State, 11 C. C. n. s. 113; 20 C. D. 445 (1908).
The exact date on which the combination was formed need not be alleged.
State v. Crystal Ice, etc., Co., 5 N. P. n. s. 149; 17 L. D. 640 (1906).

Imprisonment. Proper place of. See Lemmon v. State, 77 O. S.
427 (1908).
State v. Wirick, 81 O. S. 343 (1910).
In re Schooler, 7 N. P. n. s. 276; 19 L. D. 465 (C. P. 1908).
Improper sentence; remanding case for resentence.
Arnsmann v. State, 11 C. C. n. s. 113; 20 C. D. 445 (1908).

Corporations are subject to criminal penalties of this act.
State v. Ice Delivery Co., 6 N. P. n. s. 89; 17 L. D. 515 (C. P.
1910).

Construction of original section 4; "knowingly."
State v. Ice Delivery Co., 5 N. P. n. s. 89; 17 L. D. 515 (C. P.
1907).

Constitutionality. The imprisonment or penalty clause of this section
is not in contravention of the constitutional requirement that all laws
of a general nature shall have a uniform operation throughout the state.
State v. Hygeia Ice Co., 4 N. P. n. s. 361; 16 L. D. 735 (C. P. 1906);
affirmed, except as to prison sentence; 77 O. S. 427.

Section 6397.   (Liability for damages.)   In addition to
the civil and criminal penalties provided in this chapter, the
person injured in his business or property by another person,
or by a corporation, association or partnership, by reason of
anything forbidden or declared to be unlawful in this chapter, may sue therefor in any court having jurisdiction
thereof in the county where the defendant or his agent resides or is found, or where service may be obtained, without
respect to the amount in controversy, and recover twofold
the damages sustained by him and his costs of suit.   When
it appears to the court, before which a proceeding under
this chapter is pending, that the ends of justice require
other parties to be brought before such court, the court may
cause them to be made parties defendant and summoned
whether they reside in the county where such action is
pending, or not. ‘(April 19, 1898, 93 v. 146, § 11; R. S. Sec.
4427-11.)

Pleading.   A petition in a civil action may allege the wrongful acts
in the language authorized by § 6398.
Goode v. Ohio, etc., Assn., 3 O. L. R. 600; 16 L. D. 586 (C. P. 1906).

Cross-examination of plaintiff by deposition.   In an action to enjoin an illegal combination and for damages, the plaintiff, whose deposition is being taken before a notary, can not refuse to disclose the
names of dealers from whom he procured goods after the combination
had refused to sell to him, on the ground that it is a trade secret; but
he may refuse on the ground that the question is irrelevant in such an
examination.
Jones v. Goode, 7 C. C. n. s. 589; 18 C. D. 475 (1906); affirming
3 O. L. R. 401; 16 L. D. 404; affirmed, no report, 78 O. S. 421.

Removal to federal court. The action under this section is a civil action and may be removed to federal court.

Mahon v. Somers, 112 Fed. 174; 12 O. F. D. 433 (1901).

Section 6398. (What indictment shall contain.) In an indictment for an offense provided for in this chapter, it is sufficient to state the purpose or effects of the trust or combination, and that the accused is a member thereof, or acted with or in pursuance of it or aided or assisted in carrying out its purposes, without giving its name or description, or how, when and where it was created. (April 19, 1898, 93 v. 144, § 5; R. S. Sec. 4427-5.)

See notes §§ 6395 and 6396.

Arnsman v. State, 11 C. C. n. s. 113; 20 C. D. 445 (1908).

Hughes v. State, 9 C. C. n. s. 369; 19 C. D. 237 (1907); aff'd, no rep., 77 O. S. 640.

No overt act need be alleged. Mere membership in an unlawful combination constitutes an offense.

State v. Ice Delivery Co., 5 N. P. n. s. 89; 17 L. D. 515 (1907).

State v. Crystal Ice, etc., Co., 5 N. P. n. s. 149; 17 L. D. 640 (1906).

Section 6399. (Evidence.) In prosecutions under this chapter, it shall be sufficient to prove that a trust or combination as defined herein, exists, and that the defendant belonged to it, or acted for or in connection with it, without proving all the members belonging to it, or proving or producing an article of agreement, or a written instrument on which it may have been based; or that it was evidenced by a written instrument. The character of the trust or combination alleged may be established by proof of its general reputation as such. (April 19, 1898, 93 v. 145, § 6; R. S. Sec. 4427-6.)

Proof by general reputation unconstitutional. The last clause of this section providing that the character of a trust may be proved by general reputation is unconstitutional.

Hammond v. State, 78 O. S. 15 (1908).

Hughes v. State, 9 C. C. n. s. 369; 19 C. D. 237 (1907); aff'd, 77 O. S. 640.

Other evidence. Conversations, statements and conduct of alleged conspirators, not a part of the transactions charged in the indictment, but offered to establish the existence of the unlawful combination, are not admissible against a defendant not present nor concurring therein.

Hughes v. State, 9 C. C. n. s. 369; 19 C. D. 237 (1907); aff'd, 77 O. S. 640.

Evidence of prior acts can be considered only when it tends to show that a defendant is a member of the unlawful combination.

State v. Standard Oil Co., 51 Bull. 563 (Prob. Ct. 1906).

Charge to the jury. See Hughes v. State, 9 C. C. n. s. 369; 19 C. D. 237 (1907); 77 O. S. 640.

Section 6400. (Jurisdiction of courts. Quo warranto; injunction. Domestic corporations. Dissolution by court.) The several courts of common pleas in the state are hereby invested with jurisdiction to restrain and enjoin violators of this chapter. For a violation of any provision of this chapter by a corporation or association mentioned herein, the attorney general, or the prosecuting attorney of the proper county, shall institute proper proceedings in a court of competent jurisdiction in any county in the state where such corporation or association exists, does business or has a domicile. When such suit is instituted by the attorney general in quo warranto, he may begin the same in the supreme court of the state, or the court of appeals of Franklin county. When such suit is instituted by the attorney general to restrain and enjoin a violation of any provision of this chapter, he may begin the same in the court of common pleas of Franklin county. Such proceedings to restrain and enjoin such violation, or violations, shall be by way of petition setting forth the case, and praying that such violation shall be enjoined or otherwise prohibited.

Upon the filing of such petition, and before final decree, the court may at any time make such temporary restraining order or prohibition as shall be deemed just in the premises. In any action or proceeding in quo warranto by the attorney general or a prosecuting attorney against a corporation the court in which such action or proceeding is pending may, ancillary to such action or proceeding, restrain or enjoin the corporation and its officers and agents from continuing or committing during the pendency of the action the alleged act or acts by reason of which the action is brought. When, in a proceeding quo warranto by the attorney general or any prosecuting attorney, any corporation incorporated under the laws of this state is, on final hearing, found guilty of violating any of the provisions of this act, the court may declare a forfeiture of all its rights, privileges and franchises to the state and may order the incorporation dissolved and appoint a trustee or trustees to wind up its affairs, as is provided in other cases in quo warranto. (May 6, 1913, 103 v. 425; May 18, 1910, 101 v. 275; April 19, 1898, 93 v. 114, § 2: R. S. Sec. 4427-2.)

Quo warranto.   Proper allegations of petition.
  See State v. National, etc., Co., 13 C. C. n. s. 73; 21 C. D. 637 (1910).
  The state may inquire as to all acts committed by any participant in the alleged unlawful combination from the time it is alleged to have been formed.
  State v. National, etc., Co., 13 C. C. n. s. 74; 21 C. D. 637 (1910).
  A quo warranto proceeding may be brought in the circuit court of

any county where one or more of the defendant corporations is situated and process may issue to other counties.

It need not be brought in the county where the combination does business as a separate entity.

State v. King Bridge Co., 7 C. C. n. s. 557; 18 C. D. 147 (1906).

Where dissolution of an illegal association is decreed, the court may appoint a receiver to liquidate its affairs and distribute its funds.

Kealey v. Faulkner, 7 N. P. n. s. 49; 18 L. D. 498 (C. P. 1907).

Section 6400-1. (Parties defendant. Statute of limitation no bar to suit.)

In any action or proceeding in quo warranto, injunction or otherwise brought by the attorney-general or a prosecuting attorney under this chapter, all persons parties to or participating in the trust or conspiracy against trade violative of the provisions of this chapter, may be made parties defendant and summoned, whether they reside in the county where such action is instituted or not. Proceedings in quo warranto and in injunction may be instituted simultaneously, or while one or another of them is pending, such suits being started in the proper court as provided in this chapter, and no suit in injunction shall be a bar to a suit in quo warranto, nor shall a suit in quo warranto be a bar to one instituted to restrain and enjoin. No statute of limitation shall prevent or be a bar to any suit, or proceeding, for any violation hereafter committed of any provision of this chapter. (May 18, 1910, 101 v. 275.)

Section 6401. (Witness not excused from testifying.)

If a court of record or in vacation a judge thereof, in which is pending a civil, criminal or other action or proceeding brought or prosecuted by the attorney-general or a prosecuting attorney for the violation of any provision of this chapter, or an action or proceeding for a violation of a law, common or statute, against a conspiracy or combination in restraint of trade, so orders, no person shall be excused from attending, testifying or producing books, papers, schedules, contracts, agreements or other documents in obedience to the subpoena or order of such court or a commissioner, referee or master appointed by such court to take testimony, or a notary public or other person authorized by the laws of this state to take depositions, when the order made by such court or judge includes a witness whose deposition is being taken before such notary public or other officer, for the reason that the testimony or evidence required of him may tend to criminate him or subject him to a penalty; but no person shall be prosecuted or subjected to a penalty for or on account of a transaction, matter or thing concerning which he may so testify or produce evidence, documentary or otherwise, before such court, person or officer. (April 19, 1898, 93 v. 313, § 6a.)

The plaintiff, in a civil action under this act, being examined before a notary public under G. C. § 11497, can not refuse, on the ground that it is a trade secret, to disclose the names of dealers from whom he procured a supply of the goods which the combination had refused to furnish him, but such question is irrelevant to an examination under § 11497.

Jones v. Goode, 7 C. C. n. s. 589; 18 C. D. 475 (1906); aff'd, no rep., 78 O. S. 421; s. c., 3 O. L. R. 401.

Section 6402. (Cumulative provisions.) The provisions of this chapter shall be cumulative of each other and of all other laws in any manner affecting them. (April 19, 1898, 93 v. 145, § 9; R. S. Sec. 4427-9.)

OBSTRUCTION OF HIGHWAY BY RAILROAD CAR OR LOCOMOTIVE.

§ 7472. Obstructing roads by rail-road agents.
§ 7473. Damages.
§ 7474. Moneys collected.
§ 7475. Company liable for fines against employes.

Section 7472. (Obstructing roads by railroad agents.) A person or corporation, or a conductor of a train of rail-road cars, or other agent or servant of a railroad company, who obstructs, unnecessarily, a public road or highway authorized by any law of this state, by permitting a railroad car or locomotive to remain upon or across it for longer than five minutes, or permits timber, lumber, wood, or other obstructions to remain upon or across it to the hindrance or inconvenience of travelers, or a person passing along or upon such road or highway, shall forfeit and pay for each offense, not less than two dollars, nor more than twenty dollars. (R. S. Sec. 4748; 65 v. 14, § 31; S. & S. 669; S. & C. 1311.)

Diversion of highway during construction of railroad; duty to restore to former condition of usefulness; liability and remedies for breach of duty. See § 8773 and note.

An action to recover the penalty under this section may be maintained not only by the township trustees. but by any other person. The penalties when collected are to be applied under § 7474.

Higgins v. Grove, 40 O. S. 521.

In an action for obstruction of a highway by a railroad car it must be alleged in the petition that the obstruction was continued unnecessarily for more than five minutes. If the obstruction was caused by other agencies it need not be alleged to have been unnecessary.

Burton Twp. v. Tuttle, 30 O. S. 62.

Railroad Co. v. Mackey. 53 O. S. 370.

Section 7473. (Damages.) The company or person shall also be liable for all damages arising to a person from such obstruction, or injury to such road or highway, to be recovered by an action at the suit of the trustees of the township in which the offense is committed, or of any person suing therefor before a justice of the peace within the county where the offense is committed, or by indictment in the court of common pleas in the proper county. Each twenty-four hours the person or corporation, after being notified, permits such obstruction to remain, shall be an additional offense against the provisions of the next preceding section. (R. S. Sec. 4748; 65 v. 14, § 31; S. & S. 669; S. & C. 1311.)

See also note to § 8773.
Action by supervisor.
Hill v. Supervisor, 10 O. S. 621.
Bisher v. Richards, 9 O. S. 495.
A railroad company is not liable in a civil action for injuries sustained by its obstruction of a street, unless such obstruction is the proximate cause of the injuries.
Railroad Co. v. Staley, 41 O. S. 118.

Section 7474. (Moneys collected.) All penalties collected under section seventy-four hundred and seventy-two, shall be paid to the treasurer of the township in which the offense was committed, and be applied by the trustees to the improvement of roads and highways therein. (R. S. Sec. 4748; 65 v. 14, § 31; S. & S. 669; S. & C. 1311.)

Section 7475. (Company liable for fines against employes.) A railroad company or other corporation, the servant, agent or employe of which, in any manner, obstructs a public road or highway, shall pay all penalties which may be assessed against such servant, agent, or employe for so obstructing it. Such penalties may be enforced by execution issued against such corporation on the judgment rendered against such servant, agent, or employe. (R. S. Sec. 4749; 65 v. 14, § 32; S. & S. 669; S. & C. 1311.)

LIENS.

| §§ 8343 to 8352. | Railroad contracts and subcontracts. | §§ 8376 to 8380. | On public works, including railroads, street railroads, etc. |
| §§ 8365 to 8375. | Of carriers and warehousemen on goods. | | |

LIENS OF RAILROAD SUB-CONTRACTORS.

Section 8343. (Liens against a railroad company.) Any person, association of persons, or corporation contracting for the construction of a railroad, depot buildings, water-tanks,

or any part thereof, shall be liable to and pay to each person
performing labor or furnishing materials stipulated for in
the contract with the owner of the road, under a contract
express or implied with the original contractor, or with any
sub-contractor, for the whole or any part of the work stipulated in the original contract with the owner of the railroad. (R. S. Sec. 3207; 80 v. 99; R. S. 1880; 71 v. 51, § 1.)

The provisions of §§ 8343 to 8352 inclusive, providing for liens of
subcontractors, etc., were held unconstitutional by the U. S. Circuit
Court of Appeals.
  Shaw v. Railway Co., 8 O. L. R. 43; 173 Fed. 476 (1909).
  See Stewart v. Gardner, 10 C. C. n. s. 408; 20 C. D. 218; aff'd, 78
    O. S. 451.
  Railway Co. v. Cronin, 1 W. L. B. 315 (1876); aff'd, 38 O. S. 122
    (1882).
This section does not apply to street railroads.
  Massillon Bridge Co. v. Cambria Iron Co., 59 O. S. 179 (1898).
  It has been held that this section does not provide for an action
at law or authorize the recovery of a money judgment.
  Schneider v. Cincinnati, etc., R. Co., 20 W. L. B. 457 (C. P.)
  See Railway Co. v. Cronin, 38 O. S. 122 (1882).
  § 8350.
Where materials were delivered in another state for use in the con-
struction of a railroad in Ohio, the seller is entitled to a lien.
  Carnegie Bros. v. Lancaster, etc., Ry. Co., 1 N. P. 300; 3 L. D.
    343 (C. P. 1894).
  See Mack v. DeGraff, etc., Co., 57 O. S. 463 (1898).
Priority between mortgages and liens.
  See Toledo, etc., R. R. Co. v. Hamilton, 134 U. S. 296, 301.
  Feike v. Railroad Co., 12 C. C. 362; 5 C. D. 640 (1892); 14 C. C.
    186; 7 C. D. 652 (1897).
Act is prospective in operation.
  Feike v. Railroad Co., 12 C. C. 362; 5 C. D. 640 (1892).
Liens on railroads and bridges under general mechanics' lien law.
  See Rutherford v. Cincinnati, etc., R. R. Co., 35 O. S. 559 (1880).
  Smith Bridge Co. v. Bowman, 41 O. S. 37 (1884).
  Industrial, etc., Co. v. Supply Co., 1 O. F. D. 483 (1897).
  Bowman v. Springfield, etc., R. R. Co., 1 C. C. 64 (1885); 1 C.
    D. 39.
  Cleveland, etc., Ry. Co. v. Trust Co., 86 Fed. 73 (1898).
  Industrial, etc., Co. v. Electrical, etc., Co., 58 Fed. 732 (1893).
  In re Amherst Quarries Co., 56 O. L. B. 93 (1910).

**Section 8344. (What contracts for railroad work shall
stipulate, etc.)** A railroad company shall provide, in its
contract with any person, association of persons, or corporation for the construction of its road, or any part thereof,
that payments thereunder shall be made in the following
order of priority: First, to the persons performing labor,
furnishing materials, or boarding, on the order of any contractor or sub-contractor to persons employed by them, or
either of them, in furnishing materials or labor for or in the
construction of such railroad, without preference. Second,

to any sub-contractor, any balance due under his contract
after payment of his or their liabilities to persons performing labor or furnishing materials or boarding, under his or
their contract. Third, to any contractor, or construction
company, intervening between a sub-contractor and the railroad company, in the order of such intervention from such
sub-contractor upward to the owner of the railroad, any
balance due after payment by the company, of amounts
found due in the order of priority above provided. (R. S.
Sec. 3207; 80 v. 99; R. S. 1880; 71 v. 51, § 1.)

Section 8345. (**What lien shall have precedence.**) A
person who performs labor or furnishes materials for or in
construction of any railroad, depot buildings, water-tanks,
or any part thereof, and a person who furnishes boarding
on the order of any contractor or sub-contractor, to persons
employed by them or either of them, in furnishing materials,
or performing labor for or in construction of such railroad,
depot buildings, water-tanks, or any part thereof, in addition
to his rights under the next two preceding sections shall
have a lien for its payment upon such railroad. Such lien
shall have and maintain precedence over any lien taken, or
to be taken, and subsist for one year from the date of filing
the attested account hereafter provided for. If an action is
brought to enforce the lien within that time, it shall continue in force until finally adjudicated. (R. S. Sec. 3208; 80
v. 99; R. S. 1880; 71 v. 51, § 1.)

"Materials" in this section comprehends and includes only such
articles as are furnished for and to be used in construction of the
railroad. Hay, grain, etc., furnished for the keep of teams of a contractor or subcontractor are not "materials." Section 8351 does not
enlarge the meaning of the word "materials."
　　Penna. Co. v. Mehaffy, 75 O. S. 432 (1907).

Priority between mortgages on after acquired property and me-
chanics' lien. Reed v. Ginsburg, 64 O. S. 11 (1901).
　　Rousculp v. Railroad Co., 19 C. C. 436; 10 C. D. 621 (1899).
　　See note to § 8793.
　　Under this section the taking of a note does not waive or affect
the right to a lien, nor is it necessary to refer to or describe the note
in taking such lien.
　　Rousculp v. Ohio Southern R. R. Co., 19 C. C. 436; 10 C. D. 621
　　　(1899).
Lien not lost by extension of time.
　　Carnegie v. Lancaster, etc., Ry. Co., 1 N. P. 300; 3 L. D. 343 (1894).
Lien for materials delivered out of state.
　　Carnegie v. Lancaster, etc., Ry. Co., 1 N. P. 300; 3 L. D. 343 (1894).
　　Mack v. DeGraff, 57 O. S. 463 (1898).

Electric light plant, when not part of railroad.
  See Industrial, etc., Co. v. Electrical, etc., Co., 58 Fed. 732; 9 O. F.
    D. 483 (C. C. A. 1893).

Section 8346. (How lien perfected.) In order to perfect
such a lien, a person performing labor, or furnishing materials, or boarding, as heretofore specified, within forty days
from the date that he ceased performing labor, or furnishing
materials, or boarding on or for the railroad, shall file with
the recorder of the county where the labor was performed,
or materials, or boarding furnished, an affidavit containing
an itemized statement of the kind and amount of materials
furnished, or labor performed, the time when the contractor
or sub-contractor for whom, and the section and place where,
on the line of the road the labor was performed, or materials
furnished, and the amount due therefor, after crediting all
payments and set-offs. In case of boarding furnished, such
affidavit must have attached thereto an itemized account
thereof, showing the name of the contractor or sub-contractor on whose order it was furnished, the several persons
to whom furnished, the weekly rate of boarding, and the
several amounts unpaid by each respectively. On filing the
affidavit it shall be recorded in a separate book to be provided therefor, and then operate as a lien on the railroad,
in the manner and subject only to the limitations herein
provided. (R. S. Sec. 3208.)

Section 8347. (Proceeding after filing affidavit.). Within ten days after filing his affidavit with the recorder the
claimant shall serve a notice in writing upon the secretary,
or other officer or authorized representative of the railroad
company, by delivering or leaving a copy thereof at his
usual place of residence, or place of doing business. Such
notice shall contain a statement of the facts of his filing such
affidavit, the county wherein filed, the amount of his claim,
whether for labor, materials or boarding furnished, and the
contractor or subcontractor for whom rendered. But when
the notice can not be served in the county where the affidavit
is filed, it shall be served by the recorder upon the representative of the railroad aforesaid by depositing in the postoffice a letter containing the notice directed to his place of
residence, or place of doing business, if known to the recorder. Any person failing to file his affidavit, and serve
such notice within the time herein prescribed, shall be held
to have waived all claim under this and the next two preceding sections, against the railroad company. (R. S. Sec.
3208.)

The service of a notice under this section on a director of the company to be affected by it is sufficient.

Railway Co. v. McCoy, 42 O. S. 251 (1884).

Under this section a substantial compliance with the conditions of the statute providing for the service of written notice upon the owner of the road is essential to create any obligation.

Railway Co. v. Cronin, 38 O. S. 122 (1882).

Section 8348. (How action may be brought.) A person obtaining and holding a lien as provided for in the three preceding sections, in addition to his remedies, under this subdivision, may proceed by petition as in other cases of lien, against the owner of and all other persons interested, as lienholders or otherwise, in such a railroad, and obtain such judgment as justice and equity require. For the purposes of such suit any number of such lien-holders may join as parties plaintiffs, by separately stating and numbering their respective claims, but if several liens be obtained by several persons as aforesaid, on the same railroad, they shall have no priority among themselves; payment thereon shall be made pro rata. (R. S. Sec. 3209; 80 v. 99; R. S. 1880; 71 v. 51, § 1.)

See Schneider v. Cincinnati, etc., Ry. Co., 20 W. L. B. 457 (1888).

Section 8349. (Contractor to be notified of time of payment.) Each contractor or subcontractor shall have at least five days' notice, in writing, of the time when the lien for labor, boarding or materials furnished under a contract with him will be paid, which may be served upon him personally or upon his authorized agent or foreman, by the owner of the railroad, or any officer or agent thereof, stating therein the time of their payment. On request of such contractor or subcontractor he shall be permitted to examine such lien claims before they are paid at any time after the notice has been given. But if such notice can not be served in the county where the lien is filed, it may be given by publication in some newspaper of general circulation therein, for the period of two weeks. If he disputes any of the claims, the company or owner of the road shall withhold payment of those in dispute until they are adjusted. (R. S. Sec. 3210; 80 v. 99; R. S. 1880; 71 v. 51, § 2.)

Section 8350. (How disputed claims adjusted.) When the matter can not be adjusted between the parties interested, it may be submitted to the arbitration of three disinterested persons, one to be chosen by each of the parties, and one by the two thus chosen. Their decision, or that of any two of them, in the absence of fraud or collusion, shall be final and conclusive on the parties. If any claim be disputed and is not settled or submitted to arbitration, the claimant, in such case, shall be required to commence an action on his claim before the proper tribunal, within forty days after notice that it has been disputed, and prosecute it to final judgment without delay. The amount thus ascertained or adjudicated shall then be paid by the railroad owner. But after notice given as above provided, if no objection is filed against such claim within ten days after the expiration of the term for service of notice, then the contractor or subcontractor shall be held to have waived all objection to such claim, and, as against such contractor or subcontractor, it shall be taken to be correct. (R. S. Sec. 3210.)

The limitation of time applies to controversies arising between the contractor or subcontractor and the person furnishing materials or work, and not to right of action on the part of the latter against the owner of the road.

Railway Co. v. Cronin, 38 O. S. 122 (1882).

Section 8351. (To whom preceding sections apply.) The provisions of the next six preceding sections apply to and include any person who furnishes grain, hay, merchandise, tools or implements, or who repairs any tools or implements, on the order of any contractor or subcontractor, for their own use, or the use of persons employed by them or either of them while furnishing materials or labor for or in construction of such railroad. But the amount of such claim shall not exceed the wages of the person performing labor or furnishing materials, to whom furnished, or the amount found due such contractor, or subcontractor, under the provisions of this subdivision. In every such case the requirements, as to filing affidavits and giving notices must be strictly complied with; and the aggregate of all liens taken and perfected thereunder, shall not be in excess of the actual construction contract price of the railroad company. (R. S. Sec. 3211; 80 v. 99; R. S. 1880; 71 v. 51, § 3.)

While this section extends the provisions of § 8345 to persons furnishing hay, grain, etc., it does not enlarge the meaning of the word "materials" in § 8345.

Penna. Co. v. Mehaffy, 75 O. S. 432 (1907).
See Schneider v. Railway, 20 W. L. B. 457.

Section 8352. (Interpretation of word "owner.") The word "owner" in the sections of this subdivision of this chapter, shall be held and considered as including any lessee, receiver, corporation, company, or persons owning, operating or managing any railroad with whom or in whose behalf such contracts are made. (R. S. Sec. 3211.)

LIENS OF CARRIERS.

Section 8365. (Notice to owner of receipt of freight.) All express companies, transportation companies, forwarding and commission merchants, common carriers, warehousemen, wharfingers, and railroad companies, doing business in this state, within thirty days after the receipt of any property in their warehouse, depot, station, store or other place of deposit or doing business, when such property is plainly marked with the owner's name and place of residence, or it be otherwise known, shall notify the owner that such property is held by them subject to charges, either by leaving notice at the usual residence or place of business of the owner, or by depositing it, postage prepaid, in the proper postoffice, duly addressed to such owner. (R. S. Sec. 3221; 72 v. 17, § 1.)

Liability of warehouseman on agreement to insure stored goods.
 Storage Co. v. Cox, 74 O. S. 284 (1906).
 Refusal of consignee to accept goods. Special contract between shipper and carrier for return. Loss on line of connecting carrier. Liability of carrier.
 Railroad Co. v. Cappel, 80 O. S. 128 (1909).

Section 8366. (Register of freight.) All such persons, associations, or companies, shall keep a register, in which must be entered a list or inventory of all goods, wares, merchandise, baggage, or other property, with a pertinent description thereof by marks thereon, the size, weight, and the depot, warehouse, or other place where deposited, the time when received, and the amount of charges claimed thereon, which may be left in the possession of such person, association or company, by reason of the owner being unknown, or when such owner's residence is not known, or when such property has been refused, or the owner has neglected to receive it. (R. S. Sec. 3222; 72 v. 18, § 2.)

Section 8367. (When property may be sold.) When any such property has been conveyed to any point in this state, and remains unclaimed for six months at the place to which it is consigned, and the owner within that time fails to claim it, and pay the proper charges, if there be any against it, such person, association, or company, may sell such freight or other property, at public auction, offering each parcel separately. (R. S. Sec. 3223; 74 v. 17, § 3.)

Section 8368. (Notice of sale of property to be given.) Such property may be offered for sale either in the place where the office, station, depot, or warehouse in which it has been deposited for safe-keeping, is located, or at any other place where such person, association, or company may deem best to insure a prompt sale thereof. At least thirty days' notice of the time and place of sale, containing a descriptive list of the several articles to be sold, with names, numbers, and marks thereon, shall be given, by posting such notice at the office, station or depot of such person, association, or company in the county where the place to which the property was consigned is situated, or, if there be no such office, station, or depot, by posting such notice in three public places in such county. In addition to the posting at the place of consignment, such descriptive list must be posted at the place where the property is to be sold, and thirty days' notice of the time and place of the sale be published in a newspaper of general circulation in the county where the sale is to be. (R. S. Sec. 3224; 74 v. 18, § 4.)

Section 8369. (Disposition of proceeds of sale.) From the proceeds of such property, such person, association, or company, shall pay all the necessary costs and expenses of the sale, and all proper charges for freight and storage of the property sold, apportioning such expenses and charges, as near as may be, among the articles sold, to the amount received for each and hold any overplus, subject to the order of the owner thereof, at any time within one year after the sale, upon proof of ownership by affidavit of the claimant or his attorney. After the expiration of one year, all such sums unclaimed shall be paid into the state treasury, to be placed to the credit of the common schools. Any article remaining unsold may be again offered as above provided, until sold. (R. S. Sec. 3225; 74 v. 18, § 4.)

Section 8370. (Suit to subject freight to payment of costs.) Such person, association or company may bring suit in any court of competent jurisdiction for the amount of the freight, storage, and legal charges thereon, and subject such freight to the payment thereof, after ten days from the giving of the notice provided for in section eighty-three hundred and sixty-five, unless such cost and charges are paid, if the owner or consignee is known or can be found in the county. If such owner or consignee is unknown, a non-resident of the county, or his place of residence is unknown, then such notice shall be published for not less than ten days in a newspaper of general circulation in such county. In such case the suit may be brought after ten days from the first publication. The judgment obtained shall be a lien upon the freight, to satisfy which, with costs of suit, it shall be sold. (R. S. Sec. 3226; 74 v. 17, § 3.)

Section 8371. (Storage and the lien therefor.) Such person, association, or company, after the expiration of ten days from the receipt of goods at the place to which they are consigned, upon giving or depositing the notice provided in section eighty-three hundred and sixty-five, and the expiration of ten days, may charge a fair and reasonable cost for storage, which shall be a lien upon the goods so stored. Such person, association, or company also, after the expiration of such ten days, may deliver the goods to any warehouseman or storage merchant at the point of destination thereof, or in case there be no responsible warehouseman or storage merchant at such point willing to receive the goods, then at the most convenient point where storage can be effected, and receive from such warehouseman the freight and charges due such railroad or other company thereon, notifying the owner or consignee of such storage, when known, in the manner above provided, and the advances made. All reasonable charges for storage shall be a lien upon the goods so stored. (R. S. Sec. 3227; 74 v. 17, § 3.)

Lien for freight charges paid to other carriers.
Bennet, etc., Co. v. Robinson, 6 O. L. R. 355 (C. C. A. 1908).

Section 8372. (Copy of notice, sale bill, etc., to be kept.) Such person, association, or company shall keep a copy of the notice, a copy of the sale bill, and the expenses thereof, proportional to each article sold, and also the oath of the claimant of the residue of the proceeds, and must furnish an inspection of it, and, if required, copies thereof, to any one, on payment of the proper charges therefor. (R. S. Sec. 3228; 72 v. 19, § 5.)

Section 8373. (Sale of perishable articles.) If perishable property be so conveyed as freight, and remain unclaimed until in danger of great depreciation, or it be refused, or the owner thereof cannot be found, then such person, association or company may sell it at private sale, or auction, without giving notice, for the best price it will bring, and apply the proceeds as aforesaid. (R. S. Sec. 3229; 72 v. 19, § 6.)

Live stock is perishable property.
Trustees v. Brighton Stock Yards Co., 27 O. S. 435 (1875).

Section 8374. (Within what time property may be claimed.) If the owner of any such property, at any time within five years, reclaims it, and produces satisfactory evidence to the auditor of state of his ownership thereof, the auditor shall draw his warrant in favor of such person upon the treasurer of state for the amount paid into the state treasury. (R. S. Sec. 3230; 72 v. 20, § 9.)

Section 8375. (Penalty for neglect to comply with provisions.) Any such person, association or company who refuses or neglects to perform any of the duties required by this chapter, with the intent to avoid its provisions, shall forfeit and pay a sum not less than one hundred dollars, nor more than five hundred dollars, at the discretion of the court, to be recovered for the use of common schools in the county in which the principal office of such person, association, or company is located, and also be liable to any person injured thereby in double the value of the property. (R. S. Sec. 3231; 72 v. 20, § 7.)

LIEN ON PUBLIC WORKS.

Section 8376. (Lien for labor or material furnished.) Any person who has performed common or mechanical labor upon, or furnished supplies to any railroad, street railroad, or railroad operated wholly or in part by electric motor power, turnpike, plank road, canal or on any public structure being erected, or on any abutment, pier, culvert or foundation therefor, or for any side track, embankment, excavation, or any public work, protection, ballasting, delivering or placing ties, or track-laying, whether the labor is performed for, or the supplies or materials are furnished to any company, corporation, contractor, or subcontractor, construction company, or any individual, shall have a first and absolute lien on the whole of the property on which such work is done, or to which such supplies were contributed, and on any fund arising from a sale thereof or any part thereof under an order of any court. (95 v. 609, § 1; R. S. Sec. 3231-1; 86 v. 120.)

The provisions of this section relating to liens of subcontractors have been held unconstitutional.
Stewart v. Gardner, 10 C. C. n. s. 408; 20 C. D. 218 (1907); aff'd, 78 O. S. 451.
Shaw v. Railway, 8 O. L. R. 43; 173 Fed. 476 (C. C. A. 1909).
Section construed. New England, etc., Co. v. Railway Co., 75 Fed. 162 (1896).
Massillon Bridge Co. v. Cambria Iron Co., 59 O. S. 179 (1898).

Section 8377. (Determination of lien.) Such person shall hold the railroad, street railroad or railroad operated wholly or in part by electric motor power, canal, turnpike, plank road, or structure, to the creation or construction of which such labor or supplies were contributed, or so much thereof as in whole or part have been created by such labor or supplies, to the exclusion of any such railroads, canal, turnpike, plank road, public work or structure, as to operation, occupation or use, until the claim for such labor or supplies is properly adjusted and paid in full. (95 v. 609, § 1; R. S. Sec. 3231-1; 86 v. 120.)

Section 8378. (How lien obtained.) When it is deemed necessary for any construction company, contractor, subcontractor, mechanic, laborer, or person contributing supplies or material to secure a claim against a railroad, canal, turnpike, plank road, public work or public structure, either for work done or material furnished, they shall file a sworn itemized statement, within thirty days after the work was performed or materials furnished, of the amount of work done or material furnished, showing the balance due and claimed for labor or material furnished, with the recorder of the county or counties within which the work was done or materials furnished. If several liens be obtained by several persons on the same job, in the manner prescribed by this subdivision of this chapter, they shall have no priority among themselves, but payments thereon must be made pro rata. (86 v. 120, § 2; R. S. Sec. 3231-2.)

Section 8379. (Bond; when injunction may issue.) Any construction company, contractor, mechanic, laborer or person contributing supplies or material to any work named in section eighty-three hundred and seventy-six, at the time of filing the sworn statement of account as provided in the next preceding section, must file a good and sufficient bond of indemnity for an amount equal to the amount claimed, which bond shall be approved by the probate judge, and be so conditioned as to save and protect the defendant in any case arising under this subdivision of this chapter, and thereupon shall be entitled to a decree of the common pleas court, enjoining and prohibiting the operation, use or occupancy of the property created in whole or in part by the party or parties asking for such injunction; and the injunction shall not be dissolved until the court is satisfied that the claim has been adjusted and paid in full. (86 v. 121, § 3; R. S. Sec. 3231-3).

This section is unconstitutional.
Creech v. Railroad Co., 29 W. L. B. 112 (C. P. 1893).

But does not render the entire act invalid.
> New England, etc., Co. v. Oakwood St. Ry. Co., 75 Fed. 162; 8 O. F.
> D. 682 (C. C. 1896).

**Section 8380.   (Engineer to make measurements, esti-
mates, etc.)** Any civil engineer employed as chief or assistant engineer in the surveying, platting, or cross-section-
ing of any railroad, canal, turnpike, plank road or other
public road, before the work is commenced, shall make an
accurate measurement thereof, and prepare a profile of each
section of one mile or less of work, showing quantities of
each and every class of work to be done thereon. He also
shall designate the nearest benchmark or point from which
measurements are made, and drive stakes at top of slope,
at foot of embankments, at sides and center of grade and
around every burrow pit for each one hundred feet, showing in plain figures by feet and tenths of a foot the depths
of cut or height of fill or embankment, together with a correct showing of the quantity of overhaul beyond a given
number of feet, in cubic yards, for each section of a mile
or less. Such chief or assistant engineer, on demand, when
any work is finished, must furnish to any company, contractor, subcontractor or person a final statement of quantities in each class of work done or supplies or material furnished by parties interested. (86 v. 121, § 4; R. S. Sec.
3231-4.)

Where a construction contract requires written orders for all extra
work, an engineer has no authority to bind the company by verbal orders
therefor.
> See Railroad v. Jolly, 71 O. S. 92 (1904).
> Penalty for false measurements, see § 13181.

PART XV.

GENERAL CORPORATION LAW.

FORMATION.

Section 8623. (Purpose for which corporation may be formed.) . Except for carrying on professional business, a corporation may be formed for any purpose for which natural persons lawfully may associate themselves. (R. S. Sec. 3235; May 12, 1902, 95 v. 623; March 22, 1900, 94 v. 65; April 6, 1894, 91 v. 126; April 20, 1893, 90 v. 205; R. S. 1880.)

Section cited.
> Ehrman v. Insurance Co., 35 O. S. 342.
> Larwell v. Hanover, etc., Soc., 40 O. S. 282.
> State v. Lemert, 10 N. P. n. s. 135.
> Bachtel v. Wilson, 204 U. S. 36.

Corporations classified: (1) For profit; (2) Not for profit. Corporations organized under Ohio laws are classed as (1) corporations for profit, which must have a capital stock, and (2) corporations not for profit, which may, but need not, have a capital stock.
> State v. Standard Life Assn., 38 O. S. 281, 288 (1882).
> Snyder v. Chamber of Commerce, 53 O. S. 1 (1895).

Corporations for profit are those formed for the prosecution of business enterprises with a view to realizing gains to be distributed as dividends among the shareholders in proportion to their contributions to the capital stock.
> Snyder v. Chamber of Commerce, 53 O. S. 1, 11 (1895).

A corporation which is necessarily for profit must be so organized, with a capital stock.
> State v. Home Co-op. Union, 63 O. S. 547 (1900).

Where the real purpose of a corporation is the promotion of the pecuniary benefit of its members, it can not be organized as a corporation not for profit.
> Rep. Atty. Gen., 1911-1912, p. 127.

A corporation for profit may be organized to conduct an agricultural fair.
> State v. Long, 48 O. S. 509 (1891).

A mutual protective association organized under G. C. § 9427 is a corporation not for profit.
> State v. Standard Life Assn., 38 O. S. 281 (1882).

Purpose as a privilege, or a charter obligation. The purpose for which a corporation is organized is a privilege which need not be exercised to the full extent. The statement in articles of incorporation that the corporation is formed for the purpose of producing and furnishing natural gas to certain named cities "and to other cities, villages and places in the counties aforesaid," does not make it a charter obligation of the corporation to furnish gas to all such cities.
> East Ohio Gas Co. v. Akron, 81 O. S. 33, 51 (1909).

Professional business. A physicians defense company proposing to issue contracts whereby it agrees to defend physicians against civil actions for malpractice can not become incorporated or be authorized to do business in Ohio.

State v. Laylin, 73 O. S. 90 (1905).
Rep. Atty. Gen., 1906, p. 51.

A corporation carrying on professional business in violation of this section can not complain of unfair competition in such business.

Union Painless Dentists Co. v. Mullen, 6 O. L. R. 475; 19 L. D. 136 (Cin. Super. Ct. 1908).

A contract by a street railway corporation to perform medical services is not only ultra vires, but void. Such corporation can not be directly liable for malpractice.

Youngstown, etc., Ry. Co. v. Kessler, 84 O. S. 74 (1911).

A public accountant is not engaged in professional business.

Rep. Atty. Gen. 1909-1910, p. 84.
Rep. Atty. Gen., 1910-1911, p. 237.

Engineering is not professional business.

Rep. Atty. Gen., 1910-1911, 213.

But it is said that where the main purpose of a corporation requires that its business be transacted by agents, who are required to be qualified and licensed by public authority, such business must be deemed professional and within the prohibition of § 8623.

Rep. Atty. Gen., 1911-1912, p. 73.

It is an agency and not professional business for a corporation to arrange a contract between an individual and a professional, for a compensation to be paid by the individual, leaving the selection of the professional to the individual and leaving the amount of compensation to mutual agreement between the individual and professional.

Rep. Atty. Gen., 1911-1912, p. 73.

The making of contracts whereby a corporation, in consideration of periodical payments, agrees to furnish medical attendance in case of sickness, and to bury the remains after death, is probably professional business.

5 Opins. Attys. Gen. 975.

Single purpose rule. The use of the word "purpose" and not "purposes" implies a limitation. Except where specially authorized by statute, a corporation can be organized for one main purpose only. Several different purposes can not be united in one organization.

State v. Taylor, 55 O. S. 61, 67 (1896).
See 3 O. L. R. 187, 205.

Several purposes incident to the main purpose may be joined. A corporation organized for the main purpose of operating a street railway by electricity may also furnish electric light and power.

State v. Taylor, 55 O. S. 61, 65 (1896).

Several means may be joined to carry out the main purpose. A corporation formed to furnish light may provide, in its articles of incorporation, for both gas and electricity for such purpose.

Pickard v. Hughey, 58 O. S. 577 (1898).

A corporation may be originally organized to conduct several classes of business which one corporation, formed by consolidation of several corporations, is authorized to conduct.

Rep. Atty. Gen., 1908, pp. 62, 55, 89.
Rep. Atty. Gen., 1904, p. 78.

A corporation may be authorized to carry on both a wholesale and retail business, without violating the single purpose rule.

Rep. Atty. Gen., 1908, p 74.

The main purpose of a corporation fixes its class.   A railroad company is not a hotel company because it operates eating houses in connection with its passenger traffic, nor is a railroad company a land company because it has acquired unnecessary land. A coal company is not a railroad company because it operates a railroad from its mines to a railroad.

State v. H. V. Ry. Co., 12 C. C. n. s. 49, 60-61; 21 C. D. 175 (1909).

Special statutory provisions enlarge the powers of certain classes of corporations, such as manufacturing and mining companies.

G. C. § 10136 et seq.

A manufacturing company may deal in articles manufactured by it, but not in manufactured articles generally.

Rep. Atty. Gen., 1910-1911, pp. 214, 266.

A manufacturing company may, as an incident to its business, purchase and sell patent rights. But a corporation formed for the purpose of developing certain inventions may not include in its articles the purpose of manufacturing and selling the articles to which the patent processes are applicable.

Rep. Atty. Gen., 1911-1912, p. 72.

Illustrations of violation of single purpose rule. Articles of incorporation have been rejected by the secretary of state where it was attempted to join several unrelated purposes, as follows:

To (1) audit acounts, (2) establish a collection agency, and (3) do a mercantile agency business.

Rep. Atty. Gen. 1909-1910, p. 84.

To (1) mine, manufacture, buy and sell metals, (2) as principal, agent, factor and broker and (3) to deal in foundry supplies.

Rep. Atty. Gen. 1909-1910. p. 121.

To conduct (1) grocery stores and (2) a general invention development business.

Rep. Atty. Gen., 1908, p. 82.

To sell all merchantable articles at wholesale or retail.

Rep. Atty. Gen., 1908, p. 64.

To (1) deal in minerals and timber, (2) mineral and timber lands, and (3) engage in general mining.

Rep. Atty. Gen., 1908, p. 77.

To (1) produce oil and gas, and (2) mine coal.

Rep. Atty. Gen., 1910-1911, pp. 227, 228.

To (1) negotiate and make loans on real estate, and (2) furnish abstracts of title.

Rep. Atty. Gen., 1910-1911, p. 230.

To do (1) a general engineering, and (2) analytical, consulting and manufacturing chemistry business.

Rep. Atty. Gen., 1910-1911, p. 213.

To (1) manufacture machinery, etc., and (2) develop and sell power.

Rep. Atty. Gen., 1908-1909, p. 73.

See Rep. Atty. Gen., 1910-1911, pp. 221, 268.

To (1) do a stock and bond business, and (2) act as a trustee of corporate mortgages.

Rep. Atty. Gen. 1910-1911, p. 251.

To (1) deal in real property, (2) manage estates, and (3) act as agent and broker.

Rep. Atty. Gen., 1908-1909, p. 84; Rep. Atty. Gen. 1910-1911, p. 235.

The (1) production, smelting, etc., of minerals, (2) organizing companies to produce and smelt minerals and (3) dealing in bonds and securities of other corporations.

5 Opins. Attys. Gen., 839 (1903).

To (1) act as agent for insurance companies, (2) act as agent in employing attorneys at law, and (3) loan money to litigants.

5 Opins. Attys. Gen., 1903, p. 1022.
See Rep. Atty. Gen. 1910-1911, p. 265.
To produce and deal in lumber, building materials, and "other personal property and rights and interests of every kind and description," and "to carry on any other lawful business whatsoever which the corporation may deem proper or convenient to be carried on in connection with . . . any of the foregoing purposes, or calculated indirectly to promote the interest of the corporation or to enhance or preserve the value of its property."
Rep. Atty. Gen., 1909-1910, 146.

Purpose must be lawful. A corporation can not be formed for an unlawful purpose, nor can a foreign corporation be admitted to do an unlawful business in Ohio.
Paul v. Groene, 4 O. L. R. 632; 17 L. D. 738 (Cin. Super. Ct. 1907).
State v. Interstate Sgs. Investment Co., 64 O. S. 283, 318 (1901).
When not prohibited by local option laws a corporation may be formed to, and may, engage in the retail liquor business, regardless of the citizenship of stockholders.
Rep. Atty. Gen., 1911-1912, p. 1111.
The following purposes have been held or deemed to be unlawful:
Conducting a lottery.
Paul v. Groene, 4 O. L. R. 632; 17 L. D. 738 (1907).
State v. Interstate Sgs. Investment Co., 64 O. S. 283 (1901).
Receiving illegal rebates from railway companies.
Brundred v. Rice, 49 O. S. 640 (1892).
Purchasing franchises of corporations.
(Atty. Gen.); 24 W. L. B. 269 (1890); 4 Opins. Attys. Gen., 361.
Dealing generally in stocks of other corporations. (On the ground that under G. C. § 8683 a corporation may acquire stock in "kindred but not competing corporations" only.)
5 Opins. Attys. Gen., 924, 969 (1903); citing Bank v. Bank, 36 O. S. 354.
Rep. Atty. Gen., 1910-1911, p. 246.
Rep. Atty. Gen., 1911-1912, pp. 58, 61.
Association of unmarried persons, to establish a fund by assessment and pay stipulated sums to members upon marriage.
5 Opins. Attys. Gen., 118 (1900).
Marriage endowment association.
4 Opins. Attys. Gen., 43.
Manufacturing articles infringing patents.
See Clemshire v. Boone Co. Bank, 53 Ark. 512 (1890).
Improperly restraining trade.
In re Richmond Coal Co., 20 Phila. 251; s. c., 9 Pa. Co. Ct. Rep. 172.
Forming a military company of foreigners, presumably for an improper purpose.
Russian American Guards Charter, 3 Pa. Dist. 673 (1893); s. c., 13 Pa. Co. Ct. Rep. 148.
Assisting in war against the United States.
Chicora Co. v. Crews, 6 S. C. 243 (1874).
United States v. Insurance Co., 22 Wall. (U. S.); 99 (1874).
Importing Co. v. Locke, 50 Ala. 332 (1876).
Arranging marriages for compensation.
In re Mutual Aid Ass'n, 15 Phila. 625 (1881).
In re Helping Hand Ass'n., 15 Phila. 644 (1881).
Resisting temperance laws.
Detroit, etc., Bund v. Detroit, etc.. Verein, 44 Mich. 313 (1880).

Manipulating stocks of other corporations and thereby creating a trust.

People, ex rel., v. Gas Trust, 130 Ill. 268 (1889).

Resisting enactment of laws by lawful means has been regarded as a proper purpose.

4 Opins. Attys. Gen., 84 (1888).

Contra 2 Opins. Attys. Gen. 1070, 1086 (1882).

Banks, insurance companies, etc., can not organize under general corporation law. Where the method of incorporation of a certain class of corporations is specially provided for by statute, such companies must organize under the special statute and not under the general corporation law. G. C. § 8737.

Insurance companies.

State v. Pioneer Live Stock Co., 38 O. S. 347 (1882).

Banks.

G. C. § 9702 et seq.

Rep. of Atty. Gen., 1908-1909, p. 80.

4 Opins. Attys. Gen. 565.

In the articles of incorporation of an insurance agency company, the corporate purpose can not be expressed as a "business of general insurance underwriters."

Rep. Atty. Gen., 1911-1912, p. 60.

Corporations formed to administer trusts. A corporation formed to carry out and perpetuate a trust is subordinate and subsidiary to the objects of the trust, as declared by the donor.

State v. Toledo, 3 C. C. n. s. 468, 474; 13 C. D. 327 (1902).

Toledo v. Saiders, 15 C. C. n. s. 468; 23 C. D. 613 (1910); aff'd, no rep., 83 O. S. 495; see § 10085 et seq.

Section 8624. (Sanatoriums.) Corporations for the erection, owning and conducting of sanatoriums for receiving and caring for patients, their medical, surgical and hygienic treatment, and the instruction of nurses in the treatment of diseases and of hygiene, are not forbidden by the next preceding section. (R. S. Sec. 3235; May 12, 1902, 95 v. 623; March 22, 1900, 94 v. 65; April 6, 1894, 91 v. 126; April 20, 1893, 90 v. 205; R. S. 1880.)

Articles of incorporation of a training school for nurses may include authority to issue certificates of completion of course.

Rep. Atty. Gen. 1908, p. 64.

A corporation not for profit maintaining a charity hospital or other purely charitable institution is not liable for the negligence of its servants.

Taylor v. Protestant, etc., Assn., 85 O. S. 90 (1911).

Conner v. Sisters of Poor, 7 N. P. 514 (1900).

Johnson v. Lawrence Hospital, 12 L. D. 795 (1902).

That a hospital receives pay from a patient for lodging and care does not affect its character as a charitable institution.

Taylor v. Protestant, etc., Assn., 85 O. S. 90 (1911).

Under the "single purpose" doctrine (see note to § 8623) a corporation can not be organized to conduct both a hotel and a sanatorium.

Rep. Atty Gen., 1910-1911, p. 260.

Section 8625. (Articles of incorporation.) Any number

of persons, not less than five, a majority of whom are citizens of this state, desiring to become incorporated, shall subscribe and acknowledge articles of incorporation, which must contain:

1. The name of the corporation, which, unless it is not for profit, shall begin with the word "the" and end with the word "company", except as otherwise provided by law.

2. The place where it is to be located, or its principal business transacted.

3. The purpose for which it is formed.

4. The amount of its capital stock, if it is to have capital stock, and the number of shares into which it is divided.

5. But, if the corporation is for a purpose which includes the construction of an improvement not to be located at a single place, the articles of incorporation must also set forth—

   a. The kind of improvement intended to be constructed.

   b. Its termini, and the counties in or through which it or its branches will pass. (R. S. Secs. 3236, 3237; April 10, 1889, 86 v. 224; April 16, 1885, 82 v. 134; Rev. Stats. 1880.)

Charter, what constitutes. The charter of a corporation formed under general corporation laws consists of the articles of incorporation and the general laws of the state.
Security Trust Co. v. Ford, 75 O. S. 322, 333 (1906).
Bixler v. Summerfield, 195 Ill. 147.
People v. Chicago Gas Trust, 130 Ill. 268.
Bent v. Underdown, 156 Ill. 516, 519.
Cronin v. Potter's Co-op. Co., 29 W. L. B. 52 (1892).
The charter of a corporation, for excise tax purposes, may be determined from the nature of its business, and not exclusively from its articles of incorporation.
Railway Co. v. Poland, 10 N. P. n. s. 617 (C. P. 1910).

Unauthorized provisions in articles of incorporation. Articles of incorporation should contain only those provisions which are specified in the statute. Other provisions are void.
Security Trust Co. v. Ford, 75 O. S. 322 (1906).
People v. Chicago Gas Trust, 130 Ill. 268.
Oregon, etc., Co. v. Oregonian Ry. Co., 130 U. S. 1, 25.
State v. Anderson, 31 Ind. App. 34.
O'Brien v. Cummings, 13 Mo. App. 197.
Such unauthorized provisions do not, however, invalidate the entire instrument. If it contains the provisions required by statute, it will be held valid, and the unauthorized provisions disregarded as surplusage.
Toledo, etc., Ry. Co. v. Toledo, Elec. etc., Co., 6 C. C. 362, 391; 3
   C. D. 493, 507 (1892); aff'd, no rep., 50 O. S. 603.
Renn v. U. S. Cement Co., 36 Ind. App. 149.
State v. Anderson, 31 Ind. App. 34.
People v. Mount Shasta Mfg. Co., 107 Cal. 256.
See Hanna v. International Petroleum Co., 23 O. S. 622 (1873).
Articles containing unauthorized provisions may be refused filing by the secretary of state.
3 Opins. Attys. Gen., 699.

The following are illustrations of unauthorized provisions:
Limitation of duration of corporation (not a real estate company).
3 Opins. Attys. Gen. 241.
Designation of first board of directors or trustees.
3 Opins. Attys. Gen. 241-699.
Reformation of articles because of mistake.
See Cronin v. Potter's Co-op. Co., 29 W. L. B. 52 (C. P. 1892).
Correction of defective articles.
See § 12210 et seq.
Amendment of articles. See § 8719.

Incorporators. Only natural persons may act. Associations, firms and corporations are disqualified.
Rep. Atty. Gen., 1908, p. 72.
2 Opins. Attys. Gen., 109.
Rep. Atty. Gen. 1910-1911, p. 210.
Infants are not competent to act.
State v. Burial Assn., 8 C. C. n. s. 233, 253; 18 C. D. 397 (1906).
Articles executed by less than five incorporators are void.
State, ex rel., v. Critchett, 37 Minn. 13.
People v. Montecito Water Co., 97 Cal. 276.
Articles which failed to show that a majority of the incorporators were residents of Ohio were refused filing by the secretary of state.
3 Opins. Attys. Gen., 530.
Where, after articles have been filed and recorded, it is discovered that one of the incorporators was an infant, it is said that the articles can not be withdrawn and others substituted; but that an amendment of the articles should be filed.
Rep. Atty. Gen., 1910-1911, p. 263.
A secret intention, of illegal user, on the part of the incorporators, not expressed in the articles, does not vitiate the articles.
State v. Taylor, 25 O. S. 279 (1874).
Cronin v. Potter's Co-op. Co., 29 W. L. B. 52, 55 (C. P. 1892).
3 Opins. Attys. Gen., 1059, 1096.

(1). NAME OF CORPORATION.

See also note to § 8628.
Where the words "The" and "Company" are omitted from the name, the public is likely to be misled into the belief that it is dealing with individuals or an association of individuals.
Union Painless Dentists v. Mullen, 6 O. L. R. 475; 19 L. D. 136 (1908).

(2). LOCATION.

The statement in the articles is conclusive as to the location of the corporation, although much of its business is transacted elsewhere. The place so designated is the situs of the corporation for taxation purposes.
Pelton v. Transportation Co., 37 O. S. 450 (1882).
Mercantile Trust Co. v. Aetna Iron Works, 4 C. C. 579, 585; 2 C. D. 718, 722 (1890).
Sims v. Best, 1 C. C. n. s. 41; 15 C. D. 149 (1903);(foreign corporation).
Pomeroy Salt Co. v. Davis, 21 O. S. 555 (1871).
Booth v. Wonderly, 36 N. J. L. 250.
Union Steamboat Co. v. Buffalo, 82 N. Y. 351, §§ 10135, 8744, 9043.
The statute does not require the office building or street address to be stated. It is sufficient to specify the municipality or place. Within such municipality the corporation may, at pleasure, remove its principal

office from one building to another, although its purpose is to avoid taxation.

Pelton v. Transportation Co., 37 O. S. 450 (1882).

Mercantile Trust Co. v. Aetna Iron Works, 4 C. C. 579, 585; 2 C. D. 718, 722 (1890).

An amendment of the articles is required for a change to another municipality or place. See § 8719.

State v. Coal Co., 4 N. P. 115; 6 L. D. 180 (1897).

An order of attachment may be issued by a justice of the peace against a corporation in any county in which it is a nonresident, or has no place of business, or no officer upon whom a summons may be served. See § 10253.

Champion Machine Co. v. Huston, 24 O. S. 503 (1874).

Ruling organization—location of. See §§ 8651, 8652.

(3). PURPOSE FOR WHICH ORGANIZED.

See also note to § 8623.

The purpose should be stated in general terms. It is improper to enumerate the incidental powers which are conferred upon the corporation by general law.

Rep. Atty. Gen., 1908-1909, pp. 84, 81, 94.

Wendel v. State, 62 Wis. 300.

People v. Chicago Gas Trust, 130 Ill. 268.

Rep. Atty. Gen., 1910-1911, p. 252.

Rep. Atty. Gen. 1911-1912, p. 64.

The purpose should be clearly stated. The business to be transacted must be specified. It is not a compliance with the law to state that the company is formed to do any business it may find profitable.

In re Crown Bank L. R., 44 Ch. Div. 634.

See State, ex rel., v. Central, etc., Assn., 29 O. S. 399 (1876).

The articles of a manufacturing company should specify definitely the articles to be manufactured.

Rep. Atty. Gen., 1910-1911, pp. 229, 266.

Articles of incorporation have been refused filing and record in the office of the secretary of state because of indefinite statement of purpose. Illustrations:

Corporation formed to manufacture a certain article "and to engage in a general manufacturing and mercantile business."

Rep. Atty. Gen., 1908-1909, p. 54.

Corporation formed to manufacture brake shoes "and all other articles that may be manufactured from wood and sold at a profit."

Rep. Atty. Gen., 1908-1909, p. 54.

Contractors' association incorporated for the purpose of "promoting the business welfare of its stockholders and members."

Rep. Atty. Gen., 1911-1912, p. 70.

(4). CAPITAL STOCK.

A corporation which is necessarily for profit can not be organized without a capital stock.

State v. Home Co-op. Union, 63 O. S. 547 (1900).

A clerical error in the statement of the number or amount of shares will not invalidate articles where the amount of the capital stock is correctly stated.

Hughes v. Antietam Mfg. Co., 34 Md. 316.

Articles which failed to specify the number of shares were rejected by the secretary of state.

3 Opins. Attys. Gen., 194.

Statements in articles as to preferred stock.

See §§ 8668, 8669 and notes.

Capital stock and corporate property distinguished. In taxation and certain other statutes the term "capital stock" has been used as meaning the *capital* or property of the corporation.

Lee v. Sturges, 46 O. S. 160 (1889).
Bradley v. Bauder, 36 O. S. 34 (1880).
Jones v. Davis, 35 O. S. 476, 477 (1880).
Railway Co. v. Furnace Co., 49 O. S. 112 (1892).

But there is a distinction between the *capital stock* and the *capital* of a corporation. The amount of the capital stock remains fixed while the property or capital fluctuates in value and continually increases or diminishes in amount.

State v. Jones, 51 O. S. 510, 511 (1894).
Cleveland Trust Co. v. Lander, 62 O. S. 273 (1900).

The capital stock is not owned by the corporation, but by its shareholders. A corporation owes and not owns its stock. The capital stock is a liability of the corporation and not an asset.

Southern Gum Co. v. Laylin, 66 O. S. 578, 596 (1902).
Natl. Bank v. L. S. & M. S R. Co., 21 O. S. 221, 230 (1871).
State v. Franklin Bank, 10 Ohio 91 (1840).

A share of stock is a right which entitles its owner to participate in the profits of the corporation, in its assets upon liquidation, and to vote at elections for directors.

See Jones v. Davis, 35 O. S. 477 (1880).

(5). TERMINI AND ROUTE OF IMPROVEMENT.

See § 8745.

Articles which failed to specify the termini and route have been rejected by the secretary of state.

5 Opins. Attys. Gen., 950 (1903).

The articles of incorporation of a telephone company must set forth the termini of the improvement and the counties in or through which it or its branches shall pass.

Rep. Atty. Gen., 1904-1905, p. 74.

Definiteness of description required. The statute only requires reasonable certainty and the description of the termini and course may be somewhat indefinite in the articles of incorporation, if defined by location. The location must be made with reasonable compliance with the description in the articles of incorporation. To require a greater degree of certainty in the articles of incorporation to ensure validity would necessarily defeat the object of the statute in many, if not most, cases. Reasonable latitude must be allowed, for it is by force of such description that a company may send its engineers upon the lands of others to locate the route definitely.

Callender v. Painesville, etc., R. R. Co., 11 O. S. 516.
Cleveland, etc., R. R. Co. v. Prentice, 13 O. S. 373, 379 (1862).

A description of the termini and course of a road "from a point on the Ohio and Pennsylvania State line in the County of Trumbull, in said state of Ohio, to a point on the Ohio River in same state in the County of Brown or Adams," was held too uncertain to support condemnation proceedings.

Atlantic, etc., R. R. Co. v. Sullivant, 5 O. S. 276 (1855).

Indefiniteness of descriptions in articles of incorporation may be cured by legislative recognition or by actual location, construction and operation.

Cayuga R. R. Co. v. Kyle, 5 Thomp. & C. (N. Y.) 659 (1875).

Articles of association of a road corporation describe the termini of the projected road with sufficient certainty when the description can be rendered certain, as where the road is made to start at a point definitely described to run specified courses and distances to an end, the whole length of road being given.

Miller v. Wild Cat Gravel Road Co., 52 Ind. 51 (1875).

Where the articles of incorporation of a railroad company are defective in not specifying with sufficient certainty the terminus of the road, but are properly filed in the office of the secretary of state, such filing is notice to the state of such defect, and if the state neglects for five years (G. C. § 12340) to take advantage by quo warranto or otherwise, the right is lost.

State v. Bailey, 19 Ind. 452.

Route. This section does not require the townships to be specified. Where townships are specified, it is mere surplusage. The railroad may be extended into other townships within the counties named in the articles.

Hayes v. Toledo Ry. & Ter. Co., 6 C. C. n. s. 281; 16 C. D. 395 (1903); aff'd, no rep., 70 O. S. 425.

Contiguous counties may be named in the alternative and the terminus may be an undesignated point in a township.

Callender v. Painesville R. R. Co., 11 O. S. 516 (1860).

Termini. Both terminal points may be located in one city.

State v. Union Ter. R. Co., 72 O. S. 455 (1905).

The terminus may be an undesignated point in a township.

Callender v. Painesville, etc., R. R. Co., 11 O. S. 516 (1860).

Articles of incorporation are not invalid because the terminus of the proposed improvement is designated as "in or near the town of Lima, Allen County, state of Ohio, at a point on the Cleveland and St. Louis Railroad." The words "in or near" are sufficiently definite, meaning substantially **"in."**

Warner v. Callender, 20 O. S. 190 (1870).

Central R. R. Co. v. Penn. R. R. Co., 31 N. J. Eq. 475 (1879).

A description "from" a city or other point includes any point in such city. **See § 8745.**

Colorado, etc., Ry. Co. v. Union Pac. Ry. Co., 41 Fed. 293.

Comm. v. Erie, etc., R. R. Co., 27 Pa. St. 339, 352.

Chicago, etc., Ry. Co. v. Chicago, etc., Ry. Co., 112 Ill. 589.

St. Louis, etc., Ry. Co. v. Hannibal, etc., Co., 125 Mo. 82; 28 S. W. Rep. **483.**

Contra, Northeastern R. R. Co. v. Payne, 8 Rich. L. (s. c.), 177.

A description "to" a certain place is inclusive.

Rio Grande R. R. Co. v. Brownsville, 45 Tex. 88.

St. Louis, etc., Co. v. Hannibal, etc., Co., 125 Mo. 82; 28 S. W. Rep. 483.

See Hatry v. Painesville, etc., Ry. Co., 1 C. C. 426, 433; 1 C. D. 238, 242 (1886).

A description "at" a certain town is inclusive.

Mohawk Bridge Co. v. Utica, etc., R. R. Co., 6 Paige Ch. (N. Y.) 554.

Mason v. Brooklyn, etc., Co., 35 Barb. (N. Y.) 373.

A description "between" certain points is inclusive.

Morris, etc. R. R. Co. v. Central, etc., R. R. Co., 31 N. J. L. 205.

Section 8626. (Acknowledgment of articles; where filed.) Articles of incorporation shall be acknowledged before an officer authorized to take the acknowledgment of deeds, the form of which shall be prescribed by the secretary of state. The official character of the officer before whom articles of incorporation are acknowledged, shall be certified by the clerk of the common pleas court of the county wherein the acknowledgment is taken. Articles of incorporation shall be filed in the office of the secretary of state, who shall record them, and shall also record certificates relating to that corporation, thereafter filed in his office. (R. S. Secs. 3236, 3238; March 31, 1902, 95 v. 76; April 27, 1896, 92 v. 320; April 10, 1889, 86 v. 224; April 16, 1885, 82 v. 134; Rev. Stats. 1880.)

Execution and acknowledgment. Articles should be signed and acknowledged in this state, under the rule that the acceptance of a charter and organization of the corporation must occur in the state creating it.

3 Opins. Attys. Gen., 560.

See Myers v. Manhattan Bank, 20 Ohio 283 (1851).

Smith v. Silver, etc., Co., 64 Md. 85.

Freeman v. Machias, etc., Co., 38 Me. 343.

Heath v. Silverthorn, etc., Co., 39 Wis. 146.

A total absence of acknowledgment will render the articles void.

Doyle v. Mizner, 42 Mich. 332.

Articles signed in blank, and subject to future agreement, may be disaffirmed by the incorporators.

Dutchess R. R. Co. v. Mabbett, 58 N. Y. 397.

Richmond R. R. Co. v. Reed, 83 Ind. 9.

A material alteration, after acknowlegment, will invalidate the articles.

2 Opins. Attys. Gen., 243.

An acknowledgment made before a probate judge must be authenticated by the certificate of the clerk of the court of common pleas.

Rep. Atty. Gen., 1910-1911, p. 216.

Officers authorized to take acknowledgments in Ohio. A notary public within the county of his residence and of each county for which he is appointed, §§ 126, 8510; a judge or clerk of a court of record, a county auditor, county surveyor, mayor, a justice of the peace, § 8510; a police judge, § 4585; a probate judge, § 1582.

Acknowledgments under former law. State, ex rel., v. Lee, 21 O. S. 662 (1871).

Spinning v. Home Ass'n., 26 O. S. 483 (1875).

Warner v. Callender, 20 O. S. 190 (1870).

Lucas v. Building Ass'n., 22 O. S. 339 (1872).

Griffin v. Clinton, etc., R. R. Co., 1 W. L. M. 31 (1859).

Clarke v. Thomas. 34 O. S. 46, 59 (1877).

Hagerman v. Building Ass'n., 25 O. S. 186, 200 (1874).

Filing.

Duty of secretary of state. If the instrument is in proper form and shows compliance with the law, it is the duty of the secretary of state to file and record the same. In case of wrongful refusal, mandamus will lie to compel its filing and recording.

State v. Taylor, 55 O. S. 61 (1896).

But it is also the duty of the secretary of state to refuse to file an instrument which is defective in form, or which contains a statement of an illegal or unauthorized corporate purpose.

State v. Laylin, 73 O. S. 90 (1905).

Or in which the corporate purpose is not clearly stated.

Rep. Atty. Gen., 1908-1909, p. 54.
4 Opins. Attys. Gen., 470.
Or in which the "single purpose" rule is violated.
State v. Taylor, 55 O. S. 61 (1896).
Or in which the law is not complied with in other respects.
Security Trust Co. v. Ford, 75 O. S. 335 (1906).
Or where the corporate name violates § 8628.
The secretary of state has discretion to determine whether a name is misleading.
Rep. Atty. Gen., 1911-1912, p. 127.

Time of filing. The act of filing and not the endorsement of the instrument by the secretary of state determines the time of filing. The endorsement is merely the evidence of filing.
State v. Foulkes, 94 Ind. 493.
See King v. Penn, 43 O. S. 57 (1885).
Haines v Lindsey, 4 Ohio 88 (1829).

Withdrawal of articles. Where, after articles have been filed and recorded, it is discovered that one of the incorporators was a minor, it is said that the articles can not be withdrawn and other articles substituted; but that an amendment to the articles should be filed.
Rep. Atty. Gen. 1910-1911, p. 263.

Section 8627. (General powers.) Upon filing articles of incorporation, the persons who subscribed them, their associates, successors, and assigns, by the name and style provided therein, shall be a body corporate, with succession, power to sue and be sued, contract and be contracted with; also, unless specially limited, to acquire and hold all property, real or personal, necessary to effect the object for which it is created, and at pleasure convey it in conformity with its regulations and the laws of this state. Such corporation also may make, use, and at will alter a common seal, and do all other acts needful to accomplish the purposes of its organization. (R. S. Sec. 3239; May 1, 1852, 50 v. 274, § 3; S. & C. 273.)

POWER TO CREATE CORPORATIONS.

See Constitution of Ohio, Article XIII.
A corporation can be created only by the state acting through the instrumentality of the legislature.
Myers v. Manhattan Bank, 20 Ohio 283 (1851).
Ashley v. Ryan, 49 O. S. 504 (1892); aff'd, 153 U. S. 436; 8 O. F. D. 215.
The power of creating a corporation can not be exercised outside of the territorial limits of the state.
Myers v. Manhattan Bank, 20 Ohio 283, 295 (1851).
Before the adoption of the constitution of 1851 when the legislature had power to grant special charters, a statute which recognized the existence of a corporation in effect created the corporation.
Trustees v. Zanesville, etc., Co., 9 Ohio 203.
The state may impose such terms and conditions as it pleases upon the creation of a corporation. It may fix the filing fee of articles of incorporation and articles of consolidation.

Ashley v. Ryan, 49 O. S. 504 (1892); aff'd, 153 U. S. 436; 8 O. F. D. 215.

WHEN CORPORATE EXISTENCE BEGINS.

The filing of articles of incorporation does not create a corporation with authority to exercise all its corporate powers. Such articles merely authorize the incorporators to form the corporation. No corporation exists for the transaction of the business for which the corporation is organized until the requisite stock has been subscribed, the first instalment paid thereon and directors elected.

State v. Insurance Co., 49 O. S. 440 (1892).
Queen City Telephone Co. v. Cincinnati, 73 O. S. 64, 77 (1905).

But the existence of the corporate body begins upon the filing of the articles.

Ashtabula, etc., R. R. Co. v. Smith, 15 O. S. 328, 334 (1864).
State v. Robinson, 12 W. L. B. 269.
Milford, etc., Co. v. Brush, 10 Ohio 111, 113, 114 (1840).
See Hanna v. International Petroleum Co., 23 O. S. 622, 625 (1873).
Benninger v. Gall, 1 C. S. C. R. 331 (1871).

Its powers are divided into two classes (1) those exercisable before the election of directors, and (2) those exercisable thereafter. Before the election of directors the incorporators may receive subscriptions to the capital stock, and the stockholders may elect directors and adopt regulations; but the business for which the corporation is organized can not be transacted until after the directors are elected.

Ashtabula, etc., R. Co. v. Smith, 15 O. S. 328, 334 (1864).
Powers v. Railway Co., 33 O. S. 429, 432 (1878).
Milford, etc., Co. v. Brush, 10 Ohio 111, 113, 114 (1840).

CORPORATION AS A LEGAL ENTITY.

In contemplation of law a corporation is a legal entity, an ideal person, separate from the persons composing it. But this fiction is limited to the purposes for which it was adopted—convenience in transacting business. in suing and being sued in its corporate name, and the continuance of its rights and liabilities unaffected by change in its members.

Bank v. Trebein, 59 O. S. 316, 326 (1898).
Brown v. Hitchcock, 36 O. S. 667, 678 (1881).
Reed v. Loan Co., 68 O. S. 280 (1903).

Relation of sole stockholder to corporate property.

See 6 O. L. R. 304.

Corporate entity as instrument for fraud or illegal purpose. The fiction of corporate entity can not be abused. Fraud or illegal purposes can not be accomplished by means of the fiction of legal entity. In such cases the fiction is disregarded by the courts and the acts of the real parties dealt with.

Bank v. Trebein, 59 O. S. 316 (1898).
State v. Standard Oil Co., 49 O. S. 137 (1892).
Brundred v. Rice, 49 O. S. 640 (1892).
Sayler v. Simpson, 12 L. D. 148 (Cin. Super. Ct. 1888).
Sportsman Shot Co. v. American, etc., Co., 30 W. L. B. 87 (Cin. Super. Ct. 1893).
Cincinnati Volksblatt Co. v. Hoffmeister, 62 O. S. 189, 200 (1900).
In re Rieger, Kapner & Altmark, 8 O. L. R. 498 (D. C. Ohio 1907).

Corporations formed or controlled by failing debtors. Where the members of a partnership form a corporation, to which the entire partnership assets are transferred in exchange for its capital stock, each partner receiving shares of stock in proportion to his interest in the partnership, the partnership assets being the only consideration for the stock, the corporation is liable for the debts of the partnership.

Andres v. Morgan, 62 O. S. 236 (1900).

See Paul v. Caldwell Co., 7 C. C. n. s. 272, 276; 17 C. D. 768 (1905).

For recourse on stockholders where partnership debts exceeded the assets exchanged for stock see

Sayler v. Simpson, 12 L. D. 148 (Cin. Super. Ct. 1888).

Ford v. Lamson, 17 C. C. 539; 9 C. D. 374 (1899).

Gates v. Tippecanoe Stone Co., 57 O. S. 60 (1897).

Where a failing debtor forms a corporation, to which he transfers his assets and business in exchange for its stock, and assigns such shares of stock as security for a part of his indebtedness, and continues as manager of the business, such conveyance is a fraud on other creditors and may be set aside and the assets administered as an assignment for creditors.

Bank v. Trebein, 59 O. S. 316 (1898).

A mercantile partnership acquired 99 percent of the issued stock of a manufacturing corporation, and the partners, as directors and officers, managed the corporate business, the partnership taking and selling all its output. On bankruptcy of the partnership, the corporation was held to be merely an agency of the partnership, and the corporate property to be assets of the bankrupt estate, the respective rights of the partnership and corporate creditors being determined in the bankruptcy proceedings.

In re Rieger, Kapner & Altmark, 8 O. L. R. 498 (U. S. D. C. 1907).

Stockholders bound by judgment against corporation. In actions by or against a corporation its stockholders are represented by the corporation. A judgment against the corporation in favor of a creditor can not be impeached by a subscriber to stock in the corporation, where the judgment was not obtained by fraud or collusion.

Scofield v. Excelsior Oil Co., 6 C. C. n. s. 176; 17 C. D. 318 (1905).

Henry v. Railroad Co., 17 Ohio 187, 191.

See Toledo T. R. & P. Co. v. Smith, 58 Bull. 201 (U. S. D. C. 1913).

Non resident stockholders are represented by the corporation in a proceeding to enforce the double liability of stockholders and are bound by the finding and decree, although not served with process.

Irvine v. Putnam, 167 Fed. 174 (1909).

Francis v. Hazlett, 192 Mass. 137, 142 (1906).

Childs v. Cleaves, 95 Me. 498; 50 Atl. 714 (1901).

A stockholder may appeal from a judgment against the corporation where there is reason to believe that the officers in neglecting to appeal are actuated by an adverse interest.

Henry v. Jeanes, 47 O. S. 116 (1890).

But a stockholder not a party can not prosecute error.

Dunbar v. Casket Co., 19 C. C. 585; 10 C. D. 684 (1900).

Estoppel of corporation by action of all its stockholders.
Held not estopped.

Columbus, etc., Ry. v. Burke, 19 W. L. B. 27 (C. P. 1887).

Contra.

Central Trust Co. v. Columbus, etc., Ry., 87 Fed. 815 (1898).

DE FACTO CORPORATIONS.

Where an attempt is made to organize under a law authorizing incorporation, and the body acts as a corporation, a corporation *de facto* exists, although there are defects or irregularities in the proceedings. Its capacity can be questioned only by the state.

Society Perun v. Cleveland, 43 O. S. 481 (1885).

Shawnee, etc., Bank v. Miller, 1 C. C. n. s. 569; 14 C. D. 199 (1902).
Gaff v. Flesher, 33 O. S. 107, 113 (1877).
See Griffin v. Clinton, etc., R. Co., 3 O. F. D. 441.
State v. Toledo, etc., Assn., 8 C. C. n. s. 233; 18 C. D. 397 (1906).
In general there must be a law authorizing the formation of corporations to exercise such powers as the corporation *de facto* claims.
Gaff v. Flesher, 33 O. S. 107, 113, 114, 453 (1877).
Raccoon River Nav. Co. v. Eagle, 29 O. S. 238 (1876).
Society Perun v. Cleveland, 43 O. S. 481, 498, 499 (1885).
Where incorporation was had under a statute subsequently declared unconstitutional:
State v. Extension, etc., Co., 21 C. C. 662, 665; 12 C. D. 319 (1901).
Beck v. Rocky River, etc. District, 14 L. D. 312 (1904).
or where a judgment of ouster was rendered in a quo warranto proceeding:
Society Perun v. Cleveland, 43 O. S. 481 (1885).
Rowland v. Meader Furn. Co., 38 O. S. 271 (1882).
the private transactions prior to such adjudication were those of a corporation de facto.

De facto existence is not based upon the doctrine of estoppel. A de facto corporation is a reality. It has an actual and substantial existence.
Society Perun v. Cleveland, 43 O. S. 481, 490 (1885).
De facto existence may be proved by evidence of attempted incorporation, followed by bona fide user.
Society Perun v. Cleveland, 43 O. S. 481 (1885).
A de jure corporation does not, by an ultra vires act, lose its de jure existence and become a corporation de facto.
Dayton, etc., Ry. v. P. C. C. & St. L. Ry., 6 C. C. n. s. 537; 15 C. D. 705 (1902); aff'd, no rep., 67 O. S. 523.

Contracts of de facto corporations made through authorized agents are binding.
Beck v. Rocky River, etc., District, 14 L. D. 312 (1904); s. c., 9 C. C. n. s. 551; 19 C. D. 717; 76 O. S. 587.

Power to appropriate property. A de facto corporation can not exercise the right of eminent domain.
Powers v. Hazleton, etc., Ry. Co., 33 O. S. 429 (1878).
Queen City Telephone Co. v. Cincinnati, 73 O. S. 64 (1905).
Atlantic, etc., Co. v. Sullivant, 5 O. S. 276 (1855).

Personal liability of stockholders. Stockholders in a corporation *de facto* are liable only as stockholders; not as partners.
Rowland v. Meader Furn. Co., 38 O. S. 271 (1882).
Irregular or defective incorporation does not render the stockholders personally liable, where the statute has been substantially complied with.
Second Nat'l. Bank v. Hall, 35 O. S. 158, 166 (1878).
Bartholomew v. Bentley, 1 O. S. 37 (1852).

Estoppel to deny corporate existence. All parties to a transaction in which a de facto corporation has acted as a corporation, are estopped to deny its legal existence. No party to the transaction can escape responsibility by showing that the corporation was not duly incorporated. This rule applies to the corporation itself;
Callender v. Painesville, etc., R. Co., 11 O. S. 516 (1860).
its stockholders and subscribers to its stock;
Gaff v. Flesher, 33 O. S. 107, 113 (1877).
Clark v. Thomas, 34 O. S. 46, 59 (1877).
Callender v. Painesville, etc., R. Co., 11 O. S. 516 (1860).
Trumbull Co., etc., Co. v. Horner, 17 Ohio 407 (1848).

Vorhees v. Receivers, 19 Ohio 463 (1850).
Benninger v. Gall, 1 C. S. C. R. 331 (1871).
Ryan v. Miami Valley Ry., 10 Am. L. R. 263 (1881).
Compare Raccoon River Nav. Co. v. Eagle, 29 O. S. 238, 240 (1876).
its officers:
Second Nat'l. Bank v. Lovell, 2 C. S. C. R. 397 (1873).
and to debtors of the corporation.
Peckham Iron Co. v. Harper, 41 O. S. 100, 106 (1884).
Newburg Petroleum Co. v. Weare, 27 O. S. 343 (1875).
Hagerman v. Ohio, etc., Assn., 25 O. S. 186, 200 (1874).
Lucas v. Greenville, etc., Assn., 22 O. S. 339 (1872).
Receivers v. Renick, 15 Ohio 322 (1846).
Durrell v. Belding, 9 C. C. 74; 4 C. D. 263 (1894).
Elektron Mfg. Co. v. Jones Bros. El. Co., 8 C. C. 311; 4 C. D. 555
  (1894).
Creditors who have extended credit to a de facto corporation, as
a corporate body, are estopped from denying its corporate existence so
as to hold the stockholders liable as partners;
Second Nat'l. Bank v. Hall, 35 O. S. 158, 166 (1878).
Beebe v. Thomas, 2 W. L. B. 107 (Cin. Super. Ct. 1877).
Second Nat'l Bank v Lovell, 2 C. S. C. R. 397 (1873).
Benninger v. Gall, 1 C. S. C. R. 331 (1871).
See Rowland v. Meader Furniture Co., 38 O. S. 269 (1882).
or to invalidate a mortgage executed by the de facto corporation.
Lattimer v. Mosaic Glass Co., 13 C. C. 163; 7 C. D. 430 (1896).
Hatry v. P. & Y. Ry. Co., 1 C. C. 426; 1 C. D. 238 (1886).
Continental Trust Co. v. Toledo, etc., R. Co., 82 Fed. 642 (1897).
But the proof, in bankruptcy, of a claim against the estate of a
bankrupt corporation, and the receipt of a dividend thereon, does not
estop the creditor from subsequently bringing an action to hold the
stockholders as partners.
Ridenour v. Mayo, 29 O. S. 138, 143 (1876).
Pleading and proof of corporate existence.
See notes to § 8629. In appropriation proceedings, see note to § 11046.

"Associates" defined. Associates are such persons, other than those
specifically mentioned, as might thereafter become members of the association.
State v. Sibley, 25 Minn. 387, 399.
See also Lechmere Bank v. Boynton, 65 Mass. (11 Cush.) 369, 382.

CORPORATION AS A "PERSON."

A corporation is a "person" under G. C. § 3989 which prohibits
a municipality from granting an exclusive gas franchise to any person
or persons.
Cincinnati Gas Co. v. Avondale, 43 O. S. 257 (1885).
And under G. C. § 12940 which prohibits persons conducting hotels,
amusement places, etc., from excluding citizens because of color or race.
Johnson v. Humphrey Pop Corn Co., 4 C. C. n. s. 49; 14 C. D. 135
  (1902); aff'd, no rep., 70 O. S. 478.
And under the 14th amendment of the federal constitution for-
bidding the deprivation of property without due process of law.
Covington, etc., Co. v. Sandford, 164 U. S. 578 (1896).
Foreign corporation as a person or citizen, see note to § 194.

In criminal statutes. The word "person" in a criminal statute
has been generally held not to apply to a corporation,
State v. Cincinnati Fertilizer Co., 24 O. S. 611 (1874).

Leo Ebert Brewing Co. v. State, 2 C. C. n. s. 537; 15 C. D. 601 (1904); aff'd in part, 71 O. S. 476.
See Burke v. State, 34 O. S. 79 (1877).
except when expressly included, as in the anti-trust act.
State v. Hygeia Ice Co., 4 N. P. n. s. 361, 363; 16 L. D. 735 (1906); affirmed, except as to sentence only; 77 O. S. 427.

Since the adoption of the General Code in 1910 the word "whoever" includes "all persons, natural and artificial." G. C. § 12371,

PROMOTERS.

Fiduciary relation. Promoters occupy a fiduciary relation toward the corporation.
Shawnee, etc., Bank v. Miller, 1 C. C. n. s. 569; 14 C. D. 199 (1902).
Second N. B. v. Greenville, etc., Co., 3 C. C. n. s. 372; 13 C. D. 274 (1899); 11 O. L. R. 81 (Article by A. A. Thomas).

Sales to corporation. Promoters must truly disclose all facts relating to property which they sell to the corporation. A promoter who conceals his interest in such property, or who misrepresents its value, is liable to the corporation. He can not make a secret profit in such a transaction.
Second N. B. v. Greenville, etc., Co., 3 C. C. n. s. 372; 13 C. D. 274 (1899).
Shawnee, etc., Bank v. Miller, 1 C. C. n. s. 569; 14 C. D. 199 (1902).
Yeiser v. U. S. Board & Paper Co., 107 Fed. 340; 12 O. F. D. 678 (C. C. A. 1901).
Steamship Co. v. Shipbuilding Co., 10 O. L. R. 427; 197 Fed. 797 (D. C. 1912).
See 6 O. L. R. 307.

The corporation may rescind a contract for the purchase of property, negotiated for the corporation by the promoter, who received secret commissions from the seller of such property. The corporation may return the property to the seller and recover the purchase price paid.
Commonwealth Steamship Co. v. American Shipbuilding Co., 10 O. L. R. 395; 197 Fed. 780 (U. S. D. C. 1912).
Commonwealth Steamship Co. v. American Shipbuilding Co., 10 O. L. R. 427; 197 Fed. 797 (U. S. D. C. 1912).
Mechanic's lien on property sold to corporation.
See Burnap v. Sylvania Butter Co., 12 C. C. 639; 5 C. D. 582 (1896).
West v. Klotz, 37 O. S. 420 (1881).

Compensation for services. Where a corporation avails itself of the services and contracts of promoters, before organization, and ratifies the same, it becomes liable therefor. But the services may be shown to have been gratuitously rendered.
Third Ward Bldg. Assn. v. Lotze, 11 W. L. B. 285 (Dist. Ct.).
Ritchie v. McMullen, 79 Fed. 523 (C. C. A. Ohio 1897).

Liability. Where a corporation is formed merely as an instrumentality for the accomplishment of an illegal purpose, the promoters may be personally liable. Incorporation is no defense.
Brundred v. Rice, 49 O. S. 640 (1892).
Bank v. Trebein, 59 O. S. 316 (1898).
Andres v. Morgan, 62 O. S. 236 (1900).
Liability to purchasers of stock. Circulars as evidence.
See Russell v. Weiler, 7 C. C. n. s. 596; 18 C. D. 176 (1905).

Contracts with third persons. See below, *Transactions before incorporation.*

Sales of stock regulated.
See G. C. §§ 6373-1 to 6373-24.

TRANSACTIONS BEFORE INCORPORATION.

With third persons. Until a corporation has been organized and directors elected, no one is authorized to bind the corporation. Contracts made by promoters with third persons are not binding on the corporation.

Dayton, etc., Co. v. Coy, 13 O. S. 84 (1861).
Mosier v. Parry, 60 O. S. 388, 401, 402 (1899).

After organization such contracts may be adopted and ratified by the directors either expressly or impliedly, by accepting the benefits of the transaction.

City Bldg. Assn. v. Zahner, 6 W. L. B. 389; 10 Am. L. Rec. 181 (Dist Ct.).
Third Ward Bldg. Assn. v. Lotze, 11 W. L. B. 285 (Dist. Ct.).

But if there is a failure to incorporate, or if the corporation does not adopt or ratify such contract, the corporation is not bound, and the promoters may be personally liable.

Mosier v. Parry, 60 O. S. 388 (1899).
Magill v. Rendigs, 12 L. D. 558 (Cin. Super. Ct. 1902).

Validity of charitable bequest to corporation not yet incorporated.

See Trustees v. Zanesville, etc., Co., 9 Ohio 203 (1839).

Agreements betweeen individuals to form a corporation. An agreement between individuals for the formation of a corporation and providing for its future control is valid as between the parties.

Doan v. Rogan, 79 O. S. 372, 386 (1909).

Provisions in such an agreement are deemed waived by inconsistent provisions inserted by the parties in the charter.

Cronin v. Potters Co-op. Co., 29 W. L. B. 52, 56 (Com. Pleas 1892).

An agreement by a promoter to employ, or procure a future corporation to employ, a person is not invalid as an agreement to secure a corporate office.

Magill v. Rendigs, 12 L. D. 558 (Cin. Super. Ct. 1902).
Doan v. Rogan, 79 O. S. 372, 386 (1909).
See Mosier v. Parry, 60 O. S. 388 (1899).
Mullen v. Gaffery, 8 Am. L. R. 101 (Dist. Ct. 1879).

Where persons interested in a proposed corporation hold meetings and effect a preliminary organization, wholly in the interest of such corporation the preliminary organization does not continue as a separate and distinct organization after the corporation is organized.

Mulhauser v. Cleveland Hospital, etc., 21 C. C. 88; 11 C. D. 391 (1900); aff'd, no rep., 66 O. S. 688.

INCORPORATION OF PARTNERSHIPS.

The entire plant and assets of a partnership may be purchased by a corporation formed to engage in a like business. As a part of such a transaction it may acquire valid title to property not indispensable for its business, such as a claim for damages to partnership property caused by negligence of other persons.

Gas & Fuel Co. v. Dairy Co., 60 O. S. 96 (1899).

Where partnership assets, including good will, are sold through a receiver, and the purchaser transfers the same to a corporation, the corporation may adopt the name previously used by the partnership.

Snyder Mfg. Co. v. Snyder, 54 O. S. 86 (1896).

Liability of corporation for the partnership debts.

See Andres v. Morgan, 62 O. S. 236 (1900).

Right of partnership creditors in property transferred to the corporation.

See Bank v. Trebein, 59 O. S. 316 (1898).

Liability of partners on stock issued to them for the partnership property at an overvaluation.

See Gates v. Tippecanoe Stone Co., 57 O. S. 60 (1897).

Sayler v. Simpson, 12 L. D. 148 (Super. Ct. Cin. 1888).

Ford v. Lamson, 17 C. C. 539; 9 C. D. 374 (1899).

ULTRA VIRES ACTS.

An act of a corporation is *ultra vires* when it is beyond the chartered powers of the corporation.

Railroad Co. v. Furnace Co., 37 O. S. 321, 327 (1881).

In determining whether the act is ultra vires regard must be had to its effect and the real object in view.

Bank v. Flour Co., 41 O. S. 552, 558 (1885).

In applying the doctrine of ultra vires, in a particular case, regard must be had not only to the unauthorized agreement or transaction, but also to the relation which the litigating parties sustain to it.

Ehrman v. Ins. Co., 35 O. S. 324, 337 (1880).

Gas & Fuel Co. v. Dairy Co., 60 O. S. 96, 106 (1899).

A conveyance to a corporation to secure two debts, one valid and the other ultra vires, will be upheld to the extent of the valid debt.

Morris v. Way, 16 Ohio 469 (1847).

See also Dayton, etc., Ry. v. P. C. C. & St. L. Ry., 6 C. C. n. s. 537; 15 C. D. 705 (1902); aff'd, no rep., 67 O. S. 523.

Unauthorized act when incident or part of authorized transaction. Acts which would otherwise be ultra vires may be valid when merely incidental to, or forming part of an entire transaction that, in its general scope, is within the corporate powers. Where a corporation purchases the assets and business of a partnership, for its corporate purposes, it may acquire a valid title to its outstanding claims, including a claim for damages caused by negligence, although it would have no general power to purchase claims of that nature.

Gas & Fuel Co. v. Dairy Co., 60 O. S. 96 (1899).

When void. Where there is an absolute or total want of power in a corporation to deal in respect to a certain subject, acts done in its corporate name, in regard to such subject, may, as corporate acts, be void for all purposes and as against all persons.

Ehrman v. Insurance Co., 35 O. S. 324, 337 (1880).

But where the corporation deals with a subject within the scope of its powers, but for a purpose or in a mode not authorized, the act is not necessarily void.

Ehrman v. Insurance Co., 35 O. S. 324, 337 (1880).

White's Bank v. Toledo, etc., Co., 12 O. S. 601, 610 (1861).

Pickaway Co. Bank v. Prather. 12 O. S. 497, 511 (1861).

Effect on corporate existence and valid powers. Ultra vires acts do not per se dissolve a corporation or deprive it of its valid powers, in the absence of a proceeding by the state for that purpose.

Finnell v. Burt, 2 Handy 202 (1856).

Benninger v. Gall, 1 C. S. C. R. 331, 336 (1871).

Webb v. Moler, 8 Ohio 552 (1838).

Nor does a corporation, by an ultra vires act, lose its de jure existence and become a corporation de facto.

Dayton, etc., Ry. v. P. C. C. & St. L. Ry., 6 C. C. n. s. 537; 15 C. D. 705 (1902); aff'd, no rep., 67 O. S. 523.

Contracts performed by one party. Where a contract has been executed and fully performed on the part of the corporation or of the other party, neither may object that the contract or performance is ultra vires.

Larwell v. Hanover, etc., Society, 40 O. S. 274, 285 (1883).
Hays v. Galion, etc., Co., 29 O. S. 330, 340 (1876).
Armstrong v. Karshner, 47 O. S. 276, 296 (1890).
Dayton, etc., Ry. v. P. C. C. & St. L. Ry., 6 C. C. n. s. 537, 546;
    15 C. D. 705 (1902); aff'd, no rep., 67 O. S. 523.
Siders v. Gem City Concrete Co., 13 C. C. n. s. 481 (1910).
Newburg Petroleum Co. v. Weare, 27 O. S. 343 (1875).
Railway Co. v. Iron Co., 46 O. S. 44 (1888).
Compare Simpson v. Building, etc., Assn., 38 O. S. 349 (1882).

Guaranty of ultra vires contract. A written guaranty of the performance of a contract is valid, although the contract itself may be void as ultra vires.
Zerkle v. Price, 5 N. P. 480; 7 L. D. 465 (C. P.)

Corporate acts presumed valid. It is presumed that a corporation has acted within its powers, and its contract or note will be presumed to be valid until the contrary is shown.
Straus v. Eagle Insurance Co., 5 O. S. 59, 62 (1855).

Notice of corporate powers. Persons dealing with a corporation are charged with notice of the limits of its corporate powers.
James v. Cincinnati, etc., R. Co., 2 Dis. 261, 272 (1858).
Treadwell v. Commissioners, 11 O. S. 183, 192 (1860).
Zabriskie v. Cleveland, etc., R. Co., 64 U. S. (23 How.) 381,
    398 (1860).
Holmes v. Hayes, 32 W. L. B. 346-348 (Sup. Ct. no rep., 52 O. S.
    617 (1894)).

Who may object to ultra vires acts. *The state* may object to ultra vires acts, by quo warranto.
State v. Standard Oil Co., 49 O. S. 137 (1892).
State v. Ohio, etc., Co., 6 C. C. 412; 3 C. D. 516 (1892).
Miller v. Ratterman, 47 O. S. 141, 165 (1890).
State v. Loan Ass'n, 35 O. S. 258 (1879).

A **stockholder** may, by injunction, restrain threatened acts which are not within the express or implied powers of the corporation.
Zabriskie v. Cleveland, etc., R. Co., 64 U. S. (23 How.) 381 (1860).
Port Clinton, etc., Co. v. Cleveland, etc., Co., 13 O. S. 544, 561 (1862).
Kuhn v. Woolson Spice Co. 13 C. C. 547; 7 C. D. 294 (1897).
C. H. & D. Ry. v. Duckworth, 2 C. C. 518; 1 C. D. 618 (1887);
    affirmed, 21 W. L. B. 36.
A stockholder may in federal court enjoin the corporation from a threatened diversion of funds by illegal payment of an unconstitutional tax.
Pollock v. Farmers' Loan & Trust Co., 157 U. S. 429 (1895).
But a stockholder can not enjoin the payment of the federal income tax, as the income tax act provides a remedy at law, to-wit: the recovery of taxes paid under protest.
Straus v. Realty Co., 200 Fed. 327 (1912).
A member of a religious corporation may, by injunction, prevent a breach of trust by the corporation or a majority of its members.
Wiswell v. First Congregational Church, 14 O. S. 31 (1862).
But a stockholder must assert his rights promptly upon notice of the ultra vires act. If he delay until the act has been performed and benefits received thereunder, he will be held to have assented to the act.
Hill v. Cincinnati Hotel Co., 25 W. L. B. 425 (Cin. Super. Ct.
    1891).
Sanderson v. Aetna Iron & Nail Co., 34 O. S. 442 (1878).

Goodin v. Cincinnati, etc., Co., 18 O. S. 169 (1869).
Chapman v. Mad River, etc., R. Co., 6 O. S. 119 (1856).
Baldwin v. Hillsborough R. R., 10 W. L. J. 337 (C. P.).
Zabriskie v. Cleveland, etc., R. Co., 64 U. S. (23 How.) 381 (1860).

A stranger to the transaction can not question its validity. The maker of a note, payable to a corporation and endorsed to another corporation, can not, in an action brought by such endorsee, question the powers of the corporations to make the transfer.
Ehrman v. Insurance Co., 35 O. S. 324, 337 (1880).
Gas & Fuel Co. v. Dairy Co., 60 O. S. 96, 107 (1899).
Bank v. McIntire, 40 O. S. 528, 537 (1884).
White's Bank v. Toledo, etc., Co., 12 O. S. 601, 610 (1861).
Pickaway Co. Bank v. Prather, 12 O. S. 497, 511 (1861).
Gould v. Union, etc., Co., 8 W. L. B. 281 (Cin. Super. Ct.).

Party who has received benefits. Where a contract has been executed and fully performed on the part of one party and the other party has received the benefits, such party can not avoid liability on the ground of ultra vires. This rule applies to the corporation.
Hays v. Galion, etc., Co. 29 O. S. 330, 340 (1876).
Hill v. Cincinnati Hotel Co., 25 W. L. B. 425 (Cin. Super. Ct. 1891).
Norwalk Sgs. Bk. v. Norwalk, etc., Co., 14 C. C. 1; 7 C. D. 275 (1897); aff'd, no rep., 60 O. S. 603.
See Herrick v. Wardwell, 58 O. S. 294, 308 (1898).
And to the other party.
Newburg Petroleum Co. v. Weare, 27 O. S. 343 (1875).
Hamilton, etc., Co. v. C. H. & D. Ry., 29 O. S. 341 (1876).
Allen v. 1 N. B., 23 O. S. 97, 104 (1872).
Victoria Bldg. Assn. v. Arbeiter Bund, 6 W. L. B. 823; 10 Am. L. R. 485.
Constable Bros. Co. v. Faulhaber, 15 L. D. 700 (C. P. 1904).
The party receiving the benefits is estopped from denying the power of the corporation to make the contract.
Newburg Petroleum Co. v. Weare, 27 O. S. 343 (1875).
Tone v. Columbus, 39 O. S. 281, 308-310.
Dayton, etc., Ry. v. P. C. C. & St. L. Ry., 6 C. C. n. s. 537, 546; 15 C. D. 705 (1902); aff'd, no rep., 67 O. S. 523.

Estoppel. The doctrine that a party who has received benefits under a contract is estopped from denying the power of the corporation to make the contract does not in all cases apply to creditors. As between creditors whose claims are founded on authorized transactions and creditors relying on an ultra vires contract, the former would prevail.
Miller v. Ratterman, 47 O. S. 141, 165 (1890).
Compare Central Trust Co. v. Columbus, etc., Ry., 87 Fed. 815 (1898).
A corporation, which has made an ultra vires guaranty of the performance of a contract by another party, is not estopped from denying its power to give the guaranty, although the party to whom the guaranty was given has performed his part of the contract.
Humboldt Min. Co. v. American, etc., Co., 62 Fed. 256; 9 O. F. D. 153 (C. C. A. 1894).

Personal liability for ultra vires acts.

Directors and officers. Where the officers of a corporation transcend the corporate authority they are, under some circumstances, personally liable; but the extent of this doctrine is not clearly defined.
Medill v. Collier, 16 O. S. 599, 610 (1866).

See Manufacturers', etc., Ass'n. v. Lynchburg Drug Mills, 8 C. C.
    112; 4 C. D. 352 (1893).
Where such a liability exists it is not a bar to an action by a creditor
on stock subscriptions made by such officers.
    Dickason v. Grafton Sav. Bank, 6 C. C. n. s. 329, 335; 17 C. D. 357
    (1905); aff'd, no rep., 76 O. S. 612.
    See note to § 8674. *Irregular or incomplete incorporation.*
Officers and others actively managing the business of corporations have
been held personally liable in the following cases: For debts incurred
in carrying on a banking business in the corporate name without complying
with a statutory condition precedent, where the statute prohibited the
carrying on of such business until the condition precedent had been
complied with;
    Medill v. Collier, 16 O. S. 599 (1866).
For debts incurred in the name of a corporation incorporated under a
former statute authorizing savings societies, where the trustees made no
attempt to organize or conduct it as a savings society, but instead
carried on a general banking business:
    Ridenour v. Mayo, 40 O. S. 9 (1884).
On unauthorized bank notes:
    Kearny v. Buttles, 1 O. S. 362 (1853).
    Lawler v. Burt, 7 O. S. 340 (1857).
For debts incurred in the corporate name, where the amount of
stock required by law as a condition precedent to the election of directors
and to the transaction of business had not been subscribed.
    Trust Co. v. Floyd, 47 O. S. 525 (1890).

Stockholders are not liable unless they engage in or authorize the
prohibited **acts.**
    Medill v. Collier, 16 O. S. 599 (1866).
    Bank v. Hall, 35 O. S. 158, 166 (1878).
    Paul v. Groene, 4 O. L. R. 632 (Cin. Super. Ct. 1907).
    Morrison v. Stevens, 4 O. L. R. 671 Cin. Super. Ct. 1907).
    Kearny v. Buttles, 1 O. S. 362 (1853).
    Rainhard v. Hovey, 13 Ohio 300 (1844).

Overissue of bonds. Where a corporation, having power to issue
bonds. issues bonds in excess of the amount allowed by law, the stockholders and directors causing the issue are not liable *on the bonds.*
    Raymond v. Spring Grove, etc., Ry., 21 W. L. B. 103.

CORPORATE POWERS.

   General rule. A corporation has such powers, and such only (1) as
are expressly conferred by the statutes under which it is incorporated,
or (2) as are necessary for the purpose of carrying into effect the powers
specifically conferred.
    Straus v. Eagle Ins. Co., 5 O. S. 59 (1855).
    Gas & Fuel Co. v. Dairy Co., 60 O. S. 96 (1899).
    Franklin Bank v. Commercial Bank, 36 O. S. 350, 355 (1881).
    State v. Eagle Insurance Co., 50 O. S. 252, 267 (1893).
    Railway Co. v. Iron Co., 46 O. S. 44, 49 (1888).
    Railroad Co. v. Hinsdale, 45 O. S. 556, 572 (1888).
    Lessee of Overmyer v. Williams, 15 Ohio 26, 31 (1846).
    State v. Granville, etc., Soc., 11 Ohio 1, 12 (1841).
    Lessee of Kemper v. Cincinnati, etc., Co., 11 Ohio 392 (1842).
    State v. Washington. etc., Co., 11 Ohio 96 (1841).
    Bonham v. Taylor, 10 Ohio 108, 109 (1840).
    Bank v. Swayne, 8 Ohio 257, 286 (1838).

Implied powers. The implied powers of a corporation are not limited to those which are *indispensable* for carrying into effect the powers ex-. pressly conferred, but comprise all that are *necessary* in the sense of appropriate, convenient and suitable, including the right of reasonable choice of means to be employed.

Gas & Fuel Co. v. Dairy Co., 60 O. S. 96 (1899).

State v. Railway Co., 68 O. S. 9, 40 (1903).

Railroad Co. v. Furnace Co., 37 O. S. 321 (1881).

Power granted to a corporation to engage in a certain business carries with it the authority to act precisely as an individual would act, in carrying on such business.

Larwell v. Hanover Sgs. Fund Soc., 40 O. S. 274, 282 (1883).

Powers outside of Ohio. Foreign corporations in Ohio. Statutes conferring corporate powers apply only to domestic corporations. A foreign corporation has only the powers conferred by its charter, although it transacts business in a state where domestic corporations possess other powers.

Ewing v. Bank, 43 O. S. 31 (1885).

Humphreys v. State, 70 O. S. 67, 83 (1904).

Kit Carter Cattle Co. v. McGillin, 21 C. C. 210; 11 C. D. 413 (1900).

A foreign corporation has no greater powers in Ohio than domestic corporations of a like character.

G. C. § 5508.

See State v. Aetna Life Ins. Co., 69 O. S. 327 (1903).

Mannington v. H. V. Ry. Co., 8 O. L. R. 451, 484; 183 Fed. 133; 16 O. F. D. 552 (C. C. Ohio 1910).

G. C. § 178.

A bank authorized to make loans at a limited rate of interest can not make loans in another state at a higher rate, although the higher rate is valid in such state.

Ewing v. Bank, 43 O. S. 31 (1885).

Burden of proof as to corporate powers. Where a corporation asserts that it is clothed with a given power and the right to exercise it, the burden is on it to show where such power and right are derived.

State v. Vanderbilt, 37 O. S. 591 (1882).

Mannington v. H. V. Ry. Co., 8 O. L. R. 451, 472; 183 Fed. 133; 16 O. F. D. 552 (C. C. 1910).

Statutes conferring corporate powers. Rules of construction. Special charters granted prior to the constitution of 1851 were strictly construed against the corporations and liberally in favor of the public.

National Bank v. Insurance Co., 41 O. S. 1, 12 (1884).

See Zanesville v. Gaslight Co., 47 O. S. 1, 30-31 (1889).

The rule of strict construction is still applied to statutes which grant special privileges or immunities. Such statutes are held to carry only those privileges and exemptions which are granted expressly and without ambiguity.

State v. Eagle Insurance Co., 50 O. S. 252, 267 (1893).

State v. Vanderbilt, 37 O. S. 590, 641 (1882).

Debolt v. Ohio, etc., Trust Co., 1 O. S. 563, 573 (1853).

Matheny v. Golden, 5 O. S. 361, 417 (1856).

State v. Railway, 12 C. C. n. s. 145, 147 (1909).

But the rule of strict construction is not now invariably applied to incorporation statutes in general. Such statutes are under some circumstances interpreted under the same rules which apply to other statutes.

National Bank v. Insurance Co., 41 O. S. 1, 12 (1884).

James v. C. H. & D. Ry. Co., 2 Dis. 261, 269, 270 (1858).

Gas & Fuel Co. v. Dairy Co., 60 O. S. 96, 104 (1899).

Larwell v. Hanover, etc., Soc., 40 O. S. 274, 285 (1883).

Gaff v. Flesher, 33 O. S. 107, 114 (1877).
Contra, Humboldt Mining Co. v. American, etc., Co., 62 Fed. 356 (C. C. A. Ohio 1894).
State v. Railway, 12 C. C. n. s. 145, 147 (1909).
An act of incorporation, like any other statute, should be construed in such a manner as will best answer the intention of the legislature; and all its parts should, if possible, be made subservient to, and in harmony with, the leading purposes and objects intended to be accomplished.
Straus v. Eagle Insurance Co., 5 O. S. 59 (1855).
White's Bank v. Toledo Ins. Co., 12 O. S. 601, 605 (1861).
Shoemaker v. Goshen Twp., 14 O. S. 569, 575 (1863).

Mode of exercise. The mode or manner of exercising corporate powers rests in the sound discretion of the corporate authorities.
Railroad Co. v. Furnace Co., 37 O. S. 321 (1881).
Gas & Fuel Co. v. Dairy Co., 60 O. S. 96 (1899).
Central Trust Co. v. Columbus, etc., Ry. Co., 87 Fed. 815 (1898).

By whom exercised.

Directors. Corporate powers and business are exercised and conducted by the directors or trustees;
See § 8660.
Bradford Belting Co. v. Gibson, 68 O. S. 442 (1903).
except in certain cases where, by special statutory provisions, action by the stockholders is required.. ·
See §§ 8710 to 8718, 8698, 8700, 8720.

Stockholders. Where all or a majority of the stockholders of a corporation do an act designed to affect its property and business, and which, through their control of the corporate agencies, does affect the property and business of the company in the same manner as if done by a resolution of its directors, which act is ultra vires and illegal, and was done individually to conceal the real purpose, the act should be regarded as that of the corporation.
State v. Standard Oil Co., 49 O. S. 137 (1892).

Who may question. A person against whom a corporation may claim the right to exercise a power may call the power into question and require the corporation to show its existence.
Zanesville v. Gas-Light Co., 47 O. S. 1 (1889).
Gas-Light Co. v. Zanesville, 47 O. S. 35, 47 (1889).
See Bank v. Telegraph Co., 79 O. S. 89 (1908).
See above, ultra vires acts—who may object to.

TO SUE AND BE SUED.

Pleading and proof of corporate existence.
See note to § 8629.
A corporation may sue, or be sued by, its own stockholders.
Norton v. Norton, 43 O. S. 509 (1885).
Lamson v. Farmers' Bank, 1 O. S. 206, 211 (1853).
A corporation may sue for slander upon it in the way of its business or trade.
Brayton v. Cleveland Special Police Co., 63 O. S. 83, 85 (1900).
An insolvent corporation may be required to give security for costs.
G. C. § 11614.
Pleadings of a corporation should be verified by an officer.
Mfg. Co. v. Hedges, 76 O. S. 91 (1907).
In an action against a corporation by an administrator the general manager is not disqualified by G. C. § 11495 from testifying to facts occurring before the death of the decedent.
Cockley Milling Co. v. Bunn, 75 O. S. 270 (1906).

Criminal liability. A corporation may be indicted and prosecuted for creating a nuisance;
> Strawboard Co. v. State, 70 O. S. 140 (1904).
> See State v. Cincinnati Fertilizer Co., 24 O. S. 611 (1874).

and tor a violation of the anti-trust act.
> State v. General Fire Extinguisher Co., 9 N. P. n. s. 438; 20 L. D. 240 (1910).

The word "person" in a criminal statute has been held not to apply to a corporation.
> State v. Cincinnati Fertilizer Co., 24 O. S. 611 (1874).
> Leo Ebert Brewing Co. v. State, 2 C. C. n. s. 537; 15 C. D. 601 (1904); aff'd, in part, 71 O. S. 476.

But since the adoption of the general code in 1910 the word "whoever" in the penal code includes " all persons, natural and artificial."
> G. C. § 12371.

Civil liability. A corporation is liable, as an individual would be, for the acts of its agents within the course of their employment;
> Bank v. Blakesley, 42 O. S. 645, 652 (1885).

although the act is wilful or malicious.
> Nelson Business College Co. v. Lloyd, 60 O. S. 448 (1899).

It may be liable for punitive damages.
> Western Union Tel. Co. v. Smith, 64 O. S. 106, 117 (1901).
> Pittsburg, etc., R. Co. v. Slusser, 19 O. S. 157 (1869).
> Atlantic, etc., Co. v. Dunn, 19 O. S. 162 (1869).

A corporation may be liable for libel:
> Union, etc., Ins. Co. v. Mutual, etc., Ins. Co., 2 W. L. B. 269 (1877).

deceit;
> First N. B. v. Kehnast, 22 L. D. 15 (C. P. 1910).

false imprisonment:
> Nichols v. L. S. & M. S. Ry., 1 Cleve. L. R. 268 (1878).

assault and battery;
> Nelson Business College Co. v. Lloyd, 60 O. S. 448 (1899).
> Passenger R. R. Co. v. Young, 21 O. S. 518 (1871).
> See Little Miami R. R. Co. v. Wetmore, 19 O. S. 110 (1869).
> Contra, Orr v. Bank of U. S., 1 Ohio 36 (1822).

and negligence.
> Railway Co. v. Bank, 56 O. S. 351, 383 (1897).
> Cleveland, etc., R. Co. v. Keary, 3 O. S. 201 (1854).

A corporation not for profit maintaining a charity hospital or other purely charitable institution is not liable for negligence of its servants.
> Taylor v. Protestant, etc., Ass'n., 85 O. S. 90 (1911).
> Conner v. Sisters of Poor, 7 N. P. 514 (1900).
> Johnson v. Lawrence Hospital, 12 L. D. 795 (1902).

A street railway company can not be held directly liable for malpractice of medicine.
> Youngstown, etc., Co. v. Kessler, 84 O. S. 74 (1911).

It has been held that an action of trespass quare clausum fregit would not lie against a corporation.
> Foote v. Cincinnati, 9 Ohio 31 (1839).
> Ward v. Toledo, etc., R. Co., 10 W. L. J. 365 (1853).

Federal corporations. A national bank may be sued in a state court.
> Hade v. McVay 31 O. S. 231 (1877).
> See Zinn v. Baxter, 65 O. S. 341 (1901).

But a soldiers' home incorporated by congress for the purpose of performing a governmental function only, can not be sued in a state court in a tort action.
> Overholser v. National Home, etc., 68 O. S. 236 (1903).

TO CONTRACT AND BE CONTRACTED WITH.

The right to enter into contracts is general and is denied only when prohibited by statute or some consideration of public policy recognized by the courts.

Stafford v. Produce Exch. Bkg. Co., 61 O. S. 160, 169 (1899).

"Unless expressly restrained by its charter, every corporation has the incidental power to make any contract, and evidence it by any instrument that may be necessary and proper to accomplish the objects for which it is created."

Straus v. Eagle Insurance Co., 5 O. S. 59, 62 (1855).

But the power to contract has reference to and is limited by the nature of the corporate business.

Hays v. Galion, etc., Co., 29 O. S. 330, 338 (1876).

Contract for term of years binding future directors. A corporation may make a contract for a term of years extending beyond the term of the directors by whom it is made.

Railroad Co. v. Furnace Co., 37 O. S. 321 (1881).

Presumption as to validity of corporate contracts. The presumption is in favor of the validity of a corporate contract. A note made or received by a corporation is, prima facie, within its corporate powers and therefore valid; but it may be shown to have been made or taken for an unauthorized purpose.

Straus v. Eagle Insurance Co., 5 O. S. 59, 62 (1855).
Stone v. Traction Co., 4 N. P. n. s. 104, 107; 16 L. D. 645 (1906).

Right to contract as a constitutional right. The right to acquire property includes the right to make contracts with reference to property which can not be alienated by the legislature. The provisions of Sec. 1, bill of rights of the constitution which guarantee the liberty of acquiring property by contract apply to private corporations as well as to individuals.

Stewart v. Gardner, 10 C. C. n. s. 408; 20 C. D. 218 (1907); aff'd, no rep., 78 O. S. 451.
Shaw v. Cleveland, etc., Ry., 173 Fed. 746, 751 (C. C. A. 1909).

Form. A contract reading "I" or "we" promise, etc., but signed in the corporate name by one or more of its officers, is the contract of the corporation and not of the officers individually.

Aungst v. Creque, 72 O. S. 551 (1905).
Baldwin v. Egan, 11 C. C. n. s. 584 (1908).
See below *Form and execution of corporate deeds and instruments.*

Contracts for usurious interest. A stipulation for interest, to be received or paid by a corporation, at a rate higher than permitted by the usury laws does not render the loan or debt void. The principal may be recovered together with interest at the lawful rate.

National Bank v. Insurance Co., 41 O. S. 1 (1884).
Larwell v. Hanover, etc., Soc., 40 O. S. 274 (1883).
Ewing v. Toledo Sav. Bank, 43 O. S. 31 (1883).
State v. Urbana, etc., Co., 14 Ohio 6 (1846).
First N. B. v. Garlinghouse, 22 O. S. 492 (1872).

Under former statutes and certain special charters which expressly prohibited corporations from charging more that a certain rate of interest, it was held that a contract for a higher rate was wholly void and that neither principal nor interest could be recovered.

Bank v. Swayne, 8 Ohio 257 (1838).
Miami Exporting Co. v. Clark. 13 Ohio 1 (1853).
Preble Co. v. Russell. 1 O. S. 313 (1853).

Bank of Wooster v. Stevens, 1 O. S. 233 (1853).
Russell v. Failor, 1 O. S. 327, 329 (1853).
Union Bank v. Bell, 14 O. S. 200, 209 (1863).
Kilbreth v. Bates, 38 O. S. 187 (1882).
See Laskey v. Board of Education, 35 O. S. 519 (1880).
Southern Bank v. Gassoway, 1 Dis. 207 (1856)..
Kilbreth v. Wright, 1 W. L. B. 1; 4 Am. L. R. 449 (1876).
Creed v. Commercial, etc., Bank, 11 Ohio 489 (1842).
Spaulding v. Bank, 12 Ohio 544 (1841).
Dunkle v. Renick, 6 O. S. 527 (1856).
McLean v. LaFayette, 3 McLean (U. S.) 587; 2 O. F. D. 412.
National banks may charge interest at the same rate as individuals.
La Dow v. Bank, 51 O. S. 234 (1894).
Decisions under former statutes.
Shunk v. National Bank, 22 O. S. 508 (1872).
Bank v. Slemmons, 34 O. S. 142 (1877).
Hade v. McVay, 31 O. S. 231 (1877).
Allen v. First N. B., 23 O. S. 97 (1872).
First N. B. v. Garlinghouse, 22 O. S. 492 (1872).

Illegal contracts. For contracts in violation of anti-trust act see
§ 6393 and note.

A corporation can not enforce payment of a mortgage loan made by
it where the mortgagor, as a part of the transaction, agreed to purchase
the debentures of the corporation, which debentures were in the nature
of a lottery.
Heintz v. Sawyer, 5 C. C. n. s. 249; 17 C. D. 10 (1904); aff'd, no
rep., 72 O. S. 678.

A contract by a street railway company to perform medical services
is in violation of the laws of medicine and surgery and void.
Youngstown, etc., Ry. Co. v. Kessler, 84 O. S. 74 (1911).
For other void contracts see *ultra vires* above.

Contracts between corporations having same directors. See note to
§ 8660.

Contracts between a corporation and its directors. See note to
§ 8660.

TO ACQUIRE, HOLD AND CONVEY PROPERTY.

Constitutional property rights. The inalienable right to acquire,
hold and dispose of property, and to make contracts relating thereto,
appertains to corporations as well as to individuals.
Stewart v. Gardner, 10 C. C. n. s. 408; 20 C. D. 218 (1907); aff'd,
no rep., 78 O. S. 451.
Shaw v. Cleveland, etc., Ry., 173 Fed. 746, 751; 8 O. L. R. 43,
49 (C. C. A. 1909).
Wheeling, etc., Co. v. Gilmore. 8 C. C. 658: 4 C. D. 369 (1894).
The property of a corporation is "private property" within the meaning of Sec. 19, Art. 1 of the constitution which provides that "private
property shall ever be held inviolate."
Ohio, ex rel., v. Neff, 52 O. S. 375, 404 (1895).
A corporation is a "person" within the 14th amendment of the
federal constitution forbidding the deprivation of property without due
process of law.
Covington, etc., Co. v. Sandford, 164 U. S. 578 (1896).

Property in general. A corporation may, within the limits of its
charter, acquire and deal with property as freely as an individual might
do.

Lee v. Sturges, 46 O. S. 153, 161 (1889).
Wheeling, etc., Co. v. Gilmore, 8 C. C. 658; 4 C. D. 369 (1894).

Acquisition of property by devise or bequest. A foreign corporation may acquire property by devise or bequest, in the absence of a prohibitory statute.
American Bible Soc. v. Marshall, 15 O. S. 537 (1864).
But such devise or bequest is, in general, liable to the collateral inheritance tax.
Humphreys v. State, 70 O. S. 67 (1904).

In exchange for stock. See notes to §§ 8630, 8674.

Property not necessary for corporate business may be acquired by a corporation as a part of an entire transaction, whereby it acquired other property for its corporate purposes.
Gas & Fuel Co. v. Dairy Co., 60 O. S. 96 (1899).

Subject to police regulations. A corporation holds its property subject to all valid police regulations.
Millcreek, etc., Co. v. St. Bernard, 8 N. P. 288; 11 L. D. 454 (1901).

Corporate property as a trust fund. A corporation holds its property as trustee for the benefit of its creditors and stockholders.
Niles v. Olszak, 87 O. S. 229 (1912).
Rouse v. Bank, 46 O. S. 493, 503 (1899).
Bank v. Mfg. Co., 67 O. S. 306, 314 (1902).
See note to § 8684.

Real property. Office building. etc., companies, see § 10210.
Real estate companies, see §§ 8648-8650.
A corporation may acquire and hold such real property as may be necessary in the transaction of its business.
Lessee of Overmyer v. Williams, 15 Ohio 26 (1846).
Walsh v. Barton, 24 O. S. 28, 42 (1873).
See Baldwin v. Egan, 11 C. C. n. s. 584 (1908); aff'd, no rep., 84 O. S. 460.
It may receive a conveyance of land as security for, or in payment of, a debt.
Morris v. Way, 16 Ohio 469 (1847).

Purchase for unauthorized purpose. Where a corporation purchases unnecessary land, or acquires land for unauthorized purposes, the rules governing other *ultra vires* contracts apply. The corporation may resell such land and the title of its vendee becomes indefeasible, both the corporation and its vendor being estopped from questioning the transaction.
Walsh v. Barton, 24 O. S. 28, 42 (1873).
While the corporation holds such land its proprietary rights can not be questioned by persons with whom it has made contracts relating to the land and who have received benefits thereunder. The corporation may collect rent, and may recover damages for breach of contract.
Hamilton, etc., Co. v. C. H. & D. R. Co., 29 O. S. 341 (1876).
Rector v. Hartford Deposit Co., 190 Ill. 380; 60 N. E. Rep. 528.

Miscellaneous. A corporation having purchased land at a judicial sale and acquiesced in the confirmation of the sale can not, in error proceedings, set up its want of power to purchase.
Bank of U. S. v. White, Wright 574 (1834).
A turnpike company can not acquire the fee in land occupied by it, under an easement sufficient for its purposes, for the purpose of preventing a railroad company from building a bridge over the road.

Wooster Turnpike Co. v. C. P. & V. R. Co., 15 C. C. 268; 8 C. D. 269 (1897).

Commercial paper. A corporation may acquire commercial paper in the course of its corporate business.

Straus v. Eagle Ins. Co., 5 O. S. 59, 62 (1855).
Durrell v. Belding, 9 C. C. 74; 4 C. D. 264 (1894).
Cuyahoga, etc., Co. v. Lewis, 1 Cleve. L. Rec. 15 (Dist. Ct.).

A note received by a corporation is presumed to have been acquired in the usual course of business.

Straus v. Eagle Ins. Co., 5 O. S. 59, 62 (1855).

A corporation authorized to purchase commercial paper has no power to purchase a note for the sole purpose of assisting a third person in collecting the same by acquiring a lien on stock of the corporation owned by the maker of the note.

White's Bank v. Toledo Ins. Co., 12 O. S. 601 (1861).

An insurance company has no power to purchase a promissory note on credit for the purpose of setting off such note against a claim against the company.

Straus v. Eagle Ins. Co., 5 O. S. 59 (1855).

Sale and conveyance of corporate property. The power of disposition is a necessary incident to the power of acquiring and holding property and a corporation has, in general, the same capacity to sell and convey its property that an individual has.

Reynolds v. Commissioners, 5 Ohio 204 (1831).
Nearing v. Toledo, etc., Co., 9 C. C. 596; 6 C. D. 664 (1893).
Wiswell v. First Congregational Church, 14 O. S. 31, 43 (1862).

At a time when individuals were permitted by law to prefer certain creditors, it was held that an insolvent corporation had no such power, the corporate property being a trust fund for creditors and stockholders.

Rouse v. Bank, 46 O. S. 493 (1889).

Corporate property may be levied on by creditors and sold at judicial sale.

Coe v. Knox County Bank, 10 O. S. 412 (1859).
Coe v. Peacock, 14 O. S. 187 (1863).

Entire property. Sales of the entire property of corporations are regulated by statute.

See §§ 8710 to 8718.

Corporate franchise. A corporation has no power to sell or convey its franchise to be a corporation:

Coe v. Columbus, etc., Co., 10 O. S. 372 (1859).
Atkinson v. Marietta, etc., Co., 15 O. S. 21 (1864).
Railroad Co. v. Furnace Co., 37 O. S. 321, 330 (1881).
except when specially authorized by statute.
State v. Sherman, 22 O. S. 411, 428 (1872).

Property necessary in performance of public duty. A railroad company or other corporation which owes duties to the public can not alienate property or franchises which are essential to the performance of such duties.

Railroad Co. v. Furnace Co., 37 O. S. 321, 330 (1881).
Coe v. Columbus, etc., Co., 10 O. S. 372 (1859).

Authority of corporate officers to convey. Authority to make a sale or conveyance of corporate property is vested in the board of directors.

§ 8660 and note.

But instruments of conveyance are usually executed by one or more executive officers. A deed executed in the name of the corporation, by its

president, under the corporate seal, is presumed to have been authorized
by the directors, and is prima facie valid.

R. R. Co. v. Harter, 26 O. S. 426 (1875).
Bank v. Flour Co., 41 O. S. 552, 557 (1885).
Sheehan v. Davis, 17 O. S. 571, ,581 (1867).
Bosche v. Toledo, etc., Co., 14 C. C. 289, 295; 7 C. D. 377 (1897).

The officer who executes a deed on behalf of a corporation and
affixes its corporate seal is the proper person to acknowledge the deed.

 Sheehan v. Davis, 17 O. S. 571 (1867).

Form and execution of corporate deeds and instruments. The word
"successors" is not necessary, in a deed to a corporation, in order to
convey a fee simple.

Railway v. Bosworth, 46 O. S. 81, 84 (1888).

A conveyance by a corporation should be in the name of the corporation. A conveyance in the name of an individual, although describing
him as an officer of the corporation, is not the act of the corporation,
and does not transfer the title;

Norris v. Dains, 52 O. S. 215 (1894).
Hatch v. Barr, 1 Ohio 390 (1824).

although good as an equitable conveyance as against the corporation.

Bundy v. Iron Co., 38 O. S. 300 (1882).

Where the corporate name was not signed, but in the body of the
deed the corporation was named as grantor, and the duly authorized
officer affixed the corporate seal and subscribed his own name to the
instrument, it was held properly executed.

Sheehan v. Davis, 17 O. S. 571 (1867).
Hays v. Galion, etc., Co., 29 O. S. 330, 334 (1876).

A contract signed in the corporate name, followed by the signatures
and titles of its officers, is the contract of the corporation alone, although
the word "we" is used in the body of the instrument and the word "by"
does not precede the signatures of the officers.

Aungst v. Creque, 72 O. S. 551 (1905).

Corporate seal. Necessity of. The omission of the corporate seal
does not invalidate a corporate deed which is otherwise properly executed. The use of the corporate seal by a corporation is not compulsory.

East End Building & Loan Co. v. Hughey, 16 C. C. 19; 8 C. D.
       724 (1898).
Poyser v. Standard Paving Brick Co., 46 W. L. B. 84 (Sup. Ct. 1901).
In re Farmer's Supply Co., 170 Fed. 502 (D. C. 1909).

See below *Corporate seal.*

Stockholder or officer as witness or notary. A stockholder of a
corporation may act as notary public and take the acknowledgment of a
person executing a deed to it.

Reed v. Loan Co., 68 O. S. 280 (1903).

A stockholder may act as witness to such a deed.

Reed v. Loan Co., 68 O. S. 280 (1903).
Johnson v. Turner, 7 Ohio (pt. 2); 216 (1836).

The secretary and treasurer of a corporation may, as notary, take
the acknowledgment of a person executing a mortgage to it.

Hortón v. Columbian, etc., Soc., 6 W. L. B. 141.

Proof of execution. A corporate deed, if objected to, can not be
given in evidence without proof of its execution. The signature of the
president does not prove itself, nor is it proven by the corporate seal.

Walsh v. Barton, 24 O. S. 28, 41 (1873).
See 9 W. L. B. 253, paper by S. H. Wilder.

CORPORATE SEAL.

Necessity and effect. At common law the signature of a corporation was its corporate seal.

Tiffin v. Shawhan, 43 O. S. 178, 185 (1885).
See Railway Co. v. Lynde, 55 O. S. 23, 49 (1896).
Cincinnati v. Cameron, 33 O. S. 364 (1878).

Under present statutes a corporate deed or mortgage, when otherwise properly executed, is not rendered invalid by the omission to affix the corporate seal.

Poyser v. Standard Paving Brick Co., 46 W. L. B. 84 (Sup. Ct. 1901).
East End, etc., Co. v. Hughey, 16 C. C. 19; 8 C. D. 724 (1898).
In re Farmers' Supply Co., 170 Fed. 502 (D. C. 1909).

But the affixing of the corporate seal to an instrument affords a presumption that the instrument has been authorized by the board of directors and, when otherwise properly executed, renders the instrument prima facie valid.

Sheehan v. Davis, 17 O. S. 571 (1867).
Perin v. Cincinnati, etc., R. Co., 17 W. L. B. 261; s. c., 18 W. L. B. 382 (Super. Ct. Cin.).
R. R. Co. v. Harter, 26 O. S. 426 (1875).
Bank v. Flour Co., 41 O. S. 552, 557 (1885).
Stetson v. Durrell, 3 W. L. B. 154.
See 38 W. L. B. 204 (paper by Clement Bates).
9 W. L. B. 19 (paper by F. M. Coppock).

Negotiable bonds of a corporation do not become "sealed instruments" and nonnegotiable by the affixing of the corporate seal thereto.

Railway Co. v. Lynde, 55 O. S. 23 (1896).
G. C. § 8111.

Certain instruments are required by special statutes to be executed under the corporate seal; including the deed of a railway company (§ 8761); certificate of amendment of articles of incorporation (§ 8721); statement of a foreign corporation (§ 179), and some certificates of railroad companies (§§ 9028, 8748, 9033, 9081), and turnpike companies (§§ 9260, 9262).

Form. The seal may be an impression upon the paper on which the instrument is written, or upon wax, wafer or other adhesive substance.

G. C. § 32.

Where a corporation had no seal, an instrument signed in the corporate name by the president, with his private seal, in scrawl, attached, was held valid against the corporation.

Western Female Seminary v. Blair, 1 Dis. 370 (Cin. Super. Ct. 1857).

POWER TO ACQUIRE ITS OWN STOCK.

It has been stated as a general principle, subject to some exceptions, that an Ohio corporation can not purchase or deal in its own stock. This principle was held to rest upon a lack of power in the corporation and not upon any statutory prohibition.

Coppin v. Greenlees. 38 O. S. 275, 279 (1882).
Morgan v. Lewis, 46 O. S. 1, 6 (1888).
State v. Oberlin, etc., Ass'n., 35 O. S. 258, 263 (1879).
C. & P. R. Co. v. Kelley, 5 O. S. 180, 193.
Stunt v. Newark, etc., Co., 22 C. C. 120; 12 C. D. 175 (1901); aff'd, no rep., 67 O. S. 555.
Merchants N. B. v. Overman Carriage Co., 17 C. C. 253; 9 C. D. 738 (1898).

Shaw v. Ohio Edison Inst. Co., 19 W. L. B. 292 (Super. Ct. Cin. 1888).

Lewis v. Reed, 5 W. L. B. 79 (1880).

Hubbard v. Riley, 3 W. L. B. 434 (1878).

De La Croix v. Eid Concrete Steel Co., 8 N. P. n. s. 489 (1909).

See Holcomb v. Gibson, 39 W. L. B. 380 (58 O. S. 710).

Some doubt has been expressed as to whether the foregoing statement should be recognized as a general rule since the abrogation of the double liability of stockholders in 1903.

Siders v. Gem City Concrete Co., 13 C. C. n. s. 481, 486; 23 C. D. 552 (1910); aff'd, no rep., weight of evidence being involved, 87 O. S. 519.

Mannington v. Hocking Valley Ry. Co., 8 O. L. R. 451, 465 (U. S. C. C. 1910).

State B. & T. Co. v. Mitchell Co., 14 N. P. n. s. 49 (1913).

Contra, De La Croix v. Eid Concrete Steel Co., 8 N. P. n. s. 489, 507 (1909).

It is not doubted, however, that where the purchase by a corporation of its own stock results in injury to creditors, or is not made in good faith, it may be set aside.

Siders v. Gem City Concrete Co., 13 C. C. n. s. 481, 488, 489; 23 C. D. 552 (1910); aff'd, no rep., 87 O. S. 519.

An executory agreement for the purchase by a corporation of its own stock can not be enforced either by action for specific performance or for damages.

Coppin v. Greenles, 38 O. S. 275 (1882).

An executed transaction comes within the general rules governing other *ultra vires* contracts which have been executed. Where a corporation gave its note for the purchase price of its own stock, and thereafter sold the stock, it can not defend against the note on the ground that it had no power to purchase the stock.

Siders v. Gem City Concrete Co., 13 C. C. n. s. 481; 23 C. D. 552 (1910); aff'd, no rep., 87 O. S. 519.

See Morgan v. Lewis, 46 O. S. 1, 7, 8 (1888).

Railway Co. v. Iron Co., 46 O. S. 44 (1888).

Hubbard v. Riley, 3 W. L. B. 434 (1878).

State B. & T. Co. v. Mitchell Co., 14 N. P. n. s. 49 (1913).

Where a corporation purchased stock from a dissatisfied stockholder with the assent of all other stockholders, at a time when the corporation was free from debt and the purchase was fully executed in good faith, being made to avoid dissensions among the directors and stockholders, the transaction was upheld.

State B. & T. Co. v. Mitchell Co., 14 N. P. n. s. 49 (1913).

To secure debt due to corporation. A corporation may buy or take its own stock in order to avoid loss on a preexisting debt due to it.

Taylor v. Miami Exporting Co., 6 Ohio 176 (1833).

Coppin v. Greenles, 38 O. S. 275, 278 (1882).

Morgan v. Lewis, 46 O. S. 1, 6 (1889).

State v. Building Assn, 35 O. S. 258, 263 (1879).

State v. Franklin Bank, 10 Ohio, 91, 97 (1840).

And it may obtain and enforce a lien on the stock to secure its claim.

Stafford v. Produce Exchange Banking Co., 61 O. S. 160 (1899).

Railway Co. v. Burke, 19 W. L. B. 27 (C. P. 1887).

Bellevue Bank v. Higbee, 4 C. C. 222; 2 C. D. 512 (1889); affirmed, 28 W. L. B. 336.

Stock fraudulently issued. A corporation may, in order to avoid loss, expend money to regain stock which has been fraudulently issued by its officers.

> Cincinnati, etc., R. Co. v. Duckworth, 2 C. C. 518; 1 C. D. 618 (1887); affirmed, 21 W. L. B. 36.

Rescission of exchange of stock for property. Where a corporation issued stock in exchange for property, but, other stockholders being dissatisfied, the transaction was rescinded by agreement and in good faith, the return of such stock to the corporation is not void.

> Morgan v. Lewis, 46 O. S. 1 (1888).
> Sanderson v. Aetna, etc., Co., 34 O. S. 442 (1878).
> Biggio v. Sandheger, 8 N. P. 13; 10 L. D. 319 (1900).
> State B. & T. Co. v. Mitchell Co., 14 N. P. n. s. 49 (1913).

For power of corporation to compromise with and release subscribers to stock see notes to §§ 8630 and 8674.

Stock issued under agreement to repurchase. Where stock was issued under an agreement by the corporation to repurchase the same, such agreement to repurchase may be enforced if the rights of creditors are not impaired.

> Zerkle v. Price, 5 N. P. 480; 7 L. D. 465.
> Shoemaker v. Goshen Township, 14 O. S. 569, 583 (1863).
> Weeden v. Lake Erie, etc., Co., 14 Ohio 563 (1846).
> Fleitman v. Stone Cotton Mills, 186 Fed. 466 (C. C. A. 1911).
> Compare Stunt v. Newark, etc., Co., 22 C. C. 120; 12 C. D. 175 (1901); aff'd, no rep., 67 O. S. 555.

On retirement of officer. The retirement of the owner of stock from his corporate office does not authorize the corporation to purchase his stock.

> Merchants N. B. v. Overman Carriage Co., 17 C. C. 253, 255; 9 C. D. 738 (1898).
> See Siders v. Gem City Concrete Co., 13 C. C. n. s. 481, 489 (1910).
> State B. & T. Co. v. Mitchell Co., 14 N. P. n. s. 49 (1913).

What constitutes a purchase by a corporation of its own stock. The redemption of preferred stock issued by a railroad company under G. C. § 8817 and 8805 is not a reduction of its capital stock by a purchase of its shares.

> Mannington v. Hocking Valley Ry. Co., 183 Fed. 133; 8 O. L. R. 451; 16 O. F. D. 552 (U. S. C. C. 1910); s. c., 9 N. P. n. s. 641; 20 L. D. 468 (C. P.).

The purchase of stock by a director, as trustee for the corporation, authorized by a resolution of the directors and paid for by notes of the corporation, is a purchase by the corporation.

> Merchants N. B. v. Overman Carriage Co., 17 C. C. 253; 9 C. D. 738 (1898).

Status of stock in itself acquired by a corporation. Stock which has been transferred to the corporation by which it was issued becomes treasury stock and is held subject to control and disposition by the directors.

> See Taylor v. Miami Exporting Co., 6 Ohio 176, 220 (1833).
> Allen v. De Largerberger. 20 W. L. B. 368.

It can not be voted while held by the corporation.

> Allen v. De Largerberger. 20 W. L. B. 368.
> Ryan v. Miami Valley R. Co., 10 Am. L. R. 263, 267 (1881).

TO ACQUIRE AND HOLD STOCK OF OTHER CORPORATIONS.

See § 8683 and note.

TO EXECUTE AND INDORSE COMMERCIAL PAPER.

A corporation may become a party to commercial paper in the course of its corporate business. A note or bill of exchange made or received by a corporation is prima facie valid.

Straus v. Eagle Ins. Co., 5 O. S. 59, 62 (1855).
Larwell v. Hanover Sgs. Fund Soc., 40 O. S. 274, 282 (1883).
Andres v. Morgan, 62 O. S. 236, 248 (1900).
Hays v. Galion, etc., Co., 29 O. S. 330 (1876).
White's Bank v. Toledo Ins. Co., 12 O. S. 601 (1861).

A bona fide holder of the note of a corporation is protected to the same extent as the bona fide holder of a note made by an individual.

Holmes v. Hayes, 32 W. L. B. 346, 349 (52 O. S. 617; Sup. Ct. 1894).

Accommodation paper. A corporation has no power to become an accommodation maker or endorser of commercial paper. Such an instrument can not be enforced against the corporation by a holder having notice of its character.

Benedict v. Market N. B., 4 N. P. 231; 6 L. D. 320; s. c., 19 C. C. 408; 10 C. D. 505.
In re Continental Iron Co., 2 O. L. R. 563 (1904).
See Vos v. Building Ass'n., 9 W. L. B. 194 (Super. Ct. Cin.).

Where it did not appear that a corporation was insolvent and that it had ceased to prosecute the objects for which it was created at a time when its funds were used to pay notes, executed by its president and endorsed by the corporation, held by a bank to cover a loss by the failure of a former corporation, the funds so used are not so impressed with a trust as to be recoverable by the trustees in bankruptcy of the corporation.

Haines v. Bank, 203 Fed. 225 (C. C. A. 1913).

Corporate note payable to officer. It has been held that a note signed in the corporate name by an officer of the corporation and made payable to himself is presumptively unauthorized and that subsequent purchasers take with notice.

In re Hartwell Furniture Co., 7 O. L. R. 555 (1909).
In re Continental Iron Co., 2 O. L. R. 563 (1904).
Arnkens v. Rouse, 26 W. L. B. 221 (C. P. 1891).
Compare in re Troy, etc., Co., 136 Fed. 420 (1905); aff'd, 142 Fed. 1038.
Railway Co. v. Bank, 56 O. S. 351 (1897). (Stock certificates required by statute to be signed by president and secretary.)
See G. C. § 8147.

Form. A note reading "we promise to pay . . . " and signed "The A. B. Co., C. D., Secy. & Treas.; E. F. Pres.," is on its face the note of the corporation alone and not the note of the officers personally.

Aungst v. Creque, 72 O. S. 551 (1905).

For note held properly executed although corporate name not signed.

See Hays v. Galion, etc., Co., 29 O. S. 330, 334 (1876).
See note to § 8660. *Officers and agents. Liability.*

MISCELLANEOUS POWERS.

To act as trustee. A corporation may hold property in trust for purposes within its corporate powers.

State v. Toledo, 3 C. C. n. s. 468; 13 C. D. 327 (1902); s. c., 5 C. C. n. s. 277; 16 C. D. 628.
Chapin v. School District, 1 Warden's W. L. B. 227.
Vidal v. Girard, 43 U. S. (2 How.) 128 (187-188).
Perin v. Carey, 65 U. S. (24 How.) 465.

But it can not act as administrator or assignee for creditors unless expressly authorized by statute.

Schumacher v. McCalip, 69 O. S. 500 (1904).

In re Commercial Bank, 6 O. L. R. 682 (1909).

Where a trust company is appointed executor by a probate court having jurisdiction, the appointment can not be collaterally attacked.

Bank v. Telegraph Co., 79 O. S. 89 (1908).

Powers of trust companies, see §§ 9816 to 9819, 9828.

To enter into partnership. A corporation has no power to enter into partnership with an individual or another corporation.

Guerinck v. Alcott, 66 O. S. 94, 104 (1902).

Merchants N. B. v. Wehrmann, 69 O. S. 160, 173, 174 (1903); reversed on other grounds, 202 U. S. 295; 4 O. L. R. 344.

Merchants N. B. v. Standard Wagon Co., 6 N. P. 264; 9 L. D. 380; affirmed, 7 N. P. 539; 10 L. D. 81; affirmed, no rep., 65 O. S. 559.

See State v. Standard Oil Co., 49 O. S. 137, 185 (1892).

But a corporation may enter into a joint adventure, the purposes of which are within its corporate purposes.

Guerinck v. Alcott, 66 O. S. 94, 105 (1902).

Pomeroy Salt Co. v. Davis, 21 O. S. 555, 573 (1871).

Mestier v. Chevalier Pavement Co., 108 La. An. 562; 32 So. Rep. 520.

And may become a member of a voluntary association.

Miller, etc., Co. v. Laidlaw, etc., Co., 4 N. P. n. s. 554; 17 L. D. 499 (1905).

See Webster v. Taplin, Rice & Co., 9 C. C. n. s. 587; 19 C. D. 543 (1904); aff'd, no rep., 76 O. S. 590.

To become surety or guarantor. A corporation has, in general, no power to become surety on a bond, or to guarantee the contract or debt of an individual. A corporation engaged in sale of building materials can not guarantee the performance of a building contract, although by such guaranty it is enabled to sell materials to the contractor. Performance of such a contract by the party to whom the guaranty is given does not estop the corporation from denying its power to give the guaranty.

Humbolt Min. Co. v. American, etc., Co., 62 Fed. 356; 9 O. F. D. 153 (C. C. A. 1894).

Contra, Glenville v. Prout, 6 N. P. 152; 8 L. D. 99 (C. P.).

Builders Supply Co. v. Investment Co., 14 N. P. n. s. 383 (1913).

A corporation may give security for the debt of a third person, where it is indebted to such third person, and the real object and effect of the transaction is to secure the debt owing by the corporation.

Bank v. Flour Co., 41 O. S. 552 (1885).

A corporation selling bonds, not its own property, has no power to guarantee their payment. But, in making the sale, it may agree to repurchase the bonds on demand at the same price.

First N. B. v. Schaeffer, 16 C. C. 457; 9 C. D. 182 (1898).

A corporation has no power to become an accommodation maker or endorser of commercial paper. Such an instrument can not be enforced against the corporation by a holder having notice of its character.

Benedict v. Market N. B., 4 N. P. 231; 6 L. D. 320; s. c., 19 C. C. 408; 10 C. D. 505.

In re Continental Iron Co., 2 O. L. R. 563 (1904).

For guaranty by railroad company of bonds of coal company see note to § 8806.

To carry on professional business. A corporation can not carry on professional business.

§ 8623: State v. Laylin, 73 O. S. 90 (Law).
Union Painless Dentists Co. v. Mullen, 6 O. L. R. 475; 19 L. D. 136 (Dentistry).
Youngstown, etc., Ry. v. Kessler, 84 O. S. 74 (Medicine).

To borrow money, issue bonds, etc. See § 8705 to 8709 and notes.

Section 8628. (Same or similar names.) The secretary of state shall not file or record any articles of incorporation wherein the corporate name is likely to mislead the public as to the nature or purpose of the business its charter authorizes, nor if such name is that of an existing corporation, or so similar thereto as to be likely to mislead the public, unless the written consent of the existing corporation, signed by its president and secretary, be filed with such articles. (R. S. Sec. 3238; March 31, 1902, 95 v. 76; April 27, 1896, 92 v. 320; R. S. 1880.)

Requirement as to name of corporation for profit, see § 8625.
Change of name, § 8719.
The secretary of state has discretion to determine whether a name is misleading.
Rep. Atty. Gen. 1911-1912, p. 127.

Filing of articles not conclusive. The action of the secretary of state in receiving and filing articles of incorporation is not conclusive against another corporation having a similar name. The older corporation may enforce its rights by injunction.
Cincinnati Vici Shoe Co. v. Cincinnati Shoe Co., 7 N. P. 135; 9 L. D. 579 (1899).
Backus Oil Co. v. Backus, etc., Co., 5 W. L. B. 546 (1880).

Incorporation no defense where name infringes. The use by a corporation of a name which infringes the trade name of an individual, or of another corporation, may be enjoined. The fact of being incorporated by such name is no defense.
Thayer, etc., Co. v. Thayer Co., 6 N. P. 300; 9 L. D. 288.
Backus Oil Co. v. Backus, etc., Co., 5 W. L. B. 546 (1880).
R. W. Rogers Co. v. Wm. Rogers Mfg. Co., 70 Fed. 1017 (1895).
Bissell etc., Works v. Bissel, etc., Co., 121 Fed. 357 (1902).
Chickering v. Chickering, 120 Fed. 69 (1903).
Higgins v. Higgins Soap Co., 144 N. Y. 462.
Bear Lithia Springs Co. v. Great Bear Spring Co., 71 N. J. Eq. 595; 71 Atl. 383.

Corporation not for profit. A corporation not for profit may, by injunction, protect its name against infringement.
People v. Rose, 225 Ill. 496; 80 N. E. 293.
Salvation Army in U. S. v. American Salvation Army, 120 N. Y. Suppl. 471; 135 App. Div. 268.
B. P. O. E. v. Improved B. P. O. E. (Tenn. 1909); 118 S. W. 389.
B. P. O. E. v. Improved B. P. O. E., 111 N. Y. Suppl. 1067.

Name misleading as to nature of business. "The Trustee company" may be adopted by a real estate company proposing to sell certificates entitling the holders to undivided interests in land held by the company as agent or trustee for all of the investors.
Rep. Atty. Gen. 1910-1911, p. 218.

Right to adopt name of individual or former partnership. A corporation can not adopt or use the name of an individual so as to infringe the name of another corporation.

Thayer, etc., Co. v. Thayer, etc., Co., 6 N. P. 300; 9 L. D. 288.

L. Martin Co. v. L. Martin & Wickes Co., 75 N. J. Eq. 39; 71 Atl. 409.

See Hall's Safe Co v. Herring, etc., Co., 146 Fed. 37; 15 O. F. D. 37 (C. C. A. 1906).

Where partnership assets, including good will, are sold through a receiver, and the purchaser transfers the same to a corporation, the corporation may adopt the name previously used by the partnership.

Snyder Mfg. Co. v. Snyder, 54 O. S. 86 (1896).

A corporation may adopt and use the name of an individual connected with it provided it is not so used as to mislead the public into a belief that its products are those of another corporation having a similar name.

Hall's Safe Co. v. Herring, etc., Co., 146 Fed. 37; 15 O. F. D. 37 (C. C. A. 1906).

See Star Dist. Co. v. Mihalovitch Co., 23 L. D. 342 (C. P. 1911).

And may, by injunction, protect such name against infringement.

French Bros. Dairy Co. v. Giacin, 12 C. C. n. s. 134 (1909); affirming 8 N. P. n. s. 549.

Use of word "Edisonia" in name of corporation giving moving picture exhibitions, and authorized to use "Edison" kinetoscopes therein, held not calculated to mislead the public to believe that the manufacturer of the machines was interested in the exhibitions or the corporation.

Edison v. Mills-Edisonia, 74 N. J. Eq. 521; 70 Atl. Rep. 191.

A corporation which so adopts the name of another company, composed mainly of the same individuals, as reasonably to induce the belief that they are one and the same company, will be bound by contracts made by a common agent of the two, with parties acting in such belief, although made in the name of the other company and in its behalf.

Adams v. Brown, 16 O. S. 75 (1865).

Names held to be infringements. "National Liberty League" infringes the name "National Liberty Legion."

People v. Rose, 225 Ill. 496; 80 N. E. 293.

"Grand Lodge Knights of Pythias" is infringed by the name "Grand Lodge Knights of Pythias of North America, South America, Europe, Asia," etc.

Creswill v. Grand Lodge K. P., 133 Ga. 837; 67 S. E. 188.

"The George A. Thayer Co." is an imitation of "The George A. Thayer Carpet Cleaning and Rug Manufacturing Co."

Thayer, etc., Co. v. Thayer Co., 6 N. P. 300; 9 L. D. 288 (1899).

"The Kansas City Real Estate Exchange" is an imitation of "The Kansas City Real Estate and Stock Exchange Co."

State v. McGrath, 92 Mo. 355.

"The Holmes, Booth & Atwood Mfg. Co." is an imitation of "Holmes, Booth & Hayden."

Holmes, etc., v. Holmes, etc., Co., 37 Conn. 278.

"United States Commercial Agency & Collecting Co." is an infringement of "United States Mercantile Reporting Co."

In re U. S. Mercantile Co., 4 N. Y. Supp. 916.

Names held not to be infringements. "Corning Glass Works" held not so similar to "Corning Cut Glass Company" as to confuse the public where the companies produce different kinds of glass and cater to different customers.

Corning Glass Works v. Corning Cut Glass Co., 197 N. Y. 173;
90 N. E. 449.

"John Cashatt Company" is not so similar to the "Cashatt Cigar
Company" as to mislead the public.
Rep. Atty. Gen. 1908, p. 79.

"Bank of Michigan" does not necessarily infringe the name "Michigan Savings Bank."
Michigan Savings Bank v. Dime Sav. Bank, 162 Mich. 297; 127 N. W.
364.

Acquiring new name by usage or reputation. See Rep. Atty. Gen.
1904-1905, p. 110.

Misnomer. A devise or conveyance is not defeated by a misnomer
provided the corporation intended can be sufficiently ascertained from
the terms used.
Chapin v. School District, 1 Gaz. 227.

A stock subscription can not be avoided because of a mistake in the
corporate name, where there is no doubt as to the corporation intended.
Milford, etc., Turnpike Co. v. Brush, 10 Ohio 111, 114 (1840).
Commissioners v. Perry, 5 Ohio 56 (1831).
Royce v. Tyler, 2 C. C. 175, 183; 1 C. D. 428 (1887).
See Biggio v. Sandheger, 8 N. P. 13; 10 L. D. 316 (1900).

In a suit against a corporation, the name of which is composed of
several words, a slight mistake in the name such as the omission of one
word, will be disregarded by the court unless pleaded in abatement.
State v. Telephone Co., 36 O. S. 296 (1880).
See Cleveland, etc., R. Co. v. Fredenbur, 3 C. C. 23; 2 C. D. 15 (1887).

Section 8629.   (Certified copy evidence of incorporation.)
A copy of articles of incorporation so filed, and duly certified
by the secretary of state, shall be prima facie evidence of
the existence of the corporation therein named. (R. S. Sec.
3238; March 31, 1902, 95 v. 76; April 27, 1896, 92 v. 320;
R. S. 1880.)

Certified copy.

When not sufficient evidence of corporate existence. The filing of
articles of incorporation does not create a corporation for profit. The
articles are merely authority to the incorporators to do so. The corporate
existence does not commence until the requisite stock has been subscribed
and the first installment paid thereon and the directors chosen.
State v. Insurance Co., 49 O. S. 440 (1892).
See note to § 8627.

In appropriation proceedings by a corporation, it must prove not
only the filing of articles of incorporation, but also complete organization, by the subscription and payment of the required percentage on its
capital stock and the due and regular election of directors.
Queen City Telephone Co. v. Cincinnati, 73 O. S. 64 (1905).

Effect and admissibility. The certificate of the secretary of state
can only be as to the correctness of the copy; not that the articles are
valid.
Doyle v. Mizner, 42 Mich. 332.

Where the certified copy shows that the articles are prima facie invalid,
the instrument can not be used as evidence.
Baptist Church v. R. R. Co., 4 Mackey, 43 (D. C.).
McCallon v. Hybernia Soc., 70 Cal. 163.

Harris v. McGregor, 29 Cal. 127.

But unauthorized provisions contained in the articles do not render a certified copy inadmissible, where it contains all the provisions required by statute.

Toledo, etc., Ry. v. Toledo, etc., Ry., 6 C. C. 362, 391; 3 C. D. 493, 507 (1892).

See note to § 8625.

Imperfect articles can not be aided, varied or contradicted by evidence aliunde.

Atty. Gen. v. Lorman, 59 Mich. 157.

Hallett v. Harrower, 33 Barb. (N. Y.) 537.

People v. Selfridge, 52 Cal. 331.

Where a condition precedent to the right of incorporation is prescribed by law, a certified copy of articles is inadmissible in the absence of evidence as to performance of such condition precedent.

Raccoon River Nav. Co. v. Eagle, 29 O. S. 238 (1876).

ALLEGATION AND PROOF OF CORPORATE EXISTENCE.

In an action by a corporation, either foreign or domestic, its petition need not aver that it is a corporation. Such an averment, if made, is mere surplusage, and a general denial to the petition will not require proof of such averment.

Brady v. National Supply Co., 64 O. S. 267 (1901); affirming 19 C. C. 687; 10 C. D. 27.

Elektron Mfg. Co. v. Jones Bros. Co., 8 C. C. 311; 4 C. D. 555 (1894).

Minzey v. Marcy Mfg. Co., 6 C. C. n. s. 593; 15 C. D. 593 (1903).

Illinois, etc., Co. v. Whitman, 13 N. P. n. s. 362; 23 L. D. 12 (1911).

See Spence v. Insurance Co., 40 O. S. 517 (1884).

To raise the issue of nul tiel corporation the defendant must specially plead that the plaintiff is not a corporation, in which event the plaintiff must prove its corporate existence.

Brady v. National Supply Co., 64 O. S. 267 (1901); affirming 19 C. C. 687; 10 C. D. 27.

Smith v. Weed Sewing Machine Co., 26 O. S. 562 (1875).

Lewis v. Bank, 12 Ohio 146 (1843).

Where a corporation is defendant in an action involving its charter, powers or franchises, the same must be specially pleaded in the petition. If a foreign corporation, the name of the state of organization and the substantial terms of its charter, etc., should be set forth.

Brady v. National Supply Co., 64 O. S. 267 (1901).

Devoss v. Gray, 22 O. S. 159 (1871).

See State v. Granville, etc., Soc., 11 Ohio 9 (1841).

Streit v. Hoster Brewing Co., 12 L. D. 619 (C. P. 1902).

In appropriation proceedings by a corporation, it must prove its complete organization, including the due and regular election of directors. A general denial places the burden of proof of such organization on the plaintiff.

Queen City Telephone Co. v. Cincinnati, 73 O. S. 64 (1905).

See note to § 11046.

In criminal cases. In an indictment for burglary or larceny it is not necessary to aver or prove that the injured party was incorporated.

Murphy v. State, 36 O. S. 628 (1881).

Burke v. State, 34 O. S. 79 (1877).

Hamilton v. State. 34 O. S. 82 (1877).

See also Calkins v. State, 18 O. S. 366 (1868).

How proved. The existence of a corporation for profit may be proved by a certified copy of the articles, the certificate of subscription, and the corporate minutes showing the election and qualification of directors and officers.

> Toledo, etc., Co. v. Toledo, etc., Co., 26 W. L. B. 172 (Probate Ct. 1891); s. c., 6 C. C. 362, 391; 3 C. D. 493 (1892); affirmed, 50 O. S. 603.
> See Memphis, etc., Packet Co. v. Fogarty, 9 C. C. 418; 6 C. D. 375 (1895).

Section 8630. (Subscription books.) The persons named in the articles of incorporation of a corporation for profit, or a majority of them, shall order books to be opened for subscriptions to the capital stock of the corporation at such time or times and place or places as they deem expedient. (R. S. Sec. 3242; April 6, 1891, 88 v. 280; March 5, 1883, 80 v. 42; R. S. 1880; May 1, 1852, 50 v. 274, § 9; S. & C. 276.)

> Payment of subscriptions. See § 8632 and note.
> Enforcement of subscriptions and defenses. See § 8674 and note.
> Subscriptions to increased stock. See note to § 8698.
> The opening of subscription books, though one, is not the exclusive mode in which subscriptions to stock may be made. A subscription is not invalid because made on a separate sheet of paper.
> Ashtabula etc., R. Co. v. Smith, 15 O. S. 328, 337 (1864).

SUBSCRIPTIONS TO STOCK.

> **Before incorporation.** A mutual agreement between individuals to become stockholders in a corporation thereafter to be organized is valid.
> Doan v. Rogan, 79 O. S. 372, 386 (1909).
> But such an agreement differs from a mere subscription to stock made before incorporation. A subscription before incorporation is a continuing offer only and not a present contract. Prior to incorporation no person is authorized to accept the subscription. Such a subscription may be withdrawn by the person making it, providing he acts before the corporation is organized and his subscription accepted.
> Mill Co. v. Felt, 87 Me. 234.
> Hudson, etc., Co. v. Tower, 161 Mass. 10.
> Auburn Bolt Works v. Schultz, 143 Pa. St. 256.
> See Wallace v. Townsend, 43 O. S. 537 (1885).
> It is held in many states that where such a subscription is not withdrawn, but permitted to stand until the corporation is organized and the subscription accepted, the contract becomes complete and enforceable.
> Nebraska Chicory Co. v. Lednicky, 79 Neb. 587; 113 N. W. 245.
> McNaught v. Fisher, 96 Fed. 168 (1899).
> Athol Music Hall Co. v. Carey, 116 Mass. 471.
> Planters', etc., Co. v. Webb, 144 Ala. 666.
> Cook on Corporations, § 72.
> Thompson on Corporations, §§ 521, 522.
> In Ohio, however, it has been held that subsequent incorporation and acceptance of the subscription do not render a prior subscription enforceable.
> Dayton, etc., Co. v. Coy, 13 O. S. 84, 91 (1864).
> See Milford, etc., Co. v. Brush, 10 Ohio 111, 113, 114 (1840).
> Where the stock subscription book shows that the subscriptions were made after incorporation, evidence is not admissible to prove that in fact the subscriptions were made before incorporation.
> Royce & Pulling v. Tyler, 2 C. C. 175; 1 C. D. 428 (1887).

After incorporation.

Received by whom. After the filing of articles of incorporation the incorporators are authorized to receive subscriptions.

Sims v. Street Railroad Co., 37 O. S. 556, 565 (1882).

Subscriptions received by the incorporators after books have been opened are not void for want of mutuality but are binding.

Milford, etc., Co. v. Brush, 10 Ohio 113, 114 (1840).

Ashtabula, etc., R. R. Co. v. Smith, 15 O. S. 334, 336 (1864).

The right to dispose of stock which remains unsubscribed after the directors are elected and qualified is vested in the board of directors.

Sims v. Street Railroad Co., 37 O. S. 565 (1882).

See James v. C. H. & D. R. Co., 2 Dis. 261, 275 (Super. Ct. Cin. 1858.)

Should be in writing. A subscription for stock should be in writing. A verbal agreement to take shares is not enforceable in the absence of facts constituting an estoppel.

Fanning v. Insurance Co., 37 O. S. 339 (1881).

Hanes v. Dayton, etc., Co., 40 O. S. 98 (1883).

Persons who have not subscribed for stock but who accept certificates of stock, issued to them directly by the corporation without full payment, may be liable. An agreement to pay the par value is implied from their acceptance of the certificate.

Handley v. Stutz, 139 U. S. 417, 427 (1891).

Gates v. Tippecanoe Stone Co., 57 O. S. 60 (1897).

In re Flood-Pratt Dairy Co., 7 O. L. R. 603; 16 O. F. D. 396 (1909).

First N. B. v. Patton Co., 13 C. C. n. s. 289 (1910).

See also note to § 8674.

Where stock is exchanged for property or services at an overvaluation, the persons receiving the stock may be treated as original subscribers to such stock, credited with the actual value of the property or services and sued as debtors for the unpaid balance.

Gates v. Tippecanoe Stone Co., 57 O. S. 60 (1897).

Kiskadden v. Steinle, 203 Fed. 375 (C. C. A. 1913).

Form. The form of a subscription to stock is not prescribed by statute. It need not contain a statement of the times of payment, as payment is provided for by statute. (§ 8632).

Chamberlain v. R. R. Co., 15 O. S. 225, 249 (1864).

Ashtabula, etc., R. Co. v. Smith, 15 O. S. 328, 336 (1864).

A subscription need not be made in the subscription book provided by the incorporators. It may be made on a separate sheet of paper.

Ashtabula, etc., R. Co. v. Smith, 15 O. S. 328, 336 (1864).

See Ohio, etc., College v. Love, 16 O. S. 20 (1864).

Is a contract creating a several, not joint, liability. A subscription received by incorporators is a contract.

Gaff v. Flesher, 33 O. S. 107, 112 (1877).

An ordinary subscription is a several, and not a joint, contract.

Smith v. Johnson, 57 O. S. 486, 490 (1898).

See Burnap v. Sylvania Butter So., 7 N. P. 217 (1894); reversed on other grounds, 12 C. C. 639; 5 C. D. 582.

Withdrawal and release of subscriptions. A subscription received by the incorporators or directors is a contract which can not be rescinded without the consent of both parties. The subscriber can not relieve himself from liability by attempting to withdraw or cancel his subscription.

Gaff v. Flesher, 33 O. S. 107, 112, 113, (1877).

The corporation can not release the subscriber to the prejudice of any intervening creditor.
   Gaff v. Flesher, 33 O. S. 107, 113 (1877).
   Royce & Pulling v. Tyler, 2 C. C. 175; 1 C. D. 428 (1887).
   North Fairmount, etc., Co. v. Ashbrook, 12 L. D. 10 (Super. Ct. Cin. 1901).
   Niles v. Olszak, 87 O. S. 229 (1912).
Directors have no power to release a subscriber except with the unanimous consent of the other subscribers.
   Royce & Pulling v. Tyler, 2 C. C. 175, 187; 1 C. D. 428 (1887).
Withdrawal of unaccepted offer to subscribe or of conditional subscription.
   See Wallace v. Townsend, 43 O. S. 537 (1885).
   Armstrong v. Karshner, 47 O. S. 276, 297 (1890).
   See below *Conditional Subscriptions.*

Compromise and release of subscription. Where there is a bona fide controversy as to the liability of the subscriber, or where the subscriber is insolvent, the directors may, for a valuable consideration, compromise with and release the subscriber.
   Warner v. Callender, 20 O. S. 190, 198 (1870).
   State v. Building Assn., 35 O. S. 258, 263 (1879).
   Wangerein v. Aspell, 47 O. S. 250 (1890).
   Biggio v. Sandheger, 8 N. P. 13, 15 (1900).
   See also Morgan v. Lewis, 46 O. S. 1 (1888).
   Sanderson v. Aetna Iron & Nail Co., 34 O. S. 442 (1878).
The agreement of compromise must be fully executed.
   Frost v. Johnson, 8 Ohio 393 (1838).

Subscriptions obtained by fraud. A person is entitled to relief where he has subscribed to stock relying on material and fraudulent representations, made by authorized agents of the corporation, as to the past or present status of the corporate enterprise.
   False statements as to the future intention, purpose or expectation of the corporation do not, as a rule, entitle a subscriber to relief.
   Armstrong v. Karshner, 47 O. S. 276, 294 (1890).
   Freeman v. Muth, 3 W. L. B. 914 (Dist. Ct. 1878).
   Fraudulent representations as to the amount of stock already subscribed (Nugent v. Cincinnati, etc., Ry. Co., 2 Dis. 302), and that the soliciting agent had seen the railway plans providing for bridges and culverts over the subscriber's farm (Freeman v. Muth, 3 W. L. B. 914), were held to entitle the subscriber to relief.
   Where a subscription was made on the faith of a prior subscription by another person, a fraudulent cancellation or alteration of such prior subscription will not affect the validity of the subsequent subscription.
   Jewett v. Railway, 34 O. S. 601 (1878).
   Delay by the subscriber to take action within a reasonable time after discovery of the fraud will defeat his right to relief where the rights of creditors intervene.
   Mansfield v. Woods, Jenks & Co., 29 W. L. B. 111 (C. P.)
   Ryan v. Miami, etc., Ry. Co., 10 A. L. R. 263 (C. P. 1881).
   See Painesville N. B. v. King Varnish Co., 8 C. C. 563; 4 C. D. 511 (1894); reversed in part, 56 O. S. 774.

Remedies of subscriber. Action to rescind. A subscriber whose subscription was obtained by fraud may bring an action to set aside the subscription and to recover back the payments made by him thereon.
   Nugent v. Cincinnati, etc., R. Co., 2 Dis. 302 (1858).
   See Bank v. Greenville, etc., Co., 3 C. C. n. s. 372; 13 C. D. 274 (1899).

Defense to action on subscription. Fraud in obtaining a subscription is a defense to an action brought thereon against the subscriber except where rights of creditors have intervened.

Jewett v. Railway, 34 O. S. 601, 609 (1878).
Armstrong v. Karshner, 47 O. S. 276, 294 (1890).
Freeman v. Muth, 3 W. L. B. 914 (Dist. Ct. 1878).
James v. Cincinnati, etc., R. Co., 2 Dis. 261, 266 (1858).

Action for damages against officers or agents. The subscriber may bring an action for damages against the officers or agents of the corporation by whom the fraud was perpetrated. An officer or agent who makes material and false representations is personally liable where he had knowledge of their falsity, or where the representations were made under such circumstances that knowledge of their falsity must necessarily be imputed to him.

See Mason v. Moore, 73 O. S. 275, 291, 293 (1906).
Cable v. Bowlus, 21 C. C. 53; 11 C. D. 526 (1900); aff'd, 69 O. S. 563.
Schenck v. Knott, 13 C. C. n. s. 41 (1910).
Russell v. Weiler, 7 C. C. n. s. 596; 18 C. D. 175 (1905).
See G. C. § 6373-18.

Measure of damages. The measure of damages is the difference between the price paid for the stock and its actual value at the time of the sale.

Schenck v. Knott, 13 C. C. n. s. 41, 46 (1910).

The purchaser can not recover damages for mental suffering, disappointment or disgrace; nor in general can he recover punitive damages.

Cable v. Bowlus, 21 C. C. 53; 11 C. D. 526 (1900); aff'd, 69 O. S. 563.

Construction of subscriptions. A subscription must be construed with reference to the statutes in force at the time it was made. Such statutes enter into and form a part of the subscripion.

Armstrong v. Karshner, 47 O. S. 276, 299 (1890).
Jewett v. Railway, 34 O. S. 601, 607 (1878).
Mansfield, etc., R. Co. v. Stout, 26 O. S. 241, 254 (1875).
Compton v. Railway Co., 45 O. S. 592, 620 (1888).

Stipulation for interest to subscribers. Where interest is stipulated to be paid to subscribers on the amounts paid in on their subscriptions, such interest is not payable except out of the profits of the corporation.

Ryan v. Miami Valley Ry. Co., 10 A. L. R. 263, 265 (C. P. 1881).
Wood v. Pearce, 2 Dis. 411 (1858).
Painesville, etc., R. Co. v. King, 17 O. S. 534 (1867).
See § 8724.

Assignment of subscriptions.

By subscriber. A subscription to stock upon which installments have been paid may be assigned by the subscriber.

Railroad Co. v. Fink, 41 O. S. 321 (1884).

But an assignee is not liable for an unpaid balance on the subscription unless he accepted the assignment. The corporate books showing the transfer are, alone, not sufficient evidence of the acceptance so as to render him liable.

Tripp v. Appleman, 35 Fed. 19; 6 O. F. D. 71 (C. C. Ohio 1888).

By corporation. A corporation may assign subscriptions to its capital stock after calls have been made thereon.

Dungan v. Safford, 41 O. S. 15 (1884).
See note to § 8674.

Abandonment of subscriptions. An attempted withdrawal of his subscription, or a transfer by a subscriber to a fictitious person may perhaps be treated by the corporation as an abandonment of the subscription.

Royce v. Tyler, 2 C. C. 175, 185; 1 C. D. 428 (1887).
Muskingum, etc., Co. v. Ward, 13 Ohio 120 (1844).

But if the corporation subsequently does any act which amounts to an admission of the existence of the contract it can not thereafter elect to treat it as abandoned.

Railroad Co. v. Fink, 41 O. S. 321, 330 (1884).

CONDITIONAL SUBSCRIPTIONS.

A corporation may receive and accept conditional subscriptions to its stock at any time after its actual incorporation.

Armstrong v. Karshner, 47 O. S. 276, 295 (1890).
Ashtabula, etc., R. Co. v. Smith, 15 O. S. 328, 336 (1864).

Conditions in subscriptions may be precedent or subsequent.

Chamberlain v. Painesville, etc., Ry., 15 O. S. 247 (1864).

Conditions precedent. A subscription on a condition precedent should be accepted by the corporation and the condition must be performed by the corporation before the subscription can become absolute.

Chamberlain v. Painesville, etc., Ry., 15 O. S. 247 (1864).
Armstrong v. Karshner, 47 O. S. 276, 296 (1890).

Acceptance. Before acceptance by the corporation a subscription on a condition precedent may be revoked or withdrawn by the subscriber.

Wallace v. Townsend, 4 O. S. 537 (1885).

After acceptance by the corporation the subscriber can not, in general, withdraw or revoke the subscription, unless performance of the condition is unreasonably delayed. He is, as a rule, bound to await such performance.

Armstrong v. Karshner, 47 O. S. 276, 296 (1890).

When neither withdrawn by the subscriber nor expressly accepted by the corporation a subscription on a condition precedent is a continuing offer to subscribe, on the specified condition, which, on performance of the condition, becomes an absolute and unconditional subscription.

Armstrong v. Karshner, 47 O. S. 276, 296 (1890).
Mansfield, etc., Co. v. Stout, 26 O. S. 241 (1875).

Acceptance and performance are usually matters to be acted upon by the directors.

Ashtabula, etc., R. Co. v. Smith, 15 O. S. 328, 336 (1864).

Performance. A subscriber does not become a stockholder or liable on his subscription until the conditions precedent have been performed.

Railroad Co. v. Hinsdale, 45 O. S. 556, 570 (1888).

But on performance of the conditions the subscription becomes absolute and unconditional.

Ashtabula, etc., R. Co. v. Smith, 15 O. S. 328, 336 (1864).
Mansfield, etc., Co. v. Brown, 26 O. S. 223 (1875).

Performance of the conditions may be made by the corporation itself or by a consolidated company into which the original corporation was merged under statutes in force when the subscription was made which authorize the consolidated company to acquire debts due on subscriptions.

Mansfield, etc., Co. v. Brown, 26 O. S. 223 (1875).
Mansfield, etc., Co. v. Stout, 26 O. S. 241 (1875).

But conditional subscriptions can not be sold and transferred without statutory authority and an assignee under an unauthorized transfer can not recover although having performed the conditions.

Railroad Co. v. Hinsdale, 45 O. S. 556 (1888).

Where the corporation refuses to perform the condition the subscriber may recover back moneys paid by him on the subscription.

Weeden v. Lake Erie, etc., Co., 14 Ohio 563 (1846).

Waiver. The giving, by a subscriber, of a note in payment is prima facie a waiver of conditions precedent.

Chamberlain v. Painesville, etc., R. Co., 15 O. S. 225 (1864).

Four Mile, etc., Co. v. Bailey, 18 O. S. 208 (1868).

So also, payment of the first installment, voting the stock at an election of directors and acting as an officer of the company.

Dayton, etc., R. Co. v. Hatch, 1 Dis. 84 (Super. Ct. Cin. 1855).

Illegal conditions. A condition or stipulation in a subscription which attempts to secure to the subscriber advantages and privileges not common to other subscribers, and without their knowledge or consent, is contrary to public policy. The subscription is valid, and the condition or stipulation is no defense against its enforcement.

Jewett v. Railway, 34 O. S. 601, 609 (1878).

Stunt v. Newark, etc., Co., 22 C. C. 120; 12 C. D. 175 (1901); aff'd, no rep., 67 O. S. 555.

Rianhard v. Hovey, 13 Ohio 300 (1844).

Henry v. Vermillion, etc., Co., 17 Ohio 187 (1848).

Noble v. Callender, 20 O. S. 199 (1870).

Compare. Weeden v. Lake Erie. etc., Co., 14 Ohio 563 (1846).

Shoemaker v. Goshen Twp., 14 O. S. 569, 583 (1863).

Conditions subsequent. A subscription on a condition subsequent is not, strictly speaking, a conditional subscription.

Shoemaker v. Goshen Twp., 14 O. S. 569, 583 (1863).

It combines an absolute and unconditional subscription with an agreement by the corporation to perform one or more acts. For a breach of the agreement by the corporation the remedy is an action for damages.

Chamberlain v. Painesville, etc., R. Co., 15 O. S. 225 (1864).

Stunt v. Newark. etc., Co.. 22 C. C. 120, 123; 12 C. D. 175 (1901); aff'd, no rep., 67 O. S. 555.

Shoemaker v. Goshen Township, 14 O. S. 569 (1863).

Zerkle v. Price, 5 N. P. 480.

Conditions construed.

Precedent or subsequent. Where a subscription to the stock of a railroad company was given on condition that the road be "permanently located" on a given route and that a "freight house and depot be built" at a point named, it was held that the permanent location of the road on the specified route was a condition precedent, while the erection of the buildings was a condition subsequent.

Chamberlain v. Painesville, etc., R. Co., 15 O. S. 225 (1864).

Certain amount to be subscribed. A subscription not to be binding until subscriptions to a specified amount have been made becomes absolute and unconditional as soon as subscriptions in the required amount are obtained.

Emmitt v. Springfield, etc., R. Co., 31 O. S. 23 (1876).

Road to "pass through" or be "built" in a certain locality. Where the condition is that the road shall "pass through" or be "built" in a certain locality, the permanent location of the road, without its actual construction, is a compliance with such condition.

Ashtabula, etc., R. Co. v. Smith, 15 O. S. 328 (1864).
Mansfield, etc., R. Co. v. Stout, 26 O. S. 241, 254 (1875).
Warner v. Callender, 20 O. S. 190 (1870).
See Elder v. Bellaire, etc., Ry. Co., 1 C. C. 256; 1 C. D. 140 (1885).

Limiting amount and time of calls. A condition "that not more than ten percent shall be required at any one call, nor shall calls be made more frequently that once in sixty days" operates as a waiver of the statutory right of the directors to make calls in their discretion, and is not included in a general call for ten percent per month.
Mansfield, etc., R. Co. v. Pettis, 26 O. S. 259 (1875).

Agreement by corporation to repurchase stock. Where stock is issued by a corporation under an agreement giving the stockholder the right to return the stock and receive back the purchase money, the agreement is a condition subsequent which may be enforced if the rights of creditors are not impaired.
Zerkle v. Price, 5 N. P. 480; 7 L. D. 465.
Shoemaker v. Goshen Township, 14 O. S. 569, 583 (1863).
Fleitman v. Stone Coton Mills, 186 Fed. 466 (C. C. A. 1911).
See Weeden v. Lake Erie, etc., Co., 14 Ohio 563 (1846).
Hubbard v. Riley, 3 W. L. B. 434 (Dist. Ct. 1878).

Rules of construction of conditions. Where a subscription contract admits of two interpretations the one which facilitates the enterprise is preferred.
Ashtabula, etc., Co. v. Smith, 15 O. S. 328, 335 (1864).
And the interpretation which makes all the parts of the instrument consistent is preferred to one which makes them contradictory.
Lesher v. Karshner, 47 O. S. 302, 305 (1890).

Evidence as to conditions. Parol evidence is not admissible to annex conditions to a written subscription, in the absence of fraud or mistake.
Freeman v. Muth, 3 W. L. B. 914 (Dist. Ct. 1878).
Parol evidence is admissible to prove delivery to and acceptance of a conditional subscription by a corporation.
Mansfield, etc., R. Co. v. Brown, 26 O. S. 223, 234 (1875).

DISPOSITION OF STOCK BY CORPORATION AFTER ELECTION OF DIRECTORS.

The directors have power to dispose of the stock which remains unsubscribed after their election.
Sims v. Street Railroad Co., 37 O. S. 565 (1882).
The board may dispose of it by subscription, or may sell it outright without subscriptions;
See Peter v. Union Mfg. Co., 56 O. S. 181, 197 (1897).
exchange it for property or services;
Gates v. Tippecanoe Stone Co., 57 O. S. 75 (1897).
Orton v. Edson, etc., Co., 5 C. C. n. s. 540; 17 C. D. 107 (1905);
aff'd, no rep., 75 O. S. 580.
or use it in payment of corporate debts.
Dayton, etc., R. Co. v. Hatch, 1 Dis. 84, 96 (Super. Ct. Cin. 1855).
Sims v. Street Railroad Co., 37 O. S. 556 (1882).
Where surplus profits have arisen from the corporate business a stock dividend may be declared.
See note to § 8724.
Sales of stock and other corporate securities are regulated by statute popularly known as the "blue sky" law. G. C. §§ 6373-1 to 6373-22.

Sales below par. A corporation can not, in general, sell its stock for less than par. Purchasers from the corporation who pay less

than par for stock may be held liable to creditors for the difference between the amount paid and the par value of the stock, although the
stock was issued as full paid and nonassessable.

 Security Trust Co. v. Ford, 75 O. S. 322 (1906).
 Handley v. Stutz, 139 U. S. 417 (1891).
 In re Flood-Pratt Dairy Co., 7 O .L. R. 603; 16 O. F. D. 396
  (Referee in Bkry. 1909).
 Sturges v. Stetson, 1 Bis. (U. S.) 246 (C. C. Ohio 1858).
 Fosdick v. Sturges, 1 Bis. (U. S.) 255 (C. C. Ohio 1858).

 Under some circumstances of financial embarrassment a corporation
which is a going concern may, in order to raise money to continue its
business, make sales for less than par. Even in such cases the purchasers may be liable to subsequent creditors who have no knowledge
of the terms of such purchase.

 See Peter v. Union Mfg. Co., 56 O. S. 181, 203 (1897).
 Rickerson, etc., Co. v. Farrell, etc., Co., 75 Fed. 554 (C. C. A. 1896).

 But where the sales were made in good faith the purchasers are
not liable to the corporation, or as against other stockholders.

 Peter v. Union Mfg. Co., 56 O. S. 181 (1897).
 Kinsey v. Mt. Auburn Cable Co., 6 C. C. n. s. 305; 17 C. D. 633
  (1905); aff'd, no rep., 75 O. S. 602.
 See Security Trust Co. v. Ford, 75 O. S. 322, 335 (1906).

 Nor are they liable to creditors whose claims were incurred prior
to the purchase.

 See Peter v. Union Mfg. Co., 56 O. S. 181, 203 (1897).
 Handley v. Stutz, 139 U. S. 417 (1891).

 Nor to subsequent creditors who have knowledge of the terms of
the purchase.

 See Kinsey v. Mt. Auburn Cable Co., 6 C. C. n. s. 305, 314; 17 C. D.
  633 (1905); aff'd, no rep., 75 O. S. 602.
 Rickerson, etc., Co. v. Farrell, etc., Co., 75 Fed. 554 (C. C. A. 1896).

 Sales for less than par can be made, in general, only by corporations
engaged in conducting business and under circumstances of financial
embarrassment. They can not be made at the time of organization of a
new corporation.

 Kinsey v. Mt. Auburn, etc., Co., 6 C. C. n. s. 305, 319-320; 17 C. D.
 633 (1905); aff'd, no rep., 75 O. S. 602.

 Transferees of stock which has not been fully paid are not liable
unless they knew that it has not been paid. A transferee may rely
on the respresentation of the corporation that it has been fully paid.
The statement "full paid" on stock certificates is such a representation.

 Roeblings Sons Co. v. Shawnee, etc., Co., 4 N. P. n. s. 113, 121-122;
  17 L. D. 8 (1906); aff'd, no rep., 78 O. S. 408.

 Exchange of stock for property. The directors, acting in good faith,
may exchange stock for property or services.

 Gates v. Tippecanoe Stone Co., 57 O. S. 60, 74, 75 (1897).
 Orton v. Edson, etc., Co., 5 C. C. n. s. 540; 17 C. D. 107 (1905);
  aff'd no rep., 75 O. S. 580.
 Leman v. McLennan, 7 C. C. n. s. 205; 18 C. D. 137 (1905); aff'd,
  no rep., 75 O. S. 643.
 Sims v. Street Railroad Co., 37 O. S. 556 (1882).
 Kunz v. National Valve Co.. 9 C. C. n. s. 593; 19 C. D. 519 (1907).
 Dayton, etc., R. Co. v. Hatch, 1 Dis. 84, 96 (Super. Ct. Cin. 1855).
 See Sanderson v. Iron & Nail Co., 34 O. S. 442, 449 (1878).
 Goodin v. Evans, 18 O. S. 150 (1868).

 The property should be of a character which may be purchased by
the corporation in the prosecution of its business.

Dayton, etc., R. Co. v. Hatch, 1 Dis. 84, 96 (Super. Ct. Cin. 1855).

It should be taken at a fair and adequate valuation, and the directors must have no personal interest in the transaction. Directors can not, acting for the corporation, exchange its stock for their own property.

Gates v. Tippecanoe Stone Co., 57 O. S. 60 (1897).

As to whether the valuation placed upon the property by the directors in good faith is conclusive, the authorities in other states are conflicting. In many states it is held that the director's valuation is conclusive in the absence of fraud. This "good faith" rule has been approved by one circuit court in Ohio.

Kunz v. National Valve Co., 9 C. C. n. s. 607; 19 C. D. 519 (1907).

Property fraudulently overvalued. Liability of stockholders. (a) To the corporation. Where directors have issued stock as fully paid up in exchange for property the corporation can not thereafter treat the stock as only partially paid up and assess the stockholder with the difference between the actual value of the property and the par value of the stock. If the transaction was fraudulent the remedy of the corporation is to rescind the agreement, tender back the property and recover the stock or its market value.

Orton v. Edson, etc., Co., 5 C. C. n. s. 540; 17 C. D. 107 (1905); aff'd, no rep., 75 O. S. 580.

Leman v. McLennan, 7 C. C. n. s. 205, 208; 18 C. D. 137 (1905); aff'd, no rep., 75 O. S. 643.

See Peter v. Union Mfg. Co., 56 O. S. 181, 202 (1897).

Old Dominion, etc., Co. v. Lewisohn, 210 U. S. 206; s. c., 136 Fed. 915.

(b) To creditors. Where the property was fraudulently overvalued corporate creditors may recover the difference between the actual value of the property and the par value of the stock. The transaction is regarded as a subscription for the amount of stock issued, the actual value of the property is credited thereon, and the balance deemed a debt due from the stockholder.

Gates v. Tippecanoe Stone Co., 57 O. S. 60 (1897).

Kiskaden v. Steinle, 203 Fed. 375 (C. C. A. 1913).

If the property has no value (as where an insolvent partnership is converted into a corporation which takes the partnership assets in payment of subscriptions, and also assumes all the partnership debts), nothing is credited and the stockholders are liable to creditors for the full amount of their subscriptions.

Ford v. Lamson, 17 C. C. 539: 9 C. D. 374 (1899).

Sayler v. Simpson, 12 L. D. 148 (Super. Ct. Cin. 1888).

Preston v. Cincinnati, etc., R. Co., 36 Fed. 54 (U. S. C. C. 1888).

Transferee of stock fraudulently issued. A purchaser of such stock from the original stockholder is not liable unless he knew of its fraudulent character. He is entitled to rely on the representation of the corporation that it has been full paid.

Roeblings Sons Co. v. Shawnee, etc., Co., 4 N. P. n. s. 113; 17 L. D. 8 (C. P. 1906); aff'd, no rep., 78 O. S. 408.

President signing "full paid" certificate. The president of a corporation who signed stock certificates, which certify that the stock is "full paid and nonassessable," is not liable to a person who purchased such stock in the open market, for less than par without inquiry as to the assets of the corporation, although the president knew that such stock was issued for property at an overvaluation.

Nutt v. Wheeler, 10 C. C. n. s. 217; 20 C. D. 86 (1907).

Sales to directors and officers. A director or officer may purchase unissued or treasury stock from the corporation, when the sale is authorized by a quorum of disinterested directors and where no action has been taken to withhold the stock from sale to other stockholders or the public.

Sims v. Street Railroad Co., 37 O. S. 556 (1882).

Taylor v. Miami Exporting Co., 6 Ohio 176, 223 (1833).

Sales below par to directors have been sustained as against other stockholders, where the directors made diligent efforts to sell the stock at the same price to the public, and to the other stockholders, before purchasing themselves, and where the corporation was pressed for money to continue business.

Peter v. Union Mfg. Co., 56 O. S. 181 (1897).

Stock of a railroad company purchased below par by a director is void. G. C. § 8798.

A purchase made in order to vote at an election for directors and obtain control of the corporation is valid, when full value is paid for the stock.

Hall v. Hall, 11 C. C. n. s. 335; 20 C. D. 826 (1908); aff'd, no rep., 79 O. S. 456.

Taylor v. Miami Exporting Co., 6 Ohio 176, 223 (1833).

Directors will not be enjoined from selling treasury stock at public sale to the highest bidder although with the intention of selling to persons friendly to their management.

Loomis v. Dexter, 20 W. L. B. 5 (Super. Ct. Cin. 1888).

But sales to directors can not be made on more favorable terms than to other stockholders.

Kinsey v. Mt. Auburn Cable Co., 6 C. C. n. s. 305; 17 C. D. 633 (1905); aff'd, no rep., 75 O. S. 602.

Nor without any valuable consideration.

Straman v. North Baltimore, etc., Co., 8 C. C. 89; 4 C. D. 339 (1893).

Where stock subscribed for by directors was paid for by secret profits made by the directors on a fraudulent sale of property to the corporation, the stock may be cancelled in a suit by the corporation.

Yeiser v. U. S. Board & Paper Co., 107 Fed. 340 (C. C. A. (1901).

Section 8631. (Opening of books.) Such persons shall give at least thirty days' notice of the times and places of opening such books of subscription, by publication in a newspaper published or generally circulated in the county or counties where they are to be opened. Such notice however, may be waived in writing by all the incorporators, but the waiver shall be entered or copied in the corporate records. (R. S. Sec. 3242; April 6, 1891, 88 v. 280; March 5, 1883, 80 v. 42; R. S. 1880; May 1, 1852, 50 v. 274, § 9; S. & C. 276.)

The notice need not be published for thirty consecutive days. One notice, published at least thirty days before the day set, is sufficient.

Muskingum, etc., Co. v. Ward, 13 Ohio 120 (1844).

Craig v. Fox, 16 Ohio 563, 566 (1847).

Newport News v. Potter, 122 Fed. 321, 332 (C. C. A. 1903).

The newspaper in which the notice is inserted, should be published in the English language.

Cincinnati v. Purcell, 26 O. S. 49 (1875).

Proof of waiver of notice. Waiver of notice of publication may be proved by the corporate record in which the same was entered, the authenticity and genuineness of the record having been proved.

Toledo, etc., Ry. Co. v. Toledo, etc., Ry. Co., 6 C. C. 362, 392; 3 C. D. 493 (1892).

Section 8632. (Payment of subscription.) At the time of making a subscription to the capital stock of a corporation, ten per cent on each share subscribed for, shall be payable. The residue shall be paid in such installments at the times and places, and to such persons, as the directors require. (R. S. Sec. 3243; May 1, 1852, 50 v. 274, § 6; R. S. 1880; S. & C. 276.)

Subscriptions generally. See note to § 8630.
Subscriptions to increased stock. See note to § 8698.
Enforcement of subscriptions and defenses. See note to § 8674.

Purpose of section. This section is designed to fix the time of payment of the first installment and to provide the mode for determining the time at which the residue should become payable.

Chamberlain v. R. R. Co. 15 O. S. 225, 249 (1864).

First installment of ten percent.

Payable to incorporators. The incorporators are authorized to receive payment of the first installment on subscriptions received by them.

Sims v. Street Railway Co., 37 O. S. 556, 565 (1882).

The incorporators may, by order, designate one of their number to receive payment.

Cincinnati v. Queen City Tel. Co., 2 N. P. n. s. 349, 364; 15 L. D. 43 (1904); aff'd, 73 O. S. 64.

Payable in money. The incorporators have no authority to receive anything but money in payment of the first installment.

Dayton, etc., R. Co. v. Hatch, 1 Dis. 84, 96 (Super. Ct. Cin. 1855).

Payment by check is regarded as payment in money where sufficient funds are on deposit to meet the check.

Cincinnati v. Queen City Telephone Co., 2 N. P. n. s. 349, 357, 364; 15 L. D. 43 (1904); aff'd, 73 O. S. 64.

Payment by note is not authorized.

Kilbreath v. Gaylord, 3 W. L. B. 525 (Super. Ct. Cin. 1878); aff'd, 34 O. S. 305.

See Latham v. Union, etc., Ins. Co., 1 W. L. B. 127 (Dist. Ct. 1876).

Effect of nonpayment. Failure to pay the first installment does not release a subscriber from liability.

Henry v. Vermillion, etc., R. Co., 17 Ohio 187 (1848).
Latham v. Union, etc., Ins. Co., 1 W. L. B. 127 (Dist. Ct. 1876).
See Chamberlain v. R. R. Co., 15 O. S. 225, 249 (1864).
Ashtabula, etc., R. Co. v. Smith, 15 O. S. 328, 336 (1864).

But a subscriber in default for payment may be excluded from voting at elections for directors. § 8636.

Queen City Telephone Co. v. Cincinnati, 73 O. S. 64, 77 (1905).

Conditional subscriptions. The first installment on a conditional subscription is due at the time when the subscription becomes unconditional and absolute.

Ashtabula, etc., R. Co. v. Smith, 15 O. S. 328, 336 (1864).

Subsequent installments. After the first installment of ten percent has been paid nothing is due on a subscription until a call has been made by the directors.

Mansfield, etc., Co. v. Hall, 26 O. S. 310 (1875).
Railroad Co. v. Fink, 41 O. S. 321, 329 (1884).
Gibson v. Columbia, etc., Co., 18 O. S. 396 (1868).
Mansfield, etc., Co. v. Pettis, 26 O. S. 259 (1875).

Although demand notes have been given by subscribers in payment of their subscriptions they are not due until a call has been made.

Kilbreath v. Gaylord, 34 O. S. 305 (1877); affirming 3 W. L. B. 525.

Calls.

May be made when. Calls may be made by the directors when ten percent of the capital stock has been subscribed. It is not necessary that the entire capital stock should have been subscribed.

Jewett v. Railway, 34 O. S. 601 (1878).
Clarke v. Thomas, 34 O. S. 46 (1877).

As soon as conditional subscriptions become absolute they become subject to general calls previously made.

Mansfield, etc., Co. v. Stout, 26 O. S. 241 (1875).

A general call made by a constituent company continues for the benefit of the consolidated company, if an officer authorized to receive payment is continued at the place designated in the call.

Mansfield, etc., Co. v. Stout, 26 O. S. 241 (1875).

Calls after insolvency. Where a corporation has become insolvent and suit is brought by the receiver or a creditor, the subscriptions will either be regarded as due without a call being made, or the court will make the call.

Turnbull v. Pomeroy Salt Co., 24 W. L. B. 133.
Henry v. Vermillion R. Co., 17 Ohio 187, 191.
See Roeblings Sons Co. v. Shawnee, etc., Co., 4 N. P. n. s. 113; 17 L.
    D. 8 (1906); aff'd, no rep., 78 O. S. 408.
A court of bankruptcy may make the call.
In re Flood-Pratt Dairy Co., 7 O. L. R. 603; 16 O. F. D. 396.

Notice of calls. Whether notice of a call must be given has not been decided in Ohio except in Proprietors v. Wade, 7 W. L. J. 95 (Commercial Court of Cincinnati, 1849), in which five calls were involved and payment of the first four had been demanded before suit. It was held that demand for the fifth call was not necessary except perhaps as affecting costs.

In other states under statutes somewhat similar to §§ 8632 and 8674 the authorities are conflicting.

Cook on Corporations, §§ 117, 118.

The safer practice is to give notice.

Before stock can be forfeited for nonpayment of calls notice must be published.

See § 8675.

A notice to pay to the treasurer of a corporation implies that payment is to be made at his office, and is a sufficient designation of the place of payment.

Muskingum, etc., Co. v. Ward, 13 Ohio 120 (1844).

Waiver by corporation of right to make calls. A subscription made on condition that "not more than ten percent shall be required at any one call, nor shall calls be made more frequently that once in sixty days," was held to operate as a waiver of the statutory right of the

directors to make calls in their discretion, and a general call requiring
more frequent payments was held to not apply to such subscription.
Mansfield, etc., Co. v. Pettis, 26 O. S. 259 (1875).

Amount of payment.

Interest. A corporation is entitled to interest on installments from
the time for payment fixed in the call.
Railroad Co. v. Fink, 41 O. S. 321, 327 (1884).
Natl. Bank v. Greenville, etc., Co., 3 C. C. n. s. 372, 381; 13 C. D. 274
(1899).

Less than the amount of the subscription. Subscribers who pay
less than the full amount of their subscriptions may he held liable to
creditors for the difference between the amount paid and the full amount,
although stock is issued therefor as full paid and nonassessable.
Security Trust Co. v. Ford, 75 O. S. 322 (1906).
See note to § 8630. *Sales below par.*
Stock is not full paid until its par value has been paid in money
or its equivalent. The obligation imposed by a subscription is to pay at
the par value.
Gates v. Tippecanoe Stone Co., 57 O. S. 60, 76 (1897).
Wood v. Pearce, 2 Dis. 411 (Super. Ct. Cin. 1858).

Medium of payment.

Money. Subscriptions to the stock of corporations are *prima facie*
payable in money.
Gates v. Tippecanoe Stone Co., 57 O. S. 60, 74 (1897).

Property. Directors, acting in good faith, have power to receive
property in payment of subscriptions.
Sims v. Street Railroad Co., 37 O. S. 556 (1882).
Gates v. Tippecanoe Stone Co., 57 O. S. 60, 74, 75 (1897).
Orton v. Edson, etc., Co., 5 C. C. n. s. 540; 17 C. D. 107 (1905);
aff'd, no rep., 75 O. S. 580.
Kunz v. National Valve Co., 9 C. C. n. s. 593; 19 C. D. 519 (1907).
Goodin v. Evans, 18 O. S. 150 (1868).
For liability of subscriber where property is fraudulently overvalued
see note to § 8630. *Exchange of stock for property.*

By dividends. A subscriber is entitled to credit for dividends, both
in cash and in stock, declared after his subscription was made.
Railroad Co. v. Fink, 41 O. S. 321 (1884).
See Stewart v. Herron, 77 O. S. 130 (1907).
White v. Cooper Co., 7 C. C. n. s. 114; 17 C. D. 703 (1903); aff'd,
no rep., 72 O. S. 615, 691.
Rhodes v. Equitable Life Insurance Co., 3 C. C. 501; 2 C. D. 188
(1888); aff'd, 27 W. L. B. 160.

By note. A subscriber to stock of an insurance company who,
as authorized by a statute, gave his note and mortgage in payment
of his subscription, was held to stand in the position of a borrower
from the company, and not in the position of a subscriber.
Union, etc., Ins. Co. v. Curtis, 35 O. S. 343 (1880).
Latham v. Union, etc., Ins. Co., 1 W. L. B. 127 (Dist. Ct. 1876).
Andes Ins. Co. v. Waters, 1 W. L. B. 172 (Super. Ct. Cin. 1876).
Where a note given for a subscription is not shown to have been
given or accepted in payment, it is no defense to an action on the
subscription.
Kilbreath v. Gaylord, 3 W. L. B. 525 (Super. Ct. Cin. 1878); aff'd,
34 O. S. 305.

Set off of debt due subscriber. A subscriber may set off a bona fide debt due him from the corporation, both as against the corporation and as against its assignee for creditors.

Niles v. Olszak, 87 O. S. 229 (1912).

Dungan v. Safford, 41 O. S. 15 (1884).

Sims v. Street Railroad, 37 O. S. 556, 558 (1882).

Compare Handley v. Stutz, 139 U. S. 417 (1891).

Bank v. Varnish Co., 8 C. C. 563; 4 C. D. 511 (1894); reversed in part, 56 O. S. 744.

Union, etc., Co. v. Jones, 35 O. S. 351 (1880).

Where an officer of a corporation, who owed the corporation $750.00 on a subscription and who had a claim of $500.00 for salary, executed the note of the corporation and transferred it in payment of an individual debt, after insolvency of the corporation, it was held that the note in the hands of such creditor should be cancelled and the amount set off against the indebtedness of the officer to the corporation.

In re Empress, etc., Co., 1 N. P. n. s. 20 (C. P. 1903).

Section 8633. (Certificate when ten per cent is subscribed.) When ten per cent of the capital stock is subscribed, the subscribers to the articles of incorporation, or a majority of them at once shall so certify in writing to the secretary of state. (R. S. Sec. 3244; April 2, 1906, 98 v. 294; April 22, 1904, 97 v. 170; May 18, 1894, 91 v. 304; April 15, 1880, 77 v. 266; May 1, 1852, 50 v. 274, § 9; R. S. 1880; S. & C. 276.)

By signing a "certificate of subscription" incorporators certify, in effect, not only that ten percent of the capital stock had been subscribed but that an installment of ten percent has been paid on each share subscribed for.

Hessler v. Cleveland, etc., Co., 61 O. S. 621 (1899).

§§ 8632, 8634.

Conditional subscriptions should not be included as a part of the ten percent.

Fairview R. Co. v. Spillman, 23 Ore. 587; 32 Pac. 688.

Except subscriptions conditioned upon the securing of subscriptions to a specified amount, where the condition has been performed.

Emmitt v. Springfield, etc., R. Co., 31 O. S. 23 (1876).

Subscription of ten percent a condition precedent to corporate organization and the transaction of business. Until ten percent of the capital stock has been subscribed, directors can not be elected, nor can corporate business be transacted. nor are subscribers liable on their subscriptions beyond the first installment.

Trust Co. v. Floyd. 47 O. S. 525, 542 (1890).

Telephone Co. v. Cincinnati, 73 O. S. 64. 77 (1905).

See Jewett v. Valley Railway Co., 34 O. S. 601 (1878).

See note to 8674. Suits to collect subscriptions. *Conditions precedent.*

But subscribers may waive the right to have ten percent subscribed.

Emmitt v. Springfield, etc., Co., 31 O. S. 23 (1876).

And as against creditors subscribers are estopped from setting up such defense.

Dickason v. Grafton Sav. Bank, 6 C. C. n. s. 329; 17 C. D. 357 (1905); aff'd, no rep., 76 O. S. 612.

Certificate of subscription to increased stock. Where capital stock is increased under § 8698 a certificate of subscription to the increased stock need not be filed.

Rep. Atty. Gen. 1911-1912, p. 66.

Section 8634. (Incorporators' liability.) The incorporators shall be liable to any person affected thereby, in the amount of any deficiency in the actual payment of ten per cent on the stock subscribed for at the time of so certifying to the secretary of state. (R. S. Sec. 3244; April 2, 1906, 98 v. 294; April 22, 1904, 97 v. 170; May 18, 1894, 91 v. 304; April 15, 1880, 77 v. 266; May 1, 1852, 50 v. 274, § 9; R. S. 1880; S. & C. 276.)

The liability of incorporators is a security for corporate creditors, and it is not necessary, to entitle a creditor to its benefit, that he should have knowledge of the making of the certificate, or of its contents.

Hessler v. Cleveland, etc., Co., 61 O. S. 621 (1899).

Before the adoption of the General Code, incorporators, under Rev. Stats. §§ 3244 and 3243 (now G. C. §§ 8634 and 8632), were liable for any deficiency in the actual payment of ten percent of the entire authorized capital stock, and not merely for one-tenth of that amount.

Hessler v. Cleveland, etc., Co., 61 O. S. 621 (1899).

Ames v. McGaughey, 88 O. S. — (1913).

Under the changed language of these sections, however, incorporators are liable only for the deficiency in the payment of ten percent on the stock subscribed for.

Incorporators of a foreign corporation, who have falsely certified that a certain amount has been paid in, may be liable in damages for deceit; but it was held that the mere signing of the certificate without knowing whether the statements were true or false did not necessarily constitute a fraudulent statement, recklessly made, where there was evidence tending to show that the incorporators believed the statement to be true.

Schenck v. Knott, 13 C. C. n. s. 41 (1910).

Suit to enforce the liability of incorporators should be prosecuted for the benefit of all the creditors, and may be joined with an action to collect unpaid stock subscriptions.

Hessler v. Cleveland, etc., Co., 61 O. S. 621 (1899).

Attorneys' fees may be allowed to plaintiff's counsel out of the fund realized.

Hessler v. Cleveland, etc., Co., 61 O. S. 621 (1899).

Section 8635. (Notice of election of directors.) As soon as such certificate is made, the signers thereto, shall give notice to the stockholders, as provided in section eighty-six hundred and thirty-one, to meet at such time and place as the notice designates, for the purpose of choosing not less than five nor more than thirty directors, to continue in office until the time fixed for the annual election, and until their successors are elected and qualified. But if all subscribers to stock are present in person or by proxy, such notice may be waived by them in writing. (R. S. Sec. 3244;

April 2, 1906, 98 v. 294; April 22, 1904, 97 v. 170; May 18, 1894, 91 v. 304; April 15, 1880, 77 v. 266; May 1, 1852, 50 v. 274, § 9; R. S. 1880; S. & C. 276.)

Annual elections, terms of offices, etc., see § 8647.
Directors generally, see §§ 8660 to 8666 and notes.
The organization meeting should be held in Ohio.
Myers v. Manhattan Bank, 20 Ohio 283 (1851).
Duke v. Taylor, 37 Fla. 64 (1896).
Smith v. Silver, etc., Co., 64 Md. 85 (1885).
Hodgson v. Duluth, etc., R. Co., 46 Minn. 454 (1891).
Harding v. American Glucose Co., 182 Ill. 551 (1899).

Conditions precedent to election of directors.

Subscription of ten percent of capital stock. Directors can not be elected until ten percent of the authorized capital stock has been subscribed.
Trust Co. v. Floyd, 41 O. S. 525 (1890).
Telephone Co. v. Cincinnati, 73 O. S. 64, 77 (1905).
Powers v. Hazelton, etc., Ry. Co., 33 O. S. 429 (1878).
Directors are personally liable for acting as such and incurring debts before ten percent has been subscribed.
Trust Co. v. Floyd, 41 O. S. 525 (1890).

Notice or waiver of notice of stockholders' organization meeting. Where no notice of a meeting was given, and notice was not waived in writing, the directors elected thereat may be ousted by a proceeding in quo warranto (§§ 12303 and 12318). But persons elected at such a meeting may become *de facto* directors.
First, etc., Soo. v. First, etc., Soc., 25 O. S. 128, 133 (1874).
And the validity of their acts can not be questioned collaterally.
Chamberlain v. Painesville etc., R. Co., 15 O. S. 225, 250 (1864).
That notice was neither given nor waived is no defense to an action by creditors on stock subscriptions.
Dickason v. Grafton Sav. Bank, 6 C. C. n. s. 329, 332; 17 C. D. 357 (1905); aff'd, no rep., 76 O. S. 612.

Organization presumed to have been regular. In general it is presumed that the steps requisite to a valid organization have been taken.
Ashtabula, etc., R. Co. v. Smith, 15 O. S. 328, 334 (1864).
Except in appropriation proceedings. A corporation seeking to condemn property must prove its incorporation according to law including the due and legal election of directors.
Queen City Telephone Co. v. Cincinnati, 73 O. S. 64, 77 (1905).
Powers v. Hazelton, etc., Ry. Co.. 33 O. S. 429 (1878).
Method of proof, see note to § 8629.

Section 8636. (Conduct of election; voting.) At the time and place appointed, directors shall be chosen by ballot, by the stockholders who attend, either in person or by lawful proxies. At such and all other elections of directors, each stockholder shall have the right to vote in person or by proxy the number of shares owned by him for as many persons as there are directors to be elected, or to cumulate his shares and give one candidate as many votes as the number of directors multiplied by the number of his shares of stock equals, or to distribute them on the same principal among as many candidates as he thinks fit. Such directors shall not be elected in any other manner. A majority of the number of shares shall be necessary for a choice, but no person shall vote on a share on which an installment is due and unpaid. (R. S. Sec. 3245; April 23, 1898, 93 v. 230; May 1, 1852, 50 v. 274, § 9; S. & C. 276.)

Annual elections. See § 8647 and note.

"A majority of the number of shares shall be necessary for a choice" means a majority of the stock represented at the meeting. It does not require a majority of the entire authorized capital stock, nor a majority of the issued stock.

Lutterby v. Herancourt Brewing Co., 12 L. D. 67 (Super. Ct. Cin. 1901).

This provision applies only when the shares are voted without cumulating.

Schwartz v. State, 61 O. S. 497, 505 (1899).

Lutterby v. Herancourt Brewing Co., 12 L. D. 67 (Super. Ct. Cin. 1901).

CUMULATIVE VOTING.

Cumulative voting being authorized by this section, one receiving a majority of the votes so cast is elected a director, though he does not receive the votes of the holders of a majority of the shares.

Schwartz v. State, 61 O. S. 497 (1899).

See Hall v. Hall, 11 C. C. n. s. 335; 20 C. D. 826 (1908); aff'd, no rep., 79 O. S. 456.

In general. For each director to be elected a stockholder is entitled to one vote for each share of stock registered in his name. Where there are five directors, a person owning one share is entitled to five votes, all of which may be cast for one candidate. Or one vote may be cast for each of five candidates, or the votes may be divided among the candidates in any other manner desired.

If 500 shares are represented at a stockholders' meeting at which five directors are to elected, a minority which controls 85 shares is enabled, under the cumulative system, to elect one director. The 85 shares are entitled to 425 votes. The balance of 415 shares is entitled to 2075 votes. If the 425 minority votes are cast solidly for one candidate, it is impossible for the majority to defeat him.

The minority can not obtain control of the board of directors if the majority act together and cumulate their votes. But if the majority scatter their votes, a strong minority may obtain a majority of the board.

Schwartz v. State, 61 O. S. 497 (1899).

Not obligatory. This section authorizes two methods of voting, either by or without cumulating shares.

Schwartz v. State, 61 O. S. 497, 505 (1899).

Unauthorized prior to 1898. Prior to the amendment of this section in 1898 (93 v. 230) cumulative voting was unauthorized.

State v. Stockley, 45 O. S. 304 (1887).

Schwartz v. State, 61 O. S. 505 (1899).

State v. Halloway, 1 C. C. 157; 1 C. D. 90 (1885).

State v. Fosdick, 1 C. C. 265; 1 C. D. 145 (1885).

Corporations organized prior to 1898. Stockholders in corporations organized prior to the amendment of 1898 (93 v. 230) may cumulate their votes. The legislature, under its right to alter, amend or repeal general corporation laws, may authorize cumulative voting.

Looker v. Maynard, 179 U. S. 46 (1900).
Cross v. West Va., etc., Co., 35 W. Va. 174 (1891).
Gregg v. Granby, etc., Co., 164 Mo. 616 (1901).

Section 8637.   (Inspectors of the election.) At such first election the subscribers of the articles of incorporation present, shall be inspectors of election, certify what persons are elected directors, and appoint the time and place for holding their first meeting. (R. S. Sec. 3245; April 23, 1898, 93 v. 230; May 1, 1852, 50 v. 274, § 9; S. & C. 276.)

Subsequent elections. At elections subsequent to the first election, the right to choose the inspectors is vested in the stockholders and not in the directors.

State v. Merchant, 37 O. S. 251 (1881).
- Appointment of inspectors by common pleas court on application of holders of one-tenth of the stock.
§§ 8640 to 8645.

Powers and duties of inspectors of election. The duties of inspectors are, in general, ministerial and not judicial. An inspector may be a candidate for election.

Commonwealth v. Woelper, 3 S. & R. (Pa.) 29 (1817).
Ex parte Willcocks, 7 Cow. (N. Y.) 402 (1827).
When inspectors have once received a vote they can not afterwards reject it on the ground that it is illegal.

Hartt v. Harvey, 32 Barb. (N. Y.) 55 (1860).
People v. White, 11 Abb. Pr. (N. Y.) 168, 179 (1860).
Where the time for keeping the polls open has not been specified, the inspectors may exercise a reasonable discretion as to closing the polls.

In re Chenango, etc., Co., 19 Wend. (N. Y.) 635 (1839).
In re Mohawk, etc., R. Co., 19 Wend. (N. Y.) 135 (1838).
People v. Albany, etc., R. Co., 55 Barb. (N. Y.) 344 (1869); aff'd, 57 N. Y. 161.

Certificate of election. A certificate of election is prima facie evidence of the facts stated therein; but where it contains a statement not only of the result, but also of the facts upon which the decision was based, if the facts show the decision to be erroneous it may be set aside by the court.

Hartt v. Harvey, 32 Barb. (N. Y.) 55 (1860).
An election is valid although the inspectors fail to certify the result or certify it erroneously.

People v. Peck, 11 Wend. (N. Y.) 604 (1834).
Hartt v. Harvey, 32 Barb. (N. Y.) 55, 61 (1860).
State v. Smith, 15 Ore. 98, 115 (1887).
A certificate is valid though made long after the election.

People v. Peck, 11 Wend. (N. Y.) 604 (1834).

Section 8638.   (Limit on votes of stockholders.) A corporation may provide in the articles of incorporation that each stockholder, irrespective of the amount of stock he owns shall be entitled to one vote, and no more, at an elec-

tion of directors or upon any subject submitted at a stockholders' meeting. When such provision is made the corporation shall be governed thereby. (R. S. Sec. 3245a (1);
March 19, 1884, 81 v. 54, 55.)

This section permits corporations to adopt the common law rule that
each shareholder is entitled to but one vote irrespective of the number
of shares which he holds.
    State v. Stockley, 45 O. S. 304, 306 (1887).

**Section 8639. (Provisions to which such corporations are
subject.)** Corporations whose articles of incorporation contain the limitation provided for in the next preceding section, also shall be subject to the following:
    1. No person shall hold or own stock therein in excess
of one thousand dollars face value.
    2. Annually, within thirty days after the thirty-first day
of December, the directors shall make and file with the
recorder of the county in which the corporation is doing
business, a statement of its financial condition upon such
thirty-first day of December, plainly setting forth its assets
and liabilities in detail, the amount of its paid up capital
stock, the names of its stockholders, and the number of
shares owned by each. Such statement shall be signed and
duly sworn to before any officer authorized to administer
oaths in this state, by a majority of the directors, including
the treasurer. If the directors fail to make the statements
above required, or make a false statement, they personally
shall be liable for all claims and demands against such corporation.
    3. By-laws for the government of the corporation, and
for the distribution of its net earnings among its workmen,
patrons and shareholders, consistent with the constitution
and laws of the state, may be made by the stockholders.
(R. S. Sec. 3245b (1); March 19, 1884, 81 v. 54, 55.)

The restrictions placed by this section upon the voting power of
stockholders are intended to protect the minority and to place the workmen in a co-operative organization of employer and employee on a plane
with persons owning a great number of shares. In England, under a
similar provision, it was held possible for a person to exceed the limit
placed by the law, and to increase his voting power by placing his stock
in the hands of third persons to hold and vote according to his directions.
    In re Stranton I. & S. Co., L. R. 16 Eq. Cas. 559 (1873).
    Pender v. Lushington, L. R. 6 Ch. Div. 70 (1877).
    Moffat v. Farquhar, L. R. 7 Ch. Div. 591 (1877).
In other jurisdictions such evasions have not been sanctioned.
    Mack v. Bardelben Co., 90 Ala. 396; 9 L. R. A. 650 (1889).
    Campbell v. Poultney, 6 G. & J. (Md.) 94 (1834).
    Webb v. Ridgley, 38 Md. 364 (1873).

Where a corporation for many years acquiesced in a subscription to stock, made by a person in the name of his children, permitting them to vote and to exercise acts of ownership, the corporation was held to be estopped from claiming that the transaction was a fraudulent use of names to secure a greater number of votes that he would be entitled to, if the stock had stood in his name.

Creed v. Lancaster Bank, 1 O. S. 1 (1852).

Section 8640. (Application for appointment of inspectors of election.) Within fifteen days next before a meeting held for the election of directors or trustees, or for the determination of any question, by the stockholders of a corporation, or by the subscribers to its stock, or by its creditors and stockholders for its reorganization, any person or persons entitled to vote thereat and owning at least one-tenth interest in its stock may apply to the common pleas court of the county wherein such meeting is to be held, or, if the court be not in session, to a judge thereof, or, in case of the absence or disability of such judge, then to the probate court, for the appointment of inspectors for such meeting. No such application shall be acted upon until notice thereof has been served upon the corporation at its general office. The court or judge may require such additional notice by newspaper publication, or otherwise, as is deemed proper. (R. S. Sec. 3245a (2); March 18, 1887, 84 v. 115.)

Section 8641. (Appointment of inspectors.) Upon the hearing of such application, if deemed proper, the court or judge shall appoint three competent disinterested persons inspectors for such meeting, and for good cause may thereafter vacate the appointment of one or more and appoint another or others instead. In case an inspector fails to attend such meeting, or to act thereat, the stockholders may fill the vacancy so caused. (R. S. Sec. 3245b (2); March 18, 1887, 84 v. 115, 116.)

Section 8642. (List of stockholders for inspectors.) Before every such meeting, the officer or the agent of the corporation having charge of the transfer of its stock, under oath must make out a list of its stockholders, showing the number and classes of shares held by each, as shown by its books, on the date fixed for closing the stock transfers before its meetings; or if no time be fixed therefor, then on the tenth day prior to the date of such meeting. Such list shall be delivered to the inspectors of the meeting, and be prima facie evidence of the ownership of its stock. (R. S. Sec. 3245c; March 18, 1887, 84 v. 115, 116.)

Section 8643. (Stock ownership, how ascertained.) In case of the absence of such list the inspectors shall ascertain the ownership of stock by the corporation books, stock certificates or other proof. (R. S. Sec. 3245c; March 18, 1887, 84 v. 115, 116.)

Section 8644. (Conduct of election.) The inspectors so appointed, or if none be appointed, then those selected by the meeting, shall receive and count the votes cast at such meeting, or at any adjournment thereof, either upon an election or for the decision of any question to be decided by vote, and determine the result. Their certificate shall be prima facie evidence thereof. (R. S. Sec. 3245d; March 18, 1887, 84 v. 115, 116.)

Section 8645. (Compensation of inspectors.) The court or judge making the appointment of inspectors may fix their compensation, and require the applicants for their appointment to secure its payment; but the corporation shall be liable therefor if the meeting by vote so determines. (R. S. Sec. 3245e; March 18, 1887, 84 v. 115, 116.)

Section 8646. (Election of club-house corporation.) A corporation, the principal object of which is the owning and operating of a club-house for the use of its stockholders, which is not kept open and operated for their use during the winter season, shall hold its annual election of directors on the third Monday in July of each year. Such election shall be held at its club-house. (R. S. Sec. 3246; April 16, 1900, 94 v. 375; May 1, 1852, 50 v. 274, § 64; R. S. 1880.)

Section 8647. (Elections.) Except club-house companies, unless the regulations of a corporation otherwise provide, an annual election for trustees or directors shall be held on the first Monday in January of each year. When for any cause, trustees or directors are not elected at the annual meeting, or other meeting called for that purpose, they may be chosen at a members' or stockholders' meeting, if all the members or stockholders are present in person or by proxies, or at a meeting called by the trustees or directors, or any two members or stockholders, notice of which has been given, in writing, to each stockholder, or by publication for ten days in some newspaper printed in the county where the corporation is situated, or has its principal office. Trustees and directors in all cases shall continue in office until their successors are elected and qualified. (R. S. Sec. 3246; April 16, 1900, 94 v. 375; May 1, 1852, 50 v. 274, § 64; R. S. 1880.)

Cumulative voting. See note to § 8636.
Votes necessary to choice. See § 8636 and note.
Tellers or inspectors of election. See §§ 8637 and 8640 to 8645 inclusive.
Directors generally. See § 8660 to 8665 and notes.

The terms "annual meeting" and "annual election" are used interchangeably in this section. In general the term "annual meeting" includes the "annual election."

State v. Burial Assn., 8 C. C. n. s. 233, 250; 18 C. D. 397 (1906);
(Dismissed by Supreme Court for want of jurisdiction; 4 O. L. R. 708).

Term of office of directors. Resignation. Removal. Vacancies.

Term. The term of directors chosen at the first election continues until the time fixed for the annual election. § 8635.

The term of directors elected at an annual meeting is one year.

Lutterby v. Herancourt Brewing Co., 12 L. D. 67 (Super. Ct. Cin 1901).

See §§ 9646 and 9515 for terms of office of directors of building and loan associations and certain insurance companies.

Where no election is held at the time fixed for the annual meeting, or if an attempted election is held invalid, the directors previously elected hold over and continue in office until their successors are legally elected and qualified.

State v. Bonnell, 35 O. S. 10, 17 (1878).
State v. Smalley, 7 C. C. 400; 4 C. D. 653 (1893).
See Bartholomew v. Bentley, 1 O. S. 37, 42 (1852).

The term of office of a director can not be shortened by a decrease in the number of the directors made after his election.

Lutterby v. Herancourt Brewing Co., 12 L. D. 67 (Super. Ct. Cin. 1901).

Nor can his term be shortened by an amendment to the corporate regulations, advancing the date of the annual election, to go into immediate effect.

Toledo T. & L. P. Co., 58 Bull 201 (U. S. D. C. 1913).

But the office of trustee of a church is not one coupled with such an interest that the members can not terminate the tenure of office.

Munsel v. Boyd, 10 C. C. n. s. 121, 127; 20 C. D. 182 (1907).

Resignation. A director may resign at any time, although under the statute his term of office is for one year. Such resignation may be either oral or in writing.

Briggs v. Spaulding, 141 U. S. 132, 154 (1891).

Where a corporation is insolvent and has transacted no business for a number of years, directors elected before business was discontinued are presumed to have abandoned or resigned their offices, notwithstanding the provision that they shall continue in office until their successors are elected.

Bartholomew v. Bentley, 1 O. S. 37 (1852).

Removal. An officer can not be removed during his term of office unless the right of removal is reserved in the regulations, or unless the removal is for cause, such as embezzlement, breach of trust, etc.

State v. Bryce, 7 Ohio, pt. 2, p. 83 (1836).
Lutterby v. Herancourt Brewing Co., 12 L. D. 67 (Super. Ct. Cin. 1901).
State v. Railway Co., 6 C. C. 412; 3 C. D. 516 (1892); s. c., 49 O. S. 668.
17 W. L. B. 130 (article by W. E. Talcott).

Compare Munsel v. Boyd, 10 C. C. n. s. 121, 127; 20 C. D. 182 (1907).

Regulations can not be adopted authorizing the removal, at stock-holders' meetings, of officers or employes chosen or appointed by the directors nor to arbitrarily remove directors. Directors are entitled to hold office for the term for which they are elected, unless removed for cause upon notice and hearing.

Toledo T. L. & P. Co. v. Smith, 58 Bull 201 (U. S. D. C. 1913).

Where an officer disposes of his stock in the corporation he becomes disqualified.

G. C. § 8661.

But where he continues to act, he is recognized as a de facto officer, and his acts as to third persons held valid.

Campbell Ptg. Press Co. v. Bellman Bros. Co., 11 C. C. 360; 5 C. D. 389 (1896).

Vacancies caused by resignation, death, etc., may be filled by the remaining directors for the unexpired term unless the by-laws otherwise provide.

G. C. § 8662.

Right of stockholders to have annual election. The right of stock-holders to elect directors is not affected by the sale of the corporate property by a receiver under order of court.

State v. Merchant, 37 O. S. 251 (1881).

See Lutterby v. Herancourt Brewing Co., 12 L. D. 67, 75 (Super. Ct. Cin. 1901).

Neither the incorporators nor the first trustees of a corporation not for profit are authorized to adopt a by-law or regulation providing that the trustees shall hold office during life and, in case of vacancy, to fill the same by appointment. The members or stockholders are the elective and controlling body.

State v. Standard Life Assn., 38 O. S. 281 (1882).

See Wiswell v. First, etc., Church, 14 O. S. 31 (1862).

Remedy to compel officers to call meeting. Injunction is the proper form of remedy to compel corporate officers to call a stockholders' meeting.

State v. Unida, etc., Co., 13 C. C. n. s. 100; 22 C. D. 54 (1910).

See Cincinnati, etc., Co. v. Hoffmeister, 62 O. S. 189 (1900).

Mandamus is not a proper remedy.

State v. Unida, etc., Co., 13 C. C. n. s. 100; 22 C. D. 54 (1910).

Fraternal Mystic Circle v. State, 61 O. S. 628 (1899).

Time for annual election.

First Monday in January. The provision of this section fixing the time for annual elections is directory merely and not imperative.

State v. Lakamp, 4 C. C. 257; 2 C. D. 533 (1889).

This section applies to corporations not for profit as well as to corporations for profit.

State v. Standard Life Assn., 38 O. S. 281, 289 (1882).

Other date provided in regulations. Where the corporate regulations provide for an "annual meeting" at a time other than the first Monday in January, the time for the "annual election" is thereby changed, and the election should be held at such annual meeting.

State v. Burial Assn., 8 C. C. n. s. 233, 250; 18 C. D. 397 (1906); (Dis. by Sup. Ct. for want of jurisdiction, 4 O. L. R. 708).

Regulations which have not been properly adopted are not effective to change the time of election from the first Monday in January.

State v. Burial Assn., 8 C. C. n. s. 233, 249; 18 C. D. 397 (1906).

The term of office of a director can not be shortened by an amendment to the regulations, to go into immediate effect, advancing the date of the annual election.

Toledo T. L. & P. Co. v. Smith, 58 Bull 201 (U. S. D. C. 1913).

Where no election was held on the date fixed by corporate regulations, which provided that in such case the directors should fix the time for a special election, the fact that the president fixed the time and sent out notices, which action was ratified by the directors, does not invalidate the special election.

Lutterby v. Herancourt Brewing Co., 12 L. D. 67 (Super. Ct. Cin. 1901).

Notice of annual meeting. Where a meeting is stated and general, as where the time and place are provided for in the regulations, notice to the stockholders need not be given, unless the regulations provide for notice.

State v. Bonnell, 35 O. S. 10, 15 (1878).

Wiswell v. First, etc., Church, 14 O. S. 31 (1862).

An adjourned meeting is merely a continuation of the original meeting, and where the original meeting was properly commenced any business proper to be transacted thereat may be done at an adjourned meeting without further notice to the stockholders.

State v. Bonnell, 35 O. S. 10, 16 (1878).

Wiswell v. First, etc., Church, 14 O. S. 31 (1862).

See State v. Smalley, 7 C. C. 400; 4 C. D. 653 (1893).

Failure to give notice. Where notice is required to be given, persons elected trustees or directors at a meeting of which no notice was given may become directors *de facto*.

First, etc., Soc. v. First, etc., Soc., 25 O. S. 128, 133 (1874).

And the validity of their election can not be questioned collaterally.

Chamberlain v. Painesville, etc., R. Co., 15 O. S. 225, 250 (1864).

Stockholders may be estopped from setting up irregularities in calling or giving notice of meetings.

Lutterby v. Herancourt Brewing Co., 12 L. D. 67 (Sup. Ct. Cin. 1901).

State v. Lakamp, 4 C. C. 257; 2 C. D. 533 (1889).

Quorum. The stockholders may adopt a regulation providing for the number of stockholders constituting a quorum. (§ 8704). Where there is no regulation on the subject, the stockholders present in person or by proxy may elect officers and transact business although a majority of the stock is not represented.

Lutterby v. Herancourt Brewing Co., 12 L. D. 67, 72, 73 (Super Ct. Cin. 1901).

Who may vote stock.

Registered holders. In general only the person in whose name stock is registered on the books of the corporation is entitled to vote, although he is only a trustee. Officers in charge of the election can not take notice of the rights of third persons in the stock.

Hafer v. N. Y., etc., R. Co., 14 W. L. B. 68, 72 (Super. Ct. Cin. 1885).

Franklin v. Commercial Bank, 36 O. S. 350, 355 (1881).

See §§ 8642. 8643. 8673-3.

Closing of transfer books prior to election. See § 8642.

Stockholders in default for installment on stock. No person may vote on any stock on which an installment is due and unpaid.

See § 8636.

Queen City Telephone Co. v. Cincinnati, 73 O. S. 64, 77 (1905).

But persons elected by such votes are de facto directors and their acts can not be attacked collaterally;

Raymond v. Spring Grove, etc., Ry. Co., 21 W. L. B. 103 (Super. Ct. Cin. 1889).

except by a defendant in an appropriation proceeding.

Queen City Telephone Co. v. Cincinnati, 73 O. S. 64, 77 (1905); affirming 2 N. P. n. s. 349.

Treasury stock can not be voted while held by the corporation.

Allen v. De Lagerberger, 20 W. L. B. 368 (Super. Ct. Cin. 1888).

Ryan v. Miami Valley R. Co., 10 Am. L. R. 263, 267 (C. P. 1881).

But where the directors pledge treasury stock to secure a corporate loan, they may give pledgee the right to vote thereon.

Allen v. De Lagerberger, 20 W. L. B. 368 (Super. Ct. Cin. 1888).

Proxies. Stockholders may vote by proxy. One person may act as proxy for a number of stockholders.

Railway Co. v. State, 49 O. S. 668 (1892); affirming 6 C. C. 413; 3 C. D. 518.

See § 8636.

A written proxy may be revoked at any time by the stockholder although by its terms "irrevocable."

Griffith v. Jewett, 15 W. L. B. 419 (Super. Ct. Cin. 1886).

The holder of a proxy, in general, has discretionary power to vote as he deems best.

Burch v. Coan, 17 L. D. 717 (Super. Ct. Cin. 1907).

Where the secretary of a mutual insurance company obtains proxies from policyholders, he is not obliged to vote the same for the old directors, nor can the board control him in voting the proxies, unless the proxies were obtained under representations to that effect.

Burch v. Coan, 17 L. D. 717 (Super. Ct. Cin. 1907).

Sale of voting rights. A sale by a stockholder of the right to vote his stock is illegal.

Hafer v. N. Y., etc., R. Co., 14 W. L. B. 68 (Super. Ct. Cin. 1885).

Voting trusts. Stock pooling agreements. Where stockholders place their certificates of stock in the possession of a depositary, with instructions to vote as directed by a committee of the stockholders appointed by themselves; or where the certificates are deposited with trustees who are empowered to vote the stock, the validity of the agreement depends upon its purpose. If the purpose is a lawful one, the agreement is valid.

Railway Co. v. State, 49 O. S. 668 (1892); affirming 6 C. C. 415; 3 C. D. 518.

Griffith v. Jewett, 15 W. L. B. 419 (Super. Ct. Cin. 1886).

Article by William P. Rogers, 7 O. L. R. 561 (1910).

But if the purpose is unlawful, as for instance tending to create a monopoly, the agreement is invalid.

State v. Standard Oil Co., 49 O. S. 137 (1892).

But even a valid voting trust agreement may be revoked at any time by any one of the stockholders notwithstanding it is in terms "irrevocable."

Griffith v. Jewett, 15 W. L. B. 419 (Super. Ct. Cin. 1886).

Common law joint stock company, or voluntary association, as a means of maintaining stock control.

See article by William P. Rogers, 7 O. L. R. 561 (1910).

Cook on Corporations, § 622h.

Agreements to elect certain persons directors or officers. An agreement between individuals to form a corporation, providing for its future management and control, and specifying the future directors and officers and their compensation, is not void or illegal, where the parties to the contract subscribe for and own all the stock of the corporation.

Doan v. Rogan, 79 O. S. 372, 386 (1909).

See Mullen v. Gaffey, 8 Am. L. R. 101 (Dist. Ct. 1879).

State v. Ry. Co., 6 C. C. 415; aff'd in 49 O. S. 668.

And where in an agreement between individuals it is provided that one of the parties shall be employed for a specified time at a stipulated salary by the other parties, or by a corporation to be thereafter organized by them, on breach of such agreement an action for damages may be maintained against the individuals in default.

Doan v. Rogan, 79 O. S. 372 (1909).

Magill v. Rendigs, 12 L. D. 558 (Super. Ct. Cin. 1902).

See Mosier v. Parry, 60 O. S. 388 (1899).

But where there are other stockholders who are not parties to the agreement, or where the corporation is not a private business corporation but is one in which the public has an interest (such as an educational corporation), an agreement by a director or by one or more stockholders owning a majority of the stock to elect another person to a salaried corporate office is void as against public policy.

Jones v. Scudder, 2 C. S. C. R. 178 (1872).

West v. Camden, 135 U. S. 507 (1890).

Subscription to stock on condition that subscriber be employed by corporation. Remedy for breach of condition.

See Stunt v. Newark, etc., Co., 22 C. C. 120; 12 C. D. 175 (1901);
aff'd, 67 O. S. 555.

Right to fair election. A stockholder has a right to a fair and lawful election of directors, without regard to pecuniary injury.

Hafer v. N. Y., etc., R. Co., 14 W. L. B. 68, 71 (Super. Ct. Cin. 1885).

Unfair elections. Where a corporation was enjoined from holding an election on the day specified in the notice of the annual meeting, in consequence of which no meeting was held until several hours after the hour specified, when a small number of stockholders, without the knowledge of the others, met and adjourned until the next day, at which time an election was held by a minority, without notice to others who might readily have been notified, the election was held to be unfair and invalid.

State v. Bonnell, 35 O. S. 10 (1878).

Where a part of the stockholders assembled, but adjourned by agreement, and by a misunderstanding as to the time of the adjournment a minority met and elected directors, and subsequently the majority met and elected other directors, it was held that neither election was valid.

State v. Smalley, 7 C. C. 400; 4 C. D. 653 (1893).

Fraud by a managing officer of an insurance company in bringing about, through a misuse of proxies, an election of directors friendly to his interests, renders such election unfair.

Burch v. Coan, 4 O. L. R. 731; 17 L. D. 563 (Super. Ct. Cin. 1907).

Repeating. To vote more than once at a corporate election is not a penal offense.

Lane v. State, 39 O. S. 312 (1883).

Injunction against voting of stock. Where stock of a railroad company is illegally held by another railroad company, the voting of such stock may be enjoined by the suit of another stockholder.

Mannington v. H. V. Ry. Co., 9 N. P. n. s. 641, 687; 20 L. D. 468
(C. P. 1910): removed to U. S. Ct., see 183 Fed. 133; 8 O. L. R.
451; 16 O. F. D. 552.

Gould v. Railway, 10 N. P. n. s. 313 (C. P. 1910).

Likewise where stock is held by a trustee under an illegal agreement, in the interest of another corporation, the voting rights thereon having been sold.

Hafer v. N. Y., etc., R. Co., 14 W. L. B. 68 (Super. Ct. Cin. 1885).

See Allen v. De Lagerberger, 20 W. L. B. 368 (Super. Ct. Cin. 1888).

Injunction against election. Where there is a dispute as to whether a vacancy eists in the board of directors, it being claimed that one director has never been a stockholder, the holding of a special election to choose his successor will not be enjoined. His remedy is quo warranto after the election.

Hooe v. Hall, 9 C. C. 654; 4 C. D. 547 (1893).

Validity of election. How determined.

Quo warranto. In general the proper proceeding to test the validity of an election of directors is a proceeding in quo warranto.

§§ 12303, 12318, 12319.

Hullman v. Honcamp, 5 O. S. 237 (1855).

Presbyterian Soc. v. Smithers, 12 O. S. 248 (1861).

See State v. Bonnell, 35 O. S. 10 (1878).

Where an election is held invalid the court may, in its discretion. order a new election.

§ 12319.

Henderson v. Hogan, 1 W. L. B. 227 (Dist. Ct. 1876).

Injunction against illegal directors. Where the sole object of a suit is to test the legality of an election, it must be by proceeding in quo warranto, and a suit for injunction or other suit in equity will not lie.

Hullman v. Honcamp, 5 O. S. 237 (1855).

Hooe v. Hall, 9 C. C. 654; 4 C. D. 547 (1893).

Messenger v. Wardens, 6 W. L. B. 397 (C. P. 1881).

A restraining order may be granted, during the pendency of a quo warranto proceeding, to restrain a taking possession of the office by other than legal means.

Hooe v. Hall, 9 C. C. 654; 4 C. D. 547 (1893).

But the validity of an election may be determined in an injunction suit, or other suit in equity, where other and proper equitable relief is sought in the suit; as where the plaintiffs are members of a corporation not for profit and are wrongfully excluded from the use and enjoyment of the corporate property or privileges by persons claiming to be directors, but whose election was void or illegal.

Munsel v. Boyd, 10 C. C. n. s. 121: 20 C. D. 182 (1907).

Bartholomew v. Lutheran Cong., 35 O. S. 567 (1880).

See Presbyterian Soo. v. Smithers, 12 O. S. 248.

Messinger v. Wardens, 6 W. L. B. 397 (C. P. 1881).

Or where the suit seeks to set aside a fraudulent contract made by directors whose election was brought about by fraud.

Burch v. Coan, 4 O. L. R. 731; 17 L. D. 563, 717 (Super. Ct. Cin. 1907).

Or where the right of directors to represent the corporation arises incidentally in the course of an action.

Lutterby v. Herancourt Brewing Co., 12 L. D. 67 (Super Ct. Cin. 1901).

In such case the court may enjoin the persons illegally elected from interfering with the lawful directors in possession and control of the corporate property.

Bartholomew v. Lutheran Cong.. 35 O. S. 567 (1880).

Munsel v. Boyd, 10 C. C. n. s. 121; 20 C. D. 182 (1907).

Although it may not render a judgment of ouster against the illegal directors.

Burch v. Coan, 4 O. L. R. 731; 17 L. D. 563 (Super. Ct. Cin. 1907).

In federal courts it has been held that the remedy in equity may be invoked where the interests affected by the litigation would suffer by the delays incident necessary to a quo warranto proceeding.

Toledo T. L. & P. Co. v. Smith, 58 Bull. 201 (U. S. D. C. 1913).

Collateral attack. The title of *de jure* directors can not be questioned in a collateral proceeding. The acts of de facto directors are, as to third persons, valid, although they may have been elected by illegal votes.

Presbyterian Soc., etc., v. Smithers, 12 O. S. 248 (1861).

Chamberlain v. Painesville, etc., Co., 15 O. S. 225, 250 (1864).

Ehrman v. Ins. Co., 35 O. S. 324, 339.

Harrison v. Ellis, 15 L. D. 501 (C. P. 1905).

Raymond v. Spring Grove, etc., Ry. Co., 21 W. L. B. 103 (Super. Ct. Cin. 1889).

In a collateral proceeding the court may, however, determine who are the *de facto* directors.

Presbyterian Soc. v. Smithers, 12 O. S. 248, 251 (1861).

Corporate record or minute book as evidence. The records of a corporation are the best evidence of its officers, but it is competent to prove the existence of such officers by other evidence.

State v. Buchanan, Wright 233 (1833).

See Stillwater Turnpike Co. v. Coover, 25 O. S. 558 (1874).

Toledo, etc., Co. v. Toledo, etc., Co., 12 C. C. 367; 5 C. D. 643 (1893).

Section 8648. (Life of corporations to deal in real estate.) A corporation formed to buy or sell real estate, shall expire by limitation in twenty-five years from the date on which its articles of incorporation were issued by the secretary of state. (R. S. Sec. 3235; May 12, 1902, 95 v. 623; March 22, 1900, 94 v. 65; April 6, 1894, 91 v. 126; April 20, 1893, 90 v. 205; R. S. 1880.)

For powers of building companies to acquire and hold real estate for office, hotel, factory, etc., buildings see § 10210.

A corporation formed for the purpose of dealing in real estate is necessarily for profit and can not be organized without a capital stock.

State v. Home Co-op. Union, 63 O. S. 547 (1900).

A foreign corporation organized to deal in real estate may be admitted to do business in Ohio, but the application for admission should expressly limit its life in Ohio to twenty-five years.

5 Opins. Attys. Gen. 1002.

Although not expressly required by statute, it is proper that the articles of an Ohio corporation formed to deal in real estate should expressly limit its life to twenty-five years. The omission of such a limitation from the articles, however, does not invalidate the articles nor authorize the secretary of state to refuse to file the same.

Rep. Atty. Gen. 1911-1912, pp. 71, 61.

A real estate company may not, by amendment to its articles, acquire the powers of a building company under § 10210.

Rep. Atty. Gen. 1908-1909, p. 78.

At the expiration of twenty-five years a real estate corporation is ipso facto dissolved and should be wound up under § 8742 et seq.

People v. Anderson, etc., Road Co., 76 Cal. 190.

La Grange, etc., R. Co. v. Rainey, 7 Colw. (Tenn.) 420, 432 (1870).

Scanlan v. Crawshaw, 5 Mo. App. 337 (1878).

See Myers v. Lucas, 16 C. C. 545; 8 C. D. 431 (1898); reversed on other grounds, 63 O. S. 101.

There is no limit to the amount of land which a real estate company may hold.

Market St. Ry. Co. v. Hellman, 109 Cal. 571.

Leases for more than twenty-five years under former law.

See Beckett Paper Co. v. Hamilton, etc., Co., 18 C. C. 200; 10 C. D. 57.

Section 8649.   (Procedure if all real estate not disposed of in twenty-four years.) If within twenty-four years from the date of its articles the real estate of such a corporation is not wholly disposed of, its directors shall at once bring an action against it, and the owners of liens upon such real estate, in the common pleas court of the county wherein such realty is situated, by filing a petition praying for its sale as therein described. Should the board not begin such action within sixty days after such twenty-four years expire, the prosecuting attorney of the county in which the realty is situated, on the expiration of the sixty days at once shall begin and prosecute it. (R. S. Sec. 3235; May 12, 1902, 95 v. 623; March 22, 1900, 94 v. 65; April 6, 1894, 91 v. 126; April 20, 1893, 90 v. 205; R. S. 1880.)

Section 8650.   (Service of summons, sale and distribution.) Service of summons upon the defendants, appraisement and sale of such real estate, and distribution of the proceeds of the sale shall be made as provided in actions of foreclosure of mortgages and marshalling liens. The court may allow the plaintiff, in case he be the prosecuting attorney, a just attorney fee, to be taxed with the costs of the action. (R. S. Sec. 3235; May 12, 1902, 95 v. 623; March 22, 1900, 94 v. 65; April 6, 1894, 91 v. 126; April 20, 1893, 90 v. 205; R. S. 1880.)

Section 8651.   (Articles of incorporation not for profit.) An association of five or more persons, resident of this state, who are associated not for profit, but as the principal or ruling organization over subordinate organizations, associated, not for profit, and having a definite location or place of business in the state, may be incorporated, having its location or principal place of business therein, without naming in its articles of incorporation a permanent place where it is to be located, or its principal business transacted; but it must name therein the place where it is to be located, or its principal business transacted at the time of incorporation, with the name and places of residence of its then principal officers. (R. S. Sec. 3236; April 10, 1889, 86 v. 224; April 16, 1885, 82 v. 134; R. S. 1880.)

Articles of incorporation under this section must state the names and residences of the principal officers.
Rep. Atty. Gen. (1908-1909), 57.

Section 8652. (Duties of officers when location is changed.)

When such association changes its location, or the place where its principal business is transacted, its principal officer, under its seal, if it has one, countersigned by the officer acting as secretary of such association, shall certify the place then selected as its location, or where its principal business is to be transacted, with the name of its principal officers, and their places of residence, to the secretary of state of Ohio, which certificate he shall record for public use in the records of his office. (R. S. Sec. 3236; April 10, 1889, 86 v. 224; April 16, 1885, 82 v. 134; R. S. 1880.)

Section 8653. (Members of corporation not for profit.)

The subscribers to articles of incorporation for a purpose other than profit, shall have them copied into a book they provide, which shall be the property of the corporation. Any person who has the qualifications which the corporate body prescribes, may become a member thereof by signing his name to such copy. (R. S. Sec. 3241; March 16, 1887, 84 v. 85; May 15, 1886, 83 v. 168; R. S. 1880.)

Whether compliance with this section is indispensable to legal organization of the corporation *quaere*.
State v. Burial Assn., 8 C. C. n. s. 233, 248, 249; 18 C. D. 397 (1906);
(Dismissed by Sup. Ct. for want of jurisdiction, 4 O. L. R. 708).
This section applies to religious societies.
3 Opins. Attys. Gen. 333.
Contract of membership, what constitutes.
See notes to §§ 9468 and 9427.

Articles of incorporation. The articles of incorporation of a social club should not include in the purpose clause the terms "for mutual protection and relief," as such terms are used in the statutes to describe certain insurance business.
Rep. Atty. Gen. 1911-1912, p. 65.

Property rights of members. A member of a corporation not for profit has no severable right in its property but merely the enjoyment and use of it while he remains a member. On his withdrawal or expulsion he is not entitled to a proportionate share of the property.
Hershiser v. Williams, 24 W. L. B. 314; 4 L. D. 17 (1890); affirmed,
6 C. C. 147; 3 C. D. 389 (1892); 53 O. S. 663.
Gasely· v. Separatists Soc. of Zoar, 13 O. S. 144 (1862).
Wiswell v. First Cong. Church, 14 O. S. 31 (1863).

Secession. Members who secede from a corporation not for profit forfeit all right to its property. But the members may, by agreement. separate into two bodies and divide. the property.

Wiswell v. First Cong. Church, 14 O. S. 31 (1863).

M. E. Church v. Wood, 5 Ohio 283 (1831).

Ex parte Shoup, 16 W. L. B. 71 (C. P.).

Rike v. Floyd, 6 C. C. 80 (1891); aff'd, no rep., 53 O. S. 653.

Sale of real estate. The trustees of a religious society have no power to dispose of its real estate without the consent of its members and without authority of court under § 10051.

South Kenton, etc., Assn. v. Espy, 17 C. C. 524; 9 C. D. 695 (1899).

Liability of members. Members of a corporation not for profit are not individually liable for its debts.

See § 8666.

Myers v. Jenkins, 63 O. S. 101 (1900).

EXPULSION OF MEMBERS.

Power of corporation to expel. A corporation not for profit has inherent power to expel a member for conduct detrimental to its welfare.

State v. Aurora Relief Soc., 2 W. L. B. 125 (Dist. Ct. 1877).

Hershiser v. Williams, 24 W. L. B. 314; 4 L. D. 17 (1890); affirmed, 6 C. C. 147; 3 C. D. 389; 53 O. S. 663.

State v. Society, 8 Am. L. R. 627; 5 W. L. B. 124.

Blumenthal v. Cincinnati Chamber of Commerce, 9 W. L. B. 76 (Dist. Ct.); affirming 7 W. L. B. 327.

When organized with a capital stock a corporation not for profit may expel a member who is a stockholder.

Cheney v. Ketcham, 5 N. P. 139, 140; 7 L. D. 183.

Grounds. Causes specified in regulations or constitution. The members of a corporation are bound by the provisions of its regulations or constitution, and may be expelled or suspended for any cause specified therein.

Blumenthal v. Cincinnati Chamber of Commerce, 7 W. L. B. 327; affirmed, 9 W. L. B. 76 (Dist. Ct.).

State v. Verein, 3 W. L. B. 295 (Dist. Ct. 1878).

Hershiser v. Williams, 24 W. L. B. 314; 4 L. D. 17 (1890); affirmed, 6 C. C. 147; 3 C. D. 389; 53 O. S. 663.

Pete v. Woodmen of the World, 5 C. C. n. s. 446; 16 C. D. 653 (1904); aff'd, no rep., 74 O. S. 445.

Causes not specified. In the absence of a provision in the regulations a member may be expelled (1) for an indictable offense which renders him unfit for association, or (2) for an offense against his duty as a member of the corporation.

State v. Aurora Relief Soc., 2 W. L. B. 125 (Dist. Ct. 1877).

State v. Society, 8 Am. L. R. 627; 5 W. L. B. 124 (Dist. Ct.).

Hershiser v. Williams, 24 W. L. B. 314; 4 L. D. 17 (1890); affirmed, 6 C. C. 147; 3 C. D. 389; 53 O. S. 663.

Blumenthal v. Cincinnati Chamber of Commerce, 9 W. L. B. 76; affirming 7 W. L. B. 327.

Immoral or vicious conduct is a valid ground for the expulsion of a member of a social, fraternal or religious society.

State v. Aurora Relief Soc., 2 W. L. B. 125 (Dist. Ct. 1877).

"Unmercantile conduct," consisting of making sales by false weight, is a valid ground for the expulsion of a member of a chamber of commerce.

Blumenthal v. Chamber of Commerce, 9 W. L. B. 76 (Dist. Ct.);
affirming 7 W. L. B. 327.
See § 10144.
Unmasonic conduct.
Hershiser v. Williams, 24 W. L. B. 314; 4 L. D. 17 (1890); affirmed,
6 C. C. 147; 3 C. D. 389; 53 O. S. 663.

Trial.   A member can not be expelled without a trial, even where
the regulations contain no provisions on the subject.   Reasonable notice
of the trial must be given him and an opportunity afforded for him to
present his defense.
State v. Bryce, 7 Ohio (pt. 2) 82 (1836).
Munsel v. Boyd, 10 C. C. n. s. 121; 20 C. D. 182 (1907).
Schwartz v. Catholic Union, 9 C. C. n. s. 337; 19 C. D. 471 (1907).
Cheney v. Ketcham, 5 N. P. 139; 7 L. D. 183.
Stein v. Sherlock, 6 W. L. B. 203 (Dist. Ct. 1881).
The provisions of the regulations, if any, relating to proceedings for
expulsion must be followed.
State v. Bryce, 7 Ohio (pt. 2) 82 (1836).
Foxhever v. Order of Red Cross, 2 C. C. n. s. 394; 14 C. D. 56
(1901); aff'd, no rep., 68 O. S. 717.
But such provisions may be waived by the member on trial.
State v. Cincinnati Chamber of Commerce, 4 N. P. 244; 6 L. D.
363.
Blumenthal v. Cincinnati Chamber of Commerce, 9 W. L. B. 76
(Dist. Ct.).
Where the regulations or constitution provide for a committee or
board to hear and determine charges, the trial should be held before such
special tribunal.
Stein v. Sherlock, 6 W. L. B. 203 (Dist. Ct. 1881).
Blumenthal v. Chamber of Commerce, 9 W. L. B. 76; affirming 7
W. L. B. 327.
Where the regulations do not provide for such a tribunal the trial
must be held before the members of the corporation.
Cheney v. Ketcham, 5 N. P. 139; 7 L. D. 183.
The person by whom charges have been filed against the accused
member can not act as judge or vote.
Cheney v. Ketcham, 5 N. P. 139; 7 L. D. 183.
The strictness of judicial proceedings is not required either in the
wording of the charges against the accused member, or in the notice given
him, or in the admission of evidence.
Blumenthal v. Cincinnati Chamber of Commerce, 9 W. L. B. 76
(Dist. Ct.); affirming 7 W. L. B. 327.
State v. Aurora Relief Society, 2 W. L. B. 125 (Dist. Ct. 1877).

Remedies for wrongful expulsion.   A member unlawfully expelled
may bring an action for damages against the corporation.
State v. Slavonska Lipa, 28 O. S. 665 (1876).
Fraternal Mystic Circle v. State, 61 O. S. 628 (1899); reversing
9 C. C. 364; 6 C. D. 385
An injunction against wrongful exclusion may be granted where
the remedy at law is inadequate.
Cheney v. Ketcham, 5 N. P. 139; 7 L. D. 183.
State v. Zesch, 5 N. P. 274; 7 L. D. 298.
Mandamus is not a proper remedy.
Fraternal Mystic Circle v. State, 61 O. S. 628 (1899); reversing
9 C. C. 364; 6 C. D. 385.
A member of a chamber of commerce who is suspended until he

submits to a public reprimand is not confronted by an irreparable injury with no adequate remedy at law.

> Bishop v. Cincinnati, etc., Exchange, 5 N. P. 365.

Remedies within corporation must be exhausted before suit. A member against whom charges are preferred must submit to trial by the corporation. An injunction will not be granted against a threatened expulsion. The court will presume that a fair trial will be had within the corporation.

> Hershiser v. Williams, 6 C. C. 147; 3 C. D. 389 (1892); aff'd, no rep.; 53 O. S. 663.

Where a member has been wrongfully expelled he can not maintain an action until he has exhausted all the remedies within the corporation. If appellate tribunals exist in the corporation, he must carry his appeal to the highest tribunal.

> Hershiser v. Williams, 6 C. C. 147; 3 C. D. 389 (1892); aff'd, no rep., 53 O. S. 663.
> State v. Knights of Golden Rule, 10 W. L. B. 2 (Dist. Ct. 1883).
> Catholic Union v. Herron, 4 O. L. R. 686; 17 L. D. 789 (1907).
> Myers v. Jenkins, 63 O. S. 101 (1900).
> Supreme Court Foresters v. Herlinger, 6 C. C. n. s. 28; 17 C. D. 151 (1905).

But where the expulsion is void, as in the case of expulsion without a trial, the member may sue without resorting to the appellate tribunals.

> Cheney v. Ketcham, 5 N. P. 139; 7 L. D. 183.
> See dissenting opinion, Catholic Union v. Herron, 4 O. L. R. 686; 17 L. D. 789 (1907).

Pleading. The better practice is for the plaintiff to set out in his petition the existence of tribunals within the corporation and to aver that he has exhausted all such remedies. But the existence of appellate tribunals within the corporation, and failure to resort thereto, may be alleged in the answer.

> Myers v. Jenkins, 63 O. S. 101, 116 (1900).
> See Webster v. Taplin Rice & Co., 9 C. C. n. s. 587; 19 C. D. 543 (1904); aff'd, 76 O. S. 590.

Judicial relief granted when. Judicial relief will not be granted unless civil or property rights are involved.

> Hershiser v. Williams, 24 W. L. B. 314; 4 L. D. 17 (1890); affirmed, 6 C. C. 147; 3 C. D. 389; 53 O. S. 663.

When such a right exists, relief will be granted where the expulsion has been brought about by fraud.

> Kent v. Odd Fellows, etc., Assn., 14 W. L. B. 237 (C. P. 1885)

Or where a member has been expelled without a trial.

> Cheney v. Ketcham, 5 N. P. 139; 7 L. D. 183 (C. P.).

A court will not, as a rule, sit as a reviewing court upon the judgment of a corporate tribunal. An expulsion will not be set aside for irregularity in the proceedings, providing the cause is one for which the corporation may expel, and the accused member had notice of the trial and opportunity to defend.

> State v. Aurora Relief Society, 2 W. L. B. 125 (Dist. Ct. 1887).
> Hershiser v. Williams, 24 W. L. B. 314; 4 L. D. 17 (1890); affirmed, 6 C. C. 147; 3 C. D. 389; 53 O. S. 663.
> State v. Verein, 3 W. L. B. 295 (Dist. Ct. 1878).
> State v. Cincinnati, etc., Exchange, 4 N. P. 244; 6 L. D. 263.
> Bishop v. Cincinnati, etc., Exchange, 5 N. P. 365.

The admission of hearsay evidence does not invalidate a conviction.

> Blumenthal v. Cincinnati Chamber of Commerce, 9 W. L. B. 76 (Dist. Ct.); affirming, 7 W. L. B. 327.

Even where a member was expelled without notice or opportunity to defend, he was refused reinstatement where it clearly appeared that he had forfeited his right to membership and, if reinstated, would at once be expelled by formal proceedings.

State v. Society, 8 Am. L. R. 627; 5 W. L. B. 124.
See State v. Verein, 3 W. L. B. 295 (Dist. Ct. 1878).

Acquiescence in expulsion. A member of a fraternal benefit society, although wrongfully expelled, will be held to have acquiesced in the action taken, where he did not appeal therefrom, apply for reinstatement, and did not thereafter pay or tender dues, attend meetings or otherwise act as a member. After his death there can be no recovery on his benefit certificate or policy.

Foxhever v. Order of Red Cross, 2 C. C. n. s. 394; 14 C. D. 56 (1901); aff'd, no rep., 68 O. S. 717.
Dimmer v. Catholic Knights, 22 C. C. 366; 12 C. D. 413 (1901).
Herron v. Catholic Union, 2 O. L. R. 352; 15 L. D. 703 (1904); s. c., 4 O. L. R. 686; 17 L. D. 789.

Suspension of members. A member of a beneficial association is bound by a provision in its regulations to the effect that failure to pay dues and assessments, when due, shall ipso facto suspend the delinquent from membership.

Pete v. Woodmen of the World, 5 C. C. n. s. 446; 16 C. D. 653 (1904); aff'd, no rep., 74 O. S. 445.

Section 8654. (Members of a religious, secret or benevolent society.) When the incorporators of such a corporation now or hereafter formed, are or become members of a church, religious, secret or benevolent society, and have signed or sign articles to incorporate either thereof, any person who is or becomes a member of such church, religious, secret or benevolent society, in good standing, thereby shall be a member of such corporation, with the right to vote at all of its meetings for the election of officers or for any other purpose. (R. S. Sec. 3241; March 16, 1887, 84 v. 85; May 15, 1886, 83 v. 168; R. S. 1880.)

Where membership in a specified church is one of the qualifications of membership in a benefit society, a member of the society, on withdrawal from the church, becomes liable to expulsion.

State v. Society. 8 Am. L. R. 627; 5 W. L. B. 124 (Dist. Ct.).

Power of majority. A majority of the members of a religious corporation have a right to control the use and occupation of land purchased by it. They do not lose such right of control by any supposed error of doctrine.

Keyser v. Stansifer, 6 Ohio 363 (1834).
Brundage v. Deardorf, 92 Fed. 214 (C. C. A. 1899).

Voting rights. Where in a special charter of a religious corporation the right to vote was granted to "each member," a further provision giving to pew owners the privileges of membership was held not to restrict the right of voting to them.

Wiswell v. First Cong. Church, 14 O. S. 31 (1863).

Membership in mutual protective association. After a mutual protective association has been formed under § 9427 et seq., its members are those mutually engaged in promoting the purposes of the organization and who, by virtue of their relation to the corporation, are entitled to protection.

State v. Standard Life Assn., 38 O. S. 281 (1882).

Section 8655. (Election.) Except as otherwise provided, a majority of the subscribers to articles of incorporation not for profit, may elect not less than five trustees for such corporation, to hold their offices until the next annual meeting, or until their successors are elected and qualified. (R. S. Sec. 3240; May 10, 1902, 95 v. 547; April 6, 1888, 85 v. 166; March 26, 1883, 80 v. 79; April 20, 1881, 78 v. 200; R. S. 1880.)

Neither the incorporators nor the trustees first elected are authorized to adopt a by-law or regulation providing that they shall hold office during life, and in case of vacancy to fill the same by appointment.

State v. Standard Life Assn., 38 O. S. 281 (1882).

The provisions of § 8647 relating to the time of annual meetings apply to corporations not for profit.

State v. Standard Life Assn., 38 O. S. 281 (1882).

Validity of election; procedure to determine.

See note to § 8647.

Articles of incorporation of a religious society which recited the election of the incorporators as trustees, prior to filing the articles, were refused filing by the secretary of state.

3 Opins. Attys. Gen. 699.

Section 8656. (Term and number of trustees.) Religious corporations, and institutions incorporated for the purpose of promoting education, science or art, may prescribe the time trustees thereof may hold their offices, except that the term of none shall exceed in number of years the number of its trustees. (R. S. Sec. 3240; May 10, 1902, 95 v. 547; April 6, 1888, 85 v. 166; March 26, 1883, 80 v. 79; April 20, 1881, 78 v. 200, R. S. 1880.)

Powers of trustees of religious corporations. See note to § 10013.

The tenure of office of a trustee of a religious corporation may be terminated by the members, at a meeting properly called and held, before the expiration of the term for which he was elected.

Munsel v. Boyd, 10 C. C. n. s. 121; 20 C. D. 182 (1907).

See note to § 8647.

Section 8657. (Term and number of trustees in secret or benevolent order.) Lodges, societies, or bodies of a secret or benevolent order, incorporated under the laws of this state, may elect such number of trustees not less than three as the laws or regulations governing such lodge, society, or body, provides, and their election shall be at the time therein specified. (R. S. Sec. 3240; May 10, 1902, 95 v. 547; April 6, 1888, 85 v. 166; March 26, 1883, 80 v. 79; April 20, 1881, 78 v. 200; R. S. 1880.)

The trustees of a fraternal beneficial association, elected for the first year, have no right to adopt regulations, but they have a right to adopt by-laws relating to the conduct of its business.

Chevaliers v. Shearer, 6 C. C. n. s. 587; 17 C. D. 509 (1905).

Section 8658. (Term and number of trustees of a hospital.) Members of any corporation heretofore or hereafter organized for the purpose of owning and conducting a hospital for sick and disabled persons, may provide for the election of a board of not less than five nor more than fifteen trustees, to serve during life, and that in case of vacancy in such board by death, resignation or otherwise, the remaining members thereof shall fill the vacancy. (R. S. Sec. 3240; May 10, 1902, 95 v. 547; April 6, 1888, 85 v. 166; March 26, 1883, 80 v. 79; April 20, 1881, 78 v. 200; R. S. 1880.)

Section 8659. (Trustees of corporations organized prior to May 10th, 1902.) If such corporation was organized prior to May 10th 1902, regulations providing that its trustees are to hold office during life may be adopted at an annual meeting, or a special meeting of the association, duly and regularly called. But notice of such proposed change shall be published for three successive weeks in some newspaper published and of general circulation at the place where such hospital is located. (R. S. Sec. 3240; May 10, 1902, 95 v. 547; April 6, 1888, 85 v. 166; March 26, 1883, 80 v. 79; April 20, 1881, 78 v. 200; R. S. 1880.)

DIRECTORS AND TRUSTEES.

Section 8660. (Controlling body of a corporation.) The corporate powers, business and property of corporations formed under this title shall be exercised, conducted, and controlled by the board of directors; or, if there is no capital stock, by the board of trustees. (R. S. Sec. 3248; R. S. 1880.)

First election of directors. § 8636 and note.
Annual elections. § 8647 and note.
Term of office, resignation, removal, etc., see note to § 8647.

Meetings.

Directors must act as a board. Individual directors, as such, have no authority to represent a corporation. To bind the corporation the directors must act together as a board.

State v. People's, etc., Assn., 42 O. S. 579 (1885).
Belting Co. v. Gibson, 68 O. S. 442, 449 (1903).
State v. Railway, 6 C. C. 412; 3 C. D. 516 (1892); s. c., 49 O. S. 668.

Schot, etc., Co. v. Security, etc., Ins. Co., 7 N. P. n. s. 548; 19 L.
D. 249 (C. P. 1908); aff'd, 11 C. C. n. s. 401; 20 C. D. 656.

Tyson v. Miller-Tyson Co., 15 C. C. n. s. 177, 182, 433; 23 C. D. 418,
424 (1912).

Young, etc., Co. v. Taylor, etc., Church, 5 N. P. 378; 7 L. D. 449
(C. P. 1898).

See Ohio v. Treasurer, etc., 22 O. S. 144 (1871).

McCortle v. Bates, 29 O. S. 419, 422 (1876).

The board can not exclude minority directors from the privileges and
duties of office.

State v. Railway, 6 C. C. 412; 3 C. D. 516 (1892); s. c., 49 O. S.
668.

Notice of meeting. Where regular meetings of the board are provided for in the by-laws, no notice thereof need be given unless notice
is required by the regulations or by-laws.

Mitchell v. Bookwalter Wheel Co., 4 N. P. n. s. 609, 619 (1905);
aff'd, no rep., 75 O. S. 639.

State v. Bonnell, 35 O. S. 10, 15 (1878).

Notice of special meetings should be given to all directors. But
transactions at a special meeting, at which a quorum was present, may
be ratified by the absent members who were not notified.

Bank v. Flour Co., 41 O. S. 552, 559 (1885).

Where a meeting is adjourned no further notice of the adjourned meeting is necessary.

Mitchell v. Bookwalter Wheel Co., 4 N. P. n. s. 609, 619 (1905);
aff'd, no rep., 75 O. S. 639.

Quorum. A majority of the directors constitutes a quorum for the
transaction of business. § 8664.

Dickason v. Grafton, etc., Co., 6 C. C. n. s. 329, 333; 17 C. D. 357
(1905); aff'd, no rep., 76 O. S. 612.

Where a quorum has assembled a majority of those present may
act and bind the corporation, although a minority of the board.

Kalb v. American N. B., 21 C. C. 1, 7, 8; 11 C. D. 437 (1900); aff'd,
65 O. S. 566.

Gumaer v. Cripple Creek, etc., Co., 40 Colo. 1; 90 Pac. 81 (1907).

Sargent v. Webster, 54 Mass. 497 (1847).

Hax v. Davis Mill Co., 39 Mo. App. 453 (1889).

Buell v. Buckingham, 16 Iowa 284 (1860).

Compare Hamilton v. Hamilton Coal Co., 12 C. D. 637 (1894).

A director can not vote by proxy, nor in counting a quorum can he
be regarded as present by proxy.

Ohio, etc., Bank v. Iron Co., 30 W. L. B. 382 (Super. Ct. Cin. 1893).

It is presumed, in the absence of evidence, that a quorum was present.

Young, etc., Co. v. Taylor, etc., Church, 5 N. P. 378, 380; 7 L. D. 449,
452 (C. P. 1898).

Where less than a quorum is present, the acts of the directors present
are voidable; but may be ratified by the board either expressly or by
acquiescence and delay in taking steps to avoid the same.

U. S., etc., Co. v. Atlantic, etc., Co., 34 O. S. 450 (1878).

But an approval of the minutes of such a meeting, at a subsequent
meeting, is not a ratification. It is merely an approval of the form of
statement or correctness of the proceedings.

Ohio, etc., Bank v. Iron Co., 30 W. L. B. 382 (Super. Ct. Cin. 1893).

Proceedings and minutes. A director can not vote by proxy.

Ohio, etc., Bank v. Iron Co., 30 W. L. B. 382 (Super. Ct. Cin. 1893).

An approval of the minutes of a previous meeting is an approval of the form of statement or correctness of the previous proceedings, but not a ratification of the action of the board.

Ohio, etc., Bank v. Iron Co., 30 W. L. B. 382 (Super. Ct. Cin. 1893).

Where an action of the board is not entered in the minutes it may be proved by parol evidence.

First N. B. v. Mansfield Sav. Bank, 10 C. C. 233, 237; 6 C. D. 454 (1895).

Dixon v. Subdistrict, etc., 3 C. C. 517; 2 C. D. 298 (1888).

C. H. & D. R. Co. v. Harter, 26 O. S. 426 (1875).

Fritsch Mfg. Co. v. Elmont, etc., Co., 11 C. C. n. s. 356; 21 C. D. 47 (1908).

In construing the proceedings of directors the court will examine the entire record to ascertain the intention.

Lockwood v. Wildman, 13 Ohio 430 (1844).

Where the record is ambiguous, the proceedings will be construed so as to be consistent with all other proceedings pertaining to the same subject matter.

East Cleveland R. Co. v. Everett, 19 C. C. 205; 10 C. D. 493.

Record as evidence.

See Stillwater Turnpike Co. v. Coover, 25 O. S. 558 (1874).

Toledo, etc., Co. v. Toledo, etc., Co., 12 C. C. 367; 5 C. D. 643 (1893).

DE FACTO DIRECTORS OR OFFICERS.

A person who acts as a director or officer, after a supposed election or appointment, but which in fact is illegal, may bind the corporation. He may be ousted by proceedings in quo warranto. But so long as no proceeding is instituted nor objection made his acts as to third persons are binding on the corporation.

Clarke v. Thomas, 34 O. S. 46, 58 (1877).

Campbell Pty. Press Co. v. Bellman Bros. Co., 11 C. C. 360; 5 C. D. 389 (1896).

Lattimer v. Mosaic Glass Co., 13 C. C. 163; 7 C. D. 430 (1896).

Ehrman v. Union, etc., Ins. Co., 35 O. S. 324, 339 (1880); (affirming 2 W. L. B. 3).

First Pres. Soo. v. First Pres. Soc., 25 O. S. 128, 133 (1874).

See State v. Burial Assn., 8 C. C. n. s. 233; 18 C. D. 397 (1906).

His acts can not be collaterally attacked by creditors or debtors of the corporation.

Ehrman v. Union, etc., Ins. Co., 35 O. S. 324 (1880).

Lattimer v. Mosaic Glass Co., 13 C. C. 163; 7 C. D. 430 (1896).

Raymond v. Spring Grove, etc., Co., 21 W. L. B. 103 (Super. Ct. Cin. 1889).

Nor by stockholders.

Chamberlain v. Painesville, etc., R. Co., 15 O. S. 225, 250.

Nor by other persons claiming to be the lawful directors.

Presbyterian Soc. v. Smithers, 12 O. S. 248 (1861).

A de facto board of directors may make an assignment for creditors.

Harrison v. Ellis, 15 L. D. 501 (C. P. 1905).

DUTIES OF DIRECTORS.

Are largely supervisory. The duties of directors are, to a considerable extent, supervisory. Directors are not required to devote themselves to details of the corporate business which may be left to the executive officers and to subordinate employes.

Mason v. Moore, 73 O. S. 275, 296 (1906).

Cincinnati v. Cameron, 33 O. S. 336, 364 (1878).

Glass v. Courtright, 14 N. P. n. s. 273; 23 L. D. 253 (C. P. 1913).

To keep books. It is the duty of directors to see that proper books and accounts are kept.

Freon v. Carriage Co., 42 O. S. 30, 40 (1884).

To supervise issue of certificates of stock. Directors are charged with the duty of observing care in supervising the issue of certificates of stock.

Railway Co. v. Bank, 56 O. S. 351 (1897).

When director charged with knowledge of contents of corporate records and books. In general directors are not held, as a matter of law, to know all its affairs or what its books would show.

Mason v. Moore, 73 O. S. 275, 296 (1906).

Pugh v. City, etc., Co., 1 N. P. n. s. 253, 257, 14 L. D. 50, 53 (Super. Ct. Cin. 1901); aff'd, 68 O. S. 730.

But where a director is dealing in corporate property on his own account, he is chargeable with notice of the action of the board as to such property, whether he was present or not at the meeting which took such action.

Greenville Gas Co. v. Reis, 54 O. S. 549 (1896).

Where corporation insolvent. Where a corporation becomes insolvent it is the duty of the directors to take steps to preserve the corporate property and see that it is applied to the payment of creditors' claims.

Cheney v. Maumee Cycle Co., 20 C. C. 19; 10 C. D. 717 (1900); aff'd, 64 O. S. 205.

Delegation of duties to executive committee. The supervision and control of transactions in the usual course of business may be delegated to an executive committee of the board.

Lutterby v. Herancourt Brewing Co., 12 L. D. 67, 74 (Super. Ct. Cin. 1901).

See Bank v. Iron Co., 30 W. L. B. 382 (Super. Ct. Cin. 1893).

Whether powers involving discretion may be delegated to a committee composed of directors has not been decided in Ohio.

In other jurisdictions the authorities are conflicting but it is said that, by weight of authority, such powers may be so delegated and that the acts and contracts authorized by such committee are binding.

Cook on Corporations, § 715.

Thompson on Corporations, § 1207 (2d ed.).

Lutterby v. Herancourt Brewing Co., 12 L. D. 67, 74 (Super. Ct. Cin. 1901).

An executive committee should transact its business at a meeting of which all members should have reasonable notice.

Hayes v. Canada, etc., Co., 181 Fed. 289 (C. C. A. 1910).

Executive committee of bank directors, see §§ 9728, 9729.

Delegation of powers by directors in general. The powers of directors can not be delegated except to a committee of directors. A corporation can not enter into partnership for the reason that the powers of directors would thereby be delegated to third persons.

Miller, etc., Co. v. Laidlaw, etc., Co., 4 N. P. n. s. 554; 17 L. D. 499 (C. P. 1905).

Care required of directors. Negligence. The general management and supervision of the business of a corporation are committed to the directors. They are authorized to appoint executive officers and agents and may properly entrust the custody of the corporate property and books to such officers. This does not absolve the directors from the duty of reasonable supervision and the exercise of that degree of care which is exercised by ordinarily careful and prudent men acting under similar circumstances. But they are not insurers of the fidelity of the officers and agents. Where directors act with ordinary care, they are not liable for losses caused by dishonest or wrongful acts of such officers or agents. Directors are not, as a rule, required to devote themselves to the details of the business.

Directors of a corporation are not held, as a matter of law, to know all its affairs, or what its books and papers would show, and such knowledge can not be imputed to them for the purpose of charging them with liability.

Mason v. Moore, 73 O. S. 275, 296 (1906).

See Kalb v. American N. B., 21 C. C. 1; 11 C. D. 437; aff'd, 65 O. S. 566.

Glass v. Courtwright, 14 N. P. n. s. 273; 23 L. D. 253 (C. P. 1913).

Directors are not liable for errors or mistakes occurring while they are acting in good faith and in accordance with their best judgment as reasonably prudent men.

Baldwin v. Egan, 5 O. L. R. 476 (1907); aff'd, 11 C. C. n. s. 584.

See below *Liability of officers and agents.*

Trust relation of directors to stockholders. See Rouse v. Bank, 46 O. S. 493, 502 (1889).

Larwill v. Burke, 19 C. C. 449; 10 C. D. 579, 598 (1900).

See also note to § 8684.

Officers do not occupy a fiduciary relation toward a purchaser of their individual stock.

Cook v. Henderson, 8 Am. L. R. 429 (Dist. Ct. 1879).

POWERS OF DIRECTORS.

Controlling body of corporation. Section 8660 constitutes the directors acting as a board the controlling body of a corporation.

Bradford Belting Co. v. Gibson, 68 O. S. 442 (1903).

Sims v. Street Railroad Co., 37 O. S. 556 (1882).

Goodin v. Evans, 18 O. S. 150 (1868).

The corporate powers which are exercised by the directors are those which pertain to the ordinary transactions of the corporation. Directors can not make fundamental changes in the composition or business of the corporation.

Mannington v. H. V. Ry. Co., 9 N. P. n. s. 641, 684; 20 L. D. 468 (1910); removed to U. S. Ct., 8 O. L. R. 451; 16 O. F. D. 552.

Chicago City Railway Co. v. Allerton, 18 Wall. (U. S.) 233 (1874).

Control of directors by stockholders. The stockholders can not control the board of directors in its management of corporate affairs (except as to acts which by statute require ratification by stockholders. See §§ 8709, 8710 to 8718, 8699, 8720). Majority stockholders at a meeting can not take charge of the corporate business, or withdraw it from the control of the directors.

Dayton, etc., R. Co. v. Hatch, 1 Dis. 84, 91 (Cin. Super. Ct. 1855).

See Sims v. Street Railroad Co., 37 O. S. 556 (1882).

Donner v. Dayton, etc., R. Co., 1 C. S. C. R. 130, 140-141 (1871).

Stewart v. Little Miami, etc., Co., 14 Ohio 353, 357 (1846).

Where the directors have declared a dividend out of surplus profits, the stockholders have no power to rescind such action.

Mitchell v. Bookwalter Wheel Co., 4 N. P. n. s. 609; 17 L. D. 483 (C. P. 1905); aff'd, no rep., 75 O. S. 639.

A cognovit note executed by the president of a corporation without authority from the directors, is not rendered valid by the fact that the president was the owner of a majority of the stock.

Smead Foundry Co. v. Chesbrough, 18 C. C. 783, 787; 6 C. D. 670 (1895).

But stockholders may at a special meeting under § 8665 increase the number of directors.

See Gold Bluff, etc., Corp. v. Whitlock, 75 Conn. 669 (1903).

In re Griffing Iron Co., 63 N. J. L. 168, 357 (1898).

Control of directors by court on application of stockholders. A court of equity will not interfere with the board of directors in its management and control of corporate affairs, on the application of stockholders, while the board is acting within the scope of its authority, and in the absence of fraud or breach of trust.

Sims v. Street Railroad Co., 37 O. S. 556 (1882).

Coss v. Mansfield Lodge, 4 C. C. n. s. 11; 14 C. D. 36 (1902).

Koblitz v. W. R. U., 21 C. C. 144; 11 C. D. 515 (1901).

De Lacroix v. Eid, etc., Co., 8 N. P. n. s. 489; 19 L. D. 767 (1909).

A stockholder can not sue to enforce an active duty within the powers of directors.

Port Clinton, etc., R. Co. v. Cleveland, etc., R. Co., 13 O. S. 544, 561 (1862).

But a breach of trust may be prevented by injunction or a receivership.

Port Clinton, etc., R. Co. v. Cleveland, etc., R. Co., 13 O. S. 544, 561 (1862).

C. H. & D. R. Co. v. Duckworth, 2 C. C. 518; 1 C. D. 618 (1887).

See infra *When stockholder may sue on behalf of corporation.*

A court of equity will not interfere, at the suit of a stockholder who is acting for a competitor, to prevent directors from cutting prices or from exercising their discretion with respect thereto.

Kuhn v. Woolson Spice Co., 13 C. C. 547; 7 C. D. 289 (1897).

Contracts limiting powers of directors. A provision in a consolidation agreement which prohibits the consolidated company from issuing bonds, or making leases which entail fixed charges, without the consent of a majority in interest of holders of preferred stock, is not in conflict with § 8660.

Burke v. Cleveland, etc., Ry. Co., 22 W. L. B. 11 (C. P. 1889).

A contract for a term of years, extending beyond the term of office of the directors by whom it is made, is valid and binding upon future directors.

Railroad Co. v. Furnace Co., 37 O. S. 321 (1881).

Compare Port Clinton, etc., R. Co. v. Cleveland, etc., R. Co., 13 O. S. 544, 560 (1862).

The powers of directors can not be delegated, except to a committee composed of directors. A corporation can not enter into partnership for the reason that the powers of the directors would thereby be delegated to third persons.

Miller, etc., Co. v. Laidlaw-Gordon Co., 4 N. P. n. s. 554; 17 L. D. 499 (C. P. 1907).

See note to § 8627. *Power to enter into partnership.*

Power to dispose of unissued stock. The directors have power to dispose of the stock which remains unsubscribed after their election.

Sims v. Street Railroad Co., 37 O. S. 565 (1882).

See note to § 8630. *Disposition of stock by corporation after election of directors.*

To sell property. Directors have the right to sell corporate property.

Donner v. Dayton, etc., R. Co., 1 C. S. C. R. 130 ,140 (1871).

But a sale of the entire property of a corporation must be ratified by the stockholders.

See §§ 8710 to 8718.

The trustees of a religious society organized under §§ 8653 and 8654 have no power to dispose of its real estate without the consent of its members and without authority of the court.

South Kenton, etc., Assn. v. Espy, 17 C. C. 524; 9 C. D. 695 (1899).

To bring or defend suits. The power to bring or dispose of suits is vested in the board of directors.

Wadsworth v. Davis, 13 O. S. 123, 130 (1862).

For authority of president to bring suit see

Kalb v. American N. B., 21 C. C. 1; 11 C. D. 437 (1900); aff'd, no rep., 65 O. S. 566.

To make assignment for creditors. The directors of an insolvent corporation may make an assignment for creditors.

Commercial N. B. v. Cincinnati N. B., 3 C. C. 513, 517; 2 C. D. 295 (1889).

(*De facto* directors) Harrison v. Ellis, 15 L. D. 501 (C. P. 1905).

See Keystone Bank v. Union Oil Co., 2 C. C. n. s. 420; 15 C. D. 464. (Foreign corporation. Assignment authorized by stockholders.)

A fraudulent assignment for creditors made by directors, against the interest of stockholders, may be vacated in a stockholders' suit.

Home & Sav. Assn. v. Jones, 64 O. S. 147 (1901).

An asignment may also be vacated at the instance of stockholders upon their giving a bond to pay all the corporate debts.

Harrison v. Ellis, 15 L. D. 501 (C. P. 1905).

To release subscriptions to stock.

See notes to §§ 8630, 8674.

CORPORATE CONTRACTS.

Power to make is vested in directors. The power of making contracts on behalf of a corporation rests in the board of directors.

Bradford Belting Co. v. Gibson, 68 O. S. 442 (1903).

Authority of agents to contract. Corporate contracts are usually negotiated and executed by executive officers or agents, but the authority of such an officer or agent should in some manner be traced to the board of directors.

Bradford Belting Co. v. Gibson, 68 O. S. 442 (1903).

Minor v. Board of Control, 20 C. C. 4; 11 C. D. 16 (1899).

Tyson v. Miller-Tyson Co., 15 C. C. n. s. 177, 182; 23 C. D. 418, 424 (1912).

See note to § 8664. *Executive officers. Powers.*

In the absence of express authority, and of such a course of dealing with the world as clearly implies authority to do a controverted act, a corporation can be bound only by its board of directors.

Bradford Belting Co. v. Gibson, 68 O. S. 442 (1903).

Authority of agent to contract. How conferred. Authority may be conferred upon an executive officer or agent by the directors expressly in the by-laws, or by motion or resolution.

Dickason v. Grafton, etc., Co., 6 C. C. n. s. 329, 332, 333; 17 C. D. 357 (1905); aff'd, 76 O. S. 612.

Kalb v. American N. B., 21 C. C. 1, 7; 11 C. D. 437 (1900); aff'd, 65 O. S. 566.

When express authority to issue negotiable paper is relied on, it must be clearly proved.

Bank v. Machine Co., 9 N. P. n. s. 449 (1910).

A corporation may be bound by the acts of an agent upon whom it has conferred apparent authority. An agent of a warehouse company, authorized to receive goods for storage, may bind the corporation by an agreement to effect insurance thereon.

Storage Co. v. Cox, 74 O. S. 284 (1906).

Authority may be given informally by consent or acquiescence of the board. Unauthorized acts may be ratified by the directors.

Baldwin v. Hillsborough, etc., R. Co., 10 W. L. J. 337 (C. P. 1853).
Smead Foundry Co. v. Chesbrough, 18 C. C. 783; 6 C. D. 670 (1895).
E. Cleveland R. Co. v. Everett, 19 C. C. 205; 10 C. D. 493 (1900).
Western N. B. v. Armstrong, 152 U. S. 346; 7 O. F. D. 499 (1894).
Armstrong v. Chemical N. B., 83 Fed. 556 (1897).
Sun, etc., Assn. v. Moore, 183 U. S. 642 (1902).

Ratification may be express, by resolution, or implied from acquiescence and failure to object after knowledge of the acts.

U. S., etc., Co. v. Atlantic, etc., R. Co., 34 O. S. 450 (1878).
Marriott v. Columbus, etc., Co., 16 L. D. 135 (C. P. 1905); aff'd,
    10 C. C. n. s. 573, 575.

But knowledge by two directors only is not the knowledge of the board so as to effect a ratification of an unauthorized contract.

East Cleveland R. Co. v. Everett, 19 C. C. 205; 10 C. D. 493 (1900).

A general resolution of the board commending the officers and their official conduct is not a ratification of unlawful acts of which the board had no knowledge.

Columbus, etc., Co. v. McManigal, 6 N. P. n. s. 193 (C. P. 1907).

Where a petition for a street improvement was signed by the secretary and general manager without authority, it was held that a subsequent ratification by the directors did not render the petition valid, although it would estop the corporation.

Minor v. Board of Control, 20 C. C. 4; 11 C. D. 16 (1899).

Where a corporation, for several years, received and retained benefits of a contract entered into on its behalf by its president, making no attempt to repudiate the contract and by further corporate action expressly recognized its existence its ratification was held to be established.

Coney Island Co. v. McIntyre-Paxton Co., 200 Fed. 901 (C. C. A. 1912).

Refusal to perform contracts. The power of refusing to perform contracts is vested in the board of directors.

Bradford Belting Co. v. Gibson, 68 O. S. 442 (1903).

Stockholder not authorized to act for corporation. A stockholder as such has no authority to bind the corporation.

Hogg v. Zanesville Mfg. Co., Wright 139 (1832).
Loomis v. Eagle Bank, 1 Dis. 285, 288 (Super. Ct. Cin. 1857); aff'd,
    10 O. S. 327.
State v. Liberty Township, 22 O. S. 144 (1871).
Read v. Loan Co., 68 O. S. 280 (1903).
Trevitt v. Converse, 31 O. S. 60 (1876).

Although he may own a majority of the stock.

Smead Foundry Co. v. Chesbrough, 18 C. C. 783, 787; 6 C. D. 670 (1895).

But under some circumstances the acts of all the stockholders will be regarded as corporate acts. See note to § 8627. *Corporation as a legal entity.*

A receiver is not the agent of a corporation. A contract by the receiver of a railroad for coal for its use for a certain time is not binding on the railway company after his discharge.

Consolidated, etc., Co. v. Cincinnati, etc., R. Co., 10 W. L. B. 42 (Dist. Ct. 1883).

Contract should be in name of corporation. The contract or conveyance of a corporation should be in the corporate name.

Norris v. Dains, 52 O. S. 215 (1894).

Although a contract in the name of an individual officer may be enforced by the corporation.

Commissioners v. Perry, 5 Ohio 56, 64 (1831).

Presumptions and burden of proof as to authority of officers and agents. (1) Authority conferred by statute. Where duties are conferred on certain officers by statute, their acts in the performance of such duties are binding on the corporation. Stock certificates, required by statute to be signed by the president and secretary, are valid in the hands of innocent purchasers although fraudulently issued.

Railway Co. v. Bank, 56 O. S. 351, 378, 388.

(2) **Authority conferred by regulations.** See § 8704.

Bradford Belting Co. v. Gibson, 68 O. S. 442, 449.

Dickason v. Grafton, etc., Co., 6 C. C. n. s. 329, 333; 17 C. D. 357; aff'd, 76 O. S. 612.

(3) **Deeds and instruments under corporate seal.** A deed executed in the name of a corporation by its president, under the corporate seal, is presumed to have been authorized by the directors and is prima facie valid. The mere fact that such authority is not found on the directors' minutes will not rebut the presumption.

R. R. Co. v. Harter, 26 O. S. 426 (1875).

Bank v. Flour Co., 41 O. S. 552, 557 (1885).

Sheehan v. Davis, 17 O. S. 571, 581 (1867).

Bosche v. Toledo, etc., Co., 14 C. C. 289, 295; 7 C. D. 377.

See notes to §§ 8627 and 8664.

But, when objected to, such an instrument can not be admitted in evidence without proof of its execution. The signature of the president does not prove itself, nor is it proved by the corporate seal.

Walsh v. Barton, 24 O. S. 28, 41 (1873).

(4) **Promissory notes.** The promissory note of a corporation signed in its name by its president has been held to be prima facie valid and binding on the corporation.

Dexter Sav. Bank v. Friend, 90 Fed. 703 (C. C. Ohio 1898).

See Andres v. Morgan, 62 O. S. 236 (1900).

Security, etc., Ins. Co. v. Schott, 11 C. C. n. s. 401; aff'd, 83 O. S. 507.

But not a note payable to the president himself. There is no presumption that such a note is authorized.

In re Hartwell Furniture Co., 7 O. L. R. 555 (Ref. in Bkry. 1909).

In re Continental Iron Co., 2 O. L. R. 563 (Ref. in Bkry. 1904).

Arnkens v. Rouse, 26 W. L. B. 221 (C. P. 1891).

Compare In re Troy, etc., Co., 136 Fed. 420; aff'd, 142 Fed. 1038

A cognovit note signed by the president is not binding on the corporation in the absence of proof of authority from the directors.

Smead Foundry Co. v. Chesbrough, 18 C. C. 783; 6 C. D. 670 (1895).

(5) **Chattel mortgage.** Is has been held that a chattel mortgage executed by the president and secretary of a corporation, in its name and under its corporate seal, is presumptively authorized and valid.

Bosche v. Toledo, etc., Co., 14 C. C. 289; 7 C. D. 374 (1897).

Fritsch Mfg. Co. v. Elmont, etc., Co., 11 C. C. n. s. 356; 21 C. D. 47 (1908).

(6) **Verbal statements. Admissions.** A statement, by the secretary of a corporation, that the corporation would not perform a contract, and

that he was authorized by the directors and stockholders to so state, does not bind the corporation without further evidence showing his authority. Such a statement is not prima facie evidence that the directors had decided not to perform the contract.

Bradford Belting Co. v. Gibson, 68 O. S. 442 (1903).

A stipulation in an express contract of a corporation can not be proved merely by admissions of the president made after the transaction.

National Starch Co. v. Gruner, 13 C. C. n. s. 355 (1910).

Declarations of an officer or agent are not admissible unless made while transacting business of the corporation.

Worthington v. Cleveland City Ry., 9 C. C. n. s. 433; 19 C. D. 321 (1904); aff'd, 75 O. S. 626.

A corporation is not bound by an admission made by an officer after the transaction, unless the circumstances are such as to constitute an estoppel.

Marmet Co. v. Cincinnati, 12 C. C. n. s. 225, 227 (1909).

Cincinnati, etc., Co. v. Cincinnati, 19 C. C. 607 (1899).

Loomis v. Eagle Bank, 1 Dis. 285, 288 (Super. Ct. Cin. 1857); aff'd, 10 O. S. 327.

Sloss, etc., Co. v. Smith, 11 C. C. 213; 5 C. D. 79 (1895); reversed on other grounds, 57 O. S. 518.

Admissions of individual directors are not admissible in evidence to prove a contract alleged to have been made by the board.

Dixon v. Subdistrict, etc., 3 C. C. 517; 2 C. D. 298 (1888).

Admissions of stockholders who are not officers are not admissible in evidence to charge the corporation.

Hogg v. Zanesville Mfg. Co., Wright 139 (1832).

Duty of person dealing with agent to inquire as to action of directors. It has been held that a person dealing with executive officers need not inquire whether the directors have met and passed a resolution authorizing the transaction, where the transaction is within the corporate powers.

Bosche v. Toledo, etc., Co., 14 C. C. 289; 7 C. D. 374 (1897).

Fritsch Mfg. Co. v. Elmont, etc., Co., 11 C. C. n. s. 356; 21 C. D. 47 (1908).

Compare Bradford Belting Co. v. Gibson, 68 O. S. 442 (1903).

Fraudulent acts of agents or officers. Liability of corporation. Acts which are within the scope of the authority of an agent or officer are binding on the corporation as to innocent third persons, although a fraud upon the corporation.

Railway Co. v. Bank, 56 O. S. 351 (1897).

Citizens Sav. Bank v. Blakesley, 42 O. S. 645 (1885).

Orme v. Baker, 74 O. S. 337, 349, 354 (1906).

Notice to corporation.   (1)   Knowledge of executive officer or agent. A corporation is charged with notice of facts which are within the knowledge of its officer or agent while such officer is engaged in corporate business which he is authorized to transact.

Paul v. Caldwell Furnace Co., 7 C. C. n. s. 272; 17 C. D. 768 (1905).

Trustees v. Deposit Co., 76 O. S. 253, 265 (1907).

Burgoyne v. Clarkson, 2 W. L. J. 325 (C. P. 1845).

Holmes v. Hayes, 32 W. L. B. 346; 52 O. S. 617.

Although the agent is a special agent.

Mass, etc., Ins. Co. v. Eshelman, 30 O. S. 647 (1876).

And although the officer is acting fraudulently.

Orme v. Baker, 74 O. S. 337, 348, 354 (1906).

A corporation is chargeable with the composite knowledge which comes to it through the channels of its several agents. It is not necessary that one agent should know all the facts.

Neal v. Union Stock Yards Co., 1 C. C. n. s. 13; 15 C. D. 299 (1903).

But where the officer is dealing with the corporation, his knowledge is not imputable to it. Where a president sells land to the corporation his knowledge of equities affecting the title is not chargeable to the corporation.

Alt v. Weber, 20 W. L. B. 467 (Super. Ct. Cin. 1888).

The transaction must be within the authority of the officer or agent.

Railway Co. v. McCoy, 42 O. S. 251, 252 (1884).

Ashtabula, etc., Co. v. Stephenson, 12 C. D. 631.

Knowledge of the insolvency of a bank by its cashier and vice president is imputable to the bank so as to entitle a depositor to recover a deposit, although the insolvency was caused by the fraudulent acts of such officers and although the deposit was made after such officers had absconded.

Orme v. Baker, 74 O. S. 337 (1906).

Where a corporation takes over the business of another corporation, retaining the same officers, knowledge by the president, who is authorized to employ men, of a contract of employment of the old corporation is knowledge of the new corporation.

Paul v. Caldwell Furnace Co., 7 C. C. n. s. 272; 17 C. D. 768 (1905).

——. (2) Knowledge of director. Knowledge of one director is imputed to the corporation only while he is acting officially in the business of the corporation, unless he is acting under some special authority other than that of a director.

Railway Co. v. McCoy, 42 O. S. 251, 252 (1884).

Loomis v. Eagle Bank, 1 Dis. 285 (Super. Ct. Cin. 1857); s. c., 10 O. S. 327.

The knowledge of two directors is not the knowledge of the board so as to work a ratification of an unauthorized contract.

East Cleveland R. Co. v. Everett, 19 C. C. 205; 10 C. D. 493 (1900).

If the position of the director is adverse to that of the corporation the knowledge of such director can not be imputed to the corporation. Where a bank discounted a note for one of its directors, who was also a member of its discount committee, the bank is not charged with knowledge of such director that there was a defense to the note.

Loomis v. Eagle Bank, 1 Dis. 285 (Super. Ct. Cin. 1857); s. c., 10 O. S. 327.

Antioch College v. Carroll, 25 W. L. B. 289, 294 (Super. Ct. Cin. 1890).

Sayler v. Simpson, 12 L. D. 148, 151 (Super. Ct. Cin. 1888).

CONTRACTS BETWEEN DIRECTORS AND CORPORATION.

In general. A contract between a corporation and its directors is not void, but merely voidable at the option of the corporation within a reasonable time.

Browne v. U. S. Board & Paper Co., 20 C. C. 351 (1900); s. c., 6 N. P. 254; 1 C. C. n. s. 345; 15 C. D. 347 (1903); 7 C. C. n. s. 15; 18 C. D. 44 (1905); aff'd, 75 O. S. 604 (1906); s. c., 4 O. L. R. 539; 17 L. D. 261 (1906).

U. S., etc., Co. v. Atlantic, etc., R. Co., 34 O. S. 450, 461 (1878).

Larwell v. Burke, 19 C. C. 449; 10 C. D. 579 (1900).

Where such a contract is fair and beneficial to the corporation it will not be set aside at the suit of minority stockholders.

Sims v. Street Railroad Co., 37 O. S. 556, 566 (1882).

Roth v. St. Clair, etc., Co., 13 L. D. 154 (Super. Ct. Cin. 1902).

But the relation of the directors to the corporation being a fiduciary one, entire good faith and fair dealing are required on the part of the directors.

Yeiser v. U. S. Board, etc., Co., 7 C. C. n. s. 15, 16; 18 C. D. 44; aff'd, 75 O. S. 604.

And a contract in fraud of the corporation may be set aside at the suit of a minority stockholder.

Burch v. Coan, 4 O. L. R. 731; 17 L. D. 563 (Super. Ct. Cin. 1907).

An illegal purchase of stock in other corporations, made by a corporation from its directors who owned all its capital stock, was held invalid as to creditors.

Railway Co. v. Burke, 19 W. L. B. 27 (C. P. 1887).

A contract by a manufacturing company giving the disposal of its product to a sales agency, in which some of the directors are interested, and thereby permitting them to make profits to which the corporation is entitled, may be rescinded and cancelled by the corporation.

U. S., etc., Co. v. Browne, 1 C. C. n. s. 345; 15 C. D. 347 (1903); s. c., 7 C. C. n. s. 15; 18 C. D. 44 (1905); aff'd, 75 O. S. 604.

Where corporate property was bid in at a foreclosure sale by a director for less than its value, the sale was set aside by the court on the application of a bondholder, upon the giving of security that upon a resale the bondholder would bid at least a certain larger amount.

Secor v. Maumee, etc., Co., 1 N. P. 100; 1 L. D. 80 (1894).

Liability to corporation for profits. Secret profits made by directors in transactions with the corporation may be recovered by the corporation.

Yeiser v. U. S. Board & Paper Co., 107 Fed. 340 (C. C. A. Ohio 1901).

U. S. Board & Paper Co. v. Yeiser, 4 O. L. R. 539; 17 L. D. 261 (Super. Ct. Cin. 1906).

Where directors sell their own property to the corporation at a fraudulent overvaluation, they are liable in damages to the corporation.

Shawnee, etc., Co. v. Miller, 1 C. C. n. s. 569; 14 C. D. 199 (1902).

See Railway Co. v. Burke, 19 W. L. B. 27 (C. P. 1887).

Purchases of stock by directors. A director may purchase unissued or treasury stock when the sale is authorized by a quorum of disinterested directors and where no action has been taken to withhold the stock from sale to other stockholders or the public.

Sims v. Street Railroad Co., 37 O. S. 556 (1882).

Taylor v. Miami Exporting Co., 6 Ohio 176, 223 (1833).

Purchases below par by directors have been sustained as against other stockholders, where the corporation was pressed for money to continue business, and the stock had been previously offered at the same price to the other stockholders.

Peter v. Union Mfg. Co., 56 O. S. 181 (1897).

Under § 8798 stock of a railroad company purchased below par by a director is void.

A purchase made in order to vote at an election for directors is valid, when full value is paid for the stock.

Hall v. Hall, 11 C. C. n. s. 335; 20 C. D. 826 (1908).

Taylor v. Miami Exporting Co., 6 Ohio 176, 223 (1833).

See Loomis v. Dexter, 20 W. L. B. 5 (Super. Ct. Cin. 1888).

But sales to directors can not be made on more favorable terms than to other stockholders,

Kinsey v. Mt. Auburn Cable Co., 6 C. C. n. s. 305; 17 C. D. 33 (1905); aff'd, 75 O. S. 602.

nor without valuable consideration.

Straman v. No. Baltimore, etc., Co., 8 C. C. 89; 4 C. D. 339 (1893).

Where stock subscribed for by directors was paid for with secret profits made by the directors out of a fraudulent sale of property to the corporation, the stock was cancelled at the suit of the corporation.

Yeiser v. U. S. Board & Paper Co., 107 Fed. 340 (C. C. A. Ohio (1901).

Where directors exchanged stock for their own property at an over-valuation they were held liable for the difference between the par value of the stock and the actual value of the property.

Gates v. Tippecanoe Stone Co., 57 O. S. 60 (1897).

When directors may act for two corporations. A contract made between two corporations through their respective boards of directors is not voidable at the election of one of the corporations merely because a minority of its directors were also directors of the other company, in the absence of fraud or a breach of trust.

U. S., etc., Co. v. Atlantic, etc., Co., 34 O. S. 450 (1878).

Henry v. Pittsburg, etc., Ry. Co., 2 N. P. 118, 154 (1895).

Where one corporation sold property to another corporation for its full value, the directors of the selling company being also directors of the purchasing company, the sale being ratified by the stockholders of the vendor, and the directors thereafter incurred personal financial risks and realized large profits, it was held that stockholders in the selling corporation could not, years afterward, recover a share of the profits.

Larwill v. Burke, 19 C. C. 449; 10 C. D. 579 (1900).

That officers and directors of a burial association, not for profit, were also officers and directors of an undertaking company was held not to be a ground for the forfeiture of the charter of the burial association where it was not subsidiary to or controlled by the undertaking company.

State v. Burial Assn., 8 C. C. n. s. 233; 18 C. D. 397 (1906).

See G. C. § 666.

Unfair contracts. Where a railroad company purchased a majority of the stock of another corporation, elected a friendly board of directors, purchased property of such other corporation for less than its value, and constructed a railroad thereon, it was held that, although stockholders and creditors of such other company could not, after the road had been completed, reclaim the property or enjoin its use, they could, by action, compel the railroad company to account for its actual value.

Goodin v. Cincinnati, etc., Co., 18 O. S. 169, 182 (1868).

See Mannington v. H. V. Railway Co., 9 N. P. n. s. 641, 680; 20 L. D. 468; (removed to U. S. Ct., 8 O. L. R. 451; 16 O. F. D. 552).

WHEN STOCKHOLDER MAY SUE ON BEHALF OF CORPORATION.

See also *Liability of officers and agents,* below.

In general. Suits to remedy wrongs against the corporate property or rights should, in the first instance, be brought by the corporation itself.

Zinn v. Baxter, 65 O. S. 341, 364 (1901).

Hamilton v. Hamilton Coal Co., 12 C. D. 637 (1894).

But where the corporation fails or refuses to sue, one or more stockholders may bring suit.

Zinn v. Baxter, 65 O. S. 341, 364 (1901).

Taylor v. Miami Exporting Co., 5 Ohio 162 (1831).

Zabriskie v. Railroad Co., 64 U. S. (23 How.) 381 (1860).

The suit must be for the common benefit of all the stockholders. One stockholder can not sue the directors for his share of the common damages suffered by all stockholders in consequence of the misconduct of directors.

Zinn v. Baxter, 65 O. S. 341, 365 (1901).

Distinction between stockholders representative suits on behalf of corporation, and stockholders suits to protect individual property rights.

See Mannington v. H. V. Railway Co., 9 N. P. n. s. 641, 657-659;

20 L. D. 468 (C. P. 1910) ; (removed to U. S. Ct., 8 O. L. R. 451; 16 O. F. D. 552).

A suit against corporate officers may be in equity if an accounting is demanded.

Meisse v. Loren, 5 N. P. 307; 8 L. D. 448 (1898).

Nonconsenting stockholders may sue to rescind a contract made by the corporation in violation of the anti-trust act.

. National Salt Co. v. United Salt Co., 12 L. D. 386 (C. P. 1902).

Suits against officers of corporation. Rescission of fraudulent contracts, etc. Stockholders' suits are usually based on misconduct on the part of directors. A stockholder may sue to compel officers to account for corporate property;

Taylor v. Miami Exporting Co., 5 Ohio 162 (1831).

to recover losses occasioned by negligence or mismanagement of the directors;

Zinn v. Baxter, 65 O. S. 341 (1901).

to rescind fraudulent contracts or conveyances made by agents or officers:

Goodin v. Cincinnati, etc., Co., 18 O. S. 169, 183 (1868).

Shaw v. Edison Inst. Co., 19 W. L. B. 292 (Super. Ct. Cin. 1888).

Dye v. Hermesch, 32 W. L. B. 120 (1894).

Heintzman v. Tenacity, etc., Co., 4 O. L. R. 552; 17 L. D. 554 (Super. Ct. Cin. 1906).

or to vacate a fraudulent assignment for creditors.

Home & Sgs. Assn. v. Jones, 64 O. S. 147 (1901).

Interference with directors' management. A court of equity will not, on the application of a stockholder, interfere with the board of directors in its management and control of the corporate affairs when acting within the scope of its authority and in the absence of fraud or breach of trust.

Sims v. Street Railroad Co., 37 O. S. 556 (1882).

Coss v. Mansfield Lodge, 4 C. C. n. s. 11; 14 C. D. 36 (1902).

Koblitz v. Western Reserve University, 21 C. C. 144; 11 C. D. 515 1901).

De Lacroix v. Eid, etc., Co., 8 N. P. n. s. 489; 19 L. D. 767 (C. P. 1909).

Cronin v. Potters, etc., Co., 29 W. L. B. 52 (C. P. 1892).

A stockholder can not sue to enforce an active duty within the powers of directors.

Port Clinton R. R. Co. v. Cleveland, etc., R. Co., 13 O. S. 544, 561 (1862).

Straman v. North Baltimore, etc., Co., 8 C. C. 89, 101; 4 C. D. 339 (1893).

But fraudulent acts or a breach of trust on the part of directors may be prevented by injunction or a receivership.

Port Clinton, etc., R. Co. v. Cleveland, etc., R. Co., 13 O. S. 544, 560, 561 (1862).

C. H. & D. R. Co. v. Duckworth, 2 C. C. 518; 1 C. D. 618 (1887).

Injunction or receiver. Threatened fraudulent acts or a breach of trust on the part of directors may be enjoined.

Port Clinton, etc., R. Co. v. Cleveland, etc., R. Co., 13 O. S. 544, 560-561 (1862).

C. H. & D. R. Co. v. Duckworth, 2 C. C. 518; 1 C. D. 618 (1887).

See note to § 8627: *Who may object to ultra vires acts.*

An injunction will not be granted because of past illegal acts where there is no threatened repetition of such acts.

No. Fairmount, etc., Co. v. Rehn, 6 N. P. 185; 8 L. D. 594 (Super. Ct. Cin. 1899).

A receiver will not be appointed where injunction will afford full relief and protection. The appointment of a receiver under such circumstances would be an abuse of discretion.

C. H. & D. R. Co. v. Duckworth, 2 C. C. 518; 1 C. D. 618 (1887).

Benson v. Columbia Life Ins. Co., 7 N. P. n. s. 113; 19 L. D. 17 (Super. Ct. Cin. 1908).

Behrens v. Equality Bldg. Assn., 2 N. P. 259; 3 L. D. 275 (Super. Ct. Cin. 1895).

No. Fairmount, etc., Co. v. Rehn, 6 N. P. 185, 191; 8 L. D. 594 (Super. Ct. Cin. 1899).

Schone v. Consolidated Bldg. & Sav. Co., 4 N. P. 216; 6 L. D. 246 (Super. Ct. Cin. 1897).

A receiver will not be appointed merely because of differences of opinion in conducting the corporate business.

Straman v. No. Baltimore Water Wks. Co., 8 C. C. 89, 100; 4 C. D. 339 (1893).

Nor because of past or present irregularities or mismanagement in the absence of actual fraud.

Benson v. Columbia Life Ins. Co., 7 N. P. n. s. 113; 19 L. D. 17 (Super. Ct. Cin. 1908).

No. Fairmount, etc., Co. v. Rehn, 6 N. P. 185; 8 L. D. 594 (Super. Ct. Cin. 1899).

But a receiver will be appointed where it clearly appears that the corporate property will be fraudulently disposed of, unless taken charge of by an officer of the court;

C. H. & D. R. Co. v. Duckworth, 2 C. C. 518; 1 C. D. 618 (1887).

where both the corporation and the directors are insolvent and a fraudulent disposition of assets is threatened;

Upson v. Rocky River, etc., Co., 2 Cleve. L. R. 355 (C. P. 1879).

where the directors have made a fraudulent sale of the entire corporate property for their personal profit;

Heintzman v. Tenacity, etc., Co., 4 O. L. R. 552; 17 L. D. 554 (Super. Ct. Cin. 1906).

See Hamilton v. Hamilton Coal Co., 12 C. D. 637 (1894).

and where the corporation has no legal directors or officers to care for the property.

National Salt Co. v. United Salt Co., 8 N. P. 325; 11 L. D. 348 (C. P. 1901).

See note to § 11894.

The appointment of a receiver in a stockholders' action can not be collaterally attacked.

Egbert v. Third Ward Bldg. Assn., 8 N. P. 507; 9 L. D. 646 (Super. Ct. Cin. 1899).

Pleading and practice. Demand on directors to bring suit. A stockholder should, in his petition, allege a demand on the directors (or assignee or receiver where one has been appointed) and their refusal to bring suit; or an excuse for not making such demand.

Egbert v. Third Ward Bldg. Assn., 8 N. P. 507; 9 L. D. 646 (Super. Ct. Cin. 1899).

Reeder v. Wade, 2 C. S. C. R. 19 (1870).

It is an excuse for not making such demand that the corporation is in control of the wrongdoers.

Bates Pldg., etc., p. 1360.

Heintzman v. Tenacity, etc., Co., 4 O. L. R. 552; 17 L. D. 554 (Super. Ct. Cin. 1906).

Divine v. Auto M. C. Co., 9 N. P. n. s. 204 (C. P. 1909).

Or that there is no director or officer to whom the stockholder could apply.

Kuhn v. Woolson Spice Co., 8 N. P. 686; 10 L. D. 292 (C. P. 1897).
See Dye v. Hermesch, 32 W. L. B. 120 (C. P. 1894).

Plaintiffs. One who has transferred his stock can not sue in the
state courts, unless perhaps after dissolution of the corporation.
Zinn v. Baxter, 65 O. S. 341 (1901).
Dissette v. Lawrence Pbg. Co., 9 C. C. n. s. 118; 19 C. D. 168 (1906).
In federal courts under equity rule 94 of the U. S. Supreme Court
a transferee of stock can not sue on transactions which took place before
he acquired his stock.
See Mannington v. H. V. Ry. Co., 9 N. P. n. s. 641, 662; 20 L. D. 468
    (1910); (removed to U. S. Ct., 183 Fed. 133; 8 O. L. R. 451; 16
    O. F. D. 552).
An equitable owner—as one whose stock has not been transferred on
the corporate records—may sue.
Larwill v. Burke, 19 C. C. 449; 10 C. D. 579 (1900).
Where the corporation is insolvent and in the hands of a receiver who
refuses to sue, a creditor and stockholder may join as plaintiffs.
Miesse v. Loren, 5 N. P. 307; 8 L. D. 448 (1898).

Defendants. The corporation is a necessary party defendant.
Zinn v. Baxter, 65 O. S. 341, 364 (1901).
Taylor v. Miami Exporting Co., 5 Ohio 162 (1831).
Creditors and other stockholders may become defendants on their
application, where they allege an interest in the subject matter of the
suit.
Meisse v. Loren, 5 N. P. 307; 8 L. D. 448 (1898).
In an action to enjoin the corporation from acquiring stock in other
corporations, such other corporations are not p ope parties.
Westfall v. Lake Shore, etc., Ry., 13 N. Pr n. s. 217; 22 L. D. 75 (C.
    P. 1910).

Venue. An action by a stockholder in a railroad company to enjoin
the unlawful acquisition of stock in other corporations must be brought
in a county in which jurisdiction over the railroad company may be acquired.
Westfall v. Lake Shore, etc., Ry., 13 N. P. n. s. 217; 22 L. D. 75 (C.
    P. 1910).

Judgment. When the judgment is for the recovery of money, it
must be in favor of the corporation for the full amount of damages sustained by all stockholders combined, and when collected must be paid
to the corporation.
Zinn v. Baxter, 65 O. S. 341, 364 (1901).

Defenses.

Acquiescence of stockholders in acts complained of.   Where directors of a corporation added a new feature to its business, acting in
good faith, and the stockholders were aware of the facts and acquiesced
therein, the directors are not liable to the corporation, or stockholders.
for losses sustained thereby.
Bond v. Poe, 12 C. C. 281; 4 C. D. 10 (1893).
See De La Croix v. Eid Concrete Steel Co., 8 N. P. n. s. 489, 495; 19
    L. D. 767 (C. P. 1909).
Larwill v. Burke, 19 C. C. 513; 10 C. D. 605 (1900).
See note to § 8627: *Who may object to ultra vires acts.*
A stockholder is not barred by acquiescence unless he had knowledge
of the wrongful acts. A stockholder is not charged with knowledge of the
acts of directors or details of management, although he might have ascer-
tained such facts from the corporate books.

Heintzman v. Tenacity, etc., Co., 4 O. L. R. 552; 17 L. D. 554 (Super. Ct. Cin. 1906).

Stockholders who have no knowledge of a contract made in violation of the anti-trust act are not in pari delicto and may sue to rescind the same.

National Salt Co. v. United Salt Co., 12 L. D. 386 (C. P. 1902).

Statute of limitations. A stockholders' representative suit against the directors for loss by mismanagement is governed by the ten year statute. (G. C. § 11227.)

Glass v. Courtright, 14 N. P. n. s. 273; 23 L. D. 253 (C. P. 1913).

Laches of stockholder. A delay of ten years was held to bar a stockholder from attacking a foreclosure sale of corporate property under a judgment by confession, where the facts could have been ascertained at the time of the sale, or shortly thereafter.

Foster v. Mansfield, etc., R. Co., 36 Fed. 627 (U. S. C. C. Ohio 1888).

A delay of six weeks in bringing suit to set aside a fraudulent sale of the entire corporate property, was held not to be a defense, where the stockholders' knowledge of the transaction was incomplete.

Heintzman v. Tenacity, etc., Co., 4 O. L. R. 552; 17 L. D. 554 (Super. Ct. Cin. 1906).

Offer to sell stock. That the complaining stockholder offered to sell his stock to any one who would take it is no defense.

Heintzman v. Tenacity, etc., Co., 4 O. L. R. 552; 17 L. D. 554 (Super. Ct. Cin. 1906).

Estoppel. A decree in a foreclosure suit by the trustee of a corporate mortgage securing a bond issue does not estop the trustee, who was also a bondholder, from suing as a stockholder of the mortgagor corporation.

Henry v. Pgh., etc., Ry. Co., 2 N. P. 118, 142; 5 L. D. 41 (C. P. 1895).

Motive of stockholder. Suit not brought in good faith. If the plaintiff has a legal right which he seeks to protect in the suit, the motive which induced him to bring the action can not be inquired into.

Traction Co. v. Parish, 67 O. S. 181, 189 (1902).

Isom v. Low Fare Ry. Co., 10 C. C. n. s. 89, 102; 19 C. D. 583 (1907); aff'd, no rep., 77 O. S. 638.

Raynolds v. Cleveland, 2 C. C. n. s. 139; 14 C. D. 215 (1902); aff'd, no rep., 76 O. S. 619.

Cincinnati Volksblatt Co. v. Hoffmeister, 62 O. S. 189, 198 (1900).

Nicholson v. Franklin Brewing Co., 82 O. S. 94, 110 (1910).

These cases were not stockholders' suits on behalf of corporations, but the principle is stated as a general one in *Traction Co. v. Parish* (page 189).

In many other jurisdictions the rule is established that a stockholders' representative suit must be brought in good faith.

See Mannington v. H. V. Ry. Co., 9 N. P. n. s. 641, 659-660; 20 L. D. 468 (1910).

Dissette v. Lawrence Pbg. Co., 9 C. C. n. s. 118, 120; 19 C. D. 168 (1906).

Relief has been denied where it appeared that the complaining stockholder was acting for competitors or other persons, who have agreed to pay the costs and to indemnify him against risk.

Kuhn v. Woolson Spice Co., 13 C. C. 547; 7 C. D. 289 (1897).

Buning v. Cincinnati St. Ry. Co., 1 C. C. 323, 325; 1 C. D. 178 (1886).

Gallagher v. Johnson, 31 W. L. B. 24 (C. P. 1894).

Compare Raynolds v. Cleveland, 2 C. C. n. s. 139; 14 C. D. 215 (1902); aff'd, no rep., 76 O. S. 619.

That a stockholder has interests, other than his stock, which will be benefited by the relief sought has been held not to be a defense to his suit.
Henry v. Pgh., etc., Co., 2 N. P. 118; 5 L. D. 41 (C. P. 1895).
Sommers v. Cincinnati, 8 Am. L. Rec. 612, 624 (C. P. 1880).
Compare Stewart v. Little Miami R. Co., 14 Ohio 353, 358 (1846).

That stockholder's interest is small. That the plaintiff owns but one or two shares is no defense where his rights have been violated.
Heintzman v. Tenacity, etc., Co., 4 O. L. R. 552; 17 L. D. 554 (Super. Ct. Cin. 1906).
See C. H. & D. R. Co. v. Duckworth, 2 C. C. 518, 523; 1 C. D. 618 (1887).
Acquiescence of a majority of the stockholders is no defense, where the plaintiff did not consent.
See Goodin v. Cincinnati, etc., Co., 18 O. S. 169, 183 (1868).

That some defendants have been directors longer than others. In a suit against directors for losses occasioned by their negligence, it is not a ground of demurrer that some of the defendants have been directors longer than others. The court can fix their liability according to the circumstances.
Meisse v. Loren, 5 N. P. 307, 309; 8 L. D. 448 (C. P. 1898).
But where some of the directors were elected directors after the wrongful acts were committed, the liability may in equity be apportioned by the court according to the loss of assets resulting from their acts. Such variant liability, however, does not amount to separate causes of action.
Glass v. Courtright, 14 N. P. n. s. 273; 23 L. D. 253 (C. P. 1913).
New directors of a national bank constituting a minority of the board are not liable for mismanagement of former directors, where they relied on reports of the bank examiners and comptroller of currency although an examination would have disclosed insolvency.
Glass v. Courtright, 14 N. P. n. s. 273; 23 L. D. 253 (C. P. 1913).

Settlement. It is no defense to a stockholders' suit brought to vacate a fraudulent assignment for creditors, that the directors and the assignee have made a settlement, where the complaining stockholders do not assent thereto.
Home & Sgs. Assn. v. Jones, 64 O. S. 147 (1901).

Right of stockholder to appeal from or prosecute error proceeding to, judgment against corporation. A stockholder may appeal from a judgment against the corporation when there is reason to believe that the officers in neglecting to appeal are actuated by an adverse interest.
Henry v. Jeanes, 47 O. S. 116 (1890).
But a stockholder, not a party to the suit, can not prosecute error.
Dunbar v. American Casket Co., 19 C. C. 585; 10 C. D. 684 (1900).

Right of creditors to sue. Where directors have committed a breach of trust, and have misapplied corporate property, creditors may sue.
Columbus, etc., R. Co. v. Burke, 19 W. L. B. 27 (C. P. 1887).
See Meisse v. Loren, 4 N. P. 100; 6 L. D. 258 (C. P. 1897).
Cheney v. Maumee Cycle Co., 20 C. C. 19; 10 C. D. 717 (1900); aff'd, 64 O. S. 205.

LIABILITY OF OFFICERS AND AGENTS.

To the corporation.

(1) Secret profits from contracts with corporation. Where directors fraudulently sell their own property to the corporation for a sum greatly exceeding its actual value, they are liable in damages to the corporation.

Shawnee, etc., Co. v. Miller, 1 C. C. n. s. 569; 14 C. D. 199 (1902).
Secret profits made by directors in transactions with the corporation
may be recovered by the corporation.
Yeiser v. U. S., etc., Co., 107 Fed. 340 (C. C. A. Ohio 1901).
U. S., etc., Co. v. Yeiser, 4 O. L. R. 539; 17 L. D. 261 (Super. Ct. Cin
1906).

(2) Negligence. An officer or agent is liable to the corporation
where corporate property is lost or wasted through his negligence.
Meisse v. Loren, 5 N. P. 307; 8 L. D. 448 (1898); s. c., 4 N. P. 100;
6 L. D. 258 (1897).
Glass v. Courtright, 14 N. P. n. s. 273; 23 L. D. 253 (1913).
Directors, executive officers and agents are bound to exercise that
degree of care in the affairs of the corporation which ordinarily careful
and prudent men would exercise acting under similar circumstances.
Mason v. Moore, 73 O. S. 275 (1906).
Kalb v. American N. B., 21 C. C. 1; 11 C. D. 437 (1900); aff'd, 65
O. S. 566.
Baldwin v. Egan, 5 O. L. R. 476 (1907); aff'd, 11 C. C. n. s. 584.
See supra, *care required of directors.*
A bank cashier is liable for negligence in the matter of locking the
doors of the vault in which the funds are kept.
Kalb v. American N. B., 21 C. C. 1; 11 C. D. 437 (1900); aff'd, 65
O. S. 566.
Directors are not liable for irregularities of action, where neither the
corporation nor the stockholders have been injured.
Larwill v. Burke, 19 C. C. 513; 10 C. D. 605 (1900).
Acquiescence of stockholders in mismanagement as a bar to recovery
against directors therefor.
See Bond v. Poe, 12 C. C. 281; 4 C. D. 10 (1893).
De LaCroix v. Eid Concrete Steel Co.. 8 N. P. n. s. 489, 495; 19 L. D.
767 (C. P. 1909).

(3) Corporate property wrongfully converted by director. A director may be compelled to surrender to the corporation property belonging to the corporation which he has converted to his own use. Where a
director has disposed of such property to persons having notice of the
transaction, the corporation may recover from such persons the property
or its value.
Greenville Gas Co. v. Reis, 54 O. S. 549 (1896).
Goodin v. Cincinnati, etc., Co., 18 O. S. 169 (1868).
Columbus, etc., Ry. Co. v. Burke, 19 W. L. B. 27 (C. P. 1887).

(4) Accounting for corporate property. Directors may be required
to account for corporate funds and property in their possession or control.
Taylor v. Miami Exporting Co., 5 Ohio 162 (1831).

Liability to stockholders.

(1) In general the liability of directors for negligence, breach of
trust, etc., is to the corporation only, and individual stockholders can not
sue.
Zinn v. Baxter, 65 O. S. 341, 364 (1901).
Nor can a pledgee of stock sue.
Barnes v. Swift, 26 W. L. B. 110 (Super. Ct. Cin. 1891).
But where the corporation refuses to sue, a stockholder may bring
suit on behalf of all stockholders, making the corporation a party defend-
ant.
Zinn v. Baxter, 65 O. S. 341, 364 (1901).
Stockholders of an insolvent national bank, in the hands of a re-
ceiver appointed by the comptroller of the currency, may bring suit in a

state court in their own names against its directors for damages both under U. S. R. S. § 5239 and at common law.

Glass v. Courtright, 14 N. P. n. s. 273; 23 L. D. 253 (C. P. 1913).

A stockholders' representative suit against directors for mismanagement is governed by the ten years statute of limitations (G. C. § 11227).

Glass v. Courtright, 14 N. P. n. s. 273; 23 L. D. 253 (C. P. 1913).

(2) Share of assets on winding up. Where a corporation has ceased business, its debts have been paid, and the directors personally undertake to divide the assets among the stockholders, a stockholder, after demand, may maintain an action for his share against the directors.

Larwill v. Burke, 19 C. C. 513; 10 C. D. 605 (1900).

And where one stockholder acquires nearly all of the stock and converts the corporate property to his own use, and where the corporation has not been dissolved, but has no directors or officers, the other stockholders need not sue the corporation but may sue such stockholder individually for an accounting.

Dye v. Hermesch, 32 W. L. B. 120 (C. P. 1894).

In such case the statute of limitations begins to run against the stockholder from the time of the demand and refusal.

Larwill v. Burke, 19 C. C. 513; 10 C. D. 605 (1900).

(3) Conspiracy to depreciate price of stock. Where a stockholder has pledged his stock as collateral to secure his indebtedness to directors, and the directors enter into a conspiracy to depreciate the price of such stock, using their powers as directors, for the purpose of buying it in for less than its value, the directors are directly liable to such stockholder, the wrong being against the stockholder individually, as well as against the corporation.

Ritchie v. McMullen, 79 Fed. 522 (C. C. A. Ohio 1897).

(4) Dividends when declared by the directors become a debt of the corporation. Officers are not personally liable to stockholders therefor.

Snodgrass v. Morrison, etc., Co., 4 O. L. R. 622; 17 L. D. 497 (Super. Ct. Cin. 1907).

(5) Refusal to transfer stock. An officer is not liable to a transferee of stock for refusing to transfer the same on the corporate books.

Snodgrass v. Morrison, 4 O. L. R. 622; 17 L. D. 497 (Super. Ct. Cin. 1907).

(6) Declaring dividends otherwise than out of surplus profits. See § 8728 and note.

Dividends illegally paid by directors may, in an action by stockholders for mismanagement, be deducted from the stockholders' losses and may be adjudicated in the action.

Glass v. Courtright, 14 N. P. n. s. 273; 23 L. D. 253 (C. P. 1913).

(7) Refusal to permit inspection of corporate books. A petition by a stockholder to enforce his right to inspect the corporate books does not state a cause of action against the president individually, where the only allegation involving him is that he is president. He is entitled to be dismissed from the case, on demurrer.

Pearce v. Atkins, 13 N. P. n. s. 580 (1913).

Liability to subscribers or purchasers of stock.

(1) Fraud in inducing subscription. The liability of officers and agents of a corporation to subscribers, and purchasers of stock is controlled by the rules of law governing actions for deceit. Where an officer is applied to for information by one intending to purchase stock (Cable v. Bowlus, 21 C. C. 53; 11 C. D. 526; aff'd, 69 O. S. 563), or where an agent or officer is engaged in making sales or soliciting subscriptions, and makes material and false representations regarding the past or present status of the corporate enterprise, which are relied on by the purchasers or subscribers, to their injury, such officer or agent is personally liable if he had knowledge of the falsity of the representations, or if the same were made under such circumstances that knowledge of their falsity must necessarily be imputed to him.

Mason v. Moore, 73 O. S. 275, 291-293 (1906).

Cable v. Bowlus, 21 C. C. 53; 11 C. D. 526 (1900); aff'd, 69 O. S. 563.

See Schenck v. Knott, 13 C. C. n. s. 41 (1910).

Russell v. Weiler, 7 C. C. n. s. 596; 18 C. D. 176 (1905).

Merchants N. B. v. Thoms, 28 W. L. B. 164; s. c., 31 W. L. B. 137.

By statute directors are made personally liable to persons who purchase stock relying on untrue statements in a prospectus, etc., issued by the corporation unless they had just and reasonable grounds for believing them to be true, etc.

See G. C. § 6373-18.

Measure of damages. The measure of damages is the difference between the price paid for the stock and its actual value at the time of the sale.

Schenck v. Knott, 13 C. C. n. s. 41, 46 (1910).

The purchaser can not recover damages for mental suffering, disappointment or disgrace; nor in general can he recover punitive damages.

Cable v. Bowlus, 21 C. C. 53; 11 C. D. 526 (1900); aff'd, 69 O. S. 563.

No fiduciary relation toward **purchasers of individual stock.** Directors do not occupy a fiduciary relation toward persons to whom they sell their individual stock.

Cook v. Henderson, 8 Am. L. R. 429 (Dist. Ct. 1879).

See Hetteshimer v. Swisher, 7 O. L. R. 629 (C. P. 1909).

(2) Bank directors attesting false statements **of condition.** Where bank directors attest a report of its condition, made and published as required by statute, the statements of which were false, and a person relying on such statement purchases stock of such bank, the liability of the directors to the purchaser at common law is controlled by the law governing actions for deceit.

Mason v. Moore, 73 O. S. 275, 291 (1906).

Barnes v. Pogue, 29 W. L. B. 382 (Super. Ct. Cin. 1893).

See Barnes v. Swift, 3 N. P. 291; 3 L. D. 688 (1894).

Under the national banking act a director is not liable to third persons for mere negligence in attesting such a report. He is liable only for a knowing violation of the act.

Mason v. Moore, 73 O. S. 275, 290 (1906).

Yates v. Jones N. B., 206 U. S. 158, 178 (1906).

(3) President signing "full paid" stock certificate. A president is not liable in an action for deceit based on his having signed a stock certificate containing the statement "full paid and nonassessable" to a person who bought such stock in the open market for less than par, although the president knew that such stock had been exchanged for property at an overvaluation.

Nutt v. Wheeler, 10 C. C. n. s. 217; 20 C. D. 86 (1907).

(4) Verbal promise of dividends to subscriber. A verbal promise, by the president of the corporation, that if a person would subscribe and pay for $500.00 of stock he should, within one year, receive 15 percent on the amount invested, is valid. Such an agreement is not within the Statute of Frauds.

Moorehouse v. Crangle, 36 O. S. 130 (1880).

Liability to creditors.

(1) **Acting before ten percent of capital is subscribed.** Persons who act as directors before ten percent of the capital stock is subscribed, and incur obligations, are personally liable therefor.

Trust Co. v. Floyd, 47 O. S. 525 (1890).

(2) **Acting without authority.** A person who assumes to make a contract for a corporation, but without authority, is personally liable to the persons who contract with him, in ignorance of his want of authority.

Trust Co. v. Floyd, 47 O. S. 525 (1890).

An officer who executes notes, without authority to issue commercial paper for any purpose, is liable to a bona fide purchaser of the notes in damages for falsely representing his authority. But if authorized to issue paper for the corporate business, the notes are binding on the corporation when held by a bona fide purchaser, and the officer is liable only to the corporation and not to the purchaser.

Dexter Sav. Bank v. Friend, 90 Fed. 703 (U. S. C. C. Ohio 1898).

(3) **Conducting unauthorized business.** The officers are, under some circumstances, personally liable when they transcend the corporate authority and engage in *ultra vires* business. The limits of this doctrine are not clearly defined.

See note to § 8627, *Ultra vires acts. Personal liability.*

Medill v. Collier, 16 O. S. 599, 610.

Mfgrs., etc., Assn. v. Lynchburg Drug Mills, 8 C. C. 112; 4 C. D. 350 (1893).

Ridenour v. Mayo, 40 O. S. 9 (1883).

(4) **On notes improperly signed.** A note reading "We promise to pay" and signed "The *A. B.* Co., *C. D.*, Secy. and Treas., *E. F.*, Pres.," is on its face the note of the corporation alone and the officers who signed it are not personally liable.

Aungst v. Creque, 72 O. S. 551 (1905).

See Snyder v. Bank, 22 C. C. 624 (1897); aff'd, 60 O. S. 605.

But a note signed "*A. B.*, President," or "*A. B.*, Agent K. & O. C. Co.," is the note of the officer personally and he is liable thereon.

Robinson v. Kanawha Valley Bank, 44 O. S. 441 (1886).

Bank v. Cook, 38 O. S. 442 (1882).

Eells v. Shea, 20 C. C. 527; 11 C. D. 304 (1900); aff'd, 66 O. S. 682.

Parol evidence is not admissible, in such a case, to show that the intention of the parties was not to bind the officer but the corporation.

Robinson v. Kanawha Valley Bank, 44 O. S. 441 (1886).

Collins v. Buckeye State Ins. Co., 17 O. S. 215 (1867).

Eells v. Shea, 20 C. C. 527; 11 C. D. 304 (1900); aff'd, 66 O. S. 682.

See Barnhisel v. Commercial N. B., 14 C. C. 124; 7 C. D. 533 (1897).

A note reading "we, as directors of The *A. B.* Company promise to pay, etc.," and signed by the makers individually is the note of the individuals and they are personally liable.

Titus v. Kyle, 10 O. S. 444 (1859).

But where the intention, indicated on the face of the note, is to charge only the corporation, the officers are not liable although the note is signed "*A. B.*, President."

Second N. B. v. Wilcox, 2 C. C. 325; 1 C. D. 511 (1887).

Hays v. Galion, etc., Co., 29 O. S. 330, 334 (1876).

Sheehan v. Davis, 17 O. S. 571.

(5) **On stock exchanged for property at an overvaluation.**

Gates v. Tippecanoe Stone Co., 57 O. S. 60 (1897).

See note to § 8630. *Sales to directors and officers.*

(6) Declaring dividends otherwise than out of surplus profits.
See § 8728.

Criminal liability. An officer of a corporation may be criminally
liable, although the act was committed by an agent under his instructions,
and in conducting the corporate business.
(Violation of pure food law.)
Meyer v. State, 54 O. S. 242 (1896); affirming, 9 C. C. 714; 6 C. D.
712.

Section 8661.   (Qualifications of directors and trustees.)
A majority of such directors must be citizens of this state.
All directors and executive officers shall be holders of stock
of the company for which they are chosen, in an amount to
be fixed by the by-laws, and trustees of corporations must
be members thereof.   (R. S. Sec. 3248; R. S. 1880.)

Holders of stock. A person not a stockholder may be voted for
and elected and may, after election, qualify himself by acquiring stock.
Greenough v. Alabama, etc., R. Co., 64 Fed. 22 (C. C. 1894).
A person is not ineligible because his stock is subject to an option to
sell. Until the option is exercised he is a stockholder.
Kuhn v. Woolson Spice Co., 13 C. C. 547; 7 C. D. 289 (1897).
A director is presumed to be a stockholder.
Gates v. Tippecanoe Stone Co., 9 C. C. 99, 103; 6 C. D. 23 (1894);
aff'd, 57 O. S. 60.

Holder of "qualifying shares." It has been held that a person is
not properly qualified where a share of stock is transferred to him merely
for the purpose of qualifying him as a director, where he has no real interest in the stock.
Bartholomew v. Bentley, 1 O. S. 37 (1852).
Where a corporation issued a certificate of stock to a director to
qualify him, he agreeing to retransfer the same on ceasing to be a director,
a third person who purchased such certificate from the director, without
notice, is entitled to the stock, as against the corporation.
Dueber, etc., Co. v. Dougherty, 62 O. S. 589 (1900).
. A person to whom stock was transferred by relatives to enable him
to be elected secretary and treasurer is a trustee of the stock for such
relatives. Such trust may be established by parol.
Bonnell v. Brown, 11 C. C. n. s. 58; 20 C. D. 712 (1908).

Director ceasing to be a stockholder. Where a director parts with
all his stock he ceases to be a director *de jure.*
Commercial N. B. v. Colwell, 132 N. Y. 250 (1892).
Bartholomew v. Bentley. 1 O. S. 37 (1852.).
Henderson v. Hogan, 1 W. L. B. 227 (Dist. Ct. 1876).
See State v. Bryce, 7 Ohio (pt. 2) 82 (1836).
The vacancy may be filled immediately.
See § 8662.
Hooe v. Hall, 9 C. C. 654; 4 C. D. 547 (1893).
. But where he continues to act as a director, his acts are those of a
de facto officer and valid as to third persons.
Campbell Printing Press Co. v. Bellman Bros. Co., 11 C. C. 360; 5 C.
   D. 389 (1896).
.   Ehrman v. Insurance Co., 35 O. S. 324, 339 (1880).
See also note to § 8660.

Removal of directors from state.

Where the directors change their residence to another state, remove the plant of the corporation to such state and there continue business as an Ohio corporation, they are *de facto* officers and may bind the corporation.

Lattimer v. Mosaic Glass Co., 13 C. C. 163; 7 C. D. 430 (1896).
See State v. Bryce, 7 Ohio (pt. 2) 82 (1836).

Executive officers. The executive officers are the president, secretary and treasurer (§ 8664) and such other officers as may be provided for in the regulations. (§ 8704.)

Decisions under former statutes. In the absence of a statute requiring it, a director need not be a stockholder.

State v. McDaniel, 22 O. S. 354 (1872).

Where the special charter of a bank provided that no person should be a director who was a director of any other bank, or the partner of any director of any other bank, it was held that such provision applied to directors of banks in other states as well as in Ohio.

State. v. Buchanan, Wright 233 (1833).

Section 8662. (Vacancies.) When the office of director or trustee becomes vacant, the board may fill it for the unexpired term unless the by-laws otherwise provide. (R. S. Sec. 3248; R. S. 1880.)

Where a director ceases to own stock, his successor may be chosen immediately.

Hooe v. Hall, 9 C. C. 654; 4 C. D. 547 (1893).
Bartholomew v. Bentley, 1 O. S. 37, 43 (1852).
Henderson v. Hogan, 1 W. L. B. 227 (Dist. Ct. 1876).

Where no officers were elected for sixteen years, the corporation being insolvent, it was held that vacancies could not then be filled by the remaining directors as all directors were presumed to have resigned.

Bartholomew v. Bentley, 1 O. S. 37 (1852).

Where a majority of directors resign, or cease to be stockholders, the remaining minority have no power to fill vacancies.

Moses v. Tompkins, 84 Ala. 613 (1887).

Section 8663. (Oath.) Before entering upon his duties as such, each trustee and director must take an oath faithfully to discharge them. (R. S. Sec. 3247; March 15, 1909, 100 v. 12; R. S. 1880.)

An officer of a corporation who acts as such without being sworn is a de facto officer and his acts are binding as to third persons.

Simpson v. Garland, 76 Me. 203 (1884).

Section 8664. (Organization.) As soon thereafter as is convenient, the board of trustees or directors chosen at any election, shall select one of their number to be president thereof, and unless the regulations of the body otherwise provide for the election of such officers, also appoint a secretary and treasurer of the corporation. A majority of the directors of a corporation for profit and such a number of the trustees as the regulations of a corporation not for profit may provide, shall form a board. (R. S. Sec. 3247; March 15, 1909, 100 v. 12; R. S. 1880.)

Majority of the directors. See note to § 8660. *Quorum.*
Where, of five directors elected, only three qualified and assumed to act, their acts are binding.
> Dickason v. Grafton, etc., 6 C. C. n. s. 329, 333; 17 C. D. 357 (1905); aff'd, no rep., 76 O. S. 612.

EXECUTIVE OFFICERS.
A director is an officer.
> § 8704.
> Railway Co. v. McCoy, 42 O. S. 253 (1884).
But not an executive officer.
> See § 8661.
> State v. Peoples, etc., Assn., 42 O. S. 583 (1884).

Qualifications. All executive officers must be stockholders.
> § 8661.
> See Bonnell v. Brown, 11 C. C. n. s. 58.
> See note to § 8660. *De facto directors or officers.*
The president must be a director. See § 8664.
A corporation can not be the secretary or recording officer.
> Burch v. Trust Co., 12 N. P. n. s. 86, 91 (1911).

Election. See §§ 8704 and 8664.

Removal. Regulations can not be adopted providing for the removal at stockholders' meetings, of officers or employes chosen or appointed by the directors.
> Toledo T. L. & P. Co. v. Smith, 58 Bull 201 (U. S. D. C. 1913).
> See also note to § 8647.

Powers. (a) Derived from statute. The president and secretary are authorized and required by statute to execute stock certificates. (§ 8672.) A certificate of stock issued to the president or secretary personally is valid in the hands of a bona fide holder, although issued fraudulently.
> Railway Co. v. Bank, 56 O. S. 351 (1897).
An officer should verify pleadings of a corporation.
> Mfg. Co. v. Hedges, 76 O. S. 91 (1907).

(b) Conferred by regulations. The duties of officers may be provided for by the stockholders in the corporate regulations, except duties which are provided for by statute.
> § 8704.
> Bradford Belting Co. v. Gibson, 68 O. S. 442, 449 (1903).

(c) Conferred by directors. All authority of executive officers, except that conferred by statute or corporate regulations, must be derived from the board of directors. The active business of a corporation is managed and controlled by the board of directors. While corporate contracts are usually negotiated and executed by executive officers, the authority to do so must, in some manner, be traced to the board of directors.
> Belting Co. v. Gibson, 68 O. S. 442 (1903).
> Minor v. Board of Control, 20 C. C. 4; 11 C. D. 16 (1899).
> Tyson v. Miller-Tyson Co., 15 C. C. n. s. 177, 182; 23 C. D. 418, 424 (1912).
Executive officers are agents merely.
> Smead Foundry Co. v. Chesbrough, 18 C. C. 783; 6 C. D. 670 (1895).

For further powers of executive officers see note to § 8660, *Corporate contracts*, and see below, *President* and various other officers.

Not disqualified to testify by G. C. § 11495. In an action against a corporation by an administrator, the general manager is not disqualified by G. C. § 11495 from testifying to facts occurring before the death of the decedent.

Cockley Milling Co. v. Bunn, 75 O. S. 270 (1906).

Compensation of directors and officers.

The stockholders have a right to fix the compensation of the corporate officers by provisions in the regulations.

§ 8704.

Directors. In general, directors are entitled to reasonable compensation for their time, and reimbursement for expense incurred in attending meetings of the board.

State v. Peoples, etc., Assn., 42 O. S. 579, 583 (1885).

Where directors have accepted compensation for a period of service, they have no power, in subsequent terms, to vote themselves back pay for the same period.

State v. Peoples, etc., Assn., 42 O. S. 579 (1885).

Executive officers. Where directors elect one of their number as secretary, he is entitled to reasonable compensation for his services as secretary although no agreement was made in advance regarding compensation, where the circumstances show that it was the intention of all parties that he should be paid.

Dalton v. Brush, etc., Co., 13 C. C. 505; 7 C. D. 141 (1897).

But where there was no expectation of payment, the officer can not recover compensation.

McMullen v. Ritchie, 64 Fed. 253; 8 O. F. D. 314 (U. S. C. C. Ohio 1894).

See State v. Peoples, etc., Assn., 42 O. S. 579 (1885).

Directors and officers are not preferred creditors.

Under statute giving preferences to "operatives." The secretary of a corporation is not an "operative" under G. C. § 11138 and not entitled to priority payment from the estate of an insolvent corporation, although he at times performed manual labor.

Green v. Weller, 6 C. C. 351; 3 C. D. 488 (1892).

In In re Armleder, etc., Co., 20 C. C. 699 (1900) it was held that a person who performed manual labor was entitled to priority payment although he was a director.

Contra, Williams v. Southard, 40 W. L. B. 287 (C. P. 1898).

No right to appropriate corporate funds to payment of claim. A director or officer of a corporation has no right to appropriate corporate property or funds, in his possession for other purposes, in payment of a debt due him from the corporation.

Greenville Gas Co. v. Reis, 54 O. S. 549 (1896).

Dunbar v. Harrison, 18 O. S. 24, 38 (1868).

Where an officer, who owed the corporation $750.00 on a subscription to stock and had a claim of $500.00 for salary, executed the note of the corporation for $500.00 and transferred it in payment of an individual indebtedness, upon insolvency of the corporation it was held that the note in the hands of such creditor should be cancelled and the amount set off against the indebtedness of the officer.

In re Empress, etc., Co., 1 N. P. n. s. 20 (C. P. 1903).

Estoppel to set up unrecorded mortgage. An officer of a corporation who holds a mortgage from the corporation which he has withheld from record, is estopped from setting up such mortgage as against subsequent mortgages which have been recorded and of which he had knowledge.

Jacobs v. Jacobs, 7 L. D. 486.

Liability. See note to § 8660.

Agreements to procure corporate office. An agreement between individuals to form a corporation, providing for its future management and control and specifying the future directors and officers and their compensation, is not void or illegal where the parties to the contract become the owners of all the capital stock of the corporation.

Doan v. Rogan, 79 O. S. 372, 386 (1909).
See Mullen v. Gaffery, 8 Am. L. R. 101 (Dist. Ct. 1879).

And where, in an agreement between individuals, it is provided that one of the parties shall be employed at a specified salary for a specified time by the other parties, or by a corporation to be thereafter formed by them, on breach of such agreement an action for damages may be maintained against the individual in default.

Doan v. Rogan, 79 O. S. 372 (1909).
Magil v. Rendigs, 12 L. D. 558 (Super. Ct. Cin. 1902).
See Mosier v. Parry, 60 O. S. 388 (1899).

But where there are other stockholders who are not parties to the contract, an agreement, by a director or by one or more stockholders owning a majority of the stock, to elect another person to a salaried corporate office is void as against public policy.

Jones v. Scudder, 2 C. S. C. R. 178 (1872).
West v. Camden, 135 U. S. 507 (1890).

Where a subscription to stock was made on condition that the subscriber be employed by the corporation at a certain salary, a breach by the corporation of the employment condition was held not to constitute a defense against the subscription, but to be an independent stipulation or condition subsequent for breach of which the remedy would be an action for damages.

Stunt v. Newark, etc., Co., 22 C. C. 120; 12 C. D. 175 (1901); aff'd, 67 O. S. 555.

Where money was loaned to a corporation on a note due in two years, on condition that the son of the lender be employed by the corporation for the same time, without discharge except for specified causes, the sale by the corporation of its business, necessitating the retirement of the son, is equivalent to his discharge and renders the note due as of the date of retirement.

Benton v. Standard Carbonic Co., 6 O. L. R. 568; 19 L. D. 551 (C. P. (1908).'

Insurable interest of corporation in life of director or officer. Where a person owns a large portion of the stock of a corporation, and his skill and experience are largely relied on to make the corporate business a success, and when, in borrowing money of banks, and in dealing with creditors, and in inducing other persons to buy stock in the corporation, he represents that he has insured his life for the benefit of the corporation, such facts disclose an insurable interest in the corporation; and the insured and his legal representatives are estopped from claiming that such policies are not based upon an insurable interest, or that the amounts due thereon do not belong to the corporation.

Keckley v. Coshocton Glass Co., 86 O. S. 213 (1912); affirming, 13 C. C. n. s. 229, 240; 21 C. D. 665, 676.

Where an officer made application for insurance specifying the corporation as beneficiary, and the premiums were paid by the corporation, it is entitled to the proceeds of the policy as against the executor of

the insured, although the insured, before his death, had retired as such
officer or director.

> Insurance Co. v. Coshocton Glass Co., 13 C. C. n. s. 229; 21 C. D.
> 665 (1910); affirmed, Keckley v. Coshocton Glass Co., 86 O. S.
> 213.

And where a policy in which the widow was named as beneficiary was
assigned to a corporation in which the insured was an officer, and all
premiums were paid by the corporation, it is entitled to the proceeds of
the policy as against the widow.

> Coshocton Glass Co. v. Insurance Co., 13 C. C. n. s. 240; 21 C. D.
> 676 (1910); affirmed, Keckley v. Coshocton Glass Co., 86 O. S.
> 213.

In Schott, etc., Co. v. Insurance Co., 11 C. C. n. s. 401; 20 C. D.
656 (affirming 7 N. P. n. s. 548; 19 L. D. 249; and affirmed no report,
83 O. S. 507), is was said that a corporation has no insurable interest
in the life of an officer or director who is not indebted to it, and that
a note given for premiums on a policy on the life of a director or
officer is without consideration. The note involved in that case, however, was given by the secretary and general manager without authority
from the directors.

President.

Chosen by directors, not by stockholders. Under a Colorado statute
providing that the directors shall elect one of their number to be president, it was held that an election of a president by the stockholders
was a nullity.

> Walsenberg Water Co. v. Moore, 5 Colo. App. 144; 38 Pac. 60.

Qualifications. The president must be a stockholder (§ 8661) and
a director. (§ 8664).

Powers. The powers of the president, in the making of contracts,
as those of other executive officers, must be traced to the board of directors.

> See *Executive officers supra;* and *note to* § 8660. *Corporate con-
> tracts.*

Presumption as to. Written contracts are usually signed by the
president, and it is held that a written instrument or contract executed
in proper form under the corporate seal by the president is presumed to
have been authorized by the directors, and that the burden of proof rests
on the party denying such authority.

> Bank v. Flour Co., 41 O. S. 552, 557 (1885).
> C. H. & D. R. Co. v. Harter, 26 O. S. 426 (1875).
> Dexter Sav. Bank v. Friend, 90 Fed. 703 (1898).

The presumption is not rebutted by the mere fact that authority to
execute the instrument is not found on the minutes of the directors.

> C. H. & D. R. Co. v. Harter, 26 O. S. 426 (1875).

The presumption does not apply to unusual instruments or contracts. There is no presumption that the president is authorized to
convey the entire property of a corporation.

> De Lavergne, etc., Co. v. German Sgs. Int., 175 U. S. 40 (1889).

Nor to make an assignment for creditors.

> Commercial N. B. v. Cincinnati N. B., 3 C. C. 513, 517; 2 C. D.
> 295 (1889).

To sign notes. The promissory note of a corporation, signed in its
name by the president, is prima facie valid and binding on the corporation.

> Dexter Sav. Bank v. Friend, 90 Fed. 703 (U. S. C. C. Ohio 1898).

See Andres v. Morgan, 62 O. S. 236, 248 (1900).

But a cognovit note signed by the president is not binding on the corporation in the absence of proof of authority from the directors.

Smead Foundry Co. v. Cheesbrough, 18 C. C. 783; 6 C. D. 670 (1895).

A note signed by the president and payable to himself is not binding unless authority from the directors is shown.

In re Hartwell Furniture Co., 7 O. L. R. 555 (Referee in Bkry. 1909).

In re Continental Iron Co., 2 O. L. R. 563 (Referee in Bkry. 1904).

Arnkens v. Rouse, 26 W. L. B. 221 (C. P. 1891).

In re Empress Josephine, etc., Co., 1 N. P. n. s. 20 (C. P. 1903).

Compare In re Troy, etc., Co., 136 Fed. 420; aff'd, 142 Fed. 1038.

Where the president is authorized to sign notes, a note signed by him is valid in the hands of a bona fide holder although executed for an unauthorized purpose.

Dexter Sav. Bank v. Friend, 90 Fed. 703 (U. S. C. C. Ohio 1898).

To execute chattel mortgage. Where the president and secretary were authorized to execute notes and mortgages, a chattel mortgage executed by them to secure a preexisting debt was held valid as against other creditors, although executed without the knowledge of other directors.

Bosche v. Toledo, etc., Co., 14 C. C. 289; 7 C. D. 374 (1897).

To bring or defend suits. The president of an insolvent corporation may bring or defend suits to protect the property of the corporation, without specific authority from the directors.

Kalb v. American N. B., 21 C. C. 1; 11 C. D. 437 (1900); aff'd, no rep., 65 O. S. 566.

To appropriate corporate property in payment of debt **due him** from corporation. The president of a corporation can not, without consent of the directors, appropriate a bond of the corporation, entrusted to him for sale, in payment of a debt due him from the corporation.

Greenville Gas Co. v. Reis, 54 O. S. 549 (1896).

To sell bonds of corporation. The president of a corporation has no implied authority to sell its mortgage bonds, nor to employ another person to sell them; although the president was authorized to act as general manager in the conduct of its ordinary business.

East Cleveland R. Co. v. Everett, 19 C. C. 205; 10 C. D. 493 (1900).

But where bonds complete in form and negotiable by delivery, are placed in the custody of the president, he thereby becomes clothed with apparent authority of disposition, and a bona fide purchaser acquires a valid title although the president negotiates them wrongfully and for his own benefit.

Railway Co. v. Lynde, 55 O. S. 23 (1896); aff'd, 172 U. S. 493.

Railway Co. v. Bank, 56 O. S. 351 (1897).

To surrender franchise of corporation. It has been held that the president had no power, without special authority, to surrender or dispose of franchises granted by special charter under a former constitution.

Sebastian v. Covington, etc., Co., 21 O. S. 451 (1871).

To sign consent for street railway. The president of a corporation has no authority to execute a consent to a street railway.

Rapp v. Cincinnati, etc., R. Co., 12 W. L. B. 119 (C. P.).

Liability. Signing stock certificate representing stock to be "full paid." The president of a corporation who signed a stock certificate containing the statement "full paid and nonassessable" was held not liable to a person who purchased such stock in the open market, for less than par without inquiry as to the assets of the corporation, although the president knew that such stock had been issued for property at an over-valuation.

Nutt v. Wheeler, 10 C. C. n. s. 217; 20 C. D. 86 (1907).
See note to § 8660. *Officers and agents. Liability.*

Vice-president. Where no authority is given to the vice-president in the regulations or by-laws, and where he was not accustomed to sign notes, the corporation is not liable on notes signed by him.

Morris v. Griffith, 34 W. L. B. 191 (U. S. C. C. Ohio 1895).
The vice-president of a bank has no implied power to borrow money.
Western N. B. v. Armstrong, 152 U. S. 346; 7 O. F. D. 499 (1894).

Secretary.

A secretary has no implied authority to bind the corporation by a representation that the corporation will not perform a contract theretofore made by it.

Belting Co. v. Gibson, 68 O. S. 442 (1903).
Nor to take out insurance on the lives of directors.
Security, etc., Ins. Co. v. Schott, etc., Co., 11 C. C. n. s. 401 (1908); aff'd, no rep., 83 O. S. 507.
The secretary is authorized and required to sign stock certificates.
See § 8672.
Railway Co. v. Bank, 56 O. S. 351 (1897).
Bank v. Safe & Lock Co., 66 O. S. 367 (1902).
See further as to powers *executive officers* supra, and note to § 8660, *corporate contracts.*

The secretary of a corporation who is in possession of its books, and is acting as general manager, may be punished for contempt of court for refusal to comply with an order of court directing him to submit the books to the inspection of the adverse party, although he is acting under the order of the directors, who are nonresidents.

Arbuckle v. Woolson Spice Co., 21 C. C. 356; 11 C. D. 727 (1901).

Bond. Liability of surety. Where the duties of a secretary were to receive and deposit money, and to endorse checks for deposit only, with no authority to sign checks or pay out or withdraw money, a surety on his bond, conditioned to make good any loss occasioned by his dishonesty in connection with such duties, is not liable for the act of the secretary in inducing the corporation to make a loan on fictitious security to a fictitious person, whose name was forged to the check of the corporation by the secretary.

Trustees v. Deposit Co., 76 O. S. 253 (1907).

Treasurer.

Where a treasurer deposits corporate funds in a reputable bank, to his credit as treasurer or trustee, and not mingled with his personal funds, he is not liable if they are lost by a failure of the bank.

Odd Fellows, etc., Assn. v. Ferson, 3 C. C. 84; 2 C. D. 48 (1888).
It is the duty of the treasurer of a corporation to account for all moneys coming into his possession as treasurer, and the corporation may enforce such duty by action.

Muhlhauser v. Cleveland Hospital,, 21 C. C. 88 (1900).

Bond. Liability of surety. A surety on the bond of a treasurer, conditioned, that he shall perform his duties according to the regulations, charter, etc., is responsible for all moneys coming into the possession of such treasurer and not accounted for.

Portage, etc., Co. v. Wetmore, 17 Ohio 330 (1848).
It is no defense to the surety on a treasurer's bond that the funds were derived from an ultra vires business.

Juegling v. Arbeiter Bund, 4 W. L. B. 463; 8 Am. L. R. 94 (Dist. Ct. 1879)
See supra *secretary.*
Term of bond.
See Fancher v. Kaneen, 5 N. P. n. s. 614 (C. P. 1907).

Contempt proceeding by receiver. Where a receiver has instituted a contempt proceeding against the treasurer of a corporation for refusing to turn over the corporate funds. and the treasurer answers that there are no funds in his possession, the proceeding will be dismisssed. Such an issue can not be tried in a summary proceeding.
State v. Christy, 4 O. L. R. 64; 3 O. L. R. 430; 16 L. D. 277 (C. P. 1905).

When suit may be brought against defaulting treasurer. Suit may be brought against the treasurer of a corporation as soon as he has made default. The corporation need not wait until his successor has been appointed.
Marlborough Assn. v. Peters, 179 Mass. 61; 60 N. E. 396 (1901).

Cashier of bank. A cashier can not bind his bank by an agreement, made contemporaneously with a loan by the bank on a note signed by sureties, that he would procure bonds as collateral, and exhaust the bonds before resorting to the liability of the sureties.
Martin v. First N. B., 11 C. C. n. s. 93; 20 C. D. 398 (1907).
Nor by an agreement to defend a suit for another bank and indemnify it against loss therefrom.
First N. B. v. Mansfield Sav. Bank. 10 C. C. 233; 6 C. D. 452 (1895).
Knowledge by a cashier, of matters within his authority, is imputable to the bank.
Orme v. Baker, 74 O. S. 337 (1906).
Rangan v. Donovan, 10 O. L. R. 354; 189 Fed. 138 (U. S. D. C. 1911).
The cashier of a bank which is a creditor of a decedent's estate may be appointed administrator under G. C. § 10617 although the cashier individually is not a creditor.
McCallip v. Sharp, 13 L. D. 650 (C. P. 1903).
A cashier, authorized to sell commercial paper, has authority to guarantee that the paper is collectible.
Sturges v. Bank, 11 O. S. 153 (1860).
Where a transaction with a bank properly pertains to the business of the bank, neither the abuse or disregard of his authority by its managing officer or agent, nor his fraud or bad faith, is a defense to the bank in an action against it by an innocent party, growing out of such transaction.
Bank v. Blakesley, 42 O. S. 645 (1885).
A cashier of a bank. who is also treasurer of a building association, can not bind the bank by entering on the books of the bank a fictitious credit to the building association, on the faith of which a dividend is paid.
Webb v. Stasel, 4 N. P. n. s. 587; 17 L. D. 317 (1906); s. c., 80 O. S. 122.

Section 8665. (Change in number of directors.) By a vote of a majority of its stock, at a regular meeting of an incorporated company, it may increase the number of its directors to not more than thirty. In like manner, at any time, their number can be reduced to not less than five. At a special meeting of stockholders, also, called and of which notice was given as provided for the election of directors, by vote of a majority of its stock, the increase in the number of directors may be made. Those elected shall hold their offices until the next annual election for directors, and until their successors are elected and qualified. (R. S. Sec. 3267; April 2, 1906, 98 v. 295; May 15, 1886, 83 v. 163; R. S. 1880.)

Decrease. A director elected at an annual meeting holds office for one year. His tenure of office can not be shortened by a decrease in the number of directors made after his election.
Lutterby v. Herancourt Brewing Co., 12 L. D. 67 (Super. Ct. Cin. 1901).
But the office of trustee of a church is not one coupled with such an interest that the members can not terminate its tenure of office.
Munsel v. Boyd, 10 C. C. n. s. 121, 127; 20 C. D. 182 (1907).

Increase. Stockholders may effect a change in the policy of management by increasing the number of directors at a special meeting.
Gold Bluff, etc., Corp. v. Whitlock, 75 Conn. 669 (1903).
In re Griffing Iron Co., 63 N. J. L. 168, 357 (1898).
See Mower v. Staples, 32 Minn. 284 (1884).

Section 8666. (Liability of trustees.) The trustees of a corporation created for a purpose other than profit, shall be personally liable for all debts of the corporation by them contracted. (R. S. Sec. 3261; April 17, 1854, 52 v. 44, § 78; S. & C. 310.)

Trustees of corporation having capital stock. The trustees of a chamber of commerce, not for profit, are liable for its debts contracted by them, notwithstanding a provision in its articles of incorporation for a capital stock and a declaration that it is intended to promote the prosperity of the city in which it is located.
Snyder v. Chamber of Commerce, 53 O. S. 1 (1895).

Nature of liability. The liability of trustees under § 8666 is secondary and collateral to the principal obligation of the corporation, and can be resorted to only in case of the insolvency of the corporation, or where payment can not be enforced against it by ordinary process.
Walbrecht v. Pucketat. 9 W. L. B. 335 (Dist. Ct. 1883).
After obtaining a judgment against the corporation, the creditor can not sue the trustees on his original claim. His remedy is in the nature of a creditor's bill, on the judgment, alleging the inability of the corporation to discharge the debt.
Horstman v. Rix, 4 W. L. G. 131 (Super. Ct. Cin. 1859).
Where an action brought against the trustees was decided in their favor, on the ground that no judgment had been obtained against the corporation, and thereafter a judgment was obtained against the corporation, and another action brought against the trustees, the first judgment in favor of the trustees is not a bar to the second action against them. In such case the justice, before whom the first action was tried, may testify as to the ground on which he decided the same.
Mahaffey v. Rogers, 10 C. C. 24; 6 C. D. 88 (1894); aff'd, no rep., 37 W. L. B. 292.

For what debts trustees are liable. Where an indebtedness was incurred on behalf of the corporation, and the creditor refused to accept the note of the corporation, but accepted the personal note of the trustees therefor, which was renewed by the note of the corporation, the trustees were held liable.

> Mahaffey v. Rogers, 10 C. C. 24; 6 C. D. 88 (1894); aff'd, without report, 37 W. L. B. 292.

The claim of a member of a mutual insurance corporation organized under § 9593, for a loss under his certificate of membership and insurance, is not a debt for which the trustees are liable, although they might be liable on claims for rent, supplies, salaries, etc.

> Mfgrs. Fire Assn. v. Lynchburg Drug Mills, 8 C. C. 112; 4 C. D. 350 (1893).
> See Kelly v. Bender, 22 C. C. 144; 12 C. D. 181 (1901).
> Strobridge v. Winchell, 7 Am. L. R. 743; 4 W. L. B. 408 (1879).

Nor does the fact that the certificate of insurance is *ultra vires* render the trustees liable if the certificate was issued in good faith.

> Mfgrs. Fire Assn. v. Lynchburg Drug Mills, 8 C. C. 112; 4 C. D. 350 (1893).

Actions against trustees. See § 8690.

CAPITAL STOCK.

Section 8667.   (Classes of stock.) If a corporation be organized for profit, it must have a capital stock, which may consist of common and preferred, or common only; but at no time shall the amount of preferred stock at par value exceed two-thirds of the actual capital paid in in cash or property.   (R. S. Sec. 3235a; May 12, 1902, 95 v. 623.)

> A corporation which is necessarily for profit can not be organized without a capital stock.
> State v. Home Co-op. Union, 63 O. S. 547 (1900).
> The stock of a corporation is not its property, and is not owned by it, but by the several stockholders. It owes and not owns the stock. The stock is a liability of the corporation and not an asset.
> Southern Gum Co. v. Laylin, 66 O. S. 578, 596 (1902).
> Nat'l Bank v. Lake Shore, etc., R. Co., 21 O. S. 221, 230 (1871).
> State v. Franklin Bank, 10 Ohio 91 (1840).
> Statement of capital stock in articles of incorporation, see § 8625.

Section 8668.   (Dividends on preferred stock.) When the capital stock is to be both common and preferred, it may be provided in the articles of incorporation that the holders of the preferred stock shall be entitled to yearly dividends of not more than eight per cent, payable quarterly, half yearly, or yearly out of the surplus profits of the company each year in preference to all other stockholders. Such dividends also may be made cumulative.   (R. S. Sec. 3235a; May 12, 1902, 95 v. 623.)

> Dividends on preferred stock can be paid out of surplus profits only.
> G. C. § 8724.
> Miller v. Ratterman, 47 O. S. 141, 158 (1890).

Painesville, etc., Ry. Co. v. King, 17 O. S. 534 (1867).
Mente v. Groff, 10 N. P. n. s. 148 (1910).

Cumulative or noncumulative. Before the enactment of this section it was held that dividends on preferred stock were cumulative, in the absence of a provision making them noncumulative.
Dayton, etc., R. Co. v. Shoemaker, 3 C. C. 473, 479; 2 C. D. 270, 273 (1888); affirming 18 W. L. B. 43.

Additional dividends. Where the articles of incorporation and stock certificates are silent as to dividends on preferred stock, preferred stockholders are entitled to participate in dividends declared after the stipulated dividend has been declared on the preferred and an equal dividend on the common stock.
Ryan v. Miami Valley R. Co., 10 Am. L. R. 263, 266 (C. P. 1881).
Fidelity Trust Co. v. Railroad, 215 Pa. St. 610 (1906).
See Form No. 2.
A provision, in articles of incorporation, permitting preferred stockholders to participate in extra dividends after common stockholders have received dividends equal to the first dividend on preferred stock, is not in violation of § 8668. The limitation of this section is not violated so long as the difference between the dividend paid on preferred and that paid on other stock does not exceed eight percent.
Rep. Atty. Gen. 1911-1912, pp. 95, 115.
Rep. Atty. Gen. 1907, p. 113.

Guaranty of dividends. Mortgage to secure. A guaranty of dividends on preferred stock is not a guaranty for payment in any event, but only in the event that dividends are earned.
Miller v. Ratterman, 47 O. S. 141 (1890).
A mortgage to secure dividends on preferred stock is subject to the condition that such dividends must be earned, although such condition may be apparently inconsistent with the mortgage.
Miller v. Ratterman, 47 O. S. 141 (1890).
Warren v. King, 108 U. S. 389, 398 (1883).
The verbal promise by the president of a corporation that a subscriber should receive certain dividends, is not a promise to answer for the debt, default or miscarriage of another; dividends not being a debt.
Moorehouse v. Crangle, 36 O. S. 130 (1880).

Section 8669. (Provisions in reference to preferred stock.) A corporation issuing both common and preferred stock may create designations, preferences, and voting powers, or restrictions or qualifications thereof, in the certificate of incorporation, and if desired, preferred stock may be made subject to redemption at not less than par, at a fixed time and price, to be expressed in the stock certificates thereof. (R. S. Sec. 3235a; May 12, 1902, 95 v. 623.)
Increase of capital by preferred stock. § 8699.
Preferred stock of railroad companies, §§ 8805, 8817.

Voting restrictions. The right to vote preferred stock may be entirely withheld.
Miller v. Ratterman, 47 O. S. 141 (1890).
Or restricted to certain circumstances and conditions, as, when dividends are in default.
See Ryan v. Miami, etc., Co., 10 Am. L. R. 263 (C. P. 1881).

Preference created in unissued stock after organization. After organization, the existing stockholders, for the purpose of inducing subscriptions to the unissued stock, may, by agreement, give new subscribers a preference as to dividends.

Painesville N. B. v. King Varnish Co., 8 C. C. 563; 4 C. D. 511 (1894); reversed in part, 56 O. S. 744.

Common stock may be changed into preferred stock, by amendment to articles.

Rep. Atty. Gen. 1904-1905, p. 81.
Contra, 5 Opins. Attys. Gen. 1006 (1903).
See Rep. Atty. Gen. 1911-1912, p. 115.

Redemption. To redeem means to purchase back; to repurchase.

Miller v. Ratterman, 47 O. S. 141, 156 (1890).
Mannington v. Hocking Valley Ry. Co., 183 Fed. 133, 145; 8 O. L. R. 451, 466; 16 O. F. D. 552 (U. S. D. C. 1910).

The redemption of preferred stock, authorized by statute, is not a reduction of the corporation's capital stock by a purchase of its own shares.

Mannington v. Hocking Valley Ry. Co., 183 Fed. 133; 8 O. L. R. 451; 16 O. F. D. 552 (U. S. C. C. 1910); s. c., 9 N. P. n. s. 641; 20 L. D. 468.

Preferred stock may be redeemed and retired without filing a certificate of reduction under § 8700.

Rep. Atty. Gen. 1906, p. 46.

The right to redeem preferred stock of a railroad company under § 8817 may be exercised by the directors.

Mannington v. Hocking Valley Ry. Co., 183 Fed. 133, 142, 146; 8 O. L. R. 451, 462, 467; 16 O. F. D. 552; (U. S. C. C. 1910); s. c., 9 N. P. n. s. 641; 20 L. D. 468 (C. P.).

The redemption of preferred stock will not be enjoined where plaintiff has no interest in the stock, although it is part of a conspiracy to oppress the plaintiff.

Gould v. C. & O. Ry., 10 N. P. n. s. 129 (1910).

Issues of stock construed. Preferred stock or debt. Held to be preferred stock.

Miller v. Ratterman, 47 O. S. 141 (1890); reversing 22 W. L. B. 99.
Ryan v. Miami, etc., Co., 10 A. L. R. 263 (C. P. 1881).
Hamlin v. Toledo, etc., R. Co., 78 Fed. 664 (C. C. A. 1897).

Held to be a debt.

Burt v. Battle, 31 O. S. 116 (1876).

College endowment stock, issued by corporation not for profit.

See Ohio College, etc., v. Rosenthal, 45 O. S. 183 (1887).
Bryant v. Ohio College, etc., 1 C. S. C. R. 307 (1871).
See also note to § 9927.

Distinct rights of different classes of stockholders. Parties to actions.

See Port Clinton, etc., Co. v. Cleveland, etc., Co., 13 O. S. 544

Section 8670. (Liability of holder of preferred stock.)

Upon the insolvency of the corporation no holder of preferred stock shall be liable for its debts until after the remedy against the common stockholders upon their liability, as provided by law, has been exhausted, and then only for such amount as remains unpaid. Such liability in no event shall exceed that fixed by law for the common stock of such corporation. (R. S. Sec. 3235a; May 12, 1902, 95 v. 623.)

Section 8671.   (Rights of holders of preferred stock.) On the insolvency or dissolution of the corporation, the holders of preferred stock shall be entitled to receive from the assets remaining after paying its liabilities, the full payment of its par value, before anything is paid to the common stock. (R. S. Sec. 3235a; May 12, 1902, 95 v. 623.)

Before the enactment of this section is was held that, where not prohibited by statute, preference might be given as to assets as well as dividends.

Hamlin v. Toledo, etc., Co., 78 Fed. 664 (C. C. A. 1897).

Continental Trust Co. v. Toledo, etc., Co., 86 Fed. 929 (C. C. 1898).

Toledo, etc., Co. v. Continental Trust Co., 95 Fed. 497 (C. C. A. 1899).

But such preference could be over other stock only; not over the rights of creditors.

Warren v. King, 108 U. S. 389 (1883).

Section 8672.   (Certificate of stock.) Upon his demand therefor, of the president or secretary of the company, they shall execute and deliver to any stockholder a certificate showing the true amount of paid up stock therein, held by him. (R. S. Sec. 3254; April 14, 1884, 81 v. 196; R. S. 1880.)

A stockholder who has paid for his stock may, by a suit in equity, compel the issuance and delivery of a certificate, or he may sue for damages. But mandamus is not the proper remedy.

State v. Carpenter, 51 O. S. 83 (1894).

Freon v. Carriage Co., 42 O. S. 30 (1884).

A stockholder is only entitled to a certificate for such stock as is paid in full.

Cincinnati, etc., Co. v. Bank, 1 C. C. 199, 209; 1 C. D. 109 (1885).

This section seems to require that certificates may be issued only when the stock is fully paid up.

State v. Davis, 85 O. S. 44 (1911).

The assignee of a subscription may tender the amount due thereon and compel the corporation to issue a certificate.

Iron Railroad Co. v. Fink, 41 O. S. 321 (1884).

Certificates of stock generally, see note to § 8673.

Section 8673.   (Record of certificates of stock.) The directors of such corporation, when organized, shall keep a record of all stock subscribed and transferred, and its secretary or recording officer shall register all subscriptions and transfers of stock. For that purpose a book shall be kept, and when a certificate of stock is assigned and delivered by a stockholder, the assignee thereof on demand may have it duly transferred therein by such officer, who at the same time shall enroll also the name of the assignee as a stockholder. The books and records of such corporation at all reasonable times shall be open to the inspection of every stockholder. (R. S. Sec. 3254; April 14, 1884, 81 v. 196; R. S. 1880.)

Transfers of stock on corporate books. See note to § 8673-1.

CERTIFICATES OF STOCK.

Certificates of stock are not "moneys" or "credits."
    State v. Davis, 85 O. S. 44 (1911).

Distinguished from stock itself. There is a distinction between the stock and the certificate representing such stock. The certificate is not the stock itself but merely evidence of its ownership.
    Bank v. Towle Mfg. Co., 67 O. S. 306, 314 (1902).
    State v. Davis, 85 O. S. 44 (1911).

Person may be a stockholder without a certificate. A certificate is not necessary to constitute a person a stockholder. The person who appears on the books of a corporation as the owner of stock is entitled to vote and to receive dividends, although no certificates have been issued, or his certificates have been lost.
    Simons Hardware Co. v. Stokes, 16 C. C. 145, 150; 8 C. D. 779
        (1898).
    Bank v. Towle Mfg. Co., 67 O. S. 306, 314 (1902).
    Railroad Co. v. Robbins, 35 O. S. 483, 502 (1880).
    Franklin Bank v. Commercial Bank, 36 O. S. 350, 355 (1881).
    Norton v. Norton, 43 O. S. 509, 522 (1885).
    National Bank v. Lake Shore, etc., R. Co., 21 O. S. 221 (1871).
    Kreisser v. Ashtabula, etc., Co., 2 C. C. n. s. 597, 601; 14 C. D. 313
        (1901).
    Henderson v. Hogan, 1 W. L. B. 227 (Dist. Ct. 1876).

Officers authorized to execute certificates. The president and secretary are authorized and required to execute stock certificates. Such authority and duty are conferred by statute. (§ 8672).
    Railway Co. v. Bank, 56 O. S. 351 (1897).
It is doubtful whether a corporation may designate another corporation to act as transfer agent of its stock. This section authorizes only the secretary or recording officer to register transfers.
    Burch v. Cincinnati Trust Co., 12 N. P. n. s. 86, 91; 22 L. D. 6
        (C. P. 1911); aff'd on other grounds, 14 C. C. n. s. 346.
    Compare Robison v. Railroad, 13 L. D. 1.

LIABILITY OF CORPORATION ON CERTIFICATES ISSUED FRAUDULENTLY OR WITHOUT AUTHORITY.

Certificates issued to president or secretary. The liability of a corporation on certificates which have been fraudulently issued to an officer, who is authorized to issue certificates, depends upon its negligence. Where the president of a corporation signed certificates in blank and left them with the secretary, who fraudulently issued them to himself and the directors exercised no supervision, the corporation was held liable.
    Railway Co. v. Bank, 56 O. S. 351 (1897); affirming 29 W. L. B. 15.
But where a certificate was issued to the secretary of a corporation, who immediately pledged it back to the corporation to secure his indebtedness to it. and subsequently abstracted the certificate from the safe and pledged it to another person, the corporation was held not to be liable, there being no negligence.

Farmers Bank v. Diebold, etc., Co., 66 O. S. 367 (1902).

The same facts involved in Railway Co. v. Bank, 56 O. S. 351, were passed upon in the following cases:

Cincinnati, etc., Ry. Co. v. Third Nat. Bank, 1 C. C. 199; 1 C. D. 109 (1885).

Citizens' Nat. Bank v. Cincinnati, etc., Ry. Co., 11 W. L. B. 86 (1884).

First Nat. Bank v. Cincinnati, etc., Ry. Co., 16 W. L. B. 399 (1886).

Cincinnati, etc., Ry. Co. v. Rawson, 16 W. L. B. 423 (1886); affirmed, 25 W. L. B. 87.

Perin v. Cincinnati, etc., Ry. Co., 18 W. L. B. 382 (1887).

Cincinnati, etc., Ry. Co. v. Citizens' Nat. Bank, 22 W. L. B. 248 (1889); s. c., 56 O. S. 351.

Cincinnati, etc., Ry. Co. v. Citizens' Nat. Bank, 24 W. L. B. 198; s. c., 29 W. L. B. 15.

Overissued stock. Certificates of stock issued after the entire capital stock had been issued are spurious and void. An innocent purchaser or pledgee can not compel the corporation to transfer such stock to him. But the corporation is liable in damages to such purchaser or pledgee.

Railway Co. v. Bank, 56 O. S. 351 (1897).

Cook on Corporations, §§ 293, 426.

Certificates of stock of constituent company issued after consolidation. A certificate of stock of a corporation issued after its consolidation with another corporation is spurious. A stockholder in such constituent company who has had his stock transferred into that of the consolidated company is chargeable with knowledge of the facts, and can not be regarded as an innocent purchaser of such spurious stock, which he subsequently acquired.

Worthington v. C. C. Ry., 9 C. C. n. s. 433; 19 C. D. 321 (1904); aff'd, no rep., 75 O. S. 626.

Duty of purchaser or pledgee to make inquiry. As against the corporation, a prospective purchaser or pledgee of a certificate is not required to make inquiry beyond the genuineness of the certificate. Even where the certificate was issued to the secretary of the corporation no inquiry is necessary, in the absence of knowledge of fraud in its issue.

Railway Co. v. Bank, 56 O. S. 351, 379, 380 (1897).

Personal liability of president and secretary on certificates. A president signing a certificate which stated that the stock is "full paid and nonassessable," is not liable in damages to a person who purchased it in the open market, without inquiry, although the president knew that the stock was issued for property at an overvaluation.

Nutt v. Wheeler, 10 C. C. n. s. 217; 20 C. D. 86 (1907).

The president and secretary of a corporation are not personally liable for a refusal to transfer stock. The liability is that of the corporation.

Snodgrass v. Morrison, etc., Co., 4 O. L. R. 622; 17 L. D. 497. (Super. Ct. Cin. 1907).

CORPORATE STOCK BOOKS.

Form. Sec. 8673 does not prescribe the form in which the records shall be kept.

Freon v. Carriage Co., 42 O. S. 30, 36 (1884).

It is not necessary that a book of any special kind be adopted as a stock record; but when a book is selected and used it becomes the stock book and transfers, to be valid, must be made upon it.

Harpold v. Stobart, 46 O. S. 397, 400 (1889).

Where no stock book is kept, the stubs of the certificate book may be resorted to for the purpose of ascertaining who the stockholders are. In such case the stub of the transferred certificate should show to whom the stock has been transferred.

Herrick v. Wardwell, 58 O. S. 294 (1898).

But see State B. & T. Co. v. Mitchell Co., 14 N. P. n. s. 57, 63, 64 (1913).

Evidence as to who are stockholders. The books of a corporation are admissible in evidence to show that one who claims to be a stockholder is not in fact a stockholder.

Cincinnati, etc., Ry. Co. v. Rawson, 16 W. L. B. 423 (Super. Ct. Cin. 1886); aff'd, no rep., 25 W. L. B. 87.

See Perin v. Cincinnati, etc., R. Co., 17 W. L. B. 261 (Super. Ct. Cin.); aff'd, 18 W. L. B. 382.

Or to show that a person who claims to have transferred his stock and to be no longer a stockholder, is in fact still a stockholder.

Harpold v. Stewart, 46 O. S. 397 (1889).

Herrick v. Wardwell, 58 O. S. 294 (1898).

See Kreisser v. Ashtabula, etc., Co., 2 C. C. n. s. 597, 601; 14 C. D. 313 (1901).

But under § 8686 where a certificate is properly tendered for transfer but the entry is not made in the corporate books, the transferrer is not liable.

State B. & T. Co. v. Mitchell, 14 N. P. n. s. 49 (C. P. 1913).

As against a transferee who denies having bought the stock or authorized the transfer. the corporate records showing the transfer are not sufficient proof of acceptance of the transfer so as to render the transferee liable for calls and assessments.

Tripp v. Appleman, 35 Fed. 19; 6 O. F. D. 71 (C. C. Ohio 1888).

Who may register transfers. It is doubtful whether a corporation can appoint another corporation as a transfer agent and require certificates to be presented to such transfer agents. Section 8673 authorizes only the secretary or recording officer to register transfers.

Burch v. Cincinnati Trust Co., 12 N. P. n. s. 86, 91; 22 L. D. 6 (1911); aff'd on other grounds, 14 C. C. n. s. 346.

See G. C. § 9817, which authorizes trust companies to act as agent or trustees for registering, countersigning or transferring certificates of stock.

RIGHT OF STOCKHOLDERS TO INSPECT BOOKS OF CORPORATION.

A stockholder has the right to have the inspection made by a proper agent and to take copies from the books and records. More than one inspection may be made.

Cincinnati Volksblatt Co. v. Hoffmeister, 62 O. S. 189 (1900).

Blymyer v. Blymyer, etc., Co., 5 N. P. 71 (Super. Ct. Cin. 1898).

All the books may be examined.

Caldwell v. Hill, etc., Co., 2 O. L. R. 294; 17 L. D. 801 (Super Ct. Cin.).

Preferred stockholders are entitled to examine the corporate books.

Pearce v. Atkins, 13 N. P. n. s. 580 (1913).

The motive or purpose of a stockholder in demanding an inspection is immaterial.

Cincinnati Volksblatt Co. v. Hoffmeister, 62 O. S. 189 (1900).

Blymyer v. Blymyer, etc., Co., 5 N. P. 71 (Super. Ct. Cin. 1898).

But see Whitney v. American Shipbuilding Co., 14 N. P. n. s. 12; 23 L. D. 1 (C. P. 1912).

The only limitation of the right is that the inspection must be at rea-
sonable times.
Cincinnati Volksblatt Co. v. Hoffmeister, 62 O. S. 198 (1900).
A stockholder may inspect the books although the corporation is in the
hands of a receiver.
Rep. Atty. Gen., 1911-1912, p. 747.

What corporations are subject to inspection by stockholders.

Trust company. The word "such" in § 8673 does not limit the right
of inspection to any class of corporations. A stockholder in a trust
company may inspect its books.
Kennon v. Ohio Trust Co., 4 O. L. R. 352; 16 L. D. 733 (Super. Ct.
    Cin. 1906); s. c., 3 O. L. R. 424; 16 L. D. 339.
Except records of deposits and trusts.
See G. C. § 9795.
In a suit to enforce such right of inspection beneficiaries of trusts
administered by the trust company are not necessary or proper defend-
ants.
Kennon v. Ohio Trust Co., 4 O. L. R. 352; 16 L. D. 733 (Super. Ct.
    Cin. 1906).

Corporation not for profit. Sec. 8673 does not apply to corporations
not for profit.
Ohio Humane Soc. v. Biles, 11 C. C. n. s. 384 (1908).

Foreign corporation. Where the books of a foreign corporation were
kept in an office maintained by it in Ohio, it was held that the right
of stockholders to inspect its books, granted by a statute of its home
state, could be enforced in Ohio.
State v. Farmer, 7 C. C. 429 (1892).
Contra, Riggs v. Whippey, etc., Co., 7 O. L. R. 446 (C. P. 1909).
Compare State v. Unida, etc., Co.,   13 C. C. n. s. 100; 22 C. D. 54
    (1910).
A suit to enjoin a foreign corporation from refusing a stockholder
an inspection of its books can not be removed to federal court on the
ground of diverse citizenship, as the right of the stockholder can not be
ascertained or calculated in money.
Whitney v. American Shipbuilding Co., 10 O. L. R. 383; 197 Fed.
    777 (U. S. D. C. 1911).

National bank. The common law right, for proper purposes and
under reasonable regulations as to place and time, to inspect the books
of the corporation, may be exercised by a stockholder of a national bank.
Such right may be enforced in state courts.
Guthrie v. Harkness, 199 U. S. 148 (1905).

Remedy and pleading. Injunction, and not mandamus, is the proper
remedy.
Cincinnati Volksblatt Co. v. Hoffmeister, 62 O. S. 189 (1900).
Blymyer v. Blymyer, etc., Co., 5 N. P. 71 (Super. Ct. Cin. 1898).
A petition which alleges that the plaintiff is a stockholder; that he
has requested the corporation to allow him to inspect the books and
records of the corporation, and fix a reasonable time for the same, which
request has been refused, states a cause of action.
Cincinnati Volksblatt Co. v. Hoffmeister, 62 O. S. 189 (1900).
The details for the request for inspection, whether it was oral or
in writing, and the time, place and person upon whom made, need not
be alleged.
Kennon v. Ohio Trust Co., 3 O. L. R. 424; 16 L. D. 339 (Super. Ct.
    Cin. 1905).

A petition to enforce the right of inspection does not state a cause of action against the president individually, where the only allegation as to him is that he is president.

Pearce v. Atkins, 13 N. P. n. s. 580 (1913).

Inspection of books under § 11552.

See Arbuckle v. Woolson Spice Co., 21 C. C. 348; 11 C. D. 743 (1901).

An order under § 11552 permitting a plaintiff to inspect the books of defendant corporation is not a final order reviewable in error.

Kleybolte v. Railway Co., 11 L. D. 817 (Super. Ct. Cin. 1896).

Who are chargeable with notice of contents of corporate books and records.

Stockholders. A stockholder is not bound to have knowledge of the contents of the corporate records and books, although he had the right of inspection.

Heintzman v. Tenacity, etc., Co., 4 O. L. R. 553; 17 L. D. 554 (Super. Ct. Cin. 1906).

Greenville Gas Co. v. Reis, 54 O. S. 549, 558 (1896).

Directors. See note to § 8660. *Duties of directors.*

Section 8673-1. (Transfer of title to shares.) Title to a certificate and to the shares represented thereby can be transferred only.

(a) By delivery of the certificate indorsed either in blank or to a specified person by the person appearing by the certificate to be the owner of the shares represented thereby, or

(b) By delivery of the certificate and a separate document containing a written assignment of the certificate or a power of attorney to sell, assign, or transfer the same or the shares represented thereby signed by the person appearing by the certificate to be the owners of the shares represented thereby. Such assignment or power of attorney may be either in blank or to a specified person.

The provisions of this section shall be applicable although the charter or articles of incorporation or code of regulations or by-laws of the corporation issuing the certificate and the certificate itself, provide that the shares represented thereby shall be transferable only on the books of the corporation or shall be registered by a registrar or transferred by a transfer agent. (June 7, 1911, 102 v. 500, § 1.)

Uniform Stock Transfer Act. The Uniform Stock Transfer Act recommended by the American Bar Association for general adoption is contained in sections 8673-1 to 8673-24 inclusive. It applies only to certificates issued after July 1, 1911. Its effect is to place certificates of stock on the basis of negotiable instruments. The act has been adopted in Louisiana, Maryland, Massachussets, Michigan, New York, Ohio, Pennsylvania and Alaska.

Assignment of stock by separate instrument without transfer of certificate. It should be noted that under this section an assignment of stock by a separate instrument without a delivery of the certificate does not transfer the title. Such assignment is, in effect, merely a contract to transfer under § 8673-10.

Rep. American Bar Assn. (1910), 575, 576.

Ohio decisions as to transfer of certificates. The assignment of a certificate of stock with power of attorney to have it transferred on the books of the corporation gives to the assignee the status of a legal holder of the stock.

Dueber, etc., Co. v. Dougherty, 62 O. S. 589, 595 (1900).

Andrews v. Watson, 12 C. D. 668 (1887); s. c., 12 C. D. 692 (1890); aff'd, 51 O. S. 617.

Compare Carll v. Little Miami R. Co., 13 C. C. n. s. 598 (1911). A certificate may be assigned and an attorney appointed in blank.

Lee v. Citizens' N. B., 2 C. S. C. R. 298 (1872).

Cincinnati, etc., Ry. Co. v. Rawson, 16 W. L. B. 423 (Super. Ct. Cin. 1886); aff'd, Supreme Court, without report, 25 W. L. B. 87.

Krebs v. Forbriger, 21 W. L. B. 313 (Super. Ct. Cin. 1889).

Transfer or registry on the books of the corporation. How made. The transfer book of the corporation should be signed by the transferrer personally, or by his attorney in fact. In practice the name of the secretary or transfer agent of the corporation is usually inserted in the power of attorney on the certificate of stock.

See § 8673.

Consequences of failure to present stock for registry. As against the corporation the transferree does not become a stockholder until he presents the certificate for transfer on the corporate books. Until then he is an equitable holder merely. The registered owner is entitled to vote and to receive dividends.

§ 8673-3.

Railway Co. v. Bank, 68 O. S. 582 (1903).

Railroad Co. v. Robbins, 35 O. S. 483 (1880).

Schmuck v. Crume, etc., Co., 7 N. P. n. s. 24; 19 L. D. 819 (C. P. 1905); aff'd, 78 O. S. 409.

Norton v. Norton, 43 O. S. 509, 522-23 (1885).

Haldeman v. Hillsborough, etc., R. Co., 2 Handy 101 (Super. Ct. Cin. 1855).

Armstrong v. Herancourt Brewing Co., 26 W. L. B. 39 (C. P. 1891). Notices of proposed corporate action on such matters as a proposed consolidation, or a sale of the entire corporate property, are properly sent by the corporation to the persons registered on its books as the owners. A person who holds certificates, without transfer on the corporate books, is not entitled to be notified of, or to participate in, such proceedings.

Railway Co. v. Bank, 68 O. S. 582 (1903).

Schmuck v. Crume, etc., Co., 7 N. P. n. s. 24; 19 L. D. 819 (C. P. 1905); aff'd, 78 O. S. 409.

The lien of a corporation on stock, expressly reserved in the certificates, may be asserted against a transferee who received the certificates before, but did not present them for transfer until after the original holder become indebted to the corporation.

Stafford v. Produce Exch. Bkg. Co., 61 O. S. 160 (1899).

Effect, of § 8673-1. The intention of this section is to make the certificate I the representative of the shares and to make a transfer on the corporate books like the recording of a deed of real estate.

Rep. American Bar Assn. (1910), 574.

Right of transferee to have stock registered in his name. A purchaser or pledgee of stock, holding a certificate properly indorsed is entitled, upon presenting such certificate to the corporation, to have the stock transferred to him on the corporate books and to have a new certificate issued to him.

> Cincinnati, etc., Ry. Co. v. Rawson, 16 W. L. B. 423 (Super. Ct. Cin.); aff'd by Supreme Court without report, 25 W. L. B. 87.
> Railway Co. v. Bank, 56 O. S. 351 (1897).
> Dayton N. B. v. Merchants N. B., 37 O. S. 208, 215 (1881).

§ 8673.

What the corporation may require before registry of transfers.

Evidence of genuineness of indorsement and identity of parties. The corporation may require satisfactory evidence of the identity of the parties and the genuineness of the assignment and power of attorney. But when these are established it can not arbitrarily refuse to make the transfer.

> Krohn v. Central, etc., Co., 4 N. P. 270; 6 L. D. 552 (C. P. 1897).
> Oliver v. Cincinnati, etc., Co., 1 Hosea 457 (Super Ct. Cin.); s. c., 3 O. L. R. 53, 607; aff'd, 73 O. S. 386.
> See § 8673-11.

Where certificates of a deceased stockholder are presented for transfer, and the officers are informed of the existence of a will, they are chargeable with notice of the provisions of the will which affect the title to the stock or the right to transfer it.

> Allen v. Globe Ins. Co., 19 W. L. B. 198 (Super. Ct. Cin. 1888); aff'd, Supreme Court, 32 W. L. B. 374.

Surrender of original certificate. Where a certificate provides that the stock is transferable "on surrender of the certificate" the corporation may refuse to transfer the stock on its books and to issue new certificates, until the original certificate evidencing the same has been surrendered.

> Railroad Co. v. Robbins, 35 O. S. 483 (1880).
> Lee v. Citizens Bank, 2 C. S. C. R. 298 (1872).
> § 8673-13.

A corporation is not liable to the equitable owner of stock for its value, where certificates therefor are outstanding in the hands of a third person, who claims to be the owner.

> National Bank v. Lake Shore, etc., Ry. Co., 21 O. S. 221 (1871).

A corporation which issues a new certificate without a surrender of the original certificate, is liable to the holder of the original certificate, although the new certificate was issued under the belief that the original had been lost. The corporation must either replace the stock or account for its value.

> Railroad Co. v. Robbins, 35 O. S. 483 (1880).
> See Lee v. Citizens N. B., 2 C. S. C. R. 298 (Super. Ct. Cin. 1872).

But it is not liable for dividends paid to the registered owner before the certificate was presented for transfer.

> Railroad Co. v. Robbins, 35 O. S. 483 (1880).

Where certificates have been lost the corporation may require a bond of indemnity before issuing a new certificate.

§ 8673-17.

> Hof v. Western German Bank, 6 W. L. B. 665, 697 (Dist Ct. 1881).
> Farmers Bank v. Diebold, etc., Co., 66 O. S. 376 (1902).

Certified copy of order of probate court authorizing transfer by executor. A corporation can not require a certified copy of an order of the probate court ot the county, in which the principal office of such corporation is located, authorizing an executor to make the transfer.

Burch v. Cincinnati Trust Co., 12 N. P. n. s. 86 (1911); aff'd, 14 C. C. n. s. 346.

Remedy for refusal of corporation to register · transfers. Where a corporation wrongfully refuses to transfer stock on its books and to issue a new certificate to a person entitled thereto, his remedy is in equity to enforce the issue and delivery of such certificate, or an action against the corporation for damages, either of which he may pursue at his election.

State v. Carpenter, 51 O. S. 83 (1894).
Iron R. Co. v. Fink, 41 O. S. 321 (1884).
Krohn v. Central, etc., Co., 4 N. P. 270; 6 L. D. 552 (C. P. 1897).
Burch v. Cincinnati Trust Co., 12 N. P. n. s. 86 (C. P. 1911); aff'd, 14 C. C. n. s. 346.

The plaintiff may in his petition ask for relief in the alternative, for the issue and delivery of a certificate, or damages in lieu thereof.

State v. Carpenter, 51 O. S. 83, 89 (1894).
See Railroad Co. v. Robbins, 35 O. S. 483.

Mandamus is not the proper remedy.

State v. Carpenter, 51 O. S. 83 (1894).
Freon v. Carriage Co., 42 O. S. 30 (1884); s. c., 11 W. L. B. 103.
Richardson v. Grand View Min. Co., 1 W. L. B. 140 (Dist. Ct. 1876).

The president and secretary are not personally liable for a refusal to transfer stock. The liability is that of the corporation.

Snodgrass v. Morrison, etc., Co., 4 O. L. R. 622; 17 L. D. 497 (Super. Ct. Cin. 1907).

Wrongful refusal to transfer stock amounts to a conversion.

Andes Ins. Co. v. Waters, 1 W. L. B. 172 (Super. Ct. Cin. 1876).

Measure of damages. The damages are not limited to the market value of the stock, but the transferee may recover its actual value, which may be shown by the value of the property and business of the corporation, its good will and dividend earning capacity.

State v. Carpenter, 51 O. S. 83, 88 (1894).
Freon v. Carriage Co., 42 O. S. 30 (1884).

Presumptions and burden of proof as to validity of issue of stock. Where a certificate bears the genuine signatures of the president and secretary, and the corporate seal, the issue of such stock is presumed to be regular and valid. The burden of proving its invalidity rests on the corporation, although the certificate was issued to the secretary.

Cincinnati, etc., Ry. Co. v. Rawson, 16 W. L. B. 423 (Super. Ct. Cin. 1886); aff'd, no rep., 25 W. L. B. 87.
Railway Co. v. Bank, 56 O. S. 351.
Perin v. Railway Co., 18 W. L. B. 382 (Super. Ct. Cin. 1887).
Citizens' N. B. v. Railway Co., 11 W. L. B. 86 (Super. Ct. Cin. 1884).

Joinder of parties and actions. The transferrer of the stock is not a necessary party to a suit to compel a transfer of stock, unless he claims some interest therein.

Krohn v. Central, etc., Co., 4 N. P. 270; 6 L. D. 552 (C. P. 1897).

But the corporation may make all persons claiming any interest in the stock parties to the action.

Lahman v. Cincinnati, etc., Co., 8 N. P. 211 (Super. Ct. Cin. 1901).
See Dayton N. B. v. Merchants N. B., 37 O. S. 208 (1881).

The president and secretary are not proper parties defendant.

Snodgrass v. Morrison, etc., Co., 4 O. L. R. 622; 17 L. D. 497. (Super. Ct. Cin. 1907).

Nor a transfer agent.

Burch v. Cincinnati Trust Co., 12 N. P. n. s. 86 (1911); aff'd, 14 C. C. n. s. 346.

Other equitable relief may be sought in the same action, as, an order for the inspection of the corporate books by the stockholder.

Arbuckle v. Woolson Spice Co., 21 C. C. 356 (1901).

See Iron R. Co. v. Fink, 41 O. S. 321 (1884).

Right of corporation to join in one action all holders of certificates wrongfully issued by an officer, to remove cloud on the title of genuine certificates and to prevent a multiplicity of suits.

See Railway Co. v. Bank, 56 O. S. 351 (1897).

Defenses of corporation.

Noncompliance with by-law regulating transfers. Noncompliance with a valid by-law or regulation as to transfers, expressed in the stock certificate, is a defense to an action to enforce a transfer on the corporate books.

Nicholson v. Franklin Brewing Co., 82 O. S. 94 (1910).

§ 8673-15.

But a by-law prohibiting the transfer of stock which has been paid by note and mortgage is unreasonable and was held not to justify a refusal to transfer.

Andes Ins. Co. v. Waters, 1 W. L. B. 172 (Super. Ct. Cin. 1876).

See notes to §§ 8701 and 8702.

Certificate issued without consideration to qualify director. It is no defense against a pledgee of a stock certificate, that the certificate was issued to the pledgor to qualify·him as a director, without consideration, and under an agreement to surrender the certificate on ceasing to be a director, where the pledgee had no notice thereof.

Dueber, etc., Co. v. Dougherty, 62 O. S. 589 (1900).

Lien of corporation on stock reserved in certificate. A corporation may, by express stipulation in the certificate, reserve a lien on the stock to secure indebtedness of the original holder to it. This lien may be asserted against a purchaser who received the certificate before, but did not present it for transfer until after the original holder became indebted to the corporation.

Stafford v. Produce Exch. Bkg. Co., 61 O. S. 160 (1899).

See § 8673-15 and note.

See also State v. Davis, 85 O. S. 44 (1911).

But where the lien is not reserved in the certificate, although provided for by by-laws, a bona fide purchaser or pledgee takes the certificate free from such lien.

Lee v. Citizens N. B., 2 C. S. C. R. 298 (1872).

§ 8673-15.

Improper motive or bad faith of transferee. A corporation can not refuse to transfer stock because of the motive which prompted the transferee to acquire it.

Nicholson v. Franklin Brewing Co., 82 O. S. 94, 110 (1910).

Statute of limitations. The statute of limitations does not begin to run against a transferee of stock until a demand has been made on the corporation for a transfer, and has been refused.

Iron R. Co. v. Fink, 41 O. S. 321 (1884).

Railroad Co. v. Robbins, 35 O. S. 483 (1880).

Larwill v. Burke, 19 C. C. 449; 10 C. D. 579 (1900).

Where new certificates were issued without a surrender of the original certificates, the statute does not begin to run against the holder of the original certificates until a demand, or until he had notice of the transfer to the other parties.

Railroad Co. v. Robbins, 35 O. S. 483 (1880).

Waiver of right to damages. Where the plaintiff subsequently collected dividends, accepted a new certificate of stock and paid an assessment, the right to recover damages was held to be waived.

Andes Ins. Co. v. Waters, 1 W. L. B. 172 (Super. Ct. Cin. 1876).

That third persons claim to own the stock. Where more than one party claims to own the stock, the corporation, by refusing to assume the peril of deciding between the contending claimants, ought not to be held liable as a wrongdoer for the value of the stock.

National Bank v. Lake Shore, etc., Co., 21 O. S. 221, 232 (1871). But there must be a real controversy.

See Dayton N. B. v. Merchants N. B., 37 O. S. 208, 215 (1881).

The bankruptcy of the original stockholder, and appointment of a trustee in bankruptcy, does not justify a corporation in refusing to transfer the stock to a pledgee, who had received the certificate prior to such bankruptcy.

But where the trustee in bankruptcy became a party defendant, and contested the validity of the pledge, which was decided in favor of the pledgee, and an order of sale granted, the court can not render a deficiency judgment against the corporation.

Dayton N. B. v. Merchants N. B., 37 O. S. 208 (1881).

See Oliver v. Cincinnati, etc., Co., 1 Hosea 457 (Super. Ct. Cin.); s. c., 3 O. L. R. 53, 607; aff'd, 73 O. S. 386.

The corporation may bring in, as parties defendant, all persons claiming an interest in the stock.

Lahman v. Cincinnati, etc., Co., 8 N. P. 211 (Super. Ct. Cin. 1901).

Before the passage of the Uniform Act it was held that a corporation was bound to respect the rights of equitable owners from the time it received notice thereof.

Conant v. Reed, 1 O. S. 298 (1853).

Andrews v. Watson, 12 C. D. 686 (1887); aff'd, 51 O. S. 617.

To whom stock may be transferred on the corporate books.

Pledgee. A pledgee of stock, holding certificates properly indorsed, is entitled to have the stock registered in his name on the corporate books.

Railway Co. v. Bank, 68 O. S. 582, 599 (1903).

Dayton N. B. v. Merchants N. B., 37 O. S. 208, 215 (1881).

Cincinnati, etc., Ry. Co. v. Rawson, 16 W. L. B. 423 (Super. Ct. Cin. 1886); aff'd, 25 W. L. B. 87.

Trustee. A stockholder has the right, for a proper purpose, to transfer his stock to a trustee.

State v. Railway Co., 6 C. C. 415; 3 C. D. 518 (1892); aff'd, 49 O. S. 668.

See note to § 8647. *Voting trusts.*

A corporation. A corporation may, without liability, refuse to transfer stock on its books to another corporation which is not authorized by law to acquire or hold such stock.

Franklin Bank v. Commercial Bank, 36 O. S. 350 (1881).

Power of corporation to acquire and hold stock in other corporations. See § 8683.

Power to acquire its own stock. See note to § 8627.

Fictitious person. A transfer to a fictitious person is void, and leaves the title in the transferrer.

Krohn v. Central, etc., Co., 4 N. P. 270; 5 L. D. 113 (C. P. 1897).
Muskingum, etc., Co. v. Ward, 13 Ohio 120 (1844).
See Gaff v. Flesher, 33 O. S. 107, 112 (1877).

Guardian. A guardian, who has possession of a certificate of stock belonging to estate of the deceased mother of his wards, has no authority to exchange it for a certificate made out to himself.
First N. B. v. Merchants Bank, 7 N. P. 381 (C. P.).

Liability of transferee for unpaid balance on stock. A purchaser of stock from another person at par is not liable for an unpaid balance unless he had knowledge thereof. He is entitled to the presumption that the stock has been full paid. A statement on the certificate that it is "full paid" is a representation by the corporation to that effect and the purchaser need not inquire further.
Roebling, etc., Co. v. Shawnee, etc., Co., 4 N. P. n. s. 113; 17 L. D. 8 (C. P. 1906) ; aff'd, 78 O. S. 408.

Rights of equitable owners. Prior to the passage of the Uniform Act it was held that the corporation was bound to respect the rights of equitable owners from the time it received notice thereof.
Conant v. Reed, 1 O. S. 298 (1853).
Andrews v. Watson, 12 C. D. 686 (1887) ; s. c., 12 C. D. 692 (1890) ; aff'd, 51 O. S. 617.
Prout v. Post, 12 L. D. 141 (C. P.).
See Provident, etc., Co. v. Voight, 13 C. C. n. s. 267 (1910).
One of two conflicting equitable owners may, by acquiring the legal title, secure priority over the other where he acquired his equitable interest without notice of the earlier equity, although he had such notice at the time he acquired the legal title.
Dueber, etc., Co. v. Daugherty, 62 O. S. 589 (1900).
One who takes an assignment of stock, with notice of a prior assignment which conveyed the legal title, acquires no interest therein.
Creed v. Lancaster Bank, 1 O. S. 1 (1852).

Transfer reserving future dividends. It has been held that in a transfer of stock no valid reservation can be made of future dividends.
Marble v. Van Wert N. B., 3 C. C. 464; 2 C. D. 265 (1888).

Section 8673-2. (Powers of infant, trustee, executor, etc., not enlarged.) Nothing in this act shall be construed as enlarging the powers of an infant or other persons lacking full legal capacity, or of a trustee, executor or administrator, or other fiduciary, to make a valid indorsement, assignment or power of attorney. (June 7, 1911, 102 v. 501, § 2.)

Power of executor to transfer stock. An executor or administrator of the estate of a deceased stockholder, when properly authorized, may execute an assignment of the stock. But an executor can not execute a power of attorney for the sale of stock delegating to the attorney discretionary powers entrusted to the executor.
Allen v. Globe Ins. Co., 19 W. L. B. 198 (Super. Ct. Cin. 1888) ; aff'd, 32 W. L. B. 374.
An exchange of stock, by an executor, not authorized by the will or an order of court, is void.
Marriot v. Railway, 16 L. D. 135 (C. P. 1905) ; s. c., 10 C. C. n. s. 573, 575.
An order of the probate court directing an executor to sell stock "at

its market value" is not a sufficient compliance with G. C. § 10704 which requires a minimum price to be fixed in the order.

>Burch v. Cincinnati Trust Co., 14 C. C. n. s. 346 (1911); contra, s. c., 12 N. P. n. s. 86; 22 L. D. 6 (C. P. 1911).

But such a defect does not impair the title of a purchaser from the executor under such order, where the sale was made in good faith, at the market value, without fraud or collusion, and the proceedings in all other respects conformed to the statute.

>Burch v. Cincinnati Trust Co., 14 C. C. n. s. 346 (1911); affirming 12 N. P. n. s. 86; 22 L. D. 6.

The corporation can not require a certified copy of the order of the probate court of the county in which the principal office of the corporation is located, authorizing the transfer by the executor, before making the transfer on its books.

>Burch v. Cincinnati Trust Co., 12 N. P. n. s. 86; 22 L. D. 6 (1911); aff'd, on other grounds, 14 C. C. n. s. 346.

Pledge of certificate by trustee for his personal debt to corporation. Certificates of stock in a building and loan company were taken by M. C. in the name of her infant granddaughter, with a parenthetic clause after the name ("M. C. or other legal guardian may draw") and retained possession of the certificates. M. C. died leaving a will, wherein she named her lawyer R. as executor and trustee of her property for the use and benefit of the granddaughter, and declaring in the will an intention to make the executor her successor in the trust as to the stock. The executor sent the loan company a copy of the will, with notice that he held the certificates under the will, and requested that dividends be paid to him as trustee. Thereafter he borrowed money from the company for his personal use, pledging some of the certificates as security, and turned in other certificates for cash, signing the transfers and pledge contract as trustee. He squandered the money and died insolvent. Held, the company was a party to the breach of trust and conversion.

>Mook v. Akron Sgs. & L. Co., 87 O. S. 273 (1913).

Section 8673-3. (Corporation not forbidden to treat registered holder as owner.) Nothing in this act shall be construed as forbidding a corporation.

(a) To recognize the exclusive right of a person registered on its books as the owner of shares to receive dividends, and to vote as such owner, or

(b) To hold liable for calls and assessments a person registered on its books as the owner of shares. (June 7, 1911, 102 v. 501, § 3.)

>The person who appears on the corporate books as the owner of stock is entitled to vote and receive dividends.
>Railroad Co. v. Robbins, 35 O. S. 483 (1880).
>Norton v. Norton, 43 O. S. 509, 522-523 (1885).
>Franklin Bank v. Commercial Bank, 36 O. S. 350, 355 (1881).
>See note to § 8673-1.

Section 8673-4. (Title derived from certificate extinguishes title derived from a separate document.) The title of a transferee of a certificate under a power of attorney or assignment not written upon the certificate, and the title of any person claiming under such transferee, shall cease and determine if, at any time prior to the surrender of the certificate to the corporation issuing it, another person, for value in good faith, and without notice of the prior transfer, shall purchase and obtain delivery of such certificate with the indorsement of the person appearing by the certificate to be the owner thereof, or shall purchase and obtain delivery of such certificate and the written assignment or power of attorney of such person, though contained in a separate document. (June 7, 1911, 102 v. 501, § 4.)

Section 8673-5. (Who may deliver a certificate.) The delivery of a certificate to transfer title in accordance with the provisions of section 1 [G. C. § 8673-1], is effectual, except as provided in section 7 [G. C. § 8673-7], though made by one having no right of possession and having no authority from the owner of the certificate or from the person purporting to transfer the title. (June 7, 1911, 102 v. 501, § 5.)

Negotiability of certificates. This section is intended to give full negotiability to certificates of stock.
Rep. American Bar Assn. (1910) 576.

What must be taken notice of by purchasers or pledgees of stock.

Laws of state and by-laws regulating transfers. A purchaser or pledgee of stock is chargeable with notice of the laws of the state of incorporation and valid by-laws which impose restrictions on transfers.
Nicholson v. Franklin Brewing Co., 82 O. S. 94, 109 (1910).
See Lee v. Citizens N. B., 2 C. S. C. R. 298 (1872).
But restrictions imposed under by-laws must be stated upon the certificate.
See § 8673-15.

Genuineness of certificates and endorsement. A purchaser of stock is bound to inquire as to the genuineness of the certificates.
Railway Co. v. Bank, 56 O. S. 351, 379-380 (1897).
And of the endorsement thereon.
Krohn v. Central, etc., Co., 4 N. P. 270; 6 L. D. 552 (C. P. 1897).

Authority of executor of estate of deceased owner. Where the certificates are endorsed by the executor of a deceased owner, the transferee must take notice of the authority of such representative.
See §§ 8673-2, 8673-7.
Allen v. Globe Ins. Co., 19 W. L. B. 198 (Super. Ct. Cin. 1888); aff'd, 32 W. L. B. 374.
First N. B. v. Merchants Bank, 7 N. P. 381 (C. P.).
Marriott v. Railway, 16 L. D. 135 (C. P. 1905); s. c., 10 C. C. n. s. 573, 575.

Lien of corporation reserved in certificate. See note to § 8673-15.

Liens on stock acquired by garnishment process served on corporation. Before the passage of the Uniform Act it was held that a creditor of a stockholder could acquire a lien on his stock by garnishment process served on the corporation. Such lien was superior to the rights of a subsequent purchaser or pledgee of the stock, in good faith and without notice, who relied on the certificates.

Bank v. Towle Mfg. Co., 67 O. S. 306 (1902).

This rule is effective as to certificates issued prior to July 1, 1911.

See §§ 8673-23, 8673-24.

As to certificates issued since July 1, 1911, see § 8673-13.

Whether stock has been paid up. A purchaser who pays par for stock is entitled to assume that the stock has been paid in full. A statement in the certificate that it is "full paid" is a representation by the corporation to that effect and the purchaser need not inquire further.

Roebling, etc., Co. v. Shawnee, etc., Co., 4 N. P. n. s. 113, 121; 17 L. D. 8 (C. P. 1906); aff'd, 78 O. S. 408.

See Nutt v. Wheeler, 10 C. C. n. s. 217; 20 C. D. 86 (1907).

Pending suits affecting the stock. The doctrine of lis pendens does not apply to certificates of stock transferable by endorsement.

Krebs v. Forbriger, 21 W. L. B. 313 (Super. Ct. Cin. 1889).

NEGOTIABILITY OF CERTIFICATES ISSUED PRIOR TO JULY 1, 1911.

Prior to the passage of the Uniform Stock Transfer Act it was held that a certificate of stock was not a promise to pay money and did not possess the essentials of a negotiable instrument.

Farmers Bank v. Diebold, etc., Co., 66 O. S. 367 (1902).

Simmons Hardware Co. v. Stokes, 16 C. C. 145, 149-150; 8 C. D. 779 (1898).

A purchaser or pledgee of a certificate, although in good faith and without notice, took it subject to any lien which a creditor of the seller or pledgor may have acquired, prior to the transfer, by attachment or aid of execution served on the corporation.

Bank v. Towle Mfg. Co., 67 O. S. 306 (1902).

Certificate as evidence of title. Estoppel of corporation and former owners of stock. Prior to the passage of the Uniform Act a certificate of stock was held to be an assurance to the world that the person named therein is the owner of the number of shares stated therein and that these shares will be transferred on the corporate books to one purchasing the same, on surrender of the certificate properly assigned.

Railway Co. v. Bank, 56 O. S. 351, 383 (1897).

Bank v. Towle Mfg. Co., 67 O. S. 306, 314 (1902).

See Marble v. Van Wert N. B., 3 C. C. 464; 2 C. D. 265 (1888).

The corporation itself and former owners of the stock were, as a general rule, estopped from setting up claims to stock evidenced by certificates in the hands of an innocent purchaser for value.

Dueber, etc., Co. v. Dougherty, 62 O. S. 589, 595 (1900).

Railway Co. v. Bank, 56 O. S. 351 (1897).

Krebs v. Forbiger, 21 W. L. B. 313 (Super. Ct. Cin. 1889).

Railroad Co. v. Robbins, 35 O. S. 483 (1880).

Lee v. Citizens N. B., 2 C. S. C. R. 298 (1872).

A pledgor of certificates who had assigned the same in blank was estopped from asserting any title thereto against an innocent purchaser from the pledgee, although the pledgee had violated the contract of pledge in making the sale.

Krebs v. Forbiger, 21 W. L. B. 313 (Super. Ct. Cin. 1889).

Stolen certificates. Before the passage of the Uniform Act a purchaser of stolen certificates, endorsed in blank, acquired no title thereto, in the absence of negligence on the part of the owner, proximately contributing to the deceit.

Bank v. Safe & Lock Co., 66 O. S. 367 (1902).

Section 8673-6.   (Endorsement effectual in spite of fraud, duress, mistake, revocation, death, incapacity or lack of consideration or authority.)   The indorsement of a certificate by the person appearing by the certificate to be the owner of the shares represented thereby is effectual, except as provided in section 7 (G. C. § 8673-7) though the indorser or transferer,

(a) Was induced by fraud, duress or mistake, to make the indorsement or delivery, or

(b) Has revoked the delivery of the certificate, or the authority given by the indorsement or delivery of the certificate, or

(c) Has died or become legally incapacitated after the indorsement whether before or after the delivery of the certificate, or

(d) Has received no consideration. (June 7, 1911, 102 v. 501, § 6.)

> **Delivery by fraud, etc.** See Dueber, etc., Co. v. Dougherty, 62 O. S. 589, 595 (1900).
> Railway Co. v. Bank, 56 O. S. 351 (1897).
>
> **Death of transferrer or of attorney.** The death of the transferrer does not revoke the power of attorney.
> Culp v. Mulvane, 66 Kans. 143 (1903).
> Fraser v. Charleston, 11 S. C. 486 (1878).
> A power of attorney to transfer stock is revoked by the death of the person named as attorney. In such case a bona fide purchaser may be protected, but a donee probably not.
> Carll v. Little Miami R. Co., 13 C. C. n. s. 598 (1911).
> See Dickinson v. Central Bank, 129 Mass. 279.
> Hess v. Rau, 95 N. Y. 359.

Section 8673-7.   (Rescission of transfer.)   If the indorsement or delivery of a certificate,

(a) Was procured by fraud or duress, or

(b) Was made under such mistake as to make the indorsement or delivery inequitable; or

If the delivery of a certificate was made.

(c) Without authority from the owner, or

(d) After the owner's death or legal incapacity, the possession of the certificate may be reclaimed and the transfer thereof rescinded, unless:

(1) The certificate has been transferred to a purchaser for value in good faith without notice of any facts making the transfer wrongful, or

(2) The injured person has elected to waive the injury, or has been guilty of laches in endeavoring to enforce his rights.

Any court of appropriate jurisdiction may enforce specifically such right to reclaim the possession of the certificate or to rescind the transfer thereof and, pending litigation, may enjoin the further transfer of the certificate or impound it. (June 7, 1911, 102 v. 502, § 7.)

Section 8673-8. (Rescission of transfer of certificate does not invalidate subsequent transfer by transferee in possession.) Although the transfer of a certificate or of shares represented thereby has been rescinded or set aside, nevertheless, if the transferee has possession of the certificate or of a new certificate representing part or the whole of the same shares of stock, a subsequent transfer of such certificate by the transferee, mediately or immediately, to a purchaser for value in good faith, without notice of any facts making the transfer wrongful, shall give such purchaser an indefeasible right to the certificate and the shares represented thereby. (June 7, 1911, 102 v. 502, § 8.)

Section 8673-9. (Delivery of unendorsed certificate imposes obligation to endorse.) The delivery of a certificate by the person appearing by the certificate to be the owner thereof without the indorsement requisite for the transfer of the certificate and the shares represented thereby, but with intent to transfer such certificate or shares shall impose an obligation, in the absence of an agreement to the contrary, upon the person so delivering, to complete the transfer by making the necessary indorsement. The transfer shall take effect as of the time when the indorsement is actually made. This obligation may be specifically enforced. (June 7, 1911, 102 v. 502, § 9.)

The delivery of a certificate without written endorsement, but with the intention of transferring the title upon a valid consideration, operates as a transfer of the equitable title. The transferrer may be compelled by a suit in equity to assign the certificate.
Lawler v. Kell, 4 N. P. 218; 6 L. D. 311 (C. P. 1897).
Oliver v. Cincinnati, etc., Co., 1 Hosea 457 (Super. Ct. Cin.) ; s. c. 3 O. L. R. 53, 607; aff'd, 73 O. S. 386.

Section 8673-10. (Ineffectual attempt to transfer amounts to a promise to transfer.) An attempted transfer of title to a certificate or to the shares represented thereby without delivery of the certificate shall have the effect of a promise to transfer and the obligation, if any, imposed by such promise shall be determined by the law governing the formation, and performance of contracts. (June 7, 1911, 102 v. 502, § 10.)

See G. C. § 8385.
Bates v. Smith, 83 Mich. 347.

M. C. invested money in stock of a building and loan company, taking the certificates in the name of her infant granddaughter, with a parenthetic clause after the name ("M. C. or other legal guardian may draw") and retained possession of the certificates. This was held to be an inchoate gift in trust for the grandchild.

Mook v. Akron Sgs. & Loan Co., 87 O. S. 273 (1913).

Section 8673-11.   (Warranties on sale of a certificate.) A person who for value transfers a certificate, including one who assigns for value a claim secured by a certificate, unless a contrary intention appears, warrants:

(a) That the certificate is genuine,

(b) That he has a legal right to transfer it, and

(c) That he has no knowledge of any fact which would impair the validity of the certificate.

In the case of an assignment of a claim secured by a certificate, the liability of the assignor upon such warranty shall not exceed the amount of the claim.   (June 7, 1911, 102 v. 503, § 11.)

For similar provisions see G. C. § 8993-34 (Bills of Lading Act) and G. C. § 8500 (Warehouse Receipts Act).

Section 8673-12.   (No warranty implied from accepting payment of a debt.) A mortgagee, pledgee, or other holder for security of a certificate who in good faith demands or receives payment of the debt for which such certificate is security, whether from a party to a draft drawn for such debt, or from any other person, shall not by so doing be deemed to represent or to warrant the genuineness of such certificate, or the value of the shares represented thereby. (June 7, 1911, 102 v. 503, § 12.)

Section 8673-13.   (No attachment or levy upon shares unless certificate surrendered or transfer enjoined.) No attachment or levy upon shares of stock for which a certificate is outstanding shall be valid until such certificate be actually seized by the officer making the attachment or levy, or be surrendered to the corporation which issued it, or its transfer by the holder be enjoined.   Except where a certificate is lost or destroyed, such corporation shall not be compelled to issue a new certificate for the stock until the old certificate is surrendered to it.   (June 7, 1911, 102 v. 503, § 13.)

FORMER LAW—APPLICABLE TO STOCK EVIDENCED BY CERTIFICATES ISSUED PRIOR TO JULY 1, 1911.

Stock in a corporation may be reached by creditors of a stockholder by garnishee process served on the corporation.

Attachment.

Norton v. Norton, 43 O. S. 509 (1885).
Prout v. Post, 12 L. D. 141 (C. P. 1900).
Proceeding in aid of execution or creditor's bill.
Bank v. Mfg. Co., 67 O. S. 306 (1902).
For the purpose of seizure and subjection to legal process the situs of stock is the domicile of the corporation.
National Bank v. Lake Shore, etc., Ry. Co., 21 O. S. 221 (1871).
Ashley v. Quintard, 90 Fed. 84; 41 W. L. B. 289; 10 O. F. D. 365 (C. C. Ohio 1898).
But stock can not be reached by a judgment creditor by a bill in equity, without the return of an execution nulla bona.
Schmuck v. Pearce, 3 O. L. R. 403; 16 L. D. 287 (Super. Ct. Cin. 1905).
A corporation may, by garnishee process served upon itself, reach the stock of a shareholder indebted to it.
Norton v. Norton, 43 O. S. 509 (1885).
A corporation which, for many years, acquiesced in a subscription made by a person, in the name of his children, permitting them to vote and to exercise acts of ownership over the stock, is estopped from maintaining an action to subject such stock to the payment of its claim against the person who made the subscription.
Creed v. Lancaster Bank, 1 O. S. 1 (1852).

Dividends on attached stock. Dividends declared by a corporation, and remaining in its possession after garnishment process has been served, follow the stock and are subject to the same order of distribution.
Norton v. Norton, 43 O. S. 509 (1885).

Alimony suit against nonresident stockholder. Where, in an alimony suit against a nonresident stockholder who was served by publication only, the corporation was made a defendant and was enjoined from transferring the stock, the court has jurisdiction to award such stock as alimony and to decree a transfer of the title thereto.
Cleveland, etc., Co. v. Beeman, 12 C. C. n. s. 460 (1909); aff'd, 81 O. S. 509, 510.

Stock in foreign corporation. Stock in a foreign corporation, owned by a nonresident of Ohio, can not be attached by levying the writ upon the certificate of stock in the possession of a resident of Ohio.
Simmons Hardware Co. v. Stokes, 16 C. C. 145; 8 C. D. 776 (1898).
See §§ 8673-13 and 8673-22 "Certificate" defined.
Stock in a corporation in one state, owned by a resident of another, can not be reached by garnishment in a third state in which the corporation maintains an agent and does business, in the absence of special statutory provision therefor.
Ashley v. Quintard, 90 Fed. 84; 41 W. L. B. 289; 10 O. F. D. 365 (C. C. Ohio 1898).

Defenses of stockholder. That stock has been transferred. A stockholder can not defend against a creditor's bill on the ground that he had pledged the stock prior to the bringing of the proceeding. It is for the pledgee to make such defense. But the court may make the pledgee a party to the proceeding.
Krebs v. Forbriger, 21 W. L. B. 313 (Super. Ct. Cin. 1889).

Ulterior motive of creditor. That a creditor who seeks to reach the stock of his debtor in a corporation is induced to do so by other stockholders, with whom he has made plans for future management of the corporation, is no reason for denying him the remedy of a creditor's bill.
McMullen v. Ritchie, 64 Fed. 253; 8 O. F. D. 314 (1894).

Execution. Former law; see.

Lee v. Citizens N. B., 2 C. S. C. R. 298, 311 (1872).

Priorities between creditors of stockholder and pledgees or purchasers of stock.

Creditor and subsequent pledgee. The creditor of a stockholder acquires a lien from the time of the service of the garnishee process on the corporation. A subsequent pledge of the shares is subject to the lien, although the stock certificates were transferred to the pledgee, who advanced money thereon without notice of the lien.

Bank v. Mfg. Co., 67 O. St. 306 (1903).

Creditors' rights as against existing pledge. Where stock was pledged, and the stock certificates transferred to the pledgee, prior to the time of service of the garnishee process, the lien of the pledgee is superior to the lien of the creditor, although the pledgee has not presented the stock for transfer.

Haldeman v. Hillsborough, etc., R. Co., 2 Handy 101.

Maue v. Krell Piano Co., 7 O. L. R. 539 (Super Ct. Cin. 1909).

Krebs v. Forbriger, 21 W. L. B. 313 (Super. Ct. Cin. 1889).

Norton v. Norton, 43 O. S. 509 (1885).

The surplus after payment of the debt to the pledgee is reached by the garnishment, and if the pledgee does not exercise his right to sell, the court may order a sale and distribution of the proceeds.

Norton v. Norton, 43 O. S. 509 (1885).

Creditor and prior purchaser. A bona fide purchaser of stock has an equity superior to a subsequent attaching creditor, although the purchaser has not presented the stock for transfer.

Prout v. Post, 12 L. D. 141 (C. P. 1900).

Section 8673-14. (Creditors' remedies to reach certificate.)

A creditor whose debtor is the owner of a certificate shall be entitled to such aid from courts of appropriate jurisdiction, by injunction and otherwise, in attaching such certificate or in satisfying the claim by means thereof as is allowed at law or in equity, in regard to property which can not readily be attached or levied upon by ordinary legal process. (June 7, 1911, 102 v. 503, § 14.)

Section 8673-15. (There shall be no lien or restriction unless indicated on certificate.)

There shall be no lien in favor of a corporation upon the shares represented by a certificate issued by such corporation and there shall be no restriction upon the transfer of shares so represented by virtue of any by-law of such corporation, or otherwise, unless the right of the corporation to such lien or the restriction is stated upon the certificate. (June 7, 1911, 102 v. 503, § 15.)

Lien of corporation on stock. A corporation may, by express stipulation in a certificate of stock, reserve a lien on the stock to secure indebtedness of the holder to it. Such lien may be asserted against a transferee who received the certificate before, but did not present it for transfer until after the original holder became indebted to the corporation.

Stafford v. Produce Exch. Bkg. Co., 61 O. S. 160 (1899).

See Conant v. Reed, 1 O. S. 298 (1853).

Tomb v. Felch, 40 W. L. B. 186 (Supreme Court without report, 1898).

Franklin Bank v. Commercial Bank, 4 Am. L. R. 705 (Super. Ct. Cin. 1876); aff'd, 36 O. S. 350.

Downer v. Zanesville Bank, Wright 477 (1833).

Where a certificate of stock was transferable "subject to all conditions and stipulations in the articles of association and by-laws," a by-law passed after the certificate was issued, creating a lien in favor of the corporation, was held binding on a person who received the certificate without consideration.

Bellevue Bank v. Higbee, 4 C. C. 222; 2 C. D. 512 (1889); aff'd, 28 W. L. B. 336.

Where a certificate contains no mention of a lien in favor of the corporation, the corporation can not assert a lien against a purchaser or pledgee of such certificate.

Lee v. Citizens N. B., 2 C. S. C. R. 298 (1872).

Where there was a custom between bankers and brokers for a banker, on application of a broker, to certify as to whether the bank had a lien · on certain of its stock, an application by a broker for such a certificate will put the bank on inquiry, and charge it with notice, that a loan had been or would be made to the stockholder.

Covington, etc., Bank v. Commercial Bank, 65 Fed. 547 (C. C. Ohio 1895).

Where a corporation has a lien, by statute, on all stock owned by its debtors, and has full control over its transfer, possession of the certificates, by pledge, gives the corporation no additional rights or benefits.

State v. Davis, 85 O. S. 44 (1911).

A lien on dividends may be reserved.

Bellevue Bank v. Higbee, 4 C. C. 222; 22 C. D. 512 (1889); aff'd, 28 W. L. B. 336.

It is said that since the enactment of the Thomas Banking Act a bank has no power to reserve a lien on its stock, by stipulation on the certificate.

Rep. Atty. Gen. 1911-1912, p. 775.

G. C. § 9761.

Restriction on transfers of stock. Power of corporation to make. See notes to §§ 8702 and 8704.

Section 8673-16. (Alteration of certificate does not divest title to shares.) The alteration of a certificate, whether fraudulent or not and by whomsoever made, shall not deprive the owner of his title to the certificate and the shares originally represented thereby, and the transfer of such certificate shall convey to the transferee a good title to such certificate and to the shares originally represented thereby. (June 7, 1911, 102 v. 503, § 16.)

Section 8673-17. (Lost or destroyed certificate.) Where a certificate has been lost or destroyed, a court of competent jurisdiction may order the issue of a new certificate therefor on service of process upon the corporation and on reasonable notice by publication, and in any other way which the court may direct, to all persons interested, and upon satisfactory proof of such loss or destruction and upon the giving of a bond with sufficient surety to be approved by the court to protect the corporation or any person injured by the issue of the new certificate from any liability or expense, which it or they may incur by reason of the original certificate remaining outstanding. The court may also in its discretion order the payment of the corporation's reasonable costs and counsel fees.

The issue of a new certificate under an order of the court as provided in this section, shall not relieve the corporation from liability in damages to a person to whom the original certificate has been or shall be transferred for value without notice of the proceedings or of the issuance of the new certificate. (June 7, 1911, 102 v. 503, § 17.)

This section provides relief similar to that given by §§ 8677 to 8681, which have not been repealed. This section provides for a bond of indemnity to the corporation, which is not required under §§ 8677 to 8681.

Before the enactment of §§ 8677 to 8681, a bond was deemed proper, before a corporation was required to issue a duplicate certificate.

Hof v. Western German Bank, 6 W. L. B. 665, 697 (Dist. Ct. 1881).

See Farmers Bank v. Diebold, etc., Co., 66 O. S. 376 (1902).

Section 8673-18. (Rule for cases not provided for by this act.) In any case not provided for by this act, the rules of law and equity, including the law merchant, and in particular the rules relating to the law of principal and agent, executors, administrators and trustees, and to the effect of fraud, misrepresentation, duress or coercion, mistake, bankruptcy or other invalidating cause, shall govern. (June 7, 1911, 102 v. 504, § 18.)

Section 8673-19. (Interpretation.) This act shall be so interpreted and construed as to effectuate its general purpose to make uniform the law of those states which enact it. (June 7, 1911, 102 v. 504, § 19.)

Section 8673-20. ("Indorsement" defined.) A certificate is indorsed when an assignment or a power of attorney to sell, assign, or transfer the certificate or the shares represented thereby is written on the certificate and signed by the person appearing by the certificate to be the owner of the shares represented thereby, or when the signature of such person is written without more upon the back of the certificate. In any of such cases a certificate is indorsed though it has not been delivered. (June 7, 1911, 102 v. 504, § 20.)

Section 8673-21. ("Owner" defined.) The person to whom a certificate was originally issued is the person ap-

pearing by the certificate to be the owner thereof, and of
the shares represented thereby, until and unless he indorses
the certificate to another specified person, and thereupon
such other specified person is the person appearing by the
certificate to be the owner thereof until and unless he also
indorses the certificate to another specified person. Subsequent special indorsements may be made with like effect.
(June 7, 1911, 102 v. 504, § 21.)

Section 8673-22.   (Other definitions.)   (1) In this act,
unless the context or subject matter otherwise requires—

"Certificate" means a certificate of stock in a corporation organized under the laws of this state or of another
state whose laws are consistent with this act.

"Delivery" means voluntary transfer of possession from
one person to another.

"Person" includes a corporation or partnership or two
or more persons having a joint or common interest.

To "purchase" includes to take as mortgagee or as
pledgee.

"Purchaser" includes mortgagee and pledgee.

"Shares" means a share or shares of stock in a corporation organized under the laws of this state or of another
state whose laws are consistent with this act.

"State" includes state, territory, district and insular
possession of the United States.

"Transfer" means transfer of legal title.

"Title" means legal title and does not include a merely
equitable or beneficial ownership or interest.

"Value" is any consideration sufficient to support a simple contract, an antecedent or pre-existing obligation, whether
for money or not, constitutes value where a certificate is
taken either in satisfaction thereof or as security therefor.

(2) A thing "is done in good faith" within the meaning
of this act, when it is in fact done honestly, whether it be
done negligently or not.   (June 7, 1911, 102 v. 504, § 22.)

Pledges of stock.   Rights and remedies of pledgor and pledgee see
note to § 8682.
"Value."   For other definitions see
G. C. § 8295 (Negotiable Instruments Act).
G. C. § 8456 (Sales Act).
G. C. § 8508 (Warehouse Receipts Act).
G. C. § 8993-52 (Bills of Lading Act).
Where no extension of time was given, a pledgee to whom certificates
were transferred to secure a pre-existing debt was held to have no greater
rights therein than the pledgor.
Cleveland v. Bank, 16 O. S. 236, 269 (1865).

Section 8673-23.   The provisions of this act apply only to certificates issued after the taking effect of this act. (June 7, 1911, 102 v. 504, § 23.)

Section 8673-24. This act shall take effect on the first day of July, one thousand nine hundred and eleven. (June 7, 1911, 102 v. 505, § 24.)

Section 8674. (How payment of stock enforced.) If an installment on stock is unpaid for sixty days after the time it was to be paid, whether the stock is held by the subscriber, an assignee, or transferee, it may be collected by suit, or the directors may sell such stock at public auction for the installment then due. (R. S. Sec. 3253; March 14, 1853, 51 v. 484, § 1; May 1, 1852, 50 v. 274, § 7; S. & C. 276, 319.)

Subscriptions generally. See note to § 8630.
Payment of subscriptions. See note to § 8632.
Exchange of stock for property. See note to § 8630.

FORFEITURE OF SUBSCRIPTIONS.

Waiver of right. Until a corporation proceeds under §§ 8674 to 8676 to foreclose the interest of a subscriber, it remains the property of the subscriber. A corporation can not, without following the method authorized by these sections, forfeit the subscription and appropriate the amounts paid. Where a corporation takes no action the subscriber, or an assignee, may tender the amount due with interest, and by action compel the corporation to issue a stock certificate, and to account to him for dividends declared. The statute of limitations begins to run from the time of such tender.
Iron Railroad Co. v. Fink, 41 O. S. 321 (1884).

Injunction against forfeiture. A forfeiture of stock in an insolvent corporation by the directors so as to release solvent subscribers is fraudulent as to creditors and may be enjoined by them.
Upson v. Rocky River, etc., Co., 2 Cleve. L. R. 355 (C. P. 1879).

Irregular forfeiture. Laches of stockholder. Where there were defects in forfeiture proceedings, but the stockholder had knowledge of the assessments, and failed to pay the same for sixteen years, having knowledge of the precarious financial condition of the corporation, the stockholder is barred by laches from enforcing any rights in his stock.
Hedley v. Improvement Co., 13 N. P. n. s. 523 (C. P. 1912).

SUITS TO COLLECT SUBSCRIPTIONS.

Conditions precedent.

Calls. An action to recover on a stock subscription can not be brought until sixty days after the time of payment designated in the call. After the first installment is paid nothing is due on a subscription until a call has been made by the directors specifying the time for payment.
See § 8632.
Mansfield, etc., Co. v. Hall, 26 O. S. 310 (1875).
Railroad Co. v. Fink, 41 O. S. 321, 329 (1884).
Gibson v. Columbia, etc., Co., 18 O. S. 396 (1868).
Unless the call has been waived by agreement of the parties.
See Mansfield, etc., Co. v. Pettis, 26 O. S. 259 (1875).

The making of the call should be alleged in the petition where the action is brought by the corporation, or a consolidated company, or an assignee of the subscription.

Mansfield, etc., Co. v. Hall, 26 O. S. 310 (1875).

P. & O. Canal Co. v. Webb, 9 Ohio 136 (1839).

Notice of calls. Whether notice of a call must be given to subscribers before suit can be brought on their subscriptions has not been judicially determined in Ohio except in Proprietors, etc., v. Wade, 7 W. L. J. 95 (Commercial Court of Cincinnati, 1849) in which five installments were involved and payment of the first four had been demanded. It was held that demand of the fifth installment was not necessary except perhaps as affecting costs.

In other states under statutes somewhat similar to §§ 8632 and 8674 the authorities are conflicting.

Cook on Corporations, §§ 117, 118.

Publication of notice is a condition precedent to forfeiture of stock for nonpayment of calls.

See § 8675.

Calls after insolvency. Where the corporation is insolvent the making of a call by the directors is not a condition precedent to an action by the receiver or a creditor. In such an action the subscriptions will either be regarded as due, or the court will make the call.

Turnbull v. Pomeroy Salt Co., 24 W. L. B. 133 (C. P. 1890).

Henry v. Vermillion, etc., R. Co., 17 Ohio 187, 191 (1848).

See Roebling Sons Co. v. Shawnee, etc., Co., 4 N. P. n. s. 113; 17 L. D. 8 (1906); affirmed, 78 O. S. 408.

A court of bankruptcy may make the call.

In re Flood-Pratt Dairy Co., 7 O. L. R. 603; 16 O. F. D. 396 (Referee 1909).

In re Newfoundland Syndicate, 196 Fed. 443 (D. C. 1912).

Presentation of claim to administrator. The claim should be presented to the administrator or executor of the estate of a deceased subscriber before suit.

Roebling Sons Co. v. Shawnee, etc., Co., 4 N. P. n. s. 113, 115; 17 L. D. 8 (1906); aff'd, no rep., 78 O. S. 408.

Subscription of ten percent of capital stock. Until ten percent of the capital stock has been subscribed subscribers can not be compelled by the corporation to pay beyond the first installment.

Trust Co. v. Floyd, 47 O. S. 525, 542 (1890).

It is not necessary that the entire capital stock be subscribed. Subscriptions may be enforced after ten percent has been subscribed.

See §§ 8632 to 8635.

Jewett v. Railway, 34 O. S. 601 (1878).

Subscribers may waive the statutory right to have ten percent subscribed.

Emmitt v. Springfield, etc., R. Co., 31 O. S. 23, 26 (1876).

Performance of conditions. The petition in an action brought on a conditional subscription must allege performance of all conditions precedent.

Trott v. Sarchett, 10 O. S. 241 (1859).

Railroad Co. v. Hinsdale, 45 O. S. 556, 570 (1888).

See note to § 8630. *Conditional subscriptions.*

Tender of stock certificates to the subscriber is not required before suit. But where by the terms of a subscription the amount was payable in installments and certificates were to be issued for the several installments paid it was held that readiness and willingness to issue and deliver the certificates should be alleged in the petition.

James v. Cincinnati, etc., R. Co., 2 Dis. 261 (Super. Ct. Cin. 1858).

Who may bring suit.

The corporation may sue to enforce payment of subscriptions to its stock.

See Iron Railroad Co. v. Fink, 41 O. S. 321, 332 (1884).
Ashtabula, etc., R. Co. v. Smith, 15 O. S. 328 (1864).
Henry v. Vermillion, etc., R. Co., 17 Ohio 187 (1848).

A subscription payable to the "president and directors" of a corporation may be enforced in the name of the corporation.

Milford, etc., Co. v. Brush, 10 Ohio 111 (1840).

A consolidated company may recover on subscriptions to the stock of its constituent corporations, where the consolidation was effected under statutes in force at the time such subscriptions were made and which authorize the consolidated company to acquire debts due on subscriptions.

Mansfield, etc., Co. v. Brown, 26 O. S. 223, 238, 239 (1875).
Mansfield, etc., Co. v. Stout, 26 O. S. 241 (1875).
Compton v. Railway, 45 O. S. 592, 620 (1888).
See § 9038.

An asssignee of subscriptions may sue the subscriber where the calls have been made by the directors.

Dungan v. Safford, 41 O. S. 15 (1884).
Downie v. Hoover, 12 Wis. 174.
See Armstrong v. Karshner, 47 O. S. 276 (1890).
James v. Cincinnati, etc., Co., 2 Dis. 261 (1858).

The assignee for creditors of the corporation may sue, unpaid subscriptions being a part of the trust fund for creditors. The assignee and a creditor may join as plaintiffs in the action.

Sayler v. Simpson, 12 L. D. 148 (Super. Ct. Cin. 1888).
Turnbull v. Pomeroy Salt Co., 24 W. L. B. 133 (C. P. 1890).
See Niles v. Olszak, 87 O. S. 229 (1912).

The trustee in bankruptcy of the corporation is vested with the legal title to unpaid subscriptions and may sue thereon.

Thrall v. Union, etc., Co., 6 O. L. R. 676; 19 L. D. 732 (C. P. 1909).
Security Trust Co. v. Ford, 75 O. S. 322 (1906).
Kiskadden v. Steinle, 203 Fed. 375 (C. C. A. 1913).

A receiver appointed under § 11943 et seq. to wind up the affairs of a corporation may bring suit on stock subscriptions.

G. C. § 11946.
Smith v. Johnson, 57 O. S. 486 (1898).

After judgment against a subscriber in favor of such a receiver the court appointing the receiver has power to direct the receiver to collect on such judgment only the subscriber's fair proportion of the corporate debts.

Clarke v. Thomas, 34 O. S. 46 (1877).

An action by such a receiver is a suit at law. Subscribers residing out of the county can not be joined as defendants and served with summons issued to the county of their residence.

Smith v. Johnson, 57 O. S. 486 (1898).

A receiver of an insolvent foreign corporation appointed in its home state with no other title to its assets and property than that derived from his appointment in a suit brought to subject its property to the payment of claims of creditors can not sue in Ohio on a subscription to its stock.

Leman v. Mac Lennan, 7 C. C. n. s. 205; 18 C. D. 137 (1905); aff'd, no rep., 75 O. S. 643.

Creditors. Where a corporation has property or assets upon which execution may be levied, a creditor can not bring suit upon its stock subscriptions. But where the corporation has no such property or assets a creditor may, by a creditor's bill or proceeding in aid of execution, subject unpaid subscriptions to his claim.

Henry v. Vermillion, etc., R. Co., 17 Ohio 187 (1848).
Gilmore v. Bank of Cincinnati, 8 Ohio 62, 71 (1837).
Dunbar v. Harrison, 18 O. S. 24 (1868).
Moutray v. Connor, etc., Co., 7 O. L. R. 446 (C. P. 1909).
Ewin v. Cincinnati, etc., R. Co., 2 W. L. M. 42 (Super. Ct. Cin. 1859).
Everheart v. U. S. Investment Co., 1 Hosea 524.

By the filing of a proceeding in aid of execution, or creditor's bill, a judgment creditor acquires a lien on the fund.

Dunbar v. Harrison, 18 O. S. 24 (1868).
Miers v. Zanesville, etc., Co., 13 Ohio 197 (1844).
Kilbreath v. Gaylord, 3 W. L. B. 525 (Super. Ct. Cin. 1878); aff'd, 34 O. S. 305.

One creditor may sue on behalf of all creditors.

Turnbull v. Pomeroy Salt Co., 24 W. L. B. 133 (C. P. 1890).

But after the corporation has been adjudged a bankrupt a creditor can not sue. The trustee in bankruptcy of the corporation alone has the right to maintain the action.

Thrall v. Union, etc., Co., 6 O. L. R. 676; 19 L. D. 732 (C. P. 1909).

After the appointment of a receiver under § 11943 in a proceeding to wind up the affairs of a corporation, a creditor may intervene in the proceeding by answer and cross-petition and set up a cause of action against a subscriber.

Peter v. Farrel Foundry & Machine Co., 53 O. S. 534 (1895).

Action by creditor after assignment for creditors.

See Painesville N. B. v. King Varnish Co., 8 C. C. 563; 4 C. D. 511 (1894); reversed, without report, 56 O. S. 744.
Turnbull v. Pomeroy Salt Co., 24 W. L. B. 133 (C. P. 1890).

Subscriptions to stock in a foreign corporation may be reached in Ohio by creditor's bill.

Everheart v. U. S. Investment & Red. Co., 1 Hosea 524 (Super. Ct. Cin.).
Citing Kulp v. Fleming, 65 O. S. 321.

The petition in a creditor's action should, in general, allege that a judgment has been recovered on his claim against the corporation and that execution has been issued and returned nulla bona.

Dickason v. Grafton, etc., Co., 6 C. C. n. s. 329, 330, 331; 17 C. D. 357 (1905); aff'd, 76 O. S. 612.
Turnbull v. Pomeroy Salt Co., 24 W. L. B. 133 (C. P. 1890).
American, etc., Co. v. Dox, 4 N. P. n. s. 155; 16 L. D. 501 (Super. Ct. Cin. 1906).

But judgment and execution are unnecessary where the corporation has no property or assets subject to execution, or its assets are in the hands of a receiver.

Peter v. Farrell, etc., Co., 53 O. S. 534, 557 (1895).
Dickason v. Grafton, etc., Co., 6 C. C. n. s. 329, 330, 331; 17 C. D. 357 (1905); aff'd, 76 O. S. 612.
Moutray v. Connor, etc., Co., 7 O. L. R. 446 (C. P. 1909).
Turnbull v. Pomeroy Salt Co., 24 W. L. B. 133 (C. P. 1890).

A judgment against the corporation in favor of a creditor can not be collaterally impeached by a stockholder where it was not obtained by fraud or collusion, although the stockholder had no notice of the suit.

Scofield v. Excelsior Oil Co., 6 C. C. n. s. 176; 17 C. D. 318 (1905);
aff'd, no rep., 74 O. S. 513.
Henry v. Vermillion, etc., R. Co., 17 Ohio 187, 191.
And although obtained during the pendency of the suit to recover on
the subscription and set up in a supplemental petition.
Scofield v. Excelsior Oil Co., 6 C. C. n. s. 169, 176; 17 C. D. 347, 318
(1905); aff'd, no rep., 74 O. S. 513.
In a creditor's action directors may be enjoined from fraudulently
disposing of funds realized from stock subscriptions.
Upson v. Rocky River, etc., Co., 2 Cleve. L. R. 355 (C. P. 1879).

Who are liable.
Original subscribers are liable on their subscriptions unless they
have been released by the corporation or by a transfer in good faith.
Gaff v. Flesher, 33 O. S. 107, 112 (1877).
See below *Defenses. Withdrawal and release of subscriptions.*

Transferrers. A subscription to stock on which installments have
been paid may be assigned by the subscriber.
Iron Railroad Co. v. Fink, 41 O. S. 321 (1884).
See Peter v. Union Mfg. Co., 56 O. S. 181 (1897).
And it has been held that a subscriber who, acting in good faith, has
transferred his subscription to another and paid all calls to the time of
transfer is not further liable on his subscription, where the transfer is
properly entered in the corporate books.
Gilmore v. Bank of Cincinnati, 8 Ohio 62, 71 (1837).
Porter v. Laws, 6 Am. L. R. 756; 3 W. L. B. 384 (Dist. Ct. 1878).
A transfer to an insolvent person for the purpose of avoiding liability
does not release the transferrer, at least as against debts existing at the
time of transfer.
Gaff v. Flesher, 33 O. S. 107, 112 (1877).
Peter v. Union Mfg. Co., 56 O. S. 181 (1897).
A transfer to a fictitious person is void and does not release the
transferrer.
Muskingum, etc., Co. v. Ward, 13 Ohio 120 (1884).
Krohn v. Central, etc., Co., 4 N. P. 270; 6 L. D. 552 (C. P. 1897).
A verbal agreement made at the time of subscription between the
subscriber and the president of the corporation to the effect that a third
person would assume a part of the subscription is no defense to the sub-
scriber, where there was no transfer.
Painesville N. B. v. King Varnish Co., 8 C. C. 563; 4 C. D. 511 (1894);
reversed, in part, 56 O. S. 744.
Where a transferrer has been compelled to pay calls made after the
transfer, he may be subrogated to the rights of the corporation against
the transferee, on clear proof of acceptance of the transfer.
Tripp v. Appleman, 35 Fed. 19 (U. S. C. C. Ohio 1888).

Transferees. The transferee of stock which has not been fully paid
impliedly assumes the obligations for the unpaid balance and is liable for
calls.
Turnbull v. Pomeroy Salt Co., 24 W. L. B. 133 (C. P. 1890).
Gilmore v. Bank of Cincinnati, 8 Ohio 62, 71 (1837).
Acceptance of the transfer by the transferee must be shown.
Tripp v. Appleman, 35 Fed. 19; 6 O. F. D. 71 (U. S. C. C. Ohio
1888).
A purchaser for value of stock who has no notice that it has not been
fully paid is not liable. The purchaser may rely on the representation of
the corporation that it has been paid. The statement "full paid" on a
stock certificate is a representation by the corporation that the stock has
been paid up and the purchaser need not inquire further.

Roebling Sons Co. v. Shawnee, etc., Co., 4 N. P. n. s. 113, 121; 17 L.
D. 8 (1906); aff'd, no rep., 78 O. S. 408.

Purchasers and donees of stock after organization. Where stock
is disposed of by the directors after organization, not by means of subscriptions but by means of sales, exchanges for property or stock dividends, the persons receiving the stock from the corporation may be liable
to creditors where the stock is not fully paid in money or property. "The
fact that they did not subscribe for it or agree to take it until receipt
of the certificates is immaterial, as the acceptance of the certificates is
sufficient evidence of an agreement to pay their par value."
Handley v. Stutz, 139 U. S. 417, 427 (1891).
Gates v. Tippecanoe Stone Co., 57 O. S. 60 (1897).
In re Flood-Pratt Diary Co., 7 O. L. R. 603; 16 O. F. D. 396 (Referee
in Bkry. 1909).

——. **(a) Stock dividends.** Where a stock dividend was declared at a
time when there were no surplus profits (as required by § 8724) the
stockholders who accepted the certificates are liable. They can not be
relieved from liability by offering to return the stock after the corporation
has become insolvent and suit brought to enforce payment.
First N. B. v. Patton Co., 13 C. C. n. s. 289 (1910).
See Handley v. Stutz, 139 U. S. 417 (1891).

——. **(b) Sales below par.** A purchaser of stock from the corpora-
tion for less than par is liable to subsequent creditors who had no knowl-
edge of the terms of the purchase, for the difference between the amount
paid and the par value of the stock.
Rickerson, etc., Co. v. Farrell, etc., Co., 75 Fed. 554 (C. C. A. 1896).
Security Trust Co. v. Ford, 75 O. S. 322 (1906).
Handley v. Stutz, 139 U. S. 417 (1891).
In re Flood-Pratt Dairy Co., 7 O. L. R. 603; 16 O. F. D. 396 (Referee
in Bkry. 1909).
But under some circumstances such a purchaser is not liable to the
corporation or as against other stockholders.
Peter v. Union Mfg. Co., 56 O. S. 181 (1897).
Kinsey v. Mt. Auburn Cable Co., 6 C. C. n. s. 305; 17 C. D. 633 (1905);
aff'd, no rep., 75 O. S. 602.
See Security Trust Co. v. Ford, 75 O. S. 322, 333 (1906).
Nor to creditors whose claims were incurred prior to the purchase.
Handley v. Stutz, 139 U. S. 417 (1891).
See Peter v. Union Mfg. Co., 56 O. S. 181, 203 (1897).
Nor to subsequent creditors who have knowledge of the terms of the
purchase.
Rickerson, etc., Co. v. Farrell, etc., Co., 75 Fed. 554 (C. C. A. 1896).
Kinsey v. Mt. Auburn Cable Co., 6 C. C. n. s. 305, 314; 17 C. D. 633
(1905); aff'd, no rep., 75 O. S. 602.
See note to § 8630, *Sales below par.*

——. **(c) Exchanges of stock for property.** Where stock is exchanged
for property at a fraudulent overvaluation the persons receiving the stock
from the corporation are liable to creditors for the difference between
the actual value of the property and the par value of the stock.
Gates v. Tippecanoe Stone Co., 57 O. S. 60 (1897).
Ford v. Lamson, 17 C. C. 539; 9 C. D. 374 (1899).
Sayler v. Simpson, 12 L. D. 148 (Super. Ct. Cin. 1888).
But they are not liable to the corporation itself.
Orton v. Edson, etc., Co., 5 C. C. n. s. 540; 17 C. D. 107 (1905);
aff'd, no rep., 75 O. S. 580.

Leman v. MacLennan, 7 C. C. n. s. 205, 208; 18 C. D. 137 (1905); aff'd, no rep., 75 O. S. 643.

See note to § 8630, *Exchange of stock for property.*

Legatees. Where, under a will bequeathing all the estate to a sole legatee providing she shall first pay from the moneys of the estate all debts, the legatee did not accept stock on which there was a liability for unpaid subscriptions, she was held not to be personally liable therefor.

Roebling Sons Co. v. Shawnee, etc., Co., 4 N. P. n. s. 113, 116; 17 L. D. 8 (1906); aff'd, no rep., 78 O. S. 408.

But where such a legatee purchased the stock from herself as executrix and had it transferred to her name on the corporate books, she was held liable, although the purchase from herself was illegal.

Biggio v. Sandheger, 8 N. P. 13 (C. P. 1900).

Unauthorized agent. It has been held that a person who without authority signs the name of another person to a subscription, his own name not appearing on the paper, can not be held liable on the subscription.

Cincinnati Hotel Co. v. Marsh, 9 W. L. B. 176 (Dist. Ct. 1883).

The state. No suit can be brought against the state on a subscription.

Miers v. Zanesville, etc., Co., 11 Ohio 273 (1842).

Subscribers to stock in a foreign corporation may be sued in Ohio by a creditor.

Everheart v. U. S. Investment & Red. Co., 1 Hosea 524 (Super. Ct. Cin.)

See Kulp v. Fleming, 65 O. S. 321 (1901).

Blair v. Newbegin, 65 O. S. 425 (1901).

But not by a receiver of an insolvent foreign corporation appointed in its home state with no other title to its assets and property than that derived from his appointment in a suit brought to subject its property to the payment of creditors' claims.

Leman v. MacLennan, 7 C. C. n. s. 205; 18 C. D. 137 (1905); aff'd, no rep., 75 O. S. 643.

Joinder of actions. An action by a creditor on stock subscriptions may be joined with an action to enforce the statutory liability of stockholders.

Warner v. Callender, 20 O. S. 190 (1870).

Peter v. Farrell, etc., Co., 53 O. S. 534, 557 (1895).

Joinder of defendants. Where the suit is equitable in its nature all subscribers may be joined as defendants. Where it is merely an action at law subscribers whose liability is several can not be joined as defendants in one action.

Smith v. Johnson, 57 O. S. 486, 488 (1898).

An action by the corporation itself, or by a receiver appointed under § 11943 to wind up its affairs, is an action at law. It is not proper practice to join as defendants subscribers who reside out of the county where suit is brought and to issue summons to another county to obtain service on them.

Smith v. Johnson, 57 O. S. 486 (1898).

It has been held that such nonresident stockholders may be joined in a creditors' bill after judgment.

Ewin v. Cincinnati, etc., R. Co., 2 W. L. M. 42 (Super. Ct. Cin. 1859).

In a suit to set aside a fraudulent payment of subscriptions by property, all subscribers who participate in the fraud may be joined.

Sayler v. Simpson, 12 L. D. 148 (Super. Ct. Cin. 1888).

Pleading and practice.

Supplemental petition setting up judgment against corporation.
In an action by a creditor, where the original petition was defective in not
alleging a judgment and execution against the corporation, a supplemental
petition may be filed setting up that, during the pendency of the action,
such judgment has been recovered and execution issued.

> Scofield v. Excelsior Oil Co., 6 C. C. n. s. 169, 176; 17 C. D. 347, 318
> (1905); aff'd, 74 O. S. 513.

**Amendment of petition substituting allegation of receivership for
judgment, etc.** In an action by a creditor, where the petition alleged
a judgment against the corporation but it appeared that the judgment
was void for lack of proper service, the creditor was permitted, at the
trial, to amend and allege the appointment of a receiver and the judicial
determination of insolvency of the corporation.

> Dickason v. Grafton, etc., Co., 6 C. C. n. s. 329, 331; 17 C. D. 357
> (1905); aff'd, 76 O. S. 612.

Discovery of names of subscribers. A creditor, by creditor's bill
or proceeding in aid of execution, may compel a disclosure of the names
of subscribers and the amounts due from each.

> Miers v. Zanesville, etc., Co., 11 Ohio 273 (1842).

Evidence. As to former judgment for installments. In an action on
two subscriptions for four and ten shares respectively, which were denied
by the answer, the record of a judgment against the subscriber for installments on one subscription of a different date for fourteen shares is
not admissible.

> Hanes v. Dayton, etc., Co., 40 O. S. 95 (1883).

Prima facie case.

> See Milford, etc., Co. v. Brush, 10 Ohio 111 (1840).

Amount of recovery. Interest from the time when calls were due
may be recovered by the corporation.

> Railroad Co. v. Fink, 41 O. S. 321, 327 (1884).
> National Bank v. Greenville, etc., Co., 3 C. C. n. s. 372, 381; 13 C.
> D. 274 (1899).

On a subscription payable in land the recovery is not the par value
of the stock. If the circumstances prevent a specific performance of the
agreement, the measure of damages is the value of the land.

> Dayton, etc., R. Co. v. Hatch, 1 Dis. 84 (Super. Ct. Cin. 1855).

After judgment against a subscriber in favor of a receiver the court
appointing the receiver has power to direct the receiver to collect on such
judgment only the subscriber's fair proportion of the corporate debts.

> Clarke v. Thomas, 34 O. S. 46 (1877).

Other remedies against subscribers.

Proof of claim in bankruptcy. An unpaid subscription is a debt
provable against the estate of the bankrupt subscriber.

> Roeblings Sons Co. v. Shawnee, etc., Co., 4 N. P. n. s. 113; 17 L. D.
> 8 (1906); aff'd, no rep., 78 O. S. 408.

Corporation may apply dividends on unpaid subscriptions.

> Rhodes v. Equitable, etc., Co., 3 C. C. 501; 2 C. D. 288 (1888);
> affirmed, 27 W. L. B. 160.

Unpaid subscriptions as a trust fund for creditors.
See note to § 8684.

Statute of limitations.

An action to recover on a stock subscription is barred in fifteen
years, a subscription being a promise in writing.

Warner v. Callender, 20 O. S. 190 (1870).
Gibson v. Columbia, etc., Bridge Co., 18 O. S. 396 (1868).
See Gilmore v. Bank of Cincinnati, 8 Ohio 62, 71 (1837).
The cause of action accrues at the time of payment specified in the call made by the directors.
Gibson v. Columbia, etc., Bridge Co., 18 O. S. 396 (1868).
Warner v. Callender, 20 O. S. 190 (1870).
Railroad Co. v. Fink, 41 O. S. 321, 329 (1884).
Kilbreath v. Gaylord, 34 O. S. 305 (1877).
Where the corporation is insolvent the statute of limitations begins to run in favor of the subscriber at the time of the appointment of a receiver or other act of insolvency.
Roeblings Sons Co. v. Shawnee, etc., Co., 4 N. P. n. s. 113; 17 L. D. 8 (1906); aff'd, no rep., 78 O. S. 408.
An action against the estate of a deceased subscriber may, where the corporation is insolvent, be barred in eighteen months under G. C. § 10746.
Roebling Sons Co. v. Shawnee, etc., Co., 4 N. P. n. s. 113, 115, 116; 17 L. D. 8 (1906); aff'd, no rep., 78 O. S. 408.
An action by creditors to set aside a fraudulent exchange of property for stock is barred in four years from discovery of the fraud by the creditors.
Sayler v. Simpson, 12 L. D. 148 (Cin. Super. Ct. 1888|.)
Where demand notes were given by subscribers to the stock of an insurance company organized under a special charter, it was held that such notes were intended to be payable on call of the directors and that the statute did not begin to run until such call was made.
Kilbreath v. Gaylord, 34 O. S. 305 (1877).

DEFENSES.

Withdrawal and release of subscription. A subscriber can not relieve himself from liability by attempting to withdraw or cancel his subscription.   •
Gaff v. Flesher, 33 O. S. 107, 112-113 (1877).
Nor can the corporation release the subscriber to the prejudice of any intervening creditor.
Gaff v. Flesher, 33 O. S. 107, 113 (1877).
Directors have no power to release a subscriber except with the unanimous consent of the other subscribers.
See Royce v. Tyler, 2 C. C. 175, 187; 1 C. D. 428 (1887).

Compromise and release of subscription. The directors have power to compromise with and release a subscriber, for a valuable consideration paid by the subscriber, where there is a bona fide controversy as to his liability or where the subscriber is insolvent. When made in good faith and fully executed the compromise agreement releases the subscriber from further liability.
Warner v. Callender, 20 O. S. 190, 198 (1870).
State v. Building Assn., 35 O. S. 258, 263 (1879).
Wangerien v. Aspell, 47 O. S. 250 (1890).
Biggio v. Sandheger, 8 N. P. 13, 15 (1900).
See Morgan v. Lewis, 46 O. S. 1 (1888).
Sanderson v. Aetna Iron & Nail Co., 34 O. S. 442 (1878).

Fraud in obtaining subscription. Fraud in inducing a subscription is a defense against its enforcement.
Jewett v. Railway, 34 O. S. 601, 609 (1878).
Armstrong v. Karshner, 47 O. S. 276, 294 (1890).
Freeman v. Muth, 3 W. L. B. 914 (Dist. Ct. 1878).
James v. Cincinnati, etc., R. Co., 2 Dis. 261, 266 (1851).

But where the subscriber takes no action for an unreasonable time after discovery of the fraud and the rights of creditors intervene, he can not defend on the ground of fraud.

Mansfield v. Woods, Jenks & Co., 29 W. L. B. 111 (C. P.)
Ryan v. Miami, etc., Ry. Co., 10 A. L. R. 263 (C. P. 1881).
See Painesville N. B. v. King Varnish Co., 8 C. C. 563; 4 C. D. 511 (1894); reversed, in part, 56 O. S. 774.

False statements as to the future intentions, purpose or expectation of the corporation do not, as a rule, constitute a defense. To have that effect the statements must relate to past or present facts.

Armstrong v. Karshner, 47 O. S. 276, 294 (1890).
Freeman v. Muth, 3 W. L. B. 914 (Dist. Ct. 1878).
Nugent v. Cincinnati, etc., R. Co., 2 Dis. 302 (1858).

Alteration of subscription. Where a subscription has been materially altered by increasing the number of shares subscribed for, without the knowledge of the subscriber, the corporation can not recover on the original subscription without showing that the alteration was not fraudulently made by it.

Bery v. Marietta, etc., Co., 26 O. S. 673 (1875).

Alteration of decoy subscription made by another person. Where one was induced to subscribe on the faith of a prior subscription made by another person, a subsequent alteration of the prior subscription, the number of shares being reduced, is no defense to the persons so induced to subscribe. The alteration, being an attempted fraud on other subscribers, is a nullity.

Jewett v. Railway, 34 O. S. 601 (1878).
Bates v. Lewis, 3 O. S. 459 (1854).

Decoy subscription. That a subscription was made without any intention to pay it, but for the purpose of pretending to the public that the stock had been largely subscribed, and to prevent the predominance of certain stockholders, is no defense to the subscriber. ·

Bates v. Lewis, 3 O. S. 459 (1854).
Jewett v. Railway, 34 O. S. 601 (1878).
Royce v. Tyler, 2 C. C. 175, 183; 1 C. D. 428 (1887).

Irregular or incomplete incorporation. In an action by a creditor, or for the benefit of creditors, a subscriber is estopped from setting up as a defense that statutory requirements were not complied with in the incorporation proceedings.

Dickason v. Grafton Sav. Bank, 6 C. C. n. s. 329, 332; 17 C. D. 357 (1905); aff'd, no rep., 76 O. S. 612.
Clark v. Thomas, 34 O. S. 46, 62 (1877).
Warner v. Callender, 20 O. S. 190, 197 (1870).
Mansfield v. Woods, 29 W. L. B. 111 (C. P. 1893).
Ryan v. Miami, etc., R. Co., 10 A. L. R. 263, 273 (C. P. 1881).
See note to § 8627. *Estoppel to deny corporate existence.*

Where the corporation has a *de facto* existence the subscribers are liable to creditors regardless of defects or irregularities in its organization.

Gaff v. Flesher, 33 O. S. 107, 113 (1877).
See note to § 8627. *De facto corporations.*

Although in some cases corporate officers and others may be personally liable for carrying on business in the corporate name in violation of law, such personal liability is no defense to an action by creditors on subscriptions made by such persons.

Dickason v. Grafton Sav. Bank, 6 C. C. n. s. 329, 335; 17 C. D. 357 (1905); aff'd, no rep., 76 O. S. 612.

See note to § 8627. *Ultra vires acts. Personal liability for.*
The following irregularities or defects have been held not to release
subscribers: Failure to pay the first installment of ten percent with the
subscription as required by § 8632.
Henry v. Vermillion, etc., R. Co., 17 Ohio 187 (1848).
Chamberlain v. R. R. Co., 15 O. S. 225, 249 (1864).
Ashtabula, etc., R. Co. v. Smith, 15 O. S. 328, 336 (1864).
That a banking corporation commenced business before its entire
capital stock was subscribed and one-half paid in, as required by statute:
That the incorporators failed to give notice of the stockholders'
meeting to elect directors; or that a bare majority of the directors elected
at such irregular meeting ever qualified or acted.
Dickason v. Grafton Sav. Bank Co., 6 C. C. n. s. 329, 332; 17 C. D.
357 (1905); aff'd, no rep., 76 O. S. 612.
That the subscription was made before the articles of incorporation
were filed.
Royce v. Tyler, 2 C. C. 175; 1 C. D. 428 (1887).
That no notice was given of a meeting of stockholders at which an
increase of the capital stock of a mining company was voted; that a
part of the increased stock was declined by the stockholders without
actual apportionment; or that original stockholders were given part of
the increased stock without payment in money, as required by statute.
Clark v. Thomas, 34 O. S. 46 (1877).
Failure to obtain minimum amount of subscriptions is a defense
against the corporation.
Trust Co. v. Floyd, 47 O. S. 525, 542 (1890).

Irregular incorporation as a defense against the corporation. Where
an action is brought on a subscription by the corporation itself, it is
doubtful whether the subscriber is estopped from setting up irregular or
incomplete incorporation as a defense.
Raccoon River Nav. Co. v. Eagle, 29 O. S. 238 (1876).
Gaff v. Flesher, 33 O. S. 114-115 (1877).
Society Perun v. Cleveland, 43 O. S. 498-499 (1885).
Trust Co. v. Floyd, 47 O. S. 525, 542 (1890).

Misnomer of corporation. An error in the corporate name in the
subscription will not release the subscriber where there is no doubt as
to the corporation intended.
Milford, etc., Co. v. Brush, 10 Ohio 111, 114 (1840).
Commissioners v. Perry, 5 Ohio 56 (1831).
Royce v. Tyler, 2 C. C. 175, 183; 1 C. D. 428 (1887).
See Biggio v. Sandheger, 8 N. P. 13; 10 L. D. 316 (1900).

Forfeiture of charter. A judgment of ouster in a quo warranto
proceeding against the corporation is no defense to a subscriber in an
action brought by a creditor.
Rowland v. Meader Furniture Co., 38 O. S. 269 (1882).
Nor is it a defense to an action brought by the corporation that the
corporation has committed an act for which its charter might be forfeited
by the state.
Milford, etc., Co. v. Brush, 10 Ohio 111 (1840).

Amendments to charter. The acceptance, by a corporation organized
under a special charter, of an amendment to its charter which materially
changed the business of the corporation was held to release the subscriber.
Marietta, etc., R. Co. v. Elliott, 10 O. S. 57 (1859).

Change in character of stock. Where a corporation changes the
nature and character of its capital stock so as to make it substantially
different from the stock subscribed for, the subscriber is not liable.

James v. Cincinnati, etc., R. Co., 2 Dis. 261, 275 (Super. Ct. Cin. 1858).

Covington, etc., Co. v. Sargent, 1 C. S. C. R. 354 (1871); reversed on other grounds, 27 O. S. 233.

Delay in completion of work. Abandonment of enterprise. It is no defense that a railroad company has not completed the road in its entirety, nor that it has abandoned a part of the enterprise, where the subscription is not made on such conditions precedent.

Armstrong v. Karshner, 47 O. S. 276, 300 (1890).

See Four Mile, etc., Co. v. Bailey, 18 O. S. 208 (1868).

Where a turnpike company did not complete its enterprise until thirteen years after the date of its charter the delay was held no defense to a subscriber where the company during the entire time continued efforts to procure subscriptions and constructed the road as soon as funds were secured.

Gibson v. Columbus, etc., Co., 18 O. S. 396 (1868).

Change of route of railroad. An immaterial change of the route of a railroad or turnpike company is no defense.

Milford, etc., Turnpike Co. v. Brush, 10 Ohio 111 (1840).

Jewett v. Railway, 34 O. S. 601 (1878).

See Armstrong v. Karshner, 47 O. S. 276 (1890).

P. & O. Canal Co. v. Webb, 9 Ohio 136 (1839).

Unless the subscription was made on the faith of the original location of the road, in which case the subscriber may obtain a release by written notice.

G. C. § 8747.

Change of termini of railroad. A change of termini of a railroad may release the subscriber.

See § 8747.

Marietta, etc., R. Co. v. Elliott, 10 O. S. 57 (1859).

See Jewett v. Railway, 34 O. S. 601 (1878).

Discharge in bankruptcy. A liability on a stock subscription is not released by the discharge in bankruptcy of the subscriber where the subscriber did not schedule the liability as a debt, and the corporation had no knowledge or notice of the bankruptcy proceedings.

Roeblings Sons Co. v. Coal & Iron Co., 4 N. P. n. s. 113; 17 L. D. 8 (1906); aff'd, no rep., 78 O. S. 408.

Agreement to pay in property. A collateral agreement between a subscriber and the corporation giving the subscriber the privilege of paying his subscription in property is no defense to an action brought by a creditor, although the collateral agreement was made contemporaneously with the subscription. Such an agreement is considered a fraud on other stockholders.

Henry v. Vermillion, etc., R. Co., 17 Ohio 187 (1848).

Noble v. Callender, 20 O. S. 199 (1870).

Gates v. Tippecanoe Stone Co., 57 O. S. 60, 75 (1897).

Stunt v. Newark, etc., Co., 22 C. C. 120, 125; 12 C. D. 175 (1901); aff'd, no rep., 67 O. S. 555.

But such an agreement should be distinguished from an executed transaction in which the directors in good faith exchanged stock for property at a fair valuation, or accepted property in payment of a stock subscription.

See Gates v. Tippecanoe Stone Co., 57 O. S. 60, 75 (1897).

Orton v. Edson, etc., Co., 5 C. C. n. s. 540; 17 C. D. 107 (1905); aff'd, 75 O. S. 580.

Dayton, etc., R. Co. v. Hatch, 1 Dis. 84, 96 (Super. Ct. Cin. 1855).
Sanderson v. Iron & Nail Co., 34 O. S. 442, 449 (1878).

Payment. (a) **In money, but less than par.** Payment of a sum of money less than the full amount of the subscription is no defense against creditors although the stock has been issued as full paid and non-assessable.

Security Trust Co. v. Ford, 75 O. S. 322 (1906).
See Handley v. Stutz, 139 U. S. 417 (1891).
In re Flood-Pratt Dairy Co., 7 O. L. R. 603; 16 O. F. D. 396 (Referee in Bkry. 1909).

Although under some circumstances such payment may be a defense against the corporation or as against other stockholders.

Security Trust Co. v. Ford, 75 O. S. 322, 335 (1906).
See note to § 8630. *Sales below par.*

———. (b) **In property.** A stockholder who has received stock as fully paid up in exchange for property may under some circumstances be liable to creditors, but he is not liable to the corporation. The corporation can not treat the stock as only partially paid up and assess him with the difference between the actual value of the property and the par value of the stock. If the transaction was fraudulent the remedy of the corporation is to rescind the agreement.

Orton v. Edson, etc., Co., 5 C. C. n. s. 540; 17 C. D. 107 (1905); aff'd, no rep., 75 O. S. 580.
Leman v. MacLennan, 7 C. C. n. s. 205, 208; 18 C. D. 137 (1905); aff'd, no rep., 75 O. S. 643.

But where the property was fraudulently overvalued *creditors* may recover from the stockholder the difference between the actual value of the property and the par value of the stock.

Gates v. Tippecanoe Stone Co., 57 O. S. 60 (1897).
Sayler v. Simpson, 12 L. D. 148 (Super. Ct. Cin. 1888).
See note to § 8630.

A purchaser of such stock from the original stockholder is not liable unless he knew of its fraudulent character.

Roeblings Sons Co. v. Shawnee, etc., Co., 4 N. P. n. s. 113; 17 L. D. 8 (C. P. 1906); aff'd, no rep., 78 O. S. 408.

———. (c) **By dividends.** A subscriber is entitled to credit for dividends, both in cash and in stock, declared after his subscription was made. If in default for payments he should be charged with interest.

Railroad Co. v. Fink, 41 O. S. 321 (1884).
See Rhodes v. Equitable Life Ins. Co., 3 C. C. 501; 2 C. D. 288 (1888); aff'd, 27 W. L. B. 160.

———. (d) **By note.** See notes to § 8632.

———. (e) **To unauthorized agent of corporation.** Subscriptions should be paid to the treasurer of the corporation. Payment to an unauthorized agent is no defense.

See Natl. Bank v. Greenville, etc., Co., 3 C. C. n. s. 372, 381; 13 C. D. 274 (1899).

Breach of condition subsequent or stipulation in subscription. A breach by the corporation of a condition subsequent or stipulation in a subscription is no defense to the subscriber. His remedy is an action for damages.

Stunt v. Newark, etc., Co., 22 C. C. 120; 12 C. D. 175 (1901); aff'd, no rep., 67 O. S. 555.
Chamberlain v. Painesville, etc., R. Co., 15 O. S. 225, 247.
See note to § 8630. *Conditional subscriptions.*

Set off and counterclaim. A subscriber may set off a bona fide debt due him from the corporation against his liability on the subscription, whether the action is brought by the corporation,

Dungan v. Safford, 41 O. S. 15 (1884).
Sims v. Street Railroad, 37 O. S. 556, 558 (1882).

or by an assignee for creditors of the corporation.

Niles v. Olszak, 87 O. S. 229 (1912).
Compare Handley v. Stutz, 139 U. S. 417 (1891).
Painesville N. B. v. King Varnish Co., 8 C. C. 563; 4 C. D. 511 (1894).
Union, etc., Co. v. Jones, 35 O. S. 351 (1880).

The provisions of the bankruptcy act, as to set off of mutual debts, do not apply to the case of the creditor of a bankrupt corporation who is also indebted to the corporation on his stock subscription.

The claim of the creditor stockholder against the corporation should not be allowed until his indebtedness to the corporation has been collected by plenary suit. If found uncollectible, it should be applied on his claim as an equitable set off.

Kiskadden v. Steinle, 203 Fed. 375 (C. C. A. 1913) (distinguishing Niles v. Olszak, 87 O. S. 229.)

In an action by an assignee of the subscription a subscriber to railroad stock may set off scrip of the railroad company owned by him when notified of the assignment of his subscription, but not scrip purchased thereafter.

Dungan v. Safford, 41 O. S. 15 (1884).

Stipulation in corporate mortgage against individual liability. A stipulation in a corporate mortgage securing a bond issue to the effect that the bondholders should have no recourse to the individual liability of stockholders does not apply to a liability for unpaid subscriptions and is no defense thereto.

Raymond v. Spring Grove, etc., Co., 21 W. L. B. 103 (Super Ct. Cin. 1889).
Preston v. Cincinnati, etc., Co., 36 Fed. 54 (U. S. C. C. 1888).

Irregularities in a creditor's judgment against the corporation do not constitute a defense in favor of a subscriber, provided the judgment was not obtained by fraud or collusion.

Scofield v. Excelsior Oil Co., 6 C. C. n. s. 176; 17 C. D. 318 (1905); aff'd, no rep., 74 O. S. 513.
Henry v. Vermillion, etc., R. Co., 17 Ohio 187, 191 (1848).

Section 8675. (Notice of sale.) Before stock can so be sold, the directors shall give thirty days' notice of the time and place of sale, in some newspaper in general circulation in the county where the delinquent holder resided when he subscribed for it or became such assignee or transferee, or of his actual residence at the time of the sale. If such stockholder resides out of the state, the publication shall be made in the county where the company's principal office is located. (R. S. Sec. 3253; March 14, 1853, 51 v. 484, § 1; May 1, 1852, 50 v. 274, § 7; S. & C. 276, 319.)

Section 8676. (Distribution of proceeds of sale.) When a sale is made, if after paying from its proceeds the amount due on the stock, a balance remains, on his demand it shall be paid to the owner. But if such proceeds fail fully to pay such installment, any balance may be recovered by action against the subscriber, assignee or transferee. (R. S. Sec. 3253; March 14, 1853, 51 v. 484, § 1; May 1, 1852, 50 v. 274, § 7; S. & C. 276, 319.)

Section 8677. (Procedure when certificate of stock lost or destroyed.) In case a certificate of stock in a corporation is lost or destroyed, the owner thereof may file his petition in the probate court of the county where the principal business office of such corporation is located in this state, setting forth a pertinent description of the certificate, and a full statement of the facts relating to its destruction or loss; that he is the owner of such certificate, and was at the time of its loss or destruction; that he had not assigned, transferred or disposed of it; and that it was not pledged to any one, or if so, stating to whom, with the facts relating thereto. (R. S. Sec. 3254-1; April 23, 1891, 88 v. 336, § 1.)

Section 8678. (Parties and notice.) Such petitioner shall make the corporation and any pledgee defendants to such proceeding, and serve a certified copy of his petition on some chief officer of the corporation, and such pledgee, on which copies the probate judge over his signature shall state when the petition will be heard. Such copies shall be so served not less than twenty days before the hearing. In a newspaper published and of general circulation in the county where the proceeding is pending, and also in the county where he resides, the petitioner shall publish a notice containing the substance and prayer of his petition, for three consecutive weeks immediately before the day of hearing, and stating when and where it will be heard. (R. S. Sec. 3254-1; April 23, 1891, 88 v. 336, § 1.)

Section 8679. (Finding and order of the court.) If, upon the hearing, the probate court finds that the foregoing provisions have been complied with, that such certificate was lost or destroyed, and that at that time the petitioner was and is its owner, an order shall be made that such corporation issue and deliver a new certificate to him for the original amount and kind of stock, unless the certificate was pledged to some one at the time of its loss or destruction, and the pledgee yet has a claim against it, in which case the order shall direct that such new certificate be delivered to the pledgee on such terms as the court directs. The corporation shall comply with such orders, and it shall in no wise be prejudiced thereby, or by paying dividends on such new certificate, so long as it is not made known to it that

the original certificate is in existence and owned by a person other than the petitioner. (R. S. Sec. 3254-2; April 23,
1891, 88 v. 337, § 2.)

Under § 8673-17, which provides relief similar to that given by
§§ 8677 to 8681, a bond of indemnity must be given before a reissue
of certificates is ordered.

In the absence of other evidence, the fact that the lost certificate
was originally issued to the plaintiff would be conclusive as to his title.
But where it was shown that the real ownership was in another person
or corporation and that the plaintiff had merely the naked legal title,
the plaintiff was held not entitled to a reissue.

Provident, etc., Co. v. Voight, 13 C. C. n. s. 267 (1910).

The corporation may, in general, require surrender of original certificate before issuing a new one.

Lee v. Citizens Bank, 2 C. S. C. R. 298 (1872).
Railroad Co. v. Robbins, 35 O. S. 483 (1880).
G. C. § 8673-13.

A corporation is not liable to the equitable owner of stock for its
value, where certificates therefor are outstanding in the hands of a
third person who claims to be the owner.

National Bank v. Lake Shore, etc., Ry. Co., 21 O. S. 221 (1871).

**Section 8680. (Rights and liabilities under new certifi-
cate.)** All rights and liabilities attaching to the original
certificate shall attach to such re-issued certificate, while in
force. Upon the production of the original certificate to such
corporation by the owner or pledgee, the re-issued certificate
shall be cancelled, surrendered and void. (R. S. 3254-2;
April 23, 1891, 88 v. 337, § 2.)

Rights of holder of original certificate not affected by a reissue.
When a new certificate is, under a by-law of the corporation, issued
in lieu of a certificate represented to have been lost, the rights of the
holder of the original certificate are not affected thereby.

Railroad Co. v. Robbins, 35 O. S. 483 (1880).

A corporation which issues a new certificate, without a surrender
of the original certificate, is liable to the holder of the original certificate,
although the new certificate was issued under the belief that the original
had been lost. The corporation must either replace the stock or account
for its value.

Railroad Co. v. Robbins, 35 O. S. 483 (1880).
See Lee v. Citizens N. B., 2 C. S. C. R. 298 (Super. Ct. Cin. 1872).

But it is not liable for dividends paid to the registered owner before
the certificate was presented for transfer.

Railroad Co. v. Robbins, 35 O. S. 483 (1880).

Where a certificate issued to an officer was pledged by him, and,
while it was outstanding, he transferred the same stock on the books
to the corporation to secure his indebtedness to it, the transfer to the
corporation was held to be void. The outstanding certificate was notice
to the corporation of the rights of others.

Lee v. Citizens N. B., 2 C. S. C. R. 298 (1872).

**Section 8681. (Proceedings may be had by administra-
tors or executors.)** Executors and administrators, on be-

half of estates of deceased owners of such lost or destroyed certificates of stock, may proceed under the next three preceding sections, and have all the rights and benefits thereof. (R. S. Sec. 3254-2; April 23, 1891, 88 v. 337, § 2.)

Section 8682. (Paid up stock personal property.) Shares of stock in a corporation shall be personal property, and when fully paid up, be subject to levy and sale upon execution against the owner. (R. S. Sec. 3255; May 1, 1852, 50 v. 274, § 5; S. & C. 276.)

Certificates of stock, see §§ 8672 to 8673-24 and notes.
Capital stock, see notes to §§ 8625 and 8667.
Remedies of creditors of a stockholder, §§ 8673-13, 8673-14.

A share of stock is a right which entitles its owner to participate in the profits of the corporation, in its assets upon liquidation, and to vote at elections for directors.
See Jones v. Davis, 35 O. S. 477 (1880).
Shares of stock of a railroad company are personal property and the widow of a. stockholder is not entitled to dower therein.
Johns v. Johns, 1 O. S. 350 (1853).
Shares of stock belonging to a decedent's estate are not "debts due and owing."
Marriott v. Railway, 16 L. D. 135 (C. P. 1905); aff'd, 10 C. C. n. s. 573, 575.

Power of stockholder to dispose of stock. A stockholder has the same power of disposition over his stock as over other species of property.
Peter v. Union Mfg. Co., 56 O. S. 181, 207 (1897).
Unless restrictions are placed on his right of transfer by statute or by a valid by-law or regulation of the corporation. .
See § 8673-15.
Nicholson v. Franklin Brewing Co., 82 O. S. 94, 109 (1910).
Stafford v. Produce Exchange Bkg. Co., 61 O. S. 160 (1899).
Stock may be sold at auction.
Andrews v. Watson, 12 C. D. 686 (1887).

An assignment for creditors of all the real and personal estate. effects and credits of the assignor, includes stocks.
Haldeman v. Hillsborough, etc., R. Co., 2 C. S. C. R. 101 (1855).

Loan of stock. Where stock was loaned "to be returned on demand" the borrower was held not liable for its value until a demand therefor was made. Where no demand was made until after the corporation became insolvent and the stock worthless, only nominal damages can be recovered. Under the contract the borrower had a right to discharge his obligation by a return of an equal number of shares without regard to its market value.
Fosdick v. Greene, 27 O. S. 484 (1875).
Where stock was assigned by sisters to their brother to enable him to be elected to a salaried position in the corporation he is, in effect, a trustee. The statute of limitations does not begin to run in his favor until he disclaims the trust.
Bonnell v. Brown, 11 C. C. n. s. 58; 20 C. D. 712 (1908).
Right of borrower of stock to pledge the same.
See Brown v. Bank, 41 O. S. 445, 459 (1885).

Gift. Where a person purchases stock and places it in the name of a member of his family, the presumption is that the stock was intended as a gift or advancement, but this presumption may be rebutted.

Creed v. Lancaster Bank, 1 O. S. 1 (1852).

Bonnell v. Brown, 11 C. C. n. s. 58; 20 C. D. 712 (1908).

Mook v. Akron S. & L. Co., 87 O. S. 273 (1913).

CONTRACTS FOR SALE OF STOCK.

Payment to be made out of dividends. Sales to employees of corporation. A contract which contained an express promise by one party to sell, and by the other party to purchase, shares of stock, is not invalid for want of mutuality, although the contract further provided that the seller should receive the dividends and apply them on the purchase price; and that the purchaser had the option to make payments from other sources. No time of payment being stipulated in the contract, an agreement was implied to pay, by dividends or otherwise, within a reasonable time.

Stewart v. Herron, 77 O. S. 130 (1907) ; reversing in part, 10 C. C. n. s. 355.

Where a contract, by a large stockholder to sell stock to a skilled employee, contained no express promise by the latter to purchase (the contract providing for payment out of the dividends with an option to the employee to make other payments), but the stock was issued to the employee and by him assigned to the seller as security for payment of the purchase price, and the employee voted the stock for four years, without objection, it was held that the contract, being executed, was not invalid for want of consideration or lack of mutuality, and could not be rescinded by one party without consent of the other party.

White v. Cooper Co., 7 C. C. n. s. 114; 17 C. D. 703 (1903) ; aff'd, 72 O. S. 615, 691.

Consideration. An agreement to sell stock in a corporation, whether solvent or insolvent, imports that the stock is of some value. The seller may recover the contract price, whether the stock is valuable or not.

Van Arsdale v. Brown, 18 C. C. 52; 9 C. D. 488 (1899).

Breach of contract by buyer. Remedies of seller. Measure of damages. Where the buyer refuses to accept the stock the seller may resell the stock, within a reasonable time after such refusal, using reasonable care and judgment, and may recover from the buyer the difference between the contract price and the proceeds of such sale.

G. C. §§ 8440, 8444.

Ashley v. Walker, 15 C. C. 660; 8 C. D. 285 (1898).

Or, without a resale, the seller may bring suit for damages. In such case, where there is an available market price, the measure of damages is, ordinarily, the difference between the contract price and the market or current price at the time fixed for acceptance.

G. C. § 8444.

Andrews v. Watson, 12 C. D. 686, 692; aff'd, no rep., 51 O. S. 619.

Sullivan v. Frank, 13 N. P. n. s. 505 (1912).

Where, under the contract of sale, payment is to be made before delivery of the stock, or delivery and payment are to be concurrent acts, the seller may tender the stock, and, on refusal of the buyer to accept and pay, may bring an action for the purchase price.

G. C. § 8443.

Andrew v. Watson, 12 C. D. 692 (1890) ; aff'd, 51 O. S. 619.

Shawhan v. Van Nest, 25 O. S. 490 (1874).

When the tender is made it is not necessary that the assignment of the certificate and power of attorney should have been signed. An offer to sign and deliver, with ability to perform, is sufficient.

Hager v. Reed, 11 O. S. 626 (1860).

Where the buyer has repudiated the contract and made it certain that he does not intend to perform, actual formal tender is unnecessary. A showing of readiness and ability by the seller, to perform his part of the contract, communicated to the buyer, is sufficient.

Andrews v. Watson, 12 C. D. 692 (1890); aff'd, 51 O. S. 619.
Brewing Co. v. Maxwell, 78 O. S. 54 (1908).

SALES OF STOCK.

Sale with agreement of seller to repurchase. Where stock was sold under an agreement by the seller to repurchase the stock at par, on demand, at the end of a stipulated period, it is the duty of the purchaser, on the day specified, to tender back the certificates and to demand payment therefor.

Jones v. Jaeger, 9 N. P. n. s. 206 (C. P. 1909).

Sale of stock "short." A sale of stock "short" is a sale of that which the seller does not possess at the time, but which he expects to acquire at a lower price, subsequently, for delivery.

Lamprecht v. State, 84 O. S. 32 (1911).

Authority of agent to sell. Authority to sell stock is not authority to exchange it.

Cleveland v. State Bank, 16 O. S. 236 (1865).

An agent authorized to sell stock can not himself purchase. A bank official who gratuitously engages to find a purchaser for a customer of the bank thereby becomes the agent of the customer, and can not himself become the purchaser without the full knowledge and consent of his principal.

Telling v. Sullivan, 14 C. C. n. s. 1; 22 C. D. 312 (1911); reversed, no rep., 88 O. S. —.

Liability of broker purchasing for undisclosed principal. A stockbroker purchasing stock for an undisclosed principal is personally liable upon default of his principal.

Sullivan v. Frank, 13 N. P. n. s. 505 (1912).

Sale for illegal purpose. Where the object of a purchaser of stock is to obtain control of the corporation for illegal purposes, which were known to the seller, and the sale is made for the purpose of enabling the purchaser to carry out such illegal purpose, the sale is illegal and void.

Newark v. Elliott, 5 O. S. 113 (1855).

Evidence as to executed sale. A witness may testify that he sold stock and delivered the certificates to a person named, without producing the certificates for inspection.

Cincinnati, etc., Ry. Co. v. Rawson, 16 W. L. B. 423 (Super. Ct. Cin. 1886); aff'd, 25 W. L. B. 87.

PLEDGE OR HYPOTHECATION OF STOCK.

Stock may be hypothecated. "Strictly speaking, stock, being of an incorporeal nature, is not capable of being pledged, as there can not be a delivery of intangible property. It may be, and frequently is, hypothecated, which is a pledge in a secondary sense. An hypothecation is defined as a right which a creditor has over a thing belonging to another, and which consists in a power to cause it to be sold, in order to be paid his claim out of the proceeds."

Dueber, etc., Co. v. Dougherty, 62 O. S. 589, 593 (1900).

See Dayton N. B. v. Merchants N. B., 37 O. S. 215 (1881).

Where a corporation has a lien, by statute, on all stock owned by its debtors, and has full control over its transfer, the possession of the certificates, by pledge, gives the corporation no additional rights or benefits.

State v. Davis, 85 O. S. 44 (1911).

When note renewed, collateral becomes security for new note. Where a note secured by a pledge of stock is partly paid and a renewal note given for the balance, the stock will stand as collateral security for the balance of the debt embraced in the new note, in the absence of any agreement to the contrary.

Dayton N. B. v. Merchants N. B., 37 O. S. 208 (1881).

Agreement for pledge. Where a person became surety on a note on the agreement of the principal debtor to transfer, as indemnity, a certificate of stock which he then held, within a short time, it was held that the surety thereby acquired an equity in the stock which he could enforce against all persons having notice.

Dueber, etc., Co. v. Daugherty, 62 O. S. 589 (1900).

Purchase through stock broker. Broker as pledgee. Where a broker buys stock on the order of a customer, the customer is the owner of the stock from the time of purchase, whether purchased in his name or not, and he is entitled to its possession, on demand, subject to payment to the broker of advances and commissions, as to which the customer is the debtor of the broker. The legal relation of customer and broker is that of pledgor and pledgee. Upon such demand the broker need not deliver the identical stock purchased, but may deliver an equal number of shares of the same kind and value.

Lamprecht v. State, 84 O. S. 32 (1911).

Stolen certificates; pledge of.

See note to § 8673-5.

Pledge of fraudulently acquired stock. Where stock, fraudulently obtained, is pledged to secure a preexisting debt, without an extension of time or other consideration therefor, the pledgee has no greater rights therein than the pledgor had.

Cleveland v. Bank, 16 O. S. 236, 269 (1865).

See § 8673-22, "Value" defined.

Pledge of trust stock to secure personal debt of trustee. Where a trustee borrowed money for his own use from a building and loan company, on a pledge of certificates of its stock belonging to the trust estate, of which fact the company held notice, the company acquired no lien on such stock.

Mook v. Akron S. & L. Co., 87 O. S. 273 (1913).

Assignment of stock to be delivered to creditor after death of debtor. A certificate of stock, assigned in blank and witnessed, found among the papers of a decedent in an envelope on which was written in the handwriting of the decedent the name of the creditor and the words "collateral for whatever I owe him", was held to pass the stock to the creditor.

In re Clerke, 17 W. L. B. 369 (C. P. 1887).

Taxation of pledged stock. Where pledged stock is taxable, and no transfer to the pledgee has been made on the corporate books, it is taxed in the name of the pledgor.

Ratterman v. Ingalls, 48 O. S. 468, 491 (1891).
See notes to §§ 5372 and 192 as to what stock is taxable.

Rights of pledgee.

Transfer of stock on corporate books. A pledgee is entitled to have the stock transferred to his name on the corporate books.
Railway Co. v. Bank, 68 O. S. 582, 589 (1903).
Henkle v. Salem Mfg. Co., 39 O. S. 547 (1883).
Dayton N. B. v. Merchants N. B., 37 O. S. 208, 215 (1881).
Railway Co. v. Rawson, 16 W. L. B. 423 (Super. Ct. Cin. 1886);
    aff'd, 25 W. L. B. 87.
The bankruptcy of the pledgor does not affect this right.
Dayton N. B. v. Merchants N. B., 37 O. S. 208, 215 (1881).

Where stock not transferred to pledgee on the books of the corporation. Under the Uniform Stock Transfer Act certificates of stock are, in effect, negotiable instruments.
§§ 8673-1, 8673-5 and notes.
A bona fide pledgee, holding properly endorsed certificates, is protected against all prior holders and against third persons, without a registry of the transfer on the corporate books.
§§ 8673-1, 8673-5 ("Purchaser" includes pledgee, § 8673-22).
But as against the corporation, a pledgee is not a stockholder until he presents the certificates for transfer on the corporate books.
§ 8673-3.
Henkle v. Salem Mfg. Co., 39 O. S. 547 (1883).
He is not entitled to vote nor to receive the dividends.
Railroad Co. v. Robbins, 35 O. S. 483 (1880).
Norton v. Norton, 43 O. S. 509, 522-523 (1885).
Franklin Bank v. Commercial Bank, 36 O. S. 350, 355 (1881).
§ 8673-3.
Nor to participate in, nor be notified of, proceedings to effect a consolidation.
Railway Co. v. Bank, 68 O. S. 582 (1903).
Nor of proceedings to sell the entire corporate property.
Schmuck v. Crume, etc., Co., 7 N. P. n. s. 24; 19 L. D. 819 (1905);
    aff'd, 78 O. S. 409.
Before the enactment of the Uniform Transfer Law, where the entire corporate property was disposed of, by a sale or consolidation, and the proceeds distributed to the stockholders of record, unregistered pledgees were in danger of losing their security.
See Railway Co. v. Bank, 68 O. S. 582 (1903).
Schmuck v. Crume, etc., Co., 7 N. P. n. s. 24; 19 L. D. 819 (1905);
    aff'd, 78 O. S. 409.
But under § 8673-1, which makes registry of transfers unnecessary, it is doubtful whether a corporation may, without liability, distribute the proceeds except on a surrender of the certificates.
Before the enactment of the Uniform Transfer law it was held that as between the pledgor and pledgee the pledgee, without a transfer, held neither the equitable or legal title, but only a special property. But, by having executed the blank assignment and power of attorney, the pledgor was estopped from asserting any control over the legal title.
Krebs v. Forbriger, 21 W. L. B. 313 (Super. Ct. Cin. 1889).
Under the double liability of stockholders, by the former law, a pledgee who held the assigned certificates, without a transfer, was not liable.
Henkle v. Salem Mfg. Co., 39 O. S. 547 (1883).
A pledgee of stock in a national bank becomes liable as a stockholder,

under the national banking act, where he has the stock registered in the name of his employee, with no beneficial interest, and afterwards indorses on the note the supposed value of the stock as a credit, and presents the note, reduced by the credit, to the administrator who allows the claim in such form.

Ohio Valley N. B. v. Hulitt, 204 U. S. 162; 15 O. F. D. 530 (1907); affirming, 137 Fed. 461.

Foreclosure by judicial proceeding. A pledgee may bring suit to foreclose his lien and for a sale of the stock. In such case neither party is entitled by law to a jury trial.

Brigel v. Creed, 65 O. S. 40 (1901).

A pledgee may be made a party to a suit by a junior lienholder.

Healy v. Robinson, 21 L. D. 579 (1911).

Sale of stock without judicial proceedings. A pledgee has the right to sell the pledged stock on default of payment of the debt at maturity, without judicial proceedings, although no power of sale is contained in the collateral note or other contract of pledge.

Glidden v. Mechanics N. B., 53 O. S. 588, 598 (1895).
Robinson v. Boyd, 60 O. S. 57, 68-69 (1899).
Bates v. Wiles, 1 Handy 532 (Super. Ct. Cin. 1855).
Oliver v. Cincinnati, etc., Co., 1 Hosea 457 (Super. Ct. Cin.)

Although a receiver of the assets of the pledgor has been appointed and although the amount due is in dispute.

Harrison v. Friend, 1 N. P. 39; 1 L. D. 258 (C. P. 1893).

Where a power of sale is contained in the contract of pledge it controls the rights of the parties.

Glidden v. Mechanics N. B., 53 O. S. 588, 599 (1895).

The sale must be conducted in good faith.

Bates v. Wiles, 1 Handy 532 (Super. Ct. Cin. 1855).

The pledgee's right to sell is not affected by a suit by a creditor of the pledgor to reach the stock, to which suit the pledgee is not a party. The doctrine of lis pendens does not apply to certificates of stock.

Krebs v. Forbriger, 21 W. L. B. 313 (Super. Ct. Cin. 1889).

Notice of sale must be given. Reasonable notice of the time and place of sale must be given to the pledgor, unless notice is waived in the contract of pledge, or otherwise.

Glidden v. Mechanics N. B., 53 O. S. 588, 599 (1895).
Lee v. Citizens N. B., 2 C. S. C. R. 298 (Super. Ct. Cin. 1872).

If no notice is given, or an unreasonably short notice, the sale may be declared invalid.

Bates v. Wiles, 1 Handy 532 (Super. Ct. Cin. 1855).

A notice of sale given to the pledgor is equivalent to a demand of payment.

Harrison v. Friend, 1 N. P. 39; 1 L. D. 258 (C. P. 1893).

When pledgee may purchase. A pledgee can not become the purchaser at his own sale, either directly or indirectly, in the absence of an express agreement to that effect.

Glidden v. Mechanics N. B., 53 O. S. 588 (1895).
Moore v. Central N. B., 12 C. C. n. s. 529 (1910).

Where a collateral note authorized its *"holder"* to sell the pledged stock and to become the purchaser thereof, a bank holding the same for collection, merely, can not sell the stock nor become the purchaser.

Moore v. Central N. B., 12 C. C. n. s. 529 (1910).

An unauthorized purchase by a pledgee may be ratified by the pledgor, but ratification can not be presumed from silence where the pledgor had no notice of the sale.

Glidden v. Mechanics N. B., 53 O. S. 588, 600 (1895).

Moore v. Central N. B., 12 C. C. n. s. 529 (1910).

An unauthorized purchase by the pledgee is not a conversion while the pledgee holds the stock, unless the pledgor elects to treat it as a valid sale, in which event the pledgee is accountable for the net proceeds of sale.

Glidden v. Mechanics N. B., 53 O. S. 588 (1895).

But when the pledgee disposes of the stock, he will be liable for a conversion, without a demand and offer of performance by the pledgor.

Glidden v. Mechanics N. B., 53 O. S. 588 (1895).

Price specified in contract of pledge. Authority of negotiating agent to receive payment. Where a note and contract of pledge, stipulating the price in excess of the debt for which the payee may become the absolute owner of the stock, is delivered to the payee with knowledge that he is to obtain the consideration from another person, the payee is authorized to receive the original consideration for the note, but not authorized to receive, at the maturity of the note, a tender of the stipulated balance of the purchase price.

Rumsey v. Lentz, 59 O. S. 189 (1898).

Unauthorized sale. Statute of limitations. Measure of damages. The statute of limitations does not begin to run in favor of a pledgee, who has made an unauthorized sale, until the pledgor had notice thereof.

Moore v. Central N. B., 12 C. C. n. s. 529 (1910).

Where a pledgee, without authority, purchased stock at his own sale and subsequently disposed of it, he was held accountable for the amount received therefor, with interest, less the amount of the debt, with interest.

Moore v. Central N. B., 12 C. C. n. s. 529 (1910).

See Glidden v. Mechanics N. B., 53 O. S. 588 (1895).

Where stock was sold, without notice to the pledgor, he was held entitled to recover the highest market value at any time between the day of the sale and the commencement of the suit.

Bates v. Wiles, 1 Handy 532 (Super. Ct. Cin. 1855).

Lien of corporation on stock for indebtedness of stockholder to it. See note to § 8673-15.

Section 8683.   (May purchase stock in other companies.) A private corporation also may purchase, or otherwise acquire, and hold shares of stock in other kindred but not competing private corporations, domestic or foreign. This shall not authorize the formation of a trust or combination for the purpose of restricting trade or competition. (R. S. Sec. 3256; May 6, 1902, 95 v. 390; April 15, 1902, 95 v. 151; R. S. 1880.)

For power of corporation to acquire stock in itself see note to § 8627.

Common law rule.

A corporation has no power, at common law, to subscribe for or become the owner of stock of another corporation unless authority is clearly conferred by statute.

Franklin Bank v. Commercial Bank, 36 O. S. 350 (1881).

Ry. Co. v. Iron Co., 46 O. S. 44 (1888).

Columbus, etc., Ry. Co. v. Burke, 19 W. L. B. 27 (1887).

Hafer v. N. Y., etc., R. Co., 14 W. L. B. 68, 70 (1885).

Easun v. Buckeye Brewing Co., 51 Fed. 156; 7 O. F. D. 188 (1892).

State v. H. V. Ry. Co., 12 C. C. n. s. 49; 21 C. D. 175 (1909).

See comment in Mannington v. H. V. Ry. Co., 8 O. L. R. 481, 482; 183 Fed. 156, 157; 16 O. F. D. 577, 578 (C. C. Ohio 1910).

Exceptions.

To avoid loss. To secure itself from loss, on a debt due to it or otherwise, a corporation may acquire stock in another corporation with a view to its subsequent sale and conversion into money.

Armstrong v. Herancourt Brewing Co., 26 W. L. B. 39, 40 (C. P. 1891).

See Coppin v. Greenless, 38 O. S. 275 (1882).

Where a corporation held bonds of another corporation as security for a debt due to it, and exchanged the bonds for stock in a new corporation formed as a reorganization of the debtor corporation, it became the lawful owner of such stock.

Marriott v. Railway Co., 16 L. D. 135 (C. P. 1905); aff'd, 10 C. C. n. s. 573, 575.

Executed transaction. Where a corporation has made an *ultra vires* subscription to the capital stock of another corporation, and voluntarily made payments thereon, it can not recover back such payments.

Railway Co. v. Iron Co., 46 O. S. 44 (1888).

See Norwalk, etc., Co. v. Norwalk, etc., Co., 14 C. C. 1; 7 C. D. 275 (1897).

Mutual insurance company. A corporation may become a member of a mutual insurance company, for the purpose of its own protection.

Stone v. Traction Co., 4 N. P. n. s. 104; 16 L. D. 645 (C. P. 1906).

Stock in building and loan association. A corporation may subscribe for stock in a building and loan association in order to borrow money for its business.

Norwalk, etc., Co. v. Norwalk, etc., Co., 14 C. C. 1; 7 C. D. 275 (1897).

Effect of § 8683.

The common law rule is modified by § 8683 so as to permit a corporation to acquire stock in corporations which are (1) kindred (2) and not competing, when (3) the result of the purchase is not the formation of a trust or combination.

Mannington v. H. V. Ry. Co., 8 O. L. R. 476; 183 Fed. 152; 16 O. F. D. 572 (U. S. C. C. 1910).

Articles of incorporation which attempted to authorize the proposed corporation to own or deal generally in stocks of other companies have been rejected by the secretary of state for the reason that § 8683 authorizes only a limited dealing in stocks.

5 Opins. Attys. Gen. 969, 924 (1903).

Rep. Atty. Gen. 1911-1912, pp. 58, 61.

See page 99, Forms No. 103 and 104, for articles which have been approved.

"Kindred" corporations. A railroad company and a coal mining company are not kindred corporations. A railroad company has no power to acquire stock in a coal mining corporation.

State v. H. V. Ry. Co., 12 C. C. n. s. 49, 59; 21 C. D. 175 (1909).

"Competing" corporations.

See note to § 8807.

State v. H. V. Ry Co., 12 C. C. n. s. 145 (1909).

Mannington v. H. V. Ry. Co., 9 N. P. n. s. 675; 20 L. D. 468 (1910); removed to U. S. Ct. 8 O. L. R. 451; 183 Fed. 133; 16 O. F. D. 552 (1910).

Section 8683 applies to railroad companies. This section applies to railroad companies. Its provisions are not inconsistent with the provisions of §§ 8806 to 8809, but are cumulative.

Mannington v. H. V. Ry. Co., 8 O. L. R. 451; 183 Fed. 133.

State v. H. V. Ry. Co., 12 C. C. n. s. 49, 59; 21 C. D. 175 (1909).

Contra, Mannington v. H. V. Ry. Co., 9 N. P. n. s. 641, 668; 20 L. D. 468 (C. P. 1910).

See § 8806 et seq.

A foreign corporation may own stock in kindred but not competing Ohio corporations, when authorized by the laws of its home state, and not prohibited by statute in Ohio.

Mannington v. H. V. Ry. Co., 8 O. L. R. 451, 481 to 484; 183 Fed. 133; 16 O. F. D. 552 (C. C. Ohio 1910).

Smith v. Newark, etc., R. Co., 8 C. C. 583, 591 (1894).

Acting as a stockholder in an Ohio corporation or giving assent to changes in its regulations is not "doing business" in Ohio within the meaning of §§ 178 or 5508.

Toledo T. & L. P. Co. v. Smith, 58 Bull. 201 (U. S. D. C. 1913).

A foreign corporation organized for the sole purpose of holding the stock and securities of an Ohio corporation may exercise in Ohio all the incidents of such ownership, such as voting at stockholders' meetings and giving assent to change of regulations, provided the exercise of such incidents does not tend to foster monopoly or suppress competition.

Toledo T. L. & P. Co. v. Smith, 58 Bull. 201 (U. S. D. C. 1913).

A foreign corporation with corporate power to own and deal in stocks of other corporations generally can not be admitted to do business in Ohio, since under § 8683 Ohio corporations may acquire stock only in kindred and not competing corporations.

5 Opins. Attys. Gen. 924, 969 (1903).

Rep. Atty. Gen. 1910-1911, p. 246.

Rep. Atty. Gen. 1911-1912, p. 61.

Unless it expressly renounces the right to exercise such power in Ohio.

Rep. Atty. Gen. 1911-1912, p. 78.

Action by stockholder to enjoin acquisition of stock. Venue and parties defendant. An action by a stockholder in a railroad company to enjoin the unlawful acquisition of stock in other corporations must be brought in a county in which jurisdiction may be acquired over the railroad company. The other corporations are not proper parties defendant.

Westfall v. Lake Shore, etc., Ry., 13 N. P. n. s. 217; 22 L. D. 75, 397 (C. P. 1910).

Section 8684. (Corporate property, how employed.) No corporation shall employ its stocks, means, assets, or other property, directly or indirectly, for any other purpose than to accomplish the legitimate objects of its creation. (R. S. Sec. 3266; May 1, 1852, 50 v. 274, § 73; S. & C. 309.)

Misappropriation of property and remedies.

See note to § 8660.

Corporate property as a trust fund. Corporate property is not owned by the corporation in the sense of ownership as applied to property of an individual. Corporate property is a fund set apart to be used only for corporate purposes. It is impressed with the character of a trust fund for that purpose.

A trust relation exists between the directors and stockholders. The

duties of the directors are of a fiduciary nature. They are trustees for
the stockholders and creditors.

Rouse v. Bank, 46 O. S. 493, 501-502 (1889).
Goodin v. Cincinnati, etc., Co., 18 O. S. 169 (1868).
Cheney v. Maumee Cycle Co., 64 O. S. 205, 213 (1901).
Bank v. Mfg. Co., 67 O. S. 306, 314 (1902).
Niles v. Olszak, 87 O. S. 229 (1912).
But see Hollins v. Brierfield, etc., Co., 150 U. S. 371, 381, 383 (1893).
McDonald v. Williams, 174 U. S. 397, 401 (1899).

The trust relation exists to such an extent that when brought into
court by creditors for an accounting, the corporation may ask the instruction of the court as to its duties.

Everhardt v. U. S., etc., Co., 8 N. P. 525; 11 L. D. 687 (Super. Ct.
    Cin.)

Unpaid subscriptions to the stock of an insolvent corporation are a
part of the trust fund for creditors.

Turnbull v. Pomeroy Salt Co., 24 W. L. B. 133 (C. P. 1890).
Niles v. Olszak, 87 O. S. 229 (1912).

Fraudulent transfers of property. Where the property of a corporation has been fraudulently or wrongfully disposed of by directors, its creditors or stockholders may pursue it into the hands of purchasers with
notice.

Goodin v. Cincinnati, etc., Co., 18 O. S. 169 (1868).
Taylor v. Miami Exporting Co., 5 Ohio 162 (1831).

It is the duty of a receiver of an insolvent or dissolved corporation
to recover property fraudulently conveyed.

Monitor Furnace Co. v. Peters, 40 O. S. 575 (1884).
Sayle v. Guarantee, etc., Co., 2 C. C. n. s. 401; 15 C. D. 503 (1903).

Where it did not appear that a corporation was insolvent and that it
had ceased to prosecute the objects for which it was created at a time
when its funds were used to pay notes, executed by its president and
endorsed by the corporation, held by a bank to cover a loss by the failure
of a former corporation the funds so used are not so impressed with a
trust as to be recoverable by the trustee in bankruptcy of the corporation.

Haines v. Bank, 203 Fed. 225 (C. C. A. 1913).

Preferences by insolvent corporations. At a time when insolvent individuals were permitted to prefer certain of their creditors, it was held
that preferences by insolvent corporations were invalid.

Rouse v. Bank, 46 O. S. 493 (1889).
Smith, etc., Co. v. McGroarty, 136 U. S. 237; 24 W. L. B. 110 (1890).
Remington v. Central, etc., Co., 3 N. P. 258; 4 L. D. 337 (1896).
Benedict v. Bank, 4 N. P. 231; 6 L. D. 320 (1897); 19 C. C. 408.
Cheney v. Maumee Cycle Co., 20 C. C. 19 (1900); aff'd, 64 O. S.
    205 (1901).

Although certain mortgages and liens created or suffered by corporations, which were going concerns, were upheld as not being preferential.

Campbell, etc., Co. v. Bellman Bros. Co., 11 C. C. 360; 5 C. D. 389
    (1896).
Damarin v. Huron Iron Co., 47 O. S. 581 (1890).
Ford v. Lamson, 17 C. C. 539; 9 C. D. 374 (1899).
Bosche v. Toledo, etc., Co., 14 C. C. 289; 7 C. D. 374 (1897).
In re Winchell Mfg. Co., 1 N. P. 136; 1 L. D. 310 (1894).

Preference by foreign corporation.

See Kit Carter Cattle Co. v. McGillen, 21 C. C. 210 (1900).

STOCKHOLDERS.

Section 8685. (Annual statement to stockholders.) Every corporation organized under the laws of Ohio, annually shall make a statement of its financial condition, setting forth its assets and liabilities, and furnish to each stockholder a true copy thereof, together with a list of its stockholders, and their places of residence. (R. S. Sec. 3268; R. S. 1880.)

Section 8686. (Liability of stockholders.) The stockholders of a corporation who are holders of its shares at a time when its debts and liabilities are enforcible against them, shall be held liable, equally and ratably, but not one for another, in addition to their stock in an amount equal thereto, to the creditors of the corporation, to secure the payment of such debts and liabilities. No stockholder who transfers his stock in good faith, if such transfer is made on the books of the company or on the back of the certificate of stock properly witnessed or tendered for transfer on its books prior to the time when such debts and liabilities are so enforcible, may be held to pay any portion thereof. (R. S. Sec. 3258; April 25, 1904, 97 v. 390; April 29, 1902, 95 v. 312; May 1, 1852, 50 v. 296, §§ 78-79; March 11, 1853, 51 v. 386; April 17, 1854, 52 v. 44, § 78; April 12, 1865, 62 v. 134; March 11, 1874, 69 v. 25; R. S. 1880; S. & C. 310.)

LIABILITY OF STOCKHOLDERS IN ABSENCE OF STATUTE.

Not liable for corporate debts. A stockholder, whose stock has been paid up, is not personally liable for the debts of the corporation.
Carr v. Inglehart, 3 O. S. 457, 458 (1854).
Ireland v. Palestine, etc., Co., 19 O. S. 369, 372 (1869).

Stockholders in a corporation *de facto* are not individually liable as partners. Their liability is that of stockholders only.
Rowland v. Meader Furn. Co., 38 O. S. 271 (1882).

Irregular or defective incorporation does not render the stockholders personally liable for corporate debts, where the incorporation statute has been substantially complied with.
Second N. B. v. Hall, 35 O. S. 158 (1878).
See note to § 8627. Estoppel to deny corporate existence.

Not bound by corporate contracts. A contract made by a corporation, on a sale of its entire property and good will, that it will not re-engage in business in competition with the purchaser, is not binding upon its stockholders personally.
Hall's Safe Co. v. Herring, etc., Co., 146 Fed. 37; 15 O. F. D. 37 (C. C. A. 1906).

Not subject to injunction for acts of corporation alone. A stockholder is not individually liable, nor subject to injunction, because of unfair competition practiced by the corporation alone.
Hall's Safe Co. v. Herring, etc., Co., 146 Fed. 37; 15 O. F. D. 37 (C. C. A. 1906).

Liability on stock subscriptions.

See notes to §§ 8630 and 8674.

Agreement by stockholders to pay corporate debts. An agreement by solvent stockholders of an embarrassed corporation that they will severally contribute to raise a fund to pay the corporate indebtedness creates a valid obligation. If the share to be contributed by each is not expressly fixed by the agreement, each should contribute in the proportion that the number of shares of stock owned by him bears to the shares held by all the contributors.

Sterling Wrench Co. v. Amstutz, 50 O. S. 484 (1893).

On stock purchased from corporation for less than par.

See note to § 8630. *Disposition of stock by corporation after election of directors.*

For ultra vires or illegal acts or business.

See notes to § 8627. *Ultra vires acts; Corporation as a legal entity,* and *Promoters.*

On guaranty contracts. Rights and liabilities.

See Wise v. Miller, 45 O. S. 388 (1887).

DOUBLE STATUTORY LIABILITY.

No liability on debts incurred since 1903. Exception as to bank stockholders.

See § 8687.

Transferrer. Liability of. By the amendment of this section (95 v. 312) it was the intention of the legislature to restrict the liability of a stockholder to those debts which were incurred while the stock was held by such stockholder.

Scofield v. Excelsior Oil Co., 6 C. C. n. s. 169; 17 C. D. 347 (1905); aff'd, 74 O. S. 513.

State B. & T. Co. v. Mitchell Co., 14 N. P. n. s. 49 (1913).

The amendment (95 v. 312) was evidently intended to avoid the consequences of Herrick v. Wardwell, 58 O. S. 294 (1898).

State B. & T. Co. v. Mitchell, 14 N. P. n. s. 49, 64 (1913).

The amendment (95 v. 312) exempting transferrers from liability has been held unconstitutional.

Swift & Co. v. Youngstown, etc., Co., 6 C. C. n. s. 89; 17 C. D. 253 (1905).

Little v. Aultman, etc., Co., 15 L. D. 355 (C. P. 1905).

Contra, Scofield v. Excelsior Oil Co., 6 C. C. n. s. 169, 175; 17 C. D. 347 (1905); aff'd, no rep.. 74 O. S. 513.

See Sheets Mfg. Co. v. Neer Mfg. Co., 4 N. P. n. s. 201; 17 L. D. 119 (C. P. 1906).

State B. & T. Co. v. Mitchell Co., 14 N. P. n. s. 49, 63 (1913).

Prior to the amendment (95 v. 312) a transfer, although made in good faith, did not release the transferrer for debts incurred prior to the transfer.

Brown v. Hitchcock, 36 O. S. 678 (1881).

Harpold v. Stobart, 46 O. S. 397 (1889).

Rider v. Fritchey, 49 O. S. 285, 295 (1892).

The transferee was primarily liable. If insolvent or nonresident, resort could be had to the transferrer, after the total liability of the existing solvent and resident stockholders had been exhausted, but not before.

Poston v. Hull, 75 O. S. 502 (1907).

Wick N. B. v. Union N. B., 62 O. S. 446 (1900).

Brown v. Hitchcock, 36 O. S. 667 (1881).
The transferrer is not liable for debts incurred after transfer of the stock on the corporate books, if in good faith. But if the transferrer remained the equitable owner he remained liable.
Peter v. Union Mfg. Co., 56 O. S. 181 (1897).
Muskingum, etc., Co. v. Ward, 13 Ohio 120 (1844).
Poston v. Hull, 75 O. S. 505 (1907).
A transferrer, who has been held liable to creditors, may recover against his transferee.
Harpold v. Stobart, 46 O. S. 397, 401 (1889).
Poston v. Hull, 75 O. S. 505 (1907).
The equities between a transferrer and transferee may be adjusted in the stockholders' liability suit.
Railroad Co. v. Smith, 48 O. S. 219 (1891).
Where judgment has been rendered against the transferee, the transferrer being a party to the suit, such judgment is final, and, after failure to collect the judgment from the transferee, creditors can not hold the transferrer.
Bullock v. Kilgour, 39 O. S. 543 (1883).
The renewal of corporate notes does not release a transferrer, although after the transfer and without his knowledge.
Hauenschild v. Standard, etc., Co., 8 N. P. 124 (Super. Ct. Cin.).
Boice v. Hodge, 51 O. S. 236.
Unless the renewal note was accepted in payment of the obligation.
Wheeler v. Faurot, 37 O. S. 26 (1881).

Transferee. Liability to creditors follows the stock and a transferee of stock is primarily liable to creditors. The transferee is held to indemnify the transferrer on account of any statutory liability.
Poston v. Hull, 75 O. S. 502, 505 (1907).
Harpold v. Stobart, 46 O. S. 397, 401 (1889).
Wheeler v. Faurot, 37 O. S. 26, 28 (1881).
Brown v. Hitchcock, 36 O. S. 667, 680 (1881).
Bonewitz v. Bank, 41 O. S. 78 (1884).
R. R. Co. v. Smith, 48 O. S. 219 (1891).
Barrick v. Gifford, 47 O. S. 180 (1890).
The liability attaches to all who are stockholders at the time of the enforcement of the liability regardless of when they became stockholders.
Poston v. Hull, 75 O. S. 502' 507 (1907).
Umstaetter v. Newark, etc., Co., 4 N. P. n. s. 150; 17 L. D. 30 (1906).
A transferee is liable although he held the stock only long enough to transfer it again.
Schwill v. Beckel, 1 N. P. n. s. 1: 13 L. D. 699 (Super Ct. Cin. 1903).

Stockholders registered in the corporate books are prima facie liable.

See G. C. § 8689.
Harpold v. Stobart, 46 O. S. 397 (1889).
Herrick v. Wardwell, 58 O. S. 294 (1898).
Biles v. Looker Co., 17 C. C. 538; 9 C. D. 685 (1889).
Wehrman v. Reakirt, 1 C. S. C. R. 230 (1871).
Marriott v. Railway, 16 L. D. 135 (C. P. 1905); aff'd, 10 C. C. n. s. 573, 575.
But since the amendment of § 8686 in 1902 where a certificate properly assigned was left for transfer on the corporate books, but the transfer was not made because of omission of the officers of the corporation the transferrer is not liable.
State B. & T. Co. v. Mitchell Co., 14 N. P. n. s. 49, 64 (1913).

Debts of corporation assumed by new corporation. Where a corporation is reorganized and succeeded by a new corporation, which assumes the debts of the old corporation, the stockholders of the old corporation remain liable, but such liability is secondary to that of the new corporation and its stockholders.

> Marriott v. Railway Co., 16 L. D. 135 (C. P. 1910); s. c., 10 C. C. n. s. 573; 20 C. D. 419.
> Irvine v. Bankard, 181 Fed. 206 (1910); aff'd, no rep., 184 Fed. 986.

Nature of statutory liability. Not joint, but several.

> Mason v. Alexander, 44 O. S. 318, 333 (1886).
> Umsted v. Buskirk, 17 O. S. 113 (1866).
> Poston v. Hull, 75 O. S. 505 (1907).

Not a primary resource for the collection of corporate debts, but a secondary and collateral obligation, to be resorted to only in case of insolvency of corporation.

> Poston v. Hull, 75 O. S. 502, 505 (1907).
> Bronson v. Schneider, 49 O. S. 438 (1892).
> Younglove v. Lime Co., 49 O. S. 663, 666 (1892).
> Peter v. Union Mfg. Co., 56 O. S. 181, 197 (1897).
> Falkenback v. Patterson, 43 O. S. 359, 370 (1885).
> Swan v. Mansfield, etc., R. Co., 3 N. P. 225; 5 L. D. 297 (1896).

It is contractual in its nature.

> Dabney v. Pappenheimer Co., 20 C. C. 707 (1888).
> Cleveland Gas Co. v. Collins, 19 C. C. 247 (1899).
> Northern N. B. v. Maumee, etc., Co., 2 N. P. 260; 2 L. D. 67 (1894).
> See Kulp v. Fleming, 65 O. S. 321 (1901).
> Blair v. Newbegin, 65 O. S. 425 (1901).

The liability is a provable claim against the estate of a bankrupt stockholder.

> In re Rouse, 40 W. L. B. 220.

Control of corporation over liability. The corporation has no control over the statutory liability, which is for the exclusive benefit of creditors. It can not assign the liability even for the benefit of all creditors.

> Wright v. McCormack, 17 O. S. 86 (1866).
> Umsted v. Buskirk, 17 O. S. 113 (1866).
> White v. Ingersoll, 2 Cleve. L. R. 362 (1878).

Nor can it release a stockholder therefrom.

> No. Fairmount, etc., Co. v. Ashbrook, 12 L. D. 10 (Super. Ct. Cin. 1901).

Nor counterclaim upon it against a stockholder.

> Jungkuntz v. West Lib. Assn., 6 W. L. B. 428 (1881).

Enforcement of liability of stockholders in foreign corporations. Where the liability is contractual, and not penal, it may be enforced in Ohio.

> Kulp v. Fleming, 65 O. S. 321 (1902).
> Blair v. Newbegin, 65 O. S. 425 (1902).
> See Wyatt v. Moorehead, 4 N. P. 435; 7 L. D. 380 (1897).
> Judson v. Stewart, 7 N. P. 160 (1897).

Where the liability of stockholders of a foreign corporation is enforced in Ohio, the procedure followed is that of Ohio, and, although by the law of the home state of such corporation stockholders must be sued separately, they may in Ohio be joined in one action.

> Blair v. Newbegin, 65 O. S. 425 (1901).

Contribution between stockholders. Stockholders may require that all solvent resident stockholders be made defendants.

Harpold v. Stobart, 46 O. S. 397, 404 (1889).
Wheeler v. Faurot, 37 O. S. 26, 29 (1881).
Umsted v. Buskirk, 17 O. S. 113 (1866).
But stockholders do not bear the relation of sureties to each other.
One stockholder, having voluntarily paid the corporate debts, can not
recover contribution from other stockholders who were solvent and resident.
Burr v. Bates, 3 C. C. 1, 6; 2 C. D. 1 (1887).
See Wehrman v. Reakirt, 1 C. S. C. R. 230, 234 (1871).

Liability attaches when. The liability attaches at the time the debt
or liability is incurred.
Herrick v. Wardwell, 58 O. S. 294 (1898).
Harpold v. Stobart, 46 O. S. 397, 404 (1889).
Brown v. Hitchcock, 36 O. S. 667, 678 (1881).
Cleveland Gas Co. v. Collins, 19 C. C. 247 (1899).

Bond against liability. For rights under bond given by purchaser
of property, from stockholder, to protect stockholder against liability, see
Hatry v. Painesville, etc., Co., 1 C. C. 426; 1 C. D. 238 (1886);
aff'd, 32 W. L. B. 281.

DEFENSES OF STOCKHOLDERS.

Waiver of liability by creditors. Whether the statutory liability
may be waived by creditors, as by an express stipulation in a corporate
mortgage, has been differently decided.
Waiver held invalid.
Kreisser v. Ashtabula, etc., Co., 2 C. C. n. s. 597; 14 C. D. 313 (1901).
Held valid.
Hull v. Standard, etc., Co., 20 C. C. 533 (1900).
Hardman v. Cincinnati, etc., Co., 18 W. L. B. 264 (C. P. Referee
1887).
See Preston v. Cincinnati, etc., Co., 36 Fed. 54; 6 O. F. D. 127 (1888).
Raymond v. Spring Grove, etc., Co., 21 W. L. B. 103 (Super. Ct.
Cin. 1889).

Discharge in bankruptcy. A discharge in bankruptcy of the stockholder is no defense unless the claims of the plaintiff and other creditors
were scheduled in the bankruptcy proceeding, or they had notice or knowledge of the proceeding.
Roebling, etc., Co. v. Shawnee, etc., Co., 4 N. P. n. s. 113; 17 L. D. 8
(C. P. 1906); aff'd, 78 O. S. 408.

That corporation is not insolvent. A stockholder may deny insolvency of the corporation.
Murphy v. Alma, etc., Co., 5 O. L. R. 508 (C. P. 1907).

Settlement. Where the stockholders settled with all but one creditor,
at a discount, the one dissenting creditor can not thereafter recover more
than he would have recovered had the suit been prosecuted to a final
decree and the proceeds distributed pro rata.
Ryan v. Miami, etc., R. Co., 16 C. C. 530; 9 C. D. 401 (1898).
Where solvent stockholders agreed to severally contribute to raise a
fund to pay the corporate debts, one stockholder agreeing to surrender
and cancel a note of the corporation, the other stockholders having paid
their share may set up such agreement in defense to an action on such
note.
Sterling Wrench Co. v. Amstutz, 50 O. S. 484 (1893).
Note given to one creditor under an agreement that it shall be credited
on statutory liability. Agreement construed.
Beebe v. Thomas, 2 W. L. B. 107 (Super. Ct. Cin. 1877).

Objections to claims of creditors. Where the claim of a creditor is not in judgment, stockholders may interpose only such defenses thereto as the corporation might have pleaded.

Railroad Co. v. Smith, 48 O. S. 219 (1891).

Where the claim has been reduced to judgment it is conclusive on the stockholders, although rendered by default.

Gaw v. Glassboro, etc., Co., 20 C. C. 416 (1900).

Scofield v. Excelsior Oil Co., 6 C. C. n. s. 176; 17 C. D. 318 (1905); aff'd, 74 O. S. 513.

That the creditor has settled his claim against the corporation, or filed his claim and asserted a lien in another case is no defense, where it is not alleged that the claim has been paid.

Hardman v. Cincinnati, etc., Ry. Co., 15 W. L. B. 164 (1886).

Set off. A stockholder can not set off against his liability an indebtedness of the corporation to him.

Hardman v. Cincinnati, etc., Co., 15 W. L. B. 164 (1886).

Marriott v. Railway, 16 L. D. 135; s. c., 10 C. C. n. s. 573; 20 C. D. 419.

Painesville N. B. v. King Varnish Co., 8 C. C. 563; 4 C. D. 54 (1894); reversed, in part, 56 O. S. 744.

But see Niles v. Olszak, 87 O. S. 229 (1912).

Except to the extent of his dividend or distributive share from the fund realized for creditors.

King v. Armstrong, 50 O. S. 222 (1893).

Barber v. Leader, etc., Co., 7 C. C. 411; 4 C. D. 658 (1893).

Marriott v. Railway, 16 L. D. 135; s. c., 10 C. C. n. s. 573; 20 C. D. 419.

But a stockholder may in one pleading allege a proper defense, and also set up his claim against the corporation.

Murphy v. Alma, etc., Co., 5 O. L. R. 508 (C. P. 1907).

Insolvency of a stockholder is not a defense available to him.

Marriott v. Railway, 16 L. D. 135 (C. P. 1905); aff'd, 10 C. C. n. s. 573, 575.

That no certificate of stock has been issued is no defense.

Royce v. Tyler, 2 C. C. 175; 1 C. D. 428 (1887).

Kreisser v. Ashtabula, etc., Co., 2 C. C. n. s. 597, 601; 14 C. D. 313 (1910).

Section 8687. (**Corporations created subsequent to November 23, 1903.**) The next preceding section shall not apply to stockholders in a corporation created after the twenty-third of November, 1903, nor to debts or liabilities of a corporation incurred after such date. As to all debts and liabilities of corporations for profit incurred after such date, the stockholders thereof shall be under no liabilities other than those stated in article XIII, section three, of the constitution of Ohio. (R. S. Sec. 3258; April 25, 1904; 97 v. 390; April 29, 1902, 95 v. 312; May 1, 1852, 50 v. 296, §§ 78-79; March 11, 1853, 51 v. 386; April 17, 1854, 52 v. 44; April 12, 1865, 62 v. 134; March 11, 1874, 69 v. 25; R. S. 1880; S. & C. 310.)

Bank stockholders are subject to double liability. See Constitution, Art. XIII, Sec. 3, as amended in 1912, in effect, January 1, 1913.

The amendment of Sec. 3, Art. XIII of 1903 of the constitution is self executing. Stockholders are not subject to double liability for debts incurred by the corporation after November 23, 1903.

Sheets Mfg. Co. v. Neer Mfg. Co., 4 N. P. n. s. 201; 17 L. D. 119 (C. P. 1906).

See Little v. Aultman, etc., Co., 15 L. D. 355 (C. P. 1905).

Middletown N. B. v. Railway Co., 197 U. S. 394 (1905).

Barnes v. Wheaton, 80 Hun (N. Y.) 8 (1894).

But the amendment does not affect stockholders' liability for debts incurred prior to that date.

Poston v. Hull, 75 O. S. 502, 508 (1907).

Little v. Aultman, etc., Co., 15 L. D. 355 (1905).

Irvine v. Elliott, 203 Fed. 82, 93 (D. C. 1913).

Where a note was given after the amendment of the constitution in 1903, for an indebtedness incurred prior to the amendment, the liability of stockholders depends upon whether the note was accepted as payment of the original obligation.

First N. B. v. Patton Co., 13 C. C. n. s. 289 (1910).

See Boice v. Hodge, 51 O. S. 236 (1894).

Hauenschild v. Standard, etc., Co., 8 N. P. 124 (Super. Ct. Cin.).

Wheeler v. Faurot, 37 O. S. 26 (1881).

Section 8688. (Limitation of action to enforce liability.) An action upon the liability of stockholders under the two next preceding sections can only be brought within eighteen months after the debt or obligation shall become enforcible against stockholders. (R. S. Sec. 3258a; April 25, 1904, 97 v. 390; April 29, 1902, 95 v. 313.)

When right of action accrues. A right of action accrues when a judgment has been recovered against the corporation and an execution rendered unsatisfied in whole or in part.

Or where the corporation has done, or suffered, any act which renders judgment and process nugatory, as where it has made an assignment for creditors, or been adjudged a bankrupt, or, by the appointment of a receiver, or otherwise, its property has been put in process of application to the payment of its debts.

Younglove v. Lime Co., 49 O. S. 663 (1892).

Bronson v. Schneider, 49 O. S. 438 (1892).

Barrick v. Gifford, 47 O. S. 180 (1890).

King v. Armstrong, 50 O. S. 222, 238 (1893).

Peter v. Farrell, etc., Co., 53 O. S. 534, 557 (1895).

Morgan v. Lewis, 46 O. S. 1 (1888).

Creditors need not wait for final distribution or settlement by the assignee, etc., before commencing action.

Younglove v. Lime Co., 49 O. S. 663.

But a right of action does not accrue on the appointment of a receiver, not because of insolvency, but to carry on the business, or to subserve some other purpose of the directors or stockholders.

Nor does a right of action accrue on the mere insolvency of the corporation in the sense that its debts exceed its assets.

Younglove v. Lime Co., 49 O. S. 663 (1892).

Bronson v. Schneider, 49 O. S. 438 (1892).

Barrick v. Gilford, 47 O. S. 180 (1890).

Statute of limitations. Where a corporation, because of insolvency, was placed in the hands of a receiver on a certain date, the statute of limitations begins to run from such date.

Marriott v. Columbus, etc., R. Co., 2 N. P. n. s. 231; 15 L. D. 100
(C. P. 1904); s. c., 16 L. D. 135; aff'd, 10 C. C. n. s. 573, 575.
Roebling Sons Co. v. Shawnee, etc., Co., 4 N. P. n. s. 113; 17 L. D.
8 (C. P. 1906); aff'd, 78 O. S. 408.
Irvine v. Blackburn, 198 Fed. 360 (D. C. 1912).
The statute does not begin to run against a creditor until his claim
is due.
Hardman v. Cincinnati. etc., Ry. Co., 15 W. L. B. 164, 165 (C. P.
1886).
Harris v. Railway Co., 4 N. P. n. s. 31; 16 L. D. 653 (Super. Ct.
Cin. 1906).
Where a claim is disputed, the statute does not run until it is liqui-
dated as to amount.
Hardman v. Cincinnati, etc., Ry. Co., 15 W. L. B. 164, 165 (C. P.
1886).
A suit by one creditor on behalf of all creditors saves the running
of the statute as against all creditors who assert their claims in the suit
before its final determination.
Barrick v. Gifford, 47 O. S. 180 (1890).
Each creditor's claim is distinct, and a bar to one is no bar to others.
Hardman v. Cincinnati, etc., Ry. Co., 15 W. L. B. 164 (C. P. 1886).
Where creditors negligently fail to bring in resident, solvent stock-
holders, as defendants, until the statute has run against them, the other
stockholders' assessments can not be increased because of such neglect.
Smith v. Newark, etc., Co., 8 C. C. 583; 4 C. D. 356 (1894).
A stipulation in a contract with the corporation, limiting the time
for bringing suit thereon, does not apply to the statutory liability of its
stockholders.
. Davis v. Stewart, 26 O. S. 643 (1875).
Stewart v. Triumph Ins. Co., 1 W. L. B. 103 (1876).

Limitation of action against estate of deceased stockholder.

See Roeblings Sons Co. v. Shawnee, etc., Co., 4 N. P. n. s. 113; 17
L. D. 8 (C. P. 1906); aff'd, 78 O. S. 408.
Bevitt v. Diehl, 12 L. D. 383, 315 (1901).

Limitation of actions against nonresidents. The limitation does not
begin to run against an action brought in another jurisdiction against a
nonresident stockholder, until a decree is entered making an assessment
and appointing a receiver for its collection.
Irvine v. Putnam, 167 Fed. 174 (C. C. 1909).
Irvine v. Putnam, 190 Fed. 321 (C. C. 1911).
Irvine v. Bankard, 181 Fed. 206 (C. C. 1910); aff'd, no rep., 184
Fed. 986.
Goss v. Carter, 156 Fed. 746 (C. C. A. 1907).
Where an appeal is taken from the decree, the running of the stat-
ute is suspended during its pendency, even though the appeal is taken by
creditors.
Irvine v. Bankard, 181 Fed. 206 (C. C. 1910); aff'd, no rep., 184
Fed. 986.
A receiver is not estopped from asserting that the pendency of an
appeal from the decree suspended the running of the limitation because
during such pendency he settled and received payment of claims against
other stockholders.
Irvine v. Bankard, 181 Fed. 206 (1910).

Section 8689.   ("Stockholder" defined.) The term
"stockholder" as used in the three next preceding sections,

shall apply not only to persons who appear by the books of the corporation to be such, but also to an equitable owner of stock, although on the books it appears in the name of another. (R. S. Sec. 3259; R. S. 1880.)

This section should be construed in connection with §§ 8672 and 8673.

State B. & T. Co. v. Mitchell Co., 14 N. P. n. s. 49, 57 (1913).

What stockholders are liable.

Generally. The following have been held liable—Stockholders in de facto corporations.

Rowland v. Meader Furn. Co., 38 O. S. 269 (1882).
Gaff v. Flesher, 33 O. S. 107 (1877).
Royce v. Tyler, 2 C. C. 175, 182; 1 C. D. 428 (1887).

Corporation holding stock.

Smith v. Newark, etc., R. Co., 8 C. C. 583; 4 C. D. 356 (1894).
Marriott v. Columbus, etc., Co., 16 L. D. 135 (C. P. 1905); aff'd, 10 C. C. n. s. 573, 575.

Infant holding stock after becoming of age.

Hardman v. Cincinnati, 15 W. L. B. 164 (1886).

Preferred stockholders.

R. R. Co. v. Smith, 48 O. S. 219 (1891).

Holders of stock distributed as a stock dividend.

Aultman's Appeal, 98 Pa. St. 505 (1881).

Transferrer and Transferee.

See § 8686.

Equitable owner. The purpose of § 8689 is to give creditors a cumulative remedy and, where the legal owner is insolvent, to permit them to pursue the equitable owner.

Holcomb v. Gibson, 39 W. L. B. 380 (1898).

Under § 8689 the legal and equitable owners may be treated as co-owners.

Biggio v. Sandheger, 3 O. L. R. 470; 16 L. D. 285 (1905); s. c., 8 N. P. 13 (1900).

Where a person transfers his stock for the purpose of divesting himself of apparent ownership to escape possible liability, but really remains the beneficial owner, he is liable.

Peter v. Union Mfg. Co., 56 O. S. 181, 208 (1897).

An action may be brought against both the legal and the equitable owner and a judgment rendered against both.

Irvine v. Blackburn, 198 Fed. 360 (D. C. 1912).

Trustee. The person in whose name the stock is registered on the books of the corporation is liable. It is no defense that he is a trustee only, although he is entitled to be reimbursed by the beneficiary.

Holcomb v. Gibson, 39 W. L. B. 380 (1898).
Schwill v. Beckel, 1 N. P. n. s. 1, 104; 13 L. D. 699 (Super. Ct. Cin. 1903).
Marriott v. Columbus, etc., Co., 16 L. D. 135 (C. P. 1905); s. c., 10 C. C. n. s. 573; 20 C. D. 419.
Stewart v. Triumph Ins. Co., 1 W. L. B. 103 (1876).

But in one case where the stock books of the corporation disclosed the trust capacity in which the stock was held, the trustee was held not liable.

Biggio v. Sandheger, 8 N. P. 13 (Super. Ct. Cin. 1900); compare s. c., 3 O. L. R. 470; 16 L. D. 285 (1905).

Pledgee. A pledgee who does not have the stock transferred to his name on the corporate books is not liable.

Henkel v. Salem Mfg. Co., 39 O. S. 547 (1883).

But where it is so transferred the pledgee is liable, although as against the pledgor he is entitled to reimbursement.

Biggio v. Sandheger, 3 O. L. R. 470; 16 L. D. 285 (Super. Ct. Cin. 1905); see s. c., 8 N. P. 13.

Where a judgment is rendered against both the pledgor and pledgee it is a judgment against co-owners. A compromise by the receiver with the pledgor does not release the pledgee.

Biggio v. Sandheger, 3 O. L. R. 470; 16 L. D. 285 (Super. Ct. Cin. 1905).

A pledgee of stock in a national bank becomes liable as a stockholder, under the national banking act, where he has the stock registered in the name of his employee, with no beneficial interest, and afterwards indorses on the note the supposed value of the stock as a credit, and presents the note, reduced by the credit, to the administrator who allows the claim in such form.

Ohio Valley N. B. v. Hulitt, 204 U. S. 162; 15 O. F. D. 530 (1907); affirming 137 Fed. 461.

Legatee of stock. A person to whom stock is bequeathed by will, but the stock is not transferred on the corporate books and there is no evidence of acceptance of the bequest, is not liable. The estate of the testator is liable.

Roeblings Sons Co. v. Shawnee, etc., Co., 4 N. P. n. s. 113; 17 L. D. 8 (C. P. 1906); aff'd, 78 O. S. 408.

De Camp v. Levoy, 19 C. C. 335 (1900).

But where the legatee causes the stock to be transferred he becomes liable.

Biggio v. Sandheger, 8 N. P. 13 (Super. Ct. Cin. 1900).

Estate of deceased stockholder. The estate of a deceased stockholder is liable. In such case it is not necessary to present the claim to the administrator before suit.

Roeblings Sons Co. v. Shawnee, etc., Co., 4 N. P. n. s. 113; 17 L. D. 8; aff'd, 78 O. S. 408.

Hall v. Standard Coal Co., 7 N. P. 157 (1897).

Wanz v. Park Hotel Co., 1 C. C. 105; 1 C. D. 63 (1885).

A demurrer will lie to an answer of an executor, alleging that he has settled up the estate, but not setting up the statute of limitations.

Umstaetter v. Newark, etc., Co., 4 N. P. n. s. 150; 17 L. D. 30 (C. P. 1906).

Broker. A stock broker who purchases stock for another, on a stock exchange, and delivers the certificate to his principal, is not a "stockholder" either legal or equitable under § 8689, although he paid therefor with his own check and did not disclose the name of his principal, and although the transfer was never made on the corporate books.

Joecken v. Cuyahoga, etc., Co., 1 C. C. n. s. 342; 14 C. D. 605 (1903); affirming 13 L. D. 652.

Stockholder or creditor. See note to § 8669. *Issues of stock construed; preferred stock or debt.*

Section 8690. (Where complaint for enforcement of liability filed.)
When a creditor of a corporation seeks to charge its directors, trustees, or other superintending officers, or the stockholders thereof, on account of a liability created

by law, he may file his complaint for that purpose in any common pleas court which possesses jurisdiction to enforce such liability. (R. S. Sec. 3260; April 16, 1900, 94 v. 359; 91 v. 88; R. S. 1880.)

Nature of action. The action is equitable. The liabilities and equities of the parties as between themselves may be marshalled and adjusted in the final judgment.

Younglove v. Lime Co., 49 O. S. 663, 667 (1892).
R. R. Co. v. Smith, 48 O. S. 219 (1891).
Bullock v. Kilgour, 39 O. S. 543, 546 (1883).
Wheeler v. Faurot, 37 O. S. 26, 29 (1881).
Brown v. Hitchcock, 36 O. S. 667, 681 (1881).

It is for the benefit of all creditors. One creditor can not acquire priority.

Wright v. McCormack, 17 O. S. 86 (1866).
Umsted v. Buskirk, 17 O. S. 113 (1866).

Venue of action. Summons to other counties. The action may be brought in any county in which any defendant may be sued and served. Summons may be issued to other counties for other defendants, including the corporation.

Blair v. Newbegin, 65 O. S. 425 (1901).
Swan v. Railroad Co., 4 L. D. 71 (1895).
Hull v. Standard Coal Co., 7 N. P. 157 (1897).
See Reece v. West, etc., Co., 12 C. D. 728.

The action can not be brought in a county where a defendant does not reside and may not be summoned.

Lamont v. Home Ins. Co., 10 W. L. B. 413 (1883).

Except by consent of the parties. Such consent may be evidenced by answer and trial on the merits without objection. Objection can not be made, for the first time, on appeal.

Reece v. West, etc., Co., 12 C. D. 728.
Mason v. Alexander, 44 O. S. 318 (1886).

Parties, joinder of actions, pleading, practice, etc.

See Bates Pleading, vol. 2, p. 1364 et seq.

Consolidation of actions.

See Newberry v. Alexander, 44 O. S. 346 (1886).
Schaus v. Newark, etc., Co., 5 O. L. R. 388 (1907).

Actions in other jurisdictions.

This section contemplates an action in Ohio courts alone. An original action can not be brought in another jurisdiction for the enforcement of liability generally.

Middletown N. B. v. Railway, 197 U. S. 394 (1905).

Actions in other jurisdictions against nonresident stockholders, by receiver, see §§ 8693, 8695 and notes.

Section 8691. (Procedure by court; receiver.) The court shall proceed thereon, as in other cases, and, when necessary, cause an account to be taken of the property and obligations due to and from such corporation, and may appoint one or more receivers. (R. S. Sec. 3260a; April 16, 1900, 94 v. 360.)

Sections 8691 to 8697 inclusive were enacted to provide an efficient remedy for the enforcement of the liability against nonresident stock-holders.

Irvine v. Elliott, 203 Fed. 82 (D. C. 1913).

Section 8692. (**Enforcement of liability.**) On the filing of an answer, or the taking of such account, if it appears that such corporation is insolvent, and has not sufficient property or effects to satisfy such creditor, the court may proceed to ascertain the respective liabilities of the directors, officers and stockholders, and enforce them by its judgment, as in other cases. (R. S. Sec. 3260b; April 16, 1900, 94 v. 360.)

Practice as to creditors. The names of the creditors and the amount due to each from the corporation are usually ascertained by a reference to a master or referee, notice being published by order of the court for creditors to present their claims (§ 8696). In case of a contested claim, an issue should be ordered to be made up and tried to ascertain and fix the amount due to the creditor from the corporation. While the issue and trial as to such contested claim is a proceeding in the case, it is distinct from the proceedings against the stockholders, the one being to establish the validity of a creditor's claim against the company, and the other to collect a fund from the stockholders for the common benefit of all the creditors.

Herrick v. Wardwell, 58 O. S. 294, 307 (1898).

Burden of proof as to stockholders is on the plaintiff.

Henkle v. Salem Mfg. Co., 39 O. S. 547, 552 (1883).

Judgment. There can be but one final judgment assessing the liability.

Bullock v. Kilgour, 39 O. S. 543 (1883).

Marriott v. Railway, 16 L. D. 135; s. c., 10 C. C. n. s. 573; 20 C. D. 419.

But the court may enter an interlocutory judgment as to a part of the issues, and reserve other issues for future determination, all to be included in the final judgment.

Mason v. Alexander, 44 O. S. 318 (1886).

Marriott v. Railroad Co., 8 C. C. n. s. 495 (1906); s. c., 10 C. C. n. s. 573 (1907).

Younglove v. Lime Co., 49 O. S. 663, 667 (1892).

A final judgment is a bar to other actions against the stockholders who were parties.

Bullock v. Kilgour, 39 O. S. 543 (1883).

Herrick v. Wardwell, 58 O. S. 294, 306 (1898.)

Swan v. Mansfield, etc., Co., 3 N. P. 225; 5 L. D. 297.

See Hamilton v. Home Ins. Co., 1 N. P. 329; 3 L. D. 389 (1895).

B. & O. R. Co. v. Smith, 54 O. S. 562 (1896).

Smith v. Newark, etc., R. Co., 8 C. C. 583; 4 C. D. 356 (1894).

Judgment may be rendered against the stockholders before the court for their pro rata share of the indebtedness, taking into account the liability of all solvent stockholders.

Burr v. Bates, 3 C. C. 1, 4; 2 C. D. 1 (1887).

Marriott v. Railway, 16 L. D. 135; s. c., 10 C. C. n. s. 573; 20 C. D. 419.

The equities as between the parties may be adjusted and included in the judgment.

See R. R. Co. v. Smith, 48 O. S. 219 (1891).

Bullock v. Kilgour, 39 O. S. 543, 546 (1883).
Biggio v. Sandheger, 3 O. L. R. 470; 16 L. D. 285 (1905); s. c., 8 N. P. 13.

Interest from the beginning of the suit may be included in the judgment, although it exceeds the liability, when it is apparent at the beginning of the suit that stockholders must be assessed to the full amount of their liability.

Mason v. Alexander, 44 O. S. 318 (1886).
Taylor v. West, etc., Co., 9 Am. L. R. 28 (1880).
Wehrman v. Reakirt, 1 C. S. C. R. 230 (1871).

But if the amount is not so apparent, interest should be charged only from the confirmation of the referee's report.

Berger v. Commercial Bank, 5 N. P. 176; 5 L. D. 277.

Appeal. Where a transferrer and transferee of stock are both parties, and an issue is between the two, an appeal by one carries up the case as to the other.

Harpold v. Stobart, 46 O. S. 397 (1889).

An order of the common pleas court which determines the liability of some but not all of the defendant stockholders is interlocutory and not appealable.

Marriott v. Railroad Co., 8 C. C. n. s. 495 (1906); affirmed, no rep., 76 O. S. 599, 605, 609; s. c., 10 C. C. n. s. 573 (1907).

Section 8693.　(Notice to non-resident stockholders.)
When the directors or other officers of a corporation, or the stockholders thereof, are made parties to an action in which a judgment is rendered, if its property is insufficient to discharge its debts, the court shall give notice to non-resident stockholders as provided by law for service upon non-resident defendants in other actions, and then first proceed to compel each stockholder to pay in the amount due and unpaid on the stock held by him, or so much thereof as is necessary to satisfy the debts of the company. (R. S. Sec. 3260c; April 16, 1900, 94 v. 360.)

A proceeding under § 8690 et seq. is a proceeding in which service by publication is sufficient.

Shipman v. Treadwell, 200 N. Y. 472; 93 N. E. 1104 (1911).
Irvine v. Elliott, 203 Fed. 82, 101-102 (D. C. 1913).

Where the stockholders were not all before the court, and it did not appear that those not served with process could not have been served, it was held error to assess the entire corporate indebtedness upon the stockholders served.

Bonevitz v. Van Wert County Bank, 41 O. S. 78 (1884).

Nonresident stockholders. Nonresident stockholders are represented by the corporation, in the proceeding, and are bound by the finding and decree therein, although not served with process.

Irvine v. Putnam, 167 Fed. 174 (1909).
Francis v. Hazlett, 192 Mass. 137, 142 (1906).
Childs v. Cleaves, 95 Me. 498; 50 Atl. 114 (1901).

The decree ordering the assessment, while not binding them as a judgment or decree in personam after personal service, yet is conclusive as to the amount of the indebtedness of the corporation, and the necessity of making an assessment to the extent and in the amount specified.

Irvine v. Elliott, 203 Fed. 82, 102 (D. C. 1913).
Irvine v. Blackburn, 198 Fed. 360 (D. C. 1912).

Attachment against nonresident stockholders. An action to enforce statutory liability is upon a demand arising upon contract, and attachment will lie against nonresident stockholders.
Dabney v. Pappenheimer Co., 20 C. C. 707; 41 W. L. B. 329 (1888).
Cleveland Gas Company v. Collins, 19 C. C. 247 (1899).
Northern N. B. v. Maumee, etc., Co., 2 N. P. 260; 2 L. D. 67 (C. P. 1894).

Actions against nonresidents in other jurisdictions.

See § 8695.

Application of assets to reduce or reimburse liability.

See Morris v. Collamer, 2 Cleve. L. R. 347 (1878).
Younglove v. Lime Co., 49 O. S. 663 (1892).
Turnbull v. Pomeroy Salt Co., 24 W. L. B. 133 (1890).
Cowles v. Bartell, 3 W. L. M. 41 (1860).
Taylor v. West Liberty Wheel Co., 9 Am. L. R. 28 (1880).
An action to enforce stockholders' liability is not demurrable because brought prior to ascertainment, by the receiver, of the corporate assets.
Umsteatter v. Newark, etc., Co., 4 N. P. n. s. 150; 17 L. D. 30 (C. P. 1906).

Section 8694. (Court to ascertain and adjudge liabilities.) If its debts remain unsatisfied, the court shall proceed to ascertain the respective liabilities of the directors or other officers and of the stockholders, and to adjudge the amount payable by each, and enforce the judgment, as in other cases. (R. S. 3260d; April 16, 1900, 94 v. 360.)

No action can be maintained against nonresident stockholders in other jurisdictions until a proceeding has been brought in Ohio under § 8690 et seq. and a finding made under this section.
Middletown N. B. v. Railway Co., 197 U. S. 394 (1905).
Bank v. Sayward, 91 Fed. 443 (C. C. A. 1899).
Nimick v. Iron Works, 25 W. Va. 184 (1884).
Clark v. Knowles, 187 Mass. 35 (1904).
Rice v. Hoisery Co., 56 N. H. 114 (1875).
Barnes v. Wheaton, 80 Hun 8 (N. Y. 1894).
Cleveland, etc., Ry. v. Kent, 87 Hun 329 (N. Y. 1895).

Section 8695. (Actions by receiver.) If a receiver is appointed, the court also may authorize and direct him to prosecute such actions in his own name as receiver, in other jurisdictions as become necessary to collect the amount found due from an officer or stockholder. (R. S. Sec. 3260d; April 16, 1900, 94 v. 360.)

A receiver, directed to prosecute actions under this section, is in the position of a quasi assignee representing all of the creditors, and may maintain an action in a federal court in another state, and his own citizenship, not that of the creditors, affords the test of jurisdiction.
Irvine v. Bankard, 181 Fed. 206 (C. C. 1910); aff'd, no rep., 184 Fed. 986.

Irvine v. Putnam, 190 Fed. 321 (C. C. 1911).
Bernheimer v. Converse, 206 U. S. 516 (1907).
Converse v. Hamilton, 224 U. S. 243 (1912).
Irvine v. Elliott, 203 Fed. 82 (D. C. 1913).

A nonresident stockholder is bound by the constitution and laws of the state, under which the corporation is organized, and an assessment on stockholders, properly made by a court in the home state of such corporation, may be enforced by the receiver of the corporation in the courts of other states.

Appeal of Aultman, 98 Pa. St. 505 (1881).
Cushing v. Perot, 175 Pa. St. 66 (1896).
Howorth v. Lombard, 175 Mass. 570; 49 L. R. A. 301 (1900).
Bank v. Baker, 176 Mass. 294 (1900).
Post v. Toledo, etc., Railroad, 144 Mass. 341 (1887).
Childs v. Cleaves, 95 Me. 498; 50 Atl. 714 (1901).
Howorth v. Angle, 162 N. Y. 179; 47 L. R. A. 725.
Shipman v. Treadwell, 200 N. Y. 472; 93 N. E. 1104 (1911).

Nonresident stockholders are represented by the corporation in the proceeding under § 8690 et seq., and are bound by the finding and decree therein although not served with process.

Irvine v. Putnam, 167 Fed. 174 (1909).
Spargo v. Converse, 191 Fed. 823 (C. C. A. 1911).
Francis v. Hazlett, 192 Mass. 137, 142 (1906).
Childs v. Cleaves, 95 Me. 498; 50 Atl. 714 (1901).

Suit against a nonresident can not be founded on the finding and order of assessment as on a personal judgment, where the nonresident was not served with process in the proceeding under § 8690 et seq.

Shipman v. Willard, 194 Fed. 575 (1912).

But the decree is conclusive as to the amount of the indebtedness of the corporation and the necessity of making an assessment to the extent and in the amount specified.

Irvine v. Elliott, 203 Fed. 82, 102 (D. C. 1913).
Irvine v. Blackburn, 198 Fed. 360 (D. C. 1912).

An action against nonresident stockholders can not be brought in other states or federal courts until a proceeding has been brought in Ohio under § 8690 et seq.

Middletown N. B. v. Ry. Co., 197 U. S. 394 (1905).
Bank v. Sayward, 91 Fed. 443 (C. C. A. 1899).
Nimick v. Iron Works, 25 W. Va. 184 (1884).
Clark v. Knowles, 187 Mass. 35 (1904).
Rice v. Hoisery Co., 56 N. H. 114 (1875).
Barnes v. Wheaton, 80 Hun 8 (N. Y. 1894).
Cleve., etc., Ry. v. Kent, 87 Hun 329 (N. Y. 1895).

Limitation of actions against nonresidents. The limitation does not begin to run against an action brought in another jurisdiction against a nonresident stockholder, until a decree is entered making an assessment and appointing a receiver for its collection.

Irvine v. Putnam, 167 Fed. 174 (C. C. 1909).
Irvine v. Putnam, 190 Fed. 321 (C. C. 1911).
Irvine v. Bankard, 181 Fed. 206 (C. C. 1910); aff'd, no rep., 184 Fed. 986.
Goss v. Carter, 156 Fed. 746 (C. C. A. 1907).
Irvine v. Elliott, 203 Fed. 82, 108-110 (D. C. 1913).
Irvine v. Blackburn, 198 Fed. 360 (D. C. 1912).

Where an appeal is taken from the decree, the running of the statute is suspended during its pendency, even though the appeal is taken by creditors.

Irvine v. Bankard, 181 Fed. 206 (C. C. 1910); aff'd, no rep., 184 Fed. 986.

A receiver is not estopped from asserting that the pendency of an appeal from the decree suspended the running of the limitation because during such pendency he settled and received payment of claims against other stockholders.

Irvine v. Bankard, 181 Fed. 206 (1910).

Section 8696. (Notice to creditors.) If an action is brought against a corporation, its directors or other superintending officers, or stockholders, according to the foregoing provisions, when it appears proper, the court may order notice to be published, in such manner as it directs, requiring all the creditors of such corporation to exhibit their claims and become parties to the action, within a reasonable time, not less than six months from the first 'publication of such order, and, in default thereof, to be precluded from any benefit of the judgment rendered therein, and from any distribution made under such judgment. (R. S. Sec. 3260e; April 16, 1900, 94 v. 360.)

This section does not deprive the court of discretionary power to permit creditors to present claims after expiration of the time specified in the order, if no prejudice results.

Marriott v. Railway Co., 16 L. D. 135 (C. P. 1905).

One creditor may object to the allowance of improper claims of other creditors.

Hardman v. Cincinnati, etc., Co., 15 W. L. B. 164 (1887).

Right of creditors to reinstate action dismissed by plaintiff. An action to enforce statutory liability is for the benefit of all creditors, and where such action is dismissed by the plaintiff, other creditors may have the same reinstated.

Johnson v. Carpenter, 21 C. C. 168; 11 C. D. 457 (1900); aff'd, 66 O. S. 638.

See Dreidame v. Germania Inv. Co., 8 N. P. 405 (1901).

Section 8697. (Distribution of assets.) Upon a final judgment in such an action against an insolvent corporation, the court shall cause a just distribution of its property and assets, or the proceeds thereof, to be made among its creditors. (R. S. Sec. 3260f; April 16, 1900, 94 v. 360.)

Attorney's fees. The court may award a reasonable attorney's fee, out of the fund realized, to the plaintiff's attorney, although some creditors have employed other attorneys.

Mason v. Alexander, 44 O. S. 318, 337 (1886).

Hessler v. Cleveland, etc., Co., 61 O. S. 620 (1899).

But such attorney's fee can not be taxed as a part of the costs.

Rider v. Fritchey, 49 O. S. 285, 296 (1892).

Marriott v. Railway, 16 L. D. 135 (C. P. 1905); s. c., 10 C. C. n. s. 573; 20 C. D. 419.

Equitable setoff. Where an insolvent stockholder is also a creditor, his distributive share, as a creditor, may be set off against his liability.

King v. Armstrong, 50 O. S. 222 (1893).
Barber v. Leader, etc., Co., 7 C. C. 411; 4 C. D. 658 (1893).
Niles v. Olszak, 87 O. S. 229 (1912).
Kiskadden v. Steinle, 203 Fed. 375 (C. C. A. 1913).

Application of proceeds. A creditor having both a secured and an unsecured claim can not apply his dividend on the unsecured claim. It should be applied pro rata.
Nat. Bank v. Carn, 13 C. D. 447, 457; 3 C. C. n. s. 428, 439 (1902).

CHANGES IN CAPITAL STOCK.

Section 8698. (Increase of capital stock.) After its original capital stock is fully subscribed for, and an installment of ten per cent on each share of stock has been paid thereon, a corporation for profit, or a corporation not for profit, having a capital stock, may increase its capital stock or the number of shares into which it is divided, prior to organization, by the unanimous written consent of all original subscribers. After organization the increase may be made by a vote of the holders of a majority of its stock, at a meeting called by a majority of its directors, at least thirty days' notice of the time, place and object of which has been given by publication in some newspaper of general circulation, and by letter addressed to each stockholder whose place of residence is known. Or, the stock may be increased at a meeting of the stockholders at which all are present in person, or by proxy, and waive in writing such notice by publication and letter; and also agree in writing to such increase, naming the amount thereof to which they agree. A certificate of such action shall be filed with the secretary of state. (R. S. Sec. 3262; March 11, 1872, 69 v. 24; February 18, 1873, 70 v. 37; R. S. 1880; February 16, 1883, 80 v. 23; May 11, 1886, 83 v. 134; April 5, 1893, 90 v. 141.)

The notice need not be published for thirty consecutive days. One notice, published at least thirty days before the day set, is sufficient.
Muskingum, etc., Co. v. Ward, 13 Ohio 120 (1844).
Craig v. Fox, 16 Ohio 563, 566 (1847).
Newport News v. Potter, 122 Fed. 321, 332 (C. C. A. 1903).
It is said that the par value of shares can not be increased under this section.
Rep. Atty. Gen. 1911-1912, p. 99.

Right of stockholders to take new stock. Each stockholder is entitled to subscribe for and take new stock in proportion to his holdings of the old stock.
State v. Franklin Bank, 10 Ohio 91 (1840).
See 7 O. L. R. 345, article by Frank M. Coppock.
But this right may be waived by a stockholder. Where a stockholder fails to subscribe within a reasonable time, after opportunity is given him, he is deemed to have waived his right and the directors may dispose of the stock to others.

Hall v. Hall, 11 C. C. n. s. 335; 20 C. D. 826 (1908); aff'd, 79 O. S. 456.

7 O. L. R. 369 *ib.*

The right to take new stock may be sold by a stockholder.

See 7 O. L. R. 373 *ib.*

State v. Franklin Bank, 10 Ohio 91 (1840).

It is doubtful whether existing stockholders can be required to pay more than par for the new stock.

See 7 O. L. R. 365 *ib.*

But new stock, not taken by existing stockholders, may be sold to the public at a premium.

See State v. Franklin Bank, 10 Ohio 91, 99, 100 (1840).

Subscriptions to increased stock. Rights and liabilities of subscribers generally, see notes to §§ 8630 and 8674.

See also Clarke v. Thomas, 34 O. S. 46 (1877).

Tillinghast v. Bailey, 86 Fed. 46 (C. C. 1897).

Latham v. Union, etc., Ins. Co., 1 W. L. B. 127 (Dist. Ct. 1876).

Necessity for. There are no express statutory provisions relating to subscriptions to increased stock. The opinion has been expressed that, before corporate action is taken on the faith of the increase, at least ten percent of the entire capital stock, including the increase, must be subscribed for: but that subscriptions to the original stock may be counted.

Rep. Atty. Gen. 1906-1907, p. 52.

No certificate of subscription to the increased stock need be filed with the secretary of state.

Rep. Atty. Gen. 1911-1912, p. 66.

Liability for acting as if increased stock had been subscribed. Where an increase of stock was authorized by the stockholders, a certificate of increase filed with the secretary of state, a bond issue put forth on the faith of such increase, and no effort was made to sell the new stock, it was held that an intention was thereby shown on the part of existing stockholders to take new stock in proportion to their original holdings, and a judgment was rendered against the stockholders accordingly.

Kreisser v. Ashtabula, etc., Co., 2 C. C. n. s. 597; 14 C. D. 313 (1901).

Unissued original stock is not increased stock. The original stock which remains unsubscribed after the first election of directors is not increased stock.

Sims v. Street Railroad Co., 37 O. S. 556, 564 (1882).

Painesville N. B. v. King Varnish Co., 8 C. C. 563; 4 C. D. 511 (1894); reversed, in part, 56 O. S. 744.

Stock dividend.

See notes to § 8724.

Original stock must be fully subscribed. Where the original stock has not been fully subscribed, the capital stock can not be increased, although three-fourths of the original stock has been subscribed and paid for in cash.

Rep. Atty. Gen. (1909-10) 759.

Franchise tax on increased stock. Where its capital stock is increased within six months prior to the time for filing the annual franchise tax report under § 5495, a corporation is not required to pay the tax on the increased stock.

5 Opins. Attys. Gen. 865 (1903).

§ 5519.

831   .GENERAL CORPORATION LAW.   G. C. § 8700

Section cited.

Snyder v. Chamber of Commerce, 53 O. S. 1 (1895).
Miller v. Ratterman, 47 O. S. 157 (1890).
Mannington v. Railway Co., 9 N. P. n. s. 684 (1910).

Increases under former acts.

See Turnbull v. Pomeroy Salt Co., 24 W. L. B. 133 (1890).
Clarke v. Thomas, 34 O. S. 46 (1877) (Mining Company).
Under the former law the original capital stock was required to be
full paid before it could be increased.
Peter v. Union Mfg. Co., 56 O. S. 181, 200 (1897).

Section 8699. (Increase by preferred stock.) Upon the assent in writing of three-fourths in number of the stockholders of a corporation, representing at least three-fourths of its capital stock, to increase the capital stock, it may issue and dispose of preferred stock in the manner by law provided therefor. Upon such increase of stock, a certificate shall be filed with the secretary of state, as provided in the next preceding section. (R. S. Sec. 3263; May 12, 1902, 95 v. 624; March 6, 1874, 71 v. 19, §§ 1, 2.)

See §§ 8667 to 8671.
This section does not provide the only method of issuing preferred
stock, after organization. Without increasing the capital stock, existing
stockholders may, for the purpose of inducing subscriptions to the unissued stock, by agreement give a preference as to dividends to subscribers
to the unissued stock.
    Painesville N. B. v. King Varnish Co., 8 C. C. 563; 4 C. D. 511
        (1894) ; reversed, in part, 56 O. S. 744.
    Stockholders may change a portion of the common into preferred
stock, without increasing the stock, by amendment to articles.
    Rep. Atty. Gen. (1904-1905) 81.
    Contra, 5 Opins. Attys. Gen. 831, 1006 (1903).
    Under a statute authorizing certain corporations to increase their
capital stock by preferred stock, it was held that the increase could not
be made partly by preferred and partly by common stock.
    Covington, etc., Bridge Co. v. Sargent, 1 C. S. C. R. 354 (1871) ; re-
        versed on other grounds, 27 O. S. 233.
    Where the original articles of incorporation did not authorize the
issue of preferred stock, the articles should be amended.
    See §§ 8668, 8669, 8719.
    Rep. Atty. Gen. 1911-1912, p. 115.
    A certificate of increase by preferred stock must show that the orig-
inal capital stock is fully subscribed and ten percent paid on each share
as required by § 8698.
    Rep. Atty. Gen. 1911-1912, p. 102.

Section 8700. (Reduction of capital stock.) With the written consent of the persons in whose names a majority of the shares of the capital stock thereof stands on its books, the board of directors of such a corporation may reduce the amount of its capital stock and the nominal value of all the shares thereof, and issue certificates therefor. The

rights of creditors shall not be affected thereby; and a
certificate of such action shall be filed with the secretary of
state. (R. S. Sec. 3264; May 11, 1886, 83 v. 134; R. S. 1880;
April 3, 1868, 65 v. 51, §§ 1, 2, 3, 4, 5 [S. & C. 309; S. & S.
242]; May 1, 1852, 50 v. 274, § 74.)

Preferred stock, when issued subject to redemption, may be redeemed
and retired without filing a certificate. But common stock can be reduced
only in the manner authorized by this section.
Rep. Atty. Gen. 1906-1907, p. 46.
The redemption of preferred stock, when authorized by statute, is
not a reduction of the capital stock by a purchase of its own shares.
　　Mannington v. H. V. Ry. Co., 8 O. L. R. 451; 183 Fed. 133; 16 O. F.
　　　　D. 552 (C. C. Ohio 1910); s. c., 9 N. P. n. s. 641; 20 L. D. 468
　　　　(C. P. 1910).
See also note to § 8669.
It is not a reduction of its capital stock for a corporation to acquire
shares of its own stock, by the rescission of an exchange of stock for
property or to secure a debt, although the certificates are marked "can-
celled."
　　Morgan v. Lewis, 46 O. S. 1, 7 (1888).
See note to § 8627. *Power of corporation to acquire its own stock.*
Redemption of preferred stock. See note to § 8669.
A corporation can not reduce its capital stock by a purchase of stock
from stockholders.
Rep. Atty. Gen. 1906-1907, p. 58.
Legal reserve life and fire insurance companies can not reduce their
capital stock under this section.
Rep. Atty. Gen. 1911-1912, pp. 80, 110.
It is said that the number of shares can not be decreased under this
section.
Rep. Atty. Gen. 1911-1912, p. 99.

REGULATIONS AND BY-LAWS.

Section 8701.   (Corporation may adopt regulations.)
Every corporation may adopt a code of regulations for its
government, consistent with the constitution and laws of
the state. (R. S. Sec. 3249; R. S. 1880.)

Regulations and by-laws distinguished. Regulations constitute the
fundamental law of a corporation subordinate to the constitution and
laws of the state and must be adopted by the stockholders or members.
By-laws are adopted by directors or trustees for their own government.
　　State v. Burial Assn., 8 C. C. n. s. 233, 248; 18 C. D. 397 (1906):
　　　　dismissed by supreme court for want of jurisdiction, 4 O. L. R.
　　　　708.
　　Chevaliers v. Shearer, 6 C. C. n. s. 587; 17 C. D. 509 (1905).

Corporations not required to adopt regulations. This section is directory merely and not mandatory.
　　Proprietors v. Wade, 7 W. L. J. 95 (Com. Ct. Cincinnati 1849).

Regulations must be reasonable and consistent with laws of Ohio.
Regulations, to be valid, must be reasonable.
　　Hagerman v. Ohio, etc., Assn., 25 O. S. 186, 202 (1874).

Forest City, etc., Assn. v. Gallagher, 25 O. S. 208, 216 (1874).
They must be consistent with the statutes of the state.
Nicholson v. Franklin Brewing Co., 82 O. S. 94, 110 (1910).
And with the constitution.
State v. Cincinnati, 23 O. S. 445 (1872).
The validity of a regulation or by-law is a question of law for the court.
Holmes v. Pickering, 3 W. L. J. 222 (1845).

Knowledge of regulations imputed to stockholders. A stockholder is chargeable with knowledge of the regulations of the corporation.
Nicholson v. Franklin Brewing Co., 82 O. S. 94, 109 (1910).
Kroger Co. v. Butchers, etc., Assn., 8 N. P. n. s. 222; 20 L. D. 33 (C. P. 1909).
Where an officer of a corporation, which held stock in another corporation, was familiar with the business methods of such other corporation operating under one of its regulations, the stockholder corporation is chargeable with actual knowledge of the regulation.
Kroger Co. v. Butchers, etc., Assn., 8 N. P. n. s. 222; 20 L. D. 33 (C. P. 1909).

Estoppel to deny regulations. A member of a corporation not for profit who acquires membership under a provision of the regulations is estopped from claiming that the regulations were not legally adopted.
Cheney v. Ketcham, 5 N. P. 139; 7 L. D. 183 (C. P. 1897).
See State v. Cincinnati, etc., Exch., 4 N. P. 244; 6 L. D. 363 (1897).

Construction of regulations and by-laws. Regulations and by-laws are governed by the rules of construction which apply to statutes.
Burke v. Home Bldg. Assn., 7 W. L. B. 114 (Dist. Ct. 1882).
Practical construction by stockholders and officers will be regarded.
Kroger Co. v. Butchers, etc., Assn., 8 N. P. n. s. 222; 20 L. D. 33 (C. P. 1909).

An invalid regulation may be binding as a contract.
Nicholson v. Franklin Brewing Co., 82 O. S. 94, 110-111 (1910).
Kroger Co. v. Butchers, etc., Assn., 8 N. P. n. s. 222; 20 L. D. 33 (C. P. 1909).
Stafford v. Produce Exch. Bkg. Co., 61 O. S. 160 (1899); aff'g, 16 C. C. 50; 8 C. D. 483.
Compare Cronin v. Potters Co-op. Co., 29 W. L. B. 52 (C. P. 1892).
See note to § 8704.

Section 8702. (Trustees or directors may adopt by-laws.)

The trustees or directors of a corporation may adopt a code of by-laws for their government, consistent with the regulations of the corporation, and the constitution and laws of the state, and change it at pleasure. (R. S. Sec. 3250; R. S. 1880.)

By-laws distinguished from regulations. By-laws are adopted by directors or trustees for their own government. Regulations must be adopted by the stockholders or members.
State v. Burial Assn., 8 C. C. n. s. 233, 248; 18 C. D. 397 (1906); dismissed by supreme court for want of jurisdiction, 4 O. L. R. 708.
By-laws relating to the business of the corporation are within the powers of directors.
Chevaliers v. Shearer, 6 C. C. n. s. 587; 17 C. D. 509 (1905).

Adoption. The adoption of by-laws is sufficiently proved by showing that they appear upon the corporate records and have been uniformly acted upon and enforced as the by-laws of the corporation. The corporation may enforce rights under such by-laws, although the corporate records fail to show that they were adopted by a formal vote of its directors.

Hagerman v. Association, 25 O. S. 186, 204 (1874).

By-laws may be adopted by custom, where such custom is a uniform rule of action and is acquiesced in by all stockholders.

Stafford v. Produce Exchange Bkg. Co., 16 C. C. 50, 55; 8 C. D. 483 (1898); aff'd, 61 O. S. 160.

Regulating transfers of stock. A corporation has power to regulate the mode and manner of transferring the title of stock.

National Bank v. Lake Shore, etc., R. Co., 21 O. S. 221, 232 (1871).

Railroad Co. v. Robbins, 35 O. S. 483 (1880).

Tomb v. Felch, 40 W. L. B. 186 (Sup. Ct. without opinion).

Stafford v. Produce Exchange Banking Co., 61 O. S. 160 (1899); affirming, 16 C. C. 50; 8 C. D. 483.

See note to § 8704.

But restrictions on transfers must be stated upon the certificates.

See § 8673-15.

A by-law prohibiting the transfer of stock which has been paid with notes and mortgages is unreasonable and will not justify a refusal to transfer.

Andes Ins. Co. v. Waters, 1 W. L. B. 172 (Super. Ct. Cin. 1876).

Special act requiring by-laws of a hospital to be approved by city council. A special act requiring the rules and regulations of the trustees of a hospital to be approved by the city council is unconstitutional as a special law assuming to confer corporate power.

State v. Cincinnati, 23 O. S. 445 (1872).

Section 8703.   (How regulations adopted or changed.) Regulations may be adopted or changed by the assent thereto, in writing, of two-thirds of the stockholders, or, if there is no capital stock, of the members, or by a majority of the stockholders or members, at a meeting held for that purpose, notice of which has been given by the acting president personally to each member or stockholder, or by publication in some newspaper of general circulation in the county in which the corporation is located, or in the counties through which its improvement does or will pass.   (R. S. Sec. 3251; R. S. 1880.)

"Two-thirds of the stockholders" means "two-thirds of the stockholders in interest" and not two-thirds in number, except in the case of corporations chartered under G. C. § 8638.

Toledo T. L. & P. Co. v. Smith, 58 Bull. 201 (U. S. D. C. 1913).

Directors or trustees can not adopt or amend regulations. Regulations must be adopted by the stockholders, or, where the corporation is not for profit, by the members. Directors or trustees have no power to adopt or amend regulations.

State v. Burial Assn., 8 C. C. n. s. 233, 248; 18 C. D. 397 (1906); dismissed by supreme court for want of jurisdiction, 4 O. L. R. 708.

Farmers, etc., Co. v. Bachman, 39 W. L. B. 324 (Sup. Ct. without report 1898).

Amendments. Regulations may be amended by a majority of stockholders or members, although such regulations were originally adopted unanimously and signed by all stockholders or members.

Wangerien v. Aspell, 47 O. S. 250, 260 (1890).

Cronin v. Potters Co-op. Co., 29 W. L. B. 52 (C. P. 1892).

But a vested right acquired under a regulation or by-law can not be affected by its repeal or amendment.

Windhorst v. Germania Bldg. Assn., 7 W. L. B. 29 (Super. Ct. Cin. 1882).

A corporation may provide in its regulations that they shall not be amended without unanimous consent of all the stockholders or members. Such a provision is valid. No amendment is binding unless consent of the stipulated number is given.

Wangerien v. Aspell, 47 O. S. 250, 260 (1890).

McKeown v. Irish Bldg. Assn., 5 W. L. B. 52 (Super. Ct. Cin. 1880).

Where the regulations contain no provision as to their amendment, they are amendable under § 8703.

Wangerien v. Aspell, 47 O. S. 250, 260 (1890).

Proof of adoption. The adoption of by-laws is sufficiently proved by showing that they appear upon the records of the corporation, and have been uniformly acted upon and enforced as the by-laws of the corporation, although the corporate records do not show, and it is not otherwise proved, that they were adopted by a formal vote.

Hagerman v. Association, 25 O. S. 186, 204 (1874).

Stafford v. Banking Co., 16 C. C. 50, 55; 8 C. D. 483 (1898); aff'd, 61 O. S. 160.

Notice of stockholders' meeting. It has been held that this section requires notice to be served personally and that notice given to stockholders by mail is insufficient.

Cheney v. Ketcham, 5 N. P. 139, 142; 7 L. D. 183 (C. P. 1897).

Section 8704. (What may be provided for by regulations.) When no other provision is specially made in this title, a corporation by its regulations may provide—

1. The time, place and manner of calling and conducting its meetings.

2. The number of stockholders or members constituting a quorum.

3. The time of the annual election for trustees or directors, and the manner of giving notice thereof.

4. The duties and compensation of officers.

5. The manner of election, or appointment, and the tenure of office, of all officers other than the trustees or directors.

6. The qualifications of members, when the corporation is not for profit. (R. S. Sec. 3252; R. S. 1880.)

(1) Manner of calling meetings. Where officers refuse to call a stockholders' meeting, pursuant to the regulations, the remedy of a stockholder is injunction, not mandamus.

State v. Unida, etc., Co., 13 C. C. n. s. 100; 22 C. D. 54 (1910).

See note to § 8647.

(2) Quorum of stockholders or members. Where no regulation has been adopted on the subject, the stockholders present at a meeting, in person or by proxy, may elect officers and transact business, although a majority of the stock is not represented.

> Lutterby v. Herancourt Brewing Co., 12 L. D. 67, 72, 73 (Super. Ct. Cin. 1901).
>
> See Kalb v. American N. B., 21 C. C. 1, 7; 11 C. D. 437 (1900); ati'd, 65 O. S. 566.

(3) Time of annual election. Where the regulations provide for an "annual meeting" at a time other than the first Monday in January, as provided in § 8647, the time for the "annual election" is thereby changed and the election should be held at such annual meeting.

> State v. Burial Assn., 8 C. C. n. s. 233, 250; 18 C. D. 397 (1906); dismissed by supreme court for want of jurisdiction, 4 O. L. R. 708.

But regulations which have not been properly adopted are not effective to change the time of the annual election of directors from the first Monday in January.

> State v. Burial Assn., 8 C. C. n. s. 233, 249; 18 C. D. 397 (1906).

The term of office of a director can not be shortened by an amendment to the regulations, to go into immediate effect, advancing the date of the annual election.

> Toledo T. L. & P. Co. v. Smith, 58 Bull. 201 (U. S. D. C. 1913).

(4) Duties and compensation of officers.

See also note to § 8664. *Executive officers* and note to § 8660. *Delegation of duties to executive committee.*

A corporation may by its regulations so define the duties of its officers as to make them *alter ego* within the assigned limits.

> Bradford Belting Co. v. Gibson, 68 O. S. 442, 449 (1903).
>
> Dickason v. Grafton, etc., Co., 6 C. C. n. s. 333; 17 C. D. 357; aff'd, 76 O. S. 612.
>
> See Morris v. Griffith, 34 W. L. B. 191 (U. S. C. C. 1895).

Regulations of corporation chartered by special act under former constitution (treasurer).

> See Portage, etc., Co. v. Wetmore, 17 Ohio 330 (1848).

(5) Election of officers and tenure of office.

See note to § 8664, *Executive officers.*

The president must be elected by the directors. His election can not be otherwise provided for in the regulations.

§ 8664.

> Walsenberg Water Co. v. Moore, 5 Colo. App. 144; 38 Pac. 60.

The stockholders may determine the number of directors. §§ 8635, 8665. This is frequently done by a provision in the regulations. But the tenure of office of a director can not be shortened by a decrease in the number under § 8665.

> Lutterby v. Herancourt Brewing Co., 12 L. D. 67, 76 (Super. Ct. Cin. 1901).

Neither the incorporators of a corporation not for profit nor the trustees first elected are authorized to adopt a regulation or by-law providing that they shall hold office for life, and in case of vacancy to fill the same by appointment.

> State v. Standard Life Assn., 38 O. S. 281 (1882).

(6) Qualification of members. A corporation not for profit may provide in its regulations for the expulsion of members, and may delegate the power to try and expel to a committee or board.

> Cheney v. Ketcham, 5 N. P. 139; 7 L. D. 183 (C. P. 1897).

Blumenthal v. Chamber of Commerce, 9 W. L. B. 76 (Super. Ct. Cin.); affirming 7 W. L. B. 327.

See note to § 8653.

Regulations on other subjects. Where statutes under which a corporation is formed authorize by-laws upon specifically named subjects there is an implied denial of authority to make by-laws upon subjects not named.

But restrictive regulations upon the transfer of stock have been sustained as contracts.

Nicholson v. Franklin Brewing Co., 82 O. S. 94, 110, 111 (1911).

Transfers of stock. Specific authority is not given in § 8704 to adopt regulations as to the transfer of stock. Such regulations have been sustained as contracts in some states, although they may have been technically invalid as regulations.

Nicholson v. Franklin Brewing Co., 82 O. S. 94, 110-111 (1910).

See Stafford v. Produce Exchange Brewing Co., 61 O. S. 160 (1899); affirming 16 C. C. 50; 8 C. D. 483.

Rep. Atty. Gen. 1911-1912, p. 88.

See also note to § 8702.

Restrictions on transfers of stock must be stated in the certificates of stock.

§ 8673-15.

Power to regulate transfers of stock is not power to prohibit transfers.

Nicholson v. Franklin Brewing Co., 82 O. S. 94, 112 (1910).

See Andes Ins. Co. v. Waters, 1 W. L. B. 172 (Super. Ct. Cin. 1876).

Under a Delaware statute authorizing corporations to adopt by-laws regulating the issuance and transference of stock, a by-law was held valid which required a stockholder who desired to sell his stock, before doing so, to notify the directors and give them thirty days in which to sell the stock to certain designated classes of persons whose occupations might render them valuable in extending the corporate business.

Nicholson v. Franklin Brewing Co., 82 O. S. 94 (1910).

Limiting corporate existence. A regulation unanimously adopted, in writing, by the stockholders limiting the life of the corporation to ten years may be amended by a majority of the stockholders. And where the majority continued business beyond such period, without expressly amending such regulation, the court refused to decree a dissolution at the suit of one stockholder.

Cronin v. Potters Co-op. Co., 29 W. L. B. 52 (C. P. 1892).

Prohibiting recourse to courts. A regulation of a corporation not for profit which prohibits a member from resort to courts to assert a right, but requiring him to submit to the tribunals of the corporation, is void.

Myers v. Jenkins, 63 O. S. 101; reversing 16 C. C. 545; 8 C. D. 431.

Change of place of business.

See G. C. § 8625.

Mercantile Trust Co. v. Aetna Iron Works, 4 C. C. 579, 588; 2 C. D. 718 (1890).

Removal of directors, officers or employes. This section does not authorize regulations providing for the removal, at stockholders' meetings, of officers or employes chosen or appointed by the directors nor arbitrarily removing directors. Directors are entitled to hold office for the term for which they are elected, unless removed for cause upon notice and hearing.

Toledo T. L. & P. Co. v. Smith, 58 Bull. 201 (U. S. D. C. 1913).

Expulsion of stockholders. A regulation of a corporation for profit providing for the expulsion and suspension of stockholders is unauthorized and invalid.

Rep. Atty. Gen. 1911-1912, p. 88.

BORROWING MONEY.

Section 8705. (May borrow money on bond or mortgage.) A corporation may borrow money in any sum not exceeding the amount of its capital stock, issue its notes, or coupon or registered bonds therefor, bearing any legal rate of interest, and secure their payment by a mortgage of its property, real or personal, or both. (R. S. Sec. 3256; May 6, 1902, 95 v. 390; April 15, 1902, 95 v. 151; R. S. 1880.)

Bonds of public utility or railroad; when authority of public utilities commission required. § 614-53 et seq.

Railroad mortgages. See § 8793 et seq.

Street and interurban railway mortgages. See § 9121-1.

Power of corporations to borrow money, in general. When not prohibited by statute, a corporation may borrow money for its corporate purposes and may evidence and secure the loan by customary instruments.

Larwell v. Hanover, etc., Society, 40 O. S. 274, 282 (1883).

Hays v. Galion Gas Co., 29 O. S. 330 (1876).

Raymond v. Spring Grove, etc., Ry. Co., 21 W. L. B. 103 (1889).

Burt v. Rattle, 31 O. S. 116 (1876).

Straus v. Eagle Ins. Co., 5 O. S. 59 (1855).

Where a corporation has obtained a loan, under its apparent power to borrow, it can not escape liability therefor by setting up the defense of ultra vires.

Hays v. Galion, etc., Co., 29 O. S. 330, 340 (1876).

See Picard v. Hughey, 58 O. S. 577, 594-595 (1898).

Conant v. Reed, 1 O. S. 298 (1853).

Limitation on amount borrowed. Loans in excess of capital stock.

Section 8705 does not expressly limit loans to the amount of paid-up stock.

Kreisser v. Ashtabula, etc., Co., 2 C. C. n. s. 597, 599; 14 C. D. 313 (1901).

A mortgage by a corporation to secure a debt in excess of its capital stock is not void as to a subsequent mortgagee with notice, if upheld by the corporation and its stockholders.

Central Trust Co. v. Columbus, etc., Co., 87 Fed. 815; 10 O. F. D. 328 (C. C. 1898).

Stockholders and directors who caused an issue of bonds in excess of the amount allowed by law are not personally liable on such bonds.

Raymond v. Spring Grove, etc., Co., 21 W. L. B. 103 (Super. Ct. Cin. 1889).

Where the capital stock of a corporation was increased, and bonds issued on the faith of such increase, the stockholders and directors are estopped from questioning the validity of the mortgage on the ground that the increased stock was not subscribed for.

Kreisser v. Ashtabula, etc., Co., 2 C. C. n. s. 597; 14 C. D. 313 (1901).

Farmers Trust Co. v. Railway Co., 67 Fed. 49; 9 O. F. D. 230 (1895).

Power of a public utility or railroad to borrow in excess of capital stock when authorized by public utilities commission, see § 614-53.

Duty of lender to inquire as to authorization of loan. It has been held that a lender should know that the corporation has power to make the loan and execute the mortgage, but that he is not bound to inquire whether all the formalities have been observed, as whether the directors have had a meeting and passed a formal resolution authorizing the loan and mortgage.

Bosche v. Toledo, etc., Co., 14 C. C. 289; 7 C. D. 374 (1897).

Fritsch Mfg. Co. v. Elmont, etc., Co., 11 C. C. n. s. 356; 21 C. D. 47 (1908).

See also note to § 8660, *Corporate Contracts.*

CORPORATE MORTGAGES OR DEEDS OF TRUST.

Authorized by directors. When assent of stockholders necessary. A mortgage on the property of a corporation must be authorized by the directors.

East Cleveland R. Co. v. Everett, 19 C. C. 205; 10 C. D. 493 (1900).

And by a yea and nay vote entered in the record.

See § 8709.

Assent of the stockholders is not necessary;

Bundy v. Iron Co., 38 O. S. 300, 312 (1882).

G. C. § 8660.

Cook on Corporations, § 808.

except when specially required by statute. Mortgages by certain building companies must be assented to by a vote of the holders of two-thirds of the stock (§ 10210). Bonds or notes convertible into stock require the written assent of three-fourths of the stockholders representing three-fourths of the paid up stock (§ 8709).

Where a stockholders' meeting is held, and a mortgage authorized, the stockholders voting favorably are estopped from questioning the validity of such mortgage.

Kreisser v. Ashtabula, etc., Co., 2 C. C. n. s. 597; 14 C. D. 313 (1901).

Where, through mistake, a mortgage was executed by stockholders in their own names, it was held good as an equitable mortgage against the corporation and against a second mortgage expressly made subject to it.

Bundy v. Iron Co., 38 O. S. 300 (1882).

Where, by statute of the home state of a foreign corporation, written assent of two-thirds of the capital stock is required to be filed in the office of the "clerk," such consent may be filed with the recorder, when a mortgage is executed on property in Ohio. A guaranty of payment signed by holders of two thirds of the stock is a sufficient consent.

West v. Klotz, 37 O. S. 420, 428 (1881).

Waiver of stockholders' liability in mortgage. Validity.

See note to § 8686.

Mortgage by college incorporated under special charter. Provision in charter for permanent occupation of property.

See President, etc., v. Zeigler, 17 O. S. 52 (1866).

Execution of bonds, notes and mortgages. Authority of officers.

See notes to §§ 8627, 8660 and 8664.

An Ohio corporation which has removed its plant and business to another state, may, in such state, execute a valid mortgage on its property in Ohio. Although a majority of the directors are not residents of Ohio they are de facto directors and their acts valid.

Lattimer v. Mosaic Glass Co., 13 C. C. 163; 7 C. D. 430 (1896).

Negotiability of bonds and mortgage. The affixing of the corporate seal does not render a bond nonnegotiable.

Railway Co. v. Lynde, 55 O. S. 23 (1896); aff'd, 172 U. S. 493.

The bona fide purchaser of a bond, complete in form, and payable to bearer, acquires a valid title, although the president of the corporation, who was entrusted with its custody, negotiated it wrongfully and for his own benefit. Such purchaser is entitled to a lien under the mortgage securing the bond issue.

Railway Co. v. Lynde, 55 O. S. 23 (1896); aff'd, 172 U. S. 493.

Where a mortgage provides that a default for six months in payment of interest shall render the bonds immediately due and payable, it is doubtful whether a default alone, without steps being taken by any holder to enforce the provision, is such a dishonor as to destroy their negotiability. But where the interest is afterwards paid in full the negotiability of the bonds is restored.

Railway Co. v. Lynde, 55 O. S. 23 (1896); aff'd, 172 U. S. 493.
See G. C. § 8157.

The doctrine of *lis pendens* does not apply to negotiable bonds, transferred before due, in due course of business for value.

Railway Co. v. Lynde, 55 O. S. 23 (1896); s. c., 172 U. S. 493.

What bonds are secured by mortgage.

See note to § 8707.

Estoppel to question validity of mortgage. Stockholders and directors are estopped from denying the validity of a mortgage authorized by them.

Kreisser v. Ashtabula, etc., Co., 2 C. C. n. s. 597; 14 C. D. 313 (1901).
Farmers Trust Co. v. Toledo, etc., Ry. Co., 67 Fed. 49; 9 O. F. D. 230 (1895).

A subsequent mortgagee is estopped from questioning the validity of a prior mortgage to which his mortgage is expressly subject.

Bundy v. Iron Co., 38 O. S. 300 (1882).
Central Trust Co. v. Columbus, etc., R. Co., 87 Fed. 815 (1898).

A person who advanced money on the mortgage bonds of a corporation, and afterwards sold the same to other persons, is estopped from asserting a mechanic's lien as against the mortgage.

West v. Klotz, 37 O. S. 420 (1881).
See note to § 8793.

Consideration. A mortgage given by a corporation to secure endorsers of its notes is based on a present consideration under Bankruptcy Act, § 67d. The mortgagees became creditors of the corporation contingently at and from the time of endorsement.

In re Farmers Supply Co., 170 Fed. 502 (D. C. 1909).

Sale of bonds. The president of a corporation has no power to sell bonds without authority from the directors, nor to employ a broker to sell them.

East Cleveland R. Co. v. Everett, 19 C. C. 205, 209; 10 C. D. 493 (1900).

But where bonds, complete in form and negotiable by delivery, are placed in the custody of the president, he thereby becomes clothed with apparent authority of disposition, and a bona fide purchaser acquires a valid title although the president negotiates them wrongfully and for his own benefit.

Railway Co. v. Lynde, 55 O. S. 23 (1896); aff'd, 172 U. S. 493.
See Railway Co. v. Bank, 56 O. S. 351 (1897).

The president of a corporation, having possession of a bond for sale, has no right to appropriate the bond to the payment of a debt due to him from the corporation, without the consent of the directors.

  Greenville Gas Co. v. Reis, 54 O. S. 549 (1896).

  Where a broker is in possession of bonds of a railroad company under an agreement providing that his right to retain the same should accrue contemporaneously with actual payment therefor, an indictment for embezzlement lies for the pledging of the bonds by the broker and the conversion of the proceeds of the loan prior to a call for funds by the company.

  Hayes v. State, 14 C. C. n. s. 497 (1910); aff'd, no rep., 83 O. S. 490.

  Sale below par. A selling committee of directors, when not authorized to sell for less than par, can not authorize a broker to sell for less than par.

  East Cleveland R. Co. v. Everett, 15 C. C. 181; 8 C. D. 210 (1897);
    s. c., 19 C. C. 205, 209; 10 C. D. 493 (1900).
Sale below par by railroad company, see § 8797.

  Pledge of bonds by corporation. The power to "issue" bonds, conferred by this section, includes the power to pledge its mortgage bonds to secure other obligations, and the delivery of such bonds in pledge to a trustee is an issue of them and renders the mortgage a present incumbrance.

  Transportation Co. v. Insurance Co., 170 Fed. 279 (C. C. A. 1909).
Character of transaction, sale or loan. See note to § 8797.

  Trustee under mortgage. A statement in a bond that it shall not become obligatory until authenticated by the trustee is equivalent to a declaration that when so authenticated its obligatory character shall become complete.

  Railway Co. v. Lynde, 55 O. S. 23, 41 (1896).

  Provision in mortgage authorizing trustee to bid in property at foreclosure sale.

  See Cincinnati Trust Co. v. Miami, etc., Co., 5 O. L. R. 514 (C. P.
    1907).

  The trustee of a mortgage executed by a consolidated company, to secure a bond issue, is a necessary party to an action, by mortgage creditors of one of its constituent companies, seeking to set aside the consolidation on the ground that they were induced by fraud to surrender their lien.

  Union, etc., Co. v. Hess, 159 Fed. 889; 6 O. L. R. 372; 16 O. F. D.
    73 (C. C. A. 1908).

  Liability of trustee for certifying bonds with knowledge that the corporation did not own the property included in the mortgage.

  See Dreifus v. Union, etc., Co., 13 C. C. n. s. 441; 23 C. D. 46 (1910);
    reversed, without report, 87 O. S. 525.
  Davidge v. Trust Co., 203 N. Y. 331; 96 N. E. 751 (1911).

  Trust company as trustee. When mortgage void for failure of trust company to comply with law, see § 9780.

  Foreclosure. Where corporate property was sold under foreclosure to a director for less than its actual value, the sale was set aside on motion of a bondholder upon the giving of security that a larger sum would be bid on a resale.

  Secor v. Maumee, etc., Co., 1 N. P. 100; 1 L. D. 80 (C. P. 1894).

  Where mortgaged property is bid in by the bondholders, who, as authorized by the mortgage and the order of sale, paid therefor by surrendering the bonds, the sheriff is not entitled to poundage on the amount of bonds surrendered.

  Major v. International Coal Co., 76 O. S. 200 (1907).

Where a provision in a mortgage required the trustee to bid in the property on foreclosure and to organize a new corporation, paying the purchase price in stock of such new company, which should be distributed among the bondholders in full satisfaction of their bonds, the court refused to carry such provision into the decree of foreclosure, where it appeared that an action was pending to require stockholders to pay up their stock, which action might be prejudiced by such decree.

Cincinnati Trust Co. v. Miami, etc., Co., 5 O. L. R. 514 (C. P. 1907).

Deficiency judgment. After sale of the mortgaged property under foreclosure, the trustee under the mortgage has no legal capacity to sue on behalf of the bondholders for a personal judgment against one who had promised the corporation to assume the bonds.

Connor v. Bramble, 6 N. P. 195; 9 L. D. 516 (C. P. 1899).

See Raymond v. Spring Grove, etc., Ry. Co., 21 W. L. B. 103 (1889).

A corporation is not liable for a deficiency judgment where the loan was obtained and note and mortgage given by an individual, although for the benefit of the corporation.

De Camp v. Levoy, 19 C. C. 335 (1900).

Section 8706.   (When mortgage deemed to be duly recorded.) A mortgage of real and personal property heretofore or hereafter made by a company organized to operate a line or lines of telegraph, telephone, district telegraph messenger service, or for the purpose of supplying gas or electricity or hot water, for lighting, fuel or other purposes, or hot water, or steam, for heating or fuel purposes, shall be duly recorded in the office of the recorder of deeds in each of the counties in which the real or personal property mortgaged is situated or employed.   (R. S. Sec. 3256a; May 6, 1902, 95 v. 366.)

Section 8707.   (When lien effective.) A mortgage so recorded shall be a good and sufficient lien from the date of its filing for record in each county where it is recorded as well upon the personal as the real property of such a company.   (R. S. Sec. 3256a; May 6, 1902, 95 v. 366.)

The lien of all bonds, in the hands of bona fide holders, secured by one mortgage but issued at different times, dates from the recording of the mortgage.

Railway Co. v. Lynde, 55 O. S. 23 (1896); aff'd, 172 U. S. 493.

See Bank v. Brotherton, 78 O. S. 173 (1908).

Section 8708.   (Change of bonds authorized.) A corporation which lawfully has issued registered or coupon bonds, upon the request of a holder thereof, may change such registered into coupon bonds, or coupon into registered bonds, either by substitution or proper indorsement thereon. All liens, securities, and rights which existed on or accrued to such original bonds shall be and continue on and to such substituted or indorsed bonds.   (R. S. Sec. 3265; April 7, 1876, 73 v. 123, §§ 1, 2.)

Section 8709. (Obligations may be converted into stock.) Upon the written assent of not less than three-fourths of the stockholders, representing at least three-fourths of its capital stock actually paid, a company may borrow money not exceeding one-half of the capital stock so paid in, on such security, by way of mortgage, or otherwise, as is agreed upon, at a lawful rate of interest, and in the instrument evidencing the contract may stipulate that the holders of such instruments shall have the right to convert the amount borrowed, or a part thereof, into either common or preferred stock, this having been provided for by the proper action and certificate of the company. Any action of the directors for borrowing money, issuing bonds, or involving an expenditure of money shall be by yea and nay votes, and record thereof be made showing the vote of each director voting upon the question. (R. S. Sec. 3257; March 25, 1870, 67 v. 26, §§ 1, 2, 3, 4.)

Right to convert not severable from bond. A stipulation for conversion is inseparably connected with the bond on which it is endorsed, and is only available to the holder of the bond so long as he continues to be such holder. The holder of a bond can not assign to another the right of action for a breach of the stipulation for conversion and yet retain the bond for the benefit of himself and future assigns.

Denney v. Cleveland, etc., R. Co., 28 O. S. 108 (1875).

In an action for a refusal to convert bonds, the petition is fatally defective in not averring that the plaintiffs were, and at the commencement of the action continued to be, the holders of the bonds for the non-conversion of which they bring suit.

Denny v. Cleveland, etc., R. Co., 28 O. S. 108 (1875).

When stock deemed a debt. A corporation issued certificates of preferred stock, so called, certifying that the corporation guaranteed to holders the payment of four percent semi-annual dividends, and the final payment of the entire amount at a specified time, with the right to convert the preferred stock into common stock, and the company at the same time executed and delivered to a trustee its bond and mortgage to secure the holders of such certificates. Held, that the holders of the certificates did not thereby become stockholders of the corporation, but its creditors, and that, as such, they had a lien upon the mortgaged property superior to that of the general creditors of the corporation or of its assignees.

Burt v. Rattle, 31 O. S. 116 (1876).

See note to § 8669. *Issues of stock construed—preferred stock or debt.*

Contracts of consolidation limiting right to issue bonds. A contract of consolidation which prohibits the issuing of bonds without the consent of the majority in interest of preferred stockholders probably violates this section.

Burke v. Cleveland, etc., Co., 22 W. L. B. 11, 16 (C. P. 1889).

SALE OF ENTIRE PROPERTY.

Section 8710. (**Sale of entire property and assets.**) No corporation organized under the laws of this state shall sell its entire property and assets to any person, persons or association, or to another corporation, whether organized for the same or similar purposes or otherwise, under the laws of this or any other state, unless three-fourths of the directors of such corporation authorize the execution of an agreement therefor prescribing the terms, considerations and conditions thereof. The considerations may be money, stocks, bonds, or other instruments for the payment of money, or any valuable consideration. (R. S. Sec. 3256b; April 2, 1906, 98 v. 229.)

Power to sell corporate property generally, see note to § 8627.
Sale of stocks of merchandise in bulk, see G. C. §§ 11102 to 11103-1.

Agreement of vendor corporation and stockholders not to re-engage in business. An agreement by a corporation, on a sale of its entire property and good will, not to re-engage in business is not binding on a stockholder individually although he was an officer of the corporation and acted in the transaction.

Hall's Safe Co. v. Herring, etc., Co., 146 Fed. 37; 15 O. F. D. 37 (C. C. A. 1906).

But where the stockholders expressly agree, as individuals, not to re-engage in business, within certain limitations, they are bound.

Davis v. Booth, 2 O. L. R. 309; 131 Fed. 31 (C. C. A. 1904).

Employment contracts of corporation; when binding on purchaser. Novation.

See Paul v. Caldwell Furnace Co., 7 C. C. n. s. 272; 17 C. D. 768 (1905).

Jarmusch v. Otis, etc., Co., 3 C. C. n. s. 1; 13 C. D. 122 (1901); aff'd, 68 O. S. 720.

Rescission. Before the enactment of §§8710 to 8718 it was held that where several corporations combined by organizing a new corporation, to which the constituent companies conveyed their property in exchange for stock, one of the constituent companies could not sue for a rescission, on the ground that it was an arrangement in restraint of trade, without tendering back all the stock received by it.

Sportsman Shot Co. v. American, etc., Co., 30 W. L. B. 87 (Super. Ct. Cin. 1893).

Rights of creditors of corporation.

See Andres v. Morgan, 62 O. S. 236 (1900).
Bank v. Trebein, 59 O. S. 316 (1898).
In re Reiger, Kapner & Altmark, 8 O. L. R. 498; 187 Fed. 609.

Power of corporation to sell its entire property, independently of statute. Former law.

See Schmuck v. Crume, etc., Co., 7 N. P. n. s. 24, 32; 19 L. D. 819 (1905); aff'd, 78 O. S. 409.
Keystone Bank v. Union Oil Co., 2 C. C. n. s. 427; 15 C. D. 464 (1903).
Easum v. Buckeye Brewing Co., 51 Fed. 156 (C. C. 1892).
Donner v. Dayton, etc., Co., 1 C. S. C. R. 130, 140 (1871).

Section 8711. (Submission of agreement.) Such agreement shall be submitted to the stockholders of the corporation at a meeting called for the purpose of taking it into consideration, ten days' notice of the time and place of holding which, and the object thereof, shall be given by registered letter containing a written or printed notice addressed to each of the persons in whose names the stock of the corporation stands on its books; and also by like notice published in some newspaper in the city or village where the corporation has its principal office or place of business. But when all the stockholders are present at such meeting in person or by proxy, notice may be waived in writing. (R. S. Sec. 3256c; April 2, 1906, 98 v. 230.)

Section 8712. (Adoption of agreement.) At such meeting of stockholders the agreement of the directors shall be considered and a vote by ballot taken for its adoption or rejection. For each share of stock on which all the installments called for by the board of directors are paid, the holder thereof shall be entitled to one vote. The ballots must be cast in person or by proxy, and if three-fourths of all the votes cast at the meeting be for the adoption of the agreement, it shall be valid and binding on such corporation. Upon its adoption, the officers of the company shall execute and deliver to the purchaser good and sufficient deeds and transfers of all the property and assets of the corporation, upon the terms and conditions in the agreement provided. (R. S. Sec. 3256c; April 2, 1906, 98 v. 230.)

> Where the assets of a corporation are purchased by another corporation under §§ 8710 to 8713, the purchaser may rescind a contract of the selling corporation, entered into through the fraud of its promoter, by which a portion of the assets were acquired.
> Commonwealth Steamship Co. v. American Shipbuilding Co., 10 O. L. R. 395, 414; 197 Fed. 780 (U. S. D. C. 1912).

Section 8713. (Dissatisfied stockholder.) If a stockholder be dissatisfied with such sale and refuses to participate in the proceeds thereof, within thirty days after the adoption of such agreement, he shall state his objections thereto in writing and file them with such corporation, and in writing demand from it payment for his stock. Within sixty days thereafter such corporation shall pay to him the value thereof at the time such agreement was adopted. In case of a disagreement as to the value of the stock, it shall be ascertained by three disinterested persons, one of whom to be chosen by the stockholder, one by the directors of the corporation, and the other by the two so selected who shall conduct such arbitration as provided by the law regulating arbitrations. (R. S. Sec. 3256d; April 2, 1906, 98 v. 230.)

See § 9034.
Burke v. Cleveland, etc., Railway Co., 22 W. L. B. 11, 16 (1889).
Railway Co. v. Garrett, 50 O. S. 405 (1893).

Section 8714. (How award collected.) If the award is not paid within sixty days from its making, and notice thereof given to the stockholder and the corporation, its amount shall be evidence of the amount due from the corporation and may be collected as other debts against it. On receiving payment of the award, the stockholder shall surrender his stock to such corporation. (R. S. Sec. 3256d; April 2, 1906, 98 v. 230.)

Section 8715. (Procedure when stockholder refuses to submit question.) If such stockholder refuses to submit such question to arbitration, upon the application of a director of the company, the judge of the common pleas court shall appoint arbitrators, who shall ascertain the value of the stock as if the question had been submitted by consent of both parties. (R. S. Sec. 3256e; April 2, 1906, 98 v. 230.)

Section 8716. (Notice.) In all cases of such arbitration, the party desiring it, shall give the opposite party at least ten days' notice of his intention to apply to the judge for the appointment or arbitrators, which notice shall be served in the manner provided for the service of summons and specify the time and place of the hearing of the application. In cases of non-residents the notice shall be by publication for four consecutive weeks in some newspaper printed in the county. (R. S. Sec. 3256e; April 2, 1906, 98 v. 231.)

Section 8717. (Deposit of award.) If the party owning the stock refuses to receive the amount awarded, the company may deposit it with the clerk of the common pleas court of the county in which the arbitration was held, which deposit shall operate as if payment were made to the owner of the stock, and also as a cancellation of such stock upon the books of the company. (R. S. Sec. 3256e; April 2, 1906, 98 v. 231.)

Section 8718. (Sale to a trust prohibited.) A sale of its entire property by a corporation, as hereinbefore authorized, shall not be made for the formation of or to a trust or combination for the purpose of restricting trade or preventing competition. (R. S. Sec. 3256b; April 2, 1906, 98 v. 229.)

See Sportsman Shot Co. v. American, etc., Co., 30 W. L. B. 87 (Super. Ct. Cin. 1893).

AMENDMENTS.

Section 8719. (Power to amend.) A corporation organized under the general corporation laws of the state, may amend its articles of incorporation as follows:

1. So as to change its corporate name—but not to one already appropriated, or to one likely to mislead the public.

2. So as to change the place where it is to be located, or its principal business transacted.

3. So as to modify, enlarge or diminish the objects or purposes for which it was formed.

4. So as to add to them anything omitted from, or which lawfully might have been provided for originally, in such articles. But the capital stock of a corporation shall not be increased or diminished, by such amendment, nor the purpose of its original organization substantially changed. (R. S. Sec. 3238a; May 18, 1886, 83 v. 193.)

A fire insurance company organized under G. C. § 9510 et seq. may amend its articles under this section.
Rep. Atty. Gen. 1911-1912, p. 98.

Change of name. Corporate name generally, see note to §8628.
A corporation having changed its name, the former name was adopted by a new corporation, but most of the mail addressed to the former name was intended for the older company. Held that all mail should be opened by the former company in the presence of a representative of the new company.
Clark Carriage Co. v. Smith Eggers Co., 1 N. P. 391; 3 L. D. 77 (Cin. Super. Ct. 1894).
A casualty company may change its name under this section.
Rep. Atty. Gen. 1908-1909, p. 88.
A change of the corporate name does not release a subscriber to stock.
Royce & Pulling v. Tyler, 2 C. C. 175, 183; 1 C. D. 428 (1887).
Whether a statute, authorizing a change of name of a railroad company on certain conditions, has been complied with must be proved. Judicial notice will not be taken of a statement in a report of the commissioner of railroads, that such statute has been complied with.
Railroad Co. v. Hoffhines, 46 O. S. 643 (1889).

Capital stock. A part of the common stock may, by amendment, be changed into preferred stock.
Rep. Atty. Gen. 1904, p. 81.
Contra, 5 Opins. Atty. Gen. 1006 (1903).
See note to § 8669.

Provisions as to preferred stock may be added, by amendment, where the capital stock is neither increased nor reduced.

Rep. Atty. Gen. 1911-1912, p. 115.

A corporation not for profit, but having a capital stock, may not eliminate its capital stock by amendment, where a portion of the stock is owned by nonmembers.

Rep. Atty. Gen. 1904-1905, p. 63.

The par value of shares can not be increased by amendment under this section.

Rep. Atty. Gen. 1911-1912, pp. 99, 126.

Nor can the number of shares be increased.

Rep. Atty. Gen. 1911-1912, pp. 126, 99.

Substantial change of purpose. While the purpose may be modified, enlarged or diminished, it can not be substantially changed. A corporation organized to furnish gas and electricity can not by amendment be authorized to operate a street railway.

State ex rel. v. Taylor, 55 O. S. 61 (1896).

Where a corporation amends its articles so as to substantially change its original purpose, bonds issued in carrying out such unauthorized purposes will, in the absence of estoppel, be void in the hands of holders with notice.

Picard v. Hughey, 58 O. S. 577, 595 (1898).

A corporation organized to furnish gas for lighting purposes may, by amendment, be authorized to furnish electricity for the same purpose.

Picard v. Hughey, 58 O. S. 577 (1898).

A corporation formed to manufacture electric fixtures can not, by amendment, be authorized to furnish electric light and steam heat.

4 Opins. Attys. Gen. 580.

A company formed to conduct a farming and nursery business can not, by amendment, be authorized to deal in real estate, or to manufacture cotton and cotton paper.

Rep. Atty. Gen. 1909-1910, p. 135.

An amendment authorizing a railway company to engage in transportation by water is a fundamental change.

Marietta, etc., R. Co. v. Elliott, 10 O. S. 57 (1859).

Special charters under former constitution. Amendment of.

See note to § 8736.

Fundamental changes in special charters require the assent of all stockholders.

Chapman v. Mad River, etc., Co., 6 O. S. 119 (1856).

Marietta, etc., R. Co. v. Elliott, 10 O. S. 57 (1859).

See Dayton, etc., R. Co. v. Hatch, 1 Disn. 84 (1855).

But the rights of such stockholders may be lost by laches.

Chapman v. Mad River, etc., Co., 6 O. S. 119 (1856).

Owen v. Purdy, 12 O. S. 73 (1861).

Section 8720. (Proceedings.) Amendments to articles of incorporation may be made at any meeting of the members or stockholders thereof, of which, and of the business to come before it, thirty days' notice has been given by a majority of the directors or trustees, in a newspaper published and of general circulation in the county where the company's principal place of business is located, and by a vote of the owners of at least three-fifths of its capital stock then subscribed, if it has a capital stock, or if not, by a vote of at least three-fifths of its members. (R. S. Sec. 3238a; May 18, 1886, 83 v. 193.)

The notice need not be published for thirty consecutive days. One notice, published at least thirty days before the day set, is sufficient.

Muskingum, etc., Co. v. Ward, 13 Ohio 120 (1844).

Craig v. Fox, 16 Ohio 563, 566 (1847).

Newport News v. Potter, 122 Fed. 321, 332 (C. C. A. 1903).

Section 8721. (Copy to be filed with secretary of state.) When thus adopted, a copy of such amendment, with a certificate thereto affixed, stating the fact and date of its adoption, that such copy is a true copy thereof, signed by the president and secretary of the corporation, and if one there be, sealed with its seal, shall be recorded in the office of the secretary of state, who shall note on the margin of the record of the original articles filed by such corporation, and on the margin of the index thereto, the volume and page where such amendment is recorded. (R. S. Sec. 3238a; May 18, 1886, 83 v. 193.)

Section 8722. (When amendments take effect.) Amendments to articles of incorporation shall not take effect until filed for record with the secretary of state, nor, unless it be waived, until the corporation gives notice of them in some newspaper of general circulation in the county where its principal office is located, for three consecutive weeks. (R. S. Sec. 3238a; May 18, 1886, 83 v. 193.)

Section 8723. (How notices waived.) All the notices hereinbefore required in such proceedings to amend, may be waived when the holders of all the capital stock of a corporation, or all the members of one having no stock, consent thereto in writing. (R. S. Sec. 3238a; May 18, 1886, 83 v. 193.)

DIVIDENDS.

Section 8724. (Dividends to be paid from surplus profits only.) Directors of a corporation organized under the laws of this state shall not make dividends except from surplus profits arising from its business. (R. S. Sec. 3269-1; April 11, 1888, 85 v. 182, § 1.)

Dividends.

On preferred stock, see §§ 8668 to 8669.

Defined. Dividends consist of that portion of the profits which the directors separate from the general property and apply to the benefit of the stockholders.

State v. Farmers Bank, 11 Ohio 94 (1841).

Where the property of a corporation is divided among the stockholders, on the winding up of its affairs, the term "dividend" may be applied, although usually applied to the distribution of profits.

Larwill v. Burke, 19 C. C. 450, 513; 10 C. D. 579, 605 (1900).

Discretionary power of directors to declare dividends. In the absence of bad faith, or an arbitrary and unjustifiable withholding of the profits by the directors, the discretionary power of directors as to dividends will not be interfered with by the courts.

De La Croix v. Eid, etc., Co., 8 N. P. n. s. 489; 19 L. D. 767 (C. P. 1909).

See Arbuckle v. Woolson Spice Co., 21 C. C. 347, 356; 10 C. D. 743 (1901).

Mitchell v. Bookwalter Wheel Co., 4 N. P. n. s. 609; 17 L. D. 483 (1905); aff'd, 75 O. S. 639.

Moorehouse v. Crangle, 36 O. S. 130, 133 (1880).

Can not be declared or paid out of capital. A corporation has no power to declare or pay dividends out of its capital stock. A contract to pay dividends otherwise than out of profits is invalid and can not be enforced. Dividends can only be paid out of surplus profits.

Painesville, etc., R. Co. v. King, 17 O. S. 534 (1867).

Ohio College v. Rosenthal, 45 O. S. 183, 194 (1887).

De La Croix v. Eid, etc., Co., 8 N. P. n. s. 489; 19 L. D. 767 (C. P. 1909).

Wood v. Pearce, 2 Dis. 411 (Super. Ct. Cin. 1859).

Ryan v. Miami, etc., Ry. Co., 10 Am. L. R. 263 (1881).

Dividends on preferred stock can be paid out of surplus profits only.

Miller v. Ratterman, 47 O. S. 141, 158 (1890).

Mente v. Graff, 10 N. P. n. s. 148 (C. P. 1910).

Dividends paid out of capital, and not out of surplus profits, may be recovered from the stockholders by a trustee in bankruptcy of the corporation, although paid to preferred stockholders and received by them in good faith.

Mente v. Groff, 10 N. P. n. s. 148 (C. P. 1910).

See First N. B. v. Patton Co., 13 C. C. n. s. 289 (1910).

Railway Co. v. Burke, 19 W. L. B. 27 (C. P. 1887).

Guaranty of dividends. (a) By corporation. A general guaranty by a railroad company, of dividends on its preferred stock, was construed to be a guaranty of dividends only in the event that dividends were earned.

Miller v. Ratterman, 47 O. S. 141 (1890).

(b) Personal guaranty by officer of corporation. Where a person subscribed and paid for stock, relying on the verbal promise of the president of the corporation that the subscriber should receive fifteen percent on the amount invested, within one year, the agreement was held not to be within the statute of frauds.

Moorehouse v. Crangle, 36 O. S. 130 (1880).

Title to profits before declaration of dividend. The net earnings are the property of the corporation until a dividend is declared.

Adams v. Shields, 17 C. C. 129; 9 C. D. 558 (1898); aff'd, 61 O. S. 643.

Marble v. Van Wert N. B., 3 C. C. 464; 2 C. D. 265 (1888).

Dividend, when declared by directors, becomes a debt due to stockholders. When a dividend has been declared by the directors, it becomes a debt of the corporation to its stockholders. When declared out of profits, it can not be rescinded or revoked by the directors or by a majority of the stockholders.

Mitchell v. Bookwalter Wheel Co., 4 N. P. n. s. 609; 17 L. D. 483 (1905); aff'd, no rep., 75 O. S. 639.
See Cleveland Trust Co. v. Lander, 19 C. C. 271; 10 C. D. 452 (1900); aff'd, 62 O. S. 266.

To whom dividends payable. In general. Dividends are prima facie payable to the persons appearing on the corporate books as stockholders. The corporation is protected in paying to the registered stockholder in the absence of notice of the rights of other parties.
§ 8673-3.
Railroad Co. v. Robbins, 35 O. S. 483, 502 (1880).
Bank v. Mfg. Co., 67 O. S. 306, 314 (1902).
Norton v. Norton, 43 O. S. 509, 522 (1885).
A corporation is bound to respect the rights of equitable owners from the time it receives notice thereof.
Conant v. Seneca Co. Bank, 1 O. S. 298 (1853).
Where a corporation has paid dividends to one not entitled thereto, and has been compelled to pay the dividends a second time, it may recover the amount from the person who wrongfully obtained it.
Marble v. Van Wert N. B., 3 C. C. 464; 2 C. D. 265 (1888).

Where stock transferred. Future dividends follow the stock and are payable to the purchaser. It has been held that, on a sale of stock, no valid reservation of future dividends can be made.
Marble v. Van Wert N. B., 3 C. C. 464; 2 C. D. 265 (1888).
Dividends declared after the sale belong to the purchaser although earned prior to that time.
Dissette v. Lawrence Pub. Co., 9 C. C. n. s. 118; 19 C. D. 168 (1906).
Zinn v. Baxter, 65 O. S. 341, 366 (1901).
Where dividends have been declared by the directors and carried to the credit of the stockholder on the corporate books, the transferrer, and not the transferee, is entitled thereto.
City of Ohio v. Cleveland, etc., R. Co., 6 O. S. 489 (1856).
But where the dividends have not been declared, although earned, prior to the transfer, the transferrer has no interest in them.
See Dissette v. Lawrence Pbg. Co., 9 C. C. n. s. 118; 19 C. D. 168 (1906).
Where a creditor garnishees the interest of a stockholder in a corporation unpaid dividends follow the stock.
Norton v. Norton, 43 O. S. 509 (1885).

Application of dividends to payment of debt due from stockholder. Where a stockholder is indebted to the corporation, on a subscription to its stock, or on a valid assessment on his stock, the corporation may credit the dividends on such indebtedness.
Rhodes v. Equitable, etc., Co., 3 C. C. 501; 2 C. D. 288 (1888); aff'd, 27 W. L. B. 160.
A subscriber to stock is entitled to credit for the dividends declared thereon.
Iron Railroad Co. v. Fink, 41 O. S. 321, 326, 327 (1884).
The corporation may reserve a lien on dividends, by express stipulation in the certificate of stock.
§ 8673-15.
Bellevue Bank v. Higbee, 4 C. C. 222; 22 C. D. 512 (1889); aff'd, 28 W. L. B. 336.
Sale of stock to be paid for out of dividends.
See note to § 8682.
Stewart v. Herron, 77 O. S. 130.
White v. Cooper, 7 C. C. n. s. 114; 17 C. D. 703; aff'd, no rep., 72 O. S. 615, 691.

Stock dividends. When surplus profits exist they may be applied toward the payment of increased stock or unissued stock, and distributed among the stockholders as a stock dividend.

State v. Insurance Co., 13 C. C. n. s. 49; 22 C. D. 262 (1910); aff'd, 84 O. S. 459.

See 7 O. L. R. 352 (article by Frank M. Coppock).

Stearns v. Hibben, etc., Co., 11 C. C. n. s. 553 (1909).

Railway Co. v. Furnace Co., 49 O. S. 102 (1892).

A stock dividend, like a cash dividend, may be declared only when surplus profits exist. Where a stock dividend was declared at a time when there were no surplus profits, the stockholders who accepted the certificates may be compelled by creditors to pay for such stock.

Handley v. Stutz, 139 U. S. 417 (1891).

See note to § 8674. *Who are liable.*

An offer by stockholders to return the stock is too late after insolvency of the corporation and a suit begun to enforce liability.

First N. B. v. Patton Co., 13 C. C. n. s. 289 (1910).

As between a life tenant and remainderman stock dividends, declared out of earnings retained by the corporation and treated as part of its capital, go to the remainderman, although a part of the earnings were accumulated and carried as cash, if such funds were devoted to the extension and promotion of the corporate business.

Miller v. Miller, 15 C. C. n. s. 481; 58 Bull 125 (1912); s. c., 13 N. P. n. s. 1, 17-24.

Scrip certificates. The issuing to stockholders of scrip certificates, redeemable in the future in the stock of the corporation, is not the declaring of a dividend, nor a promise to pay money. It is merely a promise to make a future stock dividend.

Adams v. Shields, 17 C. C. 129; 9 C. D. 558 (1898); aff'd, no rep., 61 O. S. 643.

Actions to recover dividends.

Action is at law.

Larwill v. Burke, 19 C. C. 450, 513 (1900).

Moore v. Lima N. B., 8 C. C. 287, 297; 4 C. D. 529 (1894).

Before the enactment of the uniform transfer act (§ 8673-1 et seq.) it was held that an equitable owner of stock might sue for dividends.

Larwill v. Burke, 19 C. C. 449, 513; 10 C. D. 579, 605 (1900).

Conant v. Seneca County Bank, 1 O. S. 298 (1853).

Demand before suit and statute of limitations. A demand must be made on the corporation for the dividend before suit.

Stearns v. Hibben, etc., Co., 11 C. C. n. s. 553 (1908).

Larwill v. Burke, 19 C. C. 449, 513, 526, 532; 10 C. D. 579, 605 (1900).

An action to recover a dividend is barred in six years from the time when it is due and payable.

Stearns v. Hibben, etc., Co., 11 C. C. n. s. 553, 560; 21 C. D. 270 (1908).

Where no time is fixed by the directors for payment, a dividend is due and payable within a reasonable time.

Mitchell v. Bookwalter Wheel Co., 4 N. P. n. s. 609; 17 L. D. 483 (C. P. 1905); aff'd, 75 O. S. 639.

Although a demand is necessary before bringing an action to recover dividends, failure to make such demand does not suspend the operation of the statute of limitations.

Stearns v. Hibben, etc., Co., 11 C. C. n. s. 553, 560; 21 C. D. 270 (1908).

Except under circumstances where the dividends are held under a continuing trust.

Larwill v. Burke, 19 C. C. 449, 513, 526, 532; 10 C. D. 579, 605 (1900).

Officers not liable. When declared by the directors, a dividend becomes the debt of the corporation. The officers of the corporation are not personally liable therefor.

Snodgrass v. Morrison, etc., Co., 4 O. L. R. 622; 17 L. D. 497 (Super. Ct. Cin. 1907).

Miscellaneous. A bequest of dividends, without limitation as to time or other qualification, is a bequest of the stock itself.

Collier v. Collier, 3 O. S. 369 (1854).

A by-law of an incorporated co-operative sales company, making the right to certain dividends dependent on the stockholder marketing his entire product through the corporation, has been held valid.

Kroger, etc., Co. v. Butchers Hide Ass., 8 N. P. n. s. 222 (C. P. 1909).

Upon attaining their majority the daughters of R, who was their guardian and held stock inherited by them from their mother, appeared in probate court, receipted for balances shown to be due them on account of dividends collected, and in writing asked that the accounts of their father as guardian be approved. For some years thereafter they permitted him to draw and use the dividends, and then by a written agreement authorized him to draw and use the dividends during his life. After another long interval suits were filed by the daughters for a rescission of the agreement and for a judgment for the dividends drawn. Held, the action was not maintainable.

Lamkin v. Robinson, 15 C. C. n. s. 126; 34 C. D. 91; aff'd, no rep., 88 O. S. —; reversing 10 N. P. n. s. 1; 21 L. D. 13.

Section 8725. (Unpaid interest not profits.) In calculating its profits, prior to a dividend, interest then unpaid, although due, on debts owing to it, shall not be included. (R. S. Sec. 3269-2; April 11, 1888, 85 v. 182, § 2.)

Section 8726. (How profits ascertained.) In order to ascertain the surplus profits from which a dividend may be made, in the account of profit and loss there shall be charged and deducted from the actual profits—

1. All ordinary and extraordinary expenses, paid or incurred, in managing the affairs and transacting the business of the corporation.

2. Interest paid, or then due or accrued, on debts it owes.

3. All losses of the corporation. In computing its losses, debts owing to it which have been due without prosecution, or interest paid thereon, for more than one year, or upon which judgment was recovered, but has been more than two years unsatisfied, and on which also for that period, no interest was paid, shall be included. (April 10, 1889, 86 v. 228, § 3; April 11, 1888, 85 v. 182, 183.)

The profits need not have been earned during the current year. If undivided profits have been accumulated and carried over, a dividend may be declared therefrom, although no profits were earned during the current year.

Mente v. Groff, 10 N. P. n. s. 148, 157 (C. P. 1910).

Section 8727.   (What advertisements prohibited.) No such corporation shall advertise a larger amount of capital stock than actually has been subscribed and paid in, nor advertise a greater dividend than actually has been earned and credited or paid to its stockholders or members. (R. S. Sec. 3269-4; April 10, 1889, 86 v. 228; April 11, 1888, 85 v. 182, 183.)

Issuing fraudulent prospectus of financial condition, penalty, see § 13175.

Section 8728.   (Liability for violation.) Every director of such a corporation, who violates or is concerned in violating any provision of the next four preceding sections shall be personally liable to its creditors and stockholders for any loss which thereby they respectively sustain. (R. S. Sec. 3269-4; April 11, 1888, 85 v. 183, § 4.)

See notes to § 8660.
Wrongful payment of dividends.
See Excelsior Water, etc., Co. v. Pierce, 90 Cal. 131 (1891).
Braun v. Riggle, 7 Ky. Law Rep. 519 (1886).
Cornell v. Seddinger, 237 Pa. St. 389.
Where directors of a corporation caused a notice to be published that they and the stockholders were personally responsible for the debts of the company, when the charter did not make them so responsible, a creditor of the corporation who extended credit to it on the faith of such notice may maintain an action against the directors for deceit.
Westervelt v. Demorest, 46 N. J. Law, 37 (1884).
See Cross v. Sackett, 16 How. Pr. (N. Y.) 62 (1858).
Cazeaux v. Mali, 25 Barb. (N. Y.) (1857).
Morse v. Swits, 19 How. Pr. (N. Y.) 275 (1859).
Salmon v. Richardson, 30 Conn. 360 (1862).
Fenn v. Curtis, 23 Hun 384 (1881).
Dividends illegally paid by directors may, in an action by stockholders for mismanagement, be deducted from the stockholders' losses and may be adjudicated in the action.
Glass v. Courtright, 14 N. P. n. s. 273; 23 L. D. 253 (C. P. 1913).

MISCELLANEOUS.

Section 8729.   (Affidavit as to campaign contributions.) Every corporation for profit doing business in this state, except corporations required by law to file annual report with the auditor of state or the superintendent of insurance, annually during the month of May, if it be a domestic corporation, and during the month of September, if it be a foreign corporation, shall file with the secretary of state in such form as he prescribes, an affidavit subscribed and sworn to by an officer having knowledge of the facts therein set forth, setting forth that such corporation has not during the preceding year directly or indirectly paid, used or offered, consented or agreed to pay or use, any of its money or property for, or in aid, of any political party, committee or organization, or for, or in aid of, any candidate for political office or for nomination for any such office, or in any manner used any of its money or property for any political purpose whatever, or for the reimbursement or indemnification of any person or persons for moneys or property so used. Such forms of affidavits as the secretary prescribes shall be attached to or made part of the report required to be made of such corporation under the law, requiring corporations to file annual reports with the secretary of state and to pay annual fee therefor. (February 26, 1908, 99 v. 23, § 2.)

See §§ 5522, 13320.
This section does not apply to partisan newspapers.
    Rep. Atty. Gen. (1908-1909) 76.
    A corporation may pay for the insertion of an advertisement in the program of a convention of a political party.
    Rep. Atty. Gen. (1908-1909) 86.

Section 8730. (Affidavit in annual reports to auditor and superintendent of insurance.) Corporations required by law to file annual reports with the auditor of state or the superintendent of insurance, shall file with such officers similar affidavits in such form as the auditor of state or the superintendent of insurance prescribes. The form of affidavit presented by such officer shall be attached to or made a part of the report required to be made of such corporation under existing laws. The affidavit shall be made at the time when such reports are required to be made. (February 26, 1908, 99 v. 23, § 2.)

Section 8731. (By what laws corporations shall be governed.) Corporations created before the adoption of the present constitution, which have not, by election or some other act, come to be governed by laws since passed, shall be governed and controlled by the laws then in force, and the valid modifications thereof since or herein enacted. Other corporations now existing or hereafter created shall be governed and controlled by the provisions of this title. (R. S. Sec. 3232; R. S. 1880.)

A general law of the state will affect companies incorporated under special acts, as to which there was a reserved power of amendment or repeal.

State v. Cincinnati Gas, etc., Co., 18 O. S. 262.

Although the special charter is not subject to amendment or repeal, the corporation is subject to general police regulation and control.

State v. Columbus, etc., Co., 34 O. S. 572 (1878).

State v. Eagle Ins. Co., 50 O. S. 252 (1893).

Gas companies incorporated under special charters are subject to § 3982 authorizing municipalities to regulate the price of gas, where the right to fix their own rates is not expressly granted in the charters.

Zanesville v. Gas Light Co., 47 O. S. 1, 35 (1889).

A corporation organized under a special act, for a certain specified time, may be treated as a corporation where it continues to exercise its corporate powers after the expiration of the time for which it was chartered.

Myers v. Lucas, 16 C. C. 545; 8 C. D. 431 (1898); reversed on other grounds, 63 O. S. 101.

The Association of the Tobacco Trade of Cincinnati, a corporation formed under the act of April 3, 1866 (S. & S. 182), since the repeal of that act, is under this section governed by the provisions of title IX of the General Code.

State v. Casey, 38 O. S. 555 (1883).

Railroad companies organized under the act of 1848, before the adoption of the present constitution, and which have not relinquished their right to be governed by said act, are not bound by later acts reducing the rates of freight.

Iron R. R. Co. v. Lawrence Furnace Co., 29 O. S. 208 (1876).

Section 8732. (What corporations may accept the provisions of this title.) A corporation created before the adoption of the present constitution, and now actually doing business, may accept any of the provisions of this title. When a certified copy of such acceptance is filed with the secretary of state, so much of its charter as is inconsistent with the provisions of this title is hereby repealed. (R. S. Sec. 3233; May 1, 1852, 50 v. 274, § 71; S. & C. 309.)

A certificate of acceptance is merely evidence of the fact of acceptance, and is not indispensable. Acceptance may be implied from the use of privileges granted by the present law. A railroad company by taking or making leases authorized by the present law was held to thereby accept the present law and to relinquish all rights inconsistent thereith.

C. H. & D. R. Co. v. Cole, 29 O. S. 126 (1876).

Owen v. Purdy, 12 O. S. 73 (1861).

Dayton, etc., R. Co. v. Hatch, 1 Disney 84 (1855).

Zabriskie v. Cleveland, etc., R. Co., 23 How. (U. S.) 381, 396, 397 (1860).

See also, G. C. § 8736 and note.

An amendment of a charter can not be accepted in part. It must be accepted or rejected in toto.

Marietta, etc., R. Co. v. Elliott, 10 O. S. 57, 60 (1859).

Baldwin v. Hillsborough R. Co., 10 W. L. J. 337 (1853).

By adopting the provisions of this title a corporation can not acquire powers or rights inconsistent with its original charter.

Rep. Atty. Gen. 1911-1912, p. 798.

A corporation organized under special charter, which desires to change its name and at the same time preserve its corporate powers intact, should apply to the legislature for a special act changing the name.

Rep. Atty. Gen. 1911-1912, p. 1679.

Special privileges conferred by private charter under the constitution of 1802 do not so inhere in the railroad constructed under the charter as necessarily to pass to any corporation which, by subsequent legislation, may acquire the right to operate the road.

Pittsburg, etc., Ry. Co. v. Moore, 33 O. S. 384 (1878).

Section 8733. (Special charters not accepted or acted upon.) All special acts of incorporation in force in this state, which have not been accepted, or acted upon, be and the same are hereby repealed. (R. S. Sec. 3233-1; February 12, 1861, 58 v. 12.)

A special charter, being deemed merely an offer on the part of the state until acceptance, may be revoked and repealed at any time before acceptance.

State v. Damson, 16 Ind. 40 (1861).

Effect of constitution of 1851 on unaccepted charters.

See State v. Roosa, 11 O. S. 16 (1860).
Citizens Bank v. Wright, 6 O. S. 318 (1856).

Judicial notice of special charters. Held not judicially noticed; must be pleaded under G. C. § 11340 (R. S. 5092).

Pittsburg, etc., Co. v. Moore, 33 O. S. 384 (1878).
Contra, Brown v. State, 11 Ohio 276 (1842).
Jones v. Scudder, 2 C. S. C. R. 178 (1872).
See Railroad Co. v. Hoffhines, 46 O. S. 643, 650 (1889).
State v. Granville Society, 11 Ohio 1, 9 (1841).
Beaty v. Knowler, 4 Pet. 152.

Section 8734. (Duty of secretary of state; effect of charter.) When it is made to appear to the satisfaction of the secretary of state that any religious society or corporation heretofore organized or incorporated under the laws of this state has lost its charter or certificate of incorporation, or that it has been destroyed, he shall issue a new certificate of incorporation of such religious society or corporation of the date of issuing such lost or destroyed certificate as near as shall be made to appear to him. Thereupon all deeds, mortgages, or other instruments of writing for the conveyance of land, as well as all acts done by such religious society or corporation by virtue of such lost certificate or charter, shall be binding and of full force in law and in equity. But nothing herein shall be construed to make valid any act not authorized under the laws of this state which heretofore have been in force. (R. S. Sec. 3233-2; March 25, 1878, 75 v. 77.)

Section 8735. (Prima facie evidence of incorporation.) The fact that a religious society for not less than thirty

years, claiming to have been duly and legally incorporated
as such, and performing during such time duties and exercising rights as such, shall be prima facie evidence of the
original issue of such charter or certificate of incorporation
as claimed by such society. (R. S. Sec. 3233-3; March 25,
1878, 75 v. 77.)

See Congregational Church v. Webber, 54 Mich. 571.

Section 8736. (Corporations created prior to 1851.) Corporations created before the adoption of the present constitution, which take any action under or in pursuance of this
title, shall thereby and thereafter be deemed to have consented, and be held to be a corporation, and to have and
exercise all its franchises under the present constitution and
the laws passed in pursuance thereof, and not otherwise.
But any fire insurance company so created, filing annual
reports with the superintendent of insurance, as provided
by law, or complying with any police regulation contained
in chapter one of subdivision two of division three of this
title, or in chapter two of division two of title three, part
first, shall not be deemed to have consented, nor be affected
by the provisions of this section by reason of such compliance. (R. S. Sec. 3234; March 8, 1892, 89 v. 73; May 18,
1886, 83 v. 201; R. S. 1880.)

See note to § 8732.

Corporate acts constituting acceptance. Railroad company taking
or making leases.
C. H. & D. R. Co. v. Cole, 29 O. S. 126 (1876).
Consolidation of railroad companies.
Shields v. State, 26 O. S. 86 (1875); affirmed, 95 U. S. 319.
Receiving real estate in payment of subscriptions to stock of railroad
company.
Goodin v. Evans, 18 O. S. 150 (1868).
Dayton, etc., R. Co. v. Hatch, 1 Disney 84 (1855).
General course of business transacted by a bank.
Owen v. Purdy, 12 O. S. 73, 80 (1861).
Change of time of election and terms of directors.
State v. Lakamp, 4 C. C. 257; 2 C. D. 533 (1889).
Fire insurance company issuing policies authorized by general laws,
and not authorized by its charter.
Knox County Mutual Ins. Co. v. Bowersox, 6 C. C. 275; 3 C. D. 451
(1892).
5 Opins. Attys. Gen. 853, 935 (1900).
Continuing to act as a corporation after the time limited in the
special charter for its expiration.
Myers v. Lucas, 16 C. C. 545; 8 C. D. 431 (1898); reversed, on other
grounds, 63 O. S. 101.

Acceptance by directors. Where the special charter conferred such
authority on the directors, acceptance by the directors is binding upon
the corporation.

Goodin v. Evans, 18 O. S. 150, 167 (1868).
Dayton, etc., R. Co. v. Hatch, 1 Disney 84, 92 (1855).

Estoppel of stockholders to deny acceptance.
Goodin v. Evans, 18 O. S. 150, 168 (1868).
Owen v. Purdy, 12 O. S. 73, 78 (1861).

Statute imposing new liability on stockholders. A statute imposing upon stockholders, without their consent, a liability not imposed by the charter, is unconstitutional. The assent of a stockholder to such a liability is not presumed, but must be proved.
Ireland v. Palestine, etc., Turnpike Co., 19 O. S. 369 (1869).
See Owen v. Purdy, 12 O. S. 73, 79 (1861).

Fire insurance companies. A fire insurance company is not exempt from G. C. §§ 9590 to 9592 unless such exemption was clearly granted by its charter.
State v. Eagle Insurance Co., 50 O. S. 252 (1893); affirmed, 153 U. S. 446.

Section 8737.   (When provisions do not apply.) This chapter does not apply when special provision is made in subsequent chapters of this title, but the special provision shall govern, unless it clearly appears that the provision is cumulative. (R. S. Sec. 3269; R. S. 1880.)

The general corporation law (§§ 8623 to 8743 inclusive) does not apply to the organization of insurance companies, which are governed by § 9339 et seq.
State v. Pioneer Live Stock Co., 38 O. S. 347 (1882).
The provisions of § 8683 authorizing a corporation to acquire stock in certain other companies apply to railroad companies and are not inconsistent with §§ 8806 to 8809, but are cumulative.
Mannington v. H. V. Ry. Co., 8 O. L. R. 451, 477; 183 Fed. 133; 16 O. F. D. 552 (C. C. 1910).

"Unless it clearly appears that the provision is cumulative." "Clearly" means "in a clear manner; without obscurity; without entanglement or confusion; without uncertainty."
"Cumulative" means "additional; that which is superadded to another thing of the same character and not substituted for it."
Mannington v. H. V. Ry. Co., 8 O. L. R. 451, 477; 183 Fed. 133; 16 O. F. D. 552 (1910).

DISSOLUTION.

Section 8738.   (Dissolution by abandonment of objects.) When a majority of the directors, trustees, or other officers of a corporation not for profit desire to abandon its corporate existence and it has no debts, or in case of a corporation for profit when a majority of such officers become satisfied that the objects of the corporation cannot be accomplished, that no installment of its capital stock has been paid, no investments made, and that it has no debts, they, or the president of the board of directors, trustees, or other officers, may call a meeting of the members or stockholders of the corporation at such time and place as he or they designate by at least two weeks' publication in a newspaper published and of general circulation in the county wherein the principal office is located. (R. S. Sec. 5674; April 18, 1902, 95 v. 208; May 4, 1869, 66 v. 94, § 1.)

Dissolution by judicial proceedings see §§ 11938 to 11973.
Forfeiture of charter § 12304 et seq.

Section 8739.   (Filing of certificate.) If a majority of the members of such corporation not for profit present at such meeting desire such abandonment, or a majority in amount of the stockholders of such corporation for profit present in person or by proxy decide that the objects of such corporation cannot be accomplished then such corporation shall be abandoned or dissolved upon the filing of a certificate of such abandonment or dissolution with the secretary of state in the manner provided by law. (R. S. Sec. 5674; April 18, 1902, 95 v. 208; May 4, 1869, 66 v. 94, § 1.)

See § 5521.

Section 8740.   (Dissolution by corporation whose business is closed.) When a majority of the directors or other officers having the management of the concerns of a corporation for profit, which has completely closed its business, and paid all the debts and liabilities incurred by it, desire to surrender its corporate authority and franchises, they, or the president of such board of directors, may call a meeting of the stockholders at such time or place as he or they designate by publication for four weeks in some newspaper published and of general circulation in the county wherein the principal office of the corporation is located and by written notices addressed to each of the stockholders whose residence is known, of the object, time and place of the meeting. (R. S. Sec. 5674a; April 18, 1902, 95 v. 208.)

Section 8741.   (Filing of certificate.) If all the stockholders present at such meeting in person or by proxy decide to surrender and abandon its corporate authority the corporation shall be abandoned and dissolved upon the filing of a certificate of the abandonment or dissolution with the secretary of state in the manner provided by law. (R. S. Sec. 5674a; April 18, 1902, 95 v. 208.)

A certificate from tax commission that the corporation has made all reports and paid all taxes is required as a condition precedent to filing a certificate of dissolution. § 5521.

Section 8742. (Trustees to settle affairs of corporation.) Upon the dissolution of a corporation by the expiration of the term of its charter, or otherwise, and unless other persons be appointed by the legislature, or by the stockholders, directors, or trustees of the corporation, or by a court of competent authority, the directors, trustees, or managers of the affairs of such corporation, acting last before the time of its dissolution by whatever name known in law, and their survivors, shall be the trustees of the creditors and stockholders of the dissolved corporation, and have full power to settle its affairs, collect and pay outstanding debts, and divide among the stockholders the money and other property remaining, in proportion to the stock of each stockholder paid up, after payment of debts and necessary expenses. (R. S. Sec. 5675; March 21, 1850, 48 v. 90, § 5; March 7, 1842, 40 v. 67, § 14; S. & C. 363.)

Where a corporation, organized for the purpose of disposing of land, completed its business and adjourned *sine die* in 1809 it is presumed that the corporation was dissolved and that neither its stockholders nor their successors retained any interest in a strip of land which had been dedicated as a street.

Cleveland v. Railways, 8 N. P. n. s. 457 (C. P. 1909; aff'd, 15 C. C. n. s. 193; 87 O. S. 469).

Section 8743. (Powers and duties of such trustees.) The persons so constituted trustees may sue for and recover the debts and property of the dissolved corporation, by the name of trustees of the corporation, describing it by its corporate name, and jointly and severally they shall be responsible to the creditors and stockholders of the corporation, to the extent of its property and effects coming into their hands. Such trustees may be made or become parties to any action, by or against the corporation. All liens of judgments existing at the time of the dissolution either in favor of or against the corporation, shall continue in force as if the dissolution had not taken place. (R. S. Sec. 5675; March 21, 1850, 48 v. 90, § 5; March 7, 1842, 40 v. 67, § 14; S. & C. 363, 366.)

The trustees may sue in their collective names, not in their individual names.

Martin v. Trustees of Belmont Bank, 13 Ohio 250 (1844).

The trustees may have judgment entered on a cognovit note owned by the corporation at the time of its dissolution.

Martin v. Trustees of Belmont Bank, 13 Ohio 250 (1844).

Suits against defunct corporation.

See Renick v. Bank of West Union, 13 Ohio 298 (1844).

Service of process upon the members of its last acting board of directors is sufficient, under the statute, to give the court jurisdiction.

Warner v. Callender, 20 O. S. 190 (1870).

Vallette v. Kentucky Trust Co., 2 Handy 1 (1855).

Directors of a dissolved corporation may voluntarily enter their appearance in an action against the corporation.

In re Columbus Bicycle Co., 1 N. P. n. s. 461; 14 L. D. 407 (C. P. 1908).

PART XVI.

RAILROADS.

CHAPTER 1.

SPECIAL POWERS.

Section 8744. (Office of company in state.) As soon as convenient after its organization, each railway company shall establish a principal or general office at some point on the line of its road, or the line of a road within this state with which it connects or has running arrangements, but its location may be changed at pleasure. The company shall give notice of the establishment or change of such office in some newspaper published on its line in this state. The offices of its president, secretary and treasurer shall be at such general office, or some other point on its line of road in this state, and a record there kept of all the company's proceedings, to be open at reasonable hours for the inspection of any stockholder. (R. S. Sec. 3311; April 9, 1880, 77 v. 153; R. S. 1880; May 1, 1852, 50 v. 274, § 17.)

A mining company having built a railroad under § 10141 may change
the office of its railroad under this section, but not its principal office,
which can only be changed under § 8719.
  State v. Coal Co., 4 N. P. 115; 6 L. D. 178 (C. P. 1897).
  Snow Fork, etc., Co. v. Railroad Co., 7 N. P. 191; 6 L. D. 178 (C. P.
      1897).
Forfeiture of franchise for failure to maintain office.
  See Simmons v. Norfolk, etc., Co., 113 N. C. 147 (1893).
  State v. Milwaukee, etc., R. R. Co., 45 Wis. 579 (1878).
  People v. Kingston Co., 23 Wend. (N. Y.) 193 (1840).
  State v. South Pac. Co., 24 Tex. 80 (1859).

CONSTRUCTION.

Section 8745. Any railroad company may maintain and
operate, or construct, maintain and operate a railroad, with
such main tracks, not exceeding six and such side tracks,
turnouts, offices, depots, round-houses, machine shops, water
tanks, telegraph lines, and other necessary appliances, as it
deems necessary, between the points named in its articles of
incorporation, commencing at or within, and extending to
or into any city, village, or place named as a terminus of
its road. (May 10, 1910, 101 v. 323; April 7, 1908, 99 v. 71;
R. S. Sec. 3270; April 29, 1872, 69 v. 203, § 4.)

Articles of incorporation.
  See note to § 8625.

Nature of railroad companies.   Private or public corporations.
Railroad companies are not private corporations in the strict sense of the
ordinary business corporation, because they are charged with duties of a
public nature which distinguish them from the purely and strictly private
corporation, but in many respects they are private corporations in all
that the term implies.   They can not be treated as public corporations,
such as cities, counties, townships, etc.   Their foundation is private.
They are organized for gain, and their strictly private rights are as much
beyond legislative control as are the rights of the purely private corporation.
  Mannington v. Railway Co., 8 O. L. R. 451, 479; 183 Fed. 133; 16
      O. F. D. 552 (C. C. 1910).

Interurban railway when a "railroad."
  See note to § 9117.

Constitutionality of statutes applying to railroad companies. A
statute applying to railroad companies and not to other corporations is
valid where reasonable grounds exist for its application to railroad companies which do not exist as to other corporations.
  Froelich v. Railway Co., 5 C. C. n. s. 6; 14 C. D. 359 (1903).

  Termini. A railroad company is authorized by this section to construct and operate a railroad having both of its terminal points wholly
within the same city.
  State v. Railroad, 72 O. S. 455 (1905).
  Cincinnati, etc., R. Co. v. Murray, 1 N. P. n. s. 301; 51 Bull. 623 (Ct.
      of Ins. 1903).

There is nothing in this section which requires the termini to be in towns or cities.

Long Branch Com'rs v. West Line R. R. Co., 29 N. J. Eq. 566 (1878).

Attorney-General v. Delaware, etc., R. R. Co., 12 C. E. Green (N. J.) 645 (1876).

When a charter empowered a company to build a road from a town a location sixty rods outside the town is not in compliance with the charter, and the company may be compelled to extend the road.

Comm. v. Erie, etc., R. Co., 27 Pa. St. 339-352 (1856).

Where a company is empowered to build to a certain city, it is not barred from reaching such point by the fact that it made a point outside such city a temporary terminus.

Colorado, etc., Ry. Co. v. Union Pac. Ry. Co., 41 Fed. Rep. 293 (1890).

Childs v. Railroad Co., 33 N. J. L. 323 (1869).

Statements in articles of incorporation as to route and termini, see § 8625 and notes.

Change of terminus within municipality, see note to § 8747.

POWERS OF RAILROAD COMPANIES.

General powers.

See notes to §§ 8627 and 12304.

To cross streets and highways. By its articles of incorporation a railroad company is empowered to locate its tracks across streets and highways.

Commissioners v. Penna Co., 6 N. P. n. s. 141; 18 L. D. 348 (C. P. 1907); aff'd, Cir. Ct., no rep.

State v. Montclair Ry. Co., 35 N. J. L. 328 (1872).

Lewis v. Germantown, etc., R. Co., 16 Phila. (Pa.) 608 (1881).

See §§ 8763 to 8766, 8773, 8857.

To maintain side tracks. A side track constructed by a railroad company to a manufactory at the expense and over the land of the latter, solely for its advantage, under an agreement silent as to time, may not be maintained by the railroad company over the objection of the owner of the manufactory.

Rodefer v. Railroad, 72 O. S. 272 (1905).

To build and maintain bridges. Power to build a railroad between certain points implies power to bridge streams when necessary.

Fall River Iron Works Co. v. Old Colony, etc., R. Co., 5 Allen (Mass.) 221 (1862).

Hamilton v. Vicksburg, etc., R. Co., 34 La. Ann. 970 (1882); s. c., 119 U. S. 280.

Miller v. Prairie du Chien Ry. Co., 34 Wis. 533 (1874).

Works v. Junction R. Co., McLean (U. S.) 425 (1853); 3 O. F. D. 101. Power to build includes power to repair bridges.

Hamilton v. Vicksburg, etc., R. R. Co., 119 U. S. 280.

Central Trust Co. v. Wabash, etc., Ry. Co., 32 Fed. 566.

A railroad company will not be restrained from rebuilding a bridge across a stream when it will cause no greater obstruction than the old bridge.

Board of Com'rs v. Pierce, 90 Fed. 764 (1898).

A railroad bridge is a part of its line. Land may be appropriated for an approach thereto.

L. & N. Ry. v. Taylor, 50 Bull. 20 (Ct. of Insolv. 1904).

Care required in constructing bridge. Liability. In the construction, repair and maintenance of its bridges a railroad company is bound to use reasonable care.

N. Y., etc., R. Co. v. Ellis, 13 C. C. 704; 6 C. D. 304 (1895).

But in the absence of a statute, or of evidence showing that it is usual, a railroad bridge need not be constructed so as to permit a person to stand thereon while a train is passing.

Erie R. Co. v. McCormick, 69 O. S. 45 (1903).

Recovery for damages to land by flood waters can not be had from a railroad company where the flood was unprecedented, and other causes to produce the injury intervened.

B. & O. R. Co. v. Simpson, 12 C. C. n. s. 185 (1906).

To make construction contracts. A railroad company may enter into a contract with another person for the construction of its road without retaining control over the mode and manner of doing the work, and may under proper circumstances be exempt from liability for the wrongful act of its contractors.

Hughes v. Cincinnati, etc., Ry. Co., 39 O. S. 461 (1883).
Cincinnati, etc., R. Co. v. Iliff, 13 O. S. 235, 247 (1862).
Carman v. Steubenville, etc., R. Co., 4 O. S. 399 (1854).
Interpretation of construction contract.
See Cleveland, etc., R. Co. v. Kelley, 5 O. S. 180 (1855).
Mansfield, etc., R. R. Co. v. Veeder, 17 Ohio 385 (1848).

To run along and upon highways. Only in cases of necessity has a railroad power to build its road along and upon a highway.

Springfield v. Connecticut River R. R. Co., 4 Cush. (Mass.) 63 (1849).
Kenton County Bank v. Bank Lick Turnpike Co., 10 Bush. (Ky.) 529 (1874).
G. C. § 8766.

To purchase land to procure materials. A railroad company may, if necessary and convenient, purchase land for the purpose of obtaining gravel, timber, etc., for construction purposes.

Overmeyer v. Williams, 15 Ohio 26.

Power and obligation to operate. Power to purchase implies authority to operate.

Campbell v. Marietta, etc., R. Co., 23 O. S. 168 (1872).
When company compelled to operate.
See Port Clinton R. Co. v. Cleveland, etc., R. Co., 13 O. S. 544 (1862).
Chapman v. Mad River, etc., R. Co., 6 O. S. 120 (1856).

To acquire stock in other corporations.

See §§ 8806, 8683 and notes.

To purchase other railroads. Power to locate and construct branch roads does not by implication confer authority to purchase the railroad of another company.

Campbell v. Marietta, etc., R. Co., 23 O. S. 168 (1872).
See § 8807.

Eminent domain.

See §§ 8759, 8760.

Sleeping car contracts.

See Stanley v. Cleveland, etc., R. R. Co., 18 O. S. 552 (1869).

To accept donations.

See Elder v. Bellaire, etc., Ry. Co., 1 C. C. 256; 1 C. D. 140 (1885).
Sperry v. Johnson, 11 Ohio 452 (1842).

To engage in mining, telegraph, etc., business, either directly or through stock control. A railroad company may build and operate a

telegraph line, and may operate coal mines, for its own use, but can not
engage in the general telegraph, mining or other outside business.
    State v. Railway Co., 12 C. C. n. s. 49, 62; 21 C. D. 175 (1909).
    Railroad Co. v. Telegraph Co., 38 O. S. 24 (1882).
    Telegraph Co. v. Railroad Co., 1 W. L. B. 201, 309 (1876).

    To guarantee bonds of mining company. A railroad company can
not lawfully indorse and guarantee the bonds of a coal mining company.
Such an obligation may be valid in favor of the bondholders, but not as
against the state.
    State v. H. V. Ry. Co., 12 C. C. n. s. 49, 66; 21 C. D. 175 (1909).

    To operate street railway. A railroad company has no power to
engage in the street railway business.
    Rogers v. Railway Co., 12 L. D. 136 (Super. Ct. Cin. 1901).

    To locate road. All charters must be taken to allow the exercise
of a discretion in the location of the route as is incident to an ordinary
practical survey of the same, made with reference to the nature of the
country to be passed over and the obstacles to be encountered or avoided.
The courts will interfere only in cases of abuse of such discretion.
    Walker v. Mad River R. R. Co., 8 Ohio 38 (1837).
    Callender v. Painesville, etc., R. Co., 11 O. S. 524 (1860).
    Southern, etc., R. Co. v. Stoddard, 6 Minn. 150 (1861).
    Fall River Co. v. Old Colony, etc., R. Co., 5 Allen (Mass.) 221 (1862).
    Auspach v. Maganoy, etc., R. Co., 5 Phila. (Pa.) 491 (1864).
    See Baldwin v. Hillsborough, etc., R. Co., 10 W. L. J. 337 (1853).
    If the location is not in substantial compliance with the articles, the
company may be dissolved.
    State v. Railway, 40 O. S. 504 (1884).

    When road is located. A road is said to be located when a survey
is completed and accepted. The supreme court of Pennsylvania, in Wil-
liamsport R. Co. v. Railroad Co., 141 Pa. St. 407 (1891), said:
    "The successive steps contemplated as necessary to vest a title to the
railway in the corporation are these:
    "1. A preliminary entry on the lands of private owners for the pur-
pose of exploration. This is made by engineers or surveyors, who run or
work one or more experimental lines, and who report their work, with
such maps and profiles as may be necessary to represent it properly to
the company that employs them.
    "2. A selection and adoption of a line, or one of the lines so run,
as and for the location of the proposed railroad. This is done by the corporation, and it requires the action in some form of the board of directors.
This makes what was before experimental and open, a fixed and definite
location. It fastens a servitude upon the property affected thereby, and
so takes from the owner and appropriates to the use of the corporation.
    "3. Payment to the owner for what is taken and the consequences
of the taking, or security that it shall be made when the amount due
him is legally ascertained. The title of the owner is not divested until
the last of these steps has been taken. As against him the corporation
can acquire only a conditional title by its act of location, which ripens
into an absolute one upon making compensation.
    "As to third persons and rival corporations, however, the action of
the company adopting a definite location is enough to give title.

*   *   *   *   *   *   *   *   *.   *   *   *

    "In many states provision is made by law for recording the action of
the company and the line adopted by it, so as to give notice to the public
and to settle questions of priority of location. We have no such statute,
and the action of the company must be proved by other competent evi-

dence, but when proved it has the same effect upon all interested as though it had been recorded. It settles the date of actual appropriation, and shows the exact location of the line of the road proposed."

See Baldwin v. Hillsborough R. R. Co., 10 W. L. J. 356 (1853).

Agreement for location of road. An agreement for the location of the route of a railroad at a particular intermediate place is not per se void as against public policy.

Railroad Co. v. Ralston, 41 O. S. 573 (1885).

See Pittsburg, etc., Ry. Co. v. Rose, 24 O. S. 119 (1856).

Surveying and staking do not constitute a location. A line of road is not so "located" by surveying and staking without condemnation or purchase as to give the company a right to the land exclusive of another railroad company that subsequently surveys and stakes the same line, and begins appropriation proceedings. Such first company can not enjoin the second company from entering on such land. Its remedy is at law.

Columbus Terminal, etc., v. Toledo Ry. Co., 32 W. L. B. 186 (1894).

Section 8746. (Terminus on state line or boundary.) When a terminus named in the articles of incorporation is a county upon the line or boundary of the state, the president and directors of the company, upon the location of the road in that county, shall make and acknowledge a certificate definitely fixing the location in such county, and file it with the secretary of state. (R. S. Sec. 3271; 69 v. 163, § 1.)

Section 8747. (Changes of line or termini.) By a resolution adopted by a majority of its board of directors, at a meeting thereof duly called for the purpose, with the written consent of three-fourths in interest of its stockholders, a company may change the line, or any part thereof, and either of the proposed termini, of its road. No change shall be made which will involve the abandonment of any part of the road, either partly or completely constructed. Any subscription of stock made upon the faith of the location of the road, or a part thereof, upon a line abandoned by the change, shall be canceled at the written request of a subscriber who has not consented thereto, filed with the secretary or other chief officer of the company, within six months after such change. (R. S. Sec. 3272; April 7, 1876, 73 v. 115, § 1.)

History of legislation. Prior to 1848 there was no general law providing for a change of location, route, or terminus of a railroad. In that year the first statute was passed, the latest form of which is G. C. § 8753.

See Acts of Feb. 11, 1848, 46 v. 44, § 10; Acts of May 1, 1852, 50 v. 276, § 11; Acts of April 5, 1866, 63 v. 141, § 11; Acts of March 8, 1865, 62 v. 36.

In 1871 an act was passed to facilitate location of good roads by minor changes, which act, with the changes, is found in G. C. § 8750.

See Acts of May 2, 1871, 68 v. 129; Acts of March 30, 1874, 71 v. 54.

The act to provide for change in route was passed in 1876, and is found in G. C. § 8747.

See Bickerstaff v. Traction Co., 5 O. L. R. 547.

Previous to 1848 roads without special provisions in their charters were unable to adopt any changes in route or location.

Moorehead v. Little Miami R. R. Co., 17 Ohio 340 (1848).
Little Miami v. Naylor, 2 O. S. 235 (1853).
Atkinson v. Marietta, etc., R. R. Co., 15 O. S. 21 (1864).
Works v. Junction R. R. Co., 5 McLean (U. S.) 425; 3 O. F. D. 101.

Exhaustion of power to locate. In the absence of authority the completion of a location of a road exhausts the power of the company, and this principle applies whether it is attempted to relocate on private property or on a street or highway.

Moorehead v. Little Miami R. R. Co., 17 Ohio 340 (1848).
Little Miami R. R. Co. v. Naylor, 2 O. S. 235 (1853).

Construction of §§ 8747, 8750 and 8753.

These sections provide for changes in the route and location of railways in different forms and under different circumstances.

Section 8747 covers any change in the line, route or termini before the part affected is partially or completely constructed.

Section 8750 covers minor changes or divergences in the line before it is located, so as to avoid dangerous and expensive operation and construction, saving from such changes the main point of the road, the general route and located parts.

Section 8753 covers changes in a located or completed road so as to avoid dangerous operation.

Laws of this nature, being in derogation of private right, must be strictly construed, but it should not be that narrow and niggardly strictness which utterly disregards the admitted policy of the law, and gives strained and secondary meaning to its language, in order to defeat that policy. In other words, these statutes are not to be viewed with the liberality extended to enactments purely remedial, but, on the other hand, the rules applicable to penal statutes are not to be applied to them.

Jewett v. Railway, 34 O. S. 601 (1878).
Toledo, etc., Ry. Co. v. Daniels, 16 O. S. 390 (1865).

The right to change location is withheld except so far as it has been granted by these sections.

Bickerstaff v. Traction Co., 5 O. L. R. 548 (R. R. Com. 1907).

Cause of change. Before a change can be made the cause set forth must be shown to be fairly within the terms of the statute.

In re New York, etc., R. Co., 88 N. Y. 279.
Works v. Junction R. R. Co., 5 McLean (U. S.) 425; 3 O. F. D. 101.

Remedy for illegal change. Where a railroad company has received from private parties donations of lands, subscriptions of stock, and payments of money in consideration that it should locate its road at a particular place, and allow private side track and warehouse privileges in connection therewith, the company will not be permitted to effectuate a change in fact (though not in name) of the line of its road away from such a place, by getting up a new corporation and constructing a new road parallel with its old one, under a different.charter, permitting its old line to go to decay, without compensating the parties with whom it has contracted as aforesaid.

Chapman v. Mad River, etc., R. Co., 6 O. S. 119 (1856).

Indirect change of route. Whether a railroad company may construct another road entirely parallel with its own, which if owned and managed by an interest distinct from itself, must necessarily be a competing road, for the purpose and with the effect to bring about a change in its own line, rather than to create a feeder or an extension of its own line, is within the limits of such connections as are authorized by § 8806, *quaere.*

Chapman v. Mad River, etc., R. R. Co., 6 O. S. 119 (1856).
See Atlantic, etc., R. Co. v. St. Louis, 66 Mo. 228 (1890).

Injunction against change.
See Stewart v. Little Miami R. Co., 14 Ohio 353 (1846).

Extensions of line. Authority to extend a line of railroad will not authorize a company in departing from the named terminus.
Works v. Junction R. R. Co., 5 McLean (U. S.) 425; 3 O. F. D. 101; 10 W. L. J. 370 (1853).
See § 8772.

Resolution of directors. The vote of the directors need not show the particular route to be occupied in the new counties or places selected. There is a new power to locate according to the statute when the directors have by proper vote so determined.
In re New York, etc., Ry. Co. 88 N. Y. 279 (1882).

Remedy of conditional subscribers. This section adds a remedy for conditional subscribers to stock, but in no way affects the terms of their contracts. It is not necessary, therefore, for a conditional subscriber to request the cancellation of his subscription in writing. He may rely on the terms of his subscription.
Railway Co. v. Fisher, 39 O. S. 330 (1883).
A subscriber is not released unless he subscribed on the faith of the location of the road, and within six months after the change requested in writing the cancellation of his subscription.
Armstrong v. Karshner, 47 O. S. 276, 302 (1890).

Defenses of subscribers to stock.
See note to § 8674.

Change by necessity. A change of the line of a railway by necessity to adjacent property for a short distance is not such a change as is contemplated by this section.
Devou v. Cincinnati, etc., R. Co., 4 O. L. R. 313; 19 C. D. 113 (1906).

Change of terminus within municipality. Where a certain municipal corporation of the state is designated as a terminus, the point not being marked by any survey, the railroad company may extend its terminus within the municipality to procure terminal facilities, without proceeding under the statutes regulating the extension of railroads.
L. & N. Ry. v. Taylor, 50 Bull 20 (Insolv. Ct. 1904).

Abandonment of line.
See Bickerstaff v. Traction Co., 5 O. L. R. 538 (R. R. Com. 1907).

Abandonment or removal of switch or spur track. A railroad company may abandon a spur or switch track in the absence of express contract. This section does not cover such track.
Mercantile Trust Co. v. Columbus, etc., R. R. Co., 90 Fed. 148; 12 O. F. D. 157 (C. C. Ohio 1898).
Side tracks placed on the leasehold estate of a coal company, at its request, may be removed by the railroad company upon abandonment of the premises by the lessee, over the objection of the lessor, the lease providing that the lessee may remove the mining appliances.
Ambler v. Erie R. Co., 9 C. C. n. s. 81; 19 C. D. 89 (1906).
A switch constructed on the land of a manufactory, at its expense

and solely for its benefit, under an agreement silent as to the length of time it is to remain, can not be maintained by the railroad company against the objection of the owner of the manufactory.

Rodefer v. Railroad, 72 O. S. 272 (1905).

Where a track was extended about one mile beyond the terminal station, that part of the track beyond the station was regarded as a switch.

Mercantile Trust Co. v. Columbus, etc., Co., 90 Fed 148; 12 O. F. D. 157 (1898).

As between lessee and lessor, spur railway tracks and a track scale, easily removable from the land, are trade fixtures which may be removed by the lessee.

Market N. B. v. Iron Co., 13 N. P. n. s. 27; 22 L. D. 633 (1912).

Section 8748.   (Change to be certified to secretary of state.) When such change is made it shall be described in such resolution, a duly authenticated copy of which, under the seal of the company, shall be filed with the secretary of state, and by him recorded, with proper reference, on the record of the articles of incorporation of the company. When so filed, such change shall be considered as made, and be as valid and binding as if the changed line had been the line originally described in the articles. (R. S. Sec. 3273; April 7, 1876, 73 v. 115, § 2.)

Section 8749.   (Mortgage on line so changed.) When such company has issued its mortgage bonds for the construction of its road, the record of the mortgage securing them, in each county through or into which the changed line of the road passes, shall be as effectual to create a lien upon the changed line of road, and upon the property of the company, as if the mortgage contained a complete description of the changed line and of such property. (R. S. Sec. 3274; April 7, 1876, 73 v. 115, § 3.)

In Ewell v. Grand Street, etc., R. R. Co., 67 Barb. (N. Y.) 83 (1874), it is said:

"To hold that by deviating from the route laid down by the road could be pro tanto freed from the lien, would be to announce a very dangerous doctrine.

"Good faith forbids that a security should be invalidated after one party has received the full benefit, and can no longer place the other party in as good position as it originally occupied. The bondholders therefore acquired a full right to have the road, as built, sold to pay their bonds."

Meyer v. Johnston, 53 Ala. 237 (1875).

Meyer v. Stewart, 64 Ala. 603 (1879).

Section 8750.   (When and how route may be changed.) When a company, the line of whose road has not been finally located in whole or in part, finds it necessary, in order to avoid dangerous or difficult curves, grades, or dangerous or unsubstantial grounds, or foundations, or for other reasonable cause, to pass through a county not named in the articles of incorporation, or to avoid passing into or through a county named therein, other than a county in which a terminus of the road has been fixed by its articles of in-corporation, or in which is located a town or place by or through which the line of such road is to pass, its president and directors, or a majority of them, under their hands and seals, may make a certificate declaring such necessity, the cause thereof, and name therein the county, or counties, through which it is necessary to pass, or to avoid, which certificate shall be acknowledged and certified, as provided in chapter one of this title, and forwarded to the secretary of state. A copy of the certificate, duly certified by him shall be evidence of the facts therein stated. Nothing herein is to be construed to authorize the abandonment of any part of the company's line which is finally located, or a change of the general route of the line of such road, or the terminal points named in the articles of incorporation. (R. S. Sec. 3275; March 30, 1874, 71 v. 54, § 1.)

Cited, Bickerstaff v. Traction Co., 5 O. L. R. 547.
A railroad company can not change its location because of the failure of a town to contribute to the road.
Works v. Junction, etc., R. R. Co., 5 McLean (U. S.) 425; 3 O. F. D. 101; 10 W. L. J. 370 (1853).
As to change of location by directors.
See Baldwin v. Hillsborough, etc., R. R. Co., 10 W. L. J. 356 (1853).

Section 8751. (Damages for diversion.) When, under the preceding section, a company's line of road is diverted from a county named in the articles of incorporation, it shall be liable to any person owning land in the county for dam-ages caused by the change or diversion. All subscribers to the capital stock of the company, on the line of that part of its road so changed, shall be released from all obligation to pay their subscriptions. (R. S. Sec. 3276; March 30, 1874, 71 v. 54, § 2.)

Cited, Bickerstaff v. Traction Co., 5 O. L. R. 547.
Damages to landowners.
See Leisse v. St. Louis, etc., R. R. Co., 2 Mo. App. 105 (1876); s. c., 72 Mo. 561.
A defense under this section to an action on a stock subscription must show that the road was diverted from a county named in the articles of incorporation, and that the subscriber was on the line diverted.
Armstrong v. Karshner, 47 O. S. 276, 301 (1890).

Section 8752. (Limitations on actions for damages.) Saving the rights of infants, lunatics, and persons impris-oned, for six months after their disability is removed, no ac-tion shall be brought for damages caused by such change or diversion, unless it is begun within six months from the filing of the certificate therefor with the secretary of state, and the publication of notice thereof by the company, for four consecutive weeks, in some newspaper printed in such county. (R. S. Sec. 3276; 71 v. 54, § 2.)

Section 8753. (Change of location or grade.) For the purpose of avoiding annoyance to public travel, or dangerous or difficult curves or grades, or unsafe or unsubstantial grounds or foundations, or when the roadbed has been injured or destroyed by the current of a river, water-course, or other unavoidable or reasonable cause, a company may change the location or grade, of any portion of its road, but shall not depart from the general route prescribed in the articles of incorporation. (R. S. Sec. 3277; April 5, 1866, 63 v. 141, § 11; March 8, 1865, 62 v. 36, § 1.)

Section cited. Bickerstaff v. Traction Co., 5 O. L. R. 547 (R. R. Com. 1907).

This section makes no provision for the crossing of a street within a municipal corporation.

Railway Co. v. Elyria, 69 O. S. 414, 428 (1904).

No judicial determination is necessary, under this section, as to the necessity for the change, the presumption being that a railroad company would not undertake an expensive improvement unless the change is necessary. But where an appropriation of land is required to make the change, proof should be made as to the necessity of the change.

Lorain County v. Railway, 11 C. C. n. s. 419; 12 C. D. 805.

See Railway Co. v. South, 78 O. S. 10, 13 (1908).

A change under this section is valid if the general route is not departed from, and if sufficient cause exists.

Piedmont, etc., Ry. Co. v. Speelman, 67 Md. 260 (1887).

Construction of section. See note to § 8747.

Section 8754. (Appropriation of land to make such change.) For the purpose of making any such change, the company shall have all rights, powers, and privileges to enter upon and appropriate lands, and make surveys necessary to effect it, upon the terms, and subject to the obligations, rules, and regulations prescribed by law, except that, when it is necessary to appropriate property for such change, the appropriation may be had, if the probate court, in the proceedings instituted therefor, finds that it will conduce to the interests of the company and the public, and that the property and rights of those owning real estate along the portion of the road to be affected by the change will not be unreasonably injured thereby. (R. S. Sec. 3278; April 5, 1866, 63 v. 141, § 11; March 8, 1865, 62 v. 36, § 1.)

See note to § 8753.

This section and §§ 8747, 8750 and 8753 indicate that the policy of the law is against any change of location, even where the right of way may be obtained by purchase, and that the rights of residents along the line must be considered.

Bickerstaff v. Traction Co., 5 O. L. R. 548 (R. R. Com. 1907).

Section 8755. (Damages by change after completion.) When the location is changed after the road has been used for transportation of persons and property, the company shall be liable for all damages occasioned by the change to the owner of the land upon which the road was first constructed. (R. S. Sec. 3278; April 5, 1866, 63 v. 141, § 11; March 8, 1865, 62 v. 36, § 1.)

See Leisse v. St. Louis, etc., R. R. Co., 2 Mo. App. 105 (1876); s. c., 72 Mo. 561.

Chapman v. Mad River, etc., R. R. Co., 6 O. S. 119 (1856).

Section 8756. (Extension of road into other states.) A company organized for the purpose of constructing a railroad to the boundary line of this state, may extend its road into and through an adjoining state under the regulations which may be prescribed by such state. The rights, powers, and privileges of the company over the extension, in the construction and use of its road, and in controlling the property and applying the money and assets thereon, shall be the same as if the road were built wholly within this state. (R. S. Sec. 3279; April 10, 1856, 53 v. 143, § 9.)

A railroad company, by extending its lines into another state, does not cease to be a citizen of the state of Ohio, and thereby entitled to remove cases brought against it in such other state to the federal courts.

Baltimore, etc., R. R. Co. v. Cary, 28 O. S. 208 (1876).

Railway v. Stringer, 32 O. S. 468 (1877).

Railway Assurance Co. v. Pierce, 27 O. S. 155 (1875).

Section 8757. (Construction of branch road.) A company may construct branches from the main line to towns or places within the limits of a county through or into which its road passes, or to a connection with any railroad within this state, or to any coal or other mine, stone-quarry, plastic-clay, pottery-clay and fire-clay pits or banks, ore or shale banks, if, at a meeting of the stockholders called for that purpose, the holders of a majority of the capital stock of the company, by a vote, in person or by proxy, so determine. Upon such determination, the president and directors shall make and acknowledge a certificate setting forth the facts, and file it with the secretary of state. (R. S. Sec. 3280; March 22, 1894, 91 v. 87; R. S. 1880; 69 v. 203, § 4.)

The filing of the certificate required by this section is a condition precedent to the right to appropriate property for a branch railroad.

Railroad v. Tod, 72 O. S. 156 (1905).

After the steps required by this section have been taken, the railroad company has the same power to construct a branch road that it had to construct its main line. It may appropriate property for such branch.

State v. Toledo, etc., Co., 1 C. C. n. s. 513, 525; 14 C. D. 321; aff'd, no report, 69 O. S. 550.

An "industrial" track branching from a belt railway, and leading to a large plant about one mile distant, for use in the ordinary course of business, is not a branch road under this section but is a side track.

State v. Toledo, etc., Co., 1 C. C. n. s. 513, 536; 14 C. D. 321; aff'd, no rep., 69 O. S. 550.

Branches to factories, mines, etc. The authorities in other states are conflicting as to whether railroads have power to condemn land for the purpose of reaching a manufacturing plant.

In Pittsburgh, etc., R. R. Co. v. Benwood Iron Works, 31 W. Va. 710 (1888), it is said:

"It seems to us, if the railroad corporations were permitted, ad libitum, to do what this defendant in error asks to be done, no 'deadlier blow could be dealt the private rights of the citizen.' If the doctrine claimed by the defendant in error should prevail, then corporations might go to any private place they choose, to rolling mills, ice houses, tanneries, sugar refineries, brick yards, grocery stores, and in the country to stone quarries, coal mines, stock farms, etc., and if any private citizen dared to stand in the way, violently wrest his property from him for their mere private gain. In such a state of affairs the so-called protection by constitution to the rights of private property by the arbitrary ruling of the courts, would be rendered nugatory and void. The mere declaration in a petition that the property is to be appropriated to a public use does not make it so; and evidence that the public will have a right to use it amounts to nothing in the face of the fact that the only incentive to ask for condemnation was private gain, and it was apparent that the general public had no interest in it."

This view is supported by Chicago, etc., R. R. Co. v. Wiltz, 116 Ill. 449 (1886).

Denver Coal Co. v. Union Pac. R. R. Co., 34 Fed. 286 (1888).

Kyle v. Texas, etc., R. R. Co., 3 Tex. App. (Willson) 518; 4 L. R. A. 275 (1889).

Sholl v. German Coal Co., 118 Ill. 427 (1886).

Rensselaer, etc., Ry. Coal Co. v. Davis, 43 N. Y. 137 (1870).

Chattanooga, etc., Ry. Co. v. Felton, 69 Fed. 273 (1895).

See South Chicago, etc., Ry. Co. v. Dix, 109 Ill. 237 (1883).

Salt Co. v. Brown, 7 W. Va. 191 (1874).

The opposite position is held in New Central Coal Co. v. Georges Creek Coal Co., 37 Md. 357 (1872).

Railroad Co. v. Railroad Co., 72 Mich. 206; 40 N. W. 436 (1888).

Dietrich v. Murdock, 42 Mo. 279 (1868).

Brown v. Corey, 43 Pa. St. 495 (1862).

Railway Co. v. Petty, 57 Ark. 359 (1893).

National Docks R. R. Co. v. Central R. R. Co., 32 N. J. Eq. 755 (1880).

Ohio decisions.

State v. Toledo, etc., Co., 1 C. C. n. s. 513; 14 C. D. 321 (1903); aff'd, 69 O. S. 550.

State v. Railroad Co., 40 O. S. 504 (1884).

State v. Railroad Co., 50 O. S. 239 (1893).

Reeves v. Treasurer of Wood County, 8 O. S. 333 (1858).

Power to purchase branch roads. Power to construct branches to a main road does not include authority to purchase a branch road.

Campbell v. Marietta, etc., R. R. Co., 23 O. S. 168 (1872).

Location and length of branch roads. Where a special charter of an Ohio railroad granted it power to locate and construct branched roads from the main line to other towns or places in the several counties through which said road may pass, it was held that the branches must proceed from the main line and terminate at towns or places in the same county.

Works v. Junction R. R. Co., 5 McLean (U. S.) 425 (1853) ; 3 O. F. D. 101.

Section 8758. (**Electricity as motive power.**) Upon any railroad in this state, electricity may be used as a motive power in the propulsion of cars. But before a line of poles and wires may be constructed through or along the streets, alleys, or public grounds of a municipal corporation, plans of the construction must be submitted to and approved by its council. (91 v. 397, § 1; May 21, 1894; R. S. Sec. 3310-1.)

The motive power of a railroad company should be specified in the articles of incorporation.

Rep. Atty. Gen. 1908, p. 75.

A steam railroad company may amend its articles of incorporation so as to authorize the use of electricity as motive power; but may not amend so as to authorize the sale of electric light and power.

Report of Atty. Gen. 1906, p. 67.

Under the former municipal code the trustees of a hamlet were held to be included in the word "council" in this section.

In re Newburgh, 15 C. C. 78; 8 C. D. 24 (1897).

Interurban railway, when a railroad.

See note to § 9117.

Section 8759. (**Appropriation of land; entry upon for examination and survey.**) A company or municipal corporation which owns or operates a railroad may enter upon any land for the purpose of examining and surveying its railroad line, and appropriate so much thereof as is deemed necessary for its railroad including necessary side-tracks, depots, work-shops, round-houses, and water-stations, material for construction, except timber, a right of way over adjacent lands sufficient to enable it to construct and repair its road and the right to conduct water by aqueducts and to make proper drains. (R. S. Sec. 3281; May 18, 1894, 91 v. 294; R. S. 1880; May 1, 1852, 50 v. 274, § 10.)

Appropriation proceedings. See § 11038 et seq.

Appropriation of use of streets. See § 8764.

Power of foreign corporation to appropriate. § 9090.

Section cited in construing § 8764.

Rockport v. Railway, 85 O. S. 73 (1911).

Statute strictly construed. Statutes granting power to condemn land for railroad purposes must be strictly construed.

Railway Co. v. South, 78 O. S. 10 (1908).

Platt v. Pennsylvania Co., 43 O. S. 228, 244 (1885).

Currier v. Marietta, etc., R. Co., 11 O. S. 228 (1860).

Miami Coal Co. v. Wigton, 19 O. S. 560, 566 (1860).

Youngstown v. Pittsburgh, etc., R. Co., 3 C. C. 214, 222 (1888) ; 2 C. D. 121.

Harner v. Columbus, etc., Ry. Co., 29 W. L. B. 387 (1893).

Toledo Ry. Co. v. Daniels, 16 O. S. 390, 396 (1865).

Right to enter to survey. The legislature may properly and constitutionally confer the right to enter upon the lands of an individual without compensation, in order to survey and make examinations for its line of road, and the company may exercise the right, doing no unnecessary damage.

Ward v. Toledo, etc., R. Co., 10 W. L. J. 365 (1853).

Meaning of "land." The word "land" as used in this section includes all the rights and interests which may be had in lands which it may be necessary to take for railway purposes. It, therefore, includes the rights of an owner of abutting property in the street taken for the right of way, even if the fee is in the city.

Valley Ry. Co. v. Pouchet, 4 C. C. 187 (1889) ; 2 C. D. 492; aff'd, 51 O. S. 571.

See Ohio Southern R. Co. v. Hinkle, 1 N. P. 63 (1894) ; 1 L. D. 682. See § 11042.

It also includes an estate in remainder subject to a life estate.

Gorrill v. Toledo, etc., Ry., 4 C. C. 398, 403 ; 2 C. D. 617 (1890).

See Webster v. Railroad Co., 78 O. S. 87 (1908).

Quantity of land necessary. Route. Discretion of railroad company. The railroad company has primary discretion to determine how much land is necessary. But the probate judge under § 11046 may prevent abuse in the exercise of such discretion.

Railroad v. Railroad. 72 O. S. 368 (1905).

Ohio, etc., R. Co. v. Hinkle, 1 N. P. 63; 1 L. D. 682 (1894).

Where two or more ways are equally available it is not for the court to select the way. Such selection is within the discretion of the railroad company.

C. & P. Ry. v. East Liverpool, 51 Bull. 599 (Prob. Ct. 1906).

Cincinnati, etc., Co. v. Murray, 1 N. P. n. s. 301; 48 Bull. 877 (Ins. Ct. 1906).

Only so much land as is necessary can be taken.

See notes to §§ 11042 and 11046.

Interest acquired by appropriation. Rights remaining in landowner. The estate acquired by a railroad company for right of way purposes is a permanent and not a temporary interest.

Garlick v. Railway Co., 67 O. S. 223, 234 (1902).

Gorrell v. Toledo, etc., Ry., 4 C. C. 398, 403 ; 2 C. D. 617.

See Platt v. Penna. Co., 43 O. S. 228, 244 (1885).

A judgment lien attaches to the interest of the railroad company in land acquired by appropriation.

Stewart v. Railway Co., 53 O. S. 151, 172 (1895).

The possession of a right of way by a railroad company for railroad purposes is not adverse to the rights remaining in the owner of the fee.

Railway v. Wachter, 70 O. S. 113 (1904).

The owner of the fee retains, where the interest of the railroad is an easement only, all rights not inconsistent with those of the railroad company to build, repair and operate its road, and to use materials condemned.

Platt v. Penna. Co., 43 O. S. 228, 244 (1885).

Railway v. Wachter, 70 O. S. 113 (1904).

Vought v. Railroad Co., 58 O. S. 123 (1898) ; aff'd, 176 U. S. 469.

Where additional burdens are thereafter imposed, the owner is entitled to compensation therefor.

Vought v. Railroad Co., 58 O. S. 123 (1898).
Hatch v. Railway Co., 18 O. S. 92 (1868).
Hawkins v. Buckeye, etc., Co., 6 N. P. n. s. 553, 556; 16 L. D. 333 (C. P. 1905).
Newton v. Railway Co., 115 Fed. 781 (C. C. A. 1902).

Dower barred by appropriation. Where full compensation is made a widow is not entitled to dower in land appropriated pursuant to statute.

Little Miami R. Co. v. Jones, 5 W. L. G. 5 (1860).

Sale or abandonment of land acquired by appropriation. A railroad company, having acquired title to lands for railroad purposes by grant or proceedings in appropriation, may sell to another corporation for like railroad purposes all or a part of the same. Such sale is not an abandonment of the premises unless such was the intention.

Garlick v. Railway Co., 67 O. S. 223 (1902).
Compare Platt v. Penn. Co., 43 O. S. 228 (1885).
Penna. Co. v. Platt, 47 O. S. 366 (1890).

The question of abandonment is one of intention and is to be determined from the nature of the conveyance itself and the attending facts and circumstances.

Garlick v. Railway Co., 67 O. S. 223 (1902); affirming, 20 C. C. 501.
Hatch v. Railway Co., 18 O. S. 92, 121 (1868).
See Wagner v. Cleveland, etc., R. Co., 22 O. S. 563 (1872).

Nonuser for twenty-one years works an abandonment.

Platt v. Penna. Co., 43 O. S. 228, 240 (1885).
Penna. Co. v. Platt, 47 O. S. 366 (1890).
Wagner v. Cleveland, etc., R. Co., 22 O. S. 563 (1872).
See § 9059.

The ownership of a hundred foot right of way for fifty years, with only a single track in the center, does not create a presumption that the unused portion has been abandoned. Nor does the grant of a license to maintain a pipe line on the unused portion for five years establish an abandonment where the right is reserved to annul the license should the space be needed for railroad purposes.

Hawkins v. Buckeye Pipe Line Co., 6 N. P. n. s. 553; 16 L. D. 333 (C. P. 1905).

The lease of a railroad is not an abandonment.

Cincinnati, etc., Co. v. Murray, 1 N. P. n. s. 301; 48 Bull. 877 (1903).

Upon an abandonment the interest of the railroad company reverts to the landowner.

Platt v. Penna. Co., 43 O. S. 228, 240 (1885).
Vought v. Railroad Co., 58 O. S. 123 (1898).

Defenses against appropriation.

See note to § 11046.

A municipality can not appropriate for the use of a railroad.

Morehouse v. Norwalk, 6 W. L. B. 267 (1881).
See White v. Cleveland, 12 N. P. n. s. 25 (1911) ; aff'd, 14 C. C. n. s. 369.
G. C. § 3677.

For what purposes land may be appropriated.

Side tracks. Land may be appropriated for side tracks leading from the main tracks to depot buildings.

Toledo, etc., R. Co. v. Daniels, 16 O. S. 390 (1865).

Cincinnati, etc., R. Co. v. Spring Grove Ave. Co., 15 W. L. B. 384
(1886).

An "industrial" track branching from a belt railway and leading to
one or more manufacturing plants one mile distant, to be used for usual
railroad purposes is a side track within the meaning of this section.

State v. Toledo, etc., Co., 1 C. C. n. s. 513; 14 C. D. 321 (1903);
aff'd, 69 O. S. 550.

Expert testimony is competent in determining whether a proposed
track is a side track, or one to be used for a private purpose.

State v. Toledo, etc., Co., 1 C. C. n. s. 513; 14 C. D. 321 (1903);
aff'd, 69 O. S. 550.

Side track defined.

State v. Toledo, etc., Co., 1 C. C. n. s. 513, 519; 14 C. D. 321.

Depots. The legislature has constitutional power to confer upon a
corporation authorized to construct a railroad, the right to appropriate
grounds necessary for its use as a depot.

Giesy v. Cincinnati, etc., R. Co., 4 O. S. 308 (1854).

Crossings. Land occupied by a railway may be condemned, if necessary, to furnish a crossing for another road.

Lake Shore, etc., Ry. Co. v. Cincinnati, etc., Ry. Co., 30 O. S. 604
(1876).

See Railway Co. v. Traction Co., 4 C. C. n. s. 329; 16 C. D. 1 (1903);
reversed, on other grounds, 72 O. S. 429.

Appropriation for street over railroad tracks.

See § 3677 and note.

Bridges. Land may be appropriated for an approach to a railroad bridge.

L. & N. Ry. v. Taylor, 50 Bull. 20 (Ins. Ct. 1904).

Embankments. Land may be appropriated to form a basis for embankments.

Ohio, etc., R. Co. v. Henkle, 1 N. P. 63; 1 L. D. 682 (1894).

Wharves. Under this section a railroad company is not authorized
to condemn private property solely for wharf purposes.

Iron R. Co. v. Ironton, 19 O. S. 299 (1869).

Temporary right of way. A railroad company has no power to appropriate a temporary right of way to be used until its main line is ready
for use.

Currier v. Marietta, etc., Co., 11 O. S. 228 (1890).

Branch roads.

See note to § 8757.

Appropriation of property of other railroad companies. Property
of one railroad company may be appropriated by another railroad company to furnish a crossing over such road.

Railway v. Railway, 30 O. S. 604.

See §§ 8834-8836.

But a company seeking to appropriate land of another company,
longitudinally, must establish urgent necessity for the land. Where
such necessity is shown, and the other company does not require it for
immediate use, and can arrange its tracks so as to avoid using it for a
long period, the right to appropriate exists.

Railway Co. v. Railway Co., 2 N. P. n. s. 45; 49 O. L. B. 240 (Prob.
Ct. 1903).

Unfinished road bed of another company.

See §§ 11076 to 11083.

Appropriation by telegraph company of right of way of railway company.
See §§ 9175 and 9196.

Property subject to appropriation.
See note to § 11042.

Appropriation of canal lands—rights of owner of fee. Where a railroad company appropriates the lands of a canal company, the owner of the fee is entitled to recover the full value of the lands, if any, taken by the railroad company, and not covered by the former appropriation by the canal company, and, also, a full and fair compensation for such additional burdens and inconveniences, not common to the general public, as accrue to him and his entire tract on which the easement is imposed, by reason of the change of uses to which the lands appropriated have been subjected.
Hatch v. Cincinnati, etc., R. Co., 18 O. S. 92 (1868).
Vought v. Columbus, etc., R. R. Co., 58 O. S. 123 (1898).

Sale of canal lands to railways.
See Hatch v. Cincinnati, etc., Ry. Co., 18 O. S. 92 (1868).
Goodin v. Cincinnati, etc., Canal Co., 18 O. S. 180 (1868).
Cincinnati, etc., R. Co. v. Zinn, 18 O. S. 417 (1868).
Vought v. Columbus, etc., R. Co., 58 O. S. 123 (1898).

Section 8760. (Compensation for property appropriated.) The appropriation of private property provided for in the next preceding section, shall not be made until full compensation therefor, irrespective of any benefit from any improvement proposed by such company or municipal corporation, is made in money, or secured to the owner by deposit of money for him. (R. S. Sec. 3281; May 18, 1894, 91 v. 294; R. S. 1880; May 1, 1852, 50 v. 274, § 10.)

See note to § 11053.

Failure to make compensation. Remedies of landowner. A landowner may enjoin a railroad company from entering his land for the purpose of constructing a road, until compensation is made.
Gorrill v. Toledo, etc., Ry., 4 C. C. 398; 2 C. D. 617 (1890).
Where land has been occupied, tracks constructed and cars operated, without compensation having been made, the owner may recover possession of such land, unless barred by laches or acquiescence.
Bothe v. Dayton, etc., R. Co., 37 O. S. 147 (1881).
Platt v. Penna. Co., 47 O. S. 366 (1890).
Where a land owner is estopped from reclaiming the land he may recover compensation.
Penna. Co. v. Platt, 47 O. S. 366 (1890).
Goodin v. Canal Co., 18 O. S. 169.

"Owner" includes remainderman. The owner of an estate in remainder, subject to a life estate, may enjoin the construction of a railroad until compensation is made, although the owner of the life estate has granted a right of way.
Gorrill v. Toledo, etc., Ry., 4 C. C. 398, 406; 2 C. D. 617 (1890).

——. Includes owner of neighboring lots having rights under restrictive covenants as to use of property.
Kuebler v. Cleveland, etc., Ry., 10 N. P. n. s. 385; 20 L. D. 525 (1910);

(aff'd, by Cir. Ct.; reversed by Supreme Court on ground of laches, 84 O. S. 463).

Compensation.

Speculative and contingent remuneration can not be recovered. A compensatory and not a speculative remuneration is guaranteed for land taken and for the damages occasioned thereby to the rest of the property. The difference in value of the property with the appropriation and that without it is the rule of compensation. The difference must be ascertained with reference to the value of the property in view of its present character, situation, and surroundings. It can not be enhanced by proving facts of a contingent and prospective character, such as the probable rents that may be derived from the property, or its special value as a prospective monopoly of a railway to the adjoining lands of other persons.

Powers v. Hazelton, etc., R. Co., 33 O. S. 429 (1878).

Danger from fire to buildings, fences, timber or crops upon the remainder, in so far as it depreciates the value of the property is a proper element of compensation, although the railroad company is liable for all losses by fire which originate from the operation of the road.

Hayes v. Toledo, etc., Co., 6 C. C. n. s. 281; 16 C. D. 395 (1903); aff'd, 70 O. S. 425.

But the proximity of the buildings to the railway must be such as to render the danger imminent and appreciable.

Hatch v. Cincinnati, etc., R. Co., 18 O. S. 92 (1868).

Must be based on present conditions. In an appropriation proceeding preparatory to a change of grade through farm lands, the assessment of damages to the residue of the tract must be based on present conditions; not on conditions existing prior to the original location of the railway years before.

Railway Co. v. Cordry, 10 C. C. n. s. 87; 20 C. D. 830 (1907).

Railroad intersecting tract of land. Where the railroad cuts asunder an entire tract of land, the owner is entitled to compensation for the inconvenience and danger of access between the two parts of the tract when the inconvenience and danger are peculiar to the owner in the use of his property, and not common to the public at large.

See Hatch v. Cincinnati, etc., R. Co., 18 O. S. 92 (1868).
Platt v. Pennsylvania Co., 43 O. S. 244 (1885).
Lorain St. Ry. Co. v. Sinning, 17 C. C. 649; 6 C. D. 753 (1895).
Cleveland, etc., R. Co. v. Ball, 5 O. S. 568 (1856).
Schaible v. L. S., etc., Ry., 10 C. C. 334 (1895).

Damage done in making appropriation. A petition stating only that a railroad company, in locating and constructing its road on and through the plaintiff's land, appropriated about two acres of the land to its own use, and located its road through the land in a diagonal manner so as to greatly injure the same and committed other acts and trespasses upon the land to the plaintiff's damage, fails to state a cause of action, there being no allegation that unnecessary damage was done or failure to make compensation.

Cleveland, etc., R. Co. v. Stackhouse, 10 O. S. 567 (1860).

Damage of turnpike company. Where a railroad is constructed along land covered by the easement of a turnpike company, the latter is entitled to compensation to the extent of the damage accruing to it in the diminution of the productive value of its property, excepting, however, diminution caused by competition between the turnpike company and the railroad as means of transportation.

Cincinnati, etc., R. Co. v. Zinn, 18 O. S. 417 (1868).

Appropriation under constitution of 1802. Under the constitution of 1802, which was, unlike the present constitution in that respect, where lands were appropriated by a railroad company for its track, supposed benefits might be set off against the value of the land taken, and hence the land might be appropriated without the payment of any money whatever.

Platt v. Pennsylvania Co., 43 O. S. 228 (1885).

Additional burdens imposed after appropriation. Where property appropriated for one public use is subsequently appropriated for, or devoted to, another public use, and the second use imposes additional burdens on the land, the owner is entitled to compensation therefor.

Vought v. Railroad Co., 58 O. S. 123 (1898) ; aff'd, 176 U. S. 469.
Hatch v. Railway, 18 O. S. 92 (1868).
Hawkins v. Buckeye, etc., Co., 6 N. P. n. s. 553, 556; 16 L. D. 333 (C. P. 1905).
Newton v. Railway Co., 115 Fed. 781; 14 O. F. D. 156 (C. C. A. 1902).

Section 8761. (Company may acquire lands.) Such a company may acquire by purchase or gift lands in the vicinity of the line of its road, or through which it passes, so far as is deemed convenient or necessary by the company to secure a right of way, and such as are granted to aid in the construction of its road, and hold or convey them, as the directors prescribe. Conveyance made by the company shall be signed by the president under the corporate seal. (R. S. Sec. 3282; May 1, 1852, 50 v. 274, § 15.)

Right to acquire and hold land.

See also note to § 8627.

A railroad company has power to acquire real estate only when such power is granted to it by statute or by its charter.

Walsh v. Barton, 24 O. S. 28, 42 (1873).

The purpose of §§ 8761 and 8762 is to clothe the railway corporation with capacity to acquire by purchase or gift lands that are convenient or necessary to secure the right of way, or any lands granted to aid in the construction of the road.

State v. Cincinnati, etc., Ry. Co., 37 O. S. 157, 170 (1881).

The right of a railroad corporation to hold land is not an unqualified right, but it is limited to the uses and purposes of the corporation, and is to be held for the purposes of the grant for the public uses. The title which it has in its right of way is a qualified title, subject to the equal right of another railroad corporation to cross the same with its track, provided compensation be made as required in the case of individuals for the property appropriated, or the interest therein which is so appropriated.

Lake Shore, etc., Ry. Co. v. Cincinnati, etc., Ry. Co., 30 O. S. 604 (1876).

Property of a railroad company is held subject to the right of the state to adopt police regulations for public welfare and safety.

Lake Shore, etc., Ry. Co. v. Cincinnati, etc., Ry. Co., 30 O. S. 604 (1876).

Land of railroads is subject to street assessments.

Railroad Co. v. Connelly, 10 O. S. 159 (1859).
Railroad Co. v. Commissioners, 19 O. S. 589 (1869).

Purposes for which land may be purchased. Land may be purchased for the right of way.

Walsh v. Barton, 24 O. S. 28, 42 (1873).

And to obtain timber or materials.

Lessee of Overmeyer v. Williams, 15 Ohio 26 (1846).

See note to § 8759; *Purposes for which land may be appropriated.*

Where a railroad company purchases unnecessary land, a title thereto derived from such company is valid. The property would not escheat, and estoppel would operate against the parties directly concerned.

Walsh v. Barton, 24 O. S. 28, 42 (1873).

Methods of acquiring property.

Gift. §§ 8761, 8762.

Appropriation. §§ 8759, 8760.

Dedication is not a means by which property may be acquired by a railroad company. The recording of a town plat with a lot reserved for a depot is not a dedication of the lot.

Todd v. Railroad Co., 19 O. S. 514 (1869).

Property may be acquired by adverse possession for twenty-one years. But the statute of limitations does not begin to run against a remainderman until the termination of the life estate.

Webster v. Railroad Co., 78 O. S. 87 (1908).

The possession of a right of way by a railroad company for railroad purposes is not adverse to the rights remaining in the owner of the fee.

Railway v. Wachter, 70 O. S. 113 (1904).

Land granted by the state to a municipality, upon a valuable consideration, to be used for street and other purposes, may be leased by the municipality to a railroad company for its general purposes. The lease is valid where the municipality reserves the right to use the leased premises for street purposes, without compensation.

Cleveland T. & V. R. Co. v. State, 85 O. S. 251 (1912).

Subscriptions to stock payable in real estate.

See Goodin v. Evans, 18 O. S. 150 (1868).

A deed of a right of way may be held in escrow by an agent of the railroad company.

Railroad Co. v. Iliff, 13 O. S. 235 (1862).

License for side track. A written agreement, silent as to time, for the construction of a side track on the land of another, at his expense and for his advantage, is a revocable license, and the railroad company can not maintain the side track against the objection of the land owner.

Rodefer v. Railroad, 72 O. S. 272 (1905).

Right of railroad company to remove side track.

Ambler v. Erie R. Co., 9 C. C. n. s. 81; 19 C. D. 89 (1906).

Purchase by land contract.

Equitable lien of vendor. An owner agreed in writing with the railroad company to release the right of way and the right to enter upon and construct the road through his lands in consideration that the company agreed to pay a certain sum of money at a future day, and construct certain road crossings and cattle-guards. The company took possession and constructed its road before receiving a deed for the right of way, and before payment of the money or constructing the crossings or guards. Held, the owner is entitled to make an equitable lien upon the property sold as well for the damages for not constructing the road in the proper manner, as for the unpaid purchase money.

Dayton, etc., R. Co. v. Lewton, 20 O. S. 401 (1870).

Ames v. Wheeling, etc., Ry. Co., 17 C. C. 684; 9 C. D. 443 (1899).

Notice to subsequent purchasers and mortgagees. Where the owner

sells the right of way to the company on contract, and retains the legal
title, the fact is sufficient to put subsequent mortgagees and purchasers
of the road upon inquiry as to the rights of the owner.
Dayton, etc., R. Co. v. Lewton, 20 O. S. 401 (1870).
Seasongood v. Miami Valley Ry. Co., 9 W. L. B. 256 (1883).
See Day v. Railroad Co., 41 O. S. 392 (1884).
The construction and operation of a railroad on land is constructive
notice to purchasers of the rights of the railroad company.
Miller v. Railroad, 12 N. P. n. s. 683; 22 L. D. 638 (C. P. 1911).
Day v. Railroad Co., 41 O. S. 392 (1884).

Remedies of vendor. The vendor may compel specific performance
of the contract or may enforce his vendor's lien.
Dayton, etc., R. Co. v. Lewton, 20 O. S. 401 (1870).

Foreclosure of lien. Sale of entire road. Where public interests
preclude the sale of the portion of the road covered by the lien, a sale
of the entire road may be decreed.
Dayton, etc., R. Co. v. Lewton, 20 O. S. 401 (1870).
Ames v. Wheeling, etc., Ry. Co., 17 C. C. 684; 9 C. D. 443 (1899).
Stewart v. Railway, 53 O. S. 151 (1895).
Seasongood v. Miami, etc., Ry. Co., 9 W. L. B. 256 (1883).

RIGHT OF WAY.

A grant to a railroad company of a right of way, without limit as
to time, is perpetual, unless terminated by release or abandonment.
Junction R. Co. v. Ruggles, 7 O. S. 1 (1857).
Garlick v. Railway Co., 67 O. S. 223, 234 (1902).
See Bosworth v. Pittsburg, etc., Ry. Co., 1 C. C. 69, 70; 1 C. D. 42
(1885).
Where the grant is of an easement only, the grantor retains all rights
not inconsistent with those of the railroad to build, repair and operate
its road.
Railway Co. v. Wachter, 70 O. S. 113 (1904).
Platt v. Penna. Co., 43 O. S. 228, 244 (1885).
The grantor may construct a building on his remaining land, near
to the railroad, where it will not unreasonably interfere with the opera-
tion of the road, although it may cause some inconvenience to the rail-
road company.
Railway v. Baum, 15 C. C. n. s. 383 (1906); aff'd, no rep., 78 O.
S. 427.
Where a track is constructed and maintained near the center of a
right of way of definite width, such possession includes land on each side
of the track reasonably necessary for its use and maintenance, and is
constructive notice to subsequent purchasers.
Day v. Railroad Co., 41 O. S. 392 (1884).
See Happ v. Railroad Co., 1 N. P. n. s. 337; 14 L. D. 173 (C. P. 1903).
Miller v. Railroad, 12 N. P. n. s. 683; 22 L. D. 638 (C. P. 1911).
Where the terms of a right of way grant are general and indefinite,
its location and use by the grantee, acquiesced in by the grantor, will have
the same legal effect as if it had been fully described by the terms of the
grant.
Warner v. Railroad Co., 39 O. S. 70 (1883).
A lease to drill for oil and gas does not prevent the owner of the
fee from conveying a valid right of way.
Ohio Oil Co. v. Railroad Co., 4 C. C. 210; 2 C. D. 505 (1889).
Where the description of the right of way is indefinite, the grantor
by accepting the agreed compensation after construction of the railroad
thereon, with full knowledge of the facts, is estopped to deny that the actual location is the agreed location.

Railway Co. v. Williams, 53 O. S. 268 (1895).

Cleveland, etc., Ry. Co. v. Reid, 4 N. P. 127 (1896).

Where the owner of land granted to a company the right to select a strip thereof for its right of way, and from the terms of the grant and the circumstances it is clear that both parties understood that the right granted was to be exercised at the time of the final location and construction of the railroad, and not afterward, a court of equity will, by injunction, restrain such railroad company from taking possession of any additional part of said land after its railroad has been located.

Warner v. Railroad Co., 39 O. S. 70 (1883).

Where property owners agreed with a railroad company to convey land for its track, and to submit to arbitration the question of compensation to be paid them by the company for the land and damages, such arbitration does not involve the question of possession and title to real estate within the meaning of G. C. § 12148.

C. P. & V. R. R. Co. v. Duckwall (Sup. Ct.), 46 W. L. B. 92 (1901). Construction of deed for right of way.

Belmer v. Railroad Co., 10 W. L. B. 232 (Super. Ct. Cin. 1883).

Grant of right of way for specified business only. Deed of land with condition subsequent. A railroad company, having built a spur track on land of another under an agreement limiting its use to certain specified business, may be enjoined from carrying other and increased traffic without compensation to the owner.

Collins v. Craig Shipbuilding Co., 7 C. C. n. s. 350; 17 C. D. 802 (1905).

A condition subsequent in a deed, requiring the road to be completed within two years, does not operate of itself, and the right of forfeiture may be lost by waiver or estoppel.

Field v. Railway Co., 3 C. C. n. s. 130; 13 C. D. 1 (1897); aff'd, 62 O. S. 633.

A railroad company, having agreed not to locate its track in a certain manner on its right of way, and subsequently finding it necessary to disregard the agreement in order to properly discharge its duty to the public, will not be enjoined from such breach. The remedy of the owner is a suit for damages.

Miller v. Railway, 12 N. P. n. s. 683; 22 L. D. 638 (C. P. 1911).

Sale and conveyance of land by railway. A railroad company having acquired title to land for railroad purposes, by grant or appropriation, may sell all or a part of the same to another corporation for like railroad purposes.

Garlick v. Railway Co., 67 O. S. 223 (1902).

See note to § 8759.

A deed executed in the name of the corporation, by the president, under the corporate seal, is presumed to have been authorized by the directors and is prima facie valid.

Railroad Co. v. Harter, 26 O. S. 426 (1875).

But such deed is not admissible in evidence without proof of its execution.

Walsh v. Barton, 24 O. S. 28 (1873).

See note to § 8627.

A license to take gravel from the right of way need not be executed by the president.

Grene v. Trustees, 8 N. P. 491; 11 L. D. 771; aff'd, 64 O. S. 609.

Adverse possession against railroads of part of right of way. To acquire title to a right of way by adverse possession, an abutting owner must occupy and use the land in a manner inconsistent with the paramount rights of the railroad. Possession and use of part of the easement not in use and not needed for immediate railroad purposes, and consistent with its rights to reclaim it when needed, is presumed to be permissive only.

Smith v. Railway Co., 5 C. C. n. s. 194; 16 C. D. 44 (1904); aff'd, 73 O. S. 391.

Railroad v. Roseville, 76 O. S. 108 (1907).

Day v. Railroad Co., 41 O. S. 392 (1884).

Possession of a strip for more than twenty-one years does not become adverse to the railroad company by the raising of vegetables, or repair of the fence, where the original use of the land and construction of the fence were permissive on the part of the railroad company.

Happ v. Railroad Co., 1 N. P. n. s. 337; 14 L. D. 173 (C. P. 1903).

Where a railroad company maintains a way or street over its tracks and unenclosed land for forty years, for the use of its patrons, and incidentally it is used also by the public, the presumption is that the user was permissive. Such use does not establish the dedication of the way as a street, in the absence of an acceptance by proper public officials.

Railroad v. Roseville, 76 O. S. 108 (1907).

Whether exclusive occupancy is required by the necessities of the railroad, and what use by an abutting owner is an interference therewith are questions of fact.

Smith v. Railway Co., 5 C. C. n. s. 194; 16 C. D. 44 (1904); aff'd, 73 O. S. 391.

The act of an abutter in accepting and recording a deed and taking possession of disputed land is adverse.

Smith v. Railway Co., 5 C. C. n. s. 194; 16 C. D. 44 (1904); aff'd, 73 O. S. 391.

Abandonment of right of way.

See note to § 8759.

Removal of fixtures, tracks, etc., on abandonment. Stone piers built as a part of a railroad, on land acquired for its right of way, may be removed by the railroad company on abandonment.

Wagner v. Railroad Company, 22 O. S. 563 (1872).

Side tracks built on the leasehold estate of a coal mining company, at its request, may be removed by the railroad company, against the objection of the lessor on abandonment of the premises by the lessee, where the lease provided that mining appliances might be removed.

Ambler v. Erie R. Co., 9 C. C. n. s. 81; 19 C. D. 89 (1906).

Section 8762. (When conveyance to company void.) Conveyances to such companies, acquired by gift, shall be null and void, unless the company to which they are made, completes its road on the right of way so conveyed, within five years from the time of a conveyance for that purpose. (R. S. Sec. 3282; May 1, 1852, 50 v. 274, § 15.)

Where land is given to a railroad company on condition that it should be occupied for depot grounds a substantial compliance with the terms of the deed will prevent a recovery of the land for failure to perform the conditional agreement.

Pittsburg, etc., Ry. Co. v. Rose, 24 O. S. 219 (1873).

Where a railroad company has received from private parties donations of land in consideration that it should locate its road at a particular place, the company will not be permitted to effectuate a change in fact (though not in name) of the line of its road away from such place, by organizing a new corporation and constructing a new road parallel with the old one, under a different charter, and permitting its old line to go to decay, without compensating the parties with whom it has contracted as aforesaid.

Chapman v. Mad River R. Co., 6 O. S. 119 (1856).

Section 8763. (Elevated track; use of public way.) If in the location of any part of a railroad owned or operated by a domestic or foreign corporation, it be necessary to occupy with a surface or elevated track, with the necessary supports therefor, any public road, street, alley, way or ground, of any kind, or part thereof, the municipal or other corporation or public officers or authorities, owning or having charge thereof, and the company, may agree upon the manner, terms and conditions upon which it can be used or occupied. In the event of the occupancy of such ground with an elevated track, the agreement shall specify the number, character and location of all supports for the track, any part of which will be upon such public ground, and the vertical and longitudinal clearances between such supports. (R. S. Sec. 3283; May 9, 1908, 99 v. 589; April 15, 1857, 54 v. 133, § 12.)

Opening or extension of street over railroad tracks. Appropriation. § 3677 and note.

This section applies to crossings.

In re Avon Beach, etc., Ry., 3 N. P. n. s. 561, 564, 565; 16 L. D. 87, 90 (C. P. 1905).

Railroad v. Cincinnati, 8 W. L. B. 334 (Dist. Ct. 1882).

An agreement with an existing railroad for repair or alteration of a crossing or bridge is not within this section.

Railroad Co. v. Defiance, 52 O. S. 262, 313 (1895).

The grant of the right to use a street for railroad purposes does not authorize its use for other purposes.

Rogers v. Railway, 12 L. D. 136 (Super. Ct. Cin. 1901).

Exclusive occupancy of street by railroad not authorized. A municipal corporation can not by agreement permit a railroad company to occupy a street so as to exclude the public from any portion thereof, unless the municipality is authorized by statute, in express terms or by clear implication, to make such contract. General legislation authorizing the occupation of streets for railroad purposes does not authorize exclusive and permanent use.

Railway Co. v. Elyria, 69 O. S. 415 (1903); affirming, 3 C. C. n. s. 250.

Ravenna v. Penna. Co., 45 O. S. 118.

See C. & P. Ry. v. Liverpool, 51 O. L. B. 599 (Probate Ct. 1906).

Railroad Co. v. Cincinnati, 76 O. S. 481 (1907).

Change in judicial interpretation of section as to extent of use authorized, see

Railroad Co. v. Cleveland, 15 C. C. n. s. 193, 208 (1910); affirming 8 N. P. n. s. 457; 19 L. D. 372; aff'd, no rep., 87 O. S. 469.

This section contemplates a joint or common use of a street by the railroad company and public.

Railway Co. v. Elyria, 69 O. S. 415, 429 (1903); s. c., 3 C. C. n. s. 250; 14 C. C. 48; 7 C. D. 312 (1897).

And the right of the municipality to regulate the use of the street continues.

Railway Co. v. Cincinnati, 16 W. L. B. 367.

Railroad Co. v. Defiance, 52 O. S. 262, 308 (1895); s. c., 167 U. S. 88 (1897).

Ganz v. Ohio, etc., Co., 140 Fed. 692, 695 (C. C. A. 1905).

An abandonment or surrender of the street is not authorized.

Railroad Co. v. Defiance, 52 O. S. 262, 308 (1895); affirmed, 167 U. S. 88 (1897).

Railway Co. v. Elyria, 69 O. S. 415 (1903).

A person injured upon a track in a street is not a trespasser.

Smith v. Railway Co., 90 Fed. 783 (C. C. 1898).

Railroad Co. v. Anderson, 85 Fed. 413 (C. C. A. 1898).

What amounts to exclusive occupation. Two railway tracks in a street from thirty-six to forty feet wide do not amount to an exclusive occupancy.

Cincinnati, etc., Co. v. Railway Co., 14 C. C. n. s. 195; 23 C. D. 192 (1911); aff'd, no rep., 86 O. S. 343.

Before the amendment of this section and the enactment of §§ 8767 to 8771 (99 v. 589) it was held that this section did not authorize a municipality to permit permanent abutments, supporting an overhead crossing, in a street, where the public was excluded from any portion thereof.

Railway Co. v. Elyria, 69 O. S. 414 (1903); affirming 3 C. C. n. s. 250; s. c., 14 C. C. 48; 13 C. D. 482; 7 C. D. 312; 12 L. D. 609 (1897).

Railway Co. v. Steubenville (unreported), 83 O. S. 443 (1910).

Telephone Co. v. Cincinnati, 73 O. S. 81 (1905).

Control over streets not surrendered by municipality. This section does not authorize a municipality to surrender or abridge its control over a street. A city, having given a railroad company permission to cross a street below grade and to build a bridge over the railroad, is not prevented by such agreement from thereafter lowering the street so as to cross the railroad at grade.

Railroad Co. v. Defiance, 52 O. S. 262, 308 (1895).

Affirmed, Wabash R. Co. v. Defiance, 167 U. S. 88 (1897).

Ganz v. Ohio, etc., Co., 140 Fed. 692, 695 (C. C. A. 1905).

After constructing its track in a street at an agreed grade, the railroad company can not subsequently raise the grade of the street.

Railroad Co. v. Hambleton, 40 O. S. 496 (1884).

"Public road, street, alley, way or ground." A highway, outside of a municipal corporation, is a public road, and can not be occupied without agreement or appropriation under §§ 8763 or 8764.

Commissioners v. Penna. Co., 6 N. P. n. s. 141; 18 L. D. 348 (C. P. 1907); (aff'd, by Cir. Ct., without rep.).

Youngstown v. Railroad Co., 3 C. C. 214; 2 C. D. 121 (1888).

See Ritter v. Railway Co., 6 N. P. n. s. 161; 18 L. D. 846 (1907).

The word "way" or "public ground" does not include the public navigable canals of the state in express terms, nor by necessary implication. A way, in the connection in which it stands in this section, must be regarded as something of the same nature and kind as a road or street.

State v. Cincinnati, etc., Ry. Co., 37 O. S. 157 (1881).

Land acquired by a municipality for park purposes, but occupied by a railroad under an agreement for many years, and declared by municipal authorities to be unnecessary for park or municipal purposes, and never used therefor, is not park property and may be appropriated for a permanent right of way.

Railway Co. v. Cincinnati, 6 N. P. n. s. 325 (Ct. of Ins. 1908).

Likewise land dedicated for street purposes, but unsuited therefor, and having remained unimproved for many years, *ib.*

A city street can not be crossed or occupied by a railroad under § 8773; but authority must be obtained under § 8763 or § 8764.

Youngstown v. Railroad Co., 3 C. C. 214; 2 C. D. 121 (1888).

Cincinnati, etc., R. Co. v. Cincinnati, 8 W. L. B. 334 (Dist. Ct. 1882).

Where land has been granted by the state to a municipality, for a valuable consideration, to be used for street and other purposes, the municipality, reserving the right to use the property for street purposes without compensation, may make a valid lease of such land to a railroad company for its general purposes.

Cleveland T. & V. R. R. Co. v. State, 85 O. S. 251 (1912).

Prior to the amendment of this section and § 8767 (99 v. 589) a public common or landing could not be occupied with an elevated structure, by an agreement under this section.

Railroad Co. v. Cincinnati, 76 O. S. 481 (1907).

See Cincinnati v. Railway, 9 N. P. n. s. 433; 20 L. D. 440 (1910); aff'd, 82 O. S. 466.

Railway v. Cincinnati, 10 N. P. n. s. 649; 56 Bull. 317; aff'd, 88 O. S. —; 12 N. P. n. s. 65; 22 L. D. 363.

Power of municipality to lease dock to railroad company.

See G. C. § 3699-1.

White v. Cleveland, 14 C. C. n. s. 369; aff'd, no rep., 87 O. S. 482.

Agreement for occupancy of street.

By whom made. "Public officers or authorities." County commissioners are "public authorities" having charge of roads outside of municipalities.

Trust Co. v. Railway, 7 N. P. n. s. 497, 511 (Ct. of Ins. 1908).

Megrue v. Commissioners, 15 C. C. 242; 8 C. D. 262 (1897).

See Ritter v. Railway, 6 N. P. n. s. 161; 18 L. D. 846 (C. P. 1907).

To be valid under G. C. § 2445 the contract should be entered on the minutes of the commissioners. But where such a contract has been fully performed on the part of the county the other party can not evade performance on the ground that such entry was not made.

Commissioners v. Baltimore, etc., R. Co., 37 O. S. 205 (1881).

The council of a municipality has authority to agree as to the use of its streets.

Rockport v. Railway, 85 O. S. 73 (1911).

Validity. A misnomer of the street in the ordinance will not invalidate the contract where it is clear what street is intended.

Gunning v. Railway, 2 N. P. n. s. 411; 14 L. D. 660 (1904).

Provisions, terms and conditions. A restriction prohibiting the use of tracks during certain hours is valid and reasonable.

Pittsburg, etc., Ry. Co. v. Hood, 94 Fed. 618 (C. C. A. 1899).

Louisville Trust Co. v. Cincinnati, 76 Fed. 296; 10 O. F. D. 112 (C. C. A. 1896).

A municipality has no power to prescribe the rates to be charged by a belt line for hauls over its entire line, less than 30 miles long, as a condition to granting a right of way over its streets for a part of its line. Such a provision in an ordinance is ultra vires and void. In an action by an individual claiming the benefit of such provision, the railroad company is not estopped from setting up its ultra vires character as a defense.

Brick Co. v. Trust Co., 187 Fed. 63 (C. C. A. 1911).

Where permission to cross streets is granted on condition that the municipality may thereafter extend any streets across the tracks, free of damage and expense and without appropriation proceedings, the railroad company is estopped from denying the right of the municipality to extend streets.

Chicago, etc., R. Co. v. Hamilton, 3 C. C. 455; 2 C. D. 259 (1888).

In granting permission the public authorities may require a bond securing the repair and restoration of the street or highway.

Megrue v. Commissioners, 15 C. C. 242; 8 C. D. 262 (1897).

Permission to lay one track in a street does not authorize an additional track or switch.

Railroad Co. v. Hambleton, 40 O. S. 496 (1884).

Varwig v. Railroad Co., 54 O. S. 455 (1896).

Chambers v. Railway, 5 C. C. n. s. 298; 17 C. D. 193; aff'd, 73 O. S. 348.

Cleveland, etc., Co. v. Reeder, 6 C. C. 354; 3 C. D. 489 (1892).

Where the grade is specified in the agreement the railroad company can not subsequently change the grade.

Railroad Co. v. Hambleton, 40 O. S. 496 (1884).

Construction. Where a branch track was laid on an unfinished street, under an ambiguous ordinance, capable of two constructions, one that the track was laid to assist in making the street, and the other that the track was for general railroad use, the ordinance is not necessarily to be construed strictly as against the grant of a franchise. Where later ordinances recognized the track as for general use, the rule of construction by conduct may be applied.

Railway Co. v. Cincinnati, 16 W. L. B. 367 (Super. Ct. Cin. 1886; aff'd by Supreme Court without opinion).

Breach of agreement. Liability. A railroad company is liable for failure to perform an agreement to grade and gravel streets, within a reasonable time, without special notice or demand.

Railway Co. v. Carthage, 36 O. S. 631 (1881).

Revocation or rescission. The agreement authorized by this section, when fairly made, is valid and binding.

Megrue v. Commissioners, 15 C. C. 242; 8 C. D. 262 (1897).

The grant, by a municipality, of permission to use a street does not create a mere revocable license. The railroad has the same rights as if the use had been acquired by appropriation.

Pittsburg, etc., R. Co. v. Cincinnati, 16 W. L. B. 367 (Super. Ct. Cin. 1886; aff'd, Supreme Ct. no opinion).

An agreement which required the railroad company to grade and gravel the streets is not abrogated by an inoperative ordinance rescinding the original permission.

Railway Co. v. Carthage, 36 O. S. 631 (1881).

Occupation of streets without agreement or appropriation. A railroad company has no power to occupy a street until it has obtained consent or appropriated the right to do so.

In re Avon Beach, etc., Ry., 3 N. P. n. s. 561, 564; 16 L. D. 87 (C. P. 1905).

Cincinnati, etc., Ry. v. Cincinnati, 8 W. L. B. 334 (Dist. Ct.).

Youngstown v. Railroad Co., 3 C. C. 214; 2 C. D. 121 (1888).

Commissioners v. Penna. Co., 6 N. P. n. s. 141; 18 L. D. 348 (C. P. 1907); (aff'd, by Cir. Ct., without rep.).

The unauthorized occupation of a street with a permanent incumbrance is a public nuisance.

Pittsburg, etc., Ry. Co. v. Hood, 94 Fed. 618 (C. C. A. 1899).

Railroad Co. v. Railway Co., 3 N. P. n. s. 109; 16 L. D. 777 (Cin. Super. Ct. 1904).

Zanesville v. Fannan, 53 O. S. 605, 614 (1895).

Railway Co. v. Elyria, 69 O. S. 415, 433 (1903).

Such unauthorized occupation renders a railroad company a trespasser and liable for damages proximately resulting to persons or property.

Pittsburg, etc., Ry. Co. v. Hood, 94 Fed. 618 (C. C. A. 1899).

Adverse possession of street by railroad. The title of a municipality to its streets being in trust for the public, the statute of limitations does not run against a municipality, at least where the adverse possession is by structures which are unauthorized by statute.

Railroad Co. v. Cleveland, 15 C. C. n. s. 193, 205; 23 C. D. 482 (1910);
    affirming, 8 N. P. n. s. 457; 19 L. D. 372; aff'd, no rep., 87 O.
    S. 469.

Compare, Railroad Co. v. Hambleton, 40 O. S. 496 (1884).

Trust Co. v. Railway, 7 N. P. n. s. 497, 513 (1908).

Where a turnpike company was given a franchise to use a highway as a toll road, and obstructions were placed therein by a railroad while it was used by the turnpike company, the fact that the turnpike company continued to use the road for more than twenty-one years after the obstructions were placed does not give title by adverse possession to the railroad company.

Commissioners v. Railway Co., 12 N. P. n. s. 129 (1911).

Remedies for unlawful occupation. A railroad company may be enjoined from crossing or occupying a street until it has obtained authority under this section or § 8764. Such occupation may be enjoined by the municipality or county commissioners;

Commissioners v. Penna. Co., 6 N. P. n. s. 141; 18 L. D. 348; aff'd,
    by Cir. Ct., without rep.).

or by an abutting owner.

Railroad Co. v. Railway Co., 3 N. P. n. s. 109; 16 L. D. 777 (1904).

Where a railroad company has occupied a street, under an invalid agreement, with a structure which excludes the public from a portion thereof, it may be compelled by mandatory injunction to remove the structure without compensation for the expense.

Railway Co. v. Elyria, 69 O. S. 414 (1903).

An action in ejectment under § 11903 may be maintained by a municipality to recover possession of land of which the municipality has the paramount title and a railway an easement for certain purposes.

Railroad v. Cleveland, 15 C. C. n. s. 193 (1910); affirming, 8 N. P.
    n. s. 457: 19 L. D. 372: aff'd, no rep., 87 O. S. 469.

Cleveland v. Railway, 93 Fed. 113 (1899).

See Cleveland v. Railway, 147 Fed. 171.

The municipality or public authorities may maintain an action for damages.

Lawrence R. Co. v. Commissioners, 35 O. S. 1 (1878).

Where, after a spur track was constructed across a turnpike and maintained for five years, with full knowledge of the turnpike company, the turnpike company tore up the track, an injunction against relaying the track was refused, the turnpike company, having acquiesced in laying the track and having a remedy at law.

Batavia, etc., Co. v. Railroad Co., 12 C. D. 723; aff'd, 62 O. S. 635.

Spur or switch track distinguished from general tracks. A spur or switch track placed in a street for convenience of shippers differs from a track for general traffic. Such a spur track could not, in many instances, accomplish its purposes elsewhere than in a street.

Railway Co. v. Cincinnati, 16 W. L. B. 367 (Super. Ct. Cin. 1886;
    aff'd by Supreme Ct.).

Gunning v. Railway Co., 2 N. P. n. s. 411, 414; 14 L. D. 660 (C. P.
    1904).

Cincinnati v. Railway, 30 W. L. B. 137 (1893).

Cleveland Lake Front cases.

Railroad Co. v. Cleveland, 15 C. C. n. s. 193; 23 C. D. 482 (1910); affirming 8 N. P. n. s. 457; 19 L. D. 372; aff'd, no rep., 87 O. S. 469.

Holmes v. Railroad, 93 Fed. 100 (1861).

Cleveland v. Railroad, 93 Fed. 113 (1899).

Effect of § 8895 on this section. Before the amendment of this section (99 v. 589) it was held that § 8895 et seq., which require all crossings to be above or below grade, rendered this section inapplicable to grade crossings.

Ritter v. Railway, 6 N. P. n. s. 161; 18 L. D. 846 (C. P. 1907).

Compare, In re Avon Beach, etc., Ry., 3 N. P. n. s. 561; 16 L. D. 87 (C. P. 1905).

Section 8764. (Appropriation of property for elevated track.) If the parties are unable to agree thereon, and it be necessary in the judgment of the directors of such company, to use or occupy such road, street, alley, way or ground, or a part thereof, for surface tracks, or for crossing with an elevated structure when no piers, supports or obstructions are to be placed therein, the company may appropriate so much thereof as is necessary for the purposes of its road, in the manner and upon the terms provided for the appropriation of the property of individuals. (R. S. Sec. 3283; May 9, 1908, 99 v. 589; April 15, 1857, 54 v. 133, § 12.)

Appropriation of private property by railroads, §§ 8759, 8760.

Appropriation proceedings, § 11038 et seq.

No greater use can be obtained by appropriation than by agreement under § 8763.

Railroad Co. v. Defiance, 52 O. S. 262, 308 (1895); affirmed, 167 U. S. 88 (1897).

This section does not authorize appropriation for a railroad yard.

Rockport v. Railway Co., 85 O. S. 73 (1911).

Nor does it give a railroad company the right to appropriate streets for an unlimited number of tracks. The court is required to determine the reasonableness of the appropriation.

Rockport v. Railway Co., 85 O. S. 73 (1911).

Order under § 8898 et seq. as a condition precedent. An order of the court of common pleas under §§ 8898 and 8899 must be obtained before a proceeding will lie to appropriate the use of a street at grade. A petition for appropriation which does not allege such an order is subject to a motion to make definite and certain.

Railway v. East Liverpool, 10 N. P. n. s. 157; 55 Bull. 173 (Probate Ct. 1909); (aff'd, Cir. Ct., no report).

See Toledo v. Railway Co., 9 C. C. n. s. 399; 19 C. D. 658; 78 O. S. 429.

In re Avon Beach, etc., Ry., 3 N. P. n. s. 561; 16 L. D. 87 (C. P. 1905).

Ritter v. Railway, 6 N. P. n. s. 161; 18 L. D. 846 (C. P. 1907).

Public "road, street, etc."

See note to § 8763.

Necessity for use. The necessity must be expressly determined by the directors. A failure to do so is a jurisdictional defect which can not be cured.

C. & P. Ry. v. E. Liverpool, 51 O. L. B. 599 (Prob. Ct. 1906).

The directors have primary discretion to determine the necessity for the appropriation but under § 11046 the court has the final authority to determine such necessity.

Cincinnati v. Railroad Co., 88 O. S. — (1913); affirming, 12 N. P. n. s. 65; 22 L. D. 363; 10 N. P. n. s. 749; 56 Bull. 317; reversing 15 C. C. n. s. 62; 23 C. D. 464.

Railroad v. Railroad, 72 O. S. 368 (1905).

Necessity to use a street for railroad yard purposes is not a necessity within the meaning of this section.

Rockport v. Railway, 85 O. S. 73 (1911).

Inability to agree must be shown, and a finding of inability to agree made by the court.

Rockport v. Railway, 85 O. S. 73 (1911).

Section 8765. (Limitation as to action for damages.) Every company which lays a track upon or over any such street, alley, road or ground, or part thereof, shall be responsible for injuries done thereby to private or public property lying upon or near to such ground, which may be recovered by civil action brought by the owner before the proper court, at any time within two years from the completion of the track. (R. S. Sec. 3283; May 9, 1908, 99 v. 589; April 15, 1857, 54 v. 133, § 12.)

Easements or rights of abutting owners. An abutting owner has rights or easements of access, light and air.

Railway v. Lake Erie Provision Co., 9 N. P. n. s. 572 (1909).

These are property rights. (Railway v. Cumminsville, 14 O. S. 523, 524) which are not abrogated or affected in any way by an agreement between public authorities and a railroad company.

Railroad Co. v. O'Harra, 48 O. S. 343 (1891).

Lumber Co. v. Railway, 11 N. P. n. s. 289 (1911).

Railroad Co. v. Cincinnati, 76 O. S. 481 (1907).

Where land abuts upon a *cul de sac* the easement of ingress and egress extends to all that part of the street lying between such lands and the first connecting thoroughfare.

Cleveland Furnace Co. v. Ry. Co., 9 N. P. n. s. 426; 20 L. D. 188 (1909).

Lumber Co. v. Railway, 11 N. P. n. s. 289; aff'd, no rep., 86 O. S., 354 (1911).

See Railroad Co. v. Railway Co., 3 N. P. n. s. 109; 16 L. D. 777 (1904).

Furniture Co. v. Railroad, 7 N. P. 640; aff'd, no report, 65 O. S. 571.

See also below, *What property is "near to" the street.*

What constitutes an interference with access. The right of an abutting owner extends to the entire width of the street or highway. A change or obstruction which requires him to travel beyond his lot lines in order to reach the traveled way is an interference with his easement of access.

English v. Trustees, 8 W. L. B. 15 (Dist. Ct. 1882).

Madden v. Penna. Ry., 21 C. C. 73; 11 C. D. 571; aff'd, 66 O. S. 649.

Schimmelmann v. Railway Co., 83 O. S. 356 (1911).
Compare, Smedes v. Cincinnati, etc., Co., 4 O. L. R. 44; 16 L. D.
    743 (Super. Ct. Cin. 1906).

Remedies of abutting owners.

Injunction. An abutting owner may enjoin the construction of tracks
in a street, which will substantially interfere with his rights and easements, until he has been compensated. It is immaterial whether the fee
of the street is in the municipality or in the abutting owners, so long as
it is held upon the same defined uses.

Hall v. Railway, 85 O. S. 148 (1911).
Railway Co. v. Lawrence, 38 O. S. 41 (1882).
Cleveland Furnace Co. v. Ry. Co., 9 N. P. n. s. 426; 20 L. D. 188;
    aff'd, no rep., 86 O. S. 354.
Toledo Bending Co. v. Manufacturers Ry. Co., 2 N. P. 317; 3 L. D.
    430.
Taphorn v. Marietta, etc., R. Co., 4 W. L. B. 988; 11 W. L. B. 92.
Dyer v. Cincinnati, etc., Ry. Co., 7 C. C. 255; 4 C. D. 584 (1893).
Sargent v. Ohio, etc., R. Co., 1 Handy 52 (1854).
Varwig v. Railroad Co., 54 O. S. 455 (1896).

A mandatory injunction to restore the street to its former condition
will be granted, where the railroad company proceeds to tear up the street
without having first obtained the consent of abutting owners.

Toledo Bending Co. v. Manufacturers Ry. Co., 2 N. P. 317; 3 L. D.
    430 (C. P. 1895).
See Railway Co. v. Cincinnati, 8 W. L. B. 334 (1882).
Varwig v. Railway Co., 54 O. S. 455 (1896).

Tracks in the street within twenty-six feet of the entrance to a
factory, where wagons are loaded and unloaded, constitute a material interference which may be enjoined.

Cleveland, etc., Co. v. Erie Ry., 4 C. C. n. s. 365; 14 C. D. 107 (1902).
See note to § 9105.

Where the mode of construction causes the drains and gutters to fill
up and turn the surface water into the middle of the street, where gullies
have formed interfering with access, injunction will lie.

Hall v. Railway Co., 11 C. C. n. s. 97; 20 C. D. 718 (1908); reversed
    in part, 85 O. S. 148.

A spur track across the sidewalk on the opposite side of the street
from plaintiff's property, and the building of an overhead track above
it, is not a material interference.

Smedes v. Cincinnati, etc., Co., 4 O. L. R. 44; 16 L. D. 743 (Super.
    Ct. Cin. 1906).

Where the property is not opposite the track, and the outlet to other
streets are unobstructed, a track laid even with the surface of the street
is not a material interference.

Herzog v. Railway Co., 6 C. C. n. s. 527; 15 C. D. 702; aff'd, 74 O. S.
    440.
Railroad Co. v. Railway Co., 3 N. P. n. s. 109; 16 L. D. 777 (1904).
Furniture Co. v. Railroad, 7 N. P. 640; 10 L. D. 218; aff'd, 65 O. S.
    571.

But the property need not abut upon the immediate portion of the
street occupied by the railroad. The obstruction of a street near enough
to the property to materially affect its value may be enjoined.

Hall v. P. C. C. & St. L. Ry., 85 O. S. 148; modifying 11 C. C. n. s.
    97.
Madden v. Penna. Ry. Co., 21 C. C. 73; 11 C. D. 571 (1900): aff'd,
    66 O. S. 649.
Cleveland Furnace Co. v. Ry. Co., 9 N. P. n. s. 426; 20 L. D. 188 (C.
    P. 1909); aff'd, no rep., 86 O. S. 354.

An injunction will not be granted where the damages complained of by the property owner are remote and are of the same kind though different in degree than are suffered by the general public.

Herzog v. Railway Co., 6 C. C. n. s. 527; 15 C. D. 702 (1904); affirming, 2 N. P. n. s. 17; 14 L. D. 529; affirmed, 74 O. S. 440.

Furniture Co. v. Railroad, 7 N. P. 639, 640; 10 L. D. 218; aff'd, without report, 65 O. S. 571.

See Hall v. Railway Co., 85 O. S. 148 (1911).

Nor where the abutting owner is guilty of laches.

Gunning v. Railway Co., 2 N. P. n. s. 411; 14 L. D. 660 (1904).

Railway v. Duncan, 84 O. S. 463 (reversing 10 N. P. n. s. 385; 20 L. D. 525).

Nor where the abutting owner fails to show material interference with his property rights.

Railway v. Railway, 2 N. P. n. s. 237; 15 L. D. 112 (1904); aff'd, 72 O. S. 598.

Gunning v. Railway, 2 N. P. n. s. 411; 14 L. D. 660 (1904).

Nor where the abutting owner has granted a right of way over other property for a track connecting with the proposed street track.

Railway v. Railway, 2 N. P. n. s. 237; 15 L. D. 112; aff'd, 72 O. S. 598.

Nor where appropriation proceedings are pending and the proposed tracks do not constitute an exclusive occupancy of the street.

Cincinnati, etc., Co. v. Railway Co., 14 C. C. n. s. 195 (1911).

Nor where the evidence is conflicting as to whether or not the proposed track will enhance the value of the abutting property.

Lumber Co. v. Railway, 11 N. P. n. s. 289 (1911).

Action to compel appropriation. An abutting owner may bring an action under §§ 11084, 11085 to compel appropriation of his property rights.

Lawrence R. Co. v. Williams, 35 O. S. 168 (1878).

Kramer v. Toledo, etc., R. Co., 53 O. S. 436 (1895).

Railway v. Pouchot, 4 C. C. 187; 2 C. D. 492; aff'd, 51 O. S 571.

The remedy under § 8765 does not include the relief provided by the appropriation statutes. The damages recoverable under § 8765 are personal and do not pass to a grantee on a conveyance of the property. While in the case of an easement appurtenant to abutting lands the right of action passes to the grantee.

Railroad Co. v. Lersch, 58 O. S. 652 (1898).

Railroad Co. v. Campbell, 51 O. S. 328 (1894).

Railroad Co. v. O'Harra, 50 O. S. 667 (1893).

Hall v. Ry. Co., 11 C. C. n. s. 97; 20 C. D. 718 (1908); reversed in part, 85 O. S. 148.

In Grafton v. Baltimore, etc., R. Co., 12 W. L. R. 214; 21 Fed. 209; 5 O. F. D. 318 (1884) it was said that §§ 11084 and 8765 are consistent and that an abutting owner might pursue either at his election.

An action to compel appropriation is not barred in two years under this section.

Railroad Co. v. O'Harra, 48 O. S. 343 (1891).

Right of action prior to enactment of § 8765.

Parrot v. Cincinnati, etc., R. Co., 3 O. S. 330 (1854).

Little Miami R. Co. v. Naylor, 2 O. S. 235 (1853).

Columbus, etc., R. Co. v. Mowatt, 35 O. S. 284, 287 (1880).

Action under § 8765.

Limitation of two years. The track is completed when it is in a condition fit for permanent use for traffic.

Railway Co. v. Gardner, 45 O. S. 309, 325 (1887).

The limitation is waived by failure to raise it by demurrer or answer.
Baltimore, etc., R. Co. v. Lersch, 58 O. S. 639 (1898).
Where a street is occupied without consent of the public authorities
the two year limitation does not apply.
Lawrence R. Co. v. Cobb, 35 O. S. 94 (1878).
The two year limitation applies to an action based upon the common
law remedy independent of § 8765.
Railroad Co. v. Mowatt, 35 O. S. 284 (1880).
But does not apply to an action to compel appropriation under
§ 11084 et seq.
Railroad Co. v. O'Harra, 48 O. S. 343 (1891).
Where a main track occupied a street for thirty years or more and
subsequently a branch track was laid in another street, it was held that
damages were recoverable only for the branch track.
Cleveland, etc., Co. v. Reeder, 6 C. C. 354; 3 C. D. 489 (1892).

By whom action may be brought. An administrator can not sue
for compensation and damages for wrongfully taking land during the life
of the decedent. The right of action is in the heirs. But the administrator may sue for damages accruing from wrongful use of the lands,
interruption of easement, etc., for which the decedent could have maintained a personal action.
Railroad Co. v. O'Harra, 50 O. S. 667 (1893).
The right of action for damages under § 8765 remains in the grantor,
on a conveyance of the property injured. Such damages are personal in
their nature.
Railroad Co. v. Campbell, 51 O. S. 328 (1894).
Railroad Co. v. Lersch, 58 O. S. 652 (1898).
A mortgagee may bring an action for injury to the mortgage security.
Cameron v. Cincinnati, 17 W. L. B. 153 (C. P. 1886).

Against whom action brought. The lessor and lessee of a railroad
are jointly liable where the lessor raised the grade and laid an additional
track, and the lessee took possession and continued the permanent use.
Railroad Co. v. Hambleton, 40 O. S. 496 (1884).

Defenses. Unrecorded consent of plaintiff's vendor. A purchaser
of abutting property is not affected by an unrecorded consent given by his
vendor, of which he had no knowledge.
Varwig v. Railroad Co., 54 O. S. 455 (1896).
——. **Estoppel.** An abutting owner who induces a railroad to locate
on a right of way, on which his land abuts, is estopped from claiming
damages from its operation. His successors in title are also estopped,
so long as it is operated in the same manner as when originally constructed.
Kinney v. Railway, 3 O. L. R. 545; 16 L. D. 761 (Super. Ct. Cin.
    1906); aff'd, no rep., 77 O. S. 609.

Evidence. Of plaintiff's title. The plaintiff's title may be estab-
lished by proof of adverse possession.
Lawrence R. Co. v. Cobb, 35 O. S. 94 (1878).
See Shepherd v. Baltimore, etc., R. Co., 130 U. S. 426, 434; 6 O. F.
    D. 322 (1888).

——. **Of damages.** It is error to permit witnesses to testify how
much less rent was received before, than after, the track was laid; to give
opinions as to the amount of damages; and opinions as to the differences
in value of the property with the track in the street, and if it was some
other place.
Railway Co. v. Gardner, 45 O. S. 309 (1887).
See Railroad Co. v. Campbell, 4 O. S. 583 (1855).

What property is "near to" the street. Property is "near to" a street, so as to entitle the owner to avail himself of the remedy given by the statute, if the injury to it is the direct and necessary result of the occupancy of the street by the track or other structures of a railroad company. And an injury arises when the diminution of the value of the property can be fairly attributed to such use and occupancy of the street.

Shepherd v. Baltimore, etc., R. Co., 130 U. S. 426, 432; 6 O. F. D. 322 (1888).

Wheeling, etc., R. R. Co. v. McLaughlin, 15 C. C. 1 (1897); aff'd, 61 O. S. 279.

Columbus, etc., R. R. Co. v. Mowatt, 35 O. S. 284 (1880).

Madden v. Penna. Ry. Co., 21 C. C. 73; 11 C. D. 571 (1900); aff'd. 66 O. S. 649.

Property within fifty feet of that part of the street upon which the railroad is operated is "near" thereto. It is not error for the trial judge to so charge the jury.

Toledo, etc., Co. v. Meinen, 6 C. C. n. s. 377; 17 C. D. 208 (1905).

Land abutting upon a *cul de sac.*

Cleveland Furnace Co. v. Railway Co., 9 N. P. n. s. 426; 20 L. D. 188 (1909).

Lumber Co. v. Railway, 11 N. P. n. s. 289 (1911); aff'd, no rep., 86 O. S. 354.

See above, *Remedies of abutting owners. Injunction.*

Damages. Abutting owners are entitled to recover full compensation for the depreciation in value of their property. In estimating the damages the same standard is to be applied as in direct appropriation proceedings.

Grafton v. B. & O. Ry., 21 Fed. 309; 12 W. L. B. 214 (C. C. 1884).

Railway Co. v. Gardner, 45 O. S. 309, 320 (1887).

See note to § 11053.

The measure of damages is, in general, the difference in the value of the property before and after the final location and construction of the railroad.

Toledo, etc., Co. v. Meinen, 6 C. C. n. s. 377; 17 C. D. 208 (1905).

Shepherd v. B. & O. Ry., 130 U. S. 426 (1889).

Railway Co. v. Gardner, 45 O. S. 309 (1887).

The damages recoverable under § 8765 are personal in their nature.

Railroad Co. v. Campbell, 51 O. S. 328 (1894).

Railroad Co. v. Lersch, 58 O. S. 652 (1898).

Railway Co. v. Hall, 11 C. C. n. s. 97; 20 C. D. 718 (1908); reversed in part, 85 O. S. 148.

Inconvenience common to general public. Damages can not be recovered where the injury caused by the tracks and operation of the railroad is not different in kind from that suffered by the general public, although the injury may be greater in degree. The common law rule as to such injuries is not abrogated by § 8765.

Wheeling, etc., R. Co. v. McLaughlin, 15 C. C. 1; 7 C. D. 647 (1897); aff'd, 61 O. S. 279.

Herzog v. Railway Co., 6 C. C. n. s. 527; 15 C. D. 702 (1904); aff'd, 74 O. S. 440.

Railway Co. v. Railway Co., 3 N. P. n. s. 109; 16 L. D. 777.

Fliehman v. Cleveland, etc., Ry. Co., 27 W. L. B. 302.

Kinnear Mfg. Co. v. Beatty, 65 O. S. 264 (1901).

Schmidt v. Cleveland, 1 Ct. of Ap. —; 34 C. D. 7 (1913).

See Hall v. Railway Co., 85 O. S. 148 (1911).

Columbus Plow Co. v. Railway, 12 N. P. n. s. 81 (1911).

Smoke, noise, danger of fire, etc. It is competent to take into consideration evidence of substantial injury and loss to the property (not common to the community at large) caused by smoke, noises and sparks of fire, occasioned by running locomotives and cars along the track in front of the property.

Railway Co. v. Gardner, 45 O. S. 309 (1887).

Wheeling, etc., R. Co. v. McLaughlin, 15 C. C. 1; 7 C. D. 647 (1897); aff'd, 61 O. S. 279.

Nypano Ry. Co. v. Wadsworth Salt Co., 9 C. C. n. s. 114; 19 C. D. 110 (1906).

Danger of fire may be considered where the proximity of the buildings to the railroad is such as to render the danger imminent and appreciable.

Hayes v. Toledo, etc., Co., 6 C. C. n. s. 281; 16 C. D. 395 (1903); aff'd, 70 O. S. 425.

Hatch v. Railroad Co., 18 O. S. 92 (1868).

Although in actions under § 8765 noise, smoke, etc., incident to the proper operation of a railroad are proper elements of damage, yet in other actions property owners can not, in general, recover for injuries caused thereby.

Cincinnati, etc., Co. v. Burski, 4 C. C. n. s. 98; 16 C. D. 486 (1904).

Ross v. Cincinnati, etc., Ry. Co., 5 C. C. n. s. 565; 17 C. D. 135 (1905); aff'd, 74 O. S. 507.

Fliehman v. Cleveland, etc., Ry. Co., 27 W. L. B. 302 (1892).

Temporary obstruction of street. Damages caused by the temporary obstruction of a street during the construction of the railroad are not recoverable under this section unless such obstructions are unnecessarily and unreasonably interposed and prolonged.

Shepherd v. Baltimore, etc., R. Co., 130 U. S. 426; 6 O. F. D. 322 (1888).

Additional tracks. Additional tracks laid in a street, already occupied by one or more tracks, constitute an additional burden, and abutting owners are entitled to compensation and damages.

Railroad Co. v. Hambleton, 40 O. S. 496 (1884).

Varwig v. Railroad Co., 54 O. S. 455 (1896).

Chambers v. Cleveland, etc., Co., 5 C. C. n. s. 298; 17 C. D. 193; aff'd, 73 O. S. 348.

Cleveland, etc., Co. v. Reeder, 6 C. C. 354; 3 C. D. 489 (1892).

Interest. In an action under this section, an allowance may be made in the nature of interest on account of delay.

Lawrence R. Co. v. Cobb, 35 O. S. 94 (1878).

Limited to damages pleaded. Recovery is limited to the damages pleaded.

B. & O. R. Co. v. Lersch, 58 O. S. 639 (1898).

Railroad Co. v. Burski, 4 C. C. n. s. 98, 99; 16 C. D. 486 (1904).

Liability of municipality. The liability of the municipality is not affected, nor the remedy against it taken away, by this section, but in the action against the municipal corporation the plaintiff is not entitled to recover damages which are in the nature of compensation for the additional burden in the street arising from the location and construction of the tracks therein; for damages of that character the municipal corporation is not liable.

Zanesville v. Fannan, 53 O. S. 605 (1895).

See Steubenville v. McGill, 41 O. S. 235 (1884).

Dillenbach v. Xenia, 41 O. S. 207 (1884).

The liability of the railroad company is not limited to that of the municipality.

Lake Shore, etc., Ry. Co. v. Brown, 16 C. C. 269; 9 C. D. 37 (1896).

Section 8766.   (Longitudinal occupancy of way unlawful.)
Nothing herein shall authorize a grant of the right to occupy
any public street, avenue, or alley, longitudinally by an elevated track, except in so far as that is necessary to accommodate a curve in the line of the elevated track, in which
case no supports shall be placed in the roadway of the street,
avenue, or alley between the curb lines thereof, nor shall
such longitudinal occupancy of the street, avenue, or alley
exceed three hundred feet in length.   (R. S. Sec. 3283; May
9, 1908, 99 v. 589; April 15, 1857, 54 v. 133, § 12.)

In the absence of legislative authority the construction and use by a
railroad of its road longitudinally on a public highway is a public nuisance.
    Railway Co. v. Hood, 94 Fed. 618 (C. C. A. 1899).
    See Railway v. Cincinnati, 8 W. L. B. 334 (Dist. Ct. 1882).
    Railway v. Defiance, 167 U. S. 88; 10 O. F. D. 480; affirming, 52
O. S. 262.

Section 8767.   (Appropriation of easement.)   If in the
judgment of the board of directors of any domestic or foreign corporation owning or operating a railroad wholly or
partly within this state, it be necessary to use and occupy
for an elevated track any portion of any public ground lying
within the limits of a municipality and dedicated to the
public for use as a public ground, common, landing or wharf,
or for any other public purpose, excepting all streets,
avenues, alleys or public road, such company may appropriate an easement over so much of such ground as is necessary for such purpose, including the right to maintain the
necessary piers and supports for the elevated track.   Such
appropriation shall be limited to such an easement as is necessary for the construction, maintenance and uses of such
elevated track, in accordance with the plan hereinafter provided for.   Proceedings for appropriation shall be conducted
in the manner and upon the terms provided for the appropriation of the property of individuals.   (R. S. Sec. 3283a;
May 9, 1908, 99 v. 589.)

Piers in streets.
    See Railway Co. v. Elyria, 69 O. S. 414 (1903); aff'g, 3 C. C. n. s.
        250; 13 C. D. 482.
    Railway Co. v. Steubenville (unreported), 83 O. S. 443 (1910).
    See § 8763.
    Prior to the enactment of this section (99 v. 589) a public common
or landing could not be occupied with an elevated structure.
    Railroad Co. v. Cincinnati, 76 O. S. 481 (1907).
    This section authorizes the appropriation of an easement for an elevated track over a public landing.
    Cincinnati v. Railway, 9 N. P. n. s. 433; 20 L. D. 440 (1910); aff'd,
        no report, 82 O. S. 466.
    Affirmed by U. S. Supreme Court, 223 U. S. 390 (1912).

In appropriating an easement across a public landing under §§ 8767 to 8769 it is necessary to follow the procedure provided in § 11046.

Cincinnati v. Railroad Co., 88 O. S. — (1913); affirming 12 N. P. n. s. 65; 22 L. D. 363; reversing 15 C. C. n. s. 62; 23 C. D. 464.

The directors have primary discretion to determine the necessity for the appropriation under this section, but under § 11046 the court in which the proceeding is brought has the final authority to determine such necessity and whether the proposed appropriation will be an abuse of corporate power or destructive of the public purpose to which the land is devoted.

Cincinnati v. Railroad Co., 88 O. S. — (1913); affirming, 12 N. P. n. s. 65; 22 L. D. 363; 10 N. P. n. s. 749; 56 Bull. 317; reversing 15 C. C. n. s. 62; 23 C. D. 464.

Sections 8767, 8768 and 8769 are constitutional.

Cincinnati v. Railway, 223 U. S. 390 (1912); affirming, 82 O. S. 466.

Section 8768. (Submission of plans to council.) Before such appropriation may be made, there shall be submitted to the council of the municipality general plans of the proposed structure showing the manner, character and location of all supports, any part of which will be upon public ground, common, landing or wharf, and also the vertical and longitudinal clearances between the supports. No right to appropriate shall accrue to the railroad company until after it and the council have agreed upon the manner, terms and conditions upon which the property may be used or occupied and the plans submitted have been approved by ordinance duly passed by a two-thirds vote of council. Such ordinance shall be read on three separate days. The rules requiring such reading shall not be suspended. (R. S. Sec. 3283a; May 9, 1908, 99 v. 590.)

An easement across a public landing can not be appropriated until an agreement has been made as to the "manner, terms and conditions" of the occupancy.

"Manner" means method or mode—the way tracks are laid; "terms", the boundary, limit and extent of the grant; "conditions", the stipulations, precedent, the inducement to the grant.

Railway v. Cincinnati, 12 N. P. n. s. 65, 75 (C. P. 1911); aff'd, 88 O. S. —.

An ordinance, which deals with streets and a public landing, deals with two distinct subjects and is invalid.

Railway v. Cincinnati, 12 N. P. n. s. 65, 75, 76; 22 L. D. 363; (C. P. 1911); aff'd, 88 O. S. —.

Section 8769. (Control by public authorities.) Such appropriation shall not be restrictive of the control by the public officers or authorities over such public ground, common, landing or wharf, subject to the continued maintenance and use of such elevated track upon the terms and conditions agreed upon. (R. S. Sec. 3283a; May 9, 1908, 99 v. 590.)

Section 8770.   (Piers or other supports in a public way.) When it is deemed and declared necessary by two-thirds of the members of the council thereof and the mayor approving, any municipal corporation may grant the right, by ordinance duly passed, to a railroad company operating a steam railroad in such municipality to place and maintain necessary piers, or other stays or supports, in any street or way thereof, when they are provided for and included in the plans and specifications prepared for the abolishment of grade crossings therein under the provisions of an act to abolish crossings in municipal corporations, passed May 2, 1902, and all acts supplementary thereto and amendatory thereof.   Every railroad to whom a grant has been made by any municipal authority as herein provided shall notify in writing the authorities making the grant of its rejection or acceptance of the grant at a time fixed by such authorities, when making it.   After such a grant has been made, and accepted by a railroad, if within sixty days after such acceptance, there is filed with the mayor of the city or village making such grant a petition protesting against it, and signed by such a number of the electors of the city or village qualified to vote at the last preceding general election, as equals ten per cent of the number of votes cast for mayor at the last preceding election for mayor he shall certify that fact to the proper election officials.   (R. S. Sec. 3283-1; May 9, 1908, 99 v. 591.)

Prior to the enactment of this section and the amendment of § 8763 piers and supports in a street were unauthorized.
Railway Co. v. Elyria, 69 O. S. 414 (1903); affirming, 3 C. C. n. s. 250; 13 C. D. 482.
Railway Co. v. Steubenville, 83 O. S. 443 (unreported).
Sections 8770 and 8771 do not apply to § 8763 et seq. These sections are complete in themselves and do not depend upon such other sections.
Cincinnati v. Railway, 9 N. P. n. s. 433, 436; 20 L. D. 440; aff'd, no rep., 82 O. S. 466.

Section 8771.   (Submission of question to electors.)   The officials in charge of such general election, in accordance with the statutes relating to elections, shall arrange and provide for and conduct the submission of such question to such electors.   The question whether such grant shall be made shall be submitted to the electors of such city or village at the next succeeding general election occurring more than thirty days after the expiration of such sixty days. The ballots at such election shall read "Elevated Railroad Grant—Yes"; "Elevated Railroad Grant—No". If at the election a majority of the votes cast on such question is against the grant, it shall be ineffective and void.   (R. S. Sec. 3283-1; May 9, 1908, 99 v. 591.)

Blank ballots are not "votes cast on such question" under this section and can not be counted.

Brush v. Orgill, 9 N. P. n. s. 632 (C. P. 1910).

The canvassing board may be enjoined from counting ballots which did not express any vote.

Brush v. Orgill, 9 N. P. n. s. 632 (C. P. 1910).

Section 8772. (Extension of line, how authorized.) When a company desires to extend the line of its road beyond either of its previously designated termini, its president and directors may submit the question of such extension and change of termini to a meeting of its stockholders, to be called for that purpose by notice published for four consecutive weeks in some newspaper in general circulation in each county through or into which the road passes. If the holders of a majority of the stock, in person or by proxy, so determine, the president and directors, or a majority of them, shall make a certificate of the fact, naming the places of the new terminus or termini of the road, and the county or counties through or into which the extended line will pass, and file it in the office of the secretary of state. Such extension then shall be held to be a part of the original line of the road. (R. S. Sec. 3306; March 20, 1875, 72 v. 70, § 2.)

Change of line, § 8747.

The provision that an extension shall "be held to be a part of the original line" does not have the effect of including the extension in a prior mortgage on the original line, which mortgage did not in terms cover after acquired property.

Louisville Trust Co. v. Railway Co., 91 Fed. 699; 10 O. F. D. 646 (1897).

See also note to § 8793.

This section applies to completed lines and requires a vote of a majority of the stock, only, for a change of termini.

Louisville Trust Co. v. Railway Co., 91 Fed. 699, 705; 10 O. F. D. 646 (1897).

The provisions of this section are for the benefit of the public.

Metropolitan Trust Co. v. Railway Co., 91 Fed. 18, 20; 13 O. F. D. 58 (1899).

Section 8773. (Diversion of road or stream.) When it is necessary in the construction of its road to cross a road or a stream of water, a company may divert it from its location or bed, but without unnecessary delay it shall place such road or stream in such condition as not to impair its former usefulness. (R. S. Sec. 3284; May 1, 1852, 50 v. 274, § 16.)

See § 8763.

For bridges over highways, see § 8857.

This section does not authorize a railroad company to lay tracks upon or across a county road. Its purpose is confined to the diversion of a road or stream.

Commissioners v. Penna. Co., 6 N. P. n. s. 141; 18 L. D. 348 (1907);
  (aff'd Cir. Ct. without report).
This section applies only to county roads. A street in a municipal
corporation can not be crossed or occupied by a railroad under this section.
Such occupancy or crossing is governed by § 8763.
  Youngstown v. Railroad Co., 3 C. C. 214; 2 C. D. 121 (1888).
  Railroad Co. v. Cincinnati, 8 W. L. B. 334 (Dist. Ct. 1882).
  See Commissioners v. Penna. Co., 6 N. P. n. s. 141; 18 L. D. 348
  (1907); (aff'd Cir. Ct. without report).
This section is substantially the common law rule on the subject.
  Railroad Co. v. Defiance, 52 O. S. 262, 314 (1895).

Power to divert. Subject to the performance of the duty to restore,
the power or right to divert a road or stream is coextensive with the
public necessity which calls for its exercise, and the diversion may be
temporary or permanent, as the public needs or necessities require.
  Valley Ry. Co. v. Bohm, 34 O. S. 114, 119 (1877).
  See Commissioners v. Penna. Co., 6 N. P. n. s. 141; 18 L. D. 348
  (1907); (aff'd by Cir. Ct. without report).
  Trust Co. v. Railway, 7 N. P. n. s. 497.
This section authorizes a railroad company to divert the course of a
highway so as to cross the highway with an overhead bridge.
  Commissioners v. Railway, 7 N. P. n. s. 529; 17 L. D. 418 (1906);
  aff'd in part, 79 O. S. 440.
A railroad will not be enjoined from driving piling into the bed of a
stream to construct a new bridge, unless substantial damage will be caused.
  Commissioners v. Pierce, 90 Fed. 764; 12 O. F. D. 287 (C. C. 1898).

Necessity. The court may determine whether a necessity exists for
the proposed diversion.
  Commissioners v. Railway, 7 N. P. n. s. 529; 17 L. D. 418 (1908);
  aff'd in part, 79 O. S. 440.

After construction of road. A railroad company can not appropriate property for the purpose of diverting a stream after the original
construction of its road.
  Railway Co. v. South, 78 O. S. 10 (1908).
  See Lorain County v. Railway, 11 C. C. n. s. 419; 12 C. D. 805.
  Commissioners v. Railway, 7 N. P. n. s. 529; 17 L. D. 418 (1908);
  aff'd in part, 79 O. S. 440.

Duties of railroad company.

To guard pending construction. Until the highway is restored to
its former condition of usefulness, the railroad company must, by proper
barriers, prevent and guard travelers from using the highway where it is
in a dangerous condition.
  Potter v. Bunnell, 20 O. S. 150 (1870).

To restore to condition of usefulness. The requirement of this section is not to restore to its former place or conditions, but to such condition as not to affect materially its utility. It is to be left in such condition, how much so ever it may be diverted from its former course. that the
right to the public or private enjoyment, where such right exists, shall
not be materially disturbed or interfered with.
  Valley Ry. Co. v. Bohm, 34 O. S. 114 (1877).
  Little Miami R. R. Co. v. Commissioners, 31 O. S. 338 (1877).
Restoration to the former usefulness may be accomplished by the substitution of another way for the part taken.
  Commissioners v. Railway, 7 N. P. n. s. 529; 17 L. D. 418 (1906);
  aff'd in part, 79 O. S. 440.

Megrue v. Commissioners, 15 C. C. 242; 8 C. D. 262 (1897).

The duty to restore rests upon the railroad company, and can not be shifted to a contractor.

Cincinnati, etc., R. Co. v. Van Dorn, 1 C. C. 292; 1 C. D. 160 (1885).

The obligation to restore is inseparable from the right to divert.

Zanesville v. Fannan, 53 O. S. 615 (1895).

State v. Dayton, etc., R. Co., 36 O. S. 434 (1881).

A railroad may appropriate land necessary to restore the road or stream.

Valley Ry. Co. v. Bohm, 34 O. S. 114 (1877).

But the power to appropriate may be exercised only at the time of the original construction of the road.

Railway Co. v. South, 78 O. S. 10 (1908).

Before the enactment of § 8770 it was held that piers or supports for overhead tracks could not be permanently placed in a street; and that a street had not been restored to its former usefulness where such supports were maintained.

Railway Co. v. Elyria, 69 O. S. 414, 435 (1903); s. c., 3 C. C. n. s. 250; 13 C. D. 482.

To keep in repair after restoration. No duty is imposed by this section to keep the highway in repair, after it has been placed in such condition as not to impair its usefulness.

Pittsburg, etc., Ry. Co. v. Maurer, 21 O. S. 421 (1871).

Remedies on failure to restore road or stream to condition of usefulness.

Injunction. Injunction will lie to compel a railroad to perform its obligation to restore the road. Such action may be brought by the attorney general in the name of the state.

State v. Dayton, etc., R. Co., 36 O. S. 434 (1881).

Commissioners v. Railway, 7 N. P. n. s. 529, 540; 17 L. D. 418 (1906); aff'd in part, 79 O. S. 440.

Or by the county commissioners.

Little Miami R. Co. v. Commissioners, 31 O. S. 338 (1877).

The remedy given to county commissioners by G. C. § 2424 et seq. is cumulative and does not affect the right of the state.

State v. Dayton, etc., R. Co., 36 O. S. 434 (1881).

The statute of limitations is not a defense to an action brought to compel the railroad company to perform its obligation.

Little Miami R. Co. v. Commissioners, 31 O. S. 338 (1877).

Action for damages. A railroad company is liable for injuries to persons or property caused by its failure to restore the road to the former condition of usefulness.

G. C. § 7473.

Pittsburg, etc., Ry. Co. v. Maurer, 21 O. S. 421 (1871).

Potter v. Bunnell, 20 O. S. 150 (1870).

Cincinnati, etc., R. Co. v. Van Dorn, 1 C. C. 292; 1 C. D. 160 (1885).

Consent of public authorities to the change does not affect the liability of the railroad company.

McNulta v. Ralston, 5 C. C. 330; 3 C. D. 163 (1891).

Where a stream is turned into a new channel on land of the railroad company, so that, beyond the railroad land, it is thrown upon the land of another, the railroad company is under a liability, which continues until the right to cause such damage is acquired.

Valley Ry. Co. v. Frantz, 43 O. S. 623 (1885).

Damages for a diversion of a highway can not be recovered in a proceeding to appropriate land adjoining the highway. A separate action must be brought for such injury.

Schaible v. Railway Co., 10 C. C. 334; 6 C. D. 505 (1895).

Where permission to divert a highway was granted by county commissioners, and certain individuals executed a bond securing the repair of the highway, and upon default of the railroad company the commissioners completed the repairs, it was held that the cost could be recovered in an action on the bond.

Megrue v. Commissioners, 15 C. C. 242; 8 C. D. 262 (1897).

Liability of municipal corporation. The fact that the railroad company is liable does not relieve a municipal corporation from its duty to keep its streets free from nuisance, nor change its liability.

Zanesville v. Fannan, 53 O. S. 605, 615 (1895).

Where a street bridge over a railroad falls, the railroad company having assumed the repair and maintenance of the bridge, and the municipality having control over it, are jointly liable.

Toledo, etc., R. Co. v. Sweeny, 8 C. C. 298; 4 C. D. 11 (1894); (aff'd by divided court, 52 O. S. 616).

Diversion of streams generally.

See Railroad Co. v. Carr, 38 O. S. 448 (1882).
Crawford v. Rambo, 44 O. S. 279 (1886).
C. & H. C. & I. Co. v. Tucker, 48 O. S. 41 (1891).

Section 8774. (Construction of bridges; use as toll bridge.) A railroad company may so construct its bridges as to answer the ordinary purposes of travel and business, as well as for railroad purposes, and may demand and receive such rates of toll for the passage of individuals, vehicles of all kinds, or animals, as it fixes, subject to the approval of the commissioners of the county or counties in which such bridge is erected. Rates of toll shall be uniform, shall be printed or painted, and kept conspicuously posted in or near the toll-house of the bridge, and may be revised and changed in the first week of each year. The company may compound and bargain with any person or party for the use of such bridge, by the month, quarter, or year. No company shall receive toll upon such a bridge if erected within one mile of a toll bridge previously constructed over the same stream. (R. S. Sec. 3285; May 11, 1853, 51 v. 415, § 1.)

Section 8775. (Bridging of canals or navigable rivers.) When the line of the road crosses a canal or any navigable water, the company shall file with the board of public works, the plan of the bridge, and other fixtures therefor, which shall designate the place of crossing. If the board approves such plan, it shall notify the company, in writing, of such approval. If the board disapproves such plan, or fails to approve it within twenty days from the filing thereof, the company may apply to the court of common pleas, or a judge thereof in vacation, and upon reasonable notice being given to the members of the board, upon good cause shown, the court or judge shall appoint a competent, disinterested engineer, not a resident of a county through which the road passes, to examine such crossing, and prescribe the plan and conditions thereof, so as not to impede navigation. Within twenty days from his appointment, such engineer shall make his returns to the common pleas court of the county wherein such crossing is to be made, subject to exceptions by either party. At the next term after filing the return, the court shall examine, approve, and confirm it, unless good cause be shown against such approval. Its order of confirmation shall be sufficient authority for the erection, use, and occupancy of such bridge, in accordance with such plans. (R. S. Sec. 3317; May 1, 1852, 50 v. 274, § 20; 50 v. 205, §§ 4, 5.)

The words "navigable waters" are used in no restricted sense; they embrace all waters within the state, which are navigable by the works of art or nature.
Works v. Junction R. R. Co., 5 McLain (U. S.) 425; 3 O. F. D. 101 (1853).
The right to cross a navigable water by a railroad bridge must be given by the sovereign power, by special or general act. Where this is not done, the board of public works can not approve the plan of a proposed bridge. The board has no power to grant leave to cross the navigable water.
Works v. Junction R. R. Co., 5 McLain (U. S.) 425; 3 O. F. D. 101 (1853).

Remedy. See as to quo warranto in court of appeals.
Lake Shore, etc., Ry. Co. v. State (Sup. Ct.) 33 W. L. B. 169 (1894).

Power of congress. Under the power to regulate commerce, congress has power to prevent the obstruction of any navigable river, which is a means of commerce between any two or more states. The exercise of this great public right is not incompatible with the enjoyment of local rights. The public right consists in an unobstructed use of a navigable water connecting two or more states. The local right is to cross such water. The general commercial right is paramount to all state authority.
Lake Shore,. etc., Ry. Co. v. Ohio, 165 U. S. 365 (1897).
Works v. Junction R. R. Co., 5 McLain (U. S.) 425; 3 O. F. D. 101 (1853).
See Bridge Co. v. United States, 105 U. S. 470; 5 O. F. D. 67 (1882).
State v. Commissioners, 7 C. C. n. s. 469; 18 C. D. 212 (1905); (dissenting opinion) 8 C. C. n. s. 169.

Section 8776. (Height of bridges over canals.) No company shall construct over a canal any permanent bridge less than ten feet in the clear above the top water line of the canal, and the piers and abutments of such bridge must be placed so as not in any manner to contract the width of the canal, or interfere with free passage on the tow-path. This section shall not prevent the construction or continuance of draw bridges which do not interrupt navigation. (R. S. Sec. 3317; May 1, 1852, 50 v. 274, § 20; 50 v. 205, §§ 4, 5.)

The court has no power to approve a plan for the construction of a bridge where the bridge is to be less than ten feet above the top water-line of the canal, or where the piers or abutments interfere with navigation.

State ex rel. v. Railway Co., 37 O. S. 157, 173 (1881).

Section 8777. (Certain established bridges not affected.)

All railroad bridges erected prior to May 1, 1852, over any navigable canal, feeder, slack-water improvement, river, stream, lake or reservoir, not less than ten feet in the clear above the top water line, shall remain undisturbed by the board of public works. (R. S. Sec. 3318; May 1, 1852, 50 v. 205, § 4.) ·

Section 8778. (Enforcement of preceding section.)

If a company refuses to comply with any of the provisions of sections eighty-seven hundred and seventy-five and eighty-seven hundred and seventy-six, on being notified thereof, the attorney-general shall immediately institute proper legal proceedings, in the name of the state, against such company, for the purpose of enforcing such provisions. (R. S. Sec. 3319; May 1, 1852, 50 v. 205, § 5.)

Section 8779. (When companies must use same bridge.)

When it becomes necessary for two or more railroads to cross any of the navigable waters of this state at or near the same point, by draw or swing bridge, the companies or persons owning or controlling such roads, if practicable, shall use one and the same bridge, and approaches thereto. The right to use any such bridge and its approaches, or other similar structure, so situated and used as to make it necessary for the companies or persons owning or operating two or more roads to agree upon a common use thereof, in order to comply with this section, when such companies or persons can not so agree, may be appropriated by the company or persons owning or operating a road for which such use is desired, in accordance with the provisions of law authorizing the appropriation of private property to the use of corporations. (R. S. Sec. 3364; February 10, 1860, 57 v. 10, § 1.)

Section 8780. (Appropriation of use of joint bridge.)

The statement to be filed in such appropriation proceedings as near as may be, shall set forth the regulations according to which the joint use of such bridge and approaches, or other structure, are to be regulated. If their reasonableness in any part be denied by the defendant in the proceedings, the court shall hear and determine the issue, and record its findings and order thereon, confirming or altering the regulations, as it deems just and reasonable, subject to exceptions and reversal for error by the court of common pleas, on petition filed for that purpose. The order fixing the regulations shall be made before the jury is impaneled to assess the compensation for the right sought to be appropriated, which shall be a sum equal to the annual value of such use, to be paid quarterly each year, in advance, while it continues. (R. S. Sec. 3365; February 10, 1860, 57 v. 10, § 2.)

> This section applies to trestles. Whether a structure is a trestle or a bridge is a question of fact for the jury.
> Johns v. Railway, 7 N. P. 592; 10 L. D. 348 (C. P. 1900).

DIRECTORS AND OFFICERS.

Section 8781. (Opening of transfer books in other states.) When they deem it expedient for the interest or convenience of the company, its directors may open transfer books in any state of the United States, for the purpose of transferring stock purchased or held by persons out of this state, and employ suitable agents to keep such books, whose acts, done under the authority of this section, shall bind the company. (R. S. Sec. 3291; March 21, 1850, 48 v. 51, § 1.)

Section 8782. (Election of a vice-president.) The directors may elect from their number a vice-president, when, in their opinion, the interest or convenience of the company requires it. In case of the absence, death, resignation, or other disability of the president, the vice-president so elected shall exercise the powers and discharge the duties which belong to the office of president, until such vacancy is filled by a new election, or such disability removed. (R. S. Sec. 3292; March 29, 1856, 53 v. 36, § 1.)

> The office of vice-president may be made active and independent.
> Colman v. West Virginia, etc., Co., 25 W. Va. 148 (1884).
> Chicago, etc., Co. v. James, 22 Wis. 194 (1867); s. c., 24 Wis. 388 (1869).
> Richards v. Osceola, 79 Ia. 707 (1890).

Section 8783. (Election of a treasurer.) When, in their opinion, the interests or convenience of the company will be promoted thereby, the directors may elect a suitable person as treasurer of the company, to be subject to such rules and regulations as they or the company prescribe. (R. S. Sec. 3293; April 7, 1857, 54 v. 103, § 1.)

Section 8784. (Number of directors may be increased or diminished.) By a vote of a majority of its stock, at any regular annual meeting of the company, it may increase the number of directors to not more than fifteen, or decrease the number before or after such increase to not less than seven. (R. S. Sec. 3294; January 14, 1875, 72 v. 17, § 3.)

A decrease or increase in the number of directors is not such a fundamental change but that it may be done by the majority.
Mower v. Staples, 32 Minn. 284 (1884).

Section 8785. (Directors may be classified at stockholders' meeting.) The stockholders of a company, whose railroad is wholly or partly within this state, at any regular meeting, or special meeting of which at least thirty days' notice has been given by publication, by an affirmative vote of those owning a majority of the stock of the company, may direct its board of directors so to classify the members thereof, by lot or otherwise, that one-third shall terminate their official term at the first annual election thereafter, one-third at the next annual election thereafter, and the remainder at the next succeeding annual election. At the first regular election succeeding such classification, when the term of the directors of the first class expires and at each succeeding annual election thereafter, the stockholders shall elect directors for three years, to take the places of those retiring, and no more. All vacancies which otherwise occur in the board shall be filled in the manner prescribed by law. (R. S. Sec. 3295; April 30, 1869, 66 v. 77, § 1.)

Section 8786. (Classification of directors.) The stockholders of a company whose road is wholly or partly within this state, at any regular annual election of directors thereof, may so classify and elect such directors that one-third thereof shall serve for one year, one-third for two years, and the remainder for three years. At each succeeding annual election thereafter the stockholders shall elect directors to take the place of those whose terms so expire. No person shall be allowed to vote for directors unless he has been a registered stockholder of the company at· least thirty days prior to such election. The registry of such stock shall be made in the books kept at the principal office of the company. (R. S. Sec. 3296; April 30, 1869, 66 v. 77, § 2.)

Section 8787. (Rights of creditors in election of di-

rectors.) The provisions of the next two preceding sections also apply to companies whose bondholders or other creditors share with the stockholders in the election of directors. In such case the vote necessary to direct the classification provided for in those sections shall be the same as is required to elect directors of such company. (R. S. Sec. 3297; April 30, 1869, 66 v. 77, § 3.)

Section 8788. (Personal liability of directors.) Such directors shall be liable in their individual capacity to the stockholders for any damage sustained by them by reason of negligence, mismanagement, or unfaithfulness in the discharge of their duties; but a director may exonerate himself by entering his protest upon the record against an act done without his concurrence from which injury is feared, and forthwith publishing it for three weeks in some newspaper printed and of general circulation in the county in which is the principal office of the company. (R. S. Sec. 3314; May 1, 1854, 52 v. 91, § 3.)

Section 8789. (Who ineligible to office or appointment.) No person who is a stockholder, owner, or part owner of any express, dispatch, fast freight, or transportation company, whether incorporated or not, an object, or one of the objects, of which is the shipment of freight or the transportation of persons over any railroad in the United States, or who in any way is pecuniarily interested in a company or partnership formed for such or like purpose, shall perform the duties of, or be elected or appointed to, an office of profit or trust in a railroad company, or employed as freight or ticket agent thereof. All such persons shall be ineligible to any such office or appointment. (R. S. Sec. 3315; April 6, 1866, 63 v. 156, § 1.)

Similar acts are in force in Missouri, Pennsylvania and Wisconsin.

Employes of a freight despatch company are not "stockholders, owners or part owners." They are not interested in such company within the meaning of this section and are not disqualified from acting as directors.

Devou v. Cincinnati, etc., Co., 4 O. L. R. 313; 19 C. D. 113 (1906).

Section 8790. (Acts of ineligible persons void; forfeiture.) If any person be elected to an office, or appointed to a position, or performs duties, in violation of the next preceding section, all his official acts shall be null and void. For every day that he exercises or attempts to exercise the functions of such office or appointment, he shall forfeit and pay fifty dollars, to be recovered at the suit of any stockholder of the company, in its name, one-half of which shall go into the treasury of the company, and the other to the stockholder prosecuting. (R. S. Sec. 3316; April 6, 1866, 63 v. 156, § 2.)

Section 8791.   (When directors may receive subscriptions in installments.) The directors of a company which has expended in the construction of its road ten per cent of its authorized capital, and has obtained actual bona fide subscriptions to its capital stock to the amount of at least twenty per cent thereof, may receive subscriptions to its capital stock, payable in such installments, dependent upon the completion of the whole or any part of its road so that cars may pass over it, as they deem expedient, and upon full payment thereof issue certificates of stock therefor.   No subscriber to the stock hereby authorized shall be entitled to any of the privileges of a stockholder until his subscription is fully paid, nor for any purpose, be deemed a stockholder until the happening of the contingency upon which the installments on his subscription are made dependent. (R. S. Sec. 3298; April 15, 1857, 54 v. 133, § 3.)

If at the time a subscription is made it is unauthorized by this section, it may be a continuing offer to subscribe and become absolute when its conditions have been complied with, though it may be withdrawn at any time before such performance.
Armstrong v. Karshner, 47 O. S. 276 (1890).
Where a subscription is conditioned upon the completion and operation of the road between specified points, it is not necessary that the whole road should be completed before the subscription can be enforced.
Lesher v. Karshner, 47 O. S. 302 (1890).
The addition of the words "paid as donation" do not convert a conditional subscription to an agreement for a gift.
Lesher v. Karshner, 47 O. S. 302 (1890).
A subscriber to stock is entitled to no privileges until his subscription is fully paid; for instance, he can not vote if action is to be taken under §§ 8806 to 8808.
Railroad Co. v. Hinsdale, 45 O. S. 556 (1888).
For conditional subscriptions in general, see note to § 8630.

Section 8792.   (Conditional subscriptions.) A company which has begun and partly built its road, but is unable to finish and operate it for want of means, may take subscriptions conditioned that the proceeds thereof shall not be used or applied upon the debts of the company.   All money or material collected upon such subscriptions, and all material or implements purchased with such money for the construction of 'the track, houses, depots, and rolling stock of the company, shall be exempt from execution, or other process or proceedings for the payment of the debts of the company so long as such money, material or implements are used or designed for the construction of such track, houses, depots and rolling-stock. (R. S. Sec. 3299; April 16, 1867, 64 v. 192, § 1.)

Conditional subscriptions. See note to § 8630.

BORROWING MONEY.

Section 8793. (Mortgage bonds.) A railroad company may issue bonds, convertible or otherwise, bearing a rate of interest not exceeding seven per cent per annum, to an amount not exceeding two-thirds of its capital stock, actually subscribed, for one or more of the following purposes: Completing or extending its road, constructing branch roads, laying double or additional track, increasing its machinery or rolling-stock, building depots or shops, making improvements, paying its unfunded debts, or redeeming its bonds. It may secure the bonds so issued, by mortgage on its property, or otherwise, if authorized by the vote, in person or by proxy, of holders of a majority of the stock upon which all the installments called for by the board of directors have been paid. Such vote shall be taken at a meeting of stockholders, of which thirty days' notice shall be given. (R. S. Sec. 3286; March 14, 1876, 73 v. 25, § 5.)

Corporate mortgages and bond issues generally. See § 8705 et seq.
　By consolidated railroad companies, § 8801 et seq.
　By street and interurban railways, § 9121-1.
　An issue of bonds by a railroad must be authorized by the public service commission.
　See §§ 614-53 to 614-55.
　Issue of bonds regardless of amount of capital stock, when authorized by commission, see G. C. § 614-53.

Vote of stockholders. This section does not in terms require a vote of the stockholders to give the directors authority to issue bonds. Such authority is only required for the execution of a mortgage over the corporate property.
　Shoemaker v. Dayton, etc., R. Co., 19 W. L. B. 322 (1888); aff'd, 3 C. C. 473; 2 C. D. 270.

What property may be mortgaged.

　After acquired property. Where railroad mortgages contain apt language to that effect, they attach to and cover future acquisitions of property for the use of the road.
　Coopers v. Wolf, 15 O. S. 523 (1864).
　Feike v. Cincinnati, etc., Ry. Co., 14 C. C. 186; 7 C. D. 652 (1897).
　Coe v. Columbus, etc., R. Co., 10 O. S. 372 (1859).
　Coe v. Peacock, 14 O. S. 187 (1863).
　Ludlow v. Hurd, 1 Dis. 552 (1857).
　Hatry v. Painesville, etc., Ry. Co., 1 C. C. 426; 1 C. D. 238 (1886).
　Maher v. Ventilating Co., 11 C. C. 381; 5 C. D. 159.

Trust Co. v. Cincinnati, etc., Ry. Co., 91 Fed. 699; 10 O. F. D. 646 (1897).

Compton v. Jessup, 68 Fed. 263; 8 O. F. D. 452 (1895).

A railroad mortgage covering "all of the following, present and in the future to be acquired property and estate of said company" does not convey present and after acquired property generally where such description is followed by a specific reference to the property.

King v. Atlantic, etc., R. Co., 12 C. D. 551 (1886).

A conveyance of "all the right, title and interest which the said company now has or may hereafter acquire in and to its aforesaid railroad" specifies nothing and does not convey after acquired property.

King v. Atlantic, etc., R. Co., 12 C. D. 551 (1886).

Section 8772 does not operate to include an extension of line in a prior mortgage on the original line which does not, in terms, cover after acquired property.

Louisville Trust Co. v. Railway Co., 91 Fed. 699; 10 O. F. D. 646 (1897).

A railway company gave a mortgage to secure its coupon bonds, conveying all the property which it then possessed or should thereafter acquire, and subsequently executed a lease, to which the mortgagee was not a party, whereby the lessee agreed to pay the coupons at maturity, in the event the net earnings of the demised road should not be sufficient to protect the interest on the bonds. In a suit to foreclose the mortgage, held, that the lease was not after acquired property within the meaning of the mortgage.

Moran v. Pittsburg, etc., Ry. Co., 32 Fed. 878; 5 O. F. D. 712 (1887).

Where a lease is executed by a mortgagor subsequent to the mortgage, and there is no privity of estate or contract thereby created between the mortgagee and lessee, and there is no attornment by lessee to mortgagee, the mortgagee can not either before or after the mortgagor's default, demand the benefits of the lease without the consent of the lessee.

Moran v. Pittsburg, etc., Ry. Co., 32 Fed. 878; 5 O. F. D. 712 (1887).

A mortgage on "the road" of the company, "whether made or to be made, acquired or to be acquired," and all property, real or personal, "of the company, whether now owned or hereafter to be acquired, used or appropriated for the operating or maintaining the said road," is not a lien upon the real estate of the company then owned or afterward acquired which has not been used or appropriated for operating or maintaining the road.

Walsh v. Barton, 24 O. S. 28 (1873).

Hatry v. Painesville, etc., Ry. Co., 1 C. C. 426; 1 C. D. 238 (1886).

Franchise to be a corporation. A railroad company has no power to mortgage or sell its franchise to be a corporation, and a judicial sale upon mortgages executed by it would not invest the purchaser with any corporate capacity whatever.

Atkinson v. Marietta, etc., R. Co., 15 O. S. 21 (1864).

Coe v. Columbus, etc., R. Co., 10 O. S. 372 (1859).

Franchise to operate railroad. The franchise to maintain the railroad and receive compensation for transportation may be mortgaged.

Coe v. Columbus, etc., R. Co., 10 O. S. 372 (1859).

A street railway may mortgage its franchise to operate on streets.

Louisville Trust Co. v. Cincinnati, 76 Fed. 296; 10 O. F. D. 112 (C. C. A. 1896).

Rolling stock. Extra-territorial effect. A mortgage covers rolling stock, though temporarily out of the state, and a receiver may, under comity between states by an action brought in the foreign state in his own name, assert his right to the possession thereof where such right is not in conflict with the rights of citizens of such foreign state nor against the policy of its laws.

Bank v. McLeod, 38 O. S. 174 (1882).

Winslow v. Troy Iron, etc., Co., 1 Dis. 229 (1856).

Scrap. Cast-off articles. The cast-off articles, fragments and old materials, once forming part of the road, or used in its operation, still continue under the mortgage, if a proper and judicious management of the road requires that they should be recast or exchanged for new articles, for the uses of the road.

Coopers v. Wolf, 15 O. S. 523 (1864).

Construction of mortgage and bonds. Where the words or terms of a bond are equivocal or not entirely clear, the court may consider the deed of trust in connection with the bond in order to ascertain the real contract between the corporation and the bondholder.

Shoemaker v. Dayton, etc., R. Co., 18 W. L. B. 43 (1887).

A mortgage given to secure the payment of dividends to the holders of certificates of preferred stock, is an incident to the principal obligation, and the terms and purport of the certificates will be held to express the real intent of the parties, even though some of the stipulations of the mortgage may be apparently inconsistent with the intent as expressed by the certificates.

Miller v. Ratterman, 47 O. S. 141 (1890).

Interest. An interest coupon, in which no payee was designated, was held to be nonnegotiable.

Wright v. Ohio, etc., R. Co., 1 Disney 465 (1857).

But coupons payable to bearer are negotiable.

G. C. §§ 8106, 8114.

Where bonds were issued bearing interest at seven percent, per annum, payable semi-annually, and it was claimed that the corporation had no power to contract for the payment of interest either semi-annually or at any other time before the money fell due, it was held that the payment of the interest could be regulated according to the usual course of dealing in borrowing money and paying the price or compensation for its use.

Coe v. Columbus, etc., R. R. Co., 10 O. S. 372, 396 (1859).

Where interest on bonds is made payable out of net income at certain periods, a failure of income in one period does not discharge the interest, but it is payable from the income of succeeding periods.

Dayton, etc., R. Co. v. Shoemaker, 3 C. C. 473; 2 C. D. 270 (1888).

Where the mortgage provides that the bonds shall become due immediately upon a default of interest for six months, it is doubtful whether a default alone, without any steps being taken by a holder to enforce the provisions, is such a dishonor as to destroy the negotiability. But where the interest is subsequently paid in full, the negotiability of the bonds is restored.

Railway Co. v. Lynde, 55 O. S. 23 (1896); aff'd, 172 U. S. 493.

Proceeds of sale of bonds as a trust fund. Where money is held by a corporation or its directors, arising from a sale of its mortgage bonds, and the purposes for which the bonds or their proceeds are to be used by the corporation are set forth in the mortgage, and are such as are authorized by statute, it is a trust fund to be used in good faith by the corporation for the purposes stated in the mortgage.

Columbus, etc., Ry. Co. v. Burke, 19 W. L. B. 27 (1887).

Central Trust Co. v. Burke, 1 N. P. 169; 2 L. D. 96 (1895).

Upon a proper showing the bondholders are entitled to an injunction to restrain a misuse of the funds arising from the sale of bonds.

Columbus, etc., Ry. Co. v. Burke, 19 W. L. B. 27 (1887).

Estoppel to deny validity of bonds. Where a company has paid interest and principal on bonds for several years, it may be estopped to deny the validity of the issue of the bonds.

Shoemaker v. Dayton, etc., R. R. Co., 19 W. L. B. 322 (1888).
See note to § 8705.

Negotiable notes secured by bonds. A trustee appointed by a railroad company to hold bonds as collateral security for its negotiable notes is the agent of the company and not of the holders of the notes. Notice to the trustee of defenses is not notice to bona fide holders of the notes.

Central Trust Co. v. Railway Co., 7 O. L. R. 15; 169 Fed. 466 (C. C. 1908).

Convertible bonds.

See § 8709 and note.

Where convertible bonds were issued, and the interest regularly paid, the bondholders are entitled to convert their bonds into stock, but to receive only an amount of stock equal to the principal sum of the bonds, without stock or money for dividends on the stock, not being entitled to both interest and dividends.

Sutliffe v. Cleveland, etc., R. Co., 24 O. S. 147 (1873).

Where bonds are converted into stock, not in good faith, but for the purpose of keeping the control of the company in the hands of a board of directors, a court of equity may interfere on the ground of fraud.

Baldwin v. Hillsborough R. R. Co., 10 W. L. J. 356 (1853).
See note to § 8630, *Sales to directors and officers.*

Rights of general creditors, to unissued or undelivered bonds. Railroad mortgage bonds held by the company or its agents, for the use of the company before delivery, are not subject to execution as property of the company, nor can they be subjected to sale by proceedings in aid of execution.

Means v. Cincinnati, etc., R. Co., 2 Dis. 465 (1859).

A writ of mandamus will not be allowed to compel a corporation to issue its bonds to one of its creditors in order to obtain the benefit of a mortgage security, where the right of the creditor to such security is doubtful, and the property sought to be affected has passed into the hands of third parties as purchasers. The remedy in such case should be by a suit brought in equity against the parties whose interest it is sought to affect.

Ham v. Toledo, etc., Ry. Co., 29 O. S. 174 (1876).

Execution against railroad property. The levy of an execution upon personal property of a railroad, while in actual use, is invalid on the ground of public policy. But in general a railroad is not entitled to special immunity from process in favor of its creditors.

State v. Brimson, 46 W. L. B. 275 (Supreme Court without report, 1901).

A freight car in use in interstate commerce, and in transit into and from the state, can not be levied upon.

Buckeye Buggy Co. v. Railway, 3 O. L. R. 426; 16 L. D. 279 (C. P. 1905).

Pullman Co. v. Linke, 11 O. L. R. 64; 203 Fed. 1017 (D. C. 1913).

The execution of a mortgage by a railroad company can give no exemption to its personal property from liability for its debts that the execution of a like mortgage by an individual would not create.

Coe v. Columbus, etc., R. R. Co., 10 O. S. 372 (1859).
Coe v. Knox County Bank, 10 O. S. 412 (1859).
Coe v. Peacock, 14 O. S. 187.
See Carey v. Pittsburg, etc., R. Co., 1 W. L. M. 338 (1859).

But where the value of the entire mortgaged property is less than the amount of the mortgage, the removal and sale on execution of portions of such property may be enjoined.

Lane v. Bingham, 17 O. S. 642 (1867).

Ludlow v. Hurd, 1 Dis. 552 (1857).

Where the amount of mortgages exceeds the entire value of the mortgaged property, only nominal damages can be recovered against the sheriff for refusing to levy upon and sell the property on executions against the company.

Coopers v. Wolf, 15 O. S. 523 (1864).

See Coe v. Peacock, 14 O. S. 187 (1863).

When the property is inadequate security for the payment of mortgage debts, a judgment creditor's remedy is in equity, to subject the interest of the mortgagor to the payment of his judgment, or where the nature of his claim is such as to entitle him to have it paid out of the earnings of the company, by proceedings to appropriate so much thereof as may be necessary to the payment of the judgment.

Lane v. Baughman, 17 O. S. 642 (1867).

See Carey v. Pittsburg, etc., R. Co., 1 W. L. M. 338 (1859).

Stewart v. Railway Co., 53 O. S. 151 (1895).

FORECLOSURE.

By trustee. The trustee under a railroad mortgage is bound to recognize the rights of the holders of all bonds which are prima facie valid, and to act on their request to foreclose when made by the requisite number.

Central Trust Co. v. Ry. Co., 7 O. L. R. 15; 169 Fed. 466 (C. C. 1908).

A trustee under a railroad mortgage, in bringing suit to foreclose, acts for the benefit of every bondholder who may show his right to share in the proceeds of sale. The trustee is not incapacitated from maintaining the suit although there is a controversy between bondholders as to distribution of the proceeds, and although the trustee represents certain of the bondholders in a different capacity.

Central Trust Co. v. Railway Co., 7 O. L. R. 15; 169 Fed. 466 (C. C. 1908).

Suit by holder of non-negotiable coupons to compel trustee to foreclose.

See Wright v. Ohio, etc., R. Co., 1 Dis. 465 (1857).

A trustee, holding bonds for the benefit of others, can not maintain an action of deceit to recover damages suffered by his cestuis que trustent by reason of a deception practiced upon them in connection with their purchase of the bonds, nor can he maintain an equitable action on the ground of fraud.

Raymond v. Spring Grove, etc., Ry. Co., 21 W. L. B. 103 (1889).

By one bondholder on behalf of all. Where no provision is contained in the mortgage or bonds limiting the right of foreclosure to the trustee, one bondholder may bring suit on behalf of all, under G. C. § 11257. Where a special master was appointed, all who proved their claims before him were held bound by the judgment as if they had been formally made parties.

Carpenter v. Canal Co., 35 O. S. 307.

A suit by one bondholder to enforce an equitable lien of railroad equipment bonds, "on his own behalf as well as for all who may come in and contribute to the expense" is not a class suit under § 11257 and does not bind those who do not come in, unless they had notice and opportunity and refused to do so.

Adelbert College v. Toledo, etc., Ry. Co., 3 N. P. 15; 5 L. D. 14 (1896); s. c., 74 O. S. 483; reversed, 208 U. S. 38, 609 (1908).

In federal court. A suit in a federal court to foreclose a mortgage on the property of a railroad corporation, operates as constructive notice throughout the district, and all persons acquiring an interest in or lien on any part of the property during the pendency of the suit will be bound by the decree and sale made thereunder; the purchaser will take the property discharged from all such liens and interests; though the persons obtaining them be not parties to the suit, they must seek satisfaction from the proceeds of the sale, to reach which they should become parties, and bring their claims to the attention of the court by appropriate pleadings.

Stewart v. Railway Co., 53 O. S. 151 (1895).

See Railway Co. v. Lynde, 55 O. S. 23 (1896); aff'd, 172 U. S. 493.

The pendency of a foreclosure suit in federal court, in which the decree saves the rights secured by a prior mortgage, does not interfere with the negotiation of bonds secured by such prior mortgage or impair in any degree the lien thereby created.

Railway Co. v. Trust Co., 172 U. S. 493 (1899); affirming, 55 O. S. 23.

Effect of federal court proceeding on power of state courts. Where the property is in the possession of the federal court, a state court has no power to order a sale of the property, or, as an essential part of the order of sale, to adjudge that certain equipment bonds are a lien upon the property.

Wabash Railroad Co. v. Adelbert College, 208 U. S. 38, 609 (1908); reversing 74 O. S. 483.

A judgment recovered in a state court against a railroad company by a creditor who was not made a party to the foreclosure suit in federal court, remains unaffected by the decree and sale. Such judgment becomes a lien on the real property owned by the company at the time of its recovery, in the county where rendered, including lands acquired for the roadway, right of way, depots and other purposes of the company, and continues to be so against the property in the hands of the purchaser at the foreclosure sale.

Stewart v. Railway Co., 53 O. S. 151 (1895).

Sale must be of entire road. Because of the interest of the public in the operation of railroads, a railroad must, on a judicial sale, be sold in entirety and not in sections.

King v. Atlantic, etc., R. Co., 12 C. D. 551 (1886).

Stewart v. Railway Co., 53 O. S. 151 (1895).

An exception to this rule exists where the property subject to the lien is independent, as a lot of land not actually used in operation, the sale of which will not interfere with operation.

King v. Atlantic, etc., R. Co., 12 C. D. 551 (1886).

Injunction. An injunction may be allowed restraining the removal and sale on execution of portions of the mortgaged property of a railroad company on the application of the mortgagees, when the whole of the property is admitted to be inadequate security for the payment of the mortgage debts.

Lane v. Baughman, 17 O. S. 642 (1867).

Ludlow v. Hurd, 1 Dis. 552 (1857).

Possession by trustee. A power inserted in a mortgage authorizing the mortgagee, upon default of payment, to take possession of the railroad and other property connected therewith, and to use or sell the same, must be exerted upon all the property mortgaged; and does not authorize the mortgagee to detach portions thereof, either from the possession of the company or an officer succeeding to its rights by a valid levy.

Coe v. Peacock, 14 O. S. 187 (1863).

See Goodman v. Railroad Co., 2 Dis. 176 (1858).

Subrogation. The purchaser at a foreclosure sale may, when necessary for his protection, be subrogated to the rights of the mortgagee.

  Stewart v. Railway Co., 53 O. S. 151 (1895).

  Mill Creek, etc., Ry. Co. v. Carthage, 18 C. C. 216; 9 C. D. 833 (1899);
    aff'd, 62 O. S. 636.

Priorities. Where bonds, secured by one mortgage to a trustee, are issued at different times, the lien of all bonds, outstanding in the hands of bona fide holders for value, are equal in priority. The lien of each bond dates from the recording of the mortgage.

  Railway Co. v. Lynde, 55 O. S. 23 (1896); aff'd, 172 U. S. 493.

Where interest on bonds is made payable out of net income, the corporation may be enjoined from expending its net income for other purposes.

  Dayton, etc., R. Co. v. Shoemaker, 3 C. C. 473; 2 C. D. 270 (1888).

A claim for ties necessary to the preservation of a railroad, finished within six months of the appointment of a receiver, is not superior to a mortgage recorded prior to the making of the contract for furnishing the ties.

  Gregg v. Metropolitan Trust Co. (U. S. Sup. Ct. 1905); 15 O. F. D. 21;
    affirming, 124 Fed. 721; 14 O. F. D. 65; 109 Fed. 220; 13 O. F.
    D. 624.

A railroad mortgage covering after acquired property has priority over a mechanic's lien for labor and materials under § 8345, which was enacted after the execution and recording of the mortgage.

  Reed v. Ginsburg, 64 O. S. 11 (1901).

A claim against a railroad company for money advanced to pay interest and taxes is not entitled to an equitable lien as against mortgagees.

  Coe v. Columbus, etc., R. R. Co., 10 O. S. 372 (1859).

Where a party contracts to sell land to a railway company, but retains the legal title pending payment, it is sufficient to put subsequent mortgagees of the road upon inquiry as to his rights.

  Dayton, etc., R. Co. v. Lewton, 20 O. S. 401 (1870).

Priorities between vendor's lien and mortgage.

  Hatry v. Railway Co., 1 C. C. 426; 1 C. D. 238; aff'd, 23 W. L. B.
    281.

Between mortgage and lien under conditional sale agreement.

  See notes to §§ 9060, 9061.

Miscellaneous. The title to rolling stock may be determined in the foreclosure suit.

  Central Trust Co. v. Ohio Central Ry., 15 O. F. D. 843 (C. C. 1898).

In federal court, the court may order a sale before the final determination of the validity and amount of bonds held by each holder, and it is a recognized practice to postpone the final determination of such questions until after the sale. Petitioners who desire to contest the validity of certain bonds will not be allowed to intervene before the sale, but will be remanded for hearing before the master.

  Central Trust Co. v. Railway Co., 7 O. L. R. 15; 169 Fed. 466 (C. C.
    1908).

A trustee appointed by a railroad company to hold mortgage bonds pledged as security for its negotiable notes is the agent of the company only. Where such trustee is a party to a suit to foreclose the mortgage, in a different capacity, the note holders are not thereby made parties by representation.

  Central Trust Co. v. Railway Co., 7 O. L. R. 15; 169 Fed. 466 (C. C.
    1908).

Section 8794. (Aggregate indebtedness shall not exceed capital stock.) A railroad company may borrow money, at not exceeding seven per cent per annum interest for any purpose required in its business, execute bonds or promissory notes therefor in sums of not less than one hundred dollars, and secure payment thereof by a pledge of its property and income. The aggregate indebtedness authorized by this and the next preceding section shall not exceed the amount of the capital stock of the company. (R. S. Sec. 3287; May 1, 1852, 50 v. 274, § 14.)

See notes to §§ 8793, 8797 and 8705.

The income which railway corporations are authorized to pledge is their net income, not their gross earnings. It is therefore the right and duty of these companies to apply their earnings, first, to pay for all services rendered by laborers, agents and officers; for taxes, machinery, fuel, expenses of maintaining and operating their roads, and for liabilities growing thereout. Second, to pay interest on mortgages. Third, to pay liens in the order of priority.

Carey v. Pittsburg, etc., R. Co., 1 W. L. M. 338 (1859).
See McCormack v. Central Ohio R. Co., 3 W. L. G. 218 (1859).
Darst v. Pittsburg, etc., R. Co., 4 W. L. G. 377 (1859).
Railroad Co. v. Shoemaker, 3 C. C. 473; 2 C. D. 270 (1888).

A court of equity, upon application of an income bondholder for himself and others, should take cognizance of the trust, and restrain the corporation from diverting the funds, to which alone he and his associates may look for the payment of their interest.

Shoemaker v. Dayton, etc., R. R. Co., 18 W. L. B. 43; 3 C. C. 473 (1887).
Carey v. Pittsburg, etc., R. Co., 1 W. L. M. 338 (1859).
See Darst v. Pittsburg, etc., R. Co., 4 W. L. G. 377 (1859).

One lien may be put on the property after another until bonds are executed to the amount authorized and the power exhausted.

See Coe v. Columbus R. R. Co., 10 O. S., 372, 400 (1859).

Loan in excess of capital stock.

See §§ 8705, 614-53.

Railway companies have general power to issue bonds secured by mortgage and where such bonds are issued in excess of the amount allowed by law, there can be no recovery on the bonds against the individual stockholders and directors who caused the issue.

Raymond v. Spring Grove, etc., Ry. Co., 21 W. L. B. 103 (1889).

Estoppel to deny validity of issue. Where the stock of a railway company is irregularly increased, and bonds are issued based upon such increase in stock, both the corporation and the stockholders are estopped to deny the validity of the issue after they have acquiesced in the same for three years.

Farmers Trust Co. v. Toledo, etc., Ry. Co., 67 Fed. 49; 9 O. F. D. 230 (1895).
Kreisser v. Ashtabula, etc., Co., 2 C. C. n. s. 597; 14 C. D. 313 (1901).

Section 8795. (How mortgage or pledge made.) Such mortgage or pledge may be by a deed of mortgage or other instrument in writing, executed by the company, for the purpose of securing payment of money loaned to it, or the notes, bonds, or other evidences of indebtedness issued by the company, and may include both its personal and real property. (R. S. Sec. 3288; February 9, 1853, 51 v. 332, § 1.)

Section 8796. (Where mortgage recorded.) It shall be sufficient record of such mortgage or instrument, if it be recorded in the office of the recorder of deeds in each county wherein the real or personal property therein described is situated or employed. So recorded, it shall be a good and substantial lien upon all of such property, from the date of its record in each of such counties. (R. S. Sec. 3289; February 9, 1853, 51 v. 332, § 2.)

The lien of all bonds, in the hands of bona fide holders, secured by one mortgage, but issued at different times, dates from the recording of the mortgage.
Railway Co. v. Lynde, 55 O. S. 23 (1896); aff'd, 172 U. S. 493.
See Bank v. Brotherton, 78 O. S. 173 (1908).
A recorded mortgage given by a railroad company on its roadbed and other property, creates a lien whose priority can not be displaced thereafter either directly by a mortgage given by the company, or indirectly by a contract between the company and a third party for the erection of buildings or other works of original construction.
Toledo, etc., R. R. Co. v. Hamilton, 134 U. S. 296; 6 O. F. D. 537 (1890).
A creditor having been permitted to levy an execution upon a part of the personal property, including a portion acquired subsequently to the date of both second and third mortgages, but this levy having been made after the action to foreclose was brought, and while the property was in the hands of a receiver appointed in the case, he is not entitled to a preference over the equitable second mortgage.
Coe v. Columbus, etc., R. Co., 10 O. S. 372 (1859).
Where a mortgage is defective in its execution, and therefore void under our laws, it is good as against a subsequent mortgage which is made subject to it.
Coe v. Columbus, etc., R. Co., 10 O. S. 372 (1859).

Section 8797. (Disposition of securities by directors.) The directors of the company may sell, negotiate, mortgage, or pledge its own bonds or notes, as well as notes, bonds, scrip, or certificates for the payment of money or property which the company receives as donations, or in payment of subscriptions to the capital stock, or for other dues of the company, at such times and in such places, either within or without the state, and at such rates and for such prices, not less than seventy-five cents on the dollar, as, in their opinion will best advance its interests. If such notes or bonds are thus sold at a discount, without fraud, the sale shall be as valid in every respect, and the securities as binding for the respective amounts thereof, as if they were sold at their par value. (R. S. Sec. 3290; December 15, 1852, 51 v. 286, § 1; March 14, 1876, 73 v. 25, § 5.)

Character of transaction—sale or loan. The giving of a guaranty of bonds is to be looked to in determining whether the real transaction is a bona fide sale or a disguised loan. If a sale, the guaranty passes as an incident, and is, in equity, assignable to subsequent purchasers of the bonds.

Bank of Ashland v. Jones, 16 O. S. 145 (1865).
See Junction R. R. Co. v. Bank, 12 Wallace (U. S.) 226 (1870).

When a transaction would otherwise be a sale by a railroad corporation of its own bonds, the fact that their payment is guaranteed by the directors in their individual capacities does not necessarily make the transaction a loan.

Bank of Ashland v. Jones, 16 O. S. 145 (1865).

Effect on usury laws. In so far as §§ 8797 and 8794 permit railroad companies to borrow money at a rate of interest exceeding 8 percent, their effect is to exempt railroad companies from the general usury statute; and notes or lease warrants executed by a railroad company for deferred payments on equipment purchased conditionally, and which were payable monthly as rental, the title to the equipment to vest in the company on their full payment are not usurious, though their amount is greater than the stated value of the equipment with 8 percent interest until maturity, but not greater than would have been required if they had borne 7 percent interest, and had been discounted at 75 percent of par.

Metropolitan Trust Co. v. Equipment Co., 108 Fed. 913; 13 O. F. D., 643; s. c., 93 Fed. 702.

Where one contracted to perform certain services in the reorganization of a railway company, for which he was to receive certain amounts of bonds and stock in the reorganized company, it being claimed that the bonds were issued for less than 75 percent of their par value, and were therefore void under this section; held, that the stock should be taken at its actual, and not at its par, value, in computing the amount received by the company for the bonds.

Continental Trust Co. v. Toledo, etc., R. R. Co., 86 Fed. 929 (1898); s. c., 95 Fed. 497 (1899); 82 Fed. 642 (1897).

Before a sale of bonds can be declared invalid, as in contravention of the settled policy of the state where made, the repugnancy must be plain and substantial. The fact that bonds sold here bear a higher rate of interest than may be prescribed for similar bonds issued under the authority of this state, but which are authorized to be sold at any price, creates no repugnancy.

Bank of Ashland v. Jones, 16 O. S. 145 (1865).

A corporation having power to sell its bonds at less than par may exchange them for iron rails.

Coe v. Columbus, etc., R. Co., 10 O. S. 372 (1859).

Sale in foreign state. A corporation of a state, authorized to raise money by the sale of its bonds, may itself sell the bonds directly, either within or without the state, and such transaction will not be regarded as a loan.

Bank of Ashland v. Jones, 16 O. S. 145 (1865).

Foreign corporations. The law of Ohio authorizing railroad companies to sell their own bonds and notes at such prices as they may deem expedient, is extended by comity to the companies of other states authorized to transact business in Ohio.

Junction R. R. Co. v. Bank, 12 Wallace (U. S.) 226 (1870).

In McGregor v. Covington, etc., R. R. Co., 1 Dis. 509 (1857), it was held that this section applies only to domestic corporations, and a sale of bonds by a foreign corporation at less than par is usurious.

Authority of officers to sell bonds.

See note to § 8705.

Section 8798. (Securities sold to directors; when void.) All capital stock, bonds, notes, or other securities of such a company, purchased of it by a director thereof, either directly or indirectly, for less than par value, shall be null and void. (R. S. Sec. 3313; April 27, 1872, 69 v. 173, § 2.)

This section applies only to stock securities, etc., issued by a company of which the purchaser is a director. It does not apply to securities issued by one company and merely guaranteed by another company of which the purchaser is a director.

Railway Co. v. Kleybolte, 80 O. S. 311 (1909); affirming 5 N. P. n. s. 536; 18 L. D. 141.

The words "null and void" in this section are used in the sense of "voidable."

Toledo, etc., R. Co. v. Continental Trust Co., 95 Fed. 497; 13 O. F. D. 86 (C. C. A. 1899).

This section applies only to original sales, and does not apply to a subsequent purchase by a director from the original purchaser, although the original sale was for less than par.

Toledo, etc., R. Co. v. Continental Trust Co., 95 Fed. 497; 13 O. F. D. 86 (C. C. A. 1899).

Continental Trust Co. v. Toledo, etc., R. Co., 86 Fed. 929 (1898).

The issue of bonds to a syndicate of which the directors are members, for less than par, is in violation of this section.

Union Trust Co. v. Railway, 17 W. L. B. 176 (1887).

But such bonds are valid in the hands of bona fide purchasers.

Union Trust Co. v. Railway, 17 W. L. B. 176 (1887)

Railway Co. v. Lynde, 55 O. S. 23 (1896).

And the bona fide purchaser of such bonds is entitled to a lien under the mortgage.

Railway Co. v. Lynde, 55 O. S. 23 (1896).

Contra, Union Trust Co. v. Railway, 17 W. L. B. 176 (1887).

Where bonds have been purchased by a director for less than par, and the company has paid interest regularly for a long time, it can not repudiate the transaction without returning to the director the consideration paid.

Shoemaker v. Dayton, etc., R. R. Co., 19 W. L. B. 322 (1888).

Duty of directors. It is the duty of directors to use their best efforts to advance the value of the stock of their company, to restore, if lost, confidence therein, and to advise holders of the stock of its real value; and not by combinations and arrangements place themselves in a position of using their superior knowledge of its value to depress such value and purchase large quantities of stock at prices far below its real value.

Cincinnati, etc., R. Co. v. Duckworth, 2 C. C. 518; 1 C. D. 618 (1887).

Section 8799. (Narrow-gauge railroad may issue second mortgage bonds.) A railroad company having a gauge not exceeding three feet, known as a narrow-gauge road, incorporated under the laws of this state, having at least fifty miles of completed road, and not exceeding six thousand dollars per mile of first mortgage bonds issued for each mile completed, for the purpose of funding its floating debt, or for the completion of its unfinished proposed. line of road, or for the purchase of rolling stock, or for the erection of repair shops, or for the purchase of supplies necessary for the operation of such road, or for any or all of such purposes, is authorized to issue its second mortgage bonds, bearing a rate of interest not exceeding seven per cent per annum, secured by a second mortgage upon its entire property, real and personal, and its franchise, for a sum not exceeding two-thirds the amount of its authorized capital stock, and sell them at such time and places within or without the state, and at such rate as the directors of the company deem for its best interest. (77 v. 164, § 1; April 10, 1880; R. S. Sec. 3286-1.)

Section 8800. (How bonds and mortgage authorized.) Such issue of bonds and mortgage must be authorized by a vote, either in person or by proxy, of a majority of the holders of paid up stock. But previous to taking such vote thirty days' notice shall be given to the stockholders of the company, by publication in a newspaper of general circulation in each and every county through which the line of road is operated. (77 v. 164, § 1; April 10, 1880; R. S. Sec. 3286-1.)

Section 8801. (When company may borrow money.) A railroad company organized under the laws of this state, or which is or shall be consolidated with other companies, as hereinafter in this title provided, at a meeting of its stockholders, called as hereinbefore provided, instead of issuing preferred stock as provided in section eighty-eight hundred and seventeen may provide for borrowing money to locate, construct and equip its proposed line of railway, or for the purpose of leasing or purchasing and equipping branch or connecting roads constructed or in process of construction, not exceeding ten miles in length, or for redeeming or exchanging any of its previously issued bonds, or for funding its floating debt, or for any or all of such purposes, in such an amount as it deems necessary, not exceeding its authorized capital stock. (R. S. Sec. 3309a; April 14, 1880, 77 v. 206; April 19, 1881, 78 v. 230; March 13, 1883, 80 v. 55; March 20, 1884, 81 v. 57; April 11, 1890, 87 v. 181; March 10, 1892, 89 v. 82; April 27, 1896, 92 v. 415.)

Section 8802. (Bonds in excess of capital, when lawful.) Railroad companies formed by consolidation of one or more companies of this state or of this state with one or more companies of other states as hereafter in this title provided, may issue bonds in excess of such capital stock at such rates of interest as may be agreed upon between the respective parties, not exceeding seven per cent per annum, payable semiannually or quarterly, as they direct, and may execute and issue securities therefor, and to secure the payment thereof, pledge the entire property and net income of such company by mortgage or otherwise. (R. S. Sec. 3309a; April 27, 1896, 92 v. 415; March 10, 1892, 89 v. 82; April 11, 1890, 87 v. 181; March 20, 1884, 81 v. 57; March 13, 1883, 80 v. 55; April 19, 1881, 78 v. 230; April 14, 1880, 77 v. 206.)

Section 8803. (Bonds of consolidated railroad.) A railroad company formed by the consolidation of two or more railroad companies existing under the laws of this state or by the consolidation of one or more companies created by or existing under the laws of this state and any other state or states, with a railroad company or companies of this state or any other state, from time to time, if authorized by the vote in person or proxy of holders of two-thirds of the paid-up stock of such consolidated company present and voting at meetings of stockholders, called as aforesaid, may issue its bonds, convertible or otherwise, into stock, bearing a rate of interest not exceeding six per cent per annum, for one or more of the following purposes: Paying, redeeming or funding debts or obligations assumed, incurred or created by it or either of its predecessors or constituent companies, compromising claims made against it or either of its predecessors or constituent companies, purchasing the whole or a part of any railroad held by it under lease to, or operating contract with it or either of its predecessors or constituent companies acquiring the whole or a part of the stock or bonds of any company owning a railroad held by such consolidated company under lease or operating contract, acquiring the whole or any part of the bonds, notes or other obligations of any other railroad company of this or any other state, the whole or a majority of whose capital stock is held by such consolidated company, completing, extending, improving, maintaining or operating its road, branches or lines, held under lease or contract, laying double or additional track, purchasing rolling stock, building depots, elevators or shops, and generally for any purpose needed in its business, and if the directors so determine, may secure such issue or issues of bonds by mortgage or pledge of its real or personal estate, franchise or income. (R. S. Sec. 3309a; April 14, 1880, 77 v. 206; April 19, 1881, 78 v. 230; March 13, 1883, 80 v. 55; March 20, 1884, 81 v. 57; April 11, 1890, 87 v. 181; March 10, 1892, 89 v. 82; April 27, 1896, 92 v. 415.)

See notes to §§ 8793, 8794.
Application of section to street railways, before adoption of General Code.
See Massillon Bridge Co. v. Cambria Iron Co., 59 O. S. 179 (1898)

Section 8804.   (Form of disposition of such securities.) Such securities may be expressed in dollars or in the currency of the ccuntry where disposed of and be sold upon such terms, at such prices as are agreed upon between the respective parties not inconsistent with the laws of this state. The proceeds of their sale shall be applied only as now required by law. (R. S. Sec. 3309a; April 27, 1896, 92 v. 415; March 10, 1892, 89 v. 82; April 11, 1890, 87 v. 181; March 20, 1884, 81 v. 57; March 13, 1883, 80 v. 55; April 19, 1881, 78 v. 230; April 14, 1880, 77 v. 206.)

Section 8805.   (Articles of incorporation may provide for division and classification of capital stock.) At its formation, in its articles of incorporation, a railroad company may provide for the division of its capital stock into common stock and classes of preferred stock, by stating therein the amount of each kind and class of stock, the par value of the respective shares thereof, and the vote which shares of each class shall have. Such articles also may prescribe other terms and conditions of such preferred stock not inconsistent with law. (R. S. Sec. 3309b; April 2, 1891, 88 v. 267.)

See §§ 8817 and 8667 to 8671 and notes.

CONNECTING LINES.

Section 8806.   (Subscription to aid another company.) A company may aid another in the construction of its road, by means of subscription to its capital stock, or otherwise, for the purpose of forming a connection of the roads of the companies, if the road of the company so aided will not when constructed form a competing line. (R. S. Sec. 3300; March 14, 1882, 79 v. 35; R. S. 1880, § 3300; April 15, 1873, 70 v. 129, § 24; May 1, 1852, 50 v. 281.)

Purchase by mining, etc., company of stock in transportation company.
See § 10138.

What roads are competing.

See note to § 8807.

POWER TO ACQUIRE STOCK IN OTHER CORPORATIONS.

Generally under § 8683. Section 8683 applies to railroad companies. Its provisions are not inconsistent with the provisions of §§ 8806 and 8809 but are cumulative.

Mannington v. H. V. Ry. Co., 8 O. L. R. 451, 476-480; 183 Fed. 133.

State v. H. V. Ry. Co., 12 C. C. n. s. 49, 59; 21 C. D. 175 (1909).

Contra, Mannington v. H. V. Ry. Co. 9 N. P. n. s. 641, 668; 20 L. D. 468 (C. P. 1910).

Under § 8683 a railroad company may acquire stock in corporations which are (1) kindred; (2) not competing and (3) when the result of the purchase is not the formation of a trust.

Mannington v. H. V. Ry. Co., 8 O. L. R. 451, 476; 183 Fed. 133 (1910).

Stock in competing railroads can not be acquired.

State v. H. V. Ry. Co., 12 C. C. n. s. 49, 145; 21 C. D. 175 (1909).

Mannington v. Ry. Co., 9 N. P. n. s. 641; 20 L. D. 468 (1910). Removed to U. S. Court, 183 Fed. 133; 8 O. L. R. 451.

A foreign corporation may own stock in kindred but not competing Ohio corporations, when authorized by the laws of its home state, and not prohibited by statute in Ohio.

Mannington v. H. V. Ry. Co., 8 O. L. R. 451, 481 to 484; 183 Fed. 133 (1910).

Smith v. Newark, etc., R. Co., 8 C. C. 583, 591 (1894).

Under § 8806. This section authorizes only subscriptions to or purchases of stock to aid the construction of a railroad. It does not authorize a purchase of stock from stockholders of another railroad company, the road of which has been completed.

Columbus, etc., Ry. Co. v. Burke, 19 W. L. B. 27 (1887).

State v. H. V. Ry. Co., 12 C. C. n. s. 49, 60; 21 C. D. 175 (1909).

Stock in mining company. This section does not authorize a railroad company to purchase stock in a mining company.

Columbus, etc., Ry. Co. v. Burke, 19 W. L. B. 27 (1887).

A railroad company and a coal mining company are not "kindred" corporations under § 8683. A railroad company has no power to acquire stock in a coal mining company, especially to acquire or hold a controlling interest.

State v. H. V. Ry. Co., 12 C. C. n. s. 49, 59; 21 C. D. 175 (1909).

That a coal mining company has power to construct a railway from its mines to a railroad or other outlet does not constitute the mining company a railway or kindred company.

State v. H. V. Ry. Co., 12 C. C. n. s. 49; 21 C. D. 175 (1909).

Stock in miscellaneous corporations. Bridge company, § 9315. Union depot company, § 9163. Elevator company, § 10173.

Aid by traffic guaranty and purchase or guaranty of bonds. Aid may be extended by a traffic guaranty and purchase of bonds.

O. & M. R. Co. v. Short, 3 W. L. B. 1143 (1879).

Or by a guaranty of bonds.

Zabriskie v. Railroad Co., 23 How. (U. S.) 381; 3 O. F. D. 562.

Abandonment of road to which donations have been made. Construction of parallel line. A railroad company which has received from private parties, donations of lands, subscriptions of stock, and payments in money, in consideration that it should locate its road at a particular place, and allow private side track and warehouse privileges in connection

therewith, will not be permitted to effectuate a change in fact (though not in name) of the line of its road away from such place, by organizing a new corporation and constructing a new road parallel with its old one, under a different charter, and permitting its old line to go to decay, without compensating the parties with whom it has contracted as aforesaid.
Chapman v. Mad River, etc., R. R. Co., 6 O. S. 119 (1856).

Action by stockholder to enjoin acquisition of stock. Venue and parties defendant. An action by a stockholder in a railroad company to enjoin the unlawful acquisition of stock in other corporations must be brought in a county in which jurisdiction may be acquired over the railroad company. The other corporations are not proper parties defendant.
Westfall v. Lake Shore, etc., Ry., 13 N. P. n. s. 217; 22 L. D. 75, 397 (C. P. 1910).

Section 8807. (Lease or purchase of another railroad.) A company may lease or purchase any part or all of a railroad constructed, or in course of construction by another company, if the lines of their roads are continuous or connected, and not competing, upon terms agreed upon between the companies. After such purchase the purchasing company shall be vested with all the rights and powers in respect to the location, construction, completion, and operation of such railroad, and of branches thereto of the company from which it was purchased, including the power to acquire and appropriate property therefor, and be subject to all the duties, obligations, and restrictions of such company. (R. S. Sec. 3300; March 14, 1882, 79 v. 35; R. S. 1880, § 3300; April 15, 1873, 70 v. 129, § 24; May 1, 1852, 50 v. 281.)

Sale of road owned by two or more companies, § 9047 et seq.
Power to sell road, § 9054 et seq.

Connected roads. Two railroad companies owning lines of railroad connected only by other railroads, which such companies hold by lease, are not connected.
State v. Vanderbilt, 37 O. S. 590 (1882).
Where roads are connected by the tracks of a union depot and terminal company, in which each has a proprietary interest, they are connecting lines within the statute.
See Burke v. Cleveland, etc., Ry. Co., 22 W. L. B. 11 (1889).
State v. H. V. Ry. Co., 12 C. C. n. s. 145, 151 (1909).
D. & U. Ry. Co. v. Ry. Co., 6 C. C. n. s. 537, 543; 15 C. D. 705 (1902); aff'd, 67 O. S. 523.

Competing roads. Where the lines of two railroad companies are in their general features parallel they are competing roads.
State v. Vanderbilt, 37 O. S. 590 (1882).
State v. H. V. Ry. Co., 12 C. C. n. s. 49, 66, 153; 21 C. D. 175 (1909).
Chapman v. Mad River, etc., R. R. Co., 6 O. S. 119 (1856).
But where only an inconsequential part of the lines are parallel, the roads are not competing.
State v. Railway, 12 C. C. n. s. 49, 66; 21 C. D. 175 (1909).
D. & U. Ry. v. Railway, 6 C. C. n. s. 537; 15 C. D. 705 (1902); aff'd, 67 O. S. 523.

Roads running at right angles from point of connection can not be said to be competing "in their general features or from a geographical standpoint;" although there may be incidental competition on through or seaboard business.

Burke v. Cleveland, etc., Ry. Co., 22 W. L. B. 11 (1889).

Roads may be competing though they reach competing points by trackage arrangements with other lines.

Hafer v. Cincinnati, etc., R. R. Co., 29 W. L. B. 68 (1893).

Or by virtue of connections.

State v. H. V. Ry. Co., 12 C. C. n. s. 145, 152 (1909).

Roads may be competing though they do not actually cut rates.

Hafer v. Cincinnati, etc., R. R. Co., 29 W. L. B. 68 (1893).

No road or line may be deemed competing until constructed.

Mannington v. H V. Ry. Co., 183 Fed. 133; 8 O. L. R. 451; 16 O. F. O. 552 (C. C. Ohio 1910); compare s. c, 9 N. P. n. s. 641; 20 L. D. 468 (C. P. 1910).

Section 9054 does not authorize a railroad to acquire an uncompleted road which is parallel and naturally competing in character.

State v Railway Co., 13 C. C. n. s. 145; 22 C. D. 147 (1910).

Proof of illegal control of competing railroad. The control and management by a railroad of a competing road, may be shown by the circumstances. A unity of stockholding interests, together with unity of management pursuant to an established plan, is sufficient proof.

State v. H. V. Railway, 12 C. C. n. s. 49; 21 C. D. 175 (1909).

LEASE.

A lease for more than three years must be acknowledged.

Ohio, etc., R. Co. v. Indianapolis, etc., R. Co., 5 A. L. Reg. n. s 733 (1866).

The leasing of its right of way is not evidence of the abandonment of its corporate purposes and does not impair the right of a railroad company to appropriate property

Cincinnati, etc., R. Co. v. Murray, 1 N. P. n. s. 301; 48 Bull. 877 (1903).

A condition in a lease, prohibiting the lessee from receiving for transportation property from certain connecting roads, is a condition subsequent which is void as against public policy.

Metropolitan Trust Co. v Columbus, etc., Ry. Co., 95 Fed. 18 (1899).

Prior to the act of March 14, 1882, only constructed roads could be leased or purchased.

Railroad Co. v. Hinsdale, 45 O. S. 556 (1888).

A contract which, owing to defects in its execution, is invalid as a lease may be valid as a license.

D. & U. Ry. Co. v. Railway Co., 1 N. P. n. s. 577 (1900); aff'd, 6 C. C. n. s. 537; 15 C. D. 705 (1902); 67 O. S. 523.

A foreign corporation having no charter from the state of Ohio, authorizing it to construct and operate a railroad in this state, can not, by a transfer of a portion of a railroad already constructed in the state by legal authority, acquire a right to use and operate such railroad within this state.

Ohio, etc., R Co. v. Indianapolis, etc., R. Co., 5 A. L. Reg. n. s. 733 (1866).

See § 8814.

Where the lessee agreed to advance the money necessary to pay the coupons on the bonds of the lessor, such advance to be paid out of subsequent earnings and not otherwise, the agreement will not be held to be harsh, oppressive or inequitable, and not to be an agreement to loan money to an insolvent corporation, which the court will not enforce.

Henry v. Pittsburg, etc., Ry. Co., 2 N. P. 118, 5 L. D. 41 (1895).

Rescission of lease. A lease can only be rescinded by the same consent of stockholders required to authorize a lease.

Henry v. Pittsburg, etc., Ry. Co., 2 N. P. 118, 5 L. D. 41 (1895).

Specific performance. The specific performance of a lease will not be compelled by a court.

Henry v. Pittsburg, etc., Ry. Co., 2 N. P. 118, 5 L. D. 41 (1895).

See Port Clinton, etc., R. R. Co. v. Cleveland, etc., R. R. Co., 13 O. S. 544 (1862).

Effect of receivership of lessee. The receiver of a lessee company has no power to abrogate a valid lease. As between the lessor and lessee the lease stands until abrogated under some condition therein.

But the receiver has the option, under the direction of the court, to adopt or reject the lease.

Rent accruing prior to appointment of the receiver is not a preferred claim.

New York, etc., R. Co. v. Railway Co., 58 Fed. 278 (C. C. 1893).

See Investment Co. v. Railway Co., 41 Fed. 379 (C. C. 1889).

Duty of lessor to repair. At common law, in the absence of express covenant in a lease, the lessor is not bound to make repairs, additions, or improvements to the leased property, or to rebuild structures thereon which may have become unfit for use, nor is there any implied covenant that the property is fit for the purpose for which it is leased. The fact that the demised property is a railroad does not affect the application of those principles.

Felton v. Cincinnati, 95 Fed. 336; 13 O. F. D. 68 (1899).

Liability of lessor for negligence in operation.

See § 8814.

PURCHASE.

"Duties, obligations and restrictions." The purchaser takes the property subject to all limitations and restrictions, of a public nature, as to rates of fare.

Campbell v. Marietta, etc., Co., 23 O. S. 168 (1872).

Railway Co. v. Moore, 33 O. S. 384 (1878).

But not subject to private contract obligations of the seller unless assumed by the purchaser. A claim for breach of a contract, made by the selling company to transport stone for a specified rate, is not an "obligation" binding upon the purchaser.

Rice v. No o & W. Ry., 153 Fed. 497; 15 O. F. D. 478 (C. C. A. 1907). rf lk

Subscriptions to stock of vendor company. This section does not authorize a sale of stock subscriptions.

Railroad Co. v. Hinsdale, 45 O. S. 556, 557, 572 (1888).

This section becomes a part of a contract of subscription to stock, and a sale of a part of the road does not release the subscriber, unless the subscription is conditional, and the sale makes performance of the condition impossible.

Armstrong v. Karshner, 47 O. S. 276 (1890).

Control of another railroad by voting trust.

See State v. O. & M. Ry. Co., 6 C. C. 415; 3 C. D. 518 (1892); aff'd, 49 O. S. 668.

License to use tracks.

See note to § 8808, *Trackage contracts.*

Section 8808. (Companies not competing may make beneficial arrangements.) Two or more companies whose lines are connected and not competing, may enter into any arrangement for their common benefit consistent with, and calculated to promote the objects for which they were created. (R. S. Sec. 3300; March 14, 1882, 79 v. 35; R. S. 1880, § 3300; April 15, 1873, 70 v. 129, § 24; May 1, 1852, 50 v. 281.)

Trackage contracts. A trackage contract between two railroad companies, whose tracks are parallel for fifteen miles and thereafter separate widely, is authorized, and does not destroy, but rather creates, competition between them.

    D. & U. Ry. Co. v. Railway Co., 6 C. C. n. s. 537; 15 C. D. 705
    (1902); aff'd, 67 O. S. 523; s. c., 1 N. P. n. s. 577.

An agreement permitting one company to use the tracks of another company for a short distance, made in part for the purpose of enabling it to take up its parallel track, is authorized. The removal of such parallel track is a public good.

    D. & U. Ry. Co. v. Railway Co., 6 C. C. n. s. 537; 15 C. D. 705
    (1902); aff'd, 67 O. S. 523; s. c., 1 N. P. n. s. 577.

An agreement permitting one railroad company to use the tracks of the other so long as they continue to exist as chartered corporations is in the nature of a permanent license.

    D. & U. Ry. Co. v. Railway Co., 6 C. C. n. s. 537; 15 C. D. 705
    (1902); aff'd, 67 O. S. 523; s. c., 1 N. P. n. s. 577.

A company can only charge a reasonable price for use of tracks.

    See Toledo, etc., R. R. Co. v. Railway Co., 7 N. P. 376 (1894).

Interpretation. The word "road" in a trackage contract is a generic term, including present and future tracks, side tracks and structural facilities in the transaction of both local and through business.

    D. & U. Ry. Co. v. Railway Co., 6 C. C. n. s. 537; 15 C. D. 705
    (1902); aff'd, 67 O. S. 523; s. c., 1 N. P. n. s. 577.

A grant of the use of the road of another company for "all trains required in the prosecution of its business" limits the licensee to its own business. Whether business conducted is that of the licensee is to be determined by the facts, and not from the engines or crews operating the trains.

    D. & U. Ry. Co. v. Railway Co., 6 C. C. n. s. 537; 15 C. D. 705
    (1902); aff'd, 67 O. S. 523; s. c., 1 N. P. n. s. 577.

Practical construction by the parties may be considered. Where a contract for the joint use of terminal property, in fixing the basis for the division between the companies of the cost of maintenance, used the terms "wheelage" and "car and engine mileage" indiscriminately, but in the performance of the contracts the division was based on wheelage, that construction was adopted by the court.

    Columbus, etc., Ry. Co. v. Penna. Co., 143 Fed. 757; 15 O. F. D. 353
    (C. C. A. 1906).

But practical construction is not binding on successors in interest of one of the parties.

    D. & U. R. Co. v. Railway Co., 1 N. P. n. s. 577 (1900); aff'd, 6 C. C.
    n. s. 537; 15 C. D. 705; 67 O. S. 523.

Ultra vires provision. An ultra vires provision looking toward the stifling of competition which has not been acted upon, and which may be eliminated from the remainder of the contract, does not render the entire contract invalid.

> D. & U. Ry. Co. v. Railway Co., 6 C. C. n. s. 537; 15 C. D. 705 (1902); aff'd, 67 O. S. 523.

Liability for injuries. To passengers. A common carrier being the owner of its tracks is liable to its passenger for an injury received in a collision between its car and the car of another company which it admits to the joint use of its track, although the collision resulted wholly from the negligence of the latter company.

> Maumee, etc., Co. v. Montgomery, 81 O. S. 426 (1910).

——. **Liability of companies inter se.** In such a case the liability of the owning company for breach of its contract of carriage, and of the other for its negligence, may be enforced in the same action, and the facts should be so determined by interrogatories or special findings that liability for compensation may ultimately rest upon the company guilty of negligence.

> Maumee, etc., Co. v. Montgomery, 81 O. S. 426 (1910).

——. **To employee of other company.** While it is competent, in contracts to facilitate the movements of trains at crowded terminals, to incur liabilities for injuries to the employees of other companies, resulting from negligence of their own employees, such contracts may not, by implication, be extended beyond the scope of their terms.

> Ann Arbor R. Co. v. Addison, 84 O. S. 259 (1911).
> See note to § 8814.

——. **To other persons.** The defendant made an arrangement with the D. company whereby it gave to the latter company the right to construct a track on the side of defendant's roadbed for the purpose of connecting the road of the D. company with defendant's road, the connecting track passing over a bridge previously constructed by defendant for its track, and which foot-passengers had been permitted to use for the purpose of transit. The plaintiff, in passing on foot, fell through the same, between the rails of the connecting track, and was injured by reason of the defective covering; *held,* the defendant having no interest in or control over the track, can not be held liable.

> Gwathney v. Little Miami R. R. Co., 12 O. S. 92 (1861).

OTHER CONTRACTS.

Traffic agreements. A traffic agreement is not an "appurtenance" of a railroad so as to pass to the purchaser of the road from the receiver.

> Cincinnati. etc.. R. Co. v. Cincinnati, etc., Ry. Co., 6 N. P. 427; 9 L. D. 493 (1899).

An injunction will not be granted to enforce a traffic contract where there is an adequate remedy at law, or where the complainant's right is doubtful.

> B. & O. R. Co. v. Pittsburg, etc., R. Co., 1 C. C. 100; 1 C. D. 60 (1885).

Tonnage contracts, as such and without other features, are valid.

> State v. H. V. Ry. Co., 12 C. C. n. s. 145, 148 (1909).

Indorsement and guaranty of bonds of coal mining companies. The indorsement and guaranty of the bonds of a coal mining company by a railway company is *ultra vires;* and so also is an agreement between railroad companies operating parallel and naturally competing railroads to indorse and guarantee the bonds of a coal mining company, in consideration of an equal division between the railroad companies of all freight to and from the mines. Such obligations may be valid in favor of the bond-holders, but are illegal as against the state.

State v. H. V. Ry. Co., 12 C. C. n. s. 49, 66; 21 C. D. 175 (1909).

Such a guaranty can not be construed as a tonnage contract, but is in the nature of a monopoly and leads to discrimination.

State v. H. V. Ry. Co., 12 C. C. n. s. 145 (1909).

Illegal agreements. Right of state to interfere. The state is not bound by the fact that the parties are satisfied with an illegal agreement, but, if the public is prejudiced, it may proceed against the parties.

State v. H. V. Ry. Co., 12 C. C. n. s. 145 (1909).

Section 8809. (Vote of stockholders of each company requisite.) No such aid shall be furnished, nor any purchase or lease perfected, until a meeting of the stockholders of each of the companies has been called for that purpose by the directors thereof, on thirty days' notice to each stock-holder, at such place and in such manner as is provided for the annual meetings of the companies, and the holders of at least two-thirds of the stock of each company, in person or by proxy, at such meeting, assent thereto. In case of the lease of a railroad situate in whole or part within this state, the rental reserved and secured for the leased road shall be equal, at least to its net earnings for the fiscal year next preceding the one in which the lease is made. (R. S. Sec. 3301; April 17, 1892, 79 v. 111; Rev. Stats. 1880; April 15, 1873, 70 v. 129, § 24.)

The statute does not require the assent to be in any particular form, and the circumstances will be looked to for light on that question.

See Humphreys v. St. Louis, etc., Ry. Co., 37 Fed. 307 (1889).

Where a lease is made without the stockholders' assent, their acquiescence in the lease for a long period will be held to be a waiver of the requirement of the statute.

See St. Louis, etc., R. R. Co. v. Terre Haute, etc., R. R. Co., 33 Fed. 440 (1888); s. c., 145 U. S. 393.

Zabriskie v. Cleveland, etc., R. R. Co., 64 U. S. 381 (1859).

In construing a Nebraska statute similar to this section the court said: "The stockholders' meeting, and the vote in such meeting on the question of assenting to the proposed lease, are matters of essence, of substance, and not of mere form, and their assent individually obtained outside of such meeting, and in the absence of deliberation, would bind no one.

Peters v. Lincoln, etc., R. R. Co., 12 Fed. 513 (1881).

Section 8810. (Dissenting stockholder may sell stock; procedure.) A stockholder who refuses his assent to such sale, lease, or aid by subscription, and signifies it by notice, in writing, to the purchaser or lessee, within sixty days thereafter, on demand, shall be entitled to receive from such purchaser or lessee, previous to the consummation of such sale or lease, the average market value of his stock for six months next preceding the day of the meeting of the companies at which the sale or lease is approved, on surrendering the stock. If the stockholder and purchaser or lessee can not agree as to the value of the stock, the parties may submit the question to arbitration, to be conducted in accordance with the provisions of law regulating arbitrations, so far as applicable, by three disinterested persons, to be appointed upon the motion of either of the parties, by the judge of the common pleas court of the county in which the owner of the stock resides, or, in case he is a non-resident of the state, or of any county through or into which the road passes, then the county in which the principal office of the company is kept. (R. S. Sec. 3302; April 15, 1873, 70 v. 129, § 24 [§ 2].)

See as to arbitration under a similar section, Railway Co. v. Garrett, 50 O. S. 405 (1893).

Section 8811. (When court may appoint arbitrators.) If such stockholder refuses to submit the question to arbitration, upon the application of a director of either of the companies parties to the contract, the proper judge shall appoint the arbitrators, who shall proceed to ascertain the value of the stock as if the question had been submitted by consent of both parties. If the party owning the stock refuses to receive the amount awarded him, the company may deposit it with the clerk of the common pleas court of the county in which the arbitration is held, which deposit shall operate as if payment were made to the owner of the stock. (R. S. Sec. 3303; April 15, 1873, 70 v. 129, § 24 [§ 2].)

See Railway Co. v. Garrett, 50 O. S. 405 (1893).

Section 8812. (Notice of application therefor.) In all cases of arbitration under the two next preceding sections, the party desiring such arbitration shall give the opposite party at least ten days' notice of his intention to apply to the judge for the appointment of arbitrators, which notice shall be served in the manner provided for the service of a summons, and must specify the time and place of the hearing of the application. In cases of non-residents, the notice shall be by publication for four consecutive weeks, in some newspaper printed in the county. (R. S. Sec. 3304; April 15, 1873, 70 v. 129, § 24 [§ 3].)

Section 8813. (Lease of railroad; security required.) No company shall lease its road or any part thereof to another company, whether of this or any other state, as hereinbefore provided, unless the lessor receives full and adequate security for the payment of the rental and for the preservation of its property in as good condition as on entering into possession thereof. If the lessee fails to pay such rental promptly when due, such lease shall be void, at the option of the lessor. The company to whom a railroad is leased, if a corporation of any other state, shall be subject to all the restrictions, disabilities, and duties of a railroad company incorporated within this state. (R. S. Sec. 3305; April 13, 1883, 80 v. 116; R. S. 1880; April 15, 1873, 70 v. 129, § 24 [§ 4].)

A judgment ordering the cancellation of a railroad lease may be appealed from by a stockholder of the lessor under § 12224 as a person directly affected thereby when there is reason to believe that the officers of the lessor are acting in the interest of the plaintiff.

Henry v. Jeanes, 47 O. S. 116 (1890); s. c., 48 O. S. 443.

Section 8814. (Lessor and lessee jointly liable.) Notwithstanding such lease the corporation of this state lessor therein, shall remain liable as if it operated the road itself, and both the lessor and lessee shall be jointly liable upon all rights of action accruing to any person for negligence or default growing out of the operation and maintenance of such railroad, or in any wise connected therewith, and may be jointly sued in the courts of this state of proper jurisdiction, and prosecuted to final judgment therein as in other cases of joint liability. Service may be had upon such companies, or either of them by the service of process upon any officer or agent of either of the companies. (R. S. Sec. 3305; April 13, 1883, 80 v. 116; Rev. Stat. 1880; April 15, 1873, 70 v. 129, § 24 [§ 4].)

Liability of lessor.

In general. This section does not require both companies to be sued, as they are jointly and severally liable.

Stoltz v. Baltimore, etc., R. R. Co., 7 N. P. 129 (1897).

See as to removal to U. S. court, Spangler v. R. R. Co., 42 Fed. 305 (1890).

Commencing suit against one company will not save the running of the statute of limitations against the other.

Stoltz v. Baltimore, etc., R. R. Co., 7 N. P. 129 (1897).

For fires. Where damage is caused by a fire originating from the negligence of the lessee, both lessor and lessee are liable.

Fisher v. Baltimore, etc., R. Co., 3 N. P. 283; 6 L. D. 67 (1896).

For negligence of receiver of lessee. This section does not operate to give a right of action against a lessor company for negligent acts of the employes of a receiver who is operating the road as receiver of the lessee.

Chamberlain v. New York, etc. R. Co., 36 W. L. B. 81 (1896); 71 Fed. 636.

See Caldwell v. Pittsburg, etc., R. Co., 33 W. L. B. 134 (1894).

To employes of lessee. The provisions of this section apply only to the obligations of the lessor to the public. The lessor does not owe to employes of the lessee the duty of exercising ordinary care in furnishing him a safe place to work.

Powers v. Railways, 12 C. C. n. s. 230; 21 C. D. 488 (1909).

This section relates only to the duties of a carrier, and does not make the lessor liable to an employe of the lessee injured through the lessee's failure to perform its duties as master.

Axline v. Toledo, etc., R. Co., 138 Fed. 169; 15 O. F. D. 463 (C. C. 1903).

Beltz v. B. & O. R. Co., 3 O. L. R. 419; 137 Fed. 1016 (C. C. 1905).

Where a railway company leases its line without authority of law, although the lease is void, the lessor is not liable to an employe of the lessee injured through the negligence of the lessee.

Hukill v. Maysville, etc., R. Co., 72 Fed. 745 (C. C.).

At common law.

See Gwathney v. Little Miami, etc., R. Co., 12 O. S. 92 (1861).

Fisher v. Baltimore, etc., R. Co., 3 N. P. 283; 6 L. D. 67 (1896).

Under former statute.

Collins v. B. & O. R. Co., 7 N. P. 270; 7 L. D. 445 (1898).

Liability of companies using tracks jointly.

See note to § 8808. *Trackage contracts.*

Service of process. Jurisdiction over the lessee company is not obtained by the service of process upon the president of the lessor company.

Collins v. B. & O. R. Co., 7 N. P. 270; 7 L. D. 445 (1898).

Removal to federal court. Receivers of the lessee company can not remove an action brought against the lessor and receivers jointly under this section to federal court on the ground of diverse citizenship.

Central, etc., R. Co. v. Mahoney, 114 Fed. 732; 14 O. F. D. 61 (C. C. A. 1902).

But where an Ohio railroad company was joined as a defendant with a foreign railroad company, under a false allegation that the Ohio company had leased its road to the foreign company, the allegation being made to prevent the removal, the case may be removed to federal court.

Diday v. Railroad Co., 107 Fed. 565; 12 O. F. D. 734.

Removal on ground of local prejudice.

See Whelan v. Railroad, 35 Fed. 849; 6 O. F. D. 87.

INCREASE OF CAPITAL STOCK.

Section 8815.   (Purposes for which stock may be increased.) A company may increase its capital stock, as hereinafter provided, when in the opinion of the directors it is insufficient for the construction of its road, or it becomes necessary for the speedy and convenient transactions of its business to construct a second additional track, extend its line, or construct branches thereof, increase its machinery, rolling-stock, depots, or other fixtures, or for the purpose of paying any bonds issued or guaranteed by it, or for the purchase of a railroad within this state, sold by a judicial

order or decree, or for completing its line of road, or liquidating or paying off any unfunded or floating debt, or other
liabilities incurred in the construction or equipment of its
road, or for extending it, or constructing branches as authorized or for either or all of such purposes. (R. S. Sec.
3307; May 5, 1873, 70 v. 289, § 1; March 29, 1875, 72 v.
91, § 1.)

Increase of capital stock under general corporation law, § 8698.

 The sale or other disposition of unissued stock is not an increase of
capital stock.

  Sims v. Street Railroad Co., 37 O. S. 556 (1882).

 Irregularities in the proceedings to increase the stock, e. g., that no
notice of the meeting of stockholders was given, will not defeat an action
to recover on a subscription for such increased stock for the purpose of
paying debts, where such subscriber having knowledge of the facts, acquiesced until the company became insolvent.

  Clarke v. Thomas, 34 O. S. 46 (1877).

  Turnbull v. Pomeroy Salt Co., 24 W. L. B. 133 (1890).

  See Farmers' Loan, etc., Co. v. Toledo, etc., Ry. Co., 67 Fed. 49; 9
  O. F. D. 242 (1895).

 Where a railroad, having power to increase its stock, paid a stock
dividend, a holder of bonds convertible into stock, who has been paid interest on the bonds, can not on converting his bonds into stock claim the
stock dividend.

  Sutliff v. Cleveland, etc., R. Co., 24 O. S. 147 (1873).

Section 8816. **(Proceedings to increase capital stock.)**
Before any stock is issued under the next preceding section
a majority of the directors shall call a meeting of the stockholders, designating distinctly its time, place and purpose,
and the amount of stock required, which meeting shall be
held at the principal business office of the company in this
state, and notice of which shall be given for at least thirty
days previous, by continued publication in at least two
newspapers published and of general circulation in the state,
and by a like notice, mailed thirty days previous to the
time named for the meeting, to each stockholder whose residence is known. If at such meeting the consent of the
holders of a majority of the stock upon which they would
be entitled to vote at an election of directors of the company be given, the stock of the company may be increased
to such amount as is decided to be necessary for the purposes named in the preceding section. (R. S. Sec. 3308;
March 14, 1876, 73 v. 25, § 2.)

Who may vote.
 See § 8786.

Section 8817. **(Common or preferred stock may be issued; sale thereof.)** The increased stock may be "common"

or "preferred", as is designated in the call for the meeting of stockholders. If preferred stock be issued, the company may guarantee to the holders thereof semi-annual or quarterly dividends, to an amount not exceeding six per cent per annum, payable at its office, or at such other place as the directors designate. The stock may be sold at such time and place, either within or without the state, as is deemed advisable and the proceeds thereof applied to the purposes for which it is issued. The unpreferred stock of the company shall be entitled to dividends only out of the surplus of profits, after setting apart a sum sufficient to pay the dividends upon the preferred stock. The company which issues such preferred stock shall reserve the privilege of redeeming and canceling it at par, at any time after three years from the date of its issue. The preferred stock herein provided for may be convertible into bonds of the company at the option of the parties. (R. S. Sec. 3309; May 5, 1873, 70 v. 289, § 3.)

See §§ 8667 to 8671, 8699 and 8805.
The right to redeem preferred stock may be exercised by the directors.
　Mannington v. Hocking Valley Ry. Co., 183 Fed. 133, 142-146; 8 O.
　　L. R. 451, 462, 467; 16 O. F. D. 552 (U. S. D. C.).
　See s. c., 9 N. P. n. s. 641, 678 (C. P.) 20 L. D. 468.
　The redemption of preferred stock, authorized by this section, is not a reduction of the corporation's capital stock by a purchase of its own shares.
　Mannington v. Hocking Valley Ry. Co., 183 Fed. 133; 8 O. L. R. 451; 16 O. F. D. 552 (U. S. D. C.)

Section 8818. (Certificate to secretary of state.) Within ten days after such meeting the president and secretary of the company shall make an abstract, stating the whole amount of pre-existing capital stock, the amount authorized, the number of shares of stock upon which all the installments called for by the board of directors have been paid, and the vote at the meeting, and add a certificate that the provisions of the two next preceding sections have been fully complied with. They also shall make affidavit to such abstract and statement, and file it in the office of the secretary of state, who shall cause it to be recorded. (R. S. Sec. 3310; March 14, 1876, 73 v. 25, § 4.)

MISCELLANEOUS.

Section 8819. (Dissolution of certain companies.) A company which has been in existence three years, and has not begun to build the road described in its articles of in-

corporation, or whose road if commenced, has been abandoned for three years, may be dissolved by a vote of two-
thirds of its stockholders, at a meeting called for that purpose by its president, notice of which shall be published in
each county through or into which the line of the proposed
road passes at least thirty days before the meeting is held.
(R. S. Sec. 3363; April 27, 1872, 69 v. 171, §§ 1, 2.)

Section 8820.   (Owner of land leased for right of way
not to be taxed.)   Each company owning and occupying a
right of way or easement in lands, either by agreement with
the owners, or by virtue of an appropriation proceeding,
shall present to the auditor of the county in which the land
is situated a statement of the quantity embraced within the
right of way or easement.   Such quantity shall be deducted
by the auditor from the land on the tax duplicate, so that
the owners thereof shall not be required to pay taxes thereon.
A company hereafter becoming the owner and occupant of
any such right of way or easement, within six months thereafter, shall present such statement to the auditor.   Upon
the failure of the company to make the statement, the owner
of the land may make it.   (R. S. Sec. 3321; March 23, 1875,
72 v. 71, § 8.)

Section 8821.   (Taxation of land used as right of way.)
Any company using or occupying any land as a right of
way, without paper title or contract of record therefor, shall
present a correct survey and plat of such land, exhibiting
the quantity in such right of way taken from the lands of
an owner abutting thereon, as it then stands on the tax
duplicate of such county, to the auditor of the county in
which the land is situated.   Such land, so used or occupied
by any such company he shall charge to it on his duplicate,
and such relative quantity shall be deducted by him from
the land on the tax duplicate, so that the abutting owners
thereof shall not be required to pay the taxes thereon.   All
costs of such survey, plat and transfer shall be paid by the
company.   Upon the failure of a company to have such survey, plat and transfer made, the owner or owners of such
abutting land may have it made and recover the costs thereof in an action against the company before any court having
jurisdiction thereof.   (R. S. Sec. 3322a; April 1, 1902, 95 v.
73.)

Section 8822.   (Lease of right of way to be recorded.)
When the grant of such right of way or easement is not in
the form of a lawfully executed deed or lease, the recorder

of the county where the land is situated, upon the request
of the company owning the right of way or easement, shall
record such grant in the record book of leases, and index
it. Such record, or a copy thereof duly certified by the
recorder, shall be received in evidence in all courts and
places, in the same manner and to the same effect as the
original. The correctness of such record or copy may be
impeached by any interested party, by competent proof.
The recorder shall be entitled to the usual fee for recording
such grants, and certifying copies thereof. (R. S. Sec.
3322; March 23, 1875, 72 v. 71, § 8.)

This section applies to a contract for a lease. A lease is not invalid
because, by mistake of the recorder, it is recorded in a volume entitled
"miscellaneous records," instead of in the book of leases.

Cleveland, etc., Co. v. Reid, 4 N. P. 127; 6 L. D. 273 (C. P. 1896).

Where a contract for a right of way is not entitled to record because
of defective execution, the construction and operation of a railroad thereon
is constructive notice to subsequent grantees of the land.

Miller v. Railway, 12 N. P. n. s. 683; 22 L. D. 638 (C. P. 1911).

CHAPTER 2.

TRACKS AND CROSSINGS.

TRACKS.

Section 8823. (**Track to be of** uniform gauge.) Every company shall make every railroad constructed or controlled by it of one uniform gauge or width of track from end to end. When a road connects with or crosses another road, the companies owning or controlling such roads may adopt such uniform gauge or width of track as will enable each company to pass its cars over the road of the other. If roads so connecting or crossing are constructed of different gauges or widths of track, the companies controlling them may lay down, and maintain upon the whole or any portion of such road or roads, an additional rail or rails, so as to admit the passage of the same cars over both roads, and also maintain and operate either or both of such roads, upon the track or tracks originally constructed, as is deemed expedient by the company or companies owning or con-trolling either or both of the roads. (R. S. Sec. 3338; April 3, 1866, 63 v. 88, § 1.)

Section 8824. (**When tracks used in common.**) When two or more companies have two or more tracks of the same gauge in the same street, alley, public way, or opening, through a city or village, the council thereof may require such companies to use such tracks in common, and to pass their locomotives and cars over each track in one direction only. (R. S. Sec. 3339; April 15, 1857, 54 v. 133, § 4.)

It is the policy of the law to do away with unnecessary tracks.
> Dayton, etc., Ry. Co. v. Ry. Co., 6 C. C. n. s. 537, 545; 15 C. D. 705 (1902); aff'd, 67 O. S. 523.

Section 8825. (Obstructing the laying of a track.) No person or corporation shall wilfully interfere with or obstruct any company engaged in laying the track of its road across any other railroad, if such company has fully complied with the law, and obtained the right to so lay its track; nor shall any person or corporation obstruct the full operation of any road so constructed. A person or corporation violating the provisions of this section, for each day of such interference or obstruction, shall pay one thousand dollars, to be recovered by action in the name of the state, half of the recovery to go to the company so interfered with, and half to the county in which the interference occurs, and shall also be liable for damages to the party injured. (R. S. Sec. 3362; April 1876, 73 v. 160, §§ 1, 2.)

RAILROAD CROSSINGS.

Section 8826. (Railroad crossings.) When the tracks of two railroads cross each other, or in any way connect at a common grade, the crossings shall be made and kept in repair, and watchmen maintained thereat, at the joint expense of the companies owning the tracks. All trains or engines passing over such tracks must come to a full stop not nearer than two hundred feet, nor further than eight hundred feet from the crossing, and not cross until signaled so to do by the watchman, nor until the way is clear. (R. S. Sec. 3333; April 14, 1882, 79 v. 95; R. S. 1880; March 24, 1860, 57 v. 106, § 1.)

When section does not apply. See § 8833.

Constitutionality. This act is a valid exercise of the police power of the state, and is a reasonable regulation of the manner in which railroad trains shall be run so as to avoid danger to the lives and property of people using a railroad.
> Lake Shore, etc., Ry. Co. v. Cincinnati, etc., Ry. Co., 30 O. S. 604 (1876).

Every railroad company in this state accepts its charter and maintains and operates corporate property as a railroad, subject to the inherent power of the state to adopt such police regulations as this, whenever public necessity requires them.

Lake Shore, etc., Ry. Co. v. Cincinnati, etc., Ry. Co., 30 O. S. 604 (1876).

This section applies to tracks existing at the time of its enactment.

Street Ry. Co. v. Railroad Co., 32 W. L. B. 4 (1894).

Joint duty. This section imposes a joint duty and obligation of making and maintaining the crossings and keeping watchmen thereat, and requires the expense to be borne by the companies jointly. The burden is common to both companies, and where either performs the whole duty and pays the whole expense it is entitled to recover from the other its equal proportion therof.

Baltimore, etc., R. Co. v. Walker, 45 O. S. 577 (1888).

This section imposes on both companies the expense of making and keeping up such crossing as is required, without regard to the date of their respective charters, or the location or construction of their respective roads.

Lake Shore, etc., Ry. Co. v. Cincinnati, etc., Ry. Co., 30 O. S. 604 (1876).

Whether in a case under this section the expense should be apportioned according to the use of the crossing, or otherwise than equally, quaere.

Baltimore, etc., R. Co. v. Walker, 45 O. S. 577 (1888).

Duty of lessee. A railroad company which has possession and control of a railroad in this state as lessee is one "owning the tracks" of such railroad within the meaning of this section.

Baltimore, etc., R. Co. v. Walker, 45 O. S. 577 (1888).

The necessity for keeping the crossing in repair, and maintaining watchmen thereat, grows out of the use and operation of the railroads crossing each other at a common grade, and the benefits thereof accrue to the companies using and operating the roads; and as a lessee company, while operating its road, receives the benefit and security resulting from a safe crossing and the services of the watchmen, it takes them subject to the burden of their expense, as provided by the statute.

Baltimore, etc., R. Co. v. Walker, 45 O. S. 577 (1888).

Negligence in operating crossing. For a charge to a jury in a negligence case involving this section,

See Moulder v. Cleveland, etc., R. R. Co., 1 N. P. 361 (1894).

Specific performance of contract to maintain crossing.

See Columbus, etc., Ry. Co. v. Ohio Southern Ry. Co., 1 C. C. 275; 1 C. D. 151 (1885).

Right to cross tracks and manner of crossing.

See § 8834 et seq.

Street railway crossings.

See § 9124 et seq.

Stopping of electric cars at steam railroad crossings.

Order of Railroad Commission, 4 O. L. R. 668 (1906).

Section 8827. (Crossing of trains; how regulated.) When two passenger or freight trains approach the crossing at the same time, the train on the road first built shall have precedence if the tracks are both main tracks over which all passengers and freights on the road are transported. But if only one track is such main track, and the other is a side or depot track, the train on the main track shall take precedence. If one of the trains is a passenger train and the other a freight train, the former shall take precedence, and regular trains on time take precedence over trains of the same grade not on time. Engines with the cars attached, not on time, shall take precedence of engines without cars attached, not on time. (R. S. Sec. 3333; April 14, 1882, 79 v. 95; R. S. 1880; March 24, 1860, 57 v. 106, § 1.)

See note to § 8826.

Section 8828.   (Rules to be made and published.) The managing agent or superintendent of each railroad shall establish, and publish to all the employes on the road, such rules and regulations as in all cases will secure strict compliance with the provisions of the two next preceding sections, and shall republish such rules and regulations on each time table or card issued to the employes on the road. (R. S. Sec. 3334; March 24, 1860, 57 v. 106, § 2.)

Section 8829.   (Forfeiture.) If such managing agent or superintendent fails or neglects to establish and publish such rules and regulations, or to republish them on each time table or card issued to the employes on the road, he shall be personally liable, for every such failure or neglect, to a penalty of one hundred dollars, to be recovered together with costs, in an action against him in favor of the state, to be brought in the court of common pleas of any county wherein such crossing is. (R. S. Sec. 3334; March 24, 1860, 57 v. 106, § 2.)

Section 8830.   (Agent or superintendent liable.) Such agent or superintendent, and the company of which he is agent or superintendent, shall also be liable in damages to any person or company injured in person or property by an accident arising from such failure or neglect. (R. S. Sec. 3334; March 24, 1860, 57 v. 106, § 2.)

Section 8831.   (Forfeiture.) An engineer or person in charge of an engine who wilfully fails to comply with the provisions of sections eighty-eight hundred and twenty-six and eighty-eight hundred and twenty-seven, or fails to bring the engine of which he is in charge, with the train, if any, thereto attached, to a full stop at least two hundred feet before arriving at a railroad crossing, or connection, or crosses it before signaled so to do by the watchman, or before the way is clear, shall be personally liable to any person injured by reason of such failure in a penalty of one hundred dollars to be recovered by civil action, at the suit of the state, in the court of common pleas of the county wherein such crossing or connection is. (R. S. Sec. 3335; March 31, 1874, 71 v. 50, § 3.)

Section 8832. (Liability of company.) The company in whose employ such engineer or person in charge of an engine is, as well as the person himself, shall be liable in damages to any person or company injured in person or property by such neglect or act of such engineer or person. (R. S. Sec. 3335; March 31, 1874, 71 v. 50, § 3.)

Section 8833. (When trains may cross without stopping.) If such two railroads crossing each other, or in any way connecting at a common grade, by works or fixtures to be erected by them render it safe to pass over such crossings without stopping, and such works and fixtures first be approved by the state railroad commission, and the plan thereof for such crossing, designating the plan of crossing, has been filed with such commission, the provisions of the preceding sections of this chapter relating to railroad crossings, shall not apply. If the commission disapproves such plan, or fails to approve it within twenty days from the filing thereof, such companies may apply in the county where the crossing is situated, to the common pleas court or to a judge thereof in vacation, in the manner provided in section eighty-seven hundred and seventy-five. The same proceedings may be had, and with the same effect. (R. S. Sec. 3333; April 14, 1882, 79 v. 95; R. S. 1880; March 24, 1860, 57 v. 106, § 1.)

Interlocking system.

See § 592 et seq.
Where, to obtain the right to cross the track of another company, a railroad company agreed to install and maintain an interlocking system at its own expense, such company was held liable to an employee of the other company injured through the negligence of the towerman in charge. Hydell v. Railway, 74 O. S. 138 (1906).

Section 8834. (Court of common pleas, duty of.) When outside the corporate limits of a city or village it becomes necessary for the track or tracks of a steam, street, electric or interurban railroad company to cross the track or tracks of another steam, street, electric or interurban railroad company, or it is necessary within the corporate limits thereof, for the track or tracks of a steam, street, electric or inter-

urban railroad company to cross the track or tracks of
another steam, street, electric or interurban railroad company, other than within the limits of a public street or highway, unless the manner of such crossing be agreed to between such companies, the common pleas court of the county
wherein such crossing is located, or a judge thereof in vacation, on application of either party, must ascertain and define by its decree the mode of such crossing which will inflict
the least practical injury upon the rights of the company
owning or operating the road intended to be crossed. (May
9, 1908, 99 v. 358, § 1; April 23, 1904, 97 v. 548; May 10,
1902, 95 v. 530; R. S. Sec. 3333-1.)

This act is constitutional.
   Railway Co. v. Traction Co., 79 O. S. 136, 149 (1908).
A similar act has been in force in Pennsylvania since 1871.
   Railway Co. v. Traction Co., 79 O. S. 136, 150.
   Railroad v. Railroad, 14 C. C. n. s. 321, 325 (1910); aff'd, 80 O. S.
      540.
This act applies to all crossings where the companies can not agree.
   Traction Co. v. Railway Co., 11 C. C. n. s. 17; 20 C. D. 355; aff'd, 79
      O. S. 136.
   The original act (95 v. 530) applied to pending cases and it was held
that an application might be made although proceedings to appropriate
the right to cross had been commenced prior to its enactment.
   Railroad v. Railroad, 72 O. S. 368 (1905).
But the amendments do not apply to pending proceedings.
   Railroad v. Railroad, 14 C. C. n. s. 321, 322 (1907); aff'd, 80 O. S. 540.
   The original section (95 v. 530) was held not to apply to the crossing
of a steam railroad by an interurban railway.
   D. & U. Ry. Co. v. Traction Co., 4 C. C. n. s. 329; 16 C. D. 1; reversed
      on other grounds, 72 O. S. 429; s. c., 1 N. P. n. s. 218, 296; 14
      L. D. 17, 143.
   Rapid Ry. Co. v. Railroad Co., 48 O. L. B. 245 (Super. Ct. Cin.).
   The inability of two railroad companies to agree does not require
a disagreement leading to violence. It may appear in divergent views
respecting their respective rights.
   Railway Co. v. Traction Co., 79 O. S. 136, 15 (1908).

Right to cross tracks prior to enactment of § 8834 et seq. Corporate
charters and franchises are subject to the power of the state to authorize
the construction of other railroads across their tracks whenever the public
welfare may require. Neither the priority of one charter over the other,
nor the prior location or construction of a railroad thereunder, affects this
right.
   Lake Shore, etc., Ry. Co. v. Cincinnati, etc., Ry. Co., 30 O. S. 604
      (1876).
   The right of one railroad corporation to cross the track of another in
constructing and operating its road is derived by grant of the franchise
.so to do from the state, and not by purchase or appropriation from the
road first located and constructed. The latter has no vested exclusive
right to such crossing for its use against the right of the public to a crossing, provided compensation is made.
   Lake Shore, etc., Ry. Co. v. Cincinnati, etc., Ry. Co., 30 O. S. 604
      (1876).

Measure of damages. In a proceeding under the statute by a railroad corporation to appropriate a strip of land across the track of another, to be used in common by each as a railroad crossing, at a common grade, the owner of such track has no right to recover as consequential damages the additional expense rendered necessary in operating its road caused by complying with the provisions of this section.

Lake Shore, etc., Ry. Co. v. Cincinnati, etc., Ry. Co., 30 O. S. 604 (1876).

In such condemnation proceeding the company whose tracks it is sought to cross is entitled to compensation for the property or interest in its right of way and tracks actually appropriated, and for such consequential damages, not provided for by this section, as are the direct and proximate consequence of such appropriation.

Lake Shore, etc., Ry. Co. v. Cincinnati, etc., Ry. Co., 30 O. S. 604 (1876).

The jury in such condemnation proceeding can not include the additional expenses provided for by this section, nor take into account the detention of trains, loss of future business, nor additional expenses incident to the future exercise of their corporate powers.

Lake Shore, etc., Ry. Co. v. Cincinnati, etc., Ry. Co., 30 O. S. 604 (1876).

Section 8835.   (Grade crossings avoided, if practicable.) If in the judgment of such court or judge thereof, it is reasonable and practicable to avoid a grade crossing, by its process it shall prevent a crossing at grade. In determining the mode of such crossing, no grade shall be required to exceed the established maximum or ruling grade governing the operation by motive power of that division or part of the railroad on which the improvement is to be made, without the consent of the company; nor shall either company's track be required to be placed below high water mark. (May 9, 1908, 99 v. 358, § 1; April 23, 1904, 97 v. 548; May 10, 1902, 95 v. 530; R. S. Sec. 3333-1.)

This act defines the policy of the state to be that railroad tracks may cross at grade only in cases of necessity.

Railway Co. v. Traction Co., 79 O. S. 136 (1908).

The junior company may not defeat the operation of the act by voluntarily choosing a place of crossing at which the grades can not be separated, when there is a practicable place of crossing at which the grades may be separated.

Railway Co. v. Traction Co., 79 O. S. 136 (1908).

Where an interlocking device has been in use for a considerable period, with favorable results from its operation and comparatively little interruption to trains of the other road and to avoid the grade crossing would involve heavy expense and other hardships, a grade crossing will not be avoided.

Railroad Co. v. Railway Co., 14 C. C. n. s. 321; 23 C. D. 303 (1907); aff'd, 81 O. S. 540, 550.

"Reasonable and practicable." This term is not synonymous with the term "reasonably practicable" in the Pennsylvania statute.

Railway v. Railway, 14 C. C. n. s. 321, 322 to 325; 23 C. D. 303 (1907).

While one of the purposes of the act is to conserve public safety, grade crossings will not be avoided unless it is reasonable and practicable to be so. *ib.*

Street railway crossings at grade within municipalities.
  See notes to §§ 9108, 3775.
  Railway Co. v. Railway Co., 5 C. C. n. s. 597, 598; aff'd, 73 O. S. 364.

Section 8836. (Order of court.) The court by its order, shall define the manner in which the applicant is to do or let the work for such crossing and equitably apportion the initial expense of such construction or crossing and the expense of maintenance among the parties interested. (May 9, 1908, 99 v. 358, § 1; April 23, 1904, 97 v. 548; May 10, 1902, 95 v. 530; R. S. 3333-1.)

An equitable apportionment is not necessarily an equal apportionment.
  Railway v. Traction Co., 79 O. S. 136, 150 (1908).
The cost of maintenance as well as the initial cost should be apportioned.
  Traction Co. v. Railway Co., 79 O. S. 243 (1908).
  Where the junior road has projected and is constructing a double track road, the cost of a crossing sufficiently wide to carry a double track should be apportioned between the companies.
  Traction Co. v. Railway Co., 79 O. S. 243 (1908).
  The court should apportion between the roads only the cost of such a grade of approach as will be practicable. If the junior road desires a lesser grade it may be charged with the entire additional expense.
  Traction Co. v. Railway Co., 79 O. S. 243 (1908).
  The road which is first established and in operation has no proprietary rights affecting a division of the costs which are superior to those of the later company seeking a crossing.
  Traction Co. v. Railway Co., 11 C. C. n. s. 17; 20 C. D. 355; aff'd, 79
    O. S. 136 (1907).
  Lake Shore, etc., Ry. v. Cincinnati, etc., Ry. Co., 30 O. S. 604 (1876).
  But to the extent that the senior company has improved its right of way by structures and expended money, the companies do not stand on an equal footing.
  Railroad v. Railway, 14 C. C. n. s. 321, 323 (1907); aff'd, 80 O.
    S. 540.

Section 8837. (Appeal.) A party feeling aggrieved by the decision of the court shall have the right of appeal and proceedings in error as in other civil cases. (May 9, 1908, 99 v. 358, § 1; April 23, 1904, 97 v. 548; May 10, 1902, 95 v. 530; R. S. Sec. 3333-1.)

Right of appeal.
  See Railway Co. v. Traction Co., 79 O. S. 136, 137 (1908).
  D. & U. Ry. Co. v. Traction Co., 4 C. C. n. s. 329; 16 C. D. 1 (1903);
    reversed, 72 O. S. 429.
  Although the supreme court will not consider the weight of evidence, it will, in a proceeding in error to the circuit court, examine the record to see that the order of the circuit court is in accordance with a proper interpretation of the statute.
  Railway Co. v. Traction Co., 79 O. S. 136 (1908).

Section 8838. (Jury.) Unless such companies agree upon the compensation to be paid for the land occupied by

such crossing, the court shall submit that question to a
jury as provided in other cases for the appropriation of
private property. (May 9, 1908, 99 v. 359.)

Section 8839. (Exceptions.) Nothing herein shall prevent any street, electric or interurban railroad company or
steam railroad company from laying additional tracks at
existing crossings, under authority now existing by virtue
of law. (May 9, 1908, 99 v. 359, § 1; May 3, 1904, 97 v.
548, § 2.)

**Section 8840. (One steam railroad crossing another with-
in corporate limits.)** When, within the corporate limits of
a city, or village, it becomes necessary for the track of a
steam railroad company to cross the track of another steam
railroad company unless the manner of such crossings be
agreed to between such companies, the common pleas court
of the county wherein such crossing is located, or a judge
thereof in vacation, on application of either party, shall
ascertain and define by its decree the mode of such crossings which will inflict the least practical injury upon the
rights of the company owning or operating the road to be
crossed. If in the judgment of such court or the judge
thereof, it is reasonable and practicable to avoid a grade
crossing, by its process it shall prevent a crossing at grade.
(May 3, 1904, 97 v. 538, § 1a; R. S. § 3333-3.)

See notes to §§ 8834, 8835.

Section 8841. (Change of grade.) In changing the grade
of a steam railroad, no grade shall be required to exceed the
established maximum or ruling grade governing the operations by engines of that division or part of the railroad on
which the improvement is to be made, without the consent
of the railroad company, nor shall the railroad company's
tracks be required to be placed below high water mark.
(May 3, 1904, 97 v. 538, § 1a.)

Section 8842. In its order, the court shall equitably apportion the initial expense of such construction or crossing,
and the expense of such construction or crossing, and the
expense of maintenance thereof among the parties interested.
A party feeling aggrieved by the decision of the court may
appeal therefrom as in other civil cases. Nothing herein
shall prevent any railroad company from laying additional
tracks at existing crossings. (May 3, 1904, 97 v. 538, § 1a.)

See notes to §§ 8836 and 8837.

HIGHWAY CROSSINGS.

Section 8843. (Highway crossings, sidewalks, etc.) Companies operating a railroad in this state, shall build and keep in repair good and sufficient crossings over or approaches to such railway, its tracks, side-tracks and switches, at all points where any public highway, street, lane, avenue, alley, road or pike is intersected by such railway, its tracks, side-tracks or switches; also good and sufficient sidewalks on both sides of streets intersected by their roads, the full width of the right of way owned, claimed or occupied by them. Crossings and approaches outside of municipal corporations, the township trustees shall have power to fix and determine as to their kind and extent, and the time and manner of constructing them. (April 2, 1891, 88 v. 261; R. S. Sec. 3337-3.)

The power of township trustees under this section is not abridged by § 8863 et seq., which confer power on county commissioners to provide for the abolition of dangerous grade crossings.
Grinnell v. Commissioners, 6 C. C. n. s. 180; 17 C. D. 118 (1904).
Crossing defined.
Lynch v. Railway Co., 20 C. C. 248 (1899).
Constitutionality.
Lake Shore, etc., Ry. Co. v. Cincinnati, etc., Ry. Co., 30 O. S. 604 (1876).
See generally §§ 8913 to 8915, 8873.

Section 8844. (Powers of councils.) As to crossings, approaches and sidewalks within municipal corporations, the municipal councils may exercise the same powers as trustees concerning crossways and approaches outside of municipalities, and such crossways, approaches and sidewalks shall be constructed, repaired and maintained by the railroad companies as so ordered. (April 2, 1891, 88 v. 261, § 1; R. S. Sec. 3337-3.)

Section 8845. (Service of notice.) The officer or officers having charge of a public highway, street or alley intersected by a line of railway, shall serve a written notice upon the nearest station agent or section foreman having charge of that portion of the railway where such intersection occurs, that the crossing, approach or sidewalk herein described must be built or repaired, setting forth its kind and extent and the time and manner of constructing it, as ordered by the council or trustees. (April 2, 1891, 88 v. 261, § 2; R. S. Sec. 3337-4.)

Section 8846. (Failure to comply with notice.) A railway company so notified must comply with such notice within a period of thirty days after receiving it. On failure so to do, the township trustees, or council as may be the case, may cause such crossing, approach or sidewalk to be constructed or repaired as before ordered, and recover the cost of so doing with interest thereon, in a civil action against the railroad company, in the name of the trustees or municipality. (April 2, 1891, 88 v. 261, § 3; R. S. Sec. 3337-5.)

Section 8847. (Crossings must be kept clear of snow.) All railway companies owning or operating a line of railway within this state, must keep public highways crossing such line of railroad clear of snow, for a distance of fifty feet each way from the center of its railroad along such highway, so that at all times they will be in safe and convenient condition for travel. (April 2, 1891, 88 v. 261, § 4; R. S. Sec. 3337-6.)

The company is only bound to use such care as a reasonable person would use under like circumstances.
Cincinnati, etc., R. R. Co. v. Dagner, 39 W. L. B. 19 (1898).

Section 8848. (Forfeiture.) A railroad company which neglects to comply with the terms of the five next preceding sections, shall be liable to pay damage to the city, village, or township in which the highway is situated in the sum of thirty dollars for such neglect, and a further sum of ten dollars per day for each and every day such company fails to comply with the terms of such sections, to be recovered in an action brought in the name of the city, village, or township. The prosecuting attorney of the county shall prosecute to judgment any claim arising under the foregoing provisions, without charge to the city, village, or township. (April 2, 1891, 88 v. 261, § 5; R. S. Sec. 3337-7.)

The remedy provided by this section is not exclusive.
Alexander v. Railroad Co., 2 N. P. n. s. 59; 14 L. D. 102 (1903).

Section 8849. (Bridges over railroad crossings.) No person, company or corporation owning, or operating a railroad, crossing, or that may hereafter cross, over and above a street, less than seventy feet in width, in any city in this state, at an elevation above such street, sufficient to permit persons to pass and repass along such street beneath such crossing, shall place or cause to be placed, or permit to be or remain in such street, beneath such crossing or bridge, any pier or other stay or support therefor, unless the plac-

ing or maintaining thereof be authorized by the city wherein
the crossing is situated, by ordinance duly passed, or permit
such crossing or bridge to be or remain in such condition,
that iron, coal or other hard substance, or fluid or noisome
matter, can fall or drop through such crossing or bridge,
upon persons traveling or passing beneath it. (April 23,
1904, 97 v. 302, § 1; April 3, 1889, 86 v. 197; R. S. Sec.
3337-1.)

This section does not authorize a municipality to grant permission to
a railroad company to occupy a public common or landing with an elevated structure.
Railroad Co. v. Cincinnati, 76 O. S. 481 (1907); affirming, 4 N. P.
n. s. 217, 497.
See note to § 8763.
Prior to the amendment of this section in 1904 a municipal council
had no power to permit supports for an overhead bridge to be placed in
the street.
Alexander v. Railroad Co., 2 N. P. n. s. 59; 14 L. D. 102 (1903).
Railway Co. v. Elyria, 69 O. S. 414 (1903).
Railroad Co. v. Defiance, 52 O. S. 262 (1895); aff'd, 167 U. S. 88;
10 O. F. D. 480.

Section 8850. (Forfeiture.) A person, company or corporation owning or operating such railroad, that fails to
comply with the requirements of, or violates any provision
of, the next preceding section, for each and every day during the continuance of such failure or violation, and on
account thereof, shall forfeit and pay to such city the sum
of one hundred dollars, to be recovered in a civil action, in
the city's name, against the owner or operator of such railroad, or both, as the city elects. Thereafter like recovery
may be had for subsequent failures and violations. (April
23, 1904, 97 v. 302, § 1; April 3, 1889, 86 v. 197; R. S. Sec.
3337-1.)

Section 8851. (Council may regulate use of bridge.) The
council of a city may prohibit the switching of freight engines, trains, or cars, over or on such crossing or bridge,
the sounding of locomotive steam whistles, thereon or near
thereto, and the standing or stopping of a railroad engine
over or on such crossing or bridge, and by ordinance, constitute a violation thereof an offense, and provide for the
punishment of any person guilty thereof. (April 3, 1889,
86 v. 197; R. S. § 3337-2.)

Section 8852. (Signboards at road crossings.) At all
points where its road crosses a public road, at a sufficient
elevation from such public road to admit of the free passage of vehicles of every kind, each company shall erect a

sign, with large and distinct letters placed thereon, to give notice of the proximity of the railroad, and warn persons to be on the lookout for the locomotive. A company which neglects or refuses to comply with this provision shall be liable in damages for all injuries which occur to persons or property from such neglect or refusal. (R. S. Sec. 3323; May 1, 1852, 50 v. 274, § 18.)

In an action by a traveler on a public highway against a railroad company, to recover for injuries by collision with a passing train at a public crossing, alleged to have been caused by negligence in the management of the train, where the evidence tends to show that he did not exercise proper care and caution to avoid the injury, it is competent for him to show that there was no sign-board up, as required by law, as reflecting upon the question of his want of care, although the want of such sign-board is not alleged as a ground of recovery.

Baltimore, etc., R. Co. v. Whitacre, 35 O. S. 627 (1880).

Unless it is averred as a ground of negligence that a sign was omitted, he can not insist upon it as a substantive cause of action. If a party is acquainted with the crossing the absence of the warning post is not available as a proof of negligence.

New York, etc., R. R. Co. v. Kistler, 16 C. C. 316 (1894); 9 C. D. 277.

C. C. & I. Ry. Co. v. Reiss, 13 C. C. 405 (1889); 7 C. D. 450.

See Baltimore, etc., R. Co. v. Whitacre, 35 O. S. 627 (1880).

Lang v. Holiday, etc., Mining Co., 49 Ia. 469 (1878).

A violation of this section does not render the company absolutely liable for injuries to persons or property while attempting to cross the track. Evidence of such omission merely establishes the negligence of the company, and if it appear that the plaintiff's negligence contributed to the injury, he can not recover.

Dodge v. Burlington, etc., R. R. Co., 34 Ia. 276 (1872).

Section 8853. (Signals at railroad crossings.) Every company shall attach to each locomotive engine passing upon its road, a bell of the ordinary size in use on such engines, and a steam whistle. When an engine in motion and approaching a turnpike, highway or town road crossing or private crossing where the view of such crossing is obstructed by embankment, trees, curve or other obstruction to view, upon the same line therewith, and in like manner where the road crosses any other traveled place, by bridge or otherwise, the engineer or person in charge thereof, shall sound such whistle at a distance of at least eighty and not further than one hundred rods from such crossing, and ring such bell continuously until the engine passes the crossing. (R. S. Sec. 3336; April 16, 1892, 89 v. 331; May 13, 1886, 83 v. 153; R. S. 1880; March 25, 1872, 69 v. 49, § 1.)

Duty of person about to cross tracks. Ordinary prudence requires that a person in the full enjoyment of the faculties of hearing and seeing, before attempting to pass over a known railroad crossing, should use them for the purpose of discovering and avoiding danger from an approaching train; and the omission to do so without a reasonable excuse therefor is negligence, and will defeat a recovery.

B. & O. R. Co. v. McClellan, 69 O. S. 142 (1903).
Pennsylvania Co. v. Rathgeb, 32 O. S. 66 (1877).
Bellefontaine Ry. Co. v. Snyder, 24 O. S. 670 (1874).
Cleveland, etc., R. R. Co. v. Crawford, 24 O. S. 631 (1874).
Cleveland, etc., Ry. Co. v. Elliott, 28 O. S. 340 (1876).
Lake Shore, etc., Ry. Co. v. Gaffney, 9 C. C. 32 (1894); s. c., 6 C. D. 94.
Lake Shore, etc., Ry. Co. v. Schade, 15 C. C. 424 (1895); s. c., 8 C. D. 316.
Railway v. Schneider, 45 O. S. 678 (1888).
Lake Shore, etc., Ry. Co. v. Geiger, 8 C. C. 41 (1893); s. c., 4 C. D. 307.
New York, etc., Ry. Co. v. Swartout, 14 C. C. 582 (1895); s. c., 6 C. D. 768.
C. C. & I. Ry. Co. v. Reiss, 13 C. C. 405 (1889); s. c., 7 C. D. 450.
Schmidt v. Railway, 22 C. D. 539 (1911).
Traction Co. v. Smith, 15 C. C. n. s. 124 (1912).

Where a street car motorman, driving his car on railroad tracks, pursuant to a negligent direction by his conductor to "come ahead," was struck and killed by a locomotive which approached without giving signals by bell as required by this section, it was held that failure to ring the bell was at least a concurring cause of the accident, and that it was error to direct a verdict for the railroad company.

Hales v. Railroad Co., 200 Fed. 533 (C. C. A. 1912).

Where turnpike is crossed by bridge. This section requires the engineer having in charge an engine in motion to ring the bell and sound the whistle on approaching a place where the road crosses any highway or traveled place by a bridge or other structure.

Railway v. Jump, 50 O. S. 651 (1893).

Duty to persons on track. This section is intended for the protection of such persons only as are crossing the track or are about to do so; and does not inure to the benefit of persons who are on the track but not at a crossing.

Cleveland, etc., Ry. Co. v. Workman, 66 O. S. 509 (1902).
See Dick v. Railroad Co., 38 O. S. 389 (1882).
Railroad Co. v. Depew, 40 O. S. 121, 126 (1883).
Railway Co. v. Gesswine, 144 Fed. 56 (1906).
Byrket v. Railway, 10 C. C. n. s. 73; 19 C. D. 614.
Drown v. Traction Co., 76 O. S. 234.

Evidence. Though there is positive evidence that the whistle was blown before the train reached the crossing, the court can not direct a verdict for defendant where some of the witnesses testify that the whistle was blown more than 2,000 feet from the crossing instead of within 80 or 100 rods of it, as required by this section.

Griffith v. Baltimore, etc., R. R. Co., 44 Fed. 574 (1890); 6 O. F. D. 666.
Hales v. Railroad Co., 200 Fed. 533 (C. C. A. 1912).

The testimony of witnesses who testify that they were walking on the track, knew the train was coming, were giving their attention to the train, and that they heard no whistle or hell, is not negative, but positive testimony.

Lake Shore, etc., R. R. Co. v. Schade, 15 C. C. 424 (1895); 8 C. D. 316.

Other things being equal, the testimony of the engineer and fireman of the train that the whistle was blown and the bell rung as it approached the crossing is entitled to more weight than the negative testimony of other witnesses that they did not hear either or both.

Griffith v. Baltimore, etc., R. R. Co., 44 Fed. 574 (1900); 6 O. F. D. 666; affirmed, 159 U. S. 603; 8 O. F. D. 573.

Duty to trackmen. The custom of a railroad company to give signals as required by this section was for the sole benefit of persons using the crossings. A failure to give such signals does not constitute negligence as against a trackman.

Norfolk, etc., Co. v. Gesswine, 144 Fed. 56; 15 O. F. D. 426 (C. C. A. 1906).

See Railroad v. Skiles, 64 O. S. 458.

Barton v. Railway, 12 C. C. n. s. 387; 21 C. D. 441; aff'd, 74 O. S. 479.

Duty of company to take precaution in addition to bell and whistle signals. Compliance with § 8853 does not excuse a railroad company from taking other precautions if the circumstances are such as to require them.

Erie R. Co. v. Weinstein, 166 Fed. 271; 7 O. L. R. 531 (C. C. A. 1909).

Compliance with this section does not relieve a railway company from liability for injury to a traveler at a crossing resulting from negligent failure to take additional precautions by maintaining a watchman, crossing gates, etc., or from negligently running the train at a high rate of speed.

Rothe v. Penna. Co., 195 Fed. 21 (C. C. A. 1912).

In the operation of trains over a highway crosing at grade in a municipality where buildings obscure the approach of trains, care commensurate with the danger existing must be exercised, although that may exceed the giving of signals by bell and whistle; but the railroad company is not the insurer of the safety of travelers using the crossing.

Weaver v. Railway, 76 O. S. 164 (1907).

The statutory requirement as to signals at a crossing is not exclusive.

Railway Co. v. Parker, 9 C. C. n. s. 28; 19 C. D. (1907).

Section 8854. (Not to interfere with city ordinance.) The provisions of the next preceding section shall not interfere with the proper observance of an ordinance passed by a city or village council regulating the management of railroads, locomotives and steam whistles thereon, within the limits of such city or village. (R. S. Sec. 3336; April 16, 1892, 89 v. 331; May 13, 1866, 83 v. 153; R. S. 1880; March 25, 1872, 69 v. 49, § 1.)

The most that can be claimed for this section is that it by implication confers powers upon municipal corporations to regulate the management of locomotives and steam whistles and bells with reference to crossings in such municipalities. It does not enable municipalities to compel railroads to employ watchmen.

Ravena v. Pennsylvania Co., 45 O. S. 118, 125 (1887).

Rapid Transit Co. v. Erie R. Co., 7 C. C. n. s. 199; 18 C. D. 36 (1905).

An ordinance is invalid which requires the bell to be rung continuously while the train is passing through the corporate limits regardless of whether or not it is "approaching a turnpike, highway, etc."

Caskey v. Belle Center, 8 N. P. n. s. 153; 19 L. D. 726 (C. P. 1908).

Section 8855. (Penalties for violation of preceding section.) Every engineer or person in charge of such engine who fails to comply with the provisions of the two preceding sections shall be personally liable to a penalty of not less than fifty nor more than one hundred dollars, to be recovered by civil action, at the suit of the state, in the court of common pleas of a county wherein there is such a crossing. (R. S. Sec. 3337; March 25, 1872, 69 v. 49, § 2.)

Criminal penalty, see G. C. §§ 12549, 12550.

Section 8856. (Liability of company.) The company in whose employ such engineer or person in charge of an engine is, as well as the person himself, shall be liable in damages to a person or company injured in person or property by such neglect or act of such engineer or person. (R. S. Sec. 3337; March 25, 1872, 69   v. 49, § 2.)

The omission to ring the bell or sound the whistle at public crossings is not of itself sufficient ground to authorize a recovery, if the party, notwithstanding such omission, might, by the exercise of ordinary care, have avoided the accident.

Cleveland, etc., Ry. Co. v. Elliott, 28 O. S. 340 (1876).

Pennsylvania Co. v. Rathgeb, 32 O. S. 66, 72 (1877).

New York, etc., Ry. Co. v. Swartout, 14 C. C. 582 (1895); s. c., 6 C. D. 768.

Baltimore, etc., R. R. Co. v. Griffith, 159 U. S. 603, 607 (1895); s. c., 8 O. F. D. 573.

Horn v. Baltimore, etc., R. R. Co., 54 Fed. 301 (1893).

Pennsylvania Co. v. Alburn, 3 C. C. n. s. 104; 13 C. D. 130 (1901).

See Heine v. Erie R. Co., 6 C. C. n. s. 7, 9; 17 C. D. 155; reversed, 75 O. S. 629.

This section does not confer a right of action unless the omission of the signals caused the injury, nor in case the person injured is guilty of contributory negligence.

Rothe v. Penna. Co., 195 Fed. 21 (C. C. A. 1912).

It is evident from the language of this section that the failure to give signals must have occasioned the accident, that is, must have been the proximate cause of it, before a recovery can be had.

Pennsylvania Co. v. Rathgeb, 32 O. S. 66, 72 (1877).

Cincinnati, etc., R. Co. v. Murphy, 18 C. C. 298 (1899); s. c., 10 C. D. 195.

Horn v. Baltimore, etc., R. Co., 54 Fed. 301 (1893).

Where it appears that the plaintiff was struck several hundred feet from a crossing, the failure to give signals for the crossing can not be regarded as the proximate cause of the accident.

Lake Shore, etc., R. R. Co. v. Harris, 3 C. C. n. s. 599; 13 C. D. 400 (1901).

Section 8857. (Crossing of highway to cemetery.) All railroads hereafter constructed, which cross an avenue or public highway leading from a city to a public cemetery thereof, situate within or without the limits of the city, shall be constructed so as to pass under or over such avenue or highway, at an elevation or depression as the case may be, that will allow the unobstructed passage of all wagons, carriages, or other vehicles necessary for any person to use thereon. (R. S. Sec. 3284; May 1, 1852, 50 v. 274, § 16.)

The cemetery of a private association does not come within the terms of this section. It covers and protects only cemeteries owned by cities.

Youngstown v. Pittsburg, etc., R. R. Co., 3 C. C. 214; 2 C. D. 121 (1888).

PRIVATE CROSSINGS AND WAYS.

Section 8858.　(When private crossings must be built.) When a person owns fifteen or more acres of land in one body, through which a railroad passes, and which is so situated that he can not use a crossing in a public street, lane, road or other highway, in going from his land on one side of the railroad to that on the other side without great inconvenience, at his request, and within four months thereafter, the company or person operating it, at the expense of such company or person shall construct a good and sufficient private crossing across such railroad and the lands occupied by the company, between the two pieces of land to enable such landowner to pass with a loaded team, and over which he may go at all times when such railroad is not being used at the crossing, or so near to it as to render passing thereat dangerous. (R. S. Sec. 3327; April 18, 1874, 71 v. 85, § 1.)

This section was held constitutional in Mitchell, etc., Co. v. Wabash R. Co., 3 N. P. 231; 6 L. D. 135 (C. P. 1896), which case was affirmed by the supreme court (59 O. S. 607), without, however, passing on its constitutionality.

Railway Co. v. Wachter, 70 O. S. 113, 117, 121 (1904).

This section and § 8859 apply only to cases where lands, intersected by a railroad, are in one ownership at the time of the construction of the road.

Gratz v. Railroad Co., 76 O. S. 230 (1907).

But any owner of land lying on both sides of the road may, at his own expense, construct a crossing, providing it is suitably located and necessary for the convenient use of his lands and does not interfere with the movement of trains.

Gratz v. Railroad Co., 76 O. S. 230 (1907).

The right to a crossing under this section is not affected by the fact that the right of way was appropriated, and the railroad constructed, before the enactment of this section.

Mitchell, etc., Co. v. Wabash R. Co., 3 N. P. 231; 6 L. D. 135 (C. P. 1896); aff'd, 59 O. S. 607.

The omission of the word "farmer", implies an intent to provide generally for private crossings.

Mitchell v. Wabash R. Co., 3 N. P. 231; 6 L. D. 135 (C. P. 1896).

The right to a private crossing depends upon the fact that the public crossing can not be used "without great inconvenience," and that such private crossing shall be used only when not dangerous; a crossing, therefore, should be constructed at the point most convenient and least dangerous.

Mitchell v. Wabash R. R. Co., 3 N. P. 231; 6 L. D. 135 (C. P. 1896).

Where the matter is before a court of equity, if the parties can not agree as to the location, the court will fix it by means of engineers and referees.

Mitchell v. Wabash R. R. Co., 3 N. P. 231; 6 L. D. 135 (C. P. 1896).

Injunction. Where a landowner, who is entitled to a crossing at his own expense but not at the expense of the railroad company, served a notice on the company requiring it to construct such crossing, the company is not entitled to an injunction preventing such crossing.

Gratz v. Railroad Co., 76 O. S. 230 (1907).

Where a landowner has complied with this section, and the railroad company has declared its intention of preventing the construction of the crossing, an injunction may be allowed to prevent such interference.

Mitchell v. Wabash R. R. Co., 3 N. P. 231; 6 L. D. 135 (1896); aff'd, 59 O. S. 607.

See Jones, etc., Co. v. C. C. C. T. & S. Ry. Co., 7 N. P. 245 (1894).

Right to crossing in absence of statute. Where a landowner conveys to a railroad company a right of way through his land, the right to a private crossing remains in the grantor, provided such crossing is necessary for the convenient use of his lands, and will not unreasonably interfere with the use of the right of way for railroad purposes.

Railway v. Wachter, 70 O. S. 113 (1904).

See Gratz v. Railroad Co., 76 O. S. 230, 233 (1907).

Statute of limitations. The right to a crossing is not barred by the statute of limitation of twenty-one years.

Railway v. Wachter, 70 O. S. 113.

Contract for private crossing; remedies for breach.

See Bell v. Dayton, etc., R. R. Co., 3 C. C. 31; 2 C. D. 19 (1887).

Dayton, etc., R. R. Co. v. Lewton, 20 O. S. 401 (1870).

Where a contract for a right of way required the railroad company to construct a cattle pass, but the deed of the right of way was silent as to the cattle pass, which had been constructed before the execution of the deed, it was held that the purchaser of a railroad, on foreclosure, could not fill up the cattle pass, possession by the grantor constituting notice.

Lowe v. Railway, 12 C. C. 743; 4 C. D. 85 (1894).

An agreement requiring the railroad company to build a crossing within one year after completion of the road is not a covenant running with the land, specifically enforceable against a successor railroad company, several years thereafter, where the agreement contained no covenant requiring the successor to build or maintain the crossing.

Zens v. Railway, 14 N. P. n. s. 202; 23 L. D. 182 (C. P. 1912).

Section 8859. **(Owner may build at company's expense.)** If, for four months after request by such landowner for that purpose, such company or person neglects to construct a good and sufficient private crossing as provided in the next preceding section, after reasonable notice to the agent of the company for receiving and shipping freight at the station on the railroad nearest to the land where it is proposed to construct such crossing by the landowner of the time when he will proceed to construct it, he may enter upon the lands of the company, at any point he wishes between the two pieces of his land, and construct such crossing. Such company or person shall be liable to him for all the reasonable expense thereof, not exceeding the sum of fifty dollars, which he may recover in an action against it or him. (R. S. Sec. 3328; April 18, 1874, 71 v. 85, § 1.)

Section cited 30 W. L. B. 206.
Constitutionality of section.
See Railway v. Wachter, 70 O. S. 113, 117, 121 (1904).
Mitchell, etc., Co. v. Wabash R. Co., 3 N. P. 231; 6 L. D. 135 (C. P. 1896).
This section and § 8858 apply only to cases where lands are in one ownership at the time of the construction of the road. But any owner of land lying on both sides of the road may, at his own expense, build a proper crossing.
Gratz v. Railroad Co., 76 O. S. 230 (1907).

Section 8860. (When two preceding sections do not apply.) The provisions of the next two preceding sections relating to private crossings shall not apply to any case in which compensation for building a private crossing has been or may hereafter be taken into consideration, and estimated as part of the consideration to be paid for the right of way, so far as the right to private crossing, has been or may be settled or paid for; nor shall such sections be held to affect, in any manner, any contract or agreement between any railroad company, or person having control or management of a railroad, and the proprietor or occupants of lands adjoining, for the construction or maintenance of railroad crossings. (R. S. Sec. 3329; March 25, 1859, 56 v. 62, § 4; April 18, 1874, 71 v. 85, § 1.)

Where compensation for building a fence or private crossing was taken into consideration when the right of way was acquired, the company is not liable either to the landowner or the public for failure to fence or for insufficient fences.
Railway Co. v. Wood, 47 O. S. 431 (1890).
Where the defense of the company is that it has made compensation for fencing under this section, and the records of the condemnation proceedings are silent upon the subject, no presumption arises that the matter of fences was considered, even if the proceedings were had prior to the passage of this act.
Railroad Co. v. Hoffhines, 46 O. S. 643 (1888).
Mitchell, etc., Co. v. Wabash R. Co., 3 N. P. 231; 6 L. D. 135 (1896).

Contract between owner and railroad company. An agreement is not binding on a subsequent purchaser of the land who had neither actual nor constructive notice thereof at the time of the purchase.
Railway v. Bosworth, 46 O. S. 81 (1888).
A valid agreement embodied in the record of the appropriation proceeding is binding upon subsequent purchasers.
Huston v. Railroad Co., 21 O. S. 235 (1877).
See also notes to §§ 8918 and 8914.

Section 8861. (Freight ways may be constructed.) A

person owning or operating a coal or iron-ore mine, stone-quarry, rolling mill, or machine shop, who, as a means of removing the product thereof, uses or desires to use a railway, may construct one and run cars thereon, over or under any railroad or public highway, the consent of the owner of the fee in the land at such crossing first being obtained. Such railway shall be so constructed as in no wise to impede or interfere with the running of cars or the travel upon such railroad or highway, or in any manner injure or impair either, or any switch, building, or appurtenance connected therewith or belonging thereto. When such freightway is constructed over a railroad, it shall be at the height of at least eighteen and one-half feet in the clear above the rails thereof. (R. S. Sec. 3355; May 1, 1873, 70 v. 194, § 1.)

Section 8862. (Plan must be approved.) Before a person constructs such railway across a railroad he shall submit the plan of construction to the railroad commission for its approval, which at the cost of such person for traveling expenses or otherwise, must see that the structure in all respects conforms to the requirements of the next preceding section. (R. S. Sec. 3356; May 1, 1873, 70 v. 194, § 2.)

GRADE CROSSINGS.

Section 8863. (Altering or abolishing grade or other crossings.) If the council of a municipal corporation in which a railroad or railroads, and a street or other public highway cross each other at a grade or otherwise, or the commissioners of a county in which, outside of a municipal corporation, a railroad or railroads and public road or highway cross each other at grade, and the directors of the railroad company or companies are of the opinion that the security and convenience of the public require alterations in such crossing, or the approaches thereto, or in the location of the railroad or railroads or the public way, or grades thereof, so as to avoid a crossing at grade, or that such crossing should be discontinued with or without building a new way in substitution therefor, and if they agree as to the alterations they may be made as hereinafter provided. (R. S. Sec. 3337-8; April 27, 1893, 90 v. 359.)

Section cited. Ritter v. Railway, 6 N. P. n. s. 161, 163; 18 L. D. 846 (C. P. 1907).
This act (§§ 8863 to 8873), is adopted from a similar act in Massachusetts.
Stoner v. Railway, 9 N. P. n. s. 337, 348; 20 L. D. 448 (C. P. 1909).

Sections 8863 et seq. are limited to existing crossings and do not apply to proposed crossings over a railway not yet constructed.
Grinnell v. Commissioners, 6 C. C. n. s. 180; 17 C. D. 118 (1904).
The highway may be diverted from its original location for a short distance.
Stoner v. Railway, 9 N. P. n. s. 337; 20 L. D. 448 (C. P. 1909).
An owner of lands abutting upon that portion of a highway, which it is proposed to vacate or divert, may enjoin such change where the injury is different in kind from that of the general public.
Grinnell v. Commissioners, 6 C. C. n. s. 180; 17 C. D. 118 (1904).
Injunction by taxpayer.
See Stoner v. Railway, 9 N. P. n. s. 337; 20 L. D. 448 (C. P. 1909).
The authority of township trusteees under § 8843 to determine the kind, manner, etc., of construction of crossings, is not repealed or abridged by this section.
Grinnell v. Commissioners, 6 C. C. n. s. 180; 17 C. D. 118 (1904).

Section 8864. (Resolution to alter or abolish.) When it is deemed necessary by a municipality or a county to join with any railroad company or companies in the alteration or abolition of a grade or other crossing, the council of the municipality, by a two-thirds vote of all the members elected thereto, or the commissioners of the county, by a unanimous vote, by resolution, shall declare such necessity and intent, and state therein the manner in which the alterations in the crossing are to be made, giving the method of constructing the new crossing with the grades for the railroad or railroads and the public way or ways; also what land or other property it is necessary to appropriate, and how their cost is to be apportioned between the municipality or county and the railroad company or companies; also by whom the work of construction is to be done and how its cost is to be apportioned between the municipality or county and the railroad company or companies. (R. S. Sec. 3337-9; April 27, 1893, 90 v. 360, § 2.)

See note to § 8863.
Section cited. Ritter v. Railway, 6 N. P. n. s. 161, 163; 18 L. D. 846 (C. P. 1907).
Where the preliminary steps required by § 8864 et seq. have not been taken, a taxpayer may enjoin the abolition of a grade crossing, when the prosecuting attorney, after request, has refused to take action.
Stoner v. Railway, 9 N. P. n. s. 337; 20 L. D. 448 (C. D. 1909).

Section 8865. (Publication of resolution.) Such resolution shall be published and notice of its passage given to owners of property abutting on the proposed improvement, in the manner provided as to resolutions of a city council declaring the necessity of a contemplated public improvement, and claims for damages thereby caused, must be filed in the manner, and within the time prescribed in such cases. (R. S. Sec. 3337-9; April 27, 1893, 90 v. 360, § 2.)

See notes to §§ 8765 and 8885.

Where a subway is constructed under the tracks immediately adjoining the highway, which is not vacated except at the grade crossing, and a *cul de sac* thus formed between the tracks and the entrance to the subway, with the result that the main travel was diverted from the *cul de sac*, the owner of a business property, abutting on the *cul de sac*, may recover damages caused by the depreciation in value.

Schimmelmann v. Railway Co., 83 O. S. 356 (1911).

Section 8866.   (Ordinance or resolution, to proceed with improvement.)   In not less than thirty nor more than ninety days after the passage of such resolution the council or commissioners shall determine whether it or they will proceed with the proposed improvement or not.   If it is decided to proceed therewith, an ordinance by the council or resolution by the commissioners shall be passed, which ordinance or resolution must contain, in addition to the terms and conditions stated in such resolution, the plans and specifications of the proposed alteration and improvement, a statement of the damages claimed or likely to accrue by reason thereof, and how their payment is to be apportioned between the municipality or county and the railroad company or companies; also who shall supervise the work of construction. Upon the acceptance of this resolution or ordinance by resolution by the railroad company or companies through their directors, it shall constitute an agreement, valid and binding on the municipality or county and the railroad company or companies respectively.   Such agreement shall thereupon be filed in the common pleas court of the county in which the crossing is located, for entry upon its records, whereupon it shall have the same force and effect as a decree of the court.   (R. S. Sec. 3337-10; April 27, 1893, 90 v. 359.)

See State v. Amlin, 1 N. P. n. s. 517, 528; 14 L. D. 113 (1903); aff'd, 74 O. S. 447.

Where by error two crossings were omitted from an ordinance providing for the sale of bonds to pay the city's share of the cost, but such crossings had been specified in the original resolution of the council, and in the published notice of a referendum election, at which the issue of such bonds was approved by the electors, a curative ordinance, subsequently enacted, which includes such crossings renders the bond issue valid.

Cadwell v. Cleveland, 12 N. P. n. s. 483; 22 L. D. 306 (C. P. 1911).

Section 8867.   (Necessary property, how acquired.)   The land or property required to make the alteration in the street or highway necessitated by the proposed improvement, shall be purchased or appropriated by the municipality or county in the manner provided by law for the appropriation of private property for public use, and the land or property required to make the alteration in the railroad or railroads necessitated by the proposed improvement, shall be purchased or appropriated by the railroad company or companies in the manner provided for the appropriation of private property by such corporation. (R. S. Sec. 3337-11; April 27, 1893, 90 v. 361, § 4.)

Section 8868. (Apportionment of cost.) The cost of the construction of the improvement in the crossing, including the cost of land or property purchased or appropriated, and the payment of damages to abutting property shall be apportioned as follows: The railroad company or companies, if several railroads cross a public way at or near the same point, shall pay not less than sixty-five per cent and the municipality or county not more than thirty-five per cent of such cost. Within these limits the apportionment may be fixed by the agreement hereinbefore provided for. (R. S. Sec. 3337-12; April 27, 1893, 90 v. 361, § 5.)

Where the share of the county is twenty percent of the cost, and the remaining eighty percent is divided between two steam railroad companies and a street railway company, the apportionment is valid, although the share of the steam railroads aggregates less than sixty-five percent.
State v. Amlin, 1 N. P. n. s. 517; 14 L. D. 113 (1903); aff'd, 74 O. S. 417.
A certificate from the auditor, under G. C. § 3806, that money to meet the expenditure is in the municipal treasury to the credit of the fund, and not otherwise appropriated, is not required to validate a contract or obligation of the municipality to pay its share of the cost of elimination of grade crossings.
Cincinnati v. Waite, 12 N. P. n. s. 633 (1912).

Section 8869. (Repairs.) After the work is completed, the crossing and its approaches are to be kept in repair as follows: When the public way crosses the railroad by an overhead bridge, the frame work of the bridge and its abutments shall be maintained and kept in repair by the railroad company, and the surface of the bridge and its approaches, by the municipality or county in which they are situated. When the public way passes under the railroad, the bridge and its abutments shall be maintained and kept in repair by the railroad company, and the public way and its approaches, by the municipality or county in which they are situated. (R. S. Sec. 3337-13; April 27, 1893, 90 v. 361, § 6.)

Section 8870. (Bonds and tax.) For the purpose of raising money to pay its proportion of the cost of such improvement, the municipality or county may issue its bonds to the necessary amount, which bonds shall be of such denomination and payable at such place and times as the council or the commissioners determine, and bear interest not exceeding five per cent per annum, but not be sold for less than their par value. A tax on the taxable property of the municipality or county not exceeding one-half mill in each year may be levied to pay the principal and interest of the bonds as they mature. After the improvement is completed, a tax may be levied by the municipality or county to pay the cost of maintaining and keeping in repair that part of the work required to be maintained and kept in repair by it. (R. S. Sec. 3337-14; April 27, 1893, 90 v. 361, § 7.)

This act authorizes county commissioners to contract for a division of the cost of a bridge and to issue bonds, without reference to the emergency bridge fund, or the fact that sufficient funds are not in the county treasury.
State v. Amlin, 1 N. P. n. s. 517; 14 L. D. 113 (C. P. 1903); aff'd, 74 O. S. 447.
Injunction against issue of bonds by county commissioners without a referendum vote.
State v. Amlin, 1 N. P. n. s. 517; 14 L. D. 113 (1903); aff'd, 74 O. S. 447.
Sections 5635, 5636 relating to a special tax for the restoration of county bridges do not apply to bridges constructed under this act.
State v. Amlin, 1 N. P. n. s. 517; 14 L. D. 113 (1909); aff'd, 74 O. S. 447.

Section 8871. (Assessment and determination of damages.) All claims for damages by reason of such improvement, filed as hereinbefore provided, shall be assessed and determined as in other cases of public improvements within cities, wherein like claims are made, either before the beginning or after the completion of the proposed crossing improvement, as the council, or commissioners decide, when it is determined to proceed therewith. (R. S. Sec. 3337-15; April 27, 1893, 90 v. 362, § 8.)

The ascertainment of damages to property owners is provided for by this section.
Stoner v. Railway, 9 N. P. n. s. 337, 348; 20 L. D. 448 (C. P. 1909).
See East End, etc., Co. v. Cleveland, 1 N. P. n. s. 493; 14 L. D. 33 (C. P. 1903).
Elements of damage.
See notes to §§ 8885, 8865 and 8765.

Section 8872. (If company fails to comply with agreement.) If a railroad company fails to comply with any provision of an agreement entered of record in a common pleas court, as above provided, on application of a city solicitor or prosecuting attorney, stating the nature of its failure, the court shall make such orders and decrees to enforce the terms of the agreement, the requirements of law relating thereto, and to secure compliance therewith, by the railroad company, as it deems just and proper, and if necessary, may enjoin the company from the use of its track and the operation of its road on and over the crossing in question, until it complies with such order or decree as is made. (R. S. Sec. 3337-16; April 27, 1893, 90 v. 362, § 9.)

Section 8873. (Grade crossing on county line road.) When a grade crossing is on a county line road, the commissioner of the counties in which such crossing is situated may join in all the proceedings necessary for the abolition of such grade crossing as hereinbefore provided, and that part of the cost of making such change in the crossing and of keeping it in repair which is not agreed to be paid by the railroad company or companies, shall be paid by the counties in equal proportions, and the money for such purpose be raised in accordance with the above provisions as to county road crossings. (R. S. Sec. 3333-17; April 27, 1893. 90 v. 362, § 10.)

Cited, Grinnell v. Commissioners, 6 C. C. n. s. 180, 182; 17 C. D. 118 (1904).

The highway may be diverted from its original location for a short distance.

Stoner v. Railway, 9 N. P. n. s. 337; 20 L. D. 448 (C. P. 1909).

Section 8874. (Powers as to grades above or below railroad tracks, erection of piers, etc.) Any municipal corporation may raise or lower, or cause to be raised or lowered, the grade of any street or way owned by it, either within or without its municipal limits, above or below railroad tracks, and may require any railroad company operating a railroad across such streets or ways to raise or lower the grade of its tracks and may construct ways or crossings above the tracks of any railroad, or require the railroad company to construct ways or crossings that are to be passed under its tracks. The word "railroad" shall include interurban railroads and the words "railroad company" shall include interurban railroad companies engaged in the operation of cars by electricity or other lawful motive power which said companies may adopt or use. Any municipality may require such railroad company to erect permanent piers, abutments or any other appropriate supports, in the ways, crossings, streets, roads or alleys, whenever in the opinion of council, the raising or lowering of the grade of any such railroad tracks, or the raising or lowering of the construction of such ways, crossings or other supports may be necessary, upon the terms and conditions hereinafter set forth. (May 3, 1913, 103 v. 502; May 31, 1911, 102 v. 507; March 23,

1909, 100 v. 77; May 2, 1902, 95 v. 356, § 1; R. S. Sec. 3337-17a.)

This act (§ 8874 et seq.) is constitutional.
  Quinby v. Cleveland, 9 O. L. R. 313; 16 O. F. D. 583; 191 Fed. 68
    (U. S. C. C. 1911).
  Sections 8874 to 8882 relate only to streets and highways, and not
to public grounds. These sections confer power upon municipalities to
change existing occupancy of streets, but not to grant rights to occupy
streets.
  Railroad Co. v. Cincinnati, 76 O. S. 481, 499, 500 (1907).
  The general policy of the state to avoid permanent obstructions in
streets is not infringed by piers which do not interfere with travel.
  Cincinnati v. Railway, 7 N. P. n. s 81; 19 L. D. 74 (1908).
  Under this section and § 8863, a municipality may alter or reconstruct
an existing bridge, on which a railroad crosses a street above grade, to
widen the street and extend it through the embankment supporting the
tracks at the ends of the bridge.
  Cadwell v. Cleveland, 12 N. P. n. s. 483; 22 L. D. 306 (C. P. 1911).

Section 8875.   (Changes in location of public ways.)
When the council of a municipality deems it necessary in
the abolishment of such grade crossings to change the location of any street, alley, road or way such council may
relocate such street, alley, road or way or any part thereof,
may vacate the whole or any portion of such street, alley,
road or way abandoned by such relocation, and cause the
improvements above contemplated to be placed in such relocated street, alley, road or way. (May 2, 1913, 103 v. 268;
March 23, 1909, 100 v. 77, § 1; May 2, 1902, 95 v. 356, § 1;
R. S. Sec. 3337-17a.)

Streets may be altered and relocated.
  Cincinnati v. Railway, 7 N. P. n. s 81; 19 L. D. 74 (1908).

Section 8876.   (Preparations of plans and specifications.)
The council of such municipality, for the purpose of making
or causing such an improvement to be made, by ordinance
may require the railroad company, in co-operation with the
engineer of the municipality, or the engineer designated in
such ordinance, to prepare and submit to such council,
within three months, unless longer time is mutually agreed
upon in writing, plans and specifications for such improvement, specifying the number, character and location of all
piers and supports, which are to be permanently placed in
any street or way, therein, specifying the grades to be established for the streets, and the height, character and estimated cost of any viaduct or way above or below any railroad track, and the change of grade required to be made of
such tracks, including the side-tracks and switches. But
in changing the grade of any railroad, no grade shall be

required to exceed the established maximum or ruling grade governing the operations by engines of that division or part of the railroad on which the improvement is to be made, without the consent of the railroad company, nor shall the railroad company's tracks or such highway, street or way, be required to be placed below high water mark. (May 3, 1913, 103 v. 502; March 23, 1909, 100 v. 78, § 2; May 2, 1902, 95 v. 356, § 2; R. S. Sec. 3337-17b.)

The provisions of this section and § 8877, requiring that plans be prepared and agreed upon within a limited time are directory and not mandatory so far as they concern anyone except the municipality and the railroad company. The improvement can not be enjoined by a taxpayer because of failure to prepare or accept the plans within the time limited.
Cadwell v. Cleveland, 12 N. P. n. s. 483; 22 L. D. 306 (C. P. 1911).

Section 8877. (When common pleas court to determine manner of improvement.) If at the expiration of three months from the passage of such ordinance, the railroad company has refused or failed to co-operate in the preparation of such plans and specifications or if the engineer of the municipality or engineer designated in such ordinance by council, and the railroad company fail to agree upon the plans and specifications for such improvement, then either the railroad company or municipal corporation may submit the matter of determining the method by which the improvement shall be made to the court of common pleas having jurisdiction in the county in which the municipality is situated. (March 23, 1909, 100 v. 78, § 2; May 2, 1902, 95 v. 356, § 2; R. S. Sec. 3337-17b.)

A part of the original of this section (95 v. 357), which provided for submission to the circuit court, was held invalid.
Cincinnati v. Railway, 7 N. P. n. s 81; 19 L. D. 74 (1908).

Section 8878. (Who may petition the court.) Either the municipality or company after the expiration of three months from the passage of the ordinance may apply to such court of common pleas by petition accompanied by the necessary plans prepared by the municipality or railroad company asking that any grade crossing or grade crossings be abolished. Such plans must show the grades to be established for such streets, the changes to be made in the location of streets, alleys, roads or ways; the height, character and estimated cost of any viaduct or way above or below railroad tracks, and the number, character and location of piers, abutments and supports to be permanently located in the streets, alleys, roads or ways, in the municipality and the change of grade to be made in any railroad tracks, including side tracks and switches. (May 2, 1913, 103 v. 269; March

23, 1909, 100 v. 78, § 2; May 2, 1902, 95 v. 356, § 2; R. S. Sec. 3337-17b.)

Section 8879.   (Procedure.) Upon the filing of such petition, accompanied by plans, the railroad company or municipality opposed to the prayer thereof, or directly interested therein, shall have the right, within sixty days thereafter to file an answer to such petition and to present other plans for the abolition of such crossing or crossings. After the expiration of such period of sixty days the court shall proceed to a hearing upon the petition and any answers that have been filed, which hearing must be advanced upon the docket upon motion of either party. After examination of all plans presented to it and after hearing the evidence, the court shall make a finding as to whether or not the security and convenience of the public require that alterations be made in the crossing or crossings or in the approaches thereto, or in the location of the railroad or railroads or the public way, or any grades thereof, so as avoid a crossing at common grade, or that such crossings, or any of them be discontinued with or without building a new way in substitution therefor, and whether such plans or any of them are reasonable and practicable. (March 23, 1909, 100 v. 78, § 2; May 2, 1902, 95 v. 356, § 2; R. S. Sec. 3337-17b.)

Section 8880.   (Order of the court.) If the court finds that the public security and convenience require such changes to be made, and that the plans presented by the petitioner or any of the parties answering thereto are reasonable and practicable, it shall order the changes to be made in accordance with the most reasonable and practicable plan presented to the court. The municipality shall be required to make such changes in the streets, roads or highways as may be necessary, and the railroad company or companies be required to make the changes necessary in the tracks and roadbed, in order to comply with the rulings of the court. If more than one railroad company own tracks on the crossing in question, the court shall apportion the part of the expense payable by the railroad companies between or among such companies. But if the court finds that the security and convenience of the public do not require that alterations be made in such crossing or crossings, or that none of the plans are reasonable or practicable, the improvement shall not be made upon such plans. (March 23, 1909, 100 v. 78, § 2; May 2, 1902, 95 v. 356; R. S. Sec. 3337-17b.)

Section 8881. (Appeal and error.) Either party feeling aggrieved by the decision and order of the court may appeal or prosecute error as in other civil cases, the hearing of which shall be advanced upon the docket upon motion of either party. (March 23, 1909, 100 v. 78, § 2; May 2, 1902, 95 v. 356; R. S. Sec. 3337-17b.)

Section 8882. (How orders of court enforced.) If a municipality, or railroad company refuses or neglects to comply with the orders or findings made by the court under the provisions hereof, the court may enforce its orders or findings by either mandamus or mandatory injunction or as for contempt of court, as the necessity of the case may require, upon the application of either party to such proceedings. (March 23, 1909, 100 v. 78, § 2; May 2, 1902, 95 v. 356, § 2; R. S. Sec. 3337-17b.)

Section 8883. (Apportionment of cost.) The cost of constructing the improvement authorized, including the making of ways, crossings or viaducts, above or below the railroad tracks, and the raising or lowering of the grades of the railroad tracks and side tracks for such distance as may be required by such municipality and made necessary by such improvement, together with the cost of land or property purchased or appropriated, and damages to owners of abutting property, or other property, shall be borne thirty-five per cent. by the municipality and sixty-five per cent. by such railroad company or companies. The municipality shall have a right of action against any such railroad company for the recovery of the sixty-five per cent. and such costs payable by it, with interest from the time they become due. Such municipality and railroad company may agree as to what part of the work shall be done by the railroad company, and also fix the amount to be allowed or credited to the company for doing the work. Such railroad company shall be entitled to deduct from its sixty-five per cent. of the cost of the improvement the expense incurred by it in the change of its grade required by the municipality or made necessary by it under such specifications, but only in case the amount of expense has been agreed upon in writing between the municipality and the railroad company. If the amount of work done by the company, or made necessary by reason of such change of grade on lowering or raising its tracks, exceeds sixty-five per cent. of the cost of the improvement, then it shall have the right to recover the amount with interest in excess of sixty-five per cent. of the expenses, in an action at law against the municipality. (May

10, 1910, 101 v. 377; April 2, 1906, 98 v. 191, § 3; May 2, 1902, 95 v. 356, § 3; R. S. Sec. 3337-17c.)

Under an ordinance imposing 65 percent of the cost upon the railroad company and 35 percent upon the municipality, an additional credit to the railroad for the actual cost of material and labor, plus ten percent for superintendence and the use of tools, is proper.

Quinby v. Cleveland, 9 O. L. R. 313; 16 O. F. D. 583; 191 Fed. 68 (U. S. C. C. 1911).

See State v. Amlin, 1 N. P. n. s. 517; 14 L. D. 113 (1903); aff'd, 74 O. S. 417.

A certificate from the auditor, under G. C. § 3806, that money to meet the expenditure is in the municipal treasury to the credit of the fund, and not otherwise appropriated, is not required to validate a contract or obligation of the municipality to pay its share of the cost of elimination of grade crossings.

Cincinnati v. Waite, 12 N. P. n. s. 633; 23 L. D. 22 (1912).

Section 8884.   (Notice of intention to make improvement.) Before any work shall be done which may be required in the making of such proposed improvement, the council of such municipality shall by ordinance or resolution require notice of its intention to make such improvement in accordance with the plans and specifications to be given, after the manner provided by law, to the owner of each piece of property abutting upon any street, highway, or public place, the grade of which will be changed by the proposed improvement. (April 2, 1906, 98 v. 191, § 3; May 10, 1902, 95 v. 356, § 3; R. S. Sec. 3337-17c.)

See East End, etc., Co. v. Cleveland, 1 N. P. n. s. 493; 14 L. D. 33 (1903).

Section 8885.   (Claims for damages and judicial inquiry.) The provisions of law relating to the manner of service of such notices, the filing of claims for damages, and the effect of failure to file such claims, shall apply to the notice herein provided and to all claims for damages by reason of such proposed improvement. After the expiration of the time provided by law for the filing of such claims, the council of such municipality, when claims have been filed within the time limited, shall determine by ordinance or resolution whether such claims are to be judicially inquired into, as hereinafter provided, before commencing, or after the completion, of the proposed improvement. Thereupon, the mayor or solicitor shall make application for a jury, in the manner provided by law to the common pleas or probate court, of the county in which the municipality, or the larger part of it, is situated, either before commencing, or after the completion, of the improvement, as the council determines, and all proceedings upon such application shall be governed by the laws relating to the application provided for in other cases of city improvements. (April 2, 1906, 98 v. 191, § 3; May 10, 1902, 95 v. 356, § 3; R. S. Sec. 3337-17a.)

Damages to abutting owners are of two classes: damages from change of grade of the street, and damages by reason of piers and abutments in the street.
Quinby v. Cleveland, 9 O. L. R. 313; 16 O. F. D. 583; 191 Fed. 68 (U. S. C. C. 1911).
See note to § 8765.
East End, etc., Co. v. Cleveland, 1 N. P. n. s. 493; 14 L. D. 33 (1903).
Abutting property is property abutting on the street. As to piers and abutments, § 8888 applies and the right must be acquired by purchase or appropriation. As to change of grade the law relating to change of grade for other purposes controls.
Quinby v. Cleveland, 9 O. L. R. 313; 16 O. F. D. 583; 191 Fed. 68 (U. S. C. C. 1911).
A municipality may proceed with the improvement, leaving the matter of compensation to abutting owners, for damages for the change of grade, until the improvement is completed. But the railroad company must acquire the right to erect piers and abutments before the work proceeds. *Ib.*
Damage claims may be settled and paid without judicial determination of their amount. *Ib.*
A provision in an ordinance that the municipality shall not settle damage claims without the consent of the railroad company does not render the ordinance invalid. *Ib.*
Where a subway is constructed under the track immediately adjoining the highway, which is not vacated except at the grade crossing, and a *cul de sac* thus formed between the tracks and the entrance to the subway, whereby travel was diverted from the *cul de sac*, the owner of a business property, abutting on the *cul de sac*, may recover damages caused by the depreciation in value.
Schimmelmann v. Railway Co., 83 O. S. 356 (1911).
Damages can not be recovered for less convenient means of ingress and egress, where the same inconvenience is suffered by the general public, although in less degree.
Schmidt v. Cleveland, 1 Ct. of Ap. —; 34 C. D. 7 (1913).
Columbus Plow Co. v. Railway Co., 12 N. P. n. s. 81 (C. P. 1911).
Kinnear Mfg. Co. v. Beatty, 65 O. S. 264 (1901).
See note to § 8765.

Section 8886.   (Payment of railroad company's proportion of cost.) The council of such municipality, may by ordinance prescribe the manner and time or times of payment by such railroad company or companies of the proportion of the cost of such improvement which the railroad company or companies shall be required to pay. (April 2, 1906, 98 v. 191, § 3; May 2, 1902, 95 v. 356, § 3; R. S. Sec. 3337-17c.)

Section 8887.   (Height of viaduct.) Any way, crossing or viaduct so constructed over a railroad track or tracks in any municipality shall be of such height as not to be of less than twenty-one feet in the clear from the top surface of the rails in the railroad track to the lowest point or projection of such overhead way, crossing or viaduct, unless such company consents to, or the common pleas court orders a less height. But in no event shall such court order a less height than sixteen feet and three inches. (March 23, 1909, 100 v. 80, § 4; May 2, 1902, 95 v. 356, §4; R. S. Sec. 3337-17d.)

See § 8903.

Section 8888. (How necessary land acquired.)   The land or property required to make alterations in the street, road, alley or other way or any right, title or interest in a public street, alley or other way, required for the erection of piers or supports in any municipality, necessitated by the proposed improvement, shall be purchased or appropriated by the municipality or company after the manner provided by law for the appropriation of private property for public use. The land or property required to make any alteration in a railroad or railroads or any right, title or interest in a public street, road, alley or way required to permit the erection of piers or supports in any municipality, and structure necessitated by the proposed improvements, shall be purchased or appropriated by the railroad company or companies after the manner provided for the appropriation of private property by such corporation. But the municipality shall not appropriate land held or owned by a railroad company and necessary for the use of the company in maintaining and operating this road. (May 2, 1913, 103 v. 269; March 23, 1909, 100 v. 80, § 5; May 2, 1902, 95 v. 356, § 5; R. S. Sec. 3337-17e.)

See note to § 8885.

Section 8889. (Cost of maintenance.)   After the completion of the work the crossings and approaches shall be kept in repair as follows: When the public way crosses a railroad by an overhead bridge, the cost of maintenance must be borne by the municipality. When the public way passes under the railroad, the bridge and its abutments shall be kept and maintained by the railroad company, and the public way and its approaches be maintained and kept in repair by the municipality in which they are situated. (May 2, 1902, 95 v. 359, § 6; R. S. Sec. 3337-17f.)

Section 8890. (Bond issue.)   For the purpose of raising money to pay the proportion of the cost of such improvement payable by the municipality, the bonds of the munici-

pality may be issued to the necessary amount. They shall
be of such denomination, payable at such place and times
as the council determines, and bear interest not exceeding
five per cent. per annum, and shall not be sold for less than
their par value. (May 2, 1913, 103 v. 269; March 23, 1909,
100 v. 80, § 7; May 2, 1902, 95 v. 359, § 7; R. S. Sec. 3337-
17g.)

Where the cost will raise the net indebtedness of the municipality
beyond the limit authorized by statute, bonds can not be issued without
the approval of the electorate.
Cleveland v. Cleveland, 7 N. P. n. s. 249 (1907); aff'd, 76 O. S. 594.

Section 8891. (Tax levy.) A tax on the taxable property
of the municipality in addition to all other levies now allowed by law may be levied to pay the principal and interest
of such bonds as they mature. After completion of the improvement, a tax in addition to all other levies allowed by
law may be levied by the municipality to pay the cost of
maintaining and keeping in repair that part of the work
required to be maintained and kept in repair by the municipality. (March 23, 1909, 100 v. 80, § 7; May 2, 1902, 95 v.
359, § 7; R. S. Sec. 3337-17g.)

**Section 8892. (Street railway company to bear share of
expense.)** In case the track or tracks of any street railway
company or companies within the limits of a municipality
where the improvements hereinbefore authorized are made,
cross at grade or otherwise a public street or the right of
way of any railroad company or companies at a point where,
under the plans and specifications above provided for, it has
been determined to construct such improvements, the municipality by ordinance may require such street railway company or companies to bear a reasonable proportion of the
cost assumed by it, in making the improvement, not exceeding one-half the portion payable by the municipality; and
it shall have a right of action against such street railway
company or companies for that part of the cost which the
ordinance requires it or them to bear. Such part of the
cost also shall be a lien upon all the property, real and personal, of such company or companies situated in the same
county with the municipality from and after the date of
the passage of such ordinance. (April 2, 1906, 98 v. 192,
§ 8; May 2, 1902, 95 v. 359, § 8; R. S. Sec. 3337-17h.)

See State v. Amlin, 1 N. P. n. s. 517; 14 L. D. 113 (1903); aff'd, 74
O. S. 417.

Section 8893. (Time and manner of payment of propor-

tion.)   The council of such municipality may by ordinance provide the mode and time or times of payment for the proportion of the cost of such improvement to be borne by such street railway company or companies.   (April 2, 1906, 98 v. 192, § 8; May 2, 1902, 95 v. 359, § 8; R. S. Sec. 3337-17h.)

Section 8894.   (Repairs.)   Such street railway company or companies shall keep in repair at its or their own expense all tracks affected by such improvement and all construction work of whatever character, necessary to support such tracks. (April 2, 1906, 98 v. 192, § 8; May 2, 1902, 95 v. 359, § 8; R. S. Sec. 3337-17h.)

Section 8895.   (Crossings to be above or below grade.) Except as hereinafter provided, all crossings, hereafter constructed, whether of highways by railroads, or of railroads by highways, shall be above or below the grade thereof. (April 25, 1904, 97 v. 546, § 1; R. S. Sec. 3337-17j.)

This act (§ 8895 et seq.) does not apply to interurban railways.
  Commissioners v. Traction Co., 75 O. S. 548 (1907).
  In re Avon Beach, etc., R. Co., 3 N. P. n. s. 561; 16 L. D. 87 (1905).
  This act does not authorize a municipality to grant to a railroad company the right to occupy a public common or landing with an elevated railroad structure.
  Railroad Co. v. Cincinnati, 76 O. S. 481 (1907).

Section 8896.   (Railroad crossings.)   Every railroad company building a new line of road, under its charter powers, across a highway, shall construct it above or below the grade of the highway, unless in the manner hereinafter provided, allowed to build it at grade.   Such company may exercise the power contained in its charter and the general laws, for altering the grade and location of highways in order to avoid grade crossings.   (April 25, 1904, 97 v. 546, § 2; R. S. Sec. 3337-17k.)

Section 8897.   (Highway crossings.)   Every municipality or other authority hereafter building a highway across an existing railroad, shall construct it above or below the grade thereof, unless in the manner hereinafter provided allowed to build at grade.   The cost of such work shall be paid, thirty-five per cent. by such municipality or other authority, and sixty-five per cent. by the company owning the railroad. The word "railroad" shall include interurban railroads and the words "railroad company" shall include interurban railroad companies engaged in the operation of cars by electricity or other lawful motive power which said companies may adopt or use. The method or procedure for the construction of such highway and the manner of construction thereof shall be governed by the statutes regulating the abolition of grade crossings. (May 3, 1913, 103 v. 502; April 25, 1904, 97 v. 546, § 3; R. S. Sec. 3337-17l.)

Prior to the amendment of 103 v. 502, this section was held to be unconstitutional, as it contained no provision for notice with opportunity to be heard, as in other assessment cases.

Cincinnati v. Railway, 13 N. P. n. s. 276 (C. P. 1912).

A certificate from the auditor, under G. C. § 3806, that money to meet the expenditure is in the municipal treasury to the credit of the fund, and not otherwise apropriated, is not required to validate a contract or obligation of the municipality to pay its share of the cost of elimination of grade crossings.

Cincinnati v. Waite, 12 N. P. n. s. 633 (1912).

Section 8898. (Grade crossings.) When it is desired by a railroad company constructing a new railroad, or in changing or in altering the location of one heretofore constructed, or by any municipality or authority constructing a new highway that the railroad or highway should be so constructed that the railroad and highway will cross each other at the same grade or if it is desired to divert, change or alter an existing public highway, a petition shall be presented by the party desiring such construction or diversion, to the common pleas court of the county within which the crossing or diversion is situated, and if it is a highway asking for the right to cross a railroad, the railroad company shall be the defendant. If it is a railroad company asking for the right to cross a highway, or divert, change or alter any existing public highway, in a municipality, such municipality shall be the defendant. If outside the municipality, the trustees of the township and the board of county commissioners of the county shall be the defendants. Summons shall be served and the rule days and the rights of the defendants to plead shall be the same as in civil actions in such court. (April 25, 1904, 97 v. 546, § 4; April 3, 1908, 99 v. 58, § 4; R. S. Sec. 3337-17m.)

Section 8899. (Petition, what to contain.) Such petition shall set forth the reasons that are supposed to make such change or alteration necessary or desirable; and the court of common pleas thereupon shall have the jurisdiction of the parties and the subject matter of the petition, and may proceed to examine the matter, either by evidence, by reference to a master commissioner or otherwise. If satisfied that such construction is reasonably required to accommodate the public, or to avoid excessive expense, in view of the small amount of traffic on the highway or railroad, and considering the future uses to which the highway may be adapted, or in view of the difficulties of other methods of construction, or for other good and sufficient reasons, the court shall make an order or orders permitting such crossing at a grade or diversion to be established. In such order, or orders, in its' discretion, the court may prescribe that gates, signals, watchmen, or other safeguards shall be maintained by the railroad company, in addition to the signals and safeguards prescribed by statute, and all such orders shall be binding upon the parties and be observed by them. (April 25, 1904, 97 v. 546, § 4; April 3, 1908, 99 v. 58, § 4; R. S. Sec. 3337-17m.)

The court may grant permission to cross at grade, conditional upon the acquirement by the railroad company, by agreement or condemnation, of the right to do so. Such agreement or condemnation need not precede the order of the court under this section.

In re Avon Beach, etc., R. Co., 3 N. P. n. s. 561; 16 L. D. 87 (C. P. 1905).

An order of the court of common pleas under this section must be obtained before a proceeding will lie to appropriate the use of a street at grade. A petition for appropriation which does not allege such an order is subject to a motion to make definite and certain.

Railway v. East Liverpool, 10 N. P. n. s. 157; 55 O. L. B. 173 (Pr. Cr. 1909).

See Toledo v. Railway Co., 9 C. C. n. s. 399; 19 C. D. 658 (1907); aff'd, 78 O. S. 429.

In re Avon Beach, etc., R. Co., 3 N. P. n. s. 561; 16 L. D. 87 (C. P. 1905).

Ritter v. Railway, 6 N. P. n. s. 161; 18 L. D. 846 (C. P. 1907).

Section 8900. (Costs and expenses.) All costs and expenses of the proceedings shall be ascertained and allowed by the court of common pleas and be paid by such party as it decides; or by it apportioned between the parties, and may be collected by execution out of such court. (April 25, 1904, 97 v. 546, § 4; April 3, 1908, 99 v. 58, § 4; R. S. Sec. 3337-17m.)

Section 8901. (Appeals.) Appeals may be taken and error prosecuted from the decision of the common pleas court to the court of appeals in such proceedings, as in civil actions. The decision of that court shall be final and conclusive. In both the common pleas court and court of appeals proceedings brought hereunder shall be advanced over other civil causes. (May 6, 1913, 103 v. 425; April 25, 1904, 97 v. 546, § 4; April 3, 1908, 99 v. 58, § 4; R. S. Sec. 3337-17m.)

Section 8902. (Additional tracks and switches.) Nothing in sections eighty-eight hundred and ninety-five to eighty-nine hundred and one both inclusive, shall prevent a railroad company from laying additional tracks at previously existing crossings, or from constructing switches, sidings and branch lines from their lines of road to a mill, factory, or other manufacturing establishment, or other industrial plant, or an elevator, wharf or pier, or gravel, marl, or clay bed, or any mine, or from laying additional track to increase their yard facilities at terminal or other points across public highways at the grade thereof. Such signposts and signals shall be employed for the protection of such crossings as are by law prescribed for railroad crossings of public highways. (April 25, 1904, 97 v. 547, § 6; R. S. Sec. 3337-17o.)

A crossing by a spur track leading to factories, commercial houses and docks, is within the exception as to tracks for increasing "yard facilities at terminal or other points" and such crossing may be at grade.
Toledo v. Railroad Co., 9 C. C. n. s. 399; 19 C. D. 658 (1907); aff'd, 78 O. S. 429.

In an action brought in the court of common pleas to enjoin the laying of a crossing at grade, under a judgment of the probate court, it is error to exclude testimony offered to show that the crossing is within the exception of this section.
Toledo v. Railroad Co., 9 C. C. n. s. 399; 19 C. D. 658 (1907); aff'd, 78 O. S. 429.

Section 8903. (Height of over railroads.) Except cases in which the state railroad commission finds that such construction is impracticable, bridges, viaducts, overhead roadways, foot-bridges, wire or other structure hereafter built over the track or tracks of a railroad or railroads, by a county, municipality, township, railroad company, other corporation or person, shall be not less than twenty-one feet in the clear from the top of the rails of such track or tracks, to such wire or other structure or to the bottom of the lowest sill, girder or crossbeam, and the lowest downward projection on the bridge, viaduct, overhead roadway or foot-bridge. (April 16, 1900, 94 v. 297, § 1; May 21, 1894, 91 v. 365; R. S. Sec. 3337-18.)

See § 8887.
Penalty for violation.
See § 12546.
The jurisdiction of the utilities commission extends to regulating the overhead structures in city street railroad crossings, independent of any interlocking device connected therewith.
Opin. Atty. Gen., 39 W. L. B. 115 (1898).
Duty of railroad to employes.
Lake Shore, etc., Ry. Co. v. Shook, 16 C. C. 665; 9 C. D. 9 (1895).
In the absence of a statute requiring it, or of evidence showing that it is usual, a railroad company is not required to construct its bridges

so as to permit a person to stand upon them in safety while a train is passing.

> Erie R. Co. v. McCormick, 69 O. S. 45 (1903).

Power to close bridge for repairs. Where it is the duty of a railroad company to erect and maintain a bridge in a street under which its road is passing, and such bridge becomes dangerous and out of repair, the company has the same right as the city to close the bridge for repairs, although it constitutes part of the public street.

> Toledo, etc., Ry. Co. v. Mammet, 13 C. C. 591; s. c., 6 C. D. 244 (1895).

Duty to maintain bridge. Although there may be some doubt as to the original liability of a company to build a bridge across its road, if it in fact builds a bridge and maintains it for forty years, it will be held liable to continue to maintain the same.

> Toledo v. Lake Shore, etc., Ry. Co., 17 C. C. 265; 9 C. D. 135 (1893).

Bridges over right of way—removal by municipal authorities. Where a railroad is constructed in a cut across a highway, and the highway is restored by bridging across, such bridge constitutes a part of the highway and may be removed, when the council deem it necessary for the public convenience to make the crossing at grade.

> Railroad Co. v. Defiance, 52 O. S. 262 (1895); aff'd, 167 U. S. 88.

Low bridge over highway—remedy. Where an injunction is asked to restrain a railroad from building a bridge over a turnpike which would leave only a space between the surface of the road and the bridge not sufficient for the purposes of the public using such road, and it appears that much work has been done in building such bridge before objection was made, and that the cost of raising such bridge would involve a heavy expense, and that the difficulty could be remedied at much less expense and trouble by lowering the surface of the road at the point in question, the court will order that the latter be done at the expense of the railroad company.

> Wooster Turnpike Co. v. Railroad Co., 15 C. C. 268; 8 C. D. 269 (1897).

Section 8904. (Exceptions.) The exception in the next preceding section shall not apply to the structures therein named when built over the main tracks of railroads; and in cases wherein it is allowed, the railroad commission shall file in its office a written statement of the facts upon which it relied in finding the required construction impracticable. (April 16, 1900, 94 v. 297, § 1; May 21, 1894, 91 v. 365; R. S. Sec. 3337-18.)

Section 8905. (Costs.) In case of the rebuilding of bridges or the other structures above provided for, if the structure is at or in line with a public street or highway, and a cross-street or streets, the cost of making such streets or highways conform to a new grade, with all damages to owners of property abutting thereon because of such change, shall be determined and paid, as follows: The railroad company or its assigns shall pay all costs or damages resulting from the raising or building of its bridges or structures in the line of a street or highway at a greater height than heretofore was required. If such company is only part owner of such structure it shall pay its proportionate share of the cost of such change in grade and damages. Should a railroad company, or its assigns, hereafter raise the grade of its track or tracks under any of such structures not owned by it, thereby causing a bridge or structure to be put at a higher grade when rebuilt, the company shall pay all costs and damages thereby made necessary. (April 16, 1900, 94 v. 297, § 1; May 21, 1894, 91 v. 365; R. S. Sec. 3337-18.)

Section 8906. (Plans and specifications to be filed with railroad commission.) Every railroad company, public or private corporation, or person building or permitting to be built, any such bridge, viaduct, overhead roadway, foot bridge, wire and other structure, before proceeding therewith, shall file with the state railroad commission, plans and specifications therefor, and have its permit for the erection of such structure or wire. (May 21, 1894, 91 v. 366, § 2; R. S. Sec. 3337-19.)

Section 8907. (How enforced.) Observance of the provisions of the four next preceding sections may be enforced by an injunction on complaint of any person, corporation or board interested therein. (May 21, 1894, 91 v. 366, § 2; R. S. Sec. 3337-19.)

Penalty for violation.
See § 12546.

CHAPTER 3.

DRAINAGE AND FENCES.

DRAINAGE.

Section 8908. (Waterways must be provided.) Except where the road-bed of a railroad extends through or by swamp land, the company or person operating the road shall made and keep open ditches or drains along such road-bed of depth, width, and grade sufficient to conduct water accumulating at the sides of the road-bed from the building or operation of the road, to some proper outlet. (R. S. Sec. 3342; May 7, 1869, 66 v. 335, § 1.)

This section is valid in so far as the accumulation of water is injurious to the contiguous lands, or detrimental to the public, but invalid where such water is not injurious to such lands or the public.

Railroad Co. v. Keith, 67 O. S. 279 (1902); reversing 21 C. C. 669.

Railway Co. v. Eby, 67 O. S. 552 (1903).

Only the company owning the railroad, and not the lessees thereof, can be subjected to ditch assessments.

Baltimore, etc., R. Co. v. Pausch, 35 W. L. B. 1 (1896).

Agreement to maintain ditch. Where a county ditch was constructed over and along the ditch which a railroad company had agreed to open and maintain along the right of way granted by the plaintiff, under a contract made when the grant was made, the railroad company was released from further obligation.

Railway Co. v. Henry, 14 C. C. n. s. 97 (1910).

In an action for damages against the railroad company for failure to maintain such ditch, the question of whether the construction of the county ditch, with the consent of plaintiff, had not carried a large amount of water which did not naturally flow there should be submitted to the jury.

Railway Co. v. Henry, 14 C. C. n. s. 97 (1910).

Under an agreement to maintain a culvert and crossings necessary to enable the parties "to reasonably occupy their lands, to carry off surplus water," etc.: and to keep open on the hillside of the road a sufficient drain "for the discharge of the drainage," the company was held liable for damages caused by an obstruction of a lower drain through which the drainage of such parties was discharged.

Madden v. Railway Co., 36 O. S. 46 (1880).

Specific performance of a contract for the maintenance of a waterway may be decreed against the railway company.

Bell v. Railroad Co., 3 C. C. 31; 2 C. D. 19 (1887).

Liability for damages by flood waters. Damages for injury to land by flood waters can not be recovered from a railroad company where the flood was unprecedented, and other causes to produce the injury intervened.

B. & O. R. Co. v. Simpson, 12 C. C. n. s. 185 (1906).

An owner of land, abutting on a river, through which a creek flows and empties into the river, may, as against proprietors on the opposite side of the river, change the channel and mouth of the creek upon his own land and for his own protection or convenience, if, in so doing, he exercises reasonable care not to injure the rights of others.

Railroad Co. v. Carr, 38 O. S. 448 (1882).

If the opposite bank of the river be subject to inundation and overflow in case of unusual but not unprecedented floods in the river, such change in the mouth of the creek can not be made if increased danger of inundation and overflow on the opposite bank of the river might be anticipated, in the exercise of ordinary care and prudence.

Railroad Co. v. Carr, 38 O. S. 448 (1882).

Where such change is made without fault or carelessness, and a levee on the opposite bank is broken or washed away by an unusual, but not unprecedented flood, whereby the crops growing on adjacent lands are destroyed, it is *damnum sine injuria*, notwithstanding a sandbar in the river at the new mouth of the creek may have contributed to the damage.

Railroad Co. v. Carr, 38 O. S. 448 (1882).

Liability for assessments for county ditch. A railroad company may enjoin the levy of an assessment against its right of way for a county ditch, where the right of way has sufficient drainage and the county ditch would be of no benefit.

Railway v. Commissioners, 15 C. C. n. s. 236 (1912).

Section 8909. (Proceedings to enforce company to provide a waterway.) After ten days' notice or request to a ticket or other agent of the company or person operating a railroad, to provide such drain or ditch, preferred by a person authorized to institute the proceedings hereinafter provided for, if the requirements of the foregoing section are not complied with, any owner or tenant of land contiguous to such railroad aggrieved by such neglect may give notice of the fact, in writing, to the probate judge of the county in which it occurs designating therein the place or places on such road where drains or ditches have not been made. Upon receipt of such notice the probate judge shall appoint a commission, of three disinterested freeholders of such county, who with the county surveyor, shall proceed to the places designated in the notice, and, if upon inspection, it is found that such requirements are not complied with, the commission or a majority thereof, shall report the fact to the judge who shall keep a record of such proceedings. He also shall designate a time within which such ditches or drains shall be made or opened and forthwith notify the company or person operating such road, in writing, whose duty it shall be to make or open such ditches or drains within the time specified. (R. S. Sec. 3343; May 7, 1869, 66 v. 335, § 2.)

This section was held unconstitutional in
    Railroad Co. v. Keith, 67 O. S. 279 (1902); reversing 21 C. C. 669.

Section 8910.   (When probate judge may let work.) If such company or person neglects to comply with the notification of the probate judge, he shall forthwith give notice that the work of making or opening the ditches or drains will be let to the lowest bidder at the time and place designated in the advertisement. Such advertisement shall be for three consecutive weeks, in one or more of the weekly newspapers published in such county. (R. S. Sec. 3344; May 7, 1869, 66 v. 335, § 3.)

This section was held unconstitutional in
    Railroad Co. v. Keith, 67 O. S. 279 (1902); reversing 21 C. C. 669.

Section 8911.   (Sale of work and proceedings.) At the time and place so specified, such judge shall sell the job or jobs of making or opening such ditches or drains to the lowest bidder, and take from him a sufficient bond, with surety, for the performance thereof. Upon its completion to his satisfaction, he shall give the bidder a certificate therefor, stating the amount due for the work. On its presentation to the auditor of the county, he forthwith shall place the amount so certified upon the county tax duplicate, against the company, together with all costs and expenses for inspection by the commission and surveyor, notices, advertisements, sale of work, making contract therefor, approval of the work, and other costs, and interest on the amount certified to be due, from the time the work is approved until the amount can be collected by the county treasurer. Such tax shall be collected as other taxes, and be paid to the persons entitled thereto on the warrant of the auditor on the treasurer. (R. S. Sec. 3345; May 7, 1869, 66 v. 335, § 4.)

This section was held unconstitutional in
    Railroad Co. v. Keith, 67 O. S. 279 (1902); reversing 21 C. C. 669.

Section 8912.   (Fees of officers.) The probate judge, commissioners, and surveyor shall be paid for their services such costs, fees and expenses as are provided by law for costs, fees, and expenses of county commissioners and others under proceedings relating to ditches. (R. S. Sec. 3346; May 7, 1869, 66 v. 335, § 5.)

This section was held unconstitutional in
Railroad Co. v. Keith, 67 O. S. 279 (1902); reversing 21 C. C. 669.

FENCES.

Section 8913. (Fences.) A company or person having control or management of a railroad shall construct and maintain in good repair on each side of such road, along the line of the lands of the company owning or operating it, a fence sufficient to turn stock. When such fence is constructed of barbed wire, or separate lateral strands not connected by interwoven wire, or cross perpendicular wire not more than fifteen inches apart, there shall be securely fastened to the posts, at the top thereof, at right angles thereto, at least one board, not less than one and one-eighth inches thick and five inches wide, and extending the entire length thereof. (R. S. Sec. 3324; April 3, 1908, 99 v. 58; May 18, 1894, 91 v. 297; April 8, 1891, 88 v. 295; April 20, 1887, 78 v. 199; R. S. 1880; April 18, 1874, 71 v. 85, §-1.)

Section 8913 to 8915 are constitutional, founded on a sound, public policy, and equally obligatory on railroad companies whether organized under charters granted prior or laws enacted since the constitution of 1851 went into effect.
Railroad Co. v. Infirmary, 32 O. S. 566, 570 (1877).

Duty to fence. Sufficiency of fence. This section does not require railroad companies to fence against persons. The fence required is one sufficient to turn stock.
L. S. & M. S. Ry. v. Lidtke, 69 O. S. 384 (1904).
See Devereaux v. Thornton, 4 W. L. B. 355 (1879); s. c., 2 Clev. L. R. 177; 10 W. L. B. 266.
This section requires the construction and maintenance of fences within the limits of cities and villages where they do not obstruct streets, highways or other public grounds.
Cleveland, etc., R. Co. v. McConnell, 26 O. S. 57 (1875).
The duty of a railroad company is not discharged by contracting with another party to perform it, when the performance itself is insufficient.
Gill v. Atlantic, etc., Ry. Co., 27 O. S. 240 (1875).
Railway Co. v. Allen, 40 O. S. 206 (1883).
Inclosures of railroads under this act must be separate and distinct from the inclosures of adjoining proprietors.
Marietta, etc., R. Co. v. Stephenson, 24 O. S. 48 (1873).
This section does not require railroad companies to see that gates are kept closed.
Megrue v. Lennox, 59 O. S. 479 (1898).
Didman v. Railway Co., 7 N. P. 380; 5 L. D. 140; 31 W. L. B. 240.
See note to § 8914, *Defenses.*

This section does not refer to railroad land other than its line of road and right of way, and does not require such other land to be fenced.

Railroad Co. v. Kinz, 68 O. S. 210, 225 (1903).

The obligation to construct and maintain fences upon both sides of railroads, imposed by this act, is not limited to owners and occupiers of adjoining lands, but extends to the public generally.

Marietta, etc., R. R. Co. v. Stephenson, 24 O. S. 48 (1873).

Railway Co. v. Allen, 40 O. S. 206 (1883).

Gill v. Atlantic, etc., Ry. Co., 27 O. S. 240 (1875).

Railroad Co. v. Scudder, 40 O. S. 173, 175 (1883).

Where the tracks of two railroad companies are parallel and adjoining, it is the duty of the companies to maintain a fence between their respective rights of way.

Hall v. Railway Co., 14 L. D. 74 (C. P. 1903).

The duty to fence is imposed by statute only. At common law there was no duty to fence.

Railway Co. v. Phillips, 81 O. S. 453, 458 (1910).

Seymour v. Railway Co., 44 O. S. 12, 19 (1886).

Kerwhacker v. Cleveland, etc., R. Co., 3 O. S. 172 (1854).

Agreement by railroad company to fence. Where in proceedings to condemn land the parties enter into an agreement of record whereby the company bound itself to build and maintain fences, the agreement is valid and binding, and runs with the land so as to be binding on the assignees or grantees of both parties.

Huston v. Cincinnati, etc., R. R. Co., 21 O. S. 235 (1871).

Where a contract for a right of way required the railroad company to construct a cattle-pass, but the deed of the right of way was silent as to the cattle-pass, which had been constructed before the execution of the deed, it was held that the purchaser of the railroad, on foreclosure, could not fill up the cattle-pass, possession by the grantor constituting notice.

Lowe v. Railway, 12 C. C. 743; 4 C. D. 85 (1894).

Breach of agreement. Remedies. Where the owner of land, by written contract, agreed to give to a railroad company the perpetual right of way through the same, at a stipulated price, which was paid to him, with a provision in the contract that when the road should be completed the company should fence the same, *held*, that after the road is completed, the owner of the land can not, upon failure to put up the fence, eject the company from the land.

Hornback v. Cincinnati, etc., R R. Co., 20 O. S. 81 (1870).

See § 8916.

Where a landowner agreed to release a right of way in consideration of a certain sum of money and the construction of road crossings and cattle-guards, and the company took possession before receiving a deed or constructing the crossings or guards, the landowner has an equitable lien upon the property sold, as well for damages for not constructing the crossings and guards as for the unpaid purchase money, and the landowner may have a remedy by compelling specific performance or by enforcing his lien.

Dayton, etc., R. R. Co. v. Lewton, 20 O. S. 401 (1870).

——. **Damages.** In an action by the vendee of the original owner against the vendee of the company, for failure to build fences and crossings, the rule of damages is the amount of injury to the use and enjoyment of the adjoining land, occasioned by the want of such fences and crossings during the time the railroad or right of way was owned by the defendant.

Huston v. Cincinnati, etc., R. R. Co., 21 O. S. 235 (1871).

Decisions under former acts.

Railroad Co. v. M̃cElroy, 35 O. S. 147 (1878).

Railroad Co. v. Shultz, 43 O. S. 270, 274 (1885).

Partition fences under former act.

See Railroad Co. v. Miami County Infirmary, 32 O. S. 566 (1877).

Sandusky, etc., R. R. Co. v. Sloan, 27 O. S. 341 (1875).

Haxton v. Pittsburg Ry. Co., 26 O. S. 214 (1875).

Liability of railroad companies.

See § 8914 and note.

Section 8914.   (Cattle-guards and crossings.) Before operating such road, such company or person shall maintain at every point where a public road, street, lane or highway used by the public, crosses such railroad, safe and sufficient crossings, and on each side of such crossings cattle-guards sufficient to prevent domestic animals from going upon such railroad; and such company or person shall be liable for all damages sustained in person or property by reason of the want or insufficiency of such fence, crossing or cattle-guard, or neglect or carelessness in the construction thereof, or in keeping them in repair. (R. S. Sec. 3324; April 3, 1908, 99 v. 58; May 18, 1894, 91 v. 297; April 8, 1891, 88 v. 295; April 20, 1887, 78 v. 199; R. S. 1880; April 18, 1874, 71 v. 85, § 1.)

This section applies where the construction of the highway precedes that of the railroad. It does not apply where a street is extended over existing tracks.

Railway Co. v. Troy, 68 O. S. 510, 514 (1903).

This section does not refer to railroad land other than its line of road and right of way.

Railroad Co. v. Kinz, 68 O. S. 210, 225 (1903).

Crossings.

See also §§ 8763 to 8766.

Where the grade of the track is higher than that of the road the approaches need not be built by the railroad company so far on both sides of the crossing that there would be practically no incline on the approaches, so that the approaches are brought practically to a level with the railway crossing. It had a right to make inclines, and where the inclines are made safe and sufficient for ordinary and regular purposes of travel, that is a sufficient compliance with the statutes.

Lake Shore, etc., R. R. Co. v. Brazzill, 13 C. C. 622 (1895); s. c., 6 C. D. 363.

Under this section the company is liable for all damages sustained in person or property in any manner by reason of the want or insufficiency of a crossing over its tracks. The word "crossing" is used in a limited or restricted sense, and includes only that part of the structure immediately over and across the tracks, and sufficient space on either side to make a sufficient and safe way over such tracks.

Lynch v. Railway Co., 20 C. C. 248; 11 C. D. 243 (1899).

Where a private road extends across the track and right of way of a railroad company and connects with a public highway, the company is required to maintain across such private road suitable fences, or provide other protection against injuries which may result from animals passing from such highway through the private road on or along the railroad track.

Railroad Co. v. Cunnington, 39 O. S. 327 (1883).

Cattle-guards in towns and station yards. This section, so far as it relates to cattle-guards, may be construed as allowing exceptions, required by public necessity and convenience, and the proper use of a station yard by the company, but when the company is thus relieved, it is its duty to construct the guards at the first point where they will not interfere with the needs of the public and the company; and in an action against the company for damages, the question whether the guards are properly located and placed is for the jury.

Railroad Co. v. Newbrander, 40 O. S. 15 (1883).
Railroad Co. v. Cunnington, 39 O. S. 327 (1883).
Pierce v. Andrews, 13 C. C. 513; 7 C. D. 105 (1896).

To come within the above exception it is necessary that three elements be present: necessity (1) of the public, (2) of the railroad company and (3) of its employees, that the cattle-guards be omitted.

Norfolk, etc., Ry. Co. v. Vallery, 6 C. C. n. s. 348; 17 C. D. 658 (1905); aff'd, 75 O. S. 564.

A railroad company is not entitled to compensation for making or maintaining cattle-guards.

Railway Co. v. Sharpe, 38 O. S. 150 (1882).

Liability of railroad companies. Where the railroad company owning the track permits another company to run trains thereon, both companies are liable.

Berchold v. Railway, 1 Cleve. L. R. 314 (1878).

———. **To whom liable.** The liability of a railroad company under this section is not limited to owners and occupiers of abutting lands but is "for all damages sustained in person or property."

Railway Co. v. Allen, 40 O. S. 206 (1883).
Railroad Co. v. Stephenson, 24 O. S. 48 (1873).
Gill v. Railway, 27 O. S. 240 (1875).
Railroad Co. v. Scudder, 40 O. S. 173, 175 (1883).
Hall v. Railway Co., 14 L. D. 74 (C. P. 1903).

A railroad company may be liable to its employes. As a general rule a railway engineer is not chargeable as a matter of law with knowledge of a break in the fences along the line of the road through which cattle may stray upon the track. Where, after discovering that cattle are upon the track, he does all that a man of ordinary prudence would do to avoid an accident, the derailment that followed, resulting in his death, can not be said to be due to his contributory negligence.

Isley v. Railroad Co., 5 C. C. n. s. 669; 17 C. D. 785 (1905).

———. **For injuries occurring on tracks of another company.** The liability of a railroad company under this section is limited to loss or injuries occurring upon its own right of way. Where stock went through a defective fence over the tracks of the railroad company and upon the track of another company, where it was killed, the railroad company was held not liable.

Railway Co. v. Phillips, 81 O. S. 453 (1910).

As to liability of company upon whose tracks the stock was killed, see

Didman v. Railway Co., 7 N. P. 380; 5 L. D. 140; 31 W. L. B. 240 (C. P. 1894).
Railway Co. v. Wood, 47 O. S. 431 (1890).
Hall v. Railway, 14 L. D. 74 (C. P. 1903).

――――. **For injury to stock running at large.** In an action under this section, it is a sufficient answer to allege that the plaintiff did not live along the line of the railway, nor were his cattle grazing in any inclosed field adjacent thereto. That said plaintiff knowingly, willfully and unlawfully permitted his cattle to run at large on the highways and uninclosed lands adjacent to defendant's said railroad, whereby said cattle went upon said road and were accidentally killed.

Pittsburg, etc., Ry. Co. v. Methaven, 21 O. S. 586 (1871).

Railway Co. v. Wood, 47 O. S. 431, 436 (1890).

Where cattle are running at large without the fault of the owner, he is not guilty of contributory negligence in case they are injured.

Marietta, etc., R. R. Co. v. Stephenson, 24 O. S. 48 (1873).

If the owners of cattle permit them to run at large in the vicinity of an uninclosed railroad track, and do not choose to avoid danger to their cattle by keeping them within their own inclosures, they can ask no more than that the agents of the railroad company, in the legitimate conduct of its business, running its trains with a speed regulated by the grade of its road, the capacity of its locomotive power, and the safety of persons and property carried, shall, with due regard to the safety of persons and property in their charge, being the paramount consideration, exercise, what, "in that peculiar business," would be ordinary and reasonable care to avoid unnecessary injury to animals casually coming upon their uninclosed railroad. The company is not bound to take into consideration the possibility of cattle being on the track.

Central Ohio R. R. Co. v. Lawrence, 13 O. S. 66 (1861).

Cleveland, etc., R. Co. v. Elliott, 4 O. S. 474 (1855).

Kerwhacker v. Cleveland, etc., R. Co., 3 O. S. 172 (1854).

Bellefontaine, etc., R. R. Co. v. Schruyhart, 10 O. S. 116 (1859).

Bellefontaine, etc., Co. v. Bailey, 11 O. S. 333 (1860).

Didman v. Michigan, etc., R. R. Co., 31 W. L. B. 240 (1894).

Cranston v. Cincinnati, etc., R. R. Co., 1 Handy, 193 (1854).

If the road is properly fenced the company is held to the exercise of ordinary care only in the running of trains to prevent the killing of animals. Where the road is not properly fenced, a higher degree of care is required.

Gill v. Atlantic, etc., Ry. Co., 27 O. S. 240 (1875).

A railroad company in the operation of its trains, is bound to use ordinary care to avoid injury to domestic animals trespassing on the track.

Railroad Co. v. Smith, 22 O. S. 227 (1871).

Railroad Co. v. Weisel, 55 O. S. 155 (1896).

Railway Co. v. Slater, 24 W. L. B. 2 (1890).

Where the contributory negligence of the owner of the animals is the proximate cause of the injury, he can not recover, although the operation of the train was without ordinary care.

Railroad Co. v. Weisel, 55 O. S. 155 (1896).

But where the negligence of the owner of the animals was not the proximate cause of the injury, he may recover.

Railroad Co. v. Elliott, 4 O. S. 474 (1855).

The mere fact that cattle have strayed, without right, on the track of a railroad, neither establishes that character of negligence which precludes a claim for injury done by running the locomotive against them, nor justifies a want of proper care to save and preserve them from destruction.

Cranston v. Cincinnati, etc., R. R. Co., 1 Handy, 193 (1854).

Defenses.

――――. **That railroad company was not negligent.** This section is to be reasonably construed, and where damage results from defects (occurring

without the fault or neglect of such companies) in an otherwise sufficient fence, there is no liability.

Railroad Co. v. Schultz, 43 O. S. 270 (1885).
Railroad Co. v. Bailey, 11 O. S. 333 (1860).

——. **Agreement by landowner to build or repair fence.** Where the
owner of land through which a railroad runs agrees with the railroad company, for a valuable consideration, to build and keep up good and sufficient
fences, and fails to do so, and on account of the insufficiency of such
fences his animals stray upon the track and are injured, he is not entitled
to recover for such injury, although the insufficiency of the fences was
caused by casualty and without negligence on his part, unless such injury
is shown to have been intentional, or the result of gross carelessness on
the part of the agents and servants of the company.

Lake Erie, etc., R. R. Co. v. Weisel, 55 O. S. 155 (1896).
Pittsburg, etc., Ry. Co. v. Smith, 26 O. S. 124 (1875).
Cincinnati, etc., R. R. Co. v. Waterson, 4 O. S. 424 (1854).
Railway Co. v. Heiskell, 38 O. S. 666 (1883).
See Easter v. Little Miami R. R. Co., 14 O. S. 48 (1862).

And where stock of a third person gets upon the track, by reason of
the fence not being built by the landowner, the company is not liable, in
the absence of negligence.

Railway Co. v. Wood, 47 O. S. 431 (1890).
See Railway Co. v. Allen, 40 O. S. 206 (1883).
See note to § 8918.

Where the defense is that the expense of fencing was included in the
damages awarded in the appropriation proceeding (see § 8918), but the
record of the appropriation proceeding is silent on the subject, no presumption arises that the expense of fencing was so included.

Railroad Co. v. Hoffhines, 46 O. S. 643 (1889).

When a land owner is bound by an agreement made by his prede-
cessor in title,

See Hulshizer v. Railway, 13 N. P. n. s. 497 (C. P. 1912).

——. **Gates left open.** Where a company puts in a private crossing
with gates, and stock wanders through the gate upon the company's track
and is killed, the duty of keeping the same closed devolves primarily upon
the landowner, and not upon the company, and evidence showing a gate
was carelessly left open is not admissible on the issue as to the condition
of the fence.

Megrue v. Lennox, 59 O. S. 479 (1898).

Where gates to permit passage to and from fields across the track are
constructed at the request of the landowner, and where he uses them exclusively, the company owes him no duty to see that they are kept closed.

Didman v. Michigan, etc., R. R. Co., 31 W. L. B. 240 (1894); s. c., 7
    N. P. 380; 5 L. D. 140.

The same rule applies to a third person whose cattle break into a
field in which gates have been left open.

Didman v. Railway Co., 7 N. P. 380; 5 L. D. 140; 31 W. L. B. 240.
See B. & O. R. Co. v. Wood, 47 O. S. 431.

——. **Statute of limitations.** An action against a railroad company
to recover damages for killing or injuring a domestic animal which had
strayed upon its tracks, and was killed or injured without fault or negligence of the railroad company in operating its train, but solely by the
neglect to fence the road as required by law, is founded upon "a liability
created by statute, other than a forfeiture or penalty," and is barred in
six years.

Seymour v. Railway Co., 44 O. S. 12 (1886).
Roice v. Railway Co., 5 N. P. n. s. 7; 17 L. D. 505 (C. P. 1907).

——. **Knowledge by landowner of defective fence.** Where it is the duty of the railroad company to fence, it is not contributory negligence for a landowner to turn his stock into a field which he knew to be insufficiently fenced.

Railway Co. v. Smith, 38 O. S. 410 (1882).
Railroad Co. v. Scudder, 40 O. S. 173 (1883).
Pittsburg, etc., Ry. Co. v. Methven, 21 O. S. 586 (1871).
See under old partition fence act,
Railroad Co. v. Infirmary, 32 O. S. 566 (1877).
Sandusky, etc., R. Co. v. Sloan, 27 O. S. 341 (1875).

But where railroad employes, engaged in repairing or rebuilding a defective fence on the line where the fence had always been located, are ordered off the premises by the landowner, who claimed that the line of the fence was not the true line, and who continued to use the land as a pasture with knowledge that the fence is defective and dangerous, without revoking his warning to the company or taking steps to determine the true line, and his stock is injured in the loose barbed wire of the fence, he can not recover.

Railroad Co. v. McIlyar, 77 O. S. 391 (1908).

——. **That railroad company had no notice of condition of fence.** A railroad company can not escape responsibility by showing that it had no notice of the condition of a fence.

Railway Co. v. Smith, 38 O. S. 410 (1882).
Railroad Co. v. Shultz, 43 O. S. 270, 273 (1885).
Baltimore, etc., R. Co. v. Reamer, 24 W. L. B. 222 (1890).

——. **Breachy and unruly animals.** An owner of breachy and unruly animals may recover for their injury or loss provided the animals were at large without his fault, and he has used that reasonable care and precaution in restraining them which a prudent and cautious man would use under like circumstances.

Railway Co. v. Howard, 40 O. S. 6 (1883).

Pleading. The facts upon which the company's liability depends must be stated in the petition, and, if not admitted, must be established by proof. An allegation that the defendant was, by law, bound to fence and inclose its railroad, tenders an immaterial issue, and is not to be taken as true because not denied.

Baltimore, etc., R. R. Co. v. Wilson, 31 O. S. 555 (1877).

Proof. In an action against a railroad company to recover damages for killing live stock, the plaintiff must prove affirmatively that want of ordinary care on the part of the company or its employes caused the injury. Such inference does not arise from the mere fact that the animal was killed.

Railroad Co. v. McMillan, 37 O. S. 554 (1882).
Railway Co. v. Heiskell, 38 O. S. 666 (1883).
Bellefontaine, etc., R. R. Co. v. Bailey, 11 O. S. 333 (1860).

Where one of the issues in an action is whether a fence is sufficient to turn stock, it is error to permit witnesses, who show no other qualifications than that they had seen the fence, to give to the jury their opinions as to the sufficiency of the fence to turn stock.

Railroad Co. v. Schultz, 43 O. S. 270 (1885).

An expert may testify whether, in view of the distance between the cattle and the engine, it was possible to avoid injury.

Bellefontaine, etc., R. R. Co. v. Bailey, 11 O. S. 333 (1860).

The fact that an insufficient fence has for several weeks been maintained by a railroad company along its right of way is sufficient to justify a jury in finding it guilty of negligence; and the fact that the plaintiff's stock had, during all such time, been kept in a field adjoining the right of way, without escaping through such fence and passing upon the railroad track, is not sufficient to excuse the company from such neglect. Where the immediate means or cause of such stock passing over such fence and upon the railroad track is that, recently prior thereto, a board or rail had become detached and fallen from the fence, without the knowledge of the company, such company is not excused from liability where there is evidence to justify the jury in finding that such special defect was attributable to the generally defective condition of the fence.

Railroad Co. v. Schultz, 43 O. S. 270 (1885).

Section 8915. (Temporary crossings.) In the case of a road in process of construction, or a proposed road which passes through inclosed land, the company or person having control thereof during its construction, shall provide suitable crossings for the owner or occupant of each farm, and make and keep in repair fences along the line of such road through such inclosed fields, and protect crops growing thereon. When the company or person agrees with the owner of the lands through which a railroad passes, that he is to build and keep in repair any portion of the fencing, and if such fencing be destroyed or damaged by fire from passing trains or by the elements, the company or person owning or operating such road, shall rebuild or repair such fence, if the property holder demands it. If a railroad company fails or refuses to construct a fence in the manner hereinbefore provided, after having received written notice so to do from the owner or occupant of lands through which the road passes, then, after thirty days from the time of serving such notice upon the agent of such company nearest such lands, such owner or occupant may proceed to construct it, and the company shall be liable to such person for the cost thereof, together with the attorney's fees as in the next following section provided. This applies to all fences now built, as well as those hereafter constructed. (R. S. Sec. 3324; April 18, 1874, 71 v. 85, § 1; R. S. 1880; April 20, 1887, 78 v. 199; April 8, 1891, 88 v. 295; May 18, 1894, 91 v. 297; April 3, 1908, 99 v. 58.)

Section 8916. (Land owner may construct fence at company's expense.) If such company or person neglects or refuses to construct a fence, as hereinbefore provided, the owner of land abutting on the line of the land of the railroad may construct it so far as his land abuts on the railroad lands. When he has completed the fence he may present for payment a sworn itemized account of the expense thereof, including materials and labor, to the agent of the company for receiving and shipping freight at the station nearest to the tract of land so fenced. If such company or person neglects or refuses for thirty days, to pay the account, the land owner may recover from the owner or lessee of the road, the reasonable cost of such fence, and in addition thereto, if recovery is had for an amount not less than the amount of the verified itemized account as presented to such corporation or person, all reasonable attorney fees not to exceed the sum of twenty-five dollars to be assessed and awarded by the court or jury trying the issue. (R. S. Sec. 3325; April 3, 1908, 99 v. 59; April 18, 1874, 71 v. 85, § 1.)

An abutting owner who has constructed a fence may, under this section, recover of the company the reasonable cost and expense thereof, together with the value of the use and occupation of his premises during the time such fence is being constructed or repaired, but he must do all he can to confine his loss to the minimum, and he can not recover for damages he might have avoided.

Millhouse v. Railway Co., 7 C. C. 466; 4 C. D. 682 (1893); aff'd, 55 O. S. 684.

See Railway v. Bosworth, 46 O. S. 81 (1888).

Section 8917. (Owner may repair fence.) When the fence is completed the company or person shall keep it in good repair, and if such company or person permits any part of the fence on the line of its road to get out of repair, or it is damaged or destroyed by fire or the elements, so that it will not turn stock, the owner of the land abutting on the railroad lands where the fence is out of repair may notify the agent of the company for receiving and shipping freight at the station on the road nearest to the place where it is defective, that a portion of the fence on the line of the road is out of repair, stating where, how, and the probable cost of repairing it. If such company or person fails for twenty-four hours thereafter, to repair or replace the fence so that it will turn stock, the owner of the land may furnish materials and repair or replace it, and present to such agent, for payment, a sworn itemized account of the expense thereof, including materials and labor, and if this be not paid within thirty days thereafter such land owner may recover from the owner or lessee of the road the reasonable expense of such repairs, and in addition thereto, attorney's fees as is provided for in the next preceding section. (R. S. Sec. 3326; April 3, 1908, 99 v. 58; April 18, 1874, 71 v. 85, § 1.)

Section 8918. (When preceding sections do not apply.) The provisions of the preceding sections relating to fences shall not apply to any case in which compensation for building a fence has been or may hereafter be taken into consideration, and estimated as a part of the consideration to be paid for the right of way, so far as the fence has been or may be settled or paid for; nor shall such sections affect in any manner, any contract or agreement between a railroad company, or person having the control and management of a railroad, and the proprietors or occupants of lands adjoining for the construction or maintenance of fences, and cattle-guards. (R. S. Sec. 3329; April 18, 1874, 71 v. 85, § 1; March 25, 1859, 56 v. 62, § 4.)

See note to § 8860.

Agreements by landowner to build or repair fences. Occasional repairs by a company to fences, which by contract it was the duty of the landowner to repair, do not release the landowner from his duty to maintain and repair.

Railway Co. v. Heiskell, 38 O. S. 666 (1883).

——. **When covenant runs with the land.** Where a railroad company makes a deed poll of land in fee along which its right of way is located, "subject to the condition that said grantee, his heirs and assigns, shall make and maintain good and sufficient fences on each side of the right of way of the railroad as now located and built, . . . which condition and obligation shall be perpetually binding on the owners of the land." the grantee, by accepting the deed, will be deemed to have entered into an express undertaking to perform the condition contained in the deed, and such undertaking will run with the land and become obligatory upon a subsequent owner by purchase from the grantee of the company.

Hickey v. Railway Co., 51 O. S. 40 (1894).

In such case the company will not have a right of action against the grantee for failure to repair, after he has ceased to be the owner of the land by conveying it to another.

Hickey v. Railway Co., 51 O. S. 40 (1894).

A written agreement by the grantor of the right of way to a railway company to fence it on each side through his lands will not affect the right of a subsequent purchaser to require the company to fence its road, where the purchase was made without actual or constructive notice of the existence of such agreement. Such agreement not being recorded, the mere use and occupation of the right of way by the company and its successors for the purpose of a railroad will not constitute constructive notice of the existence of such agreement.

Railway v. Bosworth, 46 O. S. 81 (1888).

Where it is stipulated in a deed poll that the grantee, his heirs and assigns, shall build and perpetually maintain a fence on the line between the land granted and other lands owned by the grantor, and the parties to such deed, at the time of its execution, contemplate the subdivision of the granted premises into building or town lots, and their subsequent sale, the burden of maintaining such fence will not attach to or run with lots which do not abut on the line of the proposed fence.

Walsh v. Barton, 24 O. S. 28 (1873).

Where the covenant runs with the land the grantee of the original owner, whose duty it was to fence, can not recover the cost of fencing.

Warner v. Baltimore, etc., R. R. Co., 31 O. S. 265 (1877).

Where a landowner by duly recorded deed conveyed a right of way and covenanted for himself, his heirs and assigns, to erect and maintain a fence on each side of such way, a lessee of his grantee would be so far bound by the covenant that he could not claim from the railroad company a higher degree of care to avoid injury to a horse than if the covenant had been kept.

Easter v. Little Miami R. R. Co., 14 O. S. 48 (1862).

An agreement requiring the railroad company to build a crossing within one year after completion of the road is not a covenant running with the land, specifically enforceable against a successor railroad company, several years thereafter, where the agreement contained no covenant requiring the successor to build or maintain the crossing.

Zens v. Railway, 14 N. P. n. s. 202; 23 L. D. 182 (C. P. 1912).

Where a contract for a right of way required the railroad company to construct a cattle pass, but the deed of the right of way was silent as to the cattle pass, which had been constructed before the execution of the deed, it was held that the purchaser of the railroad, on foreclosure, could not fill up the cattle pass, possession by the grantor constituting notice.

Lowe v. Railway, 12 C. C. 743; 4 C. D. 85 (1894).

——. As a defense to railroad company in action for injury to stock.

See note to § 8914.

Compensation for fencing included in award in appropriation proceeding. Where the defense, in an action against a railroad company for failing to maintain a fence, is that the expense of fencing was included in the compensation awarded in the appropriation proceeding, but the record of the appropriation proceeding is silent on the subject, no presumption arises that the expense of fencing was so included.

Railroad Co. v. Hoffhines, 46 O. S. 643 (1889).

Section 8919. (When company may build fence at landowner's expense.) If an owner of lands abutting on the line of lands of a company, who is legally bound to build or repair the fence dividing his lands from the lands of the company, neglects or refuses to build or repair such fence within the time in which he is bound to build or repair it, the company may build or repair such fence, and present an itemized account of the cost of labor and materials so expended, to the person thus bound, for payment. If it be not settled or paid within thirty days thereafter, the company may recover from such person the reasonable cost of such labor and materials. (R. S. Sec. 3330; April 18, 1874, 71 v. 85, § 1.)

Section 8920. (Forfeitures for not constructing and repairing fences.) A company or person having the control and management of a railroad, neglecting or refusing to construct fences, cattle-guards, or public crossings, or to keep them in repair, as hereinbefore prescribed, after thirty days' previous notice or request to construct them, made in writing by any person, shall forfeit and pay, for each and every day such company or person so refuses or neglects, a sum not exceeding fifty dollars per day, to be recovered in a civil action, in the name of the state, for the use of the county in which suit is brought. (R. S. Sec. 3331; March 25, 1859, 56 v. 62, § 5.)

A state court is without power to enforce payment of the penalty under this section against a railroad out of funds, in the hands of a receiver appointed by a federal court.

Rep. Atty. Gen. 1911-1912, p. 724.

Section 8921. (Right to use culvert, etc., for cattle-way.) An owner of land through which a railroad is constructed, and upon which there is a culvert, waterway, or opening through the embankment of the railroad, of sufficient height for such purpose, may use such culvert, waterway, or opening, as a stock or cattle-way, under the track of the road, so as to permit stock to pass and re-pass. But the landowner shall build and maintain all necessary fences on both sides of the opening, and not, by use, or otherwise, permit the foundations of structures about such opening to be injured or interfered with. (R. S. Sec. 3332; R. S. 1880.)

Contract for cattle pass.
Lowe v. W. & L. E. R. R. Co., 12 C. C. 743, 4 C. D. 85 (1894).
Contract for waterway; specific performance.
See Bell v. Dayton, etc., R. R. Co., 3 C. C. 31; 2 C. D. 19 (1887).

CHAPTER 4.

TRAINS AND EQUIPMENT.

Section 8922. (Passenger trains must stop at certain stations.) Each company shall cause three, each way, of its regular trains carrying passengers, if so many are run daily, Sundays excepted, to stop at a station, city or village, containing over three thousand inhabitants, for a time sufficient to receive and let off passengers. (R. S. Sec. 3320; April 13, 1889, 86 v. 291; April 13, 1867, 64 v. 142, § 26.)

This section is a valid exercise of the police power of the state, and does not violate the interstate commerce clause of the constitution of the United States, and is valid until congress passes an act inconsistent with it.

Lake Shore, etc., Ry. Co. v. State ex rel. Lawrence, 8 C. C. 220 (1894); s. c., 4 C. D. 406; s. c., 37 W. L. B. 196.

Lake Shore, etc., Ry. Co. v. State ex rel. Lawrence, 173 U. S. 285 (1899).

This section is not inconsistent with § 5258, Rev. Stat. U. S.

Lake Shore, etc., Ry. Co. v. State ex rel. Lawrence, 8 C. C. 220 (1894); s. c., 4 C. D. 406.

In the absence of statutory provision to the contrary, a railroad company may adopt a regulation that a certain train or trains of passenger cars running regularly on its road shall not stop at designated stations or places; and one traveling as a passenger on such road is bound to inquire whether the train upon which he takes passage stops at the station or place to which he is going. A passenger who is on a train not stopping at the station he desires may be put off if he is unwilling to pay the regular fare to a station at which the train does stop.

Pennsylvania Co. v. Wentz, 37 O. S. 333 (1881).

The power of a railway company to adopt and enforce regulations that certain trains shall not stop at all places is subject to legislative control, and by this section is taken away as to cities of three thousand inhabitants.

Pennsylvania Co. v. Wentz, 37 O. S. 333 (1881).

Where the laws make provision for the stopping of trains at certain places, all tickets and contracts must be construed with reference to such laws, and a contract recognizing the validity of a regulation disregarding such laws is invalid.

Pennsylvania Co. v. Wentz, 37 O. S. 333 (1881).

Where a person who has purchased a ticket to a certain station is, by the fault of the agent of the railroad company, induced to take a train which does not stop at such station, and the passenger is ejected from the train before reaching his destination, he may recover damages in tort.

Railway v. Reynolds, 55 O. S. 370.

Decisions of railroad commission as to establishment of stations and stopping trains.

Leedon v. Railway, 7 O. L. R. 474.

Good v. Railway, 8 O. L. R. 260.

See §§ 487 to 614.

Section 8923. (Forfeiture.) A company, agent or employe thereof, which violates or causes or permits to be violated, the next preceding section, shall forfeit not more than one hundred nor less than twenty-five dollars, to be recovered in an action in the name of the state, upon the complaint of any person, before a justice of the peace of the county ·in which the violation occurs, for the benefit of the general fund of the county. In all cases of forfeiture under the preceding section, the company whose agent or employe caused or permitted such violation shall be liable for the amount of the forfeiture, and the conductor in charge of such train may be held, prima facie, to have caused the violation. (R. S. Sec. 3320; April 13, 1889, 86 v. 291; April 13, 1867, 64 v. 142, § 26.)

Section 8924. (Posting time of arrival of trains.) Each company or person operating a railroad within this state shall place a blackboard, at least four feet in length and two feet in width, in a conspicuous place in each passenger depot of such company located at any station in the state at which there is a telegraph office. Such company or person must have written upon such board, at least ten minutes before the schedule time for the arrival of each passenger train stopping regularly upon such road at such station, the fact whether such train is on schedule time or not, and if late, how much. (R. S. Sec. 3321-1, May 8, 1886, 83 v. 118, § 1.)

The discrimination in this section between stations having telegraph offices and those without such offices does not render the section unconstitutional.

Pennsylvania Co. v. State, 42 Ind. 428 (1895),

Section 8925. (Forfeiture.) For each violation of any provision of the next preceding section, such company or person so neglecting or refusing to comply therewith, shall forfeit and pay the sum of ten dollars, to recovered in a civil action in the name of the state, one-half of which shall go to the party commencing proceedings, and the remainder be paid to the treasurer of the township, village or city in which such proceedings are had. (R. S. Sec. 3321-2; May 8, 1886, 83 v. 118, § 2.)

The action to recover a penalty under this section can only be brought before a justice of the peace or a mayor.
State ex rel. McClurg v. Railroad Co., 8 C. C. 604 (1894); s. c., 4 C. D. 372.

Section 8926. (Waiting rooms must be maintained.) Every person, firm or corporation operating a steam railroad wholly or in part within this state, shall provide a suitable waiting room for the use of the traveling public, at each station where a passenger train of the road is regularly scheduled to stop. Such rooms shall be so maintained and kept, as to be conducive to the comfort, and health of the patrons of the road. (R. S. Sec. 3321-3; April 16, 1900, 94 v. 231, § 1.)

See § 519.
Greenwich v. Railway, 6 O. L. R. 51; 53 Bull. 103 (Railroad Commission).

Section 8927. (Duty of railroad commission.) Upon the written complaint of ten or more citizens of this state being filed with the state railroad commission that any provision of the next preceding section is being violated, at such station, the commission shall forthwith make investigation thereof. If upon such investigation it be found that such violation exists, it shall issue an order to the person, firm or corporation guilty thereof, setting forth the nature of the improvement required and directing that it be completed within a time to be specified therein. (R. S. Sec. 3321-4; April 16, 1900, 94 v. 231, § 2.)

Section 8928. (Forfeiture.) Any person, firm or corporation failing to comply with an order of such commission, or any of the provisions of the two next preceding sections, upon conviction therefor before a court of common pleas of the county in which such violation occurs, shall forfeit and pay any sum not less than one hundred dollars. Such forfeiture shall be recovered in a civil action in the name of the state, for the benefit of the county in which the failure or violation occurs, and such action shall be brought by the prosecuting attorney of the county, at the instance of such commission, as provided in other cases for the recovery of forfeitures against railroad companies. (R. S. Sec. 3321-5; April 16, 1900, 94 v. 231, § 3.)

Section 8929. (Movable bridge between passenger cars required.) Every company conveying passengers shall provide the passenger cars in its trains with a flexible or movable bridge or apron, of the full width of the opening between the railings attached to the platforms of such cars, with sideboards or network of strap iron, large wire, or other suitable material, at each side of the bridge or apron, of at least equal height with the ordinary railings upon the platforms, or some other apparatus or arrangement equally efficient to enable passengers to pass from car to car with safety. (R. S. Sec. 3347; March 10, 1871, 68 v. 35, § 1.)

Section 8930. (Penalties for violation of preceding section.) A company which fails to comply with the provisions of the next preceding section shall be subject to a penalty of one hundred dollars for each and every day of such failure, to be recovered in a civil action, in the name of the state, and paid into the state treasury. (R. S. Sec. 3348; March 10, 1871, 68 v. 35, § 2.)

Section 8931. (Enforcement of two preceding sections.) The state railroad commission shall see that the requirements of the two next preceding sections are enforced. Such sections shall not apply in case of passenger car attached to a freight train. (R. S. Secs. 3349, 3350; March 10, 1871, 68 v. 35, §§ 3, 4.)

Section 8932. (Heating apparatus for cars.) When necessary to heat its cars for carrying passengers, mail, baggage or express matter, each railroad company shall do so by a stove or heater so constructed and protected as will most effectually guard passengers against danger from fire, in accidents by collision, or when cars are overturned or thrown from the track. No such company shall permit any other corporation or person to use cars carrying passengers, mail, baggage or express matter, over its road, unless their heating apparatus conforms to the above requirements. (R. S. Sec. 3351; May 4, 1869, 66 v. 94, § 1; R. S. 1880; April 14, 1880, 77 v. 202.)

Constitutionality.

See People v. New York, etc., R. R. Co., 55 Hun. (N. Y.), 409 (1890).

Section 8933. (Forfeiture under preceding section.) A railroad which fails to comply with the provisions of the next preceding section shall be liable to a forfeiture of not less than one hundred nor more than five hundred dollars, to be recovered in the name of the state, for the benefit of its common schools. Such action shall be prosecuted in any county, through which the road passes, by the prosecuting attorney thereof, at his own instance, or that of the state railroad commission, as provided by law in other cases for the recovery of penalties, and forfeitures against railroad companies, after due notice given by the railroad commission to the president or managing officer of such delinquent company, and its further neglect for thirty days to comply with the requirements of such section. The prosecutor shall receive twenty-five per cent of all penalties and costs so collected. (R. S. Sec. 3354; April 14, 1880, 77 v. 202; R. S. 1880; May 4, 1869, 66 v. 94, § 4.)

Section 8934. (Lighting of passenger cars.) No passenger car on a railroad shall be lighted by naptha or any fluid made in part from it, or wholly or in part from coal or petroleum, or other substance which will ignite at a temperature of less than three hundred degrees Fahrenheit. (R. S. Sec. 3353; May 7, 1877, 74 v. 207, § 2.)

Section 8935. (Forfeiture under preceding section.) The state railroad commission or its agent at any time may enter cars running on a railroad and take from any lamp therein samples of the oil or fluid there found for the purpose of testing it. When, on trial, such oil or fluid ignites at a lower temperature than that above specified, the company or person running the car from which it was taken, shall be liable to a forfeiture of not less than one hundred nor more than five hundred dollars, which such commission shall bring suit to recover, or cause to be brought for the benefit of the state common school fund, as provided in section eighty-nine hundred and thirty-three. (R. S. Secs. 3353, 3354; April 14, 1880, 77 v. 202; R. S. 1880; May 7, 1877, 74 v. 207, § 2; May 4, 1869, 66 v. 94, § 4.)

Section 8936. (Distance from station platform to step on passenger cars.) Companies and persons operating a railroad shall so regulate the distance between station floors, or platforms and the top of the lowest step on passenger cars that it will not exceed twelve inches. When the distance is more than one foot, it shall be changed, or safe steps provided for passengers within that limit. (R. S. Sec. 3354-1; April 16, 1892, 89 v. 347, § 1.)

Section 8937. (Forfeiture under preceding section; penalty.) A company failing to comply with the next preceding section shall forfeit and pay not less than fifty nor more than five hundred dollars for each and every delinquency. On the written complaint of any citizen, the prosecuting attorney of a county wherein such default occurs at once shall begin suit against the company guilty thereof, for the recovery of such penalty. If personal injury results from failure to comply with such section, in addition to such liability for damages, the person in charge of the operation and management of the road shall be deemed to be guilty of a misdemeanor and shall be fined not less than fifty dollars nor more than five hundred dollars. (R. S. Sec. 3354-1; April 16, 1892, 89 v. 347, § 1.)

Section 8938. (Equipment of passenger trains with fire extinguishers.) If one can be bought for fifteen dollars or less, every person, company or corporation operating a railroad shall put at least one portable chemical fire extinguisher on each passenger train. Each year, one such extinguisher shall be added to every such train until all coaches carrying passengers are supplied therewith. (R. S. Sec. 3354-2; April 27, 1896, 92 v. 396, § 1.)

Section 8939. (Extinguishers to be approved by railroad commission.) Such fire extinguishers shall be of a construction which renders them durable and efficient. Before they are put on trains, the make selected shall be approved for that purpose by the state railroad commission, whose duty it is to exercise its discretion in the premises, so as to invite the fullest competition among the different makers. (R. S. Sec. 3354-3; April 27, 1896, 92 v. 396, § 2.)

Section 8940. (Designation of cars, place and manner of installing extinguisher.) The state railroad commission shall designate which car of a passenger train wherein the first and each subsequent extinguisher is to be placed, until every coach in all such trains is fully supplied. Such commission shall determine where in the car an extinguisher shall be placed, how attached so as to make it easy of access; and also see that the provisions of the two next preceding sections are carried into effect. (R. S. Sec. 3354-4; April 27, 1896, 92 v. 396, § 3.)

Section 8941. (Failure to provide fire extinguishers; penalty.) A person, company or corporation operating a railroad, or railroads, in whole or in part in this state, violating any provision of the three next preceding sections failing to comply with any of the provisions of such sections, upon conviction in any court of competent jurisdiction shall be fined not less than twenty-five dollars nor more than one hundred dollars, and each day that such person, company or corporation runs its trains in violation of such provisions shall constitute a separate offense. (R. S. Sec. 3354-4; April 27, 1896, 92 v. 396, § 3.)

Section 8942. (Telegraph and telephone wires.) Every steam railroad company operating ten miles or more of railroad for the transportation of passengers and freight, shall erect and maintain in complete working order, for use along the line of its road a telegraph or telephone wire, with an office and proper means for communication by such wire at each of its principal stations. No such company operating a road without a telegraph or telephone wire along the line thereof, shall ask, or receive any compensation for the transportation of passengers or freight thereon. (R. S. Sec. 3354-5; April 7, 1898, 93 v. 88, § 1.)

Penalty for violation, see § 12547.

Section 8943. (Forfeiture under preceding section.) The charter of a steam railroad company which fails to comply with the conditions of the next preceding section shall be declared forfeited and shall be annulled, by a civil action brought for that purpose in the name of the state by the prosecuting attorney of any county in or through which its road is operated. (R. S. Sec. 3354-6; April 7, 1898, 93 v. 89, § 2.)

Section 8944. (Self-cleaning ash dump pans.) A person, firm or corporation owning, operating or controlling any railroad running through or within this state, shall in all cases where practicable, cause each locomotive to be equipped with a self cleaning ash dump pan, of modern and approved pattern and design; and all engines or locomotives built or constructed shall be so equipped. No engineer or fireman shall be compelled to go under any locomotive for the purpose of removing ashes from it, except in cases of emergency. This section shall not apply to a person, firm or corporation which does not require engineers or firemen to go under the engine for the purpose

of removing ashes therefrom, except in cases of emergency.
(R. S. Sec. 3365-27i; March 14, 1906, 98 v. 46, § 1.)

Penalty for noncompliance, see §§ 12558, 12559.

Section 8945. (Contributory negligence.) A person, firm
or corporation failing to comply with the provisions of the
next preceding section shall not be allowed to set up or
make the defense of contributory negligence, or assumption
of risk, in an action for personal injury to, or death of, an
engineer or fireman resulting from the failure of such
person, firm or corporation to comply therewith. (R. S.
Sec. 3365-27k; March 14, 1906, 98 v. 47, § 3.)

HEADLIGHTS.

Section 8945-1. (Headlight provisions.) Every railroad
corporation operating a railroad or a part of one in this
state, shall on or before the first day of January, 1911, equip
each of its locomotives, (except locomotives used exclusively
in yard service,) with a headlight of such construction, and
with sufficient candle power to render plainly visible at a
distance of not less than three hundred and fifty feet in
advance of such engine, whistling posts, land marks and
other warning signs, and it shall be unlawful, after such
date for any such railroad to use a locomotive, (except
locomotives used exclusively in yard service) upon any part
of its road lying within this state, that is not equipped with
a headlight of such construction and candle power as will
enable the engineer, to see whistling posts, land marks and
other warning signs at a distance of not less than three
hundred and fifty feet in advance of the engine; provided
that not less than thirty per cent. of all the locomotives
hereinbefore required to be provided with such headlights
shall be so equipped on or before September 1, 1910. (May
20, 1910, 101 v. 330.)

Section 8945-2. (Inspection by railroad commission.)
The state railroad commission shall from time to time inspect or cause to be inspected the headlights of all locomotives found in use on any railroad in this state. On discovering any defective headlight the commission shall report
the fact to the superintendent or other officer having charge
of the road on which it is found, and the railroad corporation receiving such notice, shall thereupon cause such defective headlight to be immediately repaired, and if so

ordered by the railroad commission shall put the locomotive containing such defective headlight out of service until repaired and put in good working order. (May 20, 1910, 101 v. 330.)

Section 8945-3. (Penalty.) Any railroad corporation using or permitting to be used on its line in this state a locomotive, in violation of any provision of this act shall be liable to a penalty of one hundred dollars for each violation, to be recovered in a suit or suits to be brought by the prosecuting attorney in the common pleas court of the county having jurisdiction in the locality where such violation occurred. Upon duly verified information being given him of such violation such prosecuting attorney shall bring such suits. The railroad commission shall give the proper prosecuting attorney information of any such violations as may come to its knowledge. (May 20, 1910, 101 v. 330.)

COUPLERS AND BRAKES.

Section 8946. (Automatic couplers and air-brakes.) Repealed March 18, 1913, 103 v. 117. (R. S. Sec. 3364-24; April 14, 1893, 90 v. 185, § 2.)

Section 8947. (Power brakes on engines.) Repealed March 18, 1913, 103 v. 117. (R. S. Sec. 3365-25; April 14, 1893, 90 v. 185, § 3.)

Section 8948. (Forfeiture.) Repealed March 18, 1913, 103 v. 117. (R. S. Sec. 3365-27; April 14, 1893, 90 v. 185, § 5.)

Section 8949. (Power brakes for locomotives and cars. Percentage required to be so equipped.) No common carrier, engaged in moving traffic on a railroad, between points within this state, shall use on its line a locomotive therefor not equipped with power driving wheel brakes and appliauces for operating the train-brake system, or, in such business, run a train unless at least eighty-five percentum of the cars therein shall have air brakes thereon so arranged that they can be operated and used from the engine by the engineer of the locomotive drawing such train, and unless all of such cars so equipped shall be associated together. (March 18, 1913, 103 v. 117; R. S. Secs. 3365-27a, 3363-23; March 19, 1906, 98 v. 75, § 1; April 23, 1904, 97 v. 615; February 27, 1900, 94 v. 25; April 25, 1898, 93 v. 286; April 14, 1893, 90 v. 184.)

Section 8950. (Automatic couplers.) No such common carrier shall haul, or permit to be hauled or used on its line, a locomotive, car, tender, or similar vehicle used in moving state traffic, not equipped with couplers coupling automatically by impact, and which can be uncoupled, without the necessity of men going between the ends of the cars. (R. S. Sec. 3365-27b; March 19, 1906, 98 v. 76, § 2.)

This section is constitutional. It requires the same kind of automatic couplers required by the act of congress, and is not a regulation of inter-state commerce.

> Railway Co. v. State, 82 O. S. 60 (1910); affirming, 11 C. C. n. s.
> 482; 21 C. D. 20; 7 N. P. n. s. 41; 19 L. D. 285.
> State v. Railway Co., 7 N. P. n. s. 571; 19 L. D. 867 (1908).

This act is not in conflict with the federal automatic coupler act.

> Railway Co. v. State, 82 O. S. 60 (1910).
> State v. Railway Co., 7 N. P. n. s. 571; 19 L. D. 867 (1908).

The additional penalty under § 8965 for keeping defective couplers in use does not render the act invalid.

> State v. Railway, 10 N. P. n. s. 585 (C. P. 1911).

The moving of dirt from one point on the line of railway to another, for the purpose of constructing a fill, or yard, is "traffic" within the meaning of this section.

> State v. Pgh., etc., Ry., 13 N. P. n. s. 145; 23 L. D. 135 (C. P. 1912).

This section makes it the positive duty of a railroad company to provide automatic couplers. The use of cars without such equipment is unlawful.

> McGarvey v. Railway Co., 83 O. S. 273 (1911).

It is the duty of a railroad company to use ordinary care to keep the couplers in working order.

> McGarvey v. Railway Co., 83 O. S. 273 (1911).

See § 8963.

The purpose of this act is to require the use of couplers which will obviate the necessity of employes going between the ends of the cars.

> McGarvey v. Railway Co., 83 O. S. 273, 289 (1911).

While this statute is in derogation of the common law, it should receive a reasonable construction.

> McGarvey v. Railway Co., 83 O. S. 273, 292 (1911).

Under this section the car and not the train is the unit.

> Railway v. State, 11 C. C. n. s. 482; 21 C. D. 20 (1909); affirming,
> 7 N. P. n. s. 541; 19 L. D. 285 (1908); aff'd, 82 O. S. 60 (1910).

Application of former statute to interurban railways.

> See C. & E. R. Co. v. Somers, 3 C. C. n. s. 638; 14 C. D. 67 (1902);
> s. c., 74 O. S. 477.

A crane or derrick, built upon car trucks, used to unload heavy materials, and equipped with a boiler and engine to furnish power to operate the crane and move the machine about on the tracks, is not a "locomotive car, tender or similar vehicle."

> Lake Shore, etc., Co. v. Benson, 85 O. S. 215 (1912).

Section 8951. (Secure grab-irons, sill steps, ladders and running⸀boards required on locomotives, tenders and cars.) No such common carrier shall haul, or permit to be hauled or used, on its line a locomotive, car, tender, or similar vehicle, used in moving state traffic, not provided with secure grab-irons or hand-holds on the sides and ends thereof. Every locomotive shall be provided with secure sill steps, on each side of the pilot thereof and each and every tender and car used in such business shall be provided also with secure sill steps on each end of each side thereof, and efficient hand-brakes; and all cars requiring ladders and running boards shall be equipped with secure ladders and running boards, and with secure hand-holds or grab-irons on their roofs at the top of such ladders; provided, that, in the loading and hauling of long commodities requiring more than one car, the hand-brakes may be omitted on all save one of the cars while they are thus combined for such purpose. (March 18, 1913, 103 v. 117; R. S. 3365-27c; March 19, 1906, 98 v. 76, § 3.)

Section 8952. (Drawbars.) No such common carrier shall use a locomotive, tender, car, or similar vehicle used in the movement of state traffic, that is not provided with drawbars of the standard height, to-wit: Standard gauge cars, thirty-four and one-half inches; narrow gauge cars, twenty-six inches, measured perpendicularly from the level of the tops of the rails to the centers of the drawbars. The maximum variation from such standard heights between drawbars of empty and loaded cars shall be three inches. (R. S. Sec. 3365-27d; March 19, 1906, 98 v.. 76, § 4.)

Section 8953. (Cars from connecting lines.) Such common carrier may refuse to receive from connecting lines or from any shipper a car not equipped in accordance with the four next preceding sections. (R. S. Sec. 3365-27e; March 19, 1906, 98 v. 76, § 5.)

See note to § 8950.

Section 8954. (Penalty for violations of this act. Public service commission shall give information to prosecuting attorneys. Cars or trains to which act does not apply.) Such common carrier using any locomotive engine, running any train, or hauling or permitting to be hauled or used on its line any tender or car in violation of any of the provisions of this act, shall be liable to a penalty of one hundred dollars for each any every such violation thereof, to be recovered in a suit or suits to be brought by the prosecuting attorney in the common pleas court of the county having jurisdiction in the locality where such violation occurred. Upon duly verified information being given him of such violation such prosecuting attorney shall bring such suits. The public service commission of Ohio shall give the proper prosecuting attorney information of any such violations as may come to its knowledge. Nothing contained in the above provisions to common carriers shall apply to locomotives, tenders, cars, or trains, used exclusively in the movement of logs, and when the height of the drawbars of such locomotives, tenders and cars does not exceed twenty-five inches, or to street cars, or to locomotives, tenders, cars, similar vehicles, or trains, while in actual use in interstate commerce. (March 18, 1913, 103 v. 118; R. S. Sec. 3365-27f; March 19, 1906, 98 v. 76, § 6.)

Proceedings under this act are civil in their nature and guilty knowledge and intention are not essential elements of the offense.
State v. Railway Co., 7 N. P. n. s. 571; 19 L. D. 867 (C. P. 1908).
The car is made the unit; and hauling an unequipped car is penalized by this section.
Railway Co. v. State, 11 C. C. n. s. 482; 21 C. D. 20 (1909); affirming, 7 N. P. n. s. 541; 19 L. D. 285 (1908); aff'd, 82 O. S. 60 (1910).
A carrier using a car in violation of this act is not immune from the penalty because the car, or the railroad, is commonly used in interstate traffic, or because it was in a train containing cars loaded with interstate traffic.
Railway Co. v. State, 82 O. S. 60 (1910); affirming, 11 C. C. n. s. 482; 21 C. D. 20; 7 N. P. n. s. 541; 19 L. D. 285.
A car is used in interstate commerce where it is received from another company by the defendant company and hauled from one of its yards to another for the purpose of being put in a train and forwarded to its destination in another state.
U. S. v. Railway Co., 143 Fed. 360 (C. C. 1905).
See McGarvey v. Railway Co., 83 O. S. 273, 291, 292 (1911).
A proceeding may be brought against a receiver, who was acting as such at the time of the neglect of duty.
State v. Harmon, 6 O. L. R. 649; 54 O. L. B. 70 (C. P. 1909).
This section provides penalties for failure to equip cars with automatic couplers. Section 8965 provides penalties for operating cars on which the couplers are out of repair or not used.
State v. Pittsburgh, etc., Railway, 13 N. P. n. s. 145 (C. P. 1912).

Section 8955.   (Contributory negligence.) Any employe of such common carrier, who is killed or injured by a locomotive, tender, car, similar vehicle, or train, in use contrary to the provisions of sections eighty-nine hundred and forty-nine to eighty-nine hundred and fifty-four both inclusive, shall not be deemed to have assumed the risk thereby occasioned, although continuing in the employment of such carrier after the unlawful use of such locomotive, tender, car, similar vehicle, or train had been brought to his knowledge, nor shall such employe be held to have contributed to his injury in a case where the carrier violated any provision of such sections, when such violation contributed to his death or injury. (R. S. Sec. 3365-27g; March 19, 1906, 98 v. 77, § 7.)

Where an employe is injured in attempting to couple cars, not equipped with automatic couplers, the railroad company is liable in damages. Under this section he is not deemed to have assumed the risk, nor to have contributed to the injury, where the violation of § 8950 by the railroad company contributed to the injury.

McGarvey v. Railway Co., 83 O. S. 273 (1911).

See Railroad Co. v. Somers, 3 C. C. n. s. 638; 14 C. D. 67 (1902); s. c., 74 O. S. 477.

Where automatic couplers have become defective, from long use or other cause, and it became necessary for an employe to go between the cars to make the coupling, and in so doing he was injured, he may recover.

McGarvey v. Railway Co., 83 O. S. 273 (1911).

See §§ 8963, 8965.

Section 8956. (Power of railroad commission concerning brakes.) The state railroad commission after full hearing and for good cause shown, may increase the minimum proportion of cars in a train required to be operated by power or train brakes. Failure to comply with the requirements of such commission, shall be subject to a like penalty as failure to comply with any requirement herein made of such carriers. (R. S. Sec. 3365-27a; March 19, 1906, 98 v. 75, § 1.)

Section 8956-1. (Construction of caboose cars. Exception. Extension of time by railroad commission.) It shall be unlawful, from and after the first day of September, 1910, for any common carrier operating a railroad, in whole or in part, within this state, or any manager or superintendent thereof, to require or permit the use, within this state upon such railroad, of any caboose car, or other car used for like purpose, which is not provided with a door in each end thereof and an outside platform across each end of such car; each platform shall not be less than twenty-four inches in width and shall be equipped with proper guard rails, and with grab irons and steps for the safety of persons getting on and off said car. Said steps shall be equipped with a suitable rod, board or other guard at each end and at the back thereof, properly designed to prevent slipping from such step. But nothing herein provided shall affect the right of any railroad to operate a caboose car now constructed or in use having the platforms each not less than twenty inches in width and equipped with the other appliances as herein provided. The railroad commission is hereby authorized to grant to any common carrier, upon full hearing and for good cause shown, a reasonable extension of time in which to comply with the provisions of this act; provided that in no case shall such extension or extensions in the aggregate exceed the period of one year from the time herein limited for compliance with this act. (April 25, 1910, 101 v. 133.)

Section 8956-2.   (Penalty.) Any person or common carrier violating any of the provisions of section 8956-1 shall be deemed guilty of a misdemeanor and upon conviction thereof shall be fined not less than one hundred dollars nor more than five hundred dollars for each offense. (April 25, 1910, 101 v. 133.)

Section 8956-3.   (Prescribing construction and equipment of caboose cars.) Except as otherwise provided in this act, it shall be unlawful, from and after the first day of July, 1919, for any common carrier operating a railroad, in whole or in part, within this state, or any manager or division superintendent thereof to require or permit the use, upon such railroad, within this state, of any caboose car or other car used for like purpose, unless such caboose or other car shall be at least twenty-four feet in length, exclusive of platforms, and equipped with two four-wheel trucks suitable closets and cupola. (May 5, 1913, 103 v. 719, § 1.)

Section 8956-4.   (Repaired caboose cars shall conform to provisions of this act.) Whenever any such caboose car now in use upon any such railroad, shall, after this act goes into effect, be brought into any of the shops of such railroad for general repairs, it shall be unlawful to again put the same into the service of such railroad, within this state, unless it be equipped as provided in section one of this act. (May 5, 1913, 103 v. 720, § 2.)

Section 8956-5.   (Percentage of cars to be so equipped each year.) Such common carrier shall, each year, from and after the first day of July, 1914, equip, in accordance with the provisions of this act, at least fifteen per cent. of the caboose cars in use on its railroad; but the public service commission is hereby authorized to grant to any common carrier, upon full hearing and for good cause shown, a reasonable extention of time in which to comply with the provisions of this act; provided that in no case shall such extension in the aggregate exceed the period of one year from the time herein limited for compliance with this act. (May 5, 1913, 103 v. 720, § 3.)

Section 8956-6.   (Penalty.) Any person or common carrier violating any of the provisions of this act shall be deemed guilty of a misdemeanor and upon conviction thereof shall be fined not less than one hundred dollars nor more than five hundred dollars for each offense. (May 5, 1913, 103 v. 720, § 4.)

INSPECTION.

Section 8957. (Inspector of automatic couplers and brakes, etc., on locomotives and cars.) An inspector of automatic couplers, air brakes, automatic power brakes, and other safety appliances prescribed by law, on railroad locomotives, tenders, cars and similar vehicles, shall be appointed by the public service commission of Ohio. He shall hold office for two years, unless sooner removed for cause, and until his successor is appointed and qualified. When a vacancy occurs in the office such commission immediately shall fill it by appointment. (April 26, 1913, 103 v. 192, in effect July 25, 1913; R. S. Sec. 3365-23b; May 12, 1902, 95 v. 658.)

Section 8958. (Qualifications.) No person shall be eligible to the office who is an officer or employe of a railroad company or owns or is interested, directly or indirectly, in the stocks or bonds of any railroad company, or who has not had at least seven years' experience in the transportation department on some line of railroad of more than thirty miles in length, operated in this state. (R. S. Sec. 3365-23b; May 12, 1902, 95 v. 658.)

Section 8959. (Bond and oath.) Before entering on his duties, the inspector shall give bond to the state in the sum of three thousand dollars, with two or more sureties, or a bond and security company, acceptable to the state railroad commission, conditioned for the faithful performance of his duties. He also shall take the usual oath of office, which oath and bond with the approval of the commission endorsed thereon, shall be deposited with the secretary of state. (R. S. Sec. 3365-23c; May 12, 1902, 95 v. 659.)

Section 8960. (Salary and expenses.) Such inspector shall receive a salary of fifteen hundred dollars per year, and all necessary expenses, not exceeding one thousand dollars in any one year, which shall be paid in the manner now provided by law for the salary and expenses of the railroad commission. In addition to the fifteen thousand dollars now authorized for such state railroad commission, there shall be assessed yearly in the manner and upon the corporations as the law provides, the sum of two thousand, five hundred dollars to pay the salary and expenses herein provided for. (R. S. Sec. 3365-23d; May 12, 1902, 95 v. 659.)

Section 8961. (Office under supervision of railroad commission.) Such inspector shall have his office in the office of the railroad commission, and shall be under its supervision. In the performance of his duties he also shall have the right of passing upon all the railroads within the state, and upon all trains, and any part thereof free of charge. (R. S. Sec. 3365-23d; May 12, 1902, 95 v. 659.)

Section 8962. (Duties of inspector.) Such inspector shall inspect the couplers, air brakes, automatic power brakes, hand brakes, ladders, running boards, sill-steps and hand-holds or grab-irons on all locomotives, tenders, cars and similar vehicles found on any railroad in Ohio, and make weekly reports of his inspections to the public service commission, reporting all locomotives, tenders, cars and similar vehicles, giving number thereof, points of billing and final destination, road on which they are found, and the road owning them, if known, which are found to have a defective appliance, describing the defect. On discovering such defective appliance he shall also immediately report it to the superintendent of the road on which it is found, and to the agent thereof at the nearest station, describing the defect. If such defective appliance be found on any locomotive, tender, car or similar vehicle which is then being used in interstate commerce, he shall under oath lodge with the United States district attorney of the district wherein such violation shall have been committed, all information of such violation and mail a like report to the interstate commerce commission, filing a copy thereof with the public service commission of Ohio. When any one of such appliances is lacking on any locomotive, tender, car or similar vehicle, this shall be deemed to be a defective appliance. (April 24, 1913, 103 v. 193; R. S. Sec. 3365-23e; May 12, 1902, 95 v. 659.)

Section 8963. (Liability of company for failure to make repairs.) A railroad whose superintendent or station agent receives such notice of such defective appliance shall cause it to be immediately repaired. The company shall be liable in damages to any person injured, for any injury received by reason of such defective appliance. Nothing in this chapter contained shall diminish the existing legal liability of railroads for injury to persons or property. (April 24,

1913, 103 v. 193; R. S. Sec. 3365-23f; May 12, 1902, 95 v. 660.)

See McGarvey v. Railway Co., 83 O. S. 273 (1911).
State v. Railway, 10 N. P. n. s. 585 (C. P. 1911).

Section 8964. (Inspector may condemn locomotive, tender or car.) On the discovery of such defective appliance on any locomotive, tender, car or similar vehicle, such inspector may condemn such locomotive, tender, car or similar vehicle, and order it out of service until repaired and put in good working order. On receiving an order from the inspector condemning any locomotive, tender, car or similar vehicle, the employes of the road in charge thereof shall put it out of service at the first freight division terminal. (April 24, 1913, 103 v. 193; R. S. Sec. 3365-23g; May 12, 1902, 95 v. 660.)

Section 8965. (Daily forfeiture for use of defective appliance.) A railroad company which fails to comply with such order, shall forfeit and pay to the state, in addition to the penalties prescribed in section 8954 of the General Code, the sum of twenty-five dollars for each day such defective appliance is kept in use, contrary thereto, to be collected in a civil suit in any county in the state where service of process can be had on such road. On request from the inspector, the attorney general or the prosecuting attorney of any county in which the company has a line of railroad shall immediately commence and prosecute, without unnecessary delay, proceedings to collect such sum. The sum so collected less ten per cent. fees for collecting it, due such officer, shall be paid to the general revenue fund of the state. (April 24, 1913, 103 v. 193; R. S. Sec. 3365-23h; May 12, 1902, 95 v. 660.)

Penalty against officers, see § 12562.
The additional penalty imposed, for keeping defective cars in use, does not render the act invalid.
State v. Railway, 10 N. P. n. s. 585 (C. P. 1911).
It is immaterial how short the distance a defectively equipped car was moved; but if the defect was of a temporary nature, easily repairable, and was at once repaired, the use was not unlawful.
State v. Harmon, 6 O. L. R. 649; 54 O. L. B. 70 (C. P. 1909).
This section provides penalties for operating cars on which the couplers are out of repair or not used. Section 8954 provides penalties for operating cars which are not equipped with couplers.
State v. Railway Co., 13 N. P. n. s. 145; 23 L. D. 135 (C. P. 1912).

BOILERS.

Section 8965-1. (Inspection.) Every person, firm or corporation operating a steam railroad wholly or in part within this state shall require thorough inspection to be made of the boilers and appurtenances of all locomotives which shall be used by such person, firm or corporation on such railroad within this state. (May 20, 1910, 101 v. 328.)

By the enactment of the federal boiler inspection act (February 27, 1911, 36 U. S. Stat., pt. 1, p. 913) the Ohio act is superseded and is invalid in so far as it applies to a railroad company, the locomotives of which are used in transportation from Kentucky and other states into Cincinnati, and from Cincinnati to such other states, all of said locomotives being used exclusively in interstate commerce.

L. & N. R. Co. v. Hughes, 201 Fed. 727 (D. C. 1912).

See Rep. Atty. Gen. 1911-1912, p. 719.

Section 8965-2.   (Boiler requirements specified.) All such boilers so used shall comply with the following requirements: The boilers and appurtenances shall be well made of good and suitable material; the openings for the passage of water and steam respectively, and all pipes and tubes exposed to heat, shall be of proper dimensions and free from obstructions; the spaces between and around the flues shall be sufficient; the flues, boiler, furnace, safety valves, fusible plugs, low water indicators, feed water apparatus, gauge cocks, steam gauges, and means of removing mud and sediment from the boiler, and all other machinery and appurtenances thereof shall be of such construction, shape, condition, arrangement and material that the same may be safely employed in the active service of such railroad without peril to life or limb. (May 20, 1910, 101 v. 328.)

Section 8965-3.   (Duty of inspector.) Each inspector shall satisfy himself by thorough examination that said requirements have been fully complied with. No boiler, pipe, nor any connections therewith shall be approved which is made in whole or in part of bad material, or is unsafe in its form, or dangerous from defects, workmanship, age, use or other cause. (May 20, 1910, 101 v. 328.)

Section 8965-4.   (Quarterly inspection.) Said inspections shall be made at least every three months under the direction of such person, firm or corporation operating such railroad, by persons of suitable qualifications and attainments to perform the services required of inspectors of boilers and who are able to form a reliable opinion of the strength, form, workmanship and suitableness of boilers to be employed without hazard of life from imperfections in the material, workmanship or arrangement of any part of such boiler and appurtenances. (May 20, 1910, 101 v. 329.)

Section 8965-5. (Rules and regulations.) The state railroad commission shall have power to formulate rules and regulations for the uniform inspection and testing of boilers and their appurtenances, and for the qualifications and competency of inspectors of boilers under the provisions of this act. Copies of such rules and regulations shall be mailed to every person, firm or corporation operating a railroad by steam in this state. If it shall be ascertained by such inspection and test, or otherwise, that any locomotive boiler is unsafe for use, the same shall not again be used until it shall be repaired and made safe so as to comply with the requirements of this act. (May 20, 1910, 101 v. 329.)

Section 8965-6. (Appointment of inspector; salary, etc.) The railroad commission shall appoint a competent person as inspector of locomotive boilers, and such inspector shall, under the direction of the commission, have charge of the inspection of boilers and their appurtennances, of locomotives used in the operation of steam railroads within this state and shall perform such other duties in connection therewith as the commission shall direct. Said inspector shall be employed at a fixed compensation not exceeding one hundred and eighty dollars per month. (May 20, 1910, 101 v. 329.)

Section 8965-7. (Certificate of inspector.) Each inspector, if he shall approve of the boiler and the appurtenances throughout, shall make and subscribe his name to a written or printed certificate which shall contain the number of each boiler inspected, the date of its inspection, the condition of the boiler and appurtenances, and such details as may be required by the forms and regulations which shall be prescribed by the railroad commission. Every such certificate shall be verified by the oath of the inspector, and he shall cause said certificate to be filed in the office of the railroad commission within ten days after each inspection shall be made, and also a copy thereof with the officer or employee of such railroad having immediate charge of the operation of such locomotive boiler, which copy shall be placed by such officer or employee in a conspicuous place in the cab connected with the locomotive boiler inspected, and there kept framed under glass. (May 20, 1910, 101 v. 329.)

Section 8965-8. (Penalties.) Every person, firm or corporation operating such railroad and violating any of the provisions of this act shall be liable to a penalty to be paid to the general revenue fund of the state, of one hundred dollars ($100.00) for each offense, and the further penalty of one hundred dollars ($100.00) for each day it or they shall omit or neglect to comply with said provisions; and the making or filing of a false certificate shall be a misdemeanor, and every inspector who wilfully certifies falsely touching any steam boiler or appurtenances thereto belonging, or any matter or thing contained or required to be contained in any certificate signed and sworn to by him, shall be deemed guilty of a misdemeanor, and upon conviction thereof shall be fined in any sum not less than two hundred dollars ($200.00) nor more than five hundred dollars ($500.00.) (May 20, 1910, 101 v. 329.)

Section 8965-9. It shall be the duty of the state railroad commission to enforce the provisions of this act. (May 20, 1910, 101 v. 330.)

Section 8965-10. This act shall take effect and be in force on and after September 1, 1910. (May 20, 1910, 101 v. 330.)

FIRES.

Section 8966. (Spark arresters.) Except in the months of December, January and February, any company or person operating a railroad or a part of one, shall place on every locomotive engine used therefor, or in construction or repairing the road, such device or contrivance as most effectually will guard against the escape of fire or sparks that otherwise would be thrown out by such engines, and keep the device in good repair. (R. S. Sec. 3365-1; April 9, 1885, 82 v. 118, § 1.)

Character of spark arrester required. This section requires a railroad company to use a spark arrester which will most effectually guard against the emission of sparks.
  Railway Co. v. Wahlers, 1 C. C. n. s. 139; 14 C. D. 310 (1902).
  It is sufficient compliance that the spark arrester used is the best in general use.
  Railroad Co. v. Kelly, 10 C. C. 322; 6 C. D. 555 (1895); aff'd, 56 S. 785.
  See Railroad Co. v. Fredenbur, 3 C. C. 23; 2 C. D. 15 (1887).

To show that a certain netting or arrester is in general use in the United States, the company can not show its use on particular roads.

Lake Side, etc., R. R. Co. v. Kelly, 10 C. C. 322; 6 C. D. 555 (1895); aff'd, 56 O. S. 785.

Cleveland, etc., R. Co. v. Fredenbur, 3 C. C. 23; 2 C. D. 15 (1887).

Evidence.

——. **Expert testimony.** Where witnesses for the railroad company testified that the engine was equipped with the most approved kind of spark arresting device, and that it was in good condition, the plaintiff may show, in rebuttal, that on the same day other fires were caused by sparks from the same engine within two miles of plaintiff's property, and by experts that such fact would indicate that the spark arrester was not in good condition.

Toledo, etc., R. v. Star Flouring Mills, 146 Fed. 953; 15 O. F. D. 321 (C. C. A. 1906).

It is not competent to ask a witness to examine the spark arrester complained of and to state whether it was the most efficient in preventing fires. The proper way is to get all the knowledge the expert has upon the different kinds of netting used, the different classes of spark arresters, their efficiency, etc., and to submit to the jury the question as to the efficiency of the arresters.

Cleveland, etc., Ry. Co. v. McKelvey, 12 C. C. 426 (1895); 5 C. D. 561.

The testimony of expert witnesses is competent to show the different kinds of netting that were used by different roads, to enable the jury to say whether the appliance used was proper. An expert may testify as to defects in the mode of attaching a spark arrester, and as to the effect of sparks and their vitality, and the distance they will carry and still start a fire.

Cleveland, etc., Ry. Co. v. McKelvey, 12 C. C. 426 (1895); 5 C. D. 561.

Expert testimony is admissible to prove that a properly constructed locomotive will not throw sparks a long distance, although the fact that the witness has not been in the employ of a railroad for a long time may affect the weight of his testimony.

Martz v. Cincinnati, etc., R. R. Co., 12 C. C. 144 (1896); 5 C. D. 561.

——. **Fires set by other engines.** Where it is alleged that the appliances were defective and the management negligent, it is only competent to show that other engines of the company emitted sparks and coal on other occasions, when such evidence is limited and confined to a time and place not remote from the fire, and not until evidence has first been given tending to exclude the probability that the fire was communicated by any other means.

Pennsylvania Co. v. Rossman, 13 C. C. 111; 7 C. D. 119 (1896).

——. **Specimens of wire.** Specimens of wire netting can not be used as showing the netting used by the defendant, unless it is shown when it was used.

Cleveland, etc., Ry. Co. v. McKelvey, 12 C. C. 426; 5 C. D. 561 (1895).

Charge to jury. The following request and charge is proper, where the fire occurred in one of the months excepted: "The laws of Ohio expressly permit a railroad company to operate its engines during the months of December, January and February, without using a spark arresting device, and if, therefore, you find that the defendant's engine was, at the time of the fire, equipped with and using such a device, that was merely a voluntary precaution against fire taken by the defendant, and which the law did not require of it. The jury are, therefore, not concerned with the questions whether the spark arrester was or was not of the best pattern, or was or was not in repair except as the fact that it was of the

best pattern and was in good repair, if proved, may tend to show that
the engine so equipped did not and could not have started the fire."
   Railroad Co. v. Burr, 82 O. S. 129, 135, 136 (1910).
   See Railway Co. v. Kelly, 10 C. C. 322; 6 C. D. 555 (1895) ; aff'd, 56
      O. S. 785.

   **Negligence.   Decisions prior to amendment of § 8970 and repeal of
§ 8971.** A failure to comply with this section would be regarded as neg-
ligence per se.
   Continental Trust Co. v. Toledo, etc., R. Co., 89 Fed. 637; 40 W. L.
      B. 379 (1898).
   The exception in this section relative to the months of December to
February, does not relieve a company from the ordinary legal duty to
observe proper care to avoid injuring the property of others by fire.
   Toledo, etc., Ry. Co. v. Wickenden, 11 C. C. 378 (1896) ; 5 C. D. 171.
   The inspection of the locomotive and appliances before sending it
upon the road, and finding it then in good order, is not sufficient to avoid
liability; they must be kept in good order on the line of road.
   Cleveland, etc., R. R. Co. v. Fredenbur, 3 C. C. 23; 2 C. D. 15 (1887).
   The fact that a high wind caused a greater draft and fire to escape
is no defense unless it appears that a locomotive properly constructed with
suitable appliances necessarily emits fire during a high wind.
   Cleveland, etc., R. R. Co. v. Fredenbur, 3 C. C. 23 (1887) ; 2 C. D. 15;
      s. c., 23 W. L. B. 434.
   In an action against a railroad company for damages by fire emitted
from the smokestack, when it is shown by the evidence that a locomotive
properly constructed and equipped with the best appliances in general
use, will not emit sparks, and that the fire was caused by sparks from the
company's locomotive, the burden of proof is upon the company to prove
that its locomotive and appliances were properly constructed and in good
order.
   Cleveland, etc., R. Co. v. Fredenbur, 3 C. C. 23 (1887) ; 2 C. D. 15.
   An action under any of these sections involves title to real estate;
and a justice of the peace has no jurisdiction.
   Erie R. R. Co. v. Furry, 18 C. C. 880 (1894) ; s. c., 31 W. L. B. 282.

   Section 8967.   (Forfeiture under preceding section.) A
railroad company, corporation or person violating the provisions of the next preceding section, upon conviction thereof
in a court of competent jurisdiction, shall forfeit and pay
for each violation any sum not exceeding one hundred dollars.   In addition thereto the court of common pleas, in a
county through which such railroads are constructed and
operated, may enjoin such companies, corporations or persons from using on such railroads, a locomotive not provided with the device hereinbefore required.   (R. S. Sec.
3365-2; April 9, 1885, 82 v. 118, § 2.)

   **Section 8968.   (Company must keep right of way free
from combustible material.)** Every company, or person in
charge of a railroad as manager or receiver, shall keep the
right of way clear from weeds, high grass, and decayed
timber, which from nature or condition are combustible, and
liable to take or communicate fire from passing locomotives

to abutting or adjacent property. Such company shall be
liable for all damages sustained by the owner or occupant
of such property from carelessness or neglect to keep its
right of way clear of such combustible material. (R. S.
Sec. 3365-3; March 24, 1890, 87 v. 99, § 1.)

A grain elevator is not combustible material.
Martz v. Railroad Co., 12 C. C. 144; 5 C. D. 451 (1896).
Whether the fire was negligently allowed to escape or not is immaterial.
Indiana, etc., Ry. Co. v. Overman, 110 Ind. 538 (1886).
Louisville, etc., Ry. Co. v. Nitche, 126 Ind. 229 (1890).
Galveston, etc., R. R. Co. v. Polk, 28 S. W. (Tex.) 353 (1894).
See Pittsburg, etc., Ry. Co. v. Hixon, 79 Ind. 111 (1881).
The entire width of the right of way must be cleared.
Blue v. Railroad Co., 23 S. E. 275 (N. C. 1895).

Section 8969. (When abutting owner may remove combustible material.) In case of failure to comply with the
above requirements, a person owning or controlling property
abutting on or adjacent to a railroad right of way, after
twenty days' notice in writing, the default still continuing,
may cause all combustible material to be removed from the
right of way along or by such property. Upon presentation
of a reasonable account therefor to the agent at the nearest
station of such company or receiver, if it or he refuses to
pay the amount asked, within thirty days, it may be recovered before any court having jurisdiction thereof. (R. S.
Sec. 3365-4; March 24, 1890, 87 v. 99, § 2.)

**Section 8970. (Liability of railroad company for loss or
damage by fire.)** Every company, or receiver of such company, operating a railroad or a part of one shall be liable
for all loss or damage by fires originating upon the land
belonging to it caused by operating such road. Such company, or receiver of such company, further shall be liable
for all loss or damage by fires originating on lands adjacent
to its land, caused in whole or part by sparks from an engine
passing over such railroad, and the exercise by such company, or receiver of such company, of due care in equipping
and operating such engine shall not exempt such company,
or receiver of such company, from such liability, which
may be recovered before any court of competent jurisdiction
within the county in which the lands on which such loss or
damage occurs are situated. The existence of fires upon
the railroad company's lands is prima facie evidence that
they are caused by operating such railroad. Provided that
nothing herein shall invalidate or prohibit contracts of such
company or receiver now existing or hereafter made, by
which such company or receiver is indemnified against such

loss or damage by fire, or liability therefor released. (May 5, 1911, 102 v. 108; R. S. Sec. 3365-5; April 26, 1894, 91 v. 187.)

Act: history and occasion for.
 Insurance Co. v. Railway, 74 O. S. 30, 33, 35 (1906).
 Before the amendment of 1911 (102 v. 108) this section and § 8972 were held constitutional.
 Baltimore, etc., Ry. Co. v. Kreager, 61 O. S. 312 (1899).
 Martz v. Railroad Co., 12 C. C. 144; 5 C. D. 451 (1896).

Liability in absence of statute. In the absence of a statute, the decisions are generally to the effect that a railroad company is not liable for loss caused by fire, unless it was occasioned by its negligence.
 Insurance Co. v. Railway, 74 O. S. 30, 33 to 35 (1906).
 And negligence could not be inferred from the mere fact that injury to the adjacent property was caused by sparks from the locomotive.
 Ruffner v. Railroad Co., 34 O. S. 96 (1877).
 Railroad Co. v. Fredenbur, 3 C. C. 23; 2 C. D. 15 (1888).

Liability under § 8970. This section imposes upon every railroad company operating a railroad in this state an absolute liability for loss or damage by fire, originating on its land, caused by operating the road and the fact that the fire originated on the land of the company is made prima facie evidence that it was caused by operating the road. In an action for loss or damage, it is not necessary to allege or prove negligence on the part of the company; nor is the absence of such negligence a defense.
 Baltimore, etc., Ry. Co. v. Kreager, 61 O. S. 312 (1899).
 Lake Erie, etc., R. Co. v. Falk, 62 O. S. 297 (1900).
 See Martz v. Railroad Co., 12 C. C. 144; 5 C. D. 451 (1896).
 This section applies to railroad companies in existence and which obtained their right of way prior to its enactment as well as to companies organized since.
 Railway Co. v. Kreager, 61 O. S. 312 (1899).
 In an action brought by the owner of property destroyed by fire against a railroad company, an insurance company, having made payment to the owner of a portion of the loss, may intervene for the purpose of being subrogated to the extent of its payment. The amount recovered from the railroad company should be adjudged to the owner and insurer according to the interest of each.
 Railroad Co. v. Falk, 62 O. S. 297 (1900).
 A prima facie case is made out under this statute when evidence is offered tending to prove the facts set out in the statute, the fire, the loss of property, and that the fire was caused by sparks coming from an engine belonging to the defendant.
 Toledo, etc., Ry. Co. v. Wales, 11 C. C. 371; 5 C. D. 168 (1896).

Contract exempting railroad company from liability. A stipulation in a lease made by a railroad company that it shall not be liable to the lessee for damages to property on the demised premises, caused by fire accidently or negligently communicated in the operation of the road, is valid.
 Insurance Co. v. Railway, 74 O. S. 30 (1906).
 Such lessee and his insurers can not recover for loss by fire, when the fire was communicated to a part of the building located on the demised premises.
 Insurance Co. v. Railway, 74 O. S. 30 (1906).

Measure of damages. The measure of damages is the actual value of the property, and not what it would have cost to reconstruct or replace the same, with deductions for wear and tear. Under such a rule the damages might far exceed the actual value of the property and the actual loss to the plaintiffs. Where property totally destroyed has a market value, that market value is the measure of compensation for the loss.

Cleveland, etc., Ry. Co. v. McKelvey, 12 C. C. 426; 5 C. D. 561 (1895).

When the property destroyed under circumstances which make the company liable therefor is insured, the right of the owner as against the railroad company and the insurer is limited to indemnity for his loss.

Lake Erie, etc., R. R. Co. v. Falk, 62 O. S. 297 (1900).

Pleading. A petition is sufficient under this section which avers that fire and sparks were emitted by a locomotive of defendant, causing fire on the railroad right of way and plaintiff's land, the plaintiff being ignorant as to whether the fire started on his land or that of the railway company.

Railway Co. v. Anderson, 7 C. C. n. s. 17; 17 C. D. 577 (1904).

Proof.

———. **As to ownership of tracks.** It is not necessary to show ownership of the tracks. If the proof shows the defendant was the owner, and operated the engine that caused the fire, it is sufficient to make a case.

Toledo, etc., Ry. Co. v. Wales, 11 C. C. 371 (1896).

———. **As to cause of fire.** Where the proof shows that a locomotive passed a short time before the fire; that the wind was blowing in the direction of the plaintiff's land with sufficient force to carry sparks thereon, and that there were no other fires in the neighborhood at the time, the jury is warranted in finding that the fire originated from sparks from such locomotive.

Railway Co. v. Anderson, 7 C. C. n. s. 17; 17 C. D. 577 (1904).

It is competent to show that the fire started in the grass along the track soon after the passage of the engine, and that about that time and immediately after the passage of the locomotive other fires occurred in the neighborhood.

Lake Side, etc., R. R. Co. v. Kelly, 10 C. C. 322; 6 C. D. 555 (1885);
    aff'd, 56 O. S. 785.

Where the particular locomotive that is claimed to have set the fire is not traceable, it may be shown that the railway company was reckless in this particular, and it would be competent to show that every one of the company's locomotives emitted fire.

Lake Shore, etc., R. R. Co. v. Kelly, 10 C. C. 322; 6 C. D. 555 (1895);
    aff'd, 56 O. S. 785.

Martz v. Cincinnati, etc., R. R. Co., 12 C. C. 144; 5 C. D. 451 (1896).

If it is clearly established that cinders picked up and produced in evidence came from the engine, it would be competent to admit them in evidence.

Cleveland, etc., Ry. Co. v. McKelvey, 12 C. C. 426; 5 C. D. 561 (1895).

In an action under this section, it is necessary to go further than to show a mere possibility or conjecture that the fire was communicated by an engine.

Minneapolis, etc., Co. v. Great Northern Ry. Co., 86 N. W. 750 (1901) (Minn.).

A party may rest his case when he has made out a prima facie case under this statute, but he can not withhold evidence confirmatory of such prima facie case and offer it in rebuttal, unless that evidence would also actually be rebutting evidence.

Toledo, etc., Ry. Co. v. Wales, 11 C. C. 371 (1896); 5 C. D. 168.

Jurisdiction of justice of peace. A justice of the peace has no juris-

diction for the reason that the action involves the title or possession to
real estate, and not an action of trespass.

> Furry v. Erie R. R. Co., 31 W. L. B. 282 (1894); s. c., 18 C. C. 880.

Section 8971 (Repealed May 5, 1911, 102 v. 109.)

The communication of fire from a locomotive was by this section
made prima facie evidence of negligence.

> B. & O. Ry. v. Kreager, 61 O. S. 312 (1899).
> Railway Co. v. Anderson, 7 C. C. n. s. 17; 17 C. D. 577 (1904).
> Railway Co. v. Wahlers, 1 C. C. n. s. 139; 14 C. D. 310 (1902).
> Toledo, etc., R. Co. v. Star Flouring Mills, 146 Fed. 953 (C. C. A. 1906); 15 O. F. D. 321.
> Continental Trust Co. v. Railroad Co., 89 Fed. 637 (1898).

Section 8972.   (What not considered negligence.) In
no case shall it be considered as negligence on the part of
the owner or occupant of property so injured by fire, that
he used it, or permitted it to be used and remain as if no
railroad passed through or near such property. But this
rule shall not apply in cases of injury by fire to personalty
which at the time was on the property occupied by such
road. (R. S. Sec. 3365-6; April 26, 1894, 91 v. 188, § 2.)

Section 8973.   (Costs in appeal and attorney fee.) If
either party appeals from the judgment of a court in which
an action under the three next preceding sections is begun,
or carries the case up on error, the party in whose favor
judgment finally is rendered shall· have included in his bill
no case shall it be considered as negligence on the part of
of costs against the adverse party, an attorney fee of fifty
dollars, if it is not carried beyond the circuit court. But
if carried to the supreme court of Ohio an attorney fee of
one hundred dollars shall be included in his bill of costs.
(R. S. Sec. 3365-7; April 26, 1894, 91 v. 188, § 3.)

This section is unconstitutional.

> Rowland v. Railroad Co., 13 C. C. n. s. 221; 22 C. D. 93 (1910).
> See Coal Co. v. Rosser, 53 O. S. 12.

But it is severable from the other sections of the original act and
does not affect their validity.

> Baltimore, etc., R. Co. v. Kreager, 61 O. S. 312 (1899).

Section 8974.   (Application of sections.) Sections eighty-
nine hundred and seventy-one and eighty-nine hundred and
seventy-two shall apply to all cases now pending, as well as
to those hereafter to be commenced. (R. S. Sec. 3365-8;
April 26, 1894, 91 v. 188, § 4.)

WIRES OVER TRACKS.

Section 8975. (Construction of overhead wires.) Telegraph, telephone, electric light or other wires of any kind placed over the line of a steam railroad must be put on substantial poles of a size not less than twelve inches in diameter at the bottom and six inches at the top. They shall be set in the earth not less than one-sixth of their length and well tamped. Double cross-arms must be used in all cases, all wires to be insulated with glass or porcelain insulators, securely fastened to both cross-arms, and clear the top of the rails at least twenty-five feet. In trolley wire crossings, such height as is agreed upon, and approved by the railroad commission shall govern. Where there is side strain, poles must be well guyed or braced. (R. S. Sec. 3365-28; April 21, 1898, 93 v. 154, § 1.)

> See Street Railway Co. v. Railroad Co., 21 C. C. 391; 12 C. D. 113 (1898); aff'd, 64 O. S. 550.
> See also § 8903 et seq.

Section 8976. (Duty of railroad commission.) The state railroad commission shall see that the provisions of the next preceding section are enforced, and for that purpose shall have power to cause the removal of telegraph, telephone, electric light or other wires placed over a railroad, not in accordance with such section. (R. S. Sec. 3365-29, April 21, 1898, 93 v. 154, § 2.)

CHAPTER 5.

FARE AND FREIGHT.

PASSENGER FARE.

Section 8977.   (Rates of passenger fare.) A company operating a railroad in whole or in part in this state may demand and receive for the transportation of passengers on its road, not exceeding two cents per mile, for a distance of more than five miles, but the fare shall always be made that multiple of five nearest reached by multiplying the rate by the distance. (R. S. Sec. 3374; February 8, 1906, 98 v. 4; April 6, 1876, 73 v. 102, § 13.)

Schedule of fares to be posted and filed, §§ 8981, 505 et seq.
Power of public utilities commission over fares, §§ 527, 535.
Penalty for violation of this section, §§ 9002, 9003.

Unit of measurement. The unit of measurement provided by this section is one mile and fractions of a mile are not to be counted. The words "more than five miles" are equivalent to six miles. The limit of two cents per mile applies first to six miles, then to seven and so on. For any distance less than six miles the limit does not apply.

Railway Co. v. Wells, 65 O. S. 313 (1901).
See Scheidler v. Railway, 20 C. C. 712; 10 C. D. 822.

Multiple of five. A railroad company may charge as fare that multiple of five which is nearest to the product produced by multiplying the rate of two cents per mile by the distance, whether such multiple is above or below such product. If such product should be equidistant from the multiple below and the one above, the company may charge as fare either multiple.

C. C. C. & St. L. Ry. Co. v. Wells, 61 O. S. 268 (1899).
See Railroad Co. v. Skillman, 39 O. S. 444 (1883).
Heaton v. Cincinnati, etc., R. Co., 1 N. P. 433 (1894) ; s. c., 2 L. D. 47.
Scheidler v. Railway Co., 20 C. C. 712; 10 C. D. 822.

Distance less than five miles. For any distance less than six miles the limit does not apply.

Railway Co. v. Wells, 65 O. S. 313 (1901).
The railroad company may charge a reasonable rate. Whether the rate is unreasonable is a question for the jury.

Railroad Co. v. Skillman, 39 O. S. 444 (1883).
Smith v. Railway Co., 23 O. S. 10 (1872).
Peters v. Railroad Co., 42 O. S. 275 (1884).
Campbell v. Railroad Co., 23 O. S. 168, 190 (1872).

Application of section to companies organizing under special charter.

See Railroad Co. v. Cole, 29 O. S. 126 (1876).
Shields v. State, 26 O. S. 86 (1875) ; s. c., 95 U. S. 319.
Railroad Co. v. Moore, 33 O. S. 384 (1878).
See also § 8732.

Tickets.

Right to require tickets. A railroad company has a right to require passengers on freight trains to procure tickets prior to taking passage.

Railroad Co. v. Bartram, 11 O. S. 457 (1860).
Hatten v. Railroad Co., 39 O. S. 375 (1883).

Nature of ticket. A ticket is a convenient symbol to represent the fact that the bearer has paid to the company the agreed price for his conveyance upon the road to the place therein designated.

Frank v. Ingalls, 41 O. S. 560, 563 (1885).
Railroad Co. v. Campbell, 36 O. S. 647, 658 (1881).
The contract between the railroad company and passenger may be proved by parol evidence aside from the ticket.

Penna. Co. v. Loftis, 72 O. S. 288, 300 (1905).
See Penna. Co. v. O'Connell, 84 O. S. 218, 221 (1911).
Railroad Co. v. Cook, 37 O. S. 265 (1881).
Where the language of a ticket is ambiguous it should be construed most strongly against the carrier and in favor of the purchaser.

Ann Arbor Ry. v. Amos, 85 O. S. 300 (1912).

——. **Is for continuous passage.** In the absence of any agreement

or rule or regulation .to the contrary, the obligation created by a sale of
the ticket was for one continuous passage, and if the passenger voluntarily left the train at an intermediate station while the carrier was
engaged in the performance of its contract, he thereby released it from
further performance and had no right to demand such performance on
another train at another time.

Hatten v. Railroad Co., 39 O. S. 375 (1883).

Cleveland, etc., R. R. Co. v. Bartram, 11 O. S. 457 (1860).

Where a continuous passage necessitates a change of trains it must
be continued on the next available train.

Ellsworth v. Penna. Co., 2 C. C. n. s. 483; 15 C. D. 797 (1904);
aff'd, 74 O. S. 443.

But to relieve the carrier the continuity of the passage must be
broken by the holder of the ticket without the assent or fault of the carrier. Where the passenger had no information as to the time of the next
train and ignorantly allowed one train to pass, the continuity of the passage was not broken.

Ellsworth v. Penna. Co., 2 C. C. n. s. 483; 15 C. D. 797 (1904);
aff'd, 74 O. S. 443.

——. Over connecting lines. A railroad company selling a coupon
ticket over its own and connecting lines may, by contract, express or implied, make itself liable for safe carriage over the entire route, but the
mere sale of such coupon ticket does not of itself import a contract to be
responsible beyond its own line. The presumption is that the selling company acts as agent of the connecting lines.

Penna. Co. v. Loftis, 72 O. S. 288, 300 (1905).

See Railroad Co. v. Campbell, 36 O. S. 647 (1881).

——. Authority of agent to sell tickets. An agent authorized to
sell tickets, and stamp and deliver the same upon receiving pay therefor,
can not bind his company by stamping and delivering such tickets, without the knowledge or consent of its proper officers, to a third person, to
be sold by him, and to be paid for when sold.

Frank v. Ingalls, 41 O. S. 560 (1885).

Terms and conditions in tickets.

Assent of purchaser essential. The purchaser of a ticket does not,
by its mere acceptance, acquiesce in, and bind himself to, all the terms
and conditions printed therein in the absence of actual knowledge of
them.

Kent v. Railroad Co., 45 O. S. 284, 288 (1887).

Railroad Co. v. Campbell, 36 O. S. 647 (1881).

Although the ticket is sold at a reduced rate.

Kent v. Railroad Co., 45 O. S. 284, 288 (1887).

Railway Co. v. Mortal, 18 C. C. 562; 8 C. D. 134 (1897).

A passenger purchasing a ticket, immediately before the departure
of the train, is not guilty of negligence in not examining the ticket.

Ann Arbor Ry. Co. v. Amos, 85 O. S. 300 (1912).

Waiver of conditions. Conditions in a ticket may be waived by the
acts or conduct of the railroad company or its agents.

Requirement of continuous passage.

Ellsworth v. Penna. Co., 2 C. C. n. s. 483; 15 C. D. 797 (1904); aff'd,
74 O. S. 443.

Signature of purchaser in mileage book.

Kent v. Railroad Co., 45 O. S. 284 (1887).

Where a person has a ticket, purchased from a company, entitling him
to be carried from a certain station to another on the line of its road,
and is good only on trains stopping at his destination, is, by the fault of

the company's station agent, induced to take a train that does not, under the schedule stop at such place, and as a consequence is ejected by the conductor on calling for his ticket, and before reaching his destination, such facts show a right in the passenger against the company to recover as for a tort, and not merely for breach of contract.

Pittsburg, etc., Ry. Co. v. Reynolds, 55 O. S. 370 (1896).
See Pennsylvania Co. v. Wentz, 37 O. S. 333 (1881).
Haskins v. Lake Shore, etc., Ry. Co., 4 W. L. B. 951 (1879).

Special conditions. Time limit. Where a railroad company sold a ticket, which entitled the purchaser to ride upon its cars a certain number of times within a given period, for a price below the usual rate of fare, which ticket specified upon its face that it was only good during such period, the purchaser, having failed to ride the specified number of times within the period named, is not entitled to ride upon such ticket after the expiration of the period.

Powell v. Pittsburg, etc., R. R. Co., 25 O. S. 70 (1874).
Pennsylvania Co. v. Hine, 41 O. S. 276 (1884).

——. Continuous passage. A stipulation for continuous passage is reasonable.

Ellsworth v. Penna. Co., 2 C. C. n. s. 483; 15 C. D. 797 (1904);
  aff'd, 74 O. S. 443.

——. Ticket nontransferable. Stipulations, in tickets sold at reduced rates, that the tickets were to be nontransferable, and requiring the original purchasers to identify themselves by subscribing their names whenever required, are valid.

Kinner v. Railway Co., 69 O. S. 339, 340, 345 (1904); affm'g, 3 C. C.
  n. s. 401; 13 C. D. 294.

A railroad company, having sold return tickets containing such stipulation, is entitled to an injunction against ticket brokers acquiring the return portions of such tickets and selling them to others to be used by them in violation of the terms of the contract. The fact that the railway company had agreed with other carriers respecting the reduction of rates and conditions of tickets is no defense to the ticket brokers.

Kinner v. Railway Co., 69 O. S. 339 (1904).

A railroad company has no right to confiscate a nontransferable mileage book, purchased by a ticket broker in a fictitious name, when found in the hands of another person. But the conductor may refuse to accept such ticket and collect the regular fare.

Morton v. Railway Co., 20 C. C. 666; 10 C. D. 812; 35 W. L. B. 359
  (1898); affirming, 7 N. P. 605; 5 L. D. 580.

In the absence of a stipulation, restricting transfer, a ticket is transferable.

Penna. Co. v. O'Connell, 84 O. S. 218, 220, 221 (1911).

A ticket, with no limitation as to transfer on its face, is good in the hands of one who has purchased it from the original purchaser, or from a ticket broker or "scalper", when the purchase is made without knowledge of an undisclosed rule of the railroad company prohibiting such transfer.

Knecht v. Railway Co., 6 N. P. n. s. 13; 18 L. D. 202 (C. P. 1907).

——. Exempting railroad company from liability for negligence. A stipulation in a drover's ticket exempting the company from liability for negligence is void.

Cleveland, etc., R. R. Co. v. Curran, 19 O. S. 1 (1869).

The validity of a stipulation in a free pass exempting a carrier from liability for negligence must be determined by the law of the place where made.

Knowlton v. Erie Ry. Co., 19 O. S. 260 (1869).

An express messenger is not regarded as a passenger, and a contract, between the messenger and express company, exempting the railroad company from liability was held valid.

Railway v. Voight, 176 U. S. 498 (1900).

Lost tickets, rights of owner. The purchaser of a nontransferable commutation ticket, who has lost it, and refuses, on account of such loss, to pay his fare upon a train, can not maintain an action against the company for being ejected from the train.

Crawford v. Cincinnati, etc., R. R. Co., 26 O. S. 580 (1875).

Right of holder of fraudulently obtained ticket. When the possession of a railroad passenger ticket, which entitles the holder to a first-class passage between points named therein, has been fraudulently obtained from the company, a person purchasing such ticket from the holder thereof, although for value and without notice of equities, acquires no title thereto.

Frank v. Ingalls, 41 O. S. 560 (1885).

Passage on freight trains. A railroad company has the right to prescribe reasonable conditions for the admittance of way passengers upon its freight trains; and payment of fare to its office agents, or procuring a ticket prior to taking passage on such trains, is not an unreasonable condition.

Cleveland, etc., R. R. Co. v. Bartrain, 11 O. S. 457 (1860).

Expulsion from train on refusal to pay. A railway company has the right to require passengers to pay fare, and a rule directing its conductors to remove from the cars those who refuse to comply with the requirement is reasonable.

Shelton v. Lake Shore, etc., Ry. Co., 29 O. S. 214 (1876).
Traction Co. v. Rosnagle, 84 O. S. 310 (1911).
Crawford v. Cincinnati, etc., R. R. Co., 26 O. S. 580 (1875).
Railroad Co. v. Skillman, 39 O. S. 444 (1883).
Corry v. Cincinnati, etc., R. R. Co., 3 Gaz. 90 (1859).
See § 9157 and note.

A person having in charge a child of sufficient age to require payment of fare is liable for payment of the child's fare and both may be ejected for refusal to pay the same.

Railroad v. Orndorff, 55 O. S. 589 (1897).

When such person has paid fare, or purchased a ticket which has been taken up by the conductor, the unused value of the ticket or fare must be tendered back.

Railroad v. Orndorff, 55 O. S. 589 (1897).

A person refusing to pay fare acquires no right to remain on the train by offering to pay the usual fare after the train has been stopped for the purpose of ejecting him.

Railroad Co. v. Skillman, 39 O. S. 444 (1883).

An offer to pay the fare to an employe on the train unauthorized to receive the same is not an offer to the company, and does not entitle the person to passage.

Cleveland, etc., R. R. Co. v. Bartram, 11 O. S. 457 (1860).

A passenger failing to get a seat may refuse to ride, and bring suit, but if he rides he must give up his ticket or pay.

Close v. Cooper, 34 O. S. 98 (1877).
See Railway Co. v. McLean, 1 C. C. 112 (1885); 1 C. D. 67; 19 W. L. B. 217.

The fact that a ticket has been purchased by a passenger, which was afterward wrongfully taken up by a conductor of one of the defendant's trains, will not relieve the passenger from the duty of providing himself with a ticket or paying fare on another train of the defendant in which he may be a passenger. In such case the right of action of the passenger would be for the wrongful taking up of the ticket, and not for having been removed from a train by another conductor for refusing to pay fare.

Shelton v. Lake Shore, etc., Ry. Co., 29 O. S. 214 (1876).

See Railway v. Conner, 74 O. S. 225 (1906).

Wilt v. Railway Co., 21 C. C. 579; 11 C. D. 589.

A person is only entitled to compensatory damages where his object in taking passage on the train was to be ejected and to bring suit against the company.

Cincinnati, etc., R. R. Co. v. Cole, 29 O. S. 126 (1876).

Where a ticket is for passage over three lines, and calls for one exchange at the office of the intermediate line, and the agent in making the exchange negligently writes, in a coupon attached to the ticket, a wrong destination, but in the ticket itself inserts the proper destination, the passenger is entitled to be carried to the proper destination. On ejection from the train, he may recover substantial damages.

Ann Arbor Ry. v. Amos, 85 O. S. 300 (1912).

Where, by mistake of the ticket agent, the ticket is to a destination short of the proper destination, and the conductor informs the passenger that he will telegraph for instructions, which he does, it is the duty of the company to give proper instructions to the conductor.

Ann Arbor Ry. Co. v. Amos, 85 O. S. 300 (1912).

Where a conductor through an error of judgment expels a person who is entitled to ride, the company is liable.

Traction Co. v. Rosnagle, 84 O. S. 310 (1911).

Where a coin which is worn, bruised or cracked, but which is not appreciably diminished in weight, and retains evidence of genuine coinage, is tendered as fare, the passenger can not be expelled.

Traction Co. v. Rosnagle, 84 O. S. 310 (1911).

A person who was wrongfully ejected from a train between stations in the night time, and who was injured by falling into a cattle guard while making his way to the nearest highway crossing, may recover.

Railway Co. v. Willing, 5 C. C. n. s. 137; 14 C. D. 474 (1902).

A person who takes passage on a train which he knows does not stop at his destination may be ejected at any reasonably safe place between stations, upon his refusal to pay fare to the next stopping place.

Railway Co. v. Willing, 5 C. C. n. s. 137; 14 C. D. 474 (1902).

Section 8978. (**Excess fare on trains.**) Any company operating a railroad in whole or part within this state which has posted up proper notice to that effect in a conspicuous place in each waiting room and on the front of its depot building, may collect ten cents extra in addition to the fare allowed by law, when such fare is paid on the train, and if an office at the point at which the passenger boarded the train has been open for the sale of tickets at least thirty minutes next prior to the departure of such train. (R. S. Sec. 3374-a; April 7, 1908, 99 v. 65.)

A railroad company may charge a higher price for carrying passengers when the fare is paid on the train than it does at its ticket offices, provided the price thus charged is reasonable, and the fare charged on the train does not exceed the maximum allowed by law.

Railroad Co. v. Skillman, 39 O. S. 444 (1883).

See Smith v. Pittsburg, etc., Ry. Co., 23 O. S. 10 (1872).

If a railroad company fix two rates of passenger fare, to wit, a ticket rate and a car rate, the former within and the latter beyond the limits of its authority, and the conductor of the train, under the direction of the company, refuse to accept from the passenger less than the illegal and unauthorized rate, it is not necessary, to entitle the passenger to remain on the train, to tender more than the ticket rate, although the company might have fixed such ticket rate at a higher sum. Quaere, whether any tender is necessary in such case.

Smith v. Pittsburg, etc., Ry. Co., 23 O. S. 10 (1872).

Section 8979. (Bicycle as baggage.) For the purposes herein specified, bicycles, with or without lanterns or tool-boxes attached, are baggage, and shall be transported as such, for passengers, by all railroad companies, and be subject to the same charges and liabilities as other baggage. No passenger shall be required to crate, cover, or otherwise protect a bicycle. But such companies are not required to transport more than one bicycle for a single person. (R. S. Sec. 3378-2; March 3, 1898, 93 v. 24; April 27, 1896, 92 v. 372.)

The obligation of a carrier to carry the baggage of a passenger is limited to articles which are for his personal comfort and convenience.

Railway Co. v. Bowler & Burdick Co., 57 O. S. 38, 56 (1897).

It is under no obligation to carry merchandise as baggage, and is not liable for its loss if such merchandise is received by it as baggage without knowledge of its true character. But if a carrier receives merchandise as baggage, with actual knowledge on the part of its agents that it is merchandise, it is liable for the loss thereof.

Railway Co. v. Bowler & Burdick Co., 57 O. S. 38 (1897).
Smith v. Railroad Co., 2 N. P. 29; 3 L. D. 192 (1895).
Insurance Co. v. Packet Co., 1 N. P. 126; 4 L. D. 405 (1894).
See Bank v. Railroad Co., 20 O. S. 259 (1870).
Jones v. Voorhees, 10 Ohio 145 (1840).

FREIGHT CHARGES.

Section 8980. (Rates of freight.) Any railroad company may receive for transportation of property not exceeding five cents per ton per mile, when it is transported a distance of thirty miles or more; and if the quantity transported is less than one ton in weight, or any quantity is transported a less distance than thirty miles, such reasonable rate as is fixed from time to time by the corporation or prescribed by law. Until a tariff of specific rates is established by law for the transportation of property of such bulk that a quantity equal to the tonnage capacity of the car cannot be carried in it, the corporation may contract for space in a car sufficient to secure the safe transportation of such property, at a rate which shall not exceed five cents per ton per mile if such car were loaded to its tonnage capacity. For the transportation of coal, pig-iron, lime stone, iron ore, or undressed stone or lumber, not more than five cents per ton per mile shall be charged for the distance of ten miles or more, and if transported a less distance than ten miles, such reasonable rates as are fixed from time to time by the corporation or, prescribed by law. The company may charge on such freight a reasonable rate for loading and unloading, when in fact done by it. (R. S. Sec. 3375; April 6, 1876, 73 v. 102, § 13.)

Power of public utilities commission over rates, §§ 527, 535.
Schedules of rates to be filed and posted, §§ 8982, 505 et seq.

Charges for less than thirty miles. Where a company is authorized to charge for the transportation of goods for less than thirty miles such reasonable rates as it may fix from time to time, it is unreasonable, as a matter of law, to fix a greater sum for a distance less than thirty miles than the maximum for full thirty miles.
Peters v. Railroad Co., 42 O. S. 275 (1884).
Campbell v. Marietta, etc., R. R. Co., 23 O. S. 168 (1872).
Whether a freight rate fixed by a company for distances less than thirty miles is reasonable or not is a question of fact for the jury, to be determined under such instructions by the court as the circumstances of the particular case may require.
Peters v. Railroad Co., 42 O. S. 275 (1884).
See Smith v. Pittsburg, etc., Ry. Co., 23 O. S. 10 (1872).
A municipality has no power to prescribe the rates to be charged by a belt line for hauls over its entire line, less than 30 miles long as a condition to granting a right of way over its streets for a part of its line. Such a provision in an ordinance is ultra vires and void. In an action by an individual claiming the benefit of such provision, the railroad company is not estopped from setting up its ultra vires character as a defense.
Brick Co. v. Trust Co., 187 Fed. 63 (C. C. A. 1911).

Recovery of overcharges. A shipper has the right to have his goods transported at legal rates over the usual line of a common carrier of such goods; and if, to procure the services of such carrier, the shipper is compelled to pay illegal rates, the payment is not such a voluntary payment as will preclude recovering back the illegal charge, nor will it preclude such recovery, if payments, by arrangement of parties, are made at the end of each month.
Peters v. Railroad Co., 42 O. S. 275 (1884).
See § 9002.

Filing of claims with public utilities commission. Award of reparation. Procedure. §§ 579, 580.

Demurrage charges. A reasonable charge for demurrage may be made upon failure of the consignee to unload freight from its cars within a reasonable time. A railroad company may refuse to deliver cars upon the private siding of the consignee until he pays demurrage charged for the unreasonable detention of former cars delivered upon the siding.
Phillips Co. v. Erie R. Co., 6 C. C. n. s. 505; 17 C. D. 486 (1905); affirming, 14 L. D. 706.
But where the delay is caused by the acts of the railway company it is not entitled to demurrage.
Troy, etc., Co. v. Railway, 3 N. P. n. s. 412 (1903); aff'd, 72 O. S.

See Railroad v. Fisher, 3 N. P. 122; 5 L. D. 659.

Where a large part of its bill for demurrage is disputed in good faith, the railroad company can not require as a condition of continuing switching service, payment of the entire bill and an unconditional promise to pay all similar future bills.

Troy, etc., Co. v. Railway Co., 3 N. P. n. s. 412 (1903); aff'd, 72 O. S. 613.

The transferee of a bill of lading, who presents it to the railroad company and receives the goods contained in the cars, is bound by a provision in such bill of lading for demurrage, and is liable to the railroad company.

Traction Co. v. Railway Co., 8 C. C. n. s. 134; 18 C. D. 543 (1906).

A railroad company has a common law lien upon property in a car, for demurrage charges, and may refuse to deliver such property until payment is made. Such lien exists independently of any stipulation in the contract of shipment.

Railway Co. v. Mooar Lumber Co., 6 C. C. n. s. 638; 17 C. D. 588 (1905).

Forty-eight hours is a reasonable time within which a consignee may be required to remove freight from cars, after which time a demurrage charge may be imposed.

Phillips Co. v. Railroad Co., 6 C. C. n. s. 505; 17 C. D. 486 (1905); s. c., 14 L. D. 706.

Troy, etc., Co. v. Railway Co., 3 N. P. n. s. 412 (1903); aff'd, 72 O. S. 613.

Railroad v. Seiberling, 8 C. C. 593; 4 C. D. 210.

See § 8998.

Car service rules established by railroad commission.

Ohio Shippers Ass'n v. Ann Arbor R. Co., 52 O. L. B. 279 (1907).

Contracts for freight. The board of directors of a railroad company may, within the limit of the maximum rate authorized by law, make contracts for transportation for a fixed future period. Such a contract, if otherwise valid, is not ultra vires and void, for the reason that it binds the company for a fixed time.

Railroad Co. v. Furnace Co., 37 O. S. 321 (1882).

Himrod Furnace Co. v. Cleveland, etc., R. R. Co., 22 O. S. 451 (1872).

See G. C. § 513.

What companies not bound by this act. The provision in the twelfth section of the act of Feb. 11, 1848, that no reduction shall be made in the rates of fare and charges for freight allowed to companies organized under said act, unless their net profits for the previous ten years amount to ten percent on their capital, is in the nature of a contract, and binding on the state, and companies which have not lost their rights under said act and have not realized ten percent profit, are not bound by later acts reducing freight rates.

Iron R. R. Co. v. Lawrence Furnace Co., 29 O. S. 208 (1876).

Railway Co. v. Furnace Co., 49 O. S. 102 (1892).

Rights under special charters.

Campbell v. Marietta, etc., R. R. Co., 23 O. S. 168 (1872).

Section 8981.   (Points competing with public works.) Every company whose line of road extends to a place in the vicinity of, or to a point of intersection with, a navigable canal or other work of internal improvement belonging to the state, shall fix and establish a tariff of rates for the transportation of merchandise, produce, and other property consigned to or from such place or point of intersection, and not charge or receive a higher rate for transporting similar merchandise, produce, or property over a shorter distance of its road, than is charged or received according to such tariff for transportation to and from such place of intersection. (R. S. Sec. 3366; May 1, 1852, 50 v. 205, § 1.)

See §§ 564 to 568 and § 8982.

The intent of the statute was not to restrain companies subject to its provisions from charging the maximum rates allowed by their charters, but only to prevent them from fixing rates for longer distances below the maximum and below the rates fixed for shorter distances, either to the prejudice of the canals belonging to the state, or of the public whose shipments might be for the shorter distances.

Campbell v. Marietta, etc., R. R. Co., 23 O. S. 168, 191 (1872).

A railroad company whose line extends to a point of intersection with a canal of the state can not make a valid contract to repay to a shipper a portion of the freight paid by him, it being the regular rate posted by the company and received from other shippers, such contract being prohibited by this section. An action can not be maintained to enforce a promise of such repayment.

Baltimore, etc., R. R. Co. v. Diamond Coal Co., 61 O. S. 242 (1899).

Section 8982.   (Tariff of rates published; how changed.) Every such company shall publish its tariff of rates so established on property consigned to and from such places or points of intersection, and keep it conspicuously posted at the several business stations on its road. Such company, its officers or agents, shall not charge or receive, directly or indirectly, for transporting property so consigned, a less rate than is designated on such printed card, until the rate is changed by an order of its board of directors, and at least ten days' notice of the change be given by bill or card to be posted as specified above. No such company, its officers or agents, shall evade, or attempt to evade, by drawback, free warehousing, or in any other manner, the payment of full freightage, according to its printed tariff of rates, as herein provided. (R. S. Sec. 3367; May 1, 1852, 50 v. 205, § 2.)

See § 505 et seq. and §§ 564 to 568.

This section is valid as an exercise of the police power of the state.

Railroad Co. v. Fuller, 17 Wall. (U. S.) 560 (1873).

Where a railroad company, by mistake, collected less than its published rate, it may recover the deficiency from the consignee, although as between consignee and consignor the charges were to be paid by the consignor.

Railway Co. v. Magnus Co., 13 C. C. n. s. 305 (1910).

See Store Fixture Co. v. Railway Co., 1 N. P. n. s. 242; 13 L. D. 648.

Rebates.   A railroad company whose line extends to a point of intersection with a canal of the state can not make a valid contract to repay to a shipper a portion of the freight paid by him, it being the regular rate posted by the company and received from other shippers, such contract being prohibited by this section. An action can not be maintained to enforce a promise of such repayment.

Baltimore, etc., R. R. Co. v. Diamond Coal Co., 61 O. S. 242 (1899).

Where a lower rate is given by a common carrier to a favored shipper, which is intended to give and necessarily gives an exclusive monopoly to the favored shipper, affecting the business and destroying the trade of other shippers, the latter have the right to require an equal rate for all under like circumstances. An injunction may be obtained to prevent discrimination.

Scofield v. Railway Co., 43 O. S. 571 (1885).

A railroad company is not warranted in making a contract whereby it binds itself to carry for one shipper crude petroleum, or other article, at half the rate it agrees to charge all others for the same service, at the same time, and as part of the agreement, binding itself to charge all others double the amount as a fixed open rate, and to pay such favored shipper one-half of it when collected, in consideration of his agreeing to establish and maintain a system of pipe lines to its road. Money so paid by a shipper, in ignorance of the agreement, and received by the favored shipper, may be recovered back in an action for money had and received by the former against the latter.

Brundred v. Rice, 49 O. S. 640 (1892).

Where a railway company, as a common carrier, in consideration of the fact that a shipper furnished a greater quantity of freights than other shippers during a given term, agrees to make a rebate from the published tariff on such freights to the prejudice of the other shippers of like freights under the same circumstances, the contract so made is an unlawful discrimination in favor of the larger shipper, tending to create monopoly, destroy competition, injure, if not destroy, the business of smaller operators, contrary to public policy, and will be declared void at the instance of parties injured thereby.

And such a contract can not be upheld simply because the favored shipper may furnish for shipment during the year a larger freightage in the aggregate than any other shipper, or more than all others combined. A discrimination resting exclusively on such a basis will not be sustained. And such a contract will not be upheld simply because the business to be done under it is "largely profitable" to the company.

Scofield v. Railway Co., 43 O. S. 571 (1885).

A corporation created by this state, and engaged in carrying goods for hire as a common carrier, has no franchise, privilege, or right to discriminate in its freight rates in favor of one shipper, even when it is necessary to do so to secure his custom, if the discriminating rate will tend to create a monopoly by excluding from their proper markets the products of the competitors of the favored shipper.

State ex rel. v. Railway, 47 O. S. 130 (1890).

Rights of shipper when agent fraudulently overcharges.

Maple v. Railroad Co., 40 O. S. 313 (1883).

Section 8983. (Contracts prohibited.) A company whose road forms part of a line of railway between points common to another line, shall not contract or agree with any person, or other railroad company or companies, having a road or line of roads, or forming a part of a line of roads, between the same points, not to carry freight or passengers to or from such common points, nor shall it refuse to receive or

carry freight or passengers brought to it to be so carried.
(R. S. Sec. 3368; April 11, 1861, 58 v. 74, § 1.)

See Metropolitan Trust Co. v. Columbus, etc., Ry. Co., 95 Fed. 18
(1899).

**Section 8984. (Trunk roads not to discriminate between
roads.)** When a railroad is a trunk road, or in the nature
of a trunk road, and at or near the same place connects
with or is intersected by two or more other railroads tributary to or competing lines for business to or from such
trunk road, or to or from points on or beyond the same, a
company or person operating or using such trunk road shall
transport passengers and freight going to or coming from
such tributary or competing roads without discrimination
in the charges therefor, directly or indirectly, for or against
either of such roads. The company or person owning or
controlling such trunk road shall not, by lease or otherwise,
permit it to be used or operated in any manner contrary to
the foregoing provision. (R. S. Sec. 3369; April 11, 1861,
58 v. 74, § 2.)

**Section 8985. (Must forward freight by line named by
shipper.)** Every company shall ship all freight that comes
within its control by the railroads over which it is ordered
to be conveyed by the shipper. A company whose agent
knowingly diverts, or permits to be diverted, freight that
comes under his control from the railroad over which it is
ordered to be conveyed, shall forfeit and pay to the company from which such freight is diverted three times the
amount received for transporting it. (R. S. Sec. 3370;
April 11, 1861, 58 v. 74, § 3.)

Penalty for violation, § 13420.

**Section 8986. (Provisions may be enforced by injunc-
tion.)** On complaint of the violation of any provision of the
three next preceding sections by petition as in other actions,
their observance may be enforced by injunction, and the
party violating any of them, shall be liable in damages to
the person or company injured, for the injury sustained in
consequence thereof. (R. S. Sec. 3371; April 11, 1861, 58
v. 74, § 4.)

**Section 8987. (No discrimination between way and
through freight.)** Every company whose line of road is
wholly or partly within this state, shall so employ its rolling
stock used for the transportation of freight as to afford

as ample facilities for the transportation of local and way freight, delivered to or discharged by it along its line of road, as it affords for the transportation of through freight, in proportion to the amount of its rolling stock, and not give facilities for transportation to either class of freight in preference to the other. (R. S. Sec. 3372; April 14, 1863, 60 v. 93, § 1.)

Section 8988. (No discrimination against points in the state.) No company, or person owning, controlling, or operating a railroad in whole or part within this state, shall charge or receive for transportation of freight for any distance within this state a larger sum than is charged by the same company or person for the transportation in the same direction, of freight of same class or kind, for an equal or greater distance over the same road and connecting lines of road. (R. S. Sec. 3373; March 11, 1872, 69 v. 27, § 1.)

See §§ 567, 564 and notes.
Nimishilling, etc., Co. v. Railroad Co., 5 O. L. R. 455 (R. R. Commission 1907).
Campbell v. Railroad Co., 23 O. S. 168 (1872).
This section relates to freight traffic only.
Railway v. Railroad Commission, 5 N. P. n. s. 265, 274; 18 L. D. 21 (C. P. 1907); aff'd, 82 O. S. 25.
Express companies are included in the term "railroads" in this section, and its provisions may be applied to tariffs published by express companies.
Rep. Atty. Gen. 1911-1912, p. 705.
Prohibition of section considered.
Railway v. Railroad Commission, 5 N. P. n. s. 265, 274; 18 L. D. 21 (C. P. 1907); aff'd, 82 O. S. 25.

Section 8989. (Forfeiture.) Every such company or person who violates, or permits to be violated, the provisions of the next preceding section, shall forfeit and pay to the party aggrieved a sum equal to double the amount of the over-charge, but in no case less than twenty-five dollars, and also for every such unlawful act, forfeit and pay to the state a penalty of not less than one hundred nor more than one thousand dollars, to be recovered in a civil action, which shall be brought in the name of the state, by the prosecuting attorney of the county wherein such offense was committed, as his official duty, when complaint is made to him, and he is satisfied that the provisions of such section have been violated. (R. S. Sec. 3373; March 11, 1872, 69 v. 27, § 1.)

The remedy given by this section is cumulative and does not take away the remedies at common law.

Scofield v. Railway Co., 43 O. S. 571, 620 (1885).
A consignee who has purchased the property for a delivered price
can not sue. The right of action is in the consignor.
   Thompson v. Railway, 11 W. L. B. 211 (1884).

**Section 8990. (Must furnish equal facilities to same class
of shippers.)** Railroad companies and persons operating a
railroad, shall secure and extend to all persons, companies
and corporations, the same and equal opportunities and
facilities for receiving and shipping freights of all kinds,
of the same class, that such railroad company or person
operating such railroad, extends to, has used or enjoys, of
and concerning freights owned by such company, or the
person operating such road, or any officer or stockholder
therein, or in which it, they or either of them have an interest. (R. S. Sec. 3373-1; April 29, 1891, 88 v. 429, § 2.)

See §§ 535, 567, 520, 8981, 8982 and notes.
Section cited. Ohio Dairy Co. v. Railway, 7 N. P. n. s. 451, 457
   (1908).
Creamery Co. v. Railroad Co., 8 O. L. R. 10, 19 (1910).
Both under the common law and by this section it is the duty of a
railroad company to extend to all persons, without favoritism or discrimination, equal opportunities and facilities for receiving and shipping
freight of all kinds and of the same class.
Railway Co. v. Wren, 78 O. S. 137 (1908).

Terminal facilities. An unloading machine, situated on a dock belonging to a railroad company, and necessarily operated in connection
with its tracks and terminals, which was originally constructed and
jointly owned by the railroad company and a coal company for the accommodation of patrons of the railway and at prices fixed by it, is devoted to public use and is a part of terminal facilities. A grant of its
exclusive use to one patron is an unlawful discrimination and may be enjoined, although the railroad company has transferred its rights in the
machine to such patron.
Coal Co. v. Railway, 1 C. C. n. s. 333; 14 C. D. 289 (1902); dismissed in supreme court by plaintiff in error, 2 O. L. R. 280.

Duty to connect private switch. Where a railroad company had
connected with its main track switches built by several coal mining companies in the vicinity, a coal mining company having constructed a switch
from its mine, similar to these of the other companies, was held entitled
to compel the railroad company, by mandatory injunction, to permit the
switch to be connected.
Johnson, etc., Co. v. H. V. R. R. Co., 1 N. P. n. s. 385; 14 L. D. 209
   (1904).
See Mercantile Trust Co. v. Columbus, etc., Co., 90 Fed. 48; 12 O.
   F. D. 157 (1898).
Where a railroad company has made a practice of constructing and
maintaining private sidings, without restrictions as to what cars may be
placed thereon, it is unjust discrimination to require, as a condition precedent to connecting a private side track, that the owner make a written
agreement not to ask the company to switch thereon the cars of other
companies.
Gill v. Railway, 6 O. L. R. 140 (R. R. Com. 1908).

Discrimination in switching service.

See Gill v. Railway Co., 6 O. L. R. 140 (R. R. Com. 1908).
Pierce, etc., Co. v. Railroad Co., 6 O. L. R. 147 (R. R. Com. 1908).
Reinstrom v. Railway Co., 4 O. L. R. 755; 52 B. 187 (R. R. Com.).
Railway Co. v. Scofield, 2 C. C. 305 (1887).
See § 8998.

Other discrimination.

See notes to §§ 535, 567.

Section 8991. (Damages.) A railroad company or person operating a railroad failing to comply with or observe the provisions or requirements of the next preceding section, shall be liable to the party injured for the damages sustained, but for any violation of such section the recovery in such action shall be at least five hundred dollars. (R. S. Sec. 3373-1; April 29, 1891, 88 v. 429, § 2.)

In an action for damages for discrimination in giving to other shippers preference in the distribution of cars, the plaintiff is entitled to recover as damages only such sum as will compensate him for the loss actually sustained as the result of the discrimination, except that, where discrimination be proved, the recovery shall not be less than $500.
Railway Co. v. Wren, 78 O. S. 137 (1908).
Where there is no allegation of special damages, the measure of damages is the difference between the market value of the property that would have been transported in the cars which plaintiff should have received, at destination, at the time when they would have reached such destination, and the value of said property at the place of shipment, at the same time, less the cost of transportation.
Railway Co. v. Wren, 78 O. S. 137 (1908).
This section does not take away the remedies at common law.
Johnson, etc., Co. v. Railroad Co., 1 N. P. n. s. 385, 390; 14 L. D. 209 (C. P. 1903).

Section 8992. (Passengers on freight trains.) Physicians in the discharge of professional duties, sheriffs, and deputy sheriffs, in performance of official duties, officers and guards of the penitentiary or state reformatory in pursuit of escaped prisoners or returning them to their respective institutions, shall be permitted to ride at their own risk, and take a prisoner or prisoners with them on freight trains, between stations where such trains stop, paying therefor the regular passenger fare. (R. S. Sec. 3375a; April 15, 1902, 95 v. 153; April 13, 1892, 89 v. 275; April 23, 1891, 88 v. 381.)

To give a sheriff the right to ride on freight trains in the performance of his official duties, "between stations where such trains stop," it is not necessary that such trains should regularly stop at such stations, or be scheduled to stop there; it is sufficient, if they are in fact stopping there at the time the sheriff gets aboard. It is not necessary to allege that the train stopped regularly at the point the sheriff came aboard.
Allen v. Lake Shore, etc., Ry. Co., 57 O. S. 79 (1897).

The right of a sheriff to ride upon a freight train is not confined to cases in which a prisoner is taken upon such train; but the right exists whenever the sheriff is in the performance of any official duty, and complies in other respects with the statute.

Allen v. Lake Shore, etc., Ry. Co., 57 O. S. 79 (1897).

Section 8993.   (To furnish bills of lading.) Railroad companies operating a line of railway, upon demand of a person or corporation desiring to ship goods or merchandise of any kind in car lots, at any railway station or shipping point in this state, shall count or check the packages composing each lot or car load, and furnish to the shipper of such goods a receipt or bill of lading, specifying the number of packages shipped in each car. Such receipt shall bind the company so executing it to deliver the number of packages so specified, at the place of destination named in such bill of lading. (R. S. Sec. 3378-3; May 8, 1894, 91 v. 207, § 1.)

See § 8993-22.

Prior to the enactment of this section it was held in an action by a shipper against the owners of a steamboat engaged in the business of common carrier, to recover for the nondelivery of goods as per bill of lading, the defendants were liable only for so much of the goods as was actually received on the boat or delivered to some one authorized to receive freight on her account.

Dean v. King, 22 O. S. 118 (1871).

See Little Miami, etc., R. R. Co. v. Dodds, 1 C. S. C. 47 (1870).

Adams v. Brig Pilgrim, 10 W. L. J. 141.

Section 8993-1.   (Bills of lading must contain, what.) Bills of lading issued by any common carrier shall be governed by this act. Every bill must embody within its written or printed terms:

(a)   The date of its issue,

(b)   The name of the person from whom the goods have been received,

(c)   The place where the goods have been received,

(d)   The place to which the goods are to be transported,

(e)   A statement whether the goods received will be delivered to a specified person, or to the order of a specified prson,

(f)   A description of the goods or of the packages containing them which may, however, be in such general terms as are referred to in section 8993-22, and

(g)   The signature of the carrier or his agent.

A negotiable bill shall have the words "order of" printed thereon immediately before the name of the person upon whose order the goods received are deliverable.

A carrier shall be liable to any person injured thereby for the damage caused by the omission from a negotiable 'bill of any of the provisions required in this section.' (May 22, 1911, 102 v. 138.) '

The uniform bills of lading act recommended by the American Bar Association for general adoption is contained in §§ 8993-I to 8993-54 inclusive and applies to bills of lading issued after January 1, 1912.

The act has been adopted in Connecticut, Illinois, Iowa, Louisiana, Massachusetts, Maryland, Michigan, New York, Ohio and Pennsylvania.

Prior to the adoption of this act a bill of lading was defined to be a contract, including a receipt. A receipt for goods with an agreement to carry them to destination.

Wood v. Perry, Wright 240 (1833).

Babcock v. May, 4 Ohio 335 (1831).

So far as it was a receipt, as well as in its recitals of fact, it could be contradicted by parol evidence.

Page v. Railroad Co., 4 West L. M. 644 (C. P. 1863).

Dean v. King, 22 O. S. 118 (1871).

Railroad Co. v. Pontius, 19 O. S. 221 (1869).

But parol evidence was inadmissible to contradict the terms of the contract.

Babcock v. May, 4 Ohio 335 (1831).

Section 8993-2. A carrier may insert in a bill, issued by him, any other terms and conditions, provided that such terms and conditions shall not

(a) Be contrary to law or public policy, or

(b) In any wise impair his obligation to exercise at least that degree of care in the transportation and safe-keeping of the goods entrusted to him which a reasonably careful man would exercise in regard to similar goods of his own. (May 22, 1911, 102 v. 138.)

A carrier may agree with the shipper limiting the amount of the liability of the carrier to the agreed value of the property.

Railroad v. Hubbard, 72 O. S. 302, 319, 320 (1905).

Cohn-Goodman Co. v. Wells Fargo & Co., 13 C. C. n. s. 467; 22 C. D. 190 (1910); aff'd, no rep., 87 O. S. 458.

Railway Co. v. Simon, 15 C. C. 123; 8 C. D. 540 (1897).

Unless the carrier knew at the time of making the contract that the property was of greater value than stipulated.

U. S. Express Co. v. Bachman, 28 O. S. 144 (1875).

A provision in a contract between shipper and carrier requiring the shipper to make verified claim for damages within a specified time, is valid providing the time is reasonable.

Penna. Co. v. Shearer, 75 O. S. 249 (1906).

See Railroad Co. v. Hubbard, 72 O. S. 302 (1905).

Express Co. v. Gordon, 5 C. C. n. s. 563; 17 C. D. 243.

Stevenson v. Wells Fargo & Co., 33 W. L. B. 247.

The time for bringing suit for damages may be limited, if the time is reasonable.

Gatton v. Express Co., 14 C. C. n. s. 125; 22 C. D. 532 (1911).

A carrier may, by contract, restrict its liability as an insurer against losses occurring through accident or mistake. But it can not, by contract, exempt itself from liability for negligence.

Davidson v. Graham, 2 O. S. 131 (1853).

Gaines v. Transportation Co., 28 O. S. 419 (1876).

A carrier may limit its liability for loss by fire, to loss by fires caused by its negligence.

C. H. & D. Ry. Co. v. Berdan, 22 C. C. 326; 12 C. D. 481 (1901); aff'd, no rep., 68 O. S. 683.

The burden of proof is on a carrier to show that loss was due to a cause specified in the provision for exemption.

Davidson v. Graham, 2 O. S. 131 (1853).

Union Express Co. v. Graham, 26 O. S. 595 (1875).

Section 8993-3. A bill in which it is stated that the goods are consigned or destined to a specified person, is a non-negotiable or straight bill. (May 22, 1911, 102 v. 138.)

Section 8993-4. (When negotiable.) A bill in which it is stated that the goods are consigned or destined to the order of any person named in such bill, is a negotiable or order bill.

Any provision in such a bill that it is non-negotiable shall not affect its negotiability within the meaning of this act. (May 22, 1911, 102 v. 138.)

Negotiability prior to passage of this act.

See Emery's Sons v. Bank, 25 O. S. 360 (1874).

Page v. Railroad Co., 4 West L. M. 644.

Section 8993-5. (Shall not be issued in sets; to what countries.) Negotiable bills issued in this state for the transportation of goods to any place in the United States on the continent of North America, except Alaska, shall not be issued in parts or sets.

If so issued the carrier issuing them shall be liable for failure to deliver the goods described therein to any one who purchases a part for value in good faith, even though the purchase be after the delivery of the goods by the carrier to a holder of one of the other parts. (May 22, 1911, 102 v. 138.)

Section 8993-6. (When "duplicate" should appear on the face of bill.) When more than one negotiable bill is issued in this state for the same goods to be transported to any place in the United States on the continent of North America, except Alaska, the word "duplicate" or some other word or words indicating that the document is not an original bill shall be placed plainly upon the face of every such bill, except the one first issued. A carrier shall be liable for the damage caused by his failure so to do to any one who has purchased the bill for value in good faith as an original, even though the purchase be after the delivery of the goods by the carrier to the holder of the original bill. (May 22, 1911, 102 v. 139.)

Section 8993-7. (**"Non-negotiable".**) A non-negotiable bill shall have placed plainly upon its face by the carrier issuing it "non-negotiable" or "not-negotiable."

This section shall not apply, however, to memoranda or acknowledgments of an informal character. (May 22, 1911, 102 v. 139.)

Section 8993-8. (**When negotiability not limited.**) The insertion in a negotiable bill of the name of a person to be notified of the arrival of the goods shall not limit the negotiability of the bill, or constitute notice to a purchaser thereof of any rights or equities of such person in the goods. (May 22, 1911, 102 v. 139.)

Section 8993-9. (**When estopped from denial.**) Except as otherwise provided in this act, where a consignor receives a bill and makes no objection to its terms or conditions at the time he receives it, neither the consignor nor any person who accepts delivery of the goods, nor any person who seeks to enforce any provision of the bill, shall be allowed to deny that he is bound by such terms and conditions, so far as they are not contrary to law or public policy. (May 22, 1911, 102 v. 139.)

A bill of lading signed by the agent of a carrier and acquiesced in by the shipper is binding on the latter although not signed by him.
Railroad Co. v. Pontius, 19 O. S. 221 (1869).
Railroad Co. v. Berdan, 22 C. C. 326 (1901); aff'd, 68 O. S. 683.
Railway v. La Tourette, 2 C. C. 279; 1 C. D. 48 (1887).
Assent may be implied from failure to dissent within a reasonable time.
Muller v. Railway, 2 C. S. C. R. 280 (1872).
Before the enactment of this section it was held that assent of the shipper is not presumed, but must be proved.
Railroad Co. v. Barrett, 36 O. S. 448 (1881).
Gaines v. Transportation Co., 28 O. S. 418 (1876).
Mack v. Gt. Western Dispatch, 3 C. C. 36; 2 C. D. 22 (1888).
Where conditions are stamped on the bill after its execution, the assent of the shipper must be shown.
American, etc., Co. v. Packet Co., 5 N. P. 146; 8 L. D. 490 (Super. Ct. Cin.).
A shipper who fills out his own bills of lading on blanks furnished by the carrier is bound by the provisions thereof.
Shaffer v. Railway, 14 C. C. 488; 8 C. D. 66 (1897).
Cohn-Goodman Co. v. Wells Fargo & Co., 13 C. C. n. s. 467; 22 C. D. 190 (1910); aff'd, no rep., 87 O. S. 458.
See Railroad Co. v. Seiberling Co., 8 C. C. 593; 4 C. D. 210 (1894).
Where the transferee of a bill of lading presents it to the carrier and accepts the goods, he is bound by a provision in the bill of lading for demurrage charges, and may be liable to the carrier therefor.
Traction Co. v. Railway Co., 8 C. C. n. s. 134; 18 C. D. 543 (1906).

Section 8993-10. (Carrier bound to deliver goods; when.)
A carrier, in the absence of some lawful excuse, is bound
to deliver goods upon a demand made either by the consignee named in the bill for the goods, or if the bill is
negotiable, by the holder thereof, if such demand is accompanied by—

(a) An offer in good faith to satisfy the carrier's lawful lien upon the goods.

(b) An offer in good faith to surrender, properly indorsed, the bill which was issued for the goods, if the bill
is negotiable, and

(c) A readiness and willingness to sign, when the goods
are delivered, an acknowledgement that they have been delivered, if such signature is requested by the carrier.

In case the carrier refuses or fails to deliver the goods
in compliance with a demand by the consignee or holder
so accompanied, the burden shall be upon the carrier to
establish the existence of a lawful excuse for such refusal
or failure. (May 22, 1911, 102 v. 139.)

Section 8993-11. A carrier is justified, subject to the
provisions of the three following sections, in delivering
goods to one who is

(a) A person lawfully entitled to the possession of the
goods,

(b) The consignee named in a non-negotiable bill for
the goods, or

(c) A person in possession of a negotiable bill for the
goods by the terms of which the goods are deliverable to
his order, or which has been indorsed to him or in blank
by the consignee or by the mediate or immediate indorsee
of the consignee. (May 22, 1911, 102 v. 140.)

Section 8993-12. (Carrier liable for wrongful delivery.)
Where a carrier delivers goods to one who is not lawfully
entitled to the possession of them, the carrier shall be liable
to any one having a right of property or possession in the
goods, if he delivered the goods otherwise than as authorized
by subdivision (b) or (c) of the preceding section; and,
though he delivered the goods as authorized by either of
said subdivisions, he shall be so liable if prior to such delivery he—

(a) Had been requested, by or on behalf of a person
having a right of property or possession in the goods, not
to make such delivery, or

(b) Had information at the time of the delivery that

it was to a person not lawfully entitled to the possession of the goods.

A request or information to be effective within the meaning of this section must be given to an officer or agent of the carrier, the actual or apparent scope of whose duties includes action upon such a request or information, and must be given in time to enable the officer or agent to whom it is given, acting with reasonable diligence, to stop delivery of the goods. (May 22, 1911, 102 v. 140.)

Before the enactment of this section it was held that a carrier was bound to deliver the goods to the consignee. Delivery to a wrong person, not induced by some act or representation of the consignor, was not excused by any degree of care which the carrier might exercise.
Oskamp v. Southern Express Co., 61 O. S. 341 (1899).
Mere delay in delivery is not a conversion of the goods.
Wyler v. Railway, 6 N. P. n. s. 589 (1907).
See Railroad v. O'Donnell, 49 O. S. 489 (1892).

Section 8993-13.   (Delivery to purchaser of bill in good faith.) Except as provided in section 8993-26, and except when compelled by legal process, if a carrier delivers goods for which a negotiable bill had been issued, the negotiation of which would transfer the right to the possession of the goods, and fails to take up and cancel the bill, such carrier shall be liable for failure to deliver the goods to any one who for value and in good faith purchases such bill, whether such purchaser acquired title to the bill before or after the delivery of the goods by the carrier, and notwithstanding delivery was made to the person entitled thereto. (May 22, 1911, 102 v. 140.)

Section 8993-14.   (Exceptions.) Except as provided in section 8993-26, and except when compelled by legal process, if a carrier delivers part of the goods for which a negotiable bill has been issued and fails either—
(a)   To take up and cancel the bill, or
(b)   To place plainly upon it a statement that a portion of the goods has been delivered, with a description, which may be in general terms, either of the goods or packages that have been so delivered, or of the goods or packages which still remain in the carrier's possession, he shall be liable for failure to deliver all the goods specified in the bill, to any one who for value and in good faith purchases it, whether such purchaser acquired title to it before or after the delivery of any portion of the goods by the carrier, and notwithstanding such delivery was made to the person entitled thereto. (May 22, 1911, 102 v. 140.)

An intermediate carrier, which is required by statute to carry freight offered, is bound to take notice of the fact that a bill of. lading was issued, and is liable for delivery of the goods without production of the bill of lading.

Bank of Commerce v. Railroad Co., 2 N. P. n. s. 403; 15 L. D. 32 (C. P. 1904).

Section 8993-15.   (Effect of alteration.) Any alteration, addition or erasure in a bill after its issue, without authority from the carrier issuing the same, either in writing or noted on the bill, shall be void, whatever be the nature and purpose of the change, and the bill shall be enforceable according to its original tenor. (May 22, 1911, 102 v. 141.)

Section 8993-16.   (Lost or destroyed negotiable bill. Delivery under order of court does not relieve carrier from liability, without notice.) Where a negotiable bill has been lost or destroyed, a court of competent jurisdiction may order the delivery of the goods upon satisfactory proof of such loss or destruction, and upon the giving of a bond with sufficient surety to be approved by the court to protect the carrier or any person injured by such delivery from any liability or loss, incurred by reason of the original bill remaining outstanding. The court may also in its discretion order the payment of the carrier's reasonable costs and counsel fees.

The delivery of the goods under an order of the court, as provided in this section, shall not relieve the carrier from liability to a person to whom the negotiable bill has been or shall be negotiated for value without notice of the proceedings or of the delivery of the goods. (May 22, 1911, 102 v. 141.)

Section 8993-17.   (Effect of "duplicate" on face of bill.) A bill upon the face of which the word "duplicate" or some other word or words indicating that the document is not an original bill is placed plainly shall impose upon the carrier issuing the same the liability of one who represents and warrants that such bill is an accurate copy of an original bill properly issued, but no other liability. (May 22, 1911, 102 v. 141.)

Section 8993-18.   (When title no excuse from liability for refusal to deliver goods.) No title to goods or right to their possession asserted by a carrier for his own . benefit, shall excuse him from liability for refusing to deliver the goods according to the terms of a bill issued for them, unless such title or right is derived directly or indirectly from a transfer made by the consignor or consignee after the shipment, or from the carrier's lien. (May 22, 1911, 102 v. 141.)

Section 8993-19. (Interpleader.) If more than one person claims the title or possession of goods, the carrier may require all known claimants to interplead, either as a defense to an action brought against him for non-delivery of the goods, or as an original suit, whichever is appropriate. (May 22, 1911, 102 v. 141.)

Section 8993-20. (Opposing claimants.) If some one other than the consignee or person in possession of the bill has a claim to the title or possession of the goods, and the carrier has information of such claim, the carrier shall be excused from liability for refusing to deliver the goods either to the consignee or person in possession of the bill, or to the adverse claimant, until the carrier has had a reasonable time to ascertain the validity of the adverse claim or to bring legal proceedings to compel all claimants to interplead. (May 22, 1911, 102 v. 141.)

Section 8993-21. (Defense.) Except as provided in the two preceding sections and in section 8993-11, no right or title of a third person, unless enforced by legal process, shall be a defense to an action brought by the consignee of a non-negotiable bill or by the holder of a negotiable bill against the carrier for failure to deliver the goods on demand. (May 22, 1911, 102 v. 142.)

Section 8993-22. (Liability of issuing carrier.) If a bill of lading has been issued by a carrier, or on his behalf by an agent or employe, the scope of whose actual or apparent authority includes the issuing of bills of lading, the carrier shall be liable to
(a)   The consignee named in a non-negotiable bill, or
(b)   The holder of a negotiable bill,
Who has given value in good faith relying upon the description therein of the goods, for damages caused by the non-receipt by the carrier or a connecting carrier of all or part of the goods or their failure to correspond with the description thereof in the bill at the time of its issue.
If, however, the goods are described in a bill merely by a statement of marks or labels upon them, or upon packages containing them, or by a statement that the goods are said to be goods of a certain kind or quantity, or in a certain condition, or it is stated in the bill that packages are said to contain goods of a certain kind or quantity or in

a certain condition or that the contents or condition of the contents of packages are unknown, or words of like purport are contained in the bill, such statements, if true, shall not make liable the carrier issuing the bill, although the goods are not of the kind or quantity or in the condition which the marks or labels upon them indicate, or of the kind or quantity or in the condition they were said to be by the consignor. The carrier may, also, by inserting in the bills the words "shipper's load and count," or other words of like purport, indicate that the goods were loaded by the shipper and the description of them made by him; and if such statements be true, the carrier shall not be liable for damages caused by the improper loading or by the non-receipt or by the misdescription of the goods described in the bill. (May 22, 1911, 102 v. 142.)

See § 8993.
Custom of consignees to accept railway coal weight certificates.
See Nimishilling, etc., Co. v. Railway, 5 O. L. R. 455; 52 O. L. B. 569.
A carrier may refuse to receive an article not properly packed. But if received, due care must be exercised, and, if injured, the burden of proof rests on the carrier to show that the injury was due to defective packing.
Express Co. v. Graham, 26 O. S. 595 (1875).

Section 8993-23. (No attachment after delivery to carrier.) If goods are delivered to a carrier by the owner, or by a person whose act in conveying the title to them to a purchaser for value in good faith would bind the owner, and a negotiable bill is issued for them, they cannot thereafter, while in the possession of the carrier, be attached by garnishment or otherwise, or be levied upon under an execution, unless the bill be first surrendered to the carrier or its negotiation enjoined. The carrier shall in no such case be compelled to deliver the actual possession of the goods until the bill is surrendered to him or impounded by the court. (May 22, 1911, 102 v. 142.)

Section 8993-24. (Injunction.) A creditor whose debtor is the owner of a negotiable bill shall be entitled to such aid from courts of appropriate jurisdiction by injunction and otherwise in attaching such bill, or in satisfying the claim by means thereof, as is allowed at law or in equity in regard to property which cannot readily be attached or levied upon by ordinary legal process. (May 22, 1911, 102 v. 142.)

Section 8993-25. (No lien except for freight, etc.) If a negotiable bill is issued the carrier shall have no lien on the

goods therein mentioned, except for charges on those goods
for freight, storage, demurrage, terminal, and switching
charges, and expenses necessary for the preservation of the
goods or incident to their transportation subsequent to the
date of the bill, unless the bill expressly enumerates other
charges for which a lien is claimed.   In such case there
shall also be a lien for the charges enumerated so far as
they are allowed by law and the contract between the consignor and the carrier. (May 22, 1911, 102 v. 143.)

> A connecting carrier, which has paid to the initial carrier its freight
> charges and expenses of unloading and unloading, is subrogated to the
> lien of the former carrier therefor.
> Bennett Bros. Lumber Co. v. Robinson, 159 Fed. 910; 16 O. F. D. 65
> (C. C. A. 1908).

**Section 8993-26.   (Not liable for delivery, after selling
for carrier's lien.)**   After goods have been lawfully sold to
satisfy a carrier's lien, or because they have not been
claimed, or because they are perishable or hazardous, the
carrier shall not thereafter be liable for failure to deliver
the goods to the consignee or owner of the goods, or to a
holder of the bill given for the goods when they were
shipped, even if such bill be negotiable. (May 22, 1911, 102
v. 143.)

Section 8993-27.   (When bill negotiated by delivery.)   A
negotiable bill may be negotiated by delivery where, by the
terms of the bill, the carrier undertakes to deliver the goods
to the order of a specified person, and such person, or a
subsequent indorsee of the bill, has indorsed it in blank.
(May 22, 1911, 102 v. 143.)

Section 8993-28.   (Negotiated by endorsement.)   A negotiable bill may be negotiated by the indorsement of the
person to whose order the goods are deliverable by the tenor
of the bill.   Such indorsement may be in blank or to a
specified person.   If indorsed to a specified person, it may
be negotiated again by the indorsement of such person in
blank or to another specified person.   Subsequent negotiation
may be made in like manner. (May 22, 1911, 102 v. 143.)

> Former law. See Emery Sons v. Bank, 25 O. S. 360 (1874).
> Jordan v. James, 5 Ohio 88 (1831).

Section 8993-29.   (Transfer by delivery.)   A bill may
be transferred by the holder by delivery, accompanied with
an agreement, express or implied, to transfer the title to the
bill or to the goods represented thereby.   A non-negotiable

bill cannot be negotiated, and the indorsement of such a bill gives the transferee no additional right. (May 22, 1911, 102 v. 143.)

Section 8993-30. A negotiable bill may be negotiated by any person in possession of the same, however such possession may have been acquired if, by the terms of the bill, the carrier undertakes to deliver the goods to the order of such person, or if at the time of negotiation the bill is in such form that it may be negotiated by delivery. (May 22, 1911, 102 v. 143.)

Section 8993-31. (Title acquired by negotiated bill.) A person to whom a negotiable bill has been duly negotiated acquires thereby—
(a) Such title to the goods as the person negotiating the bill to him had or had ability to convey to a purchaser in good faith for value, and also such title to the goods as the consignee and consignor had or had power to convey to a purchaser in good faith for value, and
(b) The direct obligation of the carrier to hold possession of the goods for him according to the terms of the bill as fully as if the carrier had contracted directly with him. (May 22, 1911, 102 v. 143.)

See Emery Sons v. Bank, 25 O. S. 360 (1874).
Jordan v. James, 5 Ohio 88 (1831).

Section 8993-32. (Rights when bill transferred but not negotiated.) A person to whom a bill has been transferred, but not negotiated, acquires thereby as against the transferor, the title to the goods, subject to the terms of any agreement with the transferor. If the bill is non-negotiable, such person also acquires the right to notify the carrier of the transfer to him of such bill, and thereby to become the direct obligee of whatever obligations the carrier ow(n)ed to the transferor of the bill immediately before the notification.

Prior to the notification of the carrier by the transferor or transferee of a non-negotiable bill, the title of the transferee to the goods, and the right to acquire the obligation of the carrier may be defeated by garnishment or by attachment or execution upon the goods by a creditor of the transferor, or by a notification to the carrier by the transferor or a subsequent purchaser from the transferor of a subsequent sale of the goods by the transferor.

A carrier has not received notification within the meaning of this section unless an officer or agent of the carrier, the actual or apparent scope of whose duties includes action upon such a notification has been notified; and no notification shall be effective until the officer or agent to whom it is given has had time with the exercise of reasonable diligence to communicate with the agent or agents having actual possession or control of the goods. (May 22, 1911, 102 v. 144.)

Section 8993-33. (Rights when transferred for value by delivery.) Where a negotiable bill is transferred for value by delivery, and the indorsement of the transferor is essential for negotiation, the transferee acquires a right against the transferor to compel him to indorse the bill, unless a contrary intention appears. The negotiation shall take effect as of the time when the indorsement is actually made. This obligation may be specifically enforced. (May 22, 1911, 102 v. 144.)

Section 8993-34. (Warranties; when transfer for value by endorsement or delivery.) A person who negotiates or transfers for value a bill by indorsement or delivery, including one who assigns for value a claim secured by a bill, unless a contrary intention appears, warrants—

    (a)   That the bill is genuine,

    (b)   That he has a legal right to transfer it;

    (c)   That he has knowledge of no fact which would impair the validity or worth of the bill, and

    (d)   That he has a right to transfer the title to the goods, and that the goods are merchantable or fit for a particular purpose whenever such warranties would have been implied, if the contract of the parties had been to transfer without a bill the goods represented thereby.

In the case of an assignment of a claim secured by a bill, the liability of the assignor shall not exceed the amount of the claim. (May 22, 1911, 102 v. 144.)

Section 8993-35. (Previous endorsers.) The indorsement of a bill shall not make the indorser liable for any failure on the part of the carrier or previous indorsers of the bill to fulfill their respective obligations. (May 22, 1911, 102 v. 144.)

Section 8993-36. (Payment to mortgagee no warrant as to quality or quantity.) A mortgagee or pledgee, or other holder of a bill for security, who in good faith demands or receives payment of the debt for which such bill is security, whether from a party to a draft drawn for such debt, or from any other person, shall not be deemed by so doing to represent or to warrant the genuineness of such bill or the quantity or quality of the goods therein described. (May 22, 1911, 102 v. 145.)

Section 8993-37. (Validity not impaired when negotiation was by fraud, etc.) The validity of the negotiation of a bill is not impaired by the fact that such negotiation was a breach of duty on the part of the person making the negotiation, or by the fact that the owner of the bill was deprived of the possession of the same by fraud, accident, mistake, duress or conversion, if the person to whom the bill was negotiated or a person to whom the bill was subsequently negotiated gave value therefore in good faith without notice of the breach of duty or fraud, accident, duress or conversion. (May 22, 1911, 102 v. 145.)

Section 8993-38. (Effect of sale to purchaser, in good faith and for value.) Where a person having sold, mortgaged, or pledged goods which are in a carrier's possession, and for which a negotiable bill has been issued, or having sold, mortgaged, or pledged the negotiable bill representing such goods, continues in possession of the negotiable bill, the subsequent negotiation thereof by that person under any sale, pledge, or other disposition thereof to any person receiving the same in good faith, for value and without notice of the previous sale, shall have the same effect as if the first purchaser of the goods or bill had expressly authorized the subsequent negotiation. (May 22, 1911, 102 v. 145.)

Section 8993-39. (Bill shall indicate, what.) Where goods are shipped by the consignor in accordance with a contract or order for their purchase, the form in which the bill is taken by the consignor shall indicate the transfer or retention of the property or right to the possession of the goods as follows:

(a) Where by the bill the goods are deliverable to the buyer or to his agent, or to the order of the buyer or of his agent, the consignor thereby transfers the property in the goods to the buyer.

(b) Where by the bill the goods are deliverable to the seller or to his agent, or to the order of the seller or of his agent, the seller thereby reserves the property in the goods. But if, except for the form of the bill, the property would have passed to the buyer on shipment of the goods, the seller's property in the goods shall be deemed to be only for the purpose of securing performance by the buyer of his obligations under the contract.

(c) Where by the bill the goods are deliverable to the order of the buyer or of his agent, but possession of the bill is retained by the seller or his agent, the seller thereby reserves a right to the possession of the goods, as against the buyer.

(d) Where the seller draws on the buyer for the price, and transmits the draft and bill together to the buyer to secure acceptance or payment of the draft, the buyer is bound to return the bill if he does not honor the draft; and if he wrongfully retains the bill he acquires no added right thereby. If, however, the bill provides that the goods are deliverable to the buyer, or to the order of the buyer, or is indorsed in blank or to the buyer by the consignee named therein, one who purchases in good faith, for value, the bill or goods from the buyer, shall obtain the title to the goods, although the draft has not been honored, if such purchaser has received delivery of the bill indorsed by the consignee named therein, or of the goods, without notice of the facts making the transfer wrongful. (May 22, 1911, 102 v. 145.)

Section 8993-40. (Draft with bill of lading attached; assumptions.) Where the seller of goods draws on the buyer for the price of the goods, and transmits the draft and a bill of lading for the goods, either directly to the buyer or through a bank or other agency, unless a different intention on the part of the seller appears, the buyer and all other parties interested shall be justified in assuming—

(a) If the draft is by its terms or legal effect payable on demand or presentation or at sight, or not more than three days thereafter (whether such three days be termed days of grace or not), that the seller intended to require payment of the draft before the buyer should be entitled to receive or retain the bill.

(b) If the draft is by its terms payable on time, extending beyond three days after demand, presentation or sight (whether such three days be termed days of grace or not), that the seller intended to require acceptance, but not payment of the draft before the buyer should be entitled to receive or retain the bill.

The provisions of this section are applicable, whether by the terms of the bill the goods are consigned to the seller, or to his order, or to the buyer, or to his order, or to a third person, or to his order. (May 22, 1911, 102 v. 146.)

· **Section 8993-41.** (**Seller's lien nor right of stoppage in transitu, shall defeat right of purchaser for** value.) Where a negotiable bill has been issued for goods no seller's lien or right of stoppage in transitu shall defeat the rights of any purchaser for value in good faith to whom such bill has been negotiated, whether such negotiation be prior or subsequent to the notification to the carrier who issued such bill of the seller's claim to a lien or right of stoppage in transitu. Nor shall the carrier be obliged to deliver, or justified in delivering, the goods to an unpaid seller unless such bill is first surrendered for cancellation. (May 22, 1911, 102 v. 146.)

See Railroad Co. v. Koontz, 15 C. C. 288; 9 C. D. 102 (1897).
Page v. Railroad Co., 4 West L. M. 644 (C. P. 1863).
Where goods have been stopped in transit the carrier acts at his peril in delivering them to either the consignor or the consignee. It may bring the goods into court and require the claimants to determine the right of possession.
Howe v. Railway, 18 C. C. 333; 10 C. D. 182 (1899).

Section 8993-42. (**Rights of mortgagee or lien-holder.**) Except as provided in section 8993-41, nothing in this shall limit the rights and remedies of a mortgagee or lien-holder whose mortgage or lien on goods would be valid, apart from this act as against one who for value and in good faith purchased from the owner, immediately prior to the time of their delivery to the carrier, the goods which are subject to the mortgage or lien and obtained possession of them. (May 22, 1911, 102 v. 146.)

Section 8993-43. (**Fraud. Penalty.**) Any officer, agent or servant of a carrier, who, with intent to defraud, issues or aids in issuing a bill of lading knowing that all or any part of the goods for which such bill is issued have not been received by such carrier, or by an agent of such carrier, or by a connecting carrier, or are not under the carrier's control at the time of issuing such bill, shall be guilty of a crime, and, upon conviction, shall be punished for each offense by imprisonment in the penitentiary not exceeding five years, or by a fine not exceeding five thousand dollars, or by both. (May 22, 1911, 102 v. 147.)

Section 8993-44. (**False statement. Penalty.**) Any officer, agent, or servant of a carrier, who, with intent to defraud, issues or aids in issuing a bill for goods, knowing that it contains any false statement, shall be guilty of a crime, and, upon conviction, shall be punished for each of-

fense by imprisonment in the penitentiary not exceeding one
year, or by a fine not exceeding one thousand dollars, or
by both.   (May 22, 1911, 102 v. 147.)

Section 8993-45.   (Unauthorized duplicate bills.   Penalty.)
Any officer, agent, or servant of a carrier, who, with intent
to defraud, issues or aids in issuing a duplicate or additional
negotiable bill for goods in violation of the provisions of
section 8993-6, knowing that a former negotiable bill for
the same goods, or any part of them, is outstanding and
uncancelled, shall be guilty of a crime, and, upon conviction,
shall be punished for each offense by imprisonment in the
penitentiary not exceeding five years, or by a fine not exceeding five thousand dollars, or by both.   (May 22, 1911,
102 v. 147.)

**Section 8993-46.   (Penalty for transfer of negotiable bill
for value, without title or mortgaged.)**   Any person who
ships goods to which he has not title, or upon which there
is a lien or mortgage, and who takes for such goods a negotiable bill which he afterwards negotiates for value with
intent to defraud, and without disclosing his want of title
or the existence of the lien of mortgage, shall be guilty of
a crime, and, upon conviction, shall be punished for each
offense by imprisonment in the penitentiary not exceeding
one year, or by a fine not exceeding one thousand dollars,
or by both.   (May 22, 1911, 102 v. 147.)

**Section 8993-47.   (Penalty for negotiating bill for value,
for goods not in possession.)**   Any person who, with intent
to defraud, negotiates or transfers for value a bill, knowing
that any or all of the goods which, by the terms of such
bill, appear to have been received for transportation by the
carrier which issued the bill, are not in their possession or
control of such carrier, or of a connecting carrier, without
disclosing this fact, shall be guilty of a crime, and, upon
conviction, shall be punished for each offense by imprisonment in the penitentiary not exceeding five years, or by a
fine not exceeding five thousand dollars, or by both.   (May
22, 1911, 102 v. 147.)

**Section 8993-48.   (Penalty for obtaining bill falsely, when
goods not delivered to carrier.)**   Any person who, with intent to defraud, secures the issue by a carrier of a bill,
knowing that at the time of such issue, any or all of the
goods described in such bill, as received for transportation,

have not been received by such carrier, or an agent of such carrier, or a connecting carrier; or are not under the carrier's control, by inducing an officer, agent, or servant of such carrier falsely to believe that such goods have been received by such carrier, or are under its control, shall be guilty of a crime, and, upon conviction, shall be punished for each offense by imprisonment in the penitentiary not exceeding five years, or by a fine not exceeding five thousand dollars, or by both. (May 22, 1911, 102 v. 147.)

Section 8993-49. (Aid in obtaining false bills. Penalty.) Any person who, with intent to defraud, issues or aids in issuing a non-negotiable bill without the words "not-negotiable" placed plainly upon the face thereof, shall be guilty of a crime, and, upon conviction, shall be punished for each offense by imprisonment in the penitentiary not exceeding five years, or by a fine not exceeding five thousand dollars, or by both. (May 22, 1911, 102 v. 148.)

Section 8993-50. (Other laws applicable.) In any case not provided for in this act, the rules of law and equity, including the law merchant, and in particular the rules relating to the law of principal and agent, executors, administrators, and trustees, and to the effect of fraud, misrepresentation, duress, or coercion, accident, mistake, bankruptcy, or other invalidating cause, shall govern. (May 22, 1911, 102 v. 148.)

Section 8993-51. (Uniformity.) This act shall be so interpreted and construed as to effectuate its general purpose to make uniform the law of those states which enact it. (May 22, 1911, 102 v. 148.)

Section 8993-52. (Definitions.) (1) In this act, unless the context or subject matter otherwise requires—

"Action" includes counter-claim, set-off, and suit in equity.

"Bill" means bill of lading.

"Consignee" means the person named in the bill as the person to whom delivery of the goods is to be made.

"Consignor" means the person named in the bill as the person from whom the goods have been received for shipment.

"Goods" means merchandise or chattels in course of transportation, or which have been or about to be transported.

"Holder" of a bill means a person who has both actual possession of such bill and a right of property therein.

"Order" means an order by indorsement on the bill.

"Owner" does not include mortgagee or pledgee.

"Person" includes a corporation or partnership, or two or more persons having a joint or common interest.

To "purchase" includes to take as mortgagee and to take as pledgee.

"Purchaser" includes mortgagee and pledgee.

"Value" is any consideration sufficient to support a simple contract. An antecedent or pre-existing obligation, whether for money or not, constitutes value where a bill is taken either in satisfaction thereof or as security therefor.

(2) A thing is done "in good faith," within the meaning of this act, when it is in fact done honestly, whether it be done negligently or not. (May 22, 1911, 102 v. 148.)

Section 8993-53. The provisions of this act do not apply to bills made and delivered prior to the taking effect thereof. (May 22, 1911, 102 v. 150.)

Section 8993-54. This act shall take effect on the first day of January, one thousand nine hundred and twelve. (May 22, 1911, 102 v. 150.)

Section 8994. (Forfeiture.) A railroad company, or agent or officer thereof, refusing to comply with the provisions of the next preceding section (8993) shall be liable to a penalty of fifty dollars, to be recovered by civil action against the company by which such agent or officer is employed, or to which such goods are offered for shipment. (R. S. Sec. 3378-4; May 8, 1894, 91 v. 207, § 2.)

Section 8994-1. (Liability for loss or damage to freight regardless of contract or rule of common carrier.) That any common carrier, railroad or transportation company receiving property at a point within the state of Ohio for transportation to a point within the state of Ohio, shall issue a receipt or bill of lading therefor and shall be liable to the lawful holder thereof for any loss, damage, or injury to such property caused by it or by any common carrier, railroad, or transportation company to which such property may be delivered or over whose line or lines such property may pass, and no contract, receipt, rule or regulation shall exempt such common carrier, railroad, or transportation company from the liability hereby imposed: **Provided,**

that nothing in this section shall deprive any holder of such receipt or bill of lading of any remedy or right of action which he has under existing law.

That the common carrier, railroad, or transportation company issuing such receipt or bill of lading shall be entitled to recover from the common carrier, railroad, or transportation company on whose line the loss, damage, or injury shall have been sustained the amount of such loss, damage or injury as it may be required to pay the owners of such property as may be evidenced by any receipt, judgment, or transcript thereof. (May 15, 1911, 102 v. 113.)

This section is adopted from the federal interstate commerce act (34 U. S. Stat. L. 594).

This section does not prohibit a contract limiting the liability of the carrier to the agreed value of the property.

> Cohn-Goodman Co. v. Wells Fargo & Co., 13 C. C. n. s. 467, 471, 473 (1910) ; aff'd, no rep., 87 O. S. 458.
>
> Greenwald v. Barrett, 199 N. Y. 170.
>
> Travis v. Wells Fargo & Co., 79 N. J. L. 85.
>
> Bernard v. Adams Express Co., 205 Mass. 254.
>
> Larsen v. Oregon Short Line, 110 Pac. 983 (Utah).
>
> Adams Express Co. v. Croninger, 226 U. S. 491 (1912).
>
> M. K. & T. Ry. v. Harriman, 227 U. S. — (1913).

A valid limitation of liability, made by the initial carrier, inures to the benefit of succeeding carriers.

> Kansas City So. Ry. v. Carl, 227 U. S. — (1913).

Liability of initial carrier. Before the enactment of this section a carrier was liable where it contracted to transport freight over connecting lines. But where the contract was to carry freight over the initial carrier's line, only, and deliver it to connecting carriers, a stipulation in the contract was valid which exempted the initial carrier from liability for loss beyond its own line.

> Railroad Co. v. Pontius, 19 O. S. 221 (1869).

Where goods were returned to the initial carrier in a slightly damaged condition, but capable of being repaired at small cost, and were by the initial carrier placed in a warehouse and left without attention, until worthless, the shipper not having been notified, the initial carrier was held liable for the value of the goods, less the damage originally sustained.

> John Church Co. v. Railway Co., 5 N. P. n. s. 585; 18 L. D. 205 (C. P. 1907).

Where goods carried over connecting lines were refused by the consignee, and the shipper, in writing, appointed the initial carrier his agent to procure return of the goods, agreeing to indemnify the company against liability in so doing, the initial carrier was held not liable for damage to the goods on the return, without its fault and not on its own line.

> Erie Railroad Co. v. Cappell, 80 O. S. 128 (1909).

Where a consignee paid the entire freight charges to the railroad which delivered the goods, the goods having passed over several railroads and having been received in bad condition; and by agreement of the parties the consignee filed a claim for damages, the company was held to have recognized that there was but one contract for transportation, and was held liable.

> Railway Co. v. Barron, Boyle & Co., 11 C. C. n. s. 602; 21 C. D. 142 (1908) ; aff'd, 80 O. S. 707; s. c., 8 N. P. n. s. 517; 19 L. D. 710.

Duty of carrier to trace goods not delivered. On demand of the shipper, it is the duty of a carrier to trace goods which have not reached the consignee. Where a carrier apparently acquiesces in such a demand but takes no action for a long period and the goods are finally destroyed through the burning of a warehouse, the carrier is liable.

Freiberg v. Railway Co., 11 C. C. n. s. 241; 20 C. D. 669 (1908); aff'd, 83 O. S. 482.

Section 8995.   (Storage and warehouse certificate.) A railroad company, organized under the laws of this state, upon the receipt of iron ore or grain or other merchandise from any vessel, water-craft or other source for storage and deposit, duly consigned to such company, upon the request of the owner or owners of such ore, grain or other merchandise, with the written consent of the consignee, may issue to the owner or owners of such ore, grain or other merchandise, a certificate, receipt or voucher, which shall name the railway company by whom the ore or grain or other merchandise is held at the time such certificate, receipt or voucher is issued, to whom such ore, grain or other merchandise was consigned, the quantity held by such company, and so near as may be the quality or grade thereof, but not incurring any liability for the grade or quality, which certificate, receipt or voucher, shall be signed by the president or vice president of the company, and countersigned by the general agent thereof appointed for that purpose, or such other officer as may be appointed by such railroad company, and be transferable and negotiable by indorsement thereon, by the person or persons to whose order it is made payable. On the presentation of the certificate, receipt or voucher, so indorsed to such railway company at its general offices, by the holder or holders thereof and on demand, the company shall deliver to the holder or holders, the iron ore or grain or other merchandise described therein, on the payment by such person or persons to the railroad company of all proper charges thereon. (R. S. Sec. 3378-1; February 22, 1889, 86 v. 52, § 1.)

Whether a warehouse maintained by a railroad company should be taxed as real or personal property depends upon its use.

Cincinnati v. Hynicka, 9 N. P. n. s. 273 (C. P. 1909).

Section 8996.   (Rates of fare and freight on branch roads.) A company may demand and receive for the transportation of passengers on a branch road, whose length does not exceed ten miles, a fare not exceeding six cents per mile, and for transportation of property such reasonable rates as from time to time may be fixed by the company or prescribed by law. (R. S. Sec. 3378; April 29, 1872, 69 v. 203, § 4.)

Section 8997. (When connections may be made.) When the track of a company crosses, connects or intersects the track of the same gauge of another company, either company may connect the tracks of the two roads so crossing, connecting or intersecting so as to admit the passage of cars from one road to another with facility and avoid the necessity of transferring freights from such cars. (R. S. Sec. 3340; February 24, 1891, 88 v. 45; April 15, 1857, 54 v. 133, § 5.)

Section cited.
    W. Jefferson Creamery Co. v. Railroad, 8 O. L. R. 19 (R. R. Com. 1910); s. c., 10 N. P. n. s. 665.
    See § 9002.

Section 8998. (When companies must switch cars of other companies.) When the tracks of one company lie contiguous to coal mines, stone quarries, manufacturing establishments, elevators, warehouses, navigable waters or side tracks, suitable for loading or unloading, it shall switch the cars of other companies, at the request of such companies, or the shippers, over and upon the tracks so lying by such mines, quarries, manufacturing establishments, elevators, warehouses, navigable waters or side tracks, for the purpose of unloading or loading grain or other freight into or from such elevators, warehouses, boats upon such navigable waters, or side tracks without demurrage, for forty-eight hours. (R. S. Sec. 3340; February 24, 1891, 88 v. 45; April 15, 1857, 54 v. 133, § 5.)

Equal facilities to be furnished shippers. § 8990.
Penalty for violation of this section. § 9002.
    This section does not require a railroad company to throw open its public or "team" tracks to other railroads.
    Rheinstrom, etc., Co. v. Railway Co., 4 O. L. R. 755 (R. R. Com. 1907).
    Pierce, etc., Co. v. Railroad Co., 6 O. L. R. 147 (R. R. Com. 1908).

    Remedy of consignee or shipper. Mandatory injunction will lie to compel a railroad company to switch cars of other companies as required by this section.
    Troy, etc., Co. v. Railway Co., 3 N. P. n. s. 412 (1903); aff'd, 72 O. S. 613.
    See Chicago, etc., R. Co. v. Suffren, 129 Ill. 274 (1889).

    "Contiguous" tracks. The word "contiguous" in this section is limited by the phrase "suitable for loading or unloading". To be contiguous the tracks of the railroad company must be so located that the shipper or consignee may load or unload directly from car into warehouse.
    Rheinstrom, etc., Co. v. Railway Co., 4 O. L. R. 755 (R. R. Com. 1907).

A side track located wholly upon a public street, which can be reached from a grain elevator by means of a spout eighteen feet long extending over the sidewalk and over a part of the street, is not "contiguous" to the elevator.

Pierce, etc., Co. v. Railroad Co., 6 O. L. R. 147 (R. R. Com. 1908).

Demurrage. After forty-eight hours a demurrage charge may be imposed for delay in unloading.

Phillips v. Erie R. Co., 6 C. C. n. s. 505; 17 C. D. 486 (1905); affirming, 14 L. D. 706.

See note to § 8980.

A railroad company may refuse to switch cars where the consignee has refused or failed to pay proper demurrage charges for delay in unloading former cars.

Troy, etc., Co. v. Railway Co., 3 N. P. n. s. 412 (1903); aff'd, 72 O. S. 613.

Phillips v. Erie R. Co., 6 C. C. n. s. 505; 17 C. D. 486 (1905); affirming, 14 L. D. 706.

But not where the delay in unloading such former cars was caused by acts of the railway company.

Troy, etc., Co. v. Railway Co., 3 N. P. n. s. 412 (1903); aff'd, 72 O. S. 613.

Car service rules established by Railroad Commission.

Ohio Shippers Assn. v. Ann Arbor R. Co., 52 Bull. 279 (1907).

Section 8999. (When companies must transport cars of other companies.) When the tracks of two companies are so connected, either, when required, shall transport over its road to its destination thereon, any freight offered, in cars in which it is offered, at its local rates per mile as set forth in its freight tariff for the distance most nearly corresponding, and return the cars, with or without freight or unnecessary delay. (R. S. Sec. 3341; April 18, 1892, 89 v. 369; February 24, 1891, 88 v. 45; April 15, 1857, 54 v. 133, § 7.)

A railroad company must receive freight, at its regular stations, for transportation to any station on its own or connecting lines regardless of distance.

W. Jefferson, etc., Co. v. Railroad Co., 8 O. L. R. 10, 19 (R. R. Com. 1910); s. c., 10 N. P. n. s. 665.

Sections 8998 to 9000 relate only to the switching charge which the railroad companies may make each other on freight which one company receives from the other, and create no right of action against either of the companies in favor of individual shippers, if the switching charge is in excess of that provided.

Brick Co. v. Trust Co., 187 Fed. 63 (C. C. A. 1911).

Section 9000. (Rates for switching cars of other companies.) A company owning a track or tracks lying contiguous to coal mines, stone quarries, manufacturing establishments, elevators, warehouses, navigable waters or sidetracks, and within the proper terminal limits of or about a city or village, shall be entitled to receive from the company whose cars are so switched, loaded and unloaded at such mines, quarries, manufacturing establishments, elevators, warehouses, navigable waters or side-tracks, no more than one dollar per car for switching one-half mile or less on such tracks; for distances over one-half mile, and not exceeding two and one-half miles, not to exceed one dollar and fifty cents per car; for distances over two and one-half miles and not exceeding five miles, not more than two dollars per car; and for all distances of more than five miles, not more than three dollars per car. When such service is on the roads of two or more companies, then such charges shall be divided between the companies in proportion to the distances of each road. But each company shall be entitled to at least one dollar for such service, regardless of distance, but there shall be no charge for returning empty cars from such mines, quarries, manufacturing establishments, elevators, warehouses, navigable waters or side-tracks. Such company may perform the service or do the switching work herein provided for, in the daytime. Whatever private side-tracks are or may be constructed, the company must switch cars thereon at the rates herein specified. (R. S. Sec. 3341; April 18, 1892, 89 v. 369; February 24, 1891, 88 v. 45; April 15, 1857, 54 v. 133, § 7.)

Sections 8998 to 9000 relate only to the switching charge which the railroad companies may make each other on freight which one company receives from the other, and create no right of action against either of the companies in favor of individual shippers, if the switching charge is in excess of that provided.

Brick Co. v. Trust Co., 187 Fed. 63 (C. C. A. 1911).

Private side tracks. A private side track is located on private property and not on a public street.

Pierce, etc., Co. v. Railroad Co., 6 O. L. R. 147 (R. R. Com. 1908).

See Troy, etc., Co. v. Railway Co., 3 N. P. n. s. 412, 413, 415 (1903); aff'd, 72 O. S. 613.

Johnson, etc., Co. v. Railroad Co., 1 N. P. n. s. 385; 14 L. D. 209 (C. P. 1904).

A shipper having a private side track is entitled to equal service, in the switching of cars arriving over connecting lines, that is accorded to others similarly situated.

Gill v. Railway, 6 O. L. R. 140 (R. R. Com. 1908).

Car service associations. A car service association formed for the purpose of expediting the shipping business for the general public and of protecting the railroad companies composing it is legal.

Phillips v. Erie Ry., 14 L. D. 706 (C. P. 1904); aff'd, 6 C. C. n. s. 505; 17 C. D. 486 (1905).

Rules of a car service association imposing a reasonable demurrage charge for delay in unloading, and providing that the companies may refuse to switch other cars to a private siding until arrears of demurrage are paid by the owner of the siding, and that when cars are not unloaded within the time limit the charge must be paid before unloading, are reasonable and valid.

    Phillips v. Erie Ry., 14 L. D. 706 (C. P. 1904); aff'd, 6 C. C. n. s. 505; 17 C. D. 486.

    See Troy, etc., Co. v. Railway Co., 3 N. P. n. s. 412 (C. P. 1903); aff'd, 72 O. S. 613.

Section 9001.   (How distance computed.) The distance provided for in the next preceding section shall be computed from the general freight warehouse in such city or village, and from the siding used for the storage of cars nearest to where they may be required, outside municipalities. Nothing herein contained shall require a railway or railroad company now in operation to furnish its terminals and facilities at the rates herein named, to any similar company for a railroad to be built by it hereafter which does not afford similar terminals and reciprocal facilities.   (R. S. Sec. 3341; April 18, 1892, 89 v. 369; February 24, 1891, 88 v. 45; April 15, 1857, 54 v. 133, § 7.)

Section 9002.   (Penalty for overcharge.) A company which violates or permits to be violated any provision of sections eighty-nine hundred and ninety-seven to ninety hundred and one both inclusive or of sections eighty-nine hundred and seventy-seven and eighty-nine hundred and eighty, or which demands or receives a greater sum of money for the transportation of passengers or property, or for the service provided for in such sections eighty-nine hundred and ninety-seven to ninety hundred and one both inclusive than the sum allowed by law, shall pay to the party aggrieved for every such overcharge a sum equal to double the amount of the overcharge; and any officer, employe, or agent of any such company who violates, or permits to be violated, any of such provisions, or demands or receives such sum of money, shall be subject to the like penalty to the party aggrieved. In no case shall the amount paid be less than one hundred and fifty dollars to any bona fide claimant using the road of such company or demanding or receiving any such service in due course of business. (R. S. Sec. 3376; April 14, 1900, 94 v. 220; March 17, 1892, 89 v. 117; April 6, 1876, 73 v. 102, § 13.)

This section is constitutional.

    Railroad Co. v. Cook, 37 O. S. 265 (1881).

    A plaintiff in a pending action for statutory penalties has no such vested right to the penalties as to render unconstitutional as to him the repeal and amendment of the statute, when it is provided that it shall apply to all actions pending. The amendment of this section (94 v. 220) is constitutional.

Railway Co. v. Wells, 65 O. S. 313 (1901).
This section is penal in its nature and should be strictly construed.
Railway Co. v. Wells, 65 O. S. 313 (1901).

"Bona fide claimant." A "bona fide claimant" is one claiming in good faith. It is not necessary that the purchaser of a ticket should use or ride upon the ticket, in order to maintain an action under this section.
Penna. Co. v. O'Connell, 84 O. S. 218 (1911).
Railroad Co. v. Cook, 37 O. S. 265 (1881).

Amount of recovery. Jury trial. Where the facts admitted by the pleadings show that the plaintiff is entitled to recover, it is not error to refuse a jury trial to assess the damages. The statute fixes the amount of the recovery.
Railroad Co. v. Cook, 37 O. S. 265 (1881).
Before judgment, the penalty does not bear interest.
Railway Co. v. Furnace Co., 49 O. S. 102 (1892).
Penalties charged in each case.
See Railway Co. v. Moore, 33 O. S. 384 (1878).

Involuntary payment. Where a shipper is compelled to pay illegal rates to procure the transportation of his property, the payment is not such a voluntary payment as will preclude a recovery of the illegal charge, although paid monthly.
Peters v. Railroad Company, 42 O. S. 275 (1884).

Section 9003. (Separate actions for each violation.) A separate action shall be brought for each overcharge mentioned in the next preceding section, unless the party aggrieved give notice in writing at the time of such overcharge, except the first one, to the officer, agent or employe, of such railroad making or receiving such overcharge, of his intention to bring such action; and no judgment shall be rendered in any action for the penalties above provided, for more than one overcharge unless such written notice shall have been given by the party aggrieved. (R. S. Sec. 3376; April 14, 1900, 94 v. 220; March 17, 1892, 89 v. 117; April 6, 1876, 73 v. 102, § 13.)

This section was substituted for a prior provision for exemplary damages.
Railway Co. v. Wells, 65 O. S. 314 (1901).
The judgment can be rendered in any action for more than one overcharge, unless written notice is given.
Railway Co. v. Wells, 65 O. S. 313, 315 (1901).
Prior to the enactment of this section several causes of action for penalties could be joined.
Railroad Co. v. Cook, 37 O. S. 265 (1881).

Venue. An action brought by a passenger to recover the penalty under § 9002 for overcharge in the sale of a ticket should, under G. C. § 11271, be brought in the county where the ticket was purchased. The court of common pleas of the county of the passenger's destination has no jurisdiction.
Penna. Co. v. O'Connell, 84 O. S. 218 (1911).
The objection to the jurisdiction of the court is not waived by failure

to raise it by demurrer or answer. It may be raised for the first time in a proceeding in error.

Railroad Co. v. Hollenberger, 76 O. S. 177 (1907).

Section 9004. (When provisions do not apply.) The provisions of sections eighty-nine hundred and seventy-seven, eighty-nine hundred and eighty, ninety hundred and two, and ninety hundred and three shall not apply to a railroad in course of construction, the gross earnings of which are less than four thousand dollars per mile per annum, when such road is not owned or operated by companies operating another railroad. Such exemption shall not continue longer than five years after cars are run for the transportation of freight and passengers on such road. (R. S. Sec. 3377; April 6, 1876, 73 v. 102, § 13.)

See Ashley v. Railway Co., 5 O. L. R. 359, 362 (R. R. Com. 1907). Railroad v. Furnace Co., 49 O. S. 102.

CHAPTER 6.

EMPLOYES.

Section 9005. (Engineers addicted to drink not to be employed.) No person, company or corporation operating a railroad in whole or in part in this state directly, or by or through a representative, shall knowingly suffer or permit a person to run or in any capacity to operate a railroad locomotive on any part of his, their or its road in this state, who is intoxicated or in the habit of becoming intoxicated, or knowingly to continue the employment of a person in such capacity after he becomes or is intoxicated, while in charge of such locomotive. (R. S. Sec. 3365-17; April 20, 1891, 88 v. 429, § 1.)

Intoxicated employes—personal injuries.
    See Baltimore, etc., Ry. Co. v. Henthorne, 36 W. L. B. 62, 73 Fed. 634 (1896).

Section 9006. (Forfeiture under preceding section.) For every violation of the next preceding section, the company, person or corporation operating such road, shall forfeit and pay to the state two hundred dollars to be recovered in its name in an action to be prosecuted in any county through which the road runs, by the prosecuting attorney thereof, who shall be entitled to twenty-five per cent of the recovery, and the balance shall be paid into the county treasury. (R. S. Sec. 3365-17; April 20, 1891, 88 v. 429, § 1.)

Section 9007. (Hours of service of certain railroad employes.) A company operating a railroad over thirty miles in length, interurban or street railway, over four miles in length, shall not permit a conductor, engineer, fireman, brakeman, or trainman on a train, or a telegraph operator, a conductor, or motorman on a street railway, who has worked as such for fifteen consecutive hours, again to go on duty or perform work until he has had at least eight hours' rest, except in cases of detention of trains or cars caused by accident, unavoidable or otherwise. And such companies shall so regulate the hours of employment of their employees, that each employee shall have at least eight consecutive hours of rest in each period of twenty-four hours. (May 7, 1913, 103 v. 557; R. S. Sec. 3365-14; April 15, 1892, 89 v. 311, § 1; April 23, 1891, 88 v. 344; March 26, 1890, 87 v. 112.)

This section is constitutional.
    Wheeling, etc., Co. v. Gilmore, 8 C. C. 658; 4 C. D. 366 (1894).
    A part of original R. S. Sec. 3365-14 was held unconstitutional in Wheeling, etc., Co. v. Gilmore, 8 C. C. 658; 4 C. D. 366, and is omitted.
    Under an earlier form of this section it was held that the fact that trainmen had been on duty for more than fifteen consecutive hours is not a violation of this section unless the company had permitted them to undertake the run without eight hours rest, sebsequent to the next preceding run, and not then unless such preceding run occupied more than fifteen consecutive hours.
    B. & O. Ry. v. Collins, 10 C. C. n. s. 486; 20 C. D. 110 (1907); aff'd, 79 O. S. 442.
    Where a train is delayed by accident this section does not make it the duty of the company to provide other trainmen to relieve those on duty.
    B. & O. Ry. v. Collins, 10 C. C. n. s. 486; 20 C. D. 110 (1907); aff'd, 79 O. S. 442.

Section 9008. (Forfeiture under preceding section.) A

railroad company or corporation knowingly violating **the** provisions of the next preceding section shall be liable **to** a penalty of not less than five hundred nor more than one thousand dollars for the first offense, and for any subsequent offense, of not less than one thousand nor more than fifteen hundred dollars, to be recovered by civil action in the name of the state. (R. S. Sec. 3365-15; April 15, 1892, 89 v. 311, § 2; March 26, 1890, 87 v. 112.)

Section 9009. **(Blocking of frogs.)** Every railroad corporation operating a railroad or part of a railroad within this state, shall adjust, fill, or block all angles in frogs, switches and crossings on its roads and in its yards, divisional and terminal stations where trains are made up, with sheet steel, wrought or malleable iron, or other metallic appliances, which shall be so placed and be of such design as will prevent the wedging of the feet of employes and other persons in such angles; and all such appliances or devices shall before installations be approved by the state railroad commission. (May 20, 1910, 101 v. 325; R. S. Sec. 3365-18; April 25, 1898, 93 v. 342, § 1; March 23, 1888, 85 v. 105.)

Frogs need not be blocked in a new switch while it is being constructed.

See Hauss v. Lake Erie, etc., R. R. Co., 12 O. F. D. 613 (1901).

A person crossing a railroad track has the right to assume that the company has obeyed the law, unless, in the exercise of ordinary care, he learns or ought to learn that the contrary is true.

Pittsburg, etc., Ry. Co. v. Burroughs, 6 N. P. 37; 9 L. D. 324 (1899).

An employe injured by reason of a non-compliance with this section may recover damages.

Narramore v. Railway Co., 42 W. L. B. 246 (1899).

Railroad Co. v. Lambright, 5 C. C. 433; 3 C. D. 213 (1891); s. c., 29 W. L. B. 359.

Failure to comply with this section is negligence as a matter of law.

Railroad Co. v. Kountz, 168 Fed. 832 (C. C. A. 1909).

This section is intended to protect not only employes who may step into unblocked angles, but also employes who are dragged or pushed therein by an engine.

Railroad Co. v. Kountz, 168 Fed. 832 (C. C. A. 1909).

Before the amendment of this section (101 v. 325) it was held that this section was limited to frogs in yards, divisional and terminal stations where trains are made up.

Railroad Co. v. Kountz, 168 Fed. 832 (C. C. A. 1909).

Where two railway companies receive cars from each other over a delivery track at a certain point, a person employed by one of them to take the number of its cars and to inspect their seals, as trains were made up at such place by the other, is an employe of the latter within the meaning of this section.

Atkyn v. Wabash, etc., Ry. Co., 41 Fed. 193; 23 W. L. B. 151; 6 O. F. D. 395 (1890).

Defenses. Contributory negligence is a defense.

Railroad Co. v. Ullom, 20 C. C. 512; 11 C. D. 321 (1898); aff'd, no rep., 64 O. S. 582.

Assumption of risk was held to be a defense to the company.

Johns v. Railway Co., 3 C. C. n. s. 545; 13 C. D. 442 (1902); aff'd, 69 O. S. 532; s. c., 7 N. P. 592; 10 L. D. 358.

Contra, Railway Co. v. Craig, 73 Fed. 642; 9 O. F. D. 589 (1896).

Railroad Co. v. Ullom, 20 C. C. 512 (1899).

Narramore v. Railway Co., 42 W. L. B. 246 (1899).

Railway Co. v. Winslow, 10 C. C. 193; 4 C. D. 242 (1894).

The employe of the company charged with the duty of blocking the guard-rails, frogs, and switches is not a fellow servant of the other employes of the company. In such a case the acts of the servant are those of the master.

New York, etc., R. R. Co. v. Lambright, 5 C. C. 433; 3 C. D. 213 (1891); aff'd, no rep., 29 W. L. B. 359.

Impracticability of blocking.

Railway Co. v. Winslow, 10 C. C. 193; 4 C. D. 242 (1894).

Evidence. Evidence that after an accident a sufficient block was placed in the guard-rail without endangering trains is admissible to show that such block could be used with safety.

Cincinnati, etc., R. Co. v. Van Horne, 34 W. L. B. 183 (1895).

Proof of operation by company.

See Wheeling Ry. Co. v. Lewis, 33 W. L. B. 159 (1894).

Section 9009-1. (Penalty.) Whoever, owning, operating or controlling a railroad fails to comply with the provisions of the next preceding section shall be subject to a penalty of twenty-five dollars for each and every day of such failure, to be recovered in a civil action, in the name of the state, and paid into the state treasury. (May 20, 1910, 101 v. 326; see R. S. Sec. 3365-19, repealed 93 v. 343.)

Section 9010. (Relief association prohibited.) No company created, under and by virtue of the laws of this state or of any other state or country, having and operating a line or railway in this state, shall establish, maintain or assist in establishing or maintaining a relief association or society, the rules or by-laws of which require of a person or employe becoming a member thereof to enter into an agreement or stipulation, directly or indirectly, whereby he stipulates or agrees to surrender or waive a right of damages against any railroad company for personal injuries or death, or to surrender or waive, in case he asserts such claim for damages, any right whatever. (R. S. Sec. 3270; April 8, 1908, 99 v. 71; April 29, 1872, 69 v. 203, § 4.)

This section is constitutional.

State v. Railway, 13 C. C. n. s. 37 (1909).

A somewhat similar Iowa statute was held valid in C. B. & Q. Ry. v. McGuire, 219 U. S. 549 (1910).

See §§ 9012, 9013 and notes.

The establishment of an employes' relief association is not ultra vires nor contrary to public policy. Such association is not an insurance company.

State v. Railway Co., 68 O. S. 9 (1903).

Quo warranto lies to oust a relief association organized and conducted in violation of this section.

State v. Railway, 13 C. C. n. s. 37 (1909).

Section 9011. (Unlawful for railroad to limit liability as employer.) No railroad corporation or company owning and operating, or operating a railroad shall adopt or promulgate a rule or regulation for the government of its servants or employes, or make or enter into an agreement with a person engaged in or about to engage in its service, wherein such employe in any manner, promises or agrees to hold such corporation or company harmless, on account of an injury he may receive by reason of accident to, breakage, defect or insufficiency in the cars or machinery and attachments thereto belonging on cars owned, operated, or run by such corporation, or company being defective. (R. S. Sec. 3365-20; April 2, 1890, 87 v. 149, § 1.)

A rule which requires car repairers or inspectors, when at work under a car or train, to see for themselves that a certain flag or light signal is displayed at each end of the cars on which they are working, is a reasonable rule, providing for the safety of employes and not limiting the master's liability for negligence. An agreement by the employe, at the time of his employment, that he understood such rule and would obey it, is binding upon him.

Railroad Co. v. Ropp, 76 O. S. 449 (1907).

Section 9012. (Unlawful for company to compel employe to join any company or association.) No corporation directly or indirectly shall compel or require an employe to join any company or association whatsoever, or withhold any part of an employe's wages or his salary for the payment of dues or assessments in any society or organization, or demand or require either as a condition precedent to securing employment or being employed. Such railroad company shall not discharge an employe because he refuses or neglects to become a member of any society or organization. If an employe is discharged, at any time within ten days after receiving a notice thereof, he may demand the reason of such discharge, and the railroad company thereupon must give the reason to him in writing. (R. S. Sec. 3365-20; April 2, 1890, 87 v. 149, § 1.)

See § 9010.

This section does not apply where an employe voluntarily made application for membership in the company's relief department and agreed to be bound by its regulations.

Caldwell v. Railway Co., 14 L. D. 375 (C. P. 1904).

Reason of discharge. That part of this section which requires a railroad company to furnish written reasons for the discharge of an employe is probably unconstitutional.

> Railroad Co. v. Schaffer, 65 O. S. 414, 422-423 (1901); reversing 17 C. C. 77; 9 C. D. 158.
> Wallace v. Railway Co., 94 Ga. 732; 34 W. L. B. 220.
> See Mattison v. Railway Co., 2 N. P. 276; 3 L. D. 526 (1895).

A discharged employe can not recover the penalty provided in § 9014 because of the failure of the company to give a written reason for his discharge.

> Crall v. Railway Co., 7 C. C. 132; 3 C. D. 696 (1893).
> Connell v. Railway Co., 14 L. D. 400 (C. P. 1902).

Where an employe leaves the service of a company of his own accord he is not entitled to a certificate to that effect under this section.

> Editorial, 33 W. L. B. 109, 121.

Section 9013. (Companies prohibited from demanding or receiving waivers.) No railroad company insurance society or association, or other person shall demand, accept, or enter into an agreement or stipulation with a person about to enter, or in the employ of a railroad company whereby he stipulates or agrees to surrender or waive any right to damages against a railroad company, thereafter arising for personal injury or death, or whereby he agrees to surrender or waive in case he asserts such right, any other right. (R. S. Sec. 3365-20; April 2, 1890, 87 v. 149, § 1.)

> See § 9010.

This section is unconstitutional in so far as it relates to contracts voluntarily entered into by employes.

> Caldwell v. Railway Co., 14 L. D. 375 (C. P. 1904).
> Farrow v. Ry. Co., 7 N. P. 606; 5 L. D. 582 (C. P. 1895).
> Shaver v. Penna. Co., 71 Fed. 931; 9 O. F. D. 221 (C. C. 1896).
> See Pierce v. Van Dusen, 78 Fed. 693; 46 W. L. B. 102, 107; 9 O. F. D. 419 (C. C. A.).
> Cox v. Railway, 1 N. P. 213; 2 L. D. 594; aff'd, 54 O. S. 497.

This section does not apply to a release of liability for injuries received prior to the release.

> Bowers v. Railroad Co., 4 C. C. n. s. 479; 16 C. D. 518 (1904).

Relief association contracts giving option to take benefits or damages. A relief department contract which does not stipulate that all claims for damages are waived, but requires the beneficiary to elect whether he will accept benefits from the relief fund, or rely on his right to sue the company for damages, is not interdicted by this section, nor is it against public policy.

> Pittsburg, etc., Ry. Co. v. Cox, 55 O. S. 497 (1896).
> Shaver v. Pennsylvania Co., 71 Fed. 931; 9 O. F. D. 221 (1896).

Such a contract does not lack mutuality or consideration where the company as a part of the relief agreement, stipulates that it will make up deficiencies in the fund and assume the management of the fund, and do other things along that line.

> Pittsburg, etc., Ry. Co. v. Cox, 55 O. S. 497 (1896).

Where the widow of a deceased member of a relief association, being the beneficiary named by him, accepts benefits from the association. she is not barred from bringing an action as administratrix for wrongful death, although the amount she should receive in the probate court on final· distribution may be affected by her acceptance.

Baltimore, etc., R. Co. v. McCamey, 12 C. C. 543; 5 C. D. 631 (1896).

See Cullison v. Baltimore, etc., R. R. Co., 4 N. P. 360; 7 L. D. 269 (1897).

Where a member of a relief department accepts benefits and signs a release of all damages, his right of action against the company will be defeated, if at the time he signed the release he was able to read and write and was in no manner prevented from reading the release, and was capable of understanding its effect.

Farrow v. Railway Co., 5 L. D. 582 (1895).

Baltimore, etc., R. Co. v. Bryant, 9 C. C. 332 (1895); 6 C. D. 418.

A rule of the relief department of a railroad company, providing for the submission of claims to the superintendent, and on appeal to a committee, the decision of which should be final, does not prevent the beneficiary from bringing an action at law after rejection of the claim by such committee.

Railroad Co. v. Stankard, 56 O. S. 224 (1897).

Railway engaged in interstate commerce. Membership by an employe in the voluntary relief department of a railway engaged in interstate commerce, and the receipt by him of benefits, is no defense to an action by the employe for injuries. The federal law controls.

Railway v. Sheets, 15 C. C. n. s. 305 (1912); aff'd, no rep. by divided court, 87 O. S. 476.

The act of Congress of 1908 was held to apply where the cause of action and receipt of benefits occurred after its enactment, although the membership contract was made prior to its enactment.

Railway v. Sheets, 15 C. C. n. s. 305 (1912); aff'd, no rep., 87 O. S. 476.

Section 9014. (Agreements, etc., void; forfeiture.) All rules, regulations, stipulations and agreements, declared unlawful by the next three preceding sections, are void. A corporation, association or person violating, or aiding or abetting the violation of either of such sections, for each offense shall forfeit and pay to the person thus wronged or deprived of his rights thereunder, not less than fifty nor over five hundred dollars, to be recovered by a civil action. R. S. Sec. 3365-20; April 2, 1890, 87 v. 149, § 1.)

See note to § 9012. *Reason for discharge.*

Section 9015. (Defective machinery prima facie evidence of negligence.) No railroad corporation knowingly or negligently shall use or operate a car or locomotive that is defective, or upon which the machinery or attachments thereto belonging are in any manner defective. If an employe of such corporation receives injury by reason of a defect in a car or locomotive, or the machinery or attachments thereto belonging, owned and operated, or being operated by such corporation, it shall be deemed to have had knowledge of such defect before and at the time such injury is so sustained. When such defect is made to appear in the trial of any action brought by such employe, or his legal representative, against a railroad corporation for damages on account of injuries so received, that fact shall be prima facie evidence of negligence on the part of such corporation. (R. S. Sec. 3365-21; April 2, 1890, 87 v. 149, § 2.)

This section is constitutional, and provides a rule of evidence applicable to all cases on trial in this state, and to all railroad companies any part of whose line of railway extends into this state, whether the injury complained of was received within or without the state.

    Pennsylvania Co. v. McCann, 54 O. S. 10 (1896).

This section does not apply to a cause of action existing at the adoption of the act.

    Railroad Co. v. Hedges, 63 O. S. 339 (1900) ; reversing 15 C. C. 254;
        8 C. D. 265.

This section is a mere rule of evidence and applies to a cause of action, governed by federal law, which arose in another state, but on which suit is brought in Ohio.

    Railway v. Sheets, 15 C. C. n. s. 305 (1912) ; aff'd, no rep. by a divided court, 87 O. S. 476.

Presumption and burden of proof of negligence. The burden of proving, by a preponderance of the evidence, the particular negligence alleged is at all times on the plaintiff. While proof of facts sufficient under this section to create a *prima facie* presumption of negligence casts upon the defendant the burden of producing evidence of equal weight or countervailing force to control or destroy such presumption, yet proof of such facts does not impose upon the defendant the burden of establishing affirmatively, by a preponderance of the evidence, that it was not negligent.

    Klunk v. Railway, 74 O. S. 125 (1906).
    Railway Co. v. Erick, 51 O. S. 146 (1894).
    See Railroad Co. v. Schomer, 171 Fed. 798 (C. C. A. 1909).
    Shankweiler v. Railway, 148 Fed. I95; 15 O. F. D. 371 (C. C. A. 1906).
    Railway v. Burris, 111 Fed. 882; 14 O. F. D. 182 (C. C. A. 1901).
    Railway v. Stone, 2 C. C. n. s. 160; 14 C. D. 192 (1900) ; aff'd, no
        rep., 67 O. S. 528.

A company may overcome the presumption of negligence by showing that in fact it did not have such knowledge, and that it used due diligence to ascertain and remedy defects.

    Railway Co. v. Erick, 51 O. S. 146 (1894).
    Railway Co. v. Meyers, 12 C. C. 263 (1893) ; 4 C. D. 28.
    Knighton v. Baltimore, etc., R. R. Co., 33 W. L. B. 216 (1894).
    See Hill v. Lake Shore, etc., Ry. Co., 22 C. C. 291 (1901).

Inspection. The presumption of knowledge is removable by direct proof of inspection of such a character as a person of ordinary prudence would use under similar circumstances for the safety of himself or his employes.

    Rawlins v. Railway Co., 4 O. L. R. 477; 17 L. D. 344 (C. P.).

Proof of the employment of careful and competent inspectors is not sufficient to overcome the presumption of negligence. Actual and proper inspection, or its equivalent, must be shown.

    Felton v. Bullard, 94 Fed. 781; 42 W. L. B. 218 (C. C. A. 1899).
    Railway Co. v. Erick, 51 O. S. 146 (1894).
    Railway Co. v. Thompson, 82 Fed. 720 (1897).
    Railroad Co. v. Johnson, 33 W. L. B. 248 (1895).

See Railway Co. v. Gilday, 16 C. C. 649; 9 C. D. 27 (1890).
Railroad Co. v. Schomer, 171 Fed. 798 (C. C. A. 1909).
Sufficiency of the inspection is, in general, a question for the jury.
Felton v. Bullard, 94 Fed. 781; 42 W. L. B. 248 (C. C. A. 1899).
Railroad Co. v. Schomer, 171 Fed. 798 (C. C. A. 1909).
See Railroad Co. v. Johnson, 33 W. L. B. 248 (1895).
This section makes no distinction between the cars owned by the company and foreign cars which it may operate, and the duty of inspection applies to both.
Felton v. Bullard, 42 W. L. B. 218 (1899).
See Pennsylvania Co. v. Meyers, 12 C. C. 263 (1893); 4 C. D. 28.
Pennsylvania Co. v. Snyder, 55 O. S. 342 (1896).
Hunt v. Caldwell, 22 C. C. 283 (1901).

Knowledge by employe of defect. This section does not dispense with the necessity of the plaintiff's alleging and proving want of knowledge of defects, or that, having such knowledge, he informed his superior and continued in the service, relying on a promise to remedy the defects.
Hesse v. Columbus, etc., R. R. Co., 58 O. S. 167 (1898).
Where a car is inspected and has the usual three X mark upon it indicating that it is defective and is to be repaired, a brakeman is not chargeable with notice if the mark can not be seen, as at night. If he should see the mark he is chargeable only with such defects as have been discovered by the inspectors.
Michigan Central Ry. Co. v. Butler, 3 C. C. n. s. 449; 13 C. D. 459 (1902); aff'd, no rep., 68 O. S. 662.
A contract which a railroad company required its brakemen to sign when employing them, making it their duty to inspect cars and appliances on which they were to work when in fact it would be impracticable for them to make such inspection, will not relieve the company.
Lake Shore, etc., Ry. Co. v. Gilday, 16 C. C. 649; 9 C. D. 27 (1890).

What constitutes a defective car or machinery. Where an accident occurs to an employe of a railroad company, as a result of the absence of an appliance upon the locomotive which it is customary to provide, the company is placed in the same position under this act as though the appliance had been furnished and was defective.
Crumley v. Cincinnati, etc., Ry. Co., 12 C. C. 164; 5 C. D. 353; s. c., 56 O. S. 781 (1897).

——. **Held to be defective.**
Car with bent step.
O'Connell v. Penna. Co., 118 Fed. 989; 13 O. F. D. 786 (C. C. A. 1902).
Leaky valve in locomotive causing it to start.
Railway v. Raitz, 10 C. C. 70; 4 C. D. 18 (1894).
Broken tie rod, hanging over end of car in a situation likely to deceive a brakeman endeavoring to support himself on the grab iron.
Railroad Co. v. Schomer, 171 Fed. 798 (1909).

——. **Held not defective.** Flat car without sides or ends.
Railway Co. v. Beard, 20 C. C. 681; 11 C. D. 406 (1898).
Eyebolt in brake slightly longer than generally used. Brake chains longer than necessary.
Hunt v. Caldwell, 22 C. C. 283; 11 C. D. 562 (1901).
New coupling device proper in itself, although used without discarding older device.
Railway v. Henly, 48 O. S. 608 (1891).

Who is an employe. A person employed by one company to work in a yard shifting cars for it and another company under the usual arrangement between the companies for expenses is an employe of both companies.

Pittsburg, etc., R. Co. v. Johnston, 33 W. L. B. 248 (1895).

See note to § 8808.

Where the injured employe entered into the contract of employment and was injured out of the state, does this section apply when it changes the effect of the contract?

See Pittsburg, etc., Ry. Co. v. Blair, 11 C. C. 579 (1896); 5 C. D. 366; s. c., 55 O. S. 639.

Section 9016.   (Superior officer and fellow servant defined.) In actions against a railroad company for personal injury to a person while in its employ, or for death resulting from such injury, arising from the negligence of such company, or any of its officers or employes, in addition to other liability, it shall be held that every person in the employ of such company, with actual power or authority to direct or control another employe thereof is not the fellow servant, but superior of such other employe. Every person, also, in the employ of such company who has charge or control of employes in a separate branch or department, is to be held to be the superior and not fellow servant of employes in another branch or department, who have no power to·direct or control in the branch or department in which they are employed. (R. S. Sec. 3365-22; April 2, 1890, 87 v. 150, § 3.)

This section is constitutional.

B. & O. R. Co. v. Hottman, 1 C. C. n. s. 17; 15 C. D. 140 (1903); aff'd, 70 O. S. 475.

Froelich v. Railway Co., 5 C. C. n. s. 6; 14 C. D. 359 (1903).

Pierce v. Van Dusen, 78 Fed. 693; 46 W. L. B. 102; 9 O. F. D. 419 (C. C. A. 1897).

Kane v. Erie R. Co., 133 Fed. 681; 2 O. L. R. 453; 14 O. F. D. 452 (C. C. A. 1904).

Erie R. Co. v. Kane, 155 Fed. 118.

Roe v. Railway, 13 L. D. 260 (C. P. 1902); aff'd, 4 C. C. n. s. 284.

See Erie R. Co. v. McCormick, 69 O. S. 45, 56 (1903).

Maltby v. Railway Co., 13 L. D. 280 (C. P. 1902).

This section applies to receivers.

Pierce v. Van Dusen, 78 Fed. 693; 46 W. L. B. 102 (C. C.·A. 1897).

This section is in derogation of the common law and is not to be enlarged beyond its terms.

Railway Co. v. Shanower, 70 O. S. 166, 169 (1904).

A railroad company can not evade the liabilty imposed by this section by placing a dummy in nominal charge of every other employe on the train.

Kane v. Erie R. Co., 133 Fed. 681; 14 O. F. D. 452 (C. C. A. 1904).

"Authority to direct or control." Whether an employe of a company has authority to direct or control other employes of the same company is a question of fact to be determined in each case. This may be done, however, either by proof of express authority, or by showing the exercise of such authority to be customary, or according to the usual course of conducting the business of the particular company interested, or of railway companies generally.

Railroad Co. v. Margrat, 51 O. S. 130 (1894).

It seems this section would have no bearing on a case where the party alleged to have been negligent had no subordinates, and had no power to "direct or control any other employe." The existing law was not changed by this section except in so far as is specifically provided.

Felton v. Bullard, 42 W. L. B. 218 (1899).

Separate branch or department. The terms "branch" and "department" should not be limited so as to embrace merely those large divisions created for convenience in administering the affairs of the company. On the contrary, it is more reasonable to suppose that they relate to those minute ones which concern the daily duties of the employes.

Railroad Co. v. Margrat, 51 O. S. 130, 145 (1894).

An engineer in charge of a locomotive on one train of cars of a railroad company is in a branch or department of its service separate from that of a brakeman on another train of the same company, and therefore is his superior.

Railroad Co. v. Margrat, 51 O. S. 130 (1894).

See Pittsburg, etc., Ry. Co. v. Devinney, 17 O. S. 197 (1867).

But an engineer and a brakeman on the same train are in the same branch or department and are fellow servants, although by an accidental parting of the train the engineer and brakeman are left on one section of the train and the conductor on the other section.

Railway Co. v. Shanower, 70 O. S. 166 (1904).

Hill v. Railway, 22 C. C. 291; 12 C. D. 241 (1901).

Separate trains are separate branches or departments.

Kane v. Erie R. Co., 142 Fed. 682; 15 O. F. D. 188 (C. C. A. 1906); s. c., 118 Fed. 223 (C. C. A. 1902).

A station agent is in a separate branch or department from employes engaged in operating trains, and when he has no one in his department under his authority, he is not a fellow servant of an engineer.

Snyder v. Railway, 60 O. S. 487, 495 (1899).

The engineer in control of the machinery of a coal tipple and a "hooker" who hooks and unhooks the hoisting tackle are in the same department.

Froelich v. Railway Co., 5 C. C. n. s. 6; 14 C. D. 359 (1903).

It is not necessary that the superior, in the separate branch or department, should have control of all the employes in his department. A company is liable for the injury or death of a fireman through the negligence of the engineer of another train having authority over the fireman although such engineer is subject to the control of the conductor of the train.

Kane v. Erie R. Co., 142 Fed. 682, 15 O. F. D. 188 (C. C. A. 1906).

Held not to be fellow servants under this section. A "hostler," who takes charge of an engine when it arrives home, is the superior of a common laborer around the yard, assisting in caring for the engine.

Baltimore, etc., R. R. Co. v. Sutherland, 12 C. C. 309 (1894); 4 C. D. 115; s. c., 52 O. S. 676.

A yard brakeman is not the fellow servant of a conductor under whose control and direction he is placed.

Pierce v. Van Dusen, 46 W. L. B. 102 (1901).

A switchman in a yard whose duty it was to open such switches as he was notified to open by the different conductors and engineers in the yard, is acting in a separate branch or department from that of such conductors or engineers.

Lake Shore, etc., Ry. Co. v. Pero, 22 C. C. 130 (1901); aff'd, 65 O. S. 608.

A chief inspector of cars, having other inspectors under him, is not the fellow servant of a brakeman.

Railway Co. v. Erick, 51 O. S. 146 (1894); Pittsburg, etc., R. R. Co. v. Blair, 11 C. C. 579, 586 (1896); 5 C. D. 366.

See Felton v. Bullard, 94 Fed. 781 (1899); 42 W. L. B. 218.

A train dispatcher who has complete control of the movements of all trains on a division of a railroad is not a fellow servant of the engineer of a train running on such division.

Baltimore, etc., R. R. Co. v. Camp, 65 Fed. 952 (1895); 8 O. F. D. 391.

Crawford v. Railway, 12 L. D. 17; aff'd, 3 C. C. n. s. 144; 13 C. D. 207.

A yardmaster in charge of a railroad yard of the company, with full control over all its employes who have occasion to be in such yard in the discharge of their duties under their contract of employment with the company, with authority to select from the employes of such company the men who are to operate all trains sent out from such yard over the road of defendant, is by virtue of this section the "superior" and not the fellow servant of a brakeman.

McCann v. Pennsylvania Co., 10 C. C. 139 (1895); 6 C. D. 610; s. c., 54 O. S. 10.

See Pennsylvania Co. v. Fox, 10 C. C. 72 (1893; 4 C. D. 19.

A conductor of a train on which another conductor is riding on a free pass is not the fellow servant of such other conductor.

Lake Shore, etc., Ry. Co. v. Bycroft, 33 W. L. B. 160 (1895); s. c., 8 N. P. 588.

See Manville v. Cleveland, etc., R. R. Co., 11 O. S. 417 (1860).

An employe going home after a day's work stands in the same relation to the company as a person not an employe, and the defense of negligence of a fellow servant can not be interposed.

Columbus, etc., Ry. Co. v. O'Brien, 25 W. L. B. 90 (1891); s. c., 4 C. D. 515; 2 C. D. 681.

See Lake Shore, etc., Ry. Co. v. Mau, 9 C. C. 173 (1894); 4 C. D. 5.

An engineer with a fireman under him is not a fellow servant of a yard helper engaged in cleaning an ash pit.

Railway Co. v. Roe, 4 C. C. n. s. 284; 15 C. D. 628 (1903).

Nor of a brakeman on another train.

Railroad Co. v. Margrat, 51 O. S. 130 (1894).

Nor of a fireman on another train.

Kane v. Erie R. Co., 142 Fed. 682; 15 O. F. D. 188 (C. C. A. 1906).

Held to be fellow servants under this section. An engineer is the fellow servant of a brakeman on the same train.

Railway Co. v. Shanower, 70 O. S. 166 (1904).

Railway Co. v. Ranney, 37 O. S. 665 (1882).

Pittsburg, etc., Ry. Co. v. Lewis, 33 O. S. 196 (1877).

Hill v. Lake Shore, etc., Ry. Co., 22 C. C. 291 (1901).

See Railway v. Moore, 113 Fed. 269; 14 O. F. D. 35.

And of a telegraph operator at a station on the line.

Railroad Co. v. Camp, 65 Fed. 952; 8 O. F. D. 391 (1895).

See Crawford v. Railway, 12 L. D. 17; aff'd, 3 C. C. n. s. 144; 13 C. D. 207.

Snyder v. Railway, 60 O. S. 487 (1899).

The engineer in control of the machinery of a coal tipple and a hooker, who hooks and unhooks the hoisting tackle, are fellow servants where the engineer has no control over the hooker.

Froelich v. Railway Co., 5 C. C. n. s. 6; 14 C. D. 359 (1903).

OTHER LIABILITY. DECISIONS PRIOR TO ENACTMENT OF THIS SECTION.

From considerations of public policy, railroad companies are liable for injuries to their servants caused by the carelessness of those who are superior in authority and control over them.

Railway Co. v. Spangler, 44 O. S. 471, 478 (1886).
Little Miami R. R. Co. v. Stevens, 20 Ohio 415.
Cleveland, etc., R. R. Co. v. Keary, 3 O. S. 202.
Pittsburg, etc., Ry. Co. v. Lewis, 33 O. S. 196 (1877).

But for the negligence of a fellow servant a railway company was not liable, under the common law rule, where the company was free from negligence and had performed the duties imposed on it by law.

Railroad v. Fitzpatrick, 42 O. S. 318 (1884).
Railway v. Leech, 41 O. S. 388 (1884).
Railway v. Devinney, 17 O. S. 197 (1867).
Whaalen v. Railway, 8 O. S. 249 (1858).

It is against public policy for a railroad company to stipulate with its employes as a part of their contract of employment, that liability shall not attach to it for injuries caused to its servants by the carelessness of other employes who are placed in authority and control over them.

Railway Co. v. Spangler, 44 O. S. 471 (1866).

Whether or not one servant is placed by a common master under the control of another servant, thereby creating the relation of superior and subordinate between them, must be determined from the evidence in each particular case.

Pittsburg, etc., Ry. Co. v. Lewis, 33 O. S. 196 (1877).

Failure to obey rules. The failure of an employe to obey a reasonable rule providing for his own safety, which he agreed to obey, is not excused by the presence or consent of another employe, who is his superior, but is not authorized to make or change such rule or contract.

Railroad Co. v. Ropp, 76 O. S. 449 (1907).

Where an action is brought against a railroad company by one of its employes to recover damages for personal injuries sustained by the enforcement of an order, made by the superintendent of the company, as to the management of a particular tram, which order was unreasonable and the enforcement of the same was dangerous to such employe, the fact that the negligence of a fellow servant of the injured person, while executing such order, contributed in producing the injury, affords no defense to the action.

Railway Co. v. Henderson, 37 O. S. 549 (1882).
See Dick v. Railroad Co., 38 O. S. 389 (1882).

By what law governed. A contract of employment is governed by the laws of the state where made.

Alexander v. Pennsylvania Co., 48 O. S. 623 (1891).
Pittsburg. etc., Ry. Co. v. Bishop, 13 C. C. 380 (1896); 7 C. D. 73.
Ott v. Railway, 18 C. C. 395; 10 C. D. 85 (1899); aff'd, no rep., 62 O. S. 661.

Where the action is brought in Ohio the rules of evidence of this state control.

Penna. Co. v. McCann, 54 O. S. 10 (1896).

Held to be fellow servants. An engineer of a gravel train and an employe working on the same train.

Kumler v. Railroad Co., 33 O. S. 150 (1877).

A section hand and a fireman.

Whaalen v. Mad River, etc., R. R. Co., 8 O. S. 249 (1858).

Inspectors and· brakeman.

Railroad Co. v. Fitzpatrick, 42 O. S. 318 (1884).

Columbus, etc., R. R. Co. v. Webb, 12 O. S. 475 (1861).

See Lake Shore, etc., Ry. Co. v. Gilday, 16 C. C. 649 (1890); 9 C. D. 27.

Felton v. Bullard, 94 Fed. 781.

Railway v. Lamphere, 9 C. C. 263; 4 C. D. 26.

Brakemen.

Hawks v. Lake Shore, etc., Ry. Co., 16 C. C. 377 (1896); 8 C. D. 414.

Conductor and car repairer.

Johnson v. Cleveland, etc., Ry. Co., 11 C. C. 553 (1896); 5 C. D. 290.

Company can not be held for failure of section boss to look up and have knowledge of time of trains so as to avoid collisions with section handcar.

Railway Co. v. Leech, 41 O. S. 388 (1884).

Held not to be fellow servants. An engineer is a superior of his fireman.

Jenkins v. Little Miami R. R. Co., 2 Dis. 49 (1858).

Railway v. Sutherland, 12 C. C. 309; 4 C. D. 115; aff'd, no rep., 52 O. S. 676.

A car repairer is not the fellow servant of the foreman of the repair gang as concerns giving notice of dangers to those working under cars.

Lake Shore, etc., Ry. Co. v. Lavalley, 36 O. S 221 (1880).

A conductor is a superior of an engineer.

Little Miami R. R. Co. v. Stevens, 20 Oh. 415 (1851).

Lake Shore, etc., Ry. Co. v. Hunter, 13 C. C. 441 (1897); 7 C. D. 206.

Cleveland, etc., Ry. Co. v. Hudson, 22 C. C. 586 (1898).

But see Crawford v. Railway, 12 L. D. 17 (1901); aff'd, 3 C. C. n. s. 144; 13 C. D. 207.

A conductor is a superior of a brakeman.

Railway Co. v. Spangler, 44 O. S. 471 (1886).

Cleveland, etc., R. Co. v. Keary, 3 O. S. 201 (1854).

Cleveland, etc., Ry. Co. v. Hudson, 22 C. C. 586 (1898).

A yardmaster in charge of switch yards, subordinate to a general yardmaster, who in turn is subordinate to a trainmaster, and he to a superintendent, is not a vice-principal, but a fellow servant, in his relation to other employes engaged in switching in the yard.

Penna. Co. v. Fishack, 123 Fed. 465; 14 O. F. D. 86.

A railroad company is liable for the combined negligence of a superior and fellow servant of the plaintiff where the injury would not have resulted without the negligence of the superior.

Railway v. Mulcahy, 16 C. C. 204; 9 C. D. 82 (1898).

Assumed risk of negligence of superior. If an employe, with a full knowledge of an habitual and continued negligence of the company or his superior fellow employe in some particular matter, acquiesces therein, and continues in the service of the company, without any objection or effort toward a correction of the neglect, he thereby waives his right against the company and takes the risk upon himself.

Lake Shore, etc., Ry. Co. v. Knittal, 33 O. S. 468 (1878).

Section 9017. (Presumptive evidence.) Every railroad company operating a railroad which in whole or part is within this state shall be liable for all damages sustained by any of its employes by reason of personal injury or death of such employe:

1. When such injury or death is caused by a defect in

any locomotive, engine, car, hand-car, rail, track, machinery or appliance required by such company to be used by its employes in and about the business of their employment, if such defect could have been discovered by reasonable and proper care, tests or inspection. Proof of such defect shall be presumptive evidence of knowledge thereof on the part of such company. An employe of such railroad company who is injured or killed as a result of such a defect, shall not be deemed to have assumed the risk occasioned thereby, although continuing in the employment of the company after knowledge of the defect; nor shall continuance in employment after such knowledge by an employe be deemed an act of contributory negligence.

2. While such employe is engaged in operating, running, riding upon or switching passenger, freight or other trains, engines or cars, and in the performance of his duties, and when such injury was caused by the carelessness or negligence of any other employe, officer or agent of such company, in the discharge of or for failure to discharge his duties as such. (February 28, 1908, 99 v. 25, § 1.)

See also note to § 9018.
This act is unconstitutional as to all roads which are located partly in Ohio and partly in another state; but its provisions are separable and the act is valid as to roads which are wholly within the state.
Flemm v. Railway Co., 10 N. P. n. s. 273; 21 L. D. 152 (1910).
See Warren v. Hannon, 15 C. C. n. s. 289; 34 C. D. 11 (1912).
This section applies to a cause of action under §10770.
Railway Co. v. Francis, 13 C. C. n. s. 167; 22 C. D. 189 (1910);
    aff'd, 83 O. S. 520.
This section applies where death of an engineer was caused by a defective locomotive and defective track.
Railway Co. v. Francis, 13 C. C. n. s. 167; 22 C. D. 189 (1910);
    aff'd, 83 O. S. 520.
This act and the act of congress (35 Stat. at L. 65), one applying to intrastate and the other to interstate commerce, furnish a universal rule applying to all actions. These acts abrogate the defense of negligence of a fellow servant.
Warren v. Hannon, 15 C. C. n. s. 289; 34 C. D. 11 (1912).

Section 9018.   (Slight contributory negligence no bar to recovery.) In all actions hereafter brought against a railroad company operating a railroad in whole or part within this state, for personal injury to an employe or where such injuries have resulted in his death, the fact that he was guilty of contributory negligence shall not bar a recovery when such negligence was slight and that of the employer greater, in comparison. But the damages must be diminished by the jury in proportion to the amount of negligence attributable to such employe. All questions of negligence and contributory negligence shall be for the jury. (February 28, 1908, 99 v. 25, § 2.)

Constitutionality. See note to § 9017.

This section and § 9017 should be applied in the federal courts. These sections entirely abolish the defense of assumption of risk, and of contributory negligence, as an absolute defense in bar, and substitute therefor the rule of comparative negligence.

An exception to the general rule in relation to contributory negligence is not created by these sections, but a new rule is prescribed, under which the question whether such negligence bars a recovery depends on the character and extent of the contributory negligence. Where contributory negligence is pleaded as a defense, a special replication alleging its slight character is not necessary to authorize the court to apply the statute.

Railroad Co. v. White, 187 Fed. 556 (C. C. A. 1911).

SCRAP METAL.

Section 9019. (How railroad scrap metal sold.) No officer, agent, or employe of a company operating a railroad, except the superintendent, general managing agent or a receiver of the company, may sell or dispose of worn or scrap metal, iron, brass, or other metal owned by it. All sales and barter of such scraps or other metals made by any other officer, agent, or employe shall be null and void. No such superintendent, managing agent, or receiver shall sell or dispose of such scrap or other metals in quantities less than one ton, nor without delivering to the purchaser a bill of sale thereof, a copy of which shall be retained and filed in the office of such superintendent, agent, or receiver. (R. S. Sec. 3357; April 12, 1876, 73 v. 227, § 1.)

Section 9020. (Violation of preceding section.) If a superintendent, managing agent, or receiver of a company sells or disposes of railroad scrap metal in quantities less than one ton, or without delivering a bill of sale thereof to the purchaser, the company which he represents shall not thereafter be entitled to the benefit of the next three succeeding sections. (R. S. Sec. 3358; April 12, 1876, 73 v. 227, § 2.)

Section 9021. (Evidence of title of scrap.) The person, company, or firm to whom is offered for sale, pledge, or trade, worn or used links, pins, journal-bearings, or other worn, used, detached appendages of railroad equipment, or scrap metal of iron, brass, or steel appertaining thereto, or to a railroad track, before purchasing or dealing in it shall ascertain whether the ownership thereof is lawfully derived, by bill of sale, or otherwise, from a company, or the superintendent, managing agent or receiver thereof. When the right or title to such article of metal is drawn in question, in any suit, the person, company or firm dealing therein, his or its assignee, party thereto, must make prima facie proof of title and ownership so derived. (R. S. Sec. 3359; April 12, 1876, 73 v. 227, § 3.)

Section 9022. (When mixture deemed a confusion.) If it appears prima facie, from the evidence on the trial, that any of the articles or metals in controversy were unlawfully obtained, and mixed or confused with other scrap metal, it shall be deemed a confusion of goods, unless the party claiming against the title of the company establishes, prima facie, a lawful title from or through a railroad company to the residue. (R. S. Sec. 3360; April 12, 1876, 73 v. 227, § 4.)

Section 9023. (Company may replevy scrap.) By its proper officer or agent, or the receiver thereof, a company may claim to be the general owner of, and replevy any of the metals or articles mentioned in section ninety hundred and twenty-one, and metals with which they may have been confused, found in the possession of a person, firm or company, when there is good reason to believe that such metals or articles were unlawfully taken from a railroad company or its receiver. Instead of the usual averment as to ownership, in the affidavit for a writ of replevin, it shall be sufficient for the officer or agent of such company or the receiver, to aver that he believes such metals or articles were unlawfully taken from such company or some other company. The person, firm or company claiming in such action, the right or title to such metals or articles, prima facie shall prove a right or title thereto, lawfully derived as hereinbefore provided. In the absence of such proof, the company or receiver claiming such metals or articles shall be held to be the general owner thereof; but any other company or receiver, upon showing that part of such metals or articles unlawfully were taken from it or him, shall be entitled to such part, upon payment of a proper share of the cost and expenses of replevying it. (R. S. Sec. 3361; April 12, 1876, 73 v. 227, § 5.)

Section 9024. (Liability of company or receiver.) If a company, or its receiver, replevies property under the next preceding section without reasonable cause to believe that it was unlawfully taken from some company or its receiver, such company or receiver shall be liable to the party entitled thereto, in any sum not exceeding double the value of the property so replevied, in addition to such damages as such party sustains thereby. (R. S. Sec. 3361; April 12, 1876, 73 v. 227, § 5.)

CHAPTER 7.

CONSOLIDATION.

Section 9025. (When companies may consolidate.) When the lines of road of railroad companies, in this state or any portion of such lines have been or are being so constructed as to admit the passage of burthen or passenger cars over any two or more of such roads continuously, without break or interruption, such companies may consolidate themselves into a single company. (R. S. Sec. 3379; March 30, 1877, 74 v. 71, § 1.)

When roads are connected.
    See note to § 8807.
    The lines of two railroad companies, which are in their general features parallel and competing, can not be connected for the carriage of freight and passengers over both "continuously" within the meaning of this section, and hence can not consolidate.
    State v. Vanderbilt, 37 O. S. 590 (1881).
    Burke v. Cleveland, etc., Ry. Co., 22 W. L. B. 11 (1889).
    A state in granting a corporate privilege to its own citizens, or what is equivalent, in permitting a foreign corporation to become one of the constituent elements of a consolidated company, may impose such con-

ditions as it seems proper, and that the acceptance of the franchise in either case implies a submission to the conditions without which the franchise could not have been obtained.

Ashley v. Ryan, 153 U. S. 436, 443 (1893); 8 O. F. D. 215; 49 O. S. 504, 527.

Consolidated railroad companies organized in pursuance of the consolidation act are corporations formed under a general law, within the meaning of the constitution, and as such subject to the limitations and reservations of the constitution; and the general assembly has power to alter and regulate rates of fare chargeable by such companies.

Shields v. State, 26 O. S. 86 (1875); s. c., 95 U. S. 319; 4 O. F. D. 471.

Powers of constituent companies pending consolidation. Corporations, which are parties to an agreeement to consolidate, continue in the full enjoyment of their powers and franchises respectively, and may accept subscriptions to their capital stock at any time before consolidation is consummated by filing the agreement of consolidation with the secretary of state.

Mansfield, etc., R. R. Co. v. Brown, 26 O. S. 223 (1875).

Subscriptions to capital stock are to be construed with reference to consolidation statutes in force, and subscribers are bound thereby as if the statutes were a part of the contracts of subscription.

Mansfield, etc., R. R. Co. v. Brown, 26 O. S. 223 (1875).

Right of stockholders of constituent companies to enforce operation of roads.

See Port Clinton, etc., R. R. Co. v. Cleveland, etc., R. R. Co., 13 O. S. 544, 560 (1862).

Section 9026.   (Consolidation of domestic and foreign companies.) A company organized in this state for the purpose of constructing, owning and operating a line of railway, or whose line of road is made or is in process of construction to the boundary line of this state, or to a point either in or out of the state, may consolidate its capital stock with that of a company in an adjoining state, organized for a like purpose, whose line of road has been projected, constructed or is in process of construction to the same point, when the roads so united and constructed will form a continuous line for the passage of cars. Roads running or to be constructed to the bank of a river which is not bridged, or to the tracks and property of a union depot company, the use of which is enjoyed by either of the companies so proposed to be consolidated, shall be held to be continuous under this section. (R. S. Sec. 3380; April 18, 1890, 87 v. 218; April 22, 1885, 82 v. 150; March 30, 1877, 74 v. 71. § 1.)

A corporation created by the consolidation of a domestic with a foreign corporation, under co-operative legislation of the two states, becomes a corporation in each state.

Ashley v. Ryan, 49 O. S. 504, 529 (1892); s. c., 153 U. S. 436 (1893).

By a consolidation, whether of domestic corporations, or of a domestic with a foreign corporation, a new corporation is formed by the extinguishment of the old corporations.

Ashley v. Ryan, 49 O. S. 504, 529 (1892).

Notwithstanding the consolidation of two railroad corporations of different states, each retains its identity as a corporation of the state in which it was originally created; and in a suit against the consolidated corporation brought in one of such states, it can not obtain a removal to the federal courts on the ground that it is a citizen of the other state, although the consolidation was had under the laws of the latter.

Paul v. Baltimore, etc., R. R. Co., 44 Fed. 513 (1890).

Ohio, etc., R. R. Co. v. Wheeler, 1 Black (U. S.) 286 (1861).

This act may as properly be construed to mean the state adjoining the state in which the first company has its line of road, as the state adjoining the state in which the first company is incorporated, so as to enable, for example, an Ohio company to consolidate with Indiana and Illinois companies.

Adelbert College v. Toledo, etc., Ry. Co., 3 N. P. 15; 5 L. D. 14 (1894); s. c., 74 O. S. 483; reversed, 208 U. S. 38, 609.

See Union Trust Co. v. New York, etc., R. R. Co., 17 W. L. B. 176, 177 (1887).

Continental Trust Co. v. Toledo, etc., R. R. Co., 82 Fed. 642 (1897); 9 O. F. D. 321.

Toledo, etc., R. R. Co. v. Continental Trust Co., 95 Fed. 497 (1899).

"Continuous line." Where two railway companies owning lines of railroad, seeking consolidation, are connected by the tracks of a "union" company organized by several railway companies to secure union depot and terminal facilities, and where by law the interest of each company in the union company, in its capital stock, and in its property and effects of every kind, are deemed an appurtenance to the railroad of such proprietary company, and are not alienable except with and as part of the railroad of such proprietary company it will be held that the companies do unite and form a continuous line within the meaning of this section.

Burke v. Cleveland, etc., Ry. Co., 22 W. L. B. 11 (1889).

See note to § 8807.

De facto consolidation. Where two roads not coming under this section attempt and apparently complete consolidation by colorable proceedings in a formal way to the approval of the proper state officers, the certificate of incorporation, duly certified, being admitted to record in the office of the secretary of state, and its rights as a corporation having never been challenged by the state, it will be entitled to be considered at least a corporation de facto with power to mortgage its property, after it has acquired and disposed of valuable property and incurred numerous obligations.

See Toledo, etc., R. R. Co. v. Continental Trust Co., 99 Fed. 497 (1899).

Union Trust Co. v. New York, etc., R. R. Co., 17 W. L. B. 176 (1887).

A railroad company having possession of and operating property obtained through consolidation and foreclosures in which the consolidation was recognized as valid, is estopped to question the validity of the consolidation.

Adelbert College v. Toledo, etc., Ry. Co., 3 N. P. 15 (1894); s. c., 5 Dec. 14; s. c., 74 O. S. 483; reversed, 208 U. S. 38, 609.

Farmers' Loan Co. v. Toledo, etc., Ry. Co., 67 Fed. 50 (1895); s. c., 8 O. F. D. 435; 9 O. F. D. 230.

Former acts. Under the former acts the road was required to be in process of construction.

See Mansfield, etc., R. R. Co. v. Stout, 26 O. S. 241 (1875).

Union Trust Co. v. New York, etc., R. R. Co., 17 W. L. B. 176 (1887).

Section 9027. (Consolidating of railroad companies.)
A railroad company formed by the consolidation of a company or companies of this state, with a company or companies of another state, or states, may make a further consolidation with a company or companies of another state or states owning continuous, connected, but not parallel or competing lines. The constituent companies may fix by the agreement for consolidation the terms and conditions upon which it is to be made, which terms and conditions may include the payment or retirement of the preferred stock of either or any of the constituent companies, if they have such. If the new company issue preferred stock, the par value of the shares thereof may be fixed by the agreement of consolidation, or by the resolution for the issue thereof without regard to the par value of shares of the common stock of such company. (R. S. Sec. 3380a; May 2, 1902, 95 v. 354.)

Cited. Mannington v. Railway Co., 8 O. L. R. 451, 467; 183 Fed. 133 (1910).

Section 9028. (Proceedings to affect consolidation.)
Consolidation shall be made under the conditions and restrictions following:

1. The directors of the several companies may enter into a joint agreement, under the corporate seal of each company, for the consolidation of the companies, prescribing the terms and conditions thereof, the mode of carrying it into effect, the name of the new company, the number of directors and other officers thereof, their places of residence, the amount of the capital stock of the new company agreed upon, the number of shares thereof, the amount of each share, and the manner of converting the capital stock of each constituent company into that of the new company, with such other details as they deem necessary to perfect the new organization and consolidation of the companies.

2. The agreement shall be submitted to the stockholders of each of the companies, at a meeting thereof called separately for the purpose of taking it into consideration. Due notice of the time and place of holding such meeting, and the object thereof, shall be given by written or printed notices addressed to each of the persons in whose names the capital stock of the companies stand on the books thereof, and by a like notice published in some newspaper in the city or village where such company has its principal office or place of business. But if all the stockholders are present at such meeting, in person or by proxy, such notice may be waived in writing. At the meeting of stockholders the

agreement of the directors shall be considered, and a vote by ballot taken for its adoption or rejection. Each share of stock on which all the installments called for by the board of directors are paid, shall entitle the holder thereof to one vote. Ballots shall be cast in person or by proxy. If two-thirds of all the votes cast are for the adoption of the agreement, that fact shall be certified thereon by the secretary of each of the companies, and the agreement so adopted, or a certified copy thereof shall be filed in the office of the secretary of state. All consolidation agreements heretofore entered into and ratified by such companies substantially in manner as in this section prescribed, shall be as valid as if entered into and ratified by virtue of this section. (R. S. Sec. 3381; April 22, 1885, 82 v. 150; R. S. 1880; March 30, 1877, 74 v. 71, § 2.)

Consolidation of street railway companies. § 9127 et seq.
Mining, etc., companies, § 10139.
This section applies to the consolidation of a domestic corporation and a foreign corporation.
Ashley v. Ryan, 49 O. S. 504, 528 (1892).

Agreement for consolidation. The agreement of the directors of the consolidating companies is fatally defective if it does not state the number and residence of the new directors. This provision of the statute is mandatory.
State v. Vanderbilt, 37 O. S. 590, 654 (1882).
See Trester v. Mo. Pac. R. R. Co., 33 Neb. 171 (1891).
The agreement may require constituent companies to enter the consolidation free from debt.
Railway Co. v. Bank, 68 O. S. 582 (1903).
And may provide that of the stock apportioned to one of the constituent companies enough shall be sold to pay its floating debt, and the remainder distributed among the preferred and common stockholders in proportion to the relative value of each stock.
Railway Co. v. Bank, 68 O. S. 582 (1903).
A separate agreement between stockholders of the constituent companies may be incorporated by reference. A provision that all property matters, not specifically adjusted in the agreement of consolidation, should be adjusted pursuant to a separate agreement theretofore made by the holders of a majority of the stock of each constituent company, is within the powers of the directors, and such separate agreement constitutes a part of the agreement of consolidation.
Railway Co. v. Bank, 68 O. S. 582 (1903).
The directors are not only expressly empowered to agree upon the manner of converting the capital stock of each of the companies into that of the new company, but they are invested with the widest discretion as to the details of the consolidation, which may not be specifically included in the words of the statute.
Railway Co. v. Bank, 68 O. S. 582, 597 (1903).
The companies may agree upon the number and amount of shares of the proposed consolidated company, may classify such new stock into "common" and "preferred," and may issue a greater or less number of shares than that of the aggregate of the constituent companies to secure a just and equitable division of property between the shareholders of the companies.

Burke v. Cleveland, etc., Ry. Co., 22 W. L. B. 11 (1889).

Where bonds were issued by a company, which afterward was consolidated with another under a stipulation that said bonds should be protected by the new company, the holders of such bonds have a lien on the property of the company.

See Compton v. Railway Co., 45 O. S. 592 (1888).

Where a contract of consolidation provided: "The consolidated company shall not issue any evidences of funded debt, or execute any lease of railway property which may entail fixed charges, except by the consent of a majority in interest of the holders of the said preferred stock, to be expressed in writing under their signatures respectively," etc., it was held that it did not conflict with §§ 8660 or 8709.

Burke v. Cleveland, etc., Ry. Co., 22 W. L. B. 11, 15 (1889).

Where one clause of the contract of consolidation is illegal, and can be separated from the legal parts, the consolidation will not be enjoined, and the parties will be left to litigate the question as to legality of the clause when occasion requires it.

Burke v. Cleveland, etc., Ry. Co., 22 W. L. B. 11, 16 (1889).

Stockholders' meeting. This section requires notice to be given to the persons "in whose name the capital stock of the companies stands on the books thereof." It does not provide for notice to, or require participation by, a person who has a concealed equity in stock. A pledgee who has not had the stock transferred to his name on the corporate books is not entitled to notice.

Railway Co. v. Bank, 68 O. S. 582, 599 (1903).

Liability of consolidated company to unregistered pledgee. Where the joint agreement provided that certain stock of the consolidated company should be distributed to one of the constituent companies, part of which should be sold to pay the floating indebtedness of that company, and the balance distributed among the stockholders of such company, which agreement was assented to by the registered owners of certain pledged stock of such constituent company, but without the knowledge of the pledgee of their stock, who held certificates assigned in blank, without a transfer; and the agreement was performed by the consolidated company by delivering the stock to "agents and proxies" designated by the constituent company and its stockholders, to carry out the joint agreement; the consolidated company is not liable for a conversion of the stock after delivering to the "agents and proxies." A provision in the certificates of the pledged shares that they are transferable on the books of that company only on surrender of the certificates is not violated by such a distribution of stock by the consolidated company.

Railway Co. v. Bank, 68 O. S. 582.

For cases involving similar facts.

See Robison v. Railway Co., 13 L. D. 1; s. c., 5 N. P. 293; 7 L. D. 312.

Fuller v. Railway Co., 8 N. P. 605; 11 L. D. 574 (C. P. 1901).

Powers of constituent companies. Under this section the parties to a consolidation agreement continue in the full exercise of their franchises and powers, and may accept subscriptions to their capital stock at any time before consolidation is consummated by filing the agreement of consolidation with the secretary of state.

Mansfield, etc., R. R. Co. v. Brown, 26 O. S. 223 (1875).

Stock issued by a constituent company after consummation of the consolidation is spurious.

Worthington v. C. C. Ry., 9 C. C. n. s. 433; 19 C. D. 321 (1904); aff'd, 75 O. S. 626.

Section 9029.   (Effect of agreement to consolidate.) When the agreement is made and perfected, as provided in the next preceding section, and it or a copy thereof filed with the secretary of state, the several companies parties thereto shall be deemed and taken to be one company, possessing within this state all the rights, privileges, and franchises, and subject to all the restrictions, disabilities, and duties, of a railroad company.   (R. S. Sec. 3382; April 10, 1856, 53 v. 143, § 3.)

The consolidated company does not succeed to the rights, etc., of the constituent companies until the election of its first board of directors.
§ 9038.
Mansfield, etc., Co. v. Brown, 26 O. S. 223 (1875).
By the consolidation of companies, whether of Ohio companies, or Ohio and foreign companies, a new corporation is formed which succeeds to all the property of the original companies and assumes their liabilities.
Ashley v. Ryan, 49 O. S. 504, 529 (1892).
Wabash, etc., Ry. Co. v. Ham, 114 U. S. 587, 595 (1884).
Shields v. Ohio, 95 U. S. 319 (1880); s. c., 4 O. F. D. 471.
Lee v. Sturges, 46 O. S. 153, 169 (1889).
So far as concerns unpaid dissenting stockholders, the old companies may be deemed in existence after the filing of the agreement.
Railway Co. v. Garrett, 50 O. S. 405, 417 (1893).
It is only as to creditors that constituent companies remain alive. Stock issued by a constituent company, after consolidation, is spurious.
Worthington v. Railway Co., 9 C. C. n. s. 433; 19 C. D. 321 (1904); aff'd, 75 O. S. 626.
A decree against a company formed by the consolidation of companies of several states may be made against the whole road, and not merely against so much as is in the state.
Scofield v. Railway Co., 43 O. S. 571, 621 (1885).

Section 9030.   (Effect of agreement of consolidation as evidence.) A copy of the agreement and act of consolidation, duly certified by the secretary of state, shall be received in the courts of this state as prima facie evidence of the existence of the several companies parties to it, prior to and at the time of the execution of the agreement, of the consolidation of the companies, as specified in the agreement, that such consolidation was authorized by the laws of the several states within which the several companies were chartered, and into which the consolidated road extends, and of all the facts, statements, and covenants set forth and recited in the agreement and act of consolidation, and in the certificate endorsed thereon.   (R. S. Sec. 3391; February 19, 1858, 55 v. 8, § 1.)

Section 9031.   (Defects in consolidation agreements.) If the agreement for the consolidation of railroad companies heretofore filed in the office of the secretary of state is defective by reason of the omission of a statement either of the number of the directors or other officers, or their places of residence, or the number of shares of capital stock as required in such agreement by the laws of this state, such defect may be cured by filing in the office of the secretary of state a certificate signed by the president and the secretary of the consolidated company named in such agreement under its corporate seal, setting forth the omitted statements, which shall thereupon be considered a part of the agreement of consolidation, the same as if originally incorporated therein, and such agreement and all rights, remedies, powers, duties, and acts thereunder be construed accordingly. Such agreement and certificate and copies thereof, duly certified by the secretary of state, shall be held and received in all courts and other places as constituting the agreement of the consolidation of such companies to all intents and purposes, as if no such omission or defect had ever existed in such agreement. (R. S. Sec. 3282-1; April 7, 1882, 79 v. 126, § 1.)

Section 9032. (Curing defects in railroad agreements. Certificate of consolidated company.) If the agreement or certified copy thereof for the consolidation of railroad companies, heretofore filed in the office of the secretary of state, is defective by reason of the omission of a statement of the place of residence of the directors, or the number and places of residence of the other officers, as required in such agreement by the laws of this state, but when in pursuance of such agreement an election of directors has been had, and other officers have been elected or appointed, all such defects in such agreement, and any defect in the certificates thereon, may be cured by filing in the office of the secretary of state a copy of the proceedings of the election duly certified by the secretary of the consolidated company, under its corporate seal, to be such copy, and the certificate signed by the president and secretary of the consolidated company under its corporate seal, setting out the respective places of residence of the directors first elected, and of the officers first elected or appointed at the time they were so elected or appointed, which shall thereupon be considered a part of the agreement of consolidation the same as if originally incorporated therein. Upon filing such certified copy of the proceedings and certificate, all such defects existing prior to the filing of such certified copy of the proceedings and certificate, shall be cured, and the several acts of such company shall be held valid, and the agreement and all rights, remedies, powers, duties, and acts thereunder be construed accordingly. The agreement, proceedings and certificate, and copies thereof, duly certified by the secretary of state, shall be held and received in all courts and other places as constituting the agreement of consolidation of such companies, to all intents and purposes as if no omission ever existed in such agreement or the certificate thereto. (May 20, 1910, 101 v. 326; R. S. Sec. 3382-2; January 20, 1887, 84 v. 3.)

Section 9033. (How defects cured in reference to stock.) If the agreement or a certified copy thereof for the consolidation of railroad companies heretofore filed in the office of the secretary of state, states the number of shares of the capital stock of the new company, and the amount of each share, but is defective by reason of the omission of a statement of the amount of the capital stock of the new company agreed upon as required by the laws of this state in such agreement, such defect may be cured by filing in the office of the secretary of state a certificate signed by the secretary of such consolidated company, under its corporate seal, setting out the amount of the capital stock of the new company agreed upon, which shall be ascertained by multiplying the number of shares of capital stock named in the agreement by the amount of each share named in the agreement in dollars, as shown in the original agreement or the certified copy thereof filed in the office of the secretary of state, and which certificate shall thereupon be considered a part of the agreement of consolidation the same as if originally incorporated therein. Upon filing such certificate such defect shall be cured and such consolidation and the several acts of the company shall be held valid, and the agreement and all rights, remedies, powers, duties, and acts thereunder be construed accordingly. Certified copies of such certificate and the agreement of consolidation, duly certified by the secretary of state, shall be held and received in all courts and other places as constituting the agreement of consolidation of such companies, to all intents and purposes, as if no omission or defect had ever existed in such agreement. (R. S. Sec. 3382-3; February 18, 1887, 84 v. 29, § 1a.)

Section 9034. (Stockholder refusing to consolidate.) A stockholder who refuses to convert his stock into that of the consolidated company, shall be paid the highest market value of such stock at any time within two years next preceding the making of the agreement for consolidation by the directors, if, previous to such consolidation, he so requires. If a stockholder so refusing to consolidate, and the board of directors of the company desiring to consolidate, can not agree as to the value of such stock, the parties may submit the question to arbitration, to be conducted in accordance with the law regulating arbitrations, so far as applicable, by three disinterested persons, to be appointed upon the motion of either of the parties by the judge of the probate court of the county in which the person owning the stock resides, or, in case he is a non-resident, of a county through or into which the road passes, then in the county in which the principal office of the company is kept. If the person so refusing to convert his stock refuses to submit the question to arbitration, upon the application of either of the companies desiring to consolidate, the probate judge shall appoint the arbitrators. They shall ascertain the value of the stock, as if the question had been submitted by the consent of both parties. If the party owning the stock refuses to receive the amount awarded, in any case, the company may deposit it with the probate court of the county, in which the arbitration is held, which deposit shall authorize the parties to proceed to consolidate without further payment to such stockholder. But if the agreement of consolidation provides that the preferred stock of the consolidated companies, or either of them is to become and be the preferred stock of the consolidated company upon the terms and conditions upon which it was issued, then this section shall not apply thereto. (R. S. Sec. 3388; March 15, 1892, 89 v. 88; April 4, 1890, 87 v. 159; April 10, 1856, 53 v. 143, § 10.)

See § 8713.

The right to consolidate on the vote of two-thirds of the stock is a part of the contract of each stockholder and the company and other stockholders, and if a stockholder does not assent he must sell his shares as provided by statute.

Burke v. Cleveland, etc., Ry. Co., 22 W. L. B. 11, 16 (1889).

Under the act of 87 v. 159 it was held that a dissenting stockholder could compel the submission to arbitration of the question of the value of his stock, and that an agreement to arbitrate was not required.

Railway Co. v. Garrett, 50 O. S. 405 (1893).

A failure to make a demand before the consolidation agreement is filed with the secretary of state (§§ 9028, 9029) or a failure to make an attempt to agree with the company does not defeat the right of a dissenting stockholder.

Railway Co. v. Garrett, 50 O. S. 405 (1893).

It is the duty of a company proposing to consolidate to ascertain who, if any, of its stockholders refuse to convert their stock and to cause the value of the stock of dissenting stockholders to be ascertained and paid.

Railway Co. v. Garrett, 50 O. S. 405 (1893).

Section 9035. (Provision applies only to stockholders of a domestic corporation.) In cases of the consolidation of railway corporations of this with those of another state, as by law provided for, the provisions of the next preceding section shall apply only to stockholders in Ohio companies, and not to those of a foreign corporation; it being the intent to have their rights determined by the law of the states creating them. (R. S. Sec. 3388a; March 15, 1892, 89 v. 88.)

Section 9036. (Notice of application of appointment.) In all such cases of arbitration the party desiring it must give the opposite party at least ten days' notice of his intention to apply to the judge for the appointment of arbitrators which notice shall be served in the manner provided for the service of a summons and shall specify the time and place for the hearing of the application. In cases of non-residents the notice shall be by publication, for four consecutive weeks, in some newspaper printed in the county. (R. S. Sec. 3390; April 10, 1856, 53 v. 143, § 11.)

Section 9037. (Election of directors of consolidated company.) The stockholders at the meeting called to consider the agreement, after its adoption, shall appoint a time and place for the election of the directors and other officers for the new company, notice of which must be given by the secretary of each of the companies in some newspaper printed, or of general circulation at the place of the principal office of each company, at least three weeks previous thereto. But if at each meeting all the stockholders of the constituent companies are present, either in person or by proxy, in writing or by resolution they may waive such notice, and consent to hold such meeting and election at any time. It shall be conducted in the manner prescribed by the stockholders at such meeting. (R. S. Sec. 3383; April 22, 1885, 82 v. 150; 53 v. 143, § 4.)

The election of directors under this section is unauthorized until the agreement has been filed with the secretary of state. The consolidating companies continue for the purpose of holding and controlling all rights and franchises until the election is had. The divesting of the old and the investing of the new corporations are simultaneous.

Mansfield, etc., R. R. Co. v. Brown, 26 O. S. 223 (1875).

At the meeting provided for by this section the stockholders have no corporate duty to perform; therefore, the fact that some of the stockholders have been enjoined from participating in such a meeting does not constitute a ground for the appointment of a receiver of either of the consolidating companies, for such persons could act only in the capacity of stockholders.

Railway Co. v. Jewett, 37 O. S. 649 (1882).

Section 9038. (Property of old companies vests in new.) Upon the election of the first board of directors for the company created by the agreement of consolidation, all the rights, privileges, franchises of each company to the agreement, and all property, debts due on account of subscriptions for stock, or other things in action, are to be deemed transferred to and vested in such new company, without further act or deed. All property, rights of way, and other interests, shall be as effectually the property of the new company as they were of the companies parties to the agreement. Title to real estate either by deed, gift, grant, or by appropriation under the laws of this state, shall not revert or be impaired by reason of the consolidation. But rights of creditors, and liens upon the property of either company, shall be preserved unimpaired, and the respective companies deemed to be in existence to preserve them. Debts, liabilities, and duties of either company, thenceforth shall attach to the new company, and be enforced against it to the same extent as if such debts, liabilities, and duties had been contracted by it. (R. S. Sec. 3384; April 10, 1856, 53 v. 143, § 5.)

Cited, Rice v. Railway Co., 153 Fed. 497, 500 (1907).

The property of the constituent companies does not vest in the consolidated company until the election of the first directors.

Mansfield, etc., R. Co. v. Brown, 26 O. S. 223 (1875).

Liability for debts of constituent companies. It is competent for the directors to agree that the constituent companies shall enter the consolidation free from debt, although if they do not do so the liabilities of such companies will attach to the new company under this section.

Railway Co. v. Bank, 68 O. S. 582, 597 (1903).

The new consolidated company is liable for the torts of the original company.

Cincinnati, etc., Ry. Co. v. Fullbright, 7 W. L. B. 187 (1882).

See Indianapolis, etc., R. R. Co. v. Jones, 29 Ind. 465 (1868).

A dissenting stockholder may prosecute his claim against the new company which takes the property of the old company charged with the payment of its debts.

Railway Co. v. Garrett, 50 O. S. 405, 417 (1893).

An agreement by a constituent company to maintain a water course is binding on the consolidated company.

Bell v. Railway, 3 C. C. 31; 2 C. D. 19.

Under the former stockholders' double liability law, a creditor of a constituent company was entitled to subject the statutory liability of stockholders of the new corporation.

Marriott v. Railway, 16 L. D. 135 (1905) ; s. c., 8 C. C. n. s. 495; 10 C. C. n. s. 573; 20 C. C. D. 419.

How liability enforced. General creditors have no lien upon the property, of constituent companies before consolidation, nor afterward unless such lien is established by judgment and execution.

Greene v. Railroad Co., 62 O. S. 67, 79 (1900).

The consolidated company holds its property acquired by such consolidation in its own right, and not in trust for the constituent companies, and such property can not be reached by creditor's bill.

  Greene v. Woodland, etc., R. R. Co., 62 O. S. 67 (1900).

  But it has been held that an agent of the consolidated company may be guilty of contempt of court for forcibly preventing a levy on property transferred by a constituent company, under an execution issued on a judgment against such constituent company.

  State v. Brimson, 46 W. L. B. 275 (Sup. Ct. without rep., 1901).

  Equitable lien for debts of old company. On the consolidation of companies under this act the new company takes the property in its own right, subject only to the payment of the debts of the constituent companies. This liability is created by statute, and an equitable lien results as a consequence.

  Compton v. Railway Co., 45 O. S. 592 (1888).

  See Continental Trust Co. v. Toledo, etc., R. R. Co., 86 Fed. 929 (1898).

  Contra, Wabash, etc., Co. v. Ham, 114 U. S. 595 (1884).

  Wabash, etc., Co. v. Adelbert College, 208 U. S. 38 (1908).

  This equitable lien is a result of the proceedings under which the new company acquired its title to the property, and of it the creditors of the new company have, in law, the same notice they have of prior mortgages on the same property.

  Compton v. Railway Co., 45 O. S. 592 (1888).

  Where the consolidation agreement undertakes to protect certain unsecured debts of one of the constituent companies an equitable lien is established on the property of the old company to the extent of the debt.

  Compton v. Railway Co., 45 O. S. 592 (1888).

  Contra, Wabash, etc., Co. v. Ham, 114 U. S. 595 (1884).

  See Wabash, etc., Co. v. Adelbert College, 208 U. S. 38, 44 (1908).

  Compton v. Jesup, 68 Fed. 263 (1895).

  Tysen v. Wabash Ry. Co., 15 Fed. 763 (1883).

  Bonds and mortgages of constituent companies. Consolidation does not discharge the lien of a mortgage on the property of a constituent company.

  Railway Co. v. Lynde, 55 O. S. 23, 56 (1896); aff'd, 172 U. S. 493.

  Bonds of a constituent company which are negotiated after such constituent company went out of existence, but before maturity of the bonds, are protected by this section.

  Railway Co. v. Lynde, 55 O. S. 23, 56, 57 (1896); aff'd, 172 U. S. 493.

  Where mortgage creditors of a constituent company seek to set aside a transfer of its assets to the consolidated company, or to assert a first lien on such assets, on the ground that they were induced by fraud to surrender their lien, the trustee of a mortgage executed by the consolidated company, on all its assets, is a necessary party.

  Union, etc., Co. v. Hess, 6 O. L. R. 372; 159 Fed. 889; 16 O. F. D. 73 (C. C. A. 1908).

  An action to enforce a lien upon the property of a consolidated railroad company, based upon an amount alleged to be due on equipment bonds issued by a constituent company, is an action not upon a liability created by statute, nor upon a written agreement, but is solely for equitable relief and the period of limitation of such actions is ten years from the date when the cause of action accrues, and the cause of action accrues as to each installment when the same matures; the right to enforce the lien as to subsequently accruing installments of interest, or as to the principal of the bonds, can not be said to have accrued prior to the time when such installments and principal respectively matured.

  Adelbert College v. Toledo, etc., Ry. Co., 3 N. P. 15 (1894); 5 Dec. 14; s. c., 74 O. S. 483; 208 U. S. 44, 642.

Miscellaneous. Subscriptions to the stock of constituent companies made after the enactment of this section pass to the consolidated company; and suits may be brought thereon by the consolidated company.

Mansfield, etc., R. R. Co. v. Brown, 26 O. S. 223 (1875).

Mansfield, etc., R. R. Co. v. Stout, 26 O. S. 241 (1875).

It is only as to creditors that constituent companies remain alive after a consolidation is consummated. Stock issued by a constituent company after the consolidation is spurious.

Worthington v. Railway Co., 9 C. C. n. s. 433; 19 C. D. 321 (1904); aff'd, 75 O. S. 626.

Where the transfer agent of a consolidated company transfers stock in a constituent company to secure his personal debt, and promises to exchange such stock for stock in the consolidated company, such promise is not admissible against the consolidated company in an action to compel the exchange.

Worthington v. Railway, 9 C. C. n. s. 433; 19 C. D. 321 (1904); aff'd, no rep., 75 O. S. 626.

Rescission of transfer to consolidated company. Where a consolidated company executed a mortgage to a trustee, to secure a bond issue, such trustee is a necessary party to an action brought by mortgage creditors of a constituent company who allege that they were induced by fraud to surrender their lien, and seek to set aside the transfer of assets to the consolidated company, or to assert a first lien on such assets.

Union, etc., Co. v. Hess, 6 O. L. R. 372 (U. S. C. C. A. 1908).

Appointment of receiver on rescission of sale of all the capital stock of a corporation.

See National Salt Co. v. United Salt Co., 8 N. P. 325; 11 L. D. 348 (C. P. 1901); s. c., 12 L. D. 386.

Section 9039. (Companies may dispose of stocks and bonds acquired by consolidation.) A consolidated railroad company formed by the consolidation of a railroad company or companies created by or existing under the laws of this state, and any other state or states, with a railroad company or companies of this state or of another state, may take, hold, pledge or otherwise dispose of under such terms and agreements as the board of directors of such consolidated railroad company prescribes, the stock and bonds of any other company acquired upon consolidation or received by virtue of any purchase or lease or operating contract heretofore or hereafter made or executed, and may maintain and operate a railroad purchased under authority of law, and lease or contract to operate a part or all of a railroad constructed or in the course of construction by another company of this state or of another state, if the line of road covered by such lease or operating contract is connected with a line of road of such consolidated railroad company, on such terms as the companies agree upon. (R. S. Sec. 3384a; April 11, 1890, 87 v. 183.)

Section 9040. (Consolidated company may issue stock in lieu of purchase money.) When a consolidated railroad company described in the next preceding section is in possession of or operating in connection with or extension of its own railroad line or lines, any other railroads or railroad in this state, or any other state or states under purchase, conveyance, lease, contract, or agreement, such consolidated railroad company may take a surrender or transfer of the whole or a part of the capital stock of the company, conveying, leasing, or owning such railroad, from one or more stockholders, and issue in exchange therefor the like additional amount of its own capital stock at par, or on such other terms and conditions as are agreed upon by the directors of the consolidated railroad company. (R. S. Sec. 3384b; April 11, 1890, 87 v. 183.)

Section 9041. (Property of company acquired by purchase vested in consolidated company.) When the whole of such capital stock is so surrendered or transferred, and a certificate thereof filed in the office of the secretary of state, under the common seal of the consolidated railroad company to which such surrender or transfer shall have been made, the estate, property, rights, privileges, and franchises of the company whose stock was so surrendered or transferred, thereupon shall vest in and be held and enjoyed by such consolidated company to whom the surrender or transfer was made, as fully and entirely, without change or diminution, as they before were held and enjoyed and be managed and controlled by the board of directors of such consolidated company to which such surrender or transfer shall have been made. The two companies thenceforth shall be consolidated and be one company under the corporate name of such consolidated company, without any other formalities or proceedings. (R. S. Sec. 3384b; April 11, 1890, 87 v. 183.)

Section 9042. (Effect of consolidation.) Nothing in the two next preceding sections shall relieve such consolidated company from paying the fee provided by law in case a corporation files a certificate for an increase of its capital stock. The rights of a stockholder not surrendering or transferring his stock, shall not be affected hereby, nor existing liabilities or the rights of creditors of the company whose stock has been so surrendered or transferred, be affected by this or such preceding sections. (R. S. Sec. 3384b; April 11, 1890, 87 v. 183.)

This section, in requiring the consolidated company to pay a percentage fee on the capital stock acquired, is constitutional.

Ashley v. Ryan, 153 U. S. 436; 8 O. F. D. 215; s. c., 49 O. S. 504 (1892).

Where the transfer agent of a consolidated company transfers stock in a constituent company to secure his personal debt, and promises to exchange such stock for stock in the consolidated company, such promise is not admissible against the consolidated company in an action to compel the exchange.

Worthington v. Railway, 9 C. C. n. s. 433; 19 C. D. 321 (1904); aff'd, no rep., 75 O. S. 626.

Section 9043.   (To establish a principal office.)   As soon as convenient after the consolidation, the new company shall establish a principal office at some point in this state on the line of its road, but may change it at pleasure. Public notice of such establishment or change shall be given in some newspaper. This section and other laws respecting the residence of directors or corporations, the keeping of a principal or general office, and the records of corporations, shall not apply to consolidated railroad companies formed by the consolidation of a company or companies created by or existing under the laws of this state and any other state or states, with a railroad company or companies of this state or of any other state. The election for directors of such consolidated companies may be held at the principal office of the company, whether located in this or any other state under the laws of which the consolidated company was created. But at least two directors of such consolidated company must be residents of this state, and a general office of the company maintained within this state, of which notice shall be given as above provided. (R. S. Sec. 3385; April 11, 1890, 87 v. 184; April 10, 1856, 53 v. 143, § 6.)

See § 8744.

Section 9044.   (Actions against new company.)   Suits may be brought and maintained against the new company in the courts of this state, for all causes of action, in the same manner as against other companies. (R. S. Sec. 3386; April 11, 1890, 87 v. 184; April 10, 1856, 53 v. 143, § 6.)

Section 9045.   (Taxation of road partly in this state.) That part of the road of such consolidated company in this state, and all its real and personal property therein, shall be listed for taxation and taxed in the same manner as the road and property of other railroad companies in this state. To ascertain the proportion of the rolling machinery subject to taxation here, the officer listing it shall ascertain the value of all the rolling machinery of the company, and return a sum bearing such proportion to the value of the whole, as the length of the line of such road in this state bears to the length of the whole line. (R. S. Sec. 3387; April 10, 1856, 53 v. 143, § 8.)

Section 9046. (Proof dispensed with.) It shall not be necessary to produce or prove the charters of the companies, parties to such consolidation, the laws of the several states under and by virtue of which such consolidation was effected, or the original articles of consolidation, in any suit brought to charge such consolidated company with a liability of either of the companies, parties to the act of consolidation. (R. S. Sec. 3392; February 19, 1858, 55 v. 8, § 2.)

Section 9047. (Two or more companies owning a road may divide and dispose of it.) When two or more railroad companies, are owners in common of the whole or a part of a railroad situate within this state, and by reason of inequality in the amount of business done thereon by each company, require a different degree and extent of improvement and development, such companies may enter into any arrangement they agree upon, for enlarging, improving, developing or increasing the facilities of such road or any part thereof. In pursuance of such agreement, or otherwise, they may make such division of the railroad and appurtenances thereon, and execute and deliver each to the other, or to any other railroad company having authority to purchase it, such deed or deeds of conveyance for the whole or part of such railroad, as is agreed upon between such companies. Nothing herein shall impair the lawful lien of any creditor upon the railroad as conveyed. (R. S. Sec. 3392-1; April 11, 1883, 80 v. 111, § 1.)

Section 9048. (Proceedings when companies cannot agree on a division.) If such companies are unable to agree upon an equitable plan for improving and developing, or for the division and sale of the railroad and appurtenances or part thereof so owned in common, either company from time to time may file with the state railroad commission a statement, under its seal, of the ˙character and estimated cost of any addition, or change in the nature of the roadbed, right of way, main or side track or tracks, bridges, culverts, buildings, structures, fixtures, or appurtenances or either or any part thereof of such railroad, or part thereof, desired by such company, and of its inability to agree with the other joint owner or owners in respect to making them. Upon receipt of such statement the commission within thirty days of its filing, shall appoint a time when the owners of such railroad or part thereof may be heard respecting the reasonableness and necessity of such proposed additions or improvements, and give due notice in writing of the time and place of such hearing to each of the owners. Such commission may make such order in respect to the reasonableness or necessity of the whole or any part of such additions or improvements, as well as the manner in which they are to be made, and the periods within which they shall be paid for, as to it seems proper, and its decision in the matter shall be final. (R. S. Sec. 3392-2; April 11, 1883, 80 v. 111, § 2.)

Section 9049. (Cost of improvements.) The cost of such additions or improvements, unless otherwise agreed between the joint owners, shall be paid by them in proportion to their ownership in the joint property, irrespective of the amount of traffic which each owner may then have passing over such railroad. If either owner fails or refuses to pay the share of cost due from it on the basis herein fixed, or within the period or periods fixed by such commission, suit may be entered and judgment taken against that party. Such judgment shall be a valid lien upon the interest in such railroad or part thereof owned jointly of such party in default, and may be sold at public sale as in other cases upon execution. (R. S. Sec. 3392-3; April 11, 1883, 80 v. 111, § 3.)

Cited, Stewart v. Railway, 53 O. S. 151.

Section 9050. (Who may purchase.) A railroad company having authority to own or operate a railroad in this state, may purchase such interest at such sale, and enjoy and exercise in respect thereto, all the rights, privileges and franchises which were exercised or enjoyed by the company owning it up to the time of sale. The compulsory power of enforcing additions or improvements provided for in this and the two preceding sections shall not extend to local or terminal depot or shop grounds or facilities, the joint use of which is not needed by all the joint owners. (R. S. Sec. 3392-3; April 11, 1883, 80 v. 111, § 3.)

Section 9051. (Partition not compulsory.) Nothing in the four preceding sections shall be held to imply or confer a right or power of compulsory partition of the joint property against the will of either of the joint owners; but it may be sold upon execution as therein provided. (R. S. Sec. 3392-4; April 11, 1883, 80 v. 112, § 4.)

Section 9052. (Company selling interest may purchase or condemn land along route.) If, pursuant to the agreement or to the proceedings above provided for, either company sells or conveys or suffers to be sold or conveyed, its interest in the railroad or part thereof so owned in common, such company may acquire by purchase or condemnation, such land as is needed to enable it to construct, maintain and operate, a railroad along and adjacent to such part of its chartered route as was so sold or conveyed, and it shall have and enjoy all rights and franchises in respect to such newly acquired railroad as were held and enjoyed in respect to the railroad sold or conveyed. (R. S. Sec. 3392-5; April 11, 1883, 80 v. 112, § 5.)

Section 9053. (To what companies these provisions apply.) Section ninety hundred and forty-seven to ninety hundred and fifty-two both inclusive, shall apply in case one or more companies or owners in common has leased its interest in the portion of railroad owned in common, and the lessee of such interest may unite with the lessor in the agreement provided for in such section ninety-hundred and forty-seven or with such lessor and owner be compelled to make or pay for the addition and improvements contemplated therein. (R. S. Sec. 3392-6; April 11, 1883, 80 v. 112, § 6.)

CHAPTER 8.

SALES AND RECEIVERS.

PRIVATE SALE.

Section 9054. (Company may sell roadbed and right of way.) A company, owning in whole or part a roadbed and right of way for a railroad within this state, including those acquired by purchase at judicial sale, which, from lack of means, or other cause is unable to complete the construction of the proposed line of road thereon, may sell, assign and transfer it, or a part thereof, to any other company incorporated under the laws of Ohio, with authority to construct and operate a railroad over the same route, or any part thereof, which transfer shall include all work done upon such line of road, with all material furnished therefor, not exempted by the terms of the grant, and all rights, privileges, and easements, as fully as they are or may be possessed by the company making the transfer, and to the same extent, vest the title of and the right to enjoy them in such grantee. (R. S. Sec. 3409; May 5, 1868, 65 v. 142, § 1; May 7, 1869, 66 v. 334, §§ 1, 2.)

A railroad company can not acquire a parallel and naturally competing railway, although under construction and not completed.
§ 8807.
State v. Railway Co., 13 C. C. n. s. 145; 22 C. D. 147 (1910).
This section is a part of every subscription to stock, and a sale by the company of a part of its road under this section does not release the subscriber except when, and as, provision is made therefor by statute.
Armstrong v. Karshner, 47 O. S. 276 (1890).
This section confers no authority on railway companies to sell subscriptions to their stock along with their roads when they find it impossible to complete the same, from lack of means. And if it were attempted to transfer a conditional subscription to the company purchasing the road, such company could not by performing the condition precedent fix the liability of the subscriber.
Railroad Co. v. Hinsdale, 45 O. S. 556 (1888).
A railroad company, having acquired title to lands for railroad purposes by grant or proceedings in appropriation, may sell to another corporation for like railroad purposes all or a part of the same. Such a sale is not an abandonment of the premises unless such was the intention.
Garlick v. Railway Co., 67 O. S. 223 (1902).
See Platt v. Penna. Co., 43 O. S. 228 (1885).
Penna. Co. v. Platt, 47 O. S. 366 (1890).
Power to sell property generally.
See Donner v. Dayton, etc., R. Co., 1 C. S. C. R. 130 (1871).

Section 9055. (Transfer to be by deed.) Such transfer shall be by deed, executed by the president of the company grantor, in the manner provided by law for the conveyance of real estate, and for such consideration as the parties agree upon. (R. S. Sec. 3410; May 5, 1868, 65 v. 142, § 2.)

See § 8761.

Section 9056. (Two-thirds in interest of stockholders must consent.) Before such transfer may be made, the president of the company shall call a meeting of its stockholders, at some convenient point on the line, or at a terminus of the road, of which he shall cause at least thirty days' notice to be published, in some newspaper printed or in general circulation in each county in which such roadbed and right of way are situated. By a concurrent vote of two-thirds in interest of the stock represented thereat by the owners thereof, in person, or by proxy, the meeting may declare by resolution the inability of the company to complete its line of road, prescribe the terms of the proposed transfer of its roadbed and right of way, and direct the president of the company to execute the deed. All such proceedings, resolutions, and directions shall be duly recorded in the proper record of the company, and a copy thereof delivered to the grantee. They also shall be recited in the deed. (R. S. Sec. 3411; May 5, 1868, 65 v. 142, § 3.)

Section 9057. (What interest dissenting stockholder may retain.) No transfer shall be made against the dissent of any stockholder, expressly declared and filed in writing at such meeting, without the guaranty of the company grantee that it will issue to him certificates of its capital stock, equal in amount to his pro rata interest as a stockholder of the grantor, in the amount for which the property is sold. (R. S. Sec. 3412; May 5, 1868, 65 v. 142, § 4.)

Conditional subscribers to stock do not acquire any rights under this section until the happening of the contingency upon which payments on the subscription are made dependent.
Railroad Co. v. Hinsdale, 45 O. S. 573 (1888).
Armstrong v. Karshner, 47 O. S. 276, 299 (1890); § 8791.

Section 9058. (Title vests in grantee.) The title to the property transferred, with the right to use, occupy and enjoy it for all purposes proper in the construction, maintenance, and operation of a railroad thereon, shall pass to and vest in the company grantee, by the execution of such deed, to the same extent as the granting company might or could use, occupy, and enjoy it. (R. S. Sec. 3413; May 5, 1868, 65 v. 142, § 5; May 3, 1873, 70 v. 245, § 1.)

Section 9059. (Certain rights of way forfeited.) Where upon an unfinished road, a right of way, or part thereof, remains for ten years unused for railroad purposes, it shall be held forfeited, and shall revert to the owner of the land, unless at least twenty miles of the road have been completed by the company during that period, or, unless an average of one thousand dollars per mile has been expended for construction before the expiration of such period. (R. S. Sec. 3414; May 5, 1868, 65 v. 142, § 6; April 22, 1898, 93 v. 207.)

Abandonment of easement. See note to § 8759.

EQUIPMENT CONTRACTS.

Section 9060. (Certain contracts of sale void unless recorded.) No contract of, or for the sale of railroad equipment, rolling stock, or other personal property to be used in or about the operation of a railroad, by the terms of which the purchase money, in whole or part, is to be paid in the future, and wherein it is stipulated or conditioned that the title to the property sold shall not vest in the vendee, but shall remain in the vendor until the purchase money has been fully paid, shall be valid against creditors or innocent purchasers for value, unless recorded, or a copy thereof filed, in the office of the secretary of state. When the contract is so recorded, or a copy thereof so filed, the title to the property sold, or contracted to be sold, shall not vest in the vendee, but remain in the vendor until the purchase money has been fully paid; and such stipulation or condition shall be and remain valid, notwithstanding the delivery of the property to, and its possession by the vendee. (R. S. Sec. 3378a; March 16, 1882, 79 v. 45.)

The general conditional sales statutes (G. C. §§ 8568-8570) do not apply to conditional sales of railroad equipment, which are specially provided for by § 9060 et seq.

Metropolitan Trust Co. v. Railroad Co., 93 Fed. 702 (C. C. 1899).
Metropolitan Trust Co. v. Equipment Co., 108 Fed. 913; 13 O. F. D. 643 (C. C. A. 1901).

The seller of equipment to a railroad company, retaining the title as security for the purchase price, is entitled, on a foreclosure of a mortgage covering all of the railroad property, to take back the property, or, in case the mortgagee elects to retain it, to a first lien thereon for the balance due, without deduction for expenditures for preservation or improvement, made by the railroad company or its receiver.

Metropolitan Trust Co. v. Equipment Co., 108 Fed. 913; 13 O. F. D. 643 (C. C. A. 1901); s. c., 93 Fed. 702 (C. C. A. 1899).

Where the agreement states that the property described is leased at a fixed rental, and that title to the property shall not vest in the railroad company, but shall remain in said trustees until the terms of the agreement shall be fully complied with, it comes within this section as a lease or a contract of sale, or a contract for the sale of railroad equipment.

Union Trust Co. v. New York, etc., R. R. Co., 17 W. L. B. 176, 180 (1887).

Where the court appoints receivers of the property of a railroad company, and directs them to join the company in the execution of a lease, consolidating former leases of rolling stock, the terms of which have not yet expired, the purpose and provisions of which consolidated lease are to provide a lower monthly rental and extend the period of the leases —but leaving the title to the rolling stock in the lessors, with conditions of forfeiture for nonpayment of the rentals and other breaches of the covenants, such consolidated lease is not a sale of the rolling stock to the receivers, and the lessors are entitled to a preference over the bonded indebtedness of the railroad company, only for the rentals which accrue after execution of such consolidated lease and during the existence of the receivership.

Central Trust Co. v. Ohio Southern R. R. Co., 17 C. C. 633 (1898); 9 C. D. 317.

Section 9061. (Parties may provide for a conditional sale in a lease.) In any written contract for the renting, leasing, or hiring of such property to be so used, it shall be lawful to stipulate or provide for a conditional sale of the property at the termination of such renting, leasing, or hiring, and to stipulate or provide that the rental reserved as paid, or when paid in full, shall be applied and treated as purchase money. In such contract it shall be lawful to stipulate or provide that the title to such property shall remain in the lessor or vendor until the purchase money has been fully paid, notwithstanding delivery to and possession by the other party; subject, however, to the requirement as to recording or filing contained in the next preceding section. (R. S. Sec. 3378b; March 16, 1882, 79 v. 45.)

A contract purporting to be a lease of equipment to a railroad company, which executes so-called "lease warrants", on the payment of which the railroad company is to become the owner, is in legal effect a conditional sale.

Metropolitan Trust Co. v. Equipment Co., 108 Fed. 913; 13 O. F. D. 643 (C. C. A. 1901); s. c., 93 Fed. 702.

Section 9062. (Secretary of state to file contracts.) The secretary of state, when so requested, and upon being paid the proper fees, shall record any such contract, and shall file in his office a copy of any such contract, when it is delivered to him for that purpose. For every such copy so filed he shall be entitled to receive one dollar. (R. S. Sec. 3378c; March 16, 1882, 79 v. 45.)

Section 9063. (Construing application of preceding sections.) The provisions of the sections ninety hundred sixty, ninety hundred sixty-one and ninety hundred sixty-two of the General Code shall extend and apply, not only to contracts made with a railroad company, as vendee or lessee, but also to all contracts which may be made with any interurban or street railroad company or corporation, or other company, corporation, or person as vendee or lessee, by

which any such interurban or street railroad company, or
corporation, or other corporation, company or person shall
undertake to purchase, rent, lease or hire any railroad, interurban or street railroad equipment, cars, rolling stock,
or other personal property, designed for use on, or in connection with, a railroad or railroads, interurban or street
railroad or railroads, in this or other states. (May 20,
1910, 101 v. 323; R. S. Sec. 3378d; April 12, 1889, 86 v.
255.)

RECEIVER AND JUDICIAL SALES.

Section 9064. (Receiver.) When a line of railroad, the
whole or part of which lies within this state, by order of
court, has been placed in the hands of a receiver, who has
taken charge of and is operating it for the purpose of carrying passengers, freight, and doing such other things as
ordinarily belong to the running and management of railroads, in his official capacity, such receiver may sue or be
sued in the courts of this state without leave previously
granted. No person shall act as such receiver unless he is
a resident citizen of this state. (R. S. Sec. 3415; March 12,
1872, 69 v. 31, § 1.)

Cited, Cleveland, etc., R. R. Co. v. Orme, 1 C. C. 511; 1 C. D. 285
(1885).

Suits by receivers. A receiver of a railroad company is a competent
party plaintiff in a suit to restrain ditch proceedings against the company, commenced and prosecuted after his appointment as such receiver.
Caldwell v. Trustees, 2 C. C. 10 (1886); 1 C. D. 332.

A foreign receiver of a corporation, with no other title to its assets
than that derived from his appointment in a suit brought in another state
to adjudicate and enforce liens and subject its assets and property to the
claims of creditors, can not maintain an action in Ohio for the collection
of its assets, either in his own name or in that of the corporation.
Leman v. MacLennan, 7 C. C. n. s. 205; 18 C. D. 137 (1905); aff'd,
75 O. S. 643.

But where, in another state, trustees under a mortgage sought to
enforce their rights on a railroad and its equipment and pending an
application for a receiver, a creditor of the same state attached rolling
stock temporarily in Ohio; a receiver subsequently appointed on such
application, with authority to take possession of all property including
that attached, was permitted to maintain an action to recover possession.
Bank v. McLeod, 38 O. S. 174 (1882).

Suits against receivers. This section authorizes suits to be brought
against the receiver of a railroad, and the same prosecuted to final judgment without leave of court; in other words, such suits stand upon the
same footing and entitle those bringing them to the same rights and
privileges as if leave had been granted, and no more. But this section
does not authorize a levy or sale of property in possession of the receiver
without leave of court.
Croy v. Marshall, 3 C. C. 489 (1888); 2 C. D. 280.

Where property is improperly in the possession of a receiver the remedy of a creditor is by application to the court appointing such receiver for an order requiring the receiver to release it.

Croy v. Marshall, 3 C. C. 489; 2 C. D. 280 (1888).

Where a plaintiff in an action against a railroad company, whose property is then in the hands of a receiver (appointed by the same court) to which action such receiver is not a party, recovers against the company a money judgment, the same is not void or invalid on the ground that the court had no jurisdiction. Such judgment is valid as against the company, and operates as a lien on its lands, and may be, enforced after the discharge of the receiver.

Mather v. Cincinnati, etc., Ry. Co., 3 C. C. 284 (1888); 2 C. D. 161.

This section can not affect the power of a federal court to pass on a motion for leave to sue a receiver appointed by it.

Hayes v. Columbus, etc., Ry. Co., 34 W. L. B. 2; 67 Fed. 630; 9 O. F. D. 85 (1895).

Suit by state against receiver for taxes.

See Treasurer v. Dale, 60 O. S. 180 (1899).

A receiver operating a railroad is liable, in his official capacity, for negligence.

Meara v. Receivers, 20 O. S. 137 (1870).
Potter v. Bunnell, 20 O. S. 150 (1870).

Where leave to sue a receiver is required, notice of the application for such leave need not be given the parties in the action in which the receiver was appointed. Notice to the receiver is sufficient.

Potter v. Bunnell, 20 O. S. 150 (1870).

Satisfaction of judgment against receiver.

See § 9066 and note.

Miscellaneous. Nonresident receivers.

See Caldwell v. Pittsburg, etc., R. Co., 33 W. L. B. 134 (1894).
Bayne v. Brewer Pottery Co., 82 Fed. 390; 10 O. F. D. 538 (1897).

A receiver is not the agent of the corporation.

Consolidated Coal Co. v. Cincinnati, etc., R. R. Co., 10 W. L. B. 42 (1883).

Section 9065. (When action brought; service.) Actions may be brought against the receiver of a railroad in a county through or into which the road is constructed. Service of summons may be made on the receiver, or superintendent of the road, or a ticket or freight agent in the employment of or acting for the receiver. No service made upon such agent shall be valid, unless his office or place of business is in the county where suit is brought. (R. S. Sec. 3416; March 12, 1872, 69 v. 31, § 2.)

Cited, Railroad Co. v. Orme, 1 C. C. 513; 1 C. D. 285 (1885).
Service on receiver, §§ 11231, 11233.

Section 9066. (Application of funds; lien.) The earnings of a railroad in the hands of a receiver, and all other money which comes into his hands as receiver, shall be applied first to pay costs and expenses of the suit in which he was appointed, and the expenses of operating and managing the road, including materials and supplies procured

by him therefor, and liabilities incurred by him in such operation and management.   Judgments recovered against a
receiver for injuries to person or property, or for wages
of employes or work done or materials furnished while he
is operating or managing the road, shall be a lien on the
funds in his hands as receiver, but shall affect him only in
his trust capacity, and not individually.   (R. S. Sec. 3417;
March 12, 1872, 69 v. 31, § 3.)

> Satisfaction of a judgment rendered against a receiver in an action
> for the recovery of damage for personal injuries can only be obtained out
> of the fund in his hands, as may be directed by the court appointing him.
>   Meara v. Receivers, 20 O. S. 137 (1870).
>   See Mining Co. v. Railway, 10 W. L. B. 42.
>   The state is not included in this section, and the superiority of its
> claim for taxes is not thereby affected.
>   Treasurer v. Dale, 60 O. S. 180 (1899).

Section 9067.   (When receiver must deposit money.)
When the line of a railroad operated by a receiver is wholly
within this state, all money which comes into his hands,
whether from operating the road or otherwise, shall be kept
and deposited in such place within this state as the court
directs, until properly disbursed.   If a part of the road lies
in another state, the receiver shall be required to deposit in
this state at least such share of the funds in his hands as
is proportioned to the value of the property of the company
within this state.   (R. S. Sec. 3418; March 12, 1872, 69 v.
31, § 4.)

**Section 9068.   (Certain roads may be sold at judicial
sale.)**   The real and personal property, road-bed, right of
way, fixtures, and franchises of a railroad company in this
state which has not completed, nor conveyed by deed of
trust, or mortgage, any part of its road, and which is insolvent, and whose property is in the hands of a receiver
appointed by a court of competent jurisdiction, may be sold
at judicial sale; and the title thereto, with all the rights,
liberties, faculties, and franchises, shall pass by such sale,
and vest in the purchaser thereof, as fully as they had been
possessed, exercised, and enjoyed by such company.   (R. S.
Sec. 3420; May 4, 1868, 65 v. 192, § 1.)

Section 9069.   (Receiver must petition therefor.)   Before
such sale shall be ordered, the receiver shall file in such
court his petition therefor, in which he shall set forth the
names of the creditors of the company, with the sums due
to each, as nearly as can be ascertained, a statement of its
assets, exclusive of its road-bed, rights of way, and fran-

chises, and a pertinent description, in general terms, of the road-bed, right of way, and property so sought to be sold, and cause notice thereof to be published, for six consecutive weeks, in some newspaper printed and of general circulation in each of the counties wherein any part of the road-bed is situated. Before the distribution of the proceeds of the sale, any creditor may appear and set up his claim by answer, and have it determined by the court, if it is omitted from or inaccurately stated in the petition. (R. S. Sec. 3421; May 14, 1868, 65 v. 192, § 2.)

Section 9070. (Order for appraisement.) On proof of the publication of such notice, and being satisfied that a sale is necessary to pay the indebtedness of the company, the court shall order the sale of such road, road-bed, rights of way, property, and franchises, on such terms of payment as it deems proper, and issue its order to the receiver, commanding him that he cause them to be appraised by commissioners, selected by the court, skilled in the construction and value of such road-beds as they may be called upon to appraise, having the qualifications of a freeholder, not less than three in number, and consisting of at least one from each county in which any part of the road-bed is situated. Such proceedings shall be had under the order as are provided by law in sales of real estate made by judicial order in other cases, so far as they are applicable. (R. S. Sec. 3422; May 14, 1868, 65 v. 192, § 3.)

Section 9071. (Notice of sale to be published.) Before such sale is made, notice thereof shall be given by publication, for six consecutive weeks in some newspaper published and of general circulation in each of the counties through or in which such road is located, and also in some newspaper published and of general circulation in each of the cities of New York and Cincinnati, for at least thirty days prior to the day of sale. The sale shall not be made for less than two-thirds of the appraised value of the property and rights, unless, upon their having been twice offered and not sold the court in its discretion orders a reappraisement. (R. S. Sec. 3423; May 14, 1868, 65 v. 192, § 4.)

Deposits filed with bids should be returned to the bidder in case he does not buy the property.
Feike v. Cincinnati, etc., Ry. Co., 3 C. C. 72; 2 C. D. 41; s. c., 27 W. L. B. 75 (1887).

Section 9072. (Confirmation of sale and deed.) When a sale is made and reported to the court, if satisfied that it was conducted according to law, and its order, the court shall confirm the sale, and order the receiver to execute and deliver to the purchaser a deed of conveyance for the road, road-bed, rights of way, real estate, fixtures, and franchises so sold. (R. S. Sec. 3424; May 14, 1868, 65 v. 192, § 5.)

Where a tract of land was not sold, or intended to be sold, and not paid for, but, by mistake, was included in the report of sale, such mistake may be corrected in equity against the purchaser or his heirs even after confirmation of the sale and the execution of the deed.

Stites v. Wiedner, 35 O. S. 555 (1880).

Section 9073. (How proceeds distributed.) The proceeds of the sale, after paying the costs and expenses thereof and the unpaid expenses of the trust against the company, shall be distributed pro rata among all its creditors. (R. S. Sec. 3425; May 14, 1868, 65 v. 192, § 6.)

Section 9074. (Who may purchase property.) A company organized under the laws of this state may purchase such property. Any number of persons not less than five may purchase such road, road-bed, rights of way, property, and franchises at such sale, and, on filing a transcript of the decree of confirmation in the office of secretary of state, they shall become a corporation of this state, amenable to its process and, with perpetual succession by such name as they assume, be subject to the law regulating such corporations, and shall hold the property, rights, and franchises so purchased free from liability for the debts of the original corporation. (R. S. Sec. 3426; May 14, 1868, 65 v. 192, § 7.)

Cited, Rice v. Norfolk, etc., Ry. Co., 153 Fed. 497, 501 (1907).

Section 9075. (How purchaser may acquire franchise.) The purchaser of a railroad, situated wholly or partly within this state, sold pursuant to judicial proceedings, may acquire the franchise to be a corporation originally vested in the company which held the road prior to such sale, by grant of such company, under such terms and conditions as are agreed upon by the directors of the company, with the consent of stockholders owning two-thirds of the stock. Such grant shall be in the form required by law to convey real estate, and shall pass such franchise to the persons or company becoming the owner, by the purchase of such railroad. No grant may be made unless provision is made for granting to the stockholders in the original company stock in the reorganized company, upon equal terms with the stockholders thereof, and it is acceptable to the directors making it. (R. S. Sec. 3419; April 13, 1865, 62 v. 169, § 1.)

This section is a general law within the meaning of article 1, section 2 of the constitution.

Ohio v. Sherman, 22 O. S. 411 (1872).

Where a special charter, not subject to repeal or amendment, is transferred under this section, the new charter granted by implication, being granted under the present constitution, would be subject to alteration and repeal.

Ohio v. Sherman, 22 O. S. 411 (1872).

The effect of a transfer under this section is a surrender or abandonment of the old charter by the corporators, and a grant de novo of a similar charter to the so-called transferees or purchasers.

Ohio v. Sherman, 22 O. S. 411, 428 (1872).

In an action brought to determine the priority of liens on, and for the sale of a railroad, neither lienholders nor general creditors can question the legality of the incorporation of the railway company, or the validity of mortgages of such company upon the ground of such illegality.

Hatry v. Painesville, etc., Ry. Co., 1 C. C. 426 (1886); 1 C. D. 238; aff'd, 23 W. L. B. 281.

A charter can not be sold in the absence of statutory authority.

Atkinson v. Marietta, etc., R. R. Co., 15 O. S. 21 (1864).

Stockholders' liability after transfer.

See Ohio v. Sherman, 22 O. S. 411 (1872).

Section 9076.   (Purchaser at judicial sale may sell road, grant to be recorded.)   The purchaser or purchasers of the property, road-beds, rights of way, fixtures and franchises of a railroad company in this state, situated wholly or in part in this state, sold pursuant to judicial order, judgment, or decree, and which sale is confirmed by the court making the order of sale, may sell such property or any part thereof. The title thereto, with all the rights, liberties, faculties, and franchises shall pass by such sale and vest in the purchaser or purchasers thereof, as fully as if they had been possessed, exercised and enjoyed by such railroad company. The grant thereof in the form by law required to pass real estate, shall be recorded in the record of deeds of the county or counties in which such property is situated, and the rights and franchises are or may be exercised. (R. S. Sec. 3426a; March 11, 1880, 77 v. 60.)

Section 9077.   (Any number of persons may purchase, and incorporate.)   A railroad company organized or existing under the laws of this state may become the purchaser of such property, as provided in the preceding section. Any number of persons may purchase such road, roadbeds, rights of way, property and franchises, as provided herein, either directly at such judicial sale or by grant from the purchasers at such sale. On filing a copy of such deed or grant in the office of the secretary of state, with articles of incorporation executed in accordance with the law respecting the creation of corporations for profit, they, and such persons as associate with them, not less than five in number, shall become a corporation with perpetual succession by such name as they assume to themselves, with capacity to maintain and operate such railroads, whether located wholly within this state, or partly within this state and partly in another state or states. (R. S. Sec. 3426b; April 24, 1890, 87 v. 270; March 11, 1880, 77 v. 60.)

Section 9078. (May issue stock and bonds to pay purchase price.) Such corporation shall have authority to provide for the purchase price of the railroad and other property so bought by the issue of its capital stock, preferred or common, and bonds secured by mortgage or otherwise, bearing interest at a rate not exceeding seven per cent per annum. Stock and bonds heretofore or hereafter issued as such purchase price, in amounts the incorporators, in good faith, agreed on, shall be valid, and taken as fully paid for by the transfer to the corporation of such railroad and property, and also by such issue of stock or bonds, to raise the necessary means suitable to improve such railroad property and equipment for the uses and purposes for which it is employed. In the operation and maintenance of its railroad, such corporation shall be entitled to all the rights, and be subject to all the obligations and restrictions imposed upon railroad companies by the laws of this state. (R. S. Sec. 3426b; April 24, 1890, 87 v. 270; March 11, 1880, 77 v. 60.)

CHAPTER 9.

REORGANIZATION.

Section 9079. (When proceedings for reorganizations may be had.) When the proceedings are pending in any court for the sale of the road of a railroad company, under a mortgage or deed of trust, and two-thirds in interest of the creditors and two-thirds in interest of the stockholders of the company agree, in writing, upon a plan for the readjustment or capitalization of the debt and stock of the company, the court shall render judgment against the company for the amount due and in arrear upon such securities, which judgment, from its rendition, shall be a lien on all the property embraced in such securities, and all the franchises and powers of the company including its franchises to be and act as a corporation, conferred by the charter and the amendments to the charter of the company. Upon a sale had under such judgment, and a purchase at such sale by trustees, on behalf of the parties to such agreement, appointed by the agreement, all the property so bound by the judgment, including such franchises, shall vest in such trustees. But such agreement shall provide that the unsecured debts of the company incurred for repairs or running expenses, shall be paid in money, or bonds of the reorganized company, of the highest class issued, as hereinafter provided. A copy of the agreement shall be filed in such court before the rendition of the judgment. (R. S. Sec. 3393; April 11, 1861, 58 v. 70, § 1.)

The lien of a judgment recovered for injuries sustained by the misconduct of agents of the reorganized company is, under § 9085, superior to that of a mortgage executed by the company.
     King v. Atlantic, etc., Co., 12 C. D. 551 (1886).
Construction of agreement.
     Hatry v. Painesville, etc., Ry. Co., 1 C. C. 426; 1 C. D. 238 (1886); aff'd, 23 W. L. B. 281.
Constitutionality of act of 1863.
     Mather v. Cincinnati, etc., Ry. Co., 3 C. C. 284; 2 C. D. 161 (1888).

Section 9080. (Meeting of creditors and proceedings.) As soon as practicable after the sale, the trustees shall call a meeting of the parties to the agreement by a notice signed by a majority of the trustees, or of their survivors, and published not less than once a week, for four consecutive weeks in a newspaper printed in the cities of New York and Philadelphia, and in a newspaper printed in each county on the line of the railroad, specifying the day, place, and object of such meeting—the place to be on the line of the road. At such meeting, each of the parties to the agreement shall be entitled to vote according to the provisions thereof, but not exceeding one vote for every fifty dollars of the par value of the debt or stock of such party, according to a list of voters and their respective interests, which shall be prepared by the majority of the trustees, who may act as judges of the election. By a majority in interest of the persons present, in person or by proxy, such meeting may retain or change the name of the company, decide, for the time being, the amount of its capital, the number of shares into which it is to be divided, fix the number of directors, their term of office, elect such directors, a majority of whom shall be residents of the state or states, in which such railroad is situated, and do all things necessary or proper to reorganize the company. But any creditors shall be entitled to become a party to the agreement, either at or before the meeting herein provided for. A stockholder shall be entitled to become a party thereto at any time within one year after such meeting. (R. S. Sec. 3394; April 11, 1861, 58 v. 70, § 2.)

Where a railroad corporation reorganizes under the act of April 11, 1861, and, in the agreement therefor, it is stipulated that certain bonds of the original company shall be assumed by the new company, and the holder thereof entitled to vote at all meetings of stockholders, upon conditions specified, which he performs, the new company becomes liable to pay the bonds, and the holders thereof entitled to vote, without further action on the part of the new company.

State v. McDaniel, 22 O. S. 354 (1872).

In a corporation reorganized under this act, it is not necessary that the directors should be stockholders. The statute only requires them to be residents of the state, and in the absence of a statute requiring it, the discretion of the stockholders in electing directors is not limited to stockholders.

State v. McDaniel, 22 O. S. 354 (1872).

See § 8661.

Section 9081. (What to be certified to the secretary of state.) A certificate, under the common seal of the company, specifying its name, and the railroad which it is to hold, maintain, and operate, shall be filed in the office of the secretary of state. A copy thereof duly certified, in all courts and places, shall be evidence of a compliance with all the conditions and provisions of the two preceding sections, and of the due reorganization and existence of the company. (R. S. Sec. 3395; April 11, 1861, 58 v. 70, § 3.)

Section 9082. (Property of new company.) Upon such reorganization, and a conveyance by the trustees, or of such of them as are vested with the legal title, or their survivors, the railroad and other property, franchises and things purchased, and the franchises, powers, faculties, privileges, and immunities which were possessed and enjoyed by the original company, or by any company with which it had been consolidated, shall pass to and be vested in the company as reorganized; and they, and all property and things which the reorganized company thereafter acquires, except as hereinafter provided, shall be taken, held, and disposed of for the use and benefit of the creditors and stockholders of the company, who become such upon and after the reorganization, according to their respective rights, but subject to the powers of the company, and in no wise chargeable in respect to any debt, liability, or claim of any creditor or stockholder which subsisted prior to the sale and reorganization. All property of the original company not embraced in the sale, upon the reorganization shall be vested in the company as reorganized, in trust for all parties interested therein as creditors, stockholders or otherwise. (R. S. Sec. 3396; April 11, 1861, 58 v. 70, § 4.)

Cited, Rice v. Norfolk, etc., Ry., 153 Fed. 501 (1907).
Constitutionality. See note to § 9075.

Section 9083. (Powers of new company.) Such company likewise shall have power, within six months after the organization, to assume such debts or liabilities of the original company, make such adjustments or exchanges with any bondholder of the original company, and, within one year, with any stockholder, as it may deem expedient. For such purpose, the company may use bonds or stock which it is authorized to issue or create. It may make and issue such bonds, payable at times and places, and bearing rates of interest not exceeding six per cent per annum, as it deems expedient, and secure the payment of bonds which it issues or assumes to pay, by mortgages or deeds of trust of its railroad, or other property, and may include therein with its road all its cars, other rolling stock, equipments, machinery, tools, implements, fuel, materials, and other things then held or thereafter acquired for constructing, operating, or repairing the road, or for repairing or replacing its equipment or appurtenances, as part and parcel of the road, and as constituting with the road one property. It also may include in such mortgage or deeds of trust all franchises held by the company, connected with or related to the road, and all its other corporate franchises, which franchises, including the franchise to be a corporation, in case of sale by virtue of such mortgage or deed of trust, or of any judgment specified in the following section, shall pass to the purchasers, so as to enable them to reorganize the company in the manner hereinbefore provided. Such company may issue capital stock to such amount it deems proper, not exceeding a limit fixed by agreement with the trustees purchasing, and may establish preferences in respect to dividends, in favor of any class of the stock, in such order and manner as it deems expedient, not exceeding the limits fixed by such agreement. If authorized by the agreement, it may confer on holders of bonds which it issues or assumes to pay, the right to vote at meetings of stockholders, not exceeding one vote for every fifty dollars of the par amount of the bonds, as was provided for in the agreement, which right, once fixed, shall attach to and pass with such bonds, under such regulations as the by-laws may prescribe, to the successive holders thereof, but shall not subject the holder to assessment by the company, or to liability for its debts, or entitle him to dividends. (R. S. Sec. 3397; April 11, 1861, 58 v. 70, § 5.)

Section 9084. (Issue of stock or securities.) In cases of railroad companies organized or reorganized under the laws of this state, wherein the organization or reorganization agreement provides and stipulates that any class of creditors, bondholders or stockholders of the original company, shall in any wise be restricted or limited, in participation in profits, dividends, or in respect to liens or the right to vote as the holders of stock or securities in the reorganized company, such reorganized company, its directors and officers, shall issue the certificate of stock or securities into which the original stock, securities or debts may be convertible, bearing upon the face of each plainly and distinctly set forth, such restrictions or limitations so that purchasers may be advised of the terms thereof, and holders of stock or securities created under such reorganization agreements, hereafter may have only such restricted or limited rights, liens, participation in profits, dividends, and right to vote thereon, as in such agreements, certificate of stock or securities are set forth. (R. S. Sec. 3397a; March 19, 1887, 84 v. 142.)

Section 9085. (Lien of mortgages.) The lien of the mortgages and deeds of trust authorized by section ninety hundred and eighty-three shall be postponed to the lien of judgments recovered against the company, after its reorganization, for labor thereafter performed for it, or materials or supplies thereafter furnished to it, or damages, losses, or injuries thereafter suffered or sustained by the misconduct of its agents, or in any action founded on its contracts or liability as a common carrier thereafter made or incurred. (R. S. Sec. 3398; April 11, 1861, 58 v. 70, § 6.)

Cited, Stewart v. Railway Co., 53 O. S. 151, 172 (1895).
This section is constitutional.
King v. Thompson, 110 Fed. 319; 13 O. F. D. 696; 46 W. L. B. 210 (C. C. A. 1901).
This section applies to foreign corporations.

King v. Thompson, 110 Fed. 319; 13 O. F. D. 696; 46 W. L. B. 210 (C. C. A. 1901).

A judgment for personal injuries is, under this section, prior to a previously recorded mortgage.

King v. Thompson, 110 Fed. 319; 13 O. F. D. 696; 46 W. L. B. 210 (C. C. A. 1901).

A claim for personal injuries is not a lien under this section until reduced to judgment. Where such a claim is not reduced to judgment until more than a year after the property had been sold in a foreclosure proceeding under a mortgage executed under this act, the judgment does not become a lien on the property.

Jeffrey v. Moran, 101 U. S. 285 (1879).

It was further held in the above case that the judgment was not a lien on the fund arising from the sale of the property.

The lien of a judgment recovered for injuries is not extinguished by the foreclosure of a mortgage, where the judgment creditor was not made a party to the suit.

King v. Railroad Co., 12 C. D. 551 (1886).

This section should be fairly construed so as to effect the purpose for which it was enacted.

Farmers' Loan, etc., Co. v. Cincinnati, etc., R. R. Co., 21 W. L. B. 275 (1889).

Where the holder of a judgment for materials and supplies claims a priority over mortgages existing before the supplies were furnished, the burden of proof is on such claimant to show that he has obtained a judgment and that the cause of action upon which it was obtained was such as to come within the terms of this section.

Farmers' Loan, etc., Co. v. Cincinnati, etc., R. R. Co., 21 W. L. B. 275 (1889).

In an original action to obtain a judgment for the value or price of the supplies furnished, other lienholders are not necessary or proper parties. The question of priority can be properly determined in a subsequent action to marshal liens.

Farmers' Loan, etc., Co. v. Cincinnati, etc., R. R. Co., 21 W. L. B. 275 (1889).

Claims for supplies furnished under this section may be assigned and judgment thereon taken by the assignee, who thereupon obtains all the rights of the original claimant.

Farmers' Loan, etc., Co. v. Cincinnati, etc., R. R. Co., 21 W. L. B. 275 (1889).

Section 9086. (Lien for labor performed.) In an action against a railroad company, domestic or foreign, operating a railroad in this state, when it is or was for the purpose of recovering judgment against the corporation for labor done for, or supplies furnished to it, or for damages or losses, or injuries suffered or sustained by the misconduct of its agents, or the suit is founded on the company's contract or liability as a common carrier; if, when reduced to judgment by virtue of statute or the principles of equity, it would become a lien upon the property of such company, prior to the lien of a mortgage or deed of trust, legally made under the laws of this state, such judgments shall be a prior lien upon such property, notwithstanding its sale or conveyance by virtue of a judgment or decree of foreclosure for breach of the terms and conditions of such mortgage or deed of trust. (R. S. Sec. 3398a; February 17, 1882, 79 v. 11.)

See §§ 8343 et seq. and 8376 et seq.

Section 9087. (How such lien enforced.) A party prosecuting such action in order to avail himself of the provisions of the preceding section, before the day fixed for the sale of the property of such railroad under judgment or decree of foreclosure and sale, shall file with the clerk of the court wherein the judgment or decree was rendered, a notice in writing, setting forth the title of his action, the court wherein pending, the amount of his claim, the date from which he claims interest thereon, the probable amount of costs, and that he claims that the judgment sought by him to be recovered would, when obtained, become a lien prior in law or equity to the lien of the judgment or decree of foreclosure and sale. Before the day of sale, or at the time thereof, he also shall serve a certified copy of such notice upon the officer or other person making such sale, who, prior to offering the property for sale, shall read such notice publicly at the time and place of sale, and with his return of sale, return the copy of notice with the endorsement of his proceedings thereunder upon it to the court. (R. S. Sec. 3398b; February 17, 1882, 79 v. 11.)

Section 9088. (Court to retain amount of lien.) On the return of the officer or other person making such sale, before confirming it and ordering distribution of the funds arising therefrom, the court shall retain in its custody or under its control, a sufficiency of such proceeds applicable to distribution to the claimants under the liens of the mortgage or deed of trust, to satisfy any judgment which may be recovered in the action provided for in section ninety hundred and eighty-six when ended and determined. (R. S. Sec. 3398c; February 17, 1882, 79 v. 11.)

Section 9089. (In case judgment recovered.) Within sixty days after the determination of the action referred to in section ninety hundred and eighty-six, the party claiming such priority of lien, if he has recovered judgment against such railroad company, shall file his answer and cross-petition in the action pending in the court holding the fund as above provided, setting forth his claim thereto, and such court shall make the proper orders necessary to the determination of the questions of priorities and distribution

of the retained fund, as in the preceding section provided.
(R. S. Sec. 3398d; February 17, 1882, 79 v. 11.)

Section 9090. (Provisions applicable to certain other companies.) The provisions of this chapter shall extend to and apply to companies whose railroads are partly within and partly without this state. A domestic company possessing such a railroad, may exercise without this state all its powers, privileges, faculties, and franchises. A foreign corporation possessing a railroad which is partly in another state and partly within this state, may here exercise and enjoy all its powers, privileges, faculties, and franchises, for the purposes of such road and its business, not inconsistent with the laws of this state. Mortgages and deeds of trust made by such corporation upon its railroad, equipments, or other property within this state, shall operate in the manner and with like effect as provided with respect to companies so reorganized. But such part of the railroad as is within this state is subject to taxation, and to all regulations of law, as are railroads of this state in like cases, and the corporation owning it shall be subject to all duties in respect thereto imposed by law, and may sue and be sued in all cases and in the manner that a company of this state might sue or be sued. (R. S. Sec. 3399; April 11, 1861, 58 v. 70, § 7.)

There is not only no law of Ohio prohibiting the ownership and use of railroads in the state by foreign corporations, and no public policy of the state to be contravened thereby, but there is abundant legislation directly to the contrary. Where the act incorporating a foreign corporation gives it the power to condemn and appropriate private property, if its road is partly in this state and partly in a foreign state, it may exercise and enjoy within this state all its powers, privileges, faculties, and franchises, for the purpose of said railroad and its business not inconsistent with the laws of this state. This section clearly gives the right to condemn and appropriate private property in Ohio to all railroad corporations of other states, which have the power of condemnation and appropriation given them in their charters of incorporation, where their roads lie partly within this state.

State v. Sherman, 22 O. S. 411, 434 (1872).

The legislature has power to attach the conditions of this section and § 9085 to the right of foreign corporations to mortgage railroad property within the state.

King v. Thompson, 110 Fed. 319; 13 O. F. D. 696; 46 W. L. B. 210 (C. C. A. 1901).

A foreign railroad company, having acquired a connecting Ohio railroad, may appropriate property in Ohio.

Bogard v. Detroit, etc., Ry. Co., 45 W. L. B. 224 (1901).

A foreign railroad company which enters the state over a bridge owned by it, and forming a part of its line, is a railroad "partly in such other state and partly within this state" within the meaning of this section, although the bridge is used for other travel.

L. & N. Ry. v. Taylor, 50 Bull. 20 (Ins. Ct. 1904).

A foreign railroad company, by leasing and operating in this state the property of an Ohio corporation, does not thereby become an Ohio corporation.

Railroad Co. v. Cary, 28 O. S. 218 (1876).

Railroad v. Stringer, 32 O. S. 468 (1877).

Railroad Co. v. Koontz, 104 U. S. 5.

See note to § 194.

This section does not authorize a foreign telephone company to appropriate property.

Telephone Co. v. Columbus Grove, 8 C. C. n. s. 81; 18 C. D. 131 (1905).

Power of foreign railroad company to hold stock in Ohio corporations.

See Mannington v. Railway, 9 N. P. n. s. 641, 665 (1910); s. c., 183 Fed. 133; 8 O. L. R. 451; 16 O. F. D. 552.

Section 9091. (Mortgaged property may be sold without appraisement.) Railroads, and other property mortgaged therewith by such company, if the court deems it expedient, may be sold without appraisement, at judicial sales under judgments upon such mortgage. But in such case, to prevent sacrifices and protect the interests of all concerned, the court shall fix a minimum sum below which no sale shall be made. In order to fix that amount, if it deems it expedient to do so, the court may refer the subject to a master, with instructions to take testimony, and report the sum. (R. S. Sec. 3400; April 11, 1861, 58 v. 70, § 8.)

Section 9092. (Creditors may agree on capitalization.) When judicial proceedings are pending in a court for the sale of a railroad, and it is in the hands of a receiver appointed by such court, two-thirds in interest of each class of mortgagees, or holders of the bonds issued under a mortgage, and two-thirds in interest of all other classes of creditors of such company, and the owners of two-thirds of the shares of the stock thereof, may agree in writing upon a plan for the adjustment of such indebtedness, by capitalization or otherwise. (R. S. Sec. 3401; April 7, 1863, 60 v. 55, § 1.)

In so far as this section applies to debts created before its passage, it is unconstitutional.

Mather v. Cincinnati Ry. Co., 3 C. C. 284; 2 C. D. 161 (1888).

Section 9093. (Notice of agreement to be published.) When such agreement is made, and filed in the office of the secretary of state, he shall cause public notice thereof to be given in a newspaper of general circulation published in each of the cities of Columbus, Cincinnati and Cleveland, and also in a newspaper of general circulation published in each of the counties through or in which the road is lo-

cated, which publication shall be made immediately after
the agreement is filed, and be continued for six consecutive
weeks. The cost thereof shall be paid by the company. (R.
S. Sec. 3402; April 7, 1863, 60 v. 55, § 2.)

Section 9094. (Other creditors may sign the agreement.)
A duplicate of such agreement shall be kept at the principal
office of the company. All persons in interest, not parties
thereto, shall be at liberty, for four months after the date
of the first publication, to appear and become a party to
such agreement, either in person or by proxy, by signing it,
and thereby secure its benefits. (R. S. Sec. 3403; April 7,
1863, 60 v. 55, § 3.)

**Section 9095. (Rights of creditors who do not sign agree-
ment.)** Persons in interest who fail to become parties to
the agreement within such time thereafter shall be entitled
to the same rights, interest, estate, remedy, liens, and action,
and none other, which parties in interest of like class and
amount who signed the agreement obtained by, and under
it. But if a person in interest fails for six years after the
publication of the notice mentioned in the second preceding
section, to apply at the principal office of the company,
either in person or by proxy, to become a party in interest
in the agreement, such person, unless an infant, or insane,
shall be barred of all interest, claim, right or action under
the agreement, or otherwise. In case of such disability the
rights above enumerated shall be extended for two years
after the termination of the disability. (R. S. Sec. 3404;
April 7, 1863, 60 v. 55, § 4.)

Section 9096. (Court to make order as to costs.) When
such agreement is made, filed, notice of it given, and proof
thereof made, or offered to be made, in the court in which
the proceedings are pending, the court shall dismiss the
proceedings. But it may make such order or decree touching the costs and expenses thereof as it deems just. (R. S.
Sec. 3405; April 7, 1863, 60 v. 55, § 5.)

Section 9097. (Agreement may be with each interest.)
Such agreement is not required to be between the several
interests above specified, but may be between each interest
separately, and the railroad company. (R. S. Sec. 3406;
April 7, 1863, 60 v. 55, § 7.)

Section 9098. (When road used by two companies.) If
the railroad involved in such judicial proceedings is used,

in whole or part, by such company in common with another railroad company, on the same track, between points on the line common to both, and within the limits of the termini established by their charters, the company owning the railroad, if it can be done without impairing the usefulness thereof to it, for a period of years, for an annual rent, may lease or sell for a fixed sum, to the company to which the line of road, in whole or part, is common, an undivided interest in it upon such terms and conditions as they agree upon. Such lease or sale shall be reported to and approved by the court. When so made and approved, the lessee or vendee thereof shall hold such interest free from any previous lien thereon. (R. S. Sec. 3407; April 7, 1863, 60 v. 55, § 8.)

Where by the purchase of an undivided interest under this section, a tenancy in common becomes established, partition can not be compelled by either party under the statutes in relation to partition or in equity. Railway Co. v. Railroad Co., 38 O. S. 614 (1883).

Section 9099.   (Stocks or bonds held in a fiduciary capacity.) When a portion of the stock or bonds of a company is held by the state, or a county, township, city or village, or by an executor, administrator, guardian, or otherwise in a fiduciary capacity, the governor, county commissioners, township trustees, council, or other authority of the municipal corporation, or person holding in fiduciary capacity, may become parties to an agreement for the reorganization of such company, and may control, exchange, or manage such stock or bonds according to the terms of the agreement and receive new stock or bonds to be issued in place of the original stock or bonds, which shall be held on the same terms, and subject to all liens, which attached to the original stock or bonds. (R. S. Sec. 3408; April 11, 1861, 58 v. 70, § 9; April 7, 1863, 60 v. 55, § 6.)

See Commissioners v. Nichols, 14 O. S. 260.

STREET AND INTERURBAN.

Section 9100. (Authority to construct a street railway.)
Street railways, with single or double tracks, side-tracks, and turn-outs, may be constructed or extended within or without, or partly within and partly without, any municipal corporation. Offices, depots, and other necessary buildings therefor, also may be constructed. (R. S. Sec. 3437; February 10, 1870, 67 v. 10, § 1.)

Sections § 9100 et seq. relate to street railways wherever located. Sections 3768 et seq. relate to street railway lines wholly within municipalities.

In case of conflict ·between the general provisions of this chapter and the provisions of § 3768 et seq. the more specific provisions of § 3768 et seq. will prevail.

C. C. C. & St. L. Ry. v. Urbana, etc., Ry., 5 C. C. n. s. 583; 16 C. D. 180 (1903) ; aff'd, no rep., 73 O. S. 364.

See also Raynolds v. Cleveland, 2 C. C. n. s. 139, 150; 14 C. D. 215 (1902) ; aff'd. no rep., 76 O. S. 619.

Hamilton v. Street Railroad, 5 N. P. 457; 8 L. D. 174.

What is a "street railway?" The difference between a "railroad" and a "street railway" consists in the use, not in the motive power.

Clement v. Cincinnati, 16 W. L. B. 355 (1886).

To constitute a "street railway" the rails should be laid to conform to the grade and surface of the street, the space between the rails being filled in, and so constructed that the public is not excluded from any part of the street.

> McMaken v. C. & H., etc., Co., 5 N. P. 367; 5 L. D. 364.
> Williams v. City Electric St. R. Co., 41 Fed. 556 (1890).
> Schaaf v. Cleveland, etc., Co., 66 O. S. 215 (1902).
> Dietz v. C. & M. Traction Co., 4 N. P. 399; 6 L. D. 513.
> See also Street Ry. Co. v. Cumminsville, 14 O. S. 523, 545 (1863).
> Cincinnati St. Ry. Co. v. Snell, 54 O. S. 197, 205-206.
> State v. Dayton Traction Co., 18 C. C. 490; 10 C. D. 212 (1899); affirmed, 64 O. S. 272.
> Columbus D. & N. Traction Co. v. Marriot, 47 O. L. B. 347.
> G. C. § 3775.

Interurban railway as a street railway.

> See note to § 9117.

Powers of street railway companies.

To furnish medical attendance. A street railway company can not made a valid contract to perform medical services; but may agree to furnish or pay for medical attention to persons injured on its line.

> Youngstown, etc., Railway Co. v. Kessler, 84 O. S. 74 (1911).

To carry freight. An urban railway company may make a valid traffic agreement with an interurban railway company, under G. C. § 9120, for the transportation of freight over streets.

> State v. Dayton Traction Co., 64 O. S. 272 (1901); affirming, 18 C. C. 490; 10 C. D. 212.

A franchise authorizing the transportation of freight over streets does not authorize the use of a street as a station for unloading freight.

> Newark v. Ohio Electric Ry., 13 N. P. n. s. 487 (1912).

To make private agreement as to fare to resort without municipality. An agreement with the proprietor of a resort, located beyond municipal limits, to carry passengers thereto for a specified fare, while other railways are excluded from the resort, is valid.

> Humphrey Co. v. Cleveland Ry. Co., 9 N. P. n. s. 609; 20 L. D. (1910).

To appropriate property.

> §§ 9108, 9115, 9118-2.

Contracts with street railway as to operation are made in contemplation of existing laws and ordinances.

> Cemetery v. Cincinnati St. Ry. Co., 11 C. C. n. s. 429; 21 C. D. 51.

Loop on private property under agreement construed to be a revocable license.

> Cemetery v. Cincinnati St. Ry. Co., 11 C. C. n. s. 429; 21 C. D. 51 (1908).
> Mueller v. Cincinnati Traction Co., 6 O. L. R. 596; 19 L. D. 504 (1909).

Conflicting franchise rights of telephone and street railway companies. The primary purpose of streets is travel and transportation. Where the franchise rights of a telephone company conflict with those of a street railway company, the latter are, in general, paramount.

> Railway Co. v. Telephone Assn., 48 O. S. 390 (1891).

Route. The line may fork and be but one route.

> Aydelott v. Cincinnati, 11 C. C. 11, 17; 4 C. D. 86 (1893).

Extensions may run at right angles with original track.

> Belle v. Glenville, 5 C. C. n. s. 461; 17 C. D. 181 (1904); aff'd, no rep., 73 O. S. 392, 397; 75 O. S. 574.

An application for a franchise may be for two routes in the alternative, leaving it to the municipality to grant either one.
Simmons v. Toledo, 5 C. C. 124, 141; 3 C. D. 64 (1889).
See Somers v. Cincinnati, 8 Am. L. R. 612, 622.
See also note to § 3768.

Section 9101. (Who to grant right to construct.) The right to construct or extend such railway within or beyond the limits of a municipal corporation, may be granted only by its council, by ordinance; the right to construct such railway without the limits of a municipal corporation may be granted only by the county commissioners, by an order entered on their journal. (October 22, 1902, 96 v. 31, § 29; Bates' Stats. § 1536-183.)

Franchises within municipalities, see § 3768 et seq.
Franchises generally, see note to § 3714.
Section 9120 is not intended as a limitation on this section.
    Hamilton v. Railway, 5 N. P. 457; 8 L. D. 174.
    Hamlets in existence when municipal code of 1902 took effect became villages. Consent of such a village necessary to construction of street railroad.
    Railroad v. North Bend, 70 O. S. 46 (1904).
    Where the trustees of a hamlet had granted a franchise on a street, which was also a state road, the county commissioners can not enjoin operation thereunder.
    Commissioners v. A. B. & C. Ry., 21 C. C. 769; 11 C. D. 664 (1896).
    See In re Newburgh Twp., 15 C. C. 78; 8 C. D. 24 (1897).

    Over county bridge within municipality. The council may make a grant for extension over existing tracks which run over a bridge, within the municipality, but built by the county commissioners.
    State v. Cincinnati, etc., Co., 19 C. C. 79; 10 C. D. 418 (1899).

    Franchise in parks. A municipality has no power to grant a franchise for a street railway in a public park donated to the municipality for park purposes only, to revert to the donor, if used for other purposes.
    Cleveland City Cable Ry. v. Barriss, 33 W. L. B. 314 (1895).
    See Mathers v. Cincinnati, 3 W. L. B. 551, 709 (1878).

    County commissioners may recover damages under G. C. § 2424 from street railway company occupying county road without permission.
    Citizens, etc., Co. v. Commissioners, 56 O. S. 1 (1897); affirming, 9 C. C. 183; 6 C. D. 290.
    Without municipalities a franchise must be granted by the county commissioners. A franchise from a municipality permitting an extension beyond the municipal limits does not dispense with the necessity of a grant from the commissioners.
    Commissioners v. Railway, 9 C. C. 183; 6 C. D. 290 (1895); aff'd, 56 O. S. 1.
    Dietz v. Traction Co., 4 N. P. 399; 6 L. D. 513.
    A grant by the county commissioners, when accepted, is a contract.
    State v. C. E. Ry. Co., 15 C. C. 200; 8 C. D. 474 (1897).
    State v. Northern Ohio, etc., Co., 1 Ct. of App. — (1913).
    A grant made by county commissioners is not affected by the subsequent annexation of the territory to a municipality.
    Belle v. Glenville, 5 C. C. n. s. 461; 17 C. D. 181 (1904); aff'd, no rep., 73 O. S. 392; 75 O. S. 574.

A franchise granted by county commissioners may be assigned by the grantee, although the word "assignee" or "assigns" is not used.

State v. Northern Ohio, etc., Co., 1 Ct. of App. — (1913).

County commissioners have power to grant a perpetual franchise.

State v. Northern Ohio, etc., Co., 1 Ct. of App. — (1913).

Miscellaneous.

Electrolysis. The operation of a single trolley electric system, contemplated by its franchise, causing injury to municipal water pipes, will not be enjoined, unless operation is negligent.

Dayton v. City Ry. Co., 6 C. C. n. s. 41; 16 C. D. 736 (1904); affirming, 12 L. D. 258.

Building moved across tracks. Rights and liabilities.

Traction Co. v. Sterling, 9 C. C. n. s. 200; 19 C. D. 227 (1906).

Illegal contract by councilman with company. A member of a council can not recover under a contract with a street railway for services in procuring rights of way over streets.

Railroad Co. v. Morris, 10 C. C. 502; 6 C. D. 640 (1895).

Adverse possession of streets by company. Rights under.

Cincinnati v. Columbus, etc., Co., 17 W. L. B. 192 (1886).

INJUNCTIONS.

See also note to § 3714.

Solicitor or taxpayer may enjoin exercise of invalid franchise. The exercise of an invalid franchise may be enjoined, at the suit of the solicitor or a taxpayer, under G. C. § 4311 or § 4314.

Cincinnati St. R. Co. v. Smith, 29 O. S. 291 (1876).

Knorr v. Miller, 5 C. C. 609; 3 C. D. 297 (1891); affirmed, no rep., 27 W. L. B. 64.

Haskins v. Cincinnati, 4 W. L. B. 1126 (1880).

Rogers v. Railway Co., 12 L. D. 136 (1901).

See Buning v. Cincinnati St. Ry. Co., 1 C. C. 323; 1 C. D. 178 (1886).

The motive of a taxpayer in bringing such a suit is immaterial. It is no defense that he is acting for the benefit of competing railways.

Raynolds v. Cleveland, 2 C. C. n. s. 139; 14 C. D. 215 (1902); affirmed, no rep., 76 O. S. 619.

Traction Co. v. Parish, 67 O. S. 181, 189 (1902).

Isom v. Low Fare Ry. Co., 10 C. C. n. s. 89; 19 C. D. 583 (1907); affirmed, no rep., 77 O. S. 638.

Compare, Gallagher v. Johnson, 31 W. L. B. 24.

To render a grant invalid, the defects or irregularities must be in some matter which is jurisdictional, or of such a nature that equity and justice require interference by the courts.

Sloane v. Peoples, etc., Ry. Co., 7 C. C. 84; 3 C. D. 674 (1891).

Defects in a street railway franchise can not be cured by an amendment to the granting ordinance which merely sets forth the facts as to the publication of notice before bids were received, and declares that the publication was sufficient to meet the requirements of the granting ordinance.

Raynolds v. Cleveland, 8 C. C. n. s. 278; 18 C. D. 463 (1906); aff'd, on the ground of laches, 77 O. S. 631.

Failure to procure the consents required by §§ 9105 and 3770 is not such a defect as will render the grant invalid at the suit of a *taxpayer*, who is not an abutting owner. Only abutting owners may complain on that ground.

Sommers v. Cincinnati, 8 Am. L. R. 612.

Simmons v. Toledo, 5 C. C. 124; 3 C. D. 64 (1889).
Glidden v. Cincinnati, 30 W. L. B. 213.
Lima v. Cramer, 5 N. P. n. s. 113; 17 L. D. 245 (1906).
Harrison v. Mt. Auburn, etc., Co., 17 W. L. B. 265.
Hamilton v. C. & H., etc., Co., 5 N. P. 457; 8 L. D. 174.

Suit by abutting owner. An abutting owner, as such, can not complain of defects in a grant, other than failure to procure consents required by § 9105 and § 3770.

Glidden v. Cincinnati, 30 W. L. B. 213.
Barney v. Mt. Adams, etc., Ry. Co., 30 W. L. B. 286.
Raynolds v. Cleveland, 2 C. C. n. s. 139, 154; 14 C. D. 215 (1902).
Ireton Bros. v. Ft. Wayne, etc., Co., 2 N. P. n. s. 317; 15 L. D. 129 (1904).
Sloane v. Peoples, etc., Co., 7 C. C. 84, 89; 3 C. D. 674 (1891).
Dietz v. Traction Co., 4 N. P. 399; 5 L. D. 513.
See Sanfleet v. Toledo, 10 C. C. 460; 8 C. D. 711 (1893).
See note to § 9105.

Suit by railroad to prevent crossing of tracks. A steam railroad company may raise the question whether the notice required by § 3769 has been given, where the street railway proposes to cross its tracks.

C. C. C. & St. L. Ry. v. Urbana, etc., Ry., 5 C. C. n. s. 583; 16 C. D. 180 (1903); aff'd, no rep., 73 O. S. 364.

Unsuccessful bidder or competitor. An unsuccessful bidder, who does not sue as a taxpayer or an abutting owner, can not enjoin occupation of streets.

Johnson v. West Side St. Ry. Co., 10 W. L. B. 345.
Mathers v. Cincinnati, 3 W. L. B. 709 (1878).

Nor can a competing company enjoin the exercise of a franchise on the ground of interference with its franchise.

Circleville, etc., Co. v. Buckeye Gas Co., 69 O. S. 259 (1903); affirming, 1 C. C. n. s. 259; 14 C. D. 684.

Section 9102.   (Grantee not to be released from obligation.) After such grant, or the renewal of any grant has been made, by general or special ordinance, or the order of county commissioners, neither the municipality nor commissioners shall release a grantee from any obligations or liabilities imposed by the terms of the grant, or renewal of any grant, during the term for which such grant or renewal was made. (October 22, 1902, 96 v. 31, § 29; Bates' Stats. § 1536-183.)

See § 3771.

Release of obligation or liability. A modification of the contract, made in good faith for the better acommodation of the public, is not void.

Clement v. Cincinnati, 16 W. L. B. 355 (1886).
Cleveland v. Cleveland City Ry. Co., 194 U. S. 517 (1904).
Cleveland v. Cleveland Electric Ry. Co., 201 U. S. 529 (1906).

A sum due a municipality as car license fees can not be released except on payment of the full amount. The principles of account stated and accord and satisfaction, based on a less amount, do not apply.

Cincinnati St. Ry. Co. v. Cincinnati, 8 N. P. 80; 11 L. D. 15.

That operation of a railway is unprofitable is no ground for failure to give adequate service so long as the franchise is not abandoned.

Ferguson v. Transit Co., 4 O. L. R. 750; 52 W. L. B. 197 (Railroad Commission, 1907).

Remedies to enforce franchise obligations.

See note to § 3714.

Forfeiture of bidder's deposit. A deposit by grantee of franchise, to secure performance of obligations, may be forfeited to municipality as liquidated damages.

Hattersly v. Waterville, 4 C. C. n. s. 242; 16 C. D. 226 (1904); aff'd, no rep., 74 O. S. 466.

Section 9103. (Right to occupy tracks of existing companies.) No right shall be given by such municipal or county authorities to occupy the track, single or double, or other structure, of existing street railways for more than one-eighth of the distance between the termini of the route, as actually constructed, operated and run over, of the company or person to whom such grant is made. But in granting permission to extend existing routes in cities, the cities and companies owning such route shall have all the rights and powers which they possess under existing laws and contracts. (October 22, 1902, 96 v. 31, § 29; Bates' Stats. § 1536-183.)

Municipality may grant franchise over existing tracks. Subject to the limitations of this section a municipality may grant a franchise over existing tracks belonging to another company, but the grantee must appropriate the right to use such tracks before taking possession.

Street Ry. Co. v. Street Ry. Co., 50 O. S. 603 (1893).
Kinsman, etc., Co. v. Broadway, etc., Co., 36 O. S. 239 (1880).
Hamilton, etc., Co. v. Hamilton, etc., Co., 69 O. S. 402 (1903).
See note to § 3768.
For right to appropriate use of tracks, see § 9108.

Pleading compliance with this section. A petition in an appropriation proceeding which alleges that eight times the amount of track, sought to be appropriated, has been built and placed in operation, shows compliance with this section.

Toledo Cons., etc., Co. v. Toledo Elec., etc., Co., 12 C. C. 367; 5 C. D. 643 (1893).

Computation of one-eighth of trackage. The entire line, without as well as within the municipality, should be used as a basis for computation.

State v. Cincinnati, etc., Co., 19 C. C. 79, 89; 10 C. D. 418 (1899).

Abutting owners can not complain of a grant over existing tracks on the ground that the length of new track is insufficient under this section.

Sanfleet v. Toledo, 10 C. C. 460; 8 C. D. 711 (1893).

Consents of abutting owners are not necessary for a franchise to operate cars solely over existing tracks.

State v. Cincinnati, etc., Co., 19 C. C. 79; 10 C. D. 419 (1899).
Broadway, etc., Co. v. Brooklyn, etc., Co., 10 W. L. B. 72.
Mt. Auburn, etc., Co. v. Neare, 54 O. S. 153 (1896).
Lima v. Cramer, 5 N. P. n. s. 113; 17 L. D. 245 (1906).

Section 9104.   (Extensions to be constructed as new.)

No extension of a street railway located wholly outside of a city, or of one wherever located, which is built in pursuance of a right obtained from authority other than that of a municipal corporation, shall be made within the limits of such city, except as a new route. (October 22, 1902, 96 v. 31, § 29; Bates' Stats. § 1536-183.)

See Cleveland, etc., Ry. v. Urbana, etc., Ry., 5 C. C. n. s. 583; 16 C. D. 180 (1903); aff'd, no rep., 73 O. S. 364.

The validity of a grant made by county commissioners, in territory outside of a municipality, is not affected by the subsequent annexation of such territory to a municipality.

Belle v. Glenville, 5 C. C. n. s. 461; 17 C. D. 181 (1904); aff'd, no rep., 73 O. S. 392, 397; 75 O. S. 574.

Extensions within municipalities, § 3777.

Section 9105. (Consent of owners of abutting property.) No such grant shall be made until there is produced to council, or the commissioners, as the case may be, the written consent of the owners of more than one-half of the feet front of the lots and lands abutting on the street or public way, along which it is proposed to construct such railway or extension thereof; and the provisions of all ordinances of the council relating thereto, have in all respects been complied with, whether the railway proposed is an extension of an old or the granting of a new route. (R. S. Sec. 3439; April 15, 1908, 99 v. 103; April 18, 1883, 80 v. 173; R. S. 1880; April 29, 1868, 65 v. 112, § 3.)

Consents for extensions, see note to § 3777.

CONSENTS.

Statutes requiring, are constitutional. Sections 9105, 3770 and 3777, requiring the written consents of abutting owners, are constitutional.

Isom v. Low Fare Ry. Co., 10 C. C. n. s. 89, 92; 19 C. D. 583 (1907); aff'd, no rep., 77 O. S. 638.

See Forest City Ry. Co. v. Day, 73 O. S. 83, 86 (1905).

Railway v. Railway, 5 C. C. n. s. 583; 16 C. D. 180 (1903); aff'd, no rep., 73 O. S. 364.

Are jurisdictional to grant. A majority of consents by the feet front is a condition precedent to jurisdiction to pass a street railway ordinance.

Traction Co. v. Parish, 67 O. S. 181, 192 (1902).

Roberts v. Easton, 19 O. S. 78 (1869).

Sommers v. Cincinnati, 8 Am. L. R. 612.

Although tracks of another company are already in the street.

Sanfleet v. Toledo, 10 C. C. 460; 8 C. D. 711 (1893); aff'd, no rep., 54 O. S. 620.

Requisite for each street. Consents of the owners of a majority of the frontage on each street on which the railway is to be constructed are requisite.

Mt. Auburn. etc., Ry. Co. v. Neare, 54 O. S. 153 (1896); affirming, 29 W. L. B. 171.

Sommers v. Cincinnati, 8 Am. L. R. 612.
See Rapp v. Cincinnati, etc., Co., 12 W. L. B. 119.
This requirement can not be avoided by action of the council in chang-
ing the name of a street, along which consents could not be secured, to
the name of another street, along which consents were secured.
Carpenter v. Traction Co., 13 N. P. n. s. 81 (1912).

Not required to operate over existing tracks. Consents need not be
obtained where the grant is to operate solely over existing tracks.
State v. Cincinnati, etc., Co., 19 C. C. 79; 10 C. D. 418 (1899).
Broadway, etc., Co. v. Brooklyn, etc., Co., 10 W. L. B. 72.
Mt. Auburn, etc., Co. v. Neare, 54 O. S. 153 (1896).
Lima v. Cramer, 5 N. P. n. s. 113; 17 L. D. 245 (1906).
Railway v. Railway, 6 C. C. 362; 3 C. D. 493; aff'd, 50 O. S. 603.
See Sanfleet v. Toledo, 10 C. C. 460; 8 C. D. 711 (1893); affirmed, 54
  O. S. 621.
G. C. §§ 9106, 3770.
Except where the existing tracks occupy the street without right.
Isom v. Low Fare Ry. Co, 10 C. C. n. s. 89; 19 C. D. 583 (1907).

WHO ENTITLED TO BENEFIT OF CONSENTS.

**New road. Consents inure to benefit of lowest bidder. Can not be
limited to one bidder or person.** The consents of abutting owners to the
construction of a new line, by whomsoever obtained, inure to the benefit
of the lowest bidder.
Forest City Ry. Co. v. Day, 73 O. S. 83 (1905); reversing 5 C. C.
  n. s. 393.
Isom v. Low Fare Ry. Co., 10 C. C. n. s. 89, 98; 19 C. D. 583 (1907);
  aff'd, no rep., 77 O. S. 638.
State ex rel. v. Bell, 34 O. S. 194, 197 (1877).
Knorr v. Miller, 5 C. C. 609; 3 C. D. 297 (1891); affirmed, 27 W.
  L. B. 64.
Mathers v. Cincinnati, 3 W. L. B. 551.
A consent can not, by its terms, be limited to the party to whom
given. The limitation is void, and the consent good as a consent to the
construction of the road by the lowest bidder.
Forest City Ry. Co. v. Day, 73 O. S. 83 (1905).

Extension of existing line. Consents for the extension of an existing
line inure only to persons to whom given, and assigns.
Isom v. Low Fare Ry. Co., 10 C. C. n. s. 89, 99; 19 C. D. 583 (1907);
  aff'd, no rep., 77 O. S. 638.

NATURE OF CONSENTS. RIGHTS OF ABUTTING OWNERS.

Consents are not property rights, but rights personal to each abut-
ting owner, who is free to give or withhold such consent.
Traction Co. v. Parish, 67 O. S. 181 (1902); reversing 13 C. D. 527.
Forest City Ry. Co. v. Day, 73 O. S. 83 (1905).

Can not be appropriated. Consents are not property rights which
may be appropriated under the power of eminent domain.
Traction Co. v. Parish, 67 O. S. 181 (1902).

Purchased consents are valid.
Traction Co. v. Parish, 67 O. S. 181 (1902).
Cleveland v. Cleveland City Ry., 3 C. C. n. s. 563; 13 C. D. 373
  (1902); reversing 12 L. D. 623.
See Transit Co. v. Traction Co., 12 L. D. 1; s. c., 69 O. S. 402.

May be withdrawn. Consents may be withdrawn, even when induced by a money consideration, at any time before the granting ordinance has been read the second time.

G. C. § 9107.

Cleveland v. Cleveland City Ry., 3 C. C. n. s. 563; 13 C. D. 373 (1902) ; reversing 12 L. D. 623.

Simmons v. Toledo, 8 C. C. 535; 4 C. D. 69; aff'd, no rep., 51 O. S. 626.

See Hume v. Traction Co., 13 L. D. 70 (1902).

BY WHOM CONSENTS MAY BE GIVEN.

Owner or authorized agent. The "owner" must hold at least a free-hold estate. A consent signed by a tenant for years is insufficient.

Rapp v. Cincinnati, etc., Co., 12 W. L. B. 119.

Consents must be signed by the abutting owner, or in his name by his authorized agent. A consent signed by a husband, in his own name, where his wife owns the property and does not consent, is insufficient and should not be received or counted.

Simmons v. Toledo, 8 C. C. 535; 4 C. D. 69 (1890) ; aff'd, no rep., 51 O. S. 626.

Rapp v. Cincinnati, etc., Co., 12 W. L. B. 119.

See Day v. Railway, 5 C. C. n. s. 393; 17 C. D. 60; reversed, 73 O. S. 83.

A consent signed by an agent in his own name, without authority, is invalid and can not be counted, although ratified by the owner after passage of the granting ordinance.

Sommers v. Cincinnati, 8 Am. L. R. 612.

The authority of an agent may be given by parol.

Simmons v. Toledo, 8 C. C. 535; 4 C. D. 69 (1890) ; aff'd, no rep., 51 O. S. 626.

Life tenant and remainderman. A life estate is a freehold interest, and a consent signed by a life tenant is valid.

Ireton Bros. v. Ft. Wayne, etc., Co., 2 N. P. n. s. 317; 15 L. D. 129 (1904).

Rapp v. Cincinnati, etc., Co., 12 W. L. B. 119.

A consent signed by a remainderman in his own name was held valid when the remainderman had charge of the property for the life tenant.

Simmons v. Toledo, 8 C. C. 535; 4 C. D. 69 (1890).

See also *Widow* below.

Tenants in common. A tenant in common, who may desire to vote adversely to his cotenants, is entitled to vote the number of feet front which his undivided interest proportionately represents.

Simmons v. Toledo, 8 C. C. 535; 4 C. D. 69 (1890).

Day v. Railway, 5 C. C. n. s. 393; 17 C. D. 60; reversed, 73 O. S. 83.

But see Ronnebaum v. Mt. Auburn, etc., Ry., 29 W. L. B. 338.

Rapp v. Cincinnati, etc., Co., 12 W. L. B. 119.

Infants. A consent signed by a minor is of no effect.

Schwab v. Hamilton, etc., Co., 13 L. D.' 116 (1902).

Vendor and vendee. A consent given by a vendor, of which the vendee had knowledge at the time of purchase, and not withdrawn by the vendee, is valid.

Simmons v. Toledo, 8 C. C. 535; 4 C. D. 69; (1890) ; aff'd, 51 O. S. 626.

See Day v. Railway, 5 C. C. n. s. 393; 17 C. D. 60; reversed 73 O. S. 83.

A vendee in possession under a land contract may give a valid consent.

Day v. Railway, 5 C. C. n. s. 393; 17 C. D. 60 (1904) ; reversed on other grounds, 73 O. S. 83.

A consent given by a vendor with the consent of the vendee is valid.

Day v. Railway, 5 C. C. n. s. 393; 17 C. D. 60 (1904); reversed on othe.· grounds, 73 O. S. 83.

Ancestor and heir. A consent signed by an ancestor, during his life, is valid where his heirs have knowledge of the consent, but do not withdraw it.

Day v. Railway, 5 C. C. n. s. 393; 17 C. D. 60 (1904); reversed on other grounds, 73 O. S. 83.

Executor. An executor with discretionary power to convey the property, can not sign a valid consent unless the legal title of the property has been devised to him.

Rapp v. Cincinnati, 12 W. L. B. 119.

Guardian. A consent signed by a guardian, without an order of the probate court, is invalid.

Rapp v. Cincinnati, 12 W. L. B. 119.

See Day v. Railway, 5 C. C. n. s. 393; 17 C. D. 60 (1904); reversed, 73 O. S. 83.

Trustees. A consent given by trustees under a will, having full control and management of the property, is valid.

Simmons v. Toledo, 8 C. C. 535, 556; 4 C. D. 69 (1890); aff'd, 51 O. S. 626.

The omission of the word "trustee" after the signature of the trustee does not invalidate the consent.

Rapp v. Cincinnati, 12 W. L. B. 119.

Widow. Dower interest.

See Schwab v. Hamilton, etc., Co., 13 L. D. 116 (1902).

Rapp v. Cincinnati, etc., Co., 12 W. L. B. 119.

Partnership. A consent signed by one partner in the firm name is valid, although the land is not used for partnership purposes.

Schwab v. Hamilton, etc., Co., 13 L. D. 116 (1902).

Simmons v. Toledo, 8 C. C. 535; 4 C. D. 69; aff'd, no rep., 51 O. S. 626.

Corporation. Authority from the board of directors is requisite.

Rapp v. Cincinnati, etc., Co., 12 W. L. B. 119.

See Day v. Railway, 5 C. C. n. s. 393; 17 C. D. 60; reversed, 73 O. S. 83.

County property. The county commissioners have authority to execute consents for county property.

Nearing v. Toledo, etc., Ry., 9 C. C. 596; 6 C. D. 664 (1893).

Property owned by the municipality. The council may give a valid consent for a municipality, for abutting property owned by it.

Emerson v. Forest City Ry. Co., 8 C. C. n. s. 560; 14 C. C. n. s. 478; 18 C. D. 683; 23 C. D. 34 (1906); affirmed, no rep., 77 O. S. 596.

Ireton Bros. v. Traction Co., 2 N. P. n. s. 317; 15 L. D. 129 (1904).

WHEN AND HOW PRODUCED. FOR HOW LONG VALID.

Time of filing. Consents need not be obtained prior to the publication of notice of the application.

Sloane v. Peoples, etc., Co., 7 C. C. 84; 3 C. D. 674 (1891).

But they must be filed with the council before the granting ordinance is passed or becomes effective

Sommers v. Cincinnati, 8 Am. L. R. 612, 618.

Where a grant fails, as to a part of the route, for lack of proper consents, the municipality may make a new grant for that part, when proper consents are filed. Such grant is valid under the original application, notice and bids.

> Sanfleet v. Toledo, 10 C. C. 460; 8 C. D. 711 (1893); affirmed, 54 O. S. 620.

How produced. Filing with the council is sufficient. The consents need not be entered on its records.

> Sanfleet v. Toledo, 10 C. C. 460; 8 C. D. 711 (1893); affirmed, 54 O. S. 620.
> Ireton Bros. v. Traction Co., 2 N. P. n. s. 317, 325; 15 L. D. 129.

Life of consents. When once acted upon by the council, in granting a valid franchise, consents lose their vitality and can not be used again as the basis of a second grant to another company. But if the franchise is invalid, the consents may, if not withdrawn, be used again for the purpose of making a valid grant.

> Isom v. Low Fare Ry. Co., 10 C. C. n. s. 89, 99; 19 C. D. 583 (1907); affirmed, no rep., 77 O. S. 638.
> Sanfleet v. Toledo, 10 C. C. 460; 8 C. D. 711 (1893); affirmed, 54 O. S. 620
> Smith v. Columbus, etc., Co., 8 N. P. 1, 6.
> See Roberts v. Easton, 19 O. S. 78, 88 (1869).
> Day v. Railway, 5 C. C. n. s. 393; 17 C. D. 60 (1904); reversed 73 O. S. 83.

TERMS AND CONDITIONS.

Form and contents. A consent must be in writing and signed by the owner or his authorized agent. A consent by telegram is valid.

> Simmons v. Toledo, 8 C. C. 535; 4 C. D. 69; (1890); aff'd, 51 O. S. 626.
> Schwab v. Traction Co., 13 L. D. 116.

It need not specify the mode and manner of construction and operation.

> Sloane v. Peoples, etc., Ry., 7 C. C. 84; 3 C. D. 674 (1891).

Consent to single track not consent for double track railway. Consents for the construction of a single track railway can not be counted as consents for a double track.

> Roberts v. Easton, 19 O. S. 78 (1869).

Motive power. Consents for a railway with animal power are not consents for an electric railway.

> Sanfleet v. Toledo, 10 C. C. 460; 8 C. D. 711; aff'd, 54 O. S. 620.

Additional switch. Consents for the original construction of a street railway are not consents for the subsequent construction of additional switches. New consents are requisite.

> Horner v. Columbus, etc., Ry., 29 W. L. B. 387 (1893).
> Chestnut v. Railway, 15 L. D. 336; aff'd, 76 O. S. 567.
> Chambers v. Cleveland, etc., Co., 5 C. C. n. s. 298; 17 C. D. 193 (1904); aff'd, no rep., 73 O. S. 348.

Change of route after consent given. A consent for one specified route is not a consent for another and different route.

> Neare v. Mt. Auburn, etc., Co., 29 W. L. B. 171; 4 N. P. 475; aff'd, 54 O. S. 153.
> Ireton Bros. v. Traction Co., 2 N. P. n. s. 317, 321; 15 L. D. 129 (1904).
> See Day v. Railway, 5 C. C. n. s. 393; 17 C. D. 60; reversed 73 O. S. 83.

But a change by an interurban road, whereby, for one square, the street is abandoned for a private right of way to avoid sharp curves, is not fraudulent per se against abutting owners.

> Ireton Bros. v. Traction Co., 2 N. P. n. s. 317; 15 L. D. 129 (1904).

Conditional consents. A consent given upon condition that construction be commenced and completed within a certain time is upon a condition subsequent and effective only between its signer and the grantee of the franchise. Such condition does not prevent the council from acting upon the consent.

Simmons v. Toledo, 8 C. C. 535; 4 C. D. 69 (1890); aff'd, no rep., 51 O. S. 626.

Only the persons giving conditional consents may take advantage of a violation of the conditions. Abutting owners who did not consent can not complain of such violations.

Barney v. Mt. Adams, etc., Co., 30 W. L. B. 286 (Cin. Super. Ct.).

RIGHT OF ACCESS.

In absence of statute requiring consents abutting owners in municipalities have right of access only. So long as his right of ingress and egress is not materially interfered with, an abutting owner in a municipality can not prevent the construction and operation of a street railway, if permission has been duly given by the municipal authorities.

Traction Co. v. Parish, 67 O. S. 181, 191 (1902).

Isom v. Low Fare Ry. Co., 10 C. C. n. s. 91; 19 C. D. 583 (1907); aff'd, no rep., 77 O. S. 638.

Street Ry. v. Cumminsville, 14 O. S. 523 (1863).

Interference with right of access.

Held not to constitute. Tracks which leave ten feet between the curb and the nearest track.

Barney v. Mt. Adams, etc., Co., 30 W. L. B. 286, 288.

Double tracks so located that wagons can not stand at right angles with the curb while being loaded and unloaded.

Miller v. Columbus Ry. Co., 13 L. D. 418 (1902).

Sells v. Columbus St. Ry. Co., 28 W. L. B. 172 (1892).

Oviatt v. Akron St. Ry. Co., 2 N. P. 84; 3 L. D. 252 (1895).

Trolley poles.

Mt. Adams, etc., Co. v. Winslow, 3 C. C. 425; 2 C. D. 240 (1888).

See Simmons v. Toledo, 8 C. C. 535; 4 C. D. 69 (1890).

Tracks laid close to sidewalk at corner so that, in turning the corner, the body of the car extends over the sidewalk.

Powell v. Columbus, etc., Co., 10 N. P. n. s. 266; 20 L. D. 313 (1910).

Held to constitute. Water thrown upon land by construction.

A. B. & C. Ry. v. Keck, 13 C. D. 57.

Tracks laid within two or three feet from the sidewalk in front of stores.

Street Ry. v. Cumminsville, 14 O. S. 523, 543 (1863).

See Schaaf v. Railway Co., 66 O. S. 215 (1902).

Tracks laid on one side of a highway without conforming to the grade, and without filling in between the rails.

McMacken v. C. & H., etc., Co., 5 N. P. 367; 5 L. D. 358.

Temporary interference incident to the construction of a street railway can not be complained of by abutting owner.

Glidden v. Cincinnati, 30 W. L. B. 213.

Estoppel by written consent. An abutting owner, who has given his written consent, can not complain of the additional burden, but if his easement of access is interfered with in the construction of the railway he is entitled to an injunction.

Powell v. Railway Co., 10 N. P. n. s. 266; 20 L. D. 313 (1910).

Transit Co. v. Traction Co., 12 L. D. 1, 4 (1901); s. c., 69 O. S. 402.

Liability to abutting owners, for injuries to trees in highway.

A. B. & C. Ry. v. Keck, 13 C. D. 57.

Keefe v. Cleveland City R. Co., 8 N. P. 466; 11 L. D. 568.

Rights of street railway and abutting owners in streets limited. A street railway can not lawfully occupy the track in front of business premises for an unreasonable time, nor can an abutting owner occupy the tracks for an unreasonable time so as to interfere with movement of cars.

Miller v. Columbus Ry. Co., 13 L. D. 418 (1902).

See Traction Co. v. Sterling, 9 C. C. n. s. 200; 19 C. D. 227 (1906).

STREET RAILWAY AS AN ADDITIONAL BURDEN.

In municipalities. The construction and operation of a street railway upon a street is a proper street use, and not a new or additional burden entitling abutting owners to compensation.

C. C. C. & St. L. Ry. v. Urbana, etc., Ry., 5 C. C. n. s. 583; 16 C. D. 180 (1903); affirmed, no rep., 73 O. S. 364.

Street Ry. v. Cumminsville, 14 O. S. 523, 545 (1862).

Traction Co. v. Parish, 67 O. S. 181, 191 (1902).

Railway Co. v. Telegraph Assn., 48 O. S. 390 (1891).

Sanfleet v. Toledo, 10 C. C. 460; 8 C. D. 711 (1893); affirmed, 54 O. S. 620.

State v. Dayton Traction Co., 18 C. C. 490; 10 C. D. 212 (1899).

Oviatt v. Railroad, 2 N. P. 84; 3 L. D. 252 (1895).

Trolley poles do not render the use a new or additional burden.

Simmons v. Toledo, 8 C. C. 535; 4 C. D. 69 (1890).

Sells v. Columbus St. Ry., 28 W. L. B. 172 (1892).

Akron, etc., Transit Co. v. Erie R., 7 C. C. n. s. 199, 202; 18 C. D. 36 (1905).

Railway v. Winslow, 3 C. C. 425; 2 C. D. 240 (1888).

Interurban railways outside of municipalities. An interurban railway, with T rails, built entirely on one side of a highway, between improved farms and the roadway, the company having authority to operate an unlimited number of cars for passengers, mail and freight, is an additional burden similar to that of a steam railroad.

Schaaf v. Cleveland, etc., Co., 66 O. S. 215 (1902).

Chestnut v. Columbus, etc., Ry., 15 L. D. 336 (1905); affirmed, 76 O. S. 567.

Miller v. Columbus Ry. Co., 13 L. D. 418 (1902).

A steam railroad is an additional burden.

Lawrence R. R. Co. v. Williams, 35 O. S. 168 (1878).

An additional switch laid in the highway subsequent to construction of road is an additional burden.

Chambers v. Cleveland, etc., Co., 5 C. C. n. s. 298; 17 C. D. 193 (1904); aff'd, no rep., 73 O. S. 348.

Chestnut v. Columbus, etc., Ry., 15 L. D. 336 (1905); aff'd, no rep., 76 O. S. 567.

Estoppel by consent. An abutting owner, who has signed a written consent, is estopped from complaining of the additional burden.

Powell v. Columbus, etc., Co., 10 N. P. n. s. 266; 20 L. D. 313 (1910).

INJUNCTION AGAINST CONSTRUCTION OF ROAD WITHOUT VALID CONSENTS.

Suit by abutting owner. Where a franchise is granted without the required number of valid consents, the construction of the railway may be enjoined at the suit of an abutting owner.

Roberts v. Easton, 19 O. S. 78 (1869).

Mt. Auburn, etc., Ry. Co. v. Neare, 54 O. S. 153 (1896).

Lack of valid consents is, as a general rule, the only ground upon
which an abutting owner, as such, may complain. Other defects in a grant
may be attacked only by the public.
> Glidden v. Cincinnati, 30 W. L. B. 213.
> Sloane v. Peoples, etc., Co., 7 C. C. 84, 89; 3 C. D. 674 (1893).
> Barney v. Mt. Adams, etc., Ry. Co., 30 W. L. B. 286.
> Raynolds v. Cleveland, 2 C. C. n. s. 139, 154; 14 C. D. 215 (1902).
> Ireton Bros. v. Ft. Wayne, etc., Co., 2 N. P. n. s. 317; 15 L. D. 129
>   (1904).
> Dietz v. C. & M. V. Traction Co., 4 N. P. 399.

An abutting owner on one street can not complain of lack of consents
of owners of property on other streets.
> Toledo Cons., etc., Co. v. Toledo Elec., etc., Ry., 6 C. C. 362, 387;
>   3 C. D. 493; aff'd, 50 O. S. 603.
> Mathers v. Cincinnati, 3 W. L. B. 709.

An abutting owner may enjoin interference with his property right
of ingress and egress.
> Street Ry. v. Cumminsville, 14 O. S. 523 (1863).
> Powell v. Columbus, etc., Ry., 10 N. P. n. s. 266; 20 L. D. 313 (1910).

The motive of an abutting owner in bringing suit is immaterial. It
is no defense that he is acting for the benefit of competing railways.
> Traction Co. v. Parish, 67 O. S. 181, 189 (1902).
> Isom v. Low Fare Ry. Co., 10 C. C. n. s. 89; 19 C. D. 583 (1907);
>   affirmed, no rep., 77 O. S. 638.

A plaintiff, not in possession of abutting property, and whose ownership is doubtful, is not entitled to an injunction. His ownership must
first be established at law.
> Swing v. Cincinnati, etc., Traction Co., 15 L. D. 70 (Cin. Super. Ct.,
>   Gen. Term, 1904).

An abutting owner can not object to the operation of cars over existing tracks, on the ground that the length of new track is insufficient under
G. C. § 9103.
> Sanfleet v. Toledo, 10 C. C. 460; 8 C. D. 711 (1893); affirmed, 54 O.
>   S. 620.

Where an interurban road outside of municipalities constitutes an
additional burden, abutting owners may enjoin its construction until
compensation is made.
> Schaaf v. Cleveland, etc., Co., 66 O. S. 215 (1902).

Burden of proof. The action of a council in granting a franchise is
not conclusive as to the number of valid consents. An abutting owner
may raise the question.
> Roberts v. Easton, 19 O. S. 78 (1869).
> Sommers v. Cincinnati, 8 Am. L. R. 612.

But the presumption is in favor of the action of the council. The
burden of proof is upon the abutting owner to show lack of valid consents.
> Simmons v. Toledo, 8 C. C. 535; 4 C. D. 69 (1890); aff'd, 51 O. S. 626.
> Ireton Bros. v. Ft. Wayne, etc., Co., 2 N. P. n. s. 317; 15 L. D. 129
>   (1904).
> Schwab v. Traction Co., 13 L. D. 116, 120 (1902).
> Cincinnati College v. Nesmith, 2 C. S. C. R. 24 (1870).
> Hamilton v. Railroad, 5 N. P. 457; 8 L. D. 174.

Joinder of parties. Owners of property abutting on the same street
may join as plaintiffs, but they may not join with owners of property
on other streets.
> Glidden v. Cincinnati, 30 W. L. B. 213.

Suit by solicitor or taxpayer. An injunction suit by a solicitor or taxpayer can not be predicated upon a lack of valid consents. Abutting owners, only, may complain on that ground.

Glidden v. Cincinnati, 30 W. L. B. 213.

Simmons v. Toledo, 5 C. C. 124; 3 C. D. 64 (1889); aff'd, 30 W. L. B. 392.

Lima v. Cramer, 5 N. P. n. s. 113; 17 L. D. 245 (1906).

Sommers v. Cincinnati, 8 Am. L. Rec. 612.

Harrison v. Mt. Auburn, etc., Co., 17 W. L. B. 265.

Hamilton v. C. & H., etc., Co., 5 N. P. 457; 8 L. D. 174.

Nor can a solicitor base an action in quo warranto on such ground.

State v. Oakwood, etc., Ry., 11 C. C. n. s. 263; 20 C. D. 632 (1908); aff'd, no rep., 81 O. S. 502.

State v. Railway, 19 C. C. 79; 10 C. D. 418 (1899).

MISCELLANEOUS.

Right of abutting owners to prevent abandonment of part of line.

Bickerstaff v. Steubenville, etc., Co., 5 O. L. R. 539 (Railroad Commission 1907).

Cemetery v. Street Ry., 11 C. C. n. s. 429; 21 C. D. 51 (1908).

License for temporary tracks is not a grant and may be given by a municipality without consents.

Mathers v. Cincinnati, 3 W. L. B. 551, 709 (Cin. Super. Ct.).

PUBLICATION OF NOTICE.

Notice under § 3769 unnecessary for grant to construct extension.

Railway Co. v. Railway Co., 5 C. C. n. s. 583, 596, 597; 16 C. D. 180 (1903); aff'd, no rep., 73 O. S. 364.

State ex rel. v. Cincinnati, etc., Co., 19 C. C. 79 (1899).

Sommers v. Cincinnati, 8 Am. L. Rec. 612.

See § 3777.

Section 9106. (When written consent not required.) But when such grant is made by the council of a municipal corporation, either for a new route or as an extension of an existing route, on and along any part of a street or public way upon which a street railway has been operated within one year preceding under a grant or renewal of a grant which has expired or within two years will expire, it shall not be necessary to produce to the council any written consents from the owners of the lots and land abutting on such part of a street or public way; in case the number of tracks thereon or part thereof is not increased beyond the number for which consents originally were obtained. (R. S. Sec. 3439; April 15, 1908, 99 v. 103; April 18, 1883, 80 v. 173; R. S. 1880; April 29, 1868, 65 v. 112, § 3.)

Section 9107. (When property owner cannot withdraw consent.) Nothing contained in the preceding section shall permit a person owning property abutting on a street along, in or over which a street railway is about to be constructed, to withdraw his consent after an ordinance granting the right to construct and operate it has been read the second time, if at least thirty days elapsed since the first reading thereof, in the council or other body authorized to make the grant. (R. S. Sec. 3439a; May 10, 1902, 95 v. 475.)

Except as prohibited by this section, an abutting owner may withdraw his consent, even when induced by a money consideration.
> Cleveland v. Cleveland City Ry. Co., 3 C. C. n. s. 563; 13 C. D. 373 (1902); reversing, 12 L. D. 623.
> Simmons v. Toledo, 8 C. C. 535; 4 C. D. 69 (1890).
> See Hume v. Hamilton, etc., Co., 13 L. D. 70 (1902).

Section 9108. (Appropriation of property.) When the council or commissioners make such grant, the company or person to whom it is made may appropriate property necessary therefor, if the owner fails expressly to waive his claim to damages by reason of the construction and operation of the railway. (R. S. Sec. 3440; April 16, 1892, 89 v. 349; April 11, 1890, 87 v. 178; March 27, 1866, 63 v. 55, § 4; March 24, 1864, 61 v. 53, § 1; S. & S. 136; S. & S. 137.)

Procedure in appropriation cases see § 11038 et seq.
What property may be appropriated. Use of existing tracks may be.
> Street Ry. Co. v. Street Ry. Co., 50 O. S. 603 (1893).
Consents of abutting owners under §§ 9105 and 3770 can not be.
> Traction Co. v. Parish, 67 O. S. 181 (1902).
> See § 9109.
County road.
> See Railroad Co. v. Commissioners, 56 O. S. 1, 8 (1897).

APPROPRIATION OF USE OF EXISTING TRACKS.

Right of. A street railway, having a franchise to use the existing tracks of another street railway, may, under this section, appropriate such tracks to its use.
> Street Railway Co. v. Street Railway Co., 50 O. S. 603 (1893); aff'g, 6 C. C. 362; 3 C. D. 493.
> See Traction Co. v. Traction Co., 47 W. L. B. 854.
> Railway v. Railway, 26 W. L. B. 172.
Sections 9120 and 9130 conferring power to make traffic agreements do not interfere with the right to appropriate use of existing tracks.
> State v. C. & H., etc., Ry., 19 C. C. 79; 10 C. D. 418 (1899).

Successive proceedings. The appropriation of a part of existing tracks is not a bar to a proceeding to appropriate other portions.
> Toledo Consol., etc., Co. v. Toledo Elec., etc., Co., 12 C. C. 367; 5 C. D. 643 (1893).

Appropriating company not joint owner of tracks. The appropriating company does not acquire a joint ownership in the tracks, and is not entitled to compensation from another company subsequently acquiring right to use the same.
> Toledo Electric, etc., Co. v. Toledo, etc., Co., 10 C. C. 168; 6 C. D. 578 (1895); reversing 7 N. P. 211; 1 L. D. 33.

Measure of compensation.
> See Toledo Cons., etc., Co. v. Toledo Elec., etc., Co., 6 C. C. 362; 3 C. D. 493 (1892); (affirmed, 50 O. S. 603, except as to measure of compensation which was reserved for re-argument and afterwards dismissed by consent. 31 W. L. B. 348).

Toledo Cons., etc., Co. v. Toledo Elec., etc., Co., 12 C. C. 367; 5 C. D. 643 (1893).

Power of council to fix compensation. The council has no power to fix the compensation to be paid except when that right is reserved in the franchise of the owner of the tracks.

Kinsman, etc., Co. v. Broadway, etc., Co., 36 O. S. 239, 252 (1880).

Pleading and evidence.

Necessity for appropriation. The appropriating company need not show necessity for use of the tracks. The action of the council in granting the franchise is, in the absence of fraud, conclusive.

Toledo Cons., etc., Co. v. Toledo Elec,, etc., Co., 6 C. C. 362; 3 C. D. 493 (1892); affirmed, 50 O. S. 603.

Compliance with § 9103. That eight times the amount of track sought to be appropriated has been constructed and placed in operation satisfies the requirements of § 9103.

Toledo Cons., etc., Co. v. Toledo Elec., etc., Co., 12 C. C. 367; 5 C. D. 643 (1893).

Toledo Cons., etc., Co. v. Toledo Elec., etc., Co., 6 C. C. 362; 3 C. D. 493 (1892); affirmed, 50 O. S. 603.

Miscellaneous. The petition need not set out the length of time the existing tracks will be used.

Toledo Cons., etc., Co. v. Toledo Elec., etc., Co., 12 C. C. 367; 5 C. D. 643 (1893).

The appropriating company need not prove proceedings preliminary to the grant of its franchise, such as the application, notice and consents.

Toledo Cons., etc., Co. v. Toledo, Elec., etc., Co., 6 C. C. 362, 387; 3 C. D. 493 (1892); affirmed, 50 O. S. 603.

But it must show the grant of a franchise from the municipality.

Railway Co. v. Stoneware Co., 51 W. L. B. 421.

Injunction against use without appropriation. The grantee of a franchise over existing tracks may be enjoined from taking possession without appropriating the right of use.

See Hamilton, etc., Co. v. Hamilton, etc., Co., 69 O. S. 402 (1903).

Kinsman, etc., Co. v. Broadway, etc., Co., 36 O. S. 239 (1880).

But a company which has parted with its interest in the tracks is not entitled to an injunction, where the right of use has been appropriated against the company in possession.

Metropolitan, etc., Co. v. Toledo, etc., Co., 9 C. C. 664; 6 C. D. 733 (1893).

RIGHT TO CROSS TRACKS OF STEAM OR STREET RAILROADS WITHOUT APPROPRIATION.

In municipalities. A street railway, authorized to lay tracks in a street which crosses a steam railroad, may, on such streets, cross the tracks of the steam railroad without compensation.

C. & H. Electric St. Ry. v. C. H. & I. R. Co., 21 C. C. 391, 396; 12 C. D. 113 (1898); aff'd, no rep., 64 O. S. 550.

Railway Co. v. Railway Co., 5 C. C. n. s. 583, 588; 16 C. D. 180 (1903); aff'd, no rep., 73 O. S. 364.

Akron, etc., Transit Co. v. Erie R. Co., 7 C. C. n. s. 199, 201; 18 C. D. 36 (1905).

Street tracks of another street railway may be crossed without compensation.

Metropolitan, etc., Co. v. Toledo, etc., Ry., 9 C. C. 664; 6 C. D. 733 (1893).

For railroad crossings not on streets, see § 8834.

Without municipalities the right to cross railway tracks must be acquired by agreement or court decree.

G. C. § 8834 et seq.

Dayton, etc., R. Co. v. Dayton, etc., Traction Co., 1 N. P. n. s. 296; 14 L. D. 143 (1903); affirmed, 4 C. C. n. s. 329; 16 C. D. 1; reversed on other grounds, 72 O. S. 429.

Section 9109.   (Appropriation of property of turnpike or plank road.) Such power to appropriate may be exercised, for the purpose of constructing a street railway along a highway occupied by a turnpike or plank road company when the person, persons or company authorized to construct such railway cannot agree with the turnpike or plank road company on the terms and conditions upon which the highway may be occupied, and if such appropriation will not unnecessarily interfere with the reasonable use of the highway by the turnpike or plank road company. Nothing in the foregoing provisions shall affect the rights of property owners to give or withhold their consent concerning the right of way for street railways upon any street or road. (R. S. Sec. 3440; April 16, 1892, 89 v. 349; April 11, 1890, 87 v. 178; March 27, 1866, 63 v. 55, § 4; March 24, 1864, 61 v. 53, § 1.)

Consents of property owners can not be appropriated.

Traction Co. v. Parish, 67 O. S. 181 (1902).

Section 9110.   (Oath in appropriation proceedings.) In case of appropriation of property for such purpose, the oath to be administered to the jury shall be as follows: ''You and each of you do solemnly swear that you will justly and impartially assess, according to your best judgment, the amount of compensation which is due to (here name the owner or owners), by reason of the appropriation of the street or avenue (as in the statement described), irrespective of any benefit from any improvement proposed by such (here name the company, individual, or company of individuals), and that you will in assessing damages that may accrue to (here name the owner or owners), by reason of the appropriation, other than the compensation, further ascertain how much less valuable the lot or lots of such (here name the owner or owners), will be in consequence of such appropriation.'' (R. S. Sec. 3442; March 27, 1866, 63 v. 55, § 5.)

Section 9111.   (How compensation ascertained.) The jury, in ascertaining such compensation or damages, shall determine the amount thereof without reference to the distinction between a public and a private nuisance, and the effect of such distinction upon the right of such owner or owners to claim compensation or damages, and, if requested, the court shall so direct the jury. (R. S. Sec. 3442; March 27, 1866, 63 v. 55, § 5.)

Measure of compensation.
    (Land) Lorain St. Ry. Co. v. Sinning, 17 C. C. 649; 6 C. D. 753 (1895).
    Use of existing tracks, see note to § 9108.
    See also note to § 11053.

Section 9112. (Consent of authority controlling public road.) If the public road along which the railway is to be constructed is owned by a person or company, or is within the control or management of the board of public works or other public officer, such person, company, or officer may agree with the person or company constructing the railway as to the terms and conditions upon which the road may be occupied. (R. S. Sec. 3441; February 19, 1870, 67 v. 10, § 1.)

    Cited, State ex rel. v. Taylor, 55 O. S. 61, 66 (1896).
    This section applies to state and county roads under the control of county commissioners. The term "officer" includes a board of county commissioners.
    Railroad Co. v. Commissioners, 56 O. S. 1, 7 (1897).
    Where the trustees of a hamlet had, prior to 1902, granted a franchise on a street which was also a state road, the county commissioners can not enjoin operation thereunder.
    Commissioners v. A. B. & C. Ry., 21 C. C. 769; 11 C. D. 664 (1896).
    A turnpike company has no power to enter into a contract for a railway which interferes with the right of access of abutting owners.
    McMacken v. C. & H., etc., Co., 5 N. P. 367; 5 L. D. 358.

Section 9113. (Terms and conditions of construction, etc.) Council, or the commissioners, as the case may be, may fix the terms and conditions upon which such railways may be constructed, operated, extended, and consolidated. (R. S. Sec. 3443; February 19, 1870, 67 v. 10, § 1; May 7, 1869, 66 v. 140, § 1.)

    See § 3768 and 9101.
    This section does not authorize a municipality, by penal ordinance, to prescribe the qualifications of motormen and conductors.
    Columbus, etc., Co. v. Columbus, 10 N. P. n. s. 161; 20 L. D. 555 (1910).

Section 9114. (Free transportation of police and firemen.) Upon the granting of franchises to traction companies throughout this state for the use of streets, roads and highways for the transportation of passengers, it must be provided, as one of the considerations for such use of the public highways, that such traction companies shall carry free as passengers on any and all regular cars, policemen and firemen, when on duty and in uniform. (March 15, 1909, 100 v. 14, § 1.)

Section 9115. (Appropriation of property by directors.) When it is deemed necessary by a majority of the directors of a domestic or foreign corporation owning or operating a street railway in a municipality to appropriate private property therein, in order to avoid dangerous or difficult curves or grades, or unsafe or unsubstantial grounds or foundations or to extend or shorten its railway line, or to provide land on which to extend its power plant, such corporation may appropriate so much private property as is necessary for the extension of such power plant, or the construction, operation, and maintenance of the tracks, poles, supports, wires, cables and necessary appliances of such railway other than power houses, machine shops, stations or substations in the manner and subject to the provisions of law for the appropriation of private property by corporations. (April 7, 1904, 97 v. 106, § 1.)

Section 9116. (Change of location of any portion of railway.) For the purposes above provided such corporation may change the location of any part of its railway, and for the purpose of making such change, it shall have all the rights, powers, and privileges to enter upon private land and make surveys necessary to effect such change as fully as railroad companies are by law permitted to do. (April 7, 1904, 97 v. 106, § 2.)

Change of location.
 Ireton Bros. v. Traction Co., 2 N. P. n. s. 317; 15 L. D. 129 (1904).
 Bickerstaff v. Steubenville, etc., Traction Co., 5 O. L. R. 539; 53 W. L. B. 29 (Railroad Commission 1907).
 Ashley v. Railway, 5 O. L. R. 359; 52 W. L. B. 496 (1907).
 Spring Grove v. Railway, 11 C. C. n. s. 429; 21 C. D. 51 (1908).

Section 9117. (Construction of street railroads outside of municipalities.) Companies incorporated under section eighty-six hundred and twenty-five, for such purpose, may construct, maintain and operate electric street railroads, or street railroads using other than animal power as a motive power, for the transportation of passengers, packages, express matter, United States mail, baggage and freight upon the highways in this state outside of municipalities, or upon private rights of ways. (R. S. Sec. 3443-8; May 10, 1902, 95 v. 539; May 17, 1894, 91 v. 285.)

Held constitutional.
>Dietz v. C. & M. V. Traction Co., 4 N. P. 399; 6 L. D. 513.
>This section does not modify, limit or repeal §§ 9100, 9101 and 9102, nor define a different kind of street railroad.
>Hamilton v. C. & H., etc., Ry., 5 N. P. 457; 8 L. D. 174.

Motive power should be clearly stated in articles of incorporation.
>See Rep. Atty. Gen. (1909-1910) 99.

INTERURBAN RAILROAD. WHETHER A "RAILROAD" OR A "STREET RAILWAY."

Statutory classification as a "street railway." Under certain statutes interurban railroads have been classed as street railways and provisions of such statutes relating to "railroads" held not applicable to interurbans. Under sections 9117 to 9122.
>Ohio Electric Ry. Co. v. Ottawa, 85 O. S. 229 (1912); reversing, 13 C. C. n. s. 561; 22 C. D. 197.
>State v. Traction Companies, 64 O. S. 272 (1901).

Statutes imposing excise taxes.
>Electric St. R. Co. v. Lohe, 68 O. S. 101, 109, 110 (1903).
>§ 5490 (101 v. 409, orig. G. C. § 5488; R. S. 2780-17).
>See Railway v. Poland, 10 N. P. n. s. 617; 21 L. D. 630 (C. P. 1910): aff'd, no rep., 88 O. S. —.

Providing for mechanic's liens on railroads.
>Bridge Co. v. Iron Co., 59 O. S. 179 (1898).
>G. C. § 3245.

Providing for construction of railroad and highway crossings, prior to the amendment of §§ 8874 and 8897 in 1913.
>Commissioners v. Traction Co., 75 O. S. 548 (1907).
>In re Avon Beach, etc., R. Co., 3 N. P. n. s. 561; 16 L. D. 87 (C. P. 1905).

Providing for the crossing of one railroad by another.
>C. & H., etc., Co. v. C. & H., etc., Co., 21 C. C. 391; 12 C. D. 113 (1898).
>D. & U. Ry. v. D. & M. Traction Co., 4 C. C. n. s. 329; 16 C. D. 1 (1903); affirming, 1 N. P. n. s. 218, 296; 14 L. D. 17; reversed, on other grounds, 72 O. S. 429.
>Rapid Ry. Co. v. Cincinnati, etc., Ry., 48 O. L. B. 245.
>See also Cleveland, etc., Co. v. Urbana, etc., Co., 5 C. C. n. s. 597; 16 C. D. 180 (1903).
>Columbus, etc., Traction Co. v. Marriott, 47 O. L. B. 357 (Probate Court).
>Rep. Atty. Gen. (1909-10) 261.

Under § 3762 permitting municipalities to require a railroad to light a portion of its track.
>Ohio Electric Railway v. Ottawa, 85 O. S. 229 (1912); reversing, 13 C. C. n. s. 561; 22 C. D. 197 (1910).

When a "railroad." The law of negligence governing the standing on a platform of a moving interurban car outside of a municipality is the same as in the case of steam cars.
>Electric St. R. Co. v. Lohe, 68 O. S. 101, 109, 110 (1903).

The construction of an interurban railroad on one side of a highway, outside of a municipality, for the transportation of passengers, freight and mail, is an additional burden on the highway similar to that imposed by steam railroads.
>Schaaf v. Railway Co., 66 O. S. 215 (1902).
>See Railway v. Poland, 10 N. P. n. s. 617; 21 L. D. 617 (C. P. 1910).
>Weber v. Stark Electric Co., 13 L. D. 194 (1902).

In the public utilities commission acts an interurban railroad is classed as a "railroad." §§ 501, 614-2.

In the grade crossing acts the term "railroad" includes interurban railroads. §§ 8874, 8897.

Section 9118.   (Occupancy and use of public highways.)
Such companies may occupy and use for their tracks, cars, necessary fixtures and appliances, the public highways outside of cities and villages with the consent of the public authorities in charge of or controlling such highways, and with the written consent of the majority, measured by the front foot, of the property holders abutting on each of such highways.   (May 17, 1894, 91 v. 285, § 2; R. S. § 3443-9.)

When an additional burden. An interurban railway, with T rails, built entirely on one side of a highway, between improved farms and the roadway, the company having authority to run an unlimited number of cars, for passengers, mail and freight, is an additional burden similar to that of a steam railroad.

    Schaaf v. Cleveland, etc., Co., 66 O. S. 215 (1902).

    Chestnut v. Columbus, etc., Ry., 15 L. D. 336 (1905) ; aff'd, no rep., 76 O. S. 567.

    Miller v. Columbus Ry. Co., 13 L. D. 418 (1902).

An additional switch laid in the highway subsequent to construction of road is an additional burden.

    Chambers v. Cleveland, etc., Co., 5 C. C. n. s. 298; 17 C. D. 193 (1904) ; aff'd, no rep., 73 O. S. 348.

    Chestnut v. Columbus, etc., Ry., 15 L. D. 336 (1905) ; aff'd, no rep., 76 O. S. 567.

Consents, rights and remedies of abutting owners.

    See note to § 9105.

Must give adequate service. An interurban railway may be compelled to furnish adequate service, so long as its franchise is not abandoned.

    Ferguson v. Dayton, etc., Transit Co., 4 O. L. R. 750 (Railroad Commission 1907).

Crossing tracks of street, interurban or steam railroads, outside of municipalities.

    See § 8834.

Section 9118-1.   (Crossings, other than steam railway. Petition.)
Whenever it is deemed necessary by a majority of the directors of any such railway company to cross the streets, avenues, alleys, ways, or any part thereof, of any municipality, or any public highway outside of a municipality, whether the same be under the control of public authorities or a private company, or a person or persons, the council of such municipality, or the public officers or authorities owning or having charge of such highways outside of municipalities, shall have power to agree with such company as to the manner and mode of such crossing and the compensation to be paid therefor; if the parties fail to

agree, such company may file its petition in the common
pleas court of the county in which the proposed crossing is
situated, and in such cause if the crossing be within a municipality, such municipality, shall be defendant; if the
crossing be outside a municipality, the public authorities
owning or having charge of such highway, shall be defendants. Summons shall be served and the rule days and the
rights of the defendant to plead shall be the same as in
civil actions in such court. Such petition shall set forth the
action of the company declaring the necessity for crossing
the highway and the inability of the company to agree with
the council or other public officers or authorities owning or
having charge of said highway; and the court of common
pleas thereupon shall have jurisdiction of the parties and
of the subject matter of the petition and may proceed to
examine the matter offered by evidence, by reference to a
master commissioner or otherwise, and upon the final hearing of said cause the court shall enter its decree fixing the
manner and mode of such crossing and the compensation, if
any, to be paid therefor by the company, and upon compliance with the terms of said decree the company shall have
the right to construct and maintain said crossing in accordance with the order in said cause. (May 10, 1910, 101 v. 375.)

Section 9118-2. (Appropriation of real estate.) Where
the tracks of any such road extend into or through any
municipality and it is deemed necessary by such company to
enter upon and use any private property within such municipality for the construction and maintenance of either passenger stations or freight depots to be used in the operation
of such road, such company shall have the right to appropriate private property within municipalities for such purposes. (May 10, 1910, 101 v. 376.)

Section 9119. (Appropriation of property.) Street, interurban or suburban railroads using other than steam as
motive power, when necessary may enter upon and use private property in the construction, alteration and operation
of its road or any part thereof and for such purposes shall
have all of the rights and powers of appropriation, outside
of municipalities, that steam railroad companies possess.
(R. S. Sec. 3443-10; May 10, 1910, 101 v. 322; May 10, 1902,
95 v. 538; May 17, 1894, 91 v. 285.)

An interurban railway must obtain a franchise before appropriating
property.
      S. E. Ohio, etc., Co. v. Diamond, etc., Co., 51 O. L. B. 421 (Probate
Court).

Pleading and proof.

See S. E. Ohio, etc., Co. v. Diamond, etc., Co., 51 O. L. B. 421.

Columbus, etc., Co. v. Cole, 47 O. L. B. 66.

Prior to amendment of this section it was held in several probate courts that interurban railways could not appropriate private lands, except where it was impossible to use a highway.

Columbus, etc., Ry. Co. v. Cole, 47 W. L. B. 547 (1902).

Columbus, etc., Ry. Co. v. Marriott, 47 W. L. B. 357 (1902).

Power to appropriate use of urban tracks.

See §§ 3779, 9108.

State v. C. & H., etc., Ry., 19 C. C. 79; 10 C. D. 418 (1899).

Section 9120.   (Leases, purchases and traffic arrangements.) Such companies may lease, purchase, or make traffic arrangements with any other street railway company as to so much of its tracks and other property as is necessary or desirable to enable them to enter or pass through a city or village, upon the terms and conditions applicable to other street railways. Any existing street railway company, owning or operating a road shall receive the cars, freight, packages or passengers of any other road, upon the same terms and conditions as they carry for the general public. (May 17, 1894, 91 v. 286, § 4; R. S. Sec. 3443-11.)

This section is not intended as a limitation on § 9101.

Hamilton v. Railway, 5 N. P. 457; 8 L. D. 174.

Neither this section nor §§ 9130 to 9133 require an exchange of transfers between the urban and interurban railways, in the absence of an ordinance imposing such obligation.

Railway Co. v. Cincinnati, 75 O. S. 196 (1906); reversing, 3 N. P. n. s. 489; 16 L. D. 220.

Carriage of freight. This section authorizes an urban street railway company to make a traffic agreement with an interurban railway for the carriage of freight.

State v. Dayton Traction Co., 64 O. S. 272 (1901); affirming, 18 C. C. 490; 10 C. D. 212.

A franchise authorizing the transportation of freight over streets, does not authorize the use of a street as a station for unloading freight.

Newark v. Ohio Electric Ry., 13 N. P. n. s. 487 (1912).

Traffic agreements construed.

Toledo, etc., Co. v. Toledo Traction Co., 17 C. C. 22; 9 C. D. 828 (1898).

Toledo, etc., Co. v. Toledo Traction Co., 15 C. C. 190; 8 C. D. 204 (1897).

Cincinnati v. Railway, 3 N. P. n. s. 489; 16 L. D. 220 (1905); reversed, 75 O. S. 196.

Power to appropriate tracks.

See §§ 3779, 9108.

State v. C. & H., etc., Ry., 19 C. C. 79; 10 C. D. 418 (1899).

"Terms and conditions."

See Cincinnati v. Railway, 13 N. P. n. s. 265 (C. P. 1912).

Section 9121.   (Consolidation.) Such street railway companies may consolidate on the terms and conditions applicable to the consolidation of railroad companies. But no increase of fare shall be allowed on any street railway route by reason of such consolidation. (R. S. Sec. 3443-12; May 17, 1894, 91 v. 286, § 5.)

Section 9121-1. (Authority to secure loan by mortgage.) Corporations organized for the purpose of owning or operating street, interurban or electric railroads may borrow money without regard to the amount of their capital stock, and issue their notes or coupon or registered bonds therefor, bearing any rate of interest authorized by law, and may secure the payment of the same by a mortgage or other instrument in writing upon their real or personal property or both. It shall be sufficient record of such mortgage or instrument, if it be recorded in the office of the recorder of deeds in each county wherein the real or personal property therein described is situated or employed. So recorded, it shall be a good and substantial lien upon all of such property, from the date of its record in each of such counties. (May 31, 1911, 102 v. 467.)

See §§ 8705 to 8709.

Section 9122. (Regulations and powers.) Such companies shall be subject to the regulations provided for street railways and have all the powers, in so far as they are applicable, that other street railway companies possess. (May 17, 1894, 91 v. 286, § 6; R. S. Sec. 3443-13.)

Construed as showing a legislative intention to classify interurban railroads as street railways.
Ottawa Elec. Ry. Co. v. Ottawa, 85 O. S. 229 (1912).
The term "such companies" apparently refers to the companies mentioned in §§ 9115 and 9117.
Ottawa v. Electric Ry., 13 C. C. n. s. 562; 22 C. D. 197; reversed, 85 O. S. 229.
An interurban railway may construct an extension or branch within municipality.
Railway Co. v. Railway Co., 5 C. C. n. s. 583, 597; 16 C. D. 180 (1903); aff'd, no rep., 73 O. S. 364.
Right to change location to avoid dangerous grades.
Bickerstaff v. Steubenville, etc., Traction Co., 5 O. L. R. 539 (Railroad Commission, 1907).
See § 9115.

Section 9123. (Watchmen.) When street railways are operated by electricity, cable, compressed air, or motive power other than horses or mules, in a municipality, the council thereof by ordinance may require the owners or operators of such railways to place watchmen at street crossings, intersections or corners which such council deem dangerous; and also provide for the enforcement of such ordinances by penalties in the way of fine or imprisonment, or both, to be imposed upon the owner, officer, or operator of such railways, or by a penalty of not exceeding one hundred dollars per day, which may be recovered by such municipalities in a civil suit against the owners or operators of any such railway failing to place such watchman as is required. (R. S. Sec. 3443a; April 16, 1892, 89 v. 346.)

Where a traction company agreed to pay all expenses which might be "lawfully required" by the municipality or state in maintaining a flagman at a crossing, it was held not liable where the railroad company by agreement with the municipality stationed a flagman at the crossing in consideration of the repeal of a speed ordinance.

Rapid Transit Co. v. Erie R. Co., 7 C. C. n. s. 199; 18 C. D. 36 (1905).

Section 9124.   (Repairs at crossings; stopping of cars at crossings.) When the tracks of two street railways cross each other or in any way connect at a common grade, when one or both such railways use other than horse power for propelling their cars, the crossings shall be made and kept in repair at the joint expense of the companies owning the tracks. All cars used on such railways must come to a full stop, not nearer than ten feet nor further than fifty feet from the crossing, and not cross until the way is clear. When two or more cars approach the crossing at the same time the car or cars on the road first built shall have precedence. (May 4, 1891, 88 v. 581, § 1; R. S. Sec. 3443-5.)

Section 9125.   (Full stop when approaching steam railway crossing.) When the tracks of street railways cross the tracks of a steam railroad at grade, the company operating the line of street cars shall cause its cars to stop not nearer than ten nor further than fifty feet from the crossing and before they start to cross the steam railroad tracks, also cause a person in its employ to go ahead of the car or cars and see that the way is clear for the passage thereof, and free from danger. Such street railway cars shall not proceed to cross until signaled so to do by such person so employed, or the way is clear for their passage over the tracks. (May 4, 1891, 88 v. 582, § 2; R. S. Sec. 3443-6.)

This section does not relieve the motorman from the duty of exercising care.

Cincinnati, etc., Co. v. Holbrook, 12 C. C. n. s. 234 (1909).

Nor does it relieve the steam railroad from operating its gates so as to indicate to the motorman whether the track is clear.

Kopp v. B. & O. S. W. Ry., 6 C. C. n. s. 103; 1 C. C. n. s. 596 (1903); aff'd, no rep., 71 O. S. 484.

The requirements of this section apply to crossings having gates and a watchman as well as other crossings.

Street Ry. Co. v. Murray, 53 O. S. 570 (1895); affirming, 9 C. C. 291; 6 C. D. 413.

Where car is not stopped and gates are not lowered, both street railway company and railroad company are liable.

Toledo Cons., etc., Ry. v. Fuller, 17 C. C. 562; 8 C. D. 134 (1894).

Duty when car operated by one man only.

Street Ry. Co. v. Murray, 53 O. S. 570 (1895).

Collision, prima facie case.

See Toledo Cons., etc., Ry. v. Fuller, 17 C. C. 562; 8 C. D. 134 (1894). Street Ry. Co. v. Murray, 53 O. S. 570 (1895).

When not a regular stopping place, conductors and motormen are not required as a matter of law, before starting, to look for passengers getting on or off the car.

Packard v. Toledo Traction Co., 22 C. C. 578 (1901).

Requirement of crossing frogs at crossings of street railways over railroads.

§ 3775.

Railway Co. v. Railroad Co., 21 C. C. 391; 12 C. D. 113 (1898); aff'd, no rep., 64 O. S. 550.

Section 9126. (Forfeiture under preceding sections.) Every person in charge of a street car or cars who wilfully fails to comply with the provisions of the two preceding sections, or to bring the car or cars he has in charge to a stop, or before the way is clear, or signaled so to do, causes them to cross the steam railroad tracks, shall be personally liable to a person injured by reason of such failure to a penalty of one hundred dollars, to be recovered by civil action at the suit of the state, in the court of common pleas of a county wherein such crossing or connection is. The company in whose employ such person is, as well as the person himself shall be liable in damages to any person or persons so injured in person or property. (May 4, 1891, 88 v. 582, § 3; R. S. Sec. 3443-7.)

Section 9127. (Consolidation of street railway companies.) When the lines or authorized lines of road of street railway corporations or companies meet or intersect, or conveniently can be operated from one power house, or a power house or houses owned, under lease or operated by one of such corporations or companies, or when such line of a street railway corporation or company, and that of an inclined plane railway or railroad company or corporation, or any railway operated by electricity conveniently may be connected, to be operated to mutual advantage, or when such line of a street railway corporation or company and that of an inclined plane railway or railroad company or corporation or the railway of any company operated by electricity conveniently can be operated from one power

house or a power house owned, under lease or operated by
one of such street railway corporations or companies or inclined plane railway or railroad companies or corporations
or by any company or corporation, the railway of which is
operated by electricity, such corporation or companies, or
any two or more of them, if they are not competing lines,
may consolidate themselves into a single corporation. (May
10, 1902, 95 v. 510, § 2; April 22, 1896, 92 v. 277; April 18,
1892, 89 v. 406; May 1, 1891, 88 v. 493; R. S. Sec. 2505b;
Bates' Stats. § 3443-16.)

Consolidation of railroad companies.
    See § 9025 et seq.
This section is constitutional.
    Cincinnati St. R. Co. v. Horstman, 72 O. S. 93 (1905).
Rights of creditor of constituent company.
    Greene v. Woodland Ave., etc., Co., 62 O. S. 67 (1900).
Rights of pledgee of stock of constituent company.
    Railway Co. v. Bank, 68 O. S. 582 (1903).
    A corporation formed by the consolidation of two or more com-
panies holds the property acquired by such consolidation in its own right
and not in trust for the constituent companies.
    Greene v. Woodland Ave., etc., Co., 62 O. S. 67 (1900).
    Agreement of consolidation may require constituent companies to
enter consolidated company free of debt.
    Railway Co. v. Bank, 68 O. S. 582 (1903).
    Stock of constituent company issued after consolidation has been
completed is spurious.
    Worthington v. Cleveland City Ry., 9 C. C. n. s. 433; 19 C. D. 321
    (1904); affirmed, 75 O. S. 626.

**Section 9128.   (To what companies provisions do not
apply.)** The above provision as to competing lines shall
not apply to such companies or corporations whose lines are
nearby or wholly situated in a city of this state, or road of
any street railway company or corporation organized in this
state is made, or is in process of construction to the
boundary line of the state, or to a point within or without
the state. Such corporation or company may consolidate
its capital stock with that of any corporation or company,
or corporations and companies in an adjoining state, the
line or lines of whose road or roads have been made or are
in process of construction to the same point or points, in
the manner and with the effect provided by law for the
consolidation of railroad companies. (May 10, 1902, 95 v.
510; April 22, 1896, 92 v. 277; April 18, 1892, 89 v. 406;
May 1, 1891, 88 v. 493; R. S. Sec. 2505b; Bates' Stats. Sec.
3443-16.)

This section is constitutional.
    Cincinnati St. R. Co. v. Horstman, 72 O. S. 93 (1905).

Section 9129. (Consolidation of electric road companies.) When the lines of a road of any street railway or railroad company, organized under the laws of this state are constructed or in process of construction, and are or will be operated by electricity, and connect, or will or can be made to connect with the lines of another street railway or railroad company formed by the consolidation of companies organized under the laws of this state, or by the consolidation of a company organized under the laws of this state and a company organized under the laws of an adjoining state, whose lines of road are constructed or in process of construction, and are or will be operated by electricity, so that cars may pass over such lines of roads continuously, without break or interruption, such street railway or railroad company and such consolidated street railway company or railroad company, may consolidate themselves into a single company in the same manner and with like effect as is provided by law for the consolidation of railroad companies. Companies owning and operating competing lines of road shall not consolidate under the foregoing provisions, but this limitation does not apply to companies whose lines of road are nearly or wholly situated in a municipal corporation of this state. (May 6, 1904, 97 v. 570, § 2; Bates' Stats. Sec. 3443-16a.)

Section 9130. (Interurban road may contract for use of tracks in cities.) When a railway company is incorporated and organized under the laws of this state for the purpose of building, acquiring, owning, leasing, operating and maintaining a railway or railways to be operated by electricity or other motive power from one municipal corporation or point in the state, to another municipal corporation, corporations, or point in this state, it may agree with a street railway company, or companies, owning or operating a street railway or railways in such municipal corporation or corporations, and the street railway company or companies may so agree with such railway company that its passenger cars may be run and propelled over and along the track or tracks of such street railway company or companies, on such terms as may be agreed upon, in the manner, upon the conditions and for the length of time that the cars owned or operated by such street railway company or companies are operated in such municipal corporation or corporations. (R. S. Sec. 2505c; Bates' Stats. Sec. 3443-17; May 21, 1894, 91 v. 379.)

Municipal franchise to interurban railway companies.
    See §§ 3778, 3780.

Appropriation of right to use tracks of city street railway.
See § 3779.

Neither this section nor § 9120 requires an exchange of transfers between the urban and interurban railways, in the absence of an ordinance imposing such obligation.

Railway Co. v. Cincinnati, 75 O. S. 196 (1906); reversing, 3 N. P. n. s. 489; 16 L. D. 220.

An interurban road can not, under a traffic agreement to run its own cars over the tracks of an urban railway, run the cars of a third company over such tracks.

Toledo, etc., Co. v. Toledo Traction Co., 17 C. C. 22; 9 C. D. 828 (1898).

See Toledo, etc., Co. v. Toledo Traction Co., 15 C. C. 190; 8 C. D. 204 (1897).

A common carrier, owning its tracks, is liable to its passengers for an injury received in a collision between its car and the car of another company which it admits to the joint use of its track, though the collision may result wholly from the negligence of the latter company.

Light Co. v. Montgomery, 81 O. S. 426 (1910).

An interurban railway entering a municipality over the tracks of another company is bound by the rules of that company, as to speed at crossings.

Interurban, etc., Co. v. Hines, 13 C. C. n. s. 168 (1910).

Section 9131. (Privileges and obligations of the street railway apply.) While they are running and being operated over and along the track or tracks of such street railway company or companies in such municipal corporation, the cars of such railway company shall be entitled to the privileges and subject to the obligations enjoyed and imposed by and upon the cars of such street railway company or companies owning or operating its cars in such municipal corporation. They shall be operated only by the motive power which operates the cars of such street railway company or companies. When authorized by not less than two-thirds in amount of the stockholders of each company proposing to enter into such arrangement and agreement, ratified by a majority of the directors and executed by the proper officers thereof, such arrangement and agreement shall give to such railway company full authority to operate its cars on the tracks of such street railway company or companies in such municipal corporation or corporations. (R. S. Sec. 2505c; Bates' Stats. Sec. 3443-17; May 21, 1894, 91 v. 379.)

Section 9132. (Not necessary to obtain additional grant.) It shall not be necessary for such railway company, in case it uses in such municipal corporation or corporations, only the tracks of a street railway company or companies owning or operating a street railway or railways therein, to obtain an additional grant, franchise or right, except by such agreement with such street railway company or companies. (R.

S. Sec. 2505c; Bates' Stats. Sec. 3443-17; May 21, 1894, 91 v. 379.)

Section 9133. (Fare charged within city.) The fare charged by such railway company for transporting passengers within such municipal corporation or corporations, shall not be greater than that fixed in the franchise or franchises held or owned by such street railway company or companies. When there is a public park or cemetery on the line of such railway, within one mile of, and owned by, such municipal corporation, such company for such fare must so transport passengers to and from such park or cemetery the same as if either was within the limits of such corporation. (R. S. Sec. 2505c; Bates' Stats. Sec. 3443-17; May 21, 1894, 91 v. 379.)

This section does not require an exchange of transfers between urban and interurban railways, in the absence of an ordinance imposing such obligation.

Railway Co. v. Cincinnati, 75 O. S. 196 (1906); reversing, 3 N. P. n. s. 489; 16 L. D. 220.

The tender of a five dollar bill in payment of a five cent fare, change being requested, is unreasonable.

Anthony v. Cincinnati Traction Co., 3 O. L. R. 377 (1905).

Right of interurban railway to charge additional fare where municipal limits are extended so as to include its tracks.

See Cincinnati v. Railway, 13 N. P. n. s. 265 (C. P. 1912).

Section 9134. (Lease or purchase electric, or gas light, heat, power or fuel company.) A corporation or company maintaining and operating a street railway, or a railroad operated by electricity, may lease or purchase all the property, and all the franchises, rights, and privileges of any company organized for the purpose of supplying electricity, or natural or artificial gas, or both electricity and natural or artificial gas, for power, light, heat or fuel purposes, or which has been engaged in such business in whole or part in any municipality within this state, the latter being hereby vested with corresponding power to let or sell, upon such terms and conditions as may be agreed upon between the corporation and company. No such lease or purchase may be perfected until a meeting of the stockholders of each of the companies has been called for that purpose by the directors thereof, on thirty days' notice to each stockholder, at such time and place and in such manner as is provided for the annual meetings of the companies and the holders of at least two-thirds of the stock of each company in person or by proxy, at such meeting, or at any properly adjourned meeting assent thereto. (R. S. Sec. 2505e; Bates'

Stats. Sec. 3443-18; May 6, 1902, 95 v. 390; April 19, 1898, 93 v. 139.)

> A corporation may be organized to operate an interurban railway and to furnish electric light and power.
> Rep. Atty. Gen. 1910-1911, p. 261.
> See also, State v. Taylor, 55 O. S. 61 (1896).

Section 9135.   (Dissenting stockholder.) A stockholder who refuses to assent to such lease or sale and so signifies by notice in writing to the lessee or purchaser within ninety days thereafter shall be entitled to demand and receive compensation in the manner provided for the compensation of stockholders dissenting from the sale or lease of a steam railroad. (R. S. Sec. 2505e; Bates' Stats. Sec. 3443-18; May 6, 1902, 95 v. 390; April 19, 1898, 93 v. 139.)

> See §§ 8810 to 8812 and 8713 to 8717.

Section 9136.   (Liabilities of the company leased or purchased.) A company so leasing or purchasing the property, rights and franchises of an electric light and power company, or natural or artificial gas company, or electric light and power and natural or artificial gas company, shall have all the rights, power and authority of the company whose property rights and franchises are so leased or purchased. But the liability of an electric light and power company, or natural or artificial gas company, or electric light and power and natural or artificial gas company, shall in no manner be affected by such lease or sale. (R. S. Sec. 2505e; Bates' Stats. Sec. 3443-18; May 6, 1902, 95 v. 390; April 19, 1898, 93 v. 139.)

Section 9137.   (May acquire property of other companies.) A corporation or company organized for street railway purposes, may lease or purchase any street railroad, or railroads, or railroad operated as such and by electric power inclined railroad or railroads, together with all the property, and the franchises, rights and privileges respecting the use and operation of such railroad or railroads, situated or existing in whole or part in this state, constructed and held by any other corporation or company, corporations or companies, the latter being hereby invested with corresponding power to let or sell on such terms and conditions as are agreed upon between the corporations or companies. (R. S. Sec. 2505a; Bates' Stats. Sec. 3443-15; April 23, 1898, 93 v. 214; April 22, 1896, 92 v. 277; May 1, 1891, 88 v. 493.)

This section is constitutional.
    Cincinnati St. R. Co. v. Horstman, 72 O. S. 93 (1905).

Section 9138. (Agreements with other companies.) Two or more of such corporations or companies may enter into any agreement for their common benefit consistent with and calculated to promote the objects for which they were created. No such lease or purchase shall be perfected until a meeting of the stockholders of each of the companies has been called for that purpose by the directors thereof, on thirty days' notice to each stockholder at such place and in such manner, as is provided for annual meetings of the companies, and the holders of at least two-thirds of the stock of each company, in person or by proxy, at such meeting, or at any properly adjourned meeting, assent thereto. Any stockholder who refuses to assent to such lease or sale and so signifies by notice in writing to the lessee or purchaser within ninety days thereafter, shall be entitled to demand and receive compensation in the same manner and by such proceedings as are provided for the sale of stock of a stockholder dissenting to a sale or lease of a steam railroad. (R. S. Sec. 2505a; Bates' Stats. Sec. 3443-15; April 23, 1898, 93 v. 214; April 22, 1896, 92 v. 277; May 1, 1891, 88 v. 493.)

This section is constitutional.
    Cincinnati St. R. Co. v. Horstman, 72 O. S. 93 (1905).
    An agreement with the proprietor of a resort, located beyond municipal limits, to carry passengers thereto for a specified fare, while other companies are excluded from the resort, is valid.
    Humphrey Co. v. Cleveland Ry. Co., 9 N. P. n. s. 609; 20 L. D. 510 (1910).

Section 9139. (Fare can not be increased.) When a lease or purchase is made as above provided, there shall be no increase of the existing rates of fare by reason thereof, nor shall any fare be charged upon any of the separate routes so leased or purchased in excess of the fare charged over such separate routes prior to the lease or purchase thereof. When a lease or purchase is made as herein provided, the fare charged for one continuous route or ride in the same general direction over all such leased or purchased lines within any municipal corporation, shall not exceed the maximum fare charged over any one of such lines prior to such lease or purchase. (R. S. Sec. 2505a; Bates' Stats. Sec. 3443-15; April 23, 1898, 93 v. 214; April 22, 1896, 92 v. 277; May 1, 1891, 88 v. 493.)

This section is constitutional.
    Cincinnati St. R. Co. v. Horstman, 72 O. S. 93 (1905).
Remedy when excessive fares charged.
    See State v. Toledo Ry. & Lt. Co., 3 C. C. n. s. 285; 13 C. D. 603 (1904) ; reversed, 73 O. S. 356.

Section 9140. (Powers of inclined plane railway company.) An inclined plane railway company may construct, operate, and maintain an inclined plane railway, for the conveyance of passengers and freight, or either, with such offices, depots, and other buildings as it deems necessary, and also establish and maintain a park or pleasure grounds, and for such purpose acquire and hold real estate. (R. S. Sec. 3444; April 12, 1876, 73 v. 229, § 2.)

Construed.
Cincinnati v. Cincinnati Inc. Plane Ry., 30 W. L. B. 321.
Louisville Trust Co. v. Cincinnati, 73 Fed. 716.
Louisville Trust Co. v. Cincinnati, 76 Fed. 296.

Section 9141. (How street crossings to be made.) When the part of the railway of such company which is operated by steam power crosses a public street or highway, it must pass either over or under such street or highway, and shall be constructed in a manner and at such distance above or below it as not to obstruct the ordinary use of the street or highway. (R. S. Sec. 3445; April 12, 1876, 73 v. 229, § 10.)

Section 9142. (Elevated railroads.) A city owning or having charge of any public road, street, alley, way, or ground of any kind, or any part thereof, may grant to any railroad company, street railroad company, suburban railroad company or interurban railroad company the right to construct, maintain and operate by electricity, any elevated railroad along and over such public road, street, alley, way or ground, except a public landing, or across them subject to existing laws concerning crossings, so far as they are applicable, and to erect and maintain therein the necessary tracks, piers, stays, supports and stations, and the approaches therefor, which stations shall be on a level with the track, and when necessary to construct tunnels for such railroad under such roads, streets, alleys, ways or grounds or to construct, maintain and operate by electricity any underground railroad, along and under such public roads, streets, alleys, ways or grounds, and to erect and maintain stations, stairways and approaches therefor, and also to construct suitable terminals and way stations. (R. S. Sec. 3283b; March 23, 1909, 100 v. 70; May 9, 1908, 99 v. 452.)

Section 9143. (Elevated structures and crossings must not obstruct travel. Subways must not impair streets nor prevent use of sewers, etc.) Such elevated structures and crossings shall be of such height and construction as not to prevent substantially the ordinary use of, and traffic upon, such roads, streets, alleys, ways, or grounds, whether by pedestrians, vehicles, street cars or otherwise, except temporarily when necessary in the construction of the elevated structures and crossings. Such tunnels for elevated railroads or subways for underground railroads shall be constructed as not to impair the stability of the roads, streets, alleys, or public grounds, or prevent the use of any sewers, street railway tracks and appliances, pipes, wires, and conduits used for any purpose in the streets, alleys, ways or grounds except temporarily when necessary in the construction of the tunnels or subways, except as hereinafter provided. And such elevated structures and crossings and such tunnels and subways shall be constructed in accordance with general plans approved by the director of public service of the municipality. All such work of construction shall be subject to the supervision and control of the director of public service. (May 29, 1911, 102 v. 129; R. S. Sec. 3283b; March 23, 1909, 100 v. 70; May 9, 1908, 99 v. 452.)

Section 9143-1. (Changes and removals. Filing of plans and specifications required. Approval, notice, hearing, bond. Director may modify or reject plans. Sewer, water pipe, etc., may be located in subway without compensation. Cost, damage and expense.) The council may grant to the company the right to move, change, elevate, depress, relocate and reconstruct at its sole expense any sewer, sewer connection, catch-basin, water pipe, water connection, natural or artificial gas pipes or connections, hydrants, conduits, pipes, wires, street railway tracks and appliances, poles, whether for street railway, electric lighting, heating, power, telegraph, telephone, signal service, or any other purpose, or any other obstruction, which may be encountered in the construction of the underground railroad.

Any such company shall before proceeding to move, change, elevate, depress, relocate, or reconstruct any such sewer, sewer connection, catch basin, water pipe, water connection, natural or artificial gas pipes or connections, hydrants, pipes, wires, conduits, poles and street railway tracks or appliances, or other obstructions, file with the director of public service of the municipality detailed plans and specifications for all of said work. No such work shall be commenced unless such plans and specifications shall first be approved by the director of public service of such municipality, after notice and hearing, and unless such company shall file with the director of public service a bond in such amount and with such sureties as the director of public service may determine, conditioned to indemnify and save harmless the owners of any such sewer, sewer connection, catch basin, water pipe, water connection, natural or artificial gas pipes or connections, hydrants, pipes, wires, conduits, poles or street railway tracks or appliances, and the owners of any other property situated in, on, under, or near any such road, street, alley, way, or public ground, from all cost and expense of such work and damages resulting from injuries done thereby. Such director of public service may change, modify or reject any such plans or specifications, and such work of construction shall be performed under the supervision and control of the director of public service.

If such plans and specifications shall locate any such sewer, sewer connection, catch basin, water pipe, water connection, natural or artificial gas pipe or connection, hydrants, pipes, wires, conduits, or any other structures within the gallery, subway or tunnel of such underground railroad, the owners of the same shall be entitled to use such space within such gallery, subway, or tunnel, without compensation for such use and occupancy, except a reasonable charge to defray the actual cost of maintenance; provided, however, that if any such sewer, pipe, conduit or other conductor shall be of greater capacity than that existing prior to the construction of such underground railroad, the underground railroad shall be entitled to charge for the increased capacity of such conductor and not otherwise. All cost, damage, and expense, incidental to the work of removing, supporting, readjusting and reconstructing any such sewer, sewer connection, catch basin, water pipe, water connection, natural or artificial gas pipes or connections, hydrants, pipes, wires, conduits, poles, street railway tracks or appliances, or other structures, and all cost of supervision by the city shall be borne by and paid for by such elevated or underground railroad. Nothing contained in this act shall authorize the permanent removal or exclusion from any such road, street, alley, way or ground of any such sewer, sewer connection, catch basin, water pipe, water connection, natural or artificial gas pipe or connections, hydrants, pipes, wires, conduits, poles, street railway tracks or appliances, and other structures, authorized to be located therein, except when suitable facilities for such services have been otherwise provided for therein, or to prevent the practical construction, repair, operation and use of the same. (May 29, 1911, 102 v. 179.)

Section 9143-2. (When the grant of such right and privileges deemed valid.) Any ordinance of any city purporting to grant the rights or privileges, or any of them, contained in this act to any company, and which grant has been accepted and on account thereof money has been expended in good faith, is hereby declared to be as valid and effective as if the power in said city to so grant such rights and privileges had been expressly enumerated in the general municipal corporation act. (May 29, 1911, 102 v. 180.)

Section 9143-3. (Right to lease space in tunnel or subway.) The council may authorize the company to lease space in its tunnel or subway, for the purpose of placing pipes, conduits, tubes and wires for artificial or natural gas, water, sewer, heating, telegraph, telephone, signal service, United States mail, electricity for light, heat and power purposes, to any company which has been duly authorized by the municipality to engage in and which company is actually engaged in the business in connection with which the use of such space is to be made; provided that such lease shall be made and such space occupied in such manner and on such terms and conditions, as the council may determine and approve. And the council shall have the right to place, or cause to be placed in such tunnel or subway any pipes, lines and conduits for any of its service, including those above named, without charge, except for cost of construction, provided that such placing shall not interfere with the company's use of the subway. (May 29, 1911, 102 v. 180.)

Section 9144. (Terms of grant.) Such grant shall only be made upon such terms and conditions as are agreed upon by the council of the city, and the company; and every such grant shall provide that the rate of fare within the limits of such municipality shall not be in excess of five cents. (R. S. Sec. 3283b; March 23, 1909, 100 v. 71; May 9, 1908, 99 v. 452.)

Section 9145. (Appropriation of property.) After such grant has been made such company may appropriate private property necessary for the use and enjoyment of the grant, including terminals and way stations, for the purpose of constructing and operating its road in the manner and upon the terms provided by law for the appropriation of private property by corporations. (R. S. Sec. 3283b; March 23, 1909, 100 v. 71; May 9, 1908, 99 v. 452.)

Section 9146. (Damages to other property.) Every company which constructs an elevated track upon or a tunnel or an underground railroad below such roads, streets, alleys, ways or grounds, shall be responsible for injuries done thereby to private or public property, lying upon or near such streets, alleys, ways or grounds, which may be recovered by civil action brought by the owner before the proper court at any time within two years from the completion of the road. (R. S. Sec. 3283b; March 23, 1909, 100 v. 71; May 9, 1908, 99 v. 452.)

Section 9147. (Purchase of road by city.) Every city making a grant as provided in the five next preceding sections, may provide in such grant, upon such terms and conditions as are agreed upon by the council of the city, and the company, for the ultimate purchase and ownership by the city of such road or any part thereof. (R. S. Sec. 3283c; May 9, 1908, 99 v. 453.)

Section 9148. (Company to notify authorities of acceptance or rejection of grant.) Every railroad, street railroad company, suburban railroad company or interurban railroad company, to whom a grant has been made as above provided shall notify in writing the authorities making the grant of its rejection or acceptance of the grant at a time fixed by them at the time of making the grant. If after a grant has been made as above provided, and accepted by any railroad, street railroad company, suburban railroad company or interurban railroad company, within sixty days after such acceptance there is filed with the mayor of the city making the grant a petition protesting against it and signed by such a number of the electors of the city qualified to vote at the last preceding general election, as equals ten per cent of the number of votes cast for mayor at the last preceding election for mayor, he shall certify such fact to the proper election officials. (R. S. Sec. 3283d; March 23, 1909, 100 v. 71; May 9, 1908, 99 v. 453.)

Section 9149. (Submission of grant to electors.) The officials in charge of such general election, in accordance with the statutes relating to elections, shall arrange, provide for and conduct the submission of such question to such electors. The question whether the grant shall be made shall be submitted to the electors of such city at the next succeeding general election occurring more than thirty days after the expiration of such sixty days. The ballots at such election if the grant be for the construction of elevated tracks shall read "Elevated Railroad Grant—Yes". "Elevated Railroad Grant—No". If the grant be for the construction of underground tracks they shall read "Underground Railroad Grant—Yes". "Underground Railroad Grant—No". If the grant be for the construction of partly elevated and partly underground tracks, they shall read "Elevated and Underground Railroad Grant—Yes", "Elevated and Underground Railroad Grant—No". If at such election a majority of the votes cast on such question be against such grant, it shall be ineffective and void. (R. S. Sec. 3283d; March 23, 1909, 100 v. 71; May 9, 1908, 99 v. 453.)

Section 9149-1. (Power brakes.) That from and after January 1, 1913, it shall be unlawful in the state of Ohio, for any corporation, company, person or persons owning or controlling the same, to operate, use or run or permit to be run, used or operated for carrying passengers or freight on an urban or interurban railroad or street car line, any car propelled by electricity, not equipped, in addition to the hand brake in use on such car, with an air or electric power brake or apparatus, capable of applying to all the brake shoes and wheels of such car a maximum permissible braking pressure, and of automatically reducing such braking pressure, as the speed of the car decreases. Fifty per cent. of such cars to be so equipped prior to January 1, 1911, and seventy-five per cent. prior to January 1, 1912. It shall be the duty of the railroad commission of Ohio to enforce this act. (May 13, 1910, 101 v. 209.)

This section applies to cars operated wholly within a municipality. Rep. Atty. Gen. 1911-1912, p. 704.

Section 9149-2. (Penalty.) Any corporation, company, person or persons operating, using or running any car, or permitting any car to be operated, used or run, in violation of any of the provisions of this act, shall be liable to a penalty of one hundred dollars for each such violation, to be recovered in a suit or suits which it shall be the duty of the prosecuting attorney of any county where such violation shall have been committed to prosecute such suit or suits to be brought by such prosecuting attorney upon verified information being lodged with him of such violation having occurred. (May 13, 1910, 101 v. 209.)

Section 9149-3. (Electric railroads operating cars along third rail required to maintain fences, crossings and cattleguards. Exception.) That every company or person having the control or management of an electric, interurban, or street railroad, which operates its cars by electricity conducted through or along a third rail, shall construct, or cause to be constructed, and maintain in good repair on each side of its right of way through which such third rail extends, a fence sufficient to turn stock; and such company or person shall cause to be maintained at every point where any public road, street, lane, or highway crosses such railroad, safe and sufficient crossings, and on each side of such crossings cattle-guards sufficient to prevent domestic animals from going upon said railroads; and every such company or person shall be liable for all damages sustained in person or property in any manner by reason, of any neglect or carelessness in the construction or maintenance of any such fence, crossing or cattle-guard, whether such damage be sustained from the contact of said domestic animals with said cars or from contact with, or by reason of, electricity passing through or along such third rail. Provided, however, that the provisions of this act shall not require the building and maintenance of such fence between the right-of-way of such electric, interurban, or street railway, and the right-of-way of any steam or electric railway where said rights-of-way are parallel and abut upon each other, and such steam or electric railway maintains a fence on the opposite side of its right-of-way. (April 25, 1913, 103 v. 197, § 1.)

Section 9149-4. (Abutting owner may construct and maintain fence, when.) If any such company or person neglect or refuse to construct and maintain such fence as provided in the preceding section, the owner of any land abutting on the line of the right-of-way of such person or company may construct the fence thereon as herein provided for, so far as his lands abut on the right-of-way; and when he has completed the same, he may present for payment, to the ticket agent of the company at the station nearest the track so fenced, an itemized statement of the expenses thereof; and if such person or company neglect or refuse for thirty days to pay such account, such land owner may recover the reasonable cost of such fence from the owner of the road, in any court of competent jurisdiction. (April 25, 1913, 103 v. 198, § 2.)

Section 9149-5. (Injury to domestic animal prima facie evidence of failure to comply with law.) If any domestic animal shall receive any injury or be killed upon such right-of-way, either by coming in contact with a moving car, or by reason of the electricity contained in or passing through a third rail of such railroad, such injury or death shall be prima facie evidence that the person or company operating said railroad has failed to comply with the requirements of this act. (April 25, 1913, 103 v. 198, § 3.)

CHAPTER 11.

POLICEMEN.

Section 9150. (Appointment, qualification and term.) Upon the application of a company, owning or using a railroad, street railroad, suburban or interurban railroad in this state, the governor may appoint and commission such persons as the company designates or as many thereof as he may deem proper, to act as policemen for and on the premises of such railroad or elsewhere, when directly in the discharge of their duties for such railroad. Policemen so appointed shall be citizens of this state and men of good character. They shall hold office for three years, unless for good cause shown, their commission is revoked by the governor, or by the railroad company, as provided by law. Not more than one such policeman shall be appointed for each five miles of a street, suburban, or interurban railroad. (R. S. Sec. 3427; April 24, 1904, 97 v. 392; February 18, 1885, 82 v. 51; R. S. 1880; March 18, 1867, 64 v. 60, §§ 1, 2.)

Constitutionality.
See Railway Co. v. Railroad Co., 30 O. S. 604 (1877).

Section 9151. (Oath, powers and liabilities.) Before entering upon the duties of his office, each policeman so appointed shall take and subscribe an oath of office, which shall be endorsed on his commission. A certified copy of such commission, with the oath, shall be recorded in the office of the clerk of the common pleas court in each county through or into which the railroad runs for which such policeman is appointed, and intended to act. Policemen so appointed and commissioned severally shall possess and exercise the powers, and be subject to the liabilities of policemen of cities in the several counties in which they are authorized to act while discharging the duties for which they are appointed. (R. S. Sec. 3428; February 18, 1885, 82 v. 51; R. S. 1880; March 18, 1867, 64 v. 60, § 3.)

A railway police officer may make an arrest, without a warrant, for intoxication in a public place or for disorderly conduct. Such an arrest is not illegal and does render the railway company liable for false imprisonment.

Erie Railroad Co. v. Reigherd, 7 O. L. R. 485 (U. S. C. C. A. 1909).

A policeman appointed and commissioned under §§ 9150 and 9151 is a public officer, deriving his authority from the state, although his salary is paid by the railroad company; and his acts will be presumed to have been performed in his capacity as such until such presumption is overcome by sufficient evidence.

Railway Co. v. Fieback, 87 O. S. 254 (1912); reversing, 13 C C. n. s. 369; 22 C. D. 74.

A railroad company is not liable for the wrongful acts of an officer, appointed and commissioned under §§ 9150 and 9151, while acting by virtue of such office, unless such wrongful acts occurred in the performance of an act which was outside of the public duties of a policeman, and which was authorized or ratified by such company.

Railway Co. v. Fieback, 87 O. S. 254 (1912); reversing, 13 C C. n. s. 369; 22 C. D. 74.

Section 9152.   (Power of police to enforce regulations and make arrests.) A company which avails itself of the provisions of the two preceding sections may make needful regulations to promote the public convenience and safety in and about its depots, stations, and grounds, not inconsistent with law, and print and post them conspicuously upon its depots or station buildings. Such policemen shall enforce and compel obedience thereto. The keeper of jails, lockups, or station-houses in such counties shall receive persons arrested for the commission of an offense against such regulations or the laws of the state, upon or along the railroad or premises of such company to be dealt with according to law. (R. S. Sec. 3429; March 18, 1867, 64 v. 60, § 3.)

Section 9153.   (When police to wear badges.) Except while acting in the discharge of duty as a detective for such railroad, every such policeman when on duty as heretofore specified, in plain view, shall wear a metallic shield with the word "police" and the name of the railroad for which he is appointed inscribed thereon. (R. S. Sec. 3430; February 18, 1885, 82 v. 51; R. S. 1880; March 18, 1867, 64 v. 60, § 4.)

Section 9154.   (Compensation.) The compensation of such policemen shall be paid by the company for which they respectively are appointed, and at such rates as may be agreed upon by the parties. (R. S. Sec. 3431; March 18, 1867, 64 v. 60, § 5.)

Section 9155. (When powers cease.) When a company no longer requires the services of a policeman so appointed, it may file a notice to that effect, under its corporate seal, attested by its secretary, in the several offices where the commission of such policeman is recorded, which shall be noted by the clerk upon the margin of the record where the commission is recorded, and thereupon the power of such policeman shall cease. (R. S. Sec. 3432; March 18, 1867, 64 v. 60, § 6.)

Section 9156. (When conductor a policeman.) The conductor of every train carrying passengers, and the conductor of the car or cars of an interurban railroad carrying passengers, is hereby invested with the powers, duties and responsibilities of police officers, while on duty on his train or such car or cars, and he may wear the badge of a special policeman. (R. S. Sec. 3433; April 15, 1904, 97 v. 84; April 11, 1876, 73 v. 166, § 1.)

See note to § 9157.

Section 9157. (When conductor may eject passenger.) When a passenger is guilty of disorderly conduct, or uses obscene language, or plays a game of cards or chance for money or other thing of value, on a passenger train or the car or cars of an interurban railroad carrying passengers, the conductor of such train or car or cars shall stop his train, car or cars at the place where such offense is committed, or at the next stopping place therefor, and eject such passenger from the train or car or cars, using only such force as may be necessary. The conductor may command the assistance of employes of the company, person, firm or corporation owning or operating such road or roads and of the passengers on such train, car or cars, to assist in such removal. But before doing so he shall tender to the passenger such proportion of the fare he paid as the distance he then is from the place to which he paid fare bears to the whole distance for which his fare is paid. (R. S. Sec. 3434; April 15, 1904, 97 v. 84; April 11, 1876, 73 v. 166, § 2.)

Ejection from train for refusal to pay fare.
See note to § 8977.
The expulsion of a person may be at a place other than a railroad depot, or usual stopping place, provided care is taken not to expose him to serious injury or danger.
Railroad Co. v. Skillman, 39 O. S. 445 (1883).
Whether it is due and proper care to attempt to remove a person from a car, while the same is in motion, is a question of fact for the jury, and not of law for the court.
Healey v. City, etc., R. R. Co., 28 O. S. 23 (1875).

Liability of company.

See § 9158.

The provisions of §§ 9156 and this section are for the purpose of enabling a railroad company to protect other passengers as well as to protect the property of the company.

B. & O. Ry. v. Reed, 12 C. C. n. s. 177; 21 C. D. 521 (1909).

A railroad company is liable for an assault by a conductor upon a passenger whose conduct is peaceable and who is not violating any of the rules of the company.

B. & O. Ry. v. Reed, 12 C. C. n. s. 177; 21 C. D. 521 (1909).
Traction Co. v. Graybill, 8 C. C. n. s. 469; 19 C. D. 95 (1906).

When the force used to eject amounts to wanton assault, the fact as to whether the plaintiff was rightfully or wrongfully upon the train is not an element in the question of mere recovery.

Toledo, etc., Ry. Co. v. Marsh, 17 C. C. 379 (1898); 9 C. D. 548.
Cincinnati, etc., R. R. Co. v. Boyer, 18 C. C. 327 (1897); 10 C. D. 199.

Where one is wrongfully ejected from a railway train, even in the absence of use of excessive force by the servants of the railroad company, and whether or not the relation of the parties originated in contract, he may seek his remedy as for tort.

Toledo, etc., Ry. Co. v. Marsh, 17 C. C. 379 (1898); 9 C. D. 548.
See Pittsburg, etc., Ry. Co. v. Reynolds, 55 O. S. 370 (1896).

Complaints from fellow passengers, made at the time, as to the conduct of the person ejected are admissible.

United Power Co. v. Matheny, 81 O. S. 204.

Damages. Where a person is wrongfully ejected, it is error to charge that he can only recover the price of the ticket, and for the labor of walking to the place of destination. The jury may in such a case take into consideration the place where the plaintiff was left, the circumstances under which it was done, the humiliation, disgrace, and injury to his feelings, in having the train stopped and being compelled to leave the coach and train in a public manner.

Lake Shore, etc., Ry. Co. v. Teed, 14 C. C. 356 (1895); 6 C. D. 339.

Fright and terror as elements of damage.

See Traction Co. v. Rosnagle, 84 O. S. 310.

Punitive damages may be recovered when the acts of the conductor are malicious or wanton.

B. & O. Ry. v. Reed, 12 C. C. n. s. 177; 21 C. D. 521 (1909).
Traction Co. v. Graybill, 8 C. C. n. s. 469; 19 C. D. 95 (1906).

But this doctrine being capable of great practical abuse, the giving it in charge to the jury in a case clearly not warranting its application, tends to mislead them; and where, in such a case, a verdict for damages is obviously exorbitant, it is error in the court to refuse to set it aside, and award a new trial.

Pittsburg, etc., R. R. Co. v. Slusser, 19 O. S. 157 (1869).
See Atlantic, etc., Ry. Co. v. Dunn, 19 O. S. 170 (1869).
United Power Co. v. Matheny, 81 O. S. 204.

Words of provocation may be considered in mitigation of punitive but not compensatory damages.

Railway Co. v. De Pascale, 70 O. S. 179 (1904).

Section 9158. (When conductor may arrest passengers.)

When a passenger is guilty of an offense on a passenger train or the car or cars of an interurban railroad carrying passengers, the conductor of such train, car or cars, may arrest and take him before a magistrate having cognizance of such offense, in any county in which such train, car or cars runs, and file an affidavit before such magistrate, charging him with the offense. But in no case shall the liability of a railroad company for damages caused by the conduct of its conductor be affected by the provisions of this and the next preceding section. (R. S. Sec. 3435; April 15, 1904, 97 v. 84; April 11, 1876, 73 v. 166, § 3.)

Section 9159. **(Forfeiture for violation of two preceding sections.)** A conductor having charge of a passenger train or of the car or cars of any interurban railroad carrying passengers within this state, who wilfully neglects his duty as required by the two preceding sections, or fails to use all the means. in his power to carry out their requirements, shall be deemed guilty of negligence of official duty, and on conviction thereof, before any court of competent jurisdiction, shall be fined not less than five nor more than twenty-five dollars. (R. S. Sec. 3436; April 15, 1904, 97 v. 84; April 11, 1876, 73 v. 166, § 4.)

Lightning Source UK Ltd.
Milton Keynes UK
UKHW010621020119
334667UK00013B/2035/P